Law, Business, and Society

Law, Business, and Society

Ninth Edition

Tony McAdams
University of Northern Iowa

Nancy Neslund
Roger Williams University

Kiren Dosanjh Zucker
California State University, Northridge

Boston   Burr Ridge, IL   Dubuque, IA   New York   San Francisco   St. Louis
Bangkok   Bogotá   Caracas   Kuala Lumpur   Lisbon   London   Madrid   Mexico City
Milan   Montreal   New Delhi   Santiago   Seoul   Singapore   Sydney   Taipei   Toronto

McGraw-Hill
Irwin

LAW, BUSINESS, AND SOCIETY

Published by McGraw-Hill/Irwin, a business unit of The McGraw-Hill Companies, Inc., 1221 Avenue of the Americas, New York, NY, 10020. Copyright © 2009, 2007, 2004, 2001, 1998, 1995, 1992, 1989, 1986 by The McGraw-Hill Companies, Inc. All rights reserved. No part of this publication may be reproduced or distributed in any form or by any means, or stored in a database or retrieval system, without the prior written consent of The McGraw-Hill Companies, Inc., including, but not limited to, in any network or other electronic storage or transmission, or broadcast for distance learning.

Some ancillaries, including electronic and print components, may not be available to customers outside the United States.

This book is printed on acid-free paper.

1 2 3 4 5 6 7 8 9 0 WCT/WCT 0 9 8

ISBN 978-0-07-337765-0
MHID 0-07-337765-1

Vice president and editor-in-chief: *Brent Gordon*
Publisher: *Paul Ducham*
Sponsoring editor: *Dana L. Woo*
Editorial coordinator: *Sara Knox Hunter*
Executive marketing manager: *Rhonda Seelinger*
Lead project manager: *Christine A. Vaughan*
Full service project manager: *Jackie Henry, Aptara, Inc.*
Production supervisor: *Gina Hangos*
Design coordinator: *Joanne Mennemeier*
Media project manager: *Suresh Babu, Hurix Systems Pvt. Ltd.*
Cover design: *Brittany Skwierczynski*
Cover image: *©Getty Images*
Typeface: *10/12 Times Roman*
Compositor: *Aptara, Inc.*
Printer: *Quebecor World Taunton Inc.*

Library of Congress Cataloging-in-Publication Data

McAdams, Tony.
     Law, business, and society / Tony McAdams, Nancy Neslund, Kiren Dosanjh
Zucker.—9th ed.
     p. cm.
     Includes index.
     ISBN-13: 978-0-07-337765-0 (alk. paper)
     ISBN-10: 0-07-337765-1 (alk. paper)
     1. Business enterprises–Law and legislation—United States. 2. Trade
regulation—United States. 3. Business ethics—United States. 4. Industries–Social
aspects—United States. I. Neslund, Nancy. II. Zucker, Kiren Dosanjh. III. Title.
KF1355.M28 2009
346.73'065—dc22

                                                                                   2008042865

About the Authors

Tony McAdams

Tony McAdams is a professor of management at the University of Northern Iowa. He earned a B.A. in History from the University of Northern Iowa, a J.D. from the University of Iowa and an MBA from Columbia University. Professor McAdams' primary teaching interests include government regulation of business, business and society, and employment law. Professor McAdams' research interests include managerial accountability, business ethics, and employment law. His scholarly articles have appeared in such journals as *The Harvard Business Review, The Academy of Management Review, The Journal of Business Ethics,* and *The American Business Law Journal.* Professor McAdams has received the Iowa Board of Regents Award for Faculty Excellence, the Distinguished Teacher of the Year Award from the student government at the University of Kentucky, and the University of Northern Iowa College of Business Administration Excellence in Teaching Award.

Nancy Neslund, author of Chapters 9, 16, 17, and 18

Nancy Neslund is currently a Visiting Professor at Roger Williams University School of Law in Bristol, Rhode Island. She earned a B.A. in Economics from Willamette University, a J.D. from Columbia University, and an LL.M. from New York University. Prior to entering academia, she was a lawyer in private practice for 14 years. During the academic year 2004–2005, she was a visiting professor on the law faculty of Europa Universität Viadrina, in Germany on its border with Poland. She teaches business organizations, business law, and tax law. Her research interests include the World Trade Organization, international and domestic taxation of e-commerce, and international professional regulation.

Kiren Dosanjh Zucker

Kiren Dosanjh Zucker, author of Chapter 13, is an associate professor of business law and management at California State University, Northridge (CSUN) where she also serves as Faculty Development Director. She earned a B.A. in Political Science from Syracuse University and a J.D. from the University of Michigan. A member of the State Bar of California, she has served on its Committee of Bar Examiners and Committee on Professional Responsibility and Conduct. Her teaching and research interests focus primarily on employment law. In 2001, she was selected as a Master Teacher by the Academy of Legal Studies in Business, and in 2004 received the Outstanding Faculty Award from CSUN's Students with Disabilities Resources. In 2004 and 2006, she also received a CSUN University Ambassadors' Polished Apple Award.

Preface

NEW DIRECTIONS

Structurally and philosophically, this 9th edition is unchanged from its predecessors. Our adjustments on this occasion were directed to refreshing the book and achieving increased reader interest:

- Every chapter is current; reflecting a thorough updating of the law, supporting data and societal trends.
- Material added to this edition includes approximately 10 new discussion items per chapter in the form of law cases, "boxes," ethics exercises, vignettes, and case questions.
- Each chapter was carefully edited and rewritten to improve reading ease.
- Learning objectives were added to each chapter.

OVERVIEW

This text is directed to courses at both the upper-division undergraduate and masters levels in the legal environment of business, government and business, and business and society. Authors of textbooks in these areas often rely on a single discipline (for example, law, economics, or management) as the foundation for their efforts. In this text we take an interdisciplinary approach, using elements of law, political economy, international business, ethics, social responsibility, and management. This large task necessarily requires certain trade-offs, but we hope the product will more accurately capture the fullness of the business environment.

We want to emphasize that our primary goal is to produce an interesting, provocative reading experience. Naturally, accuracy and reasonable comprehensiveness cannot be sacrificed. Our feeling, however, is that a law text can be both intellectually and emotionally engaging without sacrificing substantive ends. To meet our objective we have given extensive attention to readings, provocative quotes, and factual details (surveys, data, and anecdotes) that add flesh to legal theory and practice.

The book is divided into five units as follows:

Unit I—Business and Society. We do not begin with the law. Rather, in Chapter 1 (Capitalism and the Role of Government), Chapter 2 (Business Ethics), and Chapter 3 (The Corporation and Public Policy: Expanding Responsibilities), we describe some of the economic and social forces that shape our legal system.

The goals of Unit I are to (*a*) enhance student awareness of the many societal influences on business, (*b*) establish the business context from which government regulation arose, and (*c*) explore the roles of the free market, government intervention, and individual and corporate ethics in controlling business behavior.

The student must understand not merely the law but the law in context. What forces have provoked government intervention in business? What alternatives to our current "mixed economy" might prove healthy? These considerations help the students respond to one of the critical questions of the day: To what extent, if any, *should* we regulate business?

Unit II—Introduction to Law. Chapter 4 (The American Legal System) and Chapter 5 (Constitutional Law and the Bill of Rights) survey the foundations of our legal system. Here we set out the "nuts and bolts" of law, combining cases, readings, and narrative. Then with Chapters 6 (Contracts) and 7 (Business Torts and Product Liability), we examine the foundations of business law.

Unit III—Trade Regulation and Antitrust. Chapter 8 (Government Regulation of Business) examines federal administrative law and raises the book's central policy inquiry: When should the government intervene in business practice? Chapter 9 (Business Organizations and Securities Regulation), Chapter 10 (Antitrust Law—Restraints of Trade), and Chapter 11 (Antitrust Law— Monopolies and Mergers) survey the core of government oversight of business.

Unit IV—Employer–Employee Relations. Chapter 12 (Employment Law I: Employee Rights), Chapter 13 (Employment Law II: Discrimination), and Chapter 14 (Employment Law III: Labor–Management Relations) are intended not only to survey the law in those areas, but also to introduce some of the sensitive and provocative social issues that have led to today's extensive government intervention in the employment relationship.

Unit V—Selected Topics in Government–Business Relations. Two of the closing chapters of this book—Chapter 15 (Consumer Protection) and Chapter 17 (Environmental Protection)—emphasize the dramatic expansion of the public's demands for socially responsible conduct in business. Chapter 16 (International Ethics and Law) provides an overview of the legal and ethical issues emerging from global business practice, while Chapter 18 (Internet Law and Ethics) surveys some cyberlaw and ethics problems.

ACCREDITATION

Our text conforms to AACSB International accreditation standards.

Two chapters are devoted exclusively to ethics, and ethics themes emerge throughout the book. The chapter on employment discrimination should be quite helpful in aiding students' understanding of diversity issues.

Furthermore, as required by the rapidly changing nature of commerce and as recommended by the AACSB, the text devotes extensive attention to legal and ethical issues arising from international business. Various topics throughout the text (for example, comparative economic systems, the Foreign Corrupt Practices Act, and global pollution) afford the student a sense of the worldwide implications of American business practice, and Chapter 16 is entirely devoted to international themes.

At the same time, the text's central theme remains the role of law, if any, in regulating the business and society relationship.

PHILOSOPHY

As noted, our primary goal is to provoke student thought. To that end, we place heavy emphasis on analysis. We consider the questions we ask more important than the answers to those questions. The student is acquainted with existing policy in the various areas, not merely for the purposes of understanding and retention, but also to provoke inquiry as to the desirability of those policies.

Our book takes a strong public policy orientation. Unit I's attention to political economy and ethics is a necessary foundation on which the student can build a logical understanding of the regulatory process, but the business and society themes persist throughout the book. In virtually every chapter, we look beyond the law itself to other environmental forces. For example, in the antitrust chapters economic philosophy is of great importance. Antitrust is explored as a matter of national social policy. We argue that antitrust has a good deal to do with the direction of American life generally. Law is at the heart of the fair employment practices section, but we also present material from management, sociology, history, and popular culture to treat fair employment as an issue of social policy rather than as a series of narrower technical legal disputes. These kinds of approaches characterize most chapters as we attempt to examine the various problems as a whole and in context. At the same time, the law remains the core of the book.

KEY FEATURES/DEPARTURES

Dozens of "boxes" and ethics vignettes place the law in a practical context and offer opportunities for discussion.

Journalistic and scholarly readings seek to give the book a stimulating, real-world quality.

Ethics and social responsibility are at the heart of the text rather than an afterthought to meet accreditation standards.

International issues receive extensive attention.

Law cases are long enough to clearly express the essence of the decision while challenging the reader's intellect.

The law is studied in the economic, social, and political context from which it springs.

Critics of business values and the American legal system receive attention.

Approximately 200 selected Web sites appear in this edition, and each chapter includes at least one Internet Exercise.

Perhaps the key pedagogical tactic in the book is the emphasis on questions rather than on answers.

INSTRUCTOR'S MANUAL

A package of supplementary materials is included in the instructor's manual. Those materials include (1) chapter outlines, (2) general advice regarding the goals and purposes of the chapters, (3) summaries of the law cases, (4) answers for the questions raised in the text, and (5) a test bank.

TEST BANK

Instructors can test students using a vast bank of test questions divided up by chapter. The test bank is found online at **www.mhhe.com/mcadams9e** in Word format.

POWERPOINTS

This edition's revised PowerPoints contain an easy-to-follow lecture outline summarizing key points for every chapter.

ONLINE LEARNING CENTER

This site, located at **www.mhhhe.com/mcadams9e**, enriches the PowerPoint slides. In addition to offering instructors a downloadable version of the Instructor's Manual and Test Bank, it also contains additional cases, readings, and student quizzes for the benefit of both instructors and students.

ACKNOWLEDGMENTS

Completion of the ninth edition of this book depended, in significant part, on the hard work of others.

The authors are pleased to acknowledge the contributions of these good people: Brent Gordan, editorial director; Paul Ducham, publisher; Dana Woo, sponsoring editor; Christine Vaughan, lead project manager; and Sara Hunter, editorial coordinator.

The authors also thank the 35 reviewers from past editions, and the following professors who reviewed portions of the text and otherwise provided valuable guidance for this edition: Jeanne Enders, Portland State University; Gwendolyn Yvonne Alexis, Monmouth University; Michael J. Costello, University of Missouri-St. Louis; Susan J. Helf, University of Washington; Kenneth R. Mayer, Cleveland State University; Keith D. Swim, Jr., Texas A&M University; Ivan R. Vernon, Cleveland State University; Jack E. Karns, East Carolina University; and David L. Torres, Angelo State University.

SUGGESTIONS

The authors welcome comments and criticism from all readers.

Tony McAdams

Brief Contents

xi

Contents

Chapter 3
The Corporation and Public Policy: Expanding Responsibilities   83

UNIT TWO
INTRODUCTION TO LAW   123

Chapter 4
The American Legal System   124

Chapter 5
Constitutional Law and the Bill of Rights   174

Chapter 7
Business Torts and Product Liability 257

UNIT THREE
TRADE REGULATION AND ANTITRUST 303

Chapter 8
Government Regulation of Business 304

Chapter 9
Business Organizations and Securities Regulation 354

Chapter 10
Antitrust Law—Restraints of
Trade   398

Chapter 17
Environmental Protection 677

Chapter 18
Internet Law and Ethics 714

Business and Society

CHAPTER ONE

Capitalism and the Role of Government

At the end of this chapter, students will be able to:

1. Describe capitalism and its relationship to individual rights.

2. Compare and contrast capitalism and collectivism.

3. Differentiate between communism and socialism as collectivist philosophies.

4. Evaluate arguments regarding government's proper role in the global, technology-based economy.

5. Describe the primary characteristics of a "mixed economy."

6. Analyze the impact of capitalism on equality, fairness, and community in American and global society.

7. Discuss the theory and practice of privatization.

8. Discuss the current state of capitalism in China and Russia.

9. Describe the income gap in America.

Part One—Introduction

Are you a capitalist?

Are you a capitalist? If so, what role, if any, should the law play in your business life? How much government does America need? These themes, examining the relationship between government and business in America, are the core of this text. Since the fall of the Soviet Union and the general decline of communist influence, free market reasoning has dominated worldwide economic discourse. Indeed, noted professor and theorist Francis Fukuyama has argued that capitalism and Western democracy have so thoroughly proven their worth that the capitalism/collectivism debate is over.[1] Democracy and markets, Fukuyama claims, are so clearly triumphant that no new forms of civilization are likely to emerge. Thus, he says, we are at the end of history.

On the other hand, distinguished management scholar Henry Mintzberg says we have misunderstood the lesson of the ascendance of capitalism:

"Capitalism has triumphed." That was the pat conclusion reached in the West as, one by one, the communist regimes of Eastern Europe began to fall. It has become such an article of faith that we have become blind to its effects. Those effects are highly negative—indeed, dangerous—because the conclusion itself is wrong.

*   *   *   *   *

Capitalism did not triumph at all; balance did. We in the West have been living in balanced societies with strong private sectors, strong public sectors, and great strength in the sectors in between. The countries under communism were totally out of balance. In those countries, the state controlled an enormous proportion of all organized activity. There was little or no countervailing force.

The belief that capitalism has triumphed is now throwing the societies of the West out of balance, especially the United Kingdom and the United States. That the imbalance will favor private rather than state ownership will not help society.[2]

*   *   *   *   *

Challenging Capitalism/Globalization   Whether a victory for capitalism (Fukuyama) or for balance (Mintzberg) or for something else altogether, the new global, technologically based economy is leading us in directions we can only dimly foresee. Does that uncertain future call for strengthened government controls, or are we wisest to let the market sort out our lives on a case-by-case basis? As scholar Robert Heilbroner noted, we are in an era of "warp-speed capitalism,"[3] fired by unprecedented faith in market-based decision making. That faith in the market is being severely tested, however. For example, the World Alliance of Reformed Churches [**http://www.warc.ch**], representing 75 million Christians in 107 countries, recently expanded the ideological attack on capitalism and corporations by arguing that United States–style capitalism is the biggest threat to world welfare.

> Capitalism, as currently practiced, is "unfaithful to God"

Capitalism, as currently practiced, should be blamed, the clergy claim, "for job loss and grinding poverty, an unprecedented rise in crime and violence, ecological degradation, and the spread of HIV/AIDS."[4] The alliance, in its 2004 meeting, went on to claim that capitalism, as currently practiced, is "unfaithful to God":

We live in a scandalous world that denies God's call to life for all. The annual income of the richest 1 percent is equal to that of the poorest 57 percent, and 24,000 people die each day from poverty and malnutrition.

*   *   *   *   *

The policies of unlimited growth among the most industrialized countries and the lust for profits of the multinational corporations have so badly damaged the planet that by the year 2000 one species was disappearing every hour.

This is a global system that defends and protects the interests of the powerful. . . . [I]n Biblical terms such a system of wealth accumulation at the expense of the poor is seen as unfaithful to God.[5]

Political scientist Benjamin Barber condemns the radical consumerism of contemporary capitalism; a system, he believes, that reduces our lives to finding satisfaction in brand

Capitalism drags us into decadence

names and nonstop shopping.[6] Capitalism drags us into decadence, he claims, by encouraging us to buy as many unnecessary products as we can manage thus replacing historical principles of hard work and deferred gratification with infantile hungers for anything that might promise comfort. We have replaced, he claims, capitalism based on productivity, hard work and altruism with consumer excess, fascination with "me" and lives reduced to shopping excursions. In America's version of capitalism, as Barber sees it, we find liberty in commerce. We can buy whatever we want; therefore, we are free. But that undemanding vision of liberty means we have no sense of obligation for social and political ideals greater than self-satisfaction. One of the results is a culture that threatens loyalties to faith, family, community and place.[7] Asking no more of us than unbridled consumption may undermine democracy itself, as columnist Rod Dreher argues:

> Democracy requires virtue. So does a healthy capitalism. A nation that cannot govern its own appetites will, in time, be unable to govern itself. An economy that divorces economic activity from the restraining virtues that make for good stewardship will implode.[8]

Other scholars, however, claim that the critics are simply mistaken because the world is, in fact, moving toward a "postmaterialist" era where quality of life exceeds economic achievement as our primary goal.[9] In any case, the people of the world, if we can believe the polling data, have clearly embraced free markets. A 2005 survey of citizens in 20 nations found a "striking global consensus that the free market economic system is best. . . . "[10] China showed the highest level of support for capitalism with 74 percent approval followed by the Philippines (73%), the United States (71%), and India (70%). The French were least enthusiastic with only 36 percent support for the free market economy. While all surveyed nations save France affirmed their faith in the free market, those same respondents somewhat paradoxically, and by even bigger margins, favored more government regulation of large companies. "Solid" majorities in all 20 countries favored more regulation of big business in order to protect worker rights (mean 74%), consumer rights (mean 73%) and the environment (mean 75%). Most agreed that: "The free enterprise system and free market economy work best in society's interests when accompanied by strong government regulations."[11] Thus, the survey indicates the world wants free markets, but perhaps not "too free."

Capitalism, Globalization, and September 11, 2001 The terrorist attacks on the World Trade Center and the Pentagon challenge the view that capitalism is the only meaningful economic voice for the globe. How can we conclude, as Fukuyama claims, that we are at the end of history when the terrorists have told us that they despise the current Western-dominated global culture?

Experts differ about the nature and impact of globalization; but we certainly see compelling evidence that international trade is breaching national boundaries, technology is shrinking the globe, and multinationals are increasingly viewing the globe as one giant market. As we discuss later (see Chapters 3 and 16), globalization suggests the promise of dramatic advances in worldwide prosperity. Perhaps greater social and political understanding will also emerge from our "shrinking" globe. As the following editorial suggests, however, the September 11 terrorists and doubtless millions of others around the globe see the advance of capitalist, American, Western values on all fronts as a direct assault on their way of life.

"Cultural Imperialism"? No

Omaha World-Herald, November 24, 2001

American troops don't have to take over the world. American culture—which, more accurately, is an amazingly multicultural phenomenon—is achieving conquests of its own.

"Cultural imperialism" is one of Osama bin Laden's more frequent indictments of the United States. He and others who want to beat up on this country make it sound like it is promoting an insidious plot. But what's happening is really more cultural osmosis, in many cases happily embraced. "Imperialism" implies the imposition of one nation's will upon another. The conquer-and-spread cultural imperialism practiced by Greece, for instance, was evident when its armies took over parts of the ancient Middle East and its civilizing influence and public baths "took over," in a sense, the people living there.

But cultural infiltration as it is seen these days is more subtle, traveling not via arrows or bullets but in knowledge, information, understanding. It is people listening to the music, eating the food, reading the books, watching the television shows of a foreign country—and liking them. It is attitude, atmosphere, expectations. It is the potential for change where no change is wanted, at least by the people in authority.

This kind of "imperialism" is what the United States stands accused of by bin Laden and others around the world, some less violent than he but no less contemptuous of American society.

American culture, of course, is itself an amalgam. It is portions of the cultures of all of the ethnic groups that have come here, stayed, and melted into the melting pot, adding their uniqueness. Some of the most "American" of our cultural icons—the Statue of Liberty, the ubiquitous taco, even the traditions of the Christmas season—are imports.

Americans count by using Arabic numerals (learned by Europeans from Arabs, though the numerals' origin apparently was in India). Even the tune to the national anthem is an old English drinking song.

American culture? It's a patchwork.

Unfortunately, defending some of the tackier patches exported to the world is not easy.

Baywatch is said (let us hope facetiously) to be the most popular television show on the planet. The McD-ing of the world, the homogenization of fast-food tastes, means that the people of Tokyo and Buenos Aires, Seoul and Bahrain, Canberra and Reykjavik all have the opportunity to chow down on some version of the quintessentially American burger, fries, and a shake.

The idea that so many people have enthusiastically embraced some of the worst aspects of American culture may be dismaying, but it comes with the territory. MTV, low-slung jeans, slang, and vomit-and-flatulence movies aren't necessarily what Americans might want to be known for by the people of other nations.

But that's the way it goes. When you offer up your culture for other people to see and accept, they take what they need. More significantly, they take what they like. No one forces Iranians to turn on their illicit televisions when *Baywatch* is illicitly scheduled via illicit satellite broadcast. But some—reportedly a lot of them—do.

That's free will; that's freedom. It is inherently destabilizing for the dictators of the far left and the far right and the fundamentalist mullahs of the world. It's just what the bin Laden types can't stand. In a closed, tightly controlled society, all actions are dictated by the interpretations and biases of the leaders. There is no choice, no dissent. Therefore, freedom—and the American culture that springs from it—is subversive.

It is far more comfortable for the enemies of freedom to define Americans by possessions rather than by core beliefs and ideals. How much easier it is to hate the self-indulgence of bottled water . . . and movies that swagger with exaggerated American pride than it is to deal with the depth and breadth of the American spirit. And with the virtues of tolerance, freedom and justice that have few equals in any other time or place.

Source: *Omaha World-Herald,* November 24, 2001, p. 6b. Reprinted by permission.

Questions

1. *a.* Is America deliberately seeking to convert the balance of the globe to American, free market, democratic values?

   b. Would all nations be well served if they adopt American, free market, democratic values? Explain.

2. In what ways might American culture be viewed as offensive and threatening to Muslims and others around the globe?

3. Intellectuals Michael Hardt and Antonio Negri claim that a new global economic system is emerging, which they refer to as an "empire" bound together by a network of agreements arranged and monitored by global organizations such as the World Trade Organization, the International Monetary Fund, the World Bank, and the United Nations. A reviewer explained their central ideas:

It is not a nation-state. It is not an aligned superpower bloc. It . . . has no seat like the Roman Empire. It is a distributed network, like the Internet, created by international agreements binding nations big and small into relationships that none of them fully control.[12]

What role do giant American multinational corporations, such as McDonald's, allegedly play in the emerging "empire?"

[For arguments in support of globalization, see **http://www.iccwbo.org/home/menu_case_for_the_global_economy.asp**]. [For a directory of "Critics of Globalization," see **http://newton.uor.edu/Departments&Programs/AsianStudiesDept/general-global.html**].

Our Purpose Onrushing globalization, the struggle between government intervention and free markets, and the battle between corporations and their critics provide the changing context in which American business operates. Within that context, then, the purpose of this book is to ask two questions:

1. What is the proper role of business in American and global society?
2. How much, if any, government regulation of business is necessary to secure that role?

Markets and Governments In the United States, we certainly cannot understand our system of laws without a firm appreciation for the principles of capitalism from which those laws spring. We chose a capitalist, democratic approach to life. Other cultures have placed less faith in the market and more in government planning. The legal systems in those countries reflect a preference for greater central authority.

In this chapter we will explore the full economic spectrum, moving from a laissez-faire, free market approach on the extreme right to a brief reminder of command economy principles on the far left. But the bulk of our attention will rest where the world is at this moment; that is, we will examine the notion of the *mixed economy*, a combination of markets and rules.

The pure free market approach assumes that we can operate our business structure and our society at large free of all but foundational legal mechanisms such as contract and criminal law. The wisdom of the market—our individual judgments, in combination with our individual consciences—would "regulate" American life. Most forms of government including regulatory agencies, consumer protection, environmental rules, occupational licensure, zoning restrictions, antitrust law, and all but the most basic government services (perhaps limited to the police, the courts, and the army) would be eliminated.

As noted, today's debate is no longer about capitalism versus communism but about the mixed economy—that is, about what combination of capitalism and government best serves the world's needs. Substantially open markets have shown themselves to be the stronger vehicle for productivity, efficiency, and personal freedom. But are they also the stronger vehicle for improving living conditions for all citizens, for maximizing democracy, for discouraging crime and corruption, and for building strong communities? In this era of rapid globalization, are America and the world best served by the speed and efficiency of largely unrestrained markets, or do we still need the "civilizing" influence of government rules?

Law   Finally, this chapter should be read as a foundation for the study of law that follows. Once a society settles on some broad political and economic principles, it pours a thin veneer or many heavy coats (depending on the system chosen) of social control on that foundation. The law serves as a primary method of social control. So to understand the law, we need to understand its roots in the economic, political, and social preferences of the world's people.

Questions—Part One

1. Former Secretary of Labor Robert Reich speculated about five possible scenarios for the political economy of the current century. Which do you think is the more likely direction? Explain.

   a. History is ending in bureaucratic corporatism. . . . Key decisions are shifting away from elected politicians and legislative bodies toward multinational bureaucracies (such as the G-8) and global corporations unaccountable to any single population.

   b. History alternates between periods of central control and chaos, and we are again entering the latter. The 40-year interval of superpower stability is giving way to tribal fragmentation and warfare with ethnic tensions flaring over Eastern Europe and the former Soviet Union, the Asian subcontinent, and even within advanced industrial nations.

   c. History is ending in cultural authoritarianism. Societies like Japan and Germany, which reward group loyalty and investment, are gaining economic power over societies organized around individual liberty and personal consumption. Meanwhile, much of the Third World is succumbing to Islamic fundamentalism.

   d. History is ending in liberal democracy and individual liberty. Modern economies depend on educated workforces, which in turn are demanding rights and freedoms that only liberal democracies can provide (look at Latin America).

   e. All of the above. See Robert Reich, "Is Liberal Democracy the Hallmark of Our Era?" *The Wall Street Journal*, February 6, 1992, p. A12.

2. Recent global surveys document increasing anti-American sentiments around the globe. For example, between 2002 and 2005, favorable attitudes toward the American people declined in nine of 12 leading countries for which long-term data are available. Similarly, when asked in a 2005 survey of 16 countries where a young person should go to lead a good life, no more than 10 percent of those responding in 13 of the countries recommended the United States. Australia, Canada, Great Britain, and Germany were all preferred locations. How would you explain the rising anti-Americanism around the globe? See Andrew Kohut and Bruce Stokes, "Pushing Back at U.S.; Surveys Show that Worldwide Dislike for America Has Grown in Recent Years," *The Baltimore Sun*, May 14, 2006, p. 1F.

Part Two—Capitalism

Capitalism in America was built on the strong philosophical foundation of personal freedom and private property rights. Our great natural resources and personal ambition led to extraordinary prosperity. Monopolistic abuse followed, however, and government grew to curb the power of big business. Thus, America's substantially free market was gradually constrained by government regulation. The proper balance between open markets and government intervention remains perhaps the central public policy debate in American life.

Our purpose now is to consider a return to a purer form of capitalism; largely free of government oversight. Can we, in large measure, do without government regulation of business? The controversial philosopher and novelist Ayn Rand was an uncompromising advocate of free market principles. She believed the necessary categories of government were only three in number: the police, the armed services, and the law courts. Rand's philosophy of Objectivism contends that the practice of free market principles is necessary for a rational, moral life. Rand's views are highly controversial, but she has been cited as a powerful influence by some of America's leading corporate and political figures. Her books, including *Atlas Shrugged* and *The Fountainhead,* are among the best-selling novels of all time. Indeed, *Atlas Shrugged* is one of the most influential business books in history, and according to a recent survey, has been read by over 8 percent of American adults.[13] Big business leaders, who so often are the villains of contemporary American life, are the great heroes of Rand's writing; in which she championed "the virtue of selfishness" and rejected self-sacrifice. [See The Center for the Moral Defense of Capitalism at **http://www.moraldefense.com**]

> Big business leaders are the great heroes of Rand's writing

---

Man's Rights

Ayn Rand

If one wishes to advocate a free society—that is, capitalism—one must realize that its indispensable foundation is the principle of individual rights. If one wishes to uphold individual rights, one must realize that capitalism is the only system that can uphold and protect them.

* * * * *

Every political system is based on some code of ethics. The dominant ethics of mankind's history were variants of the altruist-collectivist doctrine which subordinated the individual to some higher authority.

* * * * *

Under all such systems, morality was a code applicable to the individual, but not to society. Society was placed *outside* the moral law, and the inculcation of self-sacrificial devotion to social duty was regarded as the main purpose of ethics in man's earthly existence.

Since there is no such entity as "society," since society is only a number of individual men, this meant, in practice, that the rulers of society were exempt from moral law; subject only to traditional rituals, they held total power and exacted blind obedience—on the implicit principle of "The good is that which is good for society. . . . "

This was true of all statist systems, under all variants of the altruist-collectivist ethics . . . . As witness: the theocracy of Egypt, with the Pharaoh as an embodied god—the unlimited majority rule or *democracy* of Athens—the welfare state run by the Emperors of Rome—the Inquisition of the late Middle Ages—the absolute monarchy of France—the welfare state of Bismarck's Prussia—the gas chambers of Nazi Germany—the slaughterhouse of the Soviet Union.

All these political systems were expressions of the altruist-collectivist ethics—and their common characteristic is the fact that society stood above the moral law. . . . Thus, politically, all these systems were variants of an *amoral* society.

The most profoundly revolutionary achievement of the United States of America was *the subordination of society to moral law.*

The principle of man's individual rights represented the extension of morality into the social system—as a limitation on the power of the state. . . . The United States was the first *moral* society in history.

All previous systems had regarded man as a sacrificial means to the ends of others, and society as an end in itself. The United States regarded man as an end in himself, and society as a means to the peaceful, orderly, *voluntary* coexistence of individuals. All previous systems had held that man's life belongs to society, that society can dispose of him in any way it pleases, and that any freedom he enjoys is his only by favor, by the *permission* of society, which may be revoked at any time. The United States held that man's life is his by *right,* that a right is the property of an individual, that society as such has no rights, and that the only moral purpose of a government is the protection of individual rights.

A "right" is a moral principle defining and sanctioning a man's freedom of action in a social context. There is only *one* fundamental right (all the others are its consequences or corollaries): a man's right to his own life. . . .

America's inner contradiction was the altruist-collectivist ethics. Altruism is incompatible with freedom, with capitalism, and with individual rights. . . .

It was the concept of individual rights that had given birth to a free society. It was with the destruction of individual rights that the destruction of freedom had to begin.

A collectivist tyranny dare not enslave a country by an outright confiscation of its values, material or moral. It has to be done by a process of internal corruption. . . . The process entails such a growth of newly promulgated "rights" that people do not notice the fact that the meaning of the concept is being reversed. . . .

The Democratic Party platform of 1960 summarizes the switch boldly and explicitly. It declares that a democratic administration "will reaffirm the economic bill of rights which Franklin Roosevelt wrote into our national conscience 16 years ago."

Bear clearly in mind the meaning of the concept of *rights* when you read the list which that platform offers:

1. The right to a useful and remunerative job in the industries or shops or farms or mines of the nation.

2. The right to earn enough to provide adequate food and clothing and recreation.

3. The right of every farmer to raise and sell his products at a return which will give him and his family a decent living.

4. The right of every businessman, large and small, to trade in an atmosphere of freedom from unfair competition and domination by monopolies at home and abroad.

5. The right of every family to a decent home.

6. The right to adequate medical care and the opportunity to achieve and enjoy good health.

7. The right to adequate protection from the economic fears of old age, sickness, accidents, and unemployment.

8. The right to a good education.

A single question added to each of the above eight clauses would make the issue clear: *At whose expense?*

Jobs, food, clothing, recreation (!), homes, medical care, education, etc. do not grow in nature. These are man-made values—goods and services produced by men. *Who* is to provide them?

If some men are entitled *by right* to the products of the work of others, it means that those others are deprived of rights and condemned to slave labor.

*   *   *   *   *

Observe, in this context, the intellectual precision of the Founding Fathers: they spoke of the right to *the pursuit* of happiness—*not* of the right to happiness. It means that a man has the right to take the actions he deems necessary to achieve his happiness; it does *not* mean that others must make him happy. . . .

Property rights and the right of free trade are man's only "economic rights" (they are, in fact, *political* rights)—and there can be no such thing as "an *economic* bill of rights." . . .

And while people are clamoring about "economic rights," the concept of political rights is vanishing. . . .

Such is the state of one of today's most crucial issues: *political* rights versus "*economic*" rights." It's either-or. One destroys the other. But there are, in fact, no "economic rights," no "collective rights," no "public-interest rights." The term *individual rights* is a redundancy: there is no other kind of rights and no one else to possess them.

Those who advocate laissez-faire capitalism are the only advocates of man's rights.

Questions

1. *a.* As measured by the level of taxation and regulation, protection for property rights, the liberality of trade policy, and the like, would you say the world is increasingly free or increasingly subject to government oversight?

    b. Of all the nations of the world, does the United States enjoy the greatest level of economic freedom? Explain. [See the Index of Economic Freedom at **www .heritage.org**]

2. Gwyneth Paltrow reportedly earned $3.6 million to sing one three-minute song, "This Thing Called Love," in a cameo appearance playing singer Peggy Lee in the movie *Infamous,* a biographical treatment of the author/celebrity Truman Capote.[14] Has the market failed, or has it worked as it should when an individual is paid $3.6 million for a work product that will total three minutes? Explain.

3. Increasingly, elementary schools are banning tag, dodge ball, touch football, kickball, and other vigorous games from the playgrounds. One school banned touching altogether. Administrators fear physical injuries, reduced self-esteem, and lawsuits. As the *Los Angeles Times* editorialized, "It's hard sometimes to tell whether schools are graduating students or growing orchids."[15] Ayn Rand argued for reduced rules in life, thus relying on the market to address virtually all problems.

    a. From Rand's free market point of view, explain why we should reduce playground rules as much as possible, even at the risk of children being hurt.

    b. Would you follow the rules approach or Rand's free market approach in managing a playground? Explain.

Free Market Solution to the Baby Shortage?

The following ad appeared in *The Stanford Daily* (Stanford University):

> EGG DONOR WANTED $35,000 (PLUS ALL EXPENSES) Ivy League Professor and High-Tech CEO seek one truly exceptional woman who is attractive, athletic, under the age of 29. GPA 3.5+, SAT: 1400+.

Experts estimate that about 10,000 babies annually are born from "donated" eggs and about $38 million is spent on those eggs. Fees range from a few thousand dollars to $50,000 or more. The fertility industry is lightly regulated by the federal Centers for Disease Control and Prevention. A few states are considering their own rules. Most industrial nations have banned paid "donations."

Questions

1. Harvard Business School professor Debora Spar says, "We are selling children." a. Is she correct? b. Should we be doing so? Explain.

2. a. Does capitalism encourage us to treat people as products? b. Are people, in fact, products? Explain.

3. Should we more closely regulate the fertility industry? Explain.

Source: Jim Hopkins, "Egg-Donor Business Booms on Campus," *USA TODAY,* March 16, 2006, p. 1A.

Capitalism in Practice—"Privatization" in America and Abroad

Around the globe, from Russia to Eastern Europe and from the United Kingdom to Southeast Asia, expanded faith in the free market was the singular economic message of the past three decades. Nations increasingly embraced the free market argument that virtually all services performed by government may be more efficiently and more equitably "managed" by the private sector forces of the market; that is, those services should be *privatized.*

Most commonly, privatization follows two patterns: (1) contracting out where government, in effect, turns over a portion of its duties, such as garbage collection, to a private firm; and (2) the sale or lease of public assets, such as an airport, to a private party. Privately operated prisons, now rather common across America, are a primary example of the privatization movement that has spread to include, for example, building maintenance, computer services, welfare services, and library operation.

Price-driven, free market solutions are reaching surprising corners of American life. No longer able to maintain their parks properly, some cities are turning to private operators to find ways to make those parks more self-supporting.[16] New York City is experimenting with paying poorer residents for good behavior, such as going to parent-teacher conferences, visiting a dentist, and getting job training. About 30 nations, including Mexico, already do so with the result that school attendance and nutrition have improved.[17] Yet more controversial privatization initiatives are being considered. The mayor of Las Vegas has joined others in proposing legalized prostitution for his city, which he says would lead to "magnificent brothels" that would stimulate the local economy.[18] Some doctors and others are arguing for lifting the federal ban on organ sales as a way of addressing the current donor shortage. The resulting increase in supply would save many lives, but others fear the privatized approach would exploit the poor and vulnerable and discourage altruistic donors.[19] Professor Stephanie Coontz pushes the free market argument further by challenging the need for the state's permission to marry. For most of western history, marriage was a private contract, and Coontz wonders if the time has come to let couples, gay or straight, decide entirely on their own if they want to join together to assume the protections and obligations of a committed relationship.[20] In each of these examples, the underlying idea is that the market can make decisions more efficiently and effectively than government while also maximizing personal freedom. [For a large database supportive of privatization, see **http://www.privatization.org**]

> New York City is experimenting with paying poorer residents for good behavior

Toll Roads and Congestion Pricing Should users pay fees for access to highways? A number of states and localities are taking that direction as fuel taxes fail to keep up with road building repair costs. Private companies are building, maintaining and operating new toll roads in places such as San Antonio to Dallas, northern Virginia and suburban San Diego to the Mexican border. Taking the privatization movement a step further, state and local governments are selling or leasing existing roads to private companies. Chicago, for example, leased the Chicago Skyway, an eight-mile elevated road across the city's South

Side, to a private Spanish/Australian partnership for $1.8 billion for 99 years.[21] These deals bring quick cash to governments that do not have the political support to raise taxes to meet growing infrastructure needs. Critics worry, however, about declining service, excessive tolls, too much profit for the investors, pricing poorer drivers out of access to the roads, and trading secure government jobs with benefits for low-wage private sector jobs without benefits.[22] The record on these transformations is only beginning to emerge. Some toll roads have been successful and others less so, and with decades-long leases, only time will tell whether the privatizations were wise. [For labor union opposition to privatization, see **http://www.afscme.org/issues/76.cfm**]

The privatization movement is extending beyond toll roads to other infrastructure resources. Chicago sold control of its parking garages to Morgan Stanley for $563 million and is hoping to lease Midway Airport for as much as $3 billion.[23] Bridges, ports, utilities, and pipelines are other valuable infrastructure assets that governments are thinking about privatizing.

While adding to and upgrading infrastructure through privatization, governments and their agents are also turning to pricing/market mechanisms to reduce demand for that infrastructure. One expanding initiative is *congestion pricing* that involves making a service more expensive at times of peak demand in order to curb that demand. When the new owners took over the Chicago Skyway, they raised tolls for trucks during peak traffic hours. London now charges $16 to drive into the most heavily congested parts of the city.[24] New York City Mayor Michael Bloomberg proposed a similar plan for Manhattan south of 60th Street, but it was blocked by state legislators. Redwood City, California addressed its downtown gridlock by installing new parking meters that charge more for the prime spots.[25] Similarly, Pepco, the Washington, D.C. area electric utility, along with others, is experimenting with pricing incentives to curb electrical use at peak times by charging up to 81 cents per kilowatt hour at times of highest demand versus 9 cents at off-peak times, while the average rate is 11 cents.[26]

> New parking meters charge more for prime spots

Golf Courses Golf is a great game, beloved by many; but should nongolfing taxpayers subsidize those who choose to play? Studies show that payrolls for city-operated golf courses are about 13 percent higher than for privately operated courses.[27] According to the Reason Foundation, five of six privatized courses in Los Angeles County increased revenues "between 24 percent to 400 percent in the first year of private operation."[28] Detroit's $500,000 deficit became a $200,000 profit under private management. Similar results were reported in New York City and Chicago.[29] Reason explained,

> Should nongolfing taxpayers subsidize those who choose to play?

> [Private contractors] deliver better services at lower costs than the public sector and make a profit all at the same time . . . by increasing the number of rounds played, cutting overhead costs, purchasing materials and supplies in volume, improving golf course management techniques, and reinvesting revenues in capital improvements.[30]

Questions

1 Author Joan Didion referred to our highways as America's only communion. Would it be a social/ethical wrong to adopt widespread "congestion fees" and privately operated toll roads that would permit those with money to avoid the democracy of the highways? Explain.

2. *Governing Magazine* labeled golf courses "perhaps the most nonessential of the nonessential public services." Why do we subsidize golf, and should we continue doing so? Explain.

Schools   Is capitalism the answer to poor school performance? Can the competitive power of the market reform America's struggling public school systems? The idea was unthinkable a few decades ago, but some increasingly frustrated parents and school boards have adopted a free market "fix." Schools are experimenting with free market approaches such as open enrollment (students attend the school of their choice regardless of their place of residence), charter schools (funded by taxes but freed of much government oversight), and vouchers (students "spend" their taxpayer-provided dollars on the school of their choice). About half of the states have taken the dramatic step of contracting with private education providers, most notably New–York based Edison Schools Inc., to manage some of their more troubled schools. Edison hopes to make money running schools and improving student performance. The results to this point, however, indicate that privatization is not the hoped for magic cure for America's troubled public school system. According to the *New York Times,* "several studies have shown that on the whole, charter schools perform no better than other public schools."[31] Likewise, the value of vouchers was challenged by a large federal Department of Education study, indicating that public school students perform just as well as those in private schools, when scores are adjusted for differences in race, socioeconomic conditions, and other factors.[32] Finally, a major study of Philadelphia schools managed by private operators, including Edison, found that students in the privately managed schools performed no better than those in the other schools.[33] Edison, however, argues that its presence in the Philadelphia educational "market" has generated a sense of competition that pushes all schools to higher levels of achievement.[34]

Privatization in Sum   Much of the world has joined the United States and Great Britain in embracing the privatization movement. Pakistan, for example, has attracted billions in private sector investment to take over a few dozen state-controlled companies including telecommunications, banking and steel.[35] The result is a rapidly expanding economy. On the other hand, some countries, including India, China, and many in Latin America, have slowed their privatization efforts following concerns about moving too fast, selling assets too cheaply, lost jobs and other problems.

As is the case throughout our lives, the success of privatization efforts seems to depend to a considerable extent on how well the process is handled. Privatization often brings substantially reduced costs and improved expertise, but sometimes the transition does not work well. Many American cities, for example, have turned their water systems over to private sector, mainly European conglomerates, and many are happy with the results, but some ranging from Indianapolis, New Orleans and Atlanta to Monterey, California, Chattanooga, Tennessee, Urbana, Illinois and Lexington, Kentucky are angry about problems including increased rates, corruption, environmental violations and slow response to customer complaints.[36] The result is that one of those European conglomerates, REW AG of Germany, has decided to leave the United States and to dismantle its more than forty-nation global operations.[37] Water service privatization, expected to be a financial bonanza in the United States, has stalled with about 15 to 20 percent of the systems privately owned.[38] As one expert said, "If privatization is going to work, there really needs to be clear protection of the public good and clear standards for performance."[39]

As we have seen, privatization brings worries about job losses, reduced services, reduced responsiveness to consumers, corruption, and so on, but on balance privatization has proven efficient and useful in many instances. Nonetheless, Americans certainly are not turning their backs on government. Scholars Daniel Yergin and Joseph Stanislaw remind us of our insecurities:

> Americans are willing to tolerate more insecurity than people in other industrial nations, but there are still limits to how much insecurity they will accept. Elections and opinion polls demonstrate that while the public does not want government to extend its reach, neither does it want this rich country to abandon its American-style safety net.[40]

Privatize the Post Office?

The European Union and Japan are in the midst of postal privatization movements that will open their giant markets to mail delivery competition. Sweden, Finland, the United Kingdom, and New Zealand are among those who have already done so. Should the United States do the same? Explain.

Questions—Part Two

1. From the capitalist viewpoint, why is the private ownership of property necessary to the preservation of freedom?

2. Ayn Rand argued, "Altruism is incompatible with freedom, with capitalism, and with individual rights."

   a. Define *altruism.*

   b. Explain why Rand rejected altruism.

3. In describing life in aggressively commercialized Hong Kong, Alvin Rabushka praised the "single-minded pursuit of making money" and the "emphasis on the material things in life." Rabushka admitted to finding "Hong Kong's economic hustle and bustle more interesting, entertaining, and liberating than its lack of high opera, music, and drama."

     a. Although it is often criticized in America, is materialism the most certain and most interesting path to personal happiness? Explain.

     b. Would "sophisticated" culture (such as opera and drama) substantially disappear in America without government support? Explain.

     c. If so, how may we justify that support? If not, how may we justify that support?

4. Assume the federal government removed itself from the purchase and maintenance of its parks.

     a. Left to the private sector, what sorts of parks would develop under the profit incentive?

     b. Would Yellowstone, for example, survive in substantially its present state? Explain.

     c. Make the argument that the federal parks are an unethical, undemocratic expropriation of private resources.

5. Assume the abolition of the federal Food and Drug Administration. How would the free market protect the citizenry from dangerous food and drug products?

6. Puritan leaders felt concern over the morality of merchants selling goods for "more than their worth." That concern was particularly grave when the goods were scarce or in great demand.

     a. Should our society develop an ethic wherein goods are to be sold only "for what they are worth"? Explain.

     b. Can a seller make an accurate determination of worth? Explain.

     c. Does a product's worth differ from the price that product will bring in the marketplace? Explain.

     d. Personalize the inquiry: Assume you seek to sell your Ford car for $5,000. Assume you know of several identical Fords in a similar state of repair that can be purchased for $4,500. Assume you find a buyer at $5,000. Will you unilaterally lower your price or direct the purchaser to the other cars? Explain.

     e. If not, have you acted justly? Explain.

7. Critics of our capitalist system contend that ability and effort often are less responsible for one's success than "unearned" factors such as family background, social class, luck, and willingness to cheat. Do you agree? Explain.

8. Commentator Irving Kristol asked whether it was "just" for Ray Kroc (now deceased, formerly of McDonald's) to have made so much money by merely figuring out a new way to sell hamburgers. He concluded that capitalism says it is just because he sold a good product; people want it; it is fair.
Do you agree with Kristol? Explain.

9. Professor Robert E. Lane argued that the person who is motivated by needs for affiliation, rather than by needs for achievement, does less well in the market. Such a person is not rewarded so well as autonomous, achievement-oriented people.

     a. Is Lane correct? Explain.

     b. Is capitalism, in the long run, destructive of societal welfare in that achievement is better rewarded than affiliation? Explain.

10. How would poor people be cared for in a free market society?

11. Kevin Mattson, a researcher at Rutgers University, fears the gated community, where people shut themselves off from public life. "The privatization of everything including garbage service," he said, "disassociates people from contributing to the public good and from their responsibility to other people."

Do you agree? Explain.

Part Three—Collectivism

The term *collectivism* embraces various economic philosophies on the left of the political–economic spectrum: principally communism and socialism. Capitalism is characterized by economic individualism. Communism and the various styles of socialism feature economic cooperation and varying degrees of centralized control.

Communism

While China, Cuba, North Korea, Vietnam, and a few other nations continue to practice communism, the balance of the world has clearly rejected *Marxist-Leninist* totalitarianism, and China is rapidly and enthusiastically embracing free market practices, with continuing state oversight. Fidel Castro's departure from the Cuban presidency has permitted initial free market reforms designed to boost food production and build prosperity through self-employment and small business growth. *The Sopranos* on television, cell phones, the chance to own cars and perhaps houses; these are among the consumer promises of the "more perfect socialism" Cuba is now revealing. Of course, most Cubans cannot afford these consumer wonders, and political liberty is nowhere in sight at this writing. On the other side of the globe, the closed and aggressively hostile communist state of North Korea likewise is feeling the gradual pressure of free market forces, as evidenced by proliferating street stalls and the publication by the government of a dictionary of capitalist terms (such as interest, pawnshop, and credit) to help its citizens grasp the rudiments of capitalism.[41]

Despite the decline of communism, we need to briefly remind ourselves of some Marxist fundamentals, among which the core promise of economic justice for all remains a particularly powerful motivator. Lenin, not Marx, created the communist dictatorship in Russia. Lenin and the other communist totalitarians, most notably Stalin in the Soviet Union and Mao in China, cannot be defended. However, Marx, along with Freud and Einstein, are among the thinkers who most profoundly shaped the 20th century. For our purposes, Marx's central message concerns the severe abuses that can accompany unrestrained capitalism. Marx was particularly concerned about the growing imbalance between rich and poor. Moreover, he felt that the pursuit of wealth and self-interest would erode society's moral core. More broadly, Marx built an economic interpretation of history, arguing that "the mode of production in material life determines the general character of the social, political, and spiritual processes of life."[42] [For an introduction to Marxist thought, see **http://www.cla.purdue.edu/English/theory/marxism**]

From Communism to Capitalism

Following the fall of the Soviet Union in 1991, the newly independent eastern European nations had to make momentous decisions about how rapidly they would embrace western, free market principles. Poland, for example, while not thoroughly adopting open markets, did eliminate price controls, privatize industries and cut subsidies in the belief that the short-term pain would generate long-term rewards. The results have been enormous strides in wealth generation accompanied by, some argue, tens of millions of "discarded people" who lost their familiar places in life when state factories and protections were eliminated. Other nations, such as Slovenia, chose a go-slow transition, fearing that the capitalist shock treatment would lead to economic and social upheaval. Slovenia's slow shift, like Poland's lunge forward, has generated mixed results. Slovenian jobs have been protected and economic growth has been steady, but foreign direct investment in Slovenia has been slight and the fear is that long-term progress may have been jeopardized in a nation that continues to think of itself as substantially socialist.

Question
If you were advising a nation moving from state-domination toward free market principles, would you advocate the abrupt route favored by Poland or the slower transition of Slovenia?

Sources: Naomi Klein, "The Economic Shock Therapy of World Capitalism," *The Gazette (Montreal)*, November 25, 2007, p. A17; and Charles Goldsmith and Boris Cerni, "Slovenia Clings to Communist Past," *The International Herald Tribune*, March 29, 2007, Finance, p. 18.

Socialism

Communism appears to have run its course philosophically and pragmatically, but the problems that provoked its appeal—poverty, oppression, the rich/poor gap, and so on—remain. Hence the world continues to require government intervention. The question is: How much? We will briefly remind ourselves of the socialist response to that question. Socialists reject communist totalitarianism and embrace democracy while calling for aggressive government intervention to correct economic and social ills. Historically, socialism has often been associated with democratic governments and peaceful change, whereas communism has been characterized by totalitarianism and violent revolution.

Socialists aim to retain the benefits of industrialism while abolishing the social costs often accompanying the free market. The government is likely to be directly involved in regulating growth, inflation, and unemployment. In the contemporary Western world, Austria, Norway, Denmark, Sweden, South Africa, Finland, and France are among the nations where socialist principles have retained a significant presence. Those nations have now embraced free markets, but socialist welfare concerns remain influential.

Socialist Goals

A critical distinction between socialists and capitalists is that the former believe a society's broad directions should be carefully planned rather than left to what some take to be the whimsy of the market. Furthermore, socialists are convinced that problems of market failure (inadequate information, monopoly, externalities, public goods, and so on—see Chapter 8) mean that the free market is simply incapable of meeting the needs of all segments of society. The socialist agenda includes these elements:[43]

1. **Liberty**. To the capitalist, socialism appears to harshly restrain individual freedom. To the socialist, the freedoms of capitalism are largely an illusion, accessible only to the prosperous and powerful.

2. **Social welfare.** Socialists reserve much of their concern for the condition of the lower class—poverty, exploitation, cultural deprivation, and so on. Socialists feel that the economy must be directed toward the general interest rather than left free to multiply the welfare of successful capitalists. Hence socialists advocate income supports, free education, free health care, generous sick pay, family planning, and so on to correct the wrongs of capitalism.

3. **Fulfilling work.** Socialists object to the harshness of working life where a large segment of society is chained to degrading labor.

> Socialists seek a communitarian approach to life

4. **Community.** Socialists seek a communitarian approach to life where the excessive individualism of capitalism is muted by a concern for the welfare of all.

5. **Equality.** Class distinctions are anathema to the socialist. All humans are equally meritorious, and distinctions among them are inherently unjust.

6. **Rationality.** Socialists fear the "irrationality" of a society based on competition and unrestrained pursuit of industrial growth.

As explained in the account that follows, poverty and claims of corporate exploitation have allowed socialism to regain a tentative foothold in parts of South America.

Socialism in South America

Venezuelan president Hugo Chavez hopes to build a "21st century socialism" in South America that will elevate the poor, forgotten by "savage capitalism," while leading his country and neighbors, including Bolivia and Ecuador, away from American dominance. He wants to destroy what he sees as centuries of plundering, humiliation, and discrimination against indigenous people by monied interests, particularly American multinationals. He is clearing land in the Venezuelan interior to build new "socialist cities" where all will live in dignity enjoying parks, schools, and museums while respecting the natural environment. He has nationalized major telephone and electricity companies along with giant oil companies, driving out ExxonMobil and ConocoPhillips, and he has redistributed land from the government and private owners to the poor. Chavez's model is not communism and certainly not capitalism, but some mixture of both that embraces private capital so long as it produces "a new kind of company that dignifies the human condition." He calls for a selfless and patriotic "New Man" who creates wealth to satisfy the basic needs of the entire population.

With oil prices well over $100 per barrel at this writing, Chavez has, for now, a steady and generous revenue stream (upwards of $60 billion annually) that has allowed him to dramatically increase state funding of social projects. Chavez hit a big bump in his socialist road, however, when he lost a 2007 referendum to alter the Venezuelan constitution in a way that would have, among others things, abolished term limits for political offices and given the government more control over the economy.

Sources: *Newsday*, "Indian Rites for President-Elect Symbolize Bolivia's New Direction," *Waterloo/Cedar Falls Courier*, January 22, 2006, p. A3; Juan Forero, "Venezuela Tries to Create Its Own Kind of Socialism," *Washington Post*, August 6, 2007, p. A12; and Juan Forero, "Chavez's 'Socialist City' Rises," *Washington Post*, November 27, 2007, p. A10.

Coping with Capitalism—China and Russia

China—Economics   Business is exploding in China. The nation of 1.3 billion people is aggressively competing around the globe. Western nations have rushed to China to earn a share of the world's largest market. After 30 years of increasing capitalism, the signs of material progress are obvious: skyscrapers, cars rapidly replacing bicycles, and McDonalds, KFC, and the like on many urban corners. China's car boom is amazing. Beijing, the capital, was home to perhaps 1,100 private cars in 1985. Today, China in total has zoomed to about 20 million passenger cars.[44] China expects much more of the same in years to come, projecting a quadrupling of its gross domestic product, boosting its middle class from about five percent of today's population to over half by 2020.[45] China estimates that 400 million people have been lifted out of poverty since the shift toward open markets was initiated in the late 1970s.[46] China's spectacular growth allowed it to catch up with Germany in 2007 as the third largest economy in the world behind the United States (1st) and Japan (2nd).[47] China's per capita gross domestic product, however, was about $5,300 in 2007 while the comparable figure for the United States was $46,000.[48]

> China's car boom is amazing

China's remarkable advances are not without problems, of course. *BusinessWeek* in 2007 spoke of:

> Broken China: Beijing can't clean up the environment, rein in stock speculation, or police its companies. . . . [T]he mainland's problems could keep it from becoming the next superpower.[49]

Stunning levels of environmental pollution; stock market manipulation; rampant piracy of software, movies and music; lead-tainted toys bound for America; dangerous seafood, toothpaste, and medicine; a former commissioner of the State Food & Drug Administration executed for taking $850,000 in bribes from drug companies—these are some of the spectacular headlines that have troubled the Chinese economy. Government surveys show that nearly half of Chinese say they cannot afford to visit a doctor when they are ill.[50] Unemployment insurance (14 percent of workers) and pensions (17 percent of workers) are uncommon.[51] More broadly, China's gap between rich and poor is estimated to be the world's largest.[52] To its credit, China has instituted significant corrective measures including new environmental rules, corruption crackdowns, and social service initiatives, but the safety net that was part of China's former central planning is gone, and many Chinese are nervous about the future. An estimated 2 million Chinese try each year to kill themselves, and about 250,000 succeed.[53] Studies indicate that the nation's rapid changes and resultant stresses, including fears about grades and job losses, may have spurred the suicides.[54] Similarly, divorces, once nearly unheard of, have skyrocketed; although the divorce rate remains about one third that of the United States.[55]

> ## The Communist Party employs 30,000 "Internet security agents" to monitor online communications

China—Politics   Of course, China remains a dictatorship governed by the Communist Party. Human rights appear to have improved, but repression remains common. The Communist Party controls all media and employs 30,000 "Internet security agents" to monitor online communications. Hundreds of thousands of Chinese are confined to labor camps, and state executions are estimated to total about 4,000 annually—more than the balance of other nations combined.[56] But political progress is also evident. For the first time since 1949, party leaders were able to achieve a peaceful transfer of power in 2004 when former leader Jiang Zemin gave full control of the military to President Hu Jintao.

> ## President Hu made it clear that democracy was not in China's near future

In late 2007, President Hu made it clear, however, that democracy was not in China's near future as he insisted that the Communist Party must maintain its monopoly on power.[57] That centralized, unchecked authority has resulted in a government and economy riddled with corruption. China has put in place a series of legal reforms in contracts, property, antitrust and anticorruption that represent very big steps toward a modern, rules-based society, but they seem not yet ready to uniformly enforce and expand that system. Some notable changes are underway, nonetheless. Marxist philosophy remains enshrined in national education law, but patriotism and ethics now receive more attention in many schools than communist dogma.[58] In the same vein, interest in Confucianism has re-emerged after being suppressed during the anti-intellectual Cultural Revolution of 1966—76. Many Chinese are drawn to the 6th Century BC philosopher's ethical teachings that stress avoiding conflict and respecting others; traditional values that are attractive in this new era of corruption and materialism.[59][For the latest Chinese news, see **http://thebeijingnews.net**]

> ## Moscow has embraced consumer capitalism

Russia   A western visitor to modern Moscow must be hard-pressed to imagine that this thriving, consuming, competitive place was once the global center of communism, the dour capital of the Union of Soviet Socialist Republics and the home of America's nuclear enemy. Today after the fall of the USSR and the ideological defeat of communism, Moscow has embraced consumer capitalism, as explained by The *Christian Science Monitor:*

> The heavy, block buildings of Russia's capital are no longer covered in banners of Lenin, Marx, and Engels. Instead, enormous billboards advertise watches, cars, clothing—items unimaginable in Soviet times. Capitalism has taken hold with a vengeance.[60]

Built on soaring oil and other natural resources revenues, a growing basic economy and government budgetary restraint, Russia's recent economic performance has been remarkable: gross domestic product up 7 percent annually, personal income up 8 percent annually, the stock market up 10 percent annually.[61] Russia remains a relatively poor nation with an average per capita income of about $330 per month, about 10 percent of the U.S. average,[62] and a total economy about half the size of France.[63] Still Russia's form of capitalism has been very good for its people's material comfort and for its sense of place in the world.

Russia—Politics   Not surprisingly, Russian progress comes with some uncertainty and worry. Under former President Vladimir Putin, Russia implemented some free market reforms, but government's role in the economy was also dramatically expanded. State-controlled companies in 2006 represented 38 percent of the nation's stock market capitalization, up from 22 percent one year earlier.[64] In oil, natural gas, aluminum, cars, aerospace, and banking, Russia is creating large corporations, owned or substantially controlled by the state, that will act as international "champions" as Russia tries to build its global economic might and prestige.[65] Government's centralization of power in economics has been accompanied by tightened control over politics, courts, activists, and the mass media. Bribery and other forms of corruption in both government and the private sector are standard practice. At this writing, Russians have elected Putin's handpicked successor as president, Dmitri Medvedev, who faces very difficult strategic choices about the direction of Russia's state-influenced capitalism. Medvedev says Russia should move toward western entrepreneurship, but doing so will require enormous investments in education, health care, and infrastructure; reduced bureaucracy and strengthened legal standards; and most of all good governance;[66] a requirement it seems for successful capitalism everywhere.

> Bribery and other forms of corruption are standard practice

Questions

1. Both China and Russia have population problems; but of quite divergent natures. China has too many babies, and Russia has too few. Likewise, they are addressing their problems in quite different ways. China's government since 1979 has allowed each couple to have only one child. Heavy fines are imposed on those who violate the rule. In Russia, women who will have a second child are paid a 250,000 ruble bonus (about $10,000). China fears it cannot sustain its enormous and growing population while Russia fears its plummeting birthrate threatens the country's future.

    Can government commands, as in China, or free market incentives, as in Russia, cause people to change their childbearing practices? Explain.

2. Can China maintain its closed, centrally controlled political system while enjoying the benefits of its somewhat open economic markets? Explain.

Part Four—Middle Ground? A Mixed Economy (The Third Way)

Communism has failed. Socialist principles, to the extent that they call for central planning, bloated bureaucracies, and restraints on personal freedom, are discredited. An era
has passed, but the shape of the future is unclear. Some middle ground in free market and
welfare state principles may be the next step, but the appropriate mixture is proving elusive. For years, the Nordic states of Sweden, Norway, Denmark and Finland practiced
their market socialism or social democracy with such success that it was labeled a "third
way" between the harsher extremes of capitalism and communism. Their welfare states
provided healthy economic growth with cradle-to-grave social care for all in a system
emphasizing the collective welfare over individual preferences.

Sweden   Life expectancy in Sweden is 80.5 years, as compared with about 77.5 in the
United States. Education, health care, child care, maternity and paternity leave, unemployment protection, and more are provided by the government. To pay for its comprehensive welfare benefits, Sweden takes 50.1 percent of its national
income (gross domestic product-GDP) in taxes, the highest rate of
any industrialized nation.[67] The United States, in contrast, has one
of the lowest total tax burdens at 28.2 of GDP.[68] In order to keep
its economy healthy, Sweden has followed a policy of comparatively low corporate taxes
(about 28 percent, as compared with 35 percent in the United States).[69] As a result, Sweden's economic performance over the past 20 years has been among the strongest in the
world allowing, for example, all nine million Swedes to have health insurance, while 47
million Americans do not.[70] Even so, the pressure of globalization has been felt in Sweden where a more moderate government has pushed aside the left-leaning Social Democrats and has initiated a plan to lower taxes, privatize some state-dominated companies
and reduce unemployment by encouraging work over welfare.[71] Business regulations have
been dramatically reduced, and tens of thousands of long-term unemployed welfare recipients have been pushed back into the labor market. Sweden's 39-year-old (in 2007) finance
minister, Anders Borg, explained the new Swedish vision this way:

> Sweden takes 50.1 percent of its national income in taxes

> My idea is to combine the entrepreneurial spirit of America with the welfare of Sweden.
> That's my ideal world: the creative impulse and restructured welfare. The lowest quarter of
> our population is well educated. The United States could learn from that.[72]

Broadly, in the Nordic social democracies, government expenditures for social purposes
average about 27 percent of GDP as opposed to about 17 percent in the Anglo-Saxon states
(U.S., U.K., Canada, Australia, Ireland, and New Zealand), and yet in many ways, the
Nordic states perform better economically.[73] One expert attributes the Third Way success
to "lavish" spending on research and development and higher education.[74] Sweden, for
example, spends nearly four percent of its GDP on R&D, the highest ratio in the world.[75]
Thus, for Sweden and the other Scandinavian states, wise government spending is a key
ingredient in a successful market-based economy. To continue to provide generous cradle-
to-grave care, Sweden is committed to its Third Way path of vigorous markets and big,
smart government.

Speeding Ticket

Nokia vice president Anssi Vanjoki of Helsinki, Finland, was fined $103,600 for driving 47 miles per hour in a 30 mph zone. Consistent with its social welfare principles, Finland assesses fines based on the offender's income.

Source: Steven Landsburg, "Highway Robbery," *The Wall Street Journal,* February 11, 2002, p. A22.

American Capitalism in Europe? Globalization and the universally acknowledged power of the market have put great pressure on Sweden, Germany, France, and other European states to trim their welfare policies. Broadly, they want the benefits of aggressive capitalism, especially its proven power in wealth creation, without the problems that they observe in America: slums, poverty, the wage and wealth gaps, the uncertainties of the market, the lack of public services such as trains, and what they view as our extravagant and tasteless commercialism.

America's aggressive "cowboy capitalism"

Does the European Union have a better long-term vision for personal and societal welfare than the United States? Is America's aggressive "cowboy capitalism" better-adapted to the globe's demands than the "coordinated, stakeholder capitalism" characteristic of much of Europe? The evidence, of course, is mixed. In building entrepreneurial spirit, personal freedom, and personal wealth and income, the United States is the clear world leader, but the EU's very powerful, 27 nation, nearly 500 million person bloc produces almost one third of the global economy, as compared with 27 percent in the United States.[76] For Europeans, however, quantity seems to be less important than quality. Europeans choose to work less than Americans, and as they see it, enjoy life more. Their economy is less flexible than ours and produces fewer jobs, but it is also less harsh.[77] Universal health care, job protection and strong unemployment benefits are part of the European identity. The weight of globalization is forcing them to rethink their vision and move more in America's direction, but the differences remain pronounced. American commentator and social activist Jeremy Rifkind contrasted the American and European "Dreams:"[78]

American Dream	Versus	European Dream
Wealth/Individual success	v.	Quality of life
Growth	v.	Sustainable development
Property/Civil rights	v.	Social/Human rights
Live to work	v.	Work to live
Religiosity/Piety	v.	Declining faith
Strong military	v.	Build peace

Rifkind thinks the European strategy is the better one. What do you think? Which of those two lists of values is more comfortable and inspiring for you? Which is more likely to meet the demands of the ongoing global competition and evolution? [For an overview of "Europe vs. America," including an appraisal of Rifkind's arguments, see **http://www.nybooks.com/articles/17726**]

Is the Welfare State a Key to Personal Happiness?

To the surprise of many, including perhaps the Danes themselves, Denmark turns out to be the happiest place on Earth, according to a recent, large study of global happiness. The Happiness Top Ten includes: 1. Denmark, 2. Switzerland, 3. Austria, 4. Iceland, 5. The Bahamas, 6. Finland, 7. Sweden, 8. Bhutan, 9. Brunei, 10. Canada. The United States ranks 23rd on the list, ahead of Germany (35), United Kingdom (41), France (62), China (82), Japan (90), India (125), and Russia (167). The happiness ranking was achieved by an analysis of a number of global surveys and studies to create an estimate of subjective well-being: the first world map of happiness.

Predictably, a nation's level of happiness was found to be most closely associated with health, followed by wealth and provision of education, but a closer look at the data reveals more interesting insights. Money, it turns out, is significantly influential in producing happiness only up to the point where we are safe, warm, and well-fed. Thereafter, more money seems not to add much. Indeed, those reporting themselves as "very happy" in the United States fell from 34 percent in the early 1970s to 30 percent in the late 1990s, although the national standard of living rose markedly.

What does matter most then? Eric Weiner, author of *The Geography of Bliss: One Grump's Search for the Happiest Places in the World,* points to quantity and quality of relationships as the single biggest determinant of happiness. Simply "hanging out" with friends and family seems to be critical to the Danes' first in the world level of happiness. Ninety-two percent of Danes belong to some kind of social club, and the government encourages these get-togethers by helping to pay for them. Likewise, while Danes value nice things, they are said to be a "post-consumerist" society where consumption is not a high priority. Their extraordinarily high taxes (around 50 percent of income) may also play a role in the happiness quotient in that income is substantially leveled, allowing careers to be chosen more on the basis of interest rather than money and also allowing everyone to "hold his head high" regardless of occupational status. Finally, experts point particularly to the Danes' very high quotient of trust that may be a product of the cradle to grave security provided by the government. For example, mothers often leave their babies unattended in strollers outside restaurants. Of course, Denmark has the advantage of being a small, homogenous nation largely free of America's worldwide responsibilities. [For the "World Map of Happiness," see **http://www.le.ac.uk/users/aw57/world/sample.html**]

Questions

The tiny Himalayan kingdom (soon to be a democracy) of Bhutan has committed to measuring itself, not by Gross Domestic Product, but by Gross National Happiness; calculated from the nation's "four pillars" of sustainable development, environmental protection, cultural preservation and good governance; each of equal importance.

1. Would the United States be a better nation if we sought GNH rather than GDP?
2. Would pursuit of GNH produce a winner in today's fierce global competition? Explain.

Sources: Brook Larmer, "Bhutan's Enlightened Experiment," *National Geographic Magazine,* March 2008 [**http://ngm.nationalgeographic.com/2008/03/bhutan/larmer-text**]; Eric Weiner, "Finding Your Happy Place," *The Los Angeles Times,* January 2, 2008 [**http://www.latimes.com/news/opinion/la-oe-weiner2jan02,0,1047482.story?coll=la-tot-opinion&track=ntothtml**]; and Bill Weir and Sylvia Johnson, "Denmark: The Happiest Place on Earth," *ABC News,* January 8, 2007 [**http://abcnews.go.com/2020/story?id=40860928page=1**].

Questions—Parts Three and Four

1. Billionaire investor George Soros, in his book *Open Society,* sees "market funda-mentalism as a greater threat to open society today than communism."[79] Soros fears contemporary capitalism's extreme commitment to self-interest, which results, he says, in our greatest challenge today: "to establish a set of fundamental values."[80]

   a. What does Soros mean?

   b. Do you agree with him? Explain.

2. Americans feel a great deal of faith in the free market. Explain some of the weak-nesses in the market. That is, where is the free market likely to fail?

3. Writing in *Dissent,* Joanne Barkan says, "[A]lmost all Swedes view poverty, extreme inequalities of wealth, and the degradation that comes with unemployment as unacceptable."[81]

   a. Do you agree with the Swedes? Explain.

   b. Why are Americans more tolerant of those conditions than are the Swedes?

4. In the late 1970s, correspondent R. W. Apple of *The New York Times* reported that Sweden had willfully pursued a policy of economic leveling:

   > As a result almost every family living near the sea has a boat, but almost all are small boats. A large percentage of families have summer houses, but none of them rivals the villas of the Riviera or the stately manor houses of Britain. Virtually no one has servants.
   >
   > Even among the handful of people who might be able to afford it, conspicuous consumption is frowned upon. There are fewer than 25 Rolls Royces in Sweden.[82]

   a. Is that Swedish approach preferable to the extreme conspicuous consumption permitted—and even encouraged—in this country? Explain.

   b. Is the opportunity to garner luxuries necessary to the successful operation of the American system? Explain.

   c. Does our system generate guilt among those who enjoy its fruits in quantities well beyond the norm? Explain.

5. *a.* Should an American citizen's primary duty be to herself or himself or to all other members of society? Explain.

   b. Should all humans be regarded as of equal value and thus equally worthy of our individual support? Explain.

   c. Can social harmony be achieved in a nation whose citizens fail to regard the state as a "superfamily"? Explain.

6. *a.* In your view, is an individual's possession of extravagant wealth a moral wrong?

   b. Would economic justice require that we treat "being rich" as a social wrong? Explain.

   See George Scialabba, "Asking the Right Questions," *Dissent,* Spring 1988, p. 114.

7. In questioning Oakland Athletics general manager Billy Beane, *The Wall Street Journal* described professional football as "socialist" and baseball as "capitalist":

   > The NFL (National Football League) has been successful as a socialist league, equally divvying up the league's revenue among all the teams. Major league baseball, on the other hand, is a capitalist league, with a clear divide between big-market and small-market teams. Do you think some of baseball's financial rules have to be changed to better balance the playing field?

Is "socialism" or "capitalism" the better system for professional sports? Explain. See Jim Chairusmi, "Winning with Smaller Pockets," *The Wall Street Journal,* October 18, 2004, p. R2.

Part Five—America's Economic Future: Where Are We Going?

Greed Is Good

Michael Douglas, as Gordon Gekko in the movie *Wall Street:* "Greed is good! Greed is right! Greed works! Greed will save the USA!"

According to a United Nations report, in 2005 the world's 500 richest people had combined incomes greater than that of the poorest 416 million people.

Source: United Nations Human Development Report, 2005.

We have inspected the entire economic continuum. We know that communism has been discredited. Hence the far left has little to offer. America has led the revival of open markets both domestically and around the globe. Should we expand our faith in capitalism, or do we need to move our present mixed economy a bit closer to the welfare state model, which itself is under great pressure? Or must a new model emerge? In sum, how much government do we need?

Uncertainty

America is strong but struggling. The September 11, 2001 attacks scratched our confidence and undermined our economy. We went through a period in the middle and late 1990s when crime fell sharply, employment reached new records, gender and racial equality appeared to be improving, children were healthier than ever, and we were making at least some progress with our considerable environmental problems. Serious concerns remain, however. Economic uncertainty abounds, as the subprime mortgage meltdown of recent years indicates. In a broad sense, should we have doubts about the top-to-bottom fairness of our American system? Certainly we approve of America in the abstract, and we are generally comfortable with our overall prosperity and our expansive freedoms; but we also recognize that tens of millions are not achieving the American Dream. Let's examine a series of concerns that continue to cast a shadow on America's many free market victories.

Overall Quality of Life   The United States enjoys remarkable prosperity with occasional periods of distress, such as the recent credit crisis. Despite those bumps, most Americans seem to feel we have built the best life has to offer; and according to a United

Nations 2007/08 report on overall quality of life, we are doing well, but perhaps surprisingly, others are doing better by some important measures. The U.N. study considers educational attainment, life expectancy, and per capita gross domestic product. By that combined measure, the United States ranked 12th in the world behind, among others, Iceland (1st), Norway (2nd), Australia (3rd) and Canada (4th) and just ahead of Spain (13th) and Denmark (14th).[83] The United States slipped from a fourth place ranking in 2006.[84]

In general, the United States ranks very well on standard economic measures and not so well on standard social measures. Our GDP per capita for 2007 was an estimated $46,000, ranking 7th in the world behind smaller, more specialized economies such as Luxembourg (1st at $80,800) and well ahead of our chief industrial rivals such as Germany (23rd at $34,400) and Japan (26th at $33,800).[85] More instructive perhaps is the fact that the average American worker produces $63,885 of wealth per year (GDP divided by number of people employed), exceeding the productivity of all other nations and ranking second only to Norway (boosted by oil dollars) in productivity per hours worked.[86]

> The average American worker produces $63,885 of wealth per year

In life expectancy, on the other hand, the United States ranked 45th at 78 years (males—75.15; females — 80.97) while Japan, for example, ranked 3rd at 82.02 years.[87] Among the most discouraging U.S. performances is in the category of infant mortality (the probability of dying between birth and age one per 1,000 live births) where 42 nations (e.g., Canada, Cuba, Singapore, South Korea, and Sweden) do a better job of keeping babies alive than we do.[88] With five percent of the world's population and nearly 25 percent of the world's prisoners, the United States leads the world in producing prisoners. [For more details on imprisonment in the United States and around the world, see Adam Liptak, "Inmate Count in U.S. Dwarfs Other Nations'," *The New York Times,* April 23, 2008 **http://www.nytimes.com/2008/04/23/us/23prison.html?incamp=article_popular**]

> The United States leads the world in producing prisoners

Some trends portend a troublesome future. The United States ranks only seventh in the world, for example, in the percentage of young people who finish college,[89] and married couples with children now occupy fewer than one in four U.S. households, half the rate of 1960, and the lowest percentage ever recorded by the census.[90] Social scientists fear that the working poor increasingly reject marriage, choosing to live together and have children out of wedlock. The economically and socially productive institution of marriage with children apparently is becoming a sort of luxury item, available largely to the relatively well-off.[91]

Thus, the United States is clearly the globe's mightiest economic force, but in some important respects, we have not been successful in achieving a high quality of life for all. [For other international quality of life data, see **http://hdr.undp.org/en/reports/global/hdr2007–2008**]

Poverty   After significant improvement in the 1990s, the number of Americans living below the poverty line ($21,200 for a family of four in 2008) has since been steadily rising except for a small decline in 2006. About 37 million Americans (12.3 percent of the population) live in poverty,[92] including 18 percent of children under age 18.[93] According to the United Nations Children's Fund, the United States ranks 17th out of 21 industrial nations in the "material well-being" of its children. (Sweden ranked first and Norway second.)[94] The result is that poor people, as commentator Paul Krugman explained, live in a separate America:

> Living in or near poverty has always been a form of exile, of being cut off from the larger society. . . . To be poor in America today, even more than in the past, is to be an outcast in your own country.[95]

As critics point out, even the poor in America often live quite well compared to the balance of the world, but the suffering is real, nonetheless, and it is especially frustrating for the working poor, whose perilous life on the edge was summarized by *BusinessWeek:*

> [M]ost (of the working poor) labor in a netherworld of maximum insecurity, where one missed bus, one stalled engine, one sick kid means the difference between keeping a job and getting fired, between subsistence and setting off the financial tremors of turned-off telephones and $1,000 emergency-room bills. . . .
>
> At any moment, a boss pressured to pump profits can slash hours, shortchanging a family's grocery budget—or conversely, force employees to work off the clock, wreaking havoc on child care plans. Often, as they get close to putting in enough time to qualify for benefits, many see their schedules cut back. The time it takes to don uniforms, go to the bathroom, or take breaks routinely goes unpaid. Complain, and there is always someone younger, cheaper, and newer to the United States willing to do the work for less.[96]

Historically we have accepted difficulties for a significant share of the population in the belief that they would move up, in time, if they worked hard; but as *BusinessWeek* reports, upward mobility is slower and less likely today than in the past:

> Five of the 10 fastest-growing occupations over the next decade will be of the menial, dead-end variety, including retail clerks, janitors and cashiers.[97]

At the same time, the cost of college has "exploded" such that fewer than 5 percent of students from low-income families can now earn degrees.[98] The result is an often harsh life in this astonishingly wealthy nation. We are surprisingly unhealthy, for example. One expert recently asked, why isn't the richest country in the world also the healthiest?[99] America spends double what the British spend per person on health care, and yet Americans, even white, rich ones, are much less healthy than their peers in England.[100] Indeed, according to the highly regarded Commonwealth Fund, the United States ranks last or next to last on most measures of health care performance when compared with Australia, Canada, Germany, New Zealand, and the United Kingdom.[101] Part of the reason for our poor performance is that so many Americans (47 million in 2006) are without health insurance.[102] We are the only major industrialized nation that does not assure health care for all of its citizens. [For more data on U.S. poverty, see **www.census.gov/hhes/www/poverty.html**]

> Why isn't the richest country in the world also the healthiest?

Pets or People?

We may not take the best care of our disadvantaged fellow Americans, but we seem to be unstinting in generosity toward our pets. Americans now spend about $41 billion per year on their pets; a sum that exceeds the gross domestic product of all but 64 nations. Spending on pets has doubled in 10 years and is expected to reach $52 billion by 2009. "A dog's life" isn't all that bad these days. The American Pet Products Manufacturers Association reports that 42 percent of dogs now sleep in the same bed as their owners and almost a third receive gifts on their birthdays.

Question
Would our money for pets be more wisely spent on impoverished children? Explain.

Source: Diane Brady and Christopher Palmeri, "The Pet Economy," *BusinessWeek,* August 6, 2007, p. 45.

Good News   Of course, Americans have a great deal to be proud of. We are wealthy, adventuresome, free, and zealously democratic. Much of the world strives to achieve America's blend of entrepreneurial capitalism along with intellectual and pop culture leadership. And we should not forget that capitalist America is among the most generous of global cultures. In 2006, we likely led the world in private philanthropy, giving away about $300 billion.[103] Our federal foreign aid budget as a percentage of gross domestic product, on the other hand, is near the bottom of donor nations. So in keeping with our free market roots, we tend to give wealth privately rather than through government programs. Still the harsh side of capitalism is undeniable, and some problems continue to grow. In particular, scholars and commentators lament the expanding wealth and income gaps in America and around the world.

> America is among the most generous of global cultures

The Gaps   Extravagant wealth, side-by-side with punishing poverty, is perhaps the greatest disappointment and injustice, from the critics' point of view, in the global victory of the free market. Even the American economy is marked by large and often growing gaps in income and wealth between the top of society and the rest.

- A 2007 Internal Revenue Service study showed that the richest Americans' share of national income hit a post—World War II record with the wealthiest one percent of Americans earning 21.2 percent of all income in 2005, up from 19 percent in 2004. The bottom 50 percent earned 12.8 percent of all income, down from 13.4 percent in 2004.[104] Another study of 2005 tax data showed that the top 300,000 Americans earned almost as much income as the bottom 150 million Americans, resulting in a near doubling of the per capita income gap since 1980.[105]

- *Fortune* 500 CEOs in 2006 were making about 364 times the pay of an average employee. Forty years before they earned about 20 to 30 times what the average employee earned.[106] Steve Schwarzman head of the private equity/investment management firm, the

Steve Schwarzman spent a reported $3 million on his 60th birthday party

Blackstone Group, earned about $400 million in 2006 and spent a reported $3 million on his 60th birthday party.[107] Today of course, CEOs are hard driving, risk takers competing in a vicious global economy while yesterday's bosses were often bureaucrats in charge of big organizations in much more stable, predictable markets.

- Perhaps we can be less concerned about the big economic gaps among Americans because upward mobility, particularly for the educated, has not changed significantly over the past three decades.[108] Other rich countries, however, display greater mobility than the United States. One scholar summarized the mobility picture by saying that the United States and Britain stood out as the least mobile of the rich nations while France and Germany achieve somewhat more mobility and Canada and the Scandinavian nations are much more mobile than the United States.[109]

PRACTICING ETHICS) Are the Gaps Too Big?

Should we care about the vast and growing gaps in income and wealth in the United States and around the world? Commentator Dan Seligman says we should not be troubled because the number of poor is really all that matters, not the gap between the poor and the rich. Furthermore, the Heritage Foundation/*Wall Street Journal* Index of Economic Freedom suggests that the greater the degree of freedom in an economy, the better off the people are at *all* income levels, and that the income gap is smallest in countries with the most economic freedom. According to the 2008 Index, the United States is 5th among nations in economic freedom (with Hong Kong 1st, Australia 4th, and the United Kingdom 10th). Nonetheless, ethicist William Sundstrom argues, among other things, that fairness does matter, that the income we receive should bear some reasonable relationship to what we "deserve," and that democracy may not be able to tolerate too much social stratification.

Sources: "Index of Economic Freedom" [http://www.heritage.org/research/features/index/]; Bryan T. Johnson, Kim R. Holmes, and Melanie Kirkpatrick, "Freedom Is the Surest Path to Prosperity," *The Wall Street Journal,* December 1, 1998, p. A22; Dan Seligman, "Gap-osis," *Forbes,* August 25, 1997, p. 74; and William A. Sundstrom, "The Income Gap," *Issues in Ethics,* Fall 1998, p. 13.

Questions

1. *a.* Should income bear some reasonable relationship to what we "deserve?"

   b. How would we identify what we deserve?

   c. Based on your personal sense of fairness, is a large and growing gap in income and wealth between the rich and poor an ethical wrong? Explain.

2. The world's longest yacht (about 550 feet—approaching two football fields) is under construction at this writing at a cost of hundreds of millions of dollars. The *Eclipse* reportedly is being built for Russian tycoon, Roman Abramovich, who already owns several massive ships with the reported intention of keeping one each in the Mediterranean, the Caribbean, South America, and the Pacific. The *Eclipse* is expected to have two helicopter pads, small submarines, cinema, aquarium, disco, six hot tubs, and so on. The *Eclipse* apparently was deliberately built to be longer than the soon-to-be- runner-up in the world yacht race, the *Dubai,* owned by Sheik Mohammed of Dubai.

   Even if we have the money and we earned it legitimately, do we commit an ethical wrong when we spend our money on extravagances like colossal yachts? Explain. See "Flagship Yacht Fit for Admiral Roman Abramovich," *TimesOnline,* March 30, 2008 [http://www.timesonline.co.uk/tol/life_and_style/men/article3638066.ece].

Community Thus we see that American capitalism, despite its extraordinary success, is criticized for problems of poverty, inequality and unfairness, among others. Perhaps the more interesting concern, however, is rising evidence that our lives are increasingly solitary, distant, alone and unshared. The market is driven by and rewards individual achievement. Could that struggle for success be depriving us of the full satisfaction of our humanity? A 2006 study found that even trivial exposure to money changes our goals and behaviors such that our sense of self-sufficiency is elevated and our social interests may decline,[110] while a 2008 study showed that how people spend their money may be just as important in happiness as how much money they have. Specifically, the study demonstrated that spending money on others rather than on oneself produced greater levels of happiness.[111]

> Spending money on others rather than on oneself produced greater levels of happiness

Whether a product of capitalist impulses or not, we do have increasing evidence of declining social connections. Only 30 percent of Americans, according to a 2008 study, report a close confidant at work, down from nearly 50 percent in 1985, and workers in many other nations are much more likely to have close friends at work than are Americans. American workers report inviting 32 percent of their "close" colleagues to their homes while Polish and Indian workers report inviting more than double that percentage.[112] More worrisome perhaps are findings from a 2006 study where Americans reported an average of only two "core" confidants in their lives, down from a mean of three in 1985. Further, a quarter of Americans reported that they have no one with whom they can discuss matters of importance; a doubling of that demographic since 1985.[113] Are loneliness, social distance and declining trust somehow products of our aggressive free market? In his now famous book, *Bowling Alone,* Robert Putnam meticulously documents the decline of what he labels *social capital,* the community and commitment bonds that seem to emerge in a culture where people regularly interact with each other by volunteering, socializing, participating in clubs, engaging in group recreation, and the like.[114] The following review of *Bowling Alone* summarizes Putnam's point.[115]

> Americans report only two "core" confidants in their lives

"Bowling Alone" the New National Pastime; Author Decries Disengaged Society

Jack Cox, *Denver Post,* August 27, 2000

Thanks to cell phones, Americans appear to be doing more talking to one another than they've done in years. But ironically, they're probably less connected than ever.

That's the message that Harvard social scientist Robert Putnam rolls out in *Bowling Alone,* an influential new book that documents a steady decline in social and civic involvement over the past generation.

"It's not just that we've stopped voting. It's also that we've stopped playing cards and going to picnics," Putnam told a Denver audience recently. "Virtually every measure of social interaction is down, big time, over the last 25 years."

The most vivid illustration of the trend, Putnam suggests, may be the decrease in league bowling, which has plummeted more than 40 percent since 1980, even though the total number of bowlers in the United States has risen 10 percent—hence the notion of "bowling alone."

But regular surveys of consumer behavior, he says, chronicle similar declines in numerous other indicators of social engagement, from church attendance to charitable giving to membership in what he jokingly calls "the animal clubs" (Lions, Elks, Moose, Eagles, and so on). Even the tradition of having people over for dinner has fallen by 40 percent, he reports.

Putnam points to several factors as possible explanations for this apparent disengagement, including the migration of women from home to workplace and the increase in suburban sprawl.

"Every 10 minutes of additional commuting time," he asserts, "cuts all forms of social interaction by 10 percent, and 20 minutes more cuts it by 20 percent."

But the chief culprit, he suspects, is television. And we're not talking about public affairs shows like *Face the Nation,* he remarks. "Watching *Cheers* or *Survival* is what's really lethal in terms of social interaction."

In short, we're devoting more time to watching *Friends* than making them.

To those who see little harm in unwinding in front of the tube, Putnam points out that communities tend to work better when their inhabitants devote a fair amount of time to talking face-to-face—as he demonstrated in a 1993 book showing that local governments in Italy functioned best, oddly enough, in places where choral societies were strong.

"If you live in a community where people are connected with each other in a positive way, where there's plenty of trust and reciprocity, you are more productive," he says. "Social networks have value, and this is true whether people are organized into groups or just hanging out together."

*   *   *   *   *

Source: *Denver Post,* August 27, 2000, p. H01. Reprinted by permission.

AFTERWORD

Expanding his examination of community trust, Putnam's recent research found that ethnic diversity appears to lower the level of trust in the community, not only between members of different ethnic groups, but within those groups as well. In diverse communities, people minimize the "hits on them from society" by retreating into private space, often in front of a television. So the more diverse the community, he found, the more people tend to withdraw from social engagement, volunteer less, work less on community projects, and so on.[116] Putnam has argued, however, that diversity is highly desirable and that trust can be restored in the longer term.

Questions

1. Is Putnam correct about (a) declining social capital in America and (b) ethnic diversity as a negative force in community trust and involvement? Explain.

2. Putnam points to women in the workplace, commuting, and television as primary culprits in the decline of social capital. A 2001 study found that rising income inequality was an important force in weakening community ties. Explain that finding. See Gene Koretz, "Why Americans Grow Apart," *BusinessWeek,* July 23, 2001, p. 30.

3. Are many of us simply happier alone? Explain.

PRACTICING ETHICS) Technology and Loneliness

Since publishing *Bowling Alone,* Robert Putnam has said that we need to develop new kinds of connections when old ones die, and that electronic connections, while part of the problem currently could also be part of the solution. As we can see around us, electronic communication of all kinds has exploded in recent years. A Pew Center survey found that 55 percent of Internet users in 2006 belonged to e-mail group lists (up from 32 in 2001) as a way of maintaining ties with those sharing their interests in community, hobbies, and so on. Perhaps electronic communications, used properly, can provide the increased community that Putnam advocates. But in his book, *Interpersonal Divide: The Search for Community in a Technological Age* (Oxford University Press, 2005), Iowa State University professor

Michael Bugeja argued that excessive dependence on media technologies such as e-mail, cell phones, television, radio, and video games is destroying face-to-face relationships, causing each of us to become increasingly isolated.

Questions

1. In your view, is Bugeja correct? Explain.

2. How might our ethical standards and performances be affected by excessive reliance on media technology?

Sources: Steve Hendrix, "Offering the Nice and the Nasty, E-Mail Lists Surge in Usage," *Washington Post,* May 7, 2007, p. B1; and Steve Weinberg, "Prof Bemoans Loss of Direct Contact," *Des Moines Register,* February 20, 2005, p. 50P.

Too Much Capitalism? or Too Little?

Has America placed too much faith in the market and too little in government? Is the alleged decline in community in some sense a product of capitalism itself? Are poverty, inequality, crime, and corporate scandals such as the Enron case inevitable by-products of a "selfish, greedy" market? Even some conservatives are concerned:

> "What I'm concerned about is the idolatry of the market," says conservative intellectual William Bennett, a former education secretary and author of the *The Book of Virtues*. He worries particularly that the market for popular music and movies with sexual or violent content has a corrosive effect. "Unbridled capitalism . . . may not be a problem for production and for expansion of the economic pie, but it's a problem for human beings. It's a problem for . . . the realm of values and human relationships."[117]

> "Capitalism is more efficient . . . But it is not more fair.

The dilemma, in brief, was expressed by a 20-year-old Cuban student and communist organizer: "Capitalism is more efficient . . . But it is not more fair."[118]

The EU Dream   Fair or not, America's aggressively capitalist approach to life is the dominant model for the globe at the moment. Dramatic changes, however, seem inevitable. The rise of China and India, among others, certainly will profoundly adjust the world economic and political order. And the new European Union of 27 nations and nearly 500 million people (compared with about 305 million in the United States) suggests that our status as the world's only superpower will be challenged in the future. If so, European economic and social values will confront those of America. Author Jeremy Rifkind, in his 2004 book *The European Dream: How Europe's Vision of the Future Is Quietly Eclipsing the American Dream,*[119] raises the possibility that America's methods for achieving well-being and prosperity may someday be surpassed by the "European Dream." Rifkind explains the very dissimilar values that are leading America and Europe to differing conceptions of the good life:

> The old dream, the American Dream that made the individual the master of his fate and emphasized the personal accumulation of wealth, is faltering. . . . In today's world, the European Dream, with its emphasis on inclusivity, diversity, sustainable development, and interconnectedness, is the world's first attempt at creating a global consciousness. And it deserves our close attention.[120]

The Bill Gates Dream   Microsoft founder and perhaps the world's richest person, Bill Gates, called in early 2008 for a new vision of capitalism that can work more effectively for the poor and underprivileged.[121] Gates is not abandoning capitalism, but he is impatient with its failings. The bottom third of the world's population (two billion people), he believes, has been bypassed by the advances in technology, health care, and education that have so generously benefited the rest. He advocates a "creative capitalism" where businesses, governments, and nonprofits work together to ease the world's inequities.

Companies, Gates argues, should begin creating products and services specifically designed for the needs of the poor:

> The idea that you encourage companies to take their innovative thinkers and think about the most needy—even beyond the market opportunities—that's something that appropriately ought to be done.[122]

Skeptics want more details, and they question the profitability of focusing corporate resources on the world's poor, but for one of history's great capitalists to call into question the fairness of that system may be a good reason for reflecting on how the market can better serve the needs of all people.

Short Americans

According to a new study, white and black Americans are shrinking in height relative to Europeans. U.S. citizens through World War II were the tallest in the world, then American growth stagnated while Europeans spurted forward such that the average non-Hispanic white or black male American is about 5'10" tall as compared with, for example, Danes (6') and Dutch (6'1"). Immigrants and people of Asian or Hispanic ancestry were excluded from the study.

Questions
1. Should we be concerned that we have lost our "lead" in height? Explain.
2. Why have we fallen behind?
3. Does our slow physical growth portend a weakened position for America in the world? Explain.

Sources: John Komlos and Benjamin E. Lauderdale, "Underperformance in Affluence: The Remarkable Relative Decline in U.S. Heights in the Second Half of the 20th Century," *Social Science Quarterly* 88, Issue 2 (June 2007), p. 283; and Joshua Holland, "Are You One of the Shrinking Americans?" *AlterNet,* July 9, 2007 [**http://www.alternet.org/story/56303**].

Questions—Part Five

1. *a.* Explain the American and European Union and Bill Gates dreams for the good life of the future.
   b. Do Americans remain committed to the American Dream?
   c. Which of those dreams is most consistent with your personal values?
   d. Which of those dreams is most likely to prevail in the future? Explain.

2. *a.* What does William Bennett mean by "the idolatry of the market?"
   b. In what sense do we have a market in "values and human relationships?"
   c. What does Bennett mean about the corrosive effect of popular culture?
   d. Can we have a free market in economic affairs without harming our social values and relationships? Explain.

3. Journalist Lauren Soth said, "Let's challenge the sacred goals of economic growth, greater output of goods and services, greater productivity."[123] How could we have a better life if we were to diminish our attention to those seemingly central requirements?

Internet Exercise

The Global Policy Forum is generally critical of the globalization movement. Sample those views at [**http://www.globalpolicy.org**] and explain whether the criticisms have merit, in your judgment. Then turn to this Global Policy Forum page: "Goodbye Uncle Sam, Hello Team Europe" [**http://www.globalpolicy.org/empire/challenges/competitors/ 2005/0414byeunclesam.htm**]. Explain author John Feffer's argument that the European Union should be more influential in world affairs than the United States. Do you agree? Explain.

Chapter Questions

1. The gravestone of the late baseball great Jackie Robinson is inscribed with this advice: "A life is not important except in the impact it has on other lives." Will your life be meaningful only if you contribute to the well-being of others? Explain.

2. Commenting in *Newsweek,* economist Robert Samuelson said, "The . . . pervasive problem of capitalist economies is that almost no one fully trusts capitalists."[124]

   a. Do you agree? Why?

   b. Do you think free market capitalism is the best economic system? Explain.

   c. Do you think that multinational companies have more power than national governments? Explain.

3. In your mature years, do you expect to be as wealthy as your parents, or more so? Explain.

4. As compared with today, would you prefer a bigger U.S. government providing more services to the people, or a smaller government providing fewer services? Explain.

5. a. Noted economist Lester Thurow argued that the economic demands of the market are destroying the traditional two-parent, nuclear family. Explain his argument.

   b. Child development authority Benjamin Spock likewise blamed capitalism for the "destruction of the American family," but his reasoning differed from Thurow's:

   > The overriding problem is excessive competition and our glorification of it. It may contribute to our rapid technological advancement, but it has done so at a great price. We are taught to be rugged individualists, and we are obsessed with getting ahead. The family gets lost in this intense struggle. In a healthy society, family should come first, community second, and our outside jobs third. In this country, it is the other way around.[125]

   Comment.

   c. If Spock was correct, how did we reach this condition?

6. Barbara Ehrenreich, author of *Nickel and Dimed,* criticized Wal-Mart in a *New York Times* column. Ardent capitalist Sally Pipes summarized Ehrenreich's position:

   > This could be the central battle of the 21st century: Earth People vs. the Wal-Martians," Ehrenreich wrote. "No one knows exactly when the pod landed on our planet," but when it did Wal-Mart began to experience "recklessly metastatic growth." Wal-Mart, contends Ehrenreich, is "a creature afflicted with the appetite of a starved hyena."[126]

   a. Ehrenreich certainly is not alone in complaining about Wal-Mart. List some of those criticisms.

   b. Explain how a capitalist like Pipes would respond to the Wal-Mart critique.

7. We often read that many college professors actively criticize capitalism and support welfare state principles.

   a. Has that been your experience? Explain.

   b. If that assessment is accurate, how do you account for the leftist inclinations among intellectuals?

8. As noted in the readings, privatization is enjoying immense popularity.

   a. Make the arguments for and against turning our prisons and jails over to private enterprise.

   b. Would you favor a penal system operated for profit? Explain.

9. If we are fundamentally selfish, must we embrace capitalism as the most accurate and, therefore, most efficient expression of human nature? Explain.

10. According to *The New York Times*, in 2007 for the first time in American history, more than one in 100 American adults (over 2.3 million Americans) were behind bars. One in 36 Hispanic adults, one in 15 black adults, and one in nine black men between the ages of 20 and 34 were behind bars in 2006. According to FBI data, violent crime rates have fallen by about 25 percent in the past 20 years.[127]

    a. In your opinion, does our free market approach to life produce greater levels of crime than would be the case in a more cooperative economic system? Explain.

    b. Does our justice system favor rich, white people over poor people of color? Explain.

11. Is capitalism a necessary condition for successful democracy? Or, put another way, in a democracy will increasing state control necessarily result in the destruction of that democracy? Explain.

12. Commentator Thomas Friedman reflects on the Islamic terrorists' hatred for America:

    > Their constant refrain is that America is a country with wealth and power but "no values." The Islamic terrorists think our wealth and power is unrelated to anything in the soul of this country. . . . Of course, what this view of America completely misses is that American power and wealth flow directly from a deep spiritual source—a spirit of respect for the individual, a spirit of tolerance for differences of faith or politics, a respect for freedom of thought as the necessary foundation for all creativity, and a spirit of unity that encompasses all kinds of differences. Only a society with a deep spiritual energy, that welcomes immigrants and worships freedom, could constantly renew itself and its sources of power and wealth.[128]

    * * * * *

    a. Do you agree that the "spiritual source" Friedman cites is the foundation for American success? Explain.

    b. Is America without a meaningful "soul"? Explain.

13. Socialist Michael Harrington argued for life "freed of the curse of money":

    > [A]s long as access to goods and pleasures is rationed according to the possession of money, there is a pervasive venality, an invitation to miserliness and hostility to one's neighbor.[129]

    Should we strive to make more goods and services "free?" Raise the competing arguments.

14. The intellectual Adolph Berle once said, "A day may come when national glory and prestige, perhaps even national safety, are best established by a country's being the most beautiful, the best socially organized, or culturally the most advanced in the world."[130]

    a. Is government intervention necessary to achieving Berle's goal? Explain.
    b. If faced with a choice, would most Americans opt for Berle's model or for a nation preeminent in consumer goods, sports, and general comfort? Explain.

15. Edward Luttwak, in his book, *Turbo Capitalism,* says it is dangerous for the United States to export its mostly unregulated capitalism around the world because many other nations do not have firmly in place two central forces that balance capitalist power in the United States.

    a. What are those two forces?
    b. Do you agree with Luttwak that many other nations are not ready to fully embrace our free market system? Explain.

16. Benjamin Barber, writing in *The Atlantic,* saw two possible political futures, which he labelled the "forces of Jihad" and the "forces of McWorld":

    The first is a retribalization of large swaths of humankind by war and bloodshed . . . culture is pitted against culture, people against people, tribe against tribe—a Jihad in the name of a hundred narrowly conceived faiths against every kind of interdependence. . . . The second is being borne in on us by the onrush of economic and ecological forces that demand integration and uniformity and that mesmerize the world with fast music, fast computers, and fast food—with MTV, Macintosh, and McDonald's pressing nations into one commercially homogeneous global network: One McWorld tied together by technology, ecology, communications, and commerce.[131]

    a. Do either of these scenarios make sense to you? Explain.
    b. Which would you prefer? Explain.

17. Critics argue that socialism requires a uniformity, a "sameness" that would destroy the individuality Americans prize.

    a. Are Americans notably independent and individualistic? Explain.
    b. Explore the argument that socialism would actually enhance meaningful individualism.

18. Hilda Scott wrote a book to which she affixed the provocative title *Does Socialism Liberate Women?*

    a. Answer her question. Explain.
    b. Are minority oppression and oppression of women inevitable by-products of capitalism? Explain.

19. In Wisconsin, members of the Old Order Amish religion declined to formally educate their children beyond the eighth grade. The U.S. Supreme Court held that their First Amendment right to freedom of religion was violated by the Wisconsin compulsory education statute, which required school attendance until the age of 16. Chief Justice Burger explained:

    They object to the high school, and higher education generally, because the values they teach are in marked variance with Amish values and the Amish way of life; they view secondary school education as an impermissible exposure of their children to a "worldly" influence in conflict with their beliefs. The high school tends to emphasize intellectual and scientific accomplishments, self-distinction, competitiveness, worldly success, and social life with other students. Amish society emphasizes informal learning-through-doing; a life of "goodness," rather than a life of intellect; wisdom, rather than technical knowledge; community welfare, rather than competition; and separation from, rather than integration with, contemporary worldly society.[132]

   a. Have the Amish taken the course we should all follow? Explain.
   b. Could we do so? Explain.

20. Distinguished economist Gary Becker argued for a free market approach to America's immigration difficulties:

   In a market economy, the way to deal with excess demand for a product or service is to raise the price. This reduces the demand and stimulates the supply. I suggest that the United States adopt a similar approach to help solve its immigration problems. Under my proposal, anyone willing to pay a specified price could enter the United States immediately.[133]

   Comment.

21. Management scholars Rabindra Kanungo and Jay Conger remark that "'Altruism' is a word rarely associated with the world of business," but they ask, "Does altruism have a place in our business lives? And does it make good economic sense?"[134] Answer their questions.

Notes

1. Francis Fukuyama, "Are We at the End of History?" *Fortune,* January 15, 1990, p. 75.
2. Henry Mintzberg, "Managing Government—Governing Management," *Harvard Business Review* 74, no. 3 (May–June 1996), p. 75.
3. Robert Heilbroner, "Warp-Speed Capitalism," *Los Angeles Times Book Review,* February 8, 1998, p. 5.
4. Editorial, "The Manchurian Multinational," *The Wall Street Journal,* August 20, 2004, p. A12.
5. "Covenanting on a Matter of Life and Death," October 7, 2004 [**http://warc.jalb.de/warcajsp/ side.jsp?news_id=159navi=1**].
6. Benjamin R. Barber, *Consumed: How Markets Corrupt Children, Infantilize Adults, and Swallow Citizens Whole* (New York: W.W. Norton & Company, 2007).
7. Rod Dreher, "Big Business Can Be as Dangerous a Threat as Big Government," *The Waterloo/Cedar Falls Courier,* July 23, 2007, p. A 6
8. Ibid.
9. See Ronald Inglehart, "Globalization and Postmodern Values," *The Washington Quarterly* 23, no. 1 (2000), p. 215.
10. "20 Nation Poll Finds Strong Global Consensus: Support for Free Market System, but Also More Regulation of Large Companies," *World Public Opinion.org* [**http://www.worldpublicopinion. org/pipa/articles.btglobalizationtradea/154.php?nid=&id=&pnt=154&lb=btgl**].
11. Ibid.
12. Dean Kuipers, "The Rise of the New Global 'Empire,'" *Los Angeles Times,* October 1, 2001, Part 5, p. 1.

13. "Zogby Poll: *Atlas Shrugged* by Ayn Rand Read by 8.1 Percent," *PRWeb,* October 17, 2007 [**http://www.prweb.com/releases/1969/12/prweb561836.htm?tag=poll**].

14. "It'll Be a Good Day for Gwyneth," *Des Moines Register,* September 29, 2004, p. 2A.

15. Editorial, "Tag—You're Illegal," *Los Angeles Times,* October 28, 2006 [**http://www.latimes.com/news/opinion/la-ed-tag28oct28,0,59791.story?coll=la=opinion-leftrail**].

16. Robert Lee Hotz, "Across the U.S., Public Parks Are Landing Private Operators," *The Los Angeles Times,* February 11, 2007 [**http://www.latimes.com/news/nationworld/nation/la-na-parks11feb11,0,3215039.story?track=tottext**].

17. "Pay the Poor for Good Behavior?" *The Christian Science Monitor* [**http://www.csmonitor.com/2007/0524/p08s01-comv.html**].

18. Bob Herbert, "Fantasies, Well Meant," September 11, 2007 [**http://select.nytimes.com/2007/09/11/opinion/11herbert.html?_r=1&ref=opinion&oref=slogin**].

19. Laura Meckler, "Kidney Shortage Inspires a Radical Idea: Organ Sales," *The Wall Street Journal,* November 13, 2007, p. A1.

20. Stephanie Coontz, "Taking Marriage Private," *The New York Times,* November 26, 2006 [**http://www.nytimes.com/2007/11/26/opinion/26coontz.html**].

21. Laura Meckler, "Making Public Highways Private," *The Wall Street Journal,* April 18, 2006, p. A4.

22. Emily Thornton, "Roads to Riches," *BusinessWeek,* May 7, 2007, p. 50.

23. Ibid.

24. Kerry Capell, "The Trouble with London's Traffic Tolls," *BusinessWeek,* May 7, 2007, p. 56.

25. Conor Dougherty, "The Parking Fix," *The Wall Street Journal,* February 3-4, 2007, p. P1.

26. Lisa Rein, "Off-Peak Laundry? Pricing Power by the Hour," *Washington Post,* December 12, 2007, p. A01.

27. Editorial, "City-Owned Golf Courses Cannot Be Sacred Cows," *Waterloo/Cedar Falls Courier,* July 13, 2003, p. C7.

28. Ibid.

29. Ibid.

30. Ibid.

31. Editorial, "Reining in Charter Schools," *The New York Times,* May 10, 2006 [**http://www.nytimes.com/2006/05/10/opinion/10wed1.html**].

32. Zachary M. Seward, "Long-Delayed Education Study Casts Doubt on Value of Vouchers," *The Wall Street Journal,* July 15–16, 2006, p. A5.

33. *Bloomberg News,* "Study Disputes Philadelphia School Changes," *The Washington Post,* February 2, 2007, p. A02.

34. Ibid.

35. Zahid Hussain, "Pakistan's Privatization Push Revs Up," *The Wall Street Journal,* April 17, 2006, p. A6.

36. Mike Esterl, "Great Expectations for Private Water Fail to Pan Out," *The Wall Street Journal,* June 26, 2006, p. A1.

37. Ibid.

38. Ibid.

39. Mike Hudson, "Misconduct Taints the Water in Some Privatized Systems," *Los Angeles Times,* May 29, 2006 [**http://www.latimes.com/news/local/la-me-privatewater29may29,0,770571.story?track=tottext**].

40. David Wessel and John Harwood, "Capitalism Is Giddy with Triumph; Is It Possible to Overdo It?" *The Wall Street Journal,* May 14, 1998, p. A1.

41. Geoffrey York, "The Great Leader Peddles a Limited Brand of Capitalism to His Impoverished People," *The Globe and Mail (Canada),* September 4, 2007, p. A1.

42. Henry Myers, "His Statutes Topple, His Shadow *Persists*: Marx Can't Be Ignored," *The Wall Street Journal,* November 25, 1991, p. A1.

43. Elements of this list are drawn from Agnes Heller and Ferenc Feher, "Does Socialism Have a Future?" *Dissent,* Summer 1989, p. 371.

44. Ted Conover, "Capitalist Roaders," *The New York Times Magazine,* July 2, 2006 [**http://www.nytimes.com/2006/07/02/magazine/02china.html?pagewanted=1&_r=1**].

45. Associated Press, "China Plans Middle-Class Boom by 2020," *Waterloo/Cedar Falls Courier,* December 26, 2007, p. C4.

46. Ibid.

47. Don Lee, "China to Join Top 3 Economies," *Los Angeles Times,* July 20, 2007 [**http://www.latimes.com/news/la-fi-chinaecon20july20,0,2306336.story?coll=la-tot-topstories&track=ntottext**].

48. Central Intelligence Agency, *The World Factbook, 2008* [**https://www.cia.gov/library/publications/the-world-factbook**].

49. Pete Engardio, Dexter Roberts, Frederik Balfour, and Bruce Einhorn, "Broken China," *BusinessWeek,* July 23, 2007, p. 39.

50. Ibid.

51. Robert Samuelson, "China's Trade Time Bomb," *Washington Post,* May 9, 2007, p. A17.

52. Jason Dean, "How Capitalist Transformation Exposes Holes in China's Government," *The Wall Street Journal,* December 18, 2006, p. A2.

53. "China's Rapid Changes Bring High Suicide Rates," *Waterloo/Cedar Falls Courier,* October 27, 2005, p. B1.

54. Ibid.

55. Maureen Fan, "Chinese Slough Off Old Barriers to Divorce," *Washington Post,* April 7, 2007, p. A01.

56. David Wallechinsky, "The World's 10 Worst Dictators," *Parade,* February 22, 2004, p.5.

57. Joseph Kahn, "China's Leader Closes Door to Reform," *New York Times,* October 16, 2007 [**http://www.nytimes.com/2007/10/16/world/asia/16china.html**].

58. Mitchell Landsberg, "Marx Loses Currency in New China," *Los Angeles Times,* June 26, 2007 [**http://www.latimes.com/news/la-fg-marx26jun26,0,4069827.story?coll=la-tot-topstories&track=ntottext**].

59. Maureen Fan, "Confucius Making a Comeback in Money-Driven Modern China," *Washington Post,* July 24, 2007, p. A01.

60. Melanie Stetson Freeman, "In Moscow, Capitalism Now in Full Fashion," *The Christian Science Monitor,* February 21, 2008 [**http://www.csmonitor.com/2008/0221/p13s01-woeu.html**].

61. Jason Bush, "Russia: How Long Can the Fun Last?" *BusinessWeek,* December 18, 2006, p. 50.

62. Ibid.

63. Stephen Sestanovich, "Russia by the Numbers," *The Wall Street Journal,* December 17, 2007, p. A21.

64. Bush, "Russia: How Long Can the Fun Last?," p. 50.

65. Jason Bush, "Russia's Grand Plan to Restore Its Glory," *BusinessWeek,* September 18, 2006, p. 45.

66. Stephen Kotkin, "Now Comes the Tough Part in Russia," *The New York Times,* March 2, 2008 [**http://www.nytimes.com/2008/03/02/business/worldbusiness/02shelf.html?th&emc=th**].

67. David Cay Johnston, "Taxes in Developed Nations Reach 36% of Gross Domestic Product," *The New York Times,* October 18, 2007 [**http://www.nytimes.com/2007/10/18/business/worldbusiness/18tax.html**].

68. Ibid.

69. Chris Atkins and Scott A. Hodge, "Congress Finally Considers Lower Corporate Tax Rate but Underestimates International Tax Competition," The Tax Foundation, *Fiscal Fact No. 108,* October 25, 2007 [**http://www.taxfoundation.org/research/show/22698.html**].

70. Roger Cohen "The Nordic Option," *The New York Times,* September 17, 2007 [**http://select.nytimes.com/2007/09/17/opinion/17cohen.html?_r=1&oref=slogin**].

71. Ibid.

72. Ibid.

73. Jeffrey Sachs, *Scientific American* 295, Issue 5 (November 2006), p. 42.

74. Ibid.

75. Ibid.

76. Steven Hilll, "5 Myths about Sick Old Europe," *The Washington Post,* October 7, 2007, p. B03.

77. Roger Cohen, "For Europe, A Moment to Ponder," *The New York Times,* March 25, 2007, sec. 4, p. 1.

78. Jeremy Rifkin, "Why the European Dream Is Worth Saving," *SpiegelOnline,* July 28, 2005 [**http://www.spiegel.de/international/0,1518,druck-366940,00.html**].

79. Adrian Karatnycky quoting Soros in "The Merits of the Market, the Perils of 'Market Fundamentalism,'" *The Wall Street Journal,* January 9, 2001, p. A20.

80. Ibid.

81. Joanne Barkan, "Not Yet in Paradise, But. . . ," *Dissent,* Spring 1989, pp. 147, 150.

82. R. W. Apple, Jr., "Swedes Feel They're Lumped Together in 'National Blandness,'" *Lexington Leader,* July 26, 1978, p. A15.

83. United Nations Human Development Report 2007/2008 [**http://hdr.undp.org/en/reports/global/hdr2007-2008**].

84. United Nations Human Development Report 2006 [**http://hdr.undp.org/en/reports/global/hdr2006/**].

85. Central Intelligence Agency, *The World Factbook* [**https://www.cia.gov/library/publications/the-world-factbook**].

86. Associated Press, "Americans Work Longer, Produce More Than Rest of World," *Waterloo/Cedar Falls Courier,* September 3, 2007, p. C3.

87. Central Intelligence Agency, *The World Factbook* [**https://www.cia.gov/library/publications/the-world-factbook**].

88. Ibid.

89. Jane Norman, "Vilsack, Clinton Unveil $220 Billion College Plan," *The Des Moines Register,* July 20, 2006, p. 2B.

90. Blaine Harden, "Numbers Drop for the Married with Children," *Washington Post,* March 4, 2007, p. A03.

91. Ibid.

92. Bob Herbert, "The Millions Left Out," *The New York Times,* May 12, 2007 [**http://select.nytimes.com/2007/05/12/opinion/12herbert.html?_r=1&oref=slogin**].

93. "America's Children: Key National Indicators of Well-Being, 2007" [**http://www.childstats. gov/AMERICASCHILDREN/eco1.asp**].

94. UNICEF, "Child Poverty in Perspective: An Overview of Child Well-Being in Rich Countries," *Innocenti Report Card 7,* 2007, UNICEF Innocenti Research Centre, Florence [**http://www.unicef.org/media/files/ChildPovertyReport.pdf**].

95. Paul Krugman, "Poverty Is Poison," *The New York Times,* February 18, 2008 [**http://www.nytimes.com/2008/02/18/opinion/18krugman.html?em**].

96. Michelle Conlin and Aaron Bernstein, "Working . . . and Poor," *BusinessWeek/online,* May 31, 2004 [**http://www.businessweek.com/print/magazine/content/04_22/b3885 . . .**].

97. Ibid.

98. Ibid.

99. Carla K. Johnson and Mike Stobbe, "Study Says We Aren't as Healthy as British," *The Des Moines Register,* May 3, 2006, p. 7A.

100. Ibid.

101. Editorial, "World's Best Medical Care?" *The New York Times* [**http://www.nytimes.com/ 2007/08/12/opinion/12sun1.html**].

102. N.C. Aizenman and Christopher Lee, "U.S. Poverty Rate Drops; Ranks of Uninsured Grow," *Washington Post,* August 29, 2007, p. A03.

103. Editorial, "Charity Begins in Washington," *The New York Times,* January 22, 2008 [**http://www.nytimes.com/2008/01/22/opinion/22tue4.html?_r=2&ref=opinion&oref= slogin&oref=slogin**].

104. Greg Ip, "Income-Inequality Gap Widens," *The Wall Street Journal,* October 12, 2007, p. A2.

105. David Cay Johnston, "Income Gap Is Widening, Data Shows," *The New York Times,* March 29, 2007 [**http://www.nytimes.com/2007/03/29/business/29tax.html**].

106. Robert B. Reich, "CEOs Deserve Their Pay," *The Wall Street Journal,* September 14, 2007, p. A13.

107. Daniel Gross, "Thy Neighbor's Stash," *The New York Times,* August 5, 2007 [**http://www.nytimes.com/2007/08/05/books/review/Gross-t.html?ex=1343880000 &en=d6ed4c8d594254bd&ei=5124&partner=permalink&exprod=permalink**].

108. Erik Eckholm, "Higher Education Gap May Slow Economic Mobility," *The New York Times,* February 20, 2008 [**http://www.nytimes.com/2008/02/20/us/20mobility.html?th=&emc=th**].

109. David Wessel, "As Rich-Poor Gap Widens in the U.S., Class Mobility Stalls," *The Wall Street Journal,* May 13, 2005, p. A1.

110. Kathleen Vohs, Nicole L. Mead, and Miranda R. Goode, "The Psychological Consequences of Money," *Science* 314, no. 5802 (November 17, 2006), p. 1154.

111. Elizabeth W. Dunn, Lara B. Aknin, Michael I. Norton, "Spending Money on Others Promotes Happiness," *Science* 319, no. 5870 (March 21, 2008), p. 1687.

112. "Do Co-Workers Engage or Estrange after Hours," University of Michigan [**http://www. bus.umich.edu/NewsRoom/ArticleDisplay.asp?news_id=11931**].

113. Shankar Vedantam, "Social Isolation Growing in U.S., Study Says," *Washington Post,* June 23, 2006, p. A03.

114. Robert Putnam, *Bowling Alone* (New York: Simon& Schuster, 2000).

115. For a critique of Putnam's declining social capital research, see Garry Wills, "Putnam's America," *The American Prospect,* November 30, 2002 [**http://www.prospect.org/cs/ articles?article=putnams_america**].

116. For a commentary on Putnam's diversity research, see Gregory Rodriguez, "Diversity May Not Be the Answer," *Los Angeles Times,* August 13, 2007 [**http://www.latimes.com/news/ opinion/la-oe-rodriguez13aug13,0,3984088.column?coll=la-tot-opinion&track=ntottext**].

117. Wessel and Harwood, "Capitalism Is Giddy with Triumph," p. A1.

118. Associated Press, "A Threat to Castro," *Des Moines Register,* August 30, 1994, p. 8A.

119. Jeremy Rifkind, *The European Dream* (New York: Tarcher/Penguin, 2004).

120. Jeremy Rifkin, "Whose Vision Will Prevail?" *Des Moines Register,* December 4, 2004, p. 9A.

121. Robert A. Guth, "Bill Gates Issues Call for Kinder Capitalism," *The Wall Street Journal,* January 24, 2008, p. A1.

122. Ibid.

123. Lauren Soth, "Seek Better Care of People and Earth," *Des Moines Register,* April 24, 1993, p. 5A.

124. Robert Samuelson, "Economics Made Easy," *Newsweek,* Novermber 27, 1989, p.64.

125. Carla McClain, "Dr. Spock: Restore the Family," *Des Moines Register,* November 7, 1993, p. 3E.

126. Sally Pipes, "Wal-Mart's Success Makes It Unfair Target," *Des Moines Register,* August 7, 2004, p. 17A.

127. Adam Liptak, ""1 in 100 U.S. Adults Behind Bars, New Study Says," *The New York Times,* February 28, 2008 [**http://www.nytimes.com/2008/02/28/us/28cnd-prison.html?em&ex =1204434000&en=f278697addfa4b1**].

128. Thomas L. Friedman, "Eastern Middle School," *New York Times on the Web,* October 2, 2001.

129. Michael Harrington, "Why We Need Socialism in America," *Dissent,* May—June 1970, pp. 240, 286.

130 Adolph Berle, *Power* (New York: Harcourt Brace Jovanovich, 1969), pp. 258–59.

131. Benjamin Barber, "Jihad v. McWorld," *The Atlantic* 269, no. 3 (March 1992), p. 53.

132. *Wisconsin v. Yoder,* 406 U.S. 205, 210–11 (1972).

133. Gary Becker, "Why Not Let Immigrants Pay for Speedy Entry?" *BusinessWeek,* March 2, 1987, p. 20.

134. Rabindra Kanungo and Jay Conger, "Promoting Altruism as a Corporate Goal," *The Academy of Management Executive* 8, no. 3 (August 1993), p. 37.

CHAPTER TWO

Business Ethics

At the end of this chapter, students will be able to:

1. Describe in broad terms the scandals that have tarnished the business community in recent years.

2. Describe the role of ethics in business decision making.

3. Discuss the leading ethical decision-making systems.

4. Discuss America's current moral climate.

5. Distinguish between teleological and deontological ethical systems.

6. Distinguish utilitarianism and formalism.

7. Describe some of the forces that encourage unethical behavior in the workplace.

8. Explain the general purpose of ethics codes in the workplace.

9. Explain the general requirements of the Foreign Corrupt Practices Act.

10. Discuss some of the risks and rewards of whistle blowing.

Part One—Introduction to Ethics

Can we count on self-regulation (ethics) as a useful means of controlling managerial/corporate behavior? Put another way, can we count on the free market as discussed in Chapter 1, along with managerial and corporate ethics to guide business conduct such that government regulation (law) can be significantly reduced?

This chapter will examine the ethical climate of business and the role of ethics in business decision making. Our goal here is not to *teach morality* but to sensitize the reader to the vital role honor plays in building a sound career and a responsible life that each manager can reflect upon with pride and self-respect.

PRACTICING ETHICS Baseball Bats Encourage Subprime Loan Approvals

Maggie Hardiman cringed as she heard the salesmen knocking the sides of desks with a baseball bat as they walked through her office. *Bang! Bang* "'You cut my [expletive] deal!'" she recalls one man yelling at her. "'You can't do that.'" *Bang!* The bat whacked the top of her desk.[1]

Hardiman was an appraiser for New Century Financial in 2004 and 2005. Her job was to weed out bad mortgage applications. She says most of the applications she reviewed had problems, but if she turned them down, "all hell would break loose" and "her bosses often overruled her and found another appraiser to sign off on it." She says the pressure to approve loans was immense: "The stress in the place was ungodly. It was like selling your soul." Hardiman says she was fired for refusing to approve weak loans.[2]

New Century was the nation's leading specialized subprime mortgage lender in 2006 with $51.6 billion in loans. To achieve that volume, New Century and others often sold subprime mortgages with "teaser" adjustable rates to Americans with poor credit. Then when housing values began to fall and adjustable rates went up, many new homeowners were unable to make their payments. New Century filed for bankruptcy protection in 2007, laid off over 5,000 employees, and admitted it underreported the number of bad loans it had made.[3]

Question

Do you think the pressure to produce—to approve weak loan applications in this instance—that Maggie Hardiman says she faced, is routine in American business practice, or was this episode an exception to the norm? Explain.

Subprime Mortgages: A New Corporate Scandal? Corporate misconduct has been a staple of the news in this 21st century. The current crisis in the subprime mortgage market may be the latest such disgrace. The facts are only beginning to emerge at this writing in 2008, but experts estimate that anywhere from $150 to $400 billion in losses will result from imprudent and sometimes fraudulent transactions produced, in part, by the kind of pressure that Maggie Hardiman faced. Of course, no law is broken when lenders merely show poor judgment or borrowers are unable to pay, but the current crisis allegedly involves intentionally fraudulent schemes. Litigation likely will reach across continents and drag on for years. While lawsuits will involve ordinary Americans claiming they were deceived by lenders, they will also involve the biggest banks, mortgage insurers, mortgage brokers, and more pointing powerful fingers at each other. Governments likewise are getting involved. Cleveland, Ohio, for example, is suing 21 of the nation's largest financial firms (Wells Fargo, Merrill Lynch, et al.) accusing them of knowingly flooding the local housing market with subprime loans issued to borrowers who could not reasonably be expected to repay. The result was 14,000 foreclosures in two years such that, according to the lawsuit, Cleveland as a city has been burdened with enormous additional expense in maintaining thousands of boarded-up homes and dealing with a new wave of crime.[4] The legal issues are many, but among the questions are whether lenders failed to reveal known risks to borrowers and investors and whether lenders were too aggressively "pushing" loans to borrowers.

The extent of criminal and unethical behavior, if any, in this latest meltdown will be clearer over time, but dubious lending practices are part of a recurring pattern in recent decades of corporations contorting ethical and legal standards. Today's subprime scandal is reminiscent of the savings and loan crisis of the 1980s when $150 billion evaporated, in part because of criminal behavior. More recently the corporate greed of the Enron era has played out on worldwide televisions as some of the great titans of American commerce have been shuffled off to prison. Even Martha Stewart, that paragon of propriety in the home, spent five months in federal prison for lying to the government regarding insider trading allegations.

> **Even Martha Stewart spent five months in federal prison**

Certainly we can be encouraged that the legal system has addressed these wrongs. From 2002 through 2006, corporate fraud prosecutions resulted in more than 1,000 convictions and billions of dollars in penalties.[5] Some executives were found guilty, in effect, of looting corporate funds for personal use:

> There was Tyco Chief Executive Officer [Dennis] Kozlowski with the infamous $2 million birthday bash for his wife on Sardinia, featuring an ice sculpture of Michelangelo's David that spewed vodka. There was Adelphia CEO John Rigas and his two sons who treated the company as their personal piggy bank to fund dozens of vacation homes, the Buffalo Sabres hockey team and their own golf course.[6]

Ken Lay, founder of energy-trading giant, Enron, and Jeff Skilling, Enron CEO, were convicted of conspiracy and fraud in leading Enron from its status as the nation's seventh-most-valuable company to bankruptcy as they profited immensely from its fraudulently inflated stock.

Kozlowski, Rigas, and Skilling, along with other executives, are in jail at this writing, some of them with appeals pending. Skilling, for example, was sentenced to more than 24 years in prison. Most of Skilling's remaining assets, about $45 million, will go to a fund for Enron victims. The total loss in the Enron collapse, however, is an estimated $60 billion in Enron stock, $2 billion in employee pension funds, and thousands of jobs.[7] Skilling's legal bill was expected to be at least $70 million.[8] Lay died of a heart attack while awaiting sentencing. Since his death precluded an appeal, his conviction was vacated. [For a comprehensive archive of the Enron story, see **http://archive.wn.com/2007/12/23/1400/enronfiles**]

> **Skilling's legal bill was expected to be at least $70 million**

Enron, Tyco, and the like are, of course, the disturbing exceptions in business practice. One thousand convictions, as noted above, among tens of millions of businesspersons cannot be considered an epidemic. Obviously, the problems are serious, but former General Electric CEO Jack Welch and his wife Suzy remind us that the business community is the source of much of America's greatness:

> Business is a huge source of vitality in the world and a noble enterprise. Thriving, decent companies are everywhere, and they should be celebrated. They create jobs and opportunities, provide revenue for government, and are the foundation of a free and democratic society. . . .[9]

Practicing Ethics   By the Numbers

Joe Nacchio, CEO of Qwest Communications, reportedly gathered his employees in January 2000 to convey a clear message about what mattered at Qwest. Not customers, products, or employees, he told them. Numbers—money—was what mattered at Qwest:

> It's more important than any individual product, it's more important than any individual philosophy, it's more important than any individual cultural change. We stop everything else when we don't make the numbers.[10]

Federal Securities and Exchange Commission lawyers say that Nacchio and other company bosses created a "culture of fear" and a "pressure-cooker" atmosphere. In July 2007, Nacchio was sentenced to six years in federal prison for insider trading (see Chapter 9) and was ordered to pay $71 million.[11] On appeal, however, Nacchio was granted a new trial, which is expected in 2009.

Questions

1. If you were running a company would the "numbers" be your primary concern, as they reportedly were for Nacchio? Explain.

2. WorldBlu, a business "specializing in organizational democracy," argues that: "Businesses that embrace a democratic style are building healthier workplaces—and better bottom lines." WorldBlu asks us to imagine companies that allow employees to vote on CEO performance, rotate leadership roles, and let employees determine their work projects.

   a. Would you want to work in a democratic workplace? Explain.

   b. Would democracy in the workplace produce enhanced ethical behavior? Explain.

Ethics Survey

The Ethics Officer Association and the Ethical Leadership Group sampled a cross-section of workers at large companies nationwide. How would you respond?
1. "Is it wrong to use company e-mail for personal reasons?"
2. "Is it wrong to play computer games on office equipment during the workday?"
3. "Is it OK to take a $100 holiday food basket?"
4. "Due to on-the-job pressure, have you ever abused or lied about sick days?"

Source: *"The Wall Street Journal* Workplace-Ethics Quiz," *The Wall Street Journal,* October 21, 1999, p. B1.

Ethics Theories

Ethics, of course, involves judgments as to good and bad, right and wrong, and what ought to be. *Business ethics* refers to the measurement of business behavior based on standards of right and wrong, rather than relying entirely on principles of accounting and management. (In this discussion, the word *morals* will be used interchangeably with the word *ethics.* Distinctions certainly are drawn between the two, but those distinctions are not vital for our purposes.)

Finding and following the moral course is not easy for any of us, but the difficulty may be particularly acute for the businessperson. The bottom line often is unforgiving. Hence the pressure to produce is intense, and the temptation to cheat may be great. Although the law provides useful guideposts for minimum comportment, clear moral guidelines frequently do not exist. Therefore, when the businessperson faces a difficult decision, a common tactic is simply to do what he or she takes to be correct at any given moment. Indeed, in one survey of ethical views in business, 50 percent of the respondents indicated that the word *ethical* meant "what my feelings tell me is right."[12]

Philosophers have provided powerful intellectual support for that approach. Existentialists, led by the famed Jean-Paul Sartre, believe standards of conduct cannot be rationally justified and no actions are inherently right or wrong. Thus each person may reach his or her own choice about ethical principles. That view finds its roots in the notion that humans are only what we will ourselves to be. If God does not exist, there can be no human nature, because there is no one to conceive that nature.

| Existence precedes essence |

In Sartre's famous interpretation, existence precedes essence. First humans exist; then we individually define what we are—our essence. Therefore, each of us is free, with no rules to turn to for guidance. Just as we all choose our own natures, so must we choose our own ethical precepts. Moral responsibility belongs to each of us individually.

PRACTICING ETHICS   Mike Ditka: "Wrong Is Wrong"

Outspoken former Chicago Bears head coach Mike Ditka clearly rejected the moral ambiguity that he sees in contemporary life. In announcing that he would not seek the Republican nomination for the 2004 U.S. Senate race in Illinois, Ditka responded to a question about gay marriage:

> What's the matter with right and wrong? Talk about right and wrong. It's either right or wrong. There's no in-between. And I'm not going to change, and you're not going to change me, no matter if some judge in Massachusetts says it's right. It's not right. Wrong is wrong.

Questions

1. *a.* Is your moral view as clear as Mike Ditka's? Explain.
   b. Would America be a stronger, healthier nation if we all embraced Mike Ditka's view of right and wrong? Explain.
2. Could gay marriage constitute, at one and the same time, a legally sound but morally improper public policy? Explain.

Source: Mike Ditka, "What's the Matter with Right and Wrong?" *Waterloo/Cedar Falls Courier*, July 17, 2004, p. B1.

Universal Truths?

Have we then no rules or universal standards by which to distinguish right from wrong? Have we no absolutes? Philosophers seek to provide guidance beyond the uncertainties of ethical relativism. We will survey two ethical perspectives, teleology and deontology, which form the core of ethical analysis. Before proceeding to those theories, we will note the important role of religion in ethics and take a brief look at two additional formulations—libertarianism and virtue ethics—that have been increasingly influential in contemporary moral analysis.

1. **Religion.** Judeo–Christian beliefs, Islam, Confucianism, Buddhism, and other faiths are powerful ethical voices in contemporary life. They often feature efforts such as the Golden Rule to build absolute and universal standards. Scholarly studies indicate that most American managers believe in the Golden Rule and take it to be their most meaningful moral guidepost. From a religious point of view, the deity's laws are absolutes that must shape the whole of one's life, including work. Faith, rather than reason, intuition, or secular knowledge, provides the foundation for a moral life built on religion. [For worldwide coverage of ethics issues, see "Religion & Ethics" at **http://www.bbc. co.uk/religion/ethics**]

Religion at Work

A 2004 Gallup Poll reported that 84 percent of American adults believe religion is either "very" or "fairly" important in their lives. Business scholars and reporters note a renewed interest in religion and spirituality in the workplace. In one survey, 40 percent of those responding to a *Fortune* 1,000 survey felt that "religious principles and values were an integral part of their organization's culture." Scholars Ian Mitroff and Elizabeth Denton undertook a "spiritual audit of corporate America" and concluded that managers desire a way to express their spiritual selves at work and that managers often are unable to bring their "complete selves" to work. They argue that business must acknowledge the soul to maximize performance.

Questions
1. Do you think corporate America must now make room for spirituality and the soul in the workplace to maximize success? Explain.
2. Must we believe in God to be moral? Explain.

Source: The Gallup Poll, May 2–4, 2004 [**www.pollingreport.com/religion.htm.**] Karen C. Cash and George R. Gray, "A Framework for Accommodating Religion and Spirituality in the Workplace," *Academy of Management Executive* 14, no. 3 (2000), p. 124. Ian I. Mitroff and Elizabeth A. Denton, *A Spiritual Audit of Corporate America: A Hard Look at Spirituality, Religion, and Values in the Workplace* (San Francisco: Jossey-Bass, 1999).

---

2. **Libertarianism.** Contemporary philosopher Robert Nozick built an ethical theory rooted in personal liberty. For him, morality coincided with the maximization of personal freedom. Justice and fairness, right and wrong are measured not by equality of results (such as wealth) for all, but from ensuring equal opportunity for all to engage in informed choices about their own welfare. Hence Nozick took essentially a free market stance toward ethics.

3. **Virtue ethics.** In recent years, an increasing number of philosophers have argued that the key to good ethics lies not in rules, rights, and responsibilities but in the classic notion of character. As Plato and Aristotle argued, our attention should be given to strategies for encouraging desirable character traits such as honesty, fairness, compassion, and generosity. Aristotle believed that virtue could be taught much as any other skill. Virtue ethics applauds the person who is motivated to do the right thing and who cultivates that motivation in daily conduct. A part of the argument is that such persons are more morally reliable than those who simply follow the rules but fail to inspect, strengthen, and preserve their own personal virtues. The article that follows describes a bar owner in a Des Moines, Iowa, suburb, who decided to do what he apparently thought was the "right thing," the virtuous act. [For an overview of virtue ethics, see **http://plato.stanford.edu/entries/ethics-virtue/**]

READING ▶ # Concerned Owner Closes Bar's Doors

April Goodwin, *Register* Staff Writer

Vieux Carre, the spacious West Des Moines nightclub that pioneered all-you-can-drink specials in the metro area, has closed after the owner had an attack of conscience.

Dick Davis said he had moral concerns with how the bar was being run and had fought with his managers.

"Morally, I just wanted out," he said. "I closed it up."

Davis said he thought some of the promotions, which he did not approve in advance, tarnished his reputation. "That just irritated the hell out of me," he said of the all-you-can-drink special.

Vieux Carre opened last May in a former movie theater that Davis owned.

Davis, 75, said he worried about his customers getting hurt or driving drunk.

"I'm going to sleep so good this weekend," he said Friday. . . .

Donna Mahers of Des Moines was stunned Thursday night—her 21st birthday—to discover that the club was closed. "We pulled in and there were no stinking cars," she said.

Mahers said she had trouble finding anywhere fun to go. "I didn't even puke on my 21st birthday. I wanted to go dancing. I took the whole day off today, thinking I'd have a hangover. It was kind of a waste."

Davis said he plans to reopen the bar, which he said reaped an average of $85,000 in profits monthly, under new management.

Downtown Des Moines bar owner Larry Smithson said Vieux Carre's image was hurt by a radio ad featuring a character who says he got so drunk he didn't remember the night before.

Source: *Des Moines Register,* March 16, 2002, p. 1B. Reprinted by permission.

Questions

1. *a.* Would all "virtuous" persons do as Davis did? Explain.

   b. Would you? Explain.

   c. From a libertarian perspective, would all bar owners be morally required to act as Davis did? Explain.

   d. Does religion provide any guidance for a bar owner in Davis's position? Explain.

2. Are bar owners generally, and Davis particularly, in any way responsible for the values Donna Mahers expressed in discussing her 21st birthday plans and disappointments? Explain.

Teleology or Deontology—An Overview

Teleological ethical systems (often referred to as *consequentialist ethical systems*) are concerned with the consequences of an act rather than the act itself. A teleological view of life concerns itself with ends, goals, and the ultimate good. Duty and obligation are subordinated to the production of what is good or desirable. For the teleologist/consequentialist, the end is primary and that end or result is the measure of the ethical quality of a decision or act.

To the *deontologist,* on the other hand, principle is primary and consequence is secondary or even irrelevant. Maximizing right rather than good is the deontological standard. The deontologist might well refuse to lie even if doing so would maximize good. *Deontology,* derived from the Greek word meaning *duty,* is directed toward what ought to be, toward what is right. Relationships among people are important because they give rise to duties. A father may be morally committed to saving his son from a burning building, rather than saving another person who might well do more total good for society. Similarly, deontology considers motives. For example, why a crime was committed may be more important than the actual consequences of the crime.

The distinction here is critical. Are we to guide our behavior in terms of rational evaluations of the consequences of our acts, or are we to shape our conduct in terms of duty and principle—that which ought to be? Let's take a closer look at *utilitarianism,* the principal teleological ethical theory, and *formalism,* the principal deontological ethical theory.

Teleology

Utilitarianism   In reaching an ethical decision, good is to be weighed against evil. A decision that maximizes the ratio of good over evil for all those concerned is the ethical course. Jeremy Bentham (1748–1832) and John Stuart Mill (1806–1873) were the chief intellectual forces in the development of utilitarianism. Their views and those of other utilitarian philosophers were not entirely consistent. As a result, at least two branches of utilitarianism have developed. According to *act-utilitarianism,* one's goal is to identify the consequences of a particular act to determine whether it is right or wrong. *Rule-utilitarianism* requires one to adhere to all the rules of conduct by which society reaps the greatest value. Thus the rule-utilitarian may be forced to shun a particular act that would result in greater immediate good (punishing a guilty person whose constitutional rights have been violated) in favor of upholding a broader rule that results in the greater total good over time (maintaining constitutional principles by freeing the guilty person). In sum, the principle to be followed for the utilitarian is the greatest good for the greatest number. [For an extensive database exploring utilitarianism, see **http://www.hedweb.com/philsoph/utillink.htm**]

Deontology

Formalism   The German philosopher Immanuel Kant (1724–1804) developed perhaps the most persuasive and fully articulated vision of ethics as measured not by consequences (teleology) but by the rightness of rules. In this formalistic view of ethics, the rightness of an act depends little (or, in Kant's view, not at all) on the results of the act. Kant believed in the key moral concept of "the good will." The moral person is a person of goodwill, and that person renders ethical decisions based on what is right, regardless of the consequences of the decision. Moral worth springs from one's decision to discharge one's duty. Thus the student who refuses to cheat on exams is morally worthy if his or her decision springs from duty, but morally unworthy if the decision is merely one born of self-interest, such as fear of being caught.

How does the person of goodwill know what is right? Here Kant propounded the *categorical imperative,* the notion that every person should act on only those principles that he or she, as a rational person, would prescribe as universal laws to be applied to the whole of humankind. A moral rule is "categorical" rather than "hypothetical" in that its prescriptive force is independent of its consequences. The rule guides us independent of the ends we seek. Kant believed that every rational creature can act according to his or her categorical imperative because all such persons have "autonomous, self-legislating wills" that permit them to formulate and act on their own systems of rules. To Kant, what is right for one is right for all, and each of us can discover that "right" by exercising our rational faculties.

A 50-Year-Old Construction Worker and Hero

Wesley Autry, waiting with his two young daughters in January 2007 at a New York City subway station, saw a man collapse and fall off the passenger platform into the space between the train rails. The headlight of a train appeared. Mr. Autry immediately jumped on top of the fallen man holding him down while the train passed over them, inches above Autry's head. Asked later why he jumped to the rescue, Autry said: "I did what I felt was right."

Question

What form of ethical reasoning did Autry seem to employ in making his courageous decision?

Source: Cara Buckley, "Man Is Rescued by Stranger on Subway Tracks," *nytimes.com,* January 3, 2007 [**http://www.nytimes. com/2007/01/03/nyregion/03life.html**].

Using Utilitarianism and Formalism: Layoffs, Part I

Obviously, ethical theory does not provide magical answers to life's most difficult questions. However, those theories are useful in identifying and sorting the issues that lead to better decision making. Apply those theories to the reading that follows, and think about when layoffs are ethical.

Richard Lorant, Associated Press

As he watched Malden Mills burn, Michael Lavallee was sure the factory where he had worked for 25 years was being reduced, building by building, to a memory. "We just kept staring at the place, saying, 'It's over. It's done. It's gone,'" said Lavallee, an engineer.

*   *   *   *   *

The next morning, [mill owner Aaron] Feuerstein vowed to rebuild Malden Mills Industries without layoffs, embarking on a road that would lift him to national prominence as a symbol of corporate compassion in a seemingly heartless era.

At Malden Mills, Feuerstein appears to be succeeding in his effort to rebuild after the December 11, 1995, fire that threatened 3,100 high-paying manufacturing jobs in this economically depressed region north of Boston. The blaze injured 33 people, 8 of them severely. Six have not yet returned to work, and at least one will never work again.

Feuerstein has said everything about his Jewish upbringing and his 50-year history in the local business told him to rebuild. "It was the right thing to do and there's a moral imperative to do it, irrespective of the consequences," Feuerstein said.

The new plant is scheduled to open in February. Filled with shining machinery, it was designed to boost production of the mill's patented Polartec fabric, which has become the fleece of choice for manufacturers of name-brand winter clothes. All Malden Mills' employees received full pay and benefits for three months after the fire. Since then, 85 percent have returned to work on makeshift production lines located in once and future warehouses. About 400 workers remain idle—a shortcoming Feuerstein regards as a failure—but he pledges to restore those jobs "come hell or high water" within two years.

Feuerstein has spent more than $300 million to build the new plant, replace lost machinery, and cover business losses. Insurers have paid half that amount so far. The rest has come from bank loans and from his family's savings.

After falling off because of the fire, production of Polartec and Polarfleece is back to previous levels. "Unquestionably, in the long run, it will pay dividends," he said.

But while Feuerstein defends his decision to rebuild as a good business move, it originated in the old-fashioned way his family has run the mill since it was founded by his grandfather in 1906. Despite its technical innovations, Malden Mills is in some ways a throwback to the days when a mill was like an extended family, with the owner at its head. Almost all of the many mills in the area have closed, following cheap labor to the South and then overseas.

Whole families in the immigrant-filled neighborhoods of Methuen and nearby Lawrence see the mills as their tickets into the middle class. If their $11-an-hour jobs were to disappear, many would end up with lower-paying service jobs.

If the fire provided Feuerstein with a challenge of the magnitude few business owners face, he also had two key advantages that helped him take the high road and stand by his workers. First, Malden Mills was a profitable company offering a patented product, Polartec, that had carved out a $3 billion market and a loyal customer base. Second, as a privately held company, Malden Mills Industries was free of the pressure to produce short-term profits and satisfy Wall Street analysts faced by publicly traded businesses.

"He's still pretty lonely, but the idea has appeal," said Michael Useem, a professor at the University of Pennsylvania's Wharton School. "The thinking is: employees can be seen as an ultimate competitive advantage. If you treat them well, they'll pay you back in really hard work later on."

Source: Richard Lorant, Associated Press. Reprinted in *The Chicago Tribune,* December 10, 1996, p. 8. Reprinted by permission.

Questions

1. Aaron Feuerstein became something of an overnight national hero by protecting his workers. Feuerstein said, "It was the right thing to do and there's a moral imperative to do it, irrespective of the consequences."

    a. Was Feuerstein employing utilitarian or formalist reasoning? Explain.

    b. In your view, was he correct to say that the consequences, in this instance, did not matter? Explain.

2. Commenting on Feuerstein's approach to his employees' needs, Wharton School professor Michael Useem said, "The thinking is: employees can be seen as an ultimate competitive advantage. If you treat them well, they'll pay you back in really hard work later on."

    a. Was Useem expressing formalist or utilitarian reasoning?

    b. In a 1986 pastoral letter, the U.S. Catholic bishops argued that "every economic decision and institution must be judged in light of whether it protects or undermines the dignity of the human person."[13] Does the thinking summarized by Useem undermine that dignity and as such require rejection under either utilitarian or formalist reasoning? Explain.

3. *a.* Are we in the midst of a "heartless" era as the author suggests? Explain.

b. Are you "heartless"? Explain.

4. If you were a successful entrepreneur with the flexibility of Aaron Feuerstein, would you operate your business like "an extended family"? Explain.

Layoffs, Part II

In November 2001, Malden Mills was forced to enter Chapter 11 bankruptcy proceedings (see Chapter 15) for the purpose of reorganizing its finances under court protection. At the time, Malden Mills was bearing a $140 million debt load. Lenders demanded the bankruptcy action as a condition for extending an additional $20 million to keep the company afloat. In late 2003 Malden Mills emerged from bankruptcy. Creditors controlled the board of directors with Aaron Feuerstein occupying the family's one seat. Malden's precarious financial position was the product of a variety of forces: customers were lost during the rebuilding after the fire, cheaper fleece substitutes entered the market, the company took on substantial debt in rebuilding and in keeping on its employees following the fire, and the company probably overbuilt following the fire. As a result, the Malden Mills workforce shrunk to 1,200 employees. The article that follows contrasts Feuerstein's ethical reasoning with the apparent values of those who built Enron and then led it to bankruptcy in 2001. (Remember that Aaron Feuerstein's Malden Mills was privately held, whereas Kenneth Lay's Enron was a publicly traded company.)

READING ## Tale of Two Bankruptcies

Mary McGrory

In this anxious hour of pink-slip dread, it is restoring to think of Aaron Feuerstein, a Massachusetts manufacturer who prizes his employees and risks profits on their behalf.

The CEO of Malden Mills, located in Lawrence, the 23rd poorest community in the country, stepped clear of the greedy stereotype of his kind in 1995 when, just before Christmas, his factory burned down. Rather than taking the insurance money and retiring or moving the plant to some Third World country, he promptly announced that he would rebuild. He gave bonuses to the help and paid them while they waited for the factory reopening. Last Monday, this paragon of corporate virtue held a rally at the plant he inherited from his father. The idea was to kick off a campaign for Malden Mills' special product, Polartec, a light, warm fabric that is keeping U.S. Marines cozy in the grinding cold of Afghanistan. Sen. John Kerry hailed Malden Mills as a mill with soul and a mill with heart.

Feuerstein has not had all the good fortune he may deserve. Sales dipped, and he recently filed for bankruptcy under Chapter 11 and negotiated a $20 million loan. Feuerstein would have liked the money without the Chapter 11—"I hate to put any stain on our beautiful name"—but he told cheering workers that together they would win.

Columnist Mark Shields was the first to make the striking contrast between Feuerstein and today's most celebrated bankruptcy case, that of Enron, the monstrous Texas energy outfit. Most of its 21,000 workers lost jobs. For 11,000, it was a lump of coal, the loss of life savings invested in Enron stock. Enron employees were urged to buy the stock with their retirement funds, their 401(k)s. When Enron started going south in October, however, the employees were forbidden to sell. Enron CEO Kenneth Lay and his fellow executives were exempt from the lockdown and sold, often at tremendous profits.

Stricken ex-Enron workers told the Senate Commerce Committee of being seduced, betrayed, and abandoned by their bosses. Enron lied about earnings, cooked its books, and left its employees in the lurch, while its top brass made out like bandits.

Janice Farmer, a Florida widow, had her daughter with her to help her through her testimony. A year ago, she retired with $700,000 in Enron stock. Today it is worth $4,000. When she saw that Enron was ailing, she tried to sell. She was locked out.

If Lay is sorry about all this, he hasn't said so.* Acting committee chairman Byron Dorgan, D-N.D., said Lay had been invited to testify but declined and promised to come later. Lay is a good friend to the president and is his biggest contributor. White House strategist Karl Rove owned a big bloc of Enron stock, and when Vice President Cheney was devising his strange energy plan, Lay was consulted. There are other Texas ties: Wendy Gramm, wife of Sen. Phil Gramm, is a member of the Enron board and chairman of the auditing committee.

Where Feuerstein and Lay differed most sharply was on devotion to the bottom line. To Lay, we are almost forced to conclude, it was paramount; Feuerstein put the excellence of his product above the entries in his ledgers. To Lay, employees were as disposable as Kleenex; Feuerstein thinks they are partners.

Where did Feuerstein get his extraordinary ideas about worker–management relations? "At my father's table. We all had to be there. No pizza in the kitchen. I was 7 years old when I heard my father tell a story I never forgot."

Aaron's father had watched his father, who founded the factory, go around at the end of the day and give money to every one of his workers. Aaron's father explained to his father, a Hungarian immigrant, that this was not the American way. Aaron's grandfather screamed at Aaron's father that it was against the Torah to do it any other way.

Young Aaron consulted his rabbi, who happened to be his maternal grandfather. His other grandfather, he was told, was right. In Leviticus, it is written, "You are not permitted to oppress the working man because he is poor and needy." Aaron memorized the passage in Hebrew—and lives by it.

Such a rabbi Kenneth Lay should have had.

Source: *Pittsburgh Post-Gazette,* December 22, 2001, p. A15, Reprinted by permission of the copyright holder, The Universal Press Syndicate.

AFTERWORD

Malden Mills was forced into bankruptcy again in 2007 and was purchased by Chrysalis Capital Partners, a private-equity firm, which renamed the company Polartec LLC. Aaron Feuerstein's association with the company ended with the sale.

Questions

1. *The Wall Street Journal* raised the question, "Are layoffs moral?"[14]

   a. Should we establish a universal, formalist rule forbidding layoffs of all hard-working, competent employees, or should we rely on utilitarian reasoning, libertarian thought, virtue theory, or religious beliefs to answer that question? Explain.

   b. Is morality irrelevant to the question of when layoffs are necessary? Explain.

2. Do you think it would be accurate and fair to say that Feuerstein's ethical choice to protect his employees led to the decline of his business? Explain.

3. Did Feuerstein make an error in judgment in relying on an absolute principle—that is, the protection of his workers at all costs? Explain.

4. How might Feuerstein's workers have benefited by being laid off after the fire?

5. John MacKenzie, in a letter to *The New York Times,* says he has a duty to help Aaron Feuerstein and Malden Mills: "Of course I have an ethical obligation to buy from Malden Mills if I have a choice and if my purchase can make a difference. It would reward Mr. Feuerstein for what he has done and what he is trying to do, and the system needs more of that."[15]

   Do you have a duty to buy Malden Mills products? Explain.

* Kenneth Lay died in 2006.

Loyalty Pays Off?

Sometimes employer generosity works out more favorably than has been the case at Malden Mills. The *Des Moines Register* recently applauded an Ames, Iowa, company whose boss, Roger Underwood, said, "It's the employees who made us successful, and we decided to reward them." The *Register* explained:

> Every once in a while, an employer comes along that renews one's faith in business. Becker Underwood, a 22-year-old Ames company that makes landscaping and agricultural products, last week spent $1.4 million giving bonuses to 238 employees at eight locations around the world. Each worker received $2,000 for each year worked for the company.
>
> Finally loyalty pays off.

*   *   *   *   *

That's a rare attitude in corporate America—a winning attitude, apparently, considering how well the company is doing. Is there a lesson there?

Source: "A Rare Recognition," *Des Moines Register,* September 6, 2004, p. 10A.

PRACTICING ETHICS) Career and Family

Parents are often torn between family and career considerations. Sometimes the stress of contemporary life, often including job and child care conflicts, leads to tragic consequences. Each year a small number of mothers and fathers simply forget to remove their babies from their rear-facing car seats. On warm days, the result can be the loss of that child. The following story explains one such tragic moment.

5:45 PM, June 26, 2001. Upon leaving work, Kari Engholm, a mother and chief administrator of the Dallas County Hospital in Perry, Iowa, found her seven-month-old daughter, Clare, dead in her car seat in the rear of the Engholm family van. Clare died of elevated body temperature (hyperthermia). The official death certificate declared the death an accident.

Ms. Engholm's husband, Dennis, ordinarily took Clare to the babysitter's house; but because of Dennis's work schedule at Iowa State University, Kari intended to take the Engholm's 3½-year-old son, Eric, to day care as usual and then leave Clare at her babysitter's home. She dropped Eric off at his day care on the morning of June 26, 2001, then apparently forgot that Clare was in her car seat in the back of the family minivan. After dropping Eric off, Ms. Engholm headed directly to "a tense board meeting during which members decided to sell an Adel medical practice to a doctor for $55,000 because of criticism that the hospital was not renewing the doctor's contract." Ms. Engholm completed her workday in the normal manner, and then when entering her minivan after work, discovered her daughter who had expired during the day.

Ms. Engholm was charged with criminal violations of neglect of a dependent person and involuntary manslaughter, but she was acquitted of both charges because, in the judgment of the court, the facts did not establish that Ms. Engholm's behavior met the statutory criminal standards of willfully or recklessly causing harm to her daughter.

Prior to the Engholm trial, a letter to the *Des Moines Register* criticized parents and American society for giving too much attention to career advancement and wealth at the expense of children:

> Baby Clare might be considered an extreme example of the defenseless victims of a culture of selfishness and materialism. Far too many American couples are opting for two incomes and two careers at the expense of their

children. Sending children off to be raised by $6 per hour "child care specialists" in order to have a bigger house, more vacations, an SUV, ad infinitum, is a form of child abuse in itself.

Sources: Dan Frommelt, "Children Are Victims of Parents' Careers," (Letter to the Editor) *Des Moines Register,* July 4, 2000, p. 8A, and various other *Des Moines Register* news accounts.

Questions

1. Do you agree with the letter writer? Explain.
2. Are your career and family goals ethically compatible? Explain.

AFTERWORD

According to an Associated Press study of a 10-year period beginning in the mid-1990s, about 340 children died of heat exhaustion while trapped in cars. Charges were filed in about half of the cases, with over 80 percent of those resulting in convictions or guilty pleas. Jail time was imposed in about 50 percent of the cases with a median sentence for parents of about 54 months. Mothers and fathers are charged at about the same rates, but moms are 26 percent more likely to be jailed, and their median sentences, according to the study, are two years longer than those of dads.[16]

Part Two—Managerial Ethics: Evidence and Analysis

America's Moral Climate

Perhaps more than ever, Americans are questioning the nation's moral health. Highly publicized corporate corruption, mistreatment of war prisoners in Iraq, steroid use by professional athletes, journalists making up phony stories, government officials exaggerating intelligence evidence, and so on cause us to question our decency as a society. Fairly or not, young people seem to be a particular source of concern. A 2006 survey of 36,000 high school students, reporting on their behavior in the previous year, found that

- 60 percent had cheated on a test
- 82 percent had lied to their parents about something significant
- 28 percent had stolen something from a store.[17]

Fifty-nine percent of those high school students agreed that, "In the real world, successful people do what they have to do to win, even if others consider it cheating." (65 percent males, 54 percent females) while 42 percent believe that "A person has to lie or cheat sometimes in order to succeed" (50 percent males, 33 percent females).[18]

Sociologist David Callahan's 2004 book *The Cheating Culture: Why More Americans Are Doing Wrong to Get Ahead*[19] argues that we are a society in moral decline. Reviewer Jackson Lears summarized Callahan's position:

> As economic inequalities have deepened during the last several decades, the renewed worship of money has bred temptation at all levels. Executives at Enron, World Com, and other corporations, intoxicated by the heady atmosphere of deregulation, defraud shareholders of billions and get away with little or no punishment. The little guy naturally says, if the big shots can get away with it, why not me? So he cheats on his taxes, steals from his company, and downloads music without paying for it.

These may be trivial matters, but Callahan believes they are symptomatic of a deeper disease in the body politic. The infection takes hold as early as high school or college (cheating is rampant on campus), feeding (and feeding on) the conviction that success in life requires cutting moral corners, that success is ultimately defined in monetary terms.[20]

The result of this winner-take-all ethos, Callahan thinks, is a nation increasingly falling into two groups: a "winning class" who cheated their way to the top and an "anxious class" who fear falling behind if they too do not cheat.[21]

Do you think Callahan is correct? Is America in moral decline? In fact, the discouraging news is accompanied by important evidence of improving behavior, particularly among young people. Serious violent crime by people under 25 has fallen more than 60 percent since 1994, pregnancy and abortion for girls under age 18 declined by approximately one-third from the mid-1990s, drug use is down among young people, and on the positive side, youth volunteer work is booming.[22] [For the Josephson Institute of Ethics, see **http://www.josephsoninstitute.org**]

Sex or Cell Phone?

Fourteen percent of cell phone users admit to having interrupted sex to answer their cell phones. A 2005 survey of more than 3,000 people, 15 to 35 years of age in 15 nations, found Germans and Spaniards (22 percent) most likely to answer the phone, with Italians least likely at 7 percent and Americans in the middle at 15 percent. Almost half of those responding worldwide thought their cell phones said as much about them as a car, while one-third of the Americans surveyed felt the same way.

Advertising giant BBDO commissioned the survey. Christine Hannis, BBDO head of communications explained, "People can't bear to miss a call. Getting so many calls . . . fulfills a fundamental insecurity."

Sources: Bill Hoffman, "Cell Users Put Sex on Hold," *New York Post Online Edition;* "BBDO Releases Cell Phones and Sex Acts Reports," [**http://adage.com/news.cms?newsId-44753** or **http://www.furl.net/item.jsp?id=2605994**].

College Students

The distinguished Duke University MBA program announced in May 2007 that nearly 10 percent (34 students) of its class of 2008 had been caught cheating on a take-home final examination.[23] The students were punished, some by expulsion or suspension. The scandal should not have been completely surprising since cheating seems to be common among MBA students nationwide. A large, 2006 survey found 56 percent of graduate students in business admitted to cheating at least once in the previous year, the largest percentage of any discipline surveyed.[24] Among nonbusiness graduate students, 47 percent admitted cheating.[25]

Ninety-five percent of 3,000 undergraduate business students polled in 31 universities admit they cheated in high school or college, although only 1 to 2 percent admit having done so "frequently."[26] Professor Joseph Petrick, coauthor of the study, attributes the cheating to "the academic welfare mentality. Business school students feel morally entitled to get what they need to do well in business."[27] Academic ethics expert Donald McCabe's surveys find about 75 percent of college students cheating on either a test or paper at some point, with business majors, fraternity and sorority members, and male students being among those most likely to cheat.[28] [For the Center for Academic Integrity, see **www.academicintegrity.org**]

These contemporary cheating behaviors are an interesting contrast to the views of a 1928 Princeton University freshman writing home:

> Father, you suggest that the greatest benefit from college is to be found in . . . habits of intellectual diligence and application. I am nonetheless putting my chief emphasis on the study of right and wrong.[29]

UCLA's annual survey of college first-year students provides further evidence of dramatically changing values. Responding to the 2003 survey, 73.8 percent of new freshmen identified financial success as a very important objective, whereas a record-low 39.3 percent considered developing a "meaningful philosophy of life" important.[30] Those results represent essentially a reversal of freshmen objectives from 30–40 years ago. College, however, seems to strengthen some important ethical values. A 2007 UCLA study found that interest in developing a meaningful philosophy of life rose from 41.2 percent for freshmen in 2004 to 55.4 percent when the same students were surveyed as juniors in 2007.[31] Broadly, as compared with their freshmen attitudes, college juniors are more likely to be engaged in a spiritual quest and more likely to be "caring" persons.[32] On the other hand, a 2007 study based on the Narcissistic Personality Inventory of college students nationwide, responding to such statements as "I think I am a special person," concluded that the average college student today is about 30 percent more self-absorbed than the average student in 1982.[33] One of the study leaders, Jean Twenge of San Diego State University remarked: "We need to stop endlessly repeating 'you're special,' . . . Kids are self-centered enough already."[34]

> We need to stop endlessly repeating "you're special"

My Cheating Isn't Really Cheating

An accounting professor at a prominent Midwestern university assigned a take-home problem to his 64 undergraduate students, two-thirds of whom were business majors, telling them to work alone and not to make use of computer/online resources in any way. He was unaware that another professor had posted the answer key on the Web. After reviewing the students' papers he knew that many students had violated his rules and the University's Honor Code by using the online Web site, collaborating with other students, or both. He decided to throw out the test results and examine the cheating episode with the students. He administered a voluntary questionnaire that was completed by all 64 students. By checking the University's records of students who accessed the Web site and by some students' admissions of wrongdoing on the questionnaire, he was able to identify at least 47 students who had cheated. All but two of the 47 "cheaters" wrote answers on the questionnaire indicating that they knew their behavior was wrong or could be considered wrong. The questionnaire then examined the "cheaters" explanations or rationales for their cheating.

Question

All 47 of the cheating students tried to minimize, justify or rationalize their behavior. Can you deduce what explanations/rationalizations the students offered for their cheating?

Source: Jeffrey B. Kaufmann, Tim West, Sue Pickard Ravenscroft, and Charles B. Shrader, "Ethical Distancing: Rationalizing Violations of Organizational Norms," *Business & Professional Ethics Journal* 24, no. 3 (Fall 2005), p. 101.

Corporate Conduct

As the following Gallup Poll results depict, Americans for decades have had little faith in the ethical quality of the corporate community. Respondents were asked to rate the honesty and integrity of people in various fields on a scale of very high, high, average, low, or very low.

Gallup Poll—Honesty and Ethics in Various Professions

	Percentage Saying Very High or High						
	1977	1985	1995	2000	2002	2004	2007
Nurses				79	79	79	83
Druggists/pharmacists		65	66	67	67	72	71
Medical doctors	51	58	54	63	63	67	64
Police	37	47	41	55	59	60	53
Clergy	61	67	56	60	52	56	53
Bankers	39	38	27	37	36	36	35
Lawyers	26	27	16	19	18	18	15
Business executives	19	23	19	23	17	20	14
Congressional representatives	16	20	10	21	17	20	9
Advertising practitioners	10	12	10	10	9	10	6
Car salespeople	8	5	5	7	6	9	5

Source: "Honesty/Ethics in Professions" [**http://www.gallup.com/poll/1654/Honesty-Ethics-Professions.aspx**]. Reprinted by permission.

When asked in a 2007 Harris Poll to assess their confidence in the leaders of the major American institutions, over 1,000 adult Americans ranked their confidence ("a great deal of confidence") in "Wall Street" and "Major companies" 11th and 12th in a list of 16 powerful American institutions. Small business, however, ranked 1st on that "great deal of confidence" list, just ahead of the military, higher education, and medicine. While ranking near the bottom of the list of institutions in whom the public expressed "a great deal of confidence," the corporate community did rank ahead of organized labor, law firms, the press, and Congress.[35]

Is the public mistaken in its discouraging assessment of business ethics? Employee opinion polls provide a view from inside the organization. Fifty-six percent of employees surveyed in a 2006 nationwide poll reported that their company embraces ethics in everything it does.[36] At the same time, one-fourth of those employed full-time said that in the past six months they had witnessed a colleague acting unethically (18 percent), illegally (7 percent), or in a harassing or discriminatory manner (14 percent).[37] [For "The Business Ethics Blog," see **http://www.businessethics.ca/blog**]

Why Do Some Managers Cheat?

Moral Development

Scholars argue that some individuals are better "educated" to make ethical judgments than others. Psychologist Lawrence Kohlberg built and empirically tested a comprehensive theory of moral development in which he claimed that moral judgment evolves and improves primarily as a function of age and education.

Kohlberg, via interviews with children as they aged, was able to identify moral development as movement through distinct stages, with the later stages being improvements on the earlier ones. Kohlberg identified six universal stages grouped into three levels:

1. **Preconventional level:**

   Stage 1: Obey rules to avoid punishment.

   Stage 2: Follow rules only if it is in own interest, but let others do the same. Conform to secure rewards.

2. **Conventional level:**

   Stage 3: Conform to meet the expectations of others. Please others. Adhere to stereotypical images.

   Stage 4: Doing right is one's duty. Obey the law. Uphold the social order.

3. **Postconventional or principled level:**

   Stage 5: Current laws and values are relative. Laws and duty are obeyed on rational calculations to serve the greatest number.

   Stage 6: Follow self-chosen universal ethical principles. In the event of conflicts, principles override laws.[38]

At Level 3 the individual is able to reach independent moral judgments that may or may not conform with conventional societal wisdom. Thus the Level 2 manager might refrain from sexual harassment because it constitutes a violation of company policy and the law. A manager at Level 3 might reach the same conclusion, but his or her decision would be based on independently defined universal principles of justice.

Kohlberg found that many adults never pass beyond Level 2. Consequently, if Kohlberg was correct, many managers may behave unethically simply because they have not reached the upper stages of moral maturity.

Kohlberg's model is based on extensive longitudinal and cross-cultural studies over more than three decades. For example, one set of Chicago-area boys was interviewed at 3-year intervals for 20 years. Thus the stages of moral growth exhibit "definite empirical characteristics" such that Kohlberg was able to claim that his model had been scientifically validated.[39] Although many critics remain, the evidence, in sum, supports Kohlberg's general proposition. [For an overview of moral development and moral education, see **http://tigger.uic.edu/~Inucci/MoralEd/overview.html**]

Feminine Voice   One of those lines of criticism requires a brief inspection. Carol Gilligan, a colleague of Kohlberg, contends that our conceptions of morality are, in substantial part, gender-based.[40] She claims that men typically approach morality as a function of justice, impartiality, and rights (the ethic of justice), whereas women are more likely to build a morality based on care, support, and responsiveness (the ethic of care). Men, she says, tend to take an impersonal, universal view of morality as contrasted with the feminine "voice" that rises more commonly from relationships and concern for the specific needs of others. Gilligan criticizes Kohlberg because his highest stages, 5 and 6, are structured in terms of the male approach to morality while the feminine voice falls at stage 3. Further, Kohlberg's initial experimental subjects were limited to young males. The result, in Gilligan's view, is that women are underscored. Of course, a danger in the ethic of care is that it might be interpreted to restore and legitimize the stereotype of women as caregiving subordinates not deserving of moral autonomy.[41] Subsequent research both challenges[42] and supports[43] Gilligan's view.

System I/Moral Minds? The careful reasoning and analysis employed by Kohlberg, Gilligan and most moral philosophers has been labeled "System II" cognition by scholars Daniel Kahneman and Cass Sunstein.[44] Recent evidence suggests, however, that another set of forces, "System I," is at work in the moral judgment process. System I involves intuition; automatic, nonreflective emotions/judgments that emerge spontaneously in our thought processes.[45] System I theory suggests that our minds, when confronted with a moral question, generate instant feelings of approval or disapproval. System II moral reasoning could be a method of justifying conclusions already reached automatically via System I intuitions.[46] Brain scanning experiments have provided support for the System I hypothesis.[47]

Moral theorist Marc Hauser extends the System I, intuitionist thesis in his book *Moral Minds.*[48] He claims that our brains are biologically endowed with a moral faculty that has evolved over eons and is designed to reach very rapid judgments about right and wrong based on unconscious processes that are involuntary and universal. Thus, when we judge an action to be morally right or wrong, Hauser says we are doing so instinctively, using our inborn moral faculty.

The biological/intuitionist/System I theory provides a stern challenge to Kohlberg and to our faith in moral reasoning generally. Psychologist Jonathan Haidt compares the intuitive, moral machinery of the brain (System I) to an elephant and conscious moral reasoning (System II) to be a small rider on the elephant's back.[49] Other scholarly evidence, however, continues to support a very robust role for rational moral decision making.[50]

Organizational Forces

Obviously, individual character is an important determinant of corporate misconduct, but substantial scientific evidence and scholarly opinion support the view that organizational culture is also highly influential.[51] A recent survey of human resource managers and executives shows that 70 percent of those responding to the survey blamed ethical lapses on pressure to meet unrealistic goals and deadlines while personal considerations such as furthering one's career had less reported impact.[52] As Jay Jamrog, executive director of the Human Resource Institute said, "[Y]ou still need people at the top to set the climate."[53] Indeed, 81 percent of CEOs surveyed believe that corporate ethics standards climbed following Enron and the other scandals of the early 2000s.[54] Employees also reported reduced pressure to cheat in recent years although we should particularly note that managers under 30 years of age and with less than three years in the organization were twice as likely to feel pressure to cheat (21 percent to 10 percent).[55] [For the Business Roundtable Institute for Corporate Ethics, see **www.corporate-ethics.org**]

The pressure to produce is, of course, very great for those at the bottom of the power structure; but often it does not go away with advancement. Thirty graduates of the Harvard MBA program agreed to in-depth interviews about their on-the-job ethics experiences.

One interesting conclusion from the interviews was the degree to which these younger subordinates understood and empathized with the pressure felt by their primarily middle-manager bosses:

I really feel for people who are middle management, with a wife and four kids, under financial strain. . . . You see it happen all the time, that people are indicted for fraud or larceny. You can empathize with their situation. The world is changing fast. And a lot of people have been blindsided by it—so they've done things that they don't like. I can't say that will never happen to me. It's easy for me as a single person. . . but when you're desperate, you're desperate. [My boss] was not willfully unethical. It was the pressure of the time. . . . I have no idea what pressures were on him to drive the project. It probably wasn't [his] initiative to fudge the numbers. There may have been a good intention at some point in the organization. But as it got filtered through the organization, it changed. Some executive may have said, "This is an interesting project." Unfortunately this got translated as, "The vice president really wants this project." This sort of thing can happen a lot. Things start on high. As they go down they are filtered, modified. What was a positive comment several levels above becomes "do this or die" several levels down.[56] [For a variety of business ethics links, see **http://www.ethics.ubc.ca/resources/business/**]

> [My boss] was not willfully unethical. It was the pressure of the time

The Boss

Scholarly evidence and common sense suggest that bosses are crucial in setting the ethical climate in an organization. *The Wall Street Journal* reviewed Dial Corporation (the soap company) CEO Herb Baum's leadership book:

In *The Transparent Leader,* Herb Baum argues that a climate of integrity is crucial to the success of a public company and that it begins at the top.

Mr. Baum . . . is at the top himself, but he drives a VW Beetle to work, he tells us, and doesn't have a reserved parking space. Not that he minds: He arrives at 5 AM, ahead of the crowd. He espouses straight talk, solid values, and hiring literally good people—as opposed to people who are merely good at their jobs. His catchall term for this ethos is "transparency."

How to create it? Mr. Baum rightly insists that it has to come from the chief executive's office. He emphasizes valuing people by keeping an open door, communicating honestly, listening carefully, and making sure that integrity permeates every aspect of the company. Hypocrisy is anathema: "A lot of CEOs, including me, are overpaid," he says bluntly—and at one point he distributed his annual bonus to Dial's lowest-paid employees.[57]

Flirting to Get Ahead

"You are being considered for a promotion. Would you flirt with your boss or someone else who can help you get the job?" *Money Magazine* asked this and other ethics questions in a national poll of 1,000 adults. Answer the flirting question, then go online to see how your answer compared to the poll response: "Money and Ethics: How You Stack Up," *CNNMoney.com* [**http://money.cnn.com/galleries/2007/moneymag/0705/quiz.money_ethics.moneymag/3.html?score=2**]

> **Managers are the ethics teachers of their organizations**

Ethics Teachers? Harvard business ethics professor Joseph Badaracco has said "managers are the ethics teachers of their organizations."[58] If so, we would be forced to conclude that many corporate leaders have been teaching the wrong ethics lessons. Rather than setting the ethical tone for their organizations, executives often distance themselves as much as possible when wrongdoing is discovered:

> Call it the reverse Nuremberg strategy. Chief executives of scandal-ridden companies such as WorldCom, Sotheby's Holdings Inc., Cendant Corp., and . . . Enron Corp. all have claimed that they didn't know about the alleged fraud at their businesses and blamed it largely on underlings.
>
> It is the opposite of the defense used at the Nuremberg trials, when Hitler's minions claimed they were only carrying out orders from above. In the corporate fraud cases, the argument is that the top dog was so above the fray that he didn't know what directives were being issued or carried out by those below him. . . .
>
> The Sarbanes-Oxley Act, which requires CEOs and their chief financial officers to sign all financial statements attesting to their veracity, was designed in part to short-circuit such defenses.[59]

[For the Business Roundtable Institute for Corporate Ethics, see **http://www.darden. virginia.edu/corporate-ethics**]

Keep On Cheating? Some corporate officers not only cheat stockholders, employees, and the public while in office, but they continue to loot the corporate treasury after they have left. Many of these executives have "just cause" clauses in their contracts that make firing them difficult. If they are forced out, they often have "golden parachute" arrangements that let them collect millions as severance pay. Former PeopleSoft CEO Craig Conway reportedly managed a nice deal for himself despite his dubious conduct:

> They often have "golden parachute" arrangements that let them collect millions as severance pay

> The former chief executive of PeopleSoft Inc. lied to Wall Street analysts about the company's business. So what happened to him? He got to keep his job for a year, and when he was finally fired, he walked away with a huge severance package. . . .
>
> Conway was ousted about a month ago, in part because of his clashes with other senior managers. But there was also the big lie that got him in trouble. Conway played down the effect on PeopleSoft's business when he was asked at a September 2003 meeting with Wall Street analysts whether customers were holding back purchases because of a potential sale (of PeopleSoft) to Oracle. "The last remaining customers whose business decisions were being delayed have actually completed their sales and completed their orders. So I don't see it as a disruptive factor," Conway said.[60]

Conway later admitted he knew that statement to be untrue, but he said it anyway because he was "promoting, promoting, promoting."[61] So what happened to Conway? According to newspaper accounts, his severance package probably was in the $20 million range while his accumulated stock options might have raised his total "takeaway" to more than

$60 million.[62] [For extensive data on more than 1,500 corporations, see Hoover's Online at **http://www.hoovers.com**]

Bank Robber to Boardroom

Some bosses go wrong but correct their lives—none more dramatically than James Joseph Minder, 74-year-old former chairman of Smith & Wesson Holding Corp. In his twenties, Minder was the notorious "Shotgun Bandit" of Michigan. He committed dozens of armed holdups, some while a student at the University of Michigan. On one occasion he terrorized employees before stealing $53,000 from a branch of Manufacturers National Bank. He served time in prison and was free of trouble, he says, after 1965. After release from prison in 1969, he spent 20 years successfully setting up group homes and programs for troubled children and young adults. After retiring in the 1990s, Minder got involved in the gun industry and eventually became chairman of Smith & Wesson. Then in 2004 a reporter came to his home asking about his past, a life he had not hidden but one he had not advertised either. At first he denied he was the "Bandit," but he reconsidered and decided, "I had better tell the truth." He later told the other members of the Smith & Wesson board and resigned as chairman.

Source: Vanessa O'Connell, "How Troubled Past Finally Caught Up with James Minder," *The Wall Street Journal,* March 8, 2004, p. A1.

Questions—Part Two

1. *a.* Do you think it is important for our character development to have heroes in our lives? Explain.

   b. Do you think we have fewer heroes today than in the past? Explain.

   c. Do you have a hero? Explain.

2. A Business & Media Institute study entitled "Bad Company" looked at the top 12 television dramas from May and November 2005, including shows like "CSI" and "Desperate Housewives." Thirty-nine episodes featured business-related plots, and among those shows, 77 percent projected an unfavorable image of business. The "Law & Order" episodes, for example, had businessmen committing almost 50 percent of the felonies—mostly murders.

   a. Do you think those unfavorable depictions of business are unfair? Explain.

   b. Do you think those depictions significantly harm the image of the business community? Explain. See Editorial, "TV's Killer Capitalists," *The Wall Street Journal,* July 14, 2006, p. W9.

3. Does a corporation have a conscience? Explain. See Kenneth Goodpaster and John B. Matthews, Jr., "Can a Corporation Have a Conscience?" *Harvard Business Review,* January–February 1982, p. 136.

Part Three—Business Ethics in Practice

Introduction: Ethics Codes

Having established a general ethics foundation, we turn now to ethics in practice. Most big companies have voluntarily developed ethics codes, and the 2002 federal Sarbanes-Oxley Act (SOX), encourages all publicly traded companies to do so. Sarbanes was passed after Enron and other corporate scandals as a way to discourage financial and accounting fraud, thus maintaining confidence in America's financial markets. Section 406 of Sarbanes specifically requires publicly traded companies to adopt a code of ethics for senior financial officers or to explain why they have not done so. Section 406 defines a *code of ethics* as written standards that are reasonably designed to deter wrongdoing and to promote such behaviors as honest conduct, full disclosure in reports, compliance with all applicable laws and rules, prompt reporting of violations, and methods for conforming to the code's expectations.

Responding to SOX and other pressures, many companies now have prepared more detailed and specific codes, displayed them more prominently, required employees to read and sign the codes, and created training methods to more firmly integrate ethical expectations into the company's total decision-making processes. [For the Ethics Officers Association, see **http://www.eoa.org**]

Whether the new attention to codes will prove beneficial remains to be seen. Importantly, the company that can show compliance with its own legitimate code expectations may receive more sympathetic treatment from the justice system if criminal problems do emerge. (Additional Sarbanes-Oxley discussion follows in this chapter and in Chapter 9.) [For the Ethics Resource Center, see **http://www.ethics.org**] [For information on global corporate governance and citizenship, see **http://www.conference-board.org**]

Building an Ethical Culture at General Electric

In adding 13,000 new employees each year, General Electric struggles to implement effective training methods for achieving the ethical climate worldwide that the company demands. In most cases, GE's new hires undergo compliance training soon after joining the company. Often using online training programs, GE tests employees on problems such as how to deal with unusual requests by a customer for money or to ignore a government rule. Recently, GE began requiring each business unit to provide a quarterly report to the compliance department detailing what portion of its employees completed the required ethics training and what portion read and signed off on GE's "Spirit and Letter" ethics guide. Rather than burying employees in lists of do's and don'ts, GE and others are building contextual training exercises that attempt to immerse employees in discussions of how to approach actual, on-the-job ethical dilemmas.

Question

Do you think ethics training is likely to have a significant impact on managerial and corporate misconduct? Explain.

Sources: Kathryn Kranhold, "U.S. Firms Raise Ethics Focus," *The Wall Street Journal,* November 28, 2005, p. B4; and Erin White "What Would You Do? Ethics Courses Get Context," *The Wall Street Journal,* June 12, 2006, p. B3.

Bribery Abroad

Today's closely entwined international markets mean that strategies for curbing corrupt business practices around the world have become a matter of urgency. However, that new expectation raises complex ethical dilemmas for America's multinational businesses. In many cultures, the payment of bribes—*baksheesh* (Middle East), *huilu* (China), *vzyatku* (Russia), *mordida* (South America), or *dash* (Africa)—is accepted as necessary and, in some cases, a lawful way of doing business. American firms and officers wishing to succeed abroad have faced great pressure to engage in practices that are illegal and unethical in the American culture.

The Foreign Corrupt Practices Act (FCPA), the chief federal weapon against bribery abroad was enacted in 1977 in response to disclosure of widespread bribery by American firms. In brief, the FCPA provides that U.S. nationals and businesses acting anywhere in the world, as well as foreign nationals and companies acting in U.S. territory, are engaging in criminal conduct if they offer or provide bribes to foreign government officials to obtain or retain business or otherwise secure "any improper advantage." In addition, the FCPA requires rigorous internal accounting controls and careful recordkeeping to ensure that bribes cannot be concealed via "slush funds" and other devices. The act does not forbid "grease" payments to foreign officials or political parties where the purpose of the payments is "to expedite or to secure the performance of a routine governmental action," such as processing papers (like visas), providing police protection, and securing phone service. And those accused may offer the affirmative defense that the alleged payoff was lawful in the host country or was a normal, reasonable business expenditure directed to specific marketing and contract performance activities. Criminal penalties include fines of up to $2 million for companies, while individuals may be fined $100,000 and imprisoned for as long as five years. [For a summary of the FCPA, see **http://fcpaenforcement.com/explained/explained.asp**]

Controversy

The FCPA has been controversial from the outset. Some businesspeople see it as a blessing both because it is an honorable attempt at a firm moral stance and because it is often useful for an American businessperson abroad to say, "No, our laws forbid me from doing that." On the other hand, some have seen the act as damaging to our competitiveness. Now other nations are recognizing that corruption is a great risk to the global economy. Once believing that bribery aided the poor, most industrial countries are now moving toward the zero tolerance view held by the United States. In addition to the FCPA, the United States also participates in several other anticorruption initiatives including the United Nations Convention against Corruption, the OECD Anti-Bribery Convention, and the Inter-American Convention. [For details on the OECD Anti-Bribery Convention, see **www.oecd.org**]

> The United States ranked only 19th in the 2006 Gallup Worldwide Corruption Index

United States Corruption   Although the United States has been the clear world leader in pursuing anticorruption efforts, we should not be unduly prideful. Indeed, the United States ranked only 19th in the 2006 Gallup Worldwide Corruption Index, which asked residents in 101 nations whether they believed corruption was widespread in business and/or government in their nation. The countries perceived to be least corrupt were Finland, Denmark, and New Zealand. Most of northern and western Europe as well as Canada were perceived to be less corrupt than the United States. Japan (30), Germany (48), and Russia (93) were among the nations ranking lower than the United States.[63]

Bribery in Practice

Bribery seems to be a routine cost of daily life in some countries:

> Like many Russians, Nikolai can't even count the number of bribes he has paid in his life. He remembers the big ones, like the $1,000 he paid to avoid mandatory military service or the $1,200 he gave his wife's obstetrician to ensure her a place at one of Moscow's state-run maternity hospitals. But the small ones, like the dozens of $10 to $20 bribes he's handed to traffic police over the years, are instantly forgotten.

> **Nikolai can't even count the number of bribes he has paid in his life**

* * * * *

> Whether it's getting your child into a good school, passing your driving test or even making sure you get medical treatment, there are few areas of life in Russia where a well-placed bribe isn't essential. Experts say corruption in Russia is endemic, especially in the corporate world—where big companies, both domestic and foreign, often have to shell out hundreds of thousands of dollars to get permission for a project or win a government contract.[64]

Russian think tank INDEM estimates that, on average, Russian businesses spend seven percent of their budgets on bribes.[65] German engineering and telecom giant, Siemens AG, according to a *Wall Street Journal* report, agreed to pay a fine of 201 million euros in 2007 to settle charges that it had paid about $17.5 million in bribes to government officials in Nigeria, Libya, and Russia to secure telecommunications contracts.[66] Siemens says it has identified suspicious transactions worldwide totaling 1.3 billion euros between 2000 and 2006.[67]

China executed the former head of its food and drug agency in 2007 for accepting $850,000 in bribes from Chinese pharmaceutical companies. Bribery has often been considered a cost of doing business in China, but recent product safety scandals have threatened the reputation of China's enormous export market so the government has indicated that it will crack down on corruption. Skeptics, however, believe that bribery is so deeply rooted in the Chinese system that those who give the bribes, in particular, often "get off easy."[68]

> **China executed the former head of its food and drug agency for accepting $850,000 in bribes**

In the United States, we are seeing a remarkable new zeal in attacking bribery. Foreign bribery cases filed in the United States more than doubled from 2004 to 2007.[69] Following the scandals of the early 2000s and subsequent legal reforms such as Sarbanes-Oxley, U.S. corporate officials apparently now feel increasingly threatened by the prospect of criminal charges.[70] They are believed to be digging deeper into the practices of their companies to identify and reveal wrongdoing in hopes of receiving leniency. Tyco International, for example, paid $50 million to settle civil claims over cash and gifts its Brazilian and South Korean employees gave to government officials in order to win construction and water contracts.[71]

PRACTICING ETHICS) Bribe the Terrorists?

Banadex, a subsidiary of Cincinnati-based Chiquita Brands International, paid bribes to Colombian rebels over a period of years, including $1.7 million from 1997 to 2004 to the AUC (Autodefensas Unidas de Colombia), a right-wing Colombian terrorist group. Chiquita, one of the world's leading banana producers with operations in 70 nations, learned of the payments in 2000, but allowed them to continue. Reliable reports indicated that thousands of people had been killed, tortured, raped, or "disappeared" by the AUC (now disbanded). At the time, terrorists in Colombia were holding some Americans for ransom or killing them, and years earlier four Chiquita employees had been killed by left-wing guerillas. The bribes, then lawful under American and Colombian law, were thought necessary to protect employees and company property at Chiquita's Colombian operations.

In 2003, Chiquita allegedly "stumbled across" news that the AUC had in 2001 been designated a "foreign terrorist organization" by the U.S. government, which meant payments thereafter were unlawful. The payments continued, however, despite warnings from outside counsel to discontinue them or face the risk of felony charges. Chiquita said that stopping the payments would have endangered its employees. By 2003, Chiquita's operations in Colombia were its most profitable. The bribe payments were stopped in 2004 when a new CEO arrived. Chiquita soon sold its Colombian interests. Chiquita had earned about $50 million in profits from the time AUC was designated a terrorist organization until the period when the payments ceased.

In 2007, Chiquita entered a guilty plea to the felony of engaging in transactions with terrorists. A federal judge sentenced Chiquita to $25 million in fines and five years probation. Some evidence suggests Chiquita may have delayed its decision to stop payments by nearly one year as it waited for the U.S. government to review the security implications of a Chiquita withdrawal from Colombia. U.S.

Justice Department officials denied that claim, and in 2007 they concluded their investigation by deciding not to bring criminal charges against former Chiquita officials.

Families of Colombians killed or tortured by the terrorists along with human rights groups have filed several civil lawsuits against Chiquita for supporting the terrorists who allegedly used the bribe money to buy weapons. During the period of Chiquita payments to AUC, some 4,000 Colombians were killed in the banana-growing region of Colombia. An Organization of American States investigation concluded that 3,000 Central American rifles and millions of rounds of ammunition reached the terrorists after allegedly being unloaded at a Colombian port by Banadex. Colombian officials argue that Chiquita was not a victim of extortion and that the company knew AUC was using the bribery proceeds to attack peasants, union workers and various rival groups.

Questions

1. Chiquita argued that the safety of its employees required payment of the bribes, even after learning of their illegality. What would you have done, had you been in charge? Explain.
2. Should Chiquita's corporate officers have been prosecuted by the U.S. government? Explain.

Sources: Sibylla Brodzinsky, "Chiquita Case Puts Big Firms on Notice," *The Christian Science Monitor,* April 11, 2007 [http://www.csmonitor.com/2007/0411/p01s03-woam.html]; Laurie P. Cohen, "Chiquita Ex-Officials Won't Face Charges," *The Wall Street Journal,* September 12, 2007, p. B2; Carol D. Leonnig, "In Terrorism-Law Case, Chiquita Points to U.S.," *Washington Post,* August 2, 2007, p. A01; David J.Lynch, "Murder and Payoffs Taint Business in Colombia," *USA TODAY,* October 30, 2007, sec. Money, p. 1B; and Sue Reisinger, "Blood Money Paid by Chiquita Shows Company's Hard Choices," *Corporate Counsel,* November 26, 2007[http://www.law.com/jsp/ihc/PubArticleFriendlyIHC.jsp?id= 1195639472310].

Corporate/White Collar Crime

Martha Stewart served five months in prison

Martha Stewart served five months in prison, the Enron bosses were successfully prosecuted, and dozens of other prominent executives and corporations have been punished in recent years. While great corporations have collapsed and many good people have lost their life savings, we can find some satisfaction in a system that brings the mighty to justice. The scandals, however, persist. Executives are now threatened with jail for their roles in stock option backdating schemes. (See Chapter 9.) The subprime mortgage mess, only beginning to unfold at this writing, may produce a new round of prosecutions. Accounting manipulation, bribery, inside trading, consumer fraud, price fixing, and the like continue. In late 2007, *Forbes,* the business magazine, summed up the disturbing situation with the headline: "Corporate Crime Wave Unabated."[72] The 2007 PricewaterhouseCoopers (PwC) Global Economic Crime Survey found that over 43 percent of the 5,400 companies surveyed in 40 nations reported having been victims of at least one substantial economic crime during the two previous years.[73] Significantly, the report concluded that companies cannot rely on internal fraud controls alone to stop this misconduct:

> The answer lies in establishing a corporate culture that supports control efforts and whistle-blowing systems with clear ethical guidelines. Companies need to build loyalty to the organization, give employees the confidence to do the right thing, and put in place clear sanctions for those who commit fraud, regardless of their position in the company.[74]

One of the results of the failure to control crime, as *The Wall Street Journal* reported, is that corporations and their bosses may be at greater risk of prosecution than ever before in American history:

> There may never have been a worse time to be a corporate criminal. . . . The reason: After a wave of corporate-fraud cases, prosecutors want to send a signal that executives aren't above the law. What's more, tough federal sentencing guidelines that take into account the number of investor victims and how much money they lost have resulted in extremely long recommended sentences.[75]

Is Theft Sometimes OK?

A shopper wrote a letter to the editor explaining how he felt after observing what appeared to be a theft:

> [A]t Wal-Mart I saw a person try to put an item in their jacket. At first I thought this person was a jerk. . . . But after I returned home, I became convinced that it was OK to steal. . . . When I compare the theft of a $15 item to the grand larceny by corporate America, which ran Enron into the ground, which reaps record oil profits, . . . which occupies the seats of government and takes bribes, I now see the act of stealing a small gift . . . as heroic.

Questions

1. What do you think the letter writer meant when he applied the label "heroic" to the apparent theft?
2. Should we be more aggressive in pursuing corporate fraud? Explain.

Source: Greg Wilcox, "It's All Relative," *The Des Moines Register*, December 12, 2005, p. 6A.

Punishment   Responding to public outrage as Enron and the other corporate scandals surfaced, Congress felt great pressure to strengthen federal criminal laws dealing with corporate fraud. The result was the aforementioned 2002 Sarbanes-Oxley Act (SOX), which significantly increased penalties and provided other aggressive measures for attacking corporate crime by publicly traded companies. Among its major provisions, the bill

- Establishes an independent board to oversee the accounting profession.
- Requires corporate executives to personally certify the accuracy of their financial reports.
- Creates new crimes and raises penalties to as much as 25 years imprisonment along with heavy fines.
- Requires publicly traded companies to establish internal control systems designed to assure the accuracy of financial information (Section 404, perhaps the key provision).
- Requires publicly traded companies to disclose whether they have adopted an ethics code for senior financial management, and if not, why they have not done so (see Chapter 9 for further detail).

SOX compliance costs can be quite high, but even critics have found some benefits in the increased government oversight:

> Invitrogen Corp. spent about $2.5 million and 10,000 hours of employees' time last year reviewing its inventory-counting procedures, computer-system access and other "internal controls.". . . Officials at the Carlsbad, Calif. biotechnology company think the costs are excessive. But they say Sarbanes-Oxley helped to spur other changes that made Invitrogen a better-run business. Directors meet more often without executives present. Multiple ombudsmen field employee complaints. Ethics training is more rigorous. And Chief Executive Greg Lucier requires his lieutenants to take more responsibility for their results.[76]

Sentencing   Federal sentencing guidelines, issued by the United States Sentencing Commission, provide ranges (e.g., 10–12 months imprisonment) within which judges are advised to impose sentences. Relying on the crime's "offense level" and the defendant's criminal history" the punishment range for each category of both white-collar and "street" crime is established. The guidelines are designed to provide greater predictability and consistency in punishment. Companies must develop programs to prevent and detect crime, provide ethics training and monitor the success of compliance efforts. Responsibility for compliance rests explicitly with the board of directors and top-level executives. Companies, directors and officers complying with the guidelines may receive leniency while those engaging in aggravating behaviors such as a leadership role in crime may face increased punishment.[77]

Recent Supreme Court decisions have undercut the power of the guidelines by restoring federal judges' authority to deviate from them.[78] Judges who follow the guidelines are presumed to have acted reasonably,[79] but departures from the guidelines are now permissible. One of the results of the Supreme Court rulings is that sentences, for at least some classes of crime, are likely to be somewhat more lenient than under strict conformity to the guidelines.[80] On the other hand, corporate crime clearly remains a subject of special interest to prosecutors, and as banker Ted Peters explained, the risks are now great

> I could get 20 years in jail

and highly personal: "I could get 20 years in jail and a $5 million fine if [I] do something wrong purposely."[81]

Jerome Kerviel, the "Mad Trader"

By allegedly losing over $7 billion in apparently unauthorized hedge fund trading, Jerome Kerviel set a new world record for a financial loss racked up by a single trader. Kerviel, a 31-year-old, junior employee at Société Générale, one of Europe's largest banks, was assigned to hedge trades in European stock index futures. Kerviel confessed to fraud after his scheme was uncovered in early 2008 following months of illicit trading that Kerviel apparently hid by falsifying documents and e-mail messages. If found guilty, Kerviel could be sentenced to seven years in jail and fined 750,000 euros.

At one point, Kerviel reportedly had achieved a gain of some 1.6 billion euros, but he did not know how to announce his success without revealing that he had been trading much beyond his permitted bounds. Kerviel, a product of second-tier schools, apparently sought to prove that he could match or exceed the performance of his colleagues who were graduates of France's elite universities.

Kerviel apparently did not personally profit from his dealings, and he indicated to police that all he hoped for was a big bonus and increased respect. Kerviel told prosecutors that he thought his superiors had to be aware of his scheme:

> I cannot believe that my superiors did not realize the amount I was risking. It is impossible to generate such profit with small positions. That's what leads me to say that while I was [in the black], my supervisors closed their eyes on the methods I was using and the volumes I was trading.

Previously, probably the biggest single fraudulent trader was Nick Leeson who brought down his British employer, Barings Bank, with $1.8 billion in trading losses.

Sources: Nicola Clark and David Jolly, "Fraud Costs Bank $7.1 Billion," *The New York Times,* January 25, 2008 [**http://www.nytimes.com/2008/01/25/business/worldbusiness/25bank-web.html?em&ex=1201410000&en= bfb3bdel5a38addf&ei=5087%OA**]; David Gauthier-Villars and Carrick Mollenkamp, "Portrait Emerges of Rogue Trader at French Bank," *The Wall Street Journal,* February 2–3, 2008, p. A1; and David Gauthier-Villars, "Kerviel Felt Out of His League," *The Wall Street Journal,* January 31, 2008, p. C1.

Too Much? Critics of increased goverment activism see the open market as the best protection against corporate misconduct. To those critics, the existing laws were adequate, and the new measures are a politicized overreaction to scandals affecting a relatively small part of the economy. From a free market perspective, the greatest concern is that SOX, the revised sentencing guidelines, and the other new rules are another government-inflicted drag on the economy.

The following article details an effort by business schools to educate and frighten students into compliance with the law once on the job.

Jane Porter

By the time he was 40, Walter A. Pavlo Jr. had graduated with a master's degree in business from Mercer University, worked as a manager at MCI, concocted a $6 million money laundering scheme, served a two-year sentence in federal prison, and was divorced, unemployed, and living with his parents. It's a story that should scare any MBA straight.

At least that's the hope of business school professors who bring in Pavlo (and pay him as much as $2,500 per visit) to speak to their students about corporate crime. After the Enron-era scandals, business schools quickly created ethics centers and courses. Recently some, including New York University, the University of California at Berkeley, and Purdue, have made the conversation less academic by inviting those with practical experience into the classroom.

Pavlo, who lined up his first (albeit unpaid) gig before he was released from jail in 2003, is one of the busiest convicted felons on the B-school speaking circuit. He's given 25 lectures since January and expects to keep up that pace through the year. "Here's a real person telling students what happened to his life. I don't think there is any substitute for that," says Linda K. Trevino, a professor of organizational behavior and ethics at Penn State Smeal College of Business, where Pavlo has appeared several times. He speaks at companies and conferences, too, but says that most of the $100,000 or so he earned last year came from his B-school lectures. Part of the money goes to restitution for his crime.

Of course, some think compensating ex-cons to tell their stories is unwise. "I'm disturbed that so many professors seem to be willing to invite Pavlo and other convicted felons into the classroom without verifying that the stories are true," says John C. Knapp, director of the Center for Ethics & Corporate Responsibility at Georgia State University. "Paying the ex-cons is rewarding them for committing a crime."

On campus, Pavlo tries to project an executive image. He arrived at Purdue in West Lafayette, Ind., last month in a suit and tie and carrying business cards for his one-man company, Etika. Using a PowerPoint presentation, he tells the students how easily he was seduced by the chance to make quick money. At MCI, Pavlo worked in the financial services department, where he managed the accounts of some high-risk corporate clients. Before too long he had devised a plan to con some of them into believing an angel investor would take care of their debts to MCI in return for regular payments to a Cayman Islands account. MCI never saw a penny. "All you need to know to cook the books you learn in your first semester of accounting," Pavlo tells the students.

Except that he got caught by his manager before a year was out. "Thinking about the pressures of the workplace, particularly in a not-so-great economy, you see what people might be capable of," says Wayne Shyy, a student who heard Pavlo at Purdue.

Chuck Gallagher, a former partner at a North Carolina accounting firm, is another speaker at B-schools, sharing his tale of embezzlement and tax fraud. He began making the rounds in 2006, a decade after serving an 11-month sentence for stealing $250,000 from client trust funds. Gallagher earns up to $5,000 speaking to companies but says he is paid only for travel and lodging when visiting business schools.

One ex-con out there offers another kind of cautionary tale. Barry J. Webne says he spoke to half a dozen schools last year about how he stole more than a million dollars while working as a controller for a Cleveland company. Recently, though, Webne was convicted of embezzling another million from the security company that employed him. He is awaiting sentencing.

Source: BusinessWeek, May 5, 2008, p. 58. Reprinted by permission.

Questions

1. In your judgment, is cheating in school likely to lead to cheating on the job?
2. Does the market punish corporate criminals?

Whistle Blowing

Doing the right thing sometimes pays in a big, tangible way. Former Merck sales manager, H. Dean Steinke, who "just couldn't abide" the way his employer wanted him to market Vioxx (arthritis) and Zocor (cholesterol) to doctors, received $68.2 million as his share in the settlement of his whistle-blower lawsuit under the federal False Claims Act.[82]

Merck agreed to pay more than $650 million in early 2008 to settle Steinke's case and one other charging that Merck routinely overbilled the government for Medicare payments and paid improper inducements to acquire business from doctors and hospitals.[83] Steinke's warnings to Merck reportedly were ignored, and his direct supervisor allegedly told him, "I don't care how you do it, but get the damn business."[84] Eventually government prosecutors joined the case and Steinke spent years helping them understand Merck's marketing and pricing practices while sorting through the ten thousand pages of documents that he had collected. Merck admitted no wrongdoing in the case. To Steinke the case was about principle rather than money:

> I don't care how you do it, but get the damn business

> Sometimes you just get so frustrated about things that are wrong. These are the things that drive you, and you're not going to stop until things are resolved.[85]

> Americans have long deplored "squealing"

Steinke's courage and persistence remain unusual. Americans have long deplored "squealing," and we tend to ignore violations, partly out of fear of retribution. A recent survey found that 73 percent of full-time American employees observed wrongdoing on the job, but only about 36 percent of those employees actually reported that wrongdoing to bosses.[86] Of course, irresponsible, precipitous whistle-blowing should not be encouraged since it might disclose legitimate trade secrets, cause unnecessary conflict among employees, unfairly tarnish the company image, and so on.

Sarbanes-Oxley encourages whistle-blowing in the private sector by specifically requiring auditors to set up what amounts to a whistle-blowing hotline for employees who want to report accounting and auditing complaints. SOX also forbids employer retaliation against an employee who reports information about corporate fraud, and it makes a crime of interfering with "the lawful employment or livelihood of a person" in retaliation for reporting potential federal offenses to law enforcement authorities. The Whistle-blower Protection Act of 1989 and a number of other federal and state laws help government employees, and some of those laws also protect private-sector whistle-blowers. [For an overview of whistle-blower activity and protections, see **http://www.whistleblowers.org/** and for a law firm dedicated to representing whistle-blowers as well as the stories of some of those whistle-blowers, see **http://www.phillipsandcohen.com/**]

Retribution Despite expanded legal protection, whistle-blowers often pay a high price for exercising their consciences. Whistle-blower Jack Liles wrote a letter to *The Wall Street Journal* cautioning readers about the risks.

> Folks such as whistle-blower Sherron Watkins at Enron are rarely given a special status or legal protection merely for uncovering an ugly practice or incident, legal or not.
>
> After only four months in a management position at a large *Fortune* 500 firm, I discovered within my department an unethical practice and culture of soliciting for and accepting lavish gifts from vendors and suppliers in exchange for favorable consideration and favoritism in purchasing decisions and contract negotiations.
>
> When I confronted management on the issue and its clear violation of company rules and basic business ethics standards, I was quickly escorted to the parking lot where the parking decal was scraped from my car and my company I.D. confiscated. I was history.[87]

Questions

1. Why is the role of "squealer" or whistle blower so repugnant to many Americans?
2. *a.* How would you feel about a classmate who blew the whistle on you for cheating on an examination?

   b. Would you report cheating by a classmate if it came to your attention? Explain.

| **Internet Exercise** | Can ethics be taught? Many people say no. Experts at the Markkula Center for Applied Ethics at Santa Clara University explored that question. Look for their answer at [**http://www.scu.edu/ethics/practicing/decision/canethicsbetaught.html**]. |

a. Explain their conclusion.

b. Do you agree? Explain.

Chapter Questions

1. *Business Ethics* magazine reported the following ethical dilemma submitted by an anonymous reader:

   > Mary had only a few days to earn $1,000 in sales that would allow her to reach the $1 million sales plateau where she would receive a $10,000 bonus allowing her to finance the dream home she had found. The sales climate was tough, but she had one remaining prospect, inner-city Lincoln School, which could make especially good use of new educational materials. Lincoln had no budget for discretionary purchases, but Mary considered "donating" $1,000 to the school in return for which they would make the purchases that would put her over the top. She knew her donation would help disadvantaged students and herself, but her conscience was troubled.[88] What should she do? Explain.

2. Resolve this ethical dilemma posed by Carl Kaufmann of Du Pont:[89]

   > Assume that federal health investigators are pursuing a report that one of your manufacturing plants has a higher-than-average incidence of cancer among its employees. The plant happens to keep excellent medical records on all its employees, stretching back for decades, which might help identify the source of the problem. The government demands the files. But if the company turns them over, it might be accused of violating the privacy of all those workers who had submitted to private medical exams. The company offers an abstract of the records, but the government insists on the complete files, with employee names. Then the company tries to obtain releases from all the workers, but some of them refuse. If you give the records to the feds, the company has broken its commitment of confidentiality. What would you do?

3. a. Would you say that female undergraduate business students are more ethically inclined than their male counterparts? Explain.

   b. Would you say that religious commitment correlates with a stronger ethical inclination among undergraduate business students? Explain.

4. a. In her book *Lying,*[90] Sissela Bok argues that lying by professionals is commonplace. For example, she takes the position that prescribing placebos for experimental purposes is a lie and immoral. Do you agree with her position? Explain.

b. Is the use of an unmarked police car an immoral deception? Explain.

c. One study estimates that Americans average 200 lies per day if one includes "white lies" and inaccurate excuses. On balance, do you believe Americans approve of lying? Explain.

5. *Tonight Show* host Jay Leno performed in commercials encouraging his audience to "eat your body weight in Doritos."[91] He says that he turned down alcohol ads at twice the money. "I don't drink . . . And I don't like to sell it. You don't see dead teenagers on the highway with bags of Doritos scattered around them."[92]

a. Are you in agreement with the moral distinction that Leno draws between encouraging the consumption of alcohol and encouraging the consumption of Doritos? Explain.

b. Given the influence of television and of "stars," is all television advertising by celebrities inherently unethical? Explain.

6. The following quote and questions are drawn from Leonard Lewin's "Ethical Aptitude Test."

As with other goods and services, the medical care available to the rich is superior to that available to the poor. The difference is most conspicuous in the application of new and expensive lifesaving techniques.[93]

a. Is ability to pay an acceptable way to allocate such services? Explain.

b. If not, how should such services be apportioned?

c. Many lifesaving drugs can be tested effectively only on human beings. But often subjects are exposed to such dangers that only those who feel they have nothing to lose willingly participate. Are there any circumstances in which it would be right to conduct such tests without ensuring that the persons tested clearly understood the risks they were taking? Explain.

d. How much in dollars is the average human life worth?

7. Aaron Burr said, "All things are moral to great men." Regardless of your personal point of view, defend Burr's position.

8. A pharmacist in Lexington, Kentucky, refused to stock over-the-counter weight reducers. His reasons were (1) the active ingredient is the same as that in nasal decongestants; (2) he feared their side effects, such as high blood pressure; and (3) he felt weight reduction should be achieved via self-discipline.[94] Assume the pharmacist manages the store for a group of owners who have given him complete authority about the products stocked. Was his decision ethical? Explain.

9. When *Business and Society Review* surveyed the presidents of 500 large U.S. companies, 51 responded with their reactions to hypothetical moral dilemmas. One question was this:

Assume that you are president of a firm that provides a substantial portion of the market of one of your suppliers. You find out that this supplier discriminates illegally against minorities, although no legal action has been taken. Assume further that this supplier gives you the best price for the material you require, but that the field is competitive. Do you feel that it is proper to use your economic power over this supplier to make them stop discriminating?[95]

Respond to this question.

10. a. Do you think taking office supplies home from work for personal use is unethical? Explain.

    b. Are employers committing a serious ethics breach when they monitor their employees' e-mail? Explain.

11. Commentator Robert Scheer asks, "What does it mean that a whopping 70 percent of Americans, according to a recent *New York Times*–CBS News poll, believe that mass culture is responsible for debasing our moral values?"[96]

    a. Answer Scheer's question.

    b. Scheer went on to say;

    > Worse, these national moralists—dominated these days by evangelical Christians—politicize the issue by blaming "liberal Hollywood" for what deregulation and the free market have wrought. Never mind that Arnold Schwarzenegger made all those violent movies, it is the Democrats and their ilk who are corrupting youth by promulgating our "relativistic" morality. But that's just bunk.[97]

    Do you agree with Scheer's "that's just bunk" position? If not, why? If so, who is to blame for our arguable moral decay?

12. In general, does the American value system favor "cheaters" who win in life's various competitions over virtuous individuals who "lose" with regularity? Explain.

13. If you were an executive about to hire a new manager, which of the following qualities would you consider most important/least important: verbal skills, honesty/integrity, enthusiasm, appearance, sense of humor? Explain.

14. In general, do smaller firms have higher ethical standards than larger firms? Explain.

15. a. Rank the following occupations as to your perception of their ethical quality: businesspeople, lawyers, doctors, teachers, farmers, engineers, carpenters, librarians, scientists, professional athletes, letter carriers, secretaries, journalists.

    b. In general, do you find educated professionals to be more ethical than skilled but generally less-educated laborers? Explain.

    c. Can you justify accepting an occupation that is not at or near the top of your ethical ranking? Explain how your ranking affects your career choices.

16. Can businesspeople successfully guide their conduct by the Golden Rule?

17. Comment on the following quotes from Albert Z. Carr:

    > [M]ost bluffing in business might be regarded simply as game strategy—much like bluffing in poker, which does not reflect on the morality of the bluffer.
    >
    > I quoted Henry Taylor, the British statesman who pointed out that "falsehood ceases to be falsehood when it is understood on all sides that the truth is not expected to be spoken"—an exact description of bluffing in poker, diplomacy, and business.

    *   *   *   *   *

    > [T]he ethics of business are game ethics, different from the ethics of religion.

* * * * *

An executive's family life can easily be dislocated if he fails to make a sharp distinction between the ethical systems of the home and the office—or if his wife does not grasp that distinction.[98]

18. Anthropology professor Lionel Tiger has argued for the creation of "moral quality circles" to help improve business conduct. Tiger notes,

> [O]ur species evolved in small groups of perhaps 25 to 200 hunters and gatherers, groups in which there was no place to hide. Over 200,000 generations or so we evolved great face-to-face sensitivity and a lively skill for "whites-of-their-eyes" assessments of others.

* * * * *

> These ancient but still lively emotions can be tied into the nature of organizational life to help overcome the all-too-evident capacity of large groups to yield to "if you want to get along, go along." My hunch is that moral laxity emerges when members of such groups receive little or no dignified opportunity to define their moral views on practical matters without the risk of endangering their occupational health.[99]

Tiger says that our moral systems sprang from that small-group context; but today, with complex industry replacing hunter–gatherers, those moral systems no longer correspond to contemporary needs. Tiger goes on to argue that we have a kind of "gene for morality" and that most of us have a rather clear sense of right and wrong. Given these conditions, he proposes the moral quality circle, in which workers would discuss the ethical implications of their duties and of the company's conduct in much the same manner that quality circles are now used to improve productivity and reliability. Do you see any value in Tiger's proposal? Explain.

19. Assume that you are working as manager of women's clothing in a large department store. You observe that the manager of equivalent rank to you in men's clothing is performing poorly in that she arrives late for work, she keeps her records ineptly, and she is rude to customers. However, her work has no direct impact on your department.

   a. Do you have any responsibility either to help her or to report her poor performance? Explain.

   b. If the store as a whole performs poorly, but you have performed well, do you bear any degree of personal responsibility for the store's failure when you confined your efforts exclusively to your own department even though you witnessed mismanagement in other departments? Explain.

20. We are often confronted with questions about the boundaries of our personal responsibilities.

   a. How much money, if any, must you give to satisfy your moral responsibility in the event of a famine in a foreign country? Explain.

   b. Would your responsibility be greater if the famine were in America? Explain.

Notes

1. David Cho, "Pressure at Mortgage Firm Led to Mass Approval of Bad Loans," *The Washington Post*, May 7, 2007, p. A01.

2. Ibid.

3. Ibid.

4. Christopher Maag, "Cleveland Sues 21 Lenders Over Subprime Mortgages," *The New York Times,* January 12, 2008, Sec. A, p. 9.

5. Paul Davies and Kara Scannell, "Guilty Verdicts Provide 'Red Meat' to Prosecutors Chasing Companies," *The Wall Street Journal,* May 26, 2006, p. A1.

6. Carolyn Said, "The Enron Verdict: From White Collars to Prison Blues," SFGate.com, May 26, 2006 [**http://www.sfgate.com/cgi-bin/article.cgi?file=/c/a/2006/05/26/BUGL3J2D3B33.DTL**].

7. Tom Fowler, "Skilling Gets 24 Years in Prison for Enron Fraud," Chron.com, October 23, 2006 [**http://www.chron.com/disp/story.mpl/front/4279719.html**].

8. John R. Emshwiller, "Skilling Gets 24 Years in Prison," *The Wall Street Journal,* October 24, 2006, p. C1.

9. Jack and Suzy Welch, "The Welch Way," *BusinessWeek,* June 12, 2006, p. 100.

10. Associated Press, "SEC Says 'Culture of Fear' Led to Qwest's Acts," *Des Moines Register,* March 22, 2005, p. 10C.

11. Carrie Johnson, "Former Qwest Chief Gets 6-Year Prison Term," *Washington Post,* July 28, 2007, p. D01.

12. Raymond Baumhart, *Ethics in Business* (New York: Holt, Rinehart & Winston, 1968), p. 10.

13. Timothy Schelhardt, "Are Layoffs Moral? One Firm's Answer: You Ask, We'll Sue," *The Wall Street Journal,* August 1, 1996, p. A1.

14. Ibid.

15. John P. MacKenzie, "Lending a Hand if a Company Asks," *The New York Times,* February 3, 2002, Sec. 3, p. 11.

16. Allen G. Breed, "Sentences Vary When Kids Die in Hot Cars," *Washingtonpost.com,* July 29, 2007 [**http://www.washingtonpost.com/wp-dyn/content/article/2007/07/29/AR2007072900213.html**].

17. "2006 Josephson Institute Report Card on the Ethics of American Youth: Part One—Integrity (Summary of Data)" [**http://www.josephsoninstitute.org/pdf/ReportCard_press-release?2006-1013.pdf**].

18. Ibid.

19. David Callahan, *The Cheating Culture: Why More Americans Are Doing Wrong to Get Ahead* (New York: Harcourt, 2004).

20. Jackson Lears, "Cheater, Cheater," *In These Times,* June 21, 2004, p. 28.

21. Eriq Gardner, "Cheat Sheet," *Corporate Counsel,* June 2004, p. 131.

22. Neil Howe and William Strauss, "Will the Real Gen Y Please Stand Up," *latimes.com,* March 2, 2007 [**http://www.latimes.com/news/opinion/la-oe-howe2mar02,0,4956647.story?track=ntottext**].

23. "Duke's B-School Cheating Scandal," *The Christian Science Monitor,* May 4, 2007 [**http://www.csmonitor.com/2007/0504/p08s01-comv.html**].

24. Donald L. McCabe, Kenneth D. Butterfield, and Linda Klebe Trevino, "Academic Dishonesty in Graduate Business Programs: Prevalence, Causes, and Proposed Action," *Academy of Management Learning & Education* 5, no. 3 (2006), p. 294.

25. Ibid.

26. Lee Berton, "Business Students Hope to Cheat and Prosper, New Study Shows," *The Wall Street Journal,* April 25, 1995, p. B1.

27. Ibid.

28. Susan C. Thomson, "Internet Helps Swell E-Cheating on Campuses," *The Washington Post,* March 14, 2004, p. A08.

29. Mary Rourke, "What Happened to America's Moral Climate?" *Los Angeles Times,* April 26, 2001, p. E1.

30. Shaena Engle, "Political Interest on the Rebound among the Nation's Freshmen, UCLA Survey Reveals" [**www.gseis.ucla.edu/heri/03_press_release.pdf**].

31. News Release, "Students Experience Spiritual Growth During College," December 18, 2007 [**www.spirituality.ucla.edu**].

32. Ibid.

33. "The Most-Praised Generation Goes to Work," *The Wall Street Journal,* April 20, 2007, p. W1.

34. Jonah Goldberg, "Our Centers of the Universe," *latimes.com,* August 7, 2007 [**http://www.latimes.com/news/opinion/la-oe-goldberg7aug07,0,692285.column?coll=la-tot-opinion&track=ntottext**].

35. "Confidence in Leaders of Major Institutions: Small Business Tops the List this Year," *The Harris Poll #19*, March 1, 2007 [**http://www.harrisinteractive.com/harris_poll/index.asp?PID=735**].

36. "New Research Indicates Ethical Corporate Cultures Impact the Ability to Attract, Retain and Ensure Productivity among U.S. Workers," *LRN Ethics Study,* 2006 [**http://www.lrn.com/index.php?option=com_content&task=view&id=263&Itemid=175**].

37. Ibid.

38. For an elaboration of Kohlberg's stages, see, for example, W. D. Boyce and L. C. Jensen, *Moral Reasoning* (Lincoln, NE: University of Nebraska Press, 1978), pp. 98–109.

39. Lawrence Kohlberg, "The Cognitive–Development Approach to Moral Education," *Phi Delta Kappan* 56 (June 1975), p. 670.

40. Carol Gilligan, "In A Different Voice: Women's Conceptions of Self and Morality," *Harvard Educational Review* 47, no. 4 (November 1977), p. 481.

41. For an overview of the justice versus care debate, see Grace Clement, *Care, Autonomy, and Justice* (Boulder, CO: Westview Press, 1996).

42. James Weber and David Wasieleski, "Investigating Influences on Managers' Moral Reasoning," *Business & Society* 40, no. 1 (March 2001), pp. 79, 83.

43. Diana Robertson et al., "The Neural Processing of Moral Sensitivity to Issues of Justice and Care," *Neuropsychologia* 45 (2007), pp. 755, 763.

44. Daniel Kahneman & Cass R. Sunstein, "Indignation: Psychology, Politics," Law, *University of Chicago Law & Economics Olin Working Paper No. 346* [**http://ssrn.com/abstract=1002707**].

45. For a description of the moral intuition argument, see Jonathan Haidt, "The Emotional Dog and Its Rational Tail: A Social Intuitionist Approach to Moral Judgment," *Psychological Review* 108, No. 4 (2001), p. 814.

46. See Joshua Greene & Jonathan Haidt, "How (and Where) Does Moral Judgment Work?" *Trends in Cognitive Science* 6 (2002), p. 517.

47. Joshua Greene et al., "An fMRI Investigation of Emotional Engagement in Moral Judgment," *Science* 293 (2001), p. 2105.

48. Marc Hauser, *Moral Minds* (New York: HarperCollins Publishers, 2006).

49. Nicholas Wade, "Is 'Do Unto Others' Written into Our Genes?" *The New York Times,* September 18, 2007 [**http://www.nytimes.com/2007/09/18/science/18mora.html?**].

50. See, e.g., David Pizarro and Paul Bloom, "The Intelligence of the Moral Intuitions - Comment on Haidt," *Psychological Review* 110, No. 1 (2003), p. 193.

51. Edwin M. Hartman, "Can We Teach Character? An Aristotelian Answer," *Academy of Management Learning & Education* 5, No. 1 (2006), p. 68.

52. Tom Zucco, "Ethics Issues? Check Goals," *St. Petersburg Times,* January 28, 2006, p. 1D.

53. Ibid.

54. "Business Roundtable Institute for Corporate Ethics Announces Key Findings from 'Mapping the Terrain' Survey of CEOs," *Business Wire,* June 8, 2004 [**http://web.lexis-nexis.com/ universe/document?_m=85aa4f7ae2f804…**].

55. Ethics Resource Center Research Department, "2003 National Business Ethics Survey," (Executive Summary) [**http://www.ethics.org/nbes2003/2003nbes_summary.html**].

56. Joseph L. Badaracco, Jr., and Allen P. Webb, "Business Ethics: A View from the Trenches," *California Management Review* 37, no. 2 (Winter 1995), pp. 8, 12.

57. Daniel Akst, "Room at the Top, for Improvement," *The Wall Street Journal,* October 26, 2004, p. D8.

58. Joseph L. Badaracco, Jr., *Defining Moments: When Managers Must Choose between Right and Wrong* (Boston: Harvard Business School Press, 1997), p. 65.

59. Susan Pulliam, "The 'It Wasn't Me' Defense," *The Wall Street Journal,* July 9, 2004, p. B1.

60. Rachel Beck, Associated Press, "Bucks Still Flow to Troubled CEOs," *Des Moines Register,* November 7, 2004, p. 1D.

61. Ibid.

62. Eric Lai, "Conway's Take Eclipses Severance," *East Bay Business Times,* October 22, 2004 [**http://www.bizjournals.com/eastbay/stories/2004/10/25/story1.html**].

63. Steve Crabtree and Nicole Naurath, "Gallup Launches Worldwide Corruption Index," December 1, 2006 [**http://www.hra.am/file/gallup_corruption.htm**].

64. Michael Mainville, "Bribery Thrives as Big Business in Putin's Russia," *SFGate.com,* January 2, 2007 [**http://www.sfgate.com/cgi-bin/article.cgi?file=/c/a/2007/01/02/MNG8QNBCTN1. DTL**].

65. Ibid.

66. David Crawford and Mike Esterl, "Siemens Ruling Details Bribery Across the Globe," *The Wall Street Journal,* November 16, 2007, p. A1.

67. Ibid.

68. Mark Magnier, "In China, Bribers Get Off Easy," *latimes.com,* August 10, 2007 [**http://www.latimes.com/news/la-fg-bribes10aug10,0,2674093.story?coll=la-tot-topstories& track=ntottext**]

69. Carrie Johnson, "U.S. Targets Bribery Overseas," *Washington Post,* December 5, 2007, p. D01.

70. Ibid.

71. Ibid.

72. Neil Weinberg, "Corporate Crime Wave Unabated," *Forbes.com,* October 16, 2007 [**http://www.forbes.com/2007/10/16/corporate-crime-report-cx_nw_1016.html**].

73 PricewaterhouseCoopers, "Global Economic Crime Survey 2007: US Supplement" [**http://www.pwc.com/extweb/pwcpublications.nsf/docid/7380702EC2F7BC248525736F00 5DC595**].

74. Ibid.

75. Shawn Young and Peter Grant, "More Pinstripes to Get Prison Stripes," *The Wall Street Journal,* June 20, 2005, p. C1.

76. Joann S. Lublin and Kara Scannell, "Critics See Some Good from Sarbanes-Oxley," *The Wall Street Journal,* July 30, 2007, p. B1.

77. Portions of this paragraph relied on Robert G. Morvillo and Robert J. Anello, "White-Collar Crime, Corporate Compliance Programs: No Longer Voluntary," *New York Law Journal,* December 7, 2004, p. 3.

78. See *United States v. Booker*, 125 S.Ct. 738 (2005), *Gall v. United States*, 128 S.Ct. 586 (2007), and *Kimbrough v. United States*, 128 S.Ct. 558 (2007).

79. *Rita v. United States*, 127 S.Ct. 2456 (2007).

80. Jeff Eckhoff, "Guidelines Used Less in Sentencing," *Des Moines Register*, March 19, 2006, p. 1B.

81. Ron Scherer and Kris Axtman, "Enron's Impact on the Corner Office," *The Christian Science Monitor*, May 26, 2006 [**http://www.csmonitor.com/2006/0526/p25s02-usju.html**].

82. Carrie Johnson, "Merck to Pay $650 Million in Medicaid Settlement," *Washington Post*, February 8, 2008, p. A01.

83. Ibid.

84. Ibid.

85. Ibid.

86. Pallavi Gogoi, "The Trouble with Business Ethics," *BusinessWeek Online,* June 25, 2007 [**http://www.businessweek.com/bwdaily/dnflash/content/jun2007/db20070622_221291.htm**].

87. Jack Liles, "Blow the Whistle . . . Then Watch Out," *The Wall Street Journal,* February 21, 2002, p. A19.

88. Shel Horowitz, "Should Mary Buy Her Own Bonus?" *Business Ethics.* Submitted by Anonymous, August 1, 2007 [**http://www.business-ethics.com/node/65**].

89. Carl Kaufmann, "A Five-Part Quiz on Corporate Ethics," *Washington Post*, July 1, 1979, pp. C-1, C-4.

90. Sissela Bok, *Lying: Moral Choice in Public and Private Life* (New York: Vintage Books, 1999).

91. "Short Takes," *Des Moines Register,* February 5, 1990, p. 2T.

92. Ibid.

93. Leonard C. Lewin, "Ethical Aptitude Test," *Harper's,* October 1976, p. 21.

94. Reported on WKYT TV, Channel 27, *Evening News,* Lexington, Kentucky, May 12, 1980.

95. "Business Executives and Moral Dilemmas," *Business and Society Review,* no. 13 (Spring 1975), p. 51.

96. Robert Scheer, "The Invisible Hand Holds the Remote," *Los Angeles Times,* November 30, 2004, p. B13.

97. Ibid.

98. Albert Z. Carr, "Is Business Bluffing Ethical?" *Harvard Business Review* 46, no. 1 (January–February 1968), pp. 143–52.

99. Lionel Tiger, "Stone Age Provides Model for Instilling Business Ethics," *The Wall Street Journal,* January 11, 1988, p. 22.

CHAPTER THREE

The Corporation and Public Policy: Expanding Responsibilities

At the end of this chapter, students will be able to:

1. Recognize the interdependent relationship between business and the larger society.

2. Discuss whether business should play a more or less active role in politics, education, and other public-sector activities.

3. Discuss concerns about globalization such as the increasing wealth gap.

4. List some of the critics' primary complaints about the alleged abuse of corporate power in contemporary America.

5. Make a tentative assessment regarding the proper role of business in society.

6. Explain the concept of corporate social responsibility.

7. Discuss whether socially responsible business is "good business."

8. Explain the triple bottom line/sustainability approach to corporate citizenship.

9. Contrast the stakeholder and shareholder approaches to corporate social responsibility.

PRACTICING ETHICS) Yvon Chouinard and Patagonia

Outdoor adventurer Yvon Chouinard and his wife Ellen Pennoyer, in 1972, founded Patagonia, Inc., the sports clothing and outdoor gear retailer. By 2006, Patagonia had revenues of about $270 million, the product of entrepreneurial drive and a corporate culture practicing "green" business and "management by absence."

Chouinard was an early advocate for doing business in an environmentally friendly way; including for example, placing notes in Patagonia catalogues encouraging customers to buy only what they need. Chouinard's 2005 memoir, Let My People Go Surfing, explains his commitment to a workplace where capitalism, ethics, and fun can co-exist. Chouinard minimizes workplace monitoring believing lightly supervised employees will complete their work responsibly. Good surf or fresh snow are embraced at Patagonia where employees are free to take breaks for fun. Chouinard has become famous for his sense of social responsibility and his leadership in the environmental movement. Approaching age 70, Chouinard considers Patagonia

a work in progress, as he tests his view that a company can do the right thing for its workers and the planet and still prosper. [For more detail about Chouinard and Patagonia, see, e.g., Susan Casey, "Patagonia: Blueprint for Green Business," Fortune, May 29, 2007 [**http://money.cnn.com/ magazines/fortune/fortune_archive/2007/04/02/8403423/ index.htm**].

Questions

1. Is Chouinard correct that companies can treat workers well, respect the environment and still make money? Explain.

2. If he is correct, why aren't all companies following the Patagonia model?

Sources: Brad Wieners, "The Gospel of Yvon," Men's Journal, July 2007, p. 51; and "Employees Who March to Their Own Music," BusinessWeek, December 19, 2005, p. 81.

Introduction

The Yvon Chouinard/Patagonia story expresses the central mission of this chapter; the examination of the corporation's duties, if any, beyond providing the best products and services at the lowest price. We ask in this chapter whether the corporation must make a broad contribution to the general societal welfare beyond the performance required by the market. Put another way, must the corporation fulfill the role of citizen with all of the responsibilities that corporate wealth and power suggest? Clearly, tomorrow's leaders must understand the increasingly complex and interdependent relationship between business and the larger society. We explore the changing nature of that relationship in four parts: (1) criticism of corporate America, (2) the emergence of the expectation of *corporate social responsibility,* (3) the management of social responsibility, and (4) the examination of some specific business and society issues.

Part One—Corporate Power and Corporate Critics

Corporate critics have long argued that the public interest has not been well served by America's big corporations. We recognize that colossal size and the economies of scale that accompany it have been critical to American competitiveness in today's unforgiving global market. At the same time, that very size, the critics say, permits continuing abuse of the American public. Of course, we recognize that big companies are a fixture of the American landscape. However, a reminder of the specifics may be useful.

Wal-Mart is now the largest company in America (see Table 3.1) and the first service company to hold the top spot. Wal-Mart is, by a wide margin, America's number one employer with some 1.4 million domestic workers.[1]

TABLE 3.1   America's Largest Corporations

Corporation	Location	Sales Revenue (in billions)
Wal-Mart Stores	Bentonville, AK	$351.1
Exxon Mobil	Irving, TX	347.3
General Motors	Detroit, MI	207.3
Chevron	San Ramon, CA	200.6
ConocoPhillips	Houston, TX	172.5

Source: "*Fortune* 500 2007 Annual Ranking of America's Largest Corporations.

The extraordinary wealth of America's corporate institutions is such that they tower over most countries of the world in economic might. If we compare corporate sales with gross national products, Wal-Mart, General Motors, Exxon Mobil, Ford Motor, and Chevron rank among the 60 largest economic entities in the world.[2] Ninety-five of the globe's largest 150 economic entities are corporations.[3]

> Only 18 percent of Americans expressed "a great deal" or "quite a lot" of confidence in big business.

The critics' concerns seem to be shared by many Americans. In a 2007 Gallup Poll only 18 percent of Americans expressed "a great deal" or "quite a lot" of confidence in big business. Indeed, among the 15 major institutions listed, only health maintenance organizations (15 percent) and Congress (14 percent) ranked lower than big business. The military (69 percent), small business (59 percent), the police (54 percent), organized religion (46 percent), and banks (41 percent) topped the list.[4]

The Corporate State

The extraordinary authority of the corporate community in contemporary America and in global life is undeniable. Changing American tax policy graphically reveals that influence. A 2004 study shows that the effective tax rate for America's biggest corporations has declined sharply in recent years, and one-third of those companies paid zero taxes or less in at least one of the three years of the study period.[5] Likewise, the share of all federal taxes paid by corporations has fallen dramatically from 12.1 percent of all federal taxes in 1998 to 9.9 percent in 2003.[6] As Warren Buffett, one of the world's richest men put it, "If class warfare is being waged in America, my class is clearly winning."[7]

Of course, the stunning corporate scandals of recent years (alleged fraud in sub-prime loans, Enron, WorldCom, and so on) have strengthened doubts about corporate honor. A 2007 national survey shows that Americans are "deeply worried" about America's future and that corporate misconduct is a "major source" of that anxiety.[8] Cynicism is rampant. For example, "while 74 percent believe that large corporations should give priority to being fair and responsible in dealing with their consumers and employees over looking out for the bottom line (11 percent), only 13 percent say that being fair and responsible is actually corporations' priority today while 81 percent say it's the bottom line."[9]

Likewise complaints about the corporate role in pollution, discrimination, white-collar crime, misleading advertising, and so on remain commonplace. But in a democratic, free market society like America's, presumably we all must share some of the blame for our problems. If we are not happy with, for example, Wal-Mart's treatment of its employees, we are free to shop elsewhere. Arguably, then, the role of business in American life merely reflects the values of the American people. Thus the critics' broader concern is that America has committed its very *soul* to business values in a way that is progressively undermining our national well-being. We will briefly examine that argument prior to turning to our more detailed study of corporate social responsibility and government regulation of business.

Corporations as Psychopaths?

The 2004 movie documentary, *The Corporation,* argues that the corporation has become the dominant institution in American life, exceeding the influence of both religion and government. One result is that corporations often demonstrate the "traits of the prototypical psychopath." The contemporary corporation is depicted as an "exploitative monster" driven not by the greater good but by its first responsibility to stockholders.

Source: Jim Keough, "Film Sees Evil in Corporations," *Worchester Telegram & Gazette,* September 29, 2004, p. C5.

America's Soul?

Critics contend that the power of the business community has become so encompassing that virtually all dimensions of American life have absorbed elements of the business ethic. Values commonly associated with businesspeople (competition, profit seeking, reliance on technology, faith in growth) have overwhelmed traditional humanist values (cooperation, individual dignity, human rights, meaningful service to society). In the name of wealth, efficiency and productivity, the warmth, decency, and value of life have been debased. We engage in meaningless work.

Objects dominate our existence

Objects dominate our existence. We operate as replaceable cogs in a vast, bureaucratic machine. Indeed, we lose ourselves, the critics argue. Charles Reich, former Yale University law professor, addressed the loss of self in his influential book of the Vietnam War era, *The Greening of America:*

> Of all of the forms of impoverishment that can be seen or felt in America, loss of self, or death in life, is surely the most devastating. . . . Beginning with school, if not before, an individual is systematically stripped of his imagination, his creativity, his heritage, his dreams, and his personal uniqueness, in order to style him into a productive unit for a mass, technological society. Instinct, feeling, and spontaneity are repressed by overwhelming forces. As the individual is drawn into the meritocracy, his working life is split from his home life, and both suffer from a lack of wholeness. Eventually, people virtually become their professions, roles, or occupations, and are henceforth strangers to themselves.[10]

Some interesting empirical evidence supports Reich's view that we have become hollow men and women dominated by the demands of big institutions. The Harris Alienation Index shows a generally steady rise in Americans' feelings of powerlessness from 1966 when the index stood at 29 to the 1999 poll in which the index stood at 62.[11] *Alienation,* as defined in the survey, includes feelings of economic inequity (the rich get richer, the poor get poorer), feelings of disdain about the people in power, and feelings of powerlessness (being left out and not counting for much). The results since 1999, however, have improved with the 2007 Index at 55.[12]

Actor Ben Stein lamented an increasingly divided America

Actor and conservative commentator Ben Stein, speaking in 2006, lamented an increasingly divided America where the interests of corporations and the wealthy are dominant and the well-being of others is in danger of being forgotten:

> The Saturday before Memorial Day I spoke to a gathering of widows and widowers, parents and children of men and women in uniform who have lost their lives in Iraq and Afghanistan. The person who spoke before me was a beautiful woman named Joanna Wroblewski, whose husband of less than two years—after four years of dating at Rutgers—had been killed in Iraq. She cried as she spoke. . . . She spoke of her devotion to her country and her husband's pride in the flag. . . .
>
> Are we keeping the faith with Joanna Wroblewski? . . . Are we maintaining an America that is not just a financial neighborhood, but also a brotherhood and a sisterhood worth losing your husband for? Is this still a community of the heart, or a looting opportunity? Will there even be a free America for Mrs. Wroblewski's descendants, or will we be a colony of the people [foreign lenders] to whom we have sold our soul?[13]

Question

According to some polls, nearly three-quarters of Americans think corporations have too much power. Do you agree that corporations are too powerful? Explain.

Politics

Now we turn to a more particularized examination of the corporate critics' concerns. We begin with politics, where critics charge that big money enables the business community to disproportionately influence the electoral and law-making processes.

In recent decades, the corporate community has taken an increasingly direct role in the political process. As a result, corporate critics have been concerned that the financial weight of big business will undermine our pluralist, democratic approach to governance.

Corporate funds cannot lawfully be expended for federal campaign contributions. However, corporations (as well as labor unions, special interest groups, and others) can lawfully establish *political action committees (PACs)* to solicit and disburse voluntary campaign contributions. That is, corporations can solicit contributions from employees, shareholders, and others. That money is then put in a fund, carefully segregated from general corporate accounts, and disbursed by the PAC in support of a federal election campaign. Although PAC contributions are voluntary, corporate employees often feel pressured to participate.

Those corporate donations often seem to be motivated not so much by ideological goals as by pragmatic efforts to secure influence in Washington, DC. During the 2006 election cycle, business PACs gave a total of $234 million, 66 percent of which went to Republicans who were then in control of Congress. After the Democrats regained the congressional majority in that 2006 election, 58 percent of the early, business PAC contributions for the 2008 election went to Democrats.[14] According to *BusinessWeek,* however, many businesses re-affirmed their commitment to the Republican Party:

> ExxonMobil, Halliburton, PricewaterhouseCoopers, and U.S. Bancorp have remained loyal to the Republican Party. ExxonMobil spokesman Gantt Walton says his company's contributions are "very, very consistent," no matter which party is in power. "We focus on candidates that are pro-business and want to strengthen the free enterprise system."[15]

Reform

After years of bickering, Congress and President George Bush agreed to a 2002 campaign finance reform bill. Basically, the McCain-Feingold legislation curbed "soft money" donations (those that go directly to the political parties rather than to candidates) in an effort to prevent those situations where single sources often supplied hundreds of thousands or millions of dollars. Recent Supreme Court decisions have found that key portions of McCain-Feingold violate First Amendment free speech rights. Nonetheless, corporate PAC contributions have been reduced. Some of the money, however, seems to have made an end run around the law. So-called bundlers put up their own, legally permissible $2,000 individual campaign contribution and persuade dozens of friends, family, business associates, and so on to do the same. Other big concentrations of cash are also funneled into the political stream via so-called 527s (tax exempt under Section 527 of the Internal Revenue Code), groups that are independent from the political parties and thus are allowed under the law to collect and donate special-interest money. Financial tycoon George Soros, for example, donated $15 million of his own money in the 2004 election cycle.[16]

Lobbying

Government decisions have enormous influence on business practice with the result that lobbying is an essential ingredient in big business strategy. Lobbying also often serves the very useful role of efficiently educating busy politicians about the vast array of issues they must address but cannot possibly master without assistance. Of course, lobbying is not confined to the business community. Labor unions, consumer and environmental interest groups and myriad others battle to have their voices heard. So lobbying serves a valuable role in government, but unfortunately that role is often thoroughly corrupt. The clubby, personal nature of the lobbying process with its revolving door of politicians becoming lobbyists and lobbyists taking important government roles often undermines the democratic process. The *Washington Post* recently provided a discouraging example of these problems:

> It's the kind of story that seems to confirm everything people believe is sleazy about the way Washington works. . . . Sue Ellen Wooldridge, then the head of the Justice Department's environmental division, bought a $1 million vacation home with Don R. Duncan, the top lobbyist for oil company ConocoPhillips. Nine months later, Ms. Wooldridge signed off on a settlement agreement that let ConocoPhillips delay the installation of pollution-control equipment and the payment of fines.[17]

Buy Votes?

In the end, does all of the corporate money buy votes? In most cases probably not, but it certainly buys access and returned phone calls; and we have interesting evidence that lobbying pays off in very big ways for the business community. *BusinessWeek* looked at the nearly 2,000 congressional earmarks (special funding requests outside the regular legislative process) that went to companies in 2005. The study found that companies generated "roughly $28 in earmark revenue for every dollar they spent lobbying."[18] More than 20 of those companies gained $100 or more for each dollar they spent lobbying.[19]

Curb Lobbying?

Prompted by recent lobbying scandals, the Honest Leadership and Open Government Act of 2007 is part of the most comprehensive lobbying and ethics reform effort in the federal government in many years. Among its many provisions, the bill toughens penalties, requires much more thorough reporting of lobbying activity, and prohibits members of Congress and their staffs from receiving, with some exceptions, gifts and meals and travel assistance of any value from registered lobbyists, their employers (including corporations and nonprofits) and certain others. Cozy lobbyist/politician moments will not go away soon, however. Lobbyists apparently can lawfully skirt the thrust of the law simply by making campaign contributions to politicians. Those politicians can in turn invite the lobbyists to dinner, to a ball game or whatever diversion is mutually satisfying, and their campaign funds can lawfully pay for that entertainment. [For more details on loopholes in the new lobbying law, see Robert

Pear, "Ethics Law Isn't Without Its Loopholes," *The New York Times,* April 20, 2008 [**http://www.nytimes.com/2008/04/20/washington/20lobby.html**]

The article that follows details UPS's political campaign to secure federal approval of a highly lucrative cargo air route to China. For the Center for Responsive Politics and its extensive database on money in politics, see [**http://www.opensecrets.org/**].

READING

Congress Helps UPS Win Route

Larry Margasak, Associated Press

United Parcel Service landed its first cargo planes in China last week, the culmination of a 19-month, multimillion-dollar lobbying campaign.

Known for its brown, box-shaped delivery trucks, UPS won its new China air route from the Transportation Department after persuading a remarkable two-thirds of the House and Senate to serve as company pitchmen, according to documents and interviews by The Associated Press.

UPS provided draft letters for lawmakers to sign and send to the transportation agency. And the company handed out $1.2 million in political donations to congressmen who signed the letters. Twenty-seven House and Senate members got UPS checks within a week before or after the dates on the letters they signed, and 120 had received checks within two months, an AP analysis found.

Company officials also appeared at congressional offices with Teamster Union members—reminding both pro-corporate Republicans and pro-labor Democrats that the company provides nearly 350,000 jobs in virtually every city in the nation.

The package carrier also lent its town house to lawmakers for fund-raising events.

In all, 368 of the 535 members of Congress wrote to the Transportation Department in favor of granting the Beijing and Shanghai air route to UPS.

* * * * *

The company estimates the route will be worth $300 million in new revenue annually after the first year. It will allow UPS to compete with Federal Express, which has been flying to China since 1995.

The status of Federal Express, a nonunion company, as the only U.S. cargo carrier with direct access to China helped persuade the Teamsters to put aside any bitterness from a 1997 strike against UPS and join the company in its lobbying campaign.

"It was a pretty easy decision to put on a full court press on this," said Fred McLuckie, the Teamsters' legislative director.

The lobbying campaign overwhelmed Delta, American, and Polar Air Cargo, the three rivals competing for the same route.

UPS spokesman Tad Segal said the company won "because of the strength of our arguments."

Source: *Rocky Mountain News,* April 11, 2001, p. 30A. Reprinted by permission of the copyright holder, the Associated Press.

Questions

1. How would you defend UPS's powerful influence in Congress?

2. Then-Defense Secretary William Perry repeatedly told Congress that the Pentagon did not want more B-2 Stealth bombers than the 20 planes already delivered or on order. Nonetheless, in 1995 Congress agreed to spend nearly one-half billion dollars more on the bombers. Explain why Congress would approve weapons not wanted by the Pentagon.

3. Richard Goodwin, aide to former President John F. Kennedy, spoke out on PACs:

   Morally the system is bribery. It is not criminal only because those who make the laws are themselves accomplices. Government is for sale. But the bids are sealed, and the prices are very high.

   There is an easy way out: Eliminate PACs. We should place a rigorous ceiling on all congressional campaigns, allocate public funds to finance campaigns, and require television stations—the most costly component of modern political campaigns—to give a specified amount of air time to candidates.[20]

   a. Should we forbid PACs? Explain.

   b. Would such action be constitutionally permissible? Explain.

Too Much Business?

Clearly, the business community's influence in America's political life is enormous, but the critics' concerns only begin there. The corporation is arguably the central institution in contemporary America. In every dimension of American life, business values are increasingly pervasive. To those who criticize the corporation, that near-blanket adoption of the business ethic signals a dangerous distortion of the nation's priorities. In an editorial, the *Des Moines Register* commented that commercials have become so interwoven with our total existence that they cannot effectively be "separated out." Commentator Jane Eisner laments the increasing immersion of very young children in America's commercial culture:

> The typical first grader can name 200 brands and acquires an average of 70 new toys a year. American children view an estimated 40,000 commercials annually. Teen purchasing power has risen so rapidly that teenagers spend on average $100 a week.

* * * * *

> Despite having only 4.5 percent of the world's population, the United States consumes 45 percent of global toy production—but all those toys are not buying happiness, as rates of childhood depression, anxiety, and suicide are increasing.[21]

* * * * *

Business products and business values saturate and dominate all corners of American life, the critics claim. Judge for yourself as we take a quick look at several areas of concern.

Schools

Seeking quality education for their own needs and for the nation, corporations now prepare model curricula and lesson plans, while donating money and other resources to improve school performance. Likewise the corporate community has aggressively encouraged innovative reforms designed to push schools to the performance levels required in this competitive era. As Education Secretary Margaret Spellings put it, "business is becoming the voice of reform."[22]

Likewise as explained in Chapter 1, the profit-making corporation, Edison Schools, Inc., has contracted to operate schools in a number of cities, most prominently in Philadelphia. The results thus far have not been particularly encouraging, and the free market approach along with the more vigorous corporate role in education reform has intensified critics' concerns that cash-short schools have become vulnerable to corporate marketing strategies that will further indoctrinate students in business values and practices.

Some schools sell ad space
on school buses

Some schools sell ad space on school buses and distribute free book covers with ads about major consumer products. Channel One has supplied educational programming and television sets to 12,000 schools that agreed to show the programming and accompanying ads on a regular basis. Nearly 8 million children watch Channel One. The 12-minute telecasts include two minutes of ads. Channel One says that advertisers do not influence the news content, and the programming has won awards for excellence.[23]

A 2006 study of middle school students, however, demonstrates the commercial risks of Channel One. The students remembered more of the ads than they did the news programs, and the students reported buying or having their parents buy products advertised on Channel One.[24] (The study made no effort to separate the influence of Channel One ads from other ads that the students might have encountered.) Forty-seven percent of respondents to a 2004 Harris Poll of professionals in youth advertising said that schools should be protected from advertising while 45 percent felt that young people could handle the ads.[25] [For the Channel One news, see **http://www.channelonenews.com**]

> BusRadio would have piped entertainment and ads into school buses

Many schools have actively resisted growing commercialization. The Louisville, Kentucky schools responded to parents' outrage by rejecting in 2007 the new BusRadio product that would have piped entertainment programming and ads into school buses in exchange for which the school district would have received a portion of the ad revenue.[26] Soft drink distributors, responding to concerns about childhood obesity, agreed to stop selling nondiet soft drinks in the nation's schools.

Big business is also accused of turning college campuses into marketing and development opportunities. More and more campus buildings and programs, for example, are being named after corporate donors, and students are increasingly being hired as on-campus marketing representatives for companies/products such as EA, Sports Illustrated, Nike, and Red Bull. Pharmacy benefits manager, Express Scripts, became one of the first corporations to put its headquarters directly on a college campus in 2007 when it moved into its $50 million building at the University of Missouri at St. Louis. Students welcome the opportunity to conveniently work at the on-campus company, but critics worry about blending corporate and educational interests.

From kindergarten through graduate school, education is increasingly viewed as a product to be marketed and consumed on the road to prosperity in the Corporate State. Are students buying a full life or an empty commercial dream?

Religion

The ideas of management guru Peter Drucker have become the unexpected intellectual foundation of the mega-church movement in America. The giant new churches with thousands of parishioners in cavernous halls including former professional basketball arenas have applied Drucker's business principles to their "businesses":

> Bill Hybels, the pastor of the 17,000-strong Willow Creek Community Church in South Barrington, Illinois, has a quotation from Mr. Drucker hanging outside his office: "What is our business? Who is our customer? What does the customer consider the value?"[27]

> Religion, in some sense, has become a product

Churches now routinely engage in standard business practices such as advertising, promotional giveaways, and marketing campaigns. Religion, in some sense, has become a product. The aggressive marketing of the religious message and the explicit adoption of business principles in the name of religion is, for the most part, a development of recent decades. Craig Karpel, co-creator of Jewcy, an online boutique featuring clothing linked to the Jewish faith, explains the new commerce of religion:

People that are more conservative think it is commercializing or lessening the value of religion, but that's not what we are doing. This is a very different world than it was even 30 years ago. When it comes to spreading religion, the methods have gotten a lot savvier and smarter than they ever were.[28]

To many Christians, Jesus is a pop-culture icon[29] and thus is the inspiration for a vast array of commercial expressions including T-shirts, license plates, dolls, video games, flip flops, perfume, golf balls, scripture chocolates, and much more. The marriage of religion and commerce has even reached the business of sports where "Faith Nights" have become popular promotional devices at professional ball games. The Atlanta Braves and Arizona Diamondbacks major league baseball teams have sponsored Faith Nights, but that approach has been particularly successful in the minor leagues where Christian entertainers, player testimonies, faith trivia quizzes and bobbleheads of Samson and other Biblical characters draw big crowds. [For a review of *Christianity Incorporated: How Big Business Is Buying the Church,* see **http://www.directionjournal.org/article/?1301**]

Questions

1. Do you see any risks to religion in treating it as a product to be marketed and sold? Explain.

2. *a.* Why has religion increasingly become a product in the commercial world?
   b. Is everything a product in some sense?

Culture

Does America possess a cultural life? For decades, the concern was that so-called "high" culture—classical music, opera, ballet, and the like—would give way to rock and roll, television, and video games. Now that battle is over; Americans (and the world) have clearly voted for MTV and *American Idol.*

> Americans (and the world) have clearly voted for *American Idol*

Corporate America has been generous in its financial and organizational support for the traditional intellectual culture. At the same time, corporate bottom-line concerns appear to the critics to be steadily degrading America's cultural life.

For example, a 2007 Los Angeles Museum of Contemporary Art exhibit merged art and commerce by setting up a Louis Vuitton shop in the middle of the museum. The boutique sold limited-edition handbags and small leather goods designed by Japanese artist Takashi Murakami. Of course, the museum made the decision, and the market will rule on the wisdom of that decision, but the concern of the critics is that corporate financial interests are casting a long shadow of influence across the American cultural scene.[30]

Even popular culture (rock, movies, television, hip hop, and so on), already considered a wasteland, has been further debased the critics say, not merely by a mindless market (that's us), but by limitless corporate greed and indifference to

> Can Music Survive Inside the Big Box?

quality. In 2007, *The Wall Street Journal* asked: "Can Music Survive Inside the Big Box?"[31] Big box retailers like Wal-Mart, Target, and Best Buy now account for at least 65 percent of all U.S. music sales.[32] As CD sales continue to fall sharply, those big boxes are carrying fewer and fewer titles. A typical Best Buy might stock eight to twenty thousand CD titles, while the biggest of the now defunct Tower Records retail stores might have stocked over one hundred thousand titles. New rock and hip hop acts simply have trouble finding space on the big box shelves. Music will always be a part of our lives, and perhaps online markets will rejuvenate the music industry, but current music marketing practices seem to leave little room for anything that fails to fit comfortably in the high profit mainstream. Similar problems have emerged in the television industry.

Are the Corporate Suits Ruining TV?

The *Los Angeles Times* recently asked: "Are the Corporate Suits Ruining TV?"[33] As the *Times* explained, "Your TV may receive 200 channels, but virtually every one of them is owned by one of six big companies—NBC Universal, Disney, Time Warner, Viacom/Paramount, Sony, and News Corp."[34] As a result of that consolidation and relaxed Federal Communications Commission rules, most new programming is dominated by corporate decision makers whose interest in creative ideas seems to be blinded by the bottom line. In fairness, those corporations are only doing what we ask of them.

Sports

College sports is not a business

National Collegiate Athletic Association (NCAA) president Myles Brand, speaking at an ethics conference, made the argument that: "College sports is not a business. It's about educating young men and women in the field and in the classroom."[35] Texas Tech men's basketball coach Bob Knight did not agree:

> If it isn't a business then General Motors is a charity. College sports has turned into one of the biggest businesses in the whole sports industry. I use the word industry because that's what sport is. . . .[36]

The conversion of athletics, both professional and collegiate, from sport to business is essentially an accomplished fact, but its significance remains unclear. What have we lost when the innocence and idealism of sports are forfeited in favor of profit? Or are innocence and idealism simply a myth? Perhaps we are better off when corporate and personal profit—the free market—drives sports. Or is the pursuit of profit the route to the slow but sure death of meaningful sports, as one fan lamented?

> We would be a healthier society if professional sports did not exist. The love of money, or greed, takes all the fun out of sports, demeans the integrity of the games, corrupts the athletes and belittles the fans. . . . The love of money is slowly, subtly destroying sports and America.[37]

What does the future hold for the business of sports? One critic imagines the following:

> One day, perhaps the New York Yankees may morph into the IBM Yankees, ballplayers will decorate their uniforms with soft drink brands, and the Exxon Cowboys might win the General Motors Super Bowl.[38]

Ads are plastered all over Nascar drivers and cars

Of course, we have already seen more than a glimpse of that advertising-saturated sports future. The Red Bulls are New York City's major league soccer team. Ads are plastered all over Nascar drivers and cars as well as major league soccer uniforms. Ads are beginning to show up now and then on teams such as the New York Yankees and the Boston Red Sox (at least when playing in Japan) while jockeys are feverishly trying to work out deals to make commercials out of their silks.

With business values and practices spreading from professional sports to college athletics, we should not be surprised, although perhaps we should be dismayed, that the same influences are rapidly emerging in high school sports as well. Elite high school basketball teams have recently been traveling the country to play in special games. Then in the Fall 2007 high school football season, sports marketing company Intersport organized the 11-game Burger King Kirk Herbstreit Ohio vs. USA Challenge with more than a dozen high school teams from around the country coming to play games in Ohio. Burger King paid a six-figure sum to be the lead sponsor with Nike, Gatorade, and the Marines also helping with expenses. Burger King is happy with the new commercial prospect:

> "We like the fit with our customer," Burger King chief marketing officer Russ Klein said. "We like what the sport stands for. We like the every-town authenticity and appeal that high school football represents. We think it's an underdeveloped and untapped segment, and we're going to be aggressive about building it on the national stage."[39]

Will high school football emerge as the next great sports marketing opportunity? Certainly some business leaders think so:

> "I think high school sports is the next iteration where fans are going," said Ira Stahlberger, senior vice president of strategic partnerships for Intersport . . . "The market follows where the fans are. People are extremely passionate about the NFL. They are extremely passionate about college football. Next is high school football."[40]

Adidas Invests in Ten-Year-Old Hoops Star

Baltimore youth basketball phenom, Justin Jenifer, 5'6" and age 10 in 2006, had become a big prize for shoe companies who scramble for potential future stars. According to the *Washington Post,* Adidas representative, Scottie Bowden, had invested about $20,000 in Justin and his teammates in providing shoes, travel expenses, etc. Adidas pays Bowden to find future stars and get them to wear Adidas clothing. Bowden, a high school principal, blames his pursuit of child stars on the competition between Adidas, Nike, and Reebok:

> "It's about brand loyalty." Bowden said. "If you're in my uniform at 10 or 11, maybe you will stay with me later on. I'm not always happy we're focusing on 9-, 10-, 11-year-old kids. That's so early. But this is a business. And if that's what I've got to do now, then that's what I'm going to do."

Questions
1. Justin enjoys his nearly 20 pairs of shoes, Adidas headbands, travel opportunities, and so on. In the longer term, would you expect Adidas' attention to Justin to be beneficial to him? Explain.
2. Is the commercial development of youth sports a welcome new direction, in your view? Explain.

Source: Eli Saslow, "Is There Such a Thing as a Perfect 10?" *Washington Post,* July 4, 2006, p. A01.

Globalization

The critics' concerns about the domination of American life by big corporations and business values are now being applied to the entire globe. With the fall of the Soviet Union and the triumph of capitalism, the world has come to understand that free markets are simply more efficient than government rules. As a result, national boundaries are receding in importance, technology is shrinking the world, multinational companies are treating the world as one big market, less developed countries are trying to improve living standards by connecting to that market, financial assets flow freely and almost instantaneously from one side of the globe to the other, and the world becomes one highly greased, interconnected mass market. A lot of good news emerges from globalization. In general, less developed countries have the opportunity to raise their standard of living while the benefits of competition and efficiency (better products and services at lower prices) reach more people.

Fears

America has enjoyed unprecedented prosperity; from our view, globalization simply looks like the welcome spread of capitalist values to the entire world. Not surprisingly, however, many people are alarmed. They see a world rapidly coming under the thumb of America, and more particularly, America's giant, multinational corporations. Capital, technology, goods, and services can be moved rapidly throughout the world aided by the new free trade arrangements such as the North American Free Trade Agreement, the World Trade Organization, the European Union, and so on. These free trade mechanisms, in the critics' view, have essentially nullified the regulatory power of national governments and left corporations free to do largely as they wish. They see a world ruled by corporate interests with the following results:

> They see a world rapidly coming under the thumb of America

- The rich get richer and the poor fall further behind.
- Whole ecosystems, such as the Amazon Basin, are despoiled for profit-seeking purposes.
- Rural cultures are displaced and an urban migration follows.
- Financial instability is inevitable.
- Labor is exploited to satisfy market demands.
- Consumerism swells while traditional values and cultures are submerged.

[For the World Trade Association, see **http://www.wto.org**]

Rich/Poor   Scholar James Mittelman raises perhaps the fundamental globalization question:

> Is it ethically sustainable? Morally and politically, is it possible to maintain a global system in which the world's 225 richest people have a combined wealth equal to the annual income of 2.5 billion people, the poorest 47 percent of the world's population? In which the three richest people have assets that exceed the combined GDP of the forty-eight least developed countries?[41]

Can we tolerate the world's sharp division between haves and have-nots? Consider Haiti, an example very close to home, but one that clearly has not profited from that proximity. Haiti is the poorest country in the Western Hemisphere and the fourth poorest in the world, with a life expectancy of 52 years for women and 48 for men and unemployment near 70 percent.[42] Haitian sweatshop wages are often under 50 cents per hour. American corporations control much of the Haitian economy, and about 60 percent of the small country's imports and exports involve the United States. As the U.S. Network for Economic Justice reports, those close ties between America and Haiti have meant little to the Haitian people:

> Whereas corporations receive vast incentives to set up plants in Haiti...returns to the Haitian economy are minimal. . . . Decades of public investments and policy manipulation by the World Bank, the IMF, and the U.S. government have deliberately created an environment where the exploitation of workers is hailed as an incentive to invest in Haiti.[43]

Outsourcing   As in the Haitian example, globalization critics accuse the industrial world and particularly the United States of exploitation under the banner of free trade. To many in the West, however, that so-called exploitation really represents the wholesale export of good jobs to the low-wage, underdeveloped nations. Millions of American jobs have moved or will move to India, China, Mexico, and other low-wage nations. So what looks like low-wage exploitation to some represents enormous job losses for others. To corporate managers these dramatic labor shifts reflect a healthy market that will pay off for industrial nations by providing savings that will lead to new investments and new products while putting money in the hands of new customers in the low-wage nations. But to those losing their jobs, outsourcing doesn't work as the market theorizes:

> "The consulting firm I work for is sending jobs to India," said Steve Ward, a computer programmer in Philadelphia. . . . Ward, holding a sign—"Will Code for Food"— dismissed the notion that everyone benefits from the corporate savings generated by offshore outsourcing. "Companies are predatory institutions, and they have to be controlled," he said.[44]

Corporate Duty?   Whether the criticisms are fair or not, as the market increasingly "Americanizes" or "Westernizes" the globe, do American corporations bear some responsibility for addressing the resulting conflict? Certainly these problems, to the extent they are addressed at all, have traditionally been the province of government; but as globalization has magnified corporate power, we must wonder whether corporations won't increasingly be expected to fulfill expanded and, doubtless, uncomfortable new roles. Harvard Business School professor Christopher Bartlett explains:

> [T]hose leading today's multinational corporations must become much more attuned to the ways in which their actions can and do impact the fragile social, political, and economic environments in which they operate worldwide. Yet far too often these powerful companies have been so focused on their core economic role that they have ignored the huge social and political impact they have.[45]

Bad Days Ahead? While the critics lament globalization's damages, Americans, iron-ically may not be the ultimate winners. Indeed, while Americans are generally optimistic about the future, only 31 percent of them, according to a recent Pew Global Attitudes Survey, believe their children will have better lives than their own.[46] With the United States now deeply in debt to China, Russia, and the Middle East states and mired in long wars in Iraq and Afghanistan, globalization may be building a new economy:

> "It's remarkable how few have noticed we are entering an entirely new era of history—the rise of Asia," says Kishore Mahbubani, dean of Singapore's Lee Kuan Yew School of Public Policy. "By 2050," he adds, "the world's four largest economies will be China, the United States, India, and Japan"—in that order.[47]

[See the Corporate Watch Web site for an extensive database of concerns about global-ization: **http://www.corpwatch.org**]

Questions

1. *The Wall Street Journal* recently observed that outsourcing will not destroy the Amer-ican jobs of the future, but that the real problem may be whether outsourcing (and technology) could widen the gap between good "brainpower" jobs and poorly paid physical jobs. Explain how outsourcing may exacerbate the rich–poor income gap.[48]

2. *a.* Do Americans trust the business community? Explain.

   b. Does it matter? Explain.

3. In 1980 Ted Peters, an associate professor of systematic theology at the Pacific Lutheran Seminary and the Graduate Theological Union, asked,

   How will the advancing postindustrial culture influence the course of religion? It is my forecast that religion will become increasingly treated as a consumer item.

   Because our economy produces so much wealth, we are free to consume and consume beyond the point of satisfaction. There is a limit to what we can consume in the way of material goods—new homes, new cars, new electronic gadgets, new brands of beer, new restaurants, and so on. So we go beyond material wants to consume new personal experiences—such as broader travel, exotic vacations, continuing education, exciting conventions, psychotherapy, and sky diving.

   What will come next and is already on the horizon is the consumption of spiritual experiences—personal growth cults, drug-induced ecstasy, world-traveling gurus, training in mystical meditation to make you feel better, etc. Once aware of this trend, religious entrepreneurs and mainline denominations alike will take to pandering their wares, adver-tising how much spiritual realities "can do to you." It will be subtle, and it will be cloaked in the noble language of personal growth, but nevertheless the pressure will be on to treat religious experience as a commodity for consumption.[49] . . .

   a. Is Peters's forecast coming true? Explain.

   b. Is marketing necessary to the survival and growth of religion? Explain.

   c. Is marketing a threat to the legitimacy and value of religion? Explain.

4. In your opinion, which of the following will be the biggest threat to America in the future: big government, big labor, or big business?

5. Do you think allegiance to the company will become more important than allegiance to the state? Is that a desirable direction? Raise the arguments on both sides of the latter question.

6. As expressed in *BusinessWeek,* "Increasingly, the corporation will take over the role of the mother, supplying day care facilities where children can be tended around the clock."[50] How do you feel about the corporation as mother? Explain.

Part Two—Corporate Social Responsibility (CSR)

Introduction

We have seen that the business community is the subject of intense criticism. Journalist Daniel Seligman put it this way:

> A standard view of the American corporation . . . is that it is an efficient deliverer of goods and services, yet also a wellspring of social injustice. Driven by a narrow calculus of profits, it is oblivious to the common good. And so, the litany goes, it degrades the environment, promotes unsafe products, skimps on workplace safety and . . . lays off workers who have given it years of service.[51]

That broadly shared perception of business misdeeds or indifference, in conjunction with the growing influence of business values throughout American life, has led in recent decades to the development of the notion of *corporate social responsibility* (sometimes also referred to as *corporate citizenship*). We can express the issue this way: Must business decision making include consideration not merely of the welfare of the firm but of society as a whole? For most contemporary readers, the answer is self-evident—of course business bears a social responsibility. Business has enjoyed a central and favored role in American life. As such, it must assume a measure of the burden for the welfare of the total society. Indeed, businesspeople themselves now generally endorse businesses' responsibility to help solve society's problems. Companies continue to put profits first; but responding to a *Wall Street Journal*–Harris poll, 84 percent of corporate recruiters said it is important that MBAs display an awareness and knowledge of corporate social responsibility.[52] And students themselves are increasingly interested in the social responsibility/corporate citizenship approach to business practice. Similar philosophies such as the *triple bottom line* (giving close accounting attention to social and environmental performance as well as financial performance) and the *sustainable* corporation (operating the business with a focus on environmentally sensitive practices that will husband scarce resources and maintain a healthy community now and in the future) have powerful appeal to many students and managers. Those approaches are of interest to the corporate community; and as the following article suggests, MBA programs have begun to aggressively reflect these newer goals. [For the "Global Reporting Initiative" on sustainability practices around the world, see **http://www.globalreporting.org**]

Schools Turning Out Kinder, Gentler MBAs

Associated Press

At business schools across the country, future business leaders are learning to be kinder, gentler managers. In fact, if you're thinking about getting an MBA, be prepared to learn how to use your financial analysis, accounting, and marketing skills to help the environment and the community.

While that may come as a surprise to those who think of business school as a breeding ground for hard-charging executives obsessed with bottom-line results, it also reflects the realities that businesses are dealing with today. As companies go global, their shareholders are demanding more responsible business practices.

Jen Boulden, 30, is a big believer that businesses can be powerful agents of change in the environment. After working in technology marketing for eight years, she decided to get her MBA at George Washington University, in part because the school's curriculum would allow her to combine her passion for the environment with her business skills. "I wouldn't have gone back to school if I didn't find an environmentally oriented program within an MBA structure," said Boulden.

Once relegated to the fringes of a business school's curriculum, schools are slowly integrating ethics and social and environmental management into their classes. At Stanford University, for example, classes on social and environmental issues are woven into 12 of the 14 courses that business school students are required to take. At some schools, students can choose a concentration in environmental management or sustainability, the idea that a company can meet its financial goals without hurting the environment. And outside of the classroom, schools are holding more seminars and conferences on corporate social responsibility.

The Aspen Institute's Business & Society Program and the World Resources Institute's Sustainable Enterprise Program recently issued a report on the trend titled "Beyond Gray Pinstripes 2003." The study found about 45 percent of the schools that participated require students to take one or more courses on such subjects as ethics and corporate social responsibility.

That's up from 34 percent in 2001, the last time the survey was conducted.

* * * * *

"The idea of just focusing on shareholder value isn't enough for companies," said Meghan Chapple, manager of business education at WRI. Now companies have to work with broader constituencies, such as the community, the environment, and employees, she noted.

Student interest also is rising. At UNC's Kenan-Flagler Business School, about 20 percent of students attend the school because of its concentration in sustainable enterprise.

At Michigan Business School, when Timothy Fort started teaching business ethics 10 years ago his biggest hurdle was trying to convince students it was an important issue. Today, with the number of students in his class having more than quadrupled to over 400, his biggest challenge is trying to convince them that they won't be able to solve all the world's problems immediately.

Meanwhile, participation in Net Impact, a network of MBAs with an interest in social and environmental business issues, has grown to 8,000 members today from 1,350 in 1998, while the number of chapters jumped to 85 from 45 over the same period. "It's not just the tree-huggers anymore; it's more mainstream," said Benjamin Klasky, executive director of Net Impact.

Source: *Waterloo/Cedar Falls Courier,* October 20, 2003, p. B6. Reprinted by permission of the Associated Press.

Questions

1. *a.* Would America be better off with "kinder, gentler" managers in charge of the corporate community? Explain.

   b. If you were in charge of a corporation, would you be looking for "kinder, gentler" managers? Explain.

2. Have your business school courses given sufficient attention to social responsibility issues? Explain.

3. Do consumers care whether companies are socially responsible? Explain.

A New Ideology

The ascendance of the social responsibility concept represents a striking ideological shift. Historically, business was expected to concentrate on one goal—the production and distribution of the best products and services at the lowest possible prices. Business was largely exempt from any affirmative duty for the resolution of social problems until the 1950s when business scholars and critics began to encourage a larger role for corporate America. Now in the 21st century, expectations for business in society have been radically altered. Profit seeking remains central and essential, but for most businesspeople, the sometimes awkward ingredient of social responsibility must be a consideration.

What Is Social Responsibility?

The sweeping notion of corporate social responsibility is not readily reduced to a brief definition, but Davis and Blomstrom some years ago captured the core ingredients: "The idea of social responsibility is that decision makers are obligated to take actions which protect and improve the welfare of society as a whole along with their own interests."[53] More systematically, the social role of business can be thought of as an ideological continuum, corresponding roughly to the familiar American political spectrum of conservative/Republican views on the right, moderates in the middle, and liberal/Democrats on the left. Figure 3.1 depicts that continuum and is best understood by reading "backward" from right to left. On the right side of the spectrum lies the free market view where *profit maximization* is considered the best measure of social responsibility. Across the middle lies a viewpoint that is commonly thought of as the *long-term company interest* where profits are the first consideration, but where satisfied workers, customers, and community members are also of importance, within some reasonable limits, in order to secure the firm's long-term survival. On the left side of the spectrum lies the *triple bottom line/sustainability* movement that calls for a revolutionary re-visioning of corporate goals and practices such that profit maximization is only one of three key measures of success. Triple bottom line advocates specifically call for accounting practices that measure and respect the firm's *social* and *environmental* performance just as the firm's *financial* performance is measured and respected. The goal is to ensure the long-term viability (sustainability) of the organization and the total society.

Now let's examine the continuum in a bit more detail. [For the Business for Social Responsibility home page, see **www.bsr.org**]

FIGURE 3.1
A Social Responsibility Continuum

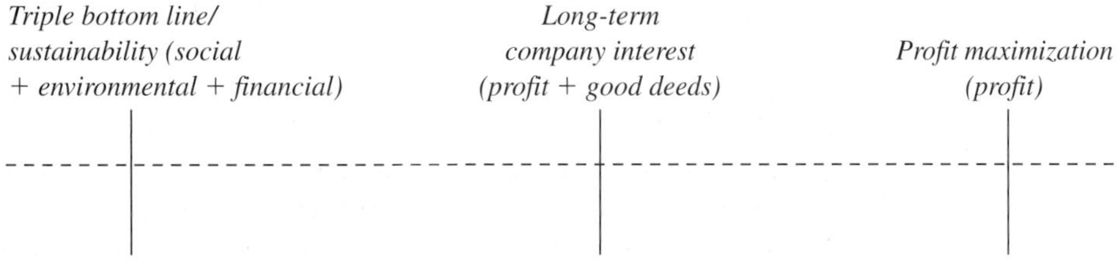

Triple bottom line/	*Long-term*	
sustainability (social	*company interest*	*Profit maximization*
+ environmental + financial)	*(profit + good deeds)*	*(profit)*

Profit Maximization Here the dominant concern lies in maximizing shareholders' interests. Those shareholders, after all, are the owners of the firm. They are taking the financial risk. Hence, from a profit maximization point of view, the only responsible and moral course of behavior is to reap the highest return possible, within the law. Nobel prize–winning economist Milton Friedman was the most prominent advocate of the profit maximization view:

> The only responsible and moral course of behavior is to reap the highest return possible, within the law

> [In a free economy] there is one and only one social responsibility of business—to use its resources and engage in activities designed to increase its profits, so long as it stays within the rules of the game, which is to say, engages in open and free competition, without deception or fraud.[54]

Friedman, employing free market reasoning, believed the firm that maximizes its profits is necessarily maximizing its contribution to society. He asked how managers can know what the public interest is. He also argued that any dilution of the profit-maximizing mode—such as charitable contributions—is a misuse of the stockholders' resources. The individual stockholder, he contended, should dispose of assets according to her or his own wishes.

Herbert Stein, former chair of the President's Council of Economic Advisers, shared Friedman's doubts about the idea of social responsibility, but Stein's concerns were of a more pragmatic nature. He argued that business is simply ill suited for solving social problems:

> Efficiency in maximizing the nation's product . . . is not the only objective of life. But it is the one that private corporations are best qualified to serve. I don't want to be a purist about this. I don't object to corporations contributing to the United Givers Fund. . . . But to rely on corporations' responsibility to solve major social problems—other than the problem of how to put our people and other resources to work most efficiently—would be a wasteful diversion from their most important function. Our other objectives can be better served in other ways, by individuals and other institutions.[55]

Long-Term Company Interest Across the broad middle ground of our social responsibility continuum lie those firms, doubtless the great majority, who believe that a strong bottom line, in many cases, requires considerations beyond the immediate, short-run, profit-maximizing interests of the firm. In a sense, these managers are merely taking a longer term view of profit maximization. They recognize the imperative of a strong return on the shareholder's investment, but they also believe that achieving that return may require heightened sensitivity to the welfare of employees, consumers, and the community. Furthermore, they often embrace the view that socially responsible behavior, within reasonable bounds, is simply the "right thing" to do. [For the United Nations' initiative to encourage responsible corporate citizenship, see **http://www.unglobalcompact.org**]

Triple Bottom Line/Sustainability Managers, whether traditional profit maximizers or those embracing the longer-term, more socially conscious attitude, are being pushed by scholars, activists, government, and often the larger community to adopt a bigger, broader conception of social responsibility—one that significantly redefines the corporate role and calls for values and tactics that will produce a sustainable, healthy global community. This redefinition is explained by Steve Rochlin:

> The new corporate citizenship challenges executives to find alternatives to zero-sum solutions that often emphasize shareholder value at the cost of social and environmental welfare. Instead, the new corporate citizenship challenges companies to deliver not just financial returns but also environmental and social value—together marking the pillars of what is called a "triple bottom line." . . .
>
> The new corporate citizenship requires business transparency and accountability regarding the ways in which business practices generate benefits and costs for issues ranging from employee diversity, community development, working conditions, clean air and water, human rights, poverty, and corruption.[56]

The triple bottom line/sustainability approach recognizes the necessity for financial success but also argues that social and environmental responsibilities are of equal importance and that corporations giving close attention to those social and economic duties have a powerful competitive advantage that will contribute to both organizational and societal sustainability. As Rochlin notes, the firm committed to triple bottom line principles and sustainability will be concerned about social equity issues such as community philanthropy, employee satisfaction, lawful corporate governance, transparency in business practices, and fair treatment of customers. In the environmental domain, sustainability will require attention to energy efficiency, waste minimization, recycling, and the total ecological agenda. All of this will be achieved via market principles, but the market is expected to work more effectively through a new spirit of cooperation between business, government, nongovernmental organizations (NGOs), and the citizenry. In sum, the idea is that the survival (sustainability) of the corporation and of the global community requires new values and new decision-making tactics that will take a balanced view of the triple bottom line while implementing accounting procedures that measure success not just in profits but in social and environmental goals as well. Figure 3.2 depicts the change in values that presumably would need to accompany a shift to the sustainability approach. [For a critique of triple bottom line thinking, see **www.businessethics.ca/3bl**]

FIGURE 3.2
Values

Who Will Satisfy the Demand for Caring Capitalism?		
Old Paradigm	→	**New Paradigm**
Careless	→	Careful, caring
Control	→	Stewardship
Me	→	We
Monocultures	→	Diversity
Growth	→	Sustainability[57]

Social Responsibility Pyramid

Another way of visualizing socially responsible business practice is depicted in Figure 3.3. Social responsibility, or corporate citizenship necessarily begins at the foundation of the pyramid with the duty to make a profit in a lawful fashion; but simultaneously the socially responsible firm moves (up the pyramid) beyond the fundamental demands of economics and law to find the ethical course of action—the behavior best suited to the demands of virtue and moral principle. In striving for profitable, lawful, ethical conduct, that company may also choose to engage in discretionary philanthropic (charitable) efforts (money, time, facilities, programs) to build a better community. While the social responsibility pyramid has been criticized, it remains a useful way of thinking about corporations' expanding duties.[58]

FIGURE 3.3

The Social Responsibility (CSR) Pyramid

Source: Archie B. Carroll, "The Pyramid of Corporate Social Responsibility: Toward the Moral Management of Organizational Stakeholders." Reprinted from *Business Horizons* 34, no. 4 (July–August 1991), pp. 39, 42. Copyright 1991 by the Foundation for the School of Business at Indiana University. Used with permission.

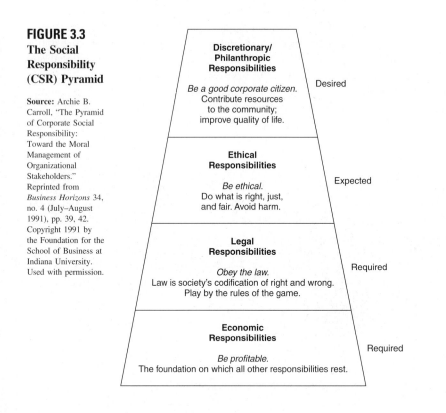

Corporations Practicing Social Responsibility

Obviously we have no shortage of social problems both domestically and globally. In recent years the corporate community has become convinced that it needs, for various reasons, to take a more active role in addressing those problems.

PRACTICING ETHICS)   Big Business—A Social Issues Leader?

Journalist Marc Gunther argues that big business is becoming a leader in addressing social problems:[59]

> Despite the understandable cynicism about the corporate world that has been fed by Enron and other scandals, many of America's big companies are becoming more socially responsible, more green, more diverse, more transparent, and more committed to the common good—as well as the bottom line.[60]

Gunther points to Hewlett-Packard, Dell, and IBM, which have agreed on a code of conduct to audit and ensure the health, safety, and human rights of the people in developing countries who work for the computer giants' electronics suppliers around the globe.[61] Likewise, Gunther notes that 227 *Fortune* 500 companies provide domestic partner benefits and that corporate America is a strong supporter of affirmative action.[62] The environmental movement clearly is influencing business practice as, for example, giant lumber retailers Home Depot and Lowe's have pledged to stop buying wood from endangered forests, and DuPont has cut its greenhouse gas emissions by 65 percent since 1990.[63] Finally, Gunther argues that leading companies have decided that they must become more open—more *transparent*—in describing their business practices. Gap recently followed that path in acknowledging that some overseas workers who make its clothes have been mistreated.

Questions

1. *a.* Do you think Gunther is correct in arguing that big business is responding in meaningful ways to the corporate social responsibility movement? Explain.

   b. Should corporations do so? Explain.

2. What forces would move corporations to give increased attention to social issues?

CSR: Smart Business from Philanthropy to Strategy   Google, through its $2 billion charitable arm, Google.org, makes many generous charitable contributions, but its version of CSR reaches beyond philanthropic efforts to attack some of the world's biggest problems (specifically, the environment, global poverty, and global health) by investing in businesses, lobbying for political causes and directing portions of its employees' time to developing business and technology solutions for those problems. Google expects to invest in small businesses in the developing world, encourage the commercial development of plug-in cars, and help make renewable energy cheaper than coal. Google is investing $10 million, for example, in eSolar, Inc., a company that is trying to develop very large scale solar power systems.[64] Google hopes to use capitalism to make life better around the world.

Google is one of many companies that have elevated their CSR efforts from giving to building. Many of those companies view social responsibility as workable only if it contributes to the strategic mission of the business and ultimately to the bottom line. Nike, for example, turned aggressively to social responsibility measures as a way of restoring its brand image after criticism for its use of global sweatshop labor. Consumers are willing to pay higher prices at Whole Foods Market, the healthy food grocery chain, in part because of the company's reputation for good works. Social responsibility can also serve the strategic advantage of encouraging innovation. The shoe manufacturer, Timberland, concerned about toxic compounds in some of the glue it used, developed new glues and reduced the amount used in order to diminish poisonous compounds in the environment, Timberland believes those zealous ethical practices also serve the purpose of inspiring its workforce, thereby benefiting the company's bottom line. Thus we see that costly social responsibility practices can generate a big return when those practices support the company's strategic goals.[65]

Finding an Employer with a Conscience

Surveys of today's teenagers suggest that employers trying to replace millions of retiring baby boomers may need to demonstrate a social commitment in order to be fully competitive in the hiring market. Seventy-eight percent of teens surveyed worldwide by Energy BBDO said that money was less important to them than personal fulfillment. The teens, who seem to have been deeply affected by 9/11, say they are committed to equality, responsible corporate behavior, and a clean environment. Today's teens are expected to be particularly interested in careers that allow them to be part of a larger social purpose. Experts mention Whole Foods Market, Inc., the Austin, Texas natural foods chain, as an example of a company that might be particularly attractive to tomorrow's new managers. Whole Foods caps CEO pay at 14 times the rate of the average employee.

Questions
1. a. Will you insist on a job with a "social purpose"?
   b. Do all jobs have a social purpose?
2. Would you expect money to replace social goals in the teen hierarchy as they age?

Source: Lindsey Gerdes, "Get Ready for a Pickier Workforce," *BusinessWeek,* September 18, 2006, p. 82.

But Is Corporate Responsibility Good Business?

The evidence is mixed, but substantially supportive of the idea that the market rewards good conduct and punishes bad conduct. A 2004 meta-analysis of 52 studies found a link between corporate social performance and corporate financial performance that is significant and varies from moderately to highly positive.[66] Looked at from another angle, however, a small global survey found that most executives think social responsibility should be taken seriously, but they do not think it has a significant impact on customer or investor decisions,[67] and a 2007 Harris Poll of nearly 2,400 Americans found only 16 percent saying that a company's reputation for social responsibility has a strong impact on their decisions about purchases and with whom to do business.[68] Similarly, a 2004 study could not establish that philanthropic giving had an effect on corporate financial performance, although "firm owners do not lose when firms contribute to charitable causes."[69]

Question

1. Construct a list of the arguments for and against social responsibility for business.

Part Three—Managing Social Responsibility

Stakeholder Approach

As the principle of social responsibility has become increasingly acceptable to the corporate community, the nature of the debate has shifted to identifying the new duties and assessing whether the corporation is meeting those duties. Many corporations, particularly those of great size, are confronting the practical notion of how best to manage the firm's response to social issues. Corporations are increasingly considering what scholars have labeled the *stakeholder model* of social responsibility. Under that model, the corporation identifies all of the groups (stockholders, customers, employees, communities, governments, unions, schools, and the like) that may affect the firm's performance or be affected by it. These are groups with a "stake" in the activities of the corporation. Of course, we have wide divisions of opinion about how expansive the list of stakeholders should be; and once identified, we have wide divisions of opinion about the extent of the corporation's duties toward those stakeholders. Certainly, scholarly advocates of the stakeholder approach see it as a redefinition of the nature of the corporation. Simply maximizing the interests of the primary stakeholders, the shareholders, would not, from the advocates' point of view, satisfy the corporation's social duties.

Building Stakeholder Relationships   Should stakeholder theory and social performance concerns significantly influence actual business practice? Business consultant Ann Svendsen points to Microsoft's enormously publicized difficulties as an example of a company harmed by poor stakeholder relations.[70] Antitrust losses in court, insensitive treatment of suppliers, efforts to manipulate the political process, and arm-twisting of corporate customers have brought storms of unfavorable publicity.

Svendsen argues that most business leaders have accepted the claim that companies have multiple stakeholders, but the difficult question lies in the attention given to each stakeholder relationship.[71] Historically, of course, shareholders towered over all other stakeholders in their perceived importance. Now that other stakeholders are asserting claims, how much attention must the firm pay to them? What sort of relationship should be developed with them? Can stakeholder relationships be regarded as opportunities for corporate growth and advantage rather than as burdensome claims on scarce resources? Recently scholars have theorized that the importance of a particular stakeholder to the corporation is determined by three factors:

- **Legitimacy.**   Does the stakeholder have some kind of legal, ethical, or moral claim on the corporation?
- **Power.**   Does the stakeholder have sufficient power to meaningfully affect the corporation?
- **Urgency.**   Is the stakeholder demanding immediate attention?[72]

Manage or Collaborate?   One plausible and common approach to stakeholders is to "manage" them—that is, to influence and perhaps control the behavior of those stakeholders. Thus the marketing department deals with consumers, human resources deals with employees, public affairs deals with the media, and so on.[73] Each department is expected to anticipate and mediate the stakeholder relationship in ways that are most advantageous to the firm. An alternative and arguably more "progressive" approach to stakeholders involves a collaborative strategy in which stakeholder relationships are regarded as being mutually defined, cooperative, reciprocal, and thus not subject to "management" by the firm.[74] The firm endeavors to understand and balance the interests and needs of all stakeholders with the view that this collaborative effort results in enhanced firm performance over the long term while building a healthier society.[75]

A. G. Lafley, Procter & Gamble Co.'s CEO, has thoroughly and personally embraced stakeholder practice. Making money remains Lafley's first job, but he leads P&G on a broader mission, partly to ensure the company's continuing success. Enron and the other scandals of the early 2000s convinced him that he had to engage in a broad dialogue with P&G's stakeholders. He now thinks of consumers as citizens who often are concerned about P&G's approach to global warming or its animal testing methods. Lafley, in fact, deals directly with groups like Greenpeace and People for the Ethical Treatment of Animals. Lafley employed that direct engagement approach to resolve a Christian conservative consumer boycott against P&G. The boycott was a protest against P&G's decision to help overturn a local ordinance considered discriminatory towards gays. Lafley also extends his stakeholder engagement to worldwide relief efforts on behalf of P&G. Those are citizenship responsibilities, he thinks, that go with P&G's big role in the new global economy and global political environment. "Honest to God, the responsibility is huge," says Lafley.[76] [For an overview of stakeholder research, see **http://www.mgmt.utoronto.ca/~stake**]

> Honest to God, the responsibility is huge

As Lafley recognized, this new complexity in business practice requires the contemporary manager to learn about a much broader range of issues than was the norm historically. Profit now rests not merely in providing the best product or service at the lowest price, but in understanding and dealing with the complex interplay between the corporation, government, and society. Thus today's manager is likely to be increasingly involved in identifying and addressing social issues and stakeholder concerns.

Stakeholder Results   Assessing the success of social responsibility efforts is very difficult, but various programs have emerged including, most prominently, Social Accountability 8000 (SA8000), the first global standard measuring companies' social and environmental records. Social Accountability Accreditation Services in New York City accredits companies that meet the SA8000 standards in the areas of child labor, forced labor, health and safety, freedom of association, discrimination, disciplinary practices, working hours, collective bargaining wages, and management systems. As of 2007, nearly 1,500 facilities employing 676,000 employees in 65 countries had been certified.[77] [For more, see **www.sa-intl.org**]

Similarly, the Global Reporting Initiative (GRI), supported by the United Nations, was established to develop consistent global guidelines for reporting the economic, environmental, and social performance of corporations (and, eventually, other organizations). GRI's specific task is to devise a generally accepted reporting system, equivalent to financial reporting, to measure and display corporations' success in achieving "sustainable" development.[78] [For more, see **www.globalreporting.org**]

Bhopal: A Social Responsibility Failure?

One way of measuring the results of stakeholder activism is to review how the business community responds when wrongs occur. The devastating 1984 chemical spill at Bhopal, India, was one of the great tragedies in global industrial history. Water accidentally entered a methyl isocyanate storage tank at a Union Carbide plant producing an uncontrollable chemical reaction and a toxic cloud that spread across nearby slums. Up to 3,000 people were killed immediately and more than 15,000 in total have perished. Nearly 600,000 people have qualified for compensation as a result of health problems attributed to the leak. Union Carbide and its parent, Dow Chemical, deny continuing responsibility for Bhopal after reaching a settlement in 1989 with the Indian government that sent over $500 million to India. Claims totaled $3 billion, and litigation continues. As explained by *The Economist* in 2004, both the corporate and governmental responses were disappointing:

> Twenty years after lethal gases from a Union Carbide pesticide factory billowed across a densely populated shanty town in the Indian city of Bhopal, both the dilapidated plant and its highly contaminated surrounding areas stand as monuments to governmental and corporate inaction. Compensation has still not been fully paid to over 500,000 victims, the plant has not been dismantled and toxic waste estimated to amount to several thousand tons remains on the site, polluting local water supplies. . . .

Nonetheless, these cataclysmic events do produce a corporate response as *The Wall Street Journal* reported about Bhopal:

> The chemical leak . . . spurred a revolution in approaches to safety, pollution, and community relations that have made chemical plants in the United States more accessible and more accountable to their neighbors. New laws forced plants to disclose safety and pollution data. And an army of community activists won new powers.

Sources: "Asia: Bhopal's Deadly Legacy; India," *The Economist,* November 27, 2004, p. 76; and Susan Warren, "Chemical Companies Keep Lessons of Bhopal Spill Fresh," *The Wall Street Journal,* February 13, 2001, p. B4.

Shareholder Approach

Stakeholder theory and corporate social performance have gained great credibility with academics and many managers. Others, however, argue that profits and shareholders must remain the consuming concerns of management, and that a skilled focus on the bottom line will, incidentally but inevitably, result in the greatest good for society. That is, the company that maximizes its profits necessarily does not only what is best for its shareholders but also what is best for society generally. The shareholder/stakeholder debate is well illustrated by the heated competition between massive retailers Wal-Mart and Costco. Each week Wal-Mart saves money for millions of Americans by its relentless focus on the bottom line and hence on the interests of its shareholders. Costco, on the other hand, has drawn great praise from management scholars for its close attention to worker welfare.

Costco workers average about $17 per hour while Wal-Mart's Sam's Club pays a reported $10 an hour.[79] Costco is a leader in providing benefits with employees often paying only a few hundred dollars annually for generous insurance coverage.[80] Wal-Mart, on the other hand, insures fewer than half of its employees, although in recent years coverage has increased and costs for workers have been reduced. As a result, Costco's employee turnover is about one-third that of Wal-Mart. The stock market has rewarded Costco in recent years with the value of Costco stock rising by more than 100 percent from 2002 to 2007 while Wal-Mart's shares have lost about 10 percent of their value during that period.[81] On the other hand, the operating profit margin at Sam's Club is about 3.5 percent, as compared with 2.8 percent at Costco;[82] one of the reasons that journalist/financial advisor Malcolm Berko believes Wal-Mart's tough, bottom-line, shareholder-focused approach will prevail in the end:

> In this business of investing, it's the bottom line that counts while kindness and goodness aren't worth a pickled herring

COST (Costco) may be a good neighbor, but WMT (Wal-Mart) is certainly a better managed company. In this business of investing, it's the bottom line that counts while kindness and goodness aren't worth a pickled herring. While COST may have a kind, empathetic, and sensitive social conscience, hard-driving, hard-hearted, and hard-headed WMT is doing precisely what its shareholders want it to do. WMT is making money, lots of money, and paying a dividend that has increased fivefold in the last eight years.[83]

Of course, Wal-Mart is the target of relentless criticism. A class action lawsuit involving 1.6 million women claims that Wal-Mart has engaged in a pattern of sex discrimination. (More than seven hundred women have also filed a sex discrimination lawsuit against Costco.)

> Entire communities have banished Wal-Mart's big boxes

Other lawsuits accuse Wal-Mart of failing to pay overtime. Entire communities have banished Wal-Mart's big boxes. In response to these public relations woes and needing a boost in the stock market, Wal-Mart has initiated new sustainable, green practices including slashing solid waste and greenhouse-gas emissions and significantly reducing energy consumption. Those efforts are part of a larger campaign to create a more positive image. Wal-Mart points to its success in providing economic opportunities for its massive and often modestly educated workforce; 61 percent of whom are women and 32 percent minorities. [84] Wal-Mart's big contribution, however, is in saving money for all Americans; an estimated $30 billion per year, or the equivalent of $270 per American family.[85]

Clearly Wal-Mart has felt harsh, market-based pressure to respond to social issues, including employee welfare and environmental sustainability. These adjustments should not be misunderstood, however. Wal-Mart's shareholder orientation is intact and remains a clear, strategic contrast to Costco's stakeholder approach.

Questions

1. Costco CEO James Sinegal says high employee pay makes for good business. How can that be so?

2. William Beaver writes, "And what of the stakeholder model? Beyond generating some academic interest, perhaps the best that can be said is that although corporations will not be unmindful of their other stakeholders, the latter's concerns will remain a distant second to those holding the share."[86] Will shareholders or other stakeholders dominate corporate thought in the coming years? Explain.

3. In 1999 Bob Thompson sold his road-building firm for $422 million. Then he divided $128 million among his 550 workers, more than 80 of whom became millionaires. Thompson explained his generosity by saying, "I wanted to go out a winner, and I wanted to go out doing the right thing."[87]

   a. Which management strategy, Wal-Mart's low wages or Thompson's bonuses, is the more socially responsible? Explain.

   b. Can Wal-Mart, a publicly traded company owned by its shareholders, practice the same kind of generosity to employees that Thompson followed in distributing money that was literally his own? Explain.

   c. Stanford professor Jeffrey Pfeffer reflecting on the bonus strategy: "It's how you look at your workforce. . . . When I look at you, do I see a cost or do I see you as the only thing that separates me from my competition?"[88] Comment.

   d. Do you agree with Thompson that he did the "right thing"? Explain.

Part Four—Social Responsibility Cases: Case One: Workplace Diversity

Corporate leaders must produce a profit, but they also must conform to society's expectations for responsible conduct. Will the business community successfully shape its own behavior, or must the government intervene? Workplace discrimination continues to require extensive government oversight (see Chapter 13). But now many corporations have moved beyond mere legal compliance to recognize the power of a diverse workforce combining the strengths of America's various demographic groups. In recent years, that attention to diversity has broadened to embrace gay, lesbian, bisexual, transsexual and transgender Americans, as employers strive to "do the right thing" and to compete in a global market that requires all of our available resources.

READING   Coming Out in Corporate America

Cliff Edwards

One chilly fall day last year, Gary Osifchin trooped into a mandatory training session at S.C. Johnson & Son Inc. The privately held company, located in Racine, Wisconsin, which was voted 2003's "all-American city" by the National Civic League, manufactures Raid insecticide and Glade air fresheners. It's the kind of place where factory workers ride to the assembly line on Harley-Davidsons, dine on local bratwurst, and chase it down with Milwaukee beer.

About 20 plant managers were seated in a circle in a drab conference room. Osifchin, an S.C. Johnson marketing exec, walked into the center and started telling stories—about his boyfriend, his romantic life, and his experiences as a homosexual. He told coworkers, for instance, that one constant source of stress was having to come out anew every time he sat down with a new supervisor or switched units. "Somebody might see a picture of a guy on my desk, and that just sparks conversation," he said.

The frank talk was the kickoff of Gay 201, the upper-level course in gay sensitivity training offered at S.C. Johnson. It's available only to graduates of Gay 101, an introductory seminar that debunks stereotypes. The classes at Johnson are hardly anomalous. Eastman Kodak Co. offers similar sessions. Lucent Technologies, Microsoft, Southern California Edison, and dozens of others, meanwhile, send executives to weeklong training courses for gay managers at the University of California–Los Angeles Anderson School of Management.

The programs are just one small piece of a growing gay, lesbian, bisexual, and transgender (GLBT) rights movement in corporate America. Following in the footsteps of African Americans, women, and other traditionally marginalized groups, corporate gays are increasingly standing up for their rights. Defense contractors such as Raytheon Co. and Lockheed Martin Corp. now sponsor gay support groups. American Express Co. and Lehman Brothers Inc. promote their gay financial advisers in GLBT publications. Even culturally conservative Wal-Mart Stores Inc., which bans racy magazines and compact disks with offensive lyrics, this year adopted a nondiscrimination policy toward gays.

GALLOPING CHANGE

Of the nation's top 500 companies, 95 percent now offer policies that preclude discrimination based on sexual orientation, and 70 percent offer domestic partner benefits for same-sex couples. In 2000 the numbers stood at 51 percent and 25 percent, respectively. "To be competitive, we need to be able to get the best from people when they're at work, and to do that they need to bring their whole selves to the table," says Marge Connelly, director of operations at credit card issuer Capital One Financial Corp. She should know—she's a lesbian. "Being out is imperative for me to be a good leader," Connelly says. "You've got to let people know you. People have to trust you."

TOUGHER AT THE TOP

Still, it comes as no surprise that, as is the case with society at large, gays still face plenty of discrimination in their jobs. In a study by researcher Harris Interactive Inc. and marketer Witeck Combs Communications Inc., 41 percent of gay employees said they had been harassed, pressured to quit, or denied a promotion because of sexual orientation. Homosexuality is still legitimate legal grounds for firing an employee in 36 states.

So while gays may have won more acceptance at work, that does not mean they have gained legal, financial, and occupational equality. Intolerance that has built up over centuries does not disappear because of the sudden emergence of harassment-training videos and rainbow flags in cubicles. Many members of the GLBT community believe that discrimination increases as they rise up the corporate hierarchy into the executive suites, boardrooms, and country clubs where true power is wielded.

Need proof? Just look at a list of openly gay corporate leaders. While there are some big names—including DreamWorks SKG cofounder David Geffen, former Quark CEO Tim Gill, and Ford vice chairman Allan D. Gilmour—it is a pretty paltry roster for a highly educated minority that comprises, by some estimates, 6 percent of the population. In fact, many corporate CEOs who are widely believed to be gay are not comfortable discussing their sexuality on the record. The price of success may be having to stay in the closet.

Ironically, many of the companies that are most progressive about GLBT rights are reluctant to stand up for them in public for fear of being identified too closely with the issue—an apprehension that is likely only to mount if gay marriage touches off a national culture battle. Several companies that were more than willing to discuss their benefits and programs were unwilling to allow gay employees to pose for photographs that might wind up prominently displayed in the pages of *BusinessWeek*. Coors Brewing Co., whose products were boycotted by the gay community in the 1970s for giving money to anti-gay groups, adopted its sexual nondiscrimination policy in 1978. Since 1988 it has offered financial support to gay community causes. But the Golden (Colorado) company would not allow Scott Coors, the gay vice president and marketing director who is the son of vice chairman William Coors, or any other spokespeople, to talk to *BusinessWeek* about its programs.

ORDINARY PEOPLE

The people driving the gay rights revolution in corporate America by and large are not working in the executive suite. They're ordinary employees like Daniel Kline. The United Parcel Service Inc. supervisor last year applied for the company's Management Initiated Transfer, which allows employees to follow spouses to other cities and keep their jobs and seniority. An employee for more than two decades, Kline wanted to move with his longtime partner, who was reassigned by United Airlines Inc. from San Francisco to Chicago. After receiving approval at district and regional levels to take an open position in Chicago, Kline was rejected at the corporate level.

UPS backed down this August after the couple enlisted Lambda Legal Defense & Education Fund, a gay advocacy organization, to sue on their behalf, contending the company violated California antidiscrimination laws. A spokesman says UPS's policy on so-called trailing partners now includes same-sex couples. "I' am not looking to change the world. I simply want to live with the person with whom I've shared the last 27 years," says Kline.

While the gay experience in corporate America is far from monolithic, most gay managers interviewed by *BusinessWeek* say it has become easier in recent years to be themselves in the workplace. Displaying a picture of a same-sex lover on a desk or bringing a partner to a corporate gathering is no longer quite as intimidating as it used to be. Many now attend events such as the Out & Equal Workplace Summit, held this year in Minneapolis in October. "I used to keep my worklife and my private life separate, never talking about what I did on the weekend," says IBM microelectronics vice president Scottie Ginn. "Once you come out, you feel a much more whole person."

Broadly speaking, there is a generational divide among gay workers. Younger employees, typically those below 35, saw Roseanne Barr kiss another woman on TV and comedian Ellen DeGeneres declare publicly that she was a lesbian. They tend to come into the workplace as unashamedly gay and to demand equal rights more aggressively. Older workers, raised in times of greater stigma, tend to be quieter about their sexual identity to both coworkers and customers. Says James Law, a gay adviser at American Express Financial Advisers Inc., "With my older clients, I'm less prone to bring it up. With my younger clients, it's a nonissue."

CONTROVERSY AWAITS

[The legal controversy over gay marriage] will surely make life more complicated for CEOs trying to navigate this contentious issue. While they may not want to alienate cultural conservatives, they will also be loath to drive away the gay community. After all, the GLBT universe in the United States includes some 15 million consumers. Many have high disposable incomes. Research from online company MarketResearch.com pegs GLBT buying power this year at $485 billion.

Of course, the path of gay rights in corporate America is not a line angling boldly upward. When Exxon bought Mobil Oil in 1999, it rescinded the target company's policy of offering medical benefits to gay partners and disowned Mobil's written policy against discrimination based on sexual orientation (arguing that gay partners are not legal spouses and that gays are covered under its broader nondiscrimination policies). But despite such setbacks, far more companies are expanding gay rights than contracting them. There's no doubt that full legal equality for gays is many years away. But for the first time, it seems reasonable for gays in corporate America to dream of a day when Gay 101 will no longer be necessary.

Source: *BusinessWeek*, December 15, 2003, p. 64, Reprinted by permission.

Questions

1. What managerial risks and problems accompany gay and lesbian diversity policies in the workplace?

2. In your view, do the gay and lesbian diversity policies described in the article constitute socially responsible corporate behavior? Explain.

3. List the issues that you would consider if you were a CEO deciding whether to extend health insurance to the same-sex partners of your employees.

4. Christopher Mossey wrote in a letter to *The Wall Street Journal*,

   > Your Oct. 11 "In Marketing to Gays, Lesbians Are Often Left Out," raises a provocative question about the direction of the gay advocacy movement: Must gay men and lesbians be "recognized" by the marketing departments of large corporations? The comments in the article by Kate Kendell, executive director of the National Center for Lesbian Rights, suggest that it is a social responsibility of corporations to pitch products to gay people.

   In your judgment, do corporations have a social responsibility to "recognize" and practice targeted marketing towards gays and lesbians? Explain. See Christopher Mossey, "Marketing to Gays: Why Is It Needed?" *The Wall Street Journal*, October 29, 1999, p. A19.

Social Responsibility Case Two: Pay Employees More Than the Market Requires?

Would the good corporate citizen, the socially responsible company, choose to pay its low-wage employees more than the market requires? The fast-food industry has been dealing with that issue and its very unfavorable publicity in recent years; not for its own employees but for the Florida tomato pickers whose notoriously low wages allow us to eat cheaper tomato-garnished hamburgers. A Florida International University study estimated the state's farm workers' wages at an average of $13,000 annually.[89] Working 10–12 hour days, migrant farm workers pick tomatoes by hand, earning about 45 cents for every 32 pound bucket picked. That long day's work typically involves picking, carrying, and unloading about two tons of tomatoes.[90] A farm workers coalition pressed the fast-food companies to raise those wages by paying an extra penny for each pound of tomatoes picked.[91]

A spokesman for the Florida tomato growers disputed the low wage claims saying pickers average $12.46 per hour plus free transportation to the fields. Angel Aguilar, a 36-year-old picker from Mexico, said that claim is a "gigantic lie." Aguilar said he generally earned $40 to $50 per day for five to seven hours of picking. Workers typically begin their day at 5 AM collecting at a parking lot in hopes of being chosen to pick, but paying work usually cannot begin until 10 or 11 AM when the dew has burned off. Workers often rent living space in trailers where they sometimes need to hang their food from wires to prevent rats from eating it.[92]

> Workers sometimes need to hang their food from wires to prevent rats from eating it

Following a fight of several years, including a boycott, Yum Brands (Taco Bell, Pizza Hut, and others), McDonald's, and Burger King have agreed to voluntarily raise tomato pickers' pay by one cent per pound, a 71-percent increase, with the result that workers are expected to earn 77 cents, instead of 45 cents, for each 32-pound bucket of tomatoes they pick. Amy Wagner, a senior Burger King vice president, estimated the company's costs would increase by about $300,000 annually, but she said, "If the Florida tomato industry is to be sustainable long term, it must become more socially responsible." At this writing, however, Florida tomato growers continue to resist the increase. [See Andrew Martin, "Burger King Grants Raise to Pickers," *The New York Times,* May 24, 2008 (**http://www.nytimes.com/2008/05/24/business/24farm.html?ref=todayspaper**).] [For more information on the pay raise campaign and the Coalition of Immokalee Workers (CIW) that led the campaign, see **http://www.ciw-online.org**]

Questions

1. a. Should the socially responsible company pay very low wage workers more than the market requires? Explain.

   b. Is the free market the best measure of a "fair" wage for all? Explain.

2. Robyn Blumner, writing in the *St. Petersburg Times,* asked: "Would you pay an extra penny per pound of tomatoes if you knew it meant farm workers . . . would nearly double their wages?"[93] Answer her question.

3. Should we, as consumers, blame ourselves for the mistreatment and low wages of Florida tomato workers? Explain.

Burger King Spying?

Eric Schlosser, author of "Fast Food Nation" and "Reefer Madness," reported in *The New York Times* that Burger King hired a private security firm, Diplomatic Tactical Services, to "spy on" the Student/Farmworker Alliance, a group dedicated to improving the lives of Florida migrants. A Burger King executive told Schlosser that the company needed to collect information about the Alliance's plans in order to prevent violence and to protect its employees and property. Soon thereafter, however, Burger King announced that it had discontinued its relationship with Diplomatic Tactical Services.

Question

Schlosser argues that we need government protection from "irresponsible" corporate power in situations like these. Do you agree? Explain. See Eric Schlosser, "Burger with a Side of Spies," *The New York Times*, May 7, 2008 [**http://www.nytimes.com/2008/05/07/opinion/07schlosser.html?th&emc=th**].

Internet Exercise

1. Many critics, activists, international scholars, and others are concerned that corporate/governmental interests threaten global human rights and the global natural environment. Using the Corporate Watch Web site [**http://www.corpwatch.org/**], explain those concerns in more detail.

2. Using the Web site opensecrets.org., find the latest campaign finance data for your congressperson or one of your senators. While there, perhaps you will want to take a look at the personal financial condition of those same politicians. See [**http://www.opensecrets.org/pfds/overview.php**].

Chapter Questions

1. a. In general, do you think employers are more concerned with profits or with delivering quality goods and services? Explain.
   b. Which *should* they be more concerned about? Explain.
   c. Are you most concerned about receiving a quality education or earning a degree? Explain.

2. Scholar Denis Goulet argued that we will find no facile resolution to the conflict between the values of a just society and the sharply opposing values of successful corporations.[94]
   a. Do you agree that the values of a just society oppose those of successful corporations? Explain.
   b. Can a solution be found? Explain.

3. *The Wall Street Journal* reported that "Alcopops"—fruit flavored, fizzy liquors such as Bacardi Breezers and Smirnoff Ice—are targeted to young women by a "barrage of ads." Heineken, for example, expanded its marketing for Amstel Light by placing ads in *Glamour* and *InStyle*. Cocktails by Jenn, a line of vodka martinis in flavors such as Blue Lagoon, Appletini, and Lemon Drop, come with small charms—a diamond ring, a purse, a high-heel shoe—on the bottles. A study found that young American and British women, in 2004, drank a third more alcohol than they did five years before.[95]
   a. Has the alcohol industry wrongly *targeted* young women to encourage them to drink more than is in their best interests?
   b. Do you personally feel targeted by the alcohol industry?
   c. Is binge drinking by young people, in part, a product of alcohol marketing? Explain.

4. During the 2007 Christmas season, millions of American children received Chinese-made toys powered by cadmium batteries. Those batteries are safe to use, save

American consumers about $1.50 on the average toy and have some performance advantages over alternatives. Producing those batteries, however, can be a dangerous practice. Inhaling toxic red cadmium dust in a factory can poison workers. The United States and other industrialized nations tightened rules for cadmium production and now all but two such factories have left the United States for less developed nations, primarily China. Cadmium safety rules in China meet World Health Organization standards and some factories are safe, but risks are common.[96]

a. Should American manufacturers refuse to sell cadmium batteries and refuse to use them in their toys and other products?

b. Would you refuse to buy such products if the alternatives cost you $1.50 more?

5. a. Under what conditions would you consider a layoff/termination to be ethically justified?

b. Do layoffs as dictated by business circumstances make good long-term sense for stockholders? Explain.

6. Worried about Junior misbehaving? Here's an answer:

Call a board meeting. As crazy as it sounds, some Americans are trying to keep tabs on the kids by bringing business strategies into the traditional family meeting. They're hashing out everything from vacations to disputes over toys with techniques that seem right out of a management textbook: mission statements, rotating chairmanships, motivational seminars, even suggestion boxes. The most corporate of clans hire professional meeting facilitators, just to smooth over family squabbles.[97]

a. List some of the strengths and weaknesses of the business approach to raising children.

b. Do you regard the business approach in the home as a promising development or another encroachment of business values into life outside of work? Explain.

7. Sam Wong, speaking during his sophomore year at Iowa State University:

Materialism, like patience, is a virtue. Ever since my parents bought me my first Transformer, almost everyone has tried to convince me that owning a lot of toys wouldn't make me happy. Oh, how wrong they were. Toys make me very, very happy. That's why today I have more of them than ever. I own every Nintendo. I own two CD-R burners. My drum set cost as much as a semester of school. I drive a Miata. What's more, I'm not ashamed to be a consumer. I consider it part of my American heritage, and I'm proud of it.[98]

Do you share Wong's values? Explain. Is materialism in America's best interests? Explain.

8. a. Do you, as a student, have a responsibility to protest if your college logo appears on sportswear made in low-wage sweatshops? Explain.

b. Have you ever inquired about the manufacturing source of a product you were considering, or have you declined, as a matter of principle, to buy certain garments or other items because you believe the manufacturer engages in unfair labor practices? Explain.

9. Should American companies refuse to do business in countries

a. That do not practice democracy?

b. That routinely practice discrimination?

c. That tolerate or even encourage the abuse of children? Explain.

10. In criticizing General Motors, Ralph Nader is reported to have said,

    > Someday we'll have a legal system that will criminally indict the president of General Motors for these outrageous crimes. But not as long as this country is populated by people who fritter away their citizenship by watching TV, playing bridge and Mah-Jongg, and just generally being slobs.[99]

    a. Is the citizenry generally unconcerned about unethical corporate conduct? Explain.
    b. To the extent that corporations engage in misdeeds, does the fault really lie with the corporate community or with society at large?

11. Journalist Michael Kinsley expresses some serious reservations about corporate social responsibility:

    > In particular, I am not impressed by corporate charity and cultural benefaction, which amount to executives playing Medici with other people's money. You wouldn't know, from the lavish parties corporate officers throw for themselves whenever they fund an art exhibit or a PBS series, that it's not costing them a penny. The shareholders, who aren't invited, pick up the tab.[100]

    Comment on Kinsley's statement.

12. The Pennsylvania garment maker AND1 developed a line of T-shirts directed to young males and adorned with sayings such as "Your game is as ugly as your girl." and "You like that move? So does your girl." A feminist group complained that the shirts "put down" girls and implied that "girls are the property of boys." JC Penney, which was selling the shirts, withdrew them after the complaints.[101] Was JC Penney's decision the socially responsible course of action, or did JC Penney cave in to "politically correct" pressure? Or did JC Penney simply make a wise business move? Explain.

13. Michael Vick, Kobe Bryant, and other high-profile athletes have been entangled in very serious legal problems. The great cycling spectacle, the Tour de France, has been plagued by allegations of drug doping by riders and many major league baseball players have been linked to steroid use. Should you refuse to watch these tarnished athletes and refuse to buy products they endorse? Explain.

14. Make the argument that corporations are not well-suited to be stakeholder driven, "do-gooders" looking out for the general welfare of society.

15. You are the sole owner of a neighborhood drugstore that stocks various brands of toothpaste. Assume that scientific testing has established that one brand is clearly superior to all others in preventing tooth decay.

    a. Would you remove from the shelves all brands except the one judged best in decay prevention? Explain.
    b. What alternative measures could you take?
    c. Should the toothpaste manufacturers be required to reveal all available data regarding the effectiveness of their products? Explain.

16. Beyond its economic efficiencies, explain how "globalization/Americanization" is valuable for personal growth in the less developed world.

17. Approximately $10 million is expended annually for alcohol ads in college newspapers. Many millions more are expended in other youth-oriented publications such as *National Lampoon* and *Rolling Stone*. The beer industry sponsors many campus

athletic contests. Brewers have established promotional relationships with rock bands. Is beer and liquor advertising directed to the youth market unethical? Explain.

18. Increasingly, U.S. corporations are farming out programming, customer support, data entry, and various back-office jobs to lower-paid workers in countries as diverse as India, Romania, and Ghana. The average programmer commands $60 an hour in the United States, six times the rate in India.

* * * * *

In a research report in mid-2003, Gartner Inc. predicted that at least 1 out of 10 technology jobs in the United States would move overseas by the end of 2004. Forrester Research predicts at least 3.3 million white-collar jobs and $136 billion in wages will shift from the United States to low-cost countries by 2015.

a. Is outsourcing good for America? Explain.

b. Are you confident that you will be competitive in the American market of the future where outsourcing seems destined to strip away big pieces of the job market? Explain. See Associated Press, "Corporations Explore New Ways to Ship Jobs Overseas," *Waterloo/Cedar Falls Courier,* January 22, 2004, p. D6.

19. Former General Motors vice president John Z. DeLorean wrote in his book, *On a Clear Day You Can See General Motors,*

It seemed to me then, and still does now, that the system of American business often produces wrong, immoral, and irresponsible decisions, even though the personal morality of the people running the business is often above reproach. The system has a different morality as a group than the people do as individuals, which permits it willfully to produce ineffective or dangerous products, deal dictatorially and often unfairly with suppliers, pay bribes for business, abrogate the rights of employment, or tamper with the democratic process of government through illegal political contributions.[102]

a. How can the corporate "group" possess values at odds with those of the individual managers?

b. Is DeLorean merely offering a convenient rationalization for corporate misdeeds? Explain.

c. Realistically, can one expect to preserve individual values when employed in a corporate group? Explain.

20. Do you agree or disagree with the following statements? Explain.

a. "Social responsibility is good business only if it is also good public relations and/or preempts government interference."

b. "The social responsibility debate is the result of the attempt of liberal intellectuals to make a moral issue of business behavior."

c. "'Profit' is really a somewhat ineffective measure of business's social effectiveness."

d. "The social responsibility of business is to 'stick to business.'"[103]

Notes

1. Ylan Q. Mui. "Wal-Mart Health Plan Gains," *Washington Post*, January 23, 2008, p. D02.

2. Rhett A. Butler, "Corporations Agree to Cut Carbon Emissions," February 20, 2006 [**http://news.mongabay.com/2007/0220-roundtable.html**].

3. "Corporations Among Largest Global Economic Entities, Rank Above Many Countries," July 18, 2005 [**http://news.mongabay.com/2005/0718-worlds_largest.html**].

4. Frank Newport, "Americans' Confidence in Congress at All-Time Low," Gallup News Service, June 21, 2007 [**http://www.gallup.com/poll/27946/Americans-Confidence-Congress-AllTime-Low.aspx**].

5. Dan Ackman, "Corporate Taxes Continue to Plummet," Forbes.com, September 23, 2004. Reprinted at ReclaimingDemocracy.org [**http://reclaimdemocracy.org/articles_2004/corporate_taxes_lower.html**].

6. Ibid.

7. Associated Press, "Buffett in Berkshire's Annual Report: Tax Cuts Favor Corporations, Wealthy," *Waterloo Courier*, March 7, 2004, p. A2.

8. Peter D. Hart Research Associates, Inc., "Civil Justice Issues and the 2008 Election" [**http://www.atla.org/pressroom/CJSPollMemo.pdf**].

9. Ibid.

10. Charles Reich, *The Greening of America* (New York: Bantam Books, 1970), pp. 7–8.

11. "Nation's Alienation Index Decreases as Fewer People Feel Powerless," *Harris Poll*, no. 96, December 1, 2004 [**http://www.harrisinteractive.com/harris_poll/index.asp?PID=525**].

12. "The Harris Poll's 'Alienation Index' Rises Slightly to Highest Level in Presidency of George W. Bush," *The Harris Poll*, no. 110, November 8, 2007 [**http://www.harrisinteractive.com/harris_poll/index.asp?PID=829**].

13. Ben Stein, "A City on a Hill, or a Looting Opportunity," *The New York Times*, July 9, 2006 [**http://www.nytimes.com**].

14. Richard S. Dunham, "As Power Shifts, So Do the Dollars," *BusinessWeek*, April 23, 2007, p. 33.

15. Ibid.

16. Editorial, "The Fat Cats Are Cozier than Ever," *BusinessWeek*, April 12, 2004, p. 120.

17. "Cozy at the Beach," *Washington Post*, February 17, 2007, p. A30.

18. Eamon Javers, "Inside the Hidden World of Earmarks," *BusinessWeek*, September 17, 2007, p. 56.

19. Ibid.

20. Richard N. Goodwin, "PACs Gobbling Up Congress," *Waterloo Courier*, December 17, 1985, p. A4.

21. Jane Eisner, "Peer Pressure, Ads Aimed at Youth Lead to Culture of Overconsumption," *Waterloo/Cedar Falls Courier*, September 19, 2004, p. C9.

22. William C. Symonds, "The Reform of School Reform," *BusinessWeek*, June 26, 2006, p. 72.

23. Carla K. Johnson, "Ads More Memorable than News, Study Says," *Des Moines Register*, March 6, 2006, p. 8A.

24. Ibid.

25. Robert Weissman, "Resisting the Commercialization of Public Schools." *Counterpunch*, May 25, 2007 [**http://www.counterpunch.org/weissman05252007.html**].

26. Ibid.

27. "Peter Drucker—Toward a More Gentle Marketplace," *Austrian Information* 59, (March/April 2006), p. 9.

28. Stacey Palevsky, "Fashion & Faith," *Waterloo/Cedar Falls Courier*, September 20, 2004, p. B4.

29. Ibid.

30. Diane Haithman, "MOCA Show Asks: Is It Business or Is It Art?" *latimes.com*, August 9, 2007 [**http://www.latimes.com/news/la-et-moca9aug09,0,5477094.story?coll=la-tot-topstories &track=ntottext**].

31. Ethan Smith, "Can Music Survive Inside the Big Box?" *The Wall Street Journal*, April 27, 2007, p. B1.

32. Ibid.

33. Marshall Herskovitz, "Are the Corporate Suits Ruining TV?" *latimes.com*, November 7, 2007 [**http://www.latimes.com/news/opinion/la-oe-herskovitz7nov07,0,5402981.story?coll=la-tot-opinion&track=ntothtml**].

34. Ibid.

35. "Knight, Big 12 Coaches Agree: College Sports Are Big Business," *USA TODAY*, February 16, 2004 [**http://www.usatoday.com/sports/college/2004-02-16-notes_x.htm**].

36. Ibid.

37. Paul Whiteley, Sr., "Fan Fears Greed Is Ruining Sports," *Des Moines Register*, August 27, 1995, p. 9D.

38. Steve Wilstein, "Let Commercialism Reign," *Waterloo/Cedar Falls Courier*, April 29, 2004, p. C2.

39. Josh Barr, "Business Embraces Prep Football," *Washington Post*, September 2, 2007, p. D05.

40. Ibid.

41. James H. Mittelman, *The Globalization Syndrome* (Princeton, NJ: Princeton University Press, 2000), p. 246.

42. Yifat Susskind, "Haiti—Insurrection in the Making," February 25, 2004 [**www.zmag.org**].

43. "50 Years Is Enough: Corporate Welfare in Haiti" [**http://www.50years.org**].

44. Associated Press, "Corporations Explore New Ways to Ship Jobs Overseas," *Waterloo/Cedar Falls Courier*, January 22, 2004, p. D6.

45. Christopher A. Bartlett, "Losing in the Court of Public Opinion," *Across the Board*, Jan.–Feb. 2002, p. 27.

46. David Wessel, "Globalization Study Moves Past Rhetoric," *The Wall Street Journal*, July 26, 2007, p. A2.

47. Trudy Rubin, "Global Economy Waits for Next 'Conductor,'" *Des Moines Register*, January 31, 2008, p. 9A.

48. David Wessel, "The Future of Jobs," *The Wall Street Journal*, March 2, 2004, p. A1.

49. Ted Peters, "The Future of Religion in a Post-Industrial Society," *The Futurist*, October 1980, pp. 20, 22.

50. "More Leisure in an Increasingly Electronic Society," *BusinessWeek*, September 3, 1979, pp. 208, 212.

51. Daniel Seligman, "Helping the Shareholder Helps the Society," *The Wall Street Journal*, June 21, 1996, p. A12.

52. Ronald Alsop, "Recruiters Seek M.B.A.s Trained in Responsibility," *The Wall Street Journal*, December 13, 2005, p. B6.

53. Keith Davis and Robert L. Blomstrom, *Business and Society: Environment and Responsibility*, 3rd ed. (New York: McGraw-Hill, 1975), p. 6.

54. Milton Friedman, *Capitalism and Freedom* (Chicago: University of Chicago Press, 1962), p. 133.

55. Herbert Stein, "Corporate America, Mind Your Own Business," *The Wall Street Journal*, July 15, 1996, p. A10.

56. Steven A. Rochlin, "The New Corporate Citizenship," *BusinessWeek*, December 13, 2003, p. 66.

57. John Elkington, *Cannibals with Forks* (Gabriola Island, British Columbia: New Society Publishers, 1998), p. 327.

58. Archie Carroll and others have pointed to some descriptive and theoretical limitations associated with his social responsibility pyramid; and Carroll has proposed a three-domain approach of economic, legal, and ethical responsibilities arrayed in a Venn framework. The newer model appears to satisfy some of the concerns of Carroll and others about Carroll's pyramid, but for both teaching and research purposes, the pyramid remains a useful construct. For Carroll's new construct, see Mark S. Schwartz and Archie B. Carroll, "Corporate Social Responsibility: A Three Domain Approach," *Business Ethics Quarterly* 13, no. 4 (October 2003), p. 503. For an example of recent research employing the Carroll pyramid and a discussion of some of the strengths and weaknesses of the pyramid, see Dane K. Peterson, "The Relationship between Perceptions of Corporate Citizenship and Organizational Commitment," *Business & Society* 43, no. 3 (September 2004), p. 296.

59. Marc Gunther, "Corporations Go for the Green," *Des Moines Register,* November 22, 2004, p. 9A.

60. Ibid.

61. Ibid.

62. Ibid.

63. Ibid.

64. Kevin Delaney, "Google: From 'Don't Be Evil' to How to Do Good," *The Wall Street Journal*, January 18, 2008, p. B1.

65. Much of the material in this paragraph is drawn from Unmesh Ker, "Getting Smart at Being Good . . . Are Companies Better Off for It?" *Time Inside Business,* January 2006, p. A1.

66. Marc Orlitzky, Frank L. Schmidt, and Sara L. Rynes, "Corporate Social and Financial Performance: A Meta Analysis," Social Investment Forum Foundation, December 2004 [**http://business.auckland.ac.nz/newstaffnet/profile/publications_upload/000000556_orlitzkyschmidtrynes2003os.pdf**].

67. "Global Reputation Survey Reflects CR's Importance," *Corporate Responsibility Management* 1, no. 3 (December 2004/January 2005), p. 14.

68. "Social Responsibility: Most People Have Good Intentions but Only a Small Minority Really Practice What They Preach," *The Harris Poll* no. 57, June 18, 2007 [**http://www.harrisinteractive. com/harris_poll/index.asp?PID=774**].

69. Bruce Seifert, Sara A. Morris, and Barbara R. Bartkus, "Having, Giving, and Getting: Slack Resources, Corporate Philanthropy, and Firm Financial Performance," *Business & Society* 43, no. 2 (June 2004), pp. 135, 154.

70. Ann Svendsen, *The Stakeholder Strategy* (San Francisco: Berrett-Koehler, 1998), p. 7.

71. Ibid., p. 49.

72. Ibid.

73. Ibid., p. 3.

74. Ibid.

75. Ibid., p. 4.

76. Alan Murray, "The CEO as Global Corporate Ambassador," *The Wall Street Journal*, March 29, 2006, p. A2.

77. Social Accountability Accreditation Services, "Certified Facilities List," September 30, 2007 [**http://www.saasaccreditation.org/certfacilieslist.htm**].

78. "A Common Framework for Sustainability Reporting" [**www.globalreporting.org/About GRI/Overview.htm**].

79. James O'Toole and Edward E. Lawler III, "Low Costs Versus High Wages?" *Forbes.com*, April 25, 2007 [**http://www.forbes.com/2007/04/24/corporate-layoffs-costs-oped-cx_jot_0425jobs_print.html**].

80. Michael Barbaro and Reed Abelson, "A Health Plan for Wal-Mart: Less Stinginess," *nytimes.com*, November 13, 2007 [**http://www.nytimes.com/2007/11/13/business/13walmart.html**].

81. Zac Bissonnette, "Costco Does Well by Doing Good - Pay Attention Wal-Mart," *Blogging Stocks*, December 3, 2007 [**http://www.bloggingstocks.com/2007/12/03/Costco-does-well-by-doing-good-pay-attention-wal-mart/**].

82. Andrew Bary, "Costco: The 'Anti-Wal-Mart'," *MSN Money*, February 16, 2007 [**http://articles.moneycentral.msn.com/Investing/Extra/CostcoTheAntiWalMart.aspx?page=all**].

83. Malcolm Berko, "Bottom Line Speaks Louder Than Employees," *Waterloo/Cedar Falls Courier*, May 25, 2004, p. C5.

84. "Wal-Mart Releases Employment Data," *Des Moines Register*, April 12, 2006, p. 6C.

85. David Vogel, "When Do 'Good' Firms Go 'Bad'?" *latimes.com*, February 13, 2007 [**http://www.latimes.com/news/opinion/la-oe-vogel13feb13,0,4670297.story?track=tottext**].

86. William Beaver, "Is the Stakeholder Model Dead?" *Business Horizons* 42, no. 2 (March–April 1999), p. 8.

87. Associated Press, "Boss Rewards Workers' Loyalty—Shares $128 Million," *Waterloo/Cedar Falls Courier*, September 12, 1999, p. B1.

88. Greg Miller, "Extreme Generosity Shocks Firm's Employees, Analysts," *Des Moines Register*, December 18, 1996, p. 1A.

89. Steven Greenhouse, "Campaign to Raise Tomato Pickers' Wages Faces Obstacles," *The New York Times*, December 24, 2007, Section A, p. 10.

90. Eric Schlosser, "Penny Foolish," *The New York Times*, November 29, 2007 [**www.newyorktimes.com**].

91. Greenhouse, "Campaign to Raise," Section A, p. 10.

92. Ibid.

93. Robyn Blumner, "At a Penny Per Pound, A Little Adds Up to a Lot," *St. Petersburg Times*, November 25, 2007, Perspective, p. 5P.

94. For an overview of Denis Goulet and his work, see [**http://www.nd.edu/~krocinst/faculty_staff/fellows/goulet.html**]

95. Deborah Ball and Vanessa O'Connell, "As Young Women Drink More, Alcohol Sales, Concerns Rise," *The Wall Street Journal*, February 15, 2006, p. A1.

96. Jane Spencer and Juliet Ye, "Toxic Factories Take Toll on China's Labor Force," *The Wall Street Journal*, January 15, 2008, p. A1.

97. Nancy Jeffrey, "Kids, Come to Order," *The Wall Street Journal*, August 10, 2001, p. W1.

98. Sam Wong, "Materialism Makes Me Feel Happy, Not Guilty," *Des Moines Register*, September 10, 2000, p. 11A.

99. Charles McCarry, *Citizen Nader* (New York: Saturday Review Press, 1972), p. 301.

100. Michael Kinsley, "Companies as Citizens: Should They Have a Conscience?" *The Wall Street Journal*, February 19, 1987, p. 29.

101. "Penney Hears Protests, Agrees to Trash T-Shirts," *Des Moines Register*, July 6, 1999, p. 2A.

102. John Z. DeLorean with J. Patrick Wright, "Bottom-Line Fever at General Motors" (excerpted from *On a Clear Day You Can See General Motors*), *The Washington Monthly*, January 1980, pp. 26–27.

103. Steven N. Brenner and Earl A. Molander, "Is the Ethics of Business Changing?" *Harvard Business Review* 55, no. 1 (January–February 1977), p. 68.

Introduction to Law

CHAPTER FOUR

The American Legal System

After completing this chapter, students will be able to:

1. Describe the importance of law to private enterprise.

2. Compare and contrast the objectives of law in society.

3. Differentiate the elements of a case brief.

4. Distinguish between substantive and procedural law.

5. Differentiate between case law and statutory law.

6. Compare and contrast civil and criminal law.

7. Describe the elements of the basic court system structure.

8. Explain the purposes of subject matter and personal jurisdiction as requirements for a court's power to hear a dispute.

9. Describe the typical steps in the civil trial process.

10. Distinguish trials and appeals.

11. Identify dispute resolution alternatives to trials.

Introduction

Presumably, we can agree that some business practices have unfavorable consequences for society. The issue, therefore, becomes: What should be done, if anything, to change those consequences? The fundamental options in the United States have been fourfold: let the market "regulate" the behavior; leave the problem to the individual decision maker's own ethical dictates; pass a law; or rely on some combination of the market, ethics, and law. Market regulation was discussed in Chapter 1. Self-regulation through ethics was explored in Chapters 2 and 3. This chapter begins the discussion of the legal regulation of business with a brief outline of the American legal system. We will also look at alternative conflict resolution processes such as negotiation, mediation, and arbitration that do not resort to the legal system. Although these alternatives are not new, they have been receiving much more attention in recent years.

Before turning to our examination of the technical dimensions of the law, we should remind ourselves of the central purpose of our legal system—the pursuit of justice. As you read this chapter, ask yourself repeatedly, "Does this rule (this procedure, this case) contribute to the search for justice?" [For a daily update of legal news, see **http://www. law.com**]

Justice

Most Americans believe we have the best civil justice system in the world. They believe we need that system to prevent and punish abuse. Nonetheless, they have some reservations. U.S. Chamber of Commerce polling, for example, shows that nine of 10 Americans believe we have too many frivolous or unfair lawsuits, that 84 percent of Americans say that meritless lawsuits clog the justice process and that 75 percent of Americans believe our justice system is most beneficial to lawyers themselves.[1] At the same time, a 2007 national poll by the American Association for Justice (formerly the American Trial Lawyers Association) found more concern about corporate abuse than about lawyers and the legal system. In identifying "extremely serious" problems facing the nation, only 34 percent of those polled cited "trial lawyers making too much money when they successfully represent a client in a lawsuit," and 24 percent cited "victims in cases involving personal injury or medical malpractice receiving too much money from juries."[2] "Corporations giving huge salaries and bonuses to CEOs, while cutting the jobs and benefits of employees" topped the list of problems, having been cited by 64 percent of those polled.[3] Broadly, those polled favored careful oversight of corporate conduct:

> They (the poll respondents) tell us that making sure corporations are held accountable when their actions harm consumers, employees, or communities (70%) should be a much higher priority for the civil justice system than limiting the amount of compensation that juries can award for pain and suffering "so that lawsuits do not cause as big a burden on our economy" (25%). Similarly, they give priority to holding corporations accountable (61%) over "reducing the number of frivolous lawsuits" and penalizing those who file them (32%).[4]

Sue Your Professor? And Your University?

Seemingly frivolous lawsuits often raise doubts about the American legal system. The *Boston Globe* described a recent lawsuit that might strike a sympathetic cord with many students while leaving many other Americans shaking their heads:

> Plenty of college students grumble when they get a mediocre grade and feel they deserved better. When Brian Marquis got a C instead of an A− at the University of Massachusetts at Amherst, he made a federal case of it.

Literally.

> Marquis, a 51-year-old paralegal seeking bachelor's degrees in legal studies and sociology, filed a 15-count lawsuit in U.S. District Court . . . after a teaching assistant

graded a political philosophy class on a curve and turned Marquis' A− into a C. Marquis contends the university violated his civil rights and contractual rights and intentionally inflicted "emotional distress."

*   *   *   *   *

"This is not something I relish," he said. . . . "This is not an issue of me walking into court and saying, 'I don't like the way this professor grades this paper,' which is purely their academic prerogative. This is an issue where the empirical data was [sic] quite clear. . . ."

Phillip Bricker, chairman of the philosophy department and one of eight defendants, said it had already caused enough damage. "I think suing over a grade is somewhat absurd," he said. "It ended up just wasting a lot of people's time and money."

Questions

1. a. Does the pursuit of justice require the legal system to hear Marquis' complaint? Explain.
   b. How would you rule? Explain.
   c. Should your answers be influenced by the fact that Marquis intended to apply for admission to law school?
2. In your judgment, are Americans too willing to file lawsuits? Explain.

Source: Jonathan Saltzman, "Student Takes His C to Federal Court," *The Boston Globe,* October 4, 2007 [http://www.boston.com/news/local/articles/2007/10/04/student_takes_his_c_to_federal_court].

Law and the Market   Whatever doubts we may share about America's pursuit of justice, the crucial role of a reliable legal system in fostering and maintaining capitalism is indisputable. The following law review excerpt explains.

READING

The Importance of Law to the Private Enterprise System

Deb Ballam

Nobel economist Frederich von Hayek describes the theoretical importance of law to private enterprise. According to Hayek, law that secures property rights in modern society is a prerequisite to private enterprise. Without the order of law enforcing private property ownership and facilitating the transfer of property rights, business enterprise in a complex, heterogeneous culture is simply infeasible.

The importance of law to the conduct of private enterprise is evident in economic developments in . . . the Republic of China. In moving from state-controlled to private enterprise, [China] faced substantial difficulties arising from the lack of a legal system that would secure property ownership and the contractual transfer of property rights.

. . . China's economy has grown steadily in recent years. Minxin Pei, a political scientist at Princeton University, explains law's contribution to that growth: "Legal reform has become one of the most important institutional changes in China since the late 1970s. . . . Within China, the changing legal institutions have begun to play an increasingly important role in governing economic activities, resolving civil disputes, enforcing law and order, and setting the boundaries between the power of the state and the autonomy of society." Pei reports that the number of lawyers in China grew threefold between 1986 and 1996 and that the number of commercial disputes adjudicated by the courts grew from about 15,000 annually in the early 1980s to some1.5 million annually in the mid-1990s. . . .

Of course, the importance of law to private enterprise goes far beyond its initial support as an institutional framework guaranteeing ownership rights. As the market system grows more complex both nationally and internationally, the legal recognition of promise keeping becomes increasingly significant in facilitating business. A condition for emerging economies entering international trade is learning how to keep promises to strangers, and whether enforced through litigation or arbitration, promise keeping in business requires the ordering presence of contract law.

In a democracy, law is important to business for another reason quite separate from its function in establishing ownership rights and facilitating promise keeping necessary to their transfer: It provides the formal expression of democratic social will. That expression implicates private enterprise in a plethora of ways, including regulation of the environment, employment laws, securities regulation, consumer protection statutes, and product liability. As contemporary society becomes increasingly diverse, law grows, not diminishes, in its importance to private enterprise; and in spite of valid concerns about the impact of law on efficiency, future business managers will need to know more, not less, about how law affects business operations. No evidence suggests any other conclusion.

Source: Deb Ballam, quoting from "The Importance of Law to the Private Enterprise System," The American Legal Studies in Business Task Force Report by O. Lee Reed. *American Business Law Journal* 36, no. 1 (Fall 1998), p. ix. Reprinted by permission.

Questions

1. *a.* Do you expect to see greater reliance on law as our society becomes increasingly complex?

   b. Can you think of any meaningful substitutes for law as we now practice it? Explain.

2. A 2001 study concludes that girls are punished more harshly than boys for minor criminal conduct. Girls arrested for more serious crimes receive fewer services and placement opportunities than boys. Girls are less likely than boys to engage in violence, and girls are less likely to be repeat offenders.[5] Why does our criminal justice system apparently treat girls more harshly than boys?

3. The police found three marijuana plants in an Iowa man's home. The man admitted smoking marijuana with his six-year-old son and was sentenced to 27 years in prison on various drug and child endangerment charges. He was to be eligible for parole in five years.[6]

   a. Does the sentence seem fair and just? Explain.

   b. Would you legalize marijuana? Explain.

Part One—Legal Foundations

Objectives of the Law

Americans differ dramatically in their views of the role the law should play in contemporary life. For some, the courts and the police primarily act as obstructions to personal freedom and to a fully efficient marketplace. Others seek much more law to ensure that everyone is cared for who is in need and everyone is sheltered from wrongdoers. We are in constant conflict about the law's precise path in our lives, but most of us can agree on some foundational expectations for a fair, efficient legal system. Certainly we expect the law to *maintain order* in our diverse, rapidly changing society. Of course, we rely on law to peacefully, fairly, and intelligently *resolve conflict*. Perhaps less obvious, but no less important, the law serves to *preserve dominant values*. Americans differ about core values, but we have reached a workable accord about our most fundamental beliefs. Some of those, such as freedom of speech, press, and religion, are guaranteed by our

Bill of Rights, thus setting a steady foundation for an enduring nation. We can see that the law is a vital force in *guaranteeing freedom*. (But freedom can be confusing: Are you free to smoke wherever you wish, or do I have a right to smoke-free air?) Broadly, we count on the law to *achieve and preserve justice*. All legal studies, in the end, must involve the search for justice. [For help with legal research on the Internet, see **http://www.virtualchase.com**]

Too Many Rules in Britain?

All societies struggle with the question of how important law should be in directing the course of affairs. Great Britain created its antisocial behavior orders (ASBOs) to discourage "loutish" conduct. The government's Antisocial Behavior Action Plan is designed to address everyday headaches from "nuisance neighbors" to begging to graffiti. Antisocial behavior interventions commonly take three progressively more serious forms: warning letters, acceptable behavior contracts, and ASBOs. A 2006 study found that 65 percent of those receiving antisocial behavior interventions did not commit further antisocial behavior, but "a hard core of persistent offenders" repeatedly violated ASBOs with one offender breaking his ASBO conditions 25 times before being sent to prison. One official summed up the frustration:

> We are not talking about high jinks from a few mischievous youngsters—we are talking about yobs whose persistent criminal activity, intimidation and plain disregard for others are making our city centres a no-go area.

Many Brits wonder, however, if the law has not gone a bit too far:

> A teenager is forbidden to say "grass" (slang for informer). A great-grandfather is banned from being sarcastic. Two record companies are told not to put up advertising posters. All have run afoul of the British government's latest weapon against petty crime, vandalism, and hooliganism: the antisocial behavior order, or ASBO. The orders have been used to ban thousands of people, some as young as 10, from associating with certain people or engaging in activities as varied as shouting, swearing, spray-painting, playing loud music, and walking down certain streets. Breaching an order is a crime, punishable by up to five years in prison.

Sources: Jill Lawless, Associated Press, "Britain Tries to Rein in Louts with Bans on Misbehavior," *Des Moines Register,* September 1, 2004, p. 5A; and Philip Johnston, "Blair's ASBO Is Failing to Tame a Hard Core of Offenders," *The Daily Telegraph* (London), December 7, 2006, p. 12 (News).

The Case Law: Locating and Analyzing

To prepare for the *Graff* case below, a bit of practical guidance should be useful. The study of law is founded largely on the analysis of judicial opinion. Except for the federal level and a few states, trial court decisions are filed locally for public inspection rather than being published. Appellate (appeals court) opinions, on the other hand, are generally published in volumes called *reports*. State court opinions are found in the reports of that state, as well as a regional reporter published by West Publishing Company that divides the United States into units, such as South Eastern (S.E.) and Pacific (P.).

Within the appropriate reporter, the cases are *cited* by case name, volume, reporter name, and page number. For example, *Royce Graff, Debra Graff, Bobby Hausmon, and Betty Hausmon v. Brett Beard and Dorothy Beard*, 858 S.W.2d 918 (Texas S.Ct. 1993) means that the opinion will be found in volume 858 of the South Western Reporter, 2nd series, at page 918 and that the decision was reached in 1993 by the Texas Supreme Court. Federal court decisions are found in several reporters, including the *Federal Reporter* and the *United States Supreme Court Reports*. In practice, of course, those cases can most readily be found via online databases such as LexisNexis and Westlaw. [For broad databases of law topics, see **http://www.findlaw.com**, **http://www.yahoo.com/law** or **www.justia.com**]

Briefing the Case

Most law students find the preparation of *case briefs* (outlines or digests) to be helpful in mastering the law. A brief should evolve into the form that best suits the individual student's needs. The following approach should be a useful starting point:

1. Parties   Identify the plaintiff and the defendant.
2. Facts   Summarize only those facts critical to the outcome of the case.
3. Procedure   Who brought the appeal? What was the outcome in the lower court(s)?
4. Issue   Note the central question or questions on which the case turns.
5. Holding   How did the court resolve the issue(s)? Who won?
6. Reasoning   Explain the logic that supported the court's decision.

Royce Graff, Debra Graff, Bobby Hausmon, and Betty Hausmon v. Brett Beard and Dorothy Beard

LEGAL BRIEFCASE   858 S.W.2d 918 (Texas S.Ct. 1993)

Justice John Cornyn

We are asked in this case to impose a common-law duty on a social host who makes alcohol available to an intoxicated adult guest who the host knows will be driving. . . .

Houston Moos consumed alcohol at a party hosted by the Graffs and Hausmons, and allegedly left in his vehicle in an intoxicated condition. En route from the party, Moos collided with a motorcycle, injuring Brett Beard. Beard sued both Moos and his hosts for his injuries. The trial court ultimately dismissed

Beard's claims against the hosts for failure to state a cause of action. An en banc divided court of appeals reversed the trial court's judgment and remanded the case, holding for the first time in Texas jurisprudence that social hosts may be liable to third parties for the acts of their intoxicated adult guests.

Under the court of appeals' standard, a social host violates a legal duty to third parties when the host makes an alcoholic beverage available to an adult guest whom the host knows is intoxicated and who will be driving. In practical effect, this duty is twofold. The first aspect of the host's duty is to prevent guests who will be driving from becoming intoxicated. If the host fails to do so, however, a second aspect of the duty comes into play—the host must prevent the intoxicated guest from driving.

The legislatures in most states, including Texas, have enacted dram shop laws that impose a statutory duty to third parties on commercial providers under specified circumstances. We have recently held that when the legislature enacted the Texas dram shop statute it also imposed a duty on the provider that extends to the patron himself. Because the dram shop statute applies only to commercial providers, however, it does not govern the duty asserted in this case.

We think it significant in appraising Beard's request to recognize common-law social host liability that the legislature has considered and declined to create such a duty. A version of the bill that eventually became our dram shop statute provided for social host liability. Although that version passed the Senate, the House rejected it. The Senate–House conference committee deleted social host liability from the bill the legislature eventually enacted.

The highest courts in only four states have done what we are asked to do today: judicially impose a duty to third parties on social hosts who make alcohol available to adult guests. In two of these states, California and Iowa, the legislatures subsequently abrogated the judicially created duty. Neither of the two remaining jurisdictions, Massachusetts and New Jersey, had dram shop statutes when their courts acted. Rather, their courts first imposed a common-law duty to third parties on commercial establishments and then extended the duty to social hosts.

* * * * *

Deciding whether to impose a new common-law duty involves complex considerations of public policy. We have said that these considerations include "'social, economic, and political questions,' and their application to the particular facts at hand." Among other factors, we consider the extent of the risk involved, "the foreseeability and likelihood of injury weighed against the social utility of the actor's conduct, the magnitude of the burden of guarding against the injury, and the consequences of placing the burden on the defendant." We have also emphasized other factors. For example, questions of duty have turned on whether one party has superior knowledge of the risk, and whether a right to control the actor whose conduct precipitated the harm exists.

Following our decisions in *Seagrams* and *Otis Engineering Corp.,* we deem it appropriate to focus on two tacit assumptions underlying the holding of the court of appeals: that the social host can reasonably know of the guest's alcohol consumption and possible intoxication, and possesses the right to control the conduct of the guest. Under Texas law, in the absence of a rela-

tionship between the parties giving rise to the right of control, one person is under no legal duty to control the conduct of another, even if there exists the practical ability to do so.

* * * * *

Instead of focusing on the host's right of control over the guest, the court of appeals conditioned a social host's duty on the host's "exclusive control" of the alcohol supply. The court defined "exclusive control," however, as nothing more than a degree of control "greater than that of the guest user." Under the court's definition, at a barbecue, a wedding reception, a backyard picnic, a pachanga, a Bar Mitzvah—or a variety of other common social settings—the host would always have exclusive control over the alcohol supply because the host chooses whether alcohol will be provided and the manner in which it will be provided. The duty imposed by the court of appeals would apparently attach in any social setting in which alcohol is available regardless of the host's right to control the guest. Thus, as a practical matter, the host has but one choice—whether to make alcohol available to guests at all.

But should the host venture to make alcohol available to adult guests, the court of appeals' standard would allow the host to avoid liability by cutting off the guest's access to alcohol at some point before the guest becomes intoxicated. Implicit in that standard is the assumption that the reasonably careful host can accurately determine how much alcohol guests have consumed and when they have approached their limit. We believe, though, that it is far from clear that a social host can reliably recognize a guest's level of intoxication. First, it is unlikely that a host can be expected to know how much alcohol, if any, a guest has consumed before the guest arrives on the host's premises. Second, in many social settings, the total number of guests present may practically inhibit the host from discovering a guest's approaching intoxication. Third, the condition may be apparent in some people but certainly not in all. . . .

* * * * *

This brings us to the second aspect of the duty implicit in the court of appeals' standard: that should the guest become intoxicated, the host must prevent the guest from driving. Unlike the court of appeals, however, we cannot assume that guests will respond to a host's attempts, verbal or physical, to prevent the guests from driving. Nor is it clear to us precisely what affirmative actions would discharge the host's duty under the court of appeals' standard. Would a simple request not to drive suffice? Or is more required? Is the host required to physically restrain the guests, take their car keys, or disable their vehicles? The problems inherent in this aspect of the court of appeals' holding are obvious.

* * * * *

Ideally, guests will drink responsibly, and hosts will monitor their social functions to reduce the likelihood of intoxication. Once a guest becomes impaired by alcohol to the point at which he becomes a threat to himself and others, we would hope that the host can persuade the guest to take public transportation, stay on the premises, or be transported home by an unimpaired driver. But we know that too often reality conflicts with ideal behavior. And, given the ultimate power of guests to control their own alcohol consumption and the absence of any legal right of the host to control the guest, we find the arguments for shifting legal responsibility from the guest to the host, who merely makes alcohol available at social gatherings, unconvincing. As the common law has long recognized, the imbiber maintains the ultimate power and thus the obligation to control his own behavior: to decide to drink or not to drink, to drive or not to drive. We therefore conclude that the common law's focus should remain on the drinker as the person primarily responsible for his own behavior and best able to avoid the foreseeable risks of that behavior.

We accordingly reverse the judgment of the court of appeals and render judgment that Beard take nothing.

DISSENTING OPINION—JUSTICE GAMMAGE JOINED BY JUSTICE DOGGETT

I respectfully dissent. The majority errs in holding that the legislature must "create" the duty for social hosts not to send intoxicated guests driving in our streets to maim and kill. Logic, legal experience, and this court's own earlier decisions dictate a contrary result. The legislature may enact a statute that creates a duty. But the legislature's failure to act does not "un-create" an existing duty. A duty created by the common law continues to exist unless and until the legislature changes it, and such an existing common law duty applies to the defendants here.

The majority confuses issues of proof with issues of whether to recognize the tort duty. The majority is concerned that the social host might not be able to persuade or control his intoxicated guest to keep him or her from driving. The host, however, clearly does control whether alcohol is being served, and in what quantities and form. The answer to the "duty" question is that the host should not let the driving guest have the alcohol in intoxicating quantities. If the guest becomes inebriated, however, just as with any other dangerous situation one helps create, the host has the duty to make every reasonable effort to keep the dangerously intoxicated guest from driving. If the guest resists those efforts, then there is a question for the factfinder to resolve whether the host's efforts were all that reasonably could be done under the circumstances.

The majority expresses concern that "the reasonably careful host" may not be able to detect when some guests are intoxicated. If that is so, then the factfinder should have no difficulty determining that the host did not serve them while they were "obviously intoxicated." The majority further asserts, without citation to authority, that the "guest . . . is in a far better position to know the amount of alcohol he has consumed" than the host.

This assertion defies common sense, because from personal observation we know that most persons, as they become intoxicated, along with losing their dexterity and responsive mental faculties, gradually become less and less cognizant of how much they've had and how badly intoxicated they are. Even if the host is also intoxicated, as a third party viewing the guest, the host is probably in a better position to evaluate the guest's intoxication. Intoxicated guests need someone to tell them not to drive. . . .

If circumstances do not permit the social host to adequately monitor and control the quantity of alcoholic beverages a guest consumes, the host still retains absolute control over whether alcoholic beverages should be served at all. . . .

* * * * *

. . . All culpable parties should be liable—the social host who knowingly intoxicated the guest and the guest who drunkenly caused the accident. I am persuaded that both should be liable to the extent of their responsibility for the accident. The television commercial says, "Friends don't let friends drive drunk." That is sound public policy. But today the majority says, "Intoxicate your friends and send them out upon the public streets and highways to drive drunk. Don't worry; you won't be liable." That is, in the kindest term I can muster, unsound policy.

AFTERWORD

Highly respected U.S. Circuit Judge Richard Posner, in his blog, argued that social host liability may sometimes be useful because the type of person who gets drunk and causes accidents is unlikely to respond rationally to deterrents while party hosts probably will do so. Posner's blog partner, distinguished economist Gary Becker, says that holding party hosts liable probably is not efficient because doing so imposes excessive costs on the hosts in relation to the amount of drunk driving that would be prevented.[7]

Questions

1. Who won this case and why?

2. What do the dissenting justices mean by saying "the majority confuses issues of proof with issues of whether to recognize the tort duty"?

3. In your judgment, does the Texas Supreme Court decision represent a just result? Explain.

4. Nichols, age 26, and Dobler, a minor, were guests at Maldonado's party. Dobler was served alcohol and, while intoxicated, repeatedly hit Nichols with a hammer. Nichols sued Maldonado for negligence in serving alcohol to a minor. The jury found for Nichols. Maldonado appealed. How would you rule on that appeal? Explain. See *Nichols v. Dobler*, 655 N.W. 2d 787 (Mich. Ct. App. 2002).

5. Richard Paul Dube suffered serious injuries when the vehicle he was driving was struck head-on by a vehicle being driven in the wrong direction on a Massachusetts highway by Ravindra Bhoge. Bhoge had earlier in the evening consumed a number of drinks with three friends at a bar. Bhoge and his friends met regularly on Fridays after work to drink at local bars. Each person took turns paying the bill, or on some occasions, payment would be equally divided. On the night of the accident Bhoge drank enough that the trial judge inferred that Bhoge's intoxication would have been apparent. Bhoge's three friends said they saw nothing to indicate that Bhoge was impaired, although Bhoge had left his coat behind in the bar on a particularly cold evening, and he was outside the bar for 45 minutes prior to his departure. Bhoge indicated to his friends that he was "okay" as they all prepared to leave in their vehicles. Dube sued Bhoge's three friends claiming they were social hosts and were negligent in permitting Bhoge to continue drinking. How would you rule on Dube's claim? Explain. See *Dube v. Lanphear & Others*, 868 N.E.2d 619 (2007).

[For the National Center for State Courts, see **http://www.ncsconline.org**]

Classifications of Law

Some elementary distinctions will make the role of law clearer.

Substantive and Procedural Law

Substantive laws create, define, and regulate legal rights and obligations. Thus, for example, the federal Civil Rights Act of 1964 forbids discrimination in employment and other matters (see Chapter 13).

Procedural law embraces the systems and methods available to enforce the rights specified in the substantive law. So procedural law includes the judicial system and the rules by which it operates. Questions of where to hear a case, what evidence to admit, and which decisions can be appealed fall within the procedural domain.

Law by Judicial Decision and Law by Enactment

In general, American rules of law are promulgated by court decisions (*case law*) or via enactments, which include constitutions, statutes, treaties, administrative rules, executive orders, and local ordinances. [For a "collaboratively built, freely available legal dictionary and encyclopedia," see **http://www.law.cornell.edu/wex**]

Case Law (Judicial Decisions)   Our case law has its roots in the early English king's courts, where rules of law gradually developed out of a series of individual dispute resolutions. That body of law was imported to America and is known as the *common law*. (This term may be confusing because it is frequently used to designate not just the law imported from England of old but also all judge-made or case law.)

The development of English common law rules and American judicial decisions into a just, ordered package is attributable in large measure to reliance on the doctrine of *stare decisis* (let the decision stand). That is, judges endeavor to follow the precedents established by previous decisions. Following precedent, however, is not mandatory.

As societal beliefs change, so does the law. For example, a United States Supreme Court decision approving racially separate but equal education was eventually overruled by a Supreme Court decision mandating integrated schools. However, the principle of stare decisis is generally adhered to because of its beneficial effect. It offers the wisdom of the past and enhances efficiency by eliminating the need for resolving every case as though it were the first of its kind. Stare decisis affords stability and predictability to the law. It promotes justice by, for example, reducing "judge-shopping" and neutralizing judges' personal prejudices.

Statutes (Enactments)   Here our primary concern is with the laws that have been adopted by the many legislative bodies—Congress, the state legislatures, city councils, and the like. These enactments are labeled *statutory law.* Some areas of law, such as torts, continue to be governed primarily by common law rules, but the direction of American law lies largely in the hands of legislators. Of course, legislators are not free of constraints. Federal legislation cannot conflict with the U.S. Constitution, and state legislation cannot violate either federal law or the constitutions of that state and the nation.

Law and Equity

Following the Norman conquest of England in 1066, a system of king's courts was established in which the king's representatives settled disputes. Those representatives were empowered to provide remedies of land, money, or personal property. The king's courts became known as *courts of law,* and the remedies were labeled *remedies of law.* Some litigants, however, sought compensation other than the three provided. They took their pleas to the king.

Typically the *chancellor,* an aide to the king, would hear these petitions and, guided by the standard of fairness, could grant a remedy (such as an injunction or specific performance—see the glossary of legal terms in the back of the book) specifically appropriate to the case. The chancellors' decisions accumulated over time such that a new body of remedies—and with it a new court system, known as *courts of equity*—evolved. Both court systems were adopted in the United States following the American Revolution, but today actions at law and equity are typically heard in the same court.

Public Law and Private Law

Public law deals with the relationship between government and the citizens. Constitutional, criminal, and administrative law (relating to such bodies as the Federal Trade Commission) fall in the public law category. *Private law* regulates the legal relationship between individuals. Contracts, agency, and commercial paper are traditional business law topics in the private category.

Civil Law and Criminal Law

The legislature or other lawmaking body normally specifies that new legislation is either *civil* or *criminal* or both. Broadly, all legislation not specifically labeled criminal law falls in the civil law category. *Civil law* addresses the legal rights and duties arising among individuals, organizations such as corporations, and governments. Thus, for example, a person might sue a company raising a civil law claim of breach of contract. *Criminal law,* on the other hand, involves wrongs against the general welfare as formulated in specific criminal statutes. Murder and theft are, of course, criminal wrongs because society has forbidden those acts in specific legislative enactments. Hence, wearing one's hat backward would be a crime if such a statute were enacted and if that statute met constitutional requirements. [For a brief discussion of business and white-collar crime and the federal sentencing guidelines, see Chapter 2.]

Crimes Crimes are of three kinds. In general, *felonies* are more serious crimes, such as murder, rape, and robbery. They are typically punishable by death or by imprisonment in a federal or state penitentiary for more than one year. In general, *misdemeanors* are less serious crimes, such as petty theft, disorderly conduct, and traffic offenses. They are typically punishable by fine or by imprisonment for no more than one year. *Treason* is the special situation in which one levies war against the United States or gives aid and comfort to its enemies.

Elements of a Crime In a broad sense, crimes consist of two elements: (1) a wrongful act or omission (*actus reus*) and (2) evil intent (*mens rea*). Thus an individual who pockets a ball-point pen and leaves the store without paying for it may be charged with petty theft. The accused may defend, however, by arguing that he or she merely absentmindedly and unintentionally slipped the pen in a pocket after picking it off the shelf to consider its merits. Intent is a state of mind, so the jury or judge must reach a determination from the objective facts as to what the accused's state of mind must have been.

Criminal Procedure In general, criminal procedure is structured as follows: For more complex, arguably more serious, crimes the process begins with the prosecuting officials bringing their charges before a grand jury or magistrate to determine whether the charges have sufficient merit to justify a trial. If so, an *indictment* or *information* is issued, charging the accused with specific crimes. (Grand juries issue indictments; magistrates issue informations.) In instances where action by a grand jury or magistrate is not required, cases are initiated by the issuance of a warrant by a judge, based on a showing of probable cause that the individual has committed or will commit a crime. Where necessity demands, arrests may be made without a warrant, but the legality of the arrest will be tested by probable cause standards.

After indictment or arrest, the individual is brought before the court for *arraignment,* where the charges are read and a plea is entered. If the individual pleads not guilty, he or she will go to trial, where guilt must be established *beyond a reasonable doubt.* (In a civil trial, the plaintiff must meet the lesser standard of *a preponderance of the evidence.*) In a criminal trial, the burden of proof is on the state. The defendant is, of course, presumed innocent. He or she is entitled to a jury trial, but many choose to have the case decided by the judge alone. If found guilty, the defendant can, among other possibilities, seek a new trial or appeal errors in the prosecution. If found innocent, the defendant may, if necessary, invoke the doctrine of *double jeopardy* under which a person cannot be prosecuted twice in the same tribunal for the same criminal offense. [For an extensive criminal justice database, see **http://www.ncjrs.org**]

North Carolina, in 2006, became the first state to create an Innocence Inquiry Commission to which inmates can turn after their court appeals have been exhausted. Noting frequent errors in the criminal justice process, including faulty eyewitness accounts, North Carolina decided to give prisoners an additional chance to prove their innocence. Legislators were particularly concerned about the possibility of executing an innocent individual. Death Penalty Information Center findings from 1973 to 2006 show that 123 inmates convicted of capital crimes have been freed from prison because they were found to have been wrongfully convicted.[8]

Criminal appeals ordinarily turn on whether an error in the judicial process can be identified. The North Carolina Commission will allow prisoners to re-assert their innocence claim regardless of whether judicial process errors occurred. Under the North Carolina system, if five of eight commission members find that a claim of innocence deserves review, they will send the case to a three-judge panel, which must unanimously agree before a conviction will be overturned. A number of other states are considering innocence programs.[9]

PRACTICING ETHICS   When Sex Becomes Rape

On December 13, 2003, J. L., an 18-year-old female attending community college in Maryland, drove Maouloud Baby, then 16, and his friend, Michael Wilson, 15, to a residential area. Wilson allegedly had sex with J.L. while Baby waited outside of the car. According to court records, Baby then said it was his turn and asked J.L.: "Are you going to let me hit that?" He also said, "I don't want to rape you." J.L. testified in court that she agreed to sex "as long as he stops when I tell him to." When asked if she felt she had a choice about agreeing to sex, J.L. testified: "Not really. I don't know. Something just clicked off and I just did whatever they said." According to J.L.'s testimony, Baby commenced intercourse, but J.L. told him to stop because he was hurting her. Baby, however, continued the sexual intercourse for "five or so" seconds, according to J.L. Baby testified that he believed J.L. had given him permission to have sex with her, and he said that he stopped when she wanted him to do so. After Baby withdrew from J.L., the trio drove to a local McDonald's where J.L. gave her phone number to Baby, at his request, and where Wilson hugged her. J.L. then went shopping for a time and thereafter went to a friend's house where she explained what happened to her friend's mother, who then called the police.[10] Prosecutors attributed J.L.'s delayed disclosure to rape trauma.

Wilson pleaded guilty to second-degree rape and was sentenced to 18 months in prison. Baby was convicted of first-degree rape, among other offenses. He was sentenced to 15 years imprisonment, with all but five years suspended, and five years probation upon his release. Baby appealed, and the conviction was reversed, but upon further appeal, Maryland's highest court ruled that a woman has a right to revoke consent during intercourse, and a man who fails to comply with that altered decision can be charged with rape.[11] Baby may, therefore, go to trial again on rape charges. Eight state courts have now concluded that consent can be withdrawn after intercourse has commenced, and Illinois passed a statute to that effect. North Carolina law explicitly provides that rape cannot occur once permission is given.

Questions

1. The law aside, was J.L. morally wronged by Baby? Explain.
2. In your view, does rape occur if permission is withdrawn and sexual intercourse continues? Explain.
3. Was Baby morally wronged by J.L.'s rape charge? Explain.

Questions—Part One

1. Jonathan Rauch argues that America is making a mistake in allowing what he calls Hidden Law to be replaced by what he calls Bureaucratic Legalism. Hidden Law refers to unwritten social codes, whereas Bureaucratic Legalism refers to state-provided due process for every problem. Thus universities formerly expected insults and epithets among students to be resolved via informal modes such as apologies, while today many universities have written codes forbidding offensive or discriminatory verbal conduct. Similarly, four kindergarten students in New Jersey were suspended from school for three days because they were observed "shooting" each other with their fingers serving as guns.

   a. Would we be better off leaving campus insults and school-yard finger "shootings" to the Hidden Law? Explain.

   b. Can you think of other examples where we have gradually replaced Hidden Law with Bureaucratic Legalism?

   c. Rauch argues that the breakdown of one Hidden Law, the rule that a man must marry a woman whom he has impregnated, may be "the most far-reaching social change of our era." Do you agree? Explain. See George Will, "Penalizing These Kids Is Zero Tolerance at a Ridiculous Extreme," *Des Moines Register,* December 27, 2000, p. 11A.

2. In 1999 Denmark legalized prostitution.

   a. Should the United States do the same?

   b. Should we remove criminal penalties from all of the so-called victimless crimes including vagrancy, pornography, and gambling? Should we regulate those practices in any way? Explain.

3. *The Wall Street Journal* commented on the criminal justice system in Japan:

   > [D]espite its image of dealing tough justice, Japan's legal system is surprisingly lenient, geared toward reinstating most suspects into the cultural mainstream. Many who are arrested for minor crimes are let off the hook before indictment if they show remorse, legal experts say. And those who are indicted tend to get much lighter sentences if they confess, show remorse, compensate victims, and demonstrate that they have a strong family to return to.
   >
   > That gives a big incentive for an indicted suspect to cooperate with prosecutors and use the trial as a stage for shows of contrition. That may explain why 60 percent of those convicted and sentenced to prison terms last year had their sentences suspended.[12]

   Should American judges and prosecutors adopt the lenient Japanese response to crime? Explain.

4. A Rhode Island man pleaded guilty to child molestation. As an alternative to imprisonment and as a condition of his probation, the judge ordered him to purchase a newspaper ad displaying his picture, identifying himself as a sex offender, and encouraging others to seek assistance. A number of courts across the country have required apologies or other forms of humiliation in criminal cases.

   a. What objections would a defendant's lawyer raise to that method of punishment?

   b. Would you impose a "humiliation sentence" if you were the judge in a case like that in Rhode Island? Explain.

Part Two—The Judicial Process

Most disputes are settled without resort to litigation, but when agreement cannot be reached, we can turn to the courts—a highly technical and sophisticated dispute resolution mechanism.

State Court Systems

While state court systems vary substantially, a general pattern can be summarized. As shown in Figure 4.1, at the base of the court pyramid in most states is a *trial court of general jurisdiction,* commonly labeled a *district court* or a *superior court.* Most trials—both civil and criminal—arising out of state law are heard here, but certain classes of

FIGURE 4.1   State and Federal Court Systems

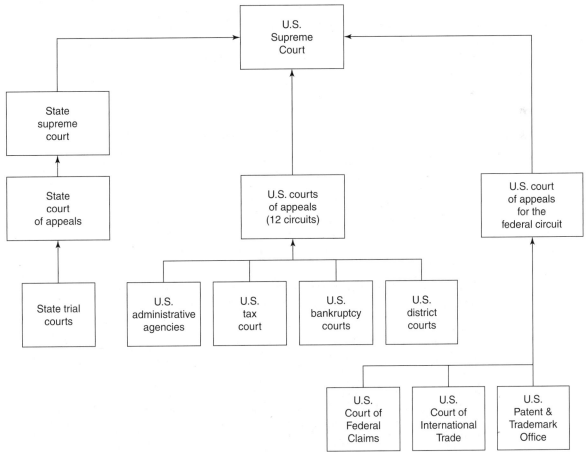

cases are reserved to courts of limited subject-matter jurisdiction or to various state administrative agencies (such as the state public utilities commission and the workers' compensation board). Family, small claims, juvenile, and traffic courts are examples of trial courts with limited jurisdiction. At the top of the judicial pyramid in all states is a court of appeals, ordinarily labeled the *supreme court.* A number of states also provide for an intermediate court of appeals located in the hierarchy between the trial courts and the highest appeals court.

Federal Court System

District Courts

The district courts serve as the foundation of the federal judicial system. The Constitution provides for a Supreme Court and such inferior courts as Congress shall authorize. Pursuant to that authority, Congress has established at least one district court for each state and territory. These are trial courts where witnesses are heard and questions of law and fact are resolved. Most federal cases begin in the district courts or in a federal administrative agency (such as the Federal Communications Commission). Congress has also provided for several courts of limited jurisdiction, including a tax court and the U.S. Court of International Trade.

[For access to all federal court Web sites, see the Federal Judicial Center at **http:// www.fjc.gov**]

Courts of Appeals

Congress has divided the United States geographically into 11 judicial circuits and the District of Columbia and has established a court of appeals for each. Those courts hear appeals from the district courts within their circuit and review decisions and enforce orders of the various federal administrative agencies. In addition, the U.S. Court of Appeals for the Federal Circuit hears, among others, all patent appeals and all appeals from the U.S. Court of Federal Claims (monetary claims against the United States).

Supreme Court

The Supreme Court consists of nine justices appointed for life by the president and confirmed by the Senate. Almost all of the Supreme Court's work consists of reviewing lower court decisions, principally from the courts of appeal with a small number from state high courts. Virtually all parties seeking Supreme Court review must petition the Court for a *writ of certiorari,* which commands the lower court to forward the trial records to the Court.

Decisions regarding those petitions are entirely discretionary with the Court. Typically it will hear those cases that will assist in resolving conflicting courts of appeal decisions, as well as those that raise questions of special significance about the Constitution or the national welfare. Petitions to the Supreme Court have grown steadily over the years and now total approximately 8,000 cases per year. Formal, written opinions, however, are issued in only about 70 to 90 cases, a decline from, for example, 175 in 1986. Thus, in terms of numbers alone, the Court has backed away from its more activist approach of the 1960s, 1970s, and 1980s.

Questions of "judicial activism," the liberal/conservative balance on the Supreme Court, the politics of the justices, and the justices' deference to big business interests have made the Court a target for criticism. President George W. Bush, in appointing a new chief justice, John Roberts, as well as a new justice, Samuel Alito, for the 2006–07 term, was able to shift the Court's political/ideological complexion more toward the conservative, probusiness, judicial restraint mode and away from the more liberal/government intervention stance that had marked the Court in recent decades. We want to believe that the Supreme Court reaches its decisions in a rational, objective fashion relying on the commands of the Constitution and precedent to maintain a consistent, fair, orderly judicial system free of political influence. The facts, however, reveal a Supreme Court that is often split along what appear to be ideological lines. During the term ending in June 2007, one-third of the Court's decisions, more than in any other term, were decided by 5–4 votes with 19 of those 24 decisions following ideological leanings, according to a *New York Times* analysis.[13] Early decisions in the term ending in June 2008, however, did not reflect that same tight division. Of course, public respect for the fairness and the rationality of Supreme Court decisions could be undermined if they come to be viewed as the product of liberal or conservative political/ideological views, rather than dispassionate, lawyerly analysis.

An apparent trend in the new, more conservative Supreme Court is to hear more business cases and to support a philosophical posture of general deference to the free market, as opposed to increased government rules and oversight. That general trend seems to reflect the thinking of both the conservative and liberal segments of the Court. *BusinessWeek* summarized the data for the 2006–07 Supreme Court term:

> Out of 15 cases in which the U.S. Chamber of Commerce filed friend-of-the-court briefs, presenting the views of its corporate members, the chamber won 13—the chamber's highest winning percentage in its 30-year history.[14]

[For an overview of the Supreme Court, see **http://www.supremecourtus.gov/ sitemap.html**].

Jurisdiction

A plaintiff may not simply proceed to trial at the court of his or her preference. The plaintiff must go to a court with *jurisdiction*—that is, a court with the necessary power and authority to hear the dispute. The court must have jurisdiction over both the subject matter and the persons (or, in some instances, the property) involved in the case.

Subject-Matter Jurisdiction

Subject-matter jurisdiction imposes bounds on the classes of cases a court may hear. The legislation or constitution creating the court will normally specify that court's jurisdictional authority. State courts of general jurisdiction, for example, may hear most types of cases, but a criminal court or probate court is limited in the subject matter it may hear.

The outer bounds of federal jurisdiction are specified in the Constitution, while Congress has further particularized that issue by statute. Essentially, the federal district courts may hear two types of cases: (1) those involving a federal question and (2) those involving diversity of citizenship and more than $75,000.

Federal question jurisdiction exists in any suit where the plaintiff's claim is based on the U.S. Constitution, a U.S. treaty, or a federal statute. Thus litigants can bring to the federal courts cases involving, for example, the federal antitrust statutes, federal criminal laws, constitutional issues such as freedom of the press, and federal tax questions. Federal question jurisdiction does not require an amount in controversy exceeding $75,000. Further, federal and state courts have *concurrent jurisdiction* for some federal questions. Thus some federal question cases are decided in state courts applying federal law. Federal courts can also hear cases involving state laws. Congress has accorded the federal courts exclusive jurisdiction over certain subjects, including federal criminal laws, bankruptcy, and copyrights. Under *diversity jurisdiction,* federal district courts may hear cases involving more than $75,000 where the plaintiff(s) and the defendant(s) are citizens of different states. (Corporations are treated as citizens both of their state of incorporation and the state in which their principal place of business is located.) Diversity cases may also be heard in state courts, but plaintiffs frequently prefer to bring their actions in federal courts. The quality of the federal judiciary is generally believed to be superior to that of the states, and the federal courts are considered less likely to be influenced by local bias. Federal court action may also have procedural advantages, such as greater capacity to secure witnesses' testimony.

Personal Jurisdiction

Judicial authority over the person is known as *in personam jurisdiction*. In general, a state court's powers are limited to the bounds of the state. While the matter is fraught with complexities, it is fair to say that state court jurisdiction can be established in three ways: (1) When the defendant is a resident of the state, a summons may be served at that residence. (2) When the defendant is not a resident, a summons may be personally served should he or she be physically present in the state. (3) Most states have legislated "long-arm" statutes that allow a state or federal court to secure jurisdiction against an out-of-state party where the defendant has committed a tort in the state or where the defendant is conducting business in the state. Hence, in an auto accident in Ohio involving both an Ohio resident and a Kentucky resident, the Ohio resident may sue in Ohio and achieve service of process over the Kentucky defendant as a consequence of the jurisdictional authority afforded by the long-arm statute.

A state court may also acquire jurisdiction via an *in rem action*. In that instance the defendant may be a nonresident, but his or her property, which must be the subject of the suit, must be located within the state.

The following case involves a dispute about the commercial use of the name of celebrated actor and California governor, Arnold Schwarzenegger.

Circuit Judge Fletcher

Arnold Schwarzenegger, an internationally known movie star and, currently, the governor of California, appeals the district court's dismissal of his suit against Fred Martin Motor Company ("Fred Martin"), an Ohio car dealership, for lack of personal jurisdiction. Fred Martin had run a series of five full-page color advertisements in the *Akron Beacon Journal,* a locally circulated Ohio newspaper. Each advertisement included a small photograph of Schwarzenegger, portrayed as the "Terminator," without his permission. Schwarzenegger brought suit in California, alleging that these unauthorized uses of his image infringed his right of publicity. We affirm the district court's dismissal for lack of personal jurisdiction.

I. BACKGROUND

Schwarzenegger is a resident of California. When Schwarzenegger brought this suit, he was a private citizen and movie star, best known for his roles as a muscle-bound hero of action films and distinctive Austrian accent. As explained in his complaint, Schwarzenegger was generally cast as the lead character in so-called star-driven films. One of Schwarzenegger's most popular and readily recognizable film roles is that of the title character in *The Terminator* (1984). . . .

Fred Martin is an automobile dealership incorporated under the laws of Ohio and located in Barberton, Ohio, a few miles southwest of Akron. There is no evidence in the record that Fred Martin has any operations or employees in California, has ever advertised in California, or has ever sold a car to anyone in California. Fred Martin maintains an Internet Web site that is available for viewing in California and, for that matter, from any Internet cafe in Istanbul, Bangkok, or anywhere else in the world.

In early 2002, Fred Martin engaged defendant Zimmerman & Partners Advertising, Inc. ("Zimmerman") to design and place a full-page color advertisement in the *Akron Beacon Journal,* a local Akron-based newspaper. The advertisement ran in the *Akron Beacon Journal* five times in April 2002. Most of the advertisement consists of small photographs and descriptions of various cars available for purchase or lease from Fred Martin. Just below a large-font promise that Fred Martin "WON'T BE BEAT," the advertise-

ment includes a small, but clearly recognizable photograph of Schwarzenegger as the Terminator. A "bubble quotation," like those found in comic strips, is drawn next to Schwarzenegger's mouth, reading, "Arnold says: 'Terminate EARLY at Fred Martin!'" This part of the advertisement refers to a special offer from Fred Martin to customers, inviting them to close out their current leases before the expected termination date, and to buy or lease a new car from Fred Martin.

Neither Fred Martin nor Zimmerman ever sought or received Schwarzenegger's permission to use his photograph in the advertisement. Schwarzenegger states in his complaint that, had such a request been made, it would have been refused. The advertisement, as far as the record reveals, was never circulated outside of Ohio.

Schwarzenegger brought suit against Fred Martin and Zimmerman in Los Angeles County Superior Court alleging six state law causes of action arising out of the unauthorized use of his image in the advertisement. He claims that the defendants caused him financial harm in that the use of his photograph to endorse Fred Martin "diminishes his hard earned reputation as a major motion picture star, and risks the potential for overexposure of his image to the public, thereby potentially diminishing the compensation he would otherwise garner from his career as a major motion picture star." According to Schwarzenegger's complaint, his compensation as the lead actor in star-driven films was based on his ability to draw crowds to the box office, and his ability to do so depended in part on the scarcity of his image. According to his complaint, if Schwarzenegger's image were to become ubiquitous—in advertisements and on television, for example—the movie-going public would be less likely to spend their money to see his films, and his compensation would diminish accordingly. Therefore, Schwarzenegger maintains, it is vital for him to avoid "over-saturation of his image." According to his complaint, he has steadfastly refused to endorse any products in the United States, despite being offered substantial sums to do so.

Defendants removed the action to federal district court in California, and Fred Martin moved to dismiss the complaint for lack of personal jurisdiction. The district court granted Fred Martin's motion, and Schwarzenegger appealed.

II. PERSONAL JURISDICTION

For a court to exercise personal jurisdiction over a nonresident defendant, that defendant must have at least "minimum contacts" with the relevant forum such that the exercise of jurisdiction "does not offend traditional notions of fair play and substantial justice." *International Shoe Co. v. Washington,* 326 U.S. 310, 316. (1945)

A. General Jusrisdiction

Schwarzenegger argues, quite implausibly, that California has general personal jurisdiction over Fred Martin. For general jurisdiction to exist over a nonresident defendant such as Fred Martin, the defendant must engage in "continuous and systematic general business contacts," *Helicopteros Nacionales de Colombia, S.A. v. Hall,* 466 U.S. 408 (1984) that "approximate physical presence" in the forum state. *Bancroft &* Masters, 223 F. 3d at 1086. This is an exacting standard, as it should be, because a finding of general jurisdiction permits a defendant to be haled into court in the forum state to answer for any of its activities anywhere in the world.

Schwarzenegger contends that Fred Martin's contacts with California are so extensive that it is subject to general jurisdiction. He points to the following contacts: Fred Martin regularly purchases Asian-made automobiles that are imported by California entities. However, in purchasing these automobiles, Fred Martin dealt directly with representatives in Illinois and New Jersey, but never dealt directly with the California-based importers. Some of Fred Martin's sales contracts with its automobile suppliers include a choice-of-law provision specifying California law. In addition, Fred Martin regularly retains the services of a California-based direct-mail marketing company; has hired a sales training company, incorporated in California, for consulting services; and maintains an Internet Web site accessible by anyone capable of using the Internet, including people living in California.

These contacts fall well short of the "continuous and systematic" contacts that the Supreme Court and this court have held to constitute sufficient "presence" to warrant general jurisdiction. Schwarzenegger has therefore failed to establish a prima facie case of general jurisdiction.

B. Specific Jurisdiction

Alternatively, Schwarzenegger argues that Fred Martin has sufficient "minimum contacts" with California arising from, or related to, its actions in creating and distributing the advertisement such that the forum may assert specific personal jurisdiction. We have established a three-prong test for analyzing a claim of specific personal jurisdiction:

(1) The nonresident defendant must purposefully direct his activities or consummate some transaction with the forum or resident thereof; or perform some act by which he purposefully avails himself of the privilege of conducting activities in the forum, thereby invoking the benefits and protections of its laws;

(2) the claim must be one which arises out of or relates to the defendant's forum-related activities; and

(3) the exercise of jurisdiction must comport with fair play and substantial justice, i.e., it must be reasonable.

The plaintiff bears the burden of satisfying the first two prongs of the test. If the plaintiff fails to satisfy either of these prongs, personal jurisdiction is not established in the forum state. If the plaintiff succeeds in satisfying both of the first two prongs, the burden then shifts to the defendant to "present a compelling case" that the exercise of jurisdiction would not be resonable. For the reasons that follow, we hold that Schwarzenegger has failed to satisfy the first prong.

1. Purposeful Availment or Direction Generally
Under the first prong of our three-part specific jurisdiction test, Schwarzenegger must establish that Fred Martin either purposefully availed itself of the privilege of conducting activities in California, or purposefully directed its activities toward California.

* * * * *

A showing that a defendant purposefully availed himself of the privilege of doing business in a forum state typically consists of evidence of the defendant's actions in the forum, such as executing or performing a contract there. By taking such actions, a defendant "purposefully avails itself of the privilege of conducting activities within the forum State, thus invoking the benefits and protections of its laws." *Hanson v. Denckla,* 357 U.S. 235, 253 (1958). In return for these "benefits and protections," a defendant must—as a quid pro quo— "submit to the burdens of litigation in that forum." *Burger King,* 471 U.S. at 476.

A showing that a defendant purposefully directed his conduct toward a forum state, by contrast, usually consists of evidence of the defendant's actions outside the forum state that are directed at the forum, such as the distribution in the forum state of goods originating elsewhere.

2. Purposeful Direction
Schwarzenegger does not point to any conduct by Fred Martin in California related to the advertisement that would be readily susceptible to a purposeful availment analysis. Rather, the conduct of which Schwarzenegger complains—

the unauthorized inclusion of the photograph in the advertisement and its distribution in the *Akron Beacon Journal*—took place in Ohio, not California. Fred Martin received no benefit, privilege, or protection from California in connection with the advertisement, and the traditional quid pro quo justification for finding purposeful availment thus does not apply. Therefore, to the extent that Fred Martin's conduct might justify the exercise of personal jurisdiction in California, that conduct must have been purposefully directed at California.

* * * * *

Here, Fred Martin's intentional act—the creation and publication of the advertisement—was expressly aimed at Ohio rather than California. The purpose of the advertisement was to entice Ohioans to buy or lease cars from Fred Martin and, in particular, to "terminate" their current car leases. The advertisement was never circulated in California, and Fred Martin had no reason to believe that any Californians would see it and pay a visit to the dealership. Fred Martin certainly had no reason to believe that a Californian had a current car lease with Fred Martin that could be "terminated" as recommended in the advertisement. It may be true that Fred Martin's intentional act eventually caused harm to Schwarzenegger in California and Fred Martin may have known that Schwarzenegger lived in California. But this does not confer jurisdiction, for Fred Martin's express aim was local. We therefore conclude that the advertisement was not expressly aimed at California.

CONCLUSION

We hold that Schwarzenegger has established neither general nor specific jurisdiction over Fred Martin in California. Schwarzenegger has not shown that Fred Martin has "continuous and systematic general business contacts," *Helicopteros,* 466 U.S. at 416, that "approximate physical presence" in California, *Bancroft & Masters,* 223 F. 3d at 1086, such that it can be sued there for any act it has committed anywhere in the world. Further, while Schwarzenegger has made out a prima facie case that Fred Martin committed intentional acts that may have caused harm to Schwarzenegger in California, he has not made out a prima facie case that Fred Martin expressly aimed its acts at California.

Affirmed.

AFTERWORD

Schwarzenegger's claim was settled out of court in 2004 when the Fred Martin Motor Company issued a written apology and agreed to pay a "substantial" sum to Arnold's All-Stars, an after-school program founded by Schwarzenegger.

Questions

1. Explain Schwarzenegger's complaint.
2. Why was Schwarzenegger unable to sue Fred Martin in California?
3. The Robinsons filed a product liability suit in an Oklahoma state court to recover for injuries sustained in an automobile accident in Oklahoma. The auto had been purchased in New York from the defendant, World-Wide Volkswagen Corp. Oklahoma's long-arm statute was used in an attempt to secure jurisdiction over the defendant. World-Wide conducted no business in Oklahoma. Nor did it solicit business there.
   a. Build an argument to support the claim of jurisdiction for the Oklahoma court.
   b. Decide. See *World-Wide Volkswagen Corp. v. Woodson,* 100 S. Ct. 559 (1980).
4. Burger King conducts a franchise, fast-food operation from its Miami, Florida, headquarters. John Rudzewicz and a partner, both residents of Michigan, secured a Burger King franchise in Michigan. Subsequently, the franchisees allegedly fell behind in payments, and after negotiations failed, Burger King ordered the franchisees to vacate the premises. They declined to do so, and continued to operate the franchise. Burger King brought suit in a federal district court in Florida. The defendant franchisees argued that the Florida court did not have personal jurisdiction over them because they were Michigan residents and because the claim did not arise in Florida. However, the district court found the defendants to be subject to the Florida long-arm statute, which extends jurisdiction to "[a]ny person, whether or not a citizen or resident of this state" who, "[b]reach[es] a contract in this state by failing to perform acts required by the contract to be performed in this state." The franchise contract provided for governance of the relationship by Florida law. Policy was set in Miami, although day-to-day supervision was managed through various district offices. The case ultimately reached the U.S. Supreme Court.
   a. What constitutional argument would you raise on behalf of the defendant franchisees?
   b. Decide. See *Burger King Corp. v. Rudzewicz,* 471 U.S. 462 (1985).

Venue

Once jurisdictional authority—that is, the power to hear the case—is established, the proper *venue* (geographic location within the court system) comes into question. Ordinarily, a case will be heard by the court geographically closest to the incident or property in question or to where the parties reside. Thus a lawsuit springing from a crime ordinarily would be filed in the county where the crime took place. Sometimes pre-trial publicity or other factors may cause one of the parties to seek a *change of venue* on the grounds that a fair trial is impossible in the original location. Former Enron Chairman Kenneth Lay and Chief Executive Jeffrey Skilling unsuccessfully asked to have their conspiracy and fraud trial moved out of Houston, Texas, where the collapse of their giant energy company cost thousands of jobs while damaging local real estate and charitable interests. The executives claimed the hatred for them in Houston was so personal and emotional that they could not receive a fair trial:

> The former Enron executives have been compared to Satan, al Quaida, Adolf Hitler, and O.J. Simpson in reports in the local media. . . . In a survey, nearly one in three Houston residents used negative statements to describe Skilling.[15]

Sometimes the choice of venue is a strategic decision reflecting the attorneys' knowledge of the tendencies of judges and juries in various locales around the nation. The pharmaceutical giant Merck & Co. has been defending itself against billions of dollars in claims linking the Merck painkilling drug Vioxx (now withdrawn from the market) to heart attacks and strokes. *The Wall Street Journal* explained that "both sides seek friendly venues":

> Whether Merck & Co. ends up winning or losing in the courts over Vioxx is going to depend in large part on the location of the playing field and the leanings of the referee. . . . [B]oth sides are battling for the courtroom advantage—seeking to have many of the cases . . . assigned to the courthouse and judge each thinks will be most open to its arguments.[16]

Merck hoped to have the federal cases heard in the conservative U.S. District Court in Maryland while the plaintiffs hoped to have those cases heard in the U.S. District Court in Houston because south Texas is often considered an attractive venue for plaintiffs.[17] Although a few Vioxx claims were litigated around the nation, judges in California, Louisiana, and New Jersey eventually oversaw nearly all of the 27,000 cases. The claims currently are moving through a settlement process, under which Merck has agreed to pay $4.85 billion.[18]

Sometimes trials, such as the one described next, are moved to avoid hardship or inconvenience (the doctrine of *forum non conveniens*).

PER CURIAM

Kia Motors America, Inc., headquartered in California; Kia Motors Corporation, headquartered in Korea (Kia Motors America, Inc., and Kia Motors Corporation are hereinafter collectively referred to as "Kia"); and Emerald Auto Sales, Inc. ("Emerald"), located in Houston County, Alabama, petition this Court to grant their motions to dismiss these cases based on the doctrine of forum non conveniens.

Facts and Procedural History

On October 16, 1999, Marilyn Elise Jeffreys, her daughter Danielle Jeffreys, Justin Valieres, and Christopher Allen Durden were in a 1998 Kia Sephia automobile when they were involved in a high-speed crash with another vehicle in Jackson County, Florida. The force of the crash caused the Sephia to leave the roadway; it came to rest in a pasture, where it caught fire and burned. The only occupant to survive the accident was Danielle Jeffreys.

On September 7, 2001, Howard Jeffreys, as the administrator of the estate of Marilyn Elise Jeffreys; Patricia Foxworth, as the administratrix of the estate of Christopher Allen Durden; and Debra Woodward, as the administratrix of the estate of Justin Valieres (Howard Jeffreys, Foxworth, and Woodward are hereinafter collectively referred to as "the respondents"), sued Kia and Emerald in the Houston Circuit Court on theories of product liability, breach of warranty, and negligence and wantonness as to Kia, and product liability and breach of warranty as to Emerald.

On October 11, 2001, Kia filed a motion to dismiss the Alabama actions on the ground of forum non conveniens. . . . [I]t requested the trial court to dismiss the actions and allow them to be filed in Jackson County, Florida. Subsequently, Kia filed an evidentiary submission in support of its motion to dismiss, presenting the affidavits of 25 witnesses who are residents of Florida and who stated that it would be more convenient if the actions were brought in Jackson County, Florida, where the crash occurred. From the facts before us, it appears that the accident site, the decedents, the plaintiffs, nonparty witnesses, rescue personnel and medical examiners who might testify, and documents related to this accident are located in Florida. The wrecked vehicle is currently being stored in Birmingham [Alabama].

* * * * *

Analysis

Kia and Emerald allege that in denying their motions to dismiss on the basis of forum non conveniens the trial court exceeded its discretion. Specifically, they argue that because the decedents were, and the plaintiffs are, residents of Florida and because the accident occurred in Florida and the majority of witnesses and accident-related documents are located in Florida, in the interests of justice the trial court should dismiss these actions so that they may be brought in Jackson County, Florida.

* * * * *

The doctrine of forum non conveniens requires a court to determine whether to accept or to decline jurisdiction of claims arising outside the state. . . . "Initially, the party seeking dismissal must show that the claims arose outside Alabama. Next, that party must show that an alternative forum exists."

* * * * *

Thus, the trial court is compelled to dismiss an action . . . if, upon a defendant's motion, it is shown that there exists a more appropriate forum outside the state, taking into account the location where the acts giving rise to the action occurred, the convenience of the parties and witnesses, and the interest of justice. . . . In addition, in determining whether a dismissal of the action on the ground of forum non conveniens should be granted, the trial court should consider "the relative ease of access to sources of proof, the location of the evidence, the availability of compulsory process for the attendance of unwilling witnesses, the cost of obtaining the attendance of willing witnesses, the possibility of a view of the premises, if a view would be appropriate to the action, and any other matter in order to assess the degree of actual difficulty and hardship that would result to the defendant in litigating the case in the forum chosen by the plaintiff." Ex parte Ben-Acadia, Ltd., 566 So. 2d 486, 488 (Ala. 1990).

* * * * *

In the instant case, for the doctrine of forum non conveniens to be applicable, the claims must have arisen outside Alabama. The respondents' complaints allege product liability and breach-of-warranty claims against both Kia and Emerald. Additionally, the respondents allege that Kia was negligent or wanton in its design and manufacture of the Sephia. It is undisputed that the product liability and negligence claims against Kia arose in Florida. However, the parties disagree as to where the breach-of-warranty claim against Emerald arose. The respondents, in their brief, state,

In this case, Florida's substantive law will apply to the product liability, negligence, and wantonness claims brought against the Defendants Kia Motors America, Inc., and Kia Motors Corporation. However, the Plaintiffs' breach of warranty claims against Emerald Auto Sales, Inc., arise under Alabama law since the subject car was purchased in Alabama.

In contrast, Kia and Emerald allege that all of the respondents' claims, including the breach-of-warranty claim against Emerald, arose in Florida.

* * * * *

In the present case, Jackson County, Florida, is clearly a more appropriate forum for these actions than is Houston County, Alabama. Applying Alabama law, we are satisfied that all of the causes of action occurred in Florida. Furthermore, 25 nonparty witnesses that Kia and Emerald plan to call on the issue of liability reside in Florida and cannot be subpoenaed and made to personally appear in the Houston Circuit Court. The inability to have live testimony in Alabama from these nonparty witnesses in the liability phase of this action, we believe, clearly favors dismissal.

* * * * *

Conclusion

We hold that the trial court exceeded its discretion in failing to dismiss the actions. Therefore, we grant the petition and order the trial court to dismiss these actions so that they can be refiled in Jackson County, Florida.

DISSENT: SEE, JUSTICE (DISSENTING)

I respectfully dissent from the majority opinion holding that the trial court exceeded its discretion in failing to dismiss this case pursuant to Alabama's forum non conveniens statute.

* * * * *

I agree with the majority that, for the forum non conveniens statute to apply, all of the claims in the present case must have arisen outside Alabama. However, I submit that Kia and Emerald have not met their burden of showing that the respondents' breach-of-warranty claim against Emerald arose outside this State.

* * * * *

In the present case, Emerald warranted the car as fit for its intended purpose when the purchaser accepted delivery of the car in Houston County. The respondents allege that the car was not fit for its intended purpose. The act giving rise to the breach-of-warranty claim against Emerald was Emerald's delivery of an allegedly defective car at its dealership in Houston County, not the accident in Florida. Therefore, the breach-of-warranty claim against Emerald arose in Houston County. . . .

* * * * *

Questions

1. *a.* Why did the court consider Florida to be the more "convenient" location for the case?

   b. Explain the dissenting opinion.

2. Why do you think the plaintiffs/respondents wanted the case heard in Alabama rather than in Florida?

Standing to Sue

All who wish to bring a claim before a court may not be permitted to do so. To receive the court's attention, the litigant must demonstrate that she or he has *standing to sue*. That is, the person must show that her or his interest in the outcome of the controversy is sufficiently direct and substantial as to justify the court's consideration. The litigant must show that she or he personally is suffering, or will be suffering, injury. Mere interest in the problem at hand is insufficient to grant standing to sue.

The significance of the standing doctrine was illustrated by a 2006 U.S. Supreme Court decision involving Ohio taxpayers who challenged their state's decision to extend $280 million in tax credits to DaimlerChrysler in return for which the auto maker was expected to create several thousand new jobs in Toledo, Ohio.[19] States routinely offer these incentives to attract corporate investment. Critics claim the incentives merely shift benefits in jobs and tax base from one state to another without actually improving the overall economic climate; a form of corporate welfare at the expense of taxpayers, they say. The Ohio taxpayers claimed that the incentives discriminated against interstate commerce in violation of the Commerce Clause of the U.S. Constitution (see Chapter 8). The Supreme Court, however, did not reach that substantive question because it ruled unanimously that the taxpayers did not have standing to sue in the case. The taxpayers had claimed that the incentives imposed a direct economic burden on them because the tax breaks depleted local and state treasuries to which they contributed. The Supreme Court, however, ruled that any such injuries were merely speculative depending upon decisions yet to be made by elected officials.

The Civil Trial Process

Civil procedure varies by jurisdiction. The following generalizations merely typify the process. (See Figure 4.2.) [For a vast "catalog" of law on the Internet, see **http://www. catalaw.com**]

Pleadings

Pleadings are the documents by which each party sets his or her initial case before the court. A civil action begins when the plaintiff files his or her first pleading, which is labeled a *complaint.* The complaint specifies (1) the parties to the suit, (2) evidence as to the court's jurisdiction in the case, (3) a statement of the facts, and (4) a prayer for relief (a remedy).

The complaint is filed with the clerk of court and a *summons* is issued, directing the defendant to appear in court to answer the claims alleged against him or her. A sheriff or some other official attempts to personally deliver the summons to the defendant. If personal delivery cannot be achieved, the summons may be left with a responsible party

FIGURE 4.2 **Stages of a Lawsuit**

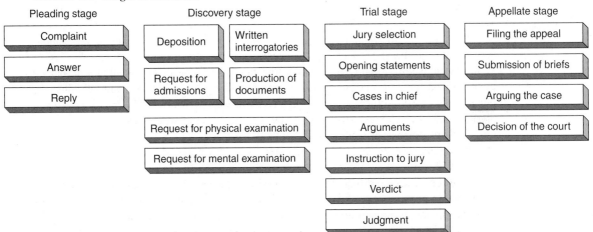

at the defendant's residence. Failing that, other modes of delivery are permissible, including a mailing. Publication of a notice in a newspaper will, in some instances, constitute good service of process. Ordinarily, a copy of the complaint accompanies the summons, so the defendant is apprised of the nature of the claim.

The defendant has several options. He or she may do nothing, but failure to respond may result in a default judgment in favor of the plaintiff. The defendant may choose to respond by filing *a demurrer* or *a motion to dismiss,* the essence of which is to argue that even if the plaintiff's recitation of the facts is accurate, a claim on which relief can be granted has not been stated. For example, a student may file suit objecting to a teacher's "bizarre" manner of dress; but, barring unusual circumstances, the student could not, as a matter of law, successfully challenge the teacher's costume.

Alternatively, the defendant may file with the court an initial pleading, called an *answer,* wherein the defendant enters a denial by setting out his or her version of the facts and law, or in which the defendant simply concedes the validity of the plaintiff's position. The answer may also contain an *affirmative defense*, such as the statute of limitations or the statute of frauds, that would bar the plaintiff's claim. The defendant's answer might include a counterclaim or cross-claim. A *counterclaim* is the defendant's assertion of a claim of action against the plaintiff. A *cross-claim* is the defendant's assertion of a claim of action against a codefendant. In some states, these would be labeled *cross-complaints*. In the event of a counterclaim or the assertion of new facts in the answer, the plaintiff will respond with a *reply*. The complaint, answer, reply, and their components are the pleadings that serve to give notice, clarify the issues, and limit the dimensions of the litigation. [For a summary of "Famous Trials" in history, see **http://www.law.umkc.edu/faculty/projects/ftrials/ftrials.htm**]

Motions

As necessary during and after the filing of the pleadings, either party may file motions with the court. For example, a party may move to clarify a pleading or to strike a portion deemed unnecessary. Of special importance is a motion for a judgment on the pleadings or a motion for summary judgment. In a *motion for a judgment on the pleadings,* either party simply asks the judge to reach a decision based on the information in the pleadings. The judge will do so only if the defendant's answer constitutes an admission of the accuracy of the plaintiff's claim, or if the plaintiff's claim clearly has no foundation in law.

In a *motion for a summary judgment,* the party filing the motion is claiming that no facts are in dispute. Therefore, the judge may make a ruling about the law without taking the case to trial. In a summary judgment hearing, the court can look beyond the pleadings to hear evidence from affidavits, depositions, and so on. These motions avoid the time and expense of trial.

Discovery

Discovery is the primary information-gathering stage in the pretrial process. That information clarifies the trial issues, promotes pretrial settlements, and helps prevent surprises at the trial, among other things. Discovery may consist of *depositions* (recorded, sworn testimony in preparation for trial), physical and mental examinations, answers to written questions (*interrogatories*), requests for access to documents and property to inspect them prior to trial, and *admissions* (agreement by the parties to stipulated issues of fact or law prior to trial).

The era of electronic communication and storage has added important new expectations and burdens to the discovery process by requiring that litigants exchange all relevant electronically stored information (ESI) during the discovery phase. Individuals and companies must be able to produce ESI from all sources, including e-mail, files, scanned handwritten notes, stored records, voice mail, fax data, instant messages, spreadsheets, video, PowerPoint presentations, and so on.

Pretrial Conference

Either party may request, and many courts require, a pretrial meeting involving the attorneys, the judge, and occasionally the parties. Usually following discovery, the conference is designed to plan the course of the trial in the interests of efficiency and justice. The participants seek to define the issues and settle the dispute in advance of trial. If no settlement is reached, a trial date is set.

The Judge and Jury

The federal Constitution and most state constitutions provide for the right to a jury trial in a civil case (excepting equity actions). Some states place dollar minimums on that guaranty. At the federal level and in most states, unless one of the parties requests a jury, the judge alone will hear the case and decide all questions of law and fact. If the case is tried before a jury, that body will resolve questions of fact; but all questions of law will be resolved by the judge, who will also instruct the jury as to the law governing the case.

Jurors are selected from a jury pool composed of a cross section of the community. A panel is drawn from that pool. The individuals in that panel are questioned by the judge, by the attorneys, or by all to determine if any individual is prejudiced about the case such that he or she could not reach an objective decision on the merits. The questioning process is called *voir dire*.

From an attorney's point of view, jury selection is often not so much a matter of finding jurors without bias as it is a matter of identifying those jurors who are most likely to reach a decision favorable to one's client. To that end, elaborate mechanisms and strategies have been employed—particularly in criminal trials—to identify desirable jurors. For example, sophisticated, computer-assisted surveys of the trial community have been conducted to develop objective evidence by which to identify jurors who would not admit to racial prejudice but whose "profile" suggests the likelihood of such prejudice.

After questioning, the attorneys may *challenge for cause,* arguing to the judge that the individual cannot exercise the necessary objectivity of judgment. Attorneys are also afforded a limited number of *peremptory challenges,* by which the attorney can have a potential juror dismissed without the judge's concurrence and without offering a reason. Peremptory challenges may not be used to reject jurors on the basis of race or gender.

Misleading the Jury?

The case that follows examines allegations of trial misconduct by the plaintiff's attorney in an apparent effort to prejudice the jury.

Judges Buckley, Rosenberger, Lerner, Rubin, Marlow

[P]laintiff alleges that he was verbally and physically abused by defendants because of his sexual orientation and then wrongfully discharged when he refused to voluntarily relinquish his position at the Supper Club.

The Supper Club is a dining and dancing establishment operated by defendant, Edison Associates, L.P. (hereinafter Edison), a limited partnership. Defendant Martin Theising is a partner in Edison and defendant Andre Cortez is the general manager of The Supper Club and is responsible for its day-to-day operations. Defendant Oliver Hoffman was an independent consultant to The Supper Club.

In November 1992, plaintiff was hired as The Supper Club's late night manager initially responsible for its disco and later for its cabaret until he was discharged in July 1995. Plaintiff alleges in his complaint, that during the course of his employment, he was repeatedly subjected to humiliation and to discriminatory epithets regarding his sexual orientation and that, two weeks before he was discharged, he was physically held down by Hoffman and another individual while Cortez threatened to cut off his ponytail with a pair of scissors.

After a lengthy trial, the jury found that plaintiff had been subjected to a hostile work environment and had been discharged because of his sexual orientation and that Cortez had committed assault and battery. The jury awarded $160,000 in lost wages, finding that plaintiff could not have mitigated his damages. It further awarded $8,000,000 for past pain, suffering, and emotional distress and $2,000,000 for such future damages. The jury also awarded punitive damages of $1,000,000 against The Supper Club, $54,000 against Cortez and $2,200,000 against Theising with respect to the discrimination claims.

Defendants contend that the damages awarded were so grossly excessive as to be the result of passion and prejudice born of plaintiff's counsel's misconduct and judicial error, that a mere reduction of the awards would not be an adequate remedy.

"When misconduct of counsel in interrogation or summation so violates the rights of the other party to the litigation that extraneous matters beyond the proper scope of the trial may have substantially influenced or been determinative of the outcome, such breaches of the rules will not be condoned." (*Kohlmann v. City of New York*, 8 AD2d 598, 598.) Although evidence of hostility and harassment to other minorities may be relevant to a claim of a hostile work environment based on sexual orientation, the cumulative effect of the many irrelevant and highly prejudicial comments made by plaintiff's counsel in the course of this trial only served to incite the jury's passion and sympathy and effectively prevented a fair and dispassionate consideration of the evidence. Plaintiff's counsel referred to Theising, a German national with an apparent accent, as someone who exhibited an "attitude of hatred" and made forced analogies to Nazi Germany and the Holocaust. While the issue of this case was sexual orientation discrimination, plaintiff's counsel presented to the jury inappropriate matters involving African Americans, Latinos, and Jews that went far beyond any permissible boundaries and served no other purpose than to incite the jury's passions. Similarly, plaintiff's counsel elicited testimony about an alleged physical attack by an assistant to Cortez on an employee dying of AIDS and extensive testimony from several witnesses regarding the consumption of alcoholic beverages by Cortez, Hoffman, and Theising which was highly prejudicial with little or no probative value.

We find that the aggregate effect of such comments and conduct of plaintiff's counsel, which cannot be characterized as inadvertent or harmless, inflamed the jury's passion and sympathy to such an extent as to render the resulting judgment meaningless. . . .

The trial court erred in refusing to allow defendants to introduce evidence that no other employees were treated abusively . . . and in denying defendants' requested jury charge on mitigation. Likewise, it was error to deny defendants a missing witness charge upon plaintiff's failure to produce his therapist, Susan Corcoran, and a treating physician, Dr. Keston, since both had provided extensive treatment to plaintiff and their testimony would not have been cumulative. Further, the trial court made a number of demeaning comments in the presence of the jury demonstrating a marked antipathy toward defense counsel which, in light of the totality of circumstances at trial, warrant a new trial.

Were this Court not to reverse and remand for a new trial for the reasons stated above, we would have nevertheless reversed on the issue of damages. The jury's grossly excessive compensatory and punitive damages awards totaling approximately $20,000,000 have no rational basis. . . . [Reversed. Remanded to "a different justice."]

Questions

1. *a.* Why did this appeals court reverse the decision of the lower court?

   b. Why was the case remanded to "a different justice"?

2. Did this decision conclude that the plaintiff had not been a victim of sexual harassment, wrongful dismissal, or the like? Explain.

3. According to this appeals court, what errors were made by the judge at trial?

Eminem Inspires Judicial Rap

A Michigan trial judge dismissed a 2003 defamation claim by DeAngelo Bailey against rapper Eminem. Bailey claimed that Eminem falsely depicted him as a bully in a song called "Brain Damage." The song's lyrics recount a childhood attack when Bailey allegedly beat up Marshall Mathers (Eminem). Perhaps inspired by the famous rapper, the judge added a rap footnote to her 13-page opinion. A portion follows:

Mr. Bailey complains that his rep is trash/so he's seeking compensation in the form of cash/Bailey thinks he's entitled to some monetary gain/Because Eminem used his name in vain."

The lyrics are stories no one would take as fact/they're an exaggeration of a childish act." It is therefore this Court's ultimate position/that Eminem is entitled to summary disposition.

The Michigan Court of Appeals affirmed the trial court decision.

Sources: "Eminem Delivered Favorable Verdict by Rap-Lovin' Judge" [**http://www.chartattack. com/damn/2003/10/2106.cfm**]; *Bailey v. Mathers,* No. 252123, 2005 WL 857242 (Michigan Ct. App., April 14, 2005).

The Trial

The trial begins with opening statements by the attorneys. Each is expected to outline what he or she intends to prove. The plaintiff, bearing the burden of proof, then presents evidence, which may include both testimony and physical evidence, such as documents and photos. Those are called *exhibits.*

The plaintiff's attorney secures testimony from his or her own witnesses via questioning labeled *direct examination.* After the plaintiff's attorney completes direct examination of a witness, the defense attorney may question that witness in a process labeled *cross-examination. Redirect* and *re-cross* may then follow. After all of the plaintiff's witnesses have been questioned, the plaintiff rests his or her case.

At this stage, the defense may make a motion for a *directed verdict,* arguing, in essence, that the plaintiff has offered insufficient evidence to justify relief, so time and expense may be saved by terminating the trial. Understandably, the judge considers the motion in the light most favorable to the plaintiff. Such motions ordinarily fail, and the trial goes forward with the defendant's presentation of evidence.

At the completion of the defendant's case, both parties may be permitted to offer *rebuttal* evidence, and either party may move for a directed verdict. Barring a directed verdict, the case goes forward, with each party making a *closing argument.* When the trial is by jury, the judge must instruct the jurors as to the law to be applied to the case. The attorneys often submit their views of the proper instructions. After deliberation, the verdict of the jury is rendered, and a judgment is entered by the court. [For a company providing a virtual jury in advance of trial, see **www.virtualjury.com**]

Experts

In this highly technological and scientific era, one of the biggest dilemmas facing judges and juries is the weight to give to expert testimony. Very often, in cases such as medical malpractice and product liability (see Chapter 7), the testimony of experts is decisive to the outcome; but that testimony varies wildly in its reliability and credibility. The golfing case that follows investigates the theme of experience as a qualification for expert testimony.

LEGAL BRIEFCASE

Nickles v. Schild   617 N.W. 2d 659
(S. D. S. Ct. 2000)

Justice Gilbertson

Larry Nickles, the guardian of Mark Nickles, appeals the trial court's admission of expert testimony.

FACTS

On May 5, 1996, Jay Schild (Schild), Mark Nickles and Schild's younger brother drove to the Human Services Golf Course in Yankton, South Dakota, to play golf. All three boys were minors. Both Nickles and Schild had previously received golf instructions and had been taught some golfing rules.

After playing five holes, Schild and Nickles proceeded to the next tee box. Schild's younger brother was still on the fifth hole green retrieving his ball, which Nickles had knocked a short distance from the green. Schild proceeded to tee up his ball at the front center of the tee box and was preparing to hit his next drive. In the meantime, Nickles moved off the tee box approximately 10 feet and was facing the previous green watching Schild's brother. Schild, who had seen Nickles walk off the tee box, stepped back from his ball and took three practice swings. On the third practice swing, Schild hit Nickles in the head, fracturing his skull and permanently injuring his left eye.

Guardian commenced a personal injury action against Schild for damages sustained as a result of Schild's negligence and failure to exercise reasonable care in swinging his golf club. Schild denied he was negligent and claimed that Nickles was contributory negligent and assumed the risk of his injuries. During trial, Schild called Robert Boldus as an expert witness. Boldus was a former member of the Professional Golfer's Association and golf professional at Fox Run Golf Course in Yankton, South Dakota. Boldus had often given golfing lessons to junior golfers while at Fox Run.

Schild asked Boldus whether "as a golf professional," he had "formed any opinions as to what had happened in this case?" Nickles immediately requested permission to briefly interrogate Boldus for purposes of objecting to his opinion. During this interrogation, the following discussion occurred:

Q: (Nickles's attorney): Mr. Boldus, as a professional golfer, a member of PGA or based upon your experience, have you had any training in evaluating liability or standards of care required in golf liability cases?

A: (Boldus): No, I haven't.

Nickles then objected to the opinion by Boldus regarding standards of care or the ultimate issue. The trial judge overruled Nickles's objection and allowed Boldus to give his opinion:

Q: (Schild's attorney): And could you tell the jury what opinions you have come to?

A: (Boldus): In my opinion it was an accident. But one of the players moved, and when you're in your preshot routine if you move, you back away from the ball six inches to a foot or one step, and then you take your practice swings. My opinion, somehow Mark Nickles had moved in the way of the swing and got hit.

Q: (Schild's attorney): In your opinion did [Schild] violate any standards of care?

A: (Boldus): No.

The jury returned a verdict in favor of Schild. Nickles appealed, raising the following issue:

Whether the trial court abused its discretion by permitting expert testimony from Boldus.

STANDARD OF REVIEW

Our standard of review in reviewing admissibility of expert testimony is well settled. We have often stated that

> we review questions of admissibility of an expert witness's testimony under an abuse of discretion standard. We have long acknowledged that the trial court has broad discretion concerning the admission of expert testimony. The trial court's decision on such matters will not be reversed absent a clear showing of an abuse of discretion.

DECISION

*   *   *   *   *

[A]n expert is not limited to testifying only upon those areas in which he or she has received formal training. Rather, when giving an opinion, an expert is allowed to draw upon all the knowledge, skill, or experience that he or she has accumulated.

[W]hile Boldus may not have had any formal classroom "training" in the applicable liability standards, it is clear Boldus was no novice at the game of golf. He was a former member of the PGA and a golf professional at Fox Run Golf Course in Yankton. While at Fox Run, he had often given golf lessons to junior golfers, which included golf etiquette and safety. He had even previously given golf lessons to Nickles. By any of these methods of acquiring the appropriate expertise or combination thereof, he could have qualified himself as an expert to testify as to "what happened."

It is quite clear from the testimony of Boldus and his vitae that he did have an opinion on the standards of care required in golf and the expertise to give such an opinion. The following testimony regarding the standard of care applicable to the game of golf was elicited from Boldus during direct testimony:

Q: When someone has addressed the ball and stepped back and they're doing their practice swings, what is the person's duty when they're doing those practice swings?

A: Well, basically there's nothing stated that says that you have to look around. You should be, when you begin your preshot routine, prior to taking your practice swings you should look and kind of [get] an idea where people are at so they are out of your way so you can take a swing. Once you begin your practice swings I think it's a duty of the other person to stay out of the way.

Q: So once, right before you start your preshot routine is when you have the duty to check what's going around?

A: Yes.

Q: And then as you start your preshot routine then it's the duty of those around you to become aware that that's what you're going to do, to watch?

A: Yes.

*   *   *   *   *

Boldus merely described, in his opinion, "what happened in this case" and that Schild's actions did not violate any standard of care concerning the game of golf. He did not invade the province of the jury as Nickles suggests. Boldus did not testify as to the ultimate issue of negligence. In fact, Boldus did not discuss the issue of liability at all until he was asked upon cross-examination, "but one party is liable, aren't they?" Boldus responded, "I wouldn't—yah—I don't know about liable, but somebody [is responsible for that]."

Nickles' objection as to the qualifications of Boldus goes in part to formal training concerning the issue of ultimate liability. The ultimate liability of one of the parties is not the same as standard of care. One can violate a standard of care and still not be held liable. There could be further potential questions of contributory negligence, assumption of the risk, financial responsibility of a minor and/or his parents, questions of duty to supervise a minor and the like, all of which can have a decisive effect on liability and which clearly are outside the expertise of a golf pro and his knowledge of golf standards of care. Boldus did not testify as to any of these issues; his testimony was limited to describing the standard of care for the game of golf.

Affirmed.

DISSENT

Justice Sabers

I dissent.

I write specially to point out that the majority opinion misses the point—not once, but several times.

Whether Boldus was qualified as an expert witness is immaterial. The point is that under the pretense of being an expert witness, Boldus cannot testify as a fact witness. He was not present at the scene. He does not know what happened. Only fact witnesses can testify "as to what happened?" Therefore, under these circumstances it was totally improper for Boldus to testify to his opinion "as to what happened in this case."

Questions

1. What were Nickles's objections to the expert, Boldus's, testimony?

2. What objection was raised by the dissenting Justice Sabers?

3. Do you agree with the expert, Boldus, that once a golfer has properly started the preshot routine the duty of care shifts to those around the golfer to be aware of what is happening and to keep themselves out of harm's way? Explain.

4. Dodge slipped leaving work and claimed that she suffered knee, ankle, and back injuries. Dodge sued the workplace cleaning service, but she provided no expert testimony to establish that the fall caused the injuries. Rather Dodge provided her own explanation of the fall and resulting injuries. Did the trial court err in admitting Dodge's lay person testimony? Explain, See *Dodge-Farrar v. American Cleaning Services Co.*, 54 P. 3d 954 (Ida. App. 2002).

Posttrial Motions

The losing party may seek a *judgment notwithstanding the verdict (judgment n.o.v)* on the grounds that the jury's decision was clearly inconsistent with the law or the evidence. Such motions are rarely granted. The judge is also empowered to enter a judgment n.o.v on his or her own initiative.

Either party may also move for a new trial. The winning party might do so on the grounds that the remedy provided was inferior to that warranted by the evidence. The losing party commonly claims an error of law to support a motion for a new trial. Other possible grounds for a new trial include jury misconduct or new evidence.

Appeals

After the judgment is rendered, either party may appeal the decision to a higher court. The winner may do so if he or she feels the remedy is inadequate. Ordinarily, of course, the losing party brings the appeal. The appealing party is the *appellant* or the *petitioner,* while the other party is the *appellee* or *respondent.* The appeals court does not try the case again. In theory, at least, its consideration is limited to mistakes of law at the trial level. The appellant will argue, for example, that a jury instruction was erroneous or that the judge erred in failing to grant a motion to strike testimony alleged to have been prejudicial. The appeals court does not hear new evidence. Its decision is based on the trial record, materials filed by the opposing attorneys, and oral arguments.

The appellate court announces its judgment and ordinarily explains that decision in an accompanying document labeled an *opinion.* (Most of the cases in this text are appellate court opinions.) If no error is found, the lower court decision is *affirmed.* In finding prejudicial error, the appellate court may simply *reverse* (overrule) the lower court. Or the judgment may be to *reverse and remand,* wherein the lower court is overruled and the case must be tried again in accordance with the law as articulated in the appeals court opinion. After the decision of the intermediate appellate court, a further appeal may be sought at the highest court of the jurisdiction. Most of those petitions are denied.

Questions—Part Two

1. What are the purposes and uses of the concept of jurisdiction? Why do we limit the courts to which a claim can be taken?

2. Law cases often read like soap operas even as they reveal important truths. A woman and man, each married to others, had engaged in a long-term love affair.

The woman's husband died, and she pleaded with her paramour to leave his New York home to visit her in Florida. She affirmed her love for the man. They made arrangements to meet in Miami, but on his arrival at the airport he was served a summons informing him that he was being sued. His Florida "lover" sought $500,000 for money allegedly loaned to him and for seduction inspired by a promise of marriage.

    a. Does the Florida court have proper jurisdiction over him?

    b. What if he had voluntarily come to Florida on vacation? See *Wyman v. Newhouse,* 93 F.2d 313 (2d Cir. 1937).

3. Sea Pines, a privately owned suburban community on Hilton Head Island, South Carolina, was designated a wildlife sanctuary by the state legislature. After study, the state Department of Natural Resources decided to issue permits to allow limited deer hunting on the land to reduce overpopulation. Various environmental groups challenged the issuance of the permits. What defense would you expect the state to offer in court? Explain. See *Sea Pines Ass'n for Protection of Wildlife v. South Carolina Dept. of Natural Resources,* 550 S.E. 2d 287 (S. C. S. Ct. 2001).

Part Three—Criticism and Alternatives

Criticism

To many Americans, our system of justice is neither systematic nor just. With more than one million lawyers in a population of 305 million people, critics argue that excessive, unproductive litigation is inevitable.

Too Many Lawyers and Lawsuits?

Many lawsuits are less a search for justice and more a pursuit of big dollars for attorneys, the critics claim. Former Enron CEO Jeffrey Skilling was found guilty in 2006 of fraud, conspiracy and other crimes in his trial involving the 2001 collapse of Enron, the Texas energy giant. (For more about Enron, see Chapter 2.) The Enron bankruptcy cost thousands of jobs, more than $60 billion in Enron stock and more than $2 billion in employee pension funds. Skilling was sentenced to 24 years in prison. Skilling's lawyer, Daniel Petrocelli, billed his services at nearly $800 per hour. Petrocelli represented Skilling for a total of five years in various civil suits, testimony before government agencies, and so on. Petrocelli said that Skilling's criminal defense required a team of 12 lawyers, five paralegals, and many temporary staffers. The total legal bill: $70 million.[20] As one attorney later quipped: "What would he have been paid if he had won?"[21] Extraordinary legal bills are only one symptom of a legal system that critics believe is harming productivity and undermining justice.

> The total legal bill: $70 million. As one attorney later quipped: "What would he have been paid if he had won?"

According to a 2006 Litigation Trends survey of corporate law departments, 89 percent of companies reported facing at least one lawsuit in the previous year; up from two thirds in the 2005 survey.[22] The survey found that U.S. companies face an average of 305 pending lawsuits worldwide with workplace disputes (pay, promotion, harassment, discrimination, etc.) and contracts being the most frequent areas of litigation.[23] More than 70 percent of companies reported that they themselves had initiated at least one lawsuit in 2005–06.[24] Notably, the 2007 survey, however, found a significant decline in litigation concerns with 17 percent reporting that they had not defended a single lawsuit in the previous year, up from 11 percent in 2005–06.[25]

Widespread criticism of litigation and lawyers seems to have had some impact; particularly in the area of tort reform (see Chapter 7) where a *BusinessWeek* cover story proclaimed: "How Business Trounced the Trial Lawyers: By focusing on litigation reform at the state level, business has won key battles. Suddenly, it's a tough time to be a plaintiffs' attorney."[26] *BusinessWeek* reported that many state governments have explicitly limited lawsuits. Twenty-three states, for example, have statutes forbidding suits against McDonald's and the like for making consumers fat.[27] Further, in some jurisdictions, jurors now seem reluctant to impose big penalties in civil suits. In Texas, a decade of spending by Texans for Lawsuit Reform and the U.S. Chamber of Commerce appears to have helped change public opinion:

> Lawyers in Texas say that after years of exposure in TV commercials, billboards, and campaign speeches, public opinion in the state has been profoundly affected. "They have demonized trial lawyers as money-hungry thugs," complains Houston litigator David Berg. "They have brainwashed jurors." The result, say Berg and others, is that they are often hesitant to bring cases before a jury.[28]

Litigation pressure remains, however. As one expert explains, dealing with legal problems is a central ingredient in management practice:

> Only a few decades ago, the law was peripheral to the core activities of doing business. When I became a business lawyer in the late 1950s, for example, our involvement was generally limited to forming a corporation or partnership for a client, providing for the investment capital, doing a lease for an office or factory, and maybe handling a key contract with a CEO or a major supplier. . . . Today the law can affect almost every action a manager takes. It has moved closer to the core activities of conducting business and succeeding in a red-hot, competitive environment. More people now have "rights" they can assert against your company, so you face claims from employees, consumers, competitors, and the government. Consequently, today's manager needs to know something about employment law, discrimination claims, sexual harassment rules, product safety issues, the rules of advertising and competition, antitrust rules, environmental law, the value of intellectual property, and more.[29]

[For a site dedicated to laughing at lawyers, see **www.power-of-attorneys.com**]

Two Big Cases: Pants and Privilege

Two of the most highly publicized cases of recent years; one civil, the other criminal, illustrate how the legal system can be abused and yet ultimately find justice.

Pants

Washington, DC administrative law judge, Roy Pearson, drew journalists from around the world by suing his neighborhood laundry for $54 million, down from an earlier claim of $67 million, over the alleged loss of the pants belonging to his $1,000 suit. Owners Soo and Jin Chung of Custom Cleaners attempted to give Pearson a pair of pants they said were the missing item, but he said the ones offered were not his. Pearson brought claims of mental suffering, inconvenience, discomfort, and fraud (based on the "Satisfaction Guaranteed" sign at Custom Cleaners). Along the way, Pearson had rejected settlement offers that reached $12,000. The Chungs won an easy trial victory with the court concluding that Pearson was unable to prove the pants offered to him were not his and that the "Satisfaction Guaranteed" sign did not require the Chungs to satisfy a customer's unreasonable demands. Pearson was ordered to pay the Chungs' court costs, and the legal fees for the Chungs' defense were covered by contributions. Pearson subsequently failed in his bid to be reappointed to his judge's position.

Source: Henri E. Cauvin, "Court Rules for Cleaners in $54 Million Pants Suit," *Washington Post,* June 26, 2007, p. A01.

Privilege

Members of Duke University's lacrosse team hired stripper and African-American North Carolina Central University student, Crystal Gail Mangum, to entertain at a March 2006 house party in Durham, North Carolina. Mangum claimed that she was raped at the party. Durham County district attorney, Mike Nifong, brought rape, kidnapping, and sexual offense charges against three of the Duke students at the party based upon Mangum's account of what occurred. Nifong, a white man, was in a close election campaign at the time, and he was accused of overreaching in the case in order to attract black voters. The three students were suspended from school, the lacrosse season was canceled and the coach resigned. Investigations in the case continued for months and Nifong's charges became increasingly suspect. Defense attorneys were able to show that Mangum's story was inconsistent and changing, that a photo lineup in the case was riddled with errors, that no one corroborated her account, including a second dancer at the party, and that DNA evidence supporting the defendants' position had been withheld from their attorneys. In January 2007, facing ethics charges and intense public criticism, Nifong turned the case over to the North Carolina attorney general. Following a three-month review of the entire case, all charges were dropped and the defendants were declared innocent. Nifong was disbarred and later sentenced to one day in jail for contempt of court. The three defendants and many of their teammates have filed lawsuits seeking damages from Durham, Nifong, Duke University and others.

The case had received extraordinary national attention because of its overtones of race, sex, and privilege. The accuser was a poor, black student and single mother at an historically black state university. The accused were young, white men from well-to-do families attending one of the most prestigious and expensive private universities in America.

Defense attorneys claimed the case was an appeal to racial and class hatred and the product of an overzealous prosecutor seeking personal, political advantage.

Question

Do these two cases strengthen or diminish your faith in America's civil and criminal justice systems? Explain.

Sources: Duff Wilson and David Barstow, "All Charges Dropped in Duke Case," *The New York Times,* April 12, 2007 [**http://www.nytimes.com/2007/04/12/us/12duke.html**]; and Michael Amon, "Nifong Gets Jail," *Newsday,* September 1, 2007, p. A07.

Law as a Global Business

Highly criticized at home, the American legal system, nonetheless, has received a rousing endorsement around the globe. Globalization has brought American-style capitalism to all corners of the world, and American-style litigation is following. An unexpected consequence of globalization is the remarkable growth in lawyers and lawsuits in nations such as Japan and China that once disdained America's litigation "mania."

Japan Globalization is changing Japan's traditionally cooperative corporate culture. Historically, the Japanese government maintained quiet order in the cartel-bound, clubby private sector, but the pressure of global competition is provoking more friction, and lawsuits are soaring in a culture that prefers working things out quietly. For most of its post–World War II era, Japan has not felt the need for lawyers, and their numbers remain among the smallest in the world with about one lawyer per 5,800 people while the comparable U.S. figure is one lawyer per 270 people.[30] Now legal pressures from the global commercial community are rising in areas such as mergers and patents. As a result in 2004, the government began allowing graduate programs in law and since that time 74 new law schools have opened with several thousand new lawyers expected to pass the bar examination annually. Still as *BusinessWeek* reports, Japan's ancient communal culture is likely to resist the legal combat that is routine in America:

> Despite the changes, it is unlikely Japan will ever fully embrace the kind of legal conflict common in the U.S. . . . But a more sophisticated, and contentious, legal system may be just what the country needs in order to keep its economic overhaul on track.[31]

China As in Japan, aggressive capitalism and globalization have brought a booming legal industry to China:

> Starting from scratch in the late 1970s, the country now has more than 200,000 judges, 100,000 lawyers, 10,000 law firms, and 400 law schools. Even so, the system remains deeply flawed. Many Chinese judges come from military backgrounds and have little legal training. Government prosecutors often lack basic skills in evidence discovery and collection.[32]

As was argued early in this chapter, a stable legal system seems to be a prerequisite to long-term success in free, global markets, but law professor Margaret Y. K. Woo notes that initial Chinese adoptions of the rule of law and the personal decision-making power of the market do not necessarily signal a blossoming of individual justice in a nation still dominated by its communist, central government.[33]

PRACTICING ETHICS   Private Law for Wal-Mart?

A portion of Wal-Mart's Ethical Standards Program demands employee welfare throughout its vast supply chain:

> We do not own, operate, or manage any factories. Instead, we purchase merchandise from suppliers located in more than 60 countries. Our Ethical Standards team is dedicated to verifying that these supplier factories are in compliance with our Standards for Suppliers. These standards cover compliance with local and national laws and regulations governing compensation, hours of labor, forced/prison labor, underage labor, discrimination, freedom of association and collective bargaining, health and safety, environment, and the right of audit by Wal-Mart Stores, Inc.[34]

Law professor Larry Cata Backer argues that Wal-Mart and other global giants are effectively legislating their own private law in the form of contract and business relationships and ethics standards governing product quality, working conditions and similar matters. Wal-Mart's Standards for Suppliers are the core of its global governance system that, according to Backer, is "an important emerging phenomenon: the development of efficient systems of private law making by nongovernmental organizations that sometimes supplement, and sometimes displace traditional legal systems."[35] Working with the media, nongovernmental organizations (NGOs), consumers, and investors, Wal-Mart and other multinationals, Backer argues, are beginning to build independent mechanisms for efficient regulation of economic behavior on a global scale that may lead to systems of law beyond governments and moderated largely by stakeholders.[36]

Question

Should we welcome and encourage the development of a private law system enforced through contractual and ethical standards by giant multinationals, or should we be concerned that strengthened, strictly enforced private law arrangements would place too much authority in the hands of already powerful organizations? Explain.

On the Other Hand—Litigation as a Last Resort

Almost everyone seems to be unhappy about lawyers and lawsuits, but at the same time Americans expect lawyers and the courts to settle disputes, preserve freedom and justice and correct problems not satisfactorily addressed by legislatures and regulators. Feeling threatened by abusive bosses, corporate fraud, dangerous drugs, defective products, environmental decline, and so on, Americans count on the justice system to protect our pecuniary interests as well as the personal freedom and democracy we prize. Lawyers and the courts often are the only available weapon to right what we believe to be a wrong. So the frustration many feel about exploding litigation may be attributable to us as much as to greedy lawyers. Furthermore, laws and lawyers are central to economic efficiency. Lawyers devise the rules, processes, and structures that permit capitalism to operate effectively. As we have read, the balance of the world is coming to recognize that law and lawyers are prerequisites to economic stability and progress.

Fewer Trials   However we may feel about lawyers and the justice system, the simple fact, as reported by *BusinessWeek,* is that civil trials have declined dramatically in recent years:

> Around the country, plenty of lawsuits are getting filed, but fewer and fewer are going to trial. The civil trial is one of the most iconic American institutions, a time-honored forum where disputes over injuries, divorces, and all manner of business disasters are resolved. Yet rising legal costs, decreasing judicial tolerance for weak lawsuits, and the surging use

of alternative dispute resolution (ADR) are combining to make courtroom showdowns exceptional occurrences.[37]

According to *BusinessWeek,* civil suits filed in federal district courts in the past 40 years soared from 66,144 to 259,541, but the number of those that eventually went to trial fell to a new low of 3,555 in 2006, down from a peak of 12,018 in 1984.[38] Likewise, in the 21 states with available data, the number of civil jury trials fell 40 percent from 1976 to 2004.[39] Trials often are an inefficient way of resolving disputes so these numbers may be considered very good news. On the other hand, trials are visible affirmations of the indispensability of justice, and they provide the careful reasoning and precedents that draw public lines identifying impermissible behavior.

One of the reasons for the declining number of trials, despite increasing disputes, is that we are developing new conflict resolution methods.

Reform: Judicial Efficiency

Governments, businesses, lawyers, judges—all are frustrated with the expense and inefficiency of our overburdened judicial system. Some small businesses are now buying legal services insurance or prepaid legal services for a flat monthly fee.

Some cities have taken novel approaches to adjudication such as business courts that hear only commercial claims, thus allowing jurists to become very efficient handling contract problems, shareholder claims, and the like. Those systems are variations on the small claims courts that have long proven effective in settling minor disputes.

Small Claims Courts

Suppose you move out of your apartment and your landlord refuses to return your $500 damage deposit even though the rooms are spotless. Hiring a lawyer doesn't make good financial sense and is beyond your means anyway, but a small claims court may provide an effective solution. Small businesses have been particularly satisfied with the small claims courts as an efficient device for collecting unpaid bills without the expense of bill collectors and lawyers. The article that follows outlines the primary features of the small claims process.

READING Small Claims Court FAQ

Nolo

CAN ANY KIND OF CASE BE RESOLVED IN SMALL CLAIMS COURT?
No. Small claims courts primarily resolve small monetary disputes. In a few states, however, small claims courts may also rule on a limited range of other types of legal disputes, such as evictions or requests for the return of an item of property (restitution). You cannot use small claims court to file a divorce, guardianship, name change, or bankruptcy, or to ask for emergency relief (such as an injunction to stop someone from doing an illegal act).

* * * * *

ARE THERE TIME LIMITS IN WHICH A SMALL CLAIMS COURT CASE MUST BE FILED?
Yes. States establish rules called "statutes of limitations" that dictate how long you may wait to initiate a lawsuit after the

key event giving rise to the lawsuit occurs or, in some instances, is discovered. Statutes of limitations rules apply to all courts, including small claims.

You'll almost always have at least one year to sue (measured from the event or, sometimes, from its discovery). Often, you'll have much longer. . . .

HOW MUCH CAN I SUE FOR IN SMALL CLAIMS COURT?

The limit is normally between $3,000 and $7,500, depending on your state. . . . Recently there has been a trend toward increasing small claims court limits. . . .

WHERE SHOULD I FILE MY SMALL CLAIMS LAWSUIT?

Assuming the other party lives or does business in your state, rules normally require that you sue in the small claims court district closest to that person's residence or headquarters. In some instances, you also may be able to sue in the location (court district) where a contract was signed or a personal injury occurred (such as an auto accident). Check with your small claims clerk for detailed rules.

If a defendant has no contact with your state, you'll generally have to sue in the state where the defendant lives or does business. . . .

WILL I GET PAID IF I WIN THE LAWSUIT?

Not necessarily. The court may decide in your favor, but it won't handle collection for you. So before you sue, always ask, "Can I collect if I win?" If not, think twice before suing.

Worrying about whether or not you can get paid is reasonable, because some people and businesses are "judgment proof"—that is, they have little money or assets and aren't likely to acquire much in the foreseeable future. If they don't pay voluntarily, you may be out of luck. Ask yourself whether the person you're suing has a steady job, valuable real property, or investments. If so, it should be reasonably easy to collect by garnishing his wages if you win. If not, try to identify another collection source, such as a bank account, before going forward. . . .

WHAT SHOULD I DO TO PREPARE MY SMALL CLAIMS CASE?

Whether you are a plaintiff (the person suing) or the defendant (person being sued), the key is to realize that it's usually what you bring with you to court to back up your story—not what you say—that determines whether you'll win or lose. This makes sense if you understand that the judge has no idea who you are and whether your oral (spoken) testimony is reliable. After all, your opponent is likely to claim that the "true story" is exactly the reverse of your version.

In short, your chances of winning will greatly increase if you carefully collect and prepare your evidence. Depending on the facts of your case, a few of the evidentiary tools you can use to convince the judge you are right include eyewitnesses, photographs, letters from experts, advertisements falsely hyping a product or service, and written contracts.

CAN I BRING A LAWYER TO SMALL CLAIMS COURT?

In a handful of states, . . . you must appear in small claims court on your own. In most states, however, you can be represented by a lawyer if you like. But even where it's allowed, hiring a lawyer is rarely cost-efficient. Most lawyers charge too much given the relatively modest amounts of money involved in small claims disputes. Happily, several studies show that people who represent themselves in small claims cases usually do just as well as those who have a lawyer.

WILL MY WITNESSES NEED TO TESTIFY IN PERSON IN SMALL CLAIMS COURT?

If possible, it's best to have key witnesses present in court. But if this isn't convenient, a clearly written memo or letter will be allowed under the rules of most small claims courts. (Be sure to check your state's rules.) Have the witness start the statement by establishing who he or she is. ("My name is John Lomox. I've owned and managed Reo's Toyota Repair Service for the last 17 years.") In clear, unemotional language, the witness should explain what he or she observed or heard. ("I carefully checked Mary Wilson's engine and found that it has been rebuilt improperly, using worn-out parts.") Finally, the witness should try to anticipate any questions a reasonable person might ask and provide the answers. ("Although it can take a few days to get new parts for older engines, such as the one Mary Wilson owned, it is easy and common practice to do so.")

IF I LOSE MY CASE IN SMALL CLAIMS COURT, CAN I APPEAL?

The answer depends on the state in which you live. Many states allow either party to appeal within a certain period of time, usually between 10 and 30 days, and obtain a new trial. In many states, appeals must be based solely on the contention that the judge made a legal mistake, and not on the facts of the case. Other states have their own unique rules. . . .

Source: Reprinted with permission from the publisher, NOLO. Copyright 2002, **http://www.nolo.com.**

Alternative Dispute Resolution (ADR)

Businesses, in particular, are increasingly looking outside the judicial system for dispute resolution strategies. Dot-com entrepreneurs are developing interesting new mechanisms on the Internet for conveniently addressing Internet-based disputes. Networks of human mediators, dispute resolution software, and an Internet version of *The People's Court* are among the online methods of settling problems outside of court. Online businesses recognize that trust is a key to their growth, so providing a quick, inexpensive, fair way for consumers to settle e-commerce grievances is an important industry goal. The leader in these developments is probably a San Francisco firm, SquareTrade, which works with eBay, customers, realtors, and others to resolve sales disputes via a password-protected tool allowing online communication. Recommendations may also be offered by a Square-Trade mediator; [See **www.squaretrade.com/cnt/jsp/odr/overview_odr.jsp**]

Cybersettle is an online system for settling insurance disputes, often of the fender-bender or slip-and-fall variety. The parties log on to Cybersettle and type in a sum they are willing to settle for. The computer compares the bids, round by round, and automatically settles the case if the bids fall within $5,000 or 30 percent of each other. Cybersettle has patented its Computerized Dispute Resolution System and says it has settled over 100,000 transactions and has facilitated over one billion dollars in settlements. [See **www.cybersettle.com**]

What Is ADR?

Of course, any form of *negotiation and settlement* would constitute an alternative to litigation, but *mediation* and *arbitration* are the most prominent of the alternatives to formal, full-blown litigation. Given the expense, frustration, and exploding numbers of lawsuits, we are seeing increasing imagination in building other ADR options including *private trials* and *minitrials*. [For many ADR links, see **www.hg.org/adr.html**]

Mediation

Mediation introduces a neutral third party into the resolution process. Ideally, the parties devise their own solution, with the mediator as a facilitator, not a decision maker. Even if the mediator does propose a solution, it will be in the nature of a compromise, not a determination of right and wrong. The bottom line is that only the disputing parties can adopt any particular outcome. The mediator may aid the parties in a number of ways, such as opening up communication between them.

Arbitration

Arbitration is a process in which a neutral third party is given the power to determine a binding resolution of the dispute. Depending on the situation, the resolution may be either a compromise solution or a determination of the rights of the parties and a win–lose solution. Even in the latter case, however, it may be quicker and less costly than a trial, and the arbitrator may be an expert in the subject area of the dispute instead of a generalist, as a judge would be. It is procedurally more formal than mediation, with the presentation of proofs and arguments by the parties, but less formal than court adjudication.

The arbitrator's decision is legally binding, although in some cases, such as labor disputes, it may be appealed to a court.

Private Trials

"rent-a-judge"

A number of states now permit private trials, sometimes labeled "rent-a-judge," where the litigants agree on that approach. Normally a third party such as a mediation firm makes the necessary arrangements, including hiring a retired judge as well as jurors to hear the case. The proceedings are conducted much as in a courtroom. Because the parties are paying, however, the dispute comes to trial more quickly, the process normally moves along more rapidly, and the proceeding may be conducted in private. Appeals to the formal judicial system are provided for in some states. Critics question the fairness of the private system and wonder if it will further erode faith in public trials, but the time and money saved can be quite substantial.

Minitrials

In recent years, some corporations have agreed to settle their disputes by holding informal hearings that clarify the facts and the issues that would emerge if the dispute were litigated. In the minitrial, each organization presents its version of the case to a panel of senior executives from each organization. The trial is presided over by a neutral third party who may be called on for an opinion as to what would happen were the case to be litigated. That opinion has no binding force. The executives then meet to attempt to negotiate a settlement. The neutral third party sometimes facilitates that discussion. Minitrials are voluntary and nonbinding, but if an agreement is reached, the parties can formalize it by entering a settlement contract.

ADR Assessed

ADR mechanisms generally have been sustained in the courts and are employed in a variety of roles across many industries and businesses. Almost all union contracts have some arbitration procedure. Many auto companies use ADR to resolve warranty claims as well as disputes with dealers. Brokerage firms as well as some banks and insurance companies require customers to arbitrate disputes over their accounts.

Ordinarily, ADR costs less and is resolved more quickly than litigation. ADR is less formal and less adversarial than the judicial process. Further, the parties have more control over the proceedings in that they can choose the facilitator, they can choose when and where the dispute will be heard, and they can keep the dispute private if they wish.

Despite those strengths, alternative dispute resolution is not without its own problems. In situations involving new or complex problems, litigation may be preferable. ADR does not provide precedent for future disputes. Lawyers are troubled that ADR, when mandatory, deprives plaintiffs of their Seventh Amendment right to a jury trial.

Further, *BusinessWeek* recently reported that arbitration is "losing its luster" in the business community:

- Arbitration can generate litigation, rather than relieving it, since parties often go to court to battle over whether arbitration is required and later over the amount and enforcement of the arbitrator's award.

- Arbitrators often allow extensive and expensive prehearing discovery.

- Judges' salaries are paid by taxes while the disputing parties must pay arbitrators' increasingly stiff fees.

- Arbitrators may have trouble being truly impartial because they seek repeat business. Not wanting to offend either side, they may too readily "split the baby" to resolve cases.[40]

Employees and consumers likewise have complaints about arbitration. In an effort to reduce costs, an estimated 15–20 percent of companies, including for example, Citigroup and Circuit City, now require arbitration for all employment disputes.[41] Critics say the arbitration approach results in meager settlements and allows problems to be "swept under the rug" even in cases involving such serious allegations as discrimination and sexual harassment.[42] (See Chapter 12 for further arbitration details.) Consumers who feel wronged by their investment brokers must turn for a hearing to securities industry mandated arbitration. Critics complain that the securities arbitration process is heavily weighted against consumers because it is "run by the industry's self-regulator under industry approved rules."[43] The case that follows examines whether McDonald's can compel arbitration in a dispute over a one million dollar prize in the company's "Who Wants to Be a Millionaire" game.

Linda James v. McDonald's Corporation

LEGAL BRIEFCASE 417 F. 3d 672 (7th Cir. 2005)

Judge Ripple

I. BACKGROUND

A.

In 2001, McDonald's was promoting sales of its food products by sponsoring a game called "Who Wants to be a Millionaire." Ms. James obtained a game card in May of 2001 when she purchased an order of french fries at the drive-thru window of a McDonald's restaurant in Franklin, Kentucky. She believed the game card to be a grand prize winner worth one million dollars. In order to redeem her prize, Ms. James sent in the original game card to the McDonald's redemption center. On June 14, 2001, however, the redemption center sent her a letter explaining that, "through security codes on your Game Card we have been able to determine that it is a Low-level Prize

Game Card. Low-level prizes included food prizes and $1 to $5 in cash."

In August 2001, the Federal Bureau of Investigation arrested eight employees of Simon Marketing who allegedly had stolen the winning game cards from the "Who Wants to be a Millionaire" game and another McDonald's promotion. Ms. James filed suit alleging that McDonald's induced her to purchase its food products by the chance to win the "Who Wants to be a Millionaire" game when it knew that, due to the theft of winning game cards, the odds of winning were less than represented. She also alleged that, as part of its fraud scheme, McDonald's had used a false pretense to refuse to honor her winning game card.

McDonald's filed a motion to compel Ms. James to arbitrate her claims. It relied on an arbitration clause contained in the rules for the "Who Wants to be a Millionaire" game ("Official Rules"), which stated:

Except where prohibited by law, as a condition of participating in this Game, participant agrees that (1) any and all disputes and causes of action arising out of or connected with this Game, or any prizes awarded, shall be resolved individually without resort to any form of class action, and exclusively by final and binding arbitration under the rules of the American Arbitration Association and held at the AAA regional office nearest the participant; (2) the Federal Arbitration Act shall govern the interpretation, enforcement and all proceedings at such arbitration; and (3) judgment upon such arbitration award may be entered in any court having jurisdiction.

McDonald's presented evidence . . . that the Official Rules were posted openly in participating restaurants.

B.

On February 4, 2003, the district court granted McDonald's motion to compel Ms. James to arbitrate her claims.

II. ANALYSIS

A. Standard of Review

We review a district court's decision, under the Federal Arbitration Act ("FAA"), to compel parties to arbitrate their disputes. . . .

B. Arbitration

Ms. James contends that the district court erred by ordering her to submit her claims to arbitration on three grounds: (1) that she did not enter into a valid agreement to arbitrate her claims; (2) that she cannot afford the costs of arbitration; and (3) that the contract is invalid because it was induced by fraud.

1. Agreement to Arbitrate

The FAA provides that a "written provision in any . . . contract . . . to settle by arbitration" any future controversy arising out of such contract "shall be valid, irrevocable, and enforceable, save upon such grounds as exist at law or in equity for the revocation of any contract." *9 U.S.C. § 2*. The FAA was designed "to reverse the longstanding judicial hostility to arbitration agreements . . . and to place [them] on the same footing as other contracts." *Gilmer v. Interstate/ Johnson Lane Corp., 500 U.S. 20, 24 (2000)*. The FAA embodies a "liberal federal policy favoring arbitration agreements." *Moses H. Cone Mem'l Hosp. v. Mercury Constr. Corp., 460 U.S. 1, 24-25 (1983)*. Any doubts with respect to arbitrability therefore should be resolved in favor of arbitration. However, a party can be compelled to arbitrate only those matters that she has agreed to submit to arbitration.

*   *   *   *   *

Ms. James contends that she should not be forced to arbitrate her claims because she never entered into an agreement to arbitrate her dispute. She submits that she was not aware of the official Rules, much less that the rules deprived her of a jury trial. For the same reasons, Ms. James contends that, if there was an agreement to arbitrate, it is unconscionable and should not be enforced. To support her position, Ms. James submits that one cannot assume that she knew of, and accepted, the arbitration clause in the Official Rules simply because she ate at a McDonald's restaurant. She maintains that customers cannot be expected to read every container of food they purchase in order to know that they are entering a contract. Rather, she submits that it was McDonald's burden to assure her understanding of, and willingness to be bound by, the arbitration provision.

Certainly, as Ms. James urges, a contract includes only terms on which the parties have agreed. However, one of the things that Ms. James agreed to by participating in the "Who Wants to be a Millionaire" game was to follow the game's rules in order to win the promised prize.

*   *   *   *   *

Ms. James cannot claim, on the one hand, that a valid contract obligates McDonald's to redeem her prize and, on the other hand, argue that no contract binds her to the contest rules. . . .

Outside the promotional-contest context, this court has held that parties are bound to an arbitration provision even if they did not read the provision. For instance, in *Hill v. Gateway 2000, 105 F.3d 1147 (7th Cir.)*, the purchasers of a computer conceded that they had noticed the terms printed inside the box in which their computer was shipped. However, they maintained that they had not read it closely enough to see the arbitration clause. We held that the arbitration clause was enforceable because the purchasers had the opportunity to return the computer after reading the terms. We stated that "[a] contract need not be read to be effective; people who accept take the risk that the unread terms may in retrospect prove unwelcome." . . .

The situation faced by McDonald's presents an apt comparison. To require McDonald's cashiers to recite to each and every customer the fourteen pages of the Official Rules, and then have each customer sign an agreement to be bound by the rules, would be unreasonable and unworkable. The Official Rules were identified to Ms. James as part of the contest, and that identification is sufficient in this case to apprise her of the contents of the rules.

2. Costs of Arbitration

Ms. James also contends that the arbitration clause should not be enforced because the high up-front costs of arbitration prohibit her from pursuing a remedy in that forum.

* * * * *

Ms. James has not made a showing that the expenses that she necessarily and definitely would incur would make arbitration prohibitive . . . Ms. James relies on the affidavit of Michael Eiben, who is a member of the Panel of Neutrals for the American Arbitration Association ("AAA"), to establish the costs of arbitration. Eiben estimated that Ms. James would have to pay $38,000 to $80,000 in fees and service costs before arbitration commenced in order to pursue her claims. Ms. James filed a sworn affidavit stating that she does not have the financial resources to advance those fees.

The AAA's Commercial Rules contain provisions to protect parties from prohibitive expenses. The Eighth Circuit has recognized that the

> AAA . . . has a fee waiver procedure. It decides whether or not to waive, in whole or in part, a fee on the basis of a claimant's financial situation. It is clear, however, from our reading of the evidentiary hearing transcript, that the [plaintiff] never fully explored the AAA's fee waiver procedures because [he] refused to provide his family's financial information to the AAA. . . .

Ms. James has submitted no evidence indicating how her financial situation would be factored into an assessment of the arbitration costs under this hardship provision. Furthermore, Ms. James has not provided any evidence concerning the comparative expense of litigating her claims. The cost differential between arbitration and litigation is evidence highly probative to Ms. James' claim that requiring her to proceed through arbitration, rather than through the courts, will effectively deny her legal recourse.

* * * * *

3. Fraud in the Inducement

Finally, Ms. James claims that the arbitration clause is unenforceable as a matter of public policy because it was part of McDonald's alleged scheme to defraud. The Supreme Court has spoken to this issue:

> If the claim is fraud in the inducement of the arbitration clause itself—an issue which goes to the "making" of the agreement to arbitrate—the federal court may proceed to adjudicate it. But the statutory language [of the FAA] does not permit the federal court to consider claims of fraud in

the inducement of the contract generally. . . . We hold, therefore, that in passing upon a § 3 [of the FAA] application for a stay while the parties arbitrate, a federal court may consider only issues relating to the making and performance of the agreement to arbitrate.

Prima Paint, 388 U.S. at 403. Thus "a court may consider a claim that a contracting party was fraudulently induced to include an arbitration provision in the agreement but not claims that the entire contract was the product of fraud." *Sweet Dreams Unlimited v. Dial-A-Mattress Int'l, Ltd. 1 F.3d 639, 641 n.4 (7 th Cir.1993).*

Ms. James' complaint alleged that she was induced into participating in the "Who Wants to be a Millionaire" game by McDonald's allegedly deceptive practices. Her allegations say nothing of fraud related uniquely to the arbitration clause. Therefore, under *Prima Paint*, Ms. James' fraud claim was a matter to be resolved by an arbitrator, not by the district court.

In sum, the district court appropriately granted McDonald's motion to compel arbitration.

* * * * *

Affirmed.

Questions

1. a. In general under the Federal Arbitration Act, are arbitration clauses in contracts considered enforceable? Explain.
   b. In approving the FAA, what message was Congress sending about the general enforceability of arbitration clauses?
2. a. Why did the court deny James' argument that she had not entered into a valid agreement to arbitrate her claims?
   b. Why did the court deny James' argument that she could not afford the costs of arbitration?
   c. Why did the court deny James' argument that the game contract, including the arbitration clause, was invalid because it was induced by fraud?
3. Kalliope and David Valchine entered court-ordered mediation to try to resolve the problems that had led them to seek a divorce. Lawyers represented both Kalliope and David at mediation. The mediation led to a marital settlement agreement between Kalliope and David. One month later, Kalliope sought to set aside the agreement, arguing that she had been coerced by her husband, her husband's attorney, and the mediator. Kalliope testified that the mediator threatened to report her to the judge for being uncooperative in refusing to sign a reasonable settlement offer. She claimed that the mediator also told her that she could sign the agreement and then object to its provisions at the final hearing.

Should the settlement be set aside? Explain.

4. Is an arbitration clause as a condition of employment a fair method of alternate dispute resolution, if entered knowingly and voluntarily? Explain.

5. In an effort to reduce legal expenses, some major banks and other businesses follow policies providing that all customer complaints will be subject to arbitration. Is mandatory arbitration fair to consumers? Explain.

6. Economist Stephen Magee argues that one way to strengthen the American economy would be to close the law schools:

> Every time you turn out one law school graduate you've got a 40-year problem on your hands, he says. These guys run around and generate a lot of spurious conflict. They're like heat-seeking missiles.[44]

Comment.

Internet Exercise

At [http://www.instituteforlegalreform.org/issues/issue.cfm?issue=TLI] study the criticism of trial lawyers. Do you agree that trial lawyers "abuse and misuse" the legal system? Explain.

Chapter Questions

1. The U.S. Supreme Court ended its first full term under new Chief Justice John Roberts in June 2007 with a series of decisions that appeared to represent a shift toward a more conservative stance; including decisions upholding abortion restrictions, cutting back on free speech rights in schools, and limiting the use of race as a consideration in school integration efforts.[45] Perhaps the most notable feature of the Court's alleged shift to the right is a philosophy that Chief Justice Roberts has called "judicial self-restraint."[46] The conservative majority on the Court repeatedly concluded that many cases simply did not belong in court at all. *The Wall Street Journal* described that change in the Court's direction as follows:

> Taken as a whole, the Supreme Court term that ended last week reflected conservatives' antipathy to what they label judicial activism—courts making decisions they believe are best left to an elected executive, a legislature or the rough and tumble of the free market. That runs counter to much of the past 50 years, during which the nation's highest court saw litigation as a way to reshape American society, leading to rulings that outlawed racial segregation, recognized individual privacy rights, and curbed police misconduct.[47]

Are you most supportive of the current judicial restraint approach championed by Chief Justice Roberts, or would you prefer the judicial activism that was more characteristic of the Court in previous decades? Explain.

2. Professor and criminal justice expert Morgan O. Reynolds argues that sterner punishment has led to reduced crime in the United States:

> This reflects a broader pattern: As our crime rates have fallen, serious crime rates in England have risen substantially, as a recent study from the U.S. Bureau of Justice Statistics found. For example, victim surveys show that
>
> • The English robbery rate was about half the U.S. rate in 1981 but was 40 percent higher than America's in 1995.

- The English assault rate was slightly higher than America's in 1981 but more than double by 1995.
- The English burglary rate was half America's in 1981 but nearly double by 1995.

Why these dramatic increases in English crime rates, while Americans' lives and property grew safer? The obvious explanation has been too often downplayed or ignored: The United States has instituted tougher, more predictable punishment for crime. The study's authors attribute the trends they note to the increasing conviction rates and longer sentences meted out in the United States versus the decreasing conviction rates and softer sentences in England and Wales. English conviction rates for rape, burglary, assault, and auto theft have plunged by half or more since 1981, while the likelihood of serving prison time for committing a serious violent crime or a burglary has increased sustantially in the United States.[48]

a. Do you agree that harsher and more certain punishment will reduce criminal behavior?

b. Do "root causes" such as being born out of wedlock affect criminal behavior? Explain.

3. Crowley, who became intoxicated at a postrace party on McRoberts's boat, was driving after the party and caused a multicar accident that resulted in serious injuries to Culver, who was driving one of the other vehicles. Culver's passenger was killed, and Crowley was later convicted of reckless homicide. Culver sued McRoberts for negligence. Crowley's drinking took place in the galley of McRoberts's 40-foot boat. McRoberts did not provide the liquor and McRoberts, who was busy with recording race results, was not aware of how much drinking Crowley had done. The Indiana Dram Shop statute provided that "it is unlawful for a person to sell, barter, deliver, or give away an alcoholic beverage to another person who is in a state of intoxication if the person knows that the other person is intoxicated." Expert testimony and a blood alcohol reading suggested that Crowley may have been visibly drunk, but several witnesses on the boat said they did not observe visible signs of intoxication. Did McRoberts violate the Indiana Dram Shop law, and was McRoberts negligent in failing to properly supervise Crowley? Explain. See *Culver v. McRoberts,* 192 F.3d 1095 (7th Cir. 1999).

4. Flanagan's, a New Jersey general contractor, ordered an irrigation pumping station from Wise, a Pennsylvania sales representative for Watertronics products. Watertronics, a Wisconsin manufacturer, completed about 15 percent of the pumping station and sent an invoice to Flanagan's seeking partial payment. When payment was not forthcoming, Watertronics asked Flanagan's to submit a credit application. Flanagan's did so and then sent a check for the agreed-upon amount. In the course of their transactions, Flanagan's had a four- to five-minute phone conversation with Watertronics. After the pump was installed problems arose, and Flanagan's made no further payments. Watertronics sued in Wisconsin to collect the balance due. Flanagan's moved to dismiss for lack of jurisdiction. Rule on that motion. See *Watertronics v. Flanagan's,* 635 N.W.2d 27 (Wis. App. 2001).

5. After drinking at the Elks Lodge, Dionne was escorted to a taxi where the driver, Grader, was told to take Dionne home because he had too much to drink. Dionne

would not give Grader directions to his home and then told Grader to take him to another bar. Dionne paid his fare and went into the second bar, and later that bar summoned the same cab to take Dionne home. On this occasion, Dionne told Grader to take him to a convenience store. Dionne conducted his business there with no overt signs of intoxication. He then returned to the cab and asked to be driven back to the Elks Lodge. Grader deposited Dionne at the Elks Lodge and watched as Dionne passed by his own car in the parking lot. Grader heard other voices in the lot, assumed Dionne would be fine, and resumed his work. Later that evening Dionne died in a single-car accident. His blood-alcohol level was .25. The facts are not clear as to whether Dionne drank more after leaving Grader's cab. The taxi service was sued for negligence for not taking Dionne home. How would you rule on that negligence claim? Explain. See *Mastriano v. Blyer,* 779 A.2d 951 (Sup. Jud. Ct. Maine 2001).

6. A letter to *The Wall Street Journal:*

   The problems with our legal system go much deeper than irresponsible plaintiffs, amoral lawyers, and inept juries. The trouble is, our system of checks and balances has been corrupted; 100 percent of the executive, 100 percent of the judicial, and 43 percent of the legislative branches have been taken over by one group—lawyers.

   The Constitution charges Congress to ordain and establish the courts. It is no wonder it has created a system that maximizes the incomes of its own kind. The system is rigged to drag out cases that are billed by the hour, or to find moochers and looters willing to bring huge civil suits against productive citizens and corporations in front of dumbed-down juries.[49]

   Do you agree? Explain.

7. Are the flaws in our legal system of such magnitude that respect for the law is threatened? Explain.

8. According to Warren Avis, founder of Avis Rent-a-Car,

   We've reached a point in this country where, in many instances, power has become more important than justice—not a matter of who is right, but of who has the most money, time, and the largest battery of lawyers to drag a case through the courts.[50]

   a. Should the rich be entitled to better legal representation, just as they have access to better food, better medical care, better education, and so on? Explain.

   b. Should we employ a nationwide legal services program sufficient to guarantee competent legal aid to all? Explain.

9. Peremptory challenges may not constitutionally be used to exclude a potential juror from a trial on racial or gender grounds.

   a. Must a criminal jury reflect the ethnic or racial diversity of the community? Explain. See *Powers v. Ohio,* 111 S.Ct. 1364 (1991).

   b. Could potential jurors lawfully be rejected on the basis of their place of residence? Explain. See *U.S. v. Bishop,* 959 F.2d 820 (9th Cir. 1992).

10. French journalist Alain Clement offered a partial explanation for Americans' increasing reliance on lawsuits to resolve conflicts:

Diverse causes explain the growth of the contentious mood in America. One could be called the devaluing of the future. In 1911, the Russian political scientist Moise Ostrgorski wrote, "Confident of the future, Americans manifest a remarkable endurance to an unhappy present, a submissive patience that is willing to bargain about not only civic rights, but even the rights of man."[51]

a. What does Clement mean?

b. How do you explain our increased reliance on litigation?

11. In 1982, a security guard was murdered during a robbery of a south Chicago McDonald's. Alton Logan was sentenced to life in prison for that murder. At the same time, two Chicago public defenders, Dale Coventry and Jamie Kunz, were representing Andrew Wilson, who was accused of murdering two police officers. Based on a tip, Coventry and Kunz suspected that Wilson was the actual murderer in the McDonald's case. They questioned Wilson who admitted that he, not Logan, was the murderer. Because of their duties under the attorney-client privilege, Coventry and Kunz felt they could not reveal what they knew. Logan, therefore, went to prison an innocent man, they believed. The public defenders decided to write the story in a notarized affidavit and lock it in a box in case something should happen that would allow them to reveal what they knew. When Wilson died in prison of natural causes in 2008, Coventry and Kunz revealed their client's confession. After 26 years, Logan was released from prison. At this writing, he is awaiting a decision by prosecutors about re-trying him for the McDonald's murder.[52]

a. Why does the legal profession expect lawyers to keep secret their clients' confidential communications?

b. Had you been Coventry and Kunz, would you have revealed what you knew in order to immediately secure justice for Logan? Explain.

12. On July 5, 1884, four sailors were cast away from their ship in a storm 1,600 miles from the Cape of Good Hope. Their lifeboat contained neither water nor much food. On the 20th day of their ordeal, Dudley and Stevens, without the assistance or agreement of Brooks, cut the throat of the fourth sailor, a 17- or 18-year-old boy. They had not eaten since day 12. Water had been available only occasionally. At the time of the death, the men were probably about 1,000 miles from land. Prior to his death, the boy was lying helplessly in the bottom of the boat. The three surviving sailors ate the boy's remains for four days, at which point they were rescued by a passing boat. They were in a seriously weakened condition.

a. Were Dudley and Stevens guilty of murder? Explain.

b. Should Brooks have been charged with a crime for eating the boy's flesh? Explain. See *The Queen v. Dudley and Stephens,* 14 Queen's Bench Division 273 (1884).

13. Tompkins was a citizen of Pennsylvania. While walking on a railroad footpath in that state, he was struck by an object protruding from a passing freight train owned by the Erie Railroad Company, a New York corporation. Tompkins, by virtue of diversity of citizenship, filed a negligence suit against Erie in a New York federal court. Erie argued for the application of Pennsylvania common law, in which case Tompkins would have been treated as a trespasser. Tompkins argued that the absence

of a Pennsylvania statute addressing the topic meant that federal common law had to be applied to the case. Should the federal court apply the relevant Pennsylvania state law, or should the court be free to exercise its independent judgment about what the common law of the state is or should be? See *Erie Railroad v. Tompkins,* 304 U.S. 64 (1938).

14. As noted in the chapter, China is rapidly training lawyers and moving toward a more Western approach to judicial systems. The following quote describes China's historic view of dispute resolution:

     Most Chinese persons engage in a large variety of economic and social activities and resolve disputes involved in those activities without coming in contact with the formal legal system. As in Japan, litigation in a court of law is not considered a normal way to resolve a dispute. Custom and extrajudicial dispute-settling mechanisms are utilized not only by private parties but by public entities. Decisions declaring someone right and someone wrong are not a desirable goal. Settlements and compromises are preferable. Even in court, Chinese litigants generally do not obtain a clear defeat or victory.[53]

In your view, would China be better off in the contemporary world to retain its traditional means of conflict settlement or should it continue its turn toward Western-style litigation? Explain.

15. Landis was employed by FINOVA. FINOVA later concluded that Landis had misrepresented certain elements of his experience that had been important in the decision to hire him. FINOVA then dismissed Landis and declared the employment contract void. That contract contained a clause requiring all employment-related disputes to be decided by arbitration. Landis sued FINOVA claiming breach of contract and defamation. FINOVA moved to compel arbitration. Landis argued that the arbitration clause was unenforceable because FINOVA had declared the agreement void. Rule on FINOVA's motion to compel arbitration. Explain. See *Landis v. FINOVA,* 2000 U.S. Dist. LEXIS 5835 (S.D.N.Y. 2000).

16. University of Chicago law professor Richard Epstein pointed out how quickly Americans turn to legal remedies rather than relying on informal social customs (negotiation, neighborhood groups, simply accepting small losses and disturbances rather than fighting about them) to resolve conflicts. In your view, why are social customs increasingly ineffective in settling disputes in this country?

17. Judicial reform advocates often argue that the United States should adopt the English rule providing that the winner in a lawsuit is entitled to recover its reasonable litigation expenses from the loser.

     a. In brief, what are the strengths and weaknesses of the English rule?

     b. Would you favor it? Explain. See Herbert Kritzer, "Searching for Winners in the Loser Pays Rule," *ABA Journal,* November 1992, p. 55.

18. Plaintiff Jonathan Gold was hired to work at defendant Deutsche Bank after completing his MBA degree at New York University. Before beginning employment, Gold signed various documents, including Form U-4 that the National Association of Securities Dealers (NASD) requires all registered representatives to sign. Form U-4 provides for arbitration for all employment disputes. Gold was fired after working about

one year. He then filed suit claiming sexual harassment based on his sexual orientation. Deutsche Bank moved to compel arbitration. Gold resisted arbitration arguing, among other things, that Form U-4 was too difficult to understand and that it raised questions in his mind. Gold also showed that Deutsche Bank had certified that it provided Gold with the relevant NASD rules when it had not. Must Gold submit his claim to arbitration? Explain. See *Gold v. Deutsche Aktiengesellschaft*, 365 F.3d 144 (2d Cir. 2004).

NOTES

1. John O'Brien, "Poll: Voters Not Worried about Tort Reform," *LegalNewsline.com*, July 12, 2007 [**http://www.legalnewsline.com/news/197868-poll-voters-not-worried-about-tort-reform**].

2. Ibid.

3. Peter Hart Research Associates, Inc., Memorandum—"Civil Justice Issues and the 2008 Election," July 11, 2007 [**http://www.atla.org/pressroom/CJSPollMemo.pdf**].

4. Ibid.

5. Martha Neil, "Gender Affects Justice," *ABA Journal*, July 2001, p. 77.

6. Paul Sisson, "Pot-Smoking Dad Gets 27-Year Term," *Waterloo/Cedar Falls Courier*, July 6, 2001, p. B1.

7. "Holding Third Parties Liable Can Do More Harm than Good," (Becker-Posner Blog, October 21, 2007), *The Wall Street Journal*, October 25, 2007, p. B7.

8. Henry Weinstein, "North Carolina to Weigh Claims of Innocence," *Los Angeles Times*, August 4, 2006 [**http://www.latimes.com/news/nationworld/nation/la-na-innocence4aug04,0, 308492.story?track=tottext**].

9. Ibid.

10. *Maouloud Baby v. State of Maryland*, 916 A.2d 410 (Md. Ct. Special App. 2007).

11. *State of Maryland v. Maouloud Baby*, 2008 Md. LEXIS 190 (Md. Ct. of Appeals).

12. Norihiko Shirouzu, "Japan Conviction Rate Dazzles, Deceives," *The Wall Street Journal*, December 19, 1995, p. A12.

13. Linda Greenhouse, "In Steps Big and Small, Supreme Court Moved Right," *The New York Times*, July 1, 2007 [**http://www.nytimes.com/2007/07/01/Washington/01scotus.html**].

14. Michael Orey, "The Supreme Court: Open for Business," *BusinessWeek*, July 9 & 16, 2007, p. 30.

15. Reuters, "Ex-Enron Execs Seek to Move Trial," *Los Angeles Times*, November 9, 2004, p. C3.

16. Barbara Martinez, "Preparing for Vioxx Suits, Both Sides Seek Friendly Venues," *The Wall Street Journal*, November 17, 2004, p. B1.

17. Ibid.

18. Alex Berenson, "Merck Agrees to Settle Vioxx Suits for $4.85 Billion," *The New York Times*, November 9, 2007 [**http://www.nytimes.com/2007/11/09/business/09merck.html**].

19. *DaimlerChrysler Corp. v. Cuno*, 126 S.Ct. 1854 (2006).

20. Christopher Palmeri, "One of Them Is Still Laughing," *BusinessWeek*, October 30, 2006, p. 13.

21. Ibid.

22. Stephen C. Dillard, "Litigation Nation," *The Wall Street Journal*, November 25, 2006, p. A9.

23. Ibid.

24. Ibid.

25. "Fulbright & Jaworski Litigation Survey Reports Drop in Number of New Lawsuits and Regulatory Actions Filed Against U.S. Companies," October 15, 2007 [**http://www.businesswire.com/portal/site/google/index.jsp?ndmViewld=news_view&newsld=20071015005270&newsLang=en**].

26. Michael Orey, "How Business Trounced the Trial Lawyers," *BusinessWeek,* January 8, 2007, p. 44.

27. Ibid.

28. Ibid.

29. Milton Bordwin, "Your Company and the Law," *Management Review,* January 2000, p. 58.

30. Ian Rowley and Kenji Hall, "Lawyers Wanted. No, Really," *BusinessWeek*, April 3, 2006, p. 46.

31. Ibid.

32. Karby Leggett, "A Trial for Chinese Justice," *The Wall Street Journal,* May 29, 2003, p. A18.

33. Margaret Y. K. Woo, "Markets, Law and Globalization," *Northeastern Law Magazine,* Summer 2006, p. 3.

34. "Becoming a Wal-Mart or Sam's Club Supplier" [**http://www.walmartstores.com/Files/Supplier_GettingStarted.pdf**].

35. Larry Cata Backer, "Economic Globalization and the Rise of Efficient Systems of Global Private Lawmaking: Wal-Mart as Global Legislator," 39 *Connecticut Law Review* 1741 (2007).

36. Ibid.

37. Michael Orey, "The Vanishing Trial," *BusinessWeek,* April 30, 2007, p. 38.

38. Ibid.

39. Ibid.

40. "Arbitration Aggravation," *BusinessWeek*, April 30, 2007, p. 38.

41. Nathan Koppel, "When Suing Your Boss Is Not an Option," *The Wall Street Journal,* December 18, 2007, p. D1.

42. Ibid.

43. Jaime Levy Pessin, "Trading Dispute? Try Mediation." *The Wall Street Journal,* November 4, 2007 [**http://online.wsj.com/public/article/SB119412615336081635.html**].

44. "An Economist Out to Be Sued," *Los Angeles Times,* October 8, 1990, p. D1.

45. Linda Greenhouse, "In Steps Big and Small, Supreme Court Moved Right," *The New York Times,* July 1, 2007 [**http://www.nytimes.com/2007/07/01/Washington/01scotus.html**].

46. Jess Bravin, "Court Under Roberts Limits Judicial Power," *The Wall Street Journal,* July 2, 2007, p. A1.

47. Ibid.

48. Morgan O. Reynolds, "Europe Surpasses America—in Crime," *The Wall Street Journal,* October 16, 1998, p. A14.

49. Darrell Dusina, "Lawyers, Everywhere," *The Wall Street Journal,* November 23, 1998, p. A23.

50. Warren Avis, "Court before Justice," *The New York Times,* July 21, 1978, p. 25.

51. Alain Clement, "Judges, Lawyers Are the Ruling Class in U.S. Society," *Washington Post,* August 22, 1980, p. A25.

52. "26-Year Secret Kept Innocent Man in Prison," *60 Minutes,* March 8, 2008 [**http://truthinjustice.org/alton-logan.htm**].

53. Percy Luney, "Traditions and Foreign Influences: Systems of Law in China and Japan," *Law and Contemporary Problems* 52 (Spring 1989), pp. 129, 136.

CHAPTER FIVE

Constitutional Law and the Bill of Rights

After completing this chapter, students will be able to:

1. Recognize the purposes of the U.S. Constitution.

2. Describe the separation of powers under the U.S. Constitution.

3. Identify the freedoms protected under the First Amendment.

4. Describe the powerful role the Bill of Rights plays in protecting personal freedoms.

5. Discuss the differences between First Amendment protections of commercial speech versus political speech.

6. Explain the "exclusionary rule."

7. Describe some of the issues arising under the Fourth Amendment "search and seizure" rules.

8. Describe the law of the Fifth Amendment "Takings Clause" and the property rights controversy associated with it.

9. Compare and contrast substantive due process and procedural due process.

10. Identify some examples of the impact of the Equal Protection Clause on business and society.

We the people of the United States, in order to form a more perfect union, establish justice, insure domestic tranquility, provide for the common defense, promote the general welfare, and secure the blessings of liberty to ourselves and our posterity, do ordain and establish this Constitution for the United States of America.

The Preamble to our Constitution summarizes the founders' lofty goals for America. The idealism embodied in the Preamble is both inspiring and touching. In reading it, we should reflect on the dream of America and the Constitution's role in molding and protecting that entirely new image of a nation. That we continue to be guided, more than 220 years later, by those rather few words is testimony to the brilliance and wisdom of its creators and to our determination to build a free, democratic, just society. Our Constitution is a remarkable document, so powerful in its ideas and images that it has reshaped the world.

Creating a Constitution—The United States

You may recall that the Constitution grew out of the Articles of Confederation as enacted by Congress in 1778. The Articles contemplated a "firm league of friendship," but each state was to maintain its "sovereignty, freedom, and independence." The Articles soon proved faulty. Seven years of war had basically bankrupted the colonies. Currency was largely worthless. The 13 new states fought over economic resources, interstate disputes were routine, and the federal union that emerged under the Articles of Confederation had little real authority. As a result of this distress, and in an effort to strengthen the Articles, the Constitutional Convention was called to order in Philadelphia on May 25, 1787.

The decision to convene the Convention may have been a first in world history in that the state leaders themselves acknowledged that the existing federal government was faulty, the citizenry calmly talked things over, violence was avoided, and the decision was made to go forward with the Convention. In the hot Philadelphia summer, with windows and curtains closed to assure secrecy (as a means of encouraging open debate), the often chubby and usually heavily clothed delegates sweated their way toward a new government. All 55 delegates, our Founding Fathers, were white males, and most of them were wealthy landowners, but they were also immensely talented with a wide range of interests and experiences.

> All 55 delegates, our Founding Fathers, were white males

The delegates agreed that a stronger central government was needed, but they were split on just how far that notion should go. Virginia, led by the brilliance of James Madison, favored a dominant central government with greatly diminished state authority. Alexander Hamilton wanted to go further yet by, among other things, instituting the Presidency as a lifetime office. On the other hand, several states, led by New Jersey, wanted to retain strong states' rights. After weeks of debate, a middle ground began to emerge that led toward our current balance of power between big states and small states and between all of the states and the central government. In the end, the delegates reached consensus on a Constitution that guaranteed the revolutionary notion of rule by the people.

On September 17, 1787, the great document, one of the most influential expressions in human history, was formally signed. Following bitter disputes in some states, the Constitution was ratified and the new government haltingly moved forward under the leadership of George Washington and John Adams.[1]

[For links to national constitutions around the globe, see **http://confinder.richmond.edu**]

A Right to Bear Arms

Addressing one of the most contentious questions in American constitutional history, the U.S. Supreme Court in a 2008 decision ruled 5–4 that the Second Amendment (see Appendix A) protects an individual's right to bear arms. The Supreme Court's four conservative justices, joined by the more moderate Justice Kennedy, ruled that individuals have a constitutional right to keep loaded firearms for self-defense, at least in the home. The majority view was based on its reading of the historical record associated with the Second Amendment, while the four dissenting, liberal justices argued that the Second Amendment guaranteed only a collective right to bear arms in a militia. The decision was the first conclusive interpretation of the Second Amendment since it was ratified in 1791.

The decision struck down a District of Columbia law that effectively banned handgun posession. Security guard Dick Heller applied for and was denied a permit for a handgun in his home located in a dangerous Washington, DC neighborhood. He sued the District arguing that the gun ban violated his individual rights under the Second Amendment. The DC law was perhaps the most stringent gun restraint in the nation, and whether the *Heller* decision will invalidate other less extreme laws, is unclear.

The Court did preserve the constitutionality of "reasonable" gun regulations and Justice Scalia, writing for the majority, said nothing in the ruling should "cast doubt on long-standing prohibitions on the possession of firearms by felons or the mentally ill, or laws forbidding the carrying of firearms in sensitive places such as schools and government buildings, or laws imposing conditions and qualifications on the commercial sale of arms." "Dangerous and unusual" weapons also could be banned.

The National Rifle Association immediately announced its intention to file lawsuits in San Francisco and Chicago challenging gun restraints. Extended litigation is sure to follow the decision as government units build arguments supporting their jurisdictions' need for gun control and the courts sort out which of those gun regulations are "reasonable."

Questions

1. As you interpret the Second Amendment, did the Supreme Court reach a *correct* decisions in the *Heller case*? Explain.
2. As a matter of public policy, did the Supreme Court reach a *wise* decision in the *Heller* case? Explain.

> *Sources: District of Columbia v. Dick Anthony Heller,* 2008 U.S. LEXIS 5268; Dina Temple-Raston, "Supreme Court: Individuals Have Right to Bear Arms," *National Public Radio,* June 27, 2008 [http://www.npr.org/templates/story.php?storyId=91911807]

Structure and Purpose

The United States Constitution is reprinted in this book's appendix. Take a moment to review its structure and purposes.

The Preamble identifies certain goals for our society, such as unity (among the various states), justice, domestic tranquility (peace), defense from outsiders, increasing general welfare, and liberty. Article I creates Congress and enumerates its powers. Article I, Section 8, Clause 3 is particularly important because it gives Congress the power to regulate commerce (the Commerce Clause). Article II sets up the executive branch, headed by the president, while Article III establishes the court system. Articles IV and VI, as well as the Fourteenth Amendment, address the relationship between the federal government and the states. Article VI provides in Clause 2 (the Supremacy Clause) for the supremacy of federal law over state law. Article V provides for amendments to the Constitution. The first 10 amendments, known as the Bill of Rights, were ratified by the states and put into effect in 1791. The remaining 16 amendments (11 through 26) were adopted at various times from 1798 through 1971.

From this review we can see that the Constitution serves a number of broad roles:

1. It establishes a national government.
2. It controls the relationship between the national government and the government of the states.
3. It defines and preserves personal liberty.
4. It contains provisions to enable the government to perpetuate itself.[2]

The Founding Fathers—Should We Move On?

Author Mark Kurlansky argues that the Founding Fathers' great accomplishment is losing its luster:

> I am sick and tired of the founding fathers and all their intents. The real American question of our times is how our country in a little over 200 years sank from the great hope to the most backward democracy in the West. The U.S. offers the worst healthcare program, one of the worst public school systems and the worst benefits for workers. The margin between rich and poor has been growing precipitously while it has been decreasing in Europe. Among the great democracies, we use military might less cautiously, show less respect for international law and are the stumbling block in international environmental cooperation. Few informed people look to the United States anymore for progressive ideas. We ought to do something. Instead, we keep worrying about the vision of a bunch of sexist, slave-owning 18th century white men in wigs and breeches.

* * * * *

> So let us stop worshiping the founding fathers and allow our minds to progress and try to build a nation of great new ideas.

Source: Mark Kurlansky, "WWFFD? Who Cares," *Los Angeles Times*, July 4, 2006 [**http://www.latimes.com/news/opinion/la-oe-kurlansky4jul04,0,2811373.story?track=totext**]

Government Power and Constitutional Restraints

Recall that the Constitution was enacted to protect the citizenry from the government. The Constitution does not protect the citizenry from purely private concentrations of power, such as large corporations. In fact, corporations themselves are often entitled to the protections of the Constitution. The Constitution formally limits the authority of the Congress to pass laws by specifically listing *enumerated powers* that are properly within congressional authority (such as the power to regulate commerce) and by providing certain checks or restraints (such as the due process clauses—discussed later in this chapter) in the Constitution that limit just how far Congress can go even with an enumerated power. In practice, the impact of the enumerated powers doctrine has been sharply reduced because the federal government, especially in the New Deal era, has chosen to aggressively regulate the American economy. But as we shall see in this and subsequent chapters, the aforementioned constitutional checks or restraints continue to limit government's power, particularly in this era of increasing respect for free market reasoning.

Separation of Powers

As a further means of controlling the power of government, the Constitution sets up the three federal branches and provides mechanisms for them to act as checks and balances on each other. The president, Congress, and the courts each have specialized areas of authority, as provided for by the Constitution. Congress has the sole power to legislate at the federal level, whereas the president, among other things, executes laws, makes treaties, and commands the armed forces; the Supreme Court and the inferior courts have judicial authority at the federal level. The result is a system of separation of powers that prevents too much authority from residing in any one branch. For example, the president has the power to veto acts of Congress, those vetoes can be overridden by a two-thirds vote of each house, and the judiciary can find those acts unconstitutional. [For the National Constitution Center, see **http:// www.constitutioncenter.org**]

Federalism

A primary role of the Constitution is to balance the central federal authority with dispersed state power. As just explained, the federal government holds only those powers explicitly designated or enumerated in the Constitution. As specified by the Tenth Amendment, the states and the people hold all powers not expressly granted to the federal government in the Constitution. The resulting division of power between the federal government and the states is a key battleground for our ongoing liberal–conservative cultural and political war. Conservatives fear big government and favor bringing power as close to the people as possible, whereas liberals fear local biases and favor a more unified national approach to many issues. Our increasingly complex and interrelated lives have led to a steady expansion in federal power; but as explained hereafter the U.S. Supreme Court continues to critically examine the constitutional balance of federal/state power.

The Constitution, the Bill of Rights, and Business

The Constitution and, in particular, the Commerce Clause (Article 1, Section 8, Clause 3) profoundly shape the practice of American business. Indeed, in some important ways, the Constitution is a commercial document reflecting the economic interests of the framers. We will defer discussion of the Commerce Clause until Chapter 8. In this chapter we will devote our attention primarily to the Bill of Rights. When we think of the Bill of Rights, corporations ordinarily do not come to mind. Extensive litigation in recent years, however, serves notice that the relationship between the corporate "person" and the fundamental freedoms is both important and unclear.

    The Bill of Rights protects our personal freedoms (speech, religion, and the like) from encroachment by the federal government. Furthermore, the Supreme Court has ruled that the Due Process Clause of the Fourteenth Amendment, which is directed at the states, absorbs or incorporates those fundamental freedoms and protects them against intrusion by state governments. [For the "Guide to Law Online," prepared by the United States Law Library of Congress, see **http://www.loc.gov/law/guide**]

The First Amendment

Congress shall make no law respecting an establishment of religion, or prohibiting the free exercise thereof; or abridging the freedom of speech, or the press; or the right of the people peaceably to assemble, and to petition the Government for a redress of grievances.

These few words constitute one of the most powerful and noble utterances in history. Much of the magnificence that we often associate with America is embodied in the protections of the First Amendment. After more than 220 years, it remains a source of wonder that our more than 305 million independent citizens continue to rely on that sentence as a cornerstone of American life. [For the First Amendment Center, see **http://www. firstamendmentcenter.org**]

1. Freedom of Religion

Christianity in the U.S. Constitution?

A 2007 national survey by the nonpartisan First Amendment Center found that 55 percent of Americans incorrectly believe that the Constitution established the United States as an explicitly Christian nation. In fact, the Constitution clearly established a nation where those of every faith as well as those with no faith are equally protected from government interference. Fifty-eight percent of the respondents said that teachers should be allowed to lead prayers. More than one-fourth of the respondents said that constitutional protection of religion does not apply to "extreme" groups. Scholars say that many Americans, especially since 9/11, consider Islam to be an "extreme" religion.

Source: Andrea Stone, "55% in Poll Say Christianity in Constitution," *Des Moines Register,* September 12, 2007, p. 1A.

The First Amendment forbids (1) the establishment of an official state religion (the Establishment Clause) and (2) undue state interference with religious practice (the Free Exercise Clause). Government may neither encourage nor discourage the practice of religion generally, nor may it give preference to one religion over another. Broadly, the idea of the First Amendment is to maintain a separation between church and state. The precise boundary of that separation, however, has become one of the more contentious social issues in contemporary life. Prayer in the schools, the words "under God" in the Pledge of Allegiance, denying state-funded scholarships to divinity students—these are some of the difficult battles in the freedom of religion debate. A highly publicized and interesting example of this conflict is the question of the constitutionality of Ten Commandments displays in government spaces. [For the Freedom Forum database on the First Amendment, see **http://www.freedomforum.org**]

Ten Commandments

In 2001 former Alabama Supreme Court Chief Justice Roy Moore designed and commissioned a 5,000-pound Ten Commandments monument and ordered it to be prominently positioned in the rotunda of the state Supreme Court building. Two federal courts ruled that the Ten Commandments monument amounted to an unconstitutional establishment of religion. The U.S. Supreme Court declined to review those rulings, the monument was wheeled away to storage, and Judge Moore was forced from the bench because he had defied court orders to remove the monument. The story is far from over, however. Perhaps hundreds of Ten Commandments displays can be found in public buildings across the United States. Indeed, the courtroom of the U.S. Supreme Court itself includes a frieze of Moses holding two tablets; but the Supreme Court frieze shows other lawgivers, including Hammurabi and Justinian, and the letters on the tablets are Hebrew.

In an effort to clarify the continuing bitter dispute, the U.S. Supreme Court handed down two Ten Commandments decisions in 2005.[3] The two 5–4 rulings offered something to both sides by allowing Texas to retain the Commandments as part of a historic display on statehouse grounds, while Kentucky officials were barred from displaying the Commandments on their courthouse walls. The essential distinctions in the two cases are matters of purpose, context, and history. The Commandments monument in Texas was set in a historical context along with 16 other monuments and 21 markers commemorating war veterans, boy scouts, pioneers, and so on, thus conveying, in total, a secular message about America's historical values—a permissible purpose that does not entwine the government in encouraging religion or favoring one religion over another. The Kentucky case, on the other hand, involved, in the judgment of the majority, the unconstitutional purpose of advancing religion. Among other things, county officials had ordered the Ten Commandments to be posted alone and had passed resolutions affirming the central role of the Ten Commandments in Kentucky life. Secular documents were added to the display only after the lawsuit was filed.

Clearly the Ten Commandments conflict will persist. Courts will decide each situation case by case.

2. Freedom of Speech

Hustler Magazine publisher Larry Flynt: "If the First Amendment will protect a scumbag like me, then it will protect all of you. Because I am the worst."

Freedom of speech is the primary guarantor of the American approach to life. Not only is it indispensable to democracy and personal dignity, but Americans believe that the free expression of ideas is the most likely path to the best ideas. We believe in a marketplace of ideas just as we believe in a marketplace of goods.

> We cannot freely yell "Fire" in a crowded theater

Freedom of speech is not absolute. Clearly we cannot freely make slanderous statements about others, publicly utter obscenities at will, speak "fighting words" that are likely to produce a clear and present danger of violence, or yell "Fire" in a crowded theater.

At the same time, in general, the state cannot tell us what we can say; that is, the state cannot, for the most part, regulate the *content* of our speech. On the other hand, the state does have greater authority to regulate the *context* of that speech; that is, the state may be able to restrict where, when, and how we say certain things if that regulation is necessary to preserve compelling state interests. We have broad free speech rights in so-called *public forums* such as downtown business districts, parks, college campuses, and public plazas. Even in those places, however, the state may need to impose reasonable time and place regulations. Thus, although the Ku Klux Klan can express hatred for black people (the content of the message), the state may restrict where and when those expressions are made (the context of the message) if necessary for the public safety. [For freedom of speech links, see **http://gjs.net/freetalk.htm**]

On the Job? The federal Constitution and the Bill of Rights protect us, as citizens, from government abuse. What happens, then, when a government employee blows the whistle on the government itself? Los Angeles Deputy District Attorney Richard Ceballos prepared a memo explaining his view that a search warrant prepared by a Los Angeles deputy sheriff for a drug case contained "serious misrepresentations" and that the case should have been dismissed. The drug prosecution went forward, however, and thereafter Ceballos says he was the victim of retaliation, including denial of a promotion. Ceballos sued, and the case reached the U.S. Supreme Court in 2006. By a 5–4 vote, the Court ruled that government employees who speak out "pursuant to their official duties" are not protected by the First Amendment. They are speaking as employees, not as citizens, and therefore, the First Amendment does not insulate them from discipline, regardless of the content of their message. The Court also pointed to the importance of the government being able to maintain efficiency and order in the workplace. The opinion did raise the possibility, however, that a government worker speaking "as a citizen" to a newspaper or legislator might be protected, but that issue awaits future litigation. Justice Souter, in dissent, argued that the Court should have retained its traditional balancing test weighing the government's need to maintain workplace discipline versus the value to the public of the employee's speech.[4]

The *Ceballos* decision affects all of the nation's approximately 20 million government employees who now must recognize that any complaints about official crimes, incompetence and inefficiency could lead to retaliation. Federal and state whistle-blower statutes offer some protection, but the much more comprehensive and powerful defense of the First Amendment is no longer available to those employees if their complaints are offered in the employment context. Government employees' personal lives separate from work, however, retain the full protection of the Constitution and Bill of Rights.

Forms of Expression Sometimes the question becomes one of what behaviors constitute speech. The First Amendment clearly extends to expression in forms other than actual verbiage or writing. In a leading case in this area, the Supreme Court extended First Amendment protection to the wearing of black armbands to high school as a protest against the Vietnam War where no evidence of disruption was presented.[5]

The U.S. Supreme Court in 2007 addressed another school speech case. Joseph Frederick, a Juneau, Alaska high school senior, and some friends unfurled a large banner reading "Bong Hits 4 Jesus." Frederick was across the street from his school with many other students watching, with school permission, an Olympic torch parade. The banner was a prank designed to attract attention from television cameras. The school principal, Deborah Morse, told Frederick to lower the banner. He refused, and he was suspended from school. Frederick sued. Does the First Amendment protect Frederick? [See *Deborah Morse v. Joseph Frederick*, 127 S.Ct. 2618 (2007).]

The Insider

The crucial role of free, open discussion in a democratic society was well illustrated by former Brown & Williamson tobacco company executive Jeffrey Wigand's decision to publicly report what he knew about the danger of cigarettes. Wigand told Mike Wallace and a *60 Minutes* national television audience that chemicals were added to tobacco to enhance its addictive quality. Wigand then became the subject of the 1999 Oscar-nominated movie *The Insider*, starring Russell Crowe and Al Pacino.

Wigand spoke to a group of Independence, Missouri, high school students about his experience in blowing the whistle on the tobacco industry. The *Kansas City Star* summarized Wigand's message to the students:

> He told them about the bullet in the mailbox and the middle-of-the-night death threats. He said Brown & Williamson squashed the First Amendment by using courts to bully CBS into postponing the *60 Minutes* segment. The tobacco industry was desperate to shut him up, he said, because he knew the secret of how cigarette companies hustled 3,000 teens each day into becoming habitual smokers. And he knew how they ensured future sales with addictive, lethal additives.

Source: Donald Bradley, "Students Hear from 'Insider,' " *Kansas City Star,* May 6, 2000, p. B1.

Politically Correct Speech

So with some exceptions, we are largely free of government restraints on what we can say. But should it be so? Is free speech often too hurtful to be tolerated? "That's some nappy-headed hos," said white radio shock jock Don Imus in talking about the 2007 Rutgers women's basketball team, made up largely of black women. Ridiculous and deplorable as those remarks were, should we be concerned that Imus was fired by his employer, CBS? (Remember the First Amendment offered no protection for Imus from the decisions of his private sector employer, CBS.) Should we continue to condemn the use of the "N word" by white people while tolerating its routine use by some black people? Should words like *fag* and *dyke* be protected in public discourse? Universities and other branches of government have often attempted to curb this "hate speech" rooted in race, sex, disability, and so on. Free speech advocates have attached the politically correct label to those efforts. College campuses have been the center of the politically correct speech debate. Hundreds of campuses developed speech codes in the 1990s. For example, Stanford University amended its student code to provide that

> Speech and other expression constitutes harassment by personal vilification if it is intended to insult or stigmatize an individual or a small number of individuals on the basis of their sex, race, color, handicap, religion, sexual orientation, or national and ethnic origin; is addressed directly to the individual or individuals whom it insults or stigmatizes; and makes use of insulting or "fighting" words or nonverbal symbols.

The Stanford speech code, as well as others around the nation, have been struck down as violations of the First Amendment and other constitutional provisions. On the other hand, recent court decisions have given universities considerable latitude in dealing with some speech issues. For example, the 5th Circuit Court of Appeals upheld the right of the University of Mississippi to ban flags, including the Confederate flag, at campus events.[6] Specifically banning only the Confederate flag presumably would not have met with the Court's approval. The virtue in maintaining a campus, community, and nation that welcome all is undeniable, but the great strength of free expression is likewise self-evident. Many First Amendment scholars believe the correct antidote to hate speech is simply more speech; that is, they place their faith in the marketplace of ideas rather than in rules, however well intended. [For a vigorous critique of campus "political correctness," see **www.shadowuniv.com**]

"That's so gay."

Santa Rosa, California high school student Rebekah Rice was teased by classmates about her Mormon family. On one occasion, Rice was asked if she had 10 mothers, to which she responded, "That's so gay." Rice was sent to the principal where she received a warning and a notation was put in her file. Her family filed suit in the Sonoma County Superior Court claiming a violation of Rice's First Amendment free speech rights.
How would you rule on Rice's claim?

Source: Lisa Leff, "'That's So Gay' Abusive? Judge to Decide," *Des Moines Register,* March 1, 2007, p. 5A.

Campus Disputes

At a 2007 "South of the Border" party at Santa Clara University, students appeared to promote ethnic stereotypes by coming to the party dressed as Hispanic gardeners, janitors, gangbangers, and pregnant women. The University of Southern California, the University of Illinois and others have reported similar parties in recent years. The decision that follows demonstrates the First Amendment's role in resolving claims of racism, sexism and general insensitivity springing from a George Mason University fraternity's "ugly woman contest."

Senior Circuit Judge Sprouse

George Mason University appeals from a summary judgment granted by the district court to the IOTA XI Chapter of Sigma Chi Fraternity in its action for declaratory judgment and an injunction seeking to nullify sanctions imposed on it by the University because it conducted an "ugly woman contest" with racist and sexist overtones. We affirm.

I

Sigma Chi has for two years held an annual "Derby Days" event, planned and conducted both as entertainment and as a source of funds for donations to charity. The "ugly woman contest," held on April 4, 1991, was one of the "Derby Days" events. The Fraternity staged the contest in the cafeteria of the student union. As part of the contest, eighteen Fraternity members were assigned to one of six sorority teams cooperating in events. The involved Fraternity members appeared in the contest dressed as caricatures of different types of women, including one member dressed as an offensive caricature of a black woman. He was painted black and wore stringy, black hair decorated with curlers, and his outfit was stuffed with pillows to exaggerate a woman's breasts and buttocks. He spoke in slang to parody African-Americans.

There is no direct evidence in the record concerning the subjective intent of the Fraternity members who conducted the contest. The Fraternity, which later apologized to the University officials for the presentation, conceded during the litigation that the contest was sophomoric and offensive.

Following the contest, a number of students protested to the University that the skit had been objectionably sexist and racist. Two hundred forty-seven students, many of them members of the foreign or minority student body, executed a petition, which stated, "[W]e are condemning the racist and sexist implications of this event in which male members dressed as women. One man in particular wore a black face, portraying a negative stereotype of black women."

On April 10, 1991, the Dean for Student Services Kenneth Bumgarner discussed the situation with representatives of the objecting students. That same day, Dean Bumgarner met with student representatives of Sigma Chi.

The Dean met again with Fraternity representatives on April 18, and the following day advised its officers of the sanctions imposed. They included suspension from all activities for the rest of the 1991 spring semester and a two-year prohibition on all social activities except preapproved pledging events

and preapproved philanthropic events with an educational purpose directly related to gender discrimination and cultural diversity. The University's sanctions also required Sigma Chi to plan and implement an educational program addressing cultural differences, diversity, and the concerns of women. A few weeks later, the University made minor modifications to the sanctions, allowing Sigma Chi to engage in selected social activities with the University's advance approval.

On June 5, 1991, Sigma Chi brought this action against the University and Dean Bumgarner. It requested declaratory judgment and injunctive relief to nullify the sanctions as violative of the First and Fourteenth Amendments. Sigma Chi moved for summary judgment on its First Amendment claims on June 28, 1991.

In addition to the affidavit of Dean Bumgarner explaining his meetings with student leaders, the University submitted the affidavits of other officials, including that of University President George W. Johnson. President Johnson, by his affidavit, presented the "mission statement" of the University:

* * * * *

(3) George Mason University is committed to promoting a culturally and racially diverse student body. . . . Education here is not limited to the classroom.

(4) We are committed to teaching the values of equal opportunity and equal treatment, respect for diversity, and individual dignity.

(5) Our mission also includes achieving the goals set forth in our affirmative action plan, a plan incorporating affirmative steps designed to attract and retain minorities to this campus.

* * * * *

(7) George Mason University is a state institution of higher education and a recipient of federal funds.

* * * * *

The district court granted summary judgment to Sigma Chi on its First Amendment claim, 773 F.Supp. 792 (E.D. Va. 1991).

II

The University urges that the district court's grant of summary judgment was premature. It stresses that there remain factual issues which the district court should have weighed in its conclusion.

* * * * *

In our view, for the reasons that follow, the district court was correct in concluding that there was no outstanding issue of material fact.

III

We initially face the task of deciding whether Sigma Chi's "ugly woman contest" is sufficiently expressive to entitle it to First Amendment protection.

* * * * *

A

First Amendment principles governing live entertainment are relatively clear: Short of obscenity, it is generally protected. As the Supreme Court announced in *Schad v. Borough of Mount Ephraim,* 452 U.S. 61 (1981), "[e]ntertainment, as well as political and ideological speech, is protected; motion pictures, programs broadcast by radio and television, and live entertainment ... fall within the First Amendment guarantee." Expression devoid of "ideas" but with entertainment value may also be protected because "[t]he line between the informing and the entertaining is too elusive." *Winters v. New York,* 333 U.S. 507, 510 (1948).

* * * * *

Even crude street skits come within the First Amendment's reach. In ... *Schacht v. United States,* 398 U.S. 58, 61–62 (1970), ... Justice Black [declared] that an actor participating in even a crude performance enjoys the constitutional right to freedom of speech.

Bearing on this dichotomy between low- and high-grade entertainment are the Supreme Court's holdings relating to nude dancing. See *Barnes v. Glen Theatre, Inc.,* 111 S.Ct. 2456, 2460 (1991).

[I]n *Barnes,* the Supreme Court conceded that nude dancing is expressive conduct entitled to First Amendment protection.

* * * * *

... [I]t appears that the low quality of entertainment does not necessarily weigh in the First Amendment inquiry. It would seem, therefore, that the Fraternity's skit, even as low-grade entertainment, was inherently expressive and thus entitled to First Amendment protection.

B

The University nevertheless contends that discovery will demonstrate that the contest does not merit characterization as a skit but only as mindless fraternity fun, devoid of any artistic expression. It argues further that entitlement to First Amendment protection exists only if the production was intended to convey a message likely to be understood by a particular audience. From the summary judgment record, the University insists, it is impossible to discern the communicative intent necessary to imbue the Fraternity's conduct with a free speech component.

As indicated, we feel that the First Amendment protects the Fraternity's skit because it is inherently expressive entertainment. Even if this were not true, however, the skit, in our view, qualifies as expressive conduct under the test articulated in *Texas v. Johnson,* 491 U.S. 397 (1989). It is true that the *Johnson* test for determining the expressiveness of conduct requires "'[a]n intent to convey a particularized message'" and a great likelihood "'that the message would be understood by those who viewed it.'"

* * * * *

[T]he affidavits establish that the punishment was meted out to the Fraternity because its boorish *message* had interfered with the described University mission. It is manifest from these circumstances that the University officials thought the Fraternity intended to convey a message. The Fraternity members' apology and postconduct contriteness suggest that they held the same view.

* * * * *

As to the second prong of the *Johnson* test, there was a great likelihood that at least some of the audience viewing the skit would understand the Fraternity's message of satire and humor. Some students paid to attend the performance and were entertained. ...

* * * * *

... [W]e are persuaded that the Fraternity's "ugly woman contest" satisfies the *Johnson* test for expressive conduct.

IV

If this were not a sufficient response to the University's argument, the principles relating to content and viewpoint discrimination recently emphasized in *R.A.V. v. City of St. Paul,* 112 S.Ct. 2538 (1992), provide a definitive answer. Although the Court in *St. Paul* reviewed the constitutional effect of a city "hate speech" ordinance, and we review the constitutionality of sanctions imposed for violating University policy, *St. Paul's* rationale applies here with equal force. Noting that St. Paul's city ordinance prohibited displays of symbols that "arouse[d] anger, alarm, or resentment in others on the basis of race, color, creed, religion, or gender," but did not prohibit displays of symbols which would advance ideas of racial or religious equality, Justice Scalia stated, "The First Amendment does not permit St. Paul to impose special prohibitions on those speakers who express views on disfavored subjects."

As evidenced by their affidavits, University officials sanctioned Sigma Chi for the message conveyed by the "ugly-woman contest" because it ran counter to the views the University sought to communicate to its students and the community. The mischief was the University's punishment of those who scoffed at its goals of racial integration and gender neutrality, while permitting, even encouraging, conduct that would further the viewpoint expressed in the University's goals and probably be embraced by a majority of society as well. "The First Amendment generally prevents government from proscribing . . . expressive conduct because of disapproval of the ideas expressed."

The University, however, urges us to weigh Sigma Chi's conduct against the substantial interests inherent in educational endeavors. We agree wholeheartedly that it is the University officials' responsibility, even their obligation, to achieve the goals they have set. On the other hand, a public university has many constitutionally permissible means to protect female and minority students. We must emphasize, as have other courts, that "the manner of [its action] cannot consist of selective limitations upon speech." The University should have accomplished its goals in some fashion other than silencing speech on the basis of its viewpoint.

Affirmed.

Questions

1. Is speech that consists merely of entertainment without benefit of meaningful ideas protected by the First Amendment? Explain.

2. Explain the Court's conclusion that the fraternity skit met the *Texas v. Johnson* test of "an intent to convey a particularized message" and a great likelihood "that the message would be understood by those who viewed it."

3. *a.* Should racist/sexist remarks be forbidden in college classrooms?

   b. As noted, the Stanford University speech code, as set out above, was ruled unconstitutional. The Superior Court judge in that case said, among other things, that the code was "overbroad." What did he mean?

   c. Do we give too much attention to freedom of speech at the expense of community civility? Explain.

4. T.W., a minor, was suspended from school for three days after he drew a picture of a Confederate flag on a piece of paper. The Kansas school, Derby Unified, suspended T.W. because it believed he had violated the district's "Racial Harassment or Intimidation" policy, which prohibits students from possessing at school "any written material, either printed or in their own handwriting, that is racially divisive or creates ill will or hatred." Confederate flags were included in a list of prohibited items. The Court found that Derby Unified had a history of racial harassment. Were T.W.'s First Amendment rights violated? Explain. See *West v. Derby Unified School District # 260,* 206 F.3d 1358 (10th Cir. 2000); cert. den. 531 U.S. 825 (2000).

5. The U.S. Supreme Court and lower federal courts have repeatedly ruled that burning the American flag is speech protected by the First Amendment. Congress often considers a flag protection amendment to the Constitution to make flag burning illegal. A 1999 Gallup Poll found 63 percent of Americans favoring that amendment. How would you vote? Explain.

6. Timothy Boomer's canoe hit a rock in Michigan's Rifle River, and he fell in. A passing mother and her young children heard Boomer cuss repeatedly (they said) or once or twice (his lawyer said). A 102-year-old Michigan law forbids swearing in front of children. Boomer was ticketed and tried.

   a. Did Boomer violate the statute?

   b. Does the First Amendment protect Boomer's outburst?

Free Speech in Cyberspace?

Phyllis Schlafly:

"Do you ever wonder why the Internet is so polluted with pornography? The Supreme Court just reminded us why: It blocks every attempt by Congress to regulate the pornographers. The court props open the floodgates for smut and graphic sex. Over the past five years, it has repeatedly found new constitutional rights for vulgarity, most recently invalidating the Child Online Protection Act."

Conservative activist Phyllis Schlafly probably spoke for most Americans in condemning the Supreme Court's 2004 decision striking down portions of the Child Online Protection Act (COPA), a congressional effort to restrict pornography on the Internet. For the third time in seven years, the Supreme Court found that a federal law aimed at online smut violated the First Amendment. Basically, the Court was concerned about the *content-based* nature of the COPA restraint on speech, and the Court considered COPA to be *overbroad* in the sense that its goal of protecting children might have been achieved with less restrictive means that would not threaten speech of interest to adults.

Congress responded to the Court's decision by writing new legislation, called the PROTECT Act, and the Court in 2008 by a 7–2 margin upheld the constitutionality of the pandering portion of that legislation that forbids, among other things, promoting online and mailed child pornography, whether the pornography actually exists or not. Michael Williams had been convicted of promoting and possessing child pornography after having an Internet chat room conversation with an undercover Secret Service agent where Williams allegedly depicted himself as "Dad of toddler has 'good' pics of her and me for swap of your toddler pics, or live cam." Later he allegedly posted some pictures of young children in sexual poses and conduct. Williams argued that the pandering portion of the PROTECT Act was unconstitutionally vague and overbroad, but the Supreme Court ruled that: "[O]ffers to provide or requests to obtain child pornography are categorically excluded from the First Amendment." The Court brushed aside fears that the ruling would threaten protected speech such as movies purporting to show underage sex.

Sources: Phyllis Schlafly, Copley News Service, "High Court Backs Pornographers," *Chattanooga Times Free Press,* July 12, 2004, p. B7; *Ashcroft v. American Civil Liberties Union,* 124 S.Ct. 2783 (2004); Robert Barnes, "Justices Uphold Child Porn Law," *Washington Post,* May 20, 2008, p. 01; and *United States v. Williams,* 2008 U.S. LEXIS 4314.

Commercial Speech

Liquor ads, the location of billboards, real estate "for sale" signs, and circulars placed on car windshields are among the many forms of commercial messages that governments may want to regulate for various reasons. Does the First Amendment protect those messages from government intervention in the same manner that it protects political speech? In 1942 the U.S. Supreme Court ruled that *commercial speech* was not entitled to First Amendment protection.[7] Subsequently the Court changed its stance and extended First Amendment rights to commercial speech, but those rights were much more limited than for political speech. In more recent years the Court has been gradually expanding protection for commercial speech, and many critics have called for full parity that would allow the government to regulate commercial speech only for compelling reasons, as has long been the case for political speech. The general rule today is that the government can regulate commercial speech where those restrictions are necessary for the public welfare.

Car for Sale

Glendale, Ohio authorities threatened Christopher Pagan with a citation when he put a small "For Sale" sign in the window of his 1970 Mercury Cougar that he parked on the street in front of his house. The sign violated a Glendale ordinance forbidding parking cars for sale on any village streets, public or private, and it forbade parking for the purpose of "any advertising." Pagan had to remove the sign, but he sued Glendale claiming the parking ordinance violated his constitutional rights.

Questions
1. What constitutional challenge was Pagan raising?
2. Defend Glendale.
3. Decide the case. Explain.

Source: Pagan v. Fruchy, 492 F.3d 766 (6th Cir. 2007).

Do-Not-Call In 2003 the Federal Trade Commission and the Federal Communications Commission together issued rules that created a national do-not-call registry, allowing consumers to indicate that they do not want to receive unsolicited calls from telemarketers. For those spared mealtime intrusions, the rule has been a blessing, but for commercial telemarketers the registry is a big financial setback. With no chance of legislative action to override the popular registry, the only recourse for direct marketers was the courts, and a key weapon in their assault on the registry was the First Amendment. Telemarketers went to court claiming the registry amounted to an unconstitutional restriction on their free speech rights. The 10th U.S. Circuit Court of Appeals, however, upheld the constitutionality of the registry, ruling that the "do-not-call registry is a valid commercial speech regulation because it directly advances the government's important interests in safeguarding personal privacy and reducing the danger of telemarketing abuse without burdening an excessive amount of speech."[8] The U.S. Supreme Court declined to review that decision.[9]

Nike

Various news reports in 1996 and thereafter harshly criticized working conditions in Nike factories in Southeast Asia. Thereafter Nike issued advertisements and press releases to tell its side of the story. Marc Kasky, a California resident, then sued Nike, saying those ads and other public defenses included either lies or deceptions about Nike's labor practices. Kasky sued Nike on behalf of the people of California under a state law forbidding unfair business practices. Nike won at both the trial and state court of appeals on the grounds that the First Amendment protected Nike's speech from government intervention. The U.S. Supreme Court then declined to resolve the commercial speech issue and sent the case back to California on procedural grounds. Thereafter Nike settled with Kasky by guaranteeing a $1.5 million payment to a Washington worker rights group. So the Kasky case failed to resolve the ongoing commercial speech debate. Honest mistakes or misleading statements made in public debate by a professor or journalist or your neighbor, for example, are protected by the First Amendment from government regulation. Deceptive or untrue commercial speech, on the other hand, may be regulated or even prohibited. So Nike feels the law puts it at a considerable disadvantage in that its critics' remarks would ordinarily be protected political speech while Nike's response would probably be commercial speech with a lesser degree of protection.[10] And in any case, doesn't our free market in ideas sufficiently protect the consumer—even in the face of inaccurate information? The *Bad Frog* decision below examines the question of free speech protection for beer advertising.

Wal-ocaust? Wal-Qaeda?

Wal-Mart demanded that Charles Smith, a 50-year-old computer store owner, stop making and selling T-shirts and other items displaying slogans such as "Wal-ocaust" and "Wal-Qaeda." Smith objected to Wal-Mart "taking over the world." Smith sold the items online, but he did not advertise or market them broadly and he offered free, downloadable copies of his designs. He sold only 62 T-shirts. Smith filed suit seeking a court order affirming his right to sell the anti-Wal-Mart items. Wal-Mart responded by arguing that Smith was engaging in trademark infringement, among other claims.

Question

Explain Smith's First Amendment response to Wal-Mart's legal claims against him.

Source: Smith v. Wal-Mart, 537 F.Supp.2d 1301 (N.D.Ga. 2008).

LEGAL BRIEFCASE

Bad Frog Brewery v. New York State Liquor Authority   134 F.3d 87 (2d Cir. 1998)

Judge Newman

BACKGROUND

Bad Frog is a Michigan corporation that manufactures and markets several different types of alcoholic beverages under its "Bad Frog" trademark. This action concerns labels used by the company in the marketing of Bad Frog Beer, Bad Frog Lemon Lager, and Bad Frog Malt Liquor. Each label prominently features an artist's rendering of a frog holding up its four-"fingered" right "hand," with the back of the "hand" shown, the second "finger" extended, and the other three "fingers" slightly curled. Bad Frog does not dispute that the frog depicted in the label artwork is making the gesture generally known as "giving the finger" and that the gesture is widely regarded as an offensive insult, conveying a message that the company has characterized as "traditionally . . . negative and nasty." Versions of the label feature slogans such as "He just don't care," "An amphibian with an attitude," "Turning bad into good," and "The beer so good . . . it's bad." Another slogan, originally used but now abandoned, was "He's mean, green and obscene."

Reprinted by permission of the trademark holder, Bad Frog Brewery.

Bad Frog's labels have been approved for use by the Federal Bureau of Alcohol, Tobacco, and Firearms, and by authorities in at least 15 states and the District of Columbia, but have been rejected by authorities in New Jersey, Ohio, and Pennsylvania.

In May 1996, Bad Frog's authorized New York distributor, Renaissance Beer Co., made an application to the New York State Liquor Authority (NYSLA) for brand label approval and registration. . . .

In September 1996, NYSLA denied Bad Frog's application. . . . Explaining its rationale for the rejection, the Authority found that the label "encourages combative behavior" and that the gesture and the slogan, "He just don't care," placed close to and in larger type than a warning concerning potential health problems,

> foster a defiance to the health warning on the label, entice underage drinkers, and invite the public not to heed conventional wisdom and to disobey standards of decorum.

In addition, the Authority said that it

> considered that approval of this label means that the label could appear in grocery and convenience stores, with obvious exposure on the shelf to children of tender age

and that it

> is sensitive to and has concern as to [the label's] adverse effects on such a youthful audience.

Finally, the Authority said that it

> has considered that within the state of New York, the gesture of "giving the finger" to someone has the insulting meaning of "**k You," or "Up Yours," . . . a confrontational, obscene gesture, known to lead to fights, shootings, and homicides . . . concludes that the encouraged use of this gesture in licensed premises is akin to yelling "fire" in a crowded theater, . . . [and] finds that to approve this admittedly obscene, provocative confrontational gesture would not be conducive to proper regulation and control and would tend to adversely affect the health, safety, and welfare of the People of the State of New York.

Bad Frog filed the present action in October 1996 and sought a preliminary injunction barring NYSLA from taking any steps to prohibit the sale of beer by Bad Frog under the controversial labels. The District Court denied the motion [and Bad Frog now appeals the District Court decision].

*   *   *   *   *

COMMERCIAL OR NONCOMMERCIAL SPEECH?

In Bad Frog's view, the commercial speech that receives reduced First Amendment protection is expression that conveys commercial information. The frog labels, it contends, do not purport to convey such information, but instead communicate only a "joke." As such, the argument continues, the labels enjoy full First Amendment protection, rather than the somewhat reduced protection accorded commercial speech.

NYSLA agrees with the District Court that the labels enjoy some First Amendment protection, but are to be assessed by the somewhat reduced standards applicable to commercial speech.

*   *   *   *   *

Bad Frog's label attempts to function, like a trademark, to identify the source of the product. The picture on a beer bottle of a frog behaving badly is reasonably to be understood as attempting to identify to consumers a product of the Bad Frog Brewery. In addition, the label serves to propose a commercial transaction. Though the label communicates no information beyond the source of the product, we think that minimal information, conveyed in the context of a proposal of a commercial transaction, suffices to invoke the protections for commercial speech. . . .

Bad Frog contends that its labels deserve full First Amendment protection because their proposal of a commercial transaction is combined with what is claimed to be political, or at least societal, commentary.

* * * * *

We are unpersuaded by Bad Frog's attempt to separate the purported social commentary in the labels from the hawking of beer. Bad Frog's labels meet the three criteria identified in *Bolger* [463 U.S. 60 (1983)]: the labels are a form of advertising, identify a specific product, and serve the economic interest of the speaker. Moreover, the purported noncommercial message is not so "inextricably intertwined" with the commercial speech as to require a finding that the entire label must be treated as "pure" speech.

* * * * *

We thus assess the prohibition of Bad Frog's labels under the commercial speech standards outlined in *Central Hudson* [447 U.S. 557 (1980)].

THE *CENTRAL HUDSON* TEST
Central Hudson sets forth the analytical framework for assessing governmental restrictions on commercial speech:

> At the outset, we must determine whether the expression is protected by the First Amendment. For commercial speech to come within that provision, it at least must concern lawful activity and not be misleading. Next, we ask whether the asserted government interest is substantial. If both inquiries yield positive answers, we must determine whether the regulation directly advances the government interest asserted, and whether it is not more extensive than is necessary to serve that interest.

* * * * *

A. Lawful Activity and Not Deceptive
We agree with the District Court that Bad Frog's labels pass *Central Hudson*'s threshold requirement that the speech "must concern lawful activity and not be misleading." The consumption of beer (at least by adults) is legal in New York, and the labels cannot be said to be deceptive, even if they are offensive.

B. Substantial State Interests
NYSLA advances two interests to support its asserted power to ban Bad Frog's labels: (i) the State's interest in "protecting children from vulgar and profane advertising," and (ii) the State's interest "in acting consistently to promote temperance, i.e., the moderate and responsible use of alcohol among those above the legal drinking age and abstention among those below the legal drinking age."

Both of the asserted interests are "substantial" within the meaning of *Central Hudson*. States have "a compelling interest in protecting the physical and psychological well-being of minors," and "[t]his interest extends to shielding minors from the influence of literature that is not obscene by adult standards."

The Supreme Court also has recognized that states have a substantial interest in regulating alcohol consumption. We agree with the District Court that New York's asserted concern for "temperance" is also a substantial state interest.

C. Direct Advancement of the State Interest
To meet the "direct advancement" requirement, a state must demonstrate that "the harms it recites are real and that its restriction will in fact alleviate them *to a material degree*" [*Edenfield v. Fane,* 507 U.S. 761, 771 (1993)].

(1) *Advancing the interest in protecting children from vulgarity.*

* * * * *

NYSLA endeavors to advance the state interest in preventing exposure of children to vulgar displays by taking only the limited step of barring such displays from the labels of alcoholic beverages. In view of the wide currency of vulgar displays throughout contemporary society, including comic books targeted directly at children, barring such displays from labels for alcoholic beverages cannot realistically be expected to reduce children's exposure to such displays to any significant degree.

* * * * *

(2) *Advancing the state interest in temperance.* We agree with the District Court that NYSLA has not established that its rejection of Bad Frog's application directly advances the state's interest in "temperance."

NYSLA maintains that the raised finger gesture and the slogan "He just don't care" urge consumers generally to defy authority and particularly to disregard the Surgeon General's warning, which appears on the label next to the gesturing frog. NYSLA also contends that the frog appeals to youngsters and promotes underage drinking.

The truth of these propositions is not so self-evident as to relieve the state of the burden of marshalling some empirical evidence to support its assumptions. All that is clear is that the gesture of "giving the finger" is offensive. Whether viewing that gesture on a beer label will encourage disregard of health warnings or encourage underage drinking remain matters of speculation.

NYSLA has not shown that its denial of Bad Frog's application directly and materially advances either of its asserted state interests.

D. Narrow Tailoring

Central Hudson's fourth criterion, sometimes referred to as "narrow tailoring," requires consideration of whether the prohibition is more extensive than necessary to serve the asserted state interest. Since NYSLA's prohibition of Bad Frog's labels has not been shown to make even an arguable advancement of the state interest in temperance, we consider here only whether the prohibition is more extensive than necessary to serve the asserted interest in insulating children from vulgarity.

* * * * *

In this case, Bad Frog has suggested numerous less intrusive alternatives to advance the asserted state interest in protecting children from vulgarity, short of a complete statewide ban on its labels. Appellant suggests "the restriction of advertising to point-of-sale locations; limitations on billboard advertising; restrictions on over-the-air advertising; and segregation of the product in the store." Even if we were to assume that the state materially advances its asserted interest by shielding children from viewing the Bad Frog labels, it is plainly excessive to prohibit the labels from all use, including placement on bottles displayed in bars and taverns where parental supervision of children is to be expected. Moreover, to whatever extent NYSLA is concerned that children will be harmfully exposed to the Bad Frog labels when wandering without parental supervision around grocery and convenience stores where beer is sold, that concern could be less intrusively dealt with by placing restrictions on the permissible locations where the appellant's products may be displayed within such stores. Or, with the labels permitted, restrictions might be imposed on placement of the frog illustration on the outside of six-packs or cases sold in such stores.

NYSLA's complete statewide ban on the use of Bad Frog's labels lacks a "reasonable fit" with the state's asserted interest in shielding minors from vulgarity, and NYSLA gave inadequate consideration to alternatives to this blanket suppression of commercial speech.

* * * * *

[W]e conclude that NYSLA has unlawfully rejected Bad Frog's application for approval of its labels.

* * * * *

[Reversed and remanded.] [For an update on Bad Frog, see **http://badfrog.com**]

Questions

1. *a.* Why did the Court of Appeals conclude that the Bad Frog label constituted commercial speech?
   b. What is the significance of that decision?

2. Why did the Court of Appeals rule in Bad Frog's favor?

3. A letter to the *Buffalo News* objecting to the *Bad Frog* decision:

   . . . The U.S. Court of Appeals' reasoning was that "vulgar materials enjoy wide currency in society today—including comic books for children." Therefore, while offensive it is not illegal. I guess this means the sickies of the world can show us anything they want, even if we don't want to see it. They have the right to offend us, but we have no rights not to be offended.

   We all know what the extended middle finger means. I personally get offended when this gesture is directed at me, whether by humans or cartoon animals. I would like to show the Court of Appeals my opinion of their decision by extending my middle finger in their direction. I hope they enjoy this gesture. After all, it's not illegal. But maybe it should be.[11]

   a. Do you agree with the letter writer that Bad Frog is an unwise decision? Explain.
   b. Should "the finger" be an illegal gesture? Explain.

4. Robert Levy, a constitutional law expert, objecting to the current First Amendment treatment of commercial speech:

   Inexplicably, advertising remains second-class speech, with less First Amendment protection than Ku Klux Klan vitriol, flag burning, even "gangsta rap." The upshot is that Time Warner can peddle rapper Ice-T's "Cop Killer" to its teen clientele. But if R. J. Reynolds were to produce a TV commercial for an adult audience featuring Tiger Woods wearing a sport coat with a Joe Camel emblem, the boot of government would come down hard on the company's neck.[12]

   Comment.

5. Two Rhode Island statutes prohibited all price advertising on liquor in the state, except for price tags and signs within a store itself which were not visible on the street. The state sought to reduce alcohol consumption. Two licensed liquor dealers challenged the statutes' constitutionality.
   a. How would you rule on that challenge? Explain.
   b. Why would the elimination of price advertising arguably contribute to reduced alcohol consumption? See *44 Liquormart, Inc. v. Rhode Island,* 116 S.Ct. 1495 (1996).

6. A U.S. statute forbade the mailing of unsolicited advertisements for contraceptives. Youngs, which sold contracep-

tives, mailed contraceptive ads to the public at large. The ads included information regarding the public health benefits of contraceptives (such as family planning and prevention of venereal disease).

a. Do the ads constitute commercial speech? Explain.

b. Does the government have a "substantial interest" in preventing the mailings where the statute shields citizens from material that they are likely to find offensive and where the statute helps parents control their chil-

dren's access to birth control information? Explain. See *Bolger v. Youngs Drug Products Corp.*, 463 U.S. 60 (1983).

7. The Township of Willingboro prohibited the posting of real estate "For Sale" or "Sold" signs. The town's purposes were to promote racial integration and to retard the flight of white homeowners. Is the Willingboro action constitutionally permissible? See *Linmark Associates, Inc. v. Willingboro*, 431 U.S. 85 (1977).

The Fourth Amendment

In an increasingly complex and interdependent society, the right of the individual to be free of unjustified governmental intrusions—that is, to a reasonable degree of privacy—has taken on new significance. The Fourth Amendment provides that

[T]he right of the people to be secure in their persons, houses, papers, and effects, against unreasonable searches and seizures, shall not be violated, and no Warrants shall issue, but upon probable cause.

Some constitutional limitations on the police powers of government officials are a necessity. The boundaries of freedom from unreasonable search and seizure are, however, the subject of continuing dispute. The police are under great pressure to cope with America's crime problems, but they must do so within the confines of the Constitution, which is designed to protect us all—including criminals—from the power of an unfair, overreaching government.

Certainly, the most controversial dimension of Fourth Amendment interpretation is the *exclusionary rule,* which provides that, as a matter of due process, no evidence secured in violation of the Fourth Amendment may be admitted as evidence in a court of law. As ultimately applied to all courts by the 1961 U.S. Supreme Court decision in *Mapp v. Ohio,*[13] we can see that the exclusionary rule, while a very effective device for discouraging illegal searches, seizures, and arrests, also from time to time has the effect of freeing guilty criminals.

The Supreme Court restricted the exclusionary rule in 2006 holding that the government need not forfeit evidence collected in constitutionally improper "no knock" searches.[14] For many years, police conducting a search have been required to knock and announce themselves then wait a reasonable time to enter. Michigan police, in executing a search warrant, announced themselves but did not wait a reasonable time before entering and finding crack cocaine in Booker T. Hudson's pockets. Hudson was convicted of drug violations, and his appeal eventually reached the U.S. Supreme Court where Justice Antonin Scalia, writing the 5–4 opinion, expressed concern about guilty defendants who have been allowed to go free because of the exclusionary rule. He concluded that the social costs of the knock and announce rule were too high as compared with the rule's added privacy value. Scalia also pointed to improved police practice since the adoption of the exclusionary rule in 1961.

In general, a search warrant issued by a judge is necessary to comply with the Constitution in making a narcotics search. However, a warrantless search is permissible where reasonable, as in association with an arrest or where probable cause exists to believe a drug-related crime has been committed but circumstances make securing a warrant impracticable. Incident to an arrest, a search may lawfully include the person, a car, and the immediate vicinity of the arrest. Further, a police officer may lawfully secure drugs that have been abandoned or that are in plain view even though a warrant has not been obtained. As the following situations attest, search/privacy problems pervade our lives.

1. **Traffic Stops.** In 1998 an Illinois police officer stopped a speeding car from Nevada. A second officer, hearing the police radio report of the stop, decided to bring his drug-sniffing dog to join the first officer. The dog led the officers to the trunk of the stopped vehicle, where the police found marijuana valued at more than $250,000. The Nevada driver, Roy I. Caballes, was convicted of drug trafficking, sentenced to 12 years' imprisonment, and fined. Caballes appealed, claiming the search was unconstitutional because the officers had no reason to believe drugs were involved. On appeal, the Illinois Supreme Court ruled for Caballes, holding that the drug-sniffing dogs can be used at a traffic stop only when the police have "specific and articulable facts" suggesting that drugs are in the vehicle.[15]

   > Sniffing by a dog did not constitute a search

   The U.S. Supreme Court in 2005 ruled for the government, concluding that sniffing by a dog trained only to identify illegal drugs did not constitute a search because the sniffing could only reveal evidence of illegal activity. We have no reasonable expectation of privacy in illegal activity, so the dog's efforts could not reveal any information that was private and protected. Because no search actually occurred, the standard of reasonableness required by the Fourth Amendment was not implicated.[16]

2. **High-Speed Chases.** Georgia deputy sheriff Tim Scott "seized" teenager Victor Harris by ramming Harris' car from the rear in a chase, sending the car into a rollover accident that rendered Harris a quadriplegic. Harris argued that the seizure violated his Fourth Amendment rights, but Justice Scalia, writing for the majority in the 8–1 decision, said that Scott's decision to force Harris off the road was reasonable given the need to protect pedestrians and other drivers. The chase, which at one time reached 83 miles per hour on two-lane roads, posed a substantial and immediate risk of serious physical injury to others.[17]

3. **Home Search.** Los Angeles sheriff's officers, with a warrant, searched a house for three African-American identity thieves, one of whom had registered a handgun. Unbeknowst to the officers, the suspects had vacated the house three months earlier. The officers knocked on the door and announced their presence. The officers entered a bedroom with guns drawn and found a white man and woman sleeping in the nude. The police ordered the couple out of bed and did not allow them to cover themselves until one or two minutes had passed. The officers, realizing their mistake, apologized and left the house within five minutes. The residents, Max Rettele and Judy Sadler, accused the officers of violating their Fourth Amendment rights by conducting the

search in an unreasonable manner. The case reached the U.S. Supreme Court where only one justice supported Rettele and Sadler's claim. The Court noted that the officers could not have known whether the suspects were elsewhere in the house or whether weapons were in the bedding. The Court noted that occupants are sometimes inconvenienced or embarrassed, but so long as police execute a valid warrant and act in a reasonable manner, the Fourth Amendment is not violated.[18]

4. **Testing Students.** In 1998 the school board in rural Tecumseh, Oklahoma, instituted a mandatory random urinalysis drug-testing program for all students participating in competitive extracurricular activities. The tests checked for illegal drugs but not for alcohol. Test results were not turned over to the police. An honor student, Lindsay Earls, challenged the program as a violation of her Fourth Amendment rights. A U.S. Court of Appeals agreed with her, ruling that school officials needed to provide evidence of an "identifiable drug abuse problem."[19] The U.S. Supreme Court, however, reversed that decision and held by a 5–4 margin that the school's interest in addressing drug problems outweighed students' privacy rights.[20] The Court reasoned that those participating in extracurricular activities are subjected to many rules and restrictions that diminish their expectation of privacy, and the Court said the program is a health and safety measure rather than an assault on personal privacy.

5. **Voyeurism and the surveillance society.** In Washington State, Richard Sorrells and Sean Glas were found guilty of violating a state voyeurism statute for taking pictures up the skirts of some women who were working and shopping in a public mall. Both men appealed their convictions and won a 2002 decision because the voyeurism law did not apply, the Washington State Supreme Court unanimously ruled, to actions in public places.[21] The women had no "reasonable expectation of privacy" in the shopping mall, so their privacy could not have been invaded. A number of states have now passed laws expanding protection against photographic voyeurism, but those laws may not meet constitutional requirements.

Meanwhile, threats to privacy are growing exponentially as new technology leads toward a surveillance society. Hidden cameras, camera phones, and other high-tech probing devices allow voyeurism, identity theft, industrial espionage, keystroke monitoring (to capture account numbers and passwords), personal spying, and much more. Of course, a lot of good can come from spying. An employee's surreptitious filming of unsafe working conditions, for example, can be much more convincing than the employee's word alone. But the risks are enormous. We have long feared government intrusions (Big Brother is watching), but now we have democratized privacy invasions by giving all of us the technological ability to intrude. Will the legal system be able to protect us from each other? [For an overview of privacy issues around the world, see **www.epic.org**]

Questions

1. A local citizen told police that Wilson was growing marijuana in a small, roofless shed at his residence. The police flew over the shed in a small plane at a legal altitude of 500 feet and observed what they believed to be marijuana growing in the shed. They

secured a warrant, conducted a search, and seized marijuana plants. Wilson moved to suppress the evidence, claiming the search was illegal. Is he correct? Explain. See *State v. Wilson,* 988 P.2d 463 (Ct. App. Wash. 1999).

2. Police stopped and arrested McFadden for riding a bicycle on a sidewalk in violation of New York City code. A search incident to the stop revealed a firearm. McFadden was later convicted of the crime of being in possession of a firearm by a previously convicted felon. McFadden appealed, claiming the search was unconstitutional. Was he correct? Explain. See *United States v. McFadden,* 238 F.3d 198 (2001); cert. den. 122 S.Ct. 223 (2001).

3. *a.* Can the police lawfully search an individual's garbage once it has been placed at the curb for disposal? A Connecticut resident, Paul DeFusco, was convicted of drug trafficking based on evidence found in his home. The police conducted the home search with a warrant secured on the basis of an informant's information as well as evidence (some short cut straws, glassine baggies, and prescription bottles) turned up in sifting through DeFusco's garbage.

   b. Explain the central issue in this case. See *State of Connecticut v. Paul DeFusco,* 620 A.2d 746 (Conn. S.Ct. 1993).

4. An informant told the police that a man, whom the informant described, was selling narcotics from the trunk of his car at a particular location. Police drove there, saw the car, and later stopped the car and arrested the driver who matched the informant's description. An officer opened the car's trunk, saw a brown bag, opened it, and found glassine bags of heroin. The car was then driven to police quarters, where another warrantless search of the trunk produced a leather pouch containing money. At trial, may the heroin and cash lawfully be introduced as evidence? Explain. See *United States v. Ross,* 456 U.S. 798 (1982).

Business Searches

Government tries to protect us from business hazards including pollution, defective products, and unsafe workplaces and business crimes such as fraud and bribery. To do so, government agents often want to enter company buildings; observe working conditions; and examine company books. We know our homes are generally protected from searches in the absence of a warrant. But for urgent circumstances such as terrorism concerns, can the same be said for a place of business? The Supreme Court has answered that question:

> The Warrant Clause of the Fourth Amendment protects commercial buildings as well as private homes. To hold otherwise would belie the origin of that Amendment, and the American colonial experience. . . . "[T]he Fourth Amendment's commands grew in large measure out of the colonists' experience with the writs of assistance. . . . [that] granted sweeping power to customs officials and other agents of the king to search at large for smuggled goods.". . . Against this background, it is untenable that the ban on warrantless searches was not intended to shield places of business as well as of residence.[22]

The following case involves a challenge to the constitutionality of a warrant to search a business for evidence of fraud and other crimes.

U.S. v. Gawrysiak 972 F. Supp. 853 (D.N.J. 1997) Affirmed 178 F.3d 1281 (3d Cir. 1999)

Judge Simandle

This matter is before the court upon the pretrial motion of defendant Edmund Danzig to suppress evidence obtained during a search conducted on October 24, 1996, at his business premises. Defendant Danzig has been charged in an indictment with one count of wire fraud, in violation of 18 U.S.C. § 1343 . . .

FACTUAL BACKGROUND

On October 18, 1996, agents from the Federal Bureau of Investigation ("FBI") obtained a warrant to search the business premises of defendant Danzig in Sarasota, Florida. The warrant was issued by United States Magistrate Judge Mark A. Pizzo of the Middle District of Florida, in Tampa, on the basis of a 24-page affidavit filed with the court by Special Agent Lynn Billings of the FBI.

By its terms, the warrant imposed four primary limitations on what items could be seized from defendant Danzig's place of business. First, the agents were only permitted to seize evidence of violations of the following federal criminal statutes: 18 U.S.C. § 371 (conspiracy), 18 U.S.C. § 1343 (wire fraud), 18 U.S.C. § 1621 (perjury), and 18 U.S.C. § 1623 (false declarations). Second, the warrant encompassed evidence concerning crimes committed by Edmund Danzig, Patrick Gawrysiak, Thomas Fox, and their co-conspirators only. Third, the warrant only encompassed evidence of these crimes committed by those individuals between 1992 and 1995. Fourth, the warrant explained that the evidence to be seized had to pertain to one of 16 enumerated persons or entities, such as "Edmund R. Danzig," "Terra Ceia Ventures, Inc.," or "Jonathan Bowers." . . .

The affidavit submitted to Magistrate Judge Pizzo, subscribed by Special Agent Lynn M. Billings, gave the details of pervasive fraud investigations being conducted by the FBI's Special Agent Wadsworth in New Jersey and Special Agent Lynn Williams in Virginia targeting Patrick Gawrysiak and identifying Danzig as a co-conspirator. Gawrysiak, using the alias Gray, claimed to be the principal of Great American Raceways International, Inc. ("GARI"), which issued forged GARI bonds falsely claimed to be backed by U.S. Treasury bonds. Danzig was described as President of Terra Ceia Ventures, Inc., a financially troubled company that had undertaken a real estate development project on Terra Ceia Island, Florida,

for which Danzig and Gawrysiak sought interim financing ("bridge financing") . . .

The affidavit laid out the contours of four known frauds allegedly involving Danzig occurring between 1992 and January 1996, which were:

1. A scheme involving misappropriation of at least $250,000 as "loans" from Moors & Cabot brokerage accounts by Thomas Fox to Edmund Danzig in 1992 and 1993.

2. A scheme involving a $60,000 loan from Jonathan Bowers in 1993 for bridge financing for the Terra Ceia project, in which Danzig allegedly falsely represented to Bowers that a $100,000 GARI bond secured repayment of Bowers's note when in fact Danzig knew the GARI bonds to be worthless

3. A scheme to gain a $1 million loan from Citizen's Bank to be collateralized by Gawrysiak's forged GARI bonds in May and June 1993.

4. A scheme to falsely represent to victim Paul Maillis that Danzig had $40 million in financing, and that Maillis's loan to Danzig would be backed by the worthless GARI bonds.

The affidavit supporting the warrant also attached numerous exhibits as examples of the forgeries and misrepresentations mentioned in the affidavit.

* * * * *

The affidavit demonstrated that evidence of Danzig's culpability for these schemes was likely to be found at his office, as well as evidence implicating others in these crimes even if Danzig is himself innocent.

* * * * *

On October 24, 1996, FBI agents executed the search, seizing from defendant's place of work approximately five boxes of various materials as well as copies of defendant's computer files.

In moving to suppress the seized items, defendant Danzig alleges primarily that (1) the search warrant issued by Judge Pizzo was overbroad and therefore invalid and (2) the law enforcement agents conducting the search acted in bad faith and with the intent to seize items beyond the scope of the warrant.

* * * * *

[FBI agent] Wadsworth testified that before commencing the search, the other five agents participating in the search met with him to discuss how to conduct the search at the Sarasota FBI at 8:00 AM. The meeting lasted approximately 30 minutes. Agent Billings gave a presentation about the search plan and made the warrant available to the others. For part of that time, Agent Wadsworth described to the other agents the type of fraudulent schemes believed to be involved in this case....

According to Agent Wadsworth, the agents also reviewed the "Search Plan" that had been drafted by Agent Billings. The Search Plan set forth the background of the government's investigation of defendants Gawrysiak and Danzig, and described the responsibilities of each of the six agents participating in the search.

* * * * *

Agent Wadsworth further testified that the agents used substantial care during the search itself. The premises before, during, and after the search were photographed by Special Agent Blake. Also, because of concern that defendant Danzig's files might contain privileged attorney/client information, Agent Huff, who is also an attorney, was assigned the responsibility of functioning as a "Chinese Wall" during the search and seizure to ensure that the other agents would not come in contact with such potentially privileged documents....

According to Agent Wadsworth, out of approximately 200 boxes of documents in defendant Danzig's office, only five boxes of documents were ultimately seized. The parties agree, however, that the agents seized approximately half of the documents in the office that pertained to the time period of 1992 through 1995. The government explains this substantial 50 percent ratio by arguing that within that time period, defendant Danzig's business affairs were pervaded by fraud.

Danzig was allowed to be present during the search. Afterward, the FBI furnished a detailed inventory of all documents taken, along with copies of same; defendant has pointed to no document that is beyond the scope permitted by the warrant, nor has defendant indicated that any seized document is within a privilege.

* * * * *

DISCUSSION

Defendant's contentions in support of his motion to suppress may be grouped into two general areas of inquiry: (1) whether Magistrate Pizzo issued a valid warrant that was sufficiently particularized and not a "general warrant" and (2) whether the government's search team acted in good faith and properly executed the warrant.

I. The Validity of the Warrant Issued by Judge Pizzo

A. Whether the Warrant Was a "General Warrant"

One of the primary arguments made by defendant on this motion is that the warrant to search defendant's premises was so overbroad as to constitute an impermissible "general warrant."

The prohibition against general warrants stems directly from the text of the Fourth Amendment to the Constitution, which requires that all warrants describe "particularly . . . the place to be searched, and the persons or things to be seized." As interpreted by the Supreme Court, this language prohibits a "'general, exploratory rummaging in a person's belongings.'"

* * * * *

In this case, the warrant imposed four significant limitations that channeled the discretion of the searching FBI agents and provided the particularized description required by the Constitution. First, the warrant provided that the agents were only permitted to seize evidence of violations of the federal criminal statutes concerning conspiracy, wire fraud, perjury, and false declarations. . . . Second, the warrant encompassed only crimes committed by Edmund Danzig, Patrick Gawrysiak, Thomas Fox [or] by the entities under their control. . . .

Third, the warrant encompassed only the enumerated crimes committed by those individuals between 1992 and 1995. Fourth, the warrant provided that the evidence to be seized had to pertain to one of the 16 persons or entities listed in Attachment B to the warrant. . . .

Because of these limitations, this was not a warrant that provided the searching agents with unbridled discretion to rummage through defendant's possessions in search of any evidence of criminal activity. That conclusion is confirmed by the small percentage of documents actually seized from defendant's premises, indicating that the warrant did have limits that could be and were applied by the agents conducting the search.

The scope of this warrant was indeed relatively broad. Broad phrasing in a warrant, however, does not necessarily render the warrant invalid. The court concludes that the breadth of the warrant in this case was justified by evidence before Judge Pizzo indicating that defendant Danzig's business operations were substantially pervaded by fraud during the time period in question.

* * * * *

B. Whether Magistrate Judge Pizzo Had Probable Cause to Issue the Warrant

Defendant also contends that the affidavit offered in support of the warrant did not provide probable cause concerning certain portions of the warrant.

* * * * *

In this case, the government has easily demonstrated that Judge Pizzo had probable cause to issue the warrant authorizing the search of defendant Danzig's premises. The affidavit and appendix of documents filed in support of the warrant provide significant detail concerning how each of the 16 entities/persons listed in Attachment B materially relates to the fraudulent schemes allegedly carried out by Gawrysiak and Danzig between 1992 and 1995. There was ample reason to believe that evidence concerning these crimes would be found in these premises at this time.

* * * * *

[The Court's discussion of the conduct of the agents in carrying out the search is omitted.] [The defendant's motion to suppress is denied.]

Questions

1. What reasoning and evidence allowed the Court to conclude that the warrant in *Gawrysiak* was sufficiently particularized as to meet constitutional requirements?

2. What reasoning and evidence supported the *Gawrysiak* court's conclusion that the magistrate had probable cause to issue the warrant?

3. Joseph Burger owned and operated an automobile junkyard where, among other things, he dismantled autos and sold the parts. A New York statute permitted police to conduct warrantless inspections of auto junkyards. Without objection by Burger, police conducted a warrantless inspection of his business. The inspection revealed stolen vehicles and stolen parts. Burger was charged with possession of stolen property. In court, Burger moved to suppress the evidence arising from the search on the grounds that the New York statute under which the search was conducted was unconstitutional.

   a. Does the statute violate the Fourth Amendment's prohibition of unreasonable searches and seizures? Explain.

   b. Why do many states, including New York, explicitly permit the warrantless inspection of automobile junkyards? See *New York v. Joseph Burger,* 482 U.S. 691 (1987).

4. Occupational Safety and Health Administration (OSHA) inspectors received permission from the Army Corps of Engineers to inspect a federal construction site where an accident had occurred. The contractor declined consent, but OSHA secured a federal district court order allowing inspection. OSHA found some obvious violations, but others were apparent only after initial observations led to follow-up interviews with employees and closer looks at equipment. The contractor objected to the search on Fourth Amendment grounds.

   a. Explain the nature of that objection.

   b. Decide the case. See *National Engineering & Contracting Co. v. Occupational Safety and Health Administration,* 928 F.2d 762 (6th Cir. 1991).

The Fifth Amendment

Takings—Eminent Domain

The Fifth Amendment prohibits the taking of private property for *public use without just compensation* for the owner. In cases where owners do not want to sell, governments often use their power of *eminent domain* to take private property for public uses such as building highways, bike trails, and parks, while providing just compensation. But what about the situation where the condemned property is to be used for a *private* purpose? Communities across America, hungry for an improved tax base and more jobs, have made the practice routine; but are they violating the Fifth Amendment rights of the property owners? The following 5–4 Supreme Court decision involves a challenge to a New London, Connecticut, plan to clear a portion of the city to make way for an office/research park along with a waterfront hotel, conference center, residences, a marina, and a riverwalk. Small businesses and residences were to make room for bigger, more successful ventures providing a stronger tax base for New London.

Kelo v. City of New London, Connecticut Supreme Court of the United States 545 U.S. 469

LEGAL BRIEFCASE

Justice Stevens

In 2000 the city of New London approved a development plan that, in the words of the Supreme Court of Connecticut, was "projected to create in excess of 1,000 jobs, to increase tax and other revenues, and to revitalize an economically distressed city, including its downtown and waterfront areas" (843 A.2d 500, 507 (2004)). In assembling the land needed for this project, the city's development agent has purchased property from willing sellers and proposes to use the power of eminent domain to acquire the remainder of the property from unwilling owners in exchange for just compensation. The question presented is whether the city's proposed disposition of this property qualifies as a "public use" within the meaning of the Takings Clause of the Fifth Amendment to the Constitution.

I

The city of New London (hereinafter City) sits at the junction of the Thames River and the Long Island Sound in southeastern Connecticut. Decades of economic decline led a state agency in 1990 to designate the City a "distressed municipality." In 1996 the Federal Government closed the Naval Undersea Warfare Center, which had been located in the Fort Trumbull area of the City and had employed over 1,500 people. In 1998 the City's unemployment rate was nearly double that of the State, and its population of just under 24,000 residents was at its lowest since 1920.

These conditions prompted state and local officials to target New London, and particularly its Fort Trumbull area, for economic revitalization. To this end, respondent New London

Development Corporation (NLDC), a private nonprofit entity established some years earlier to assist the City in planning economic development, was reactivated. In January 1998 the State authorized a $5.35 million bond issue to support the NLDC's planning activities and a $10 million bond issue toward the creation of a Fort Trumbull State Park. In February the pharmaceutical company Pfizer Inc. announced that it would build a $300 million research facility on a site immediately adjacent to Fort Trumbull; local planners hoped that Pfizer would draw new business to the area. Upon obtaining state-level approval, the NLDC finalized an integrated development plan focused on 90 acres of the Fort Trumbull area.

The Fort Trumbull area is situated on a peninsula that juts into the Thames River. The area comprises approximately 115 privately owned properties, as well as the 32 acres of land formerly occupied by the naval facility (Trumbull State Park now occupies 18 of those 32 acres). The development plan encompasses seven parcels. Parcel 1 is designated for a waterfront conference hotel at the center of a "small urban village" that will include restaurants and shopping. . . . Parcel 2 will be the site of approximately 80 new residences organized into an urban neighborhood and linked by public walkway to the remainder of the development, including the state park. This parcel also includes space reserved for a new U.S. Coast Guard Museum. Parcel 3, which is located immediately north of the Pfizer facility, will contain at least 90,000 square feet of research and development office space. Parcel 4A is a 2.4-acre site that will be used either to support the adjacent state park, by providing parking or retail services for visitors, or to support the nearby marina. Parcel 4B will include a renovated marina, as well as the final stretch of the riverwalk.

Parcels 5, 6, and 7 will provide land for office and retail space, parking, and water-dependent commercial uses.

* * * * *

The city council approved the plan in January 2000 and designated the NLDC as its development agent in charge of implementation. The city council also authorized the NLDC to purchase property or to acquire property by exercising eminent domain in the City's name. The NLDC successfully negotiated the purchase of most of the real estate in the 90-acre area, but its negotiations with petitioners failed. As a consequence, in November 2000 the NLDC initiated the condemnation proceedings that gave rise to this case.

II

Petitioner Susette Kelo has lived in the Fort Trumbull area since 1997. She has made extensive improvements to her house, which she prizes for its water view. Petitioner Wilhelmina Dery was born in her Fort Trumbull house in 1918 and has lived there her entire life. Her husband Charles has lived in the house since they married some 60 years ago. In all, the nine petitioners own 15 properties in Fort Trumbull. . . . There is no allegation that any of these properties is blighted or otherwise in poor condition; rather, they were condemned only because they happen to be located in the development area.

In December 2000 petitioners brought this action in the New London Superior Court. They claimed, among other things, that the taking of their properties would violate the "public use" restriction in the Fifth Amendment. After a seven-day bench trial, the Superior Court granted a permanent restraining order prohibiting the taking of the properties located in parcel 4A (park or marina support). It, however, denied petitioners relief as to the properties located in parcel 3 (office space).

After the Superior Court ruled, both sides took appeals to the Supreme Court of Connecticut. That court held that all of the City's proposed takings were valid.

* * * * *

III

Two polar propositions are perfectly clear. On the one hand, it has long been accepted that the sovereign may not take the property of *A* for the sole purpose of transferring it to another private party *B*, even though *A* is paid just compensation. On the other hand, it is equally clear that a State may transfer property from one private party to another if future "use by the public" is the purpose of the taking; the condemnation of land for a railroad is a familiar example. Neither of these propositions, however, determines the disposition of this case.

As for the first proposition, the City would no doubt be forbidden from taking petitioners' land for the purpose of conferring a private benefit on a particular party. Nor would the City be allowed to take property under the mere pretext of a public purpose, when its actual purpose was to bestow a private benefit. The takings before us, however, would be executed pursuant to a "carefully considered" development plan. The trial judge and all the members of the Supreme Court of Connecticut agreed that there was no evidence of an illegitimate purpose in this case.

* * * * *

On the other hand, this is not a case in which the City is planning to open the condemned land—at least not in its entirety—to use by the general public. Nor will the private lessees of the land in any sense be required to operate like common carriers, making their services available to all comers. But although such a projected use would be sufficient to satisfy the public use requirement, this "Court long ago rejected any literal requirement that condemned property be put into use for the general public." Indeed, while many state courts in the mid-19th century endorsed "use by the public" as the proper definition of public use, that narrow view steadily eroded over time. Not only was the "use by the public" test difficult to administer (e.g., what proportion of the public need have access to the property? at what price?), but it proved to be impractical given the diverse and always evolving needs of society. Accordingly, when this Court began applying the Fifth Amendment to the States at the close of the 19th century, it embraced the broader and more natural interpretation of public use as "public purpose."

* * * * *

The disposition of this case therefore turns on the question whether the City's development plan serves a "public purpose." Without exception, our cases have defined that concept broadly, reflecting our longstanding policy of deference to legislative judgments in this field.

In *Berman v. Parker,* this Court upheld a redevelopment plan targeting a blighted area of Washington, D.C., in which most of the housing for the area's 5,000 inhabitants was beyond repair. Under the plan, the area would be condemned and part of it utilized for the construction of streets, schools, and other public facilities. The remainder of the land would be leased or sold to private parties for the purpose of redevelopment, including the construction of low-cost housing.

* * * * *

IV

Those who govern the City were not confronted with the need to remove blight in the Fort Trumbull area, but their determination that the area was sufficiently distressed to justify a program of economic rejuvenation is entitled to our deference. The City has carefully formulated an economic development plan that it believes will provide appreciable benefits to the community, including—but by no means limited to—new jobs and increased tax revenue. . . . Given the comprehensive character of the plan, the thorough deliberation that preceded its adoption, and the limited scope of our review, it is appropriate for us to resolve the challenges of the individual owners, not on a piecemeal basis, but rather in light of the entire plan. Because that plan unquestionably serves a public purpose, the takings challenged here satisfy the public use requirement of the Fifth amendment.

To avoid this result, petitioners urge us to adopt a new bright-line rule that economic development does not qualify as a public use. Putting aside the unpersuasive suggestion that the City's plan will provide only purely economic benefits, neither precedent nor logic supports petitioners' proposal. Promoting economic development is a traditional and long accepted function of government.

* * * * *

In affirming the City's authority to take petitioners' properties, we do not minimize the hardship that condemnations may entail, notwithstanding the payment of just compensation. We emphasize that nothing in our opinion precludes any State from placing further restrictions on its exercise of the takings power. Indeed, many States already impose "public use" requirements that are stricter than the federal baseline.

* * * * *

Affirmed.

AFTERWORD—PROPERTY RIGHTS REVOLUTION?

The *Kelo* decision was an angry disappointment for property rights advocates. A big government taking of Americans' life-long homes, even for just compensation, is a powerful and frightening image. Clearly, however, governments need, and have long exercised, substantial authority to take property for economic development. Now in response to *Kelo,* states and localities are using their legal and democratic systems to achieve an appropriate and difficult balance between important property rights and important public purposes.

As one scholar observed, "The backlash against *Kelo* is the largest against any Supreme Court decision in decades, and the legislative response is possibly the most extensive to any Supreme Court decision in history."[23] Subsequent to *Kelo,* 28 states have passed laws to limit takings, but many of those apparently provide little actual protection for property owners.[24] Ten states, however, have approved referenda by popular vote that may offer firmer property rights protection.[25] Further, courts have shown some inclination to demand more careful justifications for takings. For example, the Ohio Supreme Court unanimously ruled that economic development alone is an insufficient justification under the Ohio Constitution for taking private property, and a City Council determination that the area was "deteriorating" was too vague, unclear and ambiguous thus violating the constitutional standard of "void for vagueness."[26] As a result, the Court stopped a $125 million redevelopment project in the Cincinnati suburb of Norwood where three owners sued to preserve their property. Most of the 70 home owners in the area had sold their property voluntarily and at prices substantially greater than their appraised value.[27] [For property rights analysis and updates, see **www.ij.org**]

Questions

1. What reasoning was offered by Justice Stevens to support the majority view that the New London development complied with due process requirements?

2. *a.* What was the issue, the central question, in this case and how did the majority answer that question?

   b. How would you expect the dissent to answer that question?

3. From the dissenting point of view, what harm is likely to emerge from this decision?

4. Marilyn and James Nollan applied for a permit to replace their beachfront home with a larger structure. The California Coastal Commission agreed on the condition that the Nollans grant an easement on their beach that would allow the public to cross that property and thus facilitate movement between the public beaches that lay on both sides of the Nollan beach. The Nollans sued, claiming a violation of the Takings Clause. Decide. Explain. See *Nollan v. California Coastal Commission,* 483 U.S. 825 (1987).

5. Tina Bennis sued when Wayne County (Detroit), Michigan, authorities took the car she jointly owned with her husband after police arrested him for receiving oral sex from a prostitute while parked in the car. A 1925 antinuisance law permitted the seizure, but Tina Bennis claimed it amounted to an unconstitutional taking because she was an innocent half owner of the 1977 Pontiac for which the couple had paid $600. Bennis's claim eventually reached the U.S. Supreme Court. Decide the case. Explain. See *Bennis v. Michigan,* 116 S. Ct. 994 (1996).

Takings—Regulatory

We have seen how the law treats situations where the government uses its power of eminent domain to condemn property for either public or private use and pays just compensation. What happens when the government does not take the property but rather *regulates* it in a manner that deprives that property of some or all of its economic usefulness? For example, without providing just compensation, can a state lawfully limit the amount a landlord can charge for rent in an effort to preserve low-income housing? Can the state forbid billboards to enhance roadside beauty?

These *regulatory takings,* whether temporary or permanent, normally do not require government compensation because doing so would severely impair the state's ability to govern in an orderly manner. Nonetheless, in recent years the courts have been more aggressive about requiring just compensation for some regulatory takings. Three broad classes of such takings have emerged in court decisions. [For an "introduction to the takings issue," see **http://www.envpoly.org/takings**]

1. **Total takings.** If a governmental body acts in a way that takes *all of the economic value* of a property or permanently physically invades the property, the taking requires just compensation unless the government is (1) preventing a nuisance or (2) the regulation was permissible under property law at the time of the purchase of the property. When the South Carolina Coastal Commission passed erosion rules having the effect of preventing David Lucas from building any permanent structure on his $975,000 beachfront lots, Lucas sued, claiming a Fifth Amendment violation. The U.S. Supreme Court agreed with Lucas and held that a taking requiring just compensation had occurred because the state had deprived Lucas of *all* economically beneficial use of the property, and the property did not fall in one of the two exceptions.[28]

> The South Carolina Coastal Commission passed erosion rules having the effect of preventing David Lucas from building any permanent structure on his $975,000 beachfront lots

2. **Exaction/mitigation.** A second class of regulatory takings involves situations where the government allows land development only if the owner dedicates some property interest (called an *exaction*) or money (called a *mitigation* or *impact fee*) to the government. Thus if you are developing land for housing, the city government might require that you devote a portion of that land to parks. Or you might be required to pay a fee to help the city meet the recreational needs of the citizens your development will be housing. The Supreme Court dealt with just such a case in *Dolan v. Tigard.*[29] Florence Dolan, owner of a plumbing and electrical supply store in Tigard, Oregon, applied for a city permit to nearly double the size of her store and to pave her parking lot. Concerned with increased traffic and water runoff due to the proposed expansion, the city granted the permit, subject to a pair of conditions: (1) Dolan was to dedicate the portion of her property that lay within the 100-year floodplain to the city to improve drainage for the creek that ran along her property, and (2) she was to dedicate an additional 15-foot strip of her land adjacent to the floodplain for use as a bicycle path/walkway to relieve traffic congestion. Dolan sought a variance from the requirements, but her petition was denied. She sued, and her case reached the U.S. Supreme Court, which ruled that government can compel a dedication of private property to public use where it can establish two factors: (1) A nexus or relationship

between the government's legitimate purpose (flood and traffic control in *Dolan*) and the condition imposed (the land Dolan was to dedicate to public purposes) and, (2) a "rough proportionality" between the burden imposed (the land given over to public use) and the impact of the development (increased water runoff and increased traffic).[30] The Supreme Court, in a firm defense of private property rights, ruled that Tigard had failed to meet those standards, and Dolan won the case.

3. **Partial takings.** Many takings problems are neither total takings nor exactions, but rather fall into a case-by-case analysis that depends greatly on the facts in each instance. The primary considerations in these cases are threefold:

1. The importance of the government interest (health, safety, or the like) that generated the regulation.
2. The economic effect on the landowner.
3. The landowner's legitimate, investment-backed expectations at the time of purchase.

Broadly here, the Court is simply asking whether the regulation goes "too far" in burdening the property owner. That is, should the property owner bear the costs of the regulation or should the public pay compensation to the property owner in exchange for the value (a public beach, a park, an unobstructed view, or whatever) derived from the regulation.[31]

Zoning in the Sixth Century

Government restraints on property development are not merely a modern imposition, as we learn from the following description of a zoning law in the Byzantine Empire:

Next came the first zoning law for the beach. Coastal vistas were so cherished, and the competition for them so keen, that by the sixth century the Emperor Justinian the Great was compelled to pass an ordinance barring construction within 100 feet of the shore to protect sea views.

Source: Lena Lencek and Gideon Bosker, *The Beach: The History of Paradise on Earth* (New York: Penguin Group, 1998). p. 31.

The Fourteenth Amendment

Due Process

The Due Process Clauses of both the Fifth Amendment (applying to the federal government) and the Fourteenth Amendment (applying to the states) forbid the government to deprive citizens of life, liberty, or property without due process of law.

Substantive Due Process

Laws that arbitrarily and unfairly infringe on fundamental personal rights and liberties such as privacy, voting, and the various freedoms specified in the Bill of Rights may be challenged on due process grounds. Basically, the purpose of the law must be so compelling as to outweigh the intrusion on personal liberty or the law will be struck down. For example, the U.S. Supreme Court ruled that a Connecticut statute forbidding the use of contraceptives violated the constitutional right to privacy (although the word *privacy* itself does not appear in the U.S. Constitution).[32] By judicial interpretation, the Fourteenth Amendment Due Process Clause "absorbs" the fundamental liberties of the *federal* Constitution and prohibits *state* laws (in this case, the Connecticut contraceptive ban) that abridge those fundamental liberties such as privacy.

Procedural Due Process

Basically, procedural due process means that the government must provide *notice* and a *fair hearing* before taking an action affecting a citizen's life, liberty, or property. A fair hearing might require, among others, the right to present evidence, the right to a decision maker free of bias, and the right to appeal. However, the precise nature of procedural due process depends on the situation. A murder trial requires meticulous attention to procedural fairness; an administrative hearing to appeal a housing officer's decision to banish a student from a dormitory, while required to meet minimal constitutional standards, can be more forgiving in its procedural niceties.

Due Process and Punitive Damages

Dr. Ira Gore purchased a new, 1990 BMW but was not told that the car had been repainted due to some minor predelivery damage. BMW's corporate policy was to advise dealers only of those predelivery repairs that exceeded 3 percent of the car's suggested retail price. Gore learned of the repainting and sued, claiming he was a victim of fraud. The Alabama jury awarded Gore $4,000 in compensatory damages and $4 million in punitive damages. The $4 million award was reduced to $2 million by the Alabama Supreme Court, but BMW took the case to the U.S. Supreme Court, which found the award "grossly excessive" in relation to the state's legitimate interest in punishing and deterring wrongful conduct. The Court employed a three-factor test to determine that the award was grossly excessive and thus violative of the Due Process Clause: (1) the reprehensibility of the defendant's conduct, (2) the ratio between the plaintiff's compensatory damages and the punitive damages, and (3) a comparison between the punitive damage award and any civil or criminal penalties the state could impose for similar misconduct. By all three standards, the award was so extreme as to violate BMW's due process rights.[33] In 1997 the Alabama Supreme Court cut Gore's award to $50,000.

> The Alabama jury awarded Gore $4,000 in compensatory damages and $4 million in punitive damages

Big punitive awards continued to rise despite *Gore,* and the Supreme Court in 2003 strengthened and clarified its *Gore* reasoning in *State Farm v. Campbell,*[34] where a $1 million compensatory award led to a $145 million punitive award. The Court found that the award violated the Due Process Clause and suggested that a 4–1 ratio between punitive and compensatory damages, while not "binding," should be "instructive," while ratios higher than 9–1 would be appropriate only in special circumstances. On remand, the lower court then reduced punitive damages in the *State Farm* case to $9 million.

The business community is encouraged by the Supreme Court rulings, but a recent study found plaintiffs winning punitive damages in only 3.3 percent of the personal injury cases studied.[35] So perhaps the issue is not as significant as claimed by corporate interests; and perhaps substantial punitive damages are necessary to correct harmful behavior.

Exxon Valdez Oil Spill

Corporate America earned a significant victory in 2008 when the United States Supreme Court by a 5-3 margin reduced the punitive damages award in the Exxon Valdez oil spill from $2.5 billion to $507.5 million, an amount approximately equal to what Exxon had already spent to compensate Alaskans for their losses. Justice Souter, writing for the majority, said that a ratio of no more than one to one between punitive and compensatory damages was appropriate under maritime law. The decision did not reach the constitutional due process question, thus the issue of whether the one-to-one ratio will apply to cases beyond maritime law is unclear. The decision does appear to reflect the Court's continuing interest in curbing punitive damages.

With interest, the reduced punitive award is expected to total about $1 billion, much of which will go to commercial fishing firms and lawyers while most of the 33,000 plaintiffs will receive about $15,000 each. Exxon says that it has already spent $3.4 billion in response to the incident that polluted 1,300 miles of coastline and killed hundreds of thousands of seabirds and marine animals. Exxon's 2007 profits totaled $40.6 billion.

The original award was intended to punish Exxon for its role in the 1989 accident where its ship, the Exxon Valdez captained by a lapsed alcoholic Joseph Hazlewood, hit a reef and spilled an estimated 11 million gallons of crude oil in the pristine fishing waters of Prince William Sound, Alaska. Witnesses reportedly indicated that Hazlewood drank five double vodkas on the night of the spill and left the bridge at a crucial moment.

Sources: Exxon Shipping Company v. Baker, 2008 U.S. LEXIS 5363; Adam Liptak, "Damages Cut Against Exxon in Valdez Case," *New York Times*, June 26, 2008 [**www.nytimes.com**]; Erika Bolstad, "Exxon Valdez Damages Cut to $507.5 Million," *Anchorage Daily News*, June 25, 2008 [**http://www.adn.com/exxonvaldez/story/446057.html**]

Equal Protection

The Fourteenth Amendment provides that no state shall "deny to any person within its jurisdiction the equal protection of the laws." The Due Process Clause of the Fifth Amendment has been interpreted to afford that same protection from the federal government. Fundamentally, these laws forbid a government from treating one person (including a corporation) differently than another without a rational basis for doing so. Most notably, the Equal Protection and Due Process Clauses have played an enormous role in attacking discrimination (see Chapter 13), but they can also significantly impact routine business practice in many ways. For example, can we lawfully impose higher taxes on a gambling casino than we impose on the sale of groceries? Or can we require the oil industry to follow more rigorous environmental standards than we expect of coal mines? In general, the answer to these questions is yes, but only if the legislation can pass the rational basis test. If not, such legislation would be unconstitutional and unenforceable.

How Many Renters?

Trying to reduce the flow of university students into certain portions of the community, Ames, Iowa, home of Iowa State University, passed a zoning ordinance that permitted only single-family residences in specified areas. Under the ordinance, "family" was defined as any number of related persons or no more than three unrelated persons. The Ames Rental Property Association challenged the constitutionality of the ordinance.

Questions
1. Describe the constitutional claim raised by the plaintiffs.
2. Criticize the Ames' standards for achieving its housing goals.
3. Decide the case. Explain.

Source: *Ames Rental Property Association v. City of Ames*, 736 N.W.2d 255 (Ia. S.Ct. 2007).

Gay and Lesbian Marriage?

Recently, the most interesting and visible equal protection dispute has been the "cultural war" over gay marriage and civil unions. The Vermont Supreme Court made headlines across America and around the world in late 1999 when it ruled that gay and lesbian couples in that state had been denied equal protection of the law under the Vermont constitution and were entitled to the same legal benefits and protections as heterosexual couples.[36] The Court did not legalize gay marriages, but it did instruct the state legislature to find a way to extend equal protection under the law to gay couples. The legislature did so in 2000 by approving *civil unions,* which are not marriages under Vermont law, but which allow same-sex couples to join in a legally recognized relationship that confers all of the legal benefits, protections, and duties of marriage—including, for example, joint property and inheritance rights and child support duties. Civil unions are not recognized under federal law, and the federal government and many states have passed "defense of marriage laws" that specifically define marriage as a union between a man and a woman.

The high courts in Massachusetts (2003) and California (2008) have both ruled that lesbian and gay couples have the same marital rights as heterosexuals. (At this writing, Californians were expected to vote on an initiative designed to reverse that state Supreme Court decision.) In recent years, Connecticut, New Jersey, and New Hampshire have approved civil union laws and a few other states have domestic partner laws or something similar that offer protections like civil unions. Now an ongoing judicial and legislative war looms. At this writing, 45 states have passed constitutional amendments or laws specifically forbidding gay marriage.[37] Congress has considered a constitutional amendment to prohibit same-sex marriage, but Republican supporters of the measure have been unable to generate the two thirds majority necessary to send the measure along for ratification by the states. A 2007 Pew Research Center poll found that 55 percent of Americans oppose same-sex marriage, but a 2006 Pew poll found 54 percent approval of civil unions.[38] At some point, perhaps the U.S. Supreme Court will address the issues. The federal Constitution along with most state constitutions could be amended to protect "traditional" marriage. If so, will gays and lesbians have been denied equal protection under the law? And at a more fundamental level, will our moral lives be stronger or weaker?

PRACTICING ETHICS) Gay and Lesbian Marriage

An editorial in the *Syracuse Post-Standard* (New York) noted the immense change portended by the gay marriage movement:

> In coming months, gay marriage ceremonies will continue in Massachusetts with the backing of that state's Supreme Court. Civil unions will proliferate in Vermont, where both sides agree the subject has become a nonissue. Time will pass as gay Americans continue to go to work, pay taxes, raise families, and participate in community and political life. And more and more Americans will get used to the idea. The times they are indeed a-changing.[39]

Morally and ethically speaking, which side is "right" about gay marriage? And how do we decide? Let's look at some questions that help us sort through this moral thicket:

1. What issues should one consider in deciding whether gay marriage is morally defensible?

2. Is a civil union arrangement like the one in Vermont an acceptable "middle ground"?

3. If the American people ultimately favor gay and lesbian marriage, could we then consider it a morally defensible practice?

4. The 2000 United States census indicated that approximately 1 million children are being raised by same-sex couples, and 47 states allow gays and lesbians to adopt children.[40] Are those children at moral risk?

5. If scholarly studies ultimately demonstrate that homosexuality and lesbianism are substantially commanded by genetic characteristics, would we be morally required to permit same-sex marriage?

Gay Marriage Abroad

In 2001, The Netherlands became the first nation to legalize gay marriage. Belgium did the same in 2002, followed by Spain and Canada in 2005 and South Africa in 2006. Denmark, France, Norway, Sweden, the United Kingdom, and Germany are among 18 European nations offering domestic partner/civil union rights.

Source: "Policies Pertaining to Same-Sex Marriages, Civil Unions, and Domestic Partnerships" [**http://www.infoplease.com/ipa/A0933870.html**].

Internet Exercise

At the First Amendment Center, read "About the First Amendment" [**http://www.firstamendmentcenter.org/about.aspx?item=about_firstamd**]. Explain the importance of the First Amendment and why Americans are divided about its application.

Chapter Questions

1. Members of the Jefferson County High School, Tennessee varsity football team circulated a petition that said: "I hate Coach Euvard [sic] and I don't want to play for him." Thereafter, all team members were asked if they were involved. Euverard dismissed

four players who admitted they signed the petition and refused to apologize for doing so. The players who signed the petition but apologized were retained on the team. The four dismissed players filed suit. (a). Explain their primary legal claim. (b). Decide the case. Explain. See *Lowery v. Euverard,* 497 F.3d 584 (6th Cir. 2007).

2. The American Civil Liberties Union of Ohio challenged the constitutionality of Ohio's state motto, "With God, All Things Are Possible."
   a. Explain the nature of that constitutional challenge.
   b. Decide the case. Explain. See *American Civil Liberties Union of Ohio v. Capitol Square Review and Advisory Board,* 243 F.3d 289 (6th Cir. 2001).

3. Several city ordinances in Arkansas made it illegal for "any person to place a handbill or advertisement on any other person's vehicle parked on public property within city limits." Church members contested the constitutionality of the ordinances, which prevented them from lawfully placing religious handbills on parked cars. Decide. Explain. See *Krantz v. City of Fort Smith,* 160 F.3d 1214 (8th Cir. 1998).

4. The Georgia Outdoor Advertising Control Act, in essence, prohibits any off-premises outdoor advertising of commercial establishments where nudity is exhibited. Cafe Erotica lawfully provides food and adult entertainment, including nude dancing, and advertises those services on billboards. Cafe Erotica challenged the constitutionality of the Advertising Control Act. Decide. Explain. See *Georgia v. Cafe Erotica,* 507 S.E.2d 732 (Ga. S. Ct. 1998).

5. Colorado School of Law Professor Pierre Schlag, summarizing the central theme raised by Ronald K. L. Collins and David M. Skover in their book *The Death of Discourse:*

   > Stated most broadly, the predicament is this: with the perfection of communications technology, the refinement of capitalist rationality, and the intensification of market-created desire, the resulting culture is one that renders its own ostensible steering mechanism—namely, reasoned discourse—impossible. This broad scale rendition of the predicament is quite bleak, for there is no exit; everyone is included. We are all living in a culture that is, quite literally, doing itself in, mindlessly devoting itself to frivolous self-amusement: the unbridled pursuit of thrills, chills, titillations, fun, and ultimately, death.[41]

   Do you agree with the argument that reasoned discourse is now impossible in our culture of advanced communications and obsessive, market-induced desire for pleasure? Explain.

6. The Labor Department conducts regular investigations of business records to ensure compliance with the wages and hours provisions (such as higher pay for overtime) of the Fair Labor Standards Act. When a compliance officer sought to inspect certain financial records at the Lone Steer restaurant/motel in Steele, North Dakota, the restaurant declined his admittance until the government detailed the scope of the investigation. Not receiving a satisfactory response, the Lone Steer demanded a search warrant prior to inspection. As provided for under the FLSA, the government secured an administrative subpoena, which, unlike a search warrant, does not require judicial approval. Once again, Lone Steer denied admission. The government then filed suit. Decide. Explain. See *Donovan v. Lone Steer,* 464 U.S. 408 (1984).

7. This chapter noted a number of decisions affording protection to commercial speech. Why are corporations unlikely to begin using their vast resources to speak out on the wide range of public issues from abortion to organized prayer in schools to the death penalty? Explain.

8. An Erie, Pennsylvania, public indecency ordinance prohibited knowingly or intentionally appearing in public in a "state of nudity." Pap's, the owners of Kandyland, an Erie establishment featuring totally nude dancers, challenged the constitutionality of the ordinance.

   a. Explain the nature of that constitutional challenge.

   b. Decide the case. Explain. See *City of Erie v. Pap's A.M.,* 529 U.S. 277 (2000).

9. An individual and a group applied to the Chicago Park District for permits to hold rallies advocating the legalization of marijuana. The Park District, a municipal agency, required a permit to conduct a public assembly, parade, or other event involving more than 50 individuals. Applications for permits had to be processed within 28 days, and denials had to be clearly explained. Denials could be appealed to the general superintendent and then to the courts. The Park District denied some of the permits for pro-marijuana rallies. Those denied filed suit, claiming the Park District permit rules were unconstitutional.

   a. What constitutional challenge was raised by the plaintiffs?

   b. Decide the case. Explain. See *Thomas and Windy City Hemp Development Board v. Chicago Park District,* 534 U.S. 316 (2002).

10. Tanner and others sought to distribute handbills in the interior mall of the Lloyd Corporation shopping center. The literature concerned an anti–Vietnam War meeting. Lloyd Corporation had a strict rule forbidding handbilling. When security guards terminated distributions within the center, Tanner, et al. claimed a violation of their First Amendment rights. Both the district court and the Court of Appeals found a violation of constitutional rights. The decision was appealed to the U.S. Supreme Court. Decide. Explain. See *Lloyd Corporation v. Tanner,* 407 U.S. 551 (1972).

11. Lancaster, California, located about 45 miles from Los Angeles, was trying to build its local economy but was tripped up by the United States Constitution. Costco, a big-box retailer, wanted to expand into next-door space leased to 99 Cents Only Stores. Costco told the city it would move to Palmdale if it could not expand. Lancaster tried to buy 99 Cents' lease, but the company refused. Lancaster then used its power of eminent domain to condemn the 99 Cents property for the purpose of making it available to Costco. The city noted that blight might follow if Costco left, and the city contrasted 99 Cents' under $40,000 per year in sales taxes generated with Costco's more than $400,000. 99 Cents then sued the city seeking an order blocking the effort to take the 99 Cents property.

   a. How would you have ruled on the case when it was tried in 2001? Explain.

   b. Would the result be any different today after the Supreme Court's 2005 decision in the New London, Connecticut, case? Explain. See *99 Cents Only Stores v. Lancaster Redevelopment Agency,* 237 F. Supp. 2d 1123 (C.D. Cal. 2001). Appeal dismissed, 2003 U.S. App. LEXIS 4197.

12. Long Island, New York, resident Stephanie Fuller was secretly videotaped by her landlord, who had installed a video camera in the smoke detector above her bed. Fuller's landlord was found guilty of trespassing and was fined $1,500 and sentenced to 280 hours of community service.
    a. Why was the landlord not charged with a more serious felony offense?
    b. After Fuller's experience, New York enacted a criminal unlawful surveillance statute; the statute includes language forbidding secret surveillance in places where the victim has "a reasonable expectation of privacy." What significance attaches to that language?

13. A California sales and use tax of 6 percent on all personal property sales was applied to the distribution of religious materials by religious organizations. The Jimmy Swaggart Ministries challenged the tax on constitutional grounds.
    a. What constitutional issue was raised by the plaintiff?
    b. Decide. Explain. See *Jimmy Swaggart Ministries v. Board of Equalization of California,* 493 U.S. 378 (1990).

14. Milwaukee prostitutes, who had been arrested on multiple occasions, sued to block the city from enforcing a court-ordered injunction that permanently enjoined them from engaging in certain specified activities in certain specified areas of the city. They were prohibited from "engaging in, beckoning to stop, or engaging male or female passersby in conversation, or stopping or attempting to stop motor vehicle operators by hailing, waving of arms or any other bodily gesture, or yelling in a loud voice" and other such activities. The women challenged the order on constitutional grounds.
    a. Explain the nature of that constitutional challenge.
    b. Decide the case. Explain. See *City of Milwaukee v. Burnette,* 637 N.W.2d 447 (Wis. App. 2001); 638 N.W.2d 590 (Wis. S. Ct. 2001).

15. Milagros Irizarry lived with the same man for more than two decades, during which time they raised two children. Irizarry, an employee of the Chicago public school system, received health benefits, but her male partner did not because the couple had not married. The school system provided health benefits to domestic partners of the same sex, but not to those of the opposite sex. Irizarry raised a constitutional challenge to the denial of benefits to her male partner.
    a. Explain the nature of that constitutional challenge.
    b. Decide the case. Explain. See *Irizarry v. Board of Education of the City of Chicago,* 251 F.3d 604 (7th Cir. 2001).

16. Fifteen-year-old Natalie Young, a lesbian, was sent to her New York City principal's office for wearing to school a T-shirt that said "Barbie is a lesbian." Young was suspended, and she sued the school.
    a. Was the suspension lawful? Explain.
    b. Could Young wear a shirt saying the war in Iraq is wrong?
    c. What about a shirt praising Osama bin Laden? Explain.

17. The sons of a murder victim brought a wrongful death/negligence action against a magazine, *Soldier of Fortune,* alleging that it had published an ad creating an unreasonable risk of violent crime. A former police officer had placed the ad offering his services as a bodyguard under the heading "Gun for Hire." The ad resulted in the

officer being hired to kill the plaintiffs' father. The ad included the phrases "professional mercenary," "very private," and a statement indicating that "all jobs" would be considered, but it also included a list of legitimate jobs that involved the use of a gun. The plaintiffs won the negligence action and were awarded a $4.3 million judgment. *Soldier of Fortune* appealed on First Amendment grounds. Decide. See *Braun v. Soldier of Fortune Magazine, Inc.*, 968 F.2d 1110 (11th Cir. 1992); cert. den. 113 S.Ct. 1028 (1993).

18. As you have read, "hate speech" (such as racist, sexist, or homophobic remarks) is generally protected by the First Amendment. Commercial speech, often in the form of intellectually empty, symbol- and emotion-laden advertisements, is also protected. The Madisonian idea of the First Amendment was to protect serious political discourse. Now the First Amendment seems often to protect hate speech and commercial babble. In a 1996 book review and commentary, lawyer Paul Reidinger raised the concern that we may have "too much" free speech. Reidinger said, "The question these days is not whether government threatens free speech, but whether free speech threatens us. . . . [T]here is a tidal wave of fetid speech washing over the American landscape." Has the marketplace of ideas failed? See Paul Reidinger, "Weighing Cost of Free Speech," *ABA Journal* 82 (January 1996), p. 88.

Notes

1. Portions of this history of the United States Constitution rely upon Gordon Lloyd, "Introduction to the Constitutional Convention," [**http://teachingamericanhistory.org/convention/intro.html**].

2. Jerre Williams, *Constitutional Analysis in a Nutshell* (St. Paul: West, 1979), p. 33.

3. *McCreary County v. ACLU*, 2005 U.S. LEXIS 5211, and *Van Orden v. Perry*, 2005 U.S. LEXIS 5215.

4. *Garcetti v. Ceballos*, 126 S.Ct. 1951 (2006).

5. *Tinker v. Des Moines School District*, 393 U.S. 503 (1969).

6. *Barrett v. University of Mississippi*, 232 F.3d 208 (5th Cir. 2000); cert. den. 531 U.S. 1052 (2000).

7. *Valentine v. Chrestensen*, 316 U.S. 52 (1942).

8. *Mainstream Marketing Services, Inc. v. Federal Trade Commission*, 358 F.3d 1228 (10th Cir. 2004).

9. *Mainstream Marketing Services, Inc. v. FTC*, 2004 U.S. LEXIS 5564 (2004).

10. See *Kasky v. Nike, Inc.*, 45 P. 3d 243 (2002). For a discussion of *Kasky* and commercial speech, see Ryan Long, "Big Foot, Big Mouth," *Legal Times*, June 23, 2003, p. 60.

11. Norman M. Cheektowaga, "And a Rude Gesture to You, Too, Judges," *Buffalo News*, February 5, 1998, p. 3B.

12. Robert Levy, "Equality for All Speech," *National Law Journal*, September 17, 2001, p. A21.

13. 367 U.S. 643.

14. *Hudson v. Michigan*, 126 S.Ct. 2159 (2006).

15. *Illinois v. Caballes*, 802 N.E. 2d 202 (Ill. S.Ct. 2003).

16. *Illinois v. Caballes*, 125 S.Ct. 834 (2005).

17. *Scott v. Harris*, 127 S.Ct. 1769 (2007).

18. *Los Angeles County, California v. Max Rettele*, 127 S.Ct. 1989 (2007).

19. *Board of Education of Pottawatomie County v. Earls,* 122 S.Ct. 2559 (2002).

20. *Earls v. Board of Education,* 242 F.3d 1264 (10th Cir. 2001).

21. *State of Washington v. Glas,* 2002 Wash. LEXIS 596.

22. *Marshall v. Barlow's,* 436 U.S. 307 (1978).

23. Ilya Somin, "The Limits of Backlash: Assessing the Political Response to Kelo," (March 2007). George Mason Law & Economics Research Paper No. 07-14. Available at SSRN: **http://ssrn.com/abstract=976298.**

24. Ibid.

25. Ibid.

26. *Norwood v. Horney*, 110 Ohio St. 3d 353 (Ohio S.Ct. 2007).

27. Ian Urbina, "Ohio Supreme Court Rejects Taking of Homes for Project," *The New York Times*, July 27, 2006 [**http://www.nytimes.com/2006/07/27/us/27ohio.html?th=&emc=th&. . . .**].

28. *Lucas v. So. Carolina Coastal Commission,* 112 S.Ct. 2886 (1992).

29. *Dolan v. City of Tigard,* 114 S.Ct. 2309 (1994).

30. Frank A. Vickory and Barry A. Diskin, "Advances in Private Property Protection Rights: The States in the Vanguard," *American Business Law Journal* 34, no. 4 (Summer 1997), p. 561.

31. See Vickory and Diskin, "Advances in Private Property," p. 561, and David L. Callies, "Regulatory Takings and the Supreme Court," *Stetson Law Review* 28 (Winter 1999), p. 523.

32. *Griswold v. Connecticut,* 381 U.S. 479 (1965).

33. 517 U.S. 559 (1996).

34. 538 U.S. 408 (2003).

35. Jess Bravin, "Surprise: Judges Hand Out Most Punitive Awards," *The Wall Street Journal,* June 12, 2000, p. B1.

36. *Baker v. State,* 744 A.2d 864 (Vt. S.Ct. 1999).

37. Human Rights Campaign [**http://www.hrc.org/documents/marriage_prohibit_20070919. pdf**].

38. Hope Lozano-Bielat and David Masci, "Same-Sex Marriage: Redefining Marriage Around the World," [**http://pewforum.org/docs/?DocID=235**].

39. Editorial, "Gay Marriage; Civil Rights Movement Slowed by Votes, But Not Halted," *Syracuse Post-Standard,* November 28, 2004, p. C2.

40. Liz Bradbury, "Same-Sex Couples Want Full Federal and State Rights, Benefits," *Morning Call* (Allentown, PA), December 5, 2004, p. D1.

41. Pierre Schlag, "This Could Be Your Culture—Junk Speech in a Time of Decadence," *Harvard Law Review* 109, no. 7 (1996), p. 1801.

CHAPTER SIX

Contracts

After completing this chapter, students will be able to:

1. Explain the importance of contracts to a capitalist free market system.

2. Determine whether the UCC or common law governs a contract dispute.

3. Identify the elements of a legally enforceable contract.

4. Classify a contract as bilateral or unilateral; express or implied; executory or executed.

5. Distinguish between valid, unenforceable, void, and voidable contracts.

6. Describe the elements of a valid offer.

7. Describe the elements of a valid acceptance.

8. Explain the significance of consideration as an element of a legally enforceable contract.

9. Compare and contrast the rights and duties arising in contractual assignment and delegation.

10. Compare and contrast different types of third-party beneficiaries to a contract.

11. Explain how a contract may be discharged.

12. Describe the remedies available for breach of contract.

Preface

A capitalist free market system cannot operate effectively and fairly without a reliable foundation in contract law. At the practical level, all buyers and sellers must have confidence that the deal they are about to make will be completed as specified or that they will have a remedy available if it is not completed. Otherwise, the legal risk in making deals would act as a drag on the commercial process, reducing certainty and depreciating the extraordinary efficiency of the free market. At the philosophical level, the fundamental point of a contract regime is personal freedom. Contract law gives each of us a reliable mechanism for freely expressing our preferences in life. From buying a tube of toothpaste, a car, or a house, to paying tuition, to accepting an employment offer, to franchising a business, to borrowing millions of dollars, to adopting a child, and so on, the direction and value of our lives are shaped and protected to a significant degree by our contractual choices. To a considerable extent, we define ourselves as persons by the contractual choices we make, and contract law protects those choices.

> To a considerable extent, we define ourselves as persons by the contractual choices we make

Contracts and Capitalism in China

Contract law has played a vital role in China's gradual movement toward free market principles and increased global commerce. Approved in 1999, China's nationwide contract law was designed to govern all forms of contractual relationships in a manner that would encourage order, confidence, and fairness in doing business in China while making Chinese commercial and legal practice compatible with international standards. Now with China's emergence in world markets, international contract disputes, loaded with cultural conflict, are inevitable:

Wahaha Group, China's largest drink maker, signed a contract in 1996 creating a joint venture with French food giant, Groupe Danone. Wahaha produces bottled mineral water, dairy products and juice packs, among other things, while Danone produces yogurt, Evian water, cereal and other products. The partnership has evolved into a bitter international feud. In 2007 Danone accused Wahaha of breaching the terms of its 1996 contract by setting up a series of independent companies in China producing products identical to those made by the joint venture. Wahaha president, Zong Qinghou, argued that the contract is not binding because it was never approved by China's trademark office. Zong also claimed that Danone had "trapped" his company into signing the joint venture with its restrictions on use of the Wahaha brand, and he claimed more broadly that Danone had failed to respect and understand Chinese customs and regulations. Zong resigned from the chairmanship of the Wahaha joint venture, and he accused Danone board members of bullying and slandering him.

Danone filed suit in Los Angeles against Wahaha seeking more than $100 million for the alleged illegal sales and also filed for arbitration in Stockholm, Sweden while Wahaha filed for arbitration with the Hangzhou Arbitration Commission. Wahaha also announced that it intended to sue Danone for up to $6.7 billion in damages for conducting illegal business in China.

Sources: China.org.cn, "Wahaha, Danone Agreement Invalid?" August 10, 2007 [**http://www. china.org.cn/english/BAT/207204.htm**]; "Danone Net Profit Falls Seven Percent Amid Ongoing Legal Dispute with Chinese Partners," *FinancialWire,* August 1, 2007; and Benjamin Morgan, "Wahaha to Sue Danone for Five Billion Euros," *Agence France Presse* (English), June 26, 2007.

Part One—Building a Binding Contract

Introduction

We make promises routinely in our lives. Some of those create binding contracts; some do not. Thus the central question in this chapter is the following: Under what circumstances do promises become enforceable contracts?

The Uniform Commercial Code

Historically, the individual states had passed a wide variety of laws to clarify contract law, but the result was a confusing, inefficient patchwork. Thus the National Conference of Commissioners on Uniform State Laws (NCCUSL) and the American Law Institute (ALI) developed for state approval the Uniform Commercial Code (UCC), a body of rules designed to render commercial law consistent across the 50 states. The UCC has been adopted in 49 states, and Louisiana has adopted portions of it. With a set of uniform, predictable rules, business can be practiced with confidence and minimal legal confusion.

The UCC is divided into a series of articles addressing the multitude of potential problems that arise in complex commercial practice. For our purposes the most important of those articles is Number 2, Sales, which governs all transactions involving the sale of goods. UCC section 2-105 defines goods as tangible, movable, things. Hence cars, clothing, appliances, and the like are covered. Real estate, stocks, bonds, money, and so forth are not covered. Nor are contracts for services governed by the UCC. Of course, many transactions involve both goods and services. Characteristically, in determining whether the UCC applies, the courts have asked whether the dominant purpose of the contract is to provide a service or to sell a good. Appendix B, at the back of the text, sets out the complete Article 2.

The first question, then, in contract disputes is whether the UCC or the common law governs the situation. Throughout this chapter, you should remember that the UCC is always controlling (1) if the transaction is addressed by the UCC—that is, it involves a contract for the sale of goods—and (2) if a UCC rule applies to the issue in question. On the other hand, the judge-made, common law of contracts continues to govern transactions (1) not involving the sale of goods or (2) involving the sale of goods but where no specific UCC provision applies. Increasingly, in non-UCC cases, the courts are analogizing to UCC reasoning to render their judgments; that is, the common law is borrowing or absorbing UCC principles. This chapter, while focusing primarily on the common law of contracts, will introduce the role of the sales article in the practice of business. At this writing, NCCUSL/ALI–recommended revisions to the sales article are being considered by the various state legislatures, most of which seem reluctant to make major changes. [For a brief overview of some of the recommended amendments to the UCC Article 2, see **http://www.nccusl.org/nccusl/ UCC2_Synopsis.pdf**]

Article 2A of the UCC governs *leases* of goods. In essence, Article 2A mimics the sales article except that it governs leases of goods rather than sales. Because of space constraints, Article 2A will not receive further attention in this text.

What Is a Contract?

Legally enforceable contracts must exhibit all of the following features:

1. **Agreement**—a meeting of the minds of the parties based on an offer by one and an acceptance by the other. The determination as to whether the parties have actually reached agreement is based on the *objective* evidence (the parties' acts, words, and so on) as a "reasonable person" would interpret it rather than on an effort to ascertain the subjective or personal intent of the parties.

2. **Consideration.** The bargained-for legal value that one party agrees to pay or provide to secure the promise of another.

3. **Capacity.** The parties must have the legal ability to enter the contract; that is, they must be sane, sober, and of legal age.

4. **Genuineness of assent.** The parties must knowingly agree to the same thing. Their minds must meet as evidenced by the objective evidence. If that meeting does not occur because of mistake, fraud, or the like, a contract does not exist because the parties' assent was not real.

5. **Legality of purpose.** The object of the contract must not violate the law or public policy.

Contracts embracing these five features are enforceable by law and hence are distinguishable from unenforceable promises. As explained later, some contracts must be in writing to be enforceable.

Classification of Contracts

Contracts fall into a series of sometimes overlapping categories. Understanding those categories helps reveal the rather well-ordered logic of our contract system (see Figure 6.1).

Contract Formation

1. **Bilateral and unilateral contracts.** A *bilateral contract* emerges from a situation in which *both* parties make promises. A *unilateral contract* ordinarily involves a situation in which one party makes a promise and the other *acts* in response to that promise. For example, in beginning to establish your new restaurant you promise a college friend that if he completes his degree, you will hire him. He can accept your offer/promise by the act of completing college.

FIGURE 6.1

Classification of Contracts

Contract formation
1. Bilateral/unilateral
    a. Bilateral contract—a promise for a promise.
    b. Unilateral contract—a promise for an act.
2. Express/implied
    a. Express contract—explicitly stated in writing or orally.
    b. Implied-in-fact contract—inferred from the conduct of the parties.
    c. Quasi-contract—implied contract created by a court to prevent unjust enrichment.

Contract performance
    1. Executory contract—not yet fully performed.
    2. Executed contract—fully performed by all parties.

Contract enforceability
    1. Valid contract—includes all of the necessary ingredients of a binding contract.
    2. Unenforceable contract—contract exists, but a legal defense prevents enforcement.
    3. Void contract—no contract at all.
    4. Voidable contract—one party has the option of either enforcing or voiding the contract.

2. **Express and implied contracts.** When parties overtly and explicitly manifest their intention to enter an agreement, either in writing or orally, the result (if other requirements are fulfilled) is an *express contract.* For example, in managing your department at an insurance firm, you sign a form contract with a local computer store ordering a new computer. In turn, the supplier's signature on the form creates an express, bilateral agreement.

If, on the other hand, you ask your local computer service to take a look at a machine that is down and one of the service's technicians does so, you have probably entered an *implied-in-fact contract.* A court would infer a promise by you to pay a reasonable price in return for the service's promise to make a commercially reasonable effort to repair the computer. The contract is inferred on the basis of the facts—that is, by the behavior of the parties.

Suppose in managing your insurance department you have received payment for insurance that was, in fact, issued by a rival firm. In these circumstances, it would be unfair for you to be able to keep the unearned money so the courts construct an implied-in-law or quasi-contract permitting the actual insurer to collect the money. This unusual situation in which the court infers the existence of a contract is employed only when necessary to prevent *unjust enrichment* (as would have been the case if you were to collect an insurance premium without having issued a policy).

Contract Performance

1. **Executory contracts.** A contract is labeled *executory* until all parties fully perform.

2. **Executed contracts.** When all parties have completed their performances, the contract is *executed.*

Contract Enforceability

1. **Valid contracts.** A *valid contract* meets all of the established legal requirements and thus is enforceable in court.

2. **Unenforceable contracts.** An *unenforceable contract* meets the basic contractual requirements but remains faulty because it fails to fulfill some other legal rule. For example, an oral contract may be unenforceable if it falls in one of those categories of contracts, such as the sale of land, that must be in writing (see the Statute of Frauds later in this chapter).

3. **Void contracts.** A *void contract* is, in fact, no contract at all because a critical legal requirement is missing; usually it is either an agreement to accomplish an illegal purpose (such as to commit a crime) or an agreement involving an incompetent (such as an individual judged by a court to be insane). In either case what is otherwise an enforceable contract is in fact void.

4. **Voidable contracts.** A *voidable contract* is enforceable but can be canceled by one or more of the parties. The most common voidable contracts are those entered by minors who have the option, under the law, of either disaffirming or fulfilling most contracts (explained later).

Can I Change My Mind?

Australian Vin Thomas placed his 1946 World War II Wirraway plane for sale on eBay. The plane reportedly is one of only five in the world still flying. Peter Smythe, also of Australia, matched the $128,640 reserve price moments before the online auction ended in 2006. Thomas then declined to convey the airplane to Smythe apparently because Thomas had already agreed to sell the plane to another party for $85,800 more than Smythe's bid. The case involved, among others, a pair of issues frequently arising in contracts law disputes: 1. Did the facts (the eBay auction) create a contract? 2. Can Thomas change his mind about selling the plane to the highest bidder?

Answer those questions according to the U.S. contract law that follows.

The Agreement: Offer

Characteristically, an offer consists of a promise to do something or to refrain from doing something in the future. A valid offer must include all of these elements:

1. Present *intent* to enter a contract.
2. Reasonable *definiteness* in the terms of the offer.
3. *Communication* of the offer to the offeree.

Intent

Assume that you are the purchasing manager for a trucking firm, and you need a small used van to do some local light hauling. Because time is of the essence, you decide to bypass the normal bidding process and go directly to the local dealers to make a quick purchase. At the first lot you find a suitable van. In discussing it, the sales manager says, "Well, we don't usually do this, but since you've been such a good customer, I'll tell you, we paid $10,000 for this one so I guess we are gonna need about $11,000 to deal with you." You say, "Fine. That's reasonable. I'll take it." The manager then says, "Now wait a minute, I was just talking off the top of my head. I'll have to punch up the numbers to be sure."

Do you have a deal at that point? The core question is whether the sales manager made an offer. Normally, language of that kind has been treated by the courts as preliminary negotiation lacking the necessary *intent* to constitute an offer. Of course, if no offer exists, you cannot accept, and no contract can emerge absent further negotiation.

Offer?

An at-will employee (can be fired at any time) asks you, his manager, about job security. You respond, "Good employees are taken care of. You are a good employee." Does that language amount to an offer of permanent employment?

Advertisements   The question of intent sometimes arises with advertisements. In buying the van for your business, suppose you were responding to an ad that said, "2007 full-size Ford cargo van, $20,000." Is that ad language an offer such that you can accept by promising to pay $20,000? Ordinarily, ads do not constitute offers, but rather are treated by the courts as invitations to deal. Were an ad actually treated as an offer, it would put the seller in the commercially impracticable position of being required to provide the advertised product at the advertised price to everyone who sought one, regardless of available supply. Presumably, that open-ended duty was not the seller's intent when issuing the ad. It follows then that the buyer, in responding to an ad, is technically making an offer, with the seller free to accept or decline.

> Suppose you were responding to an ad that said, "2007 full-size Ford cargo van, $20,000." Is that ad language an offer such that you can accept by promising to pay $20,000?

On the other hand, courts have held that some ads do manifest a present intent to make an offer. The critical terms in those ads must be highly specific and complete, leaving nothing open for negotiation.

A Jet Fighter from Pepsi?

A 1995 Pepsico promotion offered merchandise in exchange for points earned by buying Pepsi-Cola. The television ad showed a teenager modeling some of the available merchandise. A Pepsi T-shirt was displayed for 75 points and a leather jacket for 1450 points. At the end of the ad, a U.S. Marine Corps Harrier "jump jet" landed outside a school, and the boy said, "Sure beats the bus." The ad said the jet was redeemable for 7 million points. John D.R. Leonard, at the time a 21-year-old business student in Seattle, Washington, joined five investors in writing a check to Pepsi for $700,008.50 and demanded the 7 million Pepsi points. Pepsi returned the check and said it had no intention of giving Leonard the $24 million jet. Leonard sued. Who wins? Explain.

Source: John D.R. Leonard v. Pepsico, 210 F.3d 88 (2d Cir. Ct. App. 2000). [For a video of the ad, see **http://www.stcl.edu/faculty-dir/ricks/casebook/pepsi1.wmv.** Other ver-sions of the ad can be found at **pepsi2** and **pepsi3**.]

Definiteness

Suppose you have completed a management training program for a "big box" retailer. In your first assignment as an assistant manager, your boss asks you to seek bids and make the other arrangements (subject to her approval) to resurface the store's large asphalt parking lot. You secure bids, and the lowest bidder offers to complete the work "later this summer" for $120,000. You briefly explain the offer to your boss, who tells you to take care of all the details. You are busy with other matters and you put off the parking lot project for a couple of weeks. When you get back to the contractor, he says, "Sorry, man, we hadn't heard from you, and we got another deal." Can you hold that contractor to his initial offer?

One of the requirements of a binding offer is that all of its critical terms must be sufficiently clear that a court can determine both the intentions of the parties and their duties. Clearly, in the asphalt case, many critical details—such as precisely when the work would be done, the quality of the surfacing material, its thickness, and the like—had not been established. Consequently, no offer existed. In a contract for the sale of goods, UCC 2-204 relaxes the definiteness standard by providing that "one or more terms" may be missing but the court can find a contract, nonetheless, where (1) "the parties have intended to make a contract" and (2) "there is a reasonably certain basis for giving an appropriate remedy." Under the UCC, the courts can actually fill in missing terms such as specifying a reasonable price where the contract had omitted a stipulation. The following case involving Mariah Carey, the pop music star, demonstrates some of the problems that can arise when an understanding is indefinite.

LEGAL BRIEFCASE

Vian v. Carey 1993 U.S. Dist.
Lexis 5460 (U.S. Dist. Ct. S.D.N.Y. 1993)

Judge Mukasey

Defendant Mariah Carey is a famous, successful and apparently wealthy entertainer. Plaintiff Joseph Vian was her stepfather before she achieved stardom, but at the start of this litigation was in the process of becoming divorced from defendant's mother. He claims defendant agreed orally that he would have a license to market singing dolls in her likeness. . . . Plaintiff claims that he and Carey had an oral contract for him to receive a license to market "Mariah dolls." These dolls would be statuettes of the singer and would play her most popular songs. Plaintiff claims that the contract was in consideration of his financial and emotional support of defendant, including picking her up from late-night recording sessions, providing her with the use of a car, paying for dental care, allowing her to use his boat for business meetings and rehearsals, and giving her various items, including unused wedding gifts from his marriage to her mother, to help furnish her apartment.

The alleged basis of the oral contract is that on at least three occasions, twice in the family car and once on Vian's boat, Vian told Carey, "Don't forget the Mariah dolls," and "I get the Mariah dolls." According to Vian, on one occasion Carey responded "okay" and on other occasions she merely smiled and nodded. Although Carey admits Vian mentioned the dolls two or three times, she testified that she thought it was a joke. For 30 years plaintiff has been in the business of designing, producing, and marketing gift and novelty items. Although it is not clear from the evidence the parties have submitted, it will be assumed that the alleged contract was formed after defendant turned 18. Under New York law, an oral agreement can form a binding contract. . . . In de-

termining whether a contract exists, what matters are the parties' expressed intentions, the words and deeds that constitute objective signs in a given set of circumstances.

Therefore, the issue is whether the objective circumstances indicate that the parties intended to form a contract. Without such an intent, neither a contract nor a preliminary agreement to negotiate in good faith can exist. In making such a determination, a court may look at "whether the terms of the contract have been finally resolved." In addition, a court may consider "the context of the negotiations." Plaintiff has adduced no evidence that defendant ever intended by a nod of her head or the expression "okay" to enter into a complex commercial licensing agreement involving dolls in her likeness playing her copyrighted songs. The context in which this contract between an 18-year-old girl and her stepfather allegedly was made was an informal family setting, either in the car or on plaintiff's boat, while others were present. Vian's own version of events leads to the conclusion that there was no reason for Carey to think Vian was entirely serious, let alone that he intended to bind her to an agreement at that time. He admits he never told her he was serious. The objective circumstances do not indicate that Carey intended to form a contract with plaintiff. Although plaintiff's five-page memorandum of law fails to raise the possibility, plaintiff also has not shown that Carey intended to be bound to negotiate with plaintiff at some later date over the licensing of "Mariah dolls."

There can be no meeting of the minds, required for the formation of a contract, where essential material terms are missing. Thus, even if the parties both believe themselves to be bound, there is no contract when "the terms of the agreement are so vague and indefinite that there is no basis or standard for deciding whether the agreement had been kept or broken, or to fashion a remedy, and no means by which such terms may be made certain."

... The word "license" was not even used. As defendant points out, no price or royalty term was mentioned, nor was the duration or geographic scope of the license, nor was Carey's right to approve the dolls. Plaintiff admits he would not have gone ahead without defendant's approval, thus conceding the materiality of that term.

* * * * *

In sum, plaintiff has not raised a triable issue of fact as to the existence of a contract. Defendant's motion for summary judgment is granted.

Questions

1. Why did the court find for Carey?

2. As noted in the text, in UCC cases judges fill in contract terms where the parties clearly intended a deal. Should the court here fill in the missing terms to provide the necessary definiteness? Explain.

3. Pilgrim Village Company had employed Petersen as a construction manager at a specified annual salary and "a share of the profits." Petersen worked at salary for several years and then asked for a 10 percent share of the profits. The company refused, and Petersen sued seeking "some share of the profits." How should the court rule on Petersen's claim? Explain. See *Petersen v. Pilgrim Village,* 42 N.W. 2d 273 (Wis. S. Ct., 1950).

Communication

As explained, an effective offer must be the product of a present intent, it must be definite, and it must be communicated to the offeree. Communication of an offer expresses the offeror's intent to make that offer. Suppose a friend tells you that your neighbor has offered to sell his classic jukebox for $10,000. You call your neighbor and say, "I accept. I'll be right over with the $10,000." Do you have a deal? No. The owner did not communicate the offer to you. The fact that it was not communicated to you may suggest that your neighbor does not want to sell or does not want to sell to you.

Duration of an Offer Communication of an offer affords the offeree the opportunity to create a contract by accepting that offer, but how long does that opportunity last? Here are some general rules:

1. The offeror may revoke the offer anytime prior to acceptance. (Some exceptions are explained later.) Normally, revocation is effective on receipt by the offeree. Under common law the offeror has the right to revoke at any time prior to acceptance, even if he or she expressly promised to keep the offer open for a specified period.

2. The offer may specify that it is open for an express period (such as 10 days).

3. Where a time limit is not specified in the offer it will be presumed to be open for a reasonable period.

4. An offer expires if rejected or on receipt of a counteroffer.

Irrevocable Offers

Some kinds of offers may not be revoked. We will note three of them.

1. **Option contracts.** When an offeror promises to keep an offer open for a specified period and, in return, the offeree pays consideration (usually money), the parties have created an *option contract,* which is a separate agreement and is enforceable by its

terms. For example, a friend has offered to sell to you his customized car that you have long cherished, but you want to think about it for a few days. You might enter an option contract with your friend under which you pay $100 for the seller's promise to keep the offer open for seven days. You are under no obligation to buy the car, but the seller is under a binding obligation not to withdraw the offer or sell to another during the seven days.

2. **Firm offers.** Under the UCC, if the owner of that customized car is a dealer (a merchant) and he made a written, signed offer to sell that car (a good) to you, indicating that his offer would remain open for seven days, he is bound to that promise whether you paid consideration for it or not. That situation is labeled a *firm offer* as specified in UCC 2-205, which also provides that such offers will be kept open for a reasonable period if the agreement does not mention a time, but that period cannot exceed three months.

3. **Offers for unilateral contracts.** A problem sometimes arises when the offeror attempts to revoke a unilateral offer after the offeree has begun to perform. For example, your neighbor invites you to rake her leaves for $10, and then, when you are virtually done, she yells from the doorway, "Oh, sorry, I changed my mind. You go home now." Historically, the offeror (the neighbor, in this case) was free to revoke at any time; but the modern position holds that the offeror normally cannot revoke if the offeree (you) has commenced performance. If that performance is then completed (you ignore your neighbor's admonition to go home, and you finish the raking), the offeror (your neighbor) is bound to perform fully; that is, the neighbor must pay the $10.

The Agreement: Acceptance

Suppose you are in training with a large real estate firm and your boss has authorized you to enter negotiations to buy a parcel of farmland that your company hopes to develop for housing. After preliminary discussions, you extend a written offer to the owner indicating, among other terms, that your company is willing to pay $10,000 per acre for a 10-acre parcel. Assume the owner responds by writing, "I accept your offer at $10,000 per acre, but I need to keep the two-acre homesite." The offeree has used the word *accept,* but does the response constitute a legally binding acceptance?

The general rule is that an effective acceptance must be a mirror image of the offer; that is, ordinarily its terms must be the same as those in the offer. Here the offeree has changed the terms of the offer and in so doing has issued a *counteroffer,* thus extinguishing the original offer.

Communication of Acceptance

An offer may be accepted only by the offeree—that is, the person to whom the offer was directed. Because unilateral offers are accepted by performance, no communication of acceptance beyond that performance ordinarily is necessary. In the case of a bilateral contract (a promise for a promise), acceptance is not effective until communicated.

Broadly, acceptance can be accomplished by a "yes" communicated face-to-face, by a nod of the head or some other appropriate signal, by telephone, or by other unwritten means, unless the law of the state requires writing in that particular kind of transaction.

Mailbox Confusion sometimes arises when the parties are not dealing face-to-face. In general, acceptance is effective upon dispatch by whatever mode of communication has been explicitly or implicitly authorized by the offeror. This well-settled position is labeled the *mailbox rule* and means, among other things, that an acceptance is effective when sent even if never received. [For one professor's review of the mailbox rule and related rules, see **http://www.tomwbell.com/teaching/KMailbox.pdf**]

Authorization The offeror controls the acceptance process and may specify an exclusive manner in which an acceptance must be communicated. If so, a contract is not created if the acceptance is communicated in anything other than the stipulated fashion. Traditionally, if the offeror did not give an *express authorization* to a means of communication, an acceptance by the same or faster means than that used by the offeror was implied. *Implied authorization* might also arise from such factors as prior dealings between the parties and custom in their industry.

Modern View Under the UCC the rules have relaxed a bit. If no specific instructions for acceptance are included in the offer, the offeree is free to accept in any reasonable manner within a reasonable period, and acceptance is effective upon dispatch. Even when the means chosen are "unreasonable," acceptance is effective on dispatch under the UCC 1-201(38) if it is actually received in a timely manner.

Consideration

Earlier we identified the five key ingredients in an enforceable contract: agreement, consideration, capacity, genuineness of assent, and legality of purpose. Having examined the agreement (offer/acceptance) process, we turn now to consideration. As noted earlier, consideration is the bargained-for legal value that one party agrees to pay or provide to secure the promise of another. It is what the promisor demands and receives in exchange for his or her promise. Consideration is used by the courts to distinguish a contract (enforceable) from a gratuitous promise (unenforceable). The *promisee* must suffer a *legal detriment;* that is, the promisee must give up something of value (an act or a promise) or must refrain from doing something that she or he has a legal right to do in order to enforce the promise offered by the *promisor.* Each party, then, must pay a "price" for a contract to be enforceable. In sum, consideration consists of a detriment to the promisee that is bargained for by the promisor.

The classic case that follows explores the idea of consideration and demonstrates that consideration can have legal value without involving monetary loss to the promisee.

FACTS

In 1869 William E. Story Sr. promised his nephew, W. E. Story II, that he would pay the nephew $5,000 upon his 21st birthday if the nephew would refrain from drinking liquor, using tobacco, swearing, and playing cards or billiards for money until he reached that 21st birthday. The nephew agreed and performed his promise, but the uncle died in 1887 without paying the money, and the administrator of the estate, Sidway, declined to pay the $5,000 plus interest. The nephew had assigned (sold) his rights to the money to Louisa Hamer, who sued W. E. Story Sr.'s estate. Hamer, the plaintiff, won at the trial level, lost on appeal, and then appealed to the New York Court of Appeals.

* * * * *

Judge Parker

When the nephew arrived at the age of 21 years and on the 31st day of January 1875, he wrote to his uncle informing him that he had performed his part of the agreement and had thereby become entitled to the sum of $5,000. The uncle received the letter and a few days later and on the sixth of February, he wrote and mailed to his nephew the following letter:

> Buffalo, February 6, 1875
> W. E. Story, Jr.
> Dear Nephew:
> Your letter of the 31st came to hand all right, saying that you had lived up to the promise made to me several years ago. I have no doubt but you have, for which you shall have five thousand dollars as I promised you. I had the money in the bank the day you was 21 years old that I intend for you, and you shall have the money certain. Now, Willie I do not intend to interfere with this money in any way till I think you are capable of taking care of it and the sooner that time comes the better it will please me. I would hate very much to have you start out in some adventure that you thought all right and lose this money in one year. The first five thousand dollars that I got together cost me a heap of hard work. You would hardly believe me when I tell you that to obtain this I shoved a jackplane many a day, butchered three or four years, then came to this city, and after three months' perseverance I obtained a situation in a grocery store. I opened this store early, closed late, slept in the fourth story of the building in a room 30 by 40 feet and not a human being in the building but myself. All this I done to live as cheap as I could to save something. I don't want you to take up with this kind of fare. I was here in the cholera season '49 and '52 and the deaths averaged 80 to 125 daily and plenty of smallpox. I wanted to go home, but Mr. Fisk, the gentleman I was working for, told me if I left then, after it got healthy he probably would not want me. I stayed. All the money I have saved I know just how I got it. It did not come to me in any mysterious way, and the reason I speak of this is that money got in this way stops longer with a fellow that gets it with hard knocks than it does when he finds it. Willie, you are 21 and you have many a thing to learn yet. This money you have earned much easier than I did besides acquiring good habits at the same time and you are quite welcome to the money; hope you will make good use of it. I was 10 long years getting this together after I was your age. Now, hoping this will be satisfactory, I stop . . .
> Truly Yours,
> W. E. STORY
> P.S.—You can consider this money on interest.

The nephew received the letter and thereafter consented that the money should remain with his uncle in accordance with the terms and conditions of the letter. The uncle died on the 29th day of January 1887, without having paid over to his nephew any portion of the said $5,000 and interest.

* * * * *

The defendant contends that the contract was without consideration to support it, and, therefore, invalid. He asserts that the promisee by refraining from the use of liquor and tobacco was not harmed but benefited; that that which he did was best for him to do independently of his uncle's promise, and insists that it follows that unless the promisor was benefited, the contract was without consideration. A contention, which if well founded, would seem to leave open for controversy in many cases whether that which the promisee did or omitted to do was, in fact, of such benefit to him as to leave no consideration to support the enforcement of the promisor's agreement. Such a rule could not be tolerated, and is without foundation in the law.

* * * * *

"In general a waiver of any legal right at the request of another party is a sufficient consideration for a promise" (Parsons on Contracts).

Pollock, in his work on contracts, says, " . . . Consideration means not so much that one party is profiting as that the other abandons some legal right in the present or limits his legal freedom of action in the future as an inducement for the promise of the first."

Now, applying this rule to the facts before us, the promisee used tobacco, occasionally drank liquor, and had a legal right to do so. That right he abandoned for a period of years upon the strength of the promise of the testator that for such forbearance he would give him $5,000. We need not speculate on the effort which may have been required to give up the use of those stimulants. It is sufficient that he restricted his lawful freedom of action within certain prescribed limits upon the faith of his uncle's agreement, and now having fully performed the conditions imposed, it is of no moment whether such performance actually proved a benefit to the promisor, and the court will not inquire into it, but were it a proper subject of inquiry, we see nothing in this record that would permit a determination that the uncle was not benefited in a legal sense.

*   *   *   *   *

Reversed.

Questions

1. a. What detriment, if any, was sustained by the nephew?

   b. What benefit, if any, was secured by the uncle?

   c. As a matter of law, do we need to inquire into the uncle's benefit? Explain.

2. Lampley began work as an at-will (can be dismissed or can quit at any time) employee of Celebrity Homes in Denver, Colorado, in May 1975. On July 29, 1975, Celebrity announced a profit-sharing plan for all employees if the company reached its goals for the fiscal year, April 1, 1975, to March 31, 1976. Lampley was dismissed in January 1976. Celebrity distributed its profits in May 1976. Lampley sued when she did not receive a share of the profits. Celebrity argued that its promise to share its profits was a gratuity, unsupported by consideration. Decide. Explain. See *Lampley v. Celebrity Homes,* 594 P.2d 605 (Col. Ct. App. 1979).

3. An accident in the early 1960s rendered Hoffman paraplegic. At Hoffman's invitation, Thomas lived with and provided extensive physical care for Hoffman until Hoffman's death in 2004. Thomas did not pay rent and Hoffman paid for Thomas' food, provided her with a car and cellphone and made occasional cash payments to Thomas. While never married, the couple exchanged rings in 2002 and Thomas testified that she felt they "lived as man and wife." Thomas filed suit seeking $44,625 for services rendered to Hoffman. According to the trial court, her claim was based on the theories of "express or implied contract of employment" or "unjust enrichment." Thomas lost at the trial level. How would you rule on appeal? Explain. See *In Re Estate of Hoffman,* 2006 Ia. App. LEXIS 473. [For a detailed analysis of *Hamer v. Sidway,* see **http://www.law.smu.edu/firstday/contracts/case.htm**]

Adequacy of Consideration

With certain exceptions, the courts do not, as Judge Parker indicated in the *Hamer* case, inquire into the economic value of the consideration in question. Legal sufficiency depends not on the value of the consideration but on whether the promisee suffered a detriment in some way. To hold otherwise would put the courts in the place of the market in deciding the value of transactions. We are all free to make both good and bad bargains.

On the other hand, the courts will rule that consideration is found wanting in situations of pretense or sham where the parties have clearly agreed on token or nominal consideration in an effort to present the transaction as a contract rather than a gift. Likewise, an extreme inadequacy of consideration will sometimes cause the court to question a contract on the grounds of *fraud, duress,* or *unconscionability* (all are discussed later in this chapter). In these instances, the agreements would be unenforceable because of a failure of consideration. However, remember these cases are uncommon, and the courts rarely inquire into the adequacy of consideration.

Appearance of Consideration

Some agreements appear to be accompanied by consideration, but in fact, that appearance turns out to be an illusion. Hence, if one agrees to perform a preexisting duty, consideration would be found wanting. For example, if you were to pay your neighbor $50 to keep his dog chained when outdoors and a city ordinance already requires dogs to be chained if outdoors, your promise would be unenforceable because your neighbor already had a preexisting duty under the law to keep his dog chained. So performance of a pre-existing legal duty does not constitute consideration because no legal detriment or benefit has arisen.

Similarly, preexisting duties sometimes arise from contracts. Suppose you hire a contractor to resurface the parking lot at your real estate office. You agree on a price of $12,000. With a portion of the work completed, the contractor asks you to amend the agreement to add $2,000 because the project is requiring more time than anticipated. You agree. The work is completed. Could you then legally refuse to pay the additional $2,000? The answer is yes because the contractor failed to provide consideration for the modification of your contract. He was under a preexisting duty to finish the contract; hence he did not sustain a legal detriment in the modified agreement. Note, however, that UCC section 2-209(1) provides that "an agreement modifying a contract within this Article needs no consideration to be binding."

Suppose you learn from your neighbor that your friend Ames wants to sell his house. You, as a Realtor, find a buyer for the house and make all of the necessary arrangements for the sale out of regard for your friendship with Ames. Then when the transaction is complete, Ames says, "Well, this has been great of you, but I don't feel right about it. When I get my check for the sale, I'll pay you $2,000 for your hard work. I really appreciate it." What if Ames does not then pay the $2,000? Do you have recourse? No. This is a situation of *past consideration,* where the performance—arranging the sale of your friend's house—was not bargained for and was not given in exchange for the promise and thus cannot constitute consideration. In effect, the performance was a gift. Of course, past consideration is really not consideration at all. In some states, courts enforce promises to pay for benefits already received where doing so amounts to a *moral obligation* that must be enforced to prevent injustice.

Substitutes for Consideration

When necessary to achieve justice, the courts sometimes conclude that a contract exists even though consideration is clearly lacking. Moral obligation and quasi contract (discussed earlier) are two such instances; but the most prominent of these substitutes for consideration is the doctrine of *promissory estoppel,* in which the promisor is "stopped" from denying the existence of a contract where the promisee has detrimentally relied on that promise. Promissory estoppel requires the following:

1. A promise on which the promisor should expect the promisee to rely.
2. The promisee did justifiably rely on the promise.
3. Injustice can be avoided only by enforcing the promise.

Consider the following. You have been a part-time employee of a small fast-food chain restaurant while attending college. Upon graduation, you tell the manager of the restaurant that you think you could handle your own franchise. He says you need to get more experience and advises you to take a full-time position with the company. You do so. Everything goes well, and when you next approach the manager, he says, "If you can come up with the $50,000 and a good location, we will get you in a franchise right away. But you've gotta move on this. Maybe you better quit your job with us and concentrate on this thing." You take his advice and quit your job. You raise the $50,000 and find a vacant building to rent in a good location for a franchise. You show the building to the manager, and he agrees that it looks like a favorable location and one that can easily be converted to the company's needs. He says, "Looks like you have everything in place. If you can come up with $50,000 more we will make this thing happen." You refuse and decide to bring suit against the fast-food chain for breach of contract. The chain defends by saying that you did not provide consideration for its promise. No formal financing arrangement was ever agreed to, and you had not committed yourself to any franchising obligations. Under these circumstances you may well prevail using a promissory estoppel claim. In brief, you would argue that you had changed your position in reliance on the franchisor's promises and that relief is necessary to prevent injustice. (For a similar case see *Hoffman v. Red Owl Stores,* 133 N.W. 2d 267 (Wis. S. Ct. 1965).)

Capacity

Having examined two of the required ingredients in an enforceable contract, agreement and consideration, we turn now to a third, capacity to contract. To enter a binding agreement, one must have the legal ability to do so; that is, one's mental condition and maturity must be such that the agreement was entered with understanding and in recognition of one's own interests. The three primary areas of concern are intoxication, mental impairment, and minority (infancy/youthfulness), with minority being much the more common area of dispute.

> The three primary areas of concern are intoxication, mental impairment, and minority

Intoxication

Assume you have been drinking to celebrate your 21st birthday. You enter a contract with a friend to sell him your autographed Michael Jordan basketball card for $200. You receive the money and turn over the card. Later, when sober, you regret the deal. Will a court nullify that contract on the grounds of your intoxication? That decision depends on whether you were sufficiently intoxicated that you did not understand the nature and purpose of the contract. If the objective evidence suggests that you did not understand the transaction, the contract would be considered voidable, in which case you could probably disaffirm the contract and demand the return of the card, although courts are often not sympathetic with people who attempt to escape contracts made while intoxicated. In most states, if you recovered the card, you would be required to return the $200 to your friend.

If on recovering your sobriety, your friend argued that the contract was invalid because of your intoxication, and he demanded the return of his $200 in exchange for the card, you could then *ratify* (affirm) the contract and hold him to it. If the contract had been for one of life's *necessaries* (food, shelter, clothing, medical care, tools of one's trade, or the like), you would have been liable for the reasonable value of that necessary.

Mental Incompetence

In most cases an agreement involving a mentally incompetent person is either void or voidable. The transaction would be void—that is, no contract would exist—where the impaired party had been *adjudged* insane. If the impaired party was unable to understand the purpose and effect of the contract but had not been legally adjudged insane, the contract would be voidable (void in some states) at the option of the impaired party. The competent party cannot void the contract, and the impaired party would have to pay the reasonable value of any necessaries received under the contract.

Minority

> Minors may complete their contracts if they wish, but they also have an absolute right to rescind most of those contracts.

Minors may complete their contracts if they wish, but they also have an absolute right to rescind most of those contracts. They may rescind until they reach adulthood and for a reasonable time thereafter. (Many states have enacted statutes forbidding minors from disaffirming some classes of contracts such as those for marriage, student loans, and life insurance.) The minor has a right of recovery for everything given up in meeting the terms of the contract. Similarly, the minor must return everything that remains in her or his possession that was received from the contract. In many states, if nothing of the bargained-for consideration remains or if its value has been depreciated, the minor has no duty to replace it but can still recover whatever she or he put into the contract. If not disaf-firmed in a reasonable time after the minor reaches the age of majority, the contract is considered to be ratified, and the minor is bound to its terms. The minor is also liable for the reasonable value (not necessarily the contract price) of necessaries purchased from an adult. That is, a minor must pay the adult the reasonable value of contracted-for items such as food, clothing, shelter, medical care, basic education, and tools of the minor's trade.

Despite the flexibility accorded to minors entering contracts, the adults who are parties to those contracts are bound to them and do not have the power to disaffirm. Hence adults put themselves at risk when they choose to bargain with minors. As noted, in many states a minor need not make restitution if the consideration is lost, destroyed, or depreciated. On the other hand, the case that follows illustrates the growing view that minors do have some monetary obligation after disaffirming a contract.

LEGAL   BRIEFCASE

Dodson v. Shrader
824 S.W. 2d 545 (Tenn. S. Ct. 1992)

Justice O'Brien

In early April of 1987, Joseph Eugene Dodson, then 16 years of age, purchased a used 1984 pickup truck from Burns and Mary Shrader. The Shraders owned and operated Shrader's Auto Sales in Columbia, Tennessee. Dodson paid $4,900 in cash for the truck, using money he borrowed from his girlfriend's grandmother. At the time of the purchase there was no inquiry by the Shraders, and no misrepresentation by Dodson, concerning his minority. However, Shrader did testify that at the time he believed Dodson to be 18 or 19 years of age.

In December 1987, nine months after the date of purchase, the truck began to develop mechanical problems. A mechanic diagnosed the problem as a burnt valve, but could not be certain without inspecting the valves inside the engine. Dodson did not want, or did not have the money, to effect these repairs. He continued to drive the truck despite the mechanical problems. One month later, in January, the truck's engine "blew up" and the truck became inoperable.

Dodson parked the vehicle in the front yard at his parents' home, where he lived. He contacted the Shraders to rescind the purchase of the truck and requested a full refund. The Shraders refused to accept the tender of the truck or to give Dodson the refund requested.

Dodson then [sued] to rescind the contract and recover the amount paid for the truck. Before the circuit court could hear the case, the truck, while parked in Dodson's front yard, was struck on the left front fender by a hit-and-run driver. At the time of the circuit court trial, according to Shrader, the truck was worth only $500 due to the damage to the engine and the left front fender.

The case was heard in the circuit court in November 1988. The trial judge, based on previous common-law decisions, and under the doctrine of stare decisis, reluctantly granted the rescission. The Shraders were ordered, upon tender and delivery of the truck, to reimburse the $4,900 purchase price to Dodson. The Shraders appealed.

[T]he rule in Tennessee is in accord with the majority rule on the issue among our sister states. This rule is based on the underlying purpose of the "infancy doctrine," which is to protect minors from their lack of judgment and "from squandering their wealth through improvident contracts with crafty adults who would take advantage of them in the marketplace."

There is, however, a modern trend among the states, either by judicial action or by statute, in the approach to the problem of balancing the rights of minors against those of innocent merchants. As a result, two minority rules have developed that allow the other party to a contract with a minor to refund less than the full consideration paid in the event of rescission.

The first of these minority rules is called the "Benefit Rule." The rule holds that, upon rescission, recovery of the full purchase price is subject to a deduction for the minor's use of the merchandise. This rule recognizes that the traditional rule in regard to necessaries has been extended so far as to hold an infant bound by his contracts, where he failed to restore what he has received under them to the extent of the benefit actually derived by him from what he has received from the other party to the transaction.

The other minority rule holds that the minor's recovery of the full purchase price is subject to a deduction for the minor's "use" of the consideration he or she received under the contract, or for the "depreciation" or "deterioration" of the consideration in his or her possession.

We are impressed by the statement made by the Court of Appeals of Ohio:

> At a time when we see young persons between 18 and 21 years of age demanding and assuming more responsibilities in their daily lives, when we see such persons emancipated, married, and raising families; when we see such persons charged with the responsibility for committing crimes; when we see such persons being sued in tort claims for acts of negligence; when we see such persons subject to military service; when we see such persons engaged in business and acting in almost all other respects as an adult, it seems timely to reexamine the case law pertaining to contractual rights and responsibilities of infants to see if the law as pronounced and applied by the courts should be redefined.

* * * * *

We state the rule to be followed hereafter, in reference to a contract of a minor, to be where the minor has not been overreached in any way, and there has been no undue influence, and the contract is a fair and reasonable one, and the minor has actually paid money on the purchase price, and taken and used the article purchased; that he ought not be permitted to recover the amount actually paid, without allowing the vendor of the goods reasonable compensation for the use of, depreciation, and willful or negligent damage to the article purchased, while in his hands. If there has been any fraud or imposition on the part of the seller or if the contract is unfair, or any unfair advantage has been taken of the minor inducing him to make the purchase, then the rule does not apply. Whether there has been such an overreaching on the part of the seller, and the fair market value of the property returned, would always, in any case, be a question for the trier of fact. . . .

This rule is best adapted to modern conditions under which minors are permitted to, and do in fact, transact a great deal of business for themselves, long before they have reached the age of legal majority. Many young people work and earn money and collect it and spend it oftentimes without any oversight or restriction. The law does not question their right to buy if they have the money to pay for their purchases. It seems intolerably burdensome for everyone concerned if merchants and businesspeople cannot deal with them safely, in a fair and reasonable way.

* * * * *

We note that in this case, some nine months after the date of purchase, the truck purchased by the plaintiff began to develop mechanical problems. Plaintiff was informed of the probable nature of the difficulty, which apparently involved internal problems in the engine. He continued to drive the vehicle until the engine "blew up" and the truck became inoperable.

Whether or not this involved gross negligence or intentional conduct on his part is a matter for determination at the trial level. It is not possible to determine from this record whether a counterclaim for tortious damage to the vehicle was asserted. After the first tender of the vehicle was made by plaintiff, and refused by the defendant, the truck was damaged by a hit-and-run driver while parked on plaintiff's property. The amount of that damage and the liability for that amount between the purchaser and the vendor, as well as the fair market value of the vehicle at the time of tender, is also an issue for the jury.

[Reversed and remanded.]

Questions

1. What was the issue in this case?
2. Distinguish the two minority rules that are summarized in this case.
3. To achieve justice in contract cases involving a minor and an adult, what would you want to know about the adult's behavior toward the minor?

4. White, a 17-year-old high school sophomore, operated a trucking business, including hiring drivers, securing jobs, and so forth. He lived with his parents and received his food, clothing, and shelter from them. Valencia operated a garage and repaired White's equipment until they had a disagreement over replacement of a motor. White then disaffirmed his contract with Valencia and refused to pay what he owed. At trial the jury found that White had caused the damage to the motor, but the court held that White could disaffirm the contract and required Valencia to refund any money paid to White under the contract. Valencia appealed.

   a. Is the fact that White was in business for himself in any way relevant to the outcome of this case? Explain.

   b. Decide the case. Explain. See *Valencia v. White,* 654 P.2d 287 (Ariz. Ct. App. 1982).

Genuineness of Assent

Sometimes parties appear to have concluded a binding contract, but the courts will allow them to escape that obligation because they had not, in fact, achieved an agreement. They had achieved the appearance of agreement, but not the reality. That situation arises when the contract is the product of misrepresentation, fraud, duress, undue influence, or mistake. Ordinarily, such agreements are voidable and may be rescinded by the innocent party because of the absence of genuine assent, the fourth of five ingredients in a binding contract.

Misrepresentation and Fraud

An innocent untruth is a *misrepresentation*. Intentional untruths constitute *fraud*. In either case, a party to a contract who has been deceived may rescind the deal, and restitution may be secured if benefits were extended to the party issuing the untruth. The test for fraud is as follows:

1. Misrepresentation of a material fact.
2. The misrepresentation was intentional.
3. The injured party justifiably relied on the misrepresentation.
4. Injury resulted.

Note that the test requires a misrepresented fact. In general, misrepresented opinions are not grounds for action; but many courts are now recognizing exceptions to that rule, especially when the innocent party has relied on opinion coming from an expert.

Toy Yoda

Former Hooters waitress Jodee Berry sued Gulf Coast Wings for not awarding a new Toyota as a prize for her victory in an April 2001 sales contest. Berry alleged that her manager told the waitresses in their Florida Hooters that the server selling the most beer would be entered in a drawing (involving other Hooters locations) with the winner receiving a new Toyota. At one point during the contest, the manager allegedly said he did not know whether the winner would receive a Toyota car, truck or van, but he did know that the winner would be required to pay registration fees. At the close of the contest, the manager told Berry that she had won. He blindfolded her and took her to the restaurant parking lot. He laughed when Berry found, not the car she expected, but a doll based on the character Yoda in the *Star Wars* movie (a toy Yoda). Berry did not laugh, but she did sue. The case was settled out of court. The terms of that settlement were not disclosed, but Berry's lawyer did say that she would be able to afford whatever Toyota she wanted.

Questions
1. What contract-based causes of action did Berry bring in this case?
2. Defend Hooters.
3. Make the argument that the Hooters manager never actually made an offer to the waitresses.
4. If an offer was made, how did Berry accept that offer?
5. Make the argument that the offer and acceptance, if they existed, were not supported by consideration.

Source: Berry v. Gulf Coast Wings, Inc., Div. J (Fla. 14th Cir. Ct. July 24, 2001); and Keith A. Rowley, "You Asked for It, You Got It . . . Toy Yoda: Practical Jokes, Prizes, and Contract Law," 3 *Nevada Law Journal* 526 (2003).

Duress

Sometimes genuine assent is not secured and a contract may be rescinded because one of the parties was forced to agree. Fear lies at the heart of a *duress* claim. The party seeking to escape the contract would have to establish that a wrongful act was threatened or had occurred, causing the party to enter the contract out of fear of harm such that free will was precluded. Increasingly, courts are also setting aside contracts on the grounds of economic duress. For example, suppose you know that one of your regular customers depends on your timely delivery of steel to his factory and that he cannot expeditiously find an alternative supply. Therefore, you tell your customer that delivery will be delayed until he agrees to pay a higher price for the steel. If he agrees, the resulting contract probably could be rescinded on the grounds of economic duress.

Undue Influence

Under some circumstances, the first party to an apparent contract can escape its terms by demonstrating that the second party so dominated her will that she (the first party) did not act independently. These claims are most common in cases involving those who are old or infirm and who lose their independence of thought and action to the *undue-influence* of a caregiver or adviser.

Mistake

Most of us, on taking a new job, operate at least for a time in fear that we will make a mistake. Assume you are new to your job and are preparing a bid that your company will submit in hopes of securing the general maintenance contract for a large office building. In preparing the bid, you inadvertently submit a final price of $50,000 rather than $500,000. What happens? Do you lose your job?

> You inadvertently submit a final price of $50,000 rather than $500,000. What happens?

In some cases, mistakes involving critical facts can be grounds for rescinding contracts. A *mutual mistake* is one in which both parties to the contract are in error about some critical fact. With exceptions, either party can rescind those contracts because genuine assent was not achieved. Your erroneous bid, however, is a *unilateral mistake;* that is, only one party to the contract made an error. The general rule is that those contracts cannot be rescinded. However, if you are able to show that the other party to the contract knew or should have known about your mistake, many courts would allow you to rescind. Certainly you would make that argument in this instance because the $50,000 bid is presumably dramatically out of line with the other bids and at odds with reasonable business expectations about the value of the contract. In cases where an error is made in *drafting* a contract, and both parties are unaware of the error (a mutual mistake), the courts will reform the contract rather than void it. That is, the contract will be rewritten to reflect what the parties actually intended.

$4,934 Discount on Alitalia?

The Italian national airline, Alitalia, was charging more than $5,000 for trans-Atlantic, roundtrip, business class airfares in 2006, but by mistake a fare was briefly listed online at $66.00. About the same time, Marriott was offering rooms at a New York City hotel for $24.90 when the intended price was $249.00. Alitalia honored 509 reservations at an expected cost of about $2.6 million. Marriott, however, raised the $24.90 rate to the intended $249.00. Errors of this kind happen with some frequency in the travel industry.

Questions

1. As a matter of business practice, how would you have dealt with your company's error had you been in charge at Alitalia or Marriott?
2. As a matter of law, was Alitalia or Marriott obligated to honor the low prices?

Source: Scott McCartney, "When a Fare Is Too Good to Be True," *The Wall Street Journal,* April 25, 2006, p. D5.

Legality of Purpose

Having examined agreement, consideration, capacity, and genuineness of assent, we turn now to the final requirement for the creation of a binding contract: legality of purpose (see Figure 6.2). *Illegality* refers to bargains to commit a crime or a tort (such as a deal

FIGURE 6.2

Five Requirements of a Binding Contract

> 1. Agreement
> 2. Consideration
> 3. Capacity
> 4. Genuineness of assent
> 5. Legality of purpose

with a coworker to embezzle funds from one's employer); but more broadly, illegality involves bargains that are forbidden by statute or violate public policy. We can identify three general categories of illegal agreements: (1) contracts that violate statutes, (2) contracts that are unconscionable, and (3) contracts that violate public policy. In general, the effect of an illegal contract is that it cannot be enforced, and the courts will not provide a remedy if its terms are unfulfilled. With exceptions, the parties to illegal deals are left where the courts find them.

1. *Contracts violating statutes* As noted, a contract to commit a crime or a tort is illegal and unenforceable. The states have also specified certain other agreements that are illegal. Those provisions vary from state to state, but they commonly include antigambling laws, laws forbidding the conduct of certain kinds of business on Sundays (*blue laws*), laws forbidding *usury,* and laws forbidding the practice of certain professions (law, real estate, hair care) without a license.

Who Owns the BMW?

Ryno owned Bavarian Motors in Fort Worth, Texas. In 1981 Ryno agreed to sell a 1980 BMW M-l to Tyra for $125,000. Ryno then proposed a double-or-nothing coin flip for the car. Tyra agreed and won the coin flip. Ryno then handed Tyra the keys to the car, saying, "It's yours," while handing the "German title" to the car to Tyra. On several occasions Tyra took the BMW to Ryno for servicing. The car was routinely returned to Tyra until 1982 when Ryno kept the car and sold it. Tyra sued Ryno. Who wins? Explain.

Source: Ryno v. Tyra, 752 S.W.2d 148 (Tx. Ct. App. 1988).

---

2. *Unconscionable contracts.* Certain agreements are so thoroughly one-sided that fairness precludes enforcing them. Problems of *unconscionability* often arise in situations in which the bargaining power of one of the parties is much superior to the other—where one can, in effect, "twist the arm" or otherwise take advantage of the other. Both the common law of contracts and UCC 2-302 give the courts the power to modify or refuse to enforce such deals.

> Certain agreements are so thoroughly one-sided that fairness precludes enforcing them

3. ***Public policy.*** The courts may decline to enforce certain otherwise binding contracts because to do so would not be in the best interest of the public. For example, an agreement between the local convenience stores to charge $4.50 for a gallon of gasoline would be a restraint of trade (price fixing) and as such would be contrary to public policy and to antitrust laws (see Chapter 10) and thus would be unenforceable. Similarly, suppose as a condition of being hired for a job you must sign an agreement providing that you will not leave your employer to work for one of your employer's competitors. These *noncompete clauses* (see Chapter 12) are common and may be fully lawful depending largely on whether the time and geographic restrictions imposed are reasonable. If unreasonable, the courts will either not enforce the clause or will alter it to achieve a fair result.

> If you own or manage a potentially hazardous activity, you may try to protect yourself by including a release in the customer agreement

Another commonplace public policy concern is the *exculpatory clause* or *release.* If you own or manage a potentially hazardous activity such as a water slide, bungee tower, or even a health spa, you may try to protect yourself from litigation should a customer be hurt by including a release in the customer agreement. Often, such agreements are enforceable in the manner of any other contractual provision, but sometimes they are not. Many factors can influence that decision, including how sweeping the exculpation is, whether it was knowingly entered, and the relative bargaining power of the parties. The case that follows examines exculpatory clauses in greater detail.

LEGAL BRIEFCASE

Hanks v. Powder Ridge Restaurant Corporation
885 A.2d 734 (Conn. S. Ct. 2005)

Chief Justice Sullivan

* * * * *

On February 16, 2003, the plaintiff [Hanks] brought his three children and another child to Powder Ridge to snowtube. Neither the plaintiff nor the four children had ever snowtubed at Powder Ridge, but the snowtubing run was open to the public generally, regardless of prior snowtubing experience, with the restriction that only persons at least six years old or forty-four inches tall were eligible to participate. Further, in order to snowtube at Powder Ridge, patrons were required to sign a "Waiver, Defense, Indemnity and Hold Harmless Agreement, and Release of Liability" (agreement). The plaintiff read and signed the agreement on behalf of himself and the four children. While snowtubing, the plaintiff's right foot became caught between his snow tube and the man-made bank of the snowtubing run, resulting in serious injuries that required multiple surgeries to repair.

Thereafter, the plaintiff filed the present negligence action against the defendants [Powder Ridge]. Specifically, the plaintiff alleges that the defendants negligently caused his injuries by: (1) Permitting the plaintiff "to ride in a snow tube that was not of sufficient size to ensure his safety . . . "; (2) "failing to properly train, supervise, control or otherwise instruct the operators of the snow tubing run . . ."; (3) "failing to properly groom the snow tubing run . . ."; (4) "placing carpet at the end of the snow tubing run which had the tendency to cause the snow tubes to come to an abrupt halt, spin or otherwise change direction"; (5) "failing to properly landscape the snow tubing run . . ."; (6) "failing to place warning signs on said snow tubing run . . ."; and (7) "failing to place hay bales or other similar materials on the sides of the snow tubing run. . ."

The defendants denied the plaintiff's allegations of negligence and asserted two special defenses. Specifically, the defendants alleged that the plaintiff's injuries were caused by his own negligence and that the agreement relieved the defendants of liability, "even if the accident was due to the negligence of the defendants." The trial court rendered summary judgment in favor of the defendants. Specifically, the trial court determined, pursuant to our decision in *Hyson v. White Water Mountain Resorts of Connecticut, Inc.,* that the plaintiff, by signing the agreement, unambiguously had released the defendants from liability for their allegedly negligent conduct.

The plaintiff raises two claims on appeal. First, . . . the plaintiff contends that a person of ordinary intelligence reasonably would not have believed that, by signing the agreement, he or she was releasing the defendants from liability for personal injuries caused by negligence. . . . Second, the plaintiff . . . contends that a recreational operator cannot, consistent with public policy, release itself from liability for its own negligent conduct where, as in the present case, the operator offers its services to the public generally, for a fee, and requires patrons to sign a standardized exculpatory agreement as a condition of participation.

* * * * *

[The] exculpatory agreement provided:

"SNOWTUBING

"RELEASE FROM LIABILITY

"PLEASE READ CAREFULLY BEFORE SIGNING

"1. I accept use of a snowtube and accept full responsibility for the care of the snowtube while in my possession.

"2. I understand that there are inherent and other risks involved in SNOW TUBING, including the use of lifts and snowtube, and it is a dangerous activity/sport. These risks include, but are not limited to, variations in snow, steepness and terrain, ice and icy conditions, moguls, rocks, trees, and other forms of forest growth or debris (above or below the surface), bare spots, lift terminals, cables, utility lines, snowmaking equipment and component parts, and other forms [of] natural or man made obstacles on and/or off chutes, as well as collisions with equipment, obstacles or other snowtubes. Snow chute conditions vary constantly because of weather changes and snowtubing use. Be aware that snowmaking and snow grooming may be in progress at any time. These are some of the risks of SNOWTUBING. All of the inherent risks of SNOWTUBING present the risk of serious and/or fatal injury.

"3. I agree to hold harmless and indemnify Powder Ridge, White Water Mountain Resorts of Connecticut, Inc. and/or any employee of the aforementioned for loss or damage, including any loss or injuries that result from damages related to the use of a snowtube or lift.

"I, the undersigned, have read and understand the above release of liability."

I

[T]he plaintiff maintains that an ordinary person of reasonable intelligence would not understand that, by signing the agreement, he or she was releasing the defendants from liability for future negligence. We disagree.

* * * * *

We conclude that the agreement expressly and unambiguously purports to release the defendants from prospective liability for negligence. The agreement explicitly provides that the snowtuber "fully assumes all risks associated with snowtubing, even if due to the NEGLIGENCE" of the defendants. Moreover, the agreement refers to the negligence of the defendants three times and uses capital letters to emphasize the term "negligence." Accordingly, we conclude that an ordinary person of reasonable intelligence would understand that, by signing the agreement, he or she was releasing the defendants from liability for their future negligence.

* * * * *

II

We next address the issue we explicitly left unresolved in *Hyson v. White Water Mountain Resorts of Connecticut, Inc.,* namely, whether the enforcement of a well drafted exculpatory agreement purporting to release a snowtube operator from prospective liability for personal injuries sustained as a result of the operator's negligent conduct violates public policy.

Although it is well established "that parties are free to contract for whatever terms on which they may agree"; *Gibson v. Capano,* it is equally well established "that contracts that violate public policy are unenforceable." *Solomon v. Gilmore.* . . .

As previously noted, "the law does not favor contract provisions which relieve a person from his own negligence. . . ." *Hyson v. White Water Mountain Resorts of Connecticut, Inc.* This is because exculpatory provisions undermine the policy considerations governing our tort system. "The fundamental policy purposes of the tort compensation system [are] compensation of innocent parties, shifting the loss to responsible parties or distributing it among appropriate entities, and deterrence of wrongful conduct. . . .

* * * * *

The defendants are in the business of providing snowtubing services to the public generally, regardless of prior snowtubing experience, with the minimal restriction that only persons at least six years old or forty-four inches tall are eligible to participate. Given the virtually unrestricted access of the public to Powder Ridge, a reasonable person would presume that the defendants were offering a recreational activity that the whole family could enjoy safely. Indeed, this presumption is borne out by the plaintiff's own testimony. Specifically, the plaintiff testified that he "trusted that [the defendants] would, within their good conscience, operate a safe ride."

The societal expectation that family oriented recreational activities will be reasonably safe is even more important where, as in the present matter, patrons are under the care and control of the recreational operator as a result of an economic transaction. The plaintiff, in exchange for a fee, was permitted access to the defendants' snowtubing runs and was provided with snowtubing gear. As a result of this transaction, the plaintiff was under the care and control of the defendants and, thus, was subject to the risk of the defendants' carelessness. Specifically, the defendants designed and maintained the snowtubing run and, therefore, controlled the steepness of the incline, the condition of the snow and the method of slowing down or stopping patrons. Further, the defendants provided the plaintiff with the requisite snowtubing supplies and, therefore, controlled the size and quality of the snow tube as well as the provision of any necessary protective gear. Accordingly, the plaintiff voluntarily relinquished control to the defendants with the rea-

sonable expectation of an exciting, but reasonably safe, snowtubing experience.

Moreover, the plaintiff lacked the knowledge, experience and authority to discern whether, much less ensure that, the defendants' snowtubing runs were maintained in a reasonably safe condition. As the Vermont Supreme Court observed, in the context of the sport of skiing, it is consistent with public policy "to place responsibility for maintenance of the land on those who own or control it, with the ultimate goal of keeping accidents to the minimum level possible. [The] defendants, not recreational skiers, have the expertise and opportunity to foresee and control hazards, and to guard against the negligence of their agents and employees. They alone can properly maintain and inspect their premises, and train their employees in risk management. They alone can insure against risks and effectively spread the costs of insurance among their thousands of customers. Skiers, on the other hand, are not in a position to discover and correct risks of harm, and they cannot insure against the ski area's negligence.

"If the defendants were permitted to obtain broad waivers of their liability, an important incentive for ski areas to manage risk would be removed, with the public bearing the cost of the resulting injuries. . . . It is illogical, in these circumstances, to undermine the public policy underlying business invitee law and allow skiers to bear risks they have no ability or right to control." *Dalury v. S-K-I, Ltd.,* 164 Vt. 335.

* * * * *

Further, the agreement at issue was a standardized adhesion contract offered to the plaintiff on a "take it or leave it" basis. The "most salient feature [of adhesion contracts] is that they are not subject to the normal bargaining processes of ordinary contracts." *Aetna Casualty & Surety Co. v. Murphy,* 206 Conn. 409, 416, 538 A.2d 219 (1988). Not only was the plaintiff unable to negotiate the terms of the agreement, but the defendants also did not offer him the option of procuring protection against negligence at an additional reasonable cost. Moreover, the defendants did not inform prospective snowtubers prior to their arrival at Powder Ridge that they would have to waive important common-law rights as a condition of participation. Thus, the plaintiff, who traveled to Powder Ridge in anticipation of snowtubing that day, was faced with the dilemma of either signing the defendants' proffered waiver of prospective liability or forgoing completely the opportunity to snowtube at Powder Ridge. Under the present factual circumstances, it would ignore reality to conclude that the plaintiff wielded the same bargaining power as the defendants.

The defendants contend, nevertheless, that they did not have superior bargaining power because, unlike an essential public service, "snowtubing is a voluntary activity and the plaintiff could have just as easily decided not to participate." We acknowledge that snowtubing is a voluntary activity, but we do not agree that there can never be a disparity of bargaining power in the context of voluntary or elective activities. Voluntary recreational activites, such as snowtubing, skiing, basketball, soccer, football, racquetball, karate, ice skating, swimming, volleyball or yoga, are pursued by the vast majority of the population and constitute an important and healthy part of everyday life. Indeed, this court has previously recognized the public policy interest of promoting vigorous participation in such activities. In the present case, the defendants held themselves out as a provider of a healthy, fun, family activity. After the plaintiff and his family arrived at Powder Ridge eager to participate in the activity, however, the defendants informed the plaintiff that, not only would they be immune from claims arising from the inherent risks of the activity, but they would not be responsible for injuries resulting from their own carelessness and negligence in the operation of the snowtubing facility. We recognize that the plaintiff had the option of walking away. We cannot say, however, that the defendants had no bargaining advantage under these circumstances.

For the foregoing reasons, we conclude that the agreement in the present matter affects the public interest adversely and, therefore, is unenforceable because it violates public policy. Accordingly, the trial court improperly rendered summary judgment in favor of the defendants.

The defendants point out that our conclusion represents the "distinct minority view" and is inconsistent with the majority of sister state authority upholding exculpatory agreements in similar recreational settings. We acknowledge that most states uphold adhesion contracts releasing recreational operators from prospective liability for personal injuries caused by their own negligent conduct. Put simply, we disagree with these decisions for the reasons already explained in this opinion. Moreover, we find it significant that many states uphold exculpatory agreements in the context of simple negligence, but refuse to enforce such agreements in the context of *gross* negligence. Accordingly, although in some states recreational operators cannot, consistent with public policy, release themselves from prospective liability for conduct that is more egregious than *simple* negligence, in this state, were we to adopt the position advocated by the

defendants, recreational operators would be able to release their liability for such conduct unless it rose to the level of *recklessness*. As a result, recreational operators would lack the incentive to exercise even slight care, with the public bearing the costs of the resulting injuries ("'gross negligence' is commonly defined as very great or excessive negligence, or as the want of, or failure to exercise, even slight or scant care or 'slight diligence'"). Such a result would be inconsistent with the public policy of this state.

Reversed and remanded.

Questions

1. The plaintiff, Hanks, argued that the Powder Mountain release was unenforceable because the ordinary person would not have understood the release to absolve Powder Ridge of liability in the event of injury. The court rejected that argument. Explain why.

2. The court supported Hanks' public policy argument. Explain why.

3. The court labeled the release a "standardized adhesion contract." Explain what the court meant.

4. The court acknowledged that most states support the legality of releases like the one Hanks signed. Explain why such contracts are enforceable in most states.

5. a. Would a release like that in *Hanks* be enforceable if it involved a school district excusing iself from liability for any injury that might befall students on a class field trip? Explain.

    b. What if the school release sought to excuse the school not from its own negligence, but merely from events beyond the school's control? Explain.

6. Ning Yan went to Gay's fitness center to use a one-week complimentary pass. On each visit he signed in on a sheet that contained a standard exculpatory clause including this language: "I also understand that Vital Power Fitness Center assumes no responsibility for any injuries and/or sicknesses incurred to me. . . . " On February 18, 1999, Yan fell from a treadmill and sustained a severe head injury. He later died from that injury. No one witnessed that fall. Yan's estate claims that he struck his head against a window ledge because the treadmill was placed too close to the window. If he did strike the window ledge, who would likely win this case? Explain. See *Xu v. Gay*, 668 N. W. 2d 166 (Ct. App. Mich. 2003).

Part Two—Interpreting and Enforcing Contracts

We have examined the five ingredients in a binding contract: agreement, consideration, capacity, genuineness of assent, and legality of purpose. Having established those conditions, a contract may have been created, but the door to contract problems has not been closed. Contracts sometimes must fulfill writing formalities to be enforceable. Third parties may have claims against some contracts. And what happens when a party to a contract does not perform as called for by the agreement?

In Writing?

Certainly the common belief is that agreements must be in writing to be enforceable; but in most cases, oral contracts are fully enforceable. However, the exceptions are important. Oral contracts are subject to misunderstanding or to being forgotten, and fraudulent claims can readily arise from oral understandings. Consequently, our states have drawn upon the English *Statute of Frauds* in specifying that the following kinds of contracts, in most cases, must be in writing to be enforceable:

> In most cases, oral contracts are fully enforceable.

1. **Collateral contract.** Assume you have just graduated from college, and you want to get started in a small printing business. You secure a bank loan on the condition that you find a creditworthy third party as a guarantor for the loan. Jacobs, a family friend, agrees with the bank to pay the debt if you fail to do so. Jacobs's promise to pay the debt must be in writing to be enforceable.

2. **The sale of land.** Broadly, *land* is interpreted to include the surface itself, that which is in the soil (minerals) or permanently attached to it (buildings), and growing crops when accompanying the transfer of land. Thus if a building was permanently attached to a lot you seek for the aforementioned printing business, that building would need to be included in the written contract; but if you contracted to have a building constructed on your lot, you would not need (at least for the purposes of the Statute of Frauds) to execute a written agreement with the building contractor because you would not be contracting for an interest in land. A long-term lease (normally more than one year) for that land and building would, in most states, need to be in writing. All of these principles simply reflect the special role of land in our view of wealth and freedom.

3. **Promises that cannot be performed within one year.** This requirement springs from a concern about faulty memories, deaths, and other impediments to the satisfactory conclusion of long-term contracts. The courts have interpreted this provision narrowly, in effect saying that such a contract need not be in writing if it is *possible,* according to its terms, to perform it within one year from the day of its creation. It follows then that a contract for an indefinite period (such as an employment contract "for the balance of the employee's life") need not be in writing to be enforceable. (It is possible that the employee will die within one year.)

4. **Contracts for the sale of goods at a price of $500 or more.** With exceptions, under both the English-derived Statute of Frauds and UCC 2-201, contracts for the sale of goods (having a value of $500 or more under the UCC) must be in writing to be

enforceable. Under the UCC, informal writing will suffice so long as it indicates that a contract was made, it contains a quantity term, and it was signed "by the party against whom enforcement is sought." Section 2-201 provides exceptions for certain transactions of $500 or more in goods in which a contract will be enforceable even though not in writing.

5. **Contracts in consideration of marriage.**   The mutual exchange of marriage promises need not be in writing, but any contract that uses marriage as the consideration to support the contract must be in writing to be enforceable. Such contracts would include, for example, prenuptial agreements that are entered prior to marriage and serve the purpose, among others, of specifying how the couple's property will be divided in the event of a divorce. Those contracts must be in writing to be enforceable.

6. **Executor/administrator's promise.**   When an individual dies, a representative is appointed to oversee the estate. A promise by that executor/administrator to pay the estate's debts must be in writing if the payment will be made from the executor/administrator's personal funds. Thus, where the executor of an estate contracts with an auctioneer to dispose of the decedent's personal property, the executor's promise to pay the auctioneer must be in writing if the funds are to come from the executor's personal resources; the promise need not be in writing if the payment is to come from the estate.

[As we have noted, the state legislatures are considering various changes in the UCC, Article 2, including the Statute of Frauds (UCC 2-201—see the appendix) as recommended by the National Conference of Commissioners on Uniform State Laws (NCCUSL). Among the proposed changes, the $500 sale of goods standard would increase to $5,000, and electronic signatures and writings would satisfy Statute of Frauds requirements.]

Failure to Comply   A fully performed oral contract, even though not in compliance with the Statute of Frauds, will not be rescinded by the courts. However, incomplete oral contracts that fail to comply with the statute are unenforceable. If a party to an unenforceable oral contract has provided partial performance in reliance on the contract, the courts will ordinarily provide compensation under quasi-contract principles for the reasonable value of that performance. [For more on the Statute of Frauds, see **http://www.expertlaw.com/ library/business/statute_of_frauds.html**]

The Parol Evidence Rule

Suppose you are the purchasing manager for a large manufacturer. You entered a written contract for 50 new personal computers. During negotiations, the seller said they would "throw in" 10 new printers if they got the computer order, but you failed to include a provision for the printers in the contract. Is your boss about to have a fit? Perhaps, because you probably will not be able to introduce evidence of that oral understanding to alter the terms of the written contract. In general, whenever a contract has been reduced to writing with the intent that the writing represents a complete and final integration of the parties' intentions, none of the parties can introduce *parol evidence* (oral or written words outside the "four corners" of the agreement) to add to, change, or contradict that contract when that evidence was expressed/created at the time of or prior to the writing. The written agreement is presumed to be the best evidence of the parties' intentions at the time they entered the contract. (The parol evidence rule under UCC section 2-202 is essentially the same as the common-law provisions discussed here.)

Exceptions   Parol evidence may be admissible under the following exceptional circumstances:

1. To add missing terms to an incomplete written contract.
2. To explain ambiguities in a written contract.
3. To prove circumstances that would invalidate a written contract; that is, to establish one of the grounds of mistake, fraud, illegality, and so forth explained earlier in this chapter.

E-mail a "Signed Writing?"

Stevens' employment agreement with Publicis required that any modification of the agreement was to be signed by the parties. Stevens and Bloom (representing Publicis) exchanged e-mails changing Stevens' employment duties. The parties' names were typed at the end of each e-mail.

Question

Does that exchange of e-mails constitute a binding agreement?

  Explain.

Source: Stevens v. Publicis, 854 N.Y.S. 2d 690 (2008).

Third Parties

We turn now to the rights and duties of those who are not parties to a contract but hold legally recognizable interests in that contract. Those interests arise when (1) contract rights are assigned to others, (2) contract duties are delegated to others, or (3) contracts have third-party beneficiary provisions.

Assignment of Rights

Ordinarily, a party to a contract is free to transfer her or his rights under the contract to a third party. Thus, if Ames owes Jones $500 for work performed, Jones can *assign* that right to Smith, who can now assert her right to collect against Ames. That transfer of rights is labeled an *assignment* (see Figure 6.3). Jones, the party making the transfer, is

FIGURE 6.3
Assignment of Rights

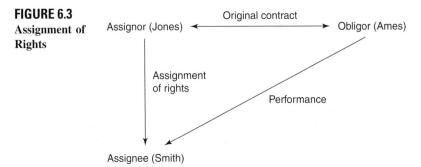

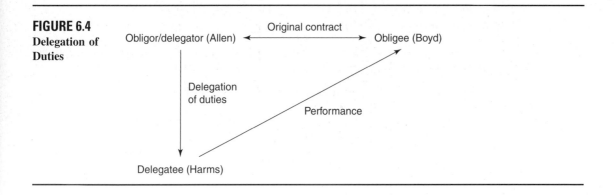

FIGURE 6.4
Delegation of Duties

the *assignor;* Smith, the one receiving the right, is the *assignee;* and Ames, the party who must perform, is the *obligor*. Ames, the obligor, must now perform the contract for the benefit of the assignee; that is, Ames must pay the $500 to Smith. The completed assignment then extinguishes the assignor's rights under the contract.

Some contracts are not assignable without consent of the obligor. That would be the case where the obligor's duties are materially altered by the assignment. For example, if you have a contract to serve as a personal fitness trainer for a busy chief executive officer, your contract could not be assigned without your consent to another CEO, or movie star, or the like because the highly personal and specific obligations under the contract would necessarily be materially altered with a different client.

Delegation of Duties

The parties to a contract may also delegate their *duties* under the contract to one or more third parties. Assume Allen has secured a contract to install windows in Boyd's new office building (see Figure 6.4). Allen could delegate that duty to another contractor, Harms (although Allen would more commonly simply enter a subcontracting arrangement without actually transferring the underlying contract). A delegation of duty leaves Harms, the *delegatee,* (the one to whom the duty is delegated) primarily responsible for performance; but Allen, the *obligor/delegator,* (the one who made the delegation) remains secondarily liable in case Harms, the delegatee, fails to fulfill the duty to Boyd, the *obligee* (the one to whom the duty is owed under both the original contract and the delegation). As with the assignment of rights, some contractual duties, particularly those of a personal service nature, cannot be delegated without consent.

The case that follows involves an employee, Burkhardt, who signed a noncompetition covenant with his employer providing that he would not work for a competitor in the area for one year. Burkhardt was later sued for violating that covenant. The district court ruled against Burkhardt, and the appeal that follows addresses the question of whether his noncompete clause was assignable.

Traffic Control Services, Inc., vs. United Rentals Northwest, Inc.; and NES Companies, L.P. 87 P.3d 1054 (Nev. S. Ct. 2004)

PER CURIAM

Philip A. Burkhardt and his current employer, Traffic Control Services, Inc., d/b/a Allied Trench Shoring Services, appeal the issuance of a preliminary injunction enforcing a noncompetition convenant in favor of United Rentals Northwest, Inc., the purchaser of the corporate assets of Burkhardt's former employer, NES Trench Shoring.

The primary issue on appeal is whether an employer in a corporate sale may assign rights under an employee's covenant not to compete without the employee's consent. . . .

FACTUAL HISTORY

Burkhardt specializes in the selling and renting of trench shoring equipment to construction contractors in the Las Vegas area. United employed Burkhardt during the years 1999 and 2000. In September 2000, he became dissatisfied with United's customer service policies and obtained a position in Las Vegas with NES, which he felt provided more specialized service and better opportunities for career advancement.

As a condition of employment with NES, and in exchange for $10,000, he signed noncompetition and nondisclosure covenants. The covenants stipulated that, if Burkhardt's employment with NES was terminated, Burkhardt would not, for a period of one year, engage in selling, leasing, marketing, distributing, or dealing with trench shoring equipment within a sixty-mile radius of his work location. . . .

On June 30, 2002, United and NES entered into an asset purchase agreement, including goodwill, under which United paid three times the concern's fair market value. The purchase agreement was limited to certain assets, providing that "all contracts and agreements that are not listed as 'Assumed Contracts' are 'Excluded Assets.'" While the agreement listed other noncompetition covenants as assumed contracts, Burkhardt's noncompetition covenant was not on the list. Notwithstanding the contract terms, NES's negotiators submitted affidavits in the proceedings below asserting that the asset sale included all of NES's noncompetition covenants, including the one with Burkhardt.

A week before closure of the asset purchase, United requested or demanded that a significant number of the listed key employees sign new one-year noncompetition and nondisclosure covenants. Consideration for the new covenants included salary packages to be paid during the noncompetition enforcement period and incentive bonuses. Nine of the eighty-one key employees, including Burkhardt, refused to sign the new covenants.

Burkhardt remained as United's Las Vegas sales manager during the transition period following the sale, but again became dissatisfied with United's customer service. He began negotiations in early August 2002 with Traffic Control, United's direct competitor. Burkhardt informed Traffic Control about his noncompetition covenant with NES, which he believed was invalid because he was terminating employment with United, not NES.

On August 5, 2002, Burkhardt accepted employment with Traffic Control. That same day, he signed United's policies and procedure bulletin, which defined confidential information and the policy regarding nondisclosure. United terminated Burkhardt's employment on August 8, 2002, after which he returned all of his work-related items to company officials.

Burkhardt commenced his new position on August 10, 2002, after signing new noncompetition and nondisclosure covenants. He began contacting companies to solicit business on behalf of Traffic Control but was mostly unsuccessful in obtaining new business.

* * * * *

PROCEDURAL HISTORY

On August 27, 2002, NES and United filed a complaint alleging that Burkhardt obtained confidential information during his employment with them and that he subsequently used and disclosed NES/United confidential information, contacted United's clients, and attempted to solicit United's customers. The district court ultimately entered a preliminary injunction enforcing the NES noncompetition covenant for a period of one year following termination and enjoining Burkhardt from using or disclosing confidential information learned during his employment with NES and United. In this, the district court concluded that Burkhardt's noncompetition covenant was reasonable in time and scope, assignable as an asset of value, and that NES validly assigned the covenant to United in the asset sale.

* * * * *

Assignability of Noncompetition Covenants

Traffic Control and Burkhardt contend that the purported assignment was invalid. We agree and hold that, absent an agreement negotiated at arm's length, which explicitly permits assignment and which is supported by separate consideration, employee noncompetition covenants are not assignable.

Employers commonly rely upon restrictive covenants, primarily nondisclosure and noncompetition covenants, to safeguard important business interests. "The non-disclosure covenant limits the dissemination of proprietary information by a former employee, while the non-competition covenant precludes the former employee from competing with his prior employer for a specified period of time and within a precise geographic area."

* * * * *

Burkhardt and Traffic Control argue that NES could not assign the noncompetition covenant to United without Burkhardt's consent because the covenant was personal to Burkhardt, that the asset purchase agreement did not contain a clause permitting the assignment, and that Burkhardt only consented to be bound to NES when he signed the covenant. They contend that NES could have included a clause in the covenant permitting assignment or negotiated for Burkhardt's consent, but chose not to do so. Burkhardt and Traffic Control also argue that the attempted assignment to United is unenforceable as against public policy, because Burkhardt was unable to assess his new employer and weigh the benefits and burdens of being bound by a noncompetition covenant with United. They argue that the district court's ruling bound Burkhardt to United, an employer for whom he did not wish to work.

In response, NES and United argue that NES validly assigned Burkhardt's covenant as an asset of

value and that a majority of courts allow enforcement of such assignments by the assignee. NES and United also argue that the covenant was not the equivalent of a personal services contract because it only required Burkhardt "to abstain from certain activities." Finally, they argue that judicial enforcement of Burkhardt's covenant does not violate public policy; rather, public policy supports enforcement of the covenant to protect the health of the business and its goodwill.

We agree with those jurisdictions holding that noncompetition covenants are personal in nature and, therefore, unassignable as a matter of law, absent the employee's express consent. When an employee enters into a covenant not to compete with his employer, he may consider the character and personality of his employer to determine whether he is willing to be held to a contract that will restrain him from future competition with his employer, even after termination of employment. This does not mean, however, that the employee is willing to suffer the same restriction with a stranger to the original obligation.

Burkhardt's covenant did not contain an assignment clause. While some courts have concluded that such an omission does not bar assignment, a reading of assignability into the covenant is contrary to the intentions of the original parties to it. As we have stated, if no ambiguity exists in a contract, "the words of the contract must be taken in their usual and ordinary signification." NES, as the drafter of the covenant, was in the best position to negotiate for an assignment clause. However, for whatever reason, it chose not to do so.

While NES and United would place the burden on the employee to request a clause prohibiting assignment, we believe the burden rests with the employer. We hold that, in Nevada, a covenant not to compete is unassignable absent an express clause permitting assignment. Recognizing that noncompetition covenants must be supported by valuable consideration, which may include continued employment after the employee's agreement to the covenant, we also hold that assignability clauses must be negotiated at arm's length and supported by additional and separate consideration from that given in exchange for the covenant itself. This places the burden on the employer to seek assignability and adequately compensates the party with the lesser bargaining power for the possibility that a stranger to the covenant may ultimately assume the right to its enforcement.

* * * * *

Reversed.

1. *a.* What was the central issue in this case? .
   b. Explain the role of consideration in this case.
2. Why did the court rule as it did?
3. Do you agree with the court that a noncompetition covenant is personal in nature and should not be assigned without the employee's consent? Explain.

Third-Party Beneficiary Contracts

Normally, those not a party to a contract have no rights with respect to it. As we have seen, however, third parties may be assigned rights or delegated duties under a contract. A third party may also enforce a contract where that contract was expressly intended to benefit the third party. An agreement of that nature is a third-party beneficiary contract. *Third-party beneficiaries* are of three kinds: creditor, donee, and incidental. In general, creditor and donee beneficiaries can enforce contracts made by others for their benefit; incidental beneficiaries cannot do so.

Creditor Beneficiary Assume you decide to expand your used car business by advertising on television. Your ads appear on TV, and you owe the local station $2,000. Rather than paying the bill directly, you transfer a used car to your friend, Gleason, with the understanding that he will pay off your bill with the television station. Thus the station becomes the *creditor beneficiary* of the contract between you and Gleason, and the station can sue Gleason for that money if necessary while you remain secondarily responsible for the payment.

Donee Beneficiary When the promisee's primary purpose in entering a contract is to make a gift to another, that third party is a *donee beneficiary* of the contract. The most common of these situations involves an ordinary life insurance policy for which the owner (the promisee) pays premiums to the life insurance company (the promisor), which is obliged to pay benefits to the third party upon the death of the promisee/policy owner. If necessary, the third-party beneficiary can sue the insurance company for payment.

Incidental Beneficiary Often a third party receives benefit from a contract although that was not the contracting parties' primary purpose or intent. For example, assume a General Motors car dealer enters into a contract to buy land adjacent to your used car lot for the purpose of opening a large dealership. You would benefit immensely from the spillover effect of the large, adjacent dealership. In such a situation, you would be an *incidental beneficiary* of the land sale contract because that contract was not intended for your benefit. If the landowner or the GM dealer failed to perform, you, as an incidental beneficiary, would have no legal rights against either of them.

At some point, obligations under a contract come to an end. When that moment arrives, we say the duties of the contracting parties have been *discharged.*

Discharge

In this section we examine some of the methods of contract discharge. Discharge can occur in many ways, but the most important of these are (1) conditions, (2) performance or breach, (3) lawful excuses, (4) agreement, and (5) operation of law.

Discharge by Conditions

Sometimes a contract is useful to one or more of the contracting parties only if some future event occurs or fails to occur. Under those circumstances, the parties may write into the contract a clause providing that performance is required only if the specified condition occurs or fails to occur. Otherwise, the duty to perform is discharged. Those conditions take three forms: conditions precedent, conditions subsequent, and conditions concurrent.

Conditions Precedent A *conditions precedent* clause specifies that an event must occur before the parties to the contract are obliged to perform. Assume you are attempting to establish a business booking rock-and-roll acts for performances. You sign a deal with the rock group Pearl Jam, providing for a performance "contingent upon obtaining satisfactory lease arrangements for the university fieldhouse within 14 days." If you are unable to achieve an acceptable lease, both parties are discharged from performance requirements under the contract.

Conditions Subsequent A *conditions subsequent* clause excuses performance if a future event transpires. Thus, in the Pearl Jam example, the band might include a clause providing that the agreement will be null and void if any member of the band is ill or otherwise unable to perform on the contracted evening. Hence in a contract with a condition subsequent the parties have bound themselves to perform *unless* a specified event occurs; whereas in a contract with a condition precedent the parties have no binding duties *until* the specified event occurs.

Conditions Concurrent Here the contract simply specifies that the parties are to perform their duties at the same time. Each performance is dependent on the other. So if Pearl Jam performs as contracted, you have a simultaneous duty to pay them for their performance. Your duty to pay is conditioned on Pearl Jam's performance and vice versa.

Express or Implied Conditions Another way of classifying the aforementioned conditions is to treat them either as express or implied. *Express conditions* are those explicitly agreed to by the parties, as in the situation where you, a concert promoter, expressly conditioned performance on your ability to secure the university fieldhouse for the concert. Express conditions are often prefaced by words such as *when, if, provided,* and so forth.

Implied-in-fact conditions are not explicitly stated in the contract but are derived by the court from the conduct of the parties and the circumstances surrounding the bargain. Suppose you contract to remove snow from your neighbor's driveway during the winter. An implied-in-fact condition of your neighbor's duty to pay would be that you would complete the work within a reasonable period.

Implied-in-law conditions (also called *constructive conditions*) are those that, although not expressly provided for in the contract or not able to be reasonably inferred from the facts, the court imposes on the contract to avoid unfairness. Hence, if you contracted to put a new roof on your neighbor's house but your written contract did not include a date for payment, the court might imply a contract clause providing that your neighbor need not pay you until the job is complete.

Whose Ring?

Barry Meyer and Robyn Mitnick became engaged on August 9, 1996, at which time Barry gave Robyn a custom-designed, $19,500 engagement ring. On November 8, 1996, Barry asked Robyn to sign a prenuptial agreement, but Robyn refused. The parties agree the engagement ended at that point, but they each blame the other for the breakup. Robyn did not return the ring, and Barry sued for its return.

Questions

1. Explain each party's argument using contract principles.
2. Does it matter who was "at fault" in the breakup? Explain.
3. Who gets the ring? Explain.

Source: Meyer v. Mitnick, 625 N.W.2d 136 (Ct. App. Mich. 2001).

Discharge by Performance or Breach of Contract

Complete performance is, of course, the normal way of discharging a contract. Failure to fully perform without a lawful excuse for that failure results in a breach of contract. The consequences of both full performance and breach of contract can be described in four parts.

Complete Performance—No Breach of Contract   Here we find the statistically normal situation in which the parties simply do precisely what the contract calls for: pay $500, provide a particular product, present the deed for a piece of land, and so on. When fully performed, a contract has been *executed*.

Substantial Performance—Nonmaterial Breach of Contract   In some cases complete performance is not achieved because of minor deviations from the agreed-upon performance. Most notably in construction contracts and in many personal or professional service contracts, the courts have recognized the doctrine of *substantial performance*. For example, assume a contractor painted a house as agreed, except that he replaced the Sears exterior paint called for in the contract with a Sherwin-Williams paint of comparable quality. Assuming the variation has not materially altered the end product and assuming that the variation was not the result of bad faith, the court will enforce the contract as written, but require a deduction for any damages sustained as a consequence of the imperfect performance.

Unacceptable Performance—Material Breach of Contract   When a party falls beneath substantial performance and does not have a lawful excuse for that failure, a *material* *breach* of contract has occurred. No clear line separates substantial performance (a non-material breach) from unacceptable performance (a material breach). Such decisions must be made case by case. We can say that material breaches are those that fall short of what the nonbreaching party should reasonably expect—that is, full performance in some cases and substantial performance in others. A material breach discharges the nonbreaching party's duties and permits that party to sue for damages or rescind the contract and seek restitution.

Advance Refusal to Perform—Anticipatory Breach of Contract Sometimes one of the parties, before performance is due, indicates by word or deed that she or he will not perform. Normally an *anticipatory breach* (also called *anticipatory repudiation*) is the equivalent of a material breach, discharging the nonbreaching party from any further obligations and allowing the nonbreaching party to sue for damages, if any.

An Alleged Breach and Public Policy The brief case that follows raises many claims, including breach of contract. The case is an interesting test of the role of law. Should sports fans be able to secure a remedy through contract law when an event does not meet their expectations? The idea seems preposterous and another instance of abuse of the legal system, but consider the facts.

> Tyson spit out his mouthpiece and bit both of Holyfield's ears

The case deals with ex-convict and former heavyweight boxing champion Mike Tyson and his famous 1997 bout with then-champion Evander Holyfield, a fight ended by disqualification in the third round when Tyson spit out his mouthpiece and bit both of Holyfield's ears. Incensed pay-per-view customers joined in a class action seeking their money back ($50–60 each) claiming they were "ripped off" or "scammed" by Tyson. They sued Tyson, fight promoters, and fight telecasters. A lower court dismissed the complaint for failure to state a cause of action. The plaintiffs appealed.

LEGAL BRIEFCASE

Castillo v. Tyson   701 N.Y.S. 2D 423
(N.Y. S. Ct. App. Div. 2000)

Judge Ramos

Plaintiffs claim that they were entitled to view a "legitimate heavyweight title fight" fought "in accordance with the applicable rules and regulations" of the governing boxing commission—that is, a fight that was to end either in an actual or technical knockout or by decision of the judges after 12 rounds—and that they are entitled to their money back because the fight ended in a disqualification. Many legal theories are invoked in support of this claim—breach of contract, breach of implied covenant of good faith and fair dealing, unjust enrichment, breach of express and implied warranties, tortious interference with contractual relations, "wantonness," fraud, negligent representation—none of which have merit. Plaintiffs are not in contractual privity with any of the defendants, and their claim that they are third-party beneficiaries of one or more of the contracts that defendants entered into among themselves was aptly rejected by the motion court as "contrived." Nothing in these contracts can be understood as promising a fight that did not end in a disqualification. The rules of the governing commission provide for disqualification, and it is a possibility that a fight fan can reasonably expect. Plaintiffs could not reasonably rule out such a possibility by the boxer's and promoters' public statements predicting a "sensational victory" and "the biggest fight of all time," and assuming other representations were made promising or implying a "legitimate fight," there can be no breach of warranty claim absent privity of contract between plaintiffs and defendants and also because defendants provided only a service. Nor is a claim of fraud supported by plaintiffs' allegations that the boxer's former trainer predicted that the boxer would get himself disqualified if he failed to achieve an early knockout and that the boxer came out without his mouthpiece in the beginning of the round that he was disqualified. Plaintiffs' claim for unjust enrichment was properly dismissed by the motion court on the ground that plaintiffs received what they paid for, namely, "the right to view whatever event transpired." We have considered plaintiffs' other arguments . . . and find them unpersuasive.

Affirmed.

Questions

1. Why did the court reject the plaintiffs' breach of contract claim?
2. What is unjust enrichment, and why was that claim denied by the court?

3. Defects discovered in the Michelin tires to be used by 14 of the 20 teams in a Formula One race at the Indianapolis Speedway caused those teams to withdraw prior to the start, leaving only six cars running in the race. The race was completed, but fans sued for breach of contract claiming the race was not what they had purchased tickets to see and that the race advertising had indicated that 20 cars would be racing. Decide the case. Explain. See *Bowers v. Federation Internationale de L'Automobile*, 489 F.3d 316 (7th Cir. 2007).

4. Pelullo promoted boxers and boxing matches through his company, Banner Productions. In 1999 Echols signed an agreement with Banner giving Echols a $30,000 bonus and giving Banner "the sole and exclusive right to secure all professional boxing bouts" for Echols. Banner was to provide no fewer than three bouts per year, and Echols was to be paid not less than a specified minimum amount for each fight, but the payments could be lowered or the whole agreement canceled, at Banner's option, if Echols lost a fight. Echols lost a championship bout, and Banner said it would thereafter negotiate each purse on a bout-by-bout basis. Echols continued to fight for Banner, but various disputes over purses arose, and Echols sued. Among other claims, Echols argued that the agreement was unenforceable for indefiniteness. Decide that claim. Explain. See *Echols v. Pelullo*, 377 F.3d 272 (3d Cir. 2004).

Discharge by Lawful Excuses (for Nonperformance)

Sometimes contracts are discharged lawfully even in the event of nonperformance. This can occur when performance is either impossible or impractical.

Impossibility   After agreement is reached but performance is not yet due, circumstances may be so altered that performance is a *legal impossibility*. In such situations nonperformance is excused. *Impossibility* here refers not simply to extreme difficulty but to objective impossibility; that is, the contracted-for performance cannot be accomplished by anyone. Notable examples of such situations are a personal service contract where the promisor has died or is incapacitated by illness, a contract where the subject of the agreement was rendered illegal by a change in the law subsequent to the agreement but prior to its performance, or a contract where an ingredient essential to performance has been destroyed and no reasonable substitutes are available. [For more on impossibility of performance, see **http://www.west.net/~smith/imposbl.htm**]

Commercial Impracticability   Akin to the doctrine of impossibility is the situation in which duties are discharged because of unforeseen events that render performance exorbitantly expensive or thoroughly impractical. *Commercial impracticability* is specifically provided for in UCC 2-615, which reads, "Delay in delivery or nondelivery in whole or in part by a seller... is not a breach of his duty under a contract for sale if performance as agreed has been made impracticable by the occurrence of a contingency the nonoccurrence of which was a basic assumption on which the contract was made. . . ."

The UCC's commercial impracticability standard is more easily established than the impossibility doctrine of the common law, but note that only exceptional and unforeseeable events fall within the impracticability excuse for nonperformance. Mere changes in market conditions do not give rise to commercial impracticability. Historically, the commercial impracticability doctrine had been applied only to transactions involving the sale of goods, but now we see courts increasingly willing to apply it to other kinds of contracts as well.

PRACTICING ETHICS) $25,000 in Dance Lessons

In November 1959 Ryland Parker, a 37-year-old, college-educated bachelor, went to the Arthur Murray Dance Studio for three free lessons. While there, he was told that he had "exceptional potential to become an accomplished dancer." Parker signed a contract for lessons, at the bottom of which in boldface capital type were the phrases "noncancellable negotiable contract" and "I understand that no refunds will be made under the terms of this contract." Parker subsequently entered and prepaid additional contracts totaling 2,734 hours of lessons and $24,812. All of those contracts had similar language boldly displayed. Parker was severely injured in a 1961 auto accident, rendering him incapable of continuing the lessons. His repeated requests for a refund were denied, and he sued Arthur Murray. The trial court found for Parker and ordered a refund for the unused lessons on the grounds of impossibility of performance. An appeals court affirmed that decision. See *Parker v. Arthur Murray, Inc.,* 295 N.E.2d 487 (1973).

Questions

1. In this case, did the law excuse Parker from an obligation he was ethically bound to honor? Explain.

2. If Parker did not have "exceptional potential to become an accomplished dancer," did the Arthur Murray Studio commit an ethical wrong in encouraging this 2,734-hour contract at a price of $24,812? Explain.

Discharge by Agreement

A contractual discharge is sometimes achieved by a new agreement arrived at after entering the original contract. These agreements take a variety of forms, but one—*accord and satisfaction*—will serve here to illustrate the general category. Parties reach an accord when they agree to a performance different from the one provided for in their contract. Performance of the accord is called *satisfaction,* at which point the original contract is discharged. A binding accord and satisfaction must spring from a genuine dispute between the parties, and it must include consideration as well as all of the other ingredients in a binding contract.

Discharge by Operation of Law

Under some circumstances, contractual duties are discharged by the legal system itself. Among those possibilities: (1) The contractual responsibilities of a debtor may be discharged by a bankruptcy decree. (2) Each state has a *statute of limitations* that specifies the time within which a performing party can initiate a lawsuit against a nonperforming party. For the UCC statute of limitations, see 2-725.

Remedies

An important ingredient in successful business practice is a rudimentary understanding of your rights in the event you are the victim of a breach of contract. We have looked at the elements of a binding contract and at those circumstances that discharge a party's duties under a contract. Now our concern is with what happens when one of the parties does not fulfill his or her contractual duties—that is, when the contract is breached. Remedies are provided in both law and in equity.

Remedies in Law

In general, a breach of contract allows the nonbreaching party to sue for money damages. The general goal of remedies law is to put the parties in the position they would have occupied had the contract been fulfilled. Normally, the best available substitute for actual performance is monetary damages.

Compensatory Damages

Fundamentally, the plaintiff in a breach of contract action is entitled to recover a sum equal to the actual damages suffered. The plaintiff is compensated for her losses by receiving a sum designed to "make her whole," to put her where she would have been had the contract not been breached.

Sale of Goods   A breach involving a sale of goods would be governed by the UCC. Typically the measure of *compensatory damages* would be the difference between the contract price and the market price of the goods at the time and place the goods were to be delivered (see UCC 2-708 and 2-713). Suppose you are working for a newly established computer manufacturer, and you have contracted with the Internal Revenue Service to deliver 1,000 laptop computers at $1,500 each, although the current market price is $1,600. If you fail to make that delivery, damages could be assessed in the amount of $100,000 ($100 × 1,000), which is the additional amount the IRS would need to pay to make the substitute purchase.

Consequential Damages   The victim of a breach may be able to recover not just the direct losses from the breach but also any indirect losses that were incurred as a consequence of that breach. Such *consequential damages* are recoverable only if they were foreseen or were reasonably foreseeable by the breaching party. For example, if you contract for a well-known local band to play for the grand opening of your new bar and dance club, you may be able to recover damages for any lost profits that you can attribute to the band's failure to appear. Those lost profits are a *consequence* of the breach. Of course, you will have some difficulty in specifying the profits lost and in proving that the loss was attributable to the band's failure to perform.

Incidental Damages The costs incurred by the nonbreaching party in arranging a substitute performance or otherwise reducing the damages sustained because of the breach are recoverable as *incidental damages.* They would include such items as phone calls and transportation expenses.

Nominal Damages In some cases of breach, the court will award only an insignificant sum, perhaps $1 (plus court costs), because the nonbreaching party has suffered no actual damages. The point of *nominal damages* is to illustrate the wrongfulness of the breach.

Punitive Damages Sometimes when the breaching party's conduct is particularly reprehensible, the court will penalize that party by awarding *punitive damages* to the injured party. The idea is to deter such conduct in the future. Normally punitive damages cannot be awarded in breach of contract cases except when provided for by statute or when the breach is accompanied by a tort such as fraud (as where one buys a defective car having reasonably relied on the falsehoods of a salesperson).

Rescission and Restitution In some instances, including a material breach, mistake, fraud, undue influence, and duress, the wronged party may rescind (undo) the contract. The effect of a contract *rescission* is to return the parties to the positions they occupied before they entered the agreement. Generally, both parties must then make *restitution* to each other by returning whatever goods, property, and so forth were transferred under the contract or an equivalent amount of money.

Mitigation Obviously the law should penalize a breaching party, as we have discussed; but you may be surprised to learn that the law also imposes expectations on the victim (the nonbreaching party). Specifically, the nonbreaching party is required to take reasonable steps toward *mitigation*—that is, to minimize her or his damages. What happens, for example, if you are wrongfully dismissed in breach of contract from your first job after college? You are required to mitigate your damages by seeking another job. You need not take an inferior job, nor must you disturb your life by moving to another state or community; but you must take reasonable measures to minimize your claim against your former employer.

Liquidated Damages We have reviewed the legal penalties for breach and the duty to mitigate. The law also offers you the opportunity to provide some control over the penalty for breach by including in your contract a *liquidated damages* clause. Here you and the other party to the contract agree in advance about the measure of damages should either of you default on your duties. That clause is fully enforceable so long as it is not designed to be a penalty but rather a good faith effort to assess in advance an accurate measure of damages. A valid liquidated damages clause limits the nonbreaching party to recovery of the amount provided for in that clause.

Remedies in Equity

Where justice cannot be achieved via money damages alone, the courts will sometimes impose *equitable remedies*. The chief forms of equitable remedy in contract cases are specific performance, injunction, reformation, and quasi-contract.

Specific Performance   In unusual circumstances the court may order the breaching party to remedy its wrong by performing its obligations precisely as provided for in the contract. Normally that *specific performance* is required only where the subject matter of the contract is unique and thus cannot be adequately compensated with money. Examples of such subject matter might include a particular piece of land, an art work, or a family heirloom. By contrast, specific performance would not be available in contracts involving conventional personal property such as a television or a car unless those items were unique (such as a one-of-a-kind Rolls Royce).

Normally the courts will not grant a specific performance remedy in personal service contracts (like an agreement by a cosmetic surgeon to perform a face-lift). If the surgeon refused to perform, specific performance probably would not be ordered. The quality of the surgery likely would not be equal to what had been bargained for; courts do not want to be in the position of supervising the completion of contracts, and as a matter of public policy, we do not want to put parties, in this case, the surgeon, in a position that amounts to involuntary servitude.

Injunction   An *injunction* is a court order that may either require or forbid a party to perform a specified act. Injunctions are granted only under exceptional circumstances. Perhaps the most common of those are the noncompetition agreements discussed earlier in this chapter. For example, you take a computer programming job that will afford you access to company secrets. To protect itself, the company expects you to sign an agreement specifying that you will not take employment with a competing firm for one year after departure from your employer. If you should quit and seek to work for a competitor within one year, your former employer might be able to secure an injunction preventing you from doing so until the year has passed.

Reformation   *Reformation* is an equitable remedy that permits the court to rewrite the contract where it imperfectly expressed the parties' true intentions. Typically such situations involve mutual mistake or fraud. Thus if the parties sign a contract to sell a lot in a housing development, but the contract is written with an incorrect street address for the lot, an equity court could simply correct the error in the contract.

Quasi-Contract   What happens if one party has conferred a benefit on another, but a contract has not been created because of a failure of consideration, the application of the statute of frauds, or something of the sort? To prevent unjust enrichment, the court might then imply a contract as a matter of law. For example, assume a lawn service mistakenly trims your shrubs and you watch them do so, knowing that they are supposed to be caring for your neighbor's lawn. You have not entered a contract with the lawn service, but a court might well require you to pay the reasonable value of trimming your shrubs. To do otherwise would unjustly enrich you.

PRACTICING ETHICS — Maytag and Jobs Gone South

In 1995 the Maytag Corporation (since absorbed by Whirlpool) reached a $16.5 million settlement with former employees at its closed Ranson, West Virginia, vending machine plant. Eight hundred former workers had filed a class action lawsuit claiming that Maytag had lied to them before stopping operations at its Dixie–Narco vending machine plant in 1991. The Dixie–Narco employees were nonunion and were not working under written contracts; however, they claimed that Maytag had repeatedly lied to them about its plans to keep the plant open. The false promises, the lawsuit claimed, added up to an oral contract that the workers relied on to their detriment.

Maytag had spent $37 million renovating a Williston, South Carolina, factory to build soft drink vending machines. Maytag told Ranson workers that the South Carolina plant (where wages were $6 per hour lower) would supplement their work and would not result in a plant closure. Then, according to Maytag, declining business conditions forced the Ranson closing. Lawyers for the plaintiffs displayed in court an internal Maytag document that, according to published reports, showed that as early as 1989 the company had expected to phase out the Ranson operation.

Questions

1. Maytag admitted no ethical or legal violations when the settlement was reached. Do you agree that Maytag was free of wrongdoing in this episode? Explain.

2. Based on what we know of the facts prior to the settlement, do you think that Maytag breached a contract with its employees?

3. How might Maytag have been able to close the plant and yet avoid the subsequent litigation?

For a detailed account of the Ranson/Maytag story, see Barry Bearak, "Lost in America: Jobs, Trust," *Los Angeles Times,* November 26, 1995, p. Al.

Internet Exercise

Go to FindLaw's "Contracts Law" [**http://library.findlaw.com/1999Jan/1/241463.html**]. (1) List the nine tips for avoiding problems in building a contract. (2) Explain the meaning of a "merger clause." [For greater detail on definitions, see **http://profs.lp.findlaw.com/contracts/contract_6.html**].

Chapter Questions

1. Wardle made a standard real estate offer to buy a house owned by Kessler. The offer contained a "time is of the essence" clause specifying that the deal had to be completed on or before 11 AM on September 26, 1997. Owen then submitted a backup purchase offer for the same price as offered by Wardle. Wardle's completed contract was not delivered to Kessler until approximately 11:20 AM on September 26, so Kessler sold to Owen. Wardle then sued Kessler. Decide. Explain. See *Owen v. Kessler,* 778 N.E. 2d 953 (App. Ct. Mass. 2002).

2. A Peoples Group representative interviewed Hawley in Missouri. Hawley and Peoples completed a contract (signed by Hawley in Missouri and Peoples' president in Florida) for Hawley to recruit students in Missouri to attend a Peoples college in Florida. Hawley was to be paid a commission for the students he recruited. Hawley was to be able to participate in the Peoples health and life insurance plans, and Peoples was to provide the appropriate payroll taxes for Social Security and so forth.

Hawley was to maintain certain licenses and insurance coverage, to exclusively represent Peoples' interests, and to complete Peoples' training program. Hawley was never physically present in Florida. Following training, Hawley was shot and killed while attempting to make one of his first calls in Missouri. Hawley's heirs sought Florida workers' compensation. Peoples said they could not be responsible for workers' compensation payments for Hawley's heirs because Peoples and Hawley had not entered a completed, binding contract.

a. Explain Peoples' contract argument.

b. Did the parties achieve a binding contract? Explain. See *Peoples Group v. Hawley,* 804 So. 2d 561 (Fla. Ct. App., 1st Dist. 2002).

3. Allen M. Campbell Co. sought a contract to build houses for the U.S. Navy. Approximately one-half hour before the housing bids were due, Virginia Metal Industries quoted Campbell Co. a price of $193,121 to supply the necessary doors and frames. Campbell, using the Virginia Metal quote, entered a bid and won the contract. Virginia Metal refused to supply the necessary doors, and Campbell had to secure an alternative source of supply at a price $45,562 higher than Virginia Metal's quote. Campbell sued. Explain Campbell's claim. Defend Virginia Metal. Decide. See *Allen M. Campbell Co. Inc. v. Virginia Metal Industries,* 708 F.2d 930 (4th Cir. 1983).

4. The Great Minneapolis Surplus Store placed a newspaper ad saying, "Saturday 9:00 AM sharp. 3 Brand New Fur Coats. Worth $100.00. First Come. First Served. $1 each." Lefkowitz was the first customer at the store that Saturday. He demanded a coat and indicated his readiness to pay the dollar, but the store refused saying it was a "house rule" that the coats were intended for women customers only. Lefkowitz sued. Express the issue(s) in this case. Defend Great Minneapolis. Decide. Explain. See *Lefkowitz v. Great Minneapolis Surplus Store,* 86 N.W.2d 689 (Minn. S. Ct. 1957).

5. Rose Elsten and Donald Cook lived together in Tucson, Arizona, from 1969 to 1981. They were not married, but Rose used Donald's last name, and they represented themselves as husband and wife. They had two joint bank accounts. They jointly owned a house, two cars, and some shares of stock. When Rose left Donald in 1981 she received a few hundred dollars and one car, and Donald retained the balance of the property. She sued Donald on the grounds that he had breached their agreement to share their assets equally. She argued, "[E]verything we did and purchased . . . was together as husband and wife. It was just something that we agreed on." If an agreement existed, did it violate public policy? Decide Rose's lawsuit. Explain. See *Cook v. Cook,* 691 P.2d 664 (Ariz. S.Ct. 1984).

6. Sherwood agreed to purchase a cow, Rose 2d of Aberlone, from Walker at a price of 5½ cents per pound (about $80). The parties believed the cow to be barren. Sherwood came to Walker's farm to collect the cow, but at that point it was obvious that Rose was pregnant. Walker refused to give over the cow, which was then worth $750–$1,000. Sherwood sued. Should he get the cow? Explain. See *Sherwood v. Walker,* 33 N.W. 919 (Mich. S. Ct. 1887).

7. Weaver leased a service station from American Oil. The lease included a clause providing that Weaver would hold American Oil harmless for any negligence by American on the premises. Weaver and an employee were burned when an American Oil employee accidentally sprayed gasoline at Weaver's station. Weaver had one and one-half years of high school education. The trial record provides no evidence that

Weaver read the lease, that American's agent asked him to read it, or that Weaver's attention was drawn to the "hold harmless" clause. The clause was in fine print and contained no title heading. Is the contract enforceable against Weaver? Explain. See *Weaver v. American Oil Co.,* 276 N.E.2d 144 (Ind. S. Ct. 1971).

8. Edward Sherman wanted to sell his business, Adgraphics. He retained V.R. Brokers as an agent for the sale. On December 5, 1985, William Lyon offered $75,000 for the business. Later that day, Sherman signed a counteroffer to sell for $80,000. On December 7 at 11:35 AM Lyon signed the counteroffer, and around noon he took it to Brokers. At about 9 AM that same day, Sherman told Brokers' principal, Robert Renault, that he had decided to cancel his counteroffer. Renault told Lyon of that decision immediately before Lyon handed the signed counteroffer to Renault. Lyon then sued for breach of contract. Decide. Explain. See *Lyon v. Adgraphics,* 540 A.2d 398 (Conn. Ct. App. 1988).

9. A building was rented "for use as a saloon" under an eight-year lease. Five years thereafter the state passed a law making the sale of liquor illegal. The renter, a brewery, argued that it no longer had any duties under the contract. Was the brewery correct? Explain. See *Heart v. East Tennessee Brewing Co.,* 113 S.W. 364 (Tenn. S. Ct. 1908).

10. The La Gasse Company contracted with the City of Fort Lauderdale to renovate one of the city's swimming pools. When the job was nearly complete, vandals severely damaged the pool and most of the work had to be redone. La Gasse sought additional compensation, which the city refused. La Gasse sued, claiming that the subject matter of the contract had been destroyed, thus discharging it from responsibility. Therefore, when it repeated the work, additional compensation was warranted. Decide. Explain. See *La Gasse Pool Construction Co. v. City of Fort Lauderdale,* 288 So. 2d 273 (Fla. Ct. App., 4th Dist. 1974).

11. Preference Personnel, a North Dakota corporation, entered a contract with Peterson to help him find employment in the tax law field. The contract provided that the employer would pay the placement fee, unless Peterson voluntarily quit within 90 days, in which case he would be responsible for the fee, which was 20 percent of one year's salary. Peterson was placed in a job with an annual salary of $60,000, but he quit after one month. Peterson refused to pay the fee, and Preference sued for breach of contract. The lower court found that Peterson breached the contract, but at the time of the contract, Preference Personnel's state-required license to operate had been allowed to lapse. The court, therefore, dismissed the Preference claim ruling that the agreement was unenforceable as a matter of public policy. Preference appealed. Rule on that appeal. Explain. See *Preference Personnel, Inc. v. Peterson,* 710 N.W. 2d 383 (N.D.S.Ct. 2006).

12. Panera, the bakery/café chain, had a clause in its lease that prevented the White City Shopping Center in Shrewsbury, Massachusetts, from renting space to another sandwich shop: "Landlord agrees not to enter into a lease, . . . for a bakery or restaurant reasonably expected to have annual sales of *sandwiches* (emphasis added) greater than ten percent (10%) of its total sales . . . " Panera asked a Massachusetts Superior Court to block the Shopping Center from leasing space to a Qdoba Mexican Grill on the grounds that a lease with the Grill would violate the terms of the Panera lease. How should the Court rule? Explain. See *White City Shopping Center, LP v. PR Restaurants, LLC,* 2006 Mass. Super. LEXIS 544.

CHAPTER SEVEN

Business Torts and Product Liability

After completing this chapter, students will be able to:

1. Compare and contrast the three fundamental kinds of torts: intentional, negligent, and strict liability.

2. Describe selected intentional torts against persons including battery, assault, fraud, invasion of privacy, intentional infliction of emotional distress, and defamation.

3. Describe selected intentional torts against property such as trespass and nuisance.

4. Identify selected intentional tort defenses.

5. Discuss the impact of product liability on business practice.

6. Identify the requirements of a successful negligence claim.

7. Differentiate between types of negligence claims emerging from defective products.

8. Analyze whether negligence defenses may be successfully asserted in a negligence claim.

9. Compare and contrast claims based on express warranties and implied warranties.

10. Identify the elements of the strict liability cause of action.

11. Identify the defenses available in strict liability cases.

12. Evaluate arguments for and against tort reform.

PRACTICING ETHICS   A Bar Stunt Turns Tragic

"It was like a gust. It just came at me." (Deanine) Busche, a former University of Iowa student, told jurors. . . . "I knew my hair had caught on fire. . . . I remember smelling it. I don't know if I was blown to the ground . . . or if I threw myself on the ground."

The Facts   Busche was testifying in her civil suit seeking $2.1 million from the owner of the Et Cetera Bar along with bartender Troy Kline. Busche, 23, was one of nine people burned or injured April 18, 2000, at the popular Iowa City, Iowa, bar when Kline ignited Everclear, high-proof alcohol, that he had poured into a stainless steel barwell on the bartender's side of the bar, about four feet from Busche. As the flames initially died down, Kline poured more alcohol into the barwell and a "fireball" followed, according to Busche's testimony. Kline said he had previously performed the flaming trick 15 to 20 times without complaints or injuries. Kline was mimicking a stunt he had seen during a spring break trip to Acapulco. Kline had earlier been sentenced to a year of probation and 100 hours of community service for a criminal charge of reckless use of fire. The bar was fined $500 for violating city fire codes.

> Kline poured more alcohol into the barwell and a "fireball" followed

The Plaintiff's Case   Busche claimed Kline was negligent and reckless in starting and accelerating the fire. Busche said she had seen Kline perform the stunt about a dozen times, and he had never issued a warning. Busche suffered third-degree burns over 13 percent of her body, including extensive facial burns. The broadcast journalism major said the injuries complicated her career pursuits, resulted in over $100,000 in medical bills, and left her extremely sensitive to cold and heat. She also suffered severe psychological trauma, including nightmares and fears of death.

The Defense   Busche's own behavior was called into question at trial. Busche said she grabbed her purse and moved close to the bar when she saw that Kline was about to ignite the alcohol. Kline testified that Busche had earlier talked to him about spitting alcohol into fire. Defense lawyer J. Ric Gass argued that Kline's conduct was not enough to cause the flames to roar across the bar as they did. Gass asked Busche if she had caused the flash fire herself by spitting alcohol at the burning alcohol. Busche denied doing so and said she had consumed only a mixed drink, but other bar patrons indicated that the fire flared when Busche attempted to "breathe fire" by spitting alcohol on the flames. Further, Kline's hand was not burned, but Busche's mouth was blistered in a manner consistent with burning alcohol. A combustion science expert testifying for the defense said that he had been unable to re-create a fireball by pouring alcohol on fire. When the expert used a plastic tube to approximate spitting, however, the fire followed the alcohol to its source. On the other hand, after 40 interviews, police were unable to confirm that Busche contributed to her own injuries. Gass also pointed out that Busche's life following the fire had included parties, camping trips, shopping, college courses, and an internship at a Chicago television station.

The Judgment   After nearly a seven-day trial and a full day of debate, the jury found the defendants 67 percent responsible for Busche's injuries, while 33 percent of the blame was attributed to the plaintiff herself. Compensatory damages and interest were set at nearly $1.4 million. The judge reduced that sum by 33 percent. The jury also awarded Busche $275,000 in punitive damages, 75 percent of which was directed to Iowa's reparations trust fund. Et Cetera was to pay $250,000 of the punitive damages, while Kline was responsible for $25,000. In the end, Busche was expected to receive a total of over $1.1 million of the $2.1 million she had sought.

Sources: Compiled from news accounts reported by the Associated Press, *The Daily Iowan,* and *The Iowa City Press-Citizen.*

Questions

1. *a.* As nearly as you can deduce from this brief rendition of the facts, did the jury reach a correct decision? Explain.

   b. Was the decision "fair"? Explain.

2. *a.* Was Kline's stunt a moral wrong? Explain.

   b. If a racing car caught on fire and crashed into the grandstand, killing spectators, did the driver or the owner commit a moral wrong?

3. *a.* Is the sale of liquor a moral wrong?

   b. Did Kline commit a moral wrong simply by working in a bar? Explain.

Part One—Torts: An Introduction

We have looked at the Et Cetera Bar story as an ethics dilemma. Now we turn to the law that resolves claims like those raised against Et Cetera. The flaming alcohol stunt involved both *torts* and *crimes*. *Torts* are civil wrongs not arising from contracts. Torts involve breaches of duty to particular persons, whereas *crimes* are regarded as public wrongs breaching duties to all of society (although, of course, they are most commonly directed at a specific person or persons). Crimes are prosecuted by the state; tort actions are initiated by individuals. Criminal law punishes wrongdoers, but the point of tort law is to make whole an injured party. At the same time, many acts can be treated either as a civil wrong (a tort) or as a crime, or both. For example, a physical attack on another can, of course, lead to criminal charges, but it can also produce civil tort claims, most commonly *assault* and *battery*.

The injured party in a tort litigation can seek *compensatory damages* to make up for the harm suffered. Those damages may consist of medical expenses, lost income, and pain and suffering, among other possibilities. In some cases, *punitive damages* may be awarded to punish the wrongdoer and to discourage others from similar behavior.

Tort Categories

Fundamentally, torts are of three kinds: (1) intentional, (2) negligent, and (3) strict liability. *Intentional* torts involve voluntary acts that harm a protected interest. Intent is established by showing the defendant meant to do the act that caused the harm. The plaintiff need not show that the harm itself was intended. The defendant would be liable for all reasonably foreseeable injuries from that intentional act.

To explain, if you run an advertisement defaming a fast-food competitor by saying its food processing does not meet government standards, but you cannot prove the truth of your allegations, you will probably be guilty of the intentional tort of *injurious false-hood* (product disparagement).

Negligence involves situations in which harm is caused accidentally. Intent is absent, but because of one party's carelessness, another has suffered injury. Thus if one of your employees is making a delivery for the printing business you are managing and carelessly runs a red light, striking another car, the employee appears to be guilty of negligent conduct for which both she and your firm may be subject to civil damages. Further, you and/or your firm might bear responsibility if, for example, you hired her knowing that she had been a careless driver in the past.

Strict liability is, in essence, a no-fault concept where an individual or organization is responsible for harm without proof of carelessness. Strict liability is limited to "unreasonably dangerous" products and practices about which we have decided, as a matter of social policy, that responsibility for injury will automatically attach without establishing blame. Thus if a product is (1) defective and (2) unreasonably dangerous and someone is hurt, strict (absolute) liability may attach even though fault is not established. Negligence and strict liability are explained in detail in Part Two of this chapter.

Tort Law

Selected Intentional Torts against Persons

Suppose you are warehouse manager for a plumbing supply business, and a subordinate does a poor job with some work, which in turn brings your boss down on you. In your frustration, you call the subordinate into your office where you chastise him and then light up a cigar and casually but pointedly blow smoke in his face. Could he file a tort claim against you for your insulting behavior? Let's look at the law in this area. (Of course, many states forbid workplace smoking.)

> In your frustration, you light up a cigar and casually but pointedly blow smoke in his face

Battery

Intentionally touching another in a harmful or offensive way without legal justification or the consent of that person is a *battery*. Merely touching another's clothing or touching an occupied car may constitute a battery. Assuming no allergic response, our example of cigar smoke in the victim's face may not be physically harmful; but could it constitute a battery, nonetheless, if the touching was offensive? Few such cases have been litigated, but some decisions suggest that recipients of smoke may, under some circumstances, be able to successfully raise battery claims. On the other hand, in a crowded world, we cannot expect the law to help us erect a glass cage around ourselves.

Assault

Intentionally causing another to reasonably believe that he or she is about to be the victim of a battery is an *assault*. The battery need not occur and the victim need not be frightened; but an assault nonetheless transpires if the victim reasonably anticipated a substantially imminent battery. Thus raising one's hand as if to strike another even though the blow never transpires constitutes the tort of assault if the victim reasonably thought herself to be in immediate danger.

False Imprisonment

If you have anticipated a career in retailing, you may have given thought to the problem of shoplifters and strategies for preserving your inventory without yourself violating customers' rights. The statutory and judge-made law of most states now protects store managers and owners from false imprisonment claims if they justifiably detain a suspected shoplifter for a reasonable period and in a reasonable manner. Broadly, *false imprisonment* occurs when someone is intentionally confined against his or her will; that is, his or her freedom of movement is restricted. That restriction might include being shut in a room, being bound, being threatened, and so on. Even a moment could conceivably constitute imprisonment, although simply sending a customer, for example, through a more distant store exit would not meet the test.

Fraud

Intentional misrepresentations of facts, sometimes identified by the formal title of *deceit,* can lead to tort claims. We discuss *fraud* in the contracts (Chapter 6) and consumer protection (Chapter 15) chapters. For now, simply note the general test for fraud:

1. A material fact was misrepresented.
2. The misrepresentation was intentional.
3. The injured party justifiably relied on the misrepresentation.
4. Injury resulted.

Defamation

Assume you are at a company party engaging in the networking that you understand to be essential to success. Still in the management trainee program, you are carefully watching your step. A coworker approaches and, after some casual talk, remarks, "I guess you have been warned about your boss, Smith. You know he can't be trusted. He lies when it serves his purposes." Language of that kind may constitute *slander,* the spoken form of the tort of *defamation. Libel* is defamation in print or some other tangible form such as a picture, movie, or video. Most courts also treat defamatory radio and television statements as forms of libel. The basic test for establishing defamation includes:

1. A false statement.
2. Harm to the victim's reputation.
3. Publication of the statement. (The statement must reach someone other than the one being defamed.)

The law's interest here is in protecting reputations. Any living person or any organization can be the victim of defamation, although public figures such as politicians or actors face the additional burden of proving malice if they are to be successful in a defamation claim. *Malice* generally requires a showing of actual knowledge of the falsehood or reckless disregard for the truth. Libel or slander about a company's products or property would constitute the tort of *injurious falsehood,* which is discussed below.

In general, a claim of slander requires a showing of actual harm, such as job loss. However, some statements are so inherently damaging that actual injury need not be shown. Those statements are labeled *slander per se* and include allegations of serious sexual misconduct, commission of a serious crime, professional incompetence, or having a loathsome disease. Similarly, libel, leaving a more permanent stain, generally does not require a showing of actual harm.

Truth acts as a complete defense to a defamation claim. Hence, if we tell the truth about others, we cannot be guilty of the tort of defamation, regardless of our evil intentions. Further, many statements are protected because of the circumstances in which they are made. We label these protections either *absolute* or *qualified privileges.* An absolute privilege to defame includes, for example, remarks by government officials in the course of their duties or by participants in a trial. A qualified privilege to defame includes statements to secure credit or a job. In those instances, the statement will not be treated as defamatory, even though false, unless it was motivated by malice. [For an overview of online defamation law for bloggers, see **http://w2.eff.org/bloggers/lg/faqdefamation.php**]

Invasion of Privacy

A key ingredient in personal freedom is the right to be left alone. Our courts recognize a right of recovery in tort law when we are the victims of some kind of unconscionable exposure of our private lives. *Invasion of privacy* takes four forms:

1. **Appropriation of a person's name or likeness:** When an individual's name or image is used without permission for commercial purposes, called an *appropriation,* that person probably has a cause of action for invasion of privacy. Typically this problem involves a company's use of a celebrity's name or picture without permission to imply that he or she has endorsed a product.
2. **Intrusion:** An intentional invasion of a person's solitude is labeled an *intrusion* if it would be highly offensive to a reasonable person. Physical intrusions such as opening an employee's mail or more subtle strategies such as an electronic probe of an employee's bank account are examples of tortious intrusion.
3. **Public disclosure of private facts:** This form of invasion of privacy bears a strong resemblance to defamation. Again, if the disclosure would be highly offensive to a reasonable person, the tort of *public disclosure of private facts* might be invoked. We believe that certain elements of one's life, such as debt payment practices or sexual preferences, are, with rare exceptions, no one else's business. In these cases truth does *not* constitute a good defense.
4. **False light:** When claims are published about another that have the effect of casting the victim in a *false light* in the public mind, a tort claim may emerge. Such a claim would be much like defamation except that false light involves one's interest in being left alone, whereas defamation involves injury to reputation. Again, the claim would need to be highly offensive to the reasonable person. So if an employee's office was wrongfully searched, and he was led from the workplace by superiors in full view of other employees and in a manner that suggested that he was engaging in dishonorable conduct, a false light tort claim might be raised. Here truth would constitute a complete defense.

Intentional Infliction of Emotional Distress

Employment terminations (firings), drug tests, and sexual harassment cases have become particularly fertile grounds for *emotional distress* claims, although it should be understood that the courts have demanded compelling evidence of outrageous conduct causing severe emotional pain.

Selected Intentional Torts against Property

We will briefly examine four prominent tort claims arising from wrongs to property.

Trespass to *real property* (land and immovable objects attached to it) occurs with the intentional entry onto the land of another without consent. Trespass to *personal property* (movable property; all property other than real property) involves an intentional interference with a person's right to enjoy his or her personal property—for example, the manager of a parking lot refuses for a day to return a car to its owner in the mistaken belief that the owner has not paid his monthly bill.

More serious and extensive interference with personal property may be labeled a *conversion*. For example, if the parking lot company kept the car for months, and it suffered damage during the impoundment, a conversion probably occurred.

Injurious falsehood is a form of defamation that is directed against the property of a person. Thus falsely claiming that a competitor's product is defective or harmful would likely constitute injurious falsehood. As with defamation, the statement must be false and it must be published. Damages must result. Often malice must also be shown.

Nuisance is the situation in which enjoyment of one's land is impaired because of some tortious interference. That interference often takes the form of light, noise, smell, or vibration. Here, the owner is not deprived of the land and the land has not been physically invaded, but the full enjoyment of the land cannot be achieved because of the interference. The case that follows involves a husband and wife seeking quiet in their home versus a neighboring bar seeking fun and profit through loud music.

Biglane and Biglane v. Under the Hill Corp.

LEGAL BRIEFCASE   949 So.2d 9 (Miss. S. Ct. 2007)

Justice Diaz

FACTS

In 1967 Nancy and James Biglane purchased a dilapidated building at 27 Silver Street [Natchez, Mississippi] that had been built in the 1840s, and opened the lower portion of the building as a gift shop in 1978. In 1973, Andre Farish, Sr., and Paul O'Malley purchased the building directly next door, at 25 Silver Street, which had been built in the 1830s; in 1975 they opened the Natchez Under the Hill Saloon. Eventually the Saloon would come to be run by the children of Mr. Farish, Melissa and Andre, Jr.

The Saloon would establish itself proudly as a welcoming haven for locals and visitors alike. . . .The Biglanes began converting the upper floors of 27 Silver Street into a large apartment, which they moved into in 2002.

Despite installing insulated walls and windows, locating their bedroom on the side of the building away from the Saloon, and placing their air conditioner unit on the side nearest the Saloon, the Biglanes quickly realized they had a problem: the raucous nature of the Saloon kept them wide awake at night.

Specifically, it was live music, a hallmark of the Saloon. During the summertime the un-air conditioned Under the Hill opened its windows and doors to lessen the heat inside, and music echoed up and down Silver Street. While the music was easier on Mr. Biglane, who had lost his hearing over the years, it was particularly difficult on Mrs. Biglane, who was frustrated by the constant rock and roll, conversation, and the clack of pool balls.

The Biglanes contacted the Saloon and asked that the music be turned down, and it was: Mr. Farish got rid of Groove Line, the band that seemed to trouble the Biglanes the most, and installed thick windows to block noise. He also purchased a sound meter by which bands could measure their output in decibels, and forbade them from going over a certain point.

Still dissatisfied, the Biglanes blocked off two nearby parking lots that served the Saloon, using a cable over the entrance of one and crafting a metal gate over another. Ultimately this classic neighborly dispute spilled into the Chancery Court of Adams County, prompted by a complaint from the Biglanes.

The couple alleged private nuisance, among other causes of action, and Under the Hill counterclaimed, alleging that the Biglanes had tortiously interfered in its business (by blocking the nearby parking lots) . . .

The [lower court] determined that Under the Hill was a private nuisance to the Biglanes, and enjoined the Saloon from leaving open any doors or windows when music was playing, and ordered it to prevent patrons from loitering in the streets.

The court also found that the Biglanes had tortiously interfered with the business relations of Under the Hill. . . .
[Both parties appealed.]

DISCUSSION

I. Is the Under the Hill Saloon a Private Nuisance to the Biglanes?

The Biglanes asserted that the Saloon was a private nuisance. "A private nuisance is a nontrespassory invasion of another's interest in the use and enjoyment of his property." *Leaf River Forest Prods., Inc. v. Ferguson, 662 So. 2d 648, 662 (Miss. 1995).* "One landowner may not use his land so as to unreasonably annoy, inconvenience, or harm others."

* * * * *

After reviewing the evidence presented the [lower court] found ample evidence that the Biglanes frequently could not use or enjoy their property—significantly, that Mrs. Biglane often slept away from the apartment on weekends to avoid the noise and that she could not have her grandchildren over on the weekends because of the noise. The audiologist who testified for the Biglanes concluded that the noise levels were excessive and unreasonable, although he also conceded that he had never measured the noise levels in the couple's bedroom. This problem was exacerbated during the summer months, when the un-airconditioned Saloon left its doors and windows open to defray the oppressive Natchez heat.

The Saloon did offer a witness who lived in back of the establishment who said he never had any problems with the noise, but the [lower court] held that he was not an impartial witness, since he was testifying for his landlord.

[T]he [lower] court weighed the fact that the Biglanes knew or should have known that there was going to be some sort of noise associated with living "within five feet of a well established saloon which provides live music on the weekends."

* * * * *

[E]ven a lawful business—which the Under the Hill Saloon certainly is—may become . . . a nuisance "by interfering with its neighbor's enjoyment of their property." We recognize that "[e]ach [private nuisance] case must be decided upon its own peculiar facts, taking into consideration the location and the surrounding circumstances." Ultimately, "[i]t is not necessary that other property owners should be driven from their dwellings," because "[i]t is enough that the enjoyment of life and property is rendered materially uncomfortable and annoying."

* * * * *

In the case at hand, the [lower] court. . . . found that the Saloon could not "operat[e] its business with its doors and windows opened during any time that amplified music is being played inside the saloon." [W]e agree that the Saloon was a private nuisance to the Biglanes.

* * * * *

II. Was There a Tortious Interference with Business Relations?

In response to the Biglanes' assertion that the Saloon was a private nuisance, the bar counterclaimed, arguing that its neighbors had interfered with the operation of their business. "There are four elements necessary to prove a claim of tortious interference with a business relationship: (1) The acts were intentional and willful; (2) The acts were calculated to cause damage to the plaintiffs in their lawful business; (3) The acts were done with the unlawful purpose of causing damage and loss, without right or justifiable cause on the part of the defendant…(4) Actual damage and loss resulted." *MBF Corp. v. Century Business Comms., Inc., 663 So. 2d 595, 598 (Miss. 1995).* In this case the Biglanes essentially concede the presence of the first two prongs, but urge that neither the third nor the fourth factors were satisfied. If any of the factors are not met, there cannot be a finding of tortious interference with business.

A. "Without Right or Justifiable Cause."

After the tensions escalated between the Biglanes and the Saloon, Mr. Biglane caused two parking areas in his control to be blocked, one with a cable gate after 6:00 p.m. and the other by an iron gate. It is undisputed that Mr. Biglane controls the former lot outright, but the ownership of the second lot—the so-called Water Street area—is more complicated. . . .

Ownership of the property is important because it speaks to the third factor of the tort—that the allegedly tortious acts must be performed without right or justifiable cause. It is a basic tenet of property law that a landowner or tenant may use the premises they control in whatever fashion they desire, so long as the law is obeyed.

Generally speaking, it cannot be malicious for a person to refuse access to others to their private property. Accordingly, blocking off the parking lot he owned in whole was not tortious conduct by Mr. Biglane.

* * * * *

It is undisputed that Mr. Biglane erected an iron gate blocking Water Street. The [lower court] found that part of the property blocked by the iron gate was owned by the city; that the gate itself partially rested upon city property; and that two of the parking spaces blocked by Mr. Biglane were city property. In light of this evidence, the [lower] court found that the third factor required for tortious interference with business was present—that Mr. Biglane did not have the right to block property which he did not own from public access.

[W]e conclude that the Biglanes acted without right in blocking the Water Street property.

B. "Actual Damage and Loss Resulted."

Next we must consider whether the Under the Hill Saloon was damaged by the actions of the Biglanes. . . .

In the case at hand, Under the Hill conceded that it could not demonstrate a loss of income from the lack of parking. In fact, business had slightly increased after the parking lots were blocked by Mr. Biglane. . . .

The Under the Hill Saloon admitted it had suffered no actual damages or loss. . . . In this type of case, there must be actual damages. Because the fourth factor was not met, there cannot be a tortious interference with business.
Reversed.

QUESTIONS

1. List the two causes of action in this case, and explain who brought each and upon what factual foundation.
2. Why did the Biglanes win their claim while Under the Hill lost its claim?
3. Had the Biglanes hired away the Under the Hill manager and several employees and started their own nearby saloon, would the Biglanes' action constitute tortious interference with business relations? Explain.
4. Rattigan and Horvitz owned a house and prime ocean front lot in Beverley Farms, Massachusetts. The house was rented during the summer months. Wile owned an adjacent undeveloped ocean front lot. The only land access to Wile's lot was through the Rattigan/Horvitz lot. Rattigan and Horvitz successfully challenged Wile's application for a building permit and thereafter Wile began a series of retaliatory acts, including putting several portable toilets on his lot immediately adjacent to the Horvitz swimming pool, landing his helicopter on his vacant lot, placing debris such as a rusted crane bucket, broken cement, and the bed of a pickup truck on his property, and holding parties (not attended by Wile) for 150–200 guests from the local youth shelter. Some of these tactics by Wile were sporadic rather than persistent. Were Rattigan and Horvitz the victims of a nuisance? Explain. See *Rattigan v. Wile*, 841 N.E.2d 680 (Mass. S. Judicial Ct. 2006).

Selected Intentional Tort Defenses

Let's take a brief look at a few of the more significant defenses to the intentional torts that we have been examining.

Consent

Clearly, if you consent to the use of your picture in an advertising campaign and you subsequently feel that your public image has been harmed, you will have difficulty in pursuing a tort claim. Of course, if you gave permission under mistake, fraud, or duress, your consent was not meaningful.

Mistake

As store security manager, you are radioed by a clerk to "stop the guy in the New York Yankees cap" on suspicion of shoplifting. After stopping someone fitting that description, you later discover that someone else, also wearing a Yankees cap, was the actual suspect. If the store is sued for false imprisonment, can it successfully raise a mistake defense? Unless protected under state law, probably not. Having acted intentionally, you and, by extension, your employer probably will bear responsibility. Of course, false imprisonment does not occur unless the detention was unreasonable.

On the other hand, mistake can be a good defense, particularly in instances in which events happen rapidly. Say, for example, a store's security personnel broke up what looked like an assault and battery in the mall parking lot, only to discover that the incident was merely horsing around by the parties. A mistake defense might be appropriate here.

Necessity

In what we would broadly label emergency situations, one may intentionally commit a tort and yet be excused. A case of public necessity might involve, for example, a person breaking into an unoccupied building late at night because he saw a fire burning inside. An example of a private necessity is when a defendant intrudes on the property of another to save himself only; he might thereafter raise a necessity defense against the tort claim of trespass.

Self-Defense

Suppose your career has taken you into retail management, and you have now decided to buy your own hardware store. You encounter the ups and downs that characterize entrepreneurial life, but you become particularly frustrated by the theft and vandalism that seem so much a part of small business. Finally, in an effort to stop the breaking, entering, and minor theft that has troubled your business, you build a trap in your store. You take up a few floorboards in a rear entryway where vandals have broken in, and you pound nails (points facing up) into those boards. Then you cover the nail points with some soft felt so they are not visible; but when stepped on, the nails will pierce the felt and stab the feet of any intruder. Suppose your trap works, and an intruder is injured. Suppose the intruder then sues you for his injury. Could you cite self-defense of your property as an excuse? What if a police officer stepped on a nail responding to an alarm at your business? The *Katko* case that follows looks at the self-defense theme.

LEGAL BRIEFCASE

Katko v. Briney 183 N.W. 2d 657 (Ia. S. Ct. 1971)

FACTS

The Brineys, defendants/appellants in this case, owned an unoccupied farmhouse. During the period from 1957 to 1967, trespassers broke into the house, broke windows, and stole some items. The Brineys boarded windows and erected "no trespassing" signs on the land. On June 11, 1967, the Brineys attached a 20-gauge, loaded shotgun to a bed in the house, pointing the barrel toward the bedroom door. They attached a wire to the trigger and the bedroom doorknob so that the gun would fire if the door were opened. At first, Mr. Briney directed the gun so that it would hit an intruder in the stomach, but agreed with Mrs. Briney's suggestion to lower the barrel so that it would strike an intruder's legs. The gun could not be seen from the outside, and no warning about it was posted.

Katko, the plaintiff/appellee, worked in an Eddyville, Iowa, gas station. He and a friend, McDonough, had found antiques—old bottles and fruit jars—on their first trip to the Briney house, which Katko considered to be abandoned. On their second trip, they entered the house through a window. Katko opened the bedroom door and was shot in the right leg. Much of that leg, including part of the tibia, was blown away. Katko was hospitalized for 40 days. His leg was in a cast for approximately one year, and he was required to wear a brace for an additional year. His leg was permanently shortened by the trauma.

Katko sued the Brineys and secured a jury verdict of $30,000. The Brineys appealed to the Iowa Supreme Court.

* * * * *

Chief Justice Moore

The primary issue presented here is whether an owner may protect personal property in an unoccupied, boarded-up farmhouse against trespassers and thieves by a spring gun capable of inflicting death or serious injury.

We are not here concerned with a man's right to protect his home and members of his family. Defendant's home was several miles from the scene of the incident to which we refer.

* * * * *

Plaintiff testified he knew he had no right to break and enter the house with intent to steal bottles and fruit jars therefrom. He further testified he had entered a plea of guilty to larceny in the nighttime of property of less than $20 value from a private building. He stated he had been fined $50 and costs and paroled during good behavior from a 60-day jail sentence. Other than minor traffic charges this was plaintiff's first brush with the law. . . .

The main thrust of the defendants' defense in the trial court and on this appeal is that "the law permits use of a spring gun in a dwelling or warehouse for the purpose of preventing the unlawful entry of a burglar or thief." . . .

In the statement of issues the trial court stated plaintiff and his companion committed a felony when they broke and entered defendant's house. In instruction 2 the court referred to the early case history of the use of spring guns and stated under the law their use was prohibited except to prevent the commission of felonies of violence and where human life is in danger. The instruction included a statement that breaking and entering is not a felony of violence.

Instruction 5 stated, "You are hereby instructed that one may use reasonable force in the protection of his property, but such right is subject to the qualification that one may not use such means of force as will take human life or inflict great bodily injury. Such is the rule even though the injured party is a trespasser and is in violation of the law himself."

Instruction 6 stated, "An owner of premises is prohibited from willfully or intentionally injuring a trespasser by means of force that either takes life or inflicts great bodily injury; and therefore a person owning a premise is prohibited from setting out 'spring guns' and like dangerous devices which will likely take life or inflict great bodily injury, for the purpose of harming trespassers. The fact that the trespasser may be acting in violation of the law does not change the rule. The only time when such conduct of setting a 'spring gun' or a like dangerous device is justified would be when the trespasser was committing a felony of violence or a felony punishable by death, or where the trespasser was endangering human life by his act." . . .

The overwhelming weight of authority, both textbook and case law, supports the trial court's statement of the applicable principles of law.

Prosser on Torts, Third Edition, pages 116–18, states,

[T]he law has always placed a higher value upon human safety than upon mere rights in property; it is the accepted rule that there is no privilege to use any force calculated to cause death or serious bodily injury to repel the threat to land or chattels, unless there is also such a threat to the defendant's personal safety as to justify a self-defense . . . spring guns and other mankilling devices are not justifiable against a mere trespasser, or even a petty thief. They are privileged only against those upon whom the landowner, if he were present in person, would be free to inflict injury of the same kind.

* * * * *

In *Hooker v. Miller*, 37 Iowa 613, we held defendant vineyard owner liable for damages resulting from a spring gun shot although plaintiff was a trespasser and there to steal grapes. At pages 614, 615, this statement is made: "This court has held that a mere trespass against property other than a dwelling is not a sufficient justification to authorize the use of a deadly weapon by the owner in its defense; and that if death results in such a case it will be murder, though the killing be actually necessary to prevent the trespass. . . ."

In Wisconsin, Oregon, and England the use of spring guns and similar devices is specifically made unlawful by statute.

* * * * *

Affirmed.

Questions

1. Why did the Iowa Supreme Court rule in favor of the criminal intruder, Katko?

2. What classes of people other than intruders are of concern to the courts in cases like *Katko?*

3. Did the Iowa Supreme Court reach a just verdict? Explain.

4. A businessman in Cordele, Georgia, troubled by small thefts from a cigarette machine in front of his store, allegedly booby-trapped the machine after hours with dynamite. A teenager then died when tampering with the machine. What legal action should be taken? Resolve.

[For a brief *Time* magazine review of "burglars and booby traps," see **http://www.time.com/time/magazine/article/ 0,9171,948174-2,00.html**]

Part Two—Product Liability

Introduction

We have examined intentional torts against both persons and property. Now we turn to tort and contract claims arising from products.

How does the law handle the situation where a wheel falls off a car, or a lighter explodes in a consumer's face? Product liability lawsuits deal with cases where buyers, users, and in some cases bystanders are injured or killed by defective products. Those harmed may have causes of action in torts (negligence or strict liability) or contracts (breach of warranty). If so, the manufacturers, distributors, and sellers of that product must then defend themselves against often enormously expensive claims. Part Two of this chapter explains product liability law and raises some of the public policy considerations that have caused critics to call for legal reforms to reduce the burden of product liability lawsuits.

Product Liability and Business Practice "The business of making small airplanes is all but dead in this country, wiped out mainly by product liability lawsuits."[1] That 1991 pronouncement by *The Wall Street Journal* powerfully depicts the influence of product liability laws in the practice of American business. Today a key ingredient in a successful business is a plan for dealing with litigation costs. Product liability law addresses situations in which injuries result from defective products.

In the early 1990s, as *The Wall Street Journal* observed, the single-engine plane industry in the United States was largely dead. The major American manufacturer, Cessna Aircraft of Wichita, Kansas, stopped making small planes in 1986. Its chief rival, Piper Aircraft, struggled with bankruptcy. Single-engine aircraft production in the United States fell from a peak of 13,000 units in 1977 to 444 in 1994.[2] The problems were, in part, attributable to poor management, overproduction, high fuel costs, and recession; but the *Journal* argued that the chief cause was the legal system:

> [W]hat is happening now, according to practically every constituency except the lawyers, is a clear case of products-liability law eating a sick industry alive.[3]

Particularly troublesome for the small plane companies was the so-called liability tail that accompanied their products. Airplanes must be built to last for many years, but because product liability claims ordinarily have no time limit, a manufacturer could be sued decades after the plane had left its control. The result was that insurance fees skyrocketed, driving up airplane prices and frightening lenders and investors.[4]

Then Congress passed the General Aviation Revitalization Act, which offered protection against serious liability claims and limited claims involving planes that are more than 18 years old.[5] The result was a near-miraculous rebirth for the small plane industry. Piper, selling fewer than 50 planes per year, was left in the early 1990s with $1,000 in the bank, 45 employees, and no way to pay its electricity bill.[6] Then, as *USA TODAY* remarked, "salvation arrived" in the form of the General Aviation Act.[7] "Piper's liability risk fell from 64,000 planes to 12,000, cutting insurance costs 90 percent."[8] The results have been good for the company and good for the American economy:

> In a dramatic turnaround sparked by 1994 legislation that limited plane makers' liability from lawsuits, the new Piper Aircraft climbed out of its tailspin and now has more than 1,500 employees. Its revenue is expected to top $291 million this year (2001), up from $182 million last year.[9]

[For a general database on defective products, see **http://consumerlawpage.com/ resource/defect.shtml**]

Justice   Although product liability law can sometimes be devastating to a company or industry, as was the case with small planes, it is often the only recourse for those wronged by defective products. The following story reminds us that product liability litigation compensates those who are harmed while applying important pressure to improve product quality.

READING

Law Student Speaks to Class about Recovery from Third-Degree Burns

James Kramer

After a chemical explosion nearly took his life, University of Iowa law student Rich Webster has recovered.

The explosion, which was caused by a solvent called acetone, occurred in an Iowa City apartment managed by Webster. The accident left him with third-degree burns that covered 65 percent of his body.

Five years later, thick red scars cover Webster's cheeks and lower lip. His arms, which he said feel like they're covered in Saran Wrap, look like leather due to extensive skin grafting.

* * * * *

Webster, an Iowa City native, was removing carpet from the apartment. After reading the acetone container's warning label and applying the chemical, he opened the apartment's windows and doors and left for 15 minutes.

When he came back, the chemical's fumes ignited from the pilot light in a water heater. He jumped out a first-floor window and got help from a neighbor.

"My immediate reaction was disbelief, then panic," Webster said. "When I got to the hospital, I didn't hurt that bad because it had burned through the nerves. I thought I was going to be able to go home."

Webster spent seven weeks in the burn unit at the UI Hospitals and Clinics, where he underwent four surgical operations to graft new skin. When he first arrived there, doctors told him he had a "50–50" chance of surviving.

Several months after the incident, Webster filed a negligence lawsuit against Sunnyside, Inc., which produced the acetone; State Industries, the producer of the water heater; and Lenoch & Cilek True Value Hardware, the store from which Webster bought the product.

The case was settled out of court in 1994. Part of the settlement required Webster not to disclose monetary figures, but he said he received "a very, very substantial amount." The money covered all of his hospital bills, which amounted to over $250,000.

* * * * *

Webster's life has changed in a number of ways since his road to recovery started. Because the chemical, acetone, was in a container without an extensive warning label, he has grown more skeptical of companies.

Since the Webster case was settled, Sunnyside increased the warning on its acetone containers. In general, Webster said he feels warning labels need to be taken more seriously.

"If I read a label that has a warning on it, I automatically think it's a watered-down version," Webster said. "I think there's a problem with people not reading labels, period."

Source: *The Daily Iowan,* March 5, 1997. Reprinted by permission of the copyright holder, *The Daily Iowan.*

Negligence

The three major product liability causes of action are negligence, breach of warranty, and strict liability. In dangerously simplified terms, *negligence* is a breach of the duty of due care. A negligent act is the failure to do what a reasonable person would do or doing what a reasonable person would not do. Thus a producer or distributor has a duty to exercise reasonable care in the entire stream of events associated with the development and sale of a product. In designing, manufacturing, testing, repairing, and warning of potential dangers, those in the chain of production and distribution must meet the standard of the reasonably prudent person. Failure to do so constitutes negligence. Some decisions also extend potential liability to situations in which a product is being put to an unintended but reasonably foreseeable *misuse.*

Historically, consumers dealt face-to-face with producers and could bring breach of contract claims if injured by a defective product. However, the development in the modern era of multilayered production and distribution systems eliminated that contractual relationship between producer and consumer, making it difficult for consumers to sue producers. Then in a famous 1916 decision (*McPherson v. Buick Motor Co.*),[10] the New York high court ruled that a consumer could bring a negligence claim against the manufacturer of a defective automobile even though the consumer did not purchase the car directly from that manufacturer. That view has since been broadly adopted, thus permitting victims of negligence to bring actions against all careless parties in the chain of production and distribution.

Donald Trump Owes a Duty?

In 1996, Mark Merrill entered a clinic for compulsive gamblers and wrote to Trump Indiana, a casino in Gary, Indiana asking that he be evicted if he ever entered to gamble. Merrill's name appeared on Trump Indiana's eviction list. Nonetheless, Merrill later gambled at the casino suffering substantial losses. In December 1998 and January 1999, Merrill robbed banks, apparently to cover his gambling losses. He was convicted of bank robbery, but while in prison he filed suit claiming Trump Indiana was negligent in failing to keep him from gambling at the casino. Rule on Merrill's negligence claim. Explain. The four-part negligence test that follows will help you resolve Merrill's claim.

Source: *Mark Merrill v. Trump Indiana, Inc.*, 320 F.3d 729 (7th Cir. 2003).

Negligence Test

To establish a successful negligence claim, the plaintiff must meet each of the following requirements:

1. **Duty:** The plaintiff must establish that the defendant owed a duty of due care to the plaintiff. In general, the standard applied is that of the fictitious reasonable man or woman. That reasonable person acts prudently, sensibly, and responsibly. The standard of reasonableness depends, of course, on the circumstances of the situation.

2. **Breach of duty:** The plaintiff must demonstrate that the defendant breached the duty of due care by engaging in conduct that did not conform to the reasonable person standard. Breach of the duty of due care may result from either the commission of a careless act or the omission of a reasonable, prudent act. Would a reasonable man or woman discharge a firearm in a public park? Would a reasonable person foresee that failure to illuminate one's front entry steps might lead to a broken bone? More formally, we might think of reasonable behavior as decision making that weighs the costs and benefits of acting or not acting. The reasonable person "takes precautions against harms when doing so costs less than the discounted value of the harms risked."[11]

3. **Causation**

    a. **Actual cause:** Did the defendant's breach of the duty of due care in fact cause the harm in question? Commonly, the "but for" test is applied to determine cause in fact. For example, but for the defendant's failure to stop at the red light, the plaintiff pedestrian would not have been struck down in the crosswalk.

    b. **Proximate cause:** The plaintiff must establish that the defendant's actions were the *proximate cause* of the injury. As a matter of policy, is the defendant's conduct sufficiently connected to the plaintiff's injury as to justify imposing liability? Many injuries arise from a series of events—some of them wildly improbable. Did the defendant's negligence lead directly to the plaintiff's harm, or did some intervening act break the causal link between the defendant's negligence and the harm? For example, the community's allegedly negligent maintenance resulted in a blocked road, forcing the plaintiff to detour. While on the detour route, the plaintiff's vehicle was struck by a plane that fell from the sky when attempting to land at a nearby airport. Was the community's negligence the proximate cause of the plaintiff's injury?[12]

4. **Injury:** The plaintiff must have sustained injury, and, due to problems of proof, that injury often must be physical. [For a tort law library, see **http://www.findlaw.com/01topics/22tort**]

The case that follows asks whether a car dealer was negligent in leaving the keys in an unlocked car that was subsequently stolen.

Justice Serna

I. FACTS AND BACKGROUND

Plaintiffs [Herrera et al.] alleged the following facts in their complaint. On May 27, 1996, an individual took his car to Defendant [Quality Pontiac] for repairs. At Defendant's direction, the owner left the keys in the car and the doors unlocked. The lot was fenced, and the gate was unlocked. After 9:00 p.m., Billy Garcia entered the lot, apparently looking inside the cars for something to steal. Garcia stole the vehicle in question. The following day, at approximately 11:00 a.m., a Bernalillo County deputy sheriff observed Garcia driving quickly through a school zone and pursued him, engaging his emergency lights and sirens. Garcia drove at a speed of up to ninety miles per hour and collided head on with Plaintiffs' car, which had pulled over onto the shoulder after hearing the sirens. One occupant was killed and the other seriously injured.

Plaintiffs presented an affidavit of a sociologist to the district court that asserted that "the Albuquerque metropolitan area's motor vehicle theft rate of 1,345.5 per 100,000 residents was the second highest rate in the nation in 1997." The expert estimated that between forty-five and eighty percent of stolen cars had been left unlocked and that between nineteen and forty-seven percent of stolen cars had the ignition keys left inside. The expert claimed that a high proportion of thefts were for the purpose of joyriding and short term transportation. The expert estimated that there is a high probability that a stolen car will be involved in traffic accidents, relying on a study which "found that nearly [seventeen percent] of all stolen cars are involved in accidents in a matter of hours or days after their theft," and another study which found "the accident rate for stolen cars [to be] approximately 200 times the accident rate for cars that have not been stolen." The expert relied on a study which found that "police pursuit was involved in [thirty-seven] percent of the motor vehicle theft cases examined [in a] national sample."

* * * * *

II. DISCUSSION

Whether Defendant Owed Plaintiffs a Common Law Duty

(a) Stare Decisis

New Mexico precedent resolves this issue in Defendant's favor. See *Bouldin*, 71 N. M. at 333. Plaintiffs ask this Court to overrule *Bouldin*.

* * * * *

(b) *Bouldin*

In *Bouldin*, the plaintiff alleged that the defendant parked his vehicle at a lounge, left it unattended, "and negligently failed to remove the ignition keys" from the vehicle. An unknown individual or group of people "borrowed or stole the truck and later abandoned it in the middle of the highway," and the plaintiff collided with it. In *Bouldin*, this Court addressed the question of whether "the owner of a car who leaves it unattended and without removing the key . . . [is] liable for injuries to persons and property suffered when the car is hit after its having been abandoned on the highway by a thief who stole it."

* * * * *

Our review of *Bouldin* indicates that the Court was hesitant to hold that a defendant who leaves his or her keys in an unattended car owes a duty to a plaintiff injured by the acts of a thief because, as a matter of policy, the theft and subsequent accident are too remote a risk. [W]e believe it is clear that *Bouldin* involved both duty and proximate cause and focused principally on duty. [W]e conclude that we must overrule *Bouldin* on its holding that there is no duty in such a case and that there is no proximate cause as a matter of law between leaving ignition keys in an unattended vehicle and an accident precipitated by a thief.

(c) The Foreseability Component of Duty

As an initial step in the establishment of a common law duty, . . . "a potential plaintiff must be reasonably foreseeable to the defendant because of defendant's actions." Kopp v. Wackenhut Corp., 113 N. M. 153, 158.

* * * * *

The present case is complicated by the fact that Plaintiffs' injuries were directly caused by Garcia's criminal operation of the stolen vehicle. As Defendant notes, "as a general rule, a person does not have a duty to protect another from harm caused by the criminal acts of third persons unless the person has a special relationship with the other giving rise to a duty." *Ciup v. Chevron U.S.A., Inc.*, 122 N.M. 537 However, "the criminal acts of a third person will not relieve a negligent defendant of liability if the defendant should have recognized that his or her actions were likely to lead to that criminal activity." *Sarracino v. Martinez*, 117 N.M. 193, 195-96 (Ct. App. 1994).

* * * * *

The present case presents a claim whereby Defendant, arguably, knew or should have known that a theft was likely to occur, and Defendant's actions may have enhanced or increased the risk of such criminal conduct. According to Plaintiffs' affidavit, Albuquerque has a high auto theft rate, and thieves are much more likely to steal vehicles to which they have ready access, as when the cars are left unlocked and unattended with the key in the ignition. Stolen cars are much more likely to be involved in automobile accidents. In this context, Defendant's alleged conduct leaving the keys in the ignition of an unlocked and unattended vehicle arguably increased the likelihood that criminal acts would occur, which ultimately led to the accident in which Plaintiffs were injured, so that we impose a duty of ordinary care.

This Court, in *Bouldin*, concluded that it did "not perceive theft of a car as a natural event to be foreseen by a person who is negligent in leaving his [or her] car unattended with the key in the ignition." Plaintiffs presented an affidavit in the district court which alleged a high rate of car thefts and the proposition that stolen vehicles are more likely to be involved in accidents. Thus, Plaintiffs in the present case have persuaded us that the theft of a car left unattended and unlocked with the key in the ignition is a natural event which can be foreseen by the tortfeasor, as is the subsequent accident and resulting injuries.

We cannot conclude that Plaintiffs' injuries were so unforeseeable that we must hold that Defendant did not owe Plaintiffs a duty as a matter of law. We conclude that Bouldin is no longer viable in its holding that such ensuing theft and subsequent negligent or criminal operation of the vehicle resulting in injury are not natural, foreseeable events attendant upon leaving one's keys in an unlocked, unattended vehicle. *Bouldin* was based on a set of facts and assumptions that no longer reflects our current situation, and we cannot ignore the connection between stolen vehicles and car accidents. . . .

We hold that Defendant's actions in directing the owner to leave the keys in the vehicle and leaving the vehicle unlocked and unattended created a duty to exercise ordinary care. Without any of these factors, the foreseeability and likelihood of theft and the risk of harm would diminish so substantially that such a claim would fail. We conclude . . . that there is a high rate of vehicle theft and that stolen vehicles are more likely to be involved in accidents, that an owner or one in possession of a vehicle reasonably can foresee that the vehicle might be stolen if he or she leaves it unattended, unlocked, and with keys in its ignition, and that he or she reasonably could anticipate that the thief might drive negligently and injure another, creating a duty to that injured party.

Other Issues

1. Breach of Duty

We recognize a duty in the present case. We do not address whether Defendant breached the duty of ordinary care. . . .

The finder of fact must determine whether Defendant breached the duty of ordinary care by considering what a reasonably prudent individual would foresee, what an unreasonable risk of injury would be, and what would consitute an exercise of ordinary care in light of all surrounding circumstances of the present case, including whether Defendant acted reasonably or negligently by keeping an unlocked, unattended vehicle with the keys in the ignition on a fenced, gated lot.

2. Proximate Cause

Defendant argues that its actions did not proximately cause Plainiffs' injuries. The issue of proximate cause is also for the jury or factfinder. . . .

While we agree wih Defendant that there is not great closeness in the connection betwen Defendant's wrongful acts and the resulting injuries, especially considering a gap in time of approximately fourteen hours and a distance of many miles, we do not believe that the connection is so tenuous that we must conclude, as a matter of law, that there is no proximate cause. We leave the fact that the accident occurred approximately fourteen hours after Garcia stole the car from Defendant's lot and the fact that the accident took place several miles away from its property for the jury's consideration on the issue of proximate cause. Thus, the finder of fact must determine whether Defendant's acts, which occurred many hours prior to the accident and many miles away, were a proximate cause of Plaintiffs' injuries.

* * * * *

[Reversed.]

Questions

1. In the *Herrera* case, the New Mexico Supreme Court overruled its own precedent (*Bouldin*). Explain the *Bouldin* reasoning, and explain why it was overruled in *Herrera*.

2. Why did the *Herrera* court find that the defendant, Quality Pontiac, had a duty to the plaintiffs?

3. Why did the New Mexico Supreme Court find that the proximate cause element of negligence claims might be present in cases like *Herrera*?

4. Jerry Colaitis, 47, went with his family to a Benihana steakhouse in Munsey Park, New York. The Benihana chain is well-known for hibachi-style cooking with diners gathered around a rectangular wooden table with a hot grill in the

middle from which the chef, as a form of entertainment, often casually tosses pieces of cooked food at the diners. Mrs. Colaitis claimed that the chef struck and burned some family members with pieces of tossed food. Mr. Colaitis asked the chef to stop, but as he was speaking a piece of shrimp was tossed his way causing Mr. Colaitis to jerk away from it resulting in two wrenched vertebrae in his neck. Mr. Colaitis underwent a corrective operation then suffered a post-operative complication that resulted in a blood-borne infection that caused Mr. Colaitis' death. The Colaitis family sued Benihana for negligence causing the death. At trial, the head chef at the Munsey Park restaurant conceded that the food tossing practice could be dangerous. The restaurant discontinued the practice. During the last year of his life, Mr. Colaitis had suffered from fevers that were not associated with his surgery. How would you rule on the Colaitis' negligence claim? Explain. See *Estate of Colaitis v. Benihana, Inc.,* 015439-2002 (Nassau County Supreme Court, 2006) and Andrew Harris, "Jury: Flying Shrimp . . . Kill Diner," **http://www.law.com/jsp/article.jsp?id=1139479516332**.

5. Johnny Burnett, described by his mother, Sheila Watters, as a devoted "Dungeons & Dragons" player, killed himself. (The record did not disclose his age at the time of death.) Watters blamed the death on her son's absorption in the game. She claimed that "he lost control of his own independent will and was driven to self-destruction."

   "Dungeons & Dragons" is an adventure game set in an imaginary ancient world; the players assume the roles of various characters as suggested by illustrated booklets. The play is orchestrated by a player labeled the "Dungeon Master." The outcome of the play is determined by using dice in conjunction with tables provided with the game. The game's materials do not mention suicide or guns. More than 1 million copies of the game have been sold, many to schools where it is used as a learning tool.

   In federal district court, Watters brought a wrongful death claim against TSR, the manufacturer of "Dungeons & Dragons." The plaintiff's complaint alleged that TSR violated its duty of care in two ways: It disseminated "Dungeons & Dragons" literature to "mentally fragile persons," and it failed to warn that the "possible consequences" of playing the game might include "loss of control of the mental processes." Decide. Explain. See *Watters v. TSR, Inc.,* 904 F.2d 378 (6th Cir. 1990).

6. Plaintiff was seven months pregnant and the mother of 17-month-old James. She was standing on the sidewalk, and James was in the street. A truck being negligently driven bore down on the boy, running him over. The shock caused the mother to miscarry and suffer actual physical and emotional injury. She brought suit against the driver for harm to herself and the infant child.

   a. What is the issue in this case?

   b. Decide the case. Explain. See *Amaya v. Home Ice, Fuel & Supply Co.,* 379 P.2d 513 (Cal. S. Ct. 1963). But also see *Dillon v. Legg,* 441 P.2d 912 (Cal. S. Ct. 1968).

7. Is a fireworks manufacturer liable for harm to children who ignited an explosive that had failed to detonate in the town public display the previous day? Explain.

8. The mother of a 12-year-old boy who died in a shooting accident when a gun he was playing with accidentally discharged sued *Boys Life,* a magazine published by the Boy Scouts of America. The mother claimed that the boy was influenced to experiment with a rifle after reading a 16-page firearms advertising section in the magazine.

   a. What product liability claims would the mother raise?

   b. What constitutional defense would the Boy Scouts raise?

   c. Decide. Explain. See *Jan Way v. Boy Scouts of America,* 856 S.W.2d 230 (Tex. 1993).

Classes of Negligence Claims

Negligence claims emerging from defective products fall into three categories of analysis: (1) manufacturing defects, (2) design defects, and (3) inadequate warnings.

Manufacturing Defects

McDonald's sells a billion cups of coffee each year, in part because its coffee is extremely hot—180 to 190 degrees—which is exactly what its customers prefer and which, McDonald's believes, produces tastier coffee than the 140–145 degrees normally achieved at home. In 1992, then 79-year-old Stella Liebeck ordered coffee at an Albuquerque, New Mexico, McDonald's drive-thru. Her grandson, who was driving, pulled forward and stopped so that Liebeck could add cream and sugar to her coffee. The dashboard of the car was slanted so that the coffee could not be set on it. Liebeck, therefore, placed the coffee between her legs, and while trying to get the top off the container, she spilled the coffee on her lap, resulting in severe burns. She was hospitalized and required skin grafts. She sought a settlement with McDonald's, but according to her family, McDonald's

> Liebeck sued, accusing McDonald's of gross negligence for selling coffee that was "unreasonably dangerous"

offered only $800.[13] Liebeck sued, accusing McDonald's of gross negligence for selling coffee that was "unreasonably dangerous" and "defectively manufactured."[14]

Liebeck was awarded $200,000 in compensatory and $2.7 million in punitive damages. The jury found Liebeck 20 percent responsible for her own injury, thus reducing her compensatory award to $160,000. The judge subsequently reduced the punitive award to $480,000. The parties then settled out of court for an undisclosed amount. According to news reports, the jury awarded Liebeck $2.7 million in punitive damages because of what it perceived to be McDonald's callous attitude toward the accident and because of the more than 700 previous coffee-burn claims that had been filed against McDonald's.[15] [For the "actual facts" on the Liebeck/McDonald's episode, see **http://www.lectlaw.com/files/cur78.htm**]

A British High Court justice, however, viewed the hot coffee situation quite differently:

> Persons generally expect tea or coffee purchased to be consumed on the premises to be hot. . . . They accordingly know that care must be taken to avoid such spills.[16]

[For a discussion of the impact of the *Liebeck* case on tort reform and the public's attitudes toward tort law, see "Taming Trouble Torts" at **http://www.sdcala.org/ CALA%20in%20the%20News/cala_in_the_news02.htm**]

Res Ipsa   As we see with the coffee cases, improper manufacturing of products often generates negligence claims. However, the extremely complex process of producing, distributing, and using a product sometimes so obscures the root of the injury in question that proof of fault is nearly impossible to establish. In those circumstances, many courts have adopted the doctrine of *res ipsa loquitur* (the thing speaks for itself), which in some cases permits the court to infer the defendant's negligence even though that negligence cannot be proven— that is, the facts suggest that the plaintiff's injury must have resulted from the defendant's negligence, but the circumstances are such that the plaintiff is unable to prove negligence. A showing of res ipsa loquitur requires that (1) the injury was caused by an instrumentality under the control of the defendant, (2) the accident ordinarily would not happen absent the defendant's negligence, and (3) there is no evidence of other causes for the accident.[17]

Design Defects

From Cessna's single-engine airplanes to five-gallon buckets (which may hold liquid sufficient to drown a child) to automobile seat belts and on across the spectrum of

American products, manufacturers must think about designing products to anticipate and avoid consumer injury. Two principal lines of analysis have emerged in these cases: (1) The *risk–utility test* holds that a product is negligently designed if the benefits of a product's design are outweighed by the risks that accompany that design. (2) The *consumer expectations test* imposes on the manufacturer a duty to design its products so that they are safe not only for their intended use but also for any reasonably foreseeable use.

In 1997 members of the American Law Institute, a group of legal experts, approved the *Restatement (Third) of Torts,* which does not constitute law but represents those experts' best judgment about what the law *should* be. They have recommended to the courts a design defect standard that supports the balancing/risk–utility model and gives much less attention to consumer expectations. Further, a product would be considered defective in design only if its foreseeable risks could have been reduced or avoided by a reasonable alternative design and if failure to include that design makes the product not reasonably safe. That is, plaintiffs would need to show that some better design was available and was not incorporated in the product in question. The case that follows involves, according to the California Supreme Court, a risk–benefit argument by the plaintiffs seeking civil damages after a mass murder.[18]

LEGAL BRIEFCASE

Marilyn Merrill v. Navegar, Inc. 28 P.3d 116 (Cal. S. Ct. 2001)

Justice Chin

On July 1, 1993, Gian Luigi Ferri killed eight people and wounded six—and then killed himself—during a shooting rampage at 101 California Street, a high-rise office building in San Francisco. Survivors and representatives of some of Ferri's victims (plaintiffs) sued defendant Navegar, Inc., which made two of the three weapons Ferri used.

We granted review to determine whether plaintiffs may hold Navegar liable on a common law negligence theory.

* * * * *

Navegar advertised the TEC-9/DC9 in a number of gun-related magazines and annuals. . . . A typical advertisement claimed that in light of the TEC-9/DC9's design features—including "32 rounds of firepower," a "'TEC-KOTE' finish," and "two-step disassembly for easy cleaning"—the weapon is "ideal for self-defense or recreation," "stands out among high-capacity 9mm assault-type pistols," and "delivers more gutsy performance and reliability than ANY other gun on the market." Navegar also distributed an advertising brochure or catalog describing its guns and accessories, which it mailed to anyone interested and, on at least one occasion, printed in special issue magazines. In a page describing the TEC-KOTE finish, Navegar claimed the finish provided "natural lubicity [*sic*] to increase bullet velocities, excellent resistance to fingerprints, sweat rust, petroleum distillates of all types, gun solvents, gun cleaners, and all powder residues. Salt spray corrosion resistance, expansion and contraction of the metal will *not* result in peeling of finish" A different brochure advertising to retailers used the slogan "Intratec: Weapons that are as tough as your toughest customer."

Navegar included a manual with each TEC-9/DC9 it sold. The 1993 manual contained safety warnings, technical information, and operating instructions. It also claimed the gun was "a radically new type of semi-automatic pistol," which was "designed to deliver a high volume of firepower" and, "thanks to its dimensions and designs," could "be used in modes of fire impossible with most handguns." Regarding the latter claim, the manual described and illustrated several recommended shooting positions, including "hipfire at shortest range," a two-handed hold with the nontrigger hand placed on the upper part of the magazine well.

In early 1993 Ferri, a Southern California resident, bought a [used] TEC-9 from the Pawn & Gun Shop in Henderson, Nevada. . . . According to the salesperson, Ferri looked at a wide variety of handguns, but seemed mainly interested in a "high-capacity type" gun, "something relatively compact that holds a lot of rounds." He gave no indication he had previously heard of the TEC-9 or the Intratec brand . . . Later that day, he returned the weapon, stating that he wanted a new gun instead.

On April 25, 1993, Ferri bought a new TEC-DC9 from Super Pawn, a gun store in Las Vegas, Nevada. . . . Ferri questioned [another] customer about the TEC-DC9. . . . The customer said that people at a shooting range would "probably laugh at" Ferri if he used a TEC-DC9 "because it wasn't really an accurate weapon" and that a .22-caliber gun was better for "plinking" than a nine-millimeter gun because ammunition for the former was much cheaper. Ferri nevertheless chose the TEC-DC9.

Ferri purchased another TEC-DC9 on May 8, 1993, at a Las Vegas gun show. . . .

To purchase the new weapons, Ferri showed an apparently valid Nevada driver's license and answered required questions about his criminal history and residency. All of the distributors and retailers were licensed by the federal Bureau of Alcohol, Tobacco, and Firearms, and [s]o far as the record shows, all of the transactions were legal . . . other than Ferri's misrepresentations as to his state of residence.

On July 1, 1993, Ferri entered 101 California Street carrying the TEC-9/DC9s and a .45-caliber Norinco Model 1911A1 pistol in a large briefcase and another bag. He had added to the TEC-DC9's Hell-Fire brand trigger systems that made the weapons fire in rapid bursts, and he was equipped with hundreds of rounds of ammunition preloaded into 40- to 50-round magazines. He went to the 34th floor, to the office of a law firm he held a grudge against, and started shooting. During his rampage, he killed eight people and wounded six on three different floors, and then killed himself.

* * * * *

PROCEDURAL BACKGROUND

Plaintiffs' first amended complaint asserted a cause of action against Navegar for "common law negligence." In this claim, plaintiffs alleged that Navegar knew or should have known that (1) the TEC-9/DC9 is a "small, easily concealable military, assault weapon; (2) it has "no legitimate sporting...or self-defense purpose and is particularly well adapted to a military-style assault on large numbers of people"; (3) it is "disproportionately associated with criminal activity"; (4) it is "more

attractive to criminals" because of its "firepower" and "other features"; (5) its "firepower was likely to be enhanced by the addition of products such as high-capacity magazines" and "the Hell-Fire trigger system"; and (6) it "would be used to kill or injure innocent persons in violent criminal acts such as the mass killing committed by Ferri." Plaintiffs also alleged that Navegar "acknowledges that publicity surrounding the [TEC-9/DC9s] reputation as a weapon favored by criminals increases its sales." Thus, plaintiffs alleged, Navegar "acted negligently by manufacturing, marketing, and making available for sale to the general public" the TEC-9/DC9.

* * * * *

Navegar moved for summary judgment. As to common law negligence, it argued it owed plaintiffs no duty not to advertise the TEC-9/DC9 and that plaintiffs had no evidence Ferri saw or was affected by a Navegar advertisement.

In opposing the motion, plaintiffs argued that Navegar had misconstrued the ordinary negligence claim. They explained that, contrary to Navegar's assertion, their negligence claim did "not depend on whether" Navegar had a "duty . . . not to advertise" or "whether there is a causal link between Navegar's advertising and plaintiffs' injuries." From the start, plaintiffs have made clear their ordinary negligence claim is not based on Navegar's negligent advertising but rather its decision to 'make available for sale to the general public guns . . . which [it] knew or should have known have "no legitimate sporting or self-defense purpose" and which are "particularly well-adapted to a military-style assault on large numbers of people." Simply put, Navegar breached a duty of care by making the TEC-9 available to the general public, i.e., "by releasing the weapons for sale to the general public even though it knew or should have known that the TEC-9 was particularly attractive to criminals and particularly suited for mass killings." Plaintiffs concluded their argument regarding duty by asserting that "Navegar breached a legal duty to forebear [*sic*] distributing the TEC-9 to the general public given the likelihood that doing so would lead to the sort of violent criminal act that occurred at the 101 California Street Building."

As to causation, plaintiffs also argued that in light of their negligence theory, "whether Ferri actually saw or was influenced by any particular Navegar advertising is immaterial." They explained, "The ordinary negligence claim is directed to Navegar's conduct in making the TEC-9 available to the public. It is *that* unreasonable conduct that was a substantial factor in causing plaintiffs' injuries, not Navegar's marketing efforts." "Navegar's advertising is only material to the ordinary negligence claim in that it underscores that the criminal use of the weapon was foreseeable to Navegar. . . . *Plaintiffs are not alleging that Ferri was induced to purchase the TEC-DC9s or to commit the 101 massacre by any particular advertisements.* The significance of the advertisements is what they say about [Navegar's] knowledge of [its] market."

* * * * *

DISCUSSION

* * * * *

[I]n the trial court, Navegar argued in effect that the Legislature, through section 1714.4, established an exception that applies in this case. Section 1714.4 provides; "(a) In a products liability action, no firearm or ammunition shall be deemed defective in design on the basis that the benefits of the product do not outweigh the risk of injury posed by its potential to cause serious injury, damage, or death when discharged. (b) For purposes of this section: (1) The potential of a firearm or ammunition to cause serious injury, damage, or death when discharged does not make the product defective in design. (2) Injuries or damages resulting from the discharge of a firearm or ammunition are not proximately caused by its potential to cause serious injury, damage, or death, but are proximately caused by the actual discharge of the product. (c) This section shall not affect a products liability cause of action based upon the improper selection of design alternatives." . . . Navegar argues that this statute, by establishing a state policy of exempting manufacturers of legal, nondefective firearms "from liability for their criminal use," bars plaintiffs' negligence claim.

Plaintiffs respond that section 1714.4 "has no application to this case because it is not a products liability action." Plaintiffs assert that they "seek to hold Navegar liable for its negligent conduct, not for making a defective product," and that they "make no assertion that Navegar should be liable because the risks posed by the TEC-9 outweigh its benefits." . . . [W]e reject plaintiffs' argument that section 1714.4 is inapplicable because this case "is not a products liability action.". . .

[C]ontrary to the assertion of plaintiffs, the record demonstrates that plaintiffs do, in fact, seek to hold Navegar liable precisely because, as the trial court stated, the TEC-9/DC9's "potential for harm substantially outweighs any possible benefit to be derived from [it]." In their brief, plaintiffs assert that Navegar is liable because it "designed and widely distributed a weapon uniquely suited for mass killing and lacking legitimate civilian uses."

Using the words of the risk–utility test for both products liability theories, plaintiffs essentially allege, argue, and hope to prove that the TEC-9/DC9 is defective in design. Thus this is a products liability action based on negligence, which asserts that the TEC-9/DC9 was defective in design because the risks of making it available to the general public outweighed the benefits of that conduct, and that defendants knew or should have known this fact.

* * * * *

Finally, we also conclude that the evidence in the record regarding Navegar's promotional activities and the literature it distributed with the TEC-9/DC9 does not save plaintiffs' negligence claim. As we have previously explained, in opposing Navegar's summary judgment motion, plaintiffs insisted that "their ordinary negligence claim" was not "directed to" or "based on Navegar's negligent advertising but rather its decision to make [the TEC-9/DC9] available for sale to the general public. . . ." Plaintiffs also insisted that it was Navegar's "unreasonable conduct" in "making the TEC-9 available to the public . . . that was a substantial factor in causing [their] injuries, not Navegar's marketing efforts." Thus, they maintained, "whether Ferri actually saw or was influenced by any particular Navegar advertising is immaterial." . . . . *Plaintiffs are not alleging that Ferri was induced to purchase the TEC-DC9s or to commit the 101 massacre by any particular advertisements.* The significance of the advertisements is what they say about [Navegar's] knowledge of [its] market."

* * * * *

In any event, the evidence in the record fails to raise a triable factual issue as to whether Navegar's advertising and literature were substantial factors in causing plaintiffs' injuries. Regarding this question, plaintiffs' counsel asserted at oral argument that "Navegar's liability does not depend on its telling the public, here's a great gun to commit a crime," but on its "communicating a message that people who want above all else in their weapons firepower, the capacity to shoot many, many rounds without the need to reload, and to use that gun in a combat fashion, this is the gun for you."

* * * * *

To the extent plaintiffs rely on allegedly more inflammatory aspects of Navegar's advertising, they fail to raise a triable factual issue regarding causation. For example, they offer no evidence, direct or circumstantial, that Ferri ever saw the promotional materials sent to dealers, which used the phrase "tough as your toughest customer," or the early version of the TEC-KOTE product brochure description, which promised "excellent resistance to fingerprints." Moreover, plaintiffs do not dispute that (1) San Francisco police inspectors did "not recall" finding "any

TEC-DC9 magazine advertisement in Ferri's apartment" and found "no evidence" that any advertisement caused Ferri to travel to Nevada to purchase the TEC-DC9s; (2) "there is otherwise no Navegar magazine advertisement in the possession of the City and County of San Francisco as evidence collected in the 101 California Street shootings"; (3) the salesman at the Pawn & Gun Shop in Henderson, Nevada, where Ferri bought the used TEC-9, "never" saw Ferri in possession of any advertisement or literature for the TEC-9 or TEC-DC9, and never heard Ferri mention he had seen any advertisement for the TEC-9 or TEC-DC9; (4) when Ferri bought the first new TEC-9/DC9, he had no firearms advertisement or other type of literature in his possession and did not ask for the TEC-9/DC9 by name; and (5) when Ferri bought the second new TEC-9/DC9, he indicated he already owned another TEC-9/DC9. Plaintiffs have failed to produce, or show that they will be able to produce at trial, substantial evidence "that Navegar's marketing style was 'a factor' in" Ferri's conduct. . . .

In arguing to the contrary, plaintiffs cite evidence that Ferri went to Nevada, where the TEC-9/DC9 was available, to buy guns for his planned attack and that the two stores where he bought TEC-9/DC9s had Las Vegas Yellow Pages advertisements picturing, among other guns, assault weapons. Although this evidence does tend to show Ferri sought to purchase high-firepower guns, it does not tend to show Ferri went to Nevada or the stores in search of a TEC-9/DC9 or other assault pistol *in response to Navegar's marketing efforts.* The existence of various high-firepower rifles and pistols would have been so widely known from other sources (especially to a reader of gun magazines as, apparently, Ferri was) as to render unjustified any inference that Navegar's marketing efforts were a substantial factor in motivating Ferri's decision to seek such a gun. Thus, we agree with the trial court that "the links plaintiffs seek to establish between advertisements and carnage amount to little more than guesswork." . . .

Accordingly, we conclude the trial court properly granted Navegar summary judgment. . . . In section 1714.4, the Legislature has set California's public policy regarding a gun manufacturer's liability under these circumstances. Given that public policy, plaintiffs may not proceed with their negligence claim.

Reversed.

DISSENTING OPINION BY JUSTICE WERDEGAR

I cannot accept the majority's conclusion that plaintiffs are statutorily barred from suing the maker of the semiautomatic assault weapon used to massacre the victims in this case.

*   *   *   *   *

Civil Code section 1714.4 bars product liability actions against gunmakers based on the risk–benefit theory of product defect.

The legislative policy behind the statute might, at most, be deemed also to encompass negligence claims that are substantially identical to risk–benefit product defect claims. Plaintiffs' claim is neither. Plaintiffs' claim of negligence is, at bottom, that defendant Navegar, Inc. acted without due care in distributing the TEC-9/DC9 to the general civilian public rather than restricting its sales to police and military units that might have a legitimate call for such a military-style assault pistol. Plaintiffs do *not* claim that the TEC-9/DC9 is defective; nor do they even claim that defendant acted negligently *simply by making* the TEC-9/DC9. Plaintiffs allege negligence, rather, in Navegar's *selling that firearm on the general civilian market knowing it would attract purchasers likely to misuse it,* rather than restricting sales to buyers with a lawful use for the tools of assaultive violence. . . . This theory of negligence, resting on the allegation that particular marketing choices by Navegar were imprudent, is not substantially identical to a claim of product defect and thus is within neither the letter nor the spirit of Civil Code section 1714.4.

Navegar's conduct was allegedly negligent not because its gun was defective but because, in light of the gun's known attractiveness to violent users and the lack of a compelling need for its availability on the civilian market, a reasonably careful distributor would have restricted sales to groups unlikely to misuse the firearm. Civil Code section 1714.4 simply does not address such a negligent distribution claim.

*   *   *   *   *

Questions

1. *a.* Why did the California Supreme Court rule in favor of Navegar in this case?
    b. Explain the plaintiffs' cause of action.
    c. Explain the dissenting opinion.
    d. Argue that the plaintiffs' claim did not involve a risk–benefit analysis of the kind forbidden by the California statute.
2. In your opinion, should gun manufacturers be liable for the criminal use of their products? Explain.
3. Some observers argued that a decision for the plaintiffs in the *Merrill/Navegar* case would have led to a product liability "slippery slope." Explain that argument. Do you agree with it? Explain.
4. Hollister was badly burned when her shirt came into contact with a burner as she leaned over her electric stove. She sued the store where she bought the shirt, claiming that it was defectively designed. What proof will Hollister need to provide to win her defective design claim? See *Hollister v. Dayton-Hudson*, 188 F.3d 414 (6th Cir. 1999).

New Law Shields Gun Industry

Congress and President Bush approved legislation in 2005 that was designed to stop lawsuits by cities and individuals against the gun industry. In general, those lawsuits claimed that the guns used in crimes were negligently marketed and that they constituted a public nuisance which resulted in heavy public sector costs (such as medical expenses paid from public funds). Many dozens of such lawsuits were introduced across the country. Most had been unsuccessful, but the bill was expected to block the remaining cases and most further such litigation. The bill contains an exception allowing some lawsuits involving defective weapons or situations such as knowingly selling a weapon to someone who has failed a background check. Critics challenged the bill as an unconstitutional special protection for a single, politically well-connected industry. [For the Brady Center to Prevent Gun Violence, see **www.bradycenter.org**; for the National Shooting Sports Foundation, see **http://www.nssf.org**]

Source: Sheryl Gay Stolberg, "Congress Passes New Legal Shield for Gun Industry," *New York Times,* October 21, 2005.

Warnings

Universal Pictures issued warnings in 2001 that we might be hurt if we tried to mimic the car-racing stunts in its movie, *The Fast and the Furious.* The studio was trying to fend off lawsuits. Warnings seem to be everywhere in our lives. Some of them seem downright silly—so much so that a nonprofit group, M-LAW, sponsors a "Wacky Warning Labels" contest. Leading recent entries included these:

> On a toilet brush: "Do not use for personal hygiene."
> On a digital thermometer: "Once used rectally, the thermometer should not be used orally."[19]

Are these warnings of value in avoiding lawsuits? Some experts think so, but others are doubtful:

> Rower McCarthy, a "human factors" engineer who studies the relationship between people and products, said that warnings simply [do] not work.
>
> He said he [has] collected more than 3,500 articles about the effectiveness of warning labels and [has] found not a single reliable study that documented a reduction in accidents resulting from a warning on a product:
>
> "Consumers who pay attention to warnings don't get hurt in the first place, and consumers who get hurt typically aren't the ones who read warnings," said McCarthy.[20]

A product may be considered defective because of inadequate warnings when reasonable warnings would have reduced or avoided the foreseeable risks and the failure to warn resulted in a product that was not reasonably safe. Courts might also consider the feasibility of an effective warning and the probable seriousness of the injury. The case that follows analyzes both design defect [under the *Restatement (Third) of Torts*] and failure to warn negligence claims. [For California's failure-to-warn law, see **http://consumerlawpage.com/article/failure.shtml**]

Justice Larson

FACTS

In June of 1999, Delbert Parish (the plaintiff's brother) and Shelley Tatro purchased a Jumpking fourteen-foot trampoline for use in their backyard. They set up the trampoline, and Delbert tried it out by attempting a somersault. He nearly fell off the trampoline, prompting Delbert and Shelley to purchase a "fun ring"—a netlike enclosure with one entry point onto the trampoline. While the plaintiff was visiting his brother on September 11, 1999, he attempted to do a back somersault on the trampoline, but he landed on his head and was rendered a quadriplegic. In August 2001 Parish filed suit against Jumpking.

The district court entered summary judgment against the plaintiff on all claims. [The plaintiff appealed.] . . .

THE DEFECTIVE DESIGN CLAIM

In Wright v. Brooke Group Ltd., 652 N.W.2d 159 (Iowa 2002), we adopted section 2 of the Restatement (Third) of Torts . . . Under a design-defect claim, a plaintiff is essentially arguing that, even though the product meets the manufacturer's design specifications, the specifications themselves create unreasonable risks. To succeed under [the Restatement] section 2(b), a plaintiff must ordinarily show the existence of a reasonable alternative design, and that this design would, at a reasonable cost, have reduced the foreseeability of harm posed by the product.

The Restatement recognizes exceptions to the requirement of a reasonable alternative design, but the plaintiff relies on only one: that the design was "manifestly unreasonable" under Restatement 2(b) comment e. Under that comment,

the designs of some products are so manifestly unreasonable, in that they have low social utility and high degree of danger, that liability should attach even absent proof of a reasonable alternative design.

The plaintiff concedes that he has not offered an alternative design; rather, he argues a trampoline is so inherently dangerous that a reasonable design alternative is not available. He contends there is no safe way to use a trampoline in a backyard, and it must be used only by properly trained and qualified participants under supervision.

The Restatement provides this illustration of a manifestly unreasonable product under comment e:

ABC Co. manufacturers novelty items. One item, an exploding cigar, is made to explode with a loud bang and the emission of smoke. Robert purchased the exploding cigar and presented it to his boss, Jack, at a birthday party arranged for him at the office. Jack lit the cigar. When it exploded, the heat from the explosion lit Jack's beard on fire causing serious burns to his face. If a court were to recognize the rule identified in this Comment, the finder of fact might find ABC liable for the defective design of the exploding cigar even if no reasonable alternative design was available that would provide similar prank characteristics. The utility of the exploding cigar is so low and the risk of injury is so high as to warrant a conclusion that the cigar is defective and should not have been marketed at all.

[T]he wording of section 2(b) and virtually all commentary on it suggest that this exception should be sparingly applied.

* * * * *

While comment e recognizes the possibility that egregiously dangerous products might be held defective for that reason alone, the Restatement has noted that "a clear majority of courts that have faced the issue have refused so to hold." [According to the Restatement:] In cases involving common and widely distributed products,

courts generally have concluded that legislatures and administrative agencies can, more appropriately than courts, consider the desirability of commercial distribution of some categories of widely used and consumed, but nevertheless dangerous, products.

It is undisputed that trampolines are common and widely distributed products. In fact, the evidence showed approximately fourteen million people use them. Even data produced by the plaintiff . . . showed that in 2002 only 2.1% of trampolines were associated with injuries, and only one-half of one percent of jumpers were injured. The Consumer Product Safety Commission concluded trampolines ranked twelfth among recreational use products in terms of injuries. They rated below such common activities as basketball, bicycle riding, football, soccer, and skating.

The benefits of trampolining include use in cardiovascular workouts and other medical treatments, including "bouncing" therapy for children with cystic fibrosis. Trampolining obviously provides valuable exercise and entertainment.

We conclude that the plaintiff has failed to generate a genuine issue of fact sufficient to except this product from the requirement of section 2(b), and the plaintiff's design-defect claim under that section must therefore be rejected.

THE WARNINGS

The plaintiff also claims the trampoline did not incorporate adequate warnings.

Under the Restatement, a product

is defective because of inadequate instructions or warnings when the foreseeable risks of harm posed by the product could have been reduced or avoided by the provision of reasonable instructions or warnings by the seller or other distributor, or a predecessor in the commercial chain of distribution, and the omission of the instructions or warnings renders the product not reasonably safe.

Restatement 2(c).

The trampoline in this case, and its surrounding fun ring, together provide numerous warnings. Three warnings are placed permanently on the pad of the trampoline and advise the user:

WARNING

Do not land on head or neck.
Paralysis or death can result, even if you land in the middle of the trampoline mat (bed).
To reduce the chance of landing on your head or neck, do not do somersaults (flips).
Only one person at a time on trampoline.
Multiple jumpers increase the chances of loss of control, collision, and falling off.
This can result in broken head, neck, back, or leg
This trampoline is not recommended for children under 6 years of age.

These warnings also include nationally recognized warning symbols cautioning against those activities. During manufacture, Jumpking also places one warning on each of the eight legs of the trampoline, and the design is such that the only way to assemble the trampoline is to have these warnings facing out so they are visible to the user. Jumpking further manufactures two printed (nonpictorial) warnings that are sewn onto the trampoline bed itself. It also provides a warning placard for the owner to affix to the trampoline that contains both the pictorial warning and the language regarding safe use of the trampoline, and it provides an owner's manual that contains the warnings as found on the trampoline as well as additional warnings regarding supervision and education. It is undisputed that these warnings exceed the warnings required by the American Society for Testing and Material (ASTM).

Warnings . . . are also provided with the fun ring.

The Restatement recognizes that users must pay some attention for their own safety:

Society does not benefit from products that are excessively safe—for example, automobiles designed with maximum speeds of 20 miles per hour—any more than its benefits

from products that are too risky. Society benefits most when the right, or optimal, amount of product safety is achieved. *From a fairness perspective, requiring individual users and consumers to bear appropriate responsibility for proper product use prevents careless users and consumers from being subsidized by more careful users and consumers, when the former are paid damages out of funds to which the latter are forced to contribute through higher product prices.*

Restatement §2 cmt. *a* (emphasis added).

In this case, it is undisputed that the three warnings affixed to the pad of the trampoline and the placards that came with both the trampoline and the fun ring warned against the specific conduct in which the plaintiff was engaged at the time of his injury, i.e., attempting somersaults or flips. We conclude that a reasonable fact finder could not conclude that the defendant's warnings were inadequate.

Affirmed.

Questions

1. *a.* Explain the plaintiff's design defect argument.
   b. Explain why that argument was rejected by the court.
2. *a.* According to the *Restatement (Third) of Torts,* when is a product design considered "manifestly unreasonable"?
   b. Explain the legal significance of a product design that is "manifestly unreasonable."
3. Explain why the Iowa Supreme Court ruled against the plaintiff's failure to warn claim.
4. Bresnahan, age 50 and 5'8" tall, was driving her Chrysler LeBaron, equipped with a driver's side air bag, at between 25 and 30 miles per hour. She was seated less than one foot from the air bag cover. Bresnahan was distracted by police lights and rear-ended a Jaguar, triggering the LeBaron air bag, which broke Bresnahan's arm and caused various abrasions. The vehicle did not include a warning about the danger of sitting too close to the air bag. Was the vehicle defective because of the absence of a warning? Explain. See *Bresnahan v. Chrysler Corp.,* 65 Cal. App. 4th 1149 (1998).
5. Laaperi installed a smoke detector in his bedroom, properly connecting it to his home's electrical system. Six months later, Laaperi's house burned and three of his children were killed. A short circuit, which caused the fire, also deprived the A.C.-powered smoke detector of electricity. Thus the detector did not sound a warning. Laaperi then claimed that Sears, Roebuck, where he purchased the detector, was guilty of negligence for failing to warn him that a fire might disable his smoke detector such that no warning would issue. How would you rule in this case? See *Laaperi v. Sears, Roebuck & Co.,* 787 F.2d 726 (1st Cir. 1986).

Negligence Defenses: Introduction

Even if the plaintiff has established all of the necessary ingredients in a negligence claim, the defendant may still prevail by asserting a good defense. The two most prominent legal defenses in these cases are (1) comparative or contributory negligence and (2) assumption of the risk.

> A trampoline at the Beta Theta Pi fraternity house at the University of Denver led to a broken neck and paralysis when a 20-year-old fraternity member, Oscar Whitlock, unsuccessfully attempted a flip at 10 PM in the dark

A trampoline at the Beta Theta Pi fraternity house at the University of Denver led to a broken neck and paralysis when a 20-year-old fraternity member, Oscar Whitlock, unsuccessfully attempted a flip at 10 PM in the dark. Whitlock had extensive experience with trampolines. The day of the accident he had slept until 2 PM after drinking that morning until 2 AM. The trampoline was located in front of the house on university land that was leased by the fraternity. The trampoline had been used over a 10-year period by students and community members. A number of injuries had resulted. The university kept its own trampoline under lock and key because of safety concerns.

At trial the jury found the university 72 percent at fault, with the remainder of the blame lying with the plaintiff/student. He recovered 72 percent of $7,300,000 ($5,256,000). On appeal the judgment was upheld; but the dissent argued that the university had no duty to warn against obvious risks, saying that "no reasonable person could conclude that the plaintiff was not at least as negligent as the defendant." Hence the dissent was saying, in effect, that the plaintiff had *assumed the risk* and, in any case, was himself arguably more *negligent* than the university.[21]

The Colorado State Supreme Court then reviewed the appeals court decision and reversed on the grounds that the university did not maintain a "special relationship" with the plaintiff that would have justified imposing a duty of due care on the university to ensure safe use of the trampoline.[22]

Questions

Assume you own an amusement park.

1. Would the dissent's reasoning in the *Whitlock* court of appeals decision apply to the trampo-line in your amusement park business? Explain.
2. Would a warning and close supervision protect you from liability under the court of appeals decision? Explain.
3. Would you have the duty of due care for your customers that the Supreme Court said the University of Denver did not have for Whitlock? Explain.

Negligence Defenses: Rules

Let's look more closely at the central defenses in negligence cases.

Comparative Negligence

Most states have adopted *comparative negligence* as a defense; an approach that involves weighing the relative negligence of the parties. Though the formula varies from state to state, typically the plaintiff's recovery is reduced by a percentage equal to the percentage of the plaintiff's fault in the case. Assume a plaintiff sustained $10,000 in injuries in an accident. If the plaintiff's own negligence is found to be 20 percent responsible for the injuries, then the plaintiff's recovery will be reduced to $8,000. In many states, however, when the plaintiff is more than 50 percent at fault, she or he will be barred from recovery.

Contributory Negligence

Rather than employing the comparative negligence doctrine, a few states continue to follow the historic rule that any contribution by the plaintiff to his or her own harm constitutes a complete bar to recovery. This is called *contributory negligence.* If the plaintiff is found to have contributed in any way to his or her injury, even if that contribution is minuscule, he or she is unable to recover.

Assumption of Risk

A plaintiff who willingly enters a dangerous situation and is injured, in many states, will be barred from recovery. For example, if a driver sees that the road ahead is flooded, he will not be compensated for the injuries sustained when he loses control as he attempts to drive through the water. His recovery is barred even though the road was flooded due to operator error in opening a floodgate. The requirements for use of the *assumption of risk* defense are (1) knowledge of the risk and (2) voluntary assumption of the risk. Assumption of the risk and contributory negligence are distinguishable in that the former is based on consent whereas the latter is rooted in carelessness. Increasingly, states that have adopted the comparative negligence doctrine do not treat assumption of the risk as a complete bar to recovery, but rather as a factor in negligence balancing.

Question

Muldovan and McEachern, two 17-year-old boys, were drinking and playing with a gun by handing it back and forth, pointing it at each other, loading and unloading it, and pulling the trigger. Others at the party warned them to stop, but they persisted. On one occasion, McEachern encouraged Muldovan to pull the trigger. He did so and killed McEachern, whose parents then sued Muldovan for negligence, among other causes of action.

1. What defense(s) would you offer on behalf of Muldovan? Explain.
2. Decide the case. Explain. See *Muldovan v. McEachern,* 523 S.E.2d 566 (Ga. S.Ct. 1999).

Warranties

As explained previously, negligence claims often are difficult to prove. For that reason and others, a wronged consumer may wish to raise a breach of warranty claim in addition to or in place of a negligence action. A warranty is simply a guarantee arising out of a contract. If the product does not conform to the standards of the warranty, the contract is violated (breached), and the wronged party is entitled to recovery. Note that a negligence claim arises from breach of the duty of due care, whereas a warranty claim arises from a breach of contract. [For the text of the Uniform Commercial Code, Article II, Sales, see Appendix B at the back of this text. For the UCC, in total, see **http://www.law. cornell.edu/ucc**]

Express Warranties

An express warranty exists if a seller of goods states a fact or makes a promise regarding the character or quality of the goods. (Some lease arrangements are also covered by warranty law, but we will limit our discussion to the sale of goods.) Warranties are governed primarily by the terms of the Uniform Commercial Code. The UCC is designed to codify and standardize the law of commercial practice.

UCC 2–313. Express Warranties by Affirmation, Promise, Description, Sample

1. Express warranties by the seller are created as follows:
   a. Any affirmation of fact or promise made by the seller to the buyer which relates to the goods and becomes part of the basis of the bargain creates an express warranty that the goods shall conform to the affirmation or promise.
   b. Any description of the goods which is made part of the basis of the bargain creates an express warranty that the goods shall conform to the description.
   c. Any sample or model which is made part of the basis of the bargain creates an express warranty that the whole of the goods shall conform to the sample or model.

The UCC 2–313 standard is straightforward: The seller who seeks to enhance the attractiveness of her product by offering representations as to the nature or quality of the product must fulfill those representations or fall in breach of contract and pay damages. [At this writing, the various state legislatures are considering changes to the UCC. For a summary of the changes recommended by the National Conference of Commissioners on Uniform State Laws for Article 2, Sales, including warranties, see **http://www. nccusl.org/Update/uniformact_summaries/uniformacts-s-ucc22003.asp**]

Puffing

Perhaps the area of greatest confusion in determining the existence and coverage of an express warranty is distinguishing a seller's promise from a mere expression of opinion. The latter, often referred to as sales talk or *puffing,* does not create an express warranty. The UCC requires an affirmation of fact or promise. Hence a statement of opinion is not covered by the code. For example, the sales clerk who says, "This is the best TV around," would not be guaranteeing that the television in question is the best available. The salesperson is expressing a view. We, as consumers, seem to be quite patient with sellers' exaggerations. If, on the other hand, the clerk said, "This TV comes with a solid walnut cabinet," when in fact it was a pine veneer stained to a walnut tone, a breach of warranty action might ultimately be in order. The reasonable expectations test is to be applied in such situations. An expression of opinion coming from an expert may well create an express warranty because the buyer should reasonably be able to rely on the expert's affirmations. That would particularly be the case if the buyer is not knowledgeable about the product.

Implied Warranties

When a seller enters a contract for the sale of goods an implied warranty arises by operation of law. That is, an implied warranty automatically attaches to the sale of goods unless the warranty is disclaimed (disavowed) by the seller.

Two types of implied warranties are provided for:

UCC 2–314. Implied Warranty: Merchantability; Usage of Trade

(1) Unless excluded or modified (Section 2–316), a warranty that the goods shall be merchantable is implied in a contract for their sale if the seller is a merchant with respect to goods of that kind. Under this section the serving for value of food or drink to be consumed either on the premises or elsewhere is a sale.

UCC 2–315. Implied Warranty: Fitness for Particular Purpose

Where the seller at the time of contracting has reason to know any particular purpose for which the goods are required and that the buyer is relying on the seller's skill or judgment to select or furnish suitable goods, there is unless excluded or modified under the next section an implied warranty that the goods shall be fit for such purpose.

The implied warranty of merchantability is a powerful tool for the wronged consumer. If the seller is a merchant regularly selling goods of the kind in question, the warranty of merchantability automatically accompanies the sale unless the warranty is excluded via a disclaimer (explained next). The warranty arises even if the seller made no certification as to the nature or quality of the goods. UCC 2–314 enshrines the consumer's reasonable expectation that only safe goods of at least ordinary quality will appear on the market.

The implied warranty of fitness for a particular purpose likewise arises by operation of law, but only when the seller (merchant or not) knows (or has reason to know) that the goods are to be used for a specific purpose, and the seller further knows that the buyer is relying on the seller's judgment. If those conditions obtain, the warranty exists automatically unless disclaimed. For example, Chris Snapp engages an audio products clerk in a discussion regarding the proper sound system for Chris's classic Austin Healey sports car. Chris explains the joy he expects to receive in driving his car along the winding Kentucky roads with the convertible top down and his songs booming. Unfortunately, the stereo selected on the clerk's advice proves insufficiently powerful to be heard clearly above the rushing wind. Should Chris recover for breach of the implied warranty of fitness for a particular purpose? Merchantability?

Disclaimers

Express warranties may be disclaimed (excluded) or modified only with great difficulty. In any contract displaying both an express warranty and language disclaiming that warranty (for example, sold "as is" or "with all faults"), the warranty will remain effective unless the warranty and the disclaimer can reasonably be read as consistent.

Implied warranties may be excluded or modified by following either of the two patterns explained in UCC sections 2–316(2) and (3)(a).

2. Subject to subsection (3), to exclude or modify the implied warranty of merchantability or any part of it the language must mention merchantability and in case of a writing must be conspicuous, and to exclude or modify any implied warranty of fitness the exclusion must be by a writing and conspicuous.

3. Notwithstanding subsection (2)

   a. unless the circumstances indicate otherwise, all implied warranties are excluded by expressions like as is, with all faults, or other language which in common understanding calls the buyer's attention to the exclusion of warranties and makes plain that there is no implied warranty.

   Finally, when a buyer, before entering a contract, inspects the goods (or a sample thereof) or declines to inspect, no implied warranty exists with regard to defects that should have been apparent on inspection UCC 2–316(3)(b).

Magnuson–Moss Warranty Act

Congress has extended and clarified the UCC warranty rules with the Magnuson–Moss Warranty Act. Congress approved the act following a study that found widespread abuse of consumers. Warranties were often vague, deceptive, or simply incomprehensible to the average purchaser. The act, administered by the FTC, applies only to consumer products and only to written warranties. It does not require offering an express written warranty, but where such a warranty is offered and the cost of the goods is more than $10, the warranty must be labeled *full* or *limited.* A full warranty requires free repair of any defect. If repair is not achieved within a reasonable time, the buyer may elect either a refund or replacement without charge. If a limited warranty is offered, the limitation must be conspicuously displayed.

   If a warranty is offered on goods costing more than $15, the warrantor must "fully and conspicuously disclose in simple and readily understandable language the terms and conditions of the warranty."

   The effect of the Magnuson–Moss Act has not been entirely consistent with Congress's hopes. In practice, many sellers have either offered limited warranties or eliminated them entirely.

   In many states, implied warranty law has been incorporated within broader product liability actions reflecting an emerging preference for treating personal injury and property damages as torts rather than contract-based (warranty) claims. The *Mitchell* case that follows demonstrates the application of some traditional warranty law reasoning (foreign-natural test and reasonable expectations test) to an injury resulting from an object in restaurant food.

LEGAL BRIEFCASE

Mitchell v. Fridays   748 N.E.2d 89
(Ohio Ct. App. 2000)

Judge Waite

This timely appeal arises from the trial court's grant of summary judgment to Appellee T.G.I. Friday's and to Appellee Pro Source Distributors. For the following reasons, we affirm the judgment of the trial court.

   On April 11, 1996, Appellant Sandra Mitchell was having dinner at Appellee Friday's restaurant. Appellant was eating a fried clam strip when she bit into a hard substance which she believed to be a piece of a clam shell. Appellant experienced immediate pain and later sought dental treatment. Some time later, the crown of a tooth came loose. It was determined that the crown could not be reattached and the remaining root of the tooth was extracted.

On September 2, 1997, Appellant filed a product liability action against both Friday's, who served the meal, and against Appellee Pro Source Distributing (hereinafter "Pro Source"), the supplier of the fried clams. Both Friday's and Pro Source filed motions for summary judgment which the trial court granted without explanation on June 18, 1999.

* * * * *

Appellant argues that in light of Ohio's product liability legislation, the trial court should have applied the "reasonable expectation test" to her claim. R.C. 2307.74 provides that "A product is defective [if] . . . it deviated in a material way from the design specifications, formula, or performance standards of the manufacturer." R.C. 2307.75(A) (2) provides that a product is defective in design or formulation if "it is more dangerous than an ordinary consumer would expect when used in an intended or reasonably foreseeable manner." According to Appellant, by the enactment of these statutes the "reasonable expectation" test supersedes the traditional "foreign–natural test" applied in cases where injury is caused by substances in food. Appellant asserts that there is a reasonable expectation that clams are completely cleaned of their shells and free of foreign materials.

* * * * *

In the present case, Friday's set forth in its motion for summary judgment Appellant's deposition testimony to the effect that while eating a clam strip, she bit down on "a hard, foreign substance." Appellant stated that she assumed it was a piece of a clam shell. Appellant described the size of the object as about a quarter of the size of a small fingernail or about a quarter of an inch or smaller and irregular in shape. Moreover, Friday's attached an affidavit from its manager, Eric Hicks, who immediately responded to Appellant's report of the incident. In that affidavit, Hicks confirmed that the object Appellant presented to him was indeed a piece of clam shell and that it was approximately one-quarter inch in length and irregularly shaped. . . .

There being no factual dispute here, we must decide whether Appellees are entitled to judgment as a matter of law. Both Friday's and Pro Source presented essentially the same argument, that regardless of whether the foreign–natural test or reasonable expectation test was applied, Appellant has no claim against Appellees. Appellant, however, has argued for the application only of the reasonable expectation test.

* * * * *

However, it does not appear necessary to determine which test applies to the present case. [A] similar argument was addressed in *Mathews v. Maysville Seafoods, Inc.* (1991). In *Mathews,* the plaintiff suffered a bowel injury when he swallowed a fish bone while eating a fish fillet served by the defendant. The trial court granted the defendant's motion for summary judgment. On appeal, the defendant argued for the adoption of the reasonable expectation test as opposed to the foreign–natural test.

The *Mathews* court set forth both tests. Under the foreign–natural test,

> Bones which are natural to the type of meat served cannot legitimately be called a foreign substance, and a consumer who eats meat dishes ought to anticipate and be on his guard against the presence of such bones.

The reasonable expectation test states,

> The test should be what is "reasonably expected" by the consumer in the food as served, not what might be natural to the ingredients of that food prior to preparation. . . . As applied to the action for common-law negligence, the test is related to the foreseeability of harm on the part of the defendant. The defendant is not an insurer but has the duty of ordinary care to eliminate or remove in the preparation of the food he serves such harmful substances as the consumer of the food, as served, would not ordinarily anticipate and guard against.

* * * * *

In the present case, it cannot be disputed that the piece of clam shell which caused Appellant's injury was natural to the clam strip which she consumed. Turning to the question of whether Appellant should have reasonably anticipated the presence of the clam shell, we are reminded of the Ohio Supreme Court's holding in *Allen* that, " . . . the possible presence of a piece of oyster shell in or attached to an oyster is so well known to anyone who eats oysters that we can say as a matter of law that one who eats oysters can reasonably anticipate and guard against eating such a piece of shell." The facts of the present case are virtually indistinguishable from *Allen* except for the type of injury and that, here, Appellant was eating fried clams rather than fried oysters. We therefore hold that as a matter of law, one who eats clams can reasonably anticipate and guard against eating such a piece of shell.

Affirmed.

Questions

1. *a.* Who won this case and why?

   b. Did the court adopt the foreign–natural test or the reasonable expectations test? Explain.

c. Is a walnut shell "natural" to, for example, maple nut ice cream? What about a cherry pit in a cherry pie? Explain.

2. In buying a new motor home, Leavitt told the dealer that he wanted to have plenty of power and braking capacity for driving in the mountains. He was assured by the dealer on both counts. He brought the motor home and found it unsatisfactory for mountain use. After many warranty repairs, he sued for breach of warranty.

   a. What warranty was breached, according to Leavitt?

   b. Decide the case. Explain. See *Leavitt v. Monaco Coach*, 616 N.W.2d 175 (Mich. Ct. App. 2000).

3. Priebe bought a used car without a warranty (sold as is). The seller, Autobarn, told Priebe that the car had not been in any accidents. After driving the car more than 30,000 miles, Priebe crashed the car. Priebe sued Autobarn claiming the car was dangerous to drive because of a previous, undisclosed accident. Priebe did not show that Autobarn had knowledge of the previous accident; nor did Priebe show that the value of the car was reduced by the previous accident. Priebe sued for breach of warranty. Decide. Explain. See *Priebe v. Autobarn,* 240 F.3d 584 (7th Cir. 2001).

4. Douglas Kolarik alleged that he used several imported, pimento-stuffed green olives in a salad. In eating the salad, he bit down on an olive pit and fractured a tooth. The olive jar label included the words "minced pimento stuffed." The defendants are importers and wholesalers of Spanish olives that reach the defendants in barrels and are then inspected for general appearance, pH and acid level and then washed and placed in glass jars suitable for distribution for the purpose of retail sales.

   a. What legal claim would be expected from the plaintiff based on the "minced pimento stuffed" language?

   b. Decide that claim. Explain. See *Kolarik v. Cory International,* 721 N.W.2d 159 (Ia. S.Ct. 2006).

It Could Have Been Worse

A piece of shell in food can be harmful and disturbing, as Sandra Mitchell discovered; but for Theresa VanHorn, a 29-year-old writer at MTV Networks, an apparent condom in her half-eaten muffin left her screaming and without an appetite. The piece of latex did not alarm the New York City Health Department, where an employee told her to throw the evidence away when she called to complain: "We won't get to your complaint for days, maybe weeks." Complaints of foreign objects in food are so common in New York City that the department reportedly does not have time to quickly investigate all of them.

Source: Lindsay Powers, "Eww!—Berry Muffin; Gal Finds Condom in Pastry," *New York Post,* October 24, 2004, p. 8.

Strict Liability

> As it turns out, your customer has been bitten by a spider

Sometimes things happen that businesses can neither prevent nor even explain and yet liability may attach. For example, imagine you are operating a clothing store. A customer enters and decides to try on a pair of slacks. You show her to the dressing room. Soon after, you hear a scream from the room. As it turns out, your customer has been bitten by a spider. Not surprisingly, she thinks the blame lies with your store. She sues, but her negligence and breach of warranty claims are rejected by the court. (Can you explain why she loses?) Finally, she raises a strict liability in tort argument, but the court denies that claim also. Read the overview of strict liability that follows and think about why the court denied her claim. See *Flippo v. Mode O'Day Frock Shops of Hollywood*, 449 S.W.2d 692 (Ark. S. Ct. 1970).

Strict Liability Overview

Negligence and warranty claims are helpful to the harmed consumer. However, rapid changes in the nature of commercial practice, as well as an increasing societal concern for consumer protection, led the legal community to gradually embrace yet another cause of action. *Strict liability in tort* offers the prospect of holding all of those in the chain of distribution liable for damages from a defective product, rather than imposing the entire burden on the injured consumer. Manufacturers and sellers are best positioned to prevent the distribution of defective products, and they are best able to bear the cost of injury by spreading the loss via pricing policies and insurance coverage.

Strict liability as an independent tort emerged in 1963 in the famous California case of *Greenman v. Yuba Power Products, Inc.*[23] In the ensuing 40 years, most states have adopted strict liability in concept. The essence of the strict liability notion is expressed in Section 402A of the *Restatement (Second) of Torts.* In brief, 402A imposes liability where a product is sold in a *defective condition, unreasonably dangerous* to the user. Here is the 402A test:

1. One who sells any product in a defective condition, unreasonably dangerous to the user or consumer or to his property, is subject to liability for physical harm thereby caused to the ultimate user or consumer, or to his property, if
   a. the seller is engaged in the business of selling such a product, and,
   b. it is expected to and does reach the user or consumer without substantial change in the condition in which it is sold.
2. The rule stated in Subsection (1) applies although
   a. the seller has exercised all possible care in the preparation and sale of his product, and
   b. the user or consumer has not bought the product from or entered into any contractual relation with the seller.

Thus, we see that strict liability does not require proof of negligence on the part of the defendant. Strict liability law focuses on the condition of the *product,* rather than the conduct of the parties. Therefore, a seller who is free of actual fault may, nonetheless, be liable for injuries caused by a defective and unreasonably dangerous product. The Aim N Flame lighter case that follows considers the conditions under which a strict liability claim may be raised.

Calles v. Scripto-Tokai

LEGAL BRIEFCASE   832 N.E.2d 409 (III. S. Ct. 2007)

Justice Burke

On March 31, 1998, plaintiff Susan Calles resided with her four daughters, Amanda, age 11, Victoria, age 5, and Jenna and Jillian, age 3. At some point that night, Calles left her home with Victoria to get videos for Amanda. When she left, the twins were in bed and Amanda was watching television. Calles returned to find fire trucks and emergency vehicles around her home. It was subsequently determined by a fire investigator, Robert Finn, that Jenna had started a fire using an Aim N Flame utility lighter Calles had purchased approximately one week earlier. The Aim N Flame was ignited by pulling a trigger after an "ON/OFF" switch was slid to the "on" position. As a result of the fire, Jillian suffered smoke inhalation. She was hospitalized and died on April 21.

Calles filed suit against Tokai, designer and manufacturer of the Aim N Flame, and Scripto-Tokai, distributor (collectively Scripto), alleging that the Aim N Flame was defectively designed and unreasonably dangerous because it did not contain a child-resistant safety device. According to the complaint, a safety device was available, inexpensive, and would have reduced the risk that children could ignite the lighter. Calles' claims sounded in strict liability.

Thereafter, Scripto filed a motion for summary judgment. . . . In her deposition, Calles admitted she was aware of the risks and dangers presented by lighters in the hands of children, and, for this reason, she stored the Aim N Flames on the top shelf of her kitchen cabinet. Calles further admitted that the Aim N Flame operated as intended and expected.

In opposition to Scripto's motion for summary judgment, Calles offered affidavits from several experts. . . . All of [the] experts opined that the Aim N Flame was defective and unreasonably dangerous because it lacked a child-resistant design. They also opined that a technologically and economically feasible alternative design, which included a child-resistant safety device, existed at the time the Aim N Flame was manufactured. Several of the experts averred that Scripto was aware of the desirability of a child-safety device because it knew children could operate the Aim N Flame. Further, according to these experts, Scripto owned the technology to make the Aim N Flame child resistant in 1994 and 1995.

With respect to the cost of an alternative design, . . . the Consumer Product Safety Commission, the regulatory body for lighters, estimated the increased cost of adding a safety device to the lighter would be $ 0.40 per unit. However, [one of Calles' experts estimated] the cost would have been negligible.

Calles also offered evidence of the dangerousness of lighters in the hands of children and Scripto's awareness of such dangers. . . . Scripto admitted they had been named as defendants in 25 lawsuits filed between 1996 and 2000 for injuries that occurred between 1992 and 1999 under circumstances similar to this case.

The trial court granted summary judgment in favor of Scripto. . . .

On appeal, the appellate court reversed [the trial court's summary judgment in favor of Scripto. . . .]

STRICT LIABILITY

This court adopted the strict liability doctrine set forth in section 402A of the Second Restatement of Torts. Under this doctrine, strict liability is imposed upon a seller of "any product in a defective condition unreasonably dangerous to the user or consumer or to his property." The test outlined in section 402A for determining whether a product is "unreasonably dangerous" is known as the consumer-expectation test. This test provides that a product is "unreasonably dangerous" when it is "dangerous to an extent beyond that which would be contemplated by the ordinary consumer who purchases it, with the ordinary knowledge common to the community as to its characteristics."

* * * * *

An ordinary consumer would expect that a child could obtain possession of the Aim N Flame and attempt to use it. Thus, a child is a reasonably foreseeable user. Likewise, an ordinary consumer would appreciate the consequences that would naturally flow when a child obtains possession of a lighter.

Under the facts of this case, the Aim N Flame performed as an ordinary consumer would expect-it produced a flame when used in a reasonably foreseeable manner, *i.e.,* by a child. This leads to the inescapable conclusion that the ordinary consumer's expectations were fulfilled. . . . Thus, as a matter of law, no fact finder could conclude that the Aim N Flame was unreasonably dangerous under the consumer-expectation test. Therefore, Calles cannot prevail under this theory.

This does not end our analysis however. Though the Aim N Flame satisfies the consumer-expectation test, it may, nonetheless, be deemed unreasonably dangerous under the risk-utility test.

RISK–UTILITY TEST

Under the risk-utility test, a plaintiff may prevail in a strict liability design-defect case if he or she demonstrates that the magnitude of the danger outweighs the utility of the product, as designed.

* * * * *

Under the risk-utility test, a court may take into consideration numerous factors. In past decisions, this court has held that a plaintiff may prove a design defect by presenting evidence of "the availability and feasability of alternate designs at the time of its manufacture, or that the design used did not conform with the design standards of the industry. . . ."

Calles presented specific and detailed evidence as to the likelihood of injury and the seriousness of injury from lighters which do not have child-safety devices.

Factors which would favor Scripto and a finding that the product is not unreasonably dangerous are the utility of the Aim N Flame and the user's awareness of the dangers. As to the utility of the Aim N Flame, it is both useful and desirable to society as a whole-it serves as an inexpensive alternative source of fire. . . . With respect to the user's awareness of the dangers, there is no question, based on Calles' deposition testimony, that it was obvious to her that the lighter could come into the hands of a child and the dangers and risks that situation would pose.

In connection with the remaining relevant factors, we find that these neither weigh for nor against a finding of unreasonably dangerous. Calles claims that a substitute product was available, but the only evidence she relies upon is the fact Bic introduced a child-resistant utility lighter in March 1998, the very same month of the incident here. This is insufficient to demonstrate that a substitute product was available at the time of the manufacture of the Aim N Flame.

Calles offered expert affidavits regarding the availability and feasibility of an alternative design, including product impairment and cost factors, along with industry standards. Each expert opined that a feasible alternative design existed.

* * * * *

There is nothing in our record showing Scripto provided any amount as to the increase in cost of incorporating a safety device. Apparently. . . . an internal Scripto memorandum estimated the cost increase would be $ 0.03 per unit. In light of the foregoing, we conclude that the question of whether there was a feasible alternative design available cannot be determined on the basis of the record as it currently stands.

Lastly, with respect to the user's ability to avoid the danger, Calles testified she put the Aim N Flames on the top shelf of her kitchen cabinet. However, she also acknowledged she could have left them on the counter.

* * * * *

Based on a review of the foregoing factors, reasonable persons could differ on the weight to be given the relevant factors and thus could differ on whether the risks of the Aim N Flame outweigh its utility. Therefore, reasonable persons could differ

as to whether the Aim N Flame is unreasonably dangerous, and we cannot say that Scripto was entitled to judgment as a matter of law. As such, we affirm the appellate court's decision reversing the trial court's decision granting summary judgment in favor of Scripto on the strict liability claims.

* * * * *

Questions

1. *a.* Explain the plaintiff Calles' claim that the Aim N Flame lighter was defective and unreasonably dangerous.

   b. Explain the court's resolution of Calles' claim.

2. What evidence must a plaintiff provide to maintain a successful defective design product liability claim?

3. Is the manufacturer excused from liability if the product's danger is obvious or if the product is used in an unintended but foreseeable fashion?

4. In a similar case [*Griggs v. Bic Corp.,* 981 F.2d 1429 (3rd Cir. 1992)] the court, employing a negligence analysis, found that the central question was whether the foreseeable risk was unreasonable. The court noted that residential fires started by children playing with lighters are estimated to take an average of 120 lives each year, and total damages amount to $300–$375 million or 60–75 cents per lighter sold.

   a. Is the foreseeable risk unreasonable, in your judgment?

   b. How did you reach your conclusion?

   c. In your view, are the parents the responsible parties in these episodes? Explain.

5. Alison Nowak, a 14-year-old girl, tried to spray her hair with Aqua Net. Because the spray valve on the recently purchased aerosol can would not work properly, she punctured the can with an opener. She was standing in her kitchen near a gas stove at the time, and the cloud of spray that gushed from the can ignited. She was severely burned. Nowak sued Faberge, the maker of the spray, on strict liability grounds. Although the back of the can contained the warnings, "Do not puncture," and "Do not use near fire or flame," the jury determined that Faberge had not adequately warned of the fire hazard and awarded her $1.5 million. Faberge appealed. Decide. Explain. See *Nowak v. Faberge USA Inc.,* 32 F.3d 755 (3d Cir. 1994).

Coverage

All of those engaged in the preparation and distribution of a defective product may be liable for any harm caused by the defect, regardless of proof of actual fault. Furthermore, the courts have extended strict liability coverage to reach injured bystanders. Coverage generally extends to both personal injuries and property damage, but in some states the latter is excluded. Some states limit strict liability recovery to new goods, and some have limited liability to a designated period (for example, 15 years) after the manufacture or sale of the product.

Furthermore, the new *Restatement (Third) of Torts* recommends applying strict liability claims to manufacturing defects but not to design and warning defect cases. Thus, in effect, the new *Restatement* calls for the reasonableness, fault-based analysis explained earlier in the negligence material in *all* defective design and failure to warn cases. Of course, the courts may choose to stick with the current expansive use of the strict liability doctrine. [For a brief overview of portions of the new *Restatement,* see **http://library.findlaw. com/1999/jun/1/127691.html**]

Defenses

Assumption of risk and product misuse are both good defenses and, if factually supported, in many states can act as a complete bar to strict liability recovery. Assumption of the risk involves the plaintiff's decision to proceed to use the product despite obvious dangers associated with that use. Thus, if a pilot decided to fly knowing that the plane's wing flaps were not operating properly, she may well have assumed the risk if she subsequently crashed. When the product is used improperly, or its directions are ignored, or it is used in an unforeseeable way, the defendant would raise the misuse defense. Presumably, crop dusting with a plane not designed for that purpose would constitute misuse. Some courts, however, hold those in the chain of distribution liable for foreseeable misuses. Because strict liability is a no-fault theory, contributory negligence ordinarily is not a recognized defense.

Video Games and *The Basketball Diaries*

Michael Carneal, a 14-year-old high school freshman in Paducah, Kentucky, brought a .22-caliber pistol and five shotguns to Heath High School on December 1, 1997, where he shot and killed three students and wounded a number of others. Carneal regularly played violent video games such as "Doom and Quake" and viewed violent Internet sites. He also watched violent movies including *The Basketball Diaries,* in which a high school student dreams of killing his teacher and other students. The parents of the dead children sued several video game, movie production, and Internet content providers raising negligence and strict liability claims. Who should win that case? Explain.

Source: James v. Meow Media, 300 F.3d 683 (6th Cir. 2002); cert. den. *James v. Meow Media,* 537 U.S. 1159 (2003).

Part Three—Product Liability and Public Policy

Giant tort awards involving products such as asbestos and breast implants have bankrupted businesses. When we hear about a $28 *billion* punitive damage award in 2002 for a 64-year-old smoker suffering from lung cancer, we may wonder if the justice system has lost its bearings.[24] We may not understand that those giant awards are almost always dramatically reduced.[25] Nonetheless, the threat of tort litigation significantly affects business decision making and, in some instances, actually prevents products from reaching the market.

Because of those problems, many critics, particularly in the business community and among free market advocates, have argued for *tort reform*. They want to change the legal system in ways that would reduce the heavy costs of personal injury claims. The proposed reforms vary widely, but common prescriptions include: limiting class actions, reducing or eliminating punitive damages, curbing attorneys' fees, penalizing frivolous lawsuits, and imposing "loser pays" rules requiring the losing party in a civil lawsuit to pay the other party's legal fees and related costs.

Are big tort judgments harming the American economy and distorting justice, or are lawsuits Americans' only effective protection against callous corporations? Consider some of the evidence.

For Tort Reform Consultants Tillinghast-Towers Perrin estimated that tort suits (not limited to product liability) cost the United States more than $260 billion in 2004; a sum more than double the average cost of other industrialized nations.[26] Put another way, that sum amounts to a "tort tax" of $900 per year for every American.[27] As a result, American businesses must struggle with rising costs, innovation is reduced, and new jobs are less plentiful. All of this comes, of course, in a fiercely competitive global market. A particular frustration to the critics is that much of the tort money goes to lawyers rather than to the injured plaintiffs. [For further criticism of tort claims and our legal system generally, see **http://www.overlawyered.com** or **www.legalreformnow.com**]

> A "tort tax" of $900 per year for every American

Against Tort Reform Can we rely on the market and managerial ethics to protect us from dangerous products? Is the threat of litigation a powerful incentive to improve business practice? And how do we calculate the societal benefits generated by a tort system that discourages negligent behavior?

More broadly, those opposing tort reform say that the tort burden simply is not of the magnitude suggested by the critics. Lawsuits, consuming less than 2 percent of spending, constitute a modest part of the cost of doing business; product liability claims are a small fraction of the total legal landscape; and studies show that insurance costs do not decline appreciably when damages are capped.[28] Furthermore, only about 3 percent of tort cases ever make it to trial; those cases that are settled before judgment often involve reasonable sums of money[29] and punitive damages are awarded in only about 3.3 percent of tort cases won by plaintiffs.[30] Even ardent defenders of tort practice often agree, however, that the system needs to be improved so that lawyers do not gobble up so much of the money themselves and so that the system produces a more consistent form of justice.[31]

> Only about 3 percent of tort cases ever make it to trial

Kids Need to Swing?

Aggressive public safety programs and the threat of lawsuits have made playground swings, particularly the tall 16 footers, a vanishing delight. Tall swings and slides along with sliding poles are rapidly being replaced by safer but less thrilling playground devices.

U.S. playground safety standards, widely adopted in the 1990s, called for new safety surfaces to cushion falls with the result that the swings became very costly. A swing set once costing $800 now costs $4,000. Thus, government rules and the threat of lawsuits have made playgrounds safer while reshaping childhood fun and virtually eliminating the challenge of overcoming the terror of big swings and slides. Are we better off?

Source: Gregg Toppo, "The Great American Swing Set Is Teetering," *USA TODAY,* March 19, 2006 [**http://www.usatoday.com/news/nation/2006-03-19-swing-sets_x.htm**].

Big Case: Lead Paint?

A helpful way to look at tort reform is to consider one of the massive claims that have emerged periodically as plaintiffs attempt to prove themselves wronged by a defective product or wrongful conduct. Tobacco smokers, Ford Explorer drivers, Vioxx users, and victims of gun violence are among those who have made headlines pursuing alleged corporate wrongdoers. Some of these claims make sense; others look like quick money grabs, a failure to accept personal responsibility or a tragedy for which the law simply does not offer a remedy. Courts across the country are struggling with an enormous problem for which the law may not be able to offer a sensible, just resolution. Lead paint, banned since 1978, often produces developmental difficulties, including IQ deficiencies, learning disabilities, hyperactivity, and impaired hearing, when ingested or inhaled by children. Ordinarily, lead paint is troublesome only when it is reduced to flakes or dust; commonly in buildings that have not been properly maintained. While the potential for exposure to lead has declined dramatically in recent years, an estimated several hundred thousand young children, often living in old, inner city housing have been victims:

> Crawling across the wooden floor of his mother's Brooklyn (New York) apartment, Jaylin paused to lick his chubby hand, swallowing flecks of toxic paint. The boy's mother had no idea the poison lurked within the cracks of the baseboard. She also had good reason to believe the apartment was safe. Documents show city officials found the home for her and even inspected it before she was allowed to move from a homeless shelter. "I came out of the shelter to be secure and start my life," Jaylin's mom, Jasmine Taylor, 23, told the *Daily News.* "If there was problems, they should have fixed it." "My son got poisoned."[32]

Should paint manufacturers be responsible for the harm caused by paint applied decades back by willing consumers before anyone fully understood the long-term hazards? What about owners and landlords who failed to properly maintain painted surfaces? Even if we can establish responsibility, how do we apportion damages when we cannot identify the specific producers of the paint in question? Or should we expect the paint manufacturers to share the damages burden according to the percentage each holds in the market (a product liability claim labeled *market share liability*)?

Lead paint lawsuits have been pursued in a number of states. In most cases, the plaintiffs have been states and municipalities who have sued paint manufacturers or landlords/property owners for creating a *public nuisance* (a significant interference with a right common to the general public such as the public health, public safety, or public peace).

Market share liability claims have also been raised in some instances. Most of those cases under both theories of recovery have failed, but litigation is ongoing. Furthermore at this writing, Mattel, the American toy company, is facing a class action lawsuit based on more than one million recalled toys that allegedly were coated with lead paint during the manufacturing process in China.

Fast Food = Fat People = Big Lawsuits?

Fortune magazine's February 2003 issue asked "Is Fat the Next Tobacco?" *Fortune* and many other publications suggested that fast-food companies, like the tobacco industry, might soon be buried in lawsuits. The American public shook its collective head at the prospect of blaming McDonald's, Wendy's and others for obese people's health problems. At this writing in 2007, however, those lawsuits, for the most part, have not materialized. Only a handful of cases have been filed, most of those have been unsuccessful, and even those that gained some traction were based in mislabeling and consumer fraud and thus did not pose a crippling financial threat. Furthermore, at least 23 states have passed "cheeseburger bills" providing at least some protection for fast-food companies facing obesity lawsuits. So the widely condemned prospect of lawyers launching a new front in the litigation wars is currently unlikely. Of course, some day new information might emerge that could endanger the fast-food companies.

Source: Lianne S. Pinchuk, "Are Fast-Food Lawsuits Likely to Be the Next 'Big Tobacco'?" *The National Law Journal*, February 28, 2007.

Too Much Law?

Perhaps, as suggested by the following analysis, the key to tort reform is simply to reduce our reliance on the law, thus providing more room for treating risk management as a matter of contractual arrangements in the free market.

READING Fundamental Reform of Tort Law

Paul H. Rubin

[T]he high costs of many goods and services can be traced to misguided attempts by federal regulators and courts to protect the public health and safety. The problems with the courts are especially serious, since they undermine more cost-effective means of achieving that goal.

A principal function of tort law is to deter manufacturers from causing excess harms, or, in the case of medical services, to deter malpractice. But this system has been under-

mined by unreasonable standards—imposed by the courts—defining parties' liability for damages.

Further, the best alternative means for securing low-cost protection has also been undermined. Before 1960, when parties agreed on an exchange of goods or services, they implicitly, if not explicitly, also agreed on the rules and limitations that would govern any liability for possible injuries. But over the past three and a half decades courts have voided such contracts, reserving for themselves the power to make determinations of liability.

* * * * *

Government intervention in the market is justified only in circumstances where the market can be expected to "fail." The most common source of market failure is the existence of some externality. An externality is said to exist when a third party, one not directly involved in a transaction, is nonetheless affected by the transaction. The classic example of a negative externality is pollution, where bystanders are harmed by the actions of polluters. Some effort at correction—by establishing or redefining property rights, by internalizing the costs of the externality, or, if all else fails, by direct government regulation—is justified by such externalities.

By this standard, much of modern tort law and much of modern government regulation purporting to protect safety and health cannot be justified, since no externalities exist that must be dealt with. Both forms of government intervention—by the courts and by regulatory agencies—stem from the fact that policymakers are unwilling to rely on private transactions to achieve efficient outcomes.

UNDERMINING CONTRACTS

Much tort law governs accidents between "strangers"— those who have no legal relationship with each other before an accident occurs. Examples include a car striking a pedestrian; two cars colliding; a passerby on the public domain being struck by a baseball flying from a stadium; a drunk punching someone for no reason in a bar. All of the above are classic tort situations, and all are cases in which there is no prior relation between the parties. In each case there is an externality, and therefore some government intervention, through regulation or through the court system, may be proper.

But many activities now governed by tort law are not of that sort. Instead, in many cases, the parties *do* have prior relations with each other, and therefore there is no externality and no need for government intervention. The major examples are product liability, where a purchaser of a product may be harmed by that product, and medical malpractice, where a patient may be harmed by some action of a physician that the patient has hired.

* * * * *

Since about 1960, as a result of a New Jersey Supreme Court case, *Henningsen v. Bloomfield Motors,* involving General Motors, courts have generally been unwilling to enforce contracts between buyers and sellers involving compensation for harms caused by accidents. No matter what terms the parties may want to govern the results of an accident, the court will decide and impose its own terms. For example, the parties may want to agree that if there is an accident, the producer of the product will pay only for lost earnings and medical costs, and will not pay anything for "pain and suffering." But if there is an injury, this voluntary agreement will have no effect. The courts will decide what level and type of damage payments from the manufacturer to the consumer are appropriate.

Source: *Regulation* 18, no. 4 (1995), p. 26. Reprinted by permission.

Questions

1. Explain Rubin's argument.

2. Why have the courts, as in the *Henningsen* case, intervened to overturn privately contracted risk and remedy arrangements?

3. Why would we want to reduce our reliance on tort law?

PRACTICING ETHICS) Invest in Merck/Vioxx?

Merck, the pharmaceutical giant, voluntarily withdrew its highly successful painkiller Vioxx from the market in 2004 after a study showed the drug doubled the risk of heart attack or stroke if taken for more than 18 months. The withdrawal was greeted by public outrage and at least 27,000 lawsuits. Merck was accused of misleading the FDA about the dangers of taking Vioxx. Merck allegedly withheld from the FDA some of its analyses of Vioxx's dangers even though it had released the underlying data. E-mail evidence showed that Merck scientists were concerned even before Vioxx entered the market.[33]

Then in 2007 Merck agreed to settle the Vioxx suits for $4.85 billion, with plaintiffs expected to recover an average of perhaps $100,000 to $200,000 each, although some will receive settlements in the millions. The settlement sum amounts to less than one year's profits for Merck.[34] Prior to the settlement, Merck had pledged to fight every individual claim to the fullness of its considerable resources. The settlement, while not cheap, seemed to vindicate Merck's tough, combative approach; so much so that Dr. Eric Topol, a cardiologist whose research raised early concerns about Vioxx, was disappointed in the settlement: "I think they've gotten off quite easily, frankly, for the problems they've engendered."[35]

Question

Given these disturbing, but not fully resolved allegations about Merck and the subsequent settlement, would an ethical, socially responsible investor continue to buy shares in Merck? Explain.

Internet Exercise

The Tillinghast-Towers Perrin studies of tort costs, noted earlier in this chapter, are the most broadly-cited source of evidence for those critical of the American tort sytem. The New York City–based Center for Justice and Democracy published its own 2007 critique of the Tillinghast findings, labeling them "bogus" "myths." Read and evaluate the CJ&D critique, "Debunking Myths about Tort Systems," at [**http://www.centerjd.org/ MB_2007costs.htm**].

Chapter Questions

1. Lydia, an adult, was intoxicated when Horton allowed Lydia to borrow his car. Lydia lost control of the car, crashed, and was rendered a quadriplegic. Lydia sued Horton for first-party negligent entrustment, claiming that Horton should have recognized that Lydia was too drunk to be entrusted with the car.
   a. Are both Lydia and Horton negligent? Explain.
   b. Who wins? Explain. See *Lydia v. Horton*, 583 S. E. 2d 750 (S. C. S. Ct. 2003).

2. Stopczynski, age 17, had used her neighbor's pool "hundreds of times." Stopczynski and her neighbor's nephew, a 34-year-old male, went to the pool. Stopczynski was noticed floating face down in the pool. She had broken her neck, apparently from diving into the four-foot deep, above-ground pool. She died a few hours later. The pool originally had stickers around the edge that said "no diving," but that edge had been replaced and the stickers were gone. Stopczynski's mother sued the property owner, Woodcox, for negligence. Decide the case. Explain. See *Stopczynski v. Woodcox*, 258 Mich. App. 226 (2003).

3. Soon after Granny's Rocker Nite Club opened in the mid-1980s, it began having a weekly "fanny" contest, which involved male and female volunteer contestants competing for cash prizes by dancing. The audience judged the contest. While attending the fanny contest on April 4, 1990, plaintiff Jeffrey Loomis, got into a fight with another patron. Loomis's right ear was bitten and torn.

   Loomis's claim against Granny's Rocker had two counts, one based on the Illinois Dramshop Act and one based on negligence. The jury found for the defendant on the dramshop count, but it found that Granny's Rocker was negligent in failing to have adequate security to stop a physical altercation on the nights of the fanny contests when it knew or should have known that such contests would result in a large and rowdy group of patrons. Granny's Rocker appealed. Decide the appeal, Explain, See *Loomis v. Granny's Rocker Nite Club.* 620 N.E.2d 664 (Ill. App. 1993).

4. Thomas Woeste died as a result of contracting a bacteria after eating about one dozen raw oysters at the Washington Platform Saloon & Restaurant. The bacteria, vibrio

vulnificus, is naturally occurring in oysters harvested in warm waters. Most people are unaffected by the bacteria, but those with weakened immune systems like Woeste can be susceptible to illness or death. Washington Platform's menu contained the following warning:

> There may be risks associated when consuming shell fish....
> If you suffer from chronic illness of the liver, stomach or blood...
> or if you have other immune disorders, you should eat these products fully cooked.

Woeste ordered and ate the oysters without opening the menu and reading the warning. A civil lawsuit was filed against Washington Platform alleging that the restaurant was both negligent and strictly liable for failure to adequately warn. Decide that case. Explain. See *Woeste v. Washington Platform Saloon & Restaurant,* 836 N.E.2d 52 (Ohio Ct. App., First App. Dist. 2005).

5. An 11-month-old child pushed on a window screen that gave way, allowing him to fall from the second story of his aunt's house. The child's parents sued the screen maker.

   a. What product liability claims could they legitimately raise?

   b. Decide. Explain. See *Brower v. Metal Industries, Inc.,* 719 A.2d 941 (Del. S.Ct. 1998).

6. Sandage loaded a car on a transport trailer. The car door could not be fully opened because of a support bar on the trailer. He suffered a back injury when he squeezed out of the car. The trailer had been modified to add several feet to its length, and support poles, including the one in question, had been added. Sandage sued the company that modified the trailer. Sandage sued in strict liability and negligence. Decide the case. Explain. See *Sandage v. Bankhead Enterprises, Inc.,* 177 F.3d 670 (8th Cir. 1999).

7. In 1995 a young Oklahoma couple shot and paralyzed a store clerk, Patsy Byers. The young couple had repeatedly viewed Oliver Stone's 1994 movie *Natural Born Killers,* which is about a young couple who go on a killing spree. The Byers family sued Stone and Warner Brothers movie studio, the film distributor. Should a film-maker and studio be liable for the alleged copycat behavior of those viewing a movie? Explain.

8. Embs was shopping in a self-serve grocery store. A carton of 7UP was on the floor about one foot from where she was standing. She was unaware of the carton. Several of the bottles exploded, severely injuring Embs's leg. Embs brought a strict liability action against the bottler.

   a. Raise a defense against the strict liability claim.

   b. Decide. Explain. See *Embs v. Pepsi-Cola Bottling Co. of Lexington, Kentucky, Inc.,* 528 S.W.2d 703 (Ky. Ct. App. 1975).

9. Plaintiffs Dr. Arthur Weisz and David and Irene Schwartz bought two paintings at auctions conducted by Parke-Bernet Galleries, Inc. The paintings were listed in the auction catalog as those of Raoul Dufy. It was later discovered that the paintings were forgeries. The plaintiffs took legal action to recover their losses. Parke-Bernet defended itself by, among other arguments, asserting that the conditions of sale included a disclaimer providing that all properties were sold "as is." The conditions of sale were 15 numbered paragraphs embracing several pages in the auction catalog. The bulk of the auction catalog was devoted to descriptions of the works of art to be sold, including artists' names, dates of birth and death, and, in some instances,

black-and-white reproductions of the paintings. It was established at trial that plaintiff Weisz had not previously entered bids at Parke-Bernet, and he had no awareness of the conditions of sale. Plaintiffs David and Irene Schwartz, however, were generally aware of the conditions of sale. Is the Parke-Bernet disclaimer legally binding on the plaintiffs? Explain. See *Weisz v. Parke-Bernet,* 325 N.Y.S.2d 576 (Civ. Ct. N.Y.C. 1971), but see *Schwartz v. Parke-Bernet,* 351 N.Y.S. 2d 911 (1974).

10. The plaintiff, born and raised in New England, was eating fish chowder at a restaurant when a fish bone lodged in her throat. The bone was removed, and the plaintiff sued the restaurant, claiming a breach of implied warranty under the UCC. Evidence was offered at trial to show that fish chowder recipes commonly did not provide for removal of bones. Decide. Explain. See *Webster v. Blue Ship Tea Room,* 198 N.E.2d 309 (Mass. S. Jud. Ct. 1964).

11. A passenger ran after a train as it was leaving a station. Two railroad employees boosted the passenger aboard, but as they did so a package carried by the passenger fell beneath the wheels of the train and exploded. The package, unbeknownst to the employees, contained fireworks. The force of that explosion caused a scale many feet away to topple over, injuring the plaintiff, Palsgraf. Palsgraf sued the railroad on negligence grounds.

    a. Defend the railroad.

    b. Decide. Explain. See *Palsgraf v. Long Island R.R.,* 162 N.E. 99 (N.Y. 1928).

12. Pat Stalter was injured when a bottle fell through the bottom of a soft drink carton and broke while she was shopping at Food City, a Little Rock, Arkansas, grocery store. A piece of glass went through her slacks, cutting her. A store employee said the carton was "mushy" and appeared to have been wet for some time. The bottles were in a display maintained by Coca-Cola Bottling Company. Two or three times a week the company cleaned the shelves and rotated the stock. Coca-Cola said that this process ensures that only minimal moisture is on bottles when they are placed in cartons. Most cartons are reused only once. Stalter sued Food City and Coca-Cola Bottling Company for damages.

    a. Explain the plaintiff's claims.

    b. Decide. See *Pat Stalter v. Coca-Cola Bottling Company of Arkansas and Geyer Springs Food City, Inc.,* 669 S.W.2d 460 (Ark. S. Ct. 1984).

13. Diane Elsroth was visiting her boyfriend, Michael Notarnicola, in the home of his parents. Diane complained of a headache, and Michael provided a Tylenol that his mother had bought earlier that week. Michael noted nothing unusual about the Tylenol packaging. After consuming two Tylenol capsules, Diane went to bed. She died during the night. The medical examiner concluded that the Tylenol had been contaminated with potassium cyanide. The murder was not solved. The evidence established that the tampering with the Tylenol occurred after the product left the manufacturer's control. The packaging included a foil seal glued to the mouth of the container, a "shrink seal" around the neck and cap of the container, and a box with its ends glued shut. The manufacturer, McNeil, a wholly owned subsidiary of Johnson & Johnson, knew through its research that a determined, sophisticated tamperer could breach the packaging and reseal it in a manner that would not be visible to the average consumer. John Elsroth sued McNeil on behalf of Diane's estate. Was

the Tylenol packaging defective in design? Explain. See *Elsroth v. Johnson & Johnson,* 700 F. Supp. 151 (S.D.N.Y. 1988).

14. In an attempt to commit suicide, Connie Daniell locked herself in the trunk of her 1973 Ford LTD automobile, where she remained for nine days before being freed. During the nine days, Daniell changed her mind and sought to escape, but she was unable to do so. She sued the Ford Motor Company for the injuries she sustained from her entrapment.

    a. What claims would she bring?

    b. Decide those claims. Explain. See *Daniell v. Ford Motor Company,* 581 F. Supp. 728 (N.Mex. 1984).

15. Plaintiff James L. Maguire was seriously injured when the motor vehicle in which he was a passenger was struck by another motor vehicle. Plaintiff alleges that Vikki Paulson, the driver of the other vehicle, was intoxicated at the time of the accident. Following the accident, Paulson entered guilty pleas to (1) operating a motor vehicle while under the influence of alcohol, (2) involuntary manslaughter as a consequence of the death of another passenger riding with Maguire, and (3) failure to stop at a stop sign. During the time in question in the case, Pabst Brewing Company had engaged in an advertising campaign promoting the sale of its products. Plaintiff claims the defendant Pabst was liable for his injuries because (among other claims) its advertising promoting the consumption of alcohol by those who drove to taverns constituted a danger to highway safety and because the brewer had failed to warn consumers of the dangers of alcohol consumption. Decide. Explain. See *Maguire v. Pabst Brewing Company,* 387 N.W.2d 565 (Iowa 1986).

16. Twenty-year-old Stephen Pavlik died from inhaling Zeus-brand butane while trying to "get high." His estate sued the Zeus maker, Lane. The fuel came in a small can with a printed warning reading, "DO NOT BREATHE SPRAY." The plaintiff argued that the can was defective because the warning inadequately expressed the hazard. A federal district court ruled that Pavlik was aware of the danger so the warning was adequate, and in any case, a warning would have had no effect so proximate cause could not exist. That decision was appealed. How would you rule on that appeal? Explain. See *Pavlik v. Lane Limited,* 135 F.3d 876 (3d Cir. 1998).

Notes

1. Timothy K. Smith, "Liability Costs Drive Small-Plane Business Back into Pilots' Barns," *The Wall Street Journal,* December 11, 1991, p. A1.

2. Mike Clancy, "Cessna Will Once Again Make Small Aircraft," *Des Moines Register,* March 15, 1995, p. 8S.

3. Smith, "Liability Costs," p. 8.

4. Smith, "Liability Costs."

5. Barbara Carton, "Cessna Says It Will Make More Small Airplanes," *The Wall Street Journal,* March 14, 1995, p. B1.

6. Thor Valdmanis, "6 Years after Nearly Collapsing, Piper Takes Off Again," *USA TODAY,* July 3, 2001, p. 6B.

7. Valdmanis, "6 Years after Nearly Collapsing."

8. Valdmanis, "6 Years after Nearly Collapsing."

9. Valdmanis, "6 Years after Nearly Collapsing."

10. 111 N.E. 1050 (N.Y. 1916).

11. Heidi Hurd, "The Deontology of Negligence," *Boston University Law Review* 76 (April 1996), p. 249.

12. *Doss v. Town of Big Stone Gap,* 134 S.E. 563 (Va. S. Ct. 1926).

13. Aric Press, Ginny Carrol, and Steven Waldman, "Are Lawyers Burning America?" *Newsweek,* March 20, 1995, p. 30.

14. Press, Carrol, and Waldman, "Are Lawyers Burning America?" p. 34.

15. "McDonald's Settles Lawsuit over Burn from Coffee," *The Wall Street Journal,* December 2, 1994, p. A14.

16. Anthony Ramirez, "Hot Coffee Justice," *National Post,* April 11, 2002, p. FP15.

17. *Pat Stalter v. Coca-Cola Bottling Company of Arkansas and Geyer Springs Food City, Inc.,* 669 S.W.2d 460 (Ark. S. Ct. 1984).

18. For more detail on the treatment of risk–utility in the *Restatement (Third) of Torts,* see **http://library.lp.findlaw.com/articles/file/00849/002259/title/subject/topic/Products%20Liability_Risk-utility/filename/productsliability_2_916.** For a brief overview of consumer expectation v. risk—utility in California, see **http://www.wilsonelser.com/files/repository/Consumer ExpectationvRisk_Spring2004.pdf**]

19. Associated Press, "Toilet Brush, Rectal Thermometer Warnings Are Deemed Wackiest," *Waterloo/Cedar Falls Courier,* January 6, 2005, p. A2.

20. John M. Broder, "Warning Labels for Every Danger," *Des Moines Register,* March 9, 1997, p. G1.

21. *Whitlock v. University of Denver,* 712 P.2d 54 (Col. Ct. App. 1985).

22. *University of Denver v. Whitlock,* 744 P.2d 54 (Col. S. Ct. 1987).

23. 27 Cal. Rptr. 697, 377 P.2d 897 (Cal. S. Ct. 1963).

24. Associated Press, "California Jury Awards Former Smoker $28 Billion," *Waterloo/Cedar Falls Courier,* October 6, 2002, p. A10.

25. Associated Press, "Huge Awards Aside, Few Companies Forced to Write Big Checks," *Waterloo/Cedar Falls Courier,* October 12, 1997, p. C5.

26. Liam Pleven, "Math Divides Critics as Starting Toll of Torts Is Added Up," *The Wall Street Journal,* March 13, 2006, p. A2.

27. Ibid.

28. Dan Zegart, "Tort Reform Advocates Play Fast and Loose with Facts," *The Seattle Post-Intelligencer,* November 21, 2004, p. F1.

29. Lou Dobbs, "Tort Reform Important to U.S. Future," *CNN,* January 6, 2005.

30. Public Citizen, "Department of Justice Study Disproves Tort 'Reform' Myths," [**http://www.citizen.org**].

31. Zegart, "Tort Reform Advocates Play Fast and Loose with Facts," p. F1.

32. Tina Moore and Benjamin Lesser, "How City Is Poisoning Kids," *New York Daily News,* January 14, 2007, p. 5.

33. Alex Berenson, "Merck Jury Adds $9 Million in Damages," *The New York Times,* April 12, 2006 (**www.nytimes.com**).

34. Alex Berenson, "Merck Agrees to Settle Vioxx Suits for $4.85 Billion," *The New York Times,* November 9, 2007 [**www.nytimes.com**].

35. Alex Berenson, "Analysts See Merck Victory in Vioxx Settlement," *The New York Times,* November 10, 2007 [**www.nytimes.com**].

Trade Regulation and Antitrust

CHAPTER EIGHT

Government Regulation of Business

After completing this chapter, students will be able to:

1. Describe the concept of market failure.

2. Explain some of the considerations involved in deciding to impose government regulations on business practice.

3. Explain the roles of the police power, the Supremacy Clause, the preemption doctrine and the Commerce Clause in regulating business practice.

4. Explain when the federal government has exceeded its authority in regulating commerce.

5. Describe some of the ways in which state and local regulation affect business practice.

6. List some of the federal agencies that regulate business practice.

7. Identify the three broad categories of federal regulatory agencies' authority.

8. Compare and contrast the federal agencies' executive, legislative and judicial roles.

9. Describe the executive, congressional and judicial controls placed on agency conduct to maintain appropriate "checks and balances."

10. Analyze the Federal Communications Commission (FCC) role in regulating indecency in broadcasting.

11. Evaluate criticisms of the federal regulatory process, including arguments for and against deregulation.

Part One—An Introduction

PRACTICING ETHICS   Violent Video Games

Prior to Christmas 2004, the *Los Angeles Times* reported on growing concerns about violence in video games:

> This holiday season, children searching for the latest video game titles could walk into a store and buy "Grand Theft Auto: San Andreas"—which lets players kill cops, steal cars, solicit prostitutes, and then beat them to get their money back. Or kids could pick up a copy of "The Guy Game" and answer questions to get busty female characters to slip out of their clothes or engage in topless rope jumping and sack races.[1]

California Assemblyman Leland Yee later proposed a state law designed to prevent those under 18 from buying or renting games depicting serious injury to people "in a manner that is especially heinous, atrocious, or cruel."[2] Yee said that numerous studies "suggest those individuals who play these ultra-violent video games do report a higher incidence of violent solutions to conflict situations."[3] Mary Wiberg, executive director of the California Women's Commission, said she believes

> She believes that some young men who play violent video games grow up to abuse women

that some young men who play violent video games grow up to abuse women.[4] Sound scientific support for those claims, however, has yet to be developed. Game makers argue that video games should be treated like other forms of entertainment with parents expected to be the primary judges of what games are appropriate for their children. They also point to evidence of intellectual challenges in game playing and, perhaps surprisingly, they find moral lessons in violent video games since they often put the game player in the hero's role fighting against overwhelming odds, much as great children's literature has done for ages.[5]

California enacted the video law proposed by Yee, but before it became effective the bill was challenged in federal court where it was struck down as an unconstitutional intrusion on the free speech rights of gamers.[6] At least eight similar laws have likewise been struck down across the nation.

Should government intervene to prevent children from having access to violent or sexually explicit video games, or will the market provide whatever protection is needed? Or perhaps we can count on the industry regulating itself as an expression of ethics and social responsibility? Indeed, the games are rated, including M for mature and AO for adults only, but authorities have been increasingly concerned about the alleged link between video games and violence by children. [For the Entertainment Software Rating Board, see **http://www.esrb.org/index.asp**]

Questions

1. *a.* In your judgment, are violent and sexually explicit videos harmful to children?

   b. Would an ethical, socially responsible video store owner decline to sell violent or sexually explicit videos if evidence revealed that those videos often reach children? Explain.

2. *a.* Will the free market and industry ethics satisfactorily protect society from any harm that may emerge from video game playing or is legal intervention necessary? Explain.

   b. Should the First Amendment protect video games from government oversight? Explain.

3. A Scottish firm, Traffic Games, released in 2004 a video game that allows players to simulate the assassination of former U.S. President John F. Kennedy. The game purportedly was designed to undermine assassination conspiracy theories by showing that one person could have killed the president. The game allows slow-motion tracking of the bullets through the president's image, and blood can be viewed by pressing a blood effects button. Is the production and sale of this game an immoral act? Explain.

How Much Government?

In this chapter and all those that follow our central question will be: How much government do we need? In the first three chapters we looked at the role of the free market and ethics as "regulators" of business behavior. Now we turn to the role the law plays in supplementing the market and ethics/self-regulation. The alleged link between video game violence and personal misconduct is one relatively small example of an enormous array of social problems springing from business practice where we have a heated debate about whether government should intervene in the market. How do we decide when a new rule is needed?

Why Regulation?

Market Failure

In theory, government intervention in a free enterprise economy would be justified only when the market is unable to serve the public interest—that is, in instances of market failure. Market failure is attributed to certain inherent imperfections in the market itself producing inefficient resource allocations.

Imperfect Information

Can the consumer choose the best pain reliever in the absence of complete information about the characteristics of the competing products? An efficient free market presumes reasoned decisions about production and consumption. Reasoned decisions require adequate information. Because we cannot have perfect information and often will not have adequate information, the government, it is argued, may impose regulations either to improve the available information or to diminish the unfavorable effect of inadequate information. Hence we have, for example, labeling mandates for consumer goods, licen-sure requirements for many occupations, and health standards for the processing and sale of goods.

The 2001 Nobel Prize for economics was awarded to three Americans whose research indicates that markets cannot behave as theorized—that is, rationally and efficiently—in part because buyers and sellers often do not have the information they need to make the best decisions. Put another way, their research demonstrates that we often face situations of asymmetric information where some parties to a transaction simply know more than the other parties to that transaction, with the result that optimal efficiency cannot be achieved. Furthermore, recent research in behavioral economics suggests that we often pursue social goals and act in other ways that are contrary to our direct, personal economic interests. Thus, while our free market system assumes rational decision making, we might more accurately recognize that we operate with limited or *bounded rationality*. Hence government intervention might be appropriate.

Monopoly

Of course, the government intervenes to thwart anticompetitive behaviors throughout the marketplace. (That process is addressed in Chapters 10 and 11.) Historically, the primary concern in this area was how to deal with the so-called natural monopoly where a single large firm, such as a utility, was more efficient (a natural monopoly) than several small ones. Today, attention in the monopoly area is largely directed to anticompetitive conduct such as price fixing and abuse of market dominance that results in a reduction of open, efficient competition.

Externalities

When all the costs and benefits of a good or service are not fully internalized or absorbed, those costs or benefits fall elsewhere as what economists have labeled *externalities, neighborhood effects,* or *spillovers.* Pollution is a characteristic example of a negative externality. The environment is used without charge as an ingredient in the production process (commonly as a receptacle for waste). Consequently, the product is underpriced. The producer and consumer do not pay the full social cost of the product, so those remaining costs are thrust on parties external to the transaction. Government regulation is sometimes considered necessary to place the full cost on those who generated it, which in turn is expected to result in less wasteful use of resources. Positive externalities are those in which a producer confers benefits not required by the market. An example of such a positive externality is a business firm that, through no direct market compulsion, landscapes its grounds and develops a sculpture garden to contribute to the aesthetic quality of its neighborhood. Positive externalities ordinarily are not the subject of regulation.

Public Goods

Some goods and services cannot be provided through the pricing system because we have no method for excluding those who choose not to pay. For such *public goods,* the added cost of benefiting one person is zero or nearly so, and, in any case, no one can effectively be denied the benefits of the activity. National defense, insect eradication, and pollution control are examples of this phenomenon. Presumably most individuals would refuse to voluntarily pay for what others would receive free. Thus, in the absence of government regulations, public goods would not be produced in adequate quantities.

Regulatory Life Cycle?

These market failures and other forces, to be explained later, sometimes lead to government intervention such as the Clean Air Act (see Chapter 17) or the Occupational Safety and Health Act (see Chapter 12). Looking at the historical record, law school dean Joseph Tomain argues that a rather predictable pattern or life cycle typically emerges when the government decides to regulate an industry. Stage One in Tomain's life cycle is the free market itself, the period when government regulation is absent from the market in question. In Stage Two a market failure is identified, suggesting the need for government intervention. In Stage Three government regulation is imposed in the form of a rule (such as a minimum drinking age). In Stage Four regulatory failure occurs because, in brief, the benefits of the rule in question no longer exceed its costs. In Stage Five the government may respond with regulatory reform to correct the failure, or it may move to Stage Six where the regulation in question is simply eliminated. The market, thus fully deregulated, has returned to Stage One (the free market) and the regulatory life cycle is complete.[7] [To read about and submit comments on proposed rules affecting small businesses, see **http://www.sba.gov/advo/laws/law_regalerts.html**]

Steroids

The steroid scandal in baseball allegedly involving Barry Bonds, Jason Giambi, and other major league stars led the *Des Moines Register* to argue for the value of regulation:

> Businesses forever complain about being regulated, but the truth is that reasonable reg-ulation is good for business. It's easier to sell insurance to people who know regulators are helping keep the insurance companies solvent. It's easier to sell stocks to investors who think the SEC is on the job and easier to sell food to shoppers who trust the labels the FDA requires. Name an industry, and a case can be made that regulation helps it.
>
> Unfortunately, the barons of baseball never figured that out. The owners and players in big-league baseball resisted any regulation of performance-enhancing chemicals in their business.

*   *   *   *   *

> Baseball had slipped in the affections of many Americans even before the scandal. Now, it's doubtful the sport can ever reclaim its good name.

Question

In your view, should the government regulate performance-enhancing drug use in sports, or will self-regulation by the sports be sufficient?

Source: Editorial, "Baseball Barons Betrayed Game," *Des Moines Register,* December 14, 2004, p. 8A.

Philosophy and Politics

Correction of market failure arguably explains the full range of government regulation of business, but an alternative or perhaps supplemental explanation lies in the political process. Three general arguments have emerged.

1. One view is that regulation is necessary for the protection and general welfare of the public. We find the government engaging in regulatory efforts designed to achieve a more equitable distribution of income and wealth (such as, Social Security and the minimum wage). Many believe government intervention in the market is necessary to stabilize the economy, thus curbing the problems of recession, inflation, and unem-ployment. Affirmative action programs seek to compensate for racism and sexism. We even find the government protecting us from ourselves, both for our benefit and for the well-being of the larger society (consider seatbelt requirements).

2. Another view is that regulation is developed at the request of industry and is oper-ated primarily for the benefit of industry. Here the various subsidies and tax advan-tages afforded to business might be cited. In numerous instances, government regu-lation has been effective in reducing or entirely eliminating the entry of competitors. Government regulation has also permitted legalized price-fixing in some industries. Of course, it may be that regulation is often initiated primarily for the public welfare, but industry eventually "captures" the regulatory process and ensures its continuation for the benefit of the industry. On the other hand, some corporations seek government standards so they can do what is best for society without being undercut by their less socially responsible competitors.

3. Finally, bureaucrats who perform government regulation are themselves a powerful force in maintaining and expanding that regulation.

Bring Back Danger?

We often count on government rules to shelter us from dangers that the market seems ill-suited to deal with. Hence, we created the federal Food and Drug Administration (FDA) to protect us from dangerous food, drugs, and medical devices. Some critics argue, however, that one of the overlooked problems with government rules is that boys, in particular, need a certain amount of danger in their lives. Brothers Conn and Hal Iggulden wrote *The Dangerous Book for Boys* as a manual of activities for boys. Their book describes how to make a bow and arrow, hunt and cook a rabbit, build a tree house, set a trip wire, and so on. They believe our "safety culture" has gone a bit too far. They point to that bygone era when every boy had a jackknife. They believe that taking risks is important to a boy's joy and maturation.

Questions
1. Do you agree with the Iggulden brothers that we should allow boys to experience a certain amount of danger in their lives?
2. How about girls? [See Andrea Buchanan and Miriam Peskowitz, *The Daring Book for Girls*.] [For an online discussion about giving children greater freedom, see **http://freerangekids.workpress.com**]

The Constitutional Foundation of Business Regulation

The Commerce Clause of the U.S. Constitution broadly specifies the power accorded to the federal government to regulate business activity. Article I, Section 8 of the Constitution provides that "The Congress shall have the power . . . to regulate Commerce with foreign Nations, and among the several States, and with the Indian Tribes." State authority to regulate commerce resides in the police power specified by the Constitution. *Police power* refers to the right of the state governments to promote the public health, safety, morals, and general welfare by regulating persons and property within each state's jurisdiction. The states have, in turn, delegated portions of the police power to local government units.

Supremacy Clause

Sometimes state or local law conflicts with federal law. Such situations are resolved by the Supremacy Clause of the Constitution, which provides that "This Constitution and the Laws of the United States . . . shall be the Supreme Law of the Land."

As explained in Chapter 5, ours is a *federalist* form of government wherein we divide authority among federal, state, and local units of government. Conflicts between the preferences of each level are inevitable. The Supremacy Clause, as interpreted by the Supreme Court, establishes that, in the event of an irreconcilable conflict, federal law will *preempt* state or local law rendering it unconstitutional. Were it not so, we would have great difficulty in achieving a unified national policy on any issue.

State regulation of commerce remains important, of course, especially in areas such as real estate, but recently the Supreme Court has emphatically affirmed the power of Congress to regulate commerce between the states. In 2007, the Court ruled that the federal National Bank Act preempts the regulations of the 50 states in governing the subsidiaries of America's federally chartered banks.[8] The result is that units of national banks are exempt from state regulations except for those state rules that are not "inconsistent or intrusive."[9] State rules, therefore, must give way if in conflict with the federal National Bank Act. At a practical level, the Supreme Court decision results in a system of uniform lending standards that provide the national banks with consistent, predictable rules across the country. Critics, however, fear that the dominance of the federal system means that consumers will not be effectively protected.

Then in 2008, the Court made its Supremacy Clause/preemption position indisputably clear with three decisions handed down on the same day wherein the Court set aside state laws in favor of broad federal oversight.[10] The result is an affirmation of Congressional power to impose uniform regulation in chosen areas of commerce, thereby freeing businesses from the burden of meeting the varying expectations of the 50 states.

Commerce Clause

The Commerce Clause, as interpreted by the judiciary, affords Congress exclusive jurisdiction over foreign commerce. States and localities, nevertheless, sometimes seek in various ways to regulate foreign commerce. For example, a state may seek, directly or indirectly, to impose a tax on foreign goods that compete with those locally grown or manufactured. Such efforts violate the Commerce Clause.

Federal authority over interstate commerce was designed to create a free market throughout the United States, wherein goods would move among the states, unencumbered by state and local tariffs and duties. The Constitution does not, however, expressly forbid state regulation of interstate commerce. As with foreign commerce, the states and localities pass laws to influence interstate commerce, often to favor local economic interests. The judiciary has aggressively curbed those efforts, and in the process, the reach of the federal government has been dramatically expanded. Even purely intrastate activities can be regulated by the federal government if they have a substantial effect on interstate commerce. In the 1942 case *Wickard v. Filburn,*[11] the U.S. Supreme Court, in interpreting a federal statute regulating the production and sale of wheat, found that one farmer's production of 23 acres of homegrown and largely home-consumed wheat, in combination with other similarly situated farmers growing and consuming wheat locally, could substantially affect interstate commerce and thus was subject to federal regulation. In 2005 the Supreme Court affirmed the *Wickard* reasoning in an interesting California case, *Gonzalez v. Raich,*[12] involving the federal government's constitutional authority to regulate the use of medical marijuana.

In 1996 California became the first of 10 states to decriminalize the doctor-approved medical use of marijuana. The federal Controlled Substances Act (CSA), on

> Angel Raich used marijuana for pain control

the other hand, forbids the use, cultivation, or possession of marijuana for any purpose. A Californian, Angel Raich, who, under a doctor's prescription, used marijuana for pain control, challenged the application of the CSA against California medical marijuana users. The heart of her claim was that the Commerce Clause does not give the federal government the authority to regulate the noncommercial cultivation and personal, medical use of marijuana that does not cross state lines. She won at the U.S. Court of Appeals for the Ninth Circuit, but the U.S. Supreme Court, by a 6–3 vote, ruled against Raich. Addressing the central question, the Court reasoned that the wholly *intrastate* use of marijuana had a substantial effect on *interstate* commerce in marijuana and thus was subject to federal regulation, as the Court had ruled decades earlier in *Wickard*. Personal consumption of marijuana, even for medical purposes, has the potential to displace demand for marijuana in the illegal interstate market, thus substantially affecting interstate commerce. To rule otherwise would hinder federal enforcement of the national drug market because authorities would not be able to determine whether marijuana in the possession of a person was grown locally or shipped across state lines.

The practical implications of the federal government's victory in the *Raich* case are becoming clearer because federal agents have recently been enforcing federal law against some California medical marijuana dispensaries. California has some 300 such establishments, but the FDA in 2006 issued an advisory affirming its stance that no sound scientific evidence supports the medicinal value of marijuana. Some medical users now worry they may have to return to street purchases to meet their needs.[13]

Too Much Federal Power?

For the long term, the significance of the medical marijuana decision lies in its Commerce Clause reasoning. The decision appears to reaffirm the broad reach of federal power over activities that are economic in some sense. Dissenting in *Raich,* Supreme Court Justice Thomas warned,

> If Congress can regulate this under the Commerce Clause, then it can regulate virtually anything—and the federal government is no longer one of limited and enumerated powers.[14]

Of course, we must remember that the case dealt with the sensitive subject of unlawful drug use, where the courts are more inclined to defer to federal policy. Furthermore, in recent years, the Supreme Court issued two important opinions clearly designed to demonstrate that the Commerce Clause does not accord unlimited power to the federal government. In the 1995 *United States v. Lopez* decision[15] the Supreme Court clearly spoke for states' rights. In 1990 the federal government approved the Gun-Free School Zones Act, which forbade "any individual knowingly to possess a firearm at a place that [he] knows . . . is a school zone."[16] Congress claimed that gun possession in school zones would increase violence, retard learning, and discourage travel, thus affecting commerce. A

A 12th-grade San Antonio, Texas, student carried an unloaded, concealed gun into his high school

12th-grade San Antonio, Texas, student carried an unloaded, concealed gun into his high school and was charged with violating the act. His case (*Lopez*) reached the Supreme Court, where he claimed and the Court agreed that Congress did not have the constitutional authority to regulate the matter. By a 5–4 vote the Court held that the possession of a gun in a local school zone is in no sense an economic activity that might, through repetition elsewhere, have a substantial effect on interstate commerce.

Strengthening its *Lopez* reasoning, the U.S. Supreme Court in the 2001 *Morrison* case[17] ruled by a 5–4 vote that Congress exceeded its Commerce Clause authority in approving some portions of the federal Violence Against Women Act (VAWA). The law allowed women who had been victims of gender-based violence to sue in federal court even though the crimes did not directly involve more than one state. In debating VAWA, Congress held hearings and developed a record on the aggregate economic impact of violence against women, including driving up medical costs and discouraging women from traveling and from holding jobs, but the Court said Congress did not have the power to regulate noneconomic violent crime simply on the basis of the total effect of that behavior on interstate commerce.

> **Brzonkala claimed she was raped by two football players**

The case involved a woman, Brzonkala, who claimed she was raped by two football players, Morrison and Crawford, when all three were students at Virginia Polytechnic Institute:

> Brzonkala alleges that soon after she met Morrison and Crawford, the two defendants pinned her down on a bed in her dormitory and forcibly raped her. Afterward, Morrison told Brzonkala, "You better not have any f* * *ing diseases." And, subsequently, Morrison announced publicly in the dormitory's dining hall, "I like to get girls drunk and f* * * the s* * * out of them."[18]

After Brzonkala complained to the university, Morrison was found guilty of abusive conduct by the VPI judicial committee and was suspended for one year, but that punishment was subsequently lifted.[19] Brzonkala then sued for civil damages in federal court, which led eventually to the Supreme Court decision. [For the federal Violence Against Women Office, see **http://www.ojp.usdoj.gov/vawo**]

Lopez and *Morrison* denote a narrow majority sentiment in the U.S. Supreme Court to at least occasionally question the limits of federal power and thus to affirm the importance of states' rights; but *Raich* and a trio of less dramatic 2005 Supreme Court decisions suggest that the Supreme Court is not currently inclined to broadly challenge the pervasive authority of the federal government. The classic decision that follows illustrates the importance of Commerce Clause reasoning. In this case Congress used its economic authority under the Commerce Clause to open public accommodations (hotels, restaurants, and the like) to all persons, thus reshaping American social and racial practices.

LEGAL BRIEFCASE

Heart of Atlanta Motel v. United States 379 U.S. 241 (1964)

Justice Clark

This is a declaratory judgment action, attacking the constitutionality of Title II of the Civil Rights Act of 1964. [The lower court found for the United States.]

1. THE FACTUAL BACKGROUND AND CONTENTIONS OF THE PARTIES

. . . Appellant owns and operates the Heart of Atlanta Motel, which has 216 rooms available to transient guests. The motel is located on Courtland Street, two blocks from downtown Peachtree Street. It is readily accessible to interstate highways 75 and 85 and state highways 23 and 41. Appellant solicits patronage from outside the State of Georgia through various national advertising media, including magazines of national circulation; it maintains over 50 billboards and highway signs within the state, soliciting patronage for the motel; it accepts convention trade from outside Georgia, and approximately 75 percent of its registered guests are from out of state. Prior to passage of the act the motel had followed a practice of refusing to rent rooms to Negroes, and it alleged that it intended to continue to do so. In an effort to perpetuate that policy this suit was filed.

The appellant contends that Congress in passing this act exceeded its power to regulate commerce under [Article I] of the Constitution of the United States. . . .

The appellees counter that the unavailability to Negroes of adequate accommodations interferes significantly with interstate travel, and that Congress, under the Commerce Clause, has power to remove such obstructions and restraints. . . .

[A]ppellees proved the refusal of the motel to accept Negro transients after the passage of the act. The district court sustained the constitutionality of the sections of the act under attack and issued a permanent injunction. . . . It restrained the appellant from "[r]efusing to accept Negroes as guests in the motel by reason of their race or color" and from "[m]aking any distinction whatever upon the basis of race or color in the availability of the goods, services, facilities, privileges, advantages, or accommodations offered or made available to the guests of the motel, or to the general public, within or upon any of the premises of the Heart of Atlanta Motel, Inc."

2. THE HISTORY OF THE ACT

. . . The act as finally adopted was most comprehensive, undertaking to prevent through peaceful and voluntary settlement discrimination in voting, as well as in places of accommodation and public facilities, federally secured programs, and in employment. Since Title II is the only portion under attack here, we confine our consideration to those public accommodation provisions.

3. TITLE II OF THE ACT

This Title is divided into seven sections beginning with § 201(a), which provides,

> "All persons shall be entitled to the full and equal enjoyment of the goods, services, facilities, privileges, advantages, and accommodations of any place of public accommodation, as defined in this section, without discrimination or segregation on the ground of race, color, religion, or national origin."

4. APPLICATION OF TITLE II TO HEART OF ATLANTA MOTEL

It is admitted that the operation of the motel brings it within the provisions of § 201(a) of the act and that appellant refused to provide lodging for transient Negroes because of their race or color and that it intends to continue that policy unless restrained.

The sole question posed is, therefore, the constitutionality of the Civil Rights Act of 1964 as applied to these facts. . . .

[Part 5 omitted.]

6. THE BASIS OF CONGRESSIONAL ACTION

While the act as adopted carried no congressional findings, the record of its passage through each house is replete with evidence of the burdens that discrimination by race or color places upon interstate commerce. . . . This testimony included the fact that our people have become increasingly mobile with millions of people of all races traveling from state to state; that Negroes in particular have been the subject of discrimination in transient accommodations, having to travel great distances to secure the same; that often they have been unable to obtain accommodations and have had to call upon friends to put them up overnight, and that these conditions have become so acute as to require the listing of available lodging for Negroes in a special guidebook which was itself "dramatic testimony to the difficulties" Negroes encounter in travel. These exclusionary practices were found to be nationwide, the Under Secretary of Commerce testifying that there is "no question that this discrimination in the North still exists to a large degree" and in the West and Midwest as well. This testimony indicated a qualitative as well as quantitative effect on interstate travel by Negroes. The former was the obvious impairment of the Negro traveler's pleasure and convenience that resulted when he continually was uncertain of finding lodging. As for the latter, there was evidence that this uncertainty stemming from racial discrimination had the effect of discouraging travel on the part of a substantial portion of the Negro community. This was the conclusion not only of the Under Secretary of Commerce but also of the Administrator of the Federal Aviation Agency, who wrote the Chairman of the Senate Commerce Committee that it was his "belief that air commerce is adversely affected by the denial to a substantial segment of the traveling public of adequate and desegregated public accommodations." We shall not burden this opinion with further details since the voluminous testimony presents overwhelming evidence that discrimination by hotels and motels impedes interstate travel.

7. THE POWER OF CONGRESS OVER INTERSTATE TRAVEL

The power of Congress to deal with these obstructions depends on the meaning of the Commerce Clause.

* * * * *

In short, the determinative test of the exercise of power by the Congress under the Commerce Clause is simply whether the activity sought to be regulated is "commerce which concerns more States than one" and has a real and substantial relation to the national interest. Let us now turn to this facet of the problem.

* * * * *

The same interest in protecting interstate commerce which led Congress to deal with segregation in interstate carriers and the white-slave traffic has prompted it to extend the exercise of its power to gambling, to criminal enterprises, to deceptive practices in the sale of products, to fraudulent security transactions, and to racial discrimination by owners and managers of terminal restaurants. . . .

That Congress was legislating against moral wrongs in many of these areas rendered its enactments no less valid. In framing Title II of this act Congress was also dealing with what it considered a moral problem. But that fact does not detract from the overwhelming evidence of the disruptive effect the racial discrimination has had on commercial intercourse. It was this burden which empowered Congress to enact appropriate legislation, and, given this basis for the exercise of its power, Congress was not restricted by the fact that the particular obstruction to interstate commerce with which it was dealing was also deemed a moral and social wrong.

It is said that the operation of the motel here is of a purely local character. But, assuming this to be true, "[i]f it is interstate commerce that feels the pinch, it does not matter how local the operation which applies the squeeze."

* * * * *

Thus the power of Congress to promote interstate commerce also includes the power to regulate the local incidents thereof, including local activities in both the states of origin and destination, which might have a substantial and harmful effect upon that commerce. One need only examine the evidence which we have discussed above to see that Congress may—as it has—prohibit racial discrimination by motels serving travelers, however "local" their operations may appear.

* * * * *

The only questions are (1) whether Congress had a rational basis for finding that racial discrimination by motels affected commerce, and (2) if it had such a basis, whether the means it selected to eliminate that evil are reasonable and appropriate. If they are, appellant has no "right" to select its guests as it sees fit, free from governmental regulation.

* * * * *

It is doubtful if in the long run appellant will suffer economic loss as a result of the act. Experience is to the contrary where discrimination is completely obliterated as to all public accommodations. But whether this be true or not is of no consequence since this Court has specifically held that the fact that a "member of the class which is regulated may suffer economic losses not shared by others . . . has never been a barrier" to such legislation. . . .

We, therefore, conclude that the action of the Congress in the adoption of the act as applied here to a motel which con-

cededly serves interstate travelers is within the power granted it by the Commerce Clause of the Constitution, as interpreted by this Court for 140 years. . . .

Affirmed.

Questions

1. In your judgment, does the Commerce Clause afford the federal government the authority to regulate a local business like the Heart of Atlanta motel? Explain.

2. Should the federal government regulate local business to further the cause of racial equity? Explain.

3. What arguments were offered by the government to establish that the Heart of Atlanta racial policy affected interstate commerce? Are you persuaded by those arguments? Explain.

4. What test did the Court articulate to determine when Congress has the power to pass legislation based on the Commerce Clause?

5. Ollie's Barbecue, a neighborhood restaurant in Birmingham, Alabama, discriminated against black customers. McClung brought suit to test the application of the public accommodations section of the Civil Rights Act of 1964 to his restaurant. In the suit, the government offered no evidence to show that the restaurant ever had served interstate customers or that it was likely to do so. Decide the case. See *Katzenbach v. McClung,* 379 U.S. 294 (1964).

6. Juan Paul Robertson was charged with various narcotics offenses and with violating the federal Racketeer Influenced and Corrupt Organizations Act (RICO) by investing the proceeds from his unlawful activities in an Alaskan gold mine. He paid for some mining equipment in Los Angeles and had it shipped to Alaska. He hired seven out-of-state employees to work in the Alaskan mine. Most of the resulting gold was sold in Alaska, although Robertson transported $30,000 in gold out of the state. He was convicted on the RICO charge, but appealed claiming that the gold mine was not engaged in or affecting interstate commerce. Was Robertson's gold mine engaged in or affecting interstate commerce? Explain. See *United States v. Juan Paul Robertson,* 115 S.Ct. 1732 (1995).

Part Two—State and Local Regulation of Interstate Commerce

As noted, the states via their constitutional *police power* have the authority to regulate commerce within their jurisdictions for the purpose of maintaining public health, safety, and morals. We have seen, however, that the Commerce Clause accords the federal government broad authority over commerce. As explained, the federal government has exclusive authority over foreign commerce. Purely intrastate commerce, having no significant effect on interstate commerce, is within the exclusive regulatory jurisdiction of the states. Of course, purely intrastate commerce is uncommon. The confusion arises in the middle ground of interstate commerce where regulation by the federal government or state governments or both may be permissible. While federal government regulation of interstate commerce is pervasive, it is not exclusive, especially in matters involving the states' police powers.

Here we are concerned with commerce that is clearly interstate but that is subjected to state and/or local regulation. The issue is whether that regulation is unconstitutional because it (1) discriminates against interstate commerce or (2) unduly burdens interstate commerce such that the burden imposed clearly exceeds the local benefits.

In the *Granholm* case that follows, we see elements of the continuing conflict between federal and state control of interstate commerce, especially in matters of health and safety (police power). At the commercial level, the case is about another

> Can states lawfully protect their local wineries from out-of-state competition?

classic conflict: free trade versus protectionism. Can states lawfully protect their local wineries from out-of-state competition? The lower courts were divided on the question of whether the Commerce Clause of the federal constitution is violated when a state permits in-state wineries to ship directly to in-state customers while not permitting out-of-state wineries to do the same. Historically only a few states had allowed wineries to ship directly to customers; but gradually about half of the states allowed direct shipments, resulting in a confusing situation where some states allowed all shipments, some permitted in-state shipments only, and some forbade all shipments. In the 5–4 decision that follows, the Supreme Court narrowly resolved the split in the lower courts. The central question facing the Court was the conflict between the requirements of the Commerce Clause versus the requirements of the Twenty-First Amendment to the United States Constitution. That Amendment ended Prohibition in 1933 and gave the states broad authority to regulate the sale of alcohol.

LEGAL BRIEFCASE

Granholm v. Heald   544 U.S. 460 (2005)

Justice Kennedy

These consolidated cases present challenges to state laws regulating the sale of wine from out-of-state wineries to consumers in Michigan and New York. The details and mechanics of the two regulatory schemes differ, but the object and effect of the laws are the same: to allow in-state wineries to sell wine directly to consumers in that state but to pro-

hibit out-of-state wineries from doing so, or, at the least, to make direct sales impractical from an economic standpoint. It is evident that the object and design of the Michigan and New York statutes is to grant in-state wineries a competitive advantage over wineries located beyond the states' borders.

* * * * *

I

Like many other states, Michigan and New York regulate the sale and importation of alcoholic beverages, including wine, through a three-tier distribution system. Separate licenses are required for producers, wholesalers, and retailers. . . . We have held previously that states can mandate a three-tier distribution scheme in the exercise of their authority under the Twenty-First Amendment. As relevant to today's cases, though, the three-tier system is, in broad terms and with refinements to be discussed, mandated by Michigan and New York only for sales from out-of-state wineries. In-state wineries, by contrast, can obtain a license for direct sales to consumers. The differential treatment between in-state and out-of-state wineries constitutes explicit discrimination against interstate commerce.

This discrimination substantially limits the direct sale of wine to consumers. . . . From 1994 to 1999, consumer spending on direct wine shipments doubled, reaching $500 million per year, or 3 percent of all wine sales. . . . [T]he number of small wineries in the United States has significantly increased. At the same time, the wholesale market has consolidated. . . . The increasing winery-to-wholesaler ratio means that many small wineries do not produce enough wine or have sufficient consumer demand for their wine to make it economical for wholesalers to carry their products. This has led many small wineries to rely on direct shipping to reach new markets. Technological improvements, in particular the ability of wineries to sell wine over the Internet, have helped make direct shipments an attractive sales channel.

Approximately 26 states allow some direct shipping of wine, with various restrictions. Thirteen of these states have reciprocity laws, which allow direct shipment from wineries outside the state, provided the state of origin affords similar nondiscriminatory treatment. In many parts of the country, however, state laws that prohibit or severely restrict direct shipments deprive consumers of access to the direct market.

The wine producers in the cases before us are small wineries that rely on direct consumer sales as an important part of their businesses. Domaine Alfred, one of the plaintiffs in the Michigan suit, is a small winery located in San Luis Obispo, California. . . . Domaine Alfred has received requests for its wine from Michigan consumers but cannot fill the orders because of the state's direct shipment ban. . . .

Similarly, Juanita Swedenburg and David Lucas, two of the plaintiffs in the New York suit, operate small wineries in Virginia (the Swedenburg Estate Vineyard) and California (the Lucas Winery). Some of their customers are tourists from other states, who purchase wine while visiting the wineries. If these customers wish to obtain Swedenburg or Lucas wines after they return home, they will be unable to do so if they reside in a state with restrictive direct shipment laws. . . .

A

We first address the background of the suit challenging the Michigan direct shipment law. Most alcoholic beverages in Michigan are distributed through the state's three-tier system. Producers or distillers of alcoholic beverages, whether located in state or out of state, generally may sell only to licensed in-state wholesalers. Wholesalers, in turn, may sell only to in-state retailers. Licensed retailers are the final link in the chain, selling alcoholic beverages to consumers at retail locations and, subject to certain restrictions, through home delivery.

Under Michigan law, wine producers, as a general matter, must distribute their wine through wholesalers. There is, however, an exception for Michigan's approximately 40 in-state wineries, which are eligible for "wine maker" licenses that allow direct shipment to in-state consumers. The cost of the license varies with the size of the winery. For a small winery, the license is $25. Out-of-state wineries can apply for a $300 "outside seller of wine" license, but this license only allows them to sell to in-state wholesalers.

* * * * *

B

New York's licensing scheme is somewhat different. It channels most wine sales through the three-tier system, but it too makes exceptions for in-state wineries. As in Michigan, the result is to allow local wineries to make direct sales to consumers in New York on terms not available to out-of-state wineries. Wineries that produce only from New York grapes can apply for a license that allows direct shipment to in-state consumers. These licensees are authorized to deliver the wines of other wineries as well, but only if the wine is made from grapes "at least seventy-five percent the volume of which were grown in New York state." An out-of-state winery may ship directly to New York consumers only if it becomes a licensed New York winery, which requires the establishment of "a branch factory, office, or storeroom within the state of New York."

* * * * *

C

We consolidated these cases and granted certiorari on the following question: "'Does a state's regulatory scheme that permits in-state wineries directly to ship alcohol to consumers but restricts the ability of out-of-state wineries to do so violate the Commerce Clause in light of § 2 of the Twenty-First Amendment?'"

II

A

Time and again this Court has held that, in all but the narrowest circumstances, state laws violate the Commerce Clause if they mandate "differential treatment of in-state and out-of-state economic interests that benefits the former and burdens the latter." This rule is essential to the foundations of the Union. The mere fact of nonresidence should not foreclose a producer in one state from access to markets in other States. States may not enact laws that burden out-of-state producers or shippers simply to give a competitive advantage to in-state businesses. This mandate "reflects a central concern of the Framers that was an immediate reason for calling the Constitutional Convention: the conviction that in order to succeed, the new Union would have to avoid the tendencies toward economic Balkanization that had plagued relations among the Colonies and later among the States under the Articles of Confederation."

*   *   *   *   *

B

The discriminatory character of the Michigan system is obvious. Michigan allows in-state wineries to ship directly to consumers, subject only to a licensing requirement. Out-of-state wineries, whether licensed or not, face a complete ban on direct shipment. The differential treatment requires all out-of-state wine, but not all in-state wine, to pass through an in-state wholesaler and retailer before reaching consumers. These two extra layers of overhead increase the cost of out-of-state wines to Michigan consumers. The cost differential, and in some cases the inability to secure a wholesaler for small shipments, can effectively bar small wineries from the Michigan market.

*   *   *   *   *

The New York scheme grants in-state wineries access to the state's consumers on preferential terms. . . . In-state producers, with the applicable licenses, can ship directly to consumers from their wineries. Out-of-state wineries must open a branch office and warehouse in New York, additional steps that drive up the cost of their wine.

*   *   *   *   *

We have no difficulty concluding that New York, like Michigan, discriminates against interstate commerce through its direct shipping laws.

III

State laws that discriminate against interstate commerce face "a virtually *per se* rule of invalidity." The Michigan and New York laws by their own terms violate this proscription. The two states, however, contend their statutes are saved by § 2 of the Twenty-First Amendment, which provides,

> The Transportation or importation into any State, Territory, or possession of the United States for delivery or use therein of intoxicating liquors, in violation of the laws thereof, is hereby prohibited.

*   *   *   *   *

State policies are protected under the Twenty-First Amendment when they treat liquor produced out of state the same as its domestic equivalent. The instant cases, in contrast, involve straightforward attempts to discriminate in favor of local producers. The discrimination is contrary to the Commerce Clause and is not saved by the Twenty-First Amendment.

IV

We still must consider whether either state regime "advances a legitimate local purpose that cannot be adequately served by reasonable nondiscriminatory alternatives." The states offer two primary justifications for restricting direct shipments from out-of-state wineries: keeping alcohol out of the hands of minors and facilitating tax collection.

The states claim that allowing direct shipment from out-of-state wineries undermines their ability to police underage drinking. Minors, the states argue, have easy access to credit cards and the Internet and are likely to take advantage of direct wine shipments as a means of obtaining alcohol illegally.

The states provide little evidence that the purchase of wine over the Internet by minors is a problem. Indeed, there is some evidence to the contrary. A recent study by the staff of the FTC found that the 26 states currently allowing direct shipments report no problems with minors' increased access to wine.

*   *   *   *   *

Even were we to credit the states' largely unsupported claim that direct shipping of wine increases the risk of underage drinking, this would not justify regulations limiting only out-of-state direct shipments. As the wineries point out, minors are just as likely to order wine from in-state producers as from out-of-state ones. Michigan, for example, already allows its licensed retailers (over 7,000 of them) to deliver alcohol directly to consumers . . .

The states' tax collection justification is also insufficient.

*   *   *   *   *

Michigan and New York benefit from provisions of federal law that supply incentives for wineries to comply with state regulations. The Tax and Trade Bureau has authority to revoke a winery's federal license if it violates state law. Without a federal license, a winery cannot operate in any state. . . .

These federal remedies, when combined with state licensing regimes, adequately protect states from lost tax revenue.

*   *   *   *   *

V

If a state chooses to allow direct shipment of wine, it must do so on evenhanded terms. Without demonstrating the need for discrimination, New York and Michigan have enacted regulations that disadvantage out-of-state wine producers. Under our Commerce Clause jurisprudence, these regulations [are unconstitutional].

*   *   *   *   *

Afterword

Thirty-six states and the District of Columbia now allow wineries to ship directly to residents, although those shipments are often limited to just a few cases or to small wineries, and the *Granholm* decision applied to wineries only so retailers, in most states, still cannot ship directly to consumers.[20] The liquor industry continues to resist an open market preferring instead the three-tier producer, wholesaler, retailer distribution system that has been in place for decades, in part, to restrict access by minors and to encourage a broader selection of products. Costco is challenging that arrangement in the courts hoping to bypass wholesalers, negotiate big discounts and make more money, while presumably reducing prices for consumers.[21]

Questions

1. *a.* Why did the *Granholm* court strike down the New York and Michigan laws?

   b. What legal and practical justifications were presented by New York and Michigan in defense of their laws?

2. *a.* What choice now faces the states that are affected by this decision?

   b. What practical effect is this decision likely to have on the wine industry?

3. In 1988, Oneida and Herkimer counties in upstate New York created a Solid Waste Management Authority and enacted a "flow control ordinance" requiring that all waste generated within their borders was to be delivered to the Authority's newly created waste processing facilities. In 1995, six waste haulers and a trade association sued the Authority and the counties claiming that the flow control ordinance and associated regulations violated the Commerce Clause by discriminating against interstate commerce. The plaintiffs provided evidence that they could dispose of the waste much less expensively at out-of-state facilities. How would you rule in this case? Explain. See *United Haulers Assn., Inc. v. Oneida-Herkimer Solid Waste Management Authority,* 127 S.Ct 1786 (2007).

4. North Dakota rules require those bringing liquor into the state to file a monthly report, and out-of-state distillers selling to federal enclaves (military bases, in this instance) must label each item indicating that it is for consumption only within the enclave. The United States challenged those rules after sellers said they would discontinue dealing with the military bases or they would raise their prices to meet the cost of dealing with the two rules.

   a. What are the constitutional foundations of the federal government's challenge?

   b. What were the state's reasons for adopting the rules?

   c. Decide. Explain. See *North Dakota v. United States,* 495 U.S. 423 (1990).

5. Premium Standard Farms, a large Missouri hog-raising operation, was pumping manure through a two-mile-long pipe into Iowa to be spread on a farm whose operator sought the manure for fertilizer. Iowa citizens objected and asked Attorney General Tom Miller to act. Can the Iowa attorney general stop the pumping? Explain.

Federalism and Free Trade

America's political structure is built on the federalist principle of a careful balance of power between the local, state, and federal governments. We prefer local control in the belief that those closest to a problem are best situated to understand and address it. At the same time, we also recognize that we cannot have a unified nation with all the benefits of that status without substantial central control. As we saw in the *Granholm* case, localities and states may pass rules to meet their needs; but the nation's needs, as expressed in the Constitution, may be undermined. If lawful, each state would be racing to erect protectionist trade barriers to benefit its citizens while burdening commerce from other states and localities. The Commerce Clause is the legal standard that prevents that kind of fracturing of the United States. Still, ample protectionism remains. Some of it, of course, may be desirable. We cannot, for example, simply move from one state to another to practice law or sell real estate. Each state sets up its own licensing rules to protect the welfare of its citizens. Of course, those rules also restrict competition.

How, for example, does a nation build an efficient, unified communications system if each local community has the power to block or increase the expense of the process of laying the necessary cables to transmit messages? Telecommunications companies are trying to spread a broadband network (the "fat" cables and equipment necessary for high-speed Internet access) across the country, but they are running into a patchwork of differing rules from community to community as they seek permission to use city streets and other rights of way for their cables. The cities, on the other hand, say the telecom companies want cheap access to valuable rights of way and that they do not fully pay for the damage they do in digging up streets.

Globalism versus Nationalism

Those protectionist tendencies that we see among our 50 states are much more pronounced around the globe. Rules are much more common in Europe, for example, than in America. We believe that tendency renders the EU nations slower and less competitive on the world scene, and we may be right.

The EU nations are questioning the wisdom of their complex web of government rules and are taking a variety of steps to reduce those rules. For example, a 2007 agreement substantially deregulated air travel between the United States and the European Union. All European carriers will be granted access to any city in the United States, and all American carriers will be permitted to fly where they wish in Europe.[22] The result is expected to be greater competition, lower fares, and expanded service. The European Union formally guarantees free movement of goods and services, and while national rules about health, labor, and safety are permissible, discriminatory rules are forbidden. Nonetheless, many obstructions remain. The American manufacturer, Caterpillar, sells tractors throughout the European Union, but in Germany it must install a louder backup horn and put lights in slightly different places than in other nations.[23] As a result of obstructions of that kind, the European Commission is taking legal steps to more firmly enforce single-market rules to attack national protectionism in areas such as accounting, insurance, and pensions.[24] The general European rethinking about the wisdom of rules has reached local, very personal considerations in Germany where weak consumer spending has convinced Berlin to eliminate its laws that had forced all retail shops to close at 8 PM. Now store owners are generally free to set their own hours, except for Sundays when stores still are generally required to be closed.[25] Much of

> There's a sign for toad crossings

Germany is expected to follow the Berlin change. Similarly, Germany is trying to eliminate up to half of its 20 million traffic signs. "Germans like clear rules," said one of the civil servants working on the sign surplus.[26] "There's a sign for toad crossings.

There's one that tells drivers when they're on a 'dirty road.' Another warns them not to drive into lakes or rivers. There are 32 different signs regulating how to park at a curb."[27]

Questions

1. Journalist Max Frankel, writing in *The New York Times,* argued that the 21st century's "Great Revolution" would be the "collapse of nationhood."[28] He said that collapse would be powered largely by technology and the global financial market.

   a. Explain what Frankel meant.

   b. Do you agree? Explain.

   c. Frankel quoted finance experts George Shultz, William Simon, and Walter Wriston, who said, "The gold standard has been replaced by the information standard, an iron discipline that no government can evade."..."No country can hide."[29] What did they mean?

2. *a.* Can you envision a time when all of the nations of the world are able to agree on the elimination of regulatory barriers? Explain.

   b. Would you favor that development? Explain.

Summary of State and Local Regulation

The federal government receives the greater attention, but state and local rules have an enormous impact on business practice. The states are primarily responsible for regulating the insurance industry and are heavily involved in regulating banking, securities, and liquor sales. Many businesses and professions—from psychology to funeral preparation to barbering to the practice of medicine—require a license from the state. Public utilities (gas, electricity, sewage disposal) are the subject of extensive regulation governing entry, rates, customer service, and virtually all of the companies' activities. All states have some form of public service commission charged with regulating utilities in the public interest. Many states seek to directly enhance competition via antitrust legislation. Many states have passed laws forbidding usury, false advertising, stock fraud, and other practices harmful to the consumer. Furthermore, Congress pushes federal activities such as welfare and highway safety rules back to the states, suggesting that state government growth is unlikely to abate. [For the "largest Internet compilation" of state government materials, see **http://www.hg.org/index.html**]

Licensure   Local regulation is much less economically significant than state regulation. Local government intervention in business typically involves various licensure requirements. For example, businesses like bars and theaters are often required to obtain a local permit to operate. Similarly, more than 1,000 of America's occupations (medicine, law, building construction, electrical work, and so on) can be practiced only by those who have secured licensure from state and/or local authorities. Licensure is to protect the public from unsafe, unhealthful, and substandard goods and services, but critics contend that the benefits of licensure are exceeded by its costs in increased prices, decreased services, and administrative overhead. *The Wall Street Journal* explained that argument:

> Overall, the level of licensing regulation in the workplace is rising precipitously, with more than 20 percent of the workforce now required to get a permit to do their jobs—up from 4.5 percent in the 1950s. . . . These requirements are essentially barriers to entry and job creation. . . .[30]

Robin Hood or a Cheat?

New York City's Taxi and Limousine Commission regulates cabs. Ray Kottner, an 80-year-old "hack" drives his unlicensed 1982 vintage Checker cab through the New York City streets picking up passengers for what he says are free rides. In July 2007, Kottner dropped off a passenger who gave him $10, which Kottner said was a tip but which the Commission said was a fare. His cab was impounded, and the passenger said that Kottner had asked for $10. Kottner says the City had been following him and trying to stop his "Robin Hood" practices, but the City says he must abide by the rules:

> "He was observed engaging in an illegal activity, and the vehicle was seized to protect the public, TLC spokesman Allan Fromberg said. The vehicle has not been TLC inspected, isn't properly registered, and does not carry adequate insurance."

Licensed drivers are likewise frustrated with Kottner:

> "This guy is nothing but a crook, and we're all glad he's finally off the streets," said David Pollack, a cabby and editor of *Taxi Insider*. "He flips his finger at our regulatory bodies; he flips his finger at taxi drivers."

The drivers say that Kottner is simply escaping all the overhead they must pay: $425,000 for a medallion (taxi license), $700 per year to renew it, $3,900 per month for insurance. They must also submit to drug testing and training that Kottner avoids.

Questions
1. Is Kottner "Robin Hood" or an unfair "free rider"? Explain.
2. Why do most cities closely regulate the cab industry?

Source: Jeremy Olshan, *New York Post,* July 21, 2007 [**http://www.nypost.com**]

Rules and Community Welfare   Most of us would say, in the abstract, that we need less government in our lives, but when we are the victims of problems that the market is ill-suited to resolve, those rules become much more attractive. The case that follows shows how Tampa, Florida, tried to apply its rules to the age-old problem of adult entertainment businesses but with a new twist—product distribution by the Internet rather than by face-to-face commerce.

Voyeur Dorm v. City of Tampa

265 F.3d 1232 (11th Cir. 2001); cert. den. 122 S.Ct. 1172 (2002)

LEGAL BRIEFCASE

Circuit Judge Dubina

This appeal arises from Voyeur Dorm L.C.'s alleged violation of Tampa's City Code based on the district court's characterization of Voyeur Dorm as an adult entertainment facility.

BACKGROUND

Voyeur Dorm operates an Internet-based Web site that provides a 24-hour-a-day Internet transmission portraying the lives of the residents of 2312 West Farwell Drive, Tampa, Florida. Throughout its existence, Voyeur Dorm has employed 25 to 30 different women, most of whom entered into a contract that specifies, among other things, that they are "employees," on a "stage and filming location," with "no reasonable expectation of privacy," for "entertainment purpose." Subscribers to "voyeurdorm.com" pay a subscription fee of $34.95 a month to watch the women employed at the premises and pay an added fee of $16.00 per month to "chat" with the women. From August 1998 to June 2000, Voyeur Dorm generated subscriptions and sales totaling $3,166,551.35.

In 1998 Voyeur Dorm learned that local law enforcement agencies had initiated an investigation into its business. In response, counsel for Voyeur Dorm sent a letter to Tampa's zoning coordinator requesting her interpretation of the city code as it applied to the activities occurring at 2312 West Farwell Drive. In February of 1999, Tampa's zoning coordinator, Gloria Moreda, replied to counsel's request and issued her interpretation of the city code:

* * * * *

It is my determination that the use occurring at 2312 W. Farwell Dr., is an adult use. Section 27-523 defines adult entertainment as "Any premises, except those businesses otherwise defined in this chapter, on which is offered to

members of the public or any person, for a consideration, entertainment featuring or in any way including specified sexual activities, as defined in this section, or entertainment featuring the displaying or depicting of specified anatomical areas, as defined in this section; 'entertainment' as used in this definition shall include, but not be limited to, books, magazines, films, newspapers, photographs, paintings, drawings, sketches or other publications or graphic media, filmed or live plays, dances or other performances distinguished by their display or depiction of specified anatomical areas or specified anatomical activities, as defined in this section."

Please be aware that the property is zoned RS-60 Residential Single Family, and an adult use business is not permitted use. You should advise your client to cease operation at that location.

Thereafter, in April of 1999, Dan and Sharon Gold Marshlack [owners of the property located at 2312 W. Farwell] appealed the zoning coordinator's decision to Tampa's Variance Review Board. On or about July 13, 1999, the Variance Review Board conducted a hearing. At the hearing, Voyeur Dorm's counsel conceded the following: that five women live in the house; that there are cameras in the corners of all the rooms of the house; that for a fee a person can join a membership to a Web site wherein a member can view the women 24 hours a day, seven days a week; that a member, at times, can see someone disrobed; that the women receive free room and board; that the women are part of a business enterprise; and that the women are paid. At the conclusion of the hearing, the Variance Review Board unanimously upheld the zoning coordinator's determination that the use occurring at 2312 West Farwell Drive was an adult use. Subsequently, Mr. and Mrs. Marshlack filed an appeal from the decision of the Variance Review Board to the City Council. The Tampa City Council . . .

unanimously affirmed the decision of the Variance Review Board.

Voyeur Dorm filed this action in the middle district of Florida. The City of Tampa and Voyeur Dorm then filed cross-motions for summary judgment. The district court granted Tampa's motion for summary judgment, from which Voyeur Dorm now appeals.

ISSUE

1. Whether the district court properly determined that the alleged activities occurring at 2312 West Farwell Drive constitute a public offering of adult entertainment as contemplated by Tampa's zoning restrictions.

[Issues 2. and 3. are omitted.—Ed.]

DISCUSSION

The threshold inquiry is whether section 27-523 of Tampa's city code applies to the alleged activities occurring at 2312 West Farwell Drive. Because of the way we answer that inquiry, it will not be necessary for us to analyze the thorny constitutional issues presented in this case.

* * * * *

Tampa argues that Voyeur Dorm is an adult use business pursuant to the express and unambiguous language of Section 27-523 and, as such, cannot operate in a residential neighborhood. In that regard, Tampa points out that members of the public pay to watch women employed on the premises; that the employment agreement refers to the premises as "a stage and filming location;" that certain anatomical areas and sexual activities are displayed for entertainment; and that the entertainers are paid accordingly. Most importantly, Tampa asserts that nothing in the city code limits its applicability to premises where the adult entertainment is actually consumed.

In accord with Tampa's arguments, the district court specifically determined that the "plain and unambiguous language of the city code . . . does not expressly state a requirement that the members of the public paying consideration be *on* the premises viewing the adult entertainment." While the public does not congregate to a specific edifice or location in order to enjoy the entertainment provided by Voyeur Dorm, the district court found 2312 West Farwell Drive to be "a premises on which is offered to members of the public for consideration entertainment featuring specified sexual activities within the plain meaning of the city code."

Moreover, the district court relied on Supreme Court and Eleventh Circuit precedent that trumpets a city's entitlement to protect and improve the quality of residential neighborhoods. *Sammy's of Mobile, Ltd.* v. *City of Mobile* (noting that it is well established that the regulation of public health, safety, and morals is a valid and substantial state interest); *Corn v. City of Lauderdale Lakes* (noting that the "Supreme Court has held [that] restrictions may be imposed to protect 'family values, youth values, and the blessings of quiet seclusion'").

In opposition, Voyeur Dorm argues that it is not an adult use business. Specifically, Voyeur Dorm contends that section 27-523 applies to locations or premises wherein adult entertainment is actually offered to the public. Because the public does not, indeed cannot, physically attend 2312 West Farwell Drive to enjoy the adult entertainment, 2312 West Farwell Drive does not fall within the purview of Tampa's zoning ordinance.

The residence of 2312 West Farwell Drive provides no "offering [of adult entertainment] to members of the public." The offering occurs when the videotaped images are dispersed over the Internet and into the public eye for consumption. The city code cannot be applied to a location that does not, itself, offer adult entertainment to the public.

* * * * *

It does not follow, then, that a zoning ordinance designed to restrict facilities that offer adult entertainment can be applied to a particular location that does not, at that location, offer adult entertainment. Moreover, the case law relied upon by Tampa and the district court concerns adult entertainment in which customers *physically attend* the premises wherein the entertainment is performed. Here, the audience or consumers of the adult entertainment do not go to 2312 West Farwell Drive or congregate anywhere else in Tampa to enjoy the entertainment. Indeed, the public offering occurs over the Internet in "virtual space." While the district court read Section 27-523 in a literal sense, finding no requirement that the paying public be *on the premises,* we hold that section 27-523 does not apply to a residence at which there is no public offering of adult entertainment.

* * * * *

Reversed.

Questions

1. *a.* Why did the court rule against Tampa?
   b. Make the argument, as the lower court did, that the Tampa statute does apply to Voyeur Dorm.
   c. Why was Tampa concerned about Voyeur Dorm operating in a residential neighborhood?
   d. Does Tampa have any additional legal grounds for challenging Voyeur Dorm? Explain.

2. The city government in Cedar Falls, Iowa, home of the University of Northern Iowa, declined to renew the liquor

license of a local bar after 58 of 100 "bar checks" over a period of nearly two years found minors drinking illegally. One hundred and seventy four alcohol-related tickets were issued over that period.[31]

a. Could the free market satisfactorily protect the public from the various risks associated with excessive drinking by college-aged students, or are rules necessary?

b. Would you vote to renew this bar's liquor license? Explain.

3. Two Dallas, Texas, ordinances were challenged in court. One gave the police very broad authority to deny licenses to "adult" businesses such as bookstores. The other, which was directed at prostitution, barred motel owners from renting rooms for fewer than 10 hours.

a. What challenges would you raise against these ordinances?

b. How would you rule? Explain. See *FW/PBS Inc v. City of Dallas,* 493 U.S. 215 (1990).

4. "Saggin'." Fashion fads come and go, but the current practice of young men wearing their oversized pants well below their waists has infuriated lots of older folks and in-

spired the city government in Delcambre, Louisiana (population 1,700) to impose a $500 fine or six months in jail on offenders. "It's just unbelievable what they do with their pants," says Carol Broussard, the town's mayor. What's next? Are they going to take their pants off completely?"[32] The fashion statement apparently originated in prison where belts are forbidden.

a. Do we need a rule forbidding young men from "saggin'"? Explain.

b. What concerns/fears motivate the opposition to "saggin'"?

c. What constitutional challenges would you raise against the Delcambre ordinance?

5. Tattoo and body piercing statutes sometimes require liability insurance, licensing, training, and health inspections, and parents are to accompany minors. Does each of those requirements seem appropriate to you? Explain.

6. a. Can we rely on the market to protect children from excessive tanning? Explain.

b. Has the market failed? Explain.

Questions—Parts One and Two

1. In 1999 Matthew Hale, a law school graduate, was denied a license to practice law in Illinois because Hale is an avowed racist and the leader of a white supremacist group. A state panel assessed the character and general fitness of all those who had passed the bar exam and graduated from law school and decided that Hale's active racism disqualified him. Illinois is one of 32 states with character and fitness standards. Hale appealed on First Amendment grounds, among others. Should Hale be excluded from the practice of law, or should we let the market decide his fitness? Explain.

2. City officials in Machesney Park, Illinois, in 1999 required nine-year-old Gregory Webb to tear down his makeshift tree house on the grounds that it was a nuisance. Webb had built the structure from lawn chairs, leftover carpet, and a pet carrier, among other objects. The city was criticized for its decision.

   a. Why would a city choose to exercise its police power over nuisances in this seemingly trivial case?

   b. What would you do if you were the city planning and zoning director and thus responsible for the situation?

3. Notwithstanding the deregulation efforts of recent years, the larger trend in the United States over the past 50 years has been that of increased government regulation of business. How do you explain that trend?

4. As a safety measure, Arizona enacted a statute that limited the length of passenger trains to 14 cars and freight trains to 70 cars. Trains of those lengths and greater were common throughout the United States. The Southern Pacific Railroad challenged the Arizona statute.

   a. What was the legal foundation of the Southern Pacific claim?

   b. Decide the case. Explain. See *Southern Pacific Railroad v. Arizona,* 325 U.S. 761 (1945).

Part Three—Administrative Agencies and the Regulatory Process

Introduction to Administrative Agencies[33]

Suppose you start a business; a small, relatively simple business, perhaps a restaurant. You quickly come to realize that the government is going to be your partner in that business. Taxes, wages, hours, sanitation, safety, advertising, zoning—at every turn a government rule shapes the conduct of your business. In many cases those rules are created and enforced by administrative agencies, a powerful subset of government little understood by the public but immensely influential in every corner of American life.

The Federal Agencies

The Federal Administrative Procedure Act defines an *agency* as any government unit other than the legislature and the courts. Thus, the *administrative law* governing those agencies technically addresses the entire executive branch of government. Our attention, however, will be directed to the prominent regulatory agencies (Federal Trade Commission, Federal Communications Commission, Securities and Exchange Commission, and the like) rather than the various executive departments (Agriculture, Defense, and so on) and nonregulatory welfare agencies (Social Security Administration and Veterans Administration). We will focus on the federal level, but administrative law principles are fully applicable to the conduct of state and local governments. At the local level, planning and zoning boards and property tax assessment appeals boards are examples of administrative agencies. At the state level, one might cite public utility commissions and the various state licensure boards for law, medicine, architecture, and the like. [To search for federal government information on the World Wide Web, see **http://www.gpoaccess.gov/index.html** or **http://www.fedworld.gov**]

History

Congress established the Interstate Commerce Commission (ICC), the first federal regulatory agency, in 1887 for the purpose of regulating railroad routes and rates. The Food and Drug Administration (FDA—1907) and the Federal Trade Commission (FTC—1914) followed, but federal regulation became pervasive only in response to the Great Depression of the 1930s. Congress created the Securities and Exchange Commission (SEC—1934), the Federal Communications Commission (FCC—1934), the Civil Aeronautics

Board (CAB—1940; abolished 1985), and the National Labor Relations Board (NLRB—1935), among others, as a response to the widely shared belief that the stock market crash and the Depression were evidence of the failure of the free market.

The next major burst of regulatory activity arrived in the 1960s and 1970s when Congress created such agencies as the Equal Employment Opportunity Commission (EEOC—1965), the Environmental Protection Agency (EPA—1970), the Occupational Safety and Health Administration (OSHA—1970), and the Consumer Product Safety Commission (CPSC—1972).

Note that the work of most of the early agencies was directed to controlling entire industries such as transportation or communications and that the primary purpose of most of those agencies was to address economic concerns. Then with the arrival of the prosperity and social turbulence of the 1960s and 1970s, Congress built a rather massive array of new agencies directed not to economic issues but to social reform in such areas as discrimination, the environment, job safety, and product safety.

As we explore later in the chapter, the free market enthusiasm of the 1980s resulted in strenuous efforts to deregulate the economy and reduce the influence of the federal agencies and the government generally. Now, in the early 21st century we appear to be in a period of great respect for the free market, tempered by concern that some government oversight remains vital to the general welfare. Current problems in the financial markets, particularly in home mortgages, make some new regulation likely.

Creating the Agencies

The so-called independent agencies (FTC, FCC, and SEC) were created by Congress via statutes labeled *enabling legislation*. The FTC for example, is empowered by its enabling legislation to pursue unfair trade practices.

In creating an agency, Congress delegates a portion of its authority to that body. Congress acknowledges the existence of a problem and recognizes that it is not the appropriate body to address the specific elements of that problem—hence the agency. The president, ordinarily with the advice and consent of the Senate, appoints the administrator or the several commissioners who direct each agency's affairs. Commissioners are appointed in staggered terms, typically of seven years' duration. The appointment of commissioners for most of the independent agencies must reflect an approximate political balance between the two major parties.

In effect, Congress has created a fourth branch of government. Possessing neither the time nor the expertise to handle issues arising from nuclear power, product safety, racial discrimination, labor unions, and much more, Congress wisely established "minigovernments" supported by the necessary technical resources and day-to-day authority to address those complicated problems.

Agency Duties

The authority of the federal regulatory agencies falls broadly into three categories.

1. Control of supply. Some agencies control entry into certain economic activities. The Federal Communications Commission grants radio and television licenses. The Food and Drug Administration decides which drugs may enter the American market. The Securities and Exchange Commission (see Chapter 9) acts as a gatekeeper, preventing the entry of new securities into the marketplace until certain standards are met. The general concern is that the market alone cannot adequately protect the public interest.

2. Control of rates. Historically, those federal agencies charged with regulating utilities and carriers (Federal Energy Regulatory Commission, ICC, and CAB) set the prices to be charged for the services offered within their jurisdictions. For example, the consumer facing an interstate change of address found little value in comparison shopping for the least expensive furniture mover because the rates, regulated by the Interstate Commerce Commission, were virtually identical. Government rate setting remains important at the state level, but at the federal level the deregulation movement resulted in the elimination of the CAB and the ICC and a general decline in agency rate-setting. The federal government decided to reduce or eliminate its authority in decisions such as the price of airline tickets, cable TV rates, and long-distance telephone rates.

3. Control of conduct

a. Information. Agencies commonly compel companies to disclose consumer information that would otherwise remain private. Warning labels, for example, may be mandated.

b. Standards. Where simply requiring information is deemed inadequate for the public need, the government may establish minimum standards that the private sector must meet. A ladder might be required to safely hold at least a specified weight, or workers might lawfully be exposed to only a specified maximum level of radiation.

c. Product Banishments. In rare circumstances, products can be banned from the market. The Consumer Product Safety Commission banned the flame retardant Tris (used in children's sleep-wear) because of evidence of the product's cancer-causing properties.

Protect Children from Food Ads?

Recent studies have measured the impact of television ads on the eating habits of young children, ages 5 to 11. The kids watched 10 ads for toys followed by a cartoon. Then they were allowed to eat from a variety of low-fat and high-fat snacks. Two weeks later the children followed the same routine, but the toy ads were replaced by ads for food of the kind commonly aired with children's television. Among five-to-seven-year-old kids, calorie consumption was 14 to 17 percent higher after viewing the food ads than after viewing the toy ads. Among 9-to 11-year-old children, calorie consumption was 84 to 134 percent higher following the food ads. The Federal Trade Commission has found that 22 percent of the ads viewed by kids are for food products.

Questions
1. Should the food companies voluntarily desist from advertising low nutrition food to young children? Explain.
2. Should the Federal Trade Commission adopt rules discouraging food ads directed to children? Explain.

Source: Tara Parker-Pope, "Watching Food Ads on TV May Program Kids to Overeat," *The Wall Street Journal,* July 10, 2007, p. D1.

Questions

1. The phrase *government regulation* embraces many functions. Define it.
2. Is the federal regulatory process limited in its goals to the correction of market failures? Should it be so limited? Explain.

Operating the Agencies

As we have noted, the administrative agencies act as minigovernments, performing quasi-executive, quasi-legislative (rule-making), and quasi-judicial (adjudicatory) roles broadly involving control of supply, rates, and conduct in large segments of American life. Let's look now at how those agencies practice their business.

Executive Functions

The basic executive duty of the various agencies is to implement the policy provided for in the enabling legislation and in the agencies' own rules and regulations. A large part of agency activity consists of performing mundane, repetitive tasks that are necessary for a smoothly operating society but do not merit day-to-day attention from Congress or the courts. Agencies enter into contracts, lease federal lands, register securities offerings, award grants, resolve tax disputes, settle workers' compensation claims, administer government benefits to the citizenry, and so on. Some agencies, such as the Food and Drug Administration, are charged with protecting the public by engaging in inspections and testing. Most agencies offer informal advice, both in response to requests and on their own initiative, to explain agency policy and positions. Each year the Federal Trade Commission, for example, receives many complaints about alleged fraud in advertising, telemarketing, identity theft, Internet commerce, and so on. Supervisory duties, including most notably the active and close attention given to the banking industry, are a further illustration of agency executive duties.

Of course, a big part of the agencies' executive duties is the protection of the public by ensuring compliance with laws and regulations. Therefore, most agencies spend a great deal of time conducting inspections and investigations and collecting information. The Occupational Safety and Health Administration, for example, regularly checks businesses for safety hazards.

PRACTICING ETHICS   Tobacco Lies?

A *Christian Science Monitor* editorial criticized continuing "lies" by the tobacco industry:

> For 50 years, big tobacco has "lied" to the American public about the devastating health effects of smoking, a U.S. judge ruled last week.

Tobacco industry executives have consistently denied manipulating nicotine to encourage addiction, but recent studies reveal steady and widespread increases in nicotine content in cigarettes. Researchers at the Harvard School of Public Health found that "nicotine yield per cigarette rose by an average of 11 percent between 1998 and

2005, a conclusion contested by the industry." The researchers believe the companies used tobacco with higher nicotine concentration and perhaps slowed the rate of cigarette burn, thus increasing puffs per cigarette.

The Food and Drug Administration does not have the authority to regulate tobacco. At this writing, Congress is considering legislation to provide that authority.

Questions

1. Has the tobacco industry lied to the American public? Explain.
2. Is a deliberate increase in nicotine yield, as alleged above, an immoral act? Explain.

3. Has the market failed to adequately protect the public from tobacco products? Explain.
4. Philip Morris, the largest tobacco company, supports FDA authority over tobacco. Why would a tobacco company favor government oversight?
5. Should Congress give the FDA authority to regulate tobacco? Explain.

Sources: Editorial, "Big Tobacco: 50 Years of Lies. Now What?" *The Christian Science Monitor,* August 22, 2006 [http://www.csmonitor.com/2006/0822/p08s02-comv.html]. Editorial, "Nicotine Manipulation Confirmed," *The New York Times,* January 23, 2007 [http://www.nytimes.com/2007/01/23/opinion/23tue3.html].

Legislative Functions

The agencies create *rules* that, in effect, are laws. These rules provide the details necessary to carry out the intentions of the enabling legislation. In day-to-day business practice, the rules are likely to be much more important than the original congressional legislation. The Occupational Safety and Health Act calls for a safe and healthful workplace, but the rules necessary for interpreting and enforcing that general mandate come, not from Congress, but from OSHA.

Rules

Agencies enact three types of rules: (1) procedural, (2) interpretive, and (3) legislative. *Procedural rules* delineate the agency's internal operating structure and methods. *Interpretive rules* offer the agency's view of the meaning of those statutes for which the agency has administrative responsibility. Internal Revenue Service regulations are an example of interpretive rules. *Legislative rules* are policy expressions having the effect of law. The agency is exercising the law-making function delegated to it by the legislature. Federal Trade Commission rules providing for a cooling-off period of three business days within which the buyer may cancel door-to-door sales contracts are an example of agency lawmaking that significantly affects business behavior.

The Rule-Making Process

The Administrative Procedure Act (APA) provides for both *informal* (often called "notice and comment") and *formal* rule-making processes for legislative rules. Under both approaches, the process begins with the publication of a Notice of Proposed Rule Making in the *Federal Register* (a daily publication of all federal rules, regulations, and orders). Thereafter, in the case of informal rule making, the agency must permit written comments on the proposal and may hold open hearings. To enhance participation in the rule-making process, the federal government provides an online portal where the public can comment on proposed rules [see **www.regulations.gov**]. Having received public comments, the agency either discontinues the process or prepares the final rule.

In the case of formal rule making, after providing notice, the agency must hold a public hearing conducted with most of the procedural safeguards of a trial, where all interested parties may call witnesses, challenge the agency evidence, and so on.

Hybrid Rule Making Although not specifically provided for in the APA, agency rule making now is often achieved by a compromise (hybrid) process that combines elements of formal and informal rule making. Hybrid rule making is informal rule making with additions in the form of some trial elements (more oral testimony and hearings) that have the effect of providing a more detailed record without all of the procedural requirements of formal rule making. In routine matters, informal rule making remains the norm; but in more complex situations, hybrid procedures now are often employed.

Whether by formal, informal, or hybrid procedures, final agency rules are published in the *Federal Register* and later compiled in the *Code of Federal Regulations*.

Challenging an Agency Rule

The power and importance of the agencies and of the agency rule-making process are evident in what at this writing is an unsettled policy debate about how closely the FCC should regulate the structure of the nation's media industry. At the behest of Congress, the FCC has imposed various rules limiting media ownership, but in 2003 the Republican majority on the FCC loosened federal restrictions on how many local television and radio stations a company could own and on newspaper and broadcast cross-ownership. Critics objected that the relaxed rules would lead to greater media consolidation and a consequent decline in diversity of programming.

They pointed to the FCC's 1996 decision to lift its limit on how many radio stations one company could own nationally. The result was the 1,200 station Clear Channel network that has been broadly criticized for "homogenizing" radio and sharply reducing local programming.

The 2003 rule changes were struck down in court,[34] but in late 2007 the three-person Republican majority on the FCC approved a new deregulation initiative by relaxing a rule that forbade, with some exceptions, one company from owning a newspaper and a television station in the same city. The new FCC position will allow a newspaper in one of the top 20 media markets to merge with a radio or television station in the same market, so long as the television station is not among the four highest rated in that market. Mergers in smaller markets would be permitted only under limited conditions, and certain waivers allow pre-existing combinations to remain in place. Twenty-five senators immediately indicated they would try to revoke or nullify the relaxed media ownership rule.[35]

Broadly, the debate is about economic policy. Will the market on its own provide for the nation's best interests? Or are restraints necessary to prevent too much concentration of power and authority in too few hands? Given the expansion of delivery systems (broadcast television, cable, Internet, satellite) and other information/entertainment sources such as newspapers, many experts believe that the government needs to take only a limited role in overseeing media ownership. Consumer advocates, on the other hand, are concerned that the media's vital free speech role will be compromised by concentrated ownership.

Judicial Functions

Although informal procedures such as settlements are preferred, agencies commonly must turn to judicial proceedings to enforce agency rules. The National Labor Relations Board may hold a hearing to determine if an employee was wrongfully dismissed for engaging in protected union activities. The Federal Communications Commission may decide whether to remove a radio license because of a failure to serve the public interest. The Federal Trade Commission may judge whether a particular ad is misleading.

Rule Making or Adjudication?

Many issues facing agencies could properly be resolved in either the rule-making or the adjudicatory format. The distinction between the two cannot be drawn vividly. Characteristically, however, an adjudication addresses specific parties involved in a specific present or past dispute. Rule making ordinarily involves standards to be applied to the future conduct of a class of unspecified parties. The rule-making/adjudication decision is discretionary with the agency (subject to judicial review) and is based on the nature of the issue and fairness to the parties. Regardless, the agencies are, in effect, "making law" either by setting a judicial-like precedent in the case of an adjudication or by passing a rule that has authority much like a law.

Administrative Hearing

Typically, after an investigation, a violation of a statute and/or rule may be alleged. Affected parties are notified. An effort is made to reach a settlement via a *consent order,* in which the party being investigated agrees to steps suitable to the agency but under which the respondent makes no admission of guilt (thus retarding the likelihood of subsequent civil liability).

ALJ

Failing a settlement, the parties proceed much as in a civil trial. Ordinarily the case is heard by an *administrative law judge (ALJ).* The respondent may be represented by counsel. Parties have the right to present their cases, cross-examine, file motions, raise objections, and so on. They do not have the right to a jury trial, however. The ALJ decides all questions of law and fact and then issues a decision (*order*). In general, that decision is final unless appealed to the agency/commission. After exhausting opportunities for review within the agency, appeal may be taken to the federal court system.

Controlling the Agencies

Although agency influence in business practice and in American life generally is enormous, none of these agencies and their thousands of employees are directly accountable to the people, and all of them operate under necessarily broad grants of power. What is to keep them from abusing their discretion? Just as with our constitutional system generally, certain checks and balances constrain agency conduct while allowing the latitude necessary to achieve effectiveness.

Executive Constraints

As noted, the president appoints the top administrators for the various agencies, thus significantly influencing the conservative or liberal slant of the agency. Further, the president obviously has great influence in the budget process.

Executive Order 12866, issued by President Clinton in 1993, was an effort to exert greater executive authority over agency rule making by, among other things, commanding cost-benefit analyses for new rules. In an effort to strengthen EO 12866, President Bush, in 2007, issued an amendment calling for agencies to cite a specific market failure (e.g., externalities, monopoly or information deficiency) before issuing a new rule. The amendment also requires each agency to designate a presidential appointee for the role of regulatory policy officer in each agency to assure that the president's policies are followed. Columbia University law professor, Peter L. Strauss, said the Bush amendment "achieves a major increase in White House control over domestic government," while William Kovacs, a vice president of the United States Chamber of Commerce, applauded the amendment as "the most serious attempt by any chief executive to get control over the regulatory process, which spews out thousands of regulations a year."[36]

Clearly, agency rules and sometimes heavy-handed enforcement practices can be inefficient and costly, but the benefits are likewise undeniable. An OMB study of major federal rules estimated that their annual benefits from 1992 to 2002 ranged from $135 billion to $218 billion, while estimated annual costs ranged from only $38 billion to $44 billion.[37] [For an OMB "watchdog" see **www.ombwatch.org**]

Congressional Constraints

Congress creates and can dissolve the agencies. Congress controls agency budgets and thus can encourage or discourage particular agency action. Broadly, Congress oversees agency action, and agencies often check with Congress before undertaking major initiatives. Congress can directly intervene by amending the enabling legislation or by passing laws that require agencies to take specific directions. The difficulty in balancing congressional and agency authority is well illustrated by an important 2001 Supreme Court decision involving the federal Clean Air Act (CAA). The case, *Whitman v. American Trucking Associations, Inc.*[38] raised the question of whether Congress had improperly delegated its authority to the Environmental Protection Agency and whether the EPA must take the cost of implementing clean air regulations into consideration when developing new rules. A unanimous Supreme Court ruled that Congress had built into the CAA constitutionally sufficient limitations on agency action, and the Court ruled that Congress clearly did not require the EPA to conduct cost–benefit analyses before establishing new rules. Thus the Court concluded that Congress can constitutionally offer agencies broad authority in carrying out Congress's general intentions.

Judicial Review

Agency rules and orders may be challenged in court. Historically, however, the courts have taken a rather narrow approach to judicial review. Two commonsense considerations support that restrained judicial stance. The first is deference to the presumed expertise of the administrative agencies. The jurists, being generalists in the field of law, have been reluctant to overrule the judgment of specialists specifically chosen to regulate within their area of expertise. Second, very crowded judicial calendars act as a natural brake on activist judicial review. For those reasons, judges have traditionally disposed of administrative law cases in an expeditious manner by readily sustaining the judgment of the agency where reasonable. Of course, the courts have overruled the agencies when appropriate, and of late we can see evidence of a firmer judicial role, including some interest in reasserting the balance of powers principle.[39]

Not surprisingly, judicial review of agency decisions raises a variety of technical issues of law. Cases turn on questions like these:

1. Does the legislature's delegation of authority meet constitutional requirements?
2. Has the agency exceeded the authority granted by the enabling legislation?
3. Are the agency's findings of fact supported by substantial evidence in the record as a whole?

These issues are close to the heart of the administrative law practitioner, but their exploration is not necessary to the layperson's understanding of the larger regulatory process. The case that follows will be our only consideration of the formalities of judicial review. This appeal from a Federal Communications Commission adjudication sheds some light on the agency regulatory process and judicial review; but, much more importantly, the case raises fundamental questions regarding freedom of speech in a technologically advanced society.

F.C.C. v. Pacifica Foundation

LEGAL BRIEFCASE 438 U.S. 726 (1978)

Justice Stevens

This case requires that we decide whether the Federal Communications Commission has any power to regulate a radio broadcast that is indecent but not obscene.

A satiric humorist named George Carlin recorded a 12-minute monologue titled "Filthy Words" before a live audience in a California theater. He began by referring to his thoughts about "the words you can't say on the public, ah, airwaves, um, the ones you definitely wouldn't say, ever." He proceeded to list those words and repeat them over and over again in a variety of colloquialisms. The transcript of the recording . . . indicates frequent laughter from the audience.

At about 2 o'clock in the afternoon on Tuesday, October 30, 1973, a New York radio station, owned by respondent Pacifica Foundation, broadcast the "Filthy Words" monologue. A few weeks later a man, who stated that he had heard the broadcast while driving with his young son, wrote a letter complaining to the commission. He stated that, although he could perhaps understand the "record's being sold for private use, I certainly cannot understand the broadcast of same over the air that, supposedly, you control."

The complaint was forwarded to the station for comment. In its response, Pacifica explained that the monologue had been played during a program about contemporary society's attitude toward language and that, immediately before its broadcast, listeners had been advised that it included "sensitive language which might be regarded as offensive to some." Pacifica characterized George Carlin as a "significant social satirist" who "like Twain and Sahl before him, examines the language of ordinary people. . . . Carlin is not mouthing obscenities; he is merely using words to satirize as harmless and essentially silly our attitudes toward those words." Pacifica stated that it was not aware of any other complaints about the broadcast.

On February 21, 1975, the commission issued a declaratory order granting the complaint and holding that Pacifica "could have been the subject of administrative sanctions." . . . The commission did not impose formal sanctions, but it did state that the order would be "associated with the station's license file, and in the event that subsequent complaints are received, the commission will then decide whether it should utilize any of the available sanctions it has been granted by Congress."

* * * * *

[T]he Commission found a power to regulate indecent broadcasting in [18 United States Code 1464] which forbids the use of "any obscene, indecent, or profane language by means of radio communications."

* * * * *

[T]he commission concluded that certain words depicted sexual and excretory activities in a patently offensive manner, noted that they "were broadcast at a time when children were undoubtedly in the audiences (in the early afternoon)" and that the prerecorded language, with these offensive words "repeated over and over," was "deliberately broadcast." . . .

In summary, the commission stated, "We therefore hold that the language as broadcast was indecent and prohibited." . . .

The United States Court of Appeals for the District of Columbia Circuit reversed, with each of the three judges on the panel writing separately. . . .

Judge Tamm concluded that the order represented censorship and was expressly prohibited by ¶ 326 of the Communications Act. Alternatively, Judge Tamm read the commission opinion as the functional equivalent of a rule and concluded that it was "overbroad." . . .

Chief Judge Bazelon's concurrence rested on the Constitution. He was persuaded that ¶ 326's prohibition against censorship is inapplicable to broadcasts forbidden by ¶ 1464. However, he concluded that ¶ 1464 must be narrowly construed to cover only language that is obscene or otherwise unprotected by the First Amendment. . . .

Judge Leventhal, in dissent, stated that the only issue was whether the commission could regulate the language "as broadcast." . . .

Emphasizing the interest in protecting children, not only from exposure to indecent language, but also from exposure to the idea that such language has official approval, . . . he

concluded that the commission had correctly condemned the daytime broadcast as indecent.

Having granted the commission's petition for certiorari, . . . we must decide (1) whether the scope of judicial review encompasses more than the commission's determination that the monologue was indecent "as broadcast"; (2) whether the commission's order was a form of censorship forbidden by ¶ 326; (3) whether the broadcast was indecent within the meaning of ¶ 1464; and (4) whether the order violates the First Amendment of the United States Constitution.

(I)

The general statements in the commission's memorandum opinion do not change the character of its order. Its action was an adjudication. . . . It did not purport to engage in formal rule making or in the promulgation of any regulations. The order "was issued in a specific factual context"; questions concerning possible action in other contexts were expressly reserved for the future. The specific holding was carefully confined to the monologue "as broadcast." . . .

(II)

The relevant statutory questions are whether the commission's action is forbidden "censorship" within the meaning of ¶ 326 and whether speech that concededly is not obscene may be restricted as "indecent" under the authority of ¶ 1464.

* * * * *

The prohibition against censorship unequivocally denies the commission any power to edit proposed broadcasts in advance and to excise material considered inappropriate for the airwaves. The prohibition, however, has never been construed to deny the commission the power to review the content of completed broadcasts in the performance of its regulatory duties.

* * * * *

Entirely apart from the fact that the subsequent review of program content is not the sort of censorship at which the statute was directed, its history makes it perfectly clear that it was not intended to limit the commission's power to regulate the broadcast of obscene, indecent, or profane language. A single section of the [Radio Act of 1927] is the source of both the anticensorship provision and the commission's authority to impose sanctions for the broadcast of indecent or obscene language. Quite plainly, Congress intended to give meaning to both provisions. Respect for that intent requires that the censorship language be read as inapplicable to the prohibition on broadcasting obscene, indecent, or profane language.

We conclude, therefore, that ¶ 326 does not limit the commission's authority to impose sanctions on licensees who engage in obscene, indecent, or profane broadcasting.

(III)

The only other statutory question presented by this case is whether the afternoon broadcast of the "Filthy Words" monologue was indecent within the meaning of ¶ 1464. . . .

The commission identified several words that referred to excretory or sexual activities or organs, stated that the repetitive, deliberate use of those words in an afternoon broadcast when children are in the audience was patently offensive, and held that the broadcast was indecent. Pacifica takes issue with the commission's definition of indecency, but does not dispute the commission's preliminary determination that each of the components of its definition was present. Specifically, Pacifica does not quarrel with the conclusion that this afternoon broadcast was patently offensive. Pacifica's claim that the broadcast was not indecent within the meaning of the statute rests entirely on the absence of prurient appeal.

The plain language of the statute does not support Pacifica's argument. The words "obscene, indecent, or profane" are written in the disjunctive, implying that each has a separate meaning. Prurient appeal is an element of the obscene, but the normal definition of "indecent" merely refers to nonconformance with accepted standards of morality.

* * * * *

Because neither our prior decisions nor the language or history of ¶ 1464 supports the conclusion that prurient appeal is an essential component of indecent language, we reject Pacifica's construction of the statute. When that construction is put to one side, there is no basis for disagreeing with the commission's conclusion that indecent language was used in this broadcast.

(IV)

Pacifica makes two constitutional attacks on the commission's order. First, it argues that the commission's construction of the statutory language broadly encompasses so much constitutionally protected speech that reversal is required even if Pacifica's broadcast of the "Filthy Words" monologue is not itself protected by the First Amendment. Second, Pacifica argues that inasmuch as the recording is not obscene, the Constitution forbids any abridgement of the right to broadcast it on the radio.

A

The first argument fails because our review is limited to the question of whether the commission has the authority to proscribe this particular broadcast. As the commission itself emphasized, its order was "issued in a specific factual context." . . .

That approach is appropriate for courts as well as the commission when regulation of indecency is at stake, for indecency is largely a function of context—it cannot be adequately judged in the abstract.

* * * * *

It is true that the commission's order may lead some broadcasters to censor themselves. At most, however, the commission's definition of indecency will deter only the broadcasting of patently offensive references to excretory and sexual organs and activities. While some of these references may be protected, they surely lie at the periphery of First Amendment concern. . . .

B

When the issue is narrowed to the facts of this case, the question is whether the First Amendment denies government any power to restrict the public broadcast of indecent language in any circumstances. For if the government has any such power, this was an appropriate occasion for its exercise.

The words of the Carlin monologue are unquestionably "speech" within the meaning of the First Amendment. It is equally clear that the commission's objections to the broadcast were based in part on its content. The order must therefore fall if, as Pacifica argues, the First Amendment prohibits all governmental regulation that depends on the content of speech. Our past cases demonstrate, however, that no such absolute rule is mandated by the Constitution.

The classic exposition of the proposition that both the content and the context of speech are critical elements of First Amendment analysis is Mr. Justice Holmes's statement . . .

> We admit that in many places and in ordinary times the defendants in saying all that was said in the circular would have been within their constitutional rights. But the character of every act depends upon the circumstances in which it was done. . . . The most stringent protection of free speech would not protect a man in falsely shouting fire in a theater and causing a panic. It does not even protect a man from an injunction against uttering words that may have all the effect of force. . . . The question in every case is whether the words used are used in such circumstances and are of such a nature as to create a clear and present danger that they will bring about the substantive evils that Congress has a right to prevent.

Other distinctions based on content have been approved. . . . The government may forbid speech calculated to provoke a fight. . . . It may pay heed to the "commonsense differences between commercial speech and other varieties.". . . It may treat libels against private citizens more severely than libels against public officials. . . . Obscenity may be wholly prohibited. . . .

The question in this case is whether a broadcast of patently offensive words dealing with sex and excretion may be regulated because of its content. Obscene materials have been denied the protection of the First Amendment because their content is so offensive to contemporary moral standards. . . . But the fact that society may find speech offensive is not a sufficient reason for suppressing it. Indeed, if it is the speaker's opinion that gives offense, that consequence is a reason for according it constitutional protection. For it is a central tenet of the First Amendment that the government must remain neutral in the marketplace of ideas. If there were any reason to believe that the commission's characterization of the Carlin monologue as offensive could be traced to its political content—or even to the fact that it satirized contemporary attitudes about four-letter words—First Amendment protection might be required. But that is simply not this case. These words offend for the same reasons that obscenity offends.

* * * * *

In this case it is undisputed that the content of Pacifica's broadcast was "vulgar," "offensive," and "shocking." Because content of that character is not entitled to absolute constitutional protection under all circumstances, we must consider its context in order to determine whether the commission's action was constitutionally permissible.

C

We have long recognized that each medium of expression presents special First Amendment problems. . . . And of all forms of communication, it is broadcasting that has received the most limited First Amendment protection. . . . The reasons for [that distinction] are complex, but two have relevance to the present case. First, the broadcast media have established a uniquely pervasive presence in the lives of all Americans. Patently offensive, indecent material presented over the airwaves confronts the citizen, not only in public, but also in the privacy of the home, where the individual's right to be left alone plainly outweighs the First Amendment rights of an intruder. . . . Because the broadcast audience is constantly tuning in and out, prior warnings cannot completely protect the listener or viewer from unexpected program content. . . .

Second, broadcasting is uniquely accessible to children, even those too young to read. . . .

It is appropriate, in conclusion, to emphasize the narrowness of our holding. This case does not involve a two-way radio conversation between a cab driver and a dispatcher, or a telecast of an Elizabethan comedy. We have not decided that an occasional expletive in either setting would justify any sanction or, indeed, that this broadcast would justify a criminal prosecution. The commission's decision rested entirely on a nuisance rationale under which context is all-important. The concept requires consideration of a host of variables. The time of day was emphasized by the commission. The content of the program in which the language is used will also affect the composition of the audience, and differences between radio, television, and perhaps closed-circuit transmissions, may also be relevant. . . .

The judgment of the court of appeals is reversed.
[The appendix containing a transcript of the "Filthy Words" monologue is omitted.]

Questions

1. *a.* Why was the question of whether the FCC's decision constituted adjudication or rule making significant to the subsequent judicial appeals?

   b. Explain the Supreme Court's resolution of that issue.

2. Why is the two-letter word *or* critical to the outcome of this case?

3. Why was the FCC's action not considered censorship?

4. Cable television operators use signal scrambling to ensure that only paying customers have access to some programming. Congress was concerned that some sexually explicit cable programming, even though scrambled, might reach children via signal "bleeding." Section 505 of the Telecommunications Act of 1996 required cable operators to fully block sexually oriented channels or to "time channel"—that is, transmit only in hours when children are unlikely to be viewing. Most cable operators adopted the latter approach, with the result that for two-thirds of the day no viewers in the operators' service areas could receive the sexually explicit programming. Section 504 of the Telecommunications Act required cable operators to block undesired channels at individual households upon request. A supplier of sexually oriented programming challenged Section 505 on First Amendment grounds. Decide the case. Explain. See *United States v. Playboy Entertainment Group,* 529 U.S. 803 (2000).

The FCC and Indecency Today

The George Carlin case, in a sense, lives on more than 30 years after it was decided. We seem to be in the midst of a cultural war over social values, none of which is more hotly contested than the public role of sex in American life. Most famously, perhaps, Janet Jackson's "wardrobe malfunction" (when her right breast was momentarily bared during the halftime show of the 2004 Super Bowl) led to a $550,000 FCC fine levied against CBS television, but a federal court of appeals panel reversed the FCC decision. [See *CBS v. FCC*, 2008 U.S. App. LEXIS 16692 (3d Cir.).] Graphic depictions of sexual and excretory functions are forbidden by FCC rules on nonsatellite radio and on noncable television between 6 AM and 10 PM—hours when children are likely to be in the audience. The 10 PM to 6 AM slot, on the other hand, offers a "safe harbor" for indecent programming.

Radio "shock jock" Howard Stern, fighting FCC sanctions for years, was the primary focus of recent FCC indecency complaints against the 1,200-station Clear Channel Communications empire. In 2004 Clear Channel agreed to pay $1.75 million in fines to settle the complaints. Stern has long argued that the government's oversight violates his First Amendment rights, but his explicit conversations about masturbation, intercourse, "spewing evil gunk all over everybody" and so on led Clear Channel to drop Stern, who has now moved to satellite radio.

> Radio "shock jock" Howard Stern was the primary focus of recent FCC indecency complaints

In perhaps its most specific indecency ruling, the FCC in 2004 overruled its own staff and its own policy of many years by declaring that Bono's phrase "f—ing brilliant" at the live, 2003 Golden Globe awards show was indecent and profane. In the past, quick, nonsexual use of the "f word" had not been interpreted to violate federal law. So the FCC's ruling apparently signaled a new, more activist, socially conservative stance.

Fox Television petitioned the federal courts after an FCC finding of indecency involving brief sexual references at broadcasts, among others, of the 2002 and 2003 Billboard Music Awards. On the 2002 show, Cher dismissed her critics with the remark: "People have been telling me I'm on the way out every year, right? So f . . . 'em," and on the 2003 show, Nicole Richie said, "Have you ever tried to get cow [excrement] out of a Prada purse? It's not so 'f. . . ing' simple."[40] A federal court of appeals panel hearing the *Fox* case held that the FCC policy to punish "fleeting expletives" was arbitrary and capricious.[41] No broadcaster had been punished in decades in similar circumstances. The court found that the agency failed to provide a reasoned analysis for its abrupt shift in policy. Thus, the FCC effort to impose a no-tolerance policy was rejected, in both the *CBS* and *Fox* cases, but a U.S. Supreme Court review is expected. Congress did strengthen FCC authority by boosting the maximum fine for broadcast indecency from $32,500 to $325,000 per utterance.

Parents' Duty?

Caroline Fredrickson explained the American Civil Liberties Union's objections to close government oversight of broadcasting:

> Congress should reject any proposals that would allow the FCC to regulate what the public sees on television. Members of the American Civil Liberties Union (ACLU) strongly believe that the government should not replace parents as decision makers in America's living rooms. There are some things the government does well, but deciding what is aired on television, and when, is not one of them. Parents already have many tools to protect their children, including blocking programs and channels, changing the channel, or (my personal favorite) turning off the television. The ACLU is not blind to the issue at hand. We can see why some parents are upset about what they see on television. But the answer lies in teaching those parents how they can limit what their children watch—not censorship. . . .

> Our concern is that imposing standards for television programming would be unconstitutional and damage important values that define America: the right to free speech, and the right of parents to decide the upbringing of their children.

Questions
1. Can we realistically expect parents to be able to fully shield their children from indecent broadcasting?
2. Should parents do so? Explain.

Source: Caroline Fredrickson, "Why Government Should Not Police TV Violence and Indecency," *The Christian Science Monitor,* September 6, 2007 [**http://www.csmonitor.com/2007/0906/p09s01-coop.html**].

Questions—Part Three

1. The Parents Television Council filed 36 indecency complaints with the FCC alleging that popular television shows, including *Friends* and *The Simpsons,* contained indecent scenes that were either sexually explicit or used indecent or profane language. How would you vote on the following scenes?

   a. In the *Gilmore Girls,* one character says to another, "You're a dick."

   b. In *The Simpsons,* students carry picket signs with the phrases "What would Jesus glue?" and "Don't cut off my pianissimo."

2. The Parents Television Council contacted sponsors of the April 6, 2005, episode of the television program *The Shield* to complain about a "graphic" scene in which a police captain was forced to perform fellatio on a gang member at gunpoint. Kia and Castrol were among those sponsors. What would you do if you were in charge of advertising for Kia or Castrol, and you received that complaint?

Part Four—The Federal Regulatory Process Evaluated

Free market advocates seek to sharply reduce government, while others favor a constrained market where the government plays an important role in preventing and correcting market failure. The economic signature of the late 1980s and 1990s was the stunning ascendance of market economics in Eastern Europe, the former Soviet Union, Great Britain, and China. (See Chapter 1.) At the same time, the Reagan administration worked to sharply reduce the regulatory role of the federal government in American life. The Bush (senior) and Clinton administrations moved back toward the center on the question of government intervention. Philosophically, the second Bush administration clearly favored a reduced government presence in business practice, environmental protection, and some other areas, but a dramatic decline in federal rules did not occur. Against that historical backdrop, the argument continues—should the government be more or less involved in American business? The regulatory process is criticized on three broad grounds: I, Too much regulation, II. Too little regulation, III. Ineffective regulation.

Criticisms

I. Excessive Regulation

In brief, the excessive regulation argument is that government rules reduce business efficiency, curb freedom, and unjustly redistribute resources. Deregulation (see below) has been a powerful force in contemporary American life, but government oversight has continued to grow even during the conservative George W. Bush presidency, as *The Wall Street Journal* explained:

> From 2001 to 2006, the number of federal regulatory personnel has risen by one-third (or 66,000 more snoopers); regulatory budgets are up by 52% after inflation; and the Federal Register—which prints all that regulatory verbiage—has climbed by more than 10,000 pages.[42]

The *Journal* reports that the biggest regulatory increases in enforcement personnel and dollars have been in "customer-friendly" agencies, such as the SEC, the FDA, and the Antitrust Division of the Justice Department.[43] The direct weight of regulation is staggering with the average American working 61.8 days per year to pay for regulatory costs, according to Americans for Tax Reform.[44] Indirect costs are the bigger concern, however. Federal regulations, according to a 2005 Small Business Administration study, reduce output in the U.S. economy by about $1 trillion per year; or about $8,000 per household.[45] Economist Robert Hahn described those "hidden" costs:

> The public never sees the factories that weren't built, the new products that didn't appear, or the entrepreneurial idea that drowned in a cumbersome regulatory process.[46]

While regulations continue to expand, we should note that President George W. Bush reportedly cut the growth of costly business regulations by about 75 percent as compared to the two previous administrations.[47] [For Americans for Tax Reform data on "Cost of Government Day," see **http://www.atr.org**]

[For more detailed criticisms of the federal regulatory process, see **http://www.heritage.org** or **http://www.cei.org** or **http://www.cato.org/pubs/regulation**]

II. Insufficient Regulation

Our society is changing, complex, and in many ways troubled. Consequently, calls for new government regulations are routine. For example, aren't most Americans pleased with the FCC's do-not-call rules that keep telemarketers at a distance? Advocates of increased regulation point to the many successes of government intervention: legal equality for minorities and women; network airways substantially free of pornography and indecency; the Auto Safety Act; child labor laws; safer workplaces; cleaner air; and so on.

At this writing, the U.S. economy is reeling from an array of problems including the subprime mortgage crisis, which is expected to produce losses of at least $150 billion. (See Chapter 2 for more details.) Should the government add new rules or step back to allow the market to sort things out? Congress seems likely to provide financial relief to the many troubled borrowers and lenders. Other proposals include licensing mortgage brokers and more closely monitoring the mortgage industry.

What about more systemic changes to the system, however? Our financial oversight structure has been in place since the 1930s, and some adjustments are needed in this era of complex, new financial products. The time may be ripe, therefore, to consolidate and streamline the half dozen federal agencies with financial system oversight to assure the government keeps an eye on conditions that might threaten the stability of our total economy. If we do so, however, financing costs likely will rise, and new rules could harm our competitiveness in international financial markets; but if we fail to do so, history suggests that more misconduct and future financial meltdowns are likely.

III. Ineffective Regulation

Critics charge that the regulatory process is corrupted by familiar bureaucratic problems including inefficiency, incompetence, and arbitrariness. Productivity, they claim, is low, and policy enforcement is weak and ineffectual. Part of that alleged regulatory weakness is attributed to inherent imbalances in the political process. The business community's financial clout allows it to exert enormous influence in the regulatory process while public opinion is diffuse, disorganized, and underfunded resulting in a muted voice for everyday Americans and a megaphone for special interests. Indeed, regulators are often recruited from the industry being regulated, and regulators, upon leaving government service, often move to the industries they were formerly charged with regulating. Of course, industry expertise is invaluable and the industry voice should be heard, but the question lies in the "volume" of that voice. Not surprisingly then, regulation sometimes is instituted at the request of industry and thereafter may be designed and operated in ways beneficial to those being regulated. Jacob Laksin, reviewing Timothy Carney's book, *The Big Ripoff,* for *The Wall Street Journal,* explains that argument:

> Another myth—debunked by Mr. Carney—holds that regulations are the scourge of the business world. In fact, as he argues, many top companies welcome these rules. The airline industry sees burdensome federal oversight as a means of discouraging upstart competition. Tobacco giant Philip Morris is only too happy to submit to government curbs on advertising, confident that the effect is to keep smaller, lesser-known manufacturers on the margins, to the benefit of its already famous Marlboro, Merit, and other brands.[48]

Deregulation

In response to the problems with the regulatory process, both Democrats and Republicans, beginning in the late 1970s, began to reduce the quantity of federal regulatory intervention in business practice. The deregulation movement consisted primarily of shrinking the federal bureaucracy, eliminating as many government rules as possible, and expediting the process of complying with rules that could not be removed. Reduced regulation has focused on key economic sectors including transportation, banking, and telecommunications, while rule making in social arenas such as discrimination and pollution has actually increased.

In cases where a government role continued to be considered necessary, deregulation advocates argued for applying free market incentives and reasoning to achieve regulatory goals. Thus, rather than forbidding undesirable conduct (such as pollution and industrial accidents), the government might impose a tax on behaviors society wants to discourage. In effect, a business would purchase the right to engage in conduct society considers injurious or inefficient. Similarly, rather than rationing portions of the radio spectrum or the right to land at airports at peak times, the government might auction those rights to the highest bidder. Market incentives would (1) encourage companies to use cost-effective compliance means and (2) raise the price of dangerous products, thus discouraging their use. However, monitoring difficulties, particularly in the case of pollution, render the taxing or auction methods inexact at best. Some object to the idea of allowing businesses to engage in undesirable conduct or highly prized conduct merely because they have the resources to pay for those privileges.

Similarly, cost–benefit analysis would be applied to all regulations. Regulations would be imposed only if added benefits equaled or exceeded added costs. Indeed, influential scholar Cass Sunstein argues that we have moved to a "cost–benefit state" to replace the New Deal regulatory approach where big government was broadly embraced with little concern for the cost–benefit equation.[49] Sunstein, however, favors a "soft" form of cost–benefit calculation where qualitative considerations that cannot be carefully measured should nonetheless be considered, especially in health and environmental regulations.[50] [For an argument in support of deregulating marriage, see **http://www.etalkinghead. com/archives/deregulation-of-marriage-2004-03-01.html**]

Your Life? $3 Million

How much is a life worth? That question is probably the crucial cost–benefit inquiry. When imposing new environmental or car safety rules, for example, we are forced to think about how much money we should spend to save an additional life. Recently the federal Environmental Protection Agency priced a life at $6 million, while the federal Department of Transportation used a $3 million value and leading scholar Kip Viscusi's most recent study put a $7 million value on human life. Should elderly people's lives be considered less valuable than those of young people? The United States spends over $37,000 annually for medical care in the average senior citizen's final year of life, versus $7,365 on average for other years. In Europe, by contrast, expensive care is routinely denied to those facing death. In the United States, several billion dollars annually is spent to keep alive those in a persistent vegetative state (estimated at 16,000 to 35,000 people nationally). Interestingly, 80 percent of Americans surveyed say they would not want to be kept alive in a vegetative state.

How much is your life worth? Should the value of lives be a consideration in federal rules and spending decisions?

Sources: John J. Fialka, "Balancing Act: Lives vs. Regulations," *The Wall Street Journal,* May 30, 2003, p. A4; Catherine Arnst, "Getting Rational about Rationing," *BusinessWeek,* November 17, 2003, p. 140.

Deregulation Assessed: The Good News

A 2003 survey of about 1,400 CEOs worldwide found 18 percent of those leaders listing "overregulation" as the biggest threat to their business, exceeding all other perils including "increased competition" (17 percent), "currency fluctuations" (15 percent), and "global terrorism" (10 percent).[51] Deregulation seems to be a success in important respects although some rough spots are evident. Scholars Robert Crandall and Jerry Ellig have identified the following "patterns" in the deregulation of trucking, railroads, airlines, telecommunications, and natural gas:

- *Lower prices:* Adjusted for inflation, prices in the five industries fell between 28 and 57 percent in the decade after the deregulation.
- *More innovation:* After deregulation, airlines developed "hub-and-spoke" routing systems, enabling them to operate more efficiently. Deregulation allowed truckers and railroads to develop "intermodal" transport systems where trucks are shipped by rail for long distances. Intermodal systems are so efficient that 28 percent of America's trucks now spend some time on a railroad.
- *More business:* Falling prices ensure more demand for products. Natural gas consumption increased 21 percent in the first decade after deregulation. Falling trucking costs were a major reason United Parcel Service doubled in size between 1980 and 1995. The number of airline flights nearly doubled after a decade of deregulation.
- *Improved lives:* Airline deregulation allowed the rise of low-cost airlines such as Southwest, making airline tickets affordable for people who would otherwise have to spend hours on a bus. Telephone deregulation lowered long-distance rates, allowing more people to spend more time talking to distant friends and relatives. Natural gas deregulation dramatically reduced the cost of heating homes.[52]

As *BusinessWeek* observed,

Deregulation dramatically increased the flexibility and responsiveness of U.S. corporations in a period of rapid technological and competitive change. Indeed, by making it easier to shift capacity where it is needed, deregulation deserves some of the credit for the current low rate of inflation.[53]

Deregulation Assessed: The Bad News

Journalist Vermont Royster argues that government is vital to civilized life:

> If I hesitate to join the hue for deregulation, even when much of the regulation is misguided, it's because I shudder at the thought of a wholly deregulated society. I prefer knowing my pharmacist has to be licensed and that somebody checks on him; so also with the butcher so that I have some assurance his scale registers a true measure.
>
> As a matter of fact, regulation to protect consumers is almost as old as civilization itself. Tourists to the ruins of Pompeii see an early version of the bureau of weights and measures, a place where the townsfolk could go to be sure they weren't cheated by the local tradesmen. Unfortunately, a little larceny is too common in the human species.
>
> So regulation in some form or other is one of the prices we pay for our complex civilization. And the more complicated society becomes, the more need for some watching over its many parts.[54]

Deregulation in practice has produced big benefits, but it has not been a painless process. Bankruptcies have been common in the airline and trucking industries. A Consumers Union study claims that deregulation has created an "increasingly Wild West marketplace" requiring some renewal of regulation in cable, phone, lending, and airline markets.[55] The recent corporate scandals and other problems are reenergizing those with doubts about the deregulation movement. A key doubt lies in fears about monopoly—that deregulated markets will allow a few firms to control vast pieces of American life. Some specific concerns:

- *Telecommunications:* The federal Telecommunications Act of 1996 substantially deregulated the phone, cable, wireless, and satellite businesses. Wireless and long-distance rates have fallen dramatically, but local phone and cable rates have been rising. Furthermore, the telecommunications merger wave since 1996 has changed the nature of music radio, *Rolling Stone* claims, resulting in homogeneous, bland, unimaginative programming:

  > The telecommunications merger wave has changed the nature of music radio

  > National playlists are in the hands of corporate programmers, who are influenced by big-label money funneled into the stations by independent radio promoters. "The airwaves are a public trust, but we have given that up and let one small group of people heist all the country's programming decisions," charges Miles Copeland III, former manager of the Police.[56]

- *Electricity:* A recent study found that electrical rates since 2000 have climbed significantly more in deregulated states than in those maintaining government oversight.[57]

- *Transportation:* Many small communities have lost airline service or seen it decline in quality, most of the remaining handful of big firms in the market are struggling to remain solvent and airline travel today is often chaotic.

- *Financial services:* The 1999 Financial Services Modernization Act deregulated the banking industry by removing barriers that had prevented banks and securities firms from competing in each other's markets. Congress had erected the walls in 1933 in the belief that risky securities speculation by banks had contributed to the Great Depression. The new open market has created the opportunity for "financial supermarkets" to provide loans, stock market advice, and investment banking (financing and advice for mergers, initial public offerings, and the like) all at one stop. *The Wall Street Journal* explained how the new freedom is changing banking practice:

> Banks have made little secret since the old restrictions crumbled that they are willing to make loans in order to win investment deals. Bank of America Corp., for instance, has indicated that if a certain borrower wants a loan, then the borrower should ante up when it is time to choose a merger or deal adviser.[58]

Enhanced efficiency and strengthened global competitiveness are the expected rewards of this reduction in rules, but big problems are inevitable, as evidenced by the subprime mortgage crisis of recent years. Indeed, in 2005, 52 percent of subprime mortgages were originated by companies with no federal supervision.[59]

Further Deregulation or Reregulation?

Historian John Steele Gordon argues that capitalism needs regulation and that regulation has made the country more stable and richer:

> Capitalism without regulation and regulators is inherently unstable, Gordon claims, "as people will usually put their short-term interests ahead of the interests of the system as a whole, and either chaos or plutocracy will result. . . . The country since the New Deal has been a far richer, far more economically secure, far more just society," Gordon writes.[60]

Government regulation in America normally arises not from ideology but from actual problems.[61] America is not committed to government regulation as a matter of political policy. Rather, regulation in this country has, in many instances, resulted from an honorable effort to correct evident wrongs. Much-maligned agencies such as the EPA, OSHA, and the FDA were not born of a desire for big government and central planning. Pollution, industrial accidents, and dangerous food and drugs were clearly the impetus for the creation of those agencies. Further, we should remember that regulation in the United States remains modest relative to the balance of the globe.

Around the Globe   While the cost of regulation in the United States is great, government rules are, in fact, less burdensome in America than in most nations. For example, a recent study found the United States just behind New Zealand among the world's nations in ease of starting and operating businesses.[62] Similarly, a recent World Bank study finds excess regulation stifling productivity in much of Africa, Latin America, and the former Soviet Union. On the other hand, the United States ranks along with Australia, Canada, New Zealand, and the United Kingdom, among a few others, as the least regulated and most efficient economies. In general, the World Bank study found that the least regulated economies are the strongest economies. Perhaps surprisingly, however, a critical factor in economic growth is the presence of an efficient legal system. For example, the creation of a private company in Australia requires two legal procedures and about two days, as contrasted with the system in Angola where 146 days and over $5,500 would be needed. Likewise a 2006 study found that countries with better regulations grow faster. Improving business regulations from the worst quartile to the best "implies a 2.3 percentage. points increase in annual growth."[63]So rules can be helpful if efficient but disastrous if excessive.[64]

But perhaps the solution does not reside in more rules. Perhaps the solution (and the blame) lies with each of us rather than with capitalism, as a student columnist from Wayne State University suggests in the following commentary about recent business scandals.

READING   Capitalism on Trial

Eric Czarnik

Is capitalism at fault for this current crisis? Despite what some Ayn Rand devotees might say, a totally unregulated capitalism isn't ideal. Although capitalism attempts to channel self-interest into safer, mutually beneficial agreements among business partners, dishonest businessmen can still satisfy their agendas while ignoring the best interests of consumers.

As we have seen, this can be successfully accomplished in many ways, such as cooking the books, insider trading, and false stock reports. These undermine the essential trust that binds suppliers and consumers together, causing capitalism to suffer immensely.

Nevertheless, acknowledging these weaknesses doesn't invalidate capitalism, which is still a far more realistic and successful economic system when compared to any other. Communism and socialism, while appealing in theory, fail to account for mankind's selfish, greedy nature. These two systems put their trust in the state while generally distrusting moral institutions like religion and the family. Amoral, self-serving, and oppressive political leaders are therefore more likely to thrive.

* * * * *

The real culprit behind these scandals isn't capitalism, per se, but shameless relativism and an arrogance that disregards the rule of law. The 1990s flourished with these two characteristics, and we're now finally reaping what we have sown.

The cultural zeitgeist of the 1990s could be summed up in one man: President Bill Clinton. During his administration, he nonchalantly sidestepped scandals, lied under oath, and debated the definition of the word "is." Meanwhile, the public collectively yawned, as it was more eager to flaunt its newfound wealth than "judge" anyone. Is it no surprise that the public's tolerance for such behavior led corporate executives to believe that they could get away with the same thing, except by manipulating numbers and figures instead of words?

We have two options for getting out of this fiasco. One option would be to have the CEOs clean up their own act—immediately. They could wisely remember the old adage, "cheaters never win." . . .

The other option would be to follow the logic of James Madison. In Federalist Paper No. 51, he proposed that "if men were angels, there would be no need for government." Because men aren't angels, Madison believed a strong central government is pertinent for our nation's stability. To executives who feel that, like Machiavelli, they're above conventional morality, tougher watchdog regulation and stiffer penalties might be necessary and fitting. Putting a few of the corrupt "suits" in orange jumpsuits would help, too.

Capitalism mostly works, and it would be a shame to abandon a system that rewards hard work and promotes social mobility. We can only hope that Wall Street listened when Bush said, "In the long run, there is no capitalism without conscience, there is no wealth without character."

Source: *The South End* via *University Wire*, July 16, 2002. Reprinted by permission.

Questions

1. Is our fundamental nature "selfish and greedy"? Explain.

2. What does Czarnik mean by "shameless relativism"?

3. *a.* Can we count on the corporate community to "clean up their own act" or must the government intervene as it did in passing the Sarbanes–Oxley Act? Explain.

   b. Do you have some other solution? Explain.

The Winner: Open Markets, But . . .

The general course of the American and world economies is clearly toward open markets, but each new disturbance reminds us that some rules in some circumstances seem to be necessary. Enron, WorldCom, Adelphia and other corporate scandals of the early 21st century raised questions about America's faith in deregulation. The result was the Sarbanes-Oxley Act (see Chapters 2 and 9). Similarly, at this writing, the Federal Reserve has responded to the collapse in the subprime mortgage market by proposing new rules designed to protect home loan borrowers by forcing mortgage lenders to fully reveal hidden sales fees while setting new standards to assure that borrowers are well-qualified for loans. Do these new government interventions suggest a revival of regulation? Former Secretary of Labor Robert Reich thinks so:

> The great pendulum in the sky, between letting [capitalism] rip and constraint in the market is certainly moving back toward regulation. . . . There is a growing sense that unlimited capitalism has its benefits. But there needs to be more regulation to protect consumers and investors.[65]

Nonetheless, any such revival seems likely to be limited to rather narrow, targeted rules that respect the need for efficiency and competitiveness in the rigorous global market.

A Concluding Case: Get Off That Phone?

Let's close this chapter about rules by asking if we need more of them:

> At least 40 nations—from Australia to Zimbabwe—have banned talking on cell phones while driving, including nearly all of Europe. Leading the crackdown, Poland has the harshest penalties, up to $1,000, while a third offense in Ireland rings up three months in jail.
>
> Almost two of three U.S. adults have a cell phone, and 43 percent of all cell phone owners say they regularly use them while driving, according to a Harris Interactive poll. Yet 76 percent of poll respondents favor banning cell phone use while driving, except in emergencies.[66]

As of late 2007, at least 15 states and the District of Columbia had imposed some form of restriction on the use of cell phones while driving, and 11 more states were considering limits.[67] Many of the laws target distracting behaviors generally including reading, grooming, and talking on the phone. The leading study to date, which followed 241 drivers as they drove more than two million miles, found that 80 percent of crashes were linked to distracted drivers, including those who were drowsy.[68] Cell phones were implicated in some fashion with about seven percent of accidents.[69] Talking by phone posed a "statistically insignificant" risk, but dialing while driving raised the risk of an accident or a close call by almost three times.[70] Some studies, however, do show increased risks associated with talking on phones while driving, whether handheld or hands-free.[71] The frequency and nature of distracting conduct while driving is difficult to measure, but obviously common. A recent study of 5,600 students reported nearly 90 percent had observed their friends driving while talking on cell phones and half had seen drivers playing handheld games, using listening devices or sending text messages.[72] In one instance not a part of the student study, an individual was seen driving while playing the flute.[73] Washington recently became the first state to ban "D.W.T."—that is, driving while texting with a cell phone or other mobile device.

Questions

1. *a.* Would you favor government rules forbidding cell phone use while driving? Explain.

   b. What about text messaging, grooming, eating, and so on? Explain.

2. From a *Des Moines Register* editorial:

   > There's talk about airline passengers soon being allowed to use cell phones. Say it isn't so. It is hard to conceive of anything more maddening than being wedged into an airline seat next to a thoughtless cell phone addict for the duration of a three-hour flight.[74]

   How would you vote on airplane cell phone use?

3. Distinguished economist Herbert Stein, perhaps best known as father of celebrity Ben Stein, said that we are desperate for cell phone conversations to ward off our loneliness:

   > It is the way of keeping contact with someone, anyone who will reassure you that you are not alone. You may think you are checking on your portfolio but deep down you are checking on your own existence.[75]

   a. Are you dependent on your cell phone?

   b. If so, should the government discourage that use by, for example, imposing higher taxes on cell phone purchases? Explain.

Guy Davenport: "The telephone is God's gift to the bore."

Source: Interview by John Jeremiah Sullivan. *The Paris Review*. Fall 2002.

Internet Exercise

Should the U.S. government impose new rules requiring all bicyclists to wear helmets? New Zealand has enforced a national mandatory all-age bicycle helmet law since 1994. To help with your recommendation for the United States, consider the evidence from the New Zealand experience at [**http://www.cycle-helmets.com/zealand_helmets.html**]

Chapter Questions

1. *a.* Has deregulation affected your life? Explain.

   b. Do you *trust* the free market? The government? Both? Neither? Explain.

   c. On balance, has business deregulation been a good direction for America? Explain.

2. The *Des Moines Register* advocated a free market approach to cable television, labeling it a "nonessential activity."

    a. Should the government be involved in regulating only those products and services that we cannot do without? Explain.

    b. Has deregulation reduced your cable television rates? Explain.

3. A 1999 study concluded that African-American youths, especially those between 18 and 29, are 50 percent less likely to wear seat belts than whites or Hispanics. The report estimated that regular use of seat belts by all African Americans would save 1,300 lives per year, prevent 26,000 injuries, and reduce societal costs by $2.6 billion.[76] According to the National Highway Transportation Safety Commission, if all Americans wore seat belts regularly, we would save 10,000 lives, 200,000 injuries, and $20 billion annually.[77] Should Congress require seat belt use? Explain.

4. The Heritage Foundation and *The Wall Street Journal* jointly publish the annual global Index of Economic Freedom. In general, the nations that have been most successful in increasing their economic freedom (by reducing taxes and so forth) have enjoyed the highest rates of economic growth. When the Index was first published in 1995, the United States ranked fifth in the world, and it ranked fourth in 2007. Hong Kong ranked first in 2007, while 12 of the 20 "freest" economies were European, with the United Kingdom and Ireland topping that group.[78]

    a. What is economic freedom?

    b. The Heritage Foundation lists 10 factors including, for example, business freedom, in its list of ingredients in measuring economic freedom. In addition to business freedom, what other factors would you include in a list designed to measure a nation's level of overall economic freedom?

    c. How does economic freedom help an economy grow?

5. Former Secretary of Labor Robert Reich: "The era of big government may be over, but the era of regulation through litigation has just begun."[79] Explain what Reich meant.

6. Sony Ericsson Mobile used actors to pose as tourists to demonstrate its camera phone at attractions in New York City and Seattle.[80] The actors asked passersby to take their photo thus demonstrating the camera's capabilities, but the actors did not identify themselves as actors representing Sony Ericsson. Advocacy groups have complained to the Federal Trade Commission about this word-of-mouth marketing campaign.

    a. Explain the objections to the Sony Ericsson approach.

    b. Should the FTC intervene in some fashion? Explain.

7. Transportation deregulation resulted in an immediate loss of bus and/or air service to some smaller communities. Some of that loss was compensated for with the entry of smaller, independent firms.

    a. Has deregulation endangered small-town America? Explain.

    b. Should we apply free market principles to the postal service, thus, among other consequences, compelling those in small and remote communities to pay the full cost of service rather than the "subsidized" cost now paid? Explain.

8. The expense of government regulation is not limited to the direct cost of administering the various agencies. Explain and offer examples of the other expenses produced by regulation.

9. To the extent the federal government achieves deregulation, what substitutes will citizens find for protection?

10. Pulitzer Prize–winning author and presidential adviser Arthur Schlesinger:

    > The assault on the national government is represented as a disinterested movement to "return" power to the people. But the withdrawal of the national government does not transfer power to the people. It transfers power to the historical rival of the national government and the prime cause of its enlargement—the great corporate interests.[81]

    a. Using 19th- and 20th-century American economic history, explain Schlesinger's claim that corporate interests are the primary cause of big government.

    b. Do you agree with Schlesinger that we continue to need big government to counteract corporate interests and achieve fairness for all in American life? Explain.

11. Make the argument that increasing government rules and jobs leads to decreasing private-sector businesses and jobs.

12. *a.* How might a student such as yourself usefully employ cost–benefit reasoning to improve academic performance?

    b. Do you do so? Explain.

13. The British government spends about $340 per year per Briton on drug costs while the United States spends about $800 per year per American. As *The Wall Street Journal* reported, Great Britain is struggling to find ways to curb rocketing health care costs:

    > Millions of patients around the world have taken drugs introduced over the past decade to delay the worsening of Alzheimer's disease. While the drugs offer no cure, studies suggest they work in some patients at least for a while. But this year, an arm of Britain's government health-care system, relying on some economists' number-crunching, said the benefit isn't worth the cost. It issued a preliminary ruling calling on doctors to stop prescribing the drugs. The ruling highlighted one of the most disputed issues in medicine today. If a treatment helps people, should governments and private insurers pay for it without question? Or should they first measure the benefit against the cost, and only pay if the cost-benefit ratio exceeds some preset standard?[82]

    Should the U.S. government and insurers employ cost-benefit calculations in deciding which illnesses and patients receive coverage? Explain.

14. Joseph Stiglitz, the chief White House economist at the time, argued in 1996 that "a huge economic literature" supports his view that "appropriately circumscribed government programs can lead to a higher-growth economy."[83] How can government programs stimulate the economy rather than act as a drag on it?

15. A major issue facing the Federal Aviation Administration is congestion in the airways caused by too many planes seeking to take off or land at peak times at high-demand airports. How might we solve that problem while maintaining reasonable service?

16. In calculating the costs and benefits of a new rule, make the argument that added regulation normally slows the economy and leads to increased deaths.

17. Eighty-three percent of teens had at least one sunburn in 1999, whereas the comparable figure in 1986 was 30 percent.[84] "Right now, we're at the apex of the 'bronze goddess era,'" said Atoosa Rubenstein, editor-in-chief of *CosmoGIRL* magazine.[85] More than a third of the 17-year-old girls in a recent survey reported going to a tanning salon in the previous year.[86] A 2002 study found that those using tanning

devices were 1.5 to 2.5 times more likely to develop common forms of skin cancer than those not using the devices.[87] The American Academy of Dermatology Association (AADA) has urged the FDA to ban the sale and use of indoor tanning equipment for non-medical purposes and has called for state or federal laws to, among other things, forbid minors from using tanning devices.[88] About 27 states have placed limits on teen tanning. Do you support limits on teen tanning? Explain?

18. *BusinessWeek:*

> How do you change the eating habits of several hundred million people? That's the daunting problem the World Health Organization (WHO) is trying to solve with a proposal for fighting obesity worldwide. It's a bold and necessary effort, but unfortunately, it may be undermined by the world's fattest nation: the United States. The U.N. estimates that 300 million people worldwide are obese and a further 750 million are overweight, including 22 million children under 5.
>
> [The United States] is charging that the WHO's conclusions that fats and sugars cause obesity are not supported by "sufficient scientific evidence."[89]

Nonetheless, the WHO has proposed a series of nonbinding actions that governments could take to encourage citizens to curb their weight gain.

a. What strategies might the WHO endorse to help us avoid weight gain?

b. Why would the United States resist the nonbinding WHO proposals?

c. Is obesity a matter of personal responsibility? Explain.

Notes

1. P.J. Huffstutter, "Illinois Seeks to Curb Explicit Video Games, *Los Angeles Times,* December 16, 2004, p. A1.

2. Edwin Garcia and Howard Mintz, " Judge Blocks Video Game Law," *San Jose Mercury News,* August 7, 2007 [**http://www.mercurynews.com**].

3. Ibid.

4. Ibid.

5. Brian C. Anderson, "The Brain Workout," *The Wall Street Journal,* June 2, 2006, p. W13.

6. *Video Software Dealers Ass'n v. Arnold Schwarzenegger,* 2007 U.S. Dist. LEXIS 57472 (N.D. Cal.).

7. Joseph P. Tomain, "American Regulatory Policy: Have We Found the 'Third Way'?" *Kansas Law Review* 48 (May 2000), p. 829.

8. *Watters v. Wachovia Bank, N.A.,* 127 S.Ct. 1559 (2007).

9. Ibid.

10. Jess Bravin, "High Court Overrules 3 State Laws," *The Wall Street Journal,* February 21, 2008, p. A8.

11. 317 U.S. 111 (1942).

12. 545 U.S. 1 (2005).

13. Heather Won Tesoriero, "Backlash Endangers California Pot Dispensaries," *The Wall Street Journal,* December 20, 2007, p. B1.

14. *Gonzalez v. Raich,* pp. 57-8.

15. 115 S.Ct. 1624 (1995).

16. 18 U.S.C. 922 (q) (1) (A).

17. *United States v. Morrison* and *Brzonkala v. Morrison,* 529 U.S. 598 (2000).

18. *Brzonkala v. Virginia Polytechnic Institute,* 169 F.3d 820, 827 (4th Cir. 1999).

19. Ibid., p. 908.

20. Jerry Hirsch, "Putting a Cork in Internet Wine Sales," *Los Angeles Times,* January 7, 2008 [**www.latimes.com**].

21. Nanette Byrnes, "Costco Starts a Barroom Brawl," *BusinessWeek,* December 31, 2007, p. 88.

22. Daniel Michaels, "Pact Ushers in Competitive Skies," *The Wall Street Journal,* March 23, 2007, p. A3.

23. G. Thomas Sims, "Corn Flakes Clash Shows the Glitches in European Union," *The Wall Street Journal,* November 1, 2005, p. A9.

24. "EU Warns 19 Nations to Stop Blocking Foreign Competition," *The Wall Street Journal,* April 20, 2006, p. A6.

25. Marcus Walker, "Longer Store Hours in Germany," *The Wall Street Journal,* January 8, 2007, p. A5.

26. Mike Esterl, "Germans Hack at Forest of Signs Distracting Drivers," *The Wall Street Journal,* July 24, 2007, p. A1.

27. Ibid.

28. Max Frankel, "The Next Great Story," *The New York Times,* March 15, 1998, sec. 6, p. 30.

29. Ibid.

30. Editorial, "Licensed to Kill," *The Wall Street Journal,* September 10, 2007, p. A14.

31. Jennifer Jacobs, "Judge Backs City's Refusal to Renew Bar's License," *Waterloo/Cedar Falls Courier,* November 22, 1998, p. C3.

32. Patrik Jonsson, "In Louisiana Town, Wearing Low-Rider Pants May Cost You," *The Christian Science Monitor,* June 18, 2007 [**http://www.csmonitor.com/2007/0618/p01s06-ussc.html**].

33. The organizational structure of the introductory administrative law materials owes a great deal to the suggestions of Professor Cynthia Srstka, Augustana College (South Dakota).

34. *Prometheus Radio Project v. Federal Communications Commission,* 373 F.3d 372 (3d Cir. 2004); *cert. denied, FCC v. Prometheus Radio Project,* 2005 U.S. LEXIS 4811.

35. Frank Ahrens, "Divided FCC Enacts Rules on Media Ownership," *Washington Post,* December 19, 2007, p. D01.

36. Robert Pear, "Bush Directive Increases Sway on Regulation," *The New York Times,* January 30, 2007 [**http://www.nytimes.com/2007/01/30/washington/30rules.html?_r=1&sq=**]

37. John D. Graham, Testimony before House Government Reform Committee, "Costs, Benefits, and Impacts of Federal Regulations," Federal Document Clearing House Congressional Testimony, March 11, 2003.

38. 531 U.S. 457.

39. See *United States v. Mead Corp.,* 533 U.S. 218 (2001).

40. *Fox Television Stations v. Federal Communications Commission,* 489 F.3d 444 (2d Cir. 2007).

41. Ibid.

42. Editorial, "Tale of the Red Tape," *The Wall Street Journal,* May 11, 2006, p. A16.

43. Ibid.

44. Americans for Tax Reform, "2007 Cost of Government Day Summary," National Press Release [**http://www.atr.org/content/html/2007/july/071107ot%20COGD%20summary.htm**].

45. Editorial, "Tale of the Red Tape," p. A16.

46. Louis Richman, "Bringing Reason to Regulation," *Fortune,* October 19, 1992, p. 94.

47. Joel Brinkley, "Out of Spotlight, Bush Overhauls U.S. Regulations," *The New York Times,* August 14, 2004 [**nytimes.com**].

48. Jacob Laksin, "Why Corporate America Needs Welfare Reform," *The Wall Street Journal,* July 29–30, 2006, p. P9.

49. Thomas O. Garrity, "A Cost-Benefit State," *Administrative Law Review* 50, no. 1 (Winter 1998), p. 7.

50. Ibid.

51. Marc Champion, "CEO's Worst Nightmares," *The Wall Street Journal,* January 21, 2004, p. A13.

52. Martin Wooster, "The Benefits of Deregulation," *The American Enterprise,* September-October 1997, p. 87.

53. Editorial, "Deregulation Is Great, But…" *BusinessWeek,* April 5, 1999, p. 130.

54. Vermont Royster, "'Regulation' Isn't a Dirty Word," *The Wall Street Journal,* September 9, 1987, p. 30.

55. Dow Jones Newswires, "Deregulation Is Likened to the 'Wild West,'" *The Wall Street Journal,* June 11, 2002, p. D3.

56. Greg Kot, "What's Wrong with Radio?" *Rolling Stone,* August 16, 2001, p. 25.

57. David Cay Johnston, "A New Push to Regulate Power Costs," *The New York Times,* September 4, 2007 [**http://www.nytimes.com**].

58. Carrick Mollenkamp and Rick Brooks, "Collapse Raises Issue of 1999 Bank Deregulation," *The Wall Street Journal,* November 30, 2001, p. A8.

59. Greg Ip and Damian Paletta, "Regulators Scrutinized in Mortgage Meltdown," *The Wall Street Journal,* March 22, 2007, p. A1.

60. John Steele Gordon, *An Empire of Wealth: The Epic History of American Economic Power* (New York: Harper Collins, 2004). Quoted by Wayne E. Yang, "The Wealth of America Is Wealth," *Christian Science Monitor,* December 7, 2004 [**http://www.csmonitor.com/2004/1207/p15s02-bogn.html**].

61. Lester Thurow, *The Zero-Sum Society* (New York: Penguin Books, 1980), p. 136.

62. Michael Schroeder, "Regulatory Rules Stifle Business in Poor Countries," *The Wall Street Journal,* September 8, 2004, p. A17.

63. Simeon Djankov, Caralee McLiesh, and Rita Maria Ramalho, "Regulation and Growth," *Social Science Research Network,* March 17, 2006. [**http://ssrn.com/abstract=893321**].

64. Michael Schroeder and Terence Roth, "World Bank Faults Tight Regulation," *The Wall Street Journal,* October 7, 2003, p. A2.

65. David R. Francis, "Government Regulation Stages a Comeback," *The Christian Science Monitor,* September 10, 2007 [**http://www.csmonitor.com/2007/0910/p14s01-wmgn.html**].

66. Editorial, "Cell Phones Not the Only Driving Distraction that Needs Attention," *Waterloo/Cedar Falls Courier,* May 11, 2004, p. A6.

67. Rachel Konrad, "States Mull Bans on Teen Drivers' Distracting Gadgets," *Des Moines Register,* September 10, 2007, p. 1A.

68. *The Baltimore Sun,* "Distractions Are Main Cause of Auto Accidents, Study Finds," *Waterloo-Cedar Falls Courier,* April 21, 2006, p. A1.

69. Ibid.

70. Ibid.

71. Jesse Drucker and Karen Lundegaard, "As Industry Pushes Headsets in Cars, U.S. Agency Sees Danger," *The Wall Street Journal,* July 19, 2004, p. A1.

72. Associated Press, "States: Drop the Flute and Drive," *Waterloo-Cedar Falls Courier,* February 11, 2007, p. A3.

73. Ibid.

74. Editorial, "On a Plane, Let Cell-Phone Silence Reign," *Des Moines Register,* December 29, 2004, p. 6A.

75. James Gleick, *The Acceleration of Just About Everything* (New York: Vintage Books, 1999), p. 89.

76. R.J. King, "U.S. Seat Belt Law Is Urged: Report: Hundreds of Lives Would Be Saved, Especially among African Americans," *Detroit News,* July 20, 1999, p. B4.

77. Ibid.

78. [**www.heritage.org**]

79. Robert Reich, "Regulation Is Out, Litigation Is In," *USA TODAY,* February 11, 1999, p. 15A.

80. Annys Shin, "FTC Moves to Unmask Word-of-Mouth Marketing," *The Washington Post,* December 12, 2006, p. D01.

81. Arthur Schlesinger, Jr., "In Defense of Government," *The Wall Street Journal,* June 7, 1995, p. A14.

82. Jeanne Wilson, "Britain Stirs Outcry by Weighing Benefits of Drugs Versus Price," *The Wall Street Journal,* November 22, 2006, p. A1.

83. Bob Davis, "In Presidential Race, the Key Question Is, 'What Causes Growth?'" *The Wall Street Journal,* September 27, 1996, p. A1.

84. Julie Sevrens Lyons, "Doctors See Growing Cancer Risk with Trendy Tans," *Milwaukee Journal,* July 29, 2002, p. 3A.

85. Lyons, "Doctors See Growing Cancer Risk."

86. Lyons, "Doctors See Growing Cancer Risk."

87. Jane E. Allen, "Young, Tan, and at Risk," *Hartford Courant,* June 25, 2002, p. D3.

88. "American Academy of Dermatology Urges Teens to Heed Warning on Dangers of Tanning," *PR Newswire,* May 3, 2004.

89. Catherine Arnst, "Let Them Eat Cake—If They Want To," *BusinessWeek,* February 23, 2004, p. 110.

CHAPTER NINE

Business Organizations and Securities Regulation

After completing this chapter, students will be able to:

1. Describe the advantages and disadvantages of the three traditional forms of business organizations: corporations, partnerships, and sole proprietorships.

2. Explain the business judgment rule.

3. Explain the relationship between limited liability and the doctrine of "piercing the corporate veil."

4. List and explain some hybrid business forms.

5. Define the term *Initial Public Offering* (IPO).

6. Describe the securities registration process.

7. Explain the differing regulatory roles of the 1933 and 1934 federal securities laws.

8. Explain the due diligence defense.

9. Define insider trading.

10. Describe the tender offer process and some defenses against it.

11. Contrast the American view of securities regulation with other philosophies around the globe.

12. Explain the crisis in the financial markets that led to the Sarbanes-Oxley Act (SOX).

13. Explain Sarbanes-Oxley's requirements and evaluate its costs and benefits.

14. Describe the backdated options scandal.

Introduction

This chapter provides a brief introduction to some of the fundamental laws governing business formation, management and capitalization. At the start we need to recognize the overlapping coverage of state and federal regulation of business. Historically, most issues—such as the creation of business entities, the powers and duties of management, and capital structure—were matters of state law. Still today, the laws that regulate the relationship of a partnership among its own partners and with outside parties are state laws; as are the laws that permit the creation of corporations; as are the laws under which limited liability companies (LLC's) have been allowed to form. The fundamental legal duties that corporations, corporate boards. and officers owe to their shareholders are those of the state of incorporation. Almost half of the *publicly held corporations* (corporations with publicly traded shares) listed on the New York Stock Exchange are incorporated in Delaware.[1] Thus, when corporate law is discussed, the corporate law of Delaware often drives the discussion. Part One of this chapter is largely devoted to an understanding of state law.

Triggered by the 1929 stock market crash and the continuing failure of our capital markets and banking system in the Great Depression of the 1930s, the federal government, largely under its powers to regulate interstate commerce, created both the Securities and Exchange Commission (SEC) to regulate our securities markets and the Federal Reserve Bank to oversee and regulate banks. Much later, in response to the spectacular and widespread corporate failures of the late '90s and early 2000s, Congress again enacted federal legislation—the Sarbanes Oxley Act of 2002 (SOX). Although much federal legislation has been passed between these two events, SOX was probably the largest incursion since the '30s into areas previously under the purview of state law. Part Two of this chapter will, therefore, focus on federal regulation of the securities markets.

Of course, many areas of corporate action are concurrently regulated by both state and federal law. This is true, for example, both of the continuing efforts of shareholders to have a say in the compensation paid to corporate officers and of the stock option backdating scandal. These issues are addressed in Part Two and Part Three, respectively.

Finally, Part Three takes a look at SOX, viewed from the perspective of nearly six years of experience. We are primarily interested in corporate governance issues—that is, the structure and obligations of management, especially those areas which have the greatest potential for impacting the investing public and the integrity of the capital markets.

Part One: Characteristics of Available Business Forms

Introduction

One of the fundamental decisions that must be made for any business venture is the legal form in which it will be conducted. Three traditional forms and several hybrids have developed in the United States. Each form has advantages and disadvantages; one must carefully evaluate which form is most suitable for a particular undertaking.

The three traditional forms, *corporations, partnerships,* and *sole proprietorships,* are discussed shortly. Each form can be distinguished along the following dimensions:

Nontax costs: The costs related to bringing a business form into existence and maintaining that existence.

Centralization of management: The degree to which control is centralized in a hierarchical structure.

Limited liability: The extent to which business owners are personally liable for business obligations.

Free transferability of interests: Whether the business owners can transfer their interests without restriction.

Duration of existence: What events, including those impacting the business owners, end the business form's existence.

Taxes: The extent to which the business form affects the taxation of the business and its owners.

Capital structure: The debt/equity trade-off and the impact of the business form on the ability to attract capital.

Circumstances Favoring a Specific Business Form: Whether a given venture's legal characteristics mandate or favor a specific business form.

[For a table summarizing the key characteristics of each business form, see **www. bizfilings.com/learning/comparison.htm**]

Corporations

> Corporations are the dominant form of business in the United States

Corporations are the dominant form of business in the United States. Although only 20 percent of all businesses are corporations, they account for 86 percent of all business revenue. Indeed, 82 percent of all businesses with revenues in excess of $1 million are corporations.[2] There are good reasons for that primacy, which will become evident in the discussion to follow.

Throughout this discussion, we must keep in mind two very different corporate realities: the publicly held corporation (or *public corporation*) previously mentioned and the *closely held corporation* (a corporation with relatively few shareholders, the stock of which has no readily available public market).

Nontax Costs

To create a corporation, a *promoter* or *incorporator* files *articles of incorporation* with the state government. A small fee is typically charged. The articles have mandatory elements, such as the corporation's name, the person designated to receive certain communications from the state (legal documents like subpoenas), and a description of the shares the corporation is permitted to issue. Discretionary content like voting rules may also appear in the articles.

Once the articles are filed, the corporation comes into existence. The owners are called *stockholders* or *shareholders* because the ownership interests are called *shares* of *stock*. An *organizational meeting* will then be held at which the issuance of stock will be authorized in exchange for contributions of capital, property or services.

The shareholders will then elect a *board of directors.* The board will meet to undertake the corporation's initial business. Among other things, it will appoint officers and adopt *bylaws.* Bylaws contain key policies and procedures, such as how meeting quorums will be determined and the percentage of shareholders that must approve major corporate actions like mergers. [For a large library of business forms, see **www.lectlaw.com/formb.htm**]

The corporation will have to make modest filings annually with the state to keep its records up-to-date, usually accompanied by a small fee. [To see how Delaware computes this fee, see **http://www.corp.delaware.gov/frtaxcalc.shtml**] At least annually, the board of directors and shareholders must meet.

Corporations are separate accounting entities. The cost of their accounting systems, however, generally reflects their scale of operation, not the decision to operate in corporate form.

Centralization of Management

Public corporations have thousands of shareholders; closely held corporations may have only one. The vast majority of shareholders do not plan to spend their time intimately involved in the company's business. They wish to entrust their resources to the stewardship of the company's management and return to their personal affairs.

To ensure the corporation is acting to further their interests, the shareholders elect a board of directors. Public corporation boards have both inside and outside directors. *Inside directors* are senior executives. *Outside directors* are not employed by the company. These boards meet at regular intervals to monitor the corporation's activities, establish corporate policies, and make major decisions. It is not uncommon for some members to attend by telephone or videoconferencing.

Boards do not operate the business on a day-to-day basis. They are policy and oversight bodies. To actually run the company, boards appoint *officers,* typically a CEO (chief executive officer) or president, secretary, treasurer, and several vice presidents. Officers hire other employees to help them operate the corporation.

Corporations have centralized management. By design, at the apex of the management pyramid is the board of directors. Immediately below is the CEO. In the next layer are the vice presidents and other top officers and executives. The pyramid further expands through layers of middle management, finally coming to the base comprised of rank-and-file employees. The recent spate of corporate failures and scandals has been ascribed, in part, to a failure of this classic management pyramid. In actual practice, the CEO rather than the Board often held the ultimate power as a consequence of the authority to nominate the Board and to control the information reaching the Board. A number of corporate governance reforms were intended to address these concerns, such as the requirement that corporate nominating committees be composed entirely of independent outside directors.

Both directors and officers have *fiduciary duties* to the corporation. A *fiduciary* is a person who acts on behalf of another (*beneficiary*) and is required to do so with great integrity. (Another fiduciary relationship is parent-to-minor child.) The *duty of loyalty* requires a fiduciary to act in the best interests of the beneficiary. This prohibits, for example, directors from authorizing the corporation to lease real estate from the board chairman unless the rental terms are consistent with the market. Directors and officers also owe the corporation a *duty of due care,* which requires that they act in good faith toward the corporation and in the manner a reasonably prudent person would employ under the same circumstances. [For an inside look at issues confronting board members today, see **http://boardmember.com**]

Business Judgment Rule

What happens if the board or CEO makes a decision which causes the stock value to decline by 30 percent? Has the duty of due care been violated? The judicial system has developed the *business judgment rule* to help make that determination. A good statement of the rule, which is explored in the *Wrigley* case below, is:

> The rule posits a powerful presumption . . . that a decision made by a loyal and informed board will not be overturned . . . unless it cannot be "attributed to any rational business purpose." [The] shareholder . . . challenging a board decision [must] rebut the . . . presumption [by] providing evidence that directors . . . breached any one of the triads of their fiduciary duty–good faith, loyalty or due care. . . . If a shareholder . . . fails to meet this. . . burden, the . . . rule attaches to protect . . . officers and directors and the decisions they make, and our courts will not second-guess these business judgments.[3]

LEGAL BRIEFCASE

Shlensky v. Wrigley
237 N.E.2d 776 (Ill. App. Ct. 1968)

FACTS

Shlensky, a minority stockholder in the Chicago Cubs, sued the directors on the grounds of mismanagement and negligence because of their refusal to install lights at Wrigley Field, then the only major league stadium without lights. One of the directors, Wrigley (80 percent owner), objected to lights because of his personal opinion that "baseball is a 'daytime sport' and that the installation of lights and night baseball games would have a deteriorating effect upon the surrounding neighborhood." The other directors deferred to Wrigley.

The Cubs were losing money. Shlensky attributed those losses to poor attendance and argued that without lights the losses would continue. His evidence was that the Chicago White Sox night games drew better than the Cubs' day games. Shlensky sought damages and an order requiring lights and night games. He lost at trial and appealed.

Justice Sullivan

[D]efendants argue that the courts will not step in and interfere with the honest business judgment of the directors unless there is a showing of fraud, illegality, or conflict of interest.

The court in *Wheeler v. The Pullman Iron & Steel Co.*, said:

> It is . . . fundamental in the law of corporations that the majority of its stockholders shall control the policy of the corporation[.] Everyone purchasing [stock] impliedly agrees that he will be bound by the [lawful acts of] a majority of the shareholders, or [of their corporate agents duly chosen,] and courts . . . will not undertake to control the policy or business methods of a corporation, although it may be seen that a wiser policy might be adopted and the business more successful if other methods were pursued.

Plaintiff . . . argues that the directors are acting for reasons unrelated to the . . . welfare of the Cubs. However, we are not satisfied that the motives assigned to . . . Wrigley [and] the other directors . . . are contrary to the best interests of the corporation[.] For example[,] the effect on the surrounding neighborhood might well be considered by a director who was considering the patrons who would or would not attend the games if the park were in a poor neighborhood. Furthermore, the long-run interest [in the] property value at Wrigley Field might demand all efforts to keep the neighborhood from deteriorating. [W]e do not mean to say . . . that the decision of the directors was a correct one. That is beyond our jurisdiction and ability. We are merely saying that the decision is one properly before the directors and the motives alleged . . . showed no fraud, illegality, or conflict of interest[.]

While all . . . courts do not insist that one or more of [these] three elements must be present for a stockholder's derivative action to lie, nevertheless we feel that unless the conduct of the defendants at least borders on one of [them], the courts should not interfere . . .

[W]e do not agree . . . that failure to follow . . . the other major league clubs in scheduling night games constituted negligence. [It] cannot be said that directors, even those of corporations that are losing money, must follow the lead of [others] in the field. Directors are elected for their business . . . judgment and the courts cannot require them to forgo their judgment because of the decisions of directors of other companies.

Affirmed.

AFTERWORD—DUTY OF CARE

Some states now require proof of *intentional misconduct* or *recklessness* to establish a breach of the duty of care.

Questions

1. What was the issue in this case?
2. The Cubs added lights in 1988. How could the board be meeting its duty of due care both in the 1960s by not erecting lights and in the 1980s by doing so?

Director, Officer, Employee Liability

Wrigley involved a *shareholder derivative suit*. That action lies where the corporation is being harmed or defrauded and neither the board nor the senior executives will take action to protect it. This often involves self-dealing by these parties. The suit is brought by a minority shareholder, but any recovery inures to the corporation.

When an employee or director commits a tort or crime while conducting corporate business, both that person and the corporation are liable for the consequences. The doctrine which makes the employer liable for an employee's acts is *respondeat superior*.

Because officers and directors are ultimately responsible for corporate acts and because corporations are frequently sued, these persons face a high risk of becoming involved in costly litigation. Most corporations, therefore, *indemnify* (pay for or reimburse) these individuals for the costs incurred to defend such suits.

PRACTICING ETHICS   Excessive Executive Compensation?

An interesting recent shareholder derivative case alleging a violation of the duty of care arose out of CEO Michael Eisner's hiring, and subsequent firing, of Michael Ovitz from his position as president of Walt Disney Co. The suit alleged that Eisner and the Disney board had violated their duty of care by hiring Ovitz (who had no previous experience as an executive of a public company in the entertainment industry), as well as when Ovitz was granted a no-fault termination. The consequence of invoking the no-fault clause in Ovitz's employment contract was that, after barely one year of employment, Ovitz received over $38 million in cash, as well as three

million stock options. Notably, the maximum salary Ovitz could have earned actually working was $11 million annually. Following a three-month trial, the Delaware court held that, "For the future, many lessons of what not to do can be learned from defendants' conduct here. Nevertheless, I conclude that . . . the defendants did not act in bad faith, and were at most ordinarily negligent, in connection with the hiring of Ovitz . . . In accordance with the business judgment rule . . . ,ordinary negligence is insufficient to constitute a violation of the fiduciary duty of care." The court also found that Ovitz could not have been fired for cause because he did not commit gross negligence or malfeasance while serving as Disney's president. Thus, Eisner did not breach his duty of care by agreeing to the no-fault termination. In 2006, 10 years after Ovitz was terminated, this decision was affirmed on appeal by the Delaware Supreme Court. See *In re Walt Disney Co. Derivative Litigation*, 907 A.2d 693 (Del. Ch. 2005), aff'd 906 A.2d 27 (Del. 2006).

Since 2007, as a result of a change in SEC disclosure rules, shareholders have been receiving more information on executive compensation packages. According to one source, severance packages typically "include a payment of three times salary and bonus, immediate vesting of options and restricted stock awards, and, in many cases,

payment of taxes owed. . . . [D]ozens of executives could have payouts of $100 million or more."

Questions
1. Apart from the legality, is it ethical for a board to agree to an executive severance package when an executive is terminated for poor performance?
2. Such packages are negotiated as part of the hiring process. Would it chill the negotiations for a board to state a corporate policy against severance payments under such circumstances?

Source: Jane Sasseen, "A Better Look at the Boss's Pay," *Business Week,* Feb. 26, 2007, p. 44.

Limited Liability

To a lawyer, there are two types of persons, natural and artificial. Natural persons are people. Artificial persons, like corporations, are entities created under the law of a state (or nation) which are considered to have separate legal existence. Corporations can own property, be sued, take on debts, and otherwise act as separate entities. They even have limited constitutional rights. One of the great advantages of this status is that the owners of the corporation are generally not responsible for the corporation's obligations. Should the corporation find that its liabilities overwhelm its assets, its creditors cannot reach the personal assets of the shareholders. This is the essence of limited liability, perhaps the most cherished characteristic of the corporate form. However, for closely held corporations, this feature can be severely restricted because lenders are well aware of limited liability and usually require the principal shareholders to *guarantee* the corporation's debts. Still, limited liability does exist for obligations like tort claims.

In closely held corporations, limited liability is sometimes lost through the application of the doctrine of *piercing the corporate veil*. This doctrine, explored in the *Wolfe* case that follows, usually has two elements: (1) misuse of the corporate form, and (2) an unjust result if limited liability is allowed to stand.

Charles E. Wolfe v. United States   612 F. Supp. 605 (D Mont 1985)

LEGAL BRIEFCASE

Aff'd 798 F.2d 1241 (9th Cir. 1986)

Judge Battin

Charles E. Wolfe was the sole shareholder and president of [the corporation,] which leased tractor-trailers. [Mr.] Wolfe

also operated a . . . proprietorship [doing] "over-the-road" trucking[.]

[T]he corporation incurred a $114,472.91 federal tax bill [. Mr.] Wolfe paid the taxes . . . after the Internal Revenue Service

(Service) [levied against him]. The Service contends . . . the corporation was the alter ego of Mr. Wolfe, thus justifying the piercing of the corporate veil. . . .

As a general rule, a corporation is treated as a legal entity, separate . . . from its shareholders[, who] enjoy limited liability. When the corporate entity is abused, however[,] limited liability may be lost[;] courts may . . . pierce the corporate veil. . . .

The facts . . . present the classic case of a shareholder so pervasively dominating corporate affairs that the shareholder and the corporation no longer have separate identities. [He] was the sole shareholder[,] a director and the president. [He] made all the corporate decisions without consulting the other directors. The corporation [had no] bank account[, telephone or separate office. All expenses were paid by the proprietor-

ship. Its] equipment was purchased on the proprietorship's credit. . . . When [it received payment,] the money was deposited into the proprietorship's bank account. . . . It is clear that the corporation and the proprietorship were operated as a single instrumentality under the sole control of Mr. Wolfe. Therefore, it was proper for the Service to look to Wolfe's personal assets to satisfy the taxes of his alter ego corporation.

[Held for the Internal Revenue Service]

Questions
1. Who owed the taxes?
2. How was the corporate form misused?
3. What injustice would have resulted if Wolfe had not been required to pay?

Free Transferability of Interests

Federal securities laws impose broad restrictions on the transfer of stock, but that topic is deferred until Part Two of this chapter. Beyond these laws, no restrictions are imposed on stock transfers. It is not uncommon, however, for dispositions to be restricted by an employment contract which might, for example, require that the stock be held until the employee leaves the company.

A common contractual restriction in closely held corporations is a *buy-sell agreement* which, at a minimum, forces a shareholder to offer his or her stock to the corporation or other shareholders before selling it to a third party. [For more on buy-sell agreements, see **http://smallbusiness.findlaw.com/business-structures/business-structures-quickstart/incorporate-shareholders-agreement.html**]

Duration of Existence

In general, a corporation has indefinite duration. Nothing that transpires in the lives of the stockholders automatically affects the corporation's existence.

The termination of a corporation, however, can occur—either voluntarily or involuntarily. Voluntary termination requires a vote by the shareholders, who might do so if business prospects are no longer favorable. On termination, the corporation is *liquidated*, which involves first satisfying all creditors and then distributing any remaining assets to the shareholders. *Articles of dissolution* are then filed, officially ending the corporation's existence.

Involuntary terminations are caused by the action of a court or of the state corporation regulator. A court might end a closely held corporation's existence if, for example, there is an irreconcilable deadlock among the shareholders. A common reason for the state to terminate a corporation is for failure to pay annual fees or make required annual filings.

Taxes

> "Taxes are what we pay for civilized society"

As Justice Oliver Wendell Holmes said, "Taxes are what we pay for civilized society."[4] But Justice Learned Hand also said, "[T]here is nothing sinister in so arranging one's affairs as to keep taxes as low as possible."[5]

Taxation transfers about one-quarter of the United States' economic output to the government. Virtually everyone wants to minimize tax payments, hopefully by legal *tax avoidance* (careful planning within the law), not by illegal *tax evasion* (committing fraud to lower taxes).

Because the corporation is a separate legal entity, it is subject to taxation in its own right. This leads to what many would say is the corporation's greatest disadvantage, *double taxation.* In the United States, a corporation pays tax on its income. When it later distributes its after-tax income to its shareholders as *dividends*, the shareholders are taxed on that amount as well; hence, "double taxation." Note, however, that dividends are not mandatory. They are paid only after the board declares them, which it cannot do if the corporation's solvency (cash flow and net worth) is insufficient.

To illustrate, assume a corporation is subject to income taxes at the rate of 40 percent and its shareholders all face a marginal rate of 35 percent (currently, the highest income tax rate for individuals), but a lower rate on corporate dividends of 15 percent. On an income of $10 million, the corporation would pay $4 million in taxes, leaving only $6 million for distribution as dividends. Upon that distribution, the shareholders would pay $900,000 in taxes. Thus, of the $10 million corporate income, only $5.1 million can actually be spent by the owners—an effective tax rate of 49 percent. Had it been possible to own the business in a form that was not subject to taxation in its own right, the total taxes would have been $3.5 million, leaving $6.5 million available for the owners to spend—27 percent more.

The 40 percent figure used above for large corporations is quite close to correct. (The largest corporations pay a flat rate of 35 percent.) Small corporations with a taxable income of less than $75,000 face a marginal tax rate of up to 25 percent, still meaningful. Thus, tax considerations are very important in deciding the form in which to house a business.

The argument that corporations are necessarily disadvantageous because of double taxation is misleading. There are many circumstances in which employing the corporate form yields clear tax advantages, especially for small- and medium-sized closely held businesses. For example, the corporation is the only form of business that comprehensively permits tax-deductible fringe benefits. [For more on fringe benefits, see **www.irs.ustreas.gov/pub/irs-pdf/p15b.pdf**]

To take advantage of lower tax rates applicable to smaller corporations, portions of a business activity can be housed in separate business entities in a fashion that lowers the overall tax rate. For example, the real estate associated with a golf course can be owned by a partnership (whose highly favorable tax characteristics are discussed later), while the golf course operation can be housed in a corporation. The taxable income of the corporation can be kept very low by purchasing fringe benefits, establishing bonus plans, timing discretionary maintenance, and the like.

Capital Structure

Businesses often need access to *capital* to finance their activities. Capital is of two types: debt and equity—two ends of the spectrum with a boundary that is challenging to identify. The providers of both debt and equity capital hold claims against the corporation's assets. However, creditors' (debtholders') claims are always satisfied before equity holders' claims.

Debt capital may be short- or long-term. Companies that provide hard disks to Dell are a source of short-term debt capital. They expect to be paid fairly quickly, although not at the moment of delivery. Therefore, they have extended credit to Dell, a very short-term form of debt. A pension plan that holds Dell's 20-year bonds provides long-term debt capital.

Equity capital (stock) has a long-term horizon. Although any given shareholder may intend to hold the stock for only a short period, the stock itself is generally expected to exist for the full life of the corporation. Three *property rights* are associated with stock ownership: the right to participate in earnings (that is, dividends), the right to participate in assets upon liquidation, and the right to participate in control. There are two principal classes of stock: preferred and common. Where only one class exists, it is *common stock*. Common stockholders share all three property rights in proportion to their holdings.

Preferred stock was created, largely for institutional investors (which hold about 50 percent of all stock[6]) like pension funds, to fill the gap on the risk-return spectrum between long-term debt and common stock. Finance professionals find it advantageous to have many different ways to combine risk and return. Preferred stock is associated with "preferences," which relate to distributions. Preferred stockholders are paid their required annual dividend in full before any dividends are distributed to the common stockholders. In addition, preferred stockholders have a preference upon the corporation's liquidation. After the creditors are satisfied, the preferred stockholders receive the next round of distributions up to their stock's *liquidation value* (also called *redemption value*).

The cost of these two preferences is the loss of the right to participate in control. Having no vote, preferred stockholders cannot elect directors to protect their interests. To help ensure that its holders regularly receive dividends, nearly all preferred stock is *cumulative*. This means that if a preferred stock dividend is missed, then before the common stockholders get any dividends, the preferred stock *arrearage* (all dividends not paid in any a prior year) must be made up. Another protection occasionally granted to preferred stockholders is a contingent right to vote if, for example, a dividend is missed twice. This voting power would continue until all arrearages have been satisfied.

Because preferred stockholders never get more than their required dividends and, upon liquidation, little more than the purchase price, all corporate growth inures to the common stockholders. If both you and Bill Gates had invested $1 million in Microsoft at the outset, you taking preferred stock and Gates taking common stock, your stock would still be worth about $1 million, whereas Gates' stock would be worth tens of billions.

Increasingly, preferred stock is being issued with both debt and equity characteristics. This poses serious classification problems for accountants and tax authorities.

Corporations carefully manage their *capital structures* (balance between debt and equity). If the debt/equity ratio is too high, it may expose a corporation to severe risk. If it is too low, opportunities for positive *financial leverage* (employing funds at a rate of return that exceeds the interest rate on the borrowed funds) may be forfeited. Executives also recognize that *interest* is tax deductible, whereas dividends are not. This places a strong emphasis on using debt capital. The capital structure must be managed to ensure that *debt covenants* are not breached. A debt covenant is a term in the lending contract that makes the debt immediately payable should the condition specified not be satisfied.

[For more on capital structure, see **http://pages.stern.nyu.edu/~adamodar/pdfiles/ovhds/capstr.pdf**]

The choice of business form must take into account the total capital needed. Large businesses need billions of dollars. Only access to global capital markets (like the New York Stock Exchange) can fulfill this need. With very few exceptions, the only form of business that has met with success in these markets is the corporation.

Circumstances Favoring a Specific Business Form

It is not rare to find someone with a great idea but insufficient resources to take the idea to market. Some investors, like *venture capitalists,* seek out such persons. They will usually insist that the venture have limited liability, as would be true with a corporation. [For more on venture capitalists, see **www.vfinance.com/home.asp?Toolpage=vencaentire.asp**]

Similarly, *franchisors* normally demand that *franchisees* operate their *franchises* in a business form with limited liability. A franchise is the right to exploit the franchisor's intangible assets (trade name and business systems) and to partake of the franchisor's marketing, purchasing and other services. The key advantages to the franchisee are a proven product or service, turn-key implementation, and access to support. The franchisor gains by earning fees and by achieving accelerated market penetration using the capital of others (franchisees). Unfortunately, franchisor fraud and oppression are not unusual, so careful investigation is essential.

Premium franchises can be expensive. The costs associated with launching a McDonald's franchise can be found at **www.mcdonalds.com/content/corp/franchise/franchisinghome.html**. [For other franchise opportunities, see **www.franchisedirect.com**]

Partnerships

This section discusses traditional, *general partnerships*. A partnership is two or more persons (*partners*) who carry on a business as co-owners. About 8 percent of all businesses are partnerships, generating 9 percent of all revenue. Only 10 percent of businesses with revenues in excess of $1 million are partnerships. Whereas corporate ownership interests are called stocks or shares, the equity interest of a partner is called a *partnership interest*.

Partnerships are *mutual agencies*. Every partner is an agent of the partnership with capacity to bind the partnership when acting within the scope of partnership's business. Knowledge held by any partner is deemed held by the partnership. As an agent, each partner is entitled to reimbursement for costs personally incurred in furtherance of the partnership's business. Each partner has the right to examine all partnership records and to demand a formal determination by a court of the value of the partner's interest (an *accounting*). Although the law of partnerships originated in the common law, all states except Louisiana have adopted the Uniform Partnership Act (UPA), originally developed by the National Conference of Commissioners on Uniform State Laws (NCCUSL). [For more on the UPA and other uniform acts, see **www.nccusl.org**]

All states except Louisiana have adopted the Uniform Partnership Act (UPA)

Nontax Costs

A partnership is not a separate legal entity. No filing with the state is required to create it. Contract law governs partnership formation. If persons intend to go into business together, and take no steps to establish a different form, they will automatically be a partnership. Thus, it is the default business form for businesses with two or more owners. Mere co-ownership of property, however, does not create a partnership. The co-owners must intend to join in the sharing of risks and rewards.

As we shall see below, the partnership relationship carries potentially grave risks. One would expect the contract which creates and governs the partnership, the *partnership agreement,* to very precisely specify the terms of that relationship. Partnership agreements may be oral or written. The vast majority are oral, which means that if disagreements arise, the partners may find it very difficult to establish conclusively what the original agreement was. This will not be helped by the fact that when important disagreements arise, the partners often discover that their interests have become adverse and that the hopeful emotions shared at the outset have been displaced by anger and a sense of betrayal.

So if the risks are great and the problems associated with a lack of clarity can be substantial, why are partnership agreements often oral and, even if written, frequently vague? The answer relates in part to the fact that to draft a quality partnership agreement, a host of touchy, even unpleasant issues must be concretely addressed. The drafters must ask, "how should the profit-sharing arrangement change if a partner becomes ill or fails to meet expectations?" And, "if the partnership does not work out, how will the relationship be unwound?" Tough questions like these are usually shied away from by the soon-to-be partners who sense that asking them will sour the high spirits in which so many partnerships are born.

> "If the partnership does not work out, how will the relationship be unwound?"

Partnership agreements also tend to be expensive to draft because of the opportunities for customization, because state law provides only a general framework for these entities, and because the personal risks of being a partner are so significant. Similarly, partnership accounting systems are the most expensive of all the business forms because of the need to keep track of extensively customized economic arrangements. However, the partnership form generally requires few or no annual recurring costs for items such as state filings or mandatory meetings of owners.

Centralization of Management

By default, management in a partnership is not centralized. Absent an agreement to the contrary, each partner has an equal right to participate in control, regardless of ownership interest. This can make partnerships unwieldy, particularly as the number of partners grows. In response, some partnerships create a central management structure by adding provisions to their partnership agreements in which the partners yield their management rights to a subset of partners (perhaps only one—a *managing partner*).

Partners owe each other the fiduciary duties of loyalty, confidentiality, sharing information, and exercising due care. The *Veale* case below explores some of these duties.

FACTS

Veal Sr., Beale Jr., Gibson, Parker, and Rose were partners in an accounting firm. The partnership agreement permitted partners to pursue other business interests so long as doing so did not conflict with the partnership practice. Rose performed accounting work for Right Away Foods and Payne, receiving the compensation personally. Rose's partners claimed that he owed them a share in that he had competed with the firm in violation of the partnership agreement. The jury held for Rose. The partners appealed.

Chief Justice Nye

The partnership agreement . . . provided[:]

> Except with the expressed approval of the other partners as to each specific instance, no partner shall perform any public accounting services . . . other than . . . on behalf of this partnership.

Partners . . . occupy a fiduciary relationship . . . which requires . . . the utmost degree of good faith and honesty in dealing with one another. . . .

It is undisputed that while a partner . . . Rose rendered accounting services for Right Away Foods for which he billed and received payment personally. [The] partnership did not share in the proceeds[.] . . . There was some testimony from which the jury could have inferred that the work which Rose did for Right Away Foods . . . was of the type which did not require the services of a CPA. However, Rose . . . admitted that there was no reason why he could not have rendered [those services] as a partner in the accounting firm. . . . [In] regard to services in connection with mergers and acquisitions, [Parker testified] that he was unaware of any [such work that was not] prepared by public accounting firms. The preponderance of all the evidence clearly establishes that Rose . . . performed accounting services for Right Away Foods . . . in competition with the partnership. The [jury] was in error.

[Rose] admitted that he performed accounting services for [Payne] for which he [was paid] personally. There is no question that those services were public accounting services. His later testimony that he performed the services, in effect, after hours, or in addition to his duties to the partnership, is of no value in light of the obligations imposed by the partnership agreement and by the common understanding of the term "competition."

Reversed and remanded.

Questions

1. *a.* Why was Rose's work for Right Away Foods considered a violation of the partnership agreement?

   b. Why did Rose's "after-hours" argument fail?

2. Could Rose operate a gas station, for instance, without violating the partnership agreement?

Limited Liability

A partnership is not a separate legal entity. Thus, it does not offer limited liability to its owners. The partners are personally liable for all of the partnership's obligations should it default. This is clearly the greatest disadvantage of the partnership form.

Partners are *jointly liable* for contract obligations, including loans. All partners must be named in the lawsuit; a verdict against them imposes an equal share of the total liability on each partner. Unfortunately for the more well-to-do partners, the victorious claimant can proceed to collect from any or all of the partners. If one partner is wealthy and liquid, the plaintiff may collect from that partner alone. Then the paying partner must sue the others to recoup, called the *right of contribution*.

Under the doctrine of respondeat superior mentioned previously, partners are *jointly and severally liable* for the torts of the partnership's employees and for the non-intentional torts of the partners. A plaintiff, such as an individual injured by the negligent driving of an employee, need sue only a subset of the partners, typically those easiest to collect from. Once again, this works to the disadvantage of the wealthier partners.

Under some circumstances, partners may be jointly and severally liable for crimes committed by partnership employees, but they ordinarily will not be liable for crimes committed by partners (unless they themselves participate in or authorize the crime).

Free Transferability of Interests

Because partnerships are mutual agencies, involve fiduciary relationships, and do not have limited liability, the law does not allow a partner to transfer a partnership interest to a third person without the unanimous consent of the other partners. However, a partnership interest can be assigned. The *assignment* entitles the *assignee* only to the distribution rights of the assigning partner (*assignor*). The assignee has no right to participate in control and does not have the status of partner.

Duration of Existence

Because partnerships entail mutual agency and fiduciary relationships, a partnership is automatically dissolved upon the death, incapacity, bankruptcy, expulsion or withdrawal of any partner. Thus, events in the private lives of the partners can seriously impact the business venture. The harm from such automatic dissolution can be minimized by placing a provision in the partnership agreement allowing a partnership to be immediately reformed by the remaining partners should such a dissolution occur. The ex-partner's partnership interest will then be valued and paid out.

Taxes

The greatest advantage of the partnership form is the extraordinary range of economic relationships that can be crafted. Whereas a 10 percent shareholder is simply entitled to 10 percent of whatever distributions are made by the corporation, a partnership agreement can detach percentage ownership from the stream of distributions and tax consequences. For example, assume L contributes land to a real estate development partnership, K contributes knowledge as the general contractor, and C contributes the cash necessary to undertake the venture. It would be acceptable to allocate the partnership cash flow as follows: C gets all of the net cash flow until C's initial cash contribution is recouped, then L gets all of the net cash flow until the value of L's contributed land has been distributed, then all three share the remaining net cash flow equally.

Double taxation does not apply to partnerships since they are not separate legal entities. The partnership's income is taxed only once—on the personal tax returns of the partners according to each's share of the partnership's income. On the downside however, partners must pay tax on that income whether or not the partnership actually distributes anything to them.

There are two important negative tax aspect of a partnership. First, fringe benefits provided to partners are not deductible (although fringes provided to employees are). Second, all of a partner's income is subject to self-employment tax (about 13 percent net).

Capital Structure

Because partnerships do not offer limited liability, free transferability of interests, indefinite life or centralized management, they are (with few exceptions) not appropriate for ventures requiring large amounts of capital accessed via the financial markets. The sole source of equity is the partners themselves.

Circumstances Favoring a Specific Business Form

With the development of such business forms as limited liability partnerships (LLPs) and LLCs, discussed below, the partnership form is not likely to be legally required for any business venture. Indeed, under most circumstances the disadvantages of the partnership form are so severe that a person is usually well advised to avoid it. Instead, such hybrid forms as S corporations (also discussed below), LLCs and LLPs will be selected.

Sole Proprietorships

The same characteristics used above to evaluate corporations and partnerships can be applied to *sole proprietorships,* business ventures undertaken by a single individual. A sole proprietorship comes into existence by the mere decision of the proprietor to pursue a venture. Thus, it is the default business form for single owners. This largely explains why more than two-thirds of all businesses are sole proprietorships, although they generate only 5 percent of all business revenue—averaging about $50,000. No legal filings or fees are required to establish the operation, but a business license, sales tax license, and/or other permits may be required by the state, county, and/or city where the business is located. Since there is only one owner, centralization of management automatically exists. Like a partnership, it is not a separate legal entity. Thus, the owner has no limited liability.

A proprietor may dispose of the proprietorship freely, but it will be deemed a transfer of the assets which underlie the business, not a transfer of the "business" in its own right. Further, the lack of a separate legal entity also means that the sole proprietorship ends if the owner becomes incapacitated or dies. Only a custodian or executor could have the power to continue operations, but either would be forced to continuously seek court approval to perform the activities required to operate the business. This impractical arrangement can destroy the business' value in short order.

A sole proprietorship is not a taxable entity. All of its revenues and expenses appear on the personal tax return of the proprietor. Like partnerships, most fringe benefits are not deductible as business expenses and all business income is subject to self-employment tax. The capital structure issues for a sole proprietorship are similar to those of a partnership—without a change in business form, new equity can only come from the sole proprietor.

No business is legally required to operate in proprietorship form.

Hybrid Business Forms

Today, where owners actively select a business form, LLCs and S corporations are the most commonly chosen forms for small business. (Remember that sole proprietorships and partnerships often exist simply because they are the default forms when no express action is taken.)

Limited Liability Companies (LLCs)

Wide displeasure with the lack of a business form that had the favorable characteristics both of partnerships (flexible tax characteristics) and corporations (limited liability) led the Wyoming legislature to create the *limited liability company* in 1977. By 1997 LLCs were available nationally—the fastest-growing business form in the United States Although a uniform act for LLCs has been established by the NCCUSL, only nine states have adopted it. Thus, there is considerable variation with regard to governing provisions from state to state.

To create an LLC, the owners (as few as one), called *members,* file *articles of organization* with the state. Their equity is called *members' interests.* An *operating agreement* will be drafted which sets forth information similar to that often found in corporate bylaws. Minor annual filings and fees will be required.

The management structure of LLCs is extremely flexible: the operating agreement generally specifies whether it will be centrally managed by managers (often one or two of the members) or member-managed (similar to a partnership). Similarly, an LLC elects on its creation whether to be taxed like a corporation or like a partnership.

LLCs are hybrids because, with regard to limited liability of the owners and the duration of existence, they most closely resemble corporations but, with regard to transferability of ownership interests and access to equity capital, they most closely resemble partnerships. In many states it is still an open question whether the limited liability of LLC members can be "pierced" as is possible with corporate shareholders. Minnesota's LLC statute expressly provides for piercing the veil of LLCs.[7] In 2002, the Wyoming Supreme Court held, "We can discern no reason, in either law or policy, to treat LLCs differently than we treat corporations. If the members and officers of an LLC fail to treat it as a separate entity . . . , they should not enjoy immunity from individual liability for the LLC's acts that cause damage to third parties."[8]

Venture capitalists and franchisors are often quite comfortable with an LLC as the business form of choice for their ventures.

S Corporations

Many would argue that the principal disadvantage of the corporate form is double taxation. In response, in 1958 Congress amended the Internal Revenue Code to establish a separate tax status for some corporations, now known as *S corporations.* An S corporation's income is taxed once—to the shareholders on their personal returns—much like partnerships. Like partnerships, S corporations may not deduct the cost of most fringe benefits provided to its owners. Unlike partnerships, however, to the extent the S corporation's income is distributed as dividends, no self-employment tax is imposed. However, the Internal Revenue Service routinely challenges attempts to distribute an excessive amount as dividends where inadequate wages have been paid to the owners.

To confine "S" status to smaller companies, significant restrictions on eligibility have been established. No more than 100 individuals and certain estates and trusts can be shareholders. Interestingly, an entire family is treated as "one" individual for these purposes. Only one class of stock is permitted. Despite these restrictions, one can find S corporations with multi-billion-dollar revenues. S corporations are popular. They represent about 55 percent of all corporations, but tend to be much smaller, generating only about 17 percent of all corporate revenue.

The "S" status is relevant only for federal (and some state) tax purposes. In all other respects, the characteristics of S corporations are like all other corporations.

Other Hybrid Forms

Limited Liability Partnerships (LLPs) At the same time LLCs were being conceived, the great multinational accounting firms were reeling from an episode in which the quality of their audits proved less than advertised—the savings and loan collapse of the 1980s. Over $1.6 billion in settlements (a staggering sum for that era) was paid out and these firms feared extinction if professional liability damages could not be brought under control. Efforts to obtain tort reform that would limit such liability failed, so a new approach was sought—the *limited liability partnership* (LLP). LLPs terminate unlimited liability for malpractice. The partner committing the tort is still personally liable, but non-tortious partners are not.

To bring an LLP into existence, a document often called *application for registration* is filed. Minor annual filings and fees are required. LLPs (and their partners) are taxed like a general partnership and in all other characteristics most closely resemble partnerships. Not all states have legislation enabling the creation of LLPs and those that do generally limit their application to professional service partnerships, such as accountants, lawyers and doctors.

Limited Partnerships   The first hybrid business form in the United States was the *limited partnership*. Partnerships have advantages: great flexibility and no double taxation. Corporations have limited liability, indefinite life, freely transferable interests and centralized management. The desire to create a business form with all of these advantages led to the limited partnership, which has two classes of partners: general and limited.

General partners are identical to the partners discussed earlier. They (often only one) make the decisions. The principal disadvantage of status as a general partner is unlimited liability. In practice, most general partners are corporations with minimal capital investment, so unlimited liability is little threat unless grounds for piercing the corporate veil exist. *Limited partners* contribute capital but do not participate in control (except to a limited extent analogous to shareholders). In exchange for limited control, they receive limited liability.

Forty-nine states have adopted either the 1976 Uniform Limited Partnership Act or its 2001 revision. Limited partnerships come into existence only upon filing a *certificate of limited partnership*. Minor annual filings and fees are required. The law of limited partnerships provides that those events which would terminate a general partnership have minimal impact on the limited partnership's existence. The income of the general partner is subject to self-employment tax; the income of the limited partners generally is not. Limited partnerships were extremely popular until the advent of limited liability companies.

International Hybrids

Dozens of other business forms exist throughout the world. For the most part, these forms are intended to achieve various combinations of the characteristics just discussed. Using these criteria, managers operating in a multinational environment should be prepared to evaluate form of business decisions under a variety of regimes.

Questions—Part One

1. Why are corporations the dominant form of business in the United States?
2. *a.* Why are sole proprietorships problematic if a proprietor dies or is disabled?

   b. Do partnerships experience similar problems? Explain.
3. *a.* What characteristics of an LLC cause it to be the fastest growing business form in the United States?

   b. What are its advantages over a corporation?

Part Two: Regulation of the Securities Markets

Introduction

To amass the capital needed to pursue global business opportunities, a large number of investors must be convinced to entrust their wealth to third parties. History shows that this trust has often been misplaced, with vast sums lost in companies with incompetent or corrupt management. As a result, the federal government has undertaken to promote the reliability of the U.S. capital markets through regulation.

Vast sums lost in companies with incompetent or corrupt management

In the past decade, two successive and widespread failures have shaken these capital markets. Although not starting with Enron, the first of these crises became undeniable with Enron's bankruptcy filing on December 2, 2001. The cumulative effect of all of the discovered corporate failures devastated the stock market. As of Monday, July 22, 2002, 100 percent of the profits earned by mutual funds in the United States since the beginning of the bull market in October 1990 had been lost. By the following Friday, losses reached $8 trillion. (This 48 percent drop was the largest since the Great Depression.[9]) About $4 trillion was volatile "paper" wealth, earned rather recently; but the remaining $4 trillion was "hard-earned" wealth. Although by the end of 2006 much of the decline had been recovered, for employees whose retirement funding was principally in the form of stock in employers which collapsed, such as Enron and Global Crossing, nearly all of their retirement security was lost, along with their jobs.

Financial Crisis   At this writing, U.S. securities markets are reacting uncertainly to a growing crisis in the financial markets. The troubles have already resulted in hundreds of billions of dollars of losses in the financial services industry (as evidenced by Citi-Group's one-quarter write-off of $18 billion[10]), with projected losses ultimately in excess of $1 trillion. Even the most creditworthy confront the availability of less credit at higher interest rates and with greater collateral requirements.[11] The problem seems to have grown out of the confluence of a number of factors: with the aforementioned stock market collapse, a substantial increase in investment dollars flooded the U.S. housing market, fueling a nearly unprecedented rise in housing prices. This investment was facilitated by the development of innovative financial products which, among other things, bundled portfolios of home mortgage loans into securitized debt obligations, shares of which could then be broadly marketed to investment funds and foreign investors, among others.

These complex arrangements, and many of the investment funds purchasing them, operated in an almost entirely unregulated environment, distributing obligations and risks globally through the use of off-balance-sheet vehicles that have made it all but impossible for market participants to assess the true risk of default. Exacerbating the problem was the use of extremely high debt-to-equity ratios (30-to-1 and higher) by such investors as unregulated hedge funds and private equity funds. The same leverage that can generate tremendous returns in trouble-free times is equally capable of magnifying losses to

> The housing bubble burst

disastrous levels when markets turn down. When the housing bubble burst, in part from rising default rates on subprime mortgages, losses quickly extinguished the equity position of highly leveraged holders and their creditors began requiring the holders to pay down the debt used to finance their investments. Some were unable to do so, such as one of the hedge funds associated with the Carlyle Group, Carlyle Capital Corp.[12] The ability of others, such as Bear Stearns, to perform was believed to be at risk, causing their own investors to withdraw their funds, in turn increasing the risk of an actual collapse.[13]

Concerned about the prospect of a widespread freeze in U.S. credit markets, the Federal Reserve Bank took aggressive and unprecedented action by backing the buyout of Bear Sterns (an unregulated private equity firm) by the Wall Street firm, J.P. Morgan; by opening its "discount window" (an emergency loan program) to investment banks; and by dropping the already low federal-funds rate. The action of the Federal Reserve in stepping in with support previously understood only to be available to regulated entities has, in turn, kicked off a heated debate on increasing regulation of the mortgage industry and the credit markets.[14] At the same time, it is unclear whether these actions will be sufficient to head off more trouble in the face of anticipated further losses on home equity and residential construction loans, credit cards, car loans and the like, as well as fears of a major recession and the possibility of a continuing devalued U.S. dollar.

Thus, both of these systemic events (the corporate failures like Enron, and the current credit market troubles) have generated considerable debate about the appropriate level of government regulation. Following the collapse of Enron and Global Crossing, Congress responded by passing SOX which, among other things, increased the regulation of corporate management and the accounting profession. A closer look at SOX, its critics and supporters, appears in Part Three. New and stronger regulation of major financial market participants may or may not result from the current market challenges.

Now we turn to an examination of how the securities markets are regulated.

Initial Public Offerings

When a corporation wants to sell a new *security* on the open market (debt or equity), it undertakes an *initial public offering* (IPO). If a corporation (*issuer*) and any of the persons to whom the security is offered for sale (*offerees*) are domiciled in different states (*interstate offering*), federal law governs the IPO. Should the corporation and all offerees be domiciled in the same state (*intrastate offering*), state law (considered later) applies.

The term *security* embraces both the instruments commonly understood to be such, like stocks and bonds, and a much broader class of interests called *investment contracts*. The *Howey* case that follows defines the term.

FACTS

[Howey] owns large tracts of citrus acreage in . . . Florida. Each prospective customer is offered both a land sales contract and a service contract [by which Howey maintains the groves and markets the produce.] Purchases are . . . narrow strips . . . arranged so that an acre consists of a row of 48 trees. . . . These tracts are not separately fenced[. The] purchaser has no right of entry [and] no right to specific fruit. . . . All the produce is pooled[.] The purchasers [are mostly] non residents of Florida[,] predominantly . . . professional people who lack the knowledge . . . and equipment necessary for the [citrus business]. They are attracted by the expectation of substantial profits. . . .

It is admitted that the mails and instrumentalities of interstate commerce are used in the sale of the land and service contracts and that no registration statement . . . has ever been filed with the Commission[.]

Justice Murphy

[T]he Act defines . . . "security" to include the commonly known [instruments like stocks and bonds. It also includes the term] "investment contract"[.] The legal issue [is whether] the land sales contract . . . and the service contract together constitute an "investment contract"[.] An affirmative answer brings into operation the registration requirements[.]

"[I]nvestment contract" is undefined by the [Act, b]ut the term was common in many state "blue sky" laws in existence prior to the adoption of the federal statute[. An] investment contract . . . means a . . . scheme whereby a person invests his money in a common enterprise and is led to expect profits solely from the efforts of . . . a third party[.]

[These] transactions clearly involve investment contracts[.] The respondent [is] offering an opportunity to contribute money and to share in the profits of a large citrus fruit enterprise managed . . . by respondent[. It is] offering this opportunity to persons who reside in distant localities and who lack the [wherewithal to deal with] citrus products. . . .

[Respondent's] failure to [register the securities] cannot be sanctioned under the Act.

Questions

1. Would an investment in Microsoft stock satisfy the definition of "investment contract"?
2. Why do you think Congress added the term "investment contract" to the definition of "security"?

1933 Act

The federal law governing IPOs is the *Securities Act of 1933* (1933 Act), which is administered by the *Securities and Exchange Commission* (SEC). The 1933 Act does not guarantee the economic merits of any investment opportunity. Rather, it seeks: (1) to ensure full disclosure of all material facts about the investment opportunity to offerees (potential investors) before they invest, and (2) to eliminate fraudulent conduct in the markets. Thus, an IPO that passes muster under the federal securities law has not been approved by the government as a good investment. [For more on the SEC, see **www.sec.gov**]

To promote full disclosure, the 1933 Act forbids any interstate offering of a new security until a *registration statement* has been filed with and approved by the SEC. The registration statement has two parts: the prospectus and the supplemental information (discussed shortly). The *prospectus* is the major component and is delivered to offerees to satisfy the requirement for preinvestment disclosure. There are three main sections in a prospectus. One contains general information about the company: the industry(ies) in which it operates, the quality of its products and services and of its management, its business plan, and so on. Another section contains a risk assessment of the business model, local operating conditions (such as political instability), and the like.

The third portion of the prospectus is the *audited financial statements*. An investor's goal is to make money. Investors want to know how well the corporation under consideration has accomplished this in the past so they can estimate its future economic potential. A corporation's ability to make a profit is shown on its *income statement,* one of the three audited financial statements.

Because the income statement seeks to measure economic income, it employs accrual accounting, which disregards cash flows in measuring revenues and expenses. Thus, a *statement of cash flows* is also presented.

The third financial statement, the *balance sheet,* shows the company's assets, liabilities and equities. Although balance sheets have numerous deficiencies (such as the use of historical cost rather than current value to measure assets), they attempt to describe the corporation's financial position as of a particular date.

Technically, the financial statements are prepared by the corporation's management. To give comfort to investors that management has prepared these statements properly and honestly, independent *certified public accountants* (CPAs) are engaged to audit them. Audits must be performed in accordance with *generally accepted auditing standards* (GAAS). GAAS are intended to ensure that the procedures used to investigate the financial statements are thorough. The objective of the investigation is to determine whether the financial statements are *not materially misleading,* in accordance with *generally accepted accounting principles* (GAAP). GAAP provides the rules for how revenues, expenses, assets, liabilities, and equity are measured and disclosed. One might paraphrase an audit: independent experts (CPAs) are supposed to "look hard" (GAAS) and decide whether the financial statements accurately measure the income, cash flow and financial position of the corporation (GAAP).

The *supplemental information* portion (the second part) of the registration statement, which is not distributed to offerees, describes such matters as how much it is costing to "float" the IPO and what major contracts exist with unions, suppliers, or customers.

The SEC vigorously enforces the 1933 Act's prescribed relationship between solicitation or sales of a security and the registration process. There are three critical stages. During the *prefiling period* (before the registration statement has been filed with the SEC), no solicitation or sales are permitted. During the *waiting period* (after the registration statement has been filed, but before it has been approved by the SEC), no sales are permitted but a limited amount of solicitation is allowed. Specifically, a *tombstone ad* (so called because of its shape) may be published in forums like *The Wall Street Journal* to make the market aware of the upcoming issuance. In addition, a *"red herring"* prospectus (name taken from the prominent red ink cautionary statement required on its first page) may be distributed. This is the draft prospectus included with the filed registration statement. Once the SEC approves the registration statement, the *posteffective period* begins. Solicitations are permitted and sales may be made, but only if the offerees have first received the final prospectus.

Some companies do *shelf registrations* which allow them to issue securities in portions over a two-year period under a single registration statement. This allows issuers to float the securities when market conditions are most favorable, without having to place the entire issue shortly after the registration statement becomes effective.

Typically not wanting to sell the securities themselves, issuers employ one of two kinds of *underwriters.* A *best-efforts underwriter* acts as the issuer's sales agent, never taking title to the securities and earning its profit from sales commissions. A *firm-commitment underwriter* purchases the securities at a discount, intending to profit by reselling them. Institutional investors and *dealers* typically purchase IPOs—the former for investment, the latter for resale to retail investors.

PRACTICING ETHICS IPO Sales to Corporate Executives in Exchange for . . . ?

Common practice among securities firms underwriting an IPO had been to allocate some IPO shares to the personal accounts of executives of the corporations with which the firm did business. This practice was known as "spinning" because IPO shares frequently increased considerably in value on their first trading day, so the corporate executive could quickly sell, or "spin," the received shares to make an immediate, and substantial, profit. The SEC outlawed the practice in 2003. A New York state judge, in holding the action to be fraudulent, referred to spinning as "a sophisticated form of bribery."

Questions

1. Is it ethically wrong for an executive to accept IPO stock in his personal name from a company with which his corporation does business?

2. Does it matter if the securities firm is not currently seeking new work from the executive's corporation? Explain.

Sources: Michael Siconolfi, "A Major Perk for Executives Takes a Big Hit," *The Wall Street Journal,* February 2, 2006, p. C1.

Exemptions

Exempt securities and *exempt transactions* do not require registration with the SEC. The most common exempt securities are those issued by governments, charities, educational institutions, and financial institutions like banks and insurance companies.

Certain transactions are also exempt from the full registration requirement. Five categories of exempt transactions were created in part as an accommodation to small issuers to lessen the financial burdens of raising capital. All intrastate offerings are exempt transactions. When creditors in a nonliquidation corporate bankruptcy exchange their debt for a new class of stock, the transaction is exempt. Corporate mergers require an exchange of securities, which are exempt transactions. Depending on the exemption, the presale disclosures and filings with the SEC range from none to something slightly less than a full registration statement. Most exemptions do not permit general advertising or solicitation.

Note that even when exemptions apply to registration under the 1933 Act, the Act's sweeping antifraud provisions, discussed later, still apply.

The Secondary Securities Markets

Once a security is issued, it can be sold repeatedly. Such sales may be accomplished on a *physical exchange,* such as the New York Stock Exchange (NYSE), where agents of buyers and sellers deal directly with each other. Others may be made on an *over-the-counter market*, where trades occur electronically over a computer network linking dealers across the nation. An example is NASDAQ, the National Association of Securities Dealers Automatic Quotation system. [For more on these exchanges, see **www.nyse.com** and **www.nasdaq.com**]

The federal law that governs these trades is the *Securities Exchange Act of 1934* (1934 Act), which also created the SEC. Its purposes are the same as those of its 1933 counterpart: to ensure full disclosure of all material information so the market can make informed investment decisions and to prevent fraudulent conduct in the markets. A company's securities are subject to the 1934 Act's registration requirements if (1) it is engaged in (or its securities are traded in) interstate commerce, and (2) it has both more than $10 million in assets and more than 500 shareholders.[15]

To promote full disclosure, the SEC requires registered corporations to file a variety of reports. Annually, each must file a *Form 10-K,* which includes information very similar to that found in an IPO registration statement, including audited financial statements. To increase the timeliness of information disclosures, the SEC requires additional reports, such as the quarterly *Form 10-Q,* which contains year-to-date information and unaudited interim financial statements. The SEC also requires corporations to file a *Form 8-K* whenever a material event occurs, such as change in control, major asset acquisitions and dispositions, bankruptcy, change in auditor and resignations of directors.[16] [To retrieve filings for specific corporations, see **www.tenkwizard.com**]

Under the 1934 Act, the SEC has the power to *suspend trading* in any security "when it serves the public interest and will protect investors." Thus, the SEC may suspend trading if it suspects price manipulation or asset misappropriation.[17] Typically, the market price of a security is devastated by a suspension, which provides a strong incentive for corporations to avoid misconduct. [For more on securities law, see **www.findlaw.com/01topics/34securities/index.html**]

Brokers and Online Trading

When an individual wants to buy or sell securities listed on an exchange, they will do so through an intermediary—a broker. Occasionally, brokers have faced charges of *churning*—repeatedly and unnecessarily engaging in trades to generate commissions. In one case, an 80-year-old woman with Alzheimer's disease entrusted $500,000 to a broker in December 1999. By February 2001, the account was worth $15,000. The broker had engaged in over 300 trades and charged the account $94,000 in fees, purchasing only high-tech stocks (versus a balanced, conservative portfolio). In addition, the broker secured a $422,000 margin loan with the account to buy more such stocks, further decimating the account when the high-tech bubble burst.[18]

> *Churning*—repeatedly and unnecessarily engaging in trades to generate commissions

One effect of widely available technology, particularly the Internet, is the disintermediation (bypassing) of full-service securities brokers through *online trading*. Whereas full-service brokers charge more and may sometimes be available only during limited hours, they typically both provide advisory services and assess the *suitability* of investments for a particular investor (that is, they take into account the investor's needs, financial situation, investment objectives, and risk tolerance). Online brokers are less expensive and have greater availability, but tend to leave investors mostly on their own.

Online trading represents about 25 percent of the total retail trades in the United States. Concerns have been expressed about the excessive use of margin trading and the extent to which many online traders are actually capable of evaluating investment opportunities. [For some advice from the SEC for trading online, see **http://www.sec.gov/ investor/pubs/onlinetips.htm**]

Matters get worse when it comes to *day trading*. Day traders rarely hold any security more than a few hours, earning profits by exploiting volatility, not inherent value. Only about 10 percent of day traders are successful.[19] The SEC has expressed great concern about advertising that suggests day trading is easy and certain to be profitable. It cautions that tips and analyses are frequently false.[20] Nonetheless, the market is moving inexorably toward global, 24-hour-a-day, electronic trading.

Violating Federal Securities Laws

The consequences for noncompliance with the securities laws are potentially staggering, including damages and civil and criminal penalties. Some of the most commonly violated provisions are discussed below.

False or Misleading Statements in Required Filings—1933 Act

Perhaps the greatest deterrent to misconduct in the securities laws is the civil liability that can be imposed upon wrongdoers by harmed investors. The 1933 Act's §11 establishes this liability with respect to false or misleading registration statements related to IPOs.

Virtually anyone with a significant role in preparing the registration statement can be sued (the issuer, its directors, its underwriters, and its accountants and other experts). The liability can be vast—essentially all damages sustained by investors while the misleading registration statements were outstanding. No proof of plaintiff reliance on the content of the registration statement is required. Accounting firms and investment bankers, because of their "deep pockets," are often at the top of the list of defendants. Accounting firms have paid hundreds of millions to settle securities fraud suits.

The principal defense against a §11 claim is *due diligence*. Every defendant, other than the issuer, can raise this defense. The defendant must show that, based on a reasonable investigation, he or she reasonably believed that the registration statement was not misleading. What constitutes "reasonable" is determined by reference to the conduct expected of a prudent person in the management of his or her own property.

The due diligence standard for experts (like accountants and lawyers) is much higher. Their inquiries must rise to the standards expected of professionals, not merely of prudent businesspersons. Thus, at an absolute minimum, an accounting firm which has audited the financial statements included in the registration statement must design its audit process to comport with GAAS and must evaluate the financial statement content in accordance with GAAP. Lawyers, actuaries, appraisers and other experts whose work has a material impact on the registration statement must adhere to analogous rules established by their professional associations and regulators. The *BarChris* case, below, explores the due diligence defense.

Escott v. BarChris Construction Corporation 283 F. Supp. 643 (S.D.N.Y. 1968)

FACTS

Bowling as a leisure activity and sport grew rapidly in the 1950s. BarChris built alleys. Its revenues grew from $800,000 in 1956 to $9,165,000 in 1960. By 1962 overbuilding caused construction to halt. BarChris ran into serious financial problems. It filed a registration statement (effective May 1961) for a bond IPO to raise cash and the bonds were issued. Circumstances were grave when the registration statement became effective. BarChris filed for bankruptcy in October 1962.

BarChris's financial statements dated December 31, 1960, were included in the prospectus. They were audited by Peat, Marwick (predecessor to KPMG) and contained material errors. Revenues and current assets were overstated and contingent liabilities were understated.

The prospectus overstated the demand for alley construction. It misrepresented how the IPO proceeds would be used (a large portion would actually go to pay overdue debts and retire loans from officers). It failed to note that because of defaults, BarChris was now operating several alleys. Escott and other bondholders sued under §11 of the 1933 Act, alleging the prospectus was materially misleading. All defendants but BarChris raised the due diligence defense.

Judge Mclean

THE "DUE DILIGENCE" DEFENSES . . .

Russo

Russo was [executive vice president and] chief executive officer[.] He was familiar with all aspects of the business. [He] knew all the relevant facts. He could not have believed that there were no untrue statements or material omissions in the prospectus. Russo has no due diligence defenses.

Vitolo and Pugliese

They were the founders[.] Despite their titles [president and vice president], their [control] over BarChris's affairs [was far less] than Russo's. [They are] men of limited education. It is not hard to believe that for them the prospectus was difficult reading, if indeed they read it at all. But [the] liability of a director who signs a registration statement does not depend upon whether or not he read it or, if he did, whether or not he understood what he was reading.

[I]n any case, [they] were not as naive as they claim[.] They were members of [the] executive committee [and] must have known what was going on. [T]hey knew of the inadequacy of cash[.] They knew of their own large advances to the company[.] They knew . . . that part of the [bond] proceeds were to be used to pay their own loans. All in all, [their situation] is not significantly different . . . from Russo's. They could not have believed that the registration statement was wholly true[.] They have not proved their due diligence defenses.

Trilling

[Trilling was . . . a CPA and former member of Peat, Marwick. He was BarChris'] controller. He signed the registration statement in that capacity, although he was not a director. [He was a] minor figure in BarChris. . . .

Trilling may well have been unaware of several of the inaccuracies in the prospectus. But he must have known of some of them. [I cannot hold] that Trilling believed the entire prospectus to be true. But even if he did, he still did not establish his due diligence defenses. He . . . failed to prove, as to the [nonaudited] parts of the prospectus[,] that he made a reasonable investigation which afforded him a reasonable ground to believe that [they were true. H]e made no investigation. . . . This would have been well enough but for the fact that he signed the registration statement. As a signer, he could not avoid responsibility[. He has not proved] his due diligence defenses.

Birnbaum

Birnbaum was a young lawyer [employed as in-house counsel. He was] secretary and a director[.] He signed the [registration statement], thereby becoming responsible for the accuracy of the prospectus[.] He did not participate in the [company's] management[. H]e attended to legal matters of a routine nature. [One of his] more important duties . . . was to keep the corporate minutes[.] This necessarily informed him to a considerable extent about the company's affairs. . . .

It seems probable that Birnbaum did not know of many of the inaccuracies in the prospectus. He must, however, have appreciated some of them. In any case, he made no investigation[. He] was entitled to rely upon Peat, Marwick for the 1960 figures[.] But he was not entitled to rely upon [anyone else] for the other portions of the prospectus. As a lawyer, he should have known his obligations[.] Having failed to make [an] investigation, he did not have reasonable ground to believe that all these statements were true. Birnbaum has not established his due diligence defenses except as to the audited 1960 figures.

Auslander

Auslander . . . was chairman . . . of Valley Stream National Bank[. He became a director shortly before the IPO. He signed the registration statement.]

As to the [financial statements], Auslander knew that Peat, Marwick had audited [them, so he] believed them to be correct[.] As to the [non-audited portions of the prospectus], however, . . . [he] made no investigation of the accuracy[.] He relied on the assurance of Vitolo and Russo[.]

It is true that Auslander became a director on the eve of the financing. He had little opportunity to familiarize himself with the company's affairs. [But S]ection 11 imposes liability . . . upon a director, no matter how new he is. . . . He can escape liability only by using that reasonable care to investigate the facts which a prudent man would employ in the management of his own property. [A] prudent man would not act in an important matter . . . in sole reliance upon representations of persons who are comparative strangers[.] To say that such minimal conduct [suffices would absolve all] new directors from responsibility[.] This is not a sensible construction of Section 11[. A]uslander has not established his due diligence defense [except as to the financial statements.]

Grant

[Grant's] law firm was counsel to BarChris[. He] drafted the registration statement[.] As the director most directly concerned with writing [it] and assuring its accuracy, more was required of him in the way of reasonable investigation than could fairly be expected of a director who had no connection with this work. . . .

I find that Grant honestly believed that the registration statement was true and [complete]. In this belief he was mistaken, and the fact is that for all his work, he never discovered any of the errors or omissions which . . . could have been detected[.] The question is whether, despite his failure to detect them, Grant made a reasonable effort to that end. [BarChris's] affairs had changed for the worse[.] Grant never discovered this. He accepted the assurances of [others] that any change . . . had been for the better[.]

It is claimed that a lawyer is entitled to rely on [his client's statements.] This is too broad[.] To require an audit would . . . be unreasonable. [T]o require a check of matters easily verifiable is not[.] Even honest clients can make mistakes. The statute imposes liability for untrue statements regardless of whether they are intentionally untrue. [H]e never asked to see the contracts[.] He did not read [all of] the minutes. . . . He knew that BarChris was short of cash, but he had no idea how short . . .

Grant was entitled to rely on Peat Marwick for the 1960 figures. [But as to the rest of the prospectus,] Grant was obliged to make a reasonable investigation. [H]e did not make one. . . . Grant has not established his due diligence defenses except as to the audited 1960 figures.

The Underwriters and Coleman

The underwriters other than Drexel made no investigation of the accuracy of the prospectus. . . . They all relied upon Drexel as the "lead" underwriter. Drexel did make an investigation [through firm member] Coleman[.] Drexel's attorneys[, led by Ballard, did the work; Ballard was] assisted by Stanton.

[C]oleman became a director[.] He signed [the] registration statement[.] He thereby assumed a responsibility as a director and signer in addition to his responsibility as an underwriter.

[Coleman] familiarized himself with general conditions in the industry[, which appeared favorable. He read the] annual reports[.] He inquired about BarChris of certain of its banks[.]

[Early underwriting discussions] were extensive[.] Coleman and Ballard asked pertinent questions and received answers which satisfied them. [However, after] Coleman was elected a director on April 17, 1961, he made no further independent investigation[.] He assumed that Ballard was taking care of this[.]

[B]allard instructed Stanton to examine BarChris's minutes [and] to look at "the major contracts[." Stanton read some minutes.] He did not examine the contracts with customers. [He] examined no accounting records[.] His visit . . . lasted one day[. He] relied on the information which he got from [others. No] effectual attempt at verification was made. [Is] it sufficient to ask questions, to obtain answers which, if true, would be thought satisfactory, and to let it go at that, without seeking to ascertain from the records whether the answers in fact are true and complete? . . . [T]he Securities Act makes no . . . distinction. The underwriters are just as responsible as the company if the prospectus is false. [P]rospective investors rely upon the reputation of the underwriters[.]

The purpose of Section 11 is to protect investors. To that end the underwriters are made responsible for the truth of the prospectus. [They] must make some reasonable attempt to verify the data submitted to them. . . .

. . . Drexel is bound by [this] failure. . . . The other underwriters, who did nothing and relied solely on Drexel[,] are also bound by it. . . . The same [applies] to Coleman [as director] . . .

Peat, Marwick . . .

The part of the registration statement . . . made upon the authority of Peat, Marwick as an expert was . . . the 1960 [audited financial statements]. But because the statute requires the court to determine Peat, Marwick's belief, and the grounds thereof, "at the time . . . the registration statement became effective," the matter must be viewed as of May 16, 1961. . . .

The 1960 Audit

[The audit] was in general charge of [partner], Cummings[.] Most of the actual work was performed by . . . Berardi[, who was about thirty.]. He was not yet a C.P.A. He had no previous experience with the bowling industry. This was his first job as a senior accountant. . . .

Capitol Lanes

First and foremost is Berardi's failure to discover that Capitol Lanes had not been sold.... Berardi did become aware [of references] in BarChris's records to ... Capitol Lanes. [He read minutes] which recited that: "the Corporation [would] operate Capitol Lanes[.]" Berardi knew ... that Capitol Lanes ... was paying rentals [and insurance, including insurance on "contents." The foregoing] should have alerted him ... that an alley existed....

The S-1 Review

The purpose of reviewing events subsequent to the date of a certified balance sheet [an S-1 review] is to ascertain whether any material change has occurred ... which should be disclosed ... to prevent the ... figures from being misleading. The scope of such a review [is not] a complete audit. Peat, Marwick prepared a written program [which] conformed to generally accepted auditing standards....

Berardi made the S-1 review in May 1961. He devoted ... 20 1/2 hours. He did not discover any of the errors or omissions[.] The question is whether, despite his failure to find out anything, his investigation was reasonable[.]

What Berardi did was [examine a] trial balance as of March 31, 1961[,] compare it with the audited December 31, 1960 figures, discuss with Trilling certain unfavorable developments[,] and read certain minutes. He did not examine any [other] "important financial records"[.] He asked questions, he got answers which he considered satisfactory, and he did

nothing to verify them. [He] had no conception of how tight the cash position was. [He] never read the prospectus....

There had been a material change for the worse in BarChris's financial position. That change was sufficiently serious so that the failure to disclose it made the 1960 figures misleading. Berardi did not discover it. As far as results were concerned, his S-1 review was useless.

Accountants should not be held to a standard higher than that recognized in their profession.... Berardi's review did not come up to that standard. He did not take some of the steps [the] written program prescribed. He did not spend an adequate amount of time on a task of this magnitude. Most important of all, he was too easily satisfied with glib answers to his inquiries. [T]here were enough danger signals in the materials which he did examine to require some further investigation on his part. [T]he burden of proof is on Peat, Marwick. [It] has not established its due diligence defense.

Questions

1. *a.* Why were so many defendants not held responsible for the misleading audited financial statements?
   b. Which defendants were not successful in claiming the due diligence defense with respect to these financial statements? Why were they denied the defense?
2. Does being "new" make any difference in terms of directoral liability for a signed registration statement?
3. What would you do differently in the future if you were Peat, Marwick?

False or Misleading Statements in Required Filings—1934 Act

§18 of the 1934 Act, relating to false or misleading statements in any filing required to maintain the registration of a security, is similar to the 1933 Act's §11. However, the only defense offered by §18 is that the defendant acted in good faith, without knowledge of the false or misleading nature of the statement. Further, unlike the 1933 Act's §11 where reliance by the plaintiff on the false or misleading statements is presumed, under the 1934 Act's §18 the plaintiff must prove that he or she relied on the statements.

Fraud

Under the 1933 Act's §17(a) and the 1934 Act's §10(b) and its related Rule 10b-5, it is illegal, in connection with the sale or purchase of any security, to employ any scheme or to engage in any practice that defrauds another person participating in the financial markets. This includes making misleading statements of material facts and failing to state material facts.

The antifraud provisions intentionally cast a "broad net" and provide a powerful basis for damage suits by harmed investors. Because bringing forward direct evidence of reliance on fraudulent statements can be difficult, the *fraud-on-the-market* theory has evolved. It is the subject of the *Basic, Inc.* case below.

Basic Inc. v. Levinson et al.

485 U.S. 224 (1988)

FACTS

Prior to December 20, 1978, Basic Inc[.] was a publicly traded company primarily engaged in the business of manufacturing chemical refractories for the steel industry. As early as 1965 or 1966, Combustion Engineering, Inc., a company producing mostly alumina-based refractories, expressed some interest in acquiring Basic, but was deterred from pursuing this inclination seriously because of antitrust concerns. Beginning in . . . 1976, Combustion . . . had meetings . . . with Basic . . . concerning the possibility of a merger. During 1977 and 1978, Basic made three public statements denying . . . merger negotiations. . . . On December 19, [1978,] Basic's board endorsed [the merger].

Respondents are former Basic shareholders who sold their stock after Basic's first public [denial], and before the . . . December 1978 [announcement. They assert] that the defendants issued three false or misleading public statements . . . in violation of § 10(b) of the 1934 Act and of Rule 10b-5 [and] that they were injured by selling Basic shares at artificially depressed prices in a market affected by petitioners' misleading statements and in reliance thereon.

Justice Blackmun

[Rule 10b-5 provides: "It shall be unlawful [t]o make any untrue statement of a material fact or to omit to state a material fact necessary . . . to make the statements made . . . not misleading. . . . in connection with the purchase or sale of any security."]

* * * * *

. . . [T]o fulfill the materiality requirement "there must be a substantial likelihood that the disclosure of the omitted fact would have been viewed by the reasonable investor as having significantly altered the 'total mix' of information made available." . . .

* * * * *

We turn to the question of reliance and the fraud-on-the-market theory. Succinctly put:

> The fraud on the market theory is based on the hypothesis that, in an open and developed securities market, the price of a company's stock is determined by the available material information regarding the company and its business. . . . Misleading statements will therefore defraud purchasers . . . even if [they] do not directly rely on the misstatements. . . . The causal connection between the defendants' fraud and the plaintiffs' purchase . . . is no less significant than in a case of direct reliance on misrepresentations.

* * * * *

. . . Requiring proof of individualized reliance from each member of the proposed plaintiff class . . . would have prevented . . . a class action, since individual issues . . . would have overwhelmed the common ones. The District Court found that the presumption of reliance created by the fraud-on-the-market theory provided "a practical resolution to the problem of balancing the [need for] proof of reliance [against] the procedural [obstacles]."

. . . Reliance provides the requisite causal connection between a defendant's misrepresentation and a plaintiff's injury. There is, however, more than one way to demonstrate the causal connection. . . .

The modern securities markets, literally involving millions of shares changing hands daily, differ from the face-to-face transactions contemplated by early fraud cases, and our understanding of Rule 10b-5's reliance requirement must encompass these differences.

". . . With the presence of a market, the market is interposed between seller and buyer and, ideally, transmits information to the investor in the processed form of a market price. Thus the market is performing a substantial part of the valuation process performed by the investor in a face-to-face transaction. The market is acting as the unpaid agent of the investor, informing him that given all the information available to it, the value of the stock is worth the market price."

Presumptions typically serve to assist courts in managing circumstances in which direct proof, for one reason or another, is rendered difficult. The courts below accepted a presumption, created by the fraud-on-the-market theory and subject to rebuttal by petitioners, that persons who had traded Basic shares had done so in reliance on the integrity of the price set by the market, but because of petitioners' material misrepresentations that price had been fraudulently depressed. Requiring a plaintiff to show . . . how he would have acted if omitted material information had been disclosed . . . or if the misrepresentation had not been made, . . . would place an unnecessarily unrealistic evidentiary burden on the Rule 10b-5 plaintiff who has traded on an impersonal market.

. . . The presumption of reliance employed in this case is consistent with . . . congressional policy[.] In drafting [the 1934] Act, Congress expressly relied on the premise that securities markets are affected by information, and enacted legislation to facilitate an investor's reliance on the integrity of those markets[.]

. . . Recent empirical studies . . . confirm Congress' premise that the market price . . . on well-developed markets reflects all publicly available information, and, hence, any material misrepresentations. . . . Because most publicly available information is reflected in market price, an investor's reliance on any public material misrepresentations, therefore, may be presumed for purposes of a Rule 10b-5 action.

Any showing that severs the link between the alleged misrepresentation and [the] decision to trade fair market price will be sufficient to rebut the presumption[.] For example, . . . if, despite petitioners' allegedly fraudulent attempt to manipulate market price, news of the merger discussions credibly entered the market and dissipated the effects of the misstatements, those who traded Basic shares after the corrective statements would have no direct or indirect connection with the fraud.

. . . It is not inappropriate to apply a presumption of reliance supported by the fraud-on-the-market theory. . . . That presumption, however, is rebuttable.

[Remanded for further proceedings consistent with the opinion.]

Questions

1. When is an item of undisclosed information about a company "material" for Rule 10b-5 purposes?
2. Is reliance on a misrepresentation essential in a Rule 10b-5 action?
3. a. Why would it be difficult for a plaintiff to demonstrate reliance in fact on a material omission?

   b. What solution did the courts create to deal with this problem?

Insider Trading

Insider trading, a securities law violation, occurs when an "insider" buys or sells a security while in possession of material, non-public information. According to the SEC enforcement director, insider trading at present appears to be "rampant."[21] Of particular concern has been the uptick in trades ahead of market moving news, especially trades by hedge funds and other institutional traders.[22] SEC cases against Wall Street professionals also have substantially increased.[23]

The 1934 Act forces the inside trader to pay damages to harmed third parties up to the extent that the insider profited on the transaction. The *Texas Gulf Sulphur* case below expresses the rule for those possessing inside information.

LEGAL BRIEFCASE

SEC v. Texas Gulf Sulphur Co. 401 F.2d 833 (2d Cir. 1968)

FACTS

On November 12, 1963, TGS drilled a "discovery hole," K-55-1, in Canada which revealed possibly one of the largest ore strikes in history. Insiders (geologists at the drill site, certain company officers, and so on) began buying TGS stock at around $18. Lab testing and further test-hole drilling fully confirmed the magnitude of the strike. Rumors began to circulate. On April 12, 1964, when the stock had passed $30 and when the best estimate was 8 million recoverable tons, TGS issued a press release naysaying the rumors. On April 16, a Canadian mining journal story, based on an April 13 site visit and interview, put the tonnage at 10 million. On the same day a Canadian government official, based on information current through April 15, put the tonnage at 25 million in a public an-

nouncement. On this day the stock passed $36. By May 15, it exceeded $58. The SEC brought an insider-trading suit.

Judge Waterman

[Rule 10b-5] is based . . . on the justifiable expectation . . . that all investors trading on impersonal exchanges have relatively equal access to material information[.] The essence of the Rule is that anyone who, trading for his own account [has access] to information intended to be available only for a corporate purpose . . . may not take "advantage of such . . . knowing it is unavailable to those with whom he is dealing," i.e., the investing public. Insiders . . . are, of course[,] precluded from so unfairly dealing, but the Rule is also applicable to one possessing the information who may not be strictly termed an "insider" [.A]nyone in possession of material inside information must either disclose it to the investing public [or] abstain from trading in or recommending the securities [while it] remains undisclosed. . . .

An insider's duty to disclose [or] abstain . . . arises only in "those situations . . . which are reasonably certain to have a substantial effect on the market price [if] disclosed." . . .

[W]hether facts are material [will depend] upon a balancing of both the indicated probability that the event will occur and the anticipated magnitude of the event[. Here,] knowledge of the possibility, which surely was more than marginal, of the existence of a mine of the vast magnitude indicated by the remarkably rich drill core . . . would certainly have been an important fact to a reasonable . . . investor[. A] major factor in determining whether the K-55-1 discovery was a material fact is the importance attached to [it] by those who knew about it. [T]he timing . . . of their stock purchases . . . virtually compels the inference that the insiders were influenced by the drilling results. . . .

We hold . . . that all transactions in TGS stock . . . by individuals apprised of the drilling results of K-55-1 were made in violation of Rule 10b-5. . . .

[Coates], who placed orders . . . immediately after the official announcement[, contends that his] purchases were not proscribed . . . for the news had already been . . . disclosed. . . . The reading of [the announcement] . . . is merely the first step in the process of dissemination [intended to provide] all investors with an equal opportunity to make informed . . . judgments. [A]t the minimum Coates should have waited until the news could reasonably have been expected to appear over the media of widest circulation, the Dow Jones broad tape, rather than hastening to insure an advantage to himself[.]

Questions

1. If you possess undisclosed inside information, what are your options for trading in the company's stock?
2. How soon after disclosure can an insider trade in the stock?

Tippees

The insider concept has been extended to include *tippees*. In some cases, the *tipper* (the insider or an "upstream" tippee) intends to improperly convey the inside information to a third party and hopes to derive personal benefit therefrom. In such a case, both the tipper and tippee are fully liable. In other cases, the tippee is deemed to "misappropriate" the inside information from the inadvertent tipper, knowing that it was confidential. This would occur, for example, if a psychiatrist learned material inside information during a session with a senior corporate executive and traded on that information. Here, the tippee, but not the tipper, would be liable. In the *O'Hagan* case, below, the U.S. Supreme Court approved the "misappropriation" theory of insider trading.

LEGAL BRIEFCASE

United States v. O'Hagan

521 U.S. 642 (1997)

FACTS

O'Hagan was a partner in the law firm of Dorsey & Whitney. In July 1988, Grand Metropolitan retained the firm to represent it in a tender offer for Pillsbury stock. O'Hagan did no work on this matter.

In August, O'Hagan began purchasing Pillsbury stock options. He also purchased Pillsbury stock at $39. When the tender offer was announced, the price rose to $60. O'Hagan sold his options and stock, making a profit of $4.3 million. He used the profits to conceal his previous embezzlement of unrelated client trust funds.

The SEC investigated. O'Hagan was convicted on securities fraud. The Eighth Circuit Court of Appeals reversed, rejecting liability under §10(b) and Rule 10b-5 under the "misappropriation theory." The Supreme Court granted certiorari.

Justice Ginsburg

Section 10(b) . . . proscribes (1) using any deceptive device (2) in connection with the purchase or sale of securities[. It] does not confine its coverage to deception of a purchaser or seller[; rather, it] reaches any deceptive device used "in connection with the purchase or sale of any security." . . .

. . . Under the . . . "classical theory" of insider trading[,] §10(b) and Rule 10b-5 are violated when [an] insider trades in the securities of his corporation on the basis of material, nonpublic information. [Such trading] qualifies as a "deceptive device" . . . because "a relationship of trust [exists] between the shareholders [and the] insiders who have obtained confidential information by reason of their position with [the] corporation." . . . That relationship . . . "gives rise to a duty to disclose [or to abstain from trading[."] The classical theory applies not only to officers, directors, and other permanent insiders[,] but also to attorneys, accountants, consultants, and others who temporarily become fiduciaries of a corporation. . . . The "misappropriation theory" holds that a person commits fraud "in connection with" a securities transaction . . . when he misappropriates confidential information for securities trading purposes, in breach of a duty owed to the source of the information. . . . Under this theory, a fiduciary's undisclosed, self-serving use of a principal's information to purchase or sell securities, in breach of a duty of loyalty and confidentiality, defrauds the principal of the exclusive use of that information. In lieu of premising liability on a fiduciary relationship between company insider and purchaser or seller of the company's stock, the misappropriation theory premises liability on a fiduciary-turned-trader's deception of those who entrusted him with access to confidential information.

The two theories are complementary, each addressing efforts to capitalize on nonpublic information through the purchase or sale of securities. . . .

In this case, the indictment alleged that O'Hagan, in breach of a duty of trust . . . owed to his law firm . . . and to its client[,] traded on the basis of nonpublic information regarding the client's tender offer[.] This conduct, the Government charged, constituted a fraudulent device in connection with the purchase and sale of securities. . . .

We agree[.] We observe, first, that misappropriators . . . deal in deception. A fiduciary who "[pretends] loyalty to the principal while secretly converting the principal's information for personal gain" . . . defrauds the principal. . . .

We turn next to the §10(b) requirement that the misappropriator's deceptive use of information be "in connection with the purchase or sale of [a] security." This element is satisfied because the fiduciary's fraud is consummated, not when the fiduciary gains the confidential information, but when, without disclosure to his principal, he uses the information to purchase or sell securities. . . .

The misappropriation theory . . . is also well-tuned to an animating purpose of the [1934] Act: to insure honest securities markets and thereby promote investor confidence. . . . Although informational disparity is inevitable in the securities markets[, an] investor's informational disadvantage vis-a-vis a misappropriator . . . stems from contrivance, not luck; it is a disadvantage that cannot be overcome with research or skill.

[Reversed and remanded.]

Questions

1. Are both insider trading theories needed to fulfill the 1934 Act's desire to keep the markets "honest?"
2. Both insider trading theories depend heavily on fiduciary relationships. Contrast the parties in the fiduciary relationships under the "classical" and "misappropriation" theories.
3. Would it have made any difference if O'Hagan had established with his broker, long before this trading, a portfolio diversification plan such that, pursuant to the plan, the identical trading would have occurred?

Short-Swing Profits

Closely related to insider trading is liability for *short-swing profits*. An insider trading case requires proof that the insider had material inside information and traded to exploit it. A short-swing profit case conclusively presumes that the insider had such information and did so trade any time the insider engages in any sale and purchase of an equity security issued by the insider's corporation within a six-month period. The insider's actual motive is irrelevant. All profits on any such trades must be remitted to the corporation (harmed third parties may sue under the insider trading rules). Here, "insider" is restricted to officers, directors and holders of at least 10 percent of any class of equity of the issuer.

Securities Law Enforcement Actions

Most of the securities laws violations just discussed can be enforced against the violators either by harmed private parties or by the government. The SEC brings civil enforcement actions; the Justice Department brings criminal enforcement actions.

Private Enforcement

In civil damage cases, harmed plaintiffs typically join together in a *class-action lawsuit*. This allows them to pool their resources and allows the judicial system to dispose of potentially thousands of cases within a single suit. The costs of these suits for defendants can be substantial—in the form of both settlement costs and adverse judgments. For example, in 2004 a record $5.4 billion was paid out in 118 settlements.[24] Since the 1990s, Congress and, more recently, the Supreme Court have acted such that bringing and prevailing in such suits has become much more difficult for injured plaintiffs.

> Major accounting firms paid out over $1.6 billion in class-action damages

As a consequence of the savings and loan debacle of the 1980s, major accounting firms paid out over $1.6 billion in class-action damages. Responding to these payouts, accounting firms and others began intense lobbying to curtail such suits. Among other things, they argued that law firms specializing in plaintiffs' securities actions groomed "professional plaintiffs" to bring damage suits in which the allegations of wrongdoing were primarily supported by a significant drop in the market price of the securities. After filing a complaint, it was argued, plaintiffs could then proceed to discovery and undertake a "fishing expedition" until sufficient facts were accumulated to motivate defendants to settle rather than endure litigation.

Some evidence of long-standing systemic abuse by plaintiffs' lawyers is now publicly available. In September 2007, William Lerach, a former partner of the law firm of Milberg Weiss, pleaded guilty to conspiracy. The allegations were that he and other lawyers of the firm had paid illegal kickbacks to individuals to serve as named plaintiffs in such securities actions, often allowing the firm to be the first to file suit with regard to a particular security, which in turn resulted in Milberg Weiss more frequently acting as attorneys for the lead plaintiff in many class action lawsuits. The firm's payoff was receipt of a larger share of the legal fees on the resolution of the suit.[25] On April 2, 2008, Melyvn Weiss, the senior securities law partner at Milberg Weiss, pleaded guilty to similar charges pursuant to a plea bargain. If the plea agreement is accepted by the court, Weiss will serve 18 to 33 months in prison and pay $10 million in fines and penalties to the government.[26]

The lobbying against runaway securities class-action suits paid off and, in December 1995, Congress enacted the *Private Securities Litigation Reform Act* (1995 Act). It significantly restricts fraud actions for civil damages. No fraudulent conduct will be presumed from the simple fact that a security's price dropped precipitously. Plaintiffs must now include concrete facts in their pleadings which create a strong inference that the defendant engaged in fraudulent conduct. In 2007, the Supreme Court clarified that the 1995 Act requires the complaint to state with particularity both the facts that constitute the alleged violation, as well as facts evidencing defendant's intention "to deceive, manipulate or defraud."[27]

The 1995 Act also restricts joint and several liability for accountants and underwriters whose deep pockets have historically attracted plaintiffs' lawyers. In early 2008, the Supreme Court further lessened the exposure of accountants, underwriters and other non-corporate defendants to liability for securities fraud violations by holding that, in instances in which plaintiffs are alleging damage based on fraudulent representations by the corporation, third parties who may have aided the fraudulent conduct, but who did not themselves make any fraudulent statements, are not liable for their actions to private plaintiffs.[28] Only the government can bring such "aided and abetted" lawsuits.

Because of the significant restraints placed on plaintiffs by the 1995 Act, plaintiffs' attorneys quickly began filing cases in state courts based on state securities laws, rather than in federal courts under federal securities laws. To stop this end-run of the 1995 Act, Congress passed the *Securities Litigation Uniform Standards Act* in 1998 (1998 Act) to require that legal actions related to *covered securities* (those traded in the national markets) be tried only in federal court under federal law, thus reimposing the 1995 Act's requirements. [For more on class-action lawsuits, see **http://securities.lerachlaw.com**]

Government Enforcement

The SEC has the power to impose civil penalties up to $750,000 for individuals and $15 million for corporations, and it can force defendants to give up ill-gotten gains. In an insider trading case, the SEC may impose a penalty of up to 300 percent of the profit gained or loss avoided by such trading.

The SEC is also empowered to issue *cease-and-desist orders,* get injunctions against persons committing securities fraud, and prohibit violators from serving as officers or directors of publicly traded companies.

Both the 1933 and 1934 Acts contain criminal sanctions for *willful* (knowing and deliberate) violations of their provisions: fines of up to $25 million and imprisonment of up to 20 years. As with criminal statutes in general, the principal problem for prosecutors is convincing the jury of guilt beyond a reasonable doubt. As a result, civil penalties are often substituted for criminal prosecutions.

Other SEC Regulatory Oversight

Tender Offers

There are several ways to acquire control of a corporation. Where mergers or direct acquisitions fail, a *tender offer* (also called a *takeover*) can be attempted. Alternatively, the person seeking to acquire control can mount a *proxy fight* by nominating an alternative slate of directors and then soliciting shareholders for their annual proxies in preference to returning proxies to current management. As this text goes to print, many are watching the developments in Microsoft's hostile offer for Yahoo. Yahoo's board rejected the initial offer, valued at $44.6 billion, and then established an enhanced severance plan for all employees, which would be triggered in any case in which an employee was terminated without cause within two years of the completion of any merger. Microsoft is said to be preparing a proxy fight, expected to cost from $20-30 million, as a less expensive way to put pressure on Yahoo's board than raising its bid price or making a tender offer directly to Yahoo's shareholders.[29]

In a tender offer, the offeror announces that it wishes to acquire a specific number of shares (often the number needed to gain control). It identifies where stockholders who want to participate must tender (that is, deliver) their shares. (Shares are returned if the tender offer fails.) It also specifies the opening bid price. If less than the desired number of shares is tendered, the tender offeror can either walk away or increase the offering price.

In dealing with a tender offer situation, the target corporation's management realizes that a change in control will likely result in its dismissal since the new controlling party will want to put its own management in place. Often the target's management will not be eager to leave. It will resist, which accounts for the term *hostile takeover*. Management has a problem, however, because it is supposed to act exclusively in the best interests of the shareholders and the tender offer may well be in their best interests. To avoid liability, management will generally try to style its resistance as "looking out for the stockholders."

Management can resist in various ways. It could launch its own tender offer (*go private*). Or it could start using corporate cash to buy back shares in the market, driving up the price to discourage the tender offeror. Here management has to worry that it could be sanctioned for violating §9 of the 1934 Act, which prohibits price manipulation. However, the SEC provides a safe harbor which allows management to purchase each day up to 25 percent of the security's average daily trading volume.

Another resistance tactic is *greenmail*, in which the target's management uses corporate cash to buy back the tender offeror's current stake, with a significant premium to "go away." Changes in the federal tax law discourage this technique.

Management sometimes puts takeover defenses in place by arranging "disasters" if a tender offer is attempted. Two notorious ones are the *crown jewel* and *poison pill* defenses. The crown jewel tactic involves arranging a stand-by agreement with a friendly third party to purchase critical corporate assets at a reasonable price should a tender offer be launched, knowing that the third party will, by lease or otherwise, continue to make these assets available to the corporation on "friendly" terms should the tender offer fail and management keep its job. The poison pill tactic involves pre-arranging with shareholders a tender offer-triggered right to buy or to redeem a significant amount of stock at very corporation-unfavorable prices. The former discourages the tender offeror by diluting the value of the stock, the latter by dissipating the cash or cash-related assets (such as overfunded pension plans) that may constitute the primary reason for the takeover.

If all else fails, the target's officers may find comfort in the *golden parachutes* (severance pay packages) they may have negotiated to protect themselves in the event of a takeover.

Shareholder Resolutions

Although shareholders are the owners of the corporation, control and management rests with the board. State law significantly restricts shareholders' ability to control management, other than through the annual election of the board. When a shareholder is dissatisfied with management's decisions, the most common shareholder response is to sell the shares. Alternatively, a wealthy shareholder might make a tender offer to gain control. Or a shareholder could engage in a proxy fight, soliciting sufficient proxies to vote out existing management.

What if a shareholder doesn't want to oust management, but rather wants to affect corporate policy on a particular issue? In publicly held corporations, management may submit resolutions for shareholder approval at the annual meeting, which proposals will be described in the proxy materials for the annual meeting. Shareholders can also submit resolutions for a vote at the annual meeting and state law determines what issues are acceptable as subjects for such resolutions. However, the cost of distributing such resolutions to the shareholders is prohibitive for most shareholders. Thus, shareholders have sought to have the corporation include shareholder resolutions in the corporation's own proxy materials. In publicly held corporations, the SEC regulates shareholders' access to corporate proxy materials for such purposes.

For the past several years, executive compensation has been a target of shareholder resolutions, spurred on by compensation information reported in the popular press and the 2007 change in SEC disclosure rules requiring more information on executive compensation to be included in the annual report to shareholders. However, SEC Rule 14a-8(i)(7) allows corporations to refuse inclusion of proposals dealing with ordinary business operations. Thus, shareholders have increasingly drafted their proposals to specify that the votes are advisory only.

State Securities Regulation

After the enactment of the Securities Act of 1933, the U.S. operated under a dual regulatory environment for securities. Both the state and federal governments were entitled to regulate IPOs and subsequent purchases and sales. However, the lack of regulatory uniformity among the states led Congress in 1996 to enact the *National Securities Markets Improvement Act*, preempting state registration requirements for securities traded on national markets. Then in 1998, as previously discussed, Congress mandated that securities fraud claims related to national market securities be litigated only in federal court under federal law. State securities regulations, known as *blue sky laws*, now are only a shadow of their former significance and are primarily applicable to solely intrastate offerings. [For more on state securities regulation, see **www.nasaa.org/About_NASAA/ Role_of_State_Securities_Regulators**]

International Securities Regulation

Critics claim the United States is losing its place as the world's leading financial center, citing such evidence as the percentage of large IPOs being listed outside of the United States. Aggressive regulation in America is often blamed for driving those IPOs abroad.

American securities regulation is the world's strongest, but whether that will continue to be true and whether it is responsible for the growth in foreign securities markets is not so certain. Other factors undoubtedly make significant contributions to the shift, such as the natural maturation of international markets, the continuing devaluation of the dollar against foreign currencies, the speed of overall economic growth elsewhere in the world and the concomitant rise in wealth, especially in Europe and Asia.[30] "Because companies want to list in the fastest-rising markets, many are staying in their home countries, which have outperformed the United States in recent years."[31] Furthermore, stringent regulation in the United States is not necessarily a net disincentive for securities registration here. Foreign securities with dual listings in the United States and elsewhere appear to enjoy an advantage in the price they command.[32] Finally, as the securities markets in other countries mature, national regulation seems to be increasing in ways that model U.S. policies.

Nothing equivalent to the SEC exists in Europe, but securities regulation there is increasing. One writer, reciting examples of recent regulations imposed in Europe, said, "if Europe is considered a model for international markets, we can expect the forces of globalization to move ever closer to the New York regulatory model, not away from it."[33] Japan is also discussing an expansion of its 15-year-old securities regulator, the Securities Exchange and Surveillance Commission.[34] Although its ability to enforce the increased regulation is an issue, Mexico's 2006 Securities Market Law is designed to attract increased investment by boosting legal standards in corporate control and accountability.[35] A 2002 study found that 87 countries of the 103 that have stock markets also have insider trading rules.[36] Other countries, including France, Japan, Canada, and China, are also adopting rules similar to some of those found in SOX.

[For more on international securities regulation, see the Web site for the International Organization of Securities Commissions at **www.iosco.org/about**]

Questions—Part Two

1. *a.* What information is contained in a registration statement under the 1933 Act?

   b. What role in the registration process is played by the prospectus?

2. Assume a midlevel manager learns that his corporation is about to go bankrupt because of about-to-be-disclosed improprieties. He calls his lawyer to ask about his personal exposure. After advising him, the lawyer immediately sells all of her holdings in that stock. Later that day, the news breaks and the stock price tumbles 60 percent.

   a. Does anyone have insider trading liability?

   b. If so, in what amount?

3. Why might it make sense to have only outside directors determine the compensation of senior executives?

Part Three: SOX

Controversy has surrounded SOX since its inception. The reading that follows explains why Congress enacted SOX and reviews some of its provisions.

Kristofer Neslund[37]

On December 2, 2001, Enron filed for bankruptcy. The collapse of the seventh largest U.S. corporation—*Fortune*'s "Most Innovative Company" for five consecutive years—cost investors $90 billion. Enron called the world's attention to extraordinary failings in corporate governance, the accounting and financial services industries, and the regulation of the markets. Its demise was not an isolated event. It had numerous predecessors that failed to alert the markets, but it was quickly followed by many scandals, at least three of which were actually larger (WorldCom, Parmalat, and Fannie Mae).

Senior managers at many corporations committed fraud and employed improper accounting methods in an effort to maximize the value of their stock options. They sought to engineer financial results, including the attainment of earnings targets, that would lead to ever-increasing stock prices. Byzantine transactions were used to hide liabilities and losses, generate phony revenues and equity, and improperly reduce taxes. Some were convicted of securities-related crimes, many others have entered plea bargains.

Financial services companies aided management in these scandalous events. For example, J.P. Morgan used its British Channel Islands company (Mahonia) to route $2 billion in loans to Enron under the guise of revenues, earning $100 million for its help.[38] The independence of stock analysts was corrupted. Instead of offering objective assessments about corporations' stocks, they promoted those stocks that would help their banks earn hundreds of millions of dollars in underwriting fees. E-mails disclosed situations in which analysts' contempt for a corporation's securities was obvious, despite their public enthusiasm for them. The country's largest investment banks paid tens of billions of dollars to settle shareholder actions.

The multinational accounting firms allegedly compromised their audits as they sought to cross-sell high-profit nonaudit services. New disclosure mandates revealed that they were generating $3 of nonaudit services for every $1 of audit services. These accounting firms paid billions of dollars in settlements. Enron's auditor, the Big 5 accounting firm Andersen, ceased to exist upon its conviction of criminal obstruction of justice related to the destruction of audit records, and KPMG nearly suffered the same fate.

Boards of directors were sued for their anemic corporate oversight. Far too frequently, boards simply abdicated authority to CEOs who, in reality, controlled board membership and compensation. Many conflicts of interest were found. At Enron, for example, some directors were personal friends of senior managers, others were academics whose institutions were receiving substantial contributions, and another was a former senior government official who had exempted Enron from regulation in its principal line of business.

By the early 2000s, the integrity of the U.S. capital markets was in jeopardy. Senior management was engaging in widespread misconduct. The "gatekeepers," especially the accounting profession and the financial services industry, were failing to safeguard the public interest and were actually complicit in furthering managements' schemes. The time was ripe for change.

CONGRESS RESPONDS

The 2002 Sarbanes-Oxley Act (SOX) was the most significant regulatory reform of the markets since the Great Depression. A summary of its key provisions appears in the box below.

Sarbanes-Oxley Act

Auditing/Accounting Provisions

New Public Company Accounting Oversight Board (PCOAB) to oversee audits of public companies (only 40 percent of members from accounting)—great investigatory and punitive powers

Audit commitee must consist of all independent directors (with at least one "financial expert")

Auditor now responsible directly to audit committee, which appoints auditor and sets compensation

Most consulting forbidden for audit clients; what consulting remains requires advance written permission from audit commitee

Mandatory audit partner rotation every five years

Enhanced scrutiny of internal control system

One-year waiting period before auditor can join senior management of audit client

Senior Executive/Officer/Director Provisions

CEO/CFO must certify accuracy of financial statements (penalties of up to $5 million plus 20 years in jail)

No loans from companies to senior executives/directors

CEO/CFO performance-based compensation forfeited if accounting results revised because of misconduct

Securities law penalties, damages and compensation forfeiture survive bankruptcy

Persons violating antifraud provisions barred from service as public company officer/director

New crime for harassing whistleblowers (fines plus up to 10 years in jail)

Other Provisions

Criminal

New destruction of evidence/obstruction of justice crime (fines plus up to 20 years in jail)

New securities fraud crime (fines plus up to 25 years in jail)

Existing securities criminal penalties increased to maximum of $25 million fine and 20 years in jail

Miscellaneous

Faster disclosure of material events and insider transactions

Starter provision granting SEC power to control conduct of lawyers practicing before it

SOX Compliance Costs

Many corporations have complained about the cost of complying with SOX, especially the rules related to internal control. Early estimates were that corporations with revenues exceeding $5 billion would pay an average of $4.7 million to implement SOX, and face an annual cost of $1.5 million to maintain compliance. Sympathy may be difficult to generate, however, given the hundreds of billions of dollars of investor losses suffered, largely related to matters an effective internal control system would have prevented (or at least detected). As Paul Volcker (former chair of the Federal Reserve Board) and Arthur Levitt (chair of the SEC immediately prior to Enron) jointly wrote in a *Wall Street Journal* editorial:

> [W]e believe that those costs are justified in light of the benefits—the price necessary to pay for more reliability in accounting, clear accountability to shareholders, and more robust and trusted markets. [T]he investment in good corporate governance, professional integrity and transparency will pay dividends in the form of investor confidence, more efficient markets, and more market participation in years to come.[39]

Inspections

The Public Company Accounting Oversight Board (PCAOB) completed its first inspections of the Big Four accounting firms in December 2003. Its August 2004 report uncovered "significant audit and accounting issues . . . missed by the firms and identified concerns about significant aspects of each firm's quality control systems."[40] [For more on the PCAOB's inspections, see **www.pcaobus.com/inspections/index.asp**]

Whistleblowers

SOX's whistleblower provisions have proven a severe disappointment thus far. Enforcement was oddly granted to the Occupational Safety and Health Administration (OSHA), which has no subpoena power, no power to place a person under oath, no budget for this enforcement, and absolutely no experience dealing with financial fraud. OSHA has ruled favorably on less than 15 percent of all claims.

Financial Statement Certification

The CEO/CFO financial statement certification requirement was enacted to preclude the "Claude Rains defense [which was] the typical defense of every CEO and CFO of every major company." In the famous film, "Casablanca," the wagering impresario played by Rains said he was "shocked, shocked" that gambling was going on around him. The certification requirement, which precludes this defense, is proving an extraordinary prosecution tool. Many senior executives have accepted plea bargains to avoid the potentially severe punishment, agreeing to help prosecutors pursue other senior executives.[41]

Evaluating SOX: The Costs and the Benefits

Has SOX been a net positive or is it just another cost of doing business? One of the oft repeated criticisms of SOX is that it has contributed to the erosion of America's position as the financial capital of the world.[42] The assumptions that (1) improper regulation has changed our position in the global financial markets and that (2) deregulation or better targeted regulation can change the trend may be faulty, as previously discussed at the end of Part Two. That said, many argue that the projected cost of compliance, particularly the cost of complying with Rule 404 which imposed new internal control processes on public corporations, was substantially understated when the legislation was under consideration.[43] Voicing yet another objection, one group in 2006 sued the PCAOB, arguing that it was unconstitutional under a variety of arguments, but that claim failed in court.[44]

Toward the other end of the continuum, an argument has been made that the act can be judged a success because it has resulted in a "rigorous new accounting discipline," as evidenced by the number of financial restatements filed in response to its tightened audit procedures.[45] Such restatements seemed to crest in 2005 and then actually fell in number in 2006,[46] suggesting that old accounting errors have been cleaned up and the act is minimizing the creation of new ones.

Finally, some assert that SOX didn't go far enough in some respects, such as in the establishment of true auditor independence.[47]

The material below takes a closer look at one of SOX's failures and then one of its unexpected successes.

Cost of Compliance

Early estimates were that the initial cost of SOX implementation would be about $4.7 million for corporations with revenues of $5 billion or more, with annual costs thereafter of $1.5 million. As acknowledged in a 2006 Government Accountability Office (GAO) report, the actual costs of compliance with Rule 404's internal control requirements were higher than expected and smaller companies suffered most.[48]

From a societal point of view, the cost still may be well worth it. A research firm estimated that the total cost of compliance for all companies through the end of 2007 would exceed $26 billion.[49] Still, Enron's losses alone cost investors $90 billion. Further, the cost of compliance for individual companies reportedly drops from the first year of compliance to the second year by 31 or 44 percent, depending on the size of the company.[50]

The SEC has acted to address the problem of the high cost of compliance for smaller companies by relaxing the guidelines.[51]

Backdated Options Scandal: An Unexpected SOX Success

SOX altered the time within which executives were required to report stock transactions between them and their corporations—from 45 days following the end of the corporation's fiscal year, to two business days after the transaction. At the time, no one connected with the legislation had any idea that its passage would lead to the uncovering of a major scandal involving over one hundred corporations.

Prior to SOX, University of Iowa finance professor Erik Lie had noticed a frequent relationship between the market price of a corporation's stock and the issuance of stock options to executives and employees: all too frequently, from a statistical standpoint, the price of the stock went up immediately after the issuance of the options. His hypothesis was that stock option grants were being deliberately backdated to dates with low market prices; that is, the stock option grant date was moved back in time to a moment when the stock's price was lower thus improving the odds of making money on the stock.[52] One example: In the weeks following 9/11, the stock market declined. While others across the United States were adjusting to a new reality, the boards of dozens of companies were busy issuing stock options. In the two weeks following the reopening of the stock markets after 9/11, 2.6 times as many top executives received stock option grants as in the same period the year before.[53]

The passage of SOX with the new provision provided a way to test the backdating hypothesis: if deliberate backdating was occurring, the new reporting rules should make it harder to accomplish with only a two-day window. If the post-SOX data showed the same rise in market price following option grants, then some other explanation would be correct. But if the phenomenon largely disappeared, deliberate backdating became a considerably more likely culprit.

The post-enactment findings? Eighty percent of the market price increases disappeared. Most of the remaining 20 percent were associated with companies that were late in filing the required reports. The results were shared with the SEC, which proceeded to investigate and ultimately brought many charges against both corporations and individuals.

Backdating of stock options can be fully lawful, but the practice becomes illegal if documents are forged, if the transactions are not fully disclosed to shareholders, or if the options are not accurately accounted for in company financial records and filings with the SEC and the IRS. In the first backdating case to go to trial, former Brocade Communications CEO Gregory Reyes was found guilty of 10 counts of conspiracy and fraud. Reyes was sentenced to 21 months in prison and fined $15 million, but he has appealed. These arrangements, whether technically lawful or not, have left the impression that corporate bosses were greedily manipulating their compensation packages at the expense of shareholders.

> Former Brocade Communications CEO Gregory Reyes was sentenced to 21 months in prison

---

PRACTICING ETHICS) "Well, If You Think That's Best"

On December 15, a CEO reviews the accounting results shaping up for the 4th quarter. The $15 million projected net income is $2 million short of the target for his $750,000 bonus. He asks the CFO to lunch. She will lose a $300,000 bonus if the target isn't achieved. The CEO casually inquires whether there might be some way to "salvage the disappointing 4th quarter performance." She ponders a moment. "What about lowering the bad debt reserve by $600,000—we can fix it next year?" She also suggests recognizing in the last week of December the income to be earned from goods actually to be shipped in the first week of January. Her "rationale" is that the contracts are already signed. That will add another $1.5 million to net income. The CEO responds, "well, if you think that's best . . ." The bonuses are awarded. Discuss the ethical issues illustrated by these facts.

Internet Exercises

Using the Frequently Asked Questions segment of **www.securitieslaw.com** answer the following questions:

1. What duties are owed by stockbrokers and brokerage firms to customers?
2. How does a customer know when he or she has been defrauded?

Chapter Questions

1. Describe the steps generally followed to bring a corporation into existence, through the election of directors.

2. Modell owned 80 percent of the Cleveland Stadium Corporation (Stadium) and 53 percent of the Cleveland Browns Football Company (Browns). Gries owned 43 percent of Browns. The Browns' board consisted of Modell, the outside lawyer for both corporations, three individuals employed by both corporations, and Gries. Modell proposed that the Browns buy the Stadium for $6 million. Gries objected, saying that the Stadium appraised for only $2 million. The Browns' board approved the purchase nonetheless (all directors other than Gries voting in favor). Gries commenced a shareholders derivative suit seeking to rescind the purchase. Who should win? See *Gries Sports Enterprises v. Cleveland Browns Football Company*, 496 N.E.2d 959 (Ohio S. Ct. 1986).

3. The Patels owned the CC Motel. They formed a partnership with their son, Raj, to own and operate the motel. Title to the motel was not transferred to the partnership. The partnership agreement required Raj to approve the motel's sale. The Patels sold the motel without telling Raj and without telling the buyers of Raj's right. He learned of the pending sale and refused to agree. The buyers asked the court to compel the sale. Who should win? See *Patel v. Patel*, 260 Cal. Rptr. 255 (Cal. Ct. App. 1989).

4. Ivan Landreth and his sons owned all of the stock in a lumber business they operated in Tonasket, Washington. The owners offered the stock for sale. During that time a fire severely damaged the business, but the owners made assurances of rebuilding and modernization. The stock was sold to Dennis and Bolten, and a new organization, Landreth Timber Company, was formed with the senior Landreth remaining as a consultant on the side. The new firm was unsuccessful and was sold at a loss. The Landreth Timber Company then filed suit against Ivan Landreth and his sons seeking rescission of the first sale, alleging, among other arguments, that Landreth and sons had widely offered and then sold their stock without registering it as required by the Securities Act of 1933. The district court acknowledged that *stocks* fit within the definition of a *security*, and that the stock in question "possessed all of the characteristics of conventional stock." However, it held that the federal securities laws do not apply to the sale of 100 percent of the stock of a closely held corporation. Here the district court found that the purchasers had not entered into the sale with the expectation of earnings secured via the labor of others. Managerial control resided with the purchasers. Thus, the sale was a commercial venture rather than a typical investment. The Court of Appeals affirmed, and the case reached the Supreme Court. Decide. See *Landreth Timber Co. v. Landreth*, 471 U.S. 681 (1985).

5. A Fortune 500 CFO admits to having deliberately treated $4 billion in operating expenses as assets, thereby allowing the corporation to show profits instead of losses. The auditor never detected this. The corporation's stock drops 95 percent and bond

covenants related to billions in debt are breached. At its peak price last year, the CFO sold stock (acquired through options) for $15 million, generating a $10 million gain.

a. Why might the corporation have to file for bankruptcy protection?

b. What provision(s) of the securities law will probably be the basis for a class-action lawsuit by the stockholders?

c. Why will the 1995 Act probably not stop a class-action lawsuit from proceeding to the discovery phase?

d. Why will the CFO be subject to criminal (as well as civil) securities sanctions?

e. Will the SEC likely ever allow the CFO to be an officer or director of a publicly traded corporation in the future?

f. Will the SEC allow the CFO to keep the $10 million gain on the stock?

g. What kind of civil penalties could the SEC impose on the CFO?

Notes

1. Jill E. Fisch, "The Peculiar Role of the Delaware Courts in the Competition for Corporate Charters, 68 U. Cin. L. Rev. 1061 (Summer 2000).

2. **www.irs.ustreas.gov/taxstats/display/0i1%3D40%26genericId%3D16810,00.html**.

3. *Cede & Co. v. Technicolor, Inc.*, 634 A.2d 345 (Del. 1993).

4. *Compania General de Tabacos de Filipinas v. Collector of Internal Revenue*, 275 U.S. 87, 100 (1927) (J. Holmes, dissenting).

5. *Commissioner v. Newman*, 159 F.2d 848, 850 (2d Cir 1947).

6. **http://corpgov.net**.

7. Minn. Stat. §322B.303, subd. 2 (1996).

8. *Kaycee Land and Livestock v. Flahive*, 46 P.2d 323 (Wyo. 2002).

9. "First the Market, Now the U.S Economy Wobbles," *Australian Financial Review*, July 27, 2002.

10. David Enrich, Robin Sidel and Susanne Craig, "World Rides to Wall Street's Rescue," *The Wall Street Journal*, January 16, 2008.

11. For a readable synopsis of the current credit crisis, see David Leonhardt, "Can't Grasp Credit Crisis? Join the Club," *New York Times*, March 19, 2008. See also, "The Financial System: What Went Wrong?," *The Economist*, May 19, 2008.

12. Peter Lattman, "Carlyle Capital Nears Collapse as Accord Can't Be Reached," *The Wall Street Journal*, March 13, 2008.

13. Jenny Anderson and Vikas Bajaj, "A Wall Street Domino Theory," *New York Times*, March 15, 2008.

14. Edmund L. Andrews and Stephen Labaton, "In Washington, a Split Over Regulation of Wall Street," *New York Times*, March 23, 2008.

15. **www.sec.gov/info/smallbus/qasbsec.htm**.

16. **http://www.sec.gov/about/forms/form8-k.pdf**.

17. **www.sec.gov/answers/tradingsuspension.htm**.

18. "Sales-Practice Complaints to SEC Increase," *The Wall Street Journal*, April 26, 2001, p. 1C.

19. "The Return of the Day Trader," **www.cbsnews.com/stories/2002/09/30/eveningnews/main523766.shtml**.

20. **www.sec.gov/investor/pubs/daytips.htm**.

21. Akerman Senterfitt, "Government Brands Insider Trading as 'Rampant'," *Corporate, Securities and White Collar Digest*, November 8, 2007 [**www.akerman.com**].

22. Karey Wutkowski and Rachelle Younglai, "Regulators Band Together to Fight Insider Trading," Reuters, August 15, 2007.

23. Christopher J. Steskal, "Insider Trading Is Back," USA (September 4, 2007).

24. Kara Scannell, "Settlements Totaled $5.4 Billion for Securities Class Actions in '04," *The Wall Street Journal*, March 2, 2005, p. C4.

25. Barry Meier, "Lawyer Pleads Guilty in Kickback Case," *New York Times,* September 19, 2007.

26. Josh Gerstein, "Weiss of Milberg Weiss Enters Guilty Plea in Deal," *New York Sun*, April 3, 2008.

27. *Tellabs, Inc. v. Makor Issues & Rights, Ltd.*, 127 S. Ct. 2499 (2007).

28. *Stoneridge Investment Partners LLC v. Scientific-Atlanta, Inc.*, 128 S. Ct. 761 (2008).

29. Andrew Ross Sorkin and Miguel Helft, "Microsoft Said to Plan Proxy Fight for Yahoo," *New York Times*, February 20, 2008.

30. Edgar Ortega and Elizabeth Hester, "IPO Fees in Europe Catch Wall Street for First Time Since WWII," May 29, 2007, at **www.bloomberg.com**.

31. Walter Hamilton, "Stock Rules Irk NYC as Wall Street Parties on," *Log Angeles Times*, April 23, 2007.

32. John C. Coffee, "Law and the Market: The Impact of Enforcement," *Columbia Law and Economics WorkingPaper No. 304*, March 7, 2007, available at **http://ssrn.com/abstract=967482**.

33. Paul Johns, "Letters to the Editor," *The Wall Street Journal,* November 6, 2006.

34. Yuka Hayashi and Andrew Morse, "Japan May Beef Up Market Oversight," *The Wall Street Journal*, January 25, 2006, p. C3.

35. "Room to Grow," *Latin Finance,* September 1, 2006, p.76.

36. Art A. Durnev and Amrita S. Nain, "Does Insider Trading Regulation Deter Private Information Trading? International Evidence," ISNIE 2006.

37. Associate Professor, School of Taxation, Golden Gate University.

38. Jathon Sapsford, Anita Raghavan, "Energy-Trading Venture Could Result in an Enormous Loss for J.P. Morgan," *Wall Street Journal*, January 25, 2002.

39. Paul Volcker, Arthur Levitt, "In Defense of Sarbanes-Oxley, *The Wall Street Journal*, June 14, 2004, p. A16.

40. "PCAOB Releases Big Four Findings," *SmartPros Ltd*, August 27, 2004, at **www.accountingnet.com/x44957.xml**.

41. Phyllis Plitch, "Scrushy Charges Show the Long Reach of Sarbanes-Oxley," *The Wall Street Journal,* November 4, 2003.

42. R. Glenn Hubbard and John L. Thornton, "Action Plan for Capital Markets," *The Wall Street Journal,* November 30, 2006, p. A16.

43. Frank B. Cross, "Economies, Capital Markets and Securities Law," *Univ. of Texas School of Law, Land and Economics Paper No. 73*, 2006, available at **http://ssn.com/abstract=908927**.

44. *Free Enterprise Fund v. PCAOB*, 2007 U.S. Dist. LEXIS 24310 (2007).

45. Diya Gullapalli, "Living With Sarbanes-Oxley," *The Wall Street Journal,* October 17, 2005, p. R1.

46. Joann S. Lublin and Kara Scannell, "Critics See Some Good from Sarbanes-Oxley," *The Wall Street Journal*, July 30, 2007, p. B1.

47. Don A. Moore, "SarbOx Doesn't Go Far Enough," *BusinessWeek*, April 17, 2006, p. 112.

48. "Report Cites High Cost of Sarbanes-Oxley Compliance," *Waterloo/Cedar Falls Courier*, May 9, 2006, p. B4.

49. Joann S. Lublin and Kara Scannell, "Critics See Some Good from Sarbanes-Oxley."

50. James H. Quigley, "Please Be Patient," *The Wall Street Journal*, May 25, 2006, p. A14.

51. Eric Dash, "SEC Revises Its Standards for Corporate Audits," *New York Times*, May 24, 2007.

52. David Henry, "A SarbOx Surprise," *BusinessWeek*, June 12, 2006, p. 38.

53. Charles Forelle, James Bandler and Mark Maremont, "Executive Pay: The 9/11 Factor," *The Wall Street Journal*, July 15, 2006, p. A1.

CHAPTER TEN

Antitrust Law— Restraints of Trade

After completing this chapter, students will be able to:

1. Recognize the changing goals of antitrust law.

2. Describe the key antitrust statutes.

3. Explain the meaning of "horizontal restraints of trade."

4. Analyze when an unlawful price-fixing arrangement has been created.

5. Identify a group boycott.

6. Define resale price maintenance.

7. Explain the requirements for establishing an unlawful tying arrangement.

8. Describe the commercial advantages and disadvantages of exclusive dealing.

9. Contrast price discrimination and predatory pricing.

10. Explain how predatory pricing may be proven.

Antitrust is a word that is only dimly recognizable to most of us, but antitrust law reaches all corners of our lives and significantly shapes our economic and social practices reaching even amateur athletics, as described below.

PRACTICING ETHICS   More "Pay" for College Athletes?

Four former college athletes representing a class of more than 20,000 former college athletes, recently sued the National Collegiate Athletic Association (NCAA) seeking to change NCAA limits on the amount of aid that student-athletes can be granted. Under long-time NCAA rules, so-called full-ride scholarships were limited to tuition, books, room and board. The athletes claimed they were denied approximately $2,500 annually because their universities were not allowed, under NCAA rules, to pay the "full cost of attendance," a package that would include money for insurance, laundry, school supplies, telephone, travel, and so on in addition to the full ride.

The class action involved all those playing "major college football" (what was Division I-A) and "major college basketball" (16 top conferences) since 2002. Total damages were estimated at several hundred million dollars. The lawsuit claimed that the NCAA rules constitute a "contract, combination and conspiracy to fix the amount of financial assistance available to student athletes" thus restraining trade in violation of section I of the Sherman Antitrust Act[1] (explained below).

As you read this chapter, think about whether the athletes' complaint appears to be a violation of antitrust law, but for our immediate purposes, think about the athletes' complaint as a matter of right and wrong; of fairness. [For more on this case, see **www.studentathleteclassaction.com**]

Question

Is it unfair to deny athletes the additional $2,500 or so that they could "earn" in the market for their services (playing "major college" football or basketball)? Detail the fairness argument for both the athletes and the NCAA.

Part One—The Foundations of Antitrust Law

Antitrust—Early Goals

Antitrust, perhaps more than any other branch of the law, is a product of changing political and economic tides. Historically, antitrust law sought to allow every American, at least in theory, the opportunity to reach the top. More specifically, antitrust advocates were concerned about the following issues:

1. **The preservation of competition.** Antitrust law was designed to provide free, open markets. The belief was (and continues to be) that competition would generate the best products and services at the lowest possible prices.

2. **The preservation of democracy.** Many businesses in competition meant that none of them could corner economic, political, or social power.

3. **The preservation of small businesses, or more generally, the preservation of the American Dream.** Antitrust was designed to preserve the opportunity for the "little people" to compete with the giants.

4. **An expression of political radicalism.** At least for a segment of society, antitrust laws were meant to be tools for reshaping America to meet the needs of all people, rather than those of big business.

During President Ronald Reagan's tenure, an aggressive free market mentality dominated, and reliance on antitrust law declined. While the federal government continued to avidly pursue collusion between competitors and certain other antitrust violations, the prevailing expectation was that the market would function most effectively in the absence of government intervention. [For professors' analyses of recent antitrust developments, see **http://lawprofessors.typepad.com/antitrustprof_blog**]

Antitrust Stability?

Today in the federal courts, conservative Reagan/Bush judges are powerful, and antitrust, while important in ensuring a competitive economy, is certainly not being used aggressively as a lever for social change. The political and sociological concerns noted, although not abandoned, have taken a back seat to efficiency considerations and to pragmatic, case-by-case consideration of the economic facts.

What we are seeing is arguably a more restrained, nuanced approach to antitrust where enforcement is limited to instances of clear market failure, but to the critics, the federal courts are simply turning their backs on antitrust enforcement. The *Los Angeles Times* recently discussed that claim:

> With a push from the Bush administration, the Supreme Court is in the midst of steady, if little noticed retreat from enforcing the antitrust laws that for decades have guarded against monopolies and price fixing. In the last year, the court has relaxed or repealed several rules designed to prevent anticompetitive schemes. . . .
>
> "The court is on a path to reshape the law to conform to the Chicago school of law and economics," said Albert Foer, president of the American Antitrust Institute, referring to the free-market theories associated with the University of Chicago. "The theory now is that markets rarely fail, and regulation of business is nearly always bad."
>
> "This is just basic economics: letting manufacturers compete in their own way," said Roy Englert Jr., a lawyer who represents the wireless industry. "This is the free market come to life."[2]

Antitrust Enforcement and Statutes

Federal government antitrust enforcement is shared by the Antitrust Division of the Department of Justice and the Federal Trade Commission. The government brings relatively few antitrust actions, but a government victory sends powerful messages to the business community about the risks of anticompetitive behavior. The government prefers to avoid litigation, and most cases are settled before going to court. Private parties may also sue under the antitrust laws. Segments of the economy, such as the securities industry, that are already closely regulated by the government can sometimes successfully claim that they are immune from the antitrust laws. [For the Justice Department Antitrust Division, see **www.usdoj.gov/atr**]

Sherman Antitrust Act, 1890

Section 1 of the Sherman Antitrust Act forbids restraints of trade, and Section 2 forbids monopolization, attempts to monopolize, and conspiracies to monopolize. Two types of enforcement options are available to the federal government:

1. Violation of the Sherman Act opens participants to criminal penalties. The maximum corporate fine is $100 million per violation, whereas individuals may be fined $1 million and/or imprisoned for 10 years.
2. Injunctive relief is provided under civil law. The government or a private party may secure a court order preventing continuing violations of the act and affording appropriate relief (such as dissolution or divestiture).

Perhaps the most important remedy is available to private parties. An individual or organization harmed by a violation of the act may bring a civil action seeking three times the actual damages (treble damages) sustained.

Clayton Act, 1914

The Clayton Act forbids price discrimination, exclusive dealing, tying arrangements, requirements contracts, mergers restraining commerce or tending to create a monopoly, and interlocking directorates. Civil enforcement of the Clayton Act is similar to the Sherman Act in that the government may sue for injunctive relief, and private parties may seek treble damages. In general, criminal law remedies are not available under the Clayton Act. [For the texts of federal antitrust laws, along with antitrust case summaries and antitrust links, see **http://www.antitrustcases.com**]

Federal Trade Commission Act (FTC)

The Federal Trade Commission Act created a powerful, independent agency designed to devote its full attention to the elimination of anticompetitive practices in American commerce. The FTC proceeds under the Sherman Act, the Clayton Act, and Section 5 of the FTC Act itself, which declares unlawful "unfair methods of competition" and "unfair or deceptive acts or practices in or affecting commerce." The commission's primary enforcement device is the cease and desist order, but fines may be imposed. [For the FTC home page, see **http://www.ftc.gov**]

Federal Antitrust Law and Other Regulatory Systems

State Law

Most states, through legislation and judicial decisions, have developed their own antitrust laws. Some states have recently become more aggressive in antitrust enforcement, as illustrated by their sucess in conjunction with the federal government in attacking Microsoft's alleged monopoly conduct. (See Chapter 11.)

Patents, Copyrights, and Trademarks

Each of these devices offers limited, government-granted market strength. As such, they frequently raise antitrust questions. Each device, however, serves to protect—and thus encourage—commercial creativity and development. The resulting antitrust problem is essentially that of limiting the patent, copyright, or trademark holder to the terms of its government-granted privilege.

Law of Other Nations

Chapter 11 addresses the immense practical and ideological significance of international antitrust issues in this era of globalization. Former U. S. antitrust chief Joel Klein explained:

> "This is a problem that is going to get much, much more serious. . . . "The worst cases of antitrust abuses take place on a global basis. . . . They're stealing money from U.S. companies and consumers."[3]

[For a guide to antitrust resources on the Internet, see **http://www.antitrustinstitute. org/Antitrust_Resources/index.ashx**]

Part Two—Horizontal Restraints

When competitors collude, conspire, or agree among themselves, they are engaging in *horizontal restraints of trade.* Instead of competing to drive prices down and quality up, they may be fixing prices, restricting output, dividing territories, and the like. The various horizontal restraints are governed by Section 1 of the Sherman Act, which forbids contracts, combinations, or conspiracies in *restraint of trade.* What is a restraint of trade? In the *Standard Oil*[4] decision of 1911, the U.S. Supreme Court articulated what has come to be known as the *rule of reason.* In essence, the Court said that the Sherman Act forbids only *unreasonable* restraints of trade. The reasonableness of a restraint of trade is largely determined by a detailed balancing of the pro- and anticompetitive effects of the situation. Thus the plaintiff must prove the existence of an anticompetitive agreement or conduct and also prove that, on balance, the agreement or conduct harms competition. [For an antitrust overview, see **http://topics.law.cornell.edu/wex/antitrust**]

Some antitrust violations, such as horizontal price fixing, are so injurious to competition that their mere existence ordinarily constitutes unlawful conduct. Plaintiffs must prove that the violation in question occurred, but they need not prove that the violation caused, or is likely to cause, competitive harm. These *per se* violations are simply unlawful on their face.

Antitrust Enforcement Produces Lower Prices?

Antitrust law is often of direct value to consumers as illustrated by a 2008 settlement between the United States Justice Department and the National Association of Realtors in which the NAR guaranteed that realtors participating in the NAR-affiliated multiple listing services (MLS—local cooperative arrangements in which realtors list all of their properties for sale in a single database) will allow online real estate agents to have full access to those MLS listings. The newer Internet-based agents claimed they had often been blocked by local MLS associations from access to listings of houses for sale thus restricting their ability to fully compete with the traditional brokers. The online brokers, often achieving productivity efficiencies, are able to charge fees about one percentage point beneath the traditional industry standard of five to six percent of the purchase price thus generating substantial consumer savings. The settlement is subject to court approval at this writing.

Sources: "Justice Department Announces Settlement with the National Association of Realtors," Department of Justice Press Release, May 27, 2008 [**http://www.usdoj.gov/opa/pr/2008/May/08-at-467.html**] and Eric Lichtblau, "Realtors Agree to Stop Blocking Web Listings," *The New York Times,* May 28, 2008 [**nytimes.com**].

Horizontal Territorial and Customer Restraints

Principal legislation—Sherman Act, Section 1.

Every contract, combination in the form of trust or otherwise, or conspiracy, in restraint of trade or commerce, among the several states, or with foreign nations, is hereby declared to be illegal.

Assume two big food wholesalers dominate the market in their small state. Could they lawfully agree between themselves to divide their state geographically with one supplying the eastern half while the other supplies only the western half? Or could they lawfully allocate their customers such that one, for example, supplies all small town grocers while the other restricts itself to grocers in the few major cities? Suppliers might want to eliminate that competition among themselves, but such arrangements ordinarily are per se violations of the Sherman Act since they attempt to nullify the powerful benefits of competition.

Horizontal Price Fixing

Principal legislation—Sherman Act, Section 1

Competitors may not lawfully agree on prices. The principle is simple and fundamental to an efficient, fair marketplace. Establishing the presence of an unlawful price-fixing arrangement, on the other hand, ordinarily is anything but simple.

Proof

The major dilemma in price fixing and all other Sherman Act Section 1 violations is the measure of proof that satisfies the requirement of a contract, combination, or conspiracy. Evidence of collusion arises in a variety of ways. Broadly, a showing of cooperative action amounting to an agreement must be established. In general, that showing may be developed by any of the following four methods of proof:

1. **Agreement with direct evidence.** In the easiest case, the government can produce direct evidence such as writings or testimony from participants proving the existence of collusion.
2. **Agreement without direct evidence.** Here the defendants directly but covertly agree, and circumstantial evidence such as company behavior must be employed to draw an inference of collusion.
3. **Agreement based on a tacit understanding.** In this situation no direct exchange of assurances occurs, but the parties employ tactics that act as surrogates for direct assurances and thus "tell" each other that they are, in fact, in agreement.
4. **Agreement based on mutual observation.** These defendants have simply observed each others' pricing behavior over time, and they are able therefore to anticipate each other's future conduct and act accordingly without any direct collusion but with results akin to those that would have resulted from a direct agreement.[5]

Parallel Conduct

An unlawful conspiracy is to be distinguished from independent but parallel business behavior by competitors. So-called *conscious parallelism* is fully lawful because the competitors have not agreed either explicitly or by implication to follow the same course of action. Rather, their business judgment has led each to independently follow parallel paths. On the other hand, a conspiracy can sometimes be established by proof that the parallel behavior in question was not arrived at independently, To do so, the plaintiff must provide enough factual matter to raise a suggestion of a preceding agreement,[6]

Aggressive Enforcement

Both government advocates and free market champions agree that price fixing cripples the market. So government intervention, at the federal and state levels, and damage claims by wronged consumers are sometimes essential to maintain effective competition. Antitrust law, including price-fixing prohibitions, is designed to protect the consumer from a variety of commercial arrangements—some well intentioned, some overt cheating—that nullify the favorable effects of competition:

- Personal computer memory chip giants, Samsung (South Korea), Infineon (Germany), and Hynix (South Korea) pleaded guilty to federal price fixing charges in 2005 and agreed to pay a total of $645 million in fines for an international price fixing conspiracy in the dynamic random access memory (DRAM) market that also sent several executives to jail.[7] Later, Samsung agreed to pay $90 million in a nationwide settlement of price fixing claims by states arising from the worldwide chip cartel.[8] At least 38 states and a variety of private parties continue to pursue the chip makers at this writing. The direct loss to consumers was probably no more than $10 per computer purchased, but the total in "excess" profit for the chip makers likely exceeded $1 billion annually.[9]

- Ending nine years of litigation over alleged conspiracies to fix corn syrup prices, Archer Daniels Midland, A. E. Staley, and others agreed in 2004 to pay $531 million to settle a class action against them.[10]

- In May 1999 the U.S. Justice Department secured a criminal fine of more than $750 million from three international vitamin manufacturers. Those three and three other companies later agreed to pay $1.1 billion to settle civil price-fixing claims. The companies' executives allegedly got together to divide the worldwide vitamin market and set prices for the vitamins, and then they allegedly policed themselves to see that all conspirators were adhering to the agreement.[11]

> The companies' executives allegedly got together to divide the worldwide vitamin market

These are only a few of the many examples in recent years of price-fixing conspiracies in America and around the world. The effect of these unlawful arrangements is to harm competition and raise prices. Price fixing is nothing new, but its aggressive pursuit both domestically and around the world does represent a change in policy, as explained by Phillip Warren, U.S. Department of Justice antitrust chief in San Francisco:

> "I think it's been going on [for a long time], and we have only recently been able to detect and prosecute them," Warren said. "There's a long tradition of cartel activity, not in the United States but around the world. Cartels were accepted." . . .
> Prosecuting international cartels is "an important development, an exciting development, and certainly it's what keeps me coming back," Warren said. "There's no sign of it trending back at all. It's the way things are going and will continue to go."[12]

Models as Price-Fixing Victims? The case that follows involves a $50 million class action by some 10,000 professional models alleging that at least 10 leading modeling agencies conspired for more than 20 years to fix prices on the fees the agencies charge models to represent them. A New York State law ("Article 11") imposed a cap of 10 percent on the fees that employment agencies could charge their clients, but the plaintiff models claimed the defendant modeling agencies' fees rose to 20 percent or more. The defendants claimed they were managing the models and thus were not simply employment agencies. The defendants moved for a summary judgment to dismiss the plaintiffs' claim.

Fears v. Wilhelmina Model Agency, et al. 2004 U.S. Dist. LEXIS 5045 (S.D. N.Y.)

LEGAL BRIEFCASE

Judge Baer

FACTUAL BACKGROUND

Plaintiffs (the models) allege that defendants (modeling agencies), through their . . . industry's trade association, IMMA (now called MMC), had the opportunity to—and indeed did—fix prices. . . . Plaintiffs assert that defendants' price-fixing conspiracy originated with "an intention and plan collectively to evade the licensing requirements and fee restrictions imposed by New York State law ("Article 11")."

CONSPIRACY TO FIX MODELS' COMMISSIONS

In Count I of their complaint, plaintiffs assert that defendants violated [the Sherman Act] Section One by (1) initially conspiring to charge the majority of their models a commission in excess of the 10 percent statutory cap imposed by Article 11, and then (2) conspiring to increase this commission to 15 percent, and finally 20 percent.

Plaintiffs allege that defendants colluded to fix models' commissions through discussions, exchanges, and agreements at IMMA meetings and outside of IMMA's formal setting. Because the alleged conspiracy, as it involves horizontal price fixing, is illegal *per se,* this Court need only determine whether plaintiffs have established a material issue of fact as to whether defendants conspired to fix models' commissions.

* * * * *

Parallel Pricing "Plus"

While plaintiffs have not uncovered direct "smoking gun" evidence to confirm that defendants operated under an agreement to fix models' commissions, it is undisputed that there is evidence of parallel pricing, both at rates exceeding 10 percent, and at rates of 20 percent. Plaintiffs' expert, Martin A. Asher, Ph.D., concluded "from data provided by defendants" that "more than

97 percent of models who had billings within the class period, from 1998 through 2003, paid commissions in excess of 10 percent." Further, Asher reports that " approximately 91 percent of the models paid commission rates of 20 percent." Similarly, plaintiffs' second expert, John C. Beyer, Ph.D., concludes that "most models (approximately 96 percent) have been charged a commission rate of 20 percent or more." While plaintiffs' experts demonstrate parallel pricing, assuming defendants were aware of each other's pricing patterns, which the evidence suggests they were, conscious parallelism alone is insufficient to create a material issue of fact as to whether an agreement was formulated. For purposes of summary judgment, additional circumstances, referred to as "plus factors," must "provide a supplemental basis to infer a conspiracy." Among recognized plus factors, two in particular have received significant exposure in case law, both of which have a strong presence in this case—a motive to conspire and a high level of interfirm communication.

* * * * *

With regard to the first plus factor, there is no question that defendants possessed a common rational motive to conspire—the ability to raise models' commissions without suffering loss of business.

Second, it is beyond peradventure that IMMA members engaged in a concentrated degree of interfirm communication, including but hardly limited to models' commissions directly.

INTERFIRM COMMUNICATIONS

Plaintiffs assert that the conspiracy began with an agreement among defendants, collectively, to transform the structure of their businesses from employment agencies to management agencies for the express purpose of avoiding the 10 percent cap imposed upon employment agencies by Article 11.

* * * * *

Plaintiffs argue that through their conspiracy to evade Article 11, or more aptly their joint agreement to become management companies, defendants were able to raise the commission that they charged to models above Article 11's 10 percent cap, and eventually agree to uniformly charge models commissions of 20 percent—a commission rate which would have been impossible under their previous configurations. While defendants hotly contest the formation of any agreements as to models' commissions, they concede that there was significant information exchanged among IMMA members about pricing. [John Casablancas, founder of Elite Model Management] noted proudly that each company "basically knew the price practices of all the agencies . . . everybody knows what everybody else is doing." He also admitted that he "knew instantly every time an agency raised or when an agency didn't raise." Dieter Esch, then President and Chief Executive Officer of Wilhelmina, admitted that he may have announced to attendees of an IMMA meeting, in the approximate timeframe of 1996 through 1998, that he was charging a 25 percent commission to models, and Casablancas made a similar, yet even more troubling, announcement at the December 12, 1991, IMMA meeting that he too "*would be*" charging 20 percent commission to all clients as a firm policy." While Casablancas's announcement does not explicitly demonstrate an agreement among IMMA members to follow course, it suggests that IMMA members were made aware of their competitors' price increases before the price increases were enacted—leaving time for others to agree to increase their fees accordingly. Further, Casablancas conceded that "the more uniformity in the prices, the more I think it was—it was something that you could then compete on the quality of your models on the service, and not just on—on rates, you know. So we were always favorable to letting everyone know as much as possible about—about our pricing policies." Casablancas also testified that "I was always hoping that as leaders, we would be followed, and that we would not be left as we were on many instances by ourselves with higher rates, and having a lot of clients segregating against us because we were too expensive." While it is possible that Elite simply took the lead in raising its commissions, with the blind hope that other members would follow, it is far more reasonable to assume that Elite sought some guarantee that the other defendants would acquiesce, to ensure that its clients would not segregate against them.

This assumption is bolstered by significant evidence of discussions and agreements concerning raising the client service fees. Elite's internal memorandum "RE: IMMA Meeting—Minutes," reports that at a January 21, 1980, IMMA meeting, trade association members acted in unison with regard to pricing decisions. The memorandum reads in part that "the suggestion of increasing client service charge from 10% which Alain Kittler

suggested I [Jo Zagami] make at this meeting *was not accepted by the Association.* The general feeling was that *with the increase of model rates,* and the agencies benefiting by models' commissions, clients would not be agreeable to a higher service charge." This memorandum reveals both that one agency sought the "acceptance" of the trade association before increasing its client service fee and also strongly suggests that the "increase of model rates" was applicable to all members and not a decision made unilaterally by each company. Similarly, a memorandum recounting a November 14, 1980, IMMA meeting, makes clear that "certain members" had made "requests" "to increase the service charge from 10 to 15%." This Court can think of no other rationale for the need for such a "request," other than that members were required to act jointly with regard to price increases.

* * * * *

The evidence suggests that the management companies did approve an increase in the client service fee to 20 percent, with Elite taking the initiative in doing so. On April 14, 1987, Casablancas sent [Monique] Pillard the letter that he intended to send to his clients, announcing the increase in the service fee, and explained that "you may show [the letter] to some people at the next IMMA meeting." He explained further that "you should say that *it is our intent to send this letter* and you should be very careful that in no way can this be construed as 'price fixing'. You are merely to inform our competitors of our intention to send this letter or a similar one." The tone and tense of this letter suggests that Casablancas provided his fellow IMMA members with advance notice of Elite's intended price increase. As further evidence that Elite actually provided its competitors with notice of its intended price increase, and secured their agreement to follow suit, plaintiffs provide a May 5, 1987, memorandum from Pillard to all Elite staff, informing them of the service charge increase from 15 to 20 percent, effective June 1, and stating that "*all other agencies will go along with this increase.* Please inform your clients accordingly so that there is no misunderstanding." Only a rich fantasy life could lead one to an inference other than that Pillard was directing her staff to inform clients that the other agencies would institute similar increases so that clients would not "misunderstand" and cease utilizing Elite's services, in hopes of moving to a management company with lower fees. . . .

At a September 16, 1986, IMMA meeting, as reflected in an internal Elite memorandum, Pillard "made a point about lowering the prices of catalogs; that we are all committing suicide, if we do not stick together. . . . [A]s usual, Bill Weinberg [of Wilhelmina] cautioned me about price fixing . . . Ha! Ha! Ha! . . . the usual bulls . . t! I warned him that by not sticking together, we would have to make 40% more volume in order to make the same figures as last year, but you know Bill, he always thinks he can get more if he acts that way." Again, it is difficult for me to escape the inference that discussions of the benefits of joint action on pricing ensued. While Wilhelmina objects to the outward discussion of price fixing, it is plausible from Pillard's reaction that Wilhelmina's objection was to the dissemination of information, not to the underlying price-fixing agreement.

* * * * *

Notably, just prior to IMMA's distribution of its standard Model Management Agreement to its members in May 1993, its counsel Edward Klagsbrun found serious antitrust problems with pertinent sections. Klagsbrun noted in an April 6, 1993, memorandum to co-IMMA counsel David Blasband that "any agreement suggested by a trade association to its members who are competitors is inherently suspect and vulnerable to attack from the point of view of federal and state antitrust law."

* * * * *

Despite advice of counsel as to the antitrust problems associated with mandating any agreement, by cover letter of August 16, 1993, Hunter circulated a draft of the model contract and wrote that he felt that it was "a very good contract for IMMA Members to *endorse.*" Similarly, draft IMMA meeting minutes from September 15, 1993, reflect that "members who had received copies of the draft agreement were in agreement that the contract was ready to be adopted." . . . Shortly after IMMA adopted its standard Model Management Agreement in 1993, plaintiffs assert that four defendants, Ford, IMG, Next, and Wilhelmina, inserted substantially identical language in the section stating that models understood that managers were also "entitled to receive a service charge from clients."

* * * * *

Sufficiency of Evidence to Establish Price-Fixing Conspiracy

Despite the artful innocent explanations that defendants have offered for their parallel pricing, . . . when analyzed together, as it must be, the evidence of parallel pricing, coupled with the evidence of discussions and agreements among association members, demonstrates a material issue of disputed fact as to whether IMMA members acted independently with regard to models' commissions.

* * * * *

Plaintiffs have established that all defendants who were members of IMMA, and therefore participated in or were privy to the conversations and agreements discussed above, "had a unity of purpose or a common design and understanding, or a

meeting of minds in an unlawful arrangement." (*Int'l Distribution Centers, Inc.,* 812 F. 2d at 793.) . . . Therefore, Ford's, G. Ford's, Wilhelmina's, Elite's, Next's, IMG's, Click's, Images, and MMC's motions for summary judgment on plaintiffs' claim of a conspiracy to fix models' commissions are *denied.*

* * * * *

AFTERWORD

As the *Fears* case was going to trial, the parties agreed to an out-of-court settlement totaling about $ 22 million.[13]

Questions
1. *a.* Explain why the Court ruled for the plaintiffs by denying the summary judgment motion.

   b. In your view, does the evidence support the judge's conclusion that the case should go to trial? Explain.

2. Does this opinion tell us that competitors cannot lawfully talk about prices? Explain.

3. Did John Casablancas of Elite Model Management appear to violate antitrust law by acting as a price leader for his industry? Explain.

4. Assume two drugstores, located across the street from each other and each involved in interstate commerce, agree to exchange a monthly list of prices charged for all nonprescription medications. Is that arrangement lawful in the absence of any further cooperation? Explain.

5. The "Three Tenors," Luciano Pavarotti, Placido Domingo, and Jose Carreras, recorded a 1990 World Cup concert, distributed by Polygram, and a 1994 World Cup concert, distributed by Warner. Polygram and Warner subsequently agreed to jointly distribute and share profits from the 1998 World Cup Three Tenors concert. The 1998 recording apparently was less "new and exciting" than had been hoped. Concerned that sales of the earlier recordings would drain interest from the 1998 recording, Polygram and Warner agreed to cease all discounting and advertising of the two earlier recordings for several weeks surrounding the release of the 1998 album. In 2001, the Federal Trade Commission issued complaints against Polygram and Warner. Those complaints eventually reached the District of Columbia Federal Circuit Court of Appeals where Polygram and Warner defended themselves by arguing that the agreement was good for competition in that it increased the joint venture's profitability from new recordings, and it eliminated free riding by each company (for the 1990 and 1994 recordings) on the joint venture's 1998 marketing.

a. What antitrust violation was alleged by the Federal Trade Commission?

b. What is free riding, and why is it a problem?

c. Decide the case. Explain. See *Polygram v. Federal Trade Commission,* 416 F.3d 29 (D.C. Cir. 2005).

6. Assume that 10 real estate firms operate in the city of Gotham. Further assume that each charges a 7 percent commission on all residential sales.

a. Does that uniformity of prices in and of itself constitute price fixing? Explain.

b. Assume we have evidence that the firms agreed to set the 7 percent level. What defense would be raised against a price-fixing charge?

c. Would that defense succeed? Explain. See *McLain v. Real Estate Board of New Orleans, Inc.,* 444 U.S. 232 (1980).

Refusal to Deal/Group Boycotts

Principal legislation—Sherman Act, Section 1.

In America we are free to do business with whomever we prefer, correct? Generally, yes; but antitrust problems sometimes emerge. When does a *refusal to deal* with another raise antitrust issues? The clearest problem is a *horizontal group boycott* where *competitors agree* not to deal with a supplier, customer, or another competitor. Ford and GM, for example, presumably could not jointly refuse to buy tires from Bridgestone/Firestone. Such arrangements so thoroughly subvert the market that they ordinarily are *per se* violations of Sherman I and thus do not require a detailed evaluation of competitive harm and benefits, although a showing of market power by those in the group may be required. A unilateral (individual) refusal to deal by a buyer or a seller sometimes raises antitrust concerns if the firm refusing to deal is a monopolist and harm to competition can be proven.[14]

A recent battle among the big bank card companies illustrates refusal to deal reasoning (although for technical reasons the case was not tried under the refusal to deal/boycott label). In 1996 American Express decided to open its own credit card network to compete with Visa and MasterCard. No bank, however, was willing to deal with American Express. Why would the banks turn down the potential to make more money by working with the respected American Express brand? They did so because Visa and MasterCard had rules forbidding their members from issuing American Express and Discover cards. Visa and MasterCard operate as nonprofit joint venture associations owned by the member banks that issue their credit cards. As long as those banks wanted to do business with Visa and MasterCard, the two giants, they could not deal with American Express and Discover. Were the Visa and MasterCard refusal to deal rules lawful? No, as it turns out. The antitrust division of the federal Department of Justice sued the two giants for their alleged exclusionary practices and won in the federal courts.[15] The six-year struggle turned largely on the finding that continued exclusion of Discover, American Express, and others from the market were horizontal restraints that would likely harm future competition. A key finding was the conclusion that Visa and MasterCard, with their collective market share exceeding 70 percent, had market power.

American Express subsequently sued Visa for damages inflicted by the alleged exclusionary practices. In 2007, Visa agreed to pay $2.1 billion to settle that lawsuit. The settlement is believed to be the largest in antitrust history. Similar American Express claims against MasterCard are pending as are Discover's claims against both Visa and MasterCard.

Clarett Boycotted by NFL?

Antitrust shapes all dimensions of our lives, as football running back Maurice Clarett learned when he tried to enter the 2004 National Football League draft. Clarett, as a freshman, led Ohio State University to an undefeated season in 2002. Clarett was ineligible for college football in his sophomore year because of allegations that he accepted improper benefits and lied about doing so. Clarett then tried to enter the NFL draft but was barred by a league rule providing that players must have been out of high school for three seasons. Clarett sued the NFL, claiming its eligibility rules violated federal antitrust laws by, in effect, allowing competing teams to agree among themselves to boycott certain players (including Clarett, who had not yet been out of high school for three years). Clarett won at the federal district court level, but he lost on appeal when the court ruled that the eligibility rule is exempt (immune from scrutiny) from the antitrust laws. The NFL eligibility rule is the product of a collective bargaining agreement between the league and the players' union, the National Football League Players Association. Antitrust promotes competition while unions restrict it in various ways; but in balancing those competing interests, Congress and the courts have long granted unions certain exemptions from antitrust laws. The Supreme Court subsequently declined to review Clarett's case.

Questions
1. Should Clarett and future football players be free to sell their services on the open market?
2. Or is the NFL correct to encourage players to stay in college and mature before seeking to become professionals? Explain.

Source: *Clarett v. National Football League,* 369 F.3d 124 (2d Cir. 2004)

Questions

1. Baptist Eye Institute, a group of nonspecialized ophthalmologists in Jacksonville, Florida, controlling approximately 15 percent of the referral market, sent nearly all of its retina cases to the Florida Retina Institute. Is BEI engaging in an unlawful group boycott against plaintiff Retina Associates, a retina care provider in competition with the Florida Retina Institute? Explain. See *Retina Associates P.A. v. Southern Baptist Hospital of Florida Inc.,* 105 F.3d 1376 (11th Cir. 1997).

2. Discon, a telephone salvage company, sold services to MECo, a subsidiary of NYNEX, a phone company for the New York/New England area. MECo switched from Discon to AT&T Technologies, a Discon competitor, and paid a higher price to AT&T than it had paid to Discon. Discon claimed that the buyer and NYNEX then received a rebate from AT&T at the end of the year. Discon argued that NYNEX was able to pass on its higher costs to its customers because NYNEX was a part of a regulated phone market. Discon claimed that NYNEX, its subsidiaries, and AT&T were engaging in a group boycott in violation of the Sherman Act in order to drive Discon out of the market. Decide. Explain. See *NYNEX Corp. v. Discon, Inc.,* 119 S.Ct. 493 (1998).

Part Three—Vertical Restraints

We have been studying unfair trade practices by competitors—that is, horizontal restraints of trade. Now we turn to antitrust violations on the vertical axis—that is, restraints involving two or more members of a supply chain (such as a manufacturer and a retailer of that manufacturer's products). *Horizontal* restraints are those arising from an agreement among the *competitors* themselves, while *vertical* restraints ordinarily are those imposed by *suppliers* on their *buyers*. Horizontal restraints, in general, are per se unlawful while vertical restraints, in general, are to be resolved under the rule of reason. Horizontal restraints eliminate competition thereby undermining the power of the market while vertical restraints sometimes are harmful and sometimes are beneficial to competition and thus ordinarily should be evaluated on a case-by-case basis. Historically, vertical restraints have been divided into price and nonprice categories, but that distinction seems to receding in significance in light of recent Supreme Court decisions.

Resale Price Maintenance

Principal legislation: Sherman Act, Section 1; Federal Trade Commission Act, Section 5.

Manufacturers and distributors often seek to specify the price at which their customers may resell their products, a policy we might think of as vertical price fixing but which is formally called *resale price maintenance*. Having sold its product, why should a manufacturer or distributor seek to influence the price at which the product is resold? The primary reasons are threefold: (1) establishing a minimum price to enhance the product's reputation for quality, (2) preventing discount stores from pricing beneath full-price retail outlets, and (3) preventing *free riders*. (Why do some manufacturers or distributors want their products to be sold by traditional, full-price retailers rather than by discounters?)

Historically, an *agreement* between a seller and a buyer dictating the price at which the buyer may resell the product was a per se violation of the law. A *unilateral* specification of a resale price, on the other hand, has been permissible since 1919. Under the Supreme Court's 1919 *Colgate*[16] decision, sellers could lawfully engage in resale price maintenance if they did nothing more than announce prices at which their products were to be resold and unilaterally refuse to deal with anyone who did not adhere to those prices. Then in 1997, the Supreme Court ruled that *agreements* specifying *maximum* resale prices would no longer be considered per se violations and must be evaluated under the rule of reason.[17] In the 2007 *Leegin* case that follows, the Supreme Court overturned a nearly 100-year-old precedent in the *Dr. Miles* case[18] to rule that *agreements* specifying *minimum* resale prices must also be analyzed under the rule of reason; that is, those agreements are no longer per se violations of the law. Rather, they must be considered on a case-by-case basis weighing their pro- and anticompetitive effects. Justice Breyer, writing for the four dissenting justices, (dissent not reproduced below) argued that the evidence did not support overturning the long-standing *Dr. Miles* precedent and that the majority's position would likely result in higher prices and reduced innovation.[19]

Justice Kennedy

I

Petitioner, Leegin Creative Leather Products, Inc. (Leegin), designs, manufactures, and distributes leather goods and accessories. In 1991, Leegin began to sell belts under the brand name "Brighton." The Brighton brand has now expanded into a variety of women's fashion accessories. It is sold across the United States in over 5,000 retail establishments, for the most part independent, small boutiques and specialty stores. . . . Leegin asserts that, at least for its products, small retailers treat customers better, provide customers more services, and make their shopping experience more satisfactory than do larger, often impersonal retailers. [Leegin's president, Jerry] Kohl explained: "[W]e want the consumers to get a different experience than they get in Sam's Club or in Wal-Mart. And you can't get that kind of experience or support or customer service from a store like Wal-Mart."

Respondent PSKS, Inc. operates Kay's Kloset, a women's apparel store in Lewisville, Texas. Kay's Kloset buys from about 75 different manufacturers and at one time sold the Brighton brand. It first started purchasing Brighton goods from Leegin in 1995. Once it began selling the brand, the store promoted Brighton. For example, it ran Brighton advertisements and had Brighton days in the store. Kay's Kloset became the destination retailer in the area to buy Brighton products. Brighton was the store's most important brand and once accounted for 40 to 50 percent of its profits.

In 1997, Leegin instituted the "Brighton retail pricing and Promotion Policy." Following the policy, Leegin refused to sell to retailers that discounted Brighton goods below suggested prices. . . . In the letter to retailers establishing the policy, Leegin stated:

> "In this age of mega stores like Macy's, Bloomingdales, May Co. and others, consumers are perplexed by promises of product quality and support of product which we believe is lacking in these large stores. Consumers are further confused by the ever popular sale, sale, sale, etc.
>
> "We, at Leegin, choose to break away from the pack by selling [at] specialty stores; specialty stores that can offer the customer great quality merchandise, superb service, and support the Brighton product 365 days a year on a consistent basis. . . .

Leegin adopted the policy to give its retailers sufficient margins to provide customers the service central to its distribution strategy. It also expressed concern that discounting harmed Brighton's brand image and reputation.

* * * * *

In December 2002, Leegin discovered Kay's Kloset had been marking down Brighton's entire line by 20 percent. Kay's Kloset contended it placed Brighton products on sale to compete with nearby retailers who also were undercutting Leegin's suggested prices. Leegin, nonetheless, requested that Kay's Kloset cease discounting. Its request refused, Leegin stopped selling to the store. The loss of the Brighton brand had a considerable negative impact on the store's revenue from sales.

PSKS sued Leegin in the United States District Court for the Eastern District of Texas. It alleged, among other claims, that Leegin had violated the antitrust laws by "enter[ing] into agreements with retailers to charge only those prices fixed by Leegin."

* * * * *

The jury agreed with PSKS and awarded it $1.2 million.

* * * * *

The Court of Appeals for the Fifth Circuit affirmed. We granted certiorari to determine whether vertical minimum resale price maintenance agreements should continue to be treated as *per se* unlawful.

* * * * *

II

Resort to *per se* rules is confined to restraints . . . "that would always or almost always tend to restrict competition and decrease output." *Business Electronics,* 485 U. S. at 723 . . .

As a consequence, the *per se* rule is appropriate only after courts have had considerable experience with the type of restraint at issue, and only if courts can predict with confidence that it would be invalidated in all or almost all instances under the rule of reason. . . .

III

The Court has interpreted *Dr. Miles Medical Co.* v. *John D. Park & Sons Co.,* 220 U. S. 373 (1911), as establishing a *per se* rule against a vertical agreement between a manufacturer and its distributor to set minimum resale prices. . . .

The reasons upon which *Dr. Miles* relied do not justify a *per se* rule. As a consequence, it is necessary to examine . . . the economic effects of vertical agreements to fix minimum resale prices, and to determine whether the *per se* rule is nonetheless appropriate.

A

Though each side of the debate can find sources to support its position, it suffices to say here that economics literature is replete with procompetitive justifications for a manufacturer's use of resale price maintenance.

* * * * *

The justifications for vertical price restraints are similar to those for other vertical restraints. Minimum resale price maintenance can stimulate interbrand competition-the competition among manufacturers selling different brands of the same type of product-by reducing intrabrand competition-the competition among retailers selling the same brand. The promotion of interbrand competition is important because "the primary purpose of the antitrust laws is to protect [this type of] competition." *Khan*, 522 U. S. at 15. . . .

Absent vertical price restraints, the retail services that enhance interbrand competition might be under-provided. This is because discounting retailers can free ride on retailers who furnish services and then capture some of the increased demand those services generate.

Resale price maintenance, in addition, can increase interbrand competition by facilitating market entry for new firms and brands. "[N]ew manufacturers and manufacturers entering new markets can use the restrictions in order to induce competent and aggressive retailers to make the kind of investment of capital and labor that is often required in the distribution of products unknown to the consumer." *GTE Sylvania*, 433 U.S. at 55; . . .

Resale price maintenance can also increase interbrand competition by encouraging retailer services that would not be provided even absent free riding. It may be difficult and inefficient for a manufacturer to make and enforce a contract with a retailer specifying the different services the retailer must perform. Offering the retailer a guaranteed margin and threatening termination if it does not live up to expectations may be the most efficient way to expand the manufacturer's market share by inducing the retailer's performance and allowing it to use its own initiative and experience in providing valuable services.

* * * * *

B

While vertical agreements setting minimum resale prices can have procompetitive justifications, they may have anticompetitive effects in other cases; and unlawful price fixing, designed solely to obtain monopoly profits, is an ever present temptation.

Resale price maintenance may, for example, facilitate a manufacturer cartel. An unlawful cartel will seek to discover if some manufacturers are undercutting the cartel's fixed prices. Resale price maintenance could assist the cartel in identifying price-cutting manufacturers who benefit from the lower prices they offer. Resale prices maintenance, furthermore, could discourage a manufacturer from cutting prices to retailers with the concomitant benefit of cheaper prices to consumers.

Vertical price restraints also "might be used to organize cartels at the retailer level." *Business Electronics,* at 725-726. A group of retailers might collude to fix prices to consumers and then compel a manufacturer to aid the unlawful arrangement with resale price maintenance.

A horizontal cartel among competing manufacturers or competing retailers that decreases output or reduces competition in order to increase price is, and ought to be, *per se* unlawful. To the extent a vertical agreement setting minimum resale prices is entered upon to facilitate either type of cartel, it, too, would need to be held unlawful under the rule of reason.

* * * * *

A manufacturer with market power . . . might use resale price maintenance to give retailers an incentive not to sell the products of smaller rivals or new entrants. As should be evident, the potential anticompetitive consequences of vertical price restraints must not be ignored or underestimated.

C

Notwithstanding the risk of unlawful conduct, it cannot be stated with any degree of confidence that resale price maintenance "always or almost always tend[s] to restrict competition and decrease output." Vertical agreements establishing minimum resale prices can have either procompetitive or anticompetitive effects, depending upon the circumstances in which they are formed.

Respondent contends, nonetheless, that . . . the *per se* rule is justified because a vertical price restraint can lead to higher prices for the manufacturer's goods. . . . Respondent is mistaken in relying on pricing effects absent a further showing of anticompetitive conduct. . . . For, as has been indicated already, the antitrust laws are designed primarily to protect interbrand competition, from which lower prices can later result. . . .

Respondent's argument, furthermore, overlooks that, in general, the interests of manufacturers and consumers are aligned with respect to retailer profit margins. . . . A manufacturer has no incentive to overcompensate retailers with unjustified margins. The retailers, not the manufacturer, gain from higher retail prices. The manufacturer often loses; interbrand competition reduces its competitiveness and market share because consumers will "substitute a different brand of the same product.", see *Business Electronics,* at 725. . . .

Resale price maintenance, it is true, does have economic dangers. If the rule of reason were to apply to vertical price restraints, courts would have to be diligent in eliminating their anticompetitive uses from the market. This is a realistic objective. . . .

As a final matter, that a dominant manufacturer or retailer can abuse resale price maintenance for anticompetitive purposes may not be a serious concern unless the relevant entity has market power. If a retailer lacks market power, manufacturers likely can sell their goods through rival retailers.

* * * * *

For all of the foregoing reasons, we think that were the Court considering the issue as an original matter, the rule of reason, not a *per se* rule of unlawfulness, would be the appropriate standard to judge vertical price restraints.

* * * * *

Reversed.

Questions

1. *a.* What potential procompetitive considerations were cited by the court in supporting a rule of reason approach to resale price maintenance?

   b. What potential anticompetitive considerations were cited by the court?

2. Could we fairly conclude from the *Leegin* decision that resale price maintenance agreements are now "per se legal"? Explain.

3. Explain why the court said the seller's market power is an important consideration in assessing the legality of a resale price maintenance agreement.

Leegin *in Practice*   Advocates of the *Leegin* decision believe it will produce more competition and better service, but critics think the decision simply allows manufacturers to pressure and cut out discounters with the result that consumers will pay higher prices. Others expect *Leegin*'s impact to be modest. Thirty-seven states supported a continuation of the nearly 100-year-old per se standard so some of them may seek legislation or judicial rulings to retain the per se rule in their states. Likewise, Canada and the European Union, for example, take the per se approach to resale price maintenance. Of course, they too might change their stances in light of *Leegin*. Further, many sellers long since found ways to achieve their pricing objectives including the use of unilateral resale pricing policies, as explained above. In any case, if anticompetitive behavior emerges, it can still be attacked under the rule of reason standard. Finally, the *Leegin* ruling seems to affirm the current court's preference for free market principles and reduced judicial intervention in business practice.

Mercedes Overpriced in South Korea?

Two weeks after the *Leegin* ruling, South Korea's Fair Trade Commission ordered Mercedes-Benz Korea to stop its resale price maintenance practices. According to the *Korea Herald,* Mercedes-Benz Korea required its dealers to confer with the company in setting prices, and dealers had to follow pricing policies included in dealership contracts. The *Herald* also reported that some dealerships were prohibited from offering discounts and gifts to buyers of certain models. Penalties were then imposed for dealerships considered to be violating the rules. According to the *Herald,* the price of a large Mercedes, the S600 model, was about $291,000 in Korea and about $140,000 in the United States.

Questions
1. Do you think the Mercedes-Benz facts, as described by the *Korea Herald,* would violate U. S. antitrust law under the *Leegin* rule of reason standard? Explain.
2. Do you think American regulators should follow the aggressive Korean approach to the Mercedes resale price maintenance scheme, or should the market be allowed to work its will as much as possible? Explain.

Source: Choi He-suk, "Mercedes-Benz Ordered to Redress Sales Policy," *The Korea Herald,* July 13, 2007.

Vertical Territorial and Customer Restraints

Principal legislation: Sherman Act, Section I; Federal Trade Commission Act, Section 5.

In addition to price restraints, manufacturers commonly impose nonprice restraints including where and to whom their product may be resold. Those restrictions typically afford an exclusive sales territory to a distributor. Similarly, manufacturers may prevent distributors from selling to some classes of customers (for example, a distributor might be forbidden to sell to an unfranchised retailer). Of course, such arrangements, necessarily retard or eliminate *intrabrand* competition. Because price and service competition among dealers in the same brand ordinarily benefits the consumer, the courts have frequently struck down such arrangements. Still, those territorial and customer allocations also have merits. The *GTE Sylvania* case[20] enunciated those virtues and established the position that vertical restrictions are to be judged case by case, balancing interbrand and intrabrand competitive effects while recognizing that interbrand competition is the primary concern of antitrust law. Thus the rule of reason is to be applied to vertical territorial and customer restraints.

Tying Arrangements

Principal legislation: Clayton Act, Section 3; Sherman Act, Sections 1 and 2; Federal Trade Commission Act, Section 5.

> Clayton act, section 3. That it shall be unlawful for any person engaged in commerce, in the course of such commerce, to lease or make a sale or contract for sale of goods . . . or other commodities . . . or fix a price charged therefore, or discount from or rebate upon, such price, on the condition, agreement, or understanding that the lessee or purchaser thereof shall not use or deal in the goods . . . or other commodities of a competitor or competitors of the lessor or seller, where the effect of such lease, sale, or contract for sale or such condition, agreement, or understanding may be to substantially lessen competition or tend to create a monopoly in any line of commerce.

Tying arrangements are another form of nonprice vertical restraints. Typically, tying arrangements permit a customer to buy or lease a desired product (the tying product) only if she or he also buys or leases another, less desirable product (the tied product).

Apple has recently been accused of tying violations both in the United States and Europe. In brief, the plaintiffs are claiming that Apple's software prevents music bought from Apple's iTunes from being played on a player other than Apple's iPod and prevents music bought from other online sources from playing on the iPod. The plaintiffs argue that Apple has monopoly power in the portable digital player market and the online music market and that it uses that power to force consumers to bundle the iPod and iTunes music. The result is fewer options and higher prices, the plaintiffs claim.[21] Do you share these concerns about Apple's iPod/iTunes strategy?

Giants Battle   In a clash of commercial titans, a large class of merchants led by Wal-Mart, Sears, and others sued Visa and MasterCard, alleging that the bank card associations engaged in unlawful tying arrangements. Merchants wanting to accept the very popular Visa and MasterCard charge cards were also required to accept the associations' debit cards. The result, the plaintiffs said, was billions in losses because they were forced to pay higher fees for Visa and MasterCard debit cards rather than the lower fees of competing debit cards. The parties reached a $3 billion out-of-court settlement in 2003, the largest class-action settlement in antitrust history.[22]

The Law   The primary antitrust concerns with trying arrangements are twofold: (1) A party who already enjoys market power over the tying product is able to extend that power into the tied product market; and (2) competitors in the tied product market are foreclosed from equal access to that market.

The basic tying violation test is as follows:

1. The existence of separate products. (That is, two products are present rather than one product consisting of two or more components, or two entirely separate products that happen to be elements in a single transaction.)
2. A requirement that the purchase of one of the products (the tying product) is conditioned on the purchase of another product (the tied product).
3. Market power in the tying product.
4. Substantial impact on commerce in the tied product. (Some courts require a substantial *anticompetitive* effect in the tied product market.)

Proof of all four of those ingredients establishes per se illegality. When all four ingredients cannot be satisfied, the analysis may proceed on a rule of reason basis, weighing pro- and anticompetitive considerations. Critics argue that tying arrangements often enhance consumer welfare and, as such, the per se approach should be overturned, as in the *Leegin* case. The following case examines tying allegations in the context of a pizza franchise. The case turns in part on market definition, a topic that we address more thoroughly in Chapter 11. In brief, in order to establish market power in the tying product, the market itself must be defined. In doing so we consider the geographic market (where the product is sold in commercially significant quantities) and the product market (those products that are interchangeable and thus compete, one with the other).

Queen City Pizza, Inc. v. Domino's Pizza, Inc.

124 F.3d 430 (3d Cir. 1997) [Cert. Denied *Baughans, Inc. v. Domino's Pizza*, 523 U.S. 1059 (1998)]

LEGAL BRIEFCASE

Circuit Judge Scirica

1. FACTS AND PROCEDURAL HISTORY

A

Domino's Pizza, Inc., is a fast-food service company that sells pizza through a national network of over 4,200 stores. Domino's Pizza owns and operates approximately 700 of these stores. Independent franchisees own and operate the remaining 3,500. Domino's Pizza, Inc., is the second largest pizza company in the United States, with revenues in excess of $1.8 billion per year.

Under the franchise agreement, the franchisee receives the right to sell pizza under the "Domino's" name and format. In return, Domino's Pizza receives franchise fees and royalties.

The essence of a successful nationwide fast-food chain is product uniformity and consistency. Uniformity benefits franchisees because customers can purchase pizza from any Domino's store and be certain the pizza will taste exactly like the Domino's pizza with which they are familiar. This means that individual franchisees need not build up their own goodwill. Uniformity also benefits the franchisor. It ensures the brand name will continue to attract and hold customers, increasing franchise fees and royalties.

For these reasons, section 12.2 of the Domino's Pizza standard franchise agreement requires that all pizza ingredients, beverages, and packaging materials used by a Domino's franchisee conform to the standards set by Domino's Pizza, Inc. Section 12.2 also provides that Domino's Pizza, Inc., "may in our sole discretion require that ingredients, supplies, and materials used in the preparation, packaging, and delivery of pizza be purchased exclusively from us or from approved suppliers or distributors." Domino's Pizza reserves the right "to impose reasonable limitations on the number of approved suppliers or distributors of any product." To enforce these rights, Domino's Pizza, Inc., retains the power to inspect franchisee stores and to test materials and ingredients. Section 12.2 is subject to a reasonableness clause providing that Domino's Pizza, Inc., must "exercise reasonable judgment with respect to all determinations to be made by us under the terms of this Agreement."

Under the standard franchise agreement, Domino's Pizza, Inc., sells approximately 90 percent of the $500 million in ingredients and supplies used by Domino's franchisees. These sales, worth some $450 million per year, form a significant part of Domino's Pizza, Inc.'s, profits. Franchisees purchase only 10 percent of their ingredients and supplies from outside sources. With the exception of fresh dough, Domino's Pizza, Inc., does not manufacture the products it sells to franchisees. Instead, it purchases these products from approved suppliers and then resells them to the franchisees at a markup.

B

The plaintiffs in this case are 11 Domino's franchisees and the International Franchise Advisory Council, Inc. ("IFAC"), a Michigan corporation consisting of approximately 40 percent of the Domino's franchisees in the United States, formed to promote their common interests.

* * * * *

[The lower court dismissed the plaintiffs' antitrust complaints. We turn now to the Appeals Court's analysis of the relevant product market—Ed.]

Plaintiffs suggest the "ingredients, supplies, materials, and distribution services used by and in the operation of Domino's pizza stores" constitutes a relevant market for antitrust purposes. We disagree.

As we have noted, the outer boundaries of a relevant market are determined by reasonable interchangeability of use.

Here, the dough, tomato sauce, and paper cups that meet Domino's Pizza, Inc., standards and are used by Domino's stores are interchangeable with dough, sauce, and cups available from other suppliers and used by other pizza companies. Indeed, it is the availability of interchangeable ingredients of comparable quality from other suppliers, at lower cost, that motivates this lawsuit. Thus, the relevant market, which is defined to include all reasonably interchangeable products, cannot be restricted solely to those products currently approved by Domino's Pizza, Inc., for use by Domino's franchisees. For that reason, we must reject plaintiffs' proposed relevant market.

Of course, Domino's-approved pizza ingredients and supplies differ from other available ingredients and supplies in one crucial manner. Only Domino's-approved products may be used by Domino's franchisees without violating section 12.2 of Domino's standard franchise agreement. Plaintiffs suggest that this difference is sufficient by itself to create a relevant market in approved products. We disagree. The test for a relevant market is not commodities reasonably interchangeable by a particular plaintiff, but "commodities reasonably interchangeable by consumers for the same purposes." A court making a relevant market determination looks not to the contractual restraints assumed by a particular plaintiff when determining whether a product is interchangeable, but to the uses to which the product is put by consumers in general. Thus, the relevant inquiry here is not whether a Domino's franchisee may reasonably use both approved or nonapproved products interchangeably without triggering liability for breach of contract, but whether pizza makers in general might use such products interchangeably. Clearly, they could. Were we to adopt plaintiffs' position that contractual restraints render otherwise identical products noninterchangeable for purposes of relevant market definition, any exclusive dealing arrangement, output or requirement contract, or franchise tying agreement would support a claim for violation of antitrust laws. Perhaps for this reason, no court has defined a relevant product market with reference to the particular contractual restraints of the plaintiff.

* * * * *

[The plaintiffs alleged that Domino's unlawfully engaged in monopolization, attempted monopolization, exclusive dealing, and predatory pricing. The Court rejected those claims. We turn now to the Court's analysis of the plaintiffs' claim that Domino's imposed unlawful tying arrangements on its franchisees—Ed.]

E
Plaintiffs allege Domino's Pizza, Inc., imposed an unlawful tying arrangement by requiring franchisees to buy ingredients and supplies from them as a condition of obtaining Domino's Pizza fresh dough, in violation of § 1 of the Sherman Act. "In a tying arrangement, the seller sells one item, known as the tying product, on the condition that the buyer also purchases another item, known as the tied product." "[T]he antitrust concern over tying arrangements is limited to those situations in which the seller can exploit its power in the market for the tying product to force buyers to purchase the tied product when they otherwise would not, thereby restraining competition in the tied product market." "Even if a seller has obtained a monopoly in the tying product legitimately (as by obtaining a patent), courts have seen the expansion of that power to other product markets as illegitimate and competition suppressing." "The first inquiry in any tying case is whether the defendant has sufficient market power over the tying product, which requires a finding that two separate product markets exist and a determination precisely what the tying and tied products markets are."

Here, plaintiffs allege Domino's Pizza, Inc., used its power in the purported market for Domino's-approved dough to force plaintiffs to buy unwanted ingredients and supplies from them. This claim fails because the proposed tying market—the market in Domino's-approved dough—is not a relevant market for antitrust purposes. Domino's dough is reasonably interchangeable with other brands of pizza dough, and does not therefore constitute a relevant market of its own. All that distinguishes this dough from other brands is that a Domino's franchisee must use it or face a suit for breach of contract. As we have noted, the particular contractual restraints assumed by a plaintiff are not sufficient by themselves to render interchangeable commodities noninterchangeable for purposes of relevant market definition. If Domino's had market power in the overall market for pizza dough and forced plaintiffs to purchase other unwanted ingredients to obtain dough, plaintiffs might possess a valid tying claim. But where the defendant's "power" to "force" plaintiffs to purchase the alleged tying product stems not from the market, but from plaintiffs' contractual agreement to purchase the tying product, no claim will lie. For that reason, plaintiffs' claim was properly dismissed.

F
Plaintiffs allege Domino's Pizza, Inc., imposed an unlawful tie-in arrangement by requiring franchisees to buy ingredients and supplies "as a condition of their continued enjoyment of rights and services under their Standard Franchise Agreement," in violation of § 1 of the Sherman Act. This claim is meritless. Though plaintiffs complain of an illegal tie-in arrangement, they have failed to point to any particular tying product or service over which Domino's Pizza, Inc., has market power. Domino's Pizza's control over plaintiffs' "continued enjoyment of rights and services under their Standard Franchise Agreement" is not a "market." Rather, it is a function of Domino's contractual powers under the franchise agreement to terminate the participation of franchisees in the franchise system if they violate the agreement. Because plaintiffs failed to plead any relevant tying market, the claim was properly dismissed.

Affirmed.

AFTERWORD
The plaintiffs in the *Queen City* case filed for a rehearing, which was denied. Circuit Judge Becker dissented from that decision:

[The majority] has endorsed the questionable theory that the kind of tying arrangements involved here "are an essential and important aspect of the franchise form of business organization." But these theories are also flawed.

I believe that the approach endorsed by the majority might have been acceptable two decades ago when franchising was in its nascent, or at least its growing, stage. But now the food franchisors are leviathans, and I am underwhelmed by the suggestion that they may be permitted with impunity to perpetuate the type of arrangements pled in the complaint. These arrangements are clearly quite onerous to the average franchisee, a relatively small businessperson whose sunk costs in the franchise represent all or most of his or her assets and who lacks the considerable resources necessary to switch or defranchise. Moreover, the amount of commerce that the franchisors are foreclosing in the tied product market—for the pizza sauce, flour, and other supplies (for which nonfranchisor–dominated suppliers, be they individual firms or a franchise cooperative, could easily meet quality control specifications) is enormous.[23] [For a franchising litigation similar to *Queen City,* see **http://www.antitrustlawblog.com/article-quiznos-franchisees-do-not-get-it-their-way.html**]

Questions

1. Describe the product market as the *Queen City* court saw it.
2. Explain the potential harm of tying arrangements.
3. Explain why the majority ruled against the plaintiffs' tying claims.

4. The *Queen City* decision can be viewed as another victory for big business over the consumers and the "little guys" generally, or it might be viewed as healthy both for business and the consumer. Explain those two points of view.
5. Judge Scirica in *Queen City* wrote, "Courts and legal commentators have long recognized that franchise tying contracts are an essential and important aspect of the franchise form of business organization because they . . . prevent franchisees from free-riding." Explain what he meant about free riding.[24]
6. When *Late Night with David Letterman* was an NBC show, the network, for some time, required those wanting to advertise on *Late Night* to also buy spots on the *Tonight Show with Johnny Carson.*
   a. Does that packaging constitute a tying arrangement?
   b. Was it lawful? Explain.
7. Chrysler included the price of a sound system in the base price of its cars. Chrysler's share of the auto market was 10 to 12 percent. Chrysler did not reveal the "subprice" for the sound systems. Independent audio dealers objected on antitrust grounds. Explain their claim. Decide. See *Town Sound and Custom Tops, Inc. v. Chrysler Motor Corp.* 959 F.2d 468 (3d Cir. 1992); cert. den., 113 S.Ct. 196 (1992).

Exclusive Dealing and Requirements Contracts

Principal legislation: Clayton Act, Section 3; Sherman Act, Section 1.

Wal-Mart haters had further reason to be furious in 2005 when country music star Garth Brooks made a deal to sell his work exclusively through the retail giant. Those critics see the deal and others like it as monopoly abuse by Wal-Mart. Brooks and Wal-Mart both see their approach as "cutting out the middleman" (music labels) resulting in lower prices for consumers. In general, a retailer has every right to negotiate with its suppliers to receive those *exclusive deals.* By its nature, however, an exclusive deal cuts competitors out of a source of supply or a market for sale. Thus antitrust issues may emerge. An *exclusive dealing contract* is an agreement in which a buyer commits itself to deal only with a specific seller, thereby cutting competing sellers out of that share of the market. A *requirements contract* is one in which a seller agrees to supply all of a buyer's needs, or a buyer agrees to purchase all of a seller's output, or both. Exclusive dealing and requirements contracts, as a matter of law, are much like the refusal to deal situations previously discussed.

Pearl Jam and the Ticket Business Exclusive dealing contracts often benefit business and consumers by ensuring a stable supply, discouraging free riders, and generally enhancing efficiency. On the other hand, those deals are sometimes anticompetitive, as the rock

Pearl Jam pursued antitrust claims against Ticketmaster

group Pearl Jam alleged in its famous mid-1990s collision with Ticketmaster. Pearl Jam and others pursued antitrust claims against Ticketmaster, claiming that the ticketing giant's market dominance and exclusive dealing arrangements allowed it to charge unfairly high service fees. Neither Congress nor the Justice Department nor the courts were supportive of Ticketmaster's critics because, among other things, new firms were entering the market to compete with Ticketmaster. The battle continued, however, with the jam band String Cheese Incident filing exclusive dealing and collusion claims against Ticketmaster in 2003. String Cheese said that Ticketmaster was blocking the band's right to sell tickets to its own shows through its own ticketing agency, SCI Ticketing. Ticketmaster said that SCI was simply trying to free-ride on Ticketmaster's vast infrastructure. Whatever the truth, the two settled their dispute out of court in 2004 with SCI (now Baseline Ticketing) then able to sell a satisfactory number of tickets to its own shows.

In its lawsuit, SCI claimed that Ticketmaster controlled 60 percent of the ticketing market. SCI further claimed that Ticketmaster controlled exclusive ticket distribution rights for 89 percent of the top 50 U.S. arenas, 88 percent of the top amphitheaters, and 70 percent of the top theaters[25]—sometimes secured, experts allege, by paybacks to the arenas. Are those exclusive deals a violation of antitrust laws? In its war with the fans, Ticketmaster is basically home free at this point. Ticket buyers may feel aggrieved, but Ticketmaster has won in court. In any case, live performances are not necessary to personal survival. Should the law intervene when customers are willing to freely spend their money for discretionary purchases?

A new Ticketmaster fight has recently emerged

NBA Basketball   A new Ticketmaster fight has recently emerged; this time involving the top of the distribution chain rather than the fans at the bottom. The Cleveland Cavaliers, a National Basketball Association franchise, and an online ticket distributor, Flash Seats, are suing Ticketmaster for exclusive dealing/monopoly behavior in trying to maintain control over the secondary ticketing market (fans reselling their tickets) for Cavaliers games. That lawsuit came in response to a Ticketmaster suit against the Cavaliers seeking a ruling that Ticketmaster alone has the contractual right to sell Cavaliers tickets in both the primary and secondary markets. The Cavaliers and many professional sports teams have exclusive dealing arrangements with Ticketmaster to sell and distribute game tickets in the primary-ticketing market, but the Cavaliers have begun to use Flash Seats (partially controlled by the Cavaliers' owner) as an online secondary market for season ticket holders to sell tickets they no longer want. Ticketmaster insists that those tickets can lawfully be transferred or resold only through its own secondary ticket market.

Price Discrimination

Principal legislation: Clayton Act, Section 2, as amended by the Robinson–Patman Act. [For the statutory language, see **http://assembler.law.cornell.edu/uscode/15/13.html**]

Price discrimination involves selling substantially identical goods (not services) at reasonably contemporaneous times to different purchasers at different prices, where the effect may substantially lessen competition or tend to create a monopoly. A seller may resist a Robinson–Patman charge by establishing one of the following defenses: (1) The price differential is attributable to cost savings. (In practice, the cost savings defense has been difficult to establish.) (2) The price differential is attributable to a good faith effort to meet the equally low price of a competitor. (3) Certain transactions are exempt from the act. Of special note is a price change made in response to a changing market. Thus prices might lawfully be altered for seasonal goods or perishables.

Upon graduation from college, suppose you decide to open a neighborhood video rental store in your hometown. Business goes well for a time, but then Blockbuster opens a superstore nearby and rents its videos at prices significantly below yours. Blockbuster is able to secure a pricing advantage from the movie studios, so you are out of business.

> A coalition of independent video stores has sued Blockbuster

In recent years, a coalition of independent video stores has sued Blockbuster claiming that the rental giant and the movie studios have conspired to drive the small stores out of business. Thus far, however, that litigation has failed.[26] The video cases are among a number in recent years pitting independent operators (such as neighborhood bookstores and local pharmacies) against chains (such as Barnes & Noble and big hospitals) where the independents claim that suppliers charge their giant rivals lower prices than those charged to the small stores. These complaints reflect the philosophical battle over the role of antitrust law in a rapidly changing global market. Should we use antitrust to protect small businesses, thus protecting small towns and an historic way of life in America? Or should we accept the dictates of the market, where the efficiency of giants like Wal-Mart brings low prices and high quality to all? [For a Web site devoted to "How to Stop Wal-Mart (and Other Superstores)," see **http://www.lawmall.com/wal-mart**]

Free market advocates condemn price discrimination law as an attack on common, consumer-friendly pricing practices that often result in reduced prices. Why, the critics ask, would we assault those who engage in vigorous price competition? The Antitrust Modernization Commission, appointed by the federal government to study whether the antitrust laws need revision, was generally supportive of the current legislative structure, but it did recommend in 2007 that the Robinson-Patman Act be repealed.[27] In fact, the federal government seldom takes an enforcement action under Robinson–Patman, and in five opinions since 1979, the Supreme Court has progressively increased the requirements for success in a Robinson–Patman litigation.[28] Furthermore, the Modernization Commission argued that the act actually hurts the small businesses it was designed to protect because some suppliers refuse to sell to those small businesses simply because they do not want to create legal problems for themselves. Nonetheless, as the following case illustrates, smaller businesses often do turn to Robinson–Patman in their ongoing struggle against what they believe to be the unfair competition of "giants."

District Judge Pauley

Defendants Barnes & Noble, Borders Group, and Walden move for summary judgment on plaintiff The Intimate Bookshop, Inc's, price discrimination claims. . . .

BACKGROUND

* * * * *

To summarize, Intimate was an independent bookseller that sold books through retail stores located in the mid-Atlantic United States from 1959 until March 31, 1999. Defendants are retailers that sell books and other goods in large stores across the United States and through Internet Web sites. Defendant Borders Group is a holding company that operates bookstores through its subsidiaries, defendants Borders and Walden. Defendant Barnes & Noble operates bookstores and has an interest in defendant B&N.com, an Internet bookseller. Intimate alleges that defendants violated Sections 2(a) and 2(f) of the act through secondary-line price discrimination because they knowingly induced and/or received illegal lower, discriminatory prices on the publishers' books, and that such discriminatory prices injured competition. . . .

Price discrimination is classified into three categories under the act: (1) primary-line price discrimination, which "occurs when a seller's price discrimination harms competition with the seller's competitors;" (2) secondary-line price discrimination, which "occurs when a seller's discrimination impacts competition among the seller's customers; i.e., the favored purchasers and disfavored purchasers;" and (3) tertiary-line price discrimination, which "occurs when the seller's price discrimination harms competition between customers of the favored and disfavored purchasers, even though the favored and disfavored purchasers do not compete directly against another." *George Haug Co. v. Rolls Royce Motor Cars Inc.,* 148 F.3d 136, 141 n.2 (2d Cir. 1988)

DISCUSSION

Sections 2(a) and 2(f) of the Act

In contrast to other antitrust laws, the Robinson–Patman Act was specifically enacted to protect small businesses from discriminatory pricing by manufacturers in favor of large chain stores. . . .

Section 2(a) of the Robinson–Patman Act makes it unlawful for anyone engaged in commerce

to discriminate in price between different purchasers of commodities of like grade and quality, where . . . the effect of such discrimination may be to substantially lessen competition . . . with any person who either grants or knowingly receives the benefits of such discrimination, or with customers of either of them.

To state a claim for secondary-line price discrimination under Section 2(a), a plaintiff must show that (i) the seller conducted sales in interstate commerce; (ii) the seller discriminated in price between two buyers; (iii) the product sold to competing buyers was of the same grade and quality; and (iv) the price discrimination had an unlawful effect on competition.

Additionally, even if Intimate establishes a prima facie case of unlawful price discrimination, defendants are not liable under Sections 2(f) or 2(a) of the act if the lower, discriminatory prices they received are protected by one of the seller's affirmative defenses to price discrimination. Indeed, Sections 2(a) and 2(b) of the act afford sellers various defenses based on cost justifications and competitive conditions.

Robinson–Patman Act Relief

Proof of a violation itself does not create a compensable private injury under the act. A plaintiff is not entitled to "automatic damages" on a successful Section 2(a) or 2(f) price discrimination claim. Instead, a plaintiff must make some showing of "actual injury attributable to something the antitrust laws were designed to prevent.". . .

In that vein, though a plaintiff need not enumerate all possible sources of its loss, it must make some showing that the injury to its business was not caused by factors unrelated to the defendant's price discrimination. . . .

1. Survey Evidence

Intimate attempts to sustain its burden of showing actual injury and causation through a survey conducted by Dr. Bruce Kardon that purports to show that Intimate lost customers to defendants. . . . In that survey, former members of Intimate's book club were contacted and asked questions about where they purchased books and the reasons for choosing that retailer. Dr. Kardon acknowledged at his deposition, however, that his survey could not be used to show any dollar value of Intimate's lost sales to any defendant. Indeed, the survey does not even question respondents whether they stopped purchasing books from Intimate and switched to another retailer. Further, the survey did not determine the year, the geographical market, or the extent to which survey respondents shopped at a defendant's store.

Finally, the survey does not provide an adequate basis to discern whether, and the extent to which, the defendants' lawful, as opposed to unlawful, competitive conduct caused injury to Intimate.

Accordingly, this Court finds that Dr. Kardon's survey is insufficient to establish a causal link between Intimate's injuries and the defendants' allegedly unlawful conduct.

2. Expert Reports

Second, Intimate cannot meet the causation requirement through any of its other experts' reports or testimony. As noted, Intimate submitted five expert reports in addition to the Kardon Report that purportedly opine on its damages claim as well as its claim that defendants violated the act. Each of Intimate's experts admitted at their deposition, however, that (i) they could not establish any causal link between Intimate's lost sales and profits and defendants' alleged receipt of unlawful discounts; and (ii) their damages calculations and opinions are based merely on an assumption that the defendants' alleged violations of the act were the sole cause of Intimate's lost sales and profits. . . .

3. Disaggregation

Third, Intimate has provided no evidence, in any form, that defendants' alleged violation of the act, as opposed to other intervening market factors, was a material cause of its [lost] sales and profits. In fact, Wallace Kuralt, one of Intimate's owners, acknowledged at his deposition that some of Intimate's business loss may be attributable to factors other than the defendants' discriminatory activity, including (i) competition with nonparties Books-a-Million and Media Play; (ii) adverse business decisions; (iii) undercapitalization; (iv) a fire at plaintiff's flagship Chapel Hill, North Carolina, location; (v) competition with franchise bookselling chains and other independent bookstores; (vi) competition with nonparty mass merchants, such as Wal-Mart and Kmart and discount warehouses, such as Price Club, Costco, and Sam's Club; and (vii) competition with specialty book retailers such as Williams Sonoma, Office Max, Staples, and Home Depot.

* * * * *

Intimate's survey and damages models are impermissibly fraught with assumptions and speculation, which unquestionably fail to show that the alleged discriminatory prices the defendants received caused Intimate actual injury.

* * * * *

[Summary judgment dismissing the Robinson–Patman claims is granted.]

Questions

1. Why did Intimate Bookshop lose this case?
2. Explain why this case involves secondary-line price discrimination.
3. In what sense does the Robinson–Patman Act arguably reduce efficiency, thus harming consumer welfare?
4. Texaco sold gasoline at its retail tank wagon prices to Hasbrouck, an independent Texaco retailer, but granted discounts to distributors Gull and Dompier. Dompier also sold at the retail level. Gull and Dompier both delivered their gas directly to retailers and did not maintain substantial storage facilities. During the period in question, sales at the stations supplied by the two distributors grew dramatically, while Hasbrouck's sales declined. Hasbrouck filed suit against Texaco, claiming that the distributor discount constituted a Robinson–Patman violation. Texaco defended, saying the discount reflected the services the distributors performed for Texaco, and that the arrangement did not harm competition. Decide. Explain. See *Texaco v. Ricky Hasbrouck,* 496 U.S. 543 (1990).
5. Utah Pie produced frozen pies in its Salt Lake City plant. Utah's competitors, Carnation, Pet, and Continental, sometimes sold pies in Salt Lake City at prices beneath those charged in other markets. Indeed, Continental's prices in Salt Lake City were beneath its direct costs plus overhead. Pet sold to Safeway using Safeway's private label at a price lower than that at which the same pies were sold under the Pet label. Pet employed an industrial spy to infiltrate Utah Pie and gather information. Utah Pie claimed that Carnation, Pet, and Continental were in violation of Robinson–Patman. Decide. Explain. See *Utah Pie Co. v. Continental Baking Co.,* 386 U.S. 685 (1967).

Predatory Pricing

Principal legislation—Sherman Act, Section 2.

Can a giant legally reduce its prices below operating costs until a competing discounter drops out of the market and then raise those prices to supracompetitive levels? Intel, the world's computer chip giant, was accused by the European Commission in 2007 of pricing its chips below cost, among other violations. Intel's smaller rival, Advance Micro Devices (AMD), has filed suit in the United States on similar grounds and investigations are being conducted by government agencies in New York, Japan, and South Korea. *Predatory pricing* charges under European precedents have some reasonable probability of success, but in the United States they are very difficult to win. The U.S. Justice Department claimed that American Airlines engaged in predatory pricing in attempting to monopolize air travel at the Dallas–Fort Worth Airport from 1995 to 1997. Justice argued that American Airlines engaged in predatory pricing by lowering its prices to drive out seven discount carriers in the expectation that it could then recover its losses by charging monopoly prices. A federal court of appeals, however, ruled for American Airlines, holding that the government was unable to prove that American had priced its flights below cost (as measured by some appropriate formulation, such as average variable cost).[29] Thus the government had failed to satisfy the standard two-part test for establishing predatory pricing:

• Pricing below cost.
• A "dangerous probability" of recouping the losses suffered from the below-cost pricing.[30]

The *American Airlines* decision could be seen as a great victory for consumers in that it supports the right to cut prices as low as possible. But consider *BusinessWeek*'s description of American's pricing practices:

> . . . Between Dallas and Kansas City, for instance, American's average one-way ticket was $108 before low-cost start-up Vanguard Airlines Inc. entered the market in early 1995. That prompted American to cut fares to $80 and almost double the number of daily flights to 14. When Vanguard gave up in December 1995, American jacked up prices to $147 and scaled back the number of flights. Justice lawyers even had memos from American execs plotting the upstart's demise.[31]

Predatory Buying Predatory pricing law also applies to situations where a dominant buyer bids up prices so high that smaller rivals are unable to compete. Plaintiff Ross-Simmons, a smaller sawmill, filed suit claiming that its giant competitor Weyerhaeuser, with a 65 percent share of the market in a particular type of timber, had deliberately paid more than necessary for lumber so that Ross-Simmons could not compete. Ross-Simmons claimed that it was driven out of business by Weyerhaeuser's bidding practices. The case reached the U.S. Supreme Court which ruled that the strict standards applied to predatory pricing would also apply to allegations of predatory buying. Ross-Simmons was unable to meet those standards and Weyerhaeuser won the case.[32]

Internet Exercise	Using the Federal Trade Commission's "Frequently Asked Questions" page [**http://www.ftc.gov/bc/compguide/question.htm**], answer these questions:

1. Shopping for a stereo loudspeaker made by Sound Corporation, I couldn't find a dealer who would sell it for less than the manufacturer's suggested retail price. Isn't that price fixing?

2. I own a retail clothing store and the Brand Company refuses to sell me any of its line of clothes. These clothes are very popular in my area, so this policy is hurting my business. Isn't it illegal for Brand to refuse to sell to me?

3. I operate two stores that sell recorded music. My business is being ruined by giant discount store chains that sell their products for less than my wholesale cost. I thought there were laws against price discrimination, but I can't afford the legal fees to fight the big corporations. Can you help?

Chapter Questions

1. After reading this chapter, what is your judgment about the antitrust system?
   a. Does it work? Explain.
   b. How might it be altered?
   c. Could we place more reliance on the market? Explain.
   d. Do the statutes and case law, as a body, seem to form a rational package? Explain.

2. Scholar and jurist Richard Posner argues,

   > T]he protection of small business whatever its intrinsic merit cannot be attained within the framework of antitrust principles and procedures. The small businessman is, in general, helped rather than hurt by monopoly, so unless the antitrust laws are stood completely on their head they are an inapt vehicle (compared, say, to tax preferences) for assisting small business.[33]

   a. Is antitrust law an inappropriate vehicle for protecting small business? Explain.
   b. Should we protect small business? Explain.
   c. How does the presence of monopolies benefit small business?
   d. If it is not the proper vehicle for protecting small business, what role should antitrust law serve? For example, should social considerations (such as the maintenance of full employment and the dispersal of political power) assume greater importance? Or should antitrust policy hew as closely as possible to economic goals? Explain.

3. Subway sandwich shops required all franchisees to employ a computerized point-of-sale (POS) system. The only approved system was provided by an unrelated company, RBS. Vendors of a competing POS system sued Subway's parent, Doctor's Associates, alleging, among other things, an unlawful tying arrangement.
   a. Describe the alleged tie.
   b. Defend Doctor's Associates (Subway).
   c. Explain what the plaintiffs would need to demonstrate in order to prevail. See *Subsolutions, Inc. v. Doctor's Associates, Inc.,* 62 F. Supp. 2d 616 (D. Conn. 1999).

4. In *Continental T.V., Inc. v. GTE Sylvania, Inc.,* 433 U.S. 36 (1977), the U.S. Supreme Court took the position that interbrand, rather than intrabrand, agreements must be the primary concern of antitrust law.
   a. Why did the Court take that view?
   b. In your opinion, is the Court correct? Explain.
   c. Explain the "free-rider" problem that frequently concerns the courts in cases involving vertical territorial restraints, among others.

5. Could Whirlpool, the appliance manufacturer, lawfully refuse to deal with any purchaser that sells the products of a competitor such as General Electric? Explain.

6. Does a businessperson create antitrust problems by joining industry trade associations, promoting common safety standards for the industry, and contributing to industry advertising campaigns such as "take the family to the movies"? Explain. See John H. Shenefield and Irwin M. Stelzer, *The Antitrust Laws—A Primer*, 2nd ed. (Washington, D.C.: The AEI Press, 1996), p. 107.

7. Tanaka played soccer at the University of Southern California, a member of the PAC 10 Conference. She became unhappy, asked if she could transfer, and was told that she could. She decided to go to another PAC 10 school, UCLA. USC, unhappy with that choice, invoked an NCAA rule limiting transfers within a conference. The rule required her to sit out one year and to lose one year of eligibility. She sued USC and the NCAA on restraint of trade grounds.

   a. Explain her claim.

   b. Decide the case. Explain your decision. See *Tanaka v. University of Southern California*, 252 F.3d 1059 (9th Cir. 2001).

8. Assume two fertilizer dealerships, Grow Quick and Fertile Fields, hold 70 percent and 30 percent, respectively, of the fertilizer business in the farm community of What Cheer, Iowa. Assume the owner of Fertile Fields learns via inquiry, hearsay, and the like of Grow Quick's price quotes. Then, each growing season the Fertile Fields owner sets her prices exactly equal to those of her competitor. Is that practice unlawful? Explain.

9. Given identical competing products, why is identical pricing virtually inevitable— at least over the long run?

10. In 1968, Business Electronics Corporation (BEC) became the exclusive retailer in the Houston, Texas, area of electronic calculators manufactured by Sharp Electronics Corporation. In 1972 Sharp appointed Hartwell as a second retailer in the Houston area. Sharp published a list of suggested minimum retail prices, but its written dealership agreements with BEC and Hartwell did not obligate either to observe them, or to charge any other specific price. BEC's retail prices were often below Sharp's suggested retail prices and generally below Hartwell's retail prices, even though Hartwell too sometimes priced below Sharp's suggested retail prices. Hartwell complained to Sharp on a number of occasions about BEC's prices. In 1973, Hartwell gave Sharp the ultimatum that Hartwell would terminate his dealership unless Sharp ended its relationship with BEC within 30 days. Sharp terminated BEC's dealership. BEC filed suit alleging that Sharp and Hartwell had unlawfully conspired to terminate BEC and that the conspiracy was illegal per se under the Sherman Act, Section I. Decide the case. Explain. See *Business Electronics Corporation v. Sharp Electronics Corporation*, 485 U.S. 717 (1988).

11. Some antitrust experts argue that a firm possessing market power should be challenged by the government with the goal of eradicating the power as quickly as possible. Others maintain that the government should be patient with short-term market power. Explain those two points of view.

12. Adidas contracts with NCAA schools and their coaches to promote its products. An NCAA rule limits the amount of advertising that may appear on uniforms and equipment. Adidas complained that those restrictions on promotional rights "artificially limit the price and quality options available to apparel manufacturers as consumers of promotional space, force manufacturers to pay additional amounts for billboard space or other advertising, decrease the selection of apparel offered to the end consumer, increase the price of the apparel for end consumers, and financially benefit the NCAA." Adidas sued the NCAA on antitrust grounds.

    a. What antitrust violations were cited by Adidas?

    b. Decide the case. Explain. See *Adidas v. NCAA*, 64 F. Supp. 2d 1097 (1999).

13. A board-certified anesthesiologist was denied admission to the Jefferson Parish Hospital staff because the hospital had an exclusive services contract with a firm of anesthesiologists. The contract required all surgery patients at the hospital to use that firm for their anesthesiology work. Seventy percent of the patients in the parish were served by hospitals other than Jefferson. The anesthesiologist who was denied admission sued the hospital, claiming the contract was unlawful.

    a. What antitrust violation was raised by the plaintiff?

    b. Decide. Explain. See *Jefferson Parish Hospital District No. 2 v. Hyde*, 466 U.S. 2 (1984).

14. In 1990 the American Institute of Certified Public Accountants agreed to enforce a change in its ethics rules that allowed its members to accept contingent fees and commissions from nonaudit clients. The agreement was the result of a consent order between the AICPA and the Federal Trade Commission. Likewise, in 1990 the American Institute of Architects signed a consent order with the Justice Department that forbade the Institute from adopting policies that would restrain architects from bidding competitively for jobs, offering discounts, or doing work without compensation.

    a. What antitrust violation was the government seeking to stem in both of these cases?

    b. What defenses were offered by the professions for their policies?

15. Starter Sportswear had a license to manufacture and sell satin professional team jackets marketed as "authentic" because they were styled in the manner of jackets actually worn by the members of the various teams. A Starter policy statement provided that it would sell only to retailers that carry a representative amount of Starter's full line of jackets. Starter also had a minimum order policy specifying that it wouldn't deal with retailers who sought quantities beneath that minimum order. Trans Sport, a retailer, began selling Starter jackets to other retailers who did not meet Starter's requirements. At that point, Starter declined to deal further with Trans Sport. Trans Sport then sued Starter.

    a. List Trans Sport's claims against Starter.

    b. Resolve those claims, raising all the relevant issues. See *Trans Sport, Inc. v. Starter Sportswear, Inc.*, 964 F. 2d 186 (2d Cir. 1992).

Notes

1. *White, Polak, Harris and Craig v. National Collegiate Athletic Association,* Case No. CV 06-0999 RGK (MANx), (U.S. District Court Central District of California, Western Division). Second Amended Complaint for Violation of Section 1 of the Sherman Act, 15 U.S.C. Section 1, p. 25, lines 3–5.

2. David G. Savage, "Antitrust Law Losing Its Teeth," *Los Angeles Times,* March 19, 2007 [**http://www.latimes.com/news/nationworld/nation/la-na-antitrust19mar19,0,3050690.story?page=2&track=ntothtml**].

3. Steven Thomas, "First President of New Century Brings Dramatic Change," *Waterloo/Cedar Falls Courier,* January 21, 2001, p. F1.

4. *Standard Oil Co. of New Jersey v. United States,* 221 U.S. 1 (1911).

5. This analysis is drawn from William Kovacic, "The Identification and Proof of Horizontal Agreements under the Antitrust Laws," *Antitrust Bulletin* 38, no. 1 (Spring 1993), p. 5.

6. *Bell Atlantic Corp. v. Twombly,* 127 S.Ct. 1955 (2007).

7. Laurie J. Flynn, "Samsung to Pay Large Fine in Price-Fixing Conspiracy," *The New York Times,* October 14, 2005 [**http://www.nytimes.com/2005/10/14/technology/14chip.htm**].

8. Press Release, "States Obtain $90 Million for Consumers Harmed by Semiconductor Price-Fixing Conspiracy" [**http://www.ag.state.il.us/pressroom/2007_02/20070206.html**].

9. Joseph Menn, "Samsung Pleads Guilty to Price Fixing," *Waterloo/Cedar Falls Courier,* October 14, 2005, p. B4.

10. Bill Myers, "$100 Million Accord in Price-Fix Lawsuit," *Chicago Daily Law Bulletin,* July 29, 2004.

11. *Washington Post,* "Vitamin Giants to Settle Antitrust Suit," *Waterloo/Cedar Falls Courier,* September 8, 1999, p. A9.

12. Jeff Chorney, "Amnesty International: S.F. Antitrust Prosecutors Are Breaking Cartels with Immunity," *The Recorder,* September 27, 2004, p. 1.

13. *Fears v. Wilhelmina,* No. 02 Civ. 4911 (HB) (HBP) (S.D.N.Y. 2005).

14. The analysis in this paragraph relies considerably on Donald M. Falk, "Antitrust and Refusals to Deal after *Nynex v. Discon,*" *Practical Lawyer* 46, no. 3 (2000), p. 25.

15. *United States v. Visa and MasterCard,* 344 F.3d 229 (2d. Cir. 2003); cert. den. *Visa v. United States,* 125 S.Ct. 45(2004).

16. *United States v. Colgate & Co.,* 250 U.S. 300 (1919).

17. *State Oil Co. v. Khan,* 118 S.Ct. 275 (1997).

18. *Dr. Miles Medical Co. v. John D. Park & Sons Co.,* 220 U.S. 373 (1911).

19. For a journalistic account of the *Leegin* case, see Stephen Labaton, "Century-Old Ban Lifted on Minimum Retail Pricing," *The New York Times,* June 29, 2007 [**http://www.nytimes.com/2007/06/29/washington/29bizcourt.html**].

20. *Continental T.V., Inc. v. GTE Sylvania, Inc.,* 433 U.S. 36 (1977).

21. Kasper Jade, "Class-Action Charges Apple with Illegally Tying iPods to iTunes," *Apple Insider,* November 7, 2007 [**http://www.appleinsider.com**].

22. *Wal-Mart v. Visa and MasterCard,* 396 F.3d 96 (2005).

23. *Queen City Pizza, Inc. v. Domino's Pizza, Inc.,* 129 F.3d 724 (3d Cir. 1997).

24. *Queen City Pizza, Inc. v. Domino's Pizza, Inc.,* 124 F.3d 430, 440 (3d Cir. 1997).

25. Steve Knopper, "Incident Fight Ticketmaster," *RollingStone.com* [**http://www.rollingstone.com/news/story/_id/5936870**].

26. *Cleveland v. Viacom,* 2003 U.S. App. LEXIS 17717 (5th Cir.); cert. den. *Cleveland v. Viacom,* 540 U.S. 1219 (2004).

27. "Panel Urges Repeal of '30s Era Antitrust Law," *Reuters,* April 3, 2007 [**http://www.reuters.com/articleousiv/idUKN0244771620070403**].

28. Elaine Foreman and Robert Skitol, "*Volvo v. Reeder*: Narrow Holding, Broad Implications," *The Antitrust Source* [**http://www.abanet.org/antitrust/at-source/06/03/Mar06-Skitol3=22f.pdf**].

29. *United States v. AMR Corp,* 335 F.3d 1109 (10th Cir. 2003).

30. *Brooke Group Ltd. v. Brown & Williamson Tobacco Corp., 509 U.S. 209 (1993).*

31. Dan Carney, "Predatory Pricing: Cleared for Takeoff," *BusinessWeek,* May 14, 2001, p. 50.

32. *Weyerhaeuser Co. v. Ross-Simmons Hardwood Lumber,* 127 S.Ct. 1069 (2007).

33. Richard Posner, *Antitrust Law* (Chicago: University of Chicago Press, 1976), p. 4.

Antitrust Law— Monopolies and Mergers

After completing this chapter, students will be able to:

1. Explain how Microsoft violated U.S. antitrust laws.

2. Analyze when a monopoly has been created.

3. Identify the potential benefits and hazards of mergers.

4. Distinguish between horizontal and vertical mergers.

5. Explain premerger notification requirements.

6. Describe remedies for mergers determined to be anticompetitive.

7. Analyze when a horizontal merger is anticompetitive.

8. Analyze when a vertical merger creates anticompetitive "market foreclosure."

9. Contrast antitrust enforcement in the United States and the European Union (EU).

Introduction—Microsoft and Monopoly

Is Microsoft an outsized, predatory law breaker, an amazing force for technological progress, or both? The U.S. Justice Department, 18 states, and the District of Columbia went to trial against Microsoft in 1998, claiming not that the software giant was too big, but that it had violated various antitrust laws in gaining and maintaining its market dominance. An epic legal struggle followed with major elements of the American justice system challenging one of the world's richest men, Bill Gates.

> An epic legal struggle followed with major elements of the American justice system challenging the world's richest man, Bill Gates

A federal district court in 2000 and later a federal court of appeals ruled that Microsoft had violated federal antitrust laws by maintaining its 95 percent share of the Intel-compatible PC operating systems market through anticompetitive means (basically using its monopoly power to coerce customers to buy other Microsoft products such as its browser, Internet Explorer).[1] The district court judge ordered Microsoft split into two companies as a remedy for its antitrust wrongs, but the court of appeals threw out that order. Thereafter, the case was settled out of court with Microsoft agreeing, among other things, to not retaliate unfairly against other software and computer makers and to disclose some software code.

The settlement, though somewhat of a victory for Microsoft, might also be regarded as a victory for common sense in allowing Microsoft to go forward with its remarkable work. The decision places considerable faith in the market, as it probably should in America; but the case also represents a powerful affirmation of the government's authority to attack monopoly behavior no matter how prominent the wrongdoer.

As it turns out, the federal antitrust charges were only the beginning of Microsoft's battles. Settlements with Novell, Sun Microsystems, AOL, RealNetworks and others cost Microsoft billions. The European Union turned up the heat on Microsoft in 2007 when its Court of First Instance affirmed earlier rulings that Microsoft had abused its near-monopoly power by illegally bundling its Windows Media Player inside the Windows operating system thus effectively shutting out media player rivals, such as RealPlayer. The court also found that Microsoft violated EU law by not sharing confidential computer code with its competitors thus limiting their ability to make their products work with Microsoft's dominant operating system. In 2007 Microsoft accepted the court's ruling along with penalties that might total $2.5 billion. At this writing, the European Commission has opened a new investigation exploring whether Microsoft harmed Opera (a Norwegian Web browser) by bundling Internet Explorer with Windows. The Microsoft struggles underline the aggressive stance of EU antitrust regulators. Since 25 percent of the global market for many products resides in the European Union, all big companies must now think more carefully about how their practices will be received by EU regulators even if those practices are not of concern to U.S. regulators.

Meanwhile, a group of 10 states, led by California, urged continued U.S. government oversight of Microsoft pointing to its 92 percent share of the PC operating systems market in 2006 along with an 85 percent share of the Web browser market.[2] At this writing, Microsoft's compliance with the U.S. settlement is to be monitored by a federal judge through late 2009. This remarkable odyssey is a powerful testament to our hunger for fairness and justice. But it also offers a less edifying message, as CNBC journalist Alan Murray explained in *The Wall Street Journal:*

> The Microsoft saga serves as a reminder of an important truth: Capitalists, for the most part, don't care much for capitalism. Their goal is to make money. And if they can do it without messy competition, so much the better. As long as it keeps its monopoly, Microsoft can afford to share the wealth with its onetime rivals. For Microsoft, those fines and payments add up to less than a year's profit from the operating system. For the others, it's easier to take Microsoft's money than fight.[3]

Power The Microsoft battle is about whether a giant bullied its rivals, but it is also about the very nature of capitalism—that is, the role of the market and government in

American life. The case obliges us to think about what we want America to be and what role the law should play in securing that ideal. By considering Microsoft and other cases, we can learn the rudiments of the law while thinking about how much faith we want to place in the free market. The excerpt that follows condemns the increasing concentration of wealth and power in the hands of a small number of corporate giants and wealthy individuals. [For links to many antitrust Web sites, see **http://www.antitrustinstitute. org/Antitrust_Resources/index.ashx**]

READING

Perspective on Antitrust: Keep an Eye on the Monopolists

Jeff Gates

* * * * *

It should come as no surprise in these market-myopic times that the (Microsoft) case turned on the narrow issue of competition. Yet that confuses the means with the end. The trust-busters of the 1890s had no idea how markets would be dominated a century later. That wasn't the issue. The target was not the monopoly but the monopolists—the economic royalists with their kingly prerogatives—and the keen dangers they pose to democracy. That's why they urged that monopolies be broken up and their forbidden fruits dispersed.

Jefferson and Madison were similarly insistent. They warned about monarchical tendencies in the marketplace and the impossibility of maintaining a robust democracy along side an economic oligarchy. Yet that's what today's market-obsessed perspective has wrought. The financial wealth of the top 1 percent of Americans now exceeds the combined net worth of the bottom 95 percent, according to New York University economist Edward Wolff. [Bill] Gates's wealth alone exceeds the net worth of the bottom 45 percent. The personal assets of Microsoft co-founders Paul Allen and Gates plus Berkshire Hathaway's Warren Buffet exceed the combined gross domestic products of the world's 41 poorest countries, with their 550 million citizens. So much for being a beacon of hope for democracy.

* * * * *

Contrary to the misplaced focus of the current debate, antitrust isn't just about monopolizing markets. Never was.

It's about redressing the antidemocratic results that accompany abuse of the market. To address only the means while leaving intact the gains mocks the very rationale for antitrust.

* * * * *

Source: *Los Angeles Times,* January 12, 2000, Metro, Part B, p. 7. Reprinted by permission.

Questions

1. *a.* Do you see increasing concentration of wealth and power as a threat to America's long-term welfare? Explain.
   b. If that concentration is a concern, is antitrust law the best remedy?
2. Jeff Gates, in this article, says antitrust is about "redressing the antidemocratic results that accompany abuse of the market." Explain what he means.
3. Does the *Microsoft* case stand simply for the view that bigness is bad? Explain.
4. Critics have argued that technology is eliminating the imperfections of the market, making antitrust law enforcement obsolete in this high-tech era.
   a. Explain that argument.
   b. Now build the argument that high-tech industries may actually be especially susceptible to antitrust problems because of the need to maintain the compatibility of equipment (like the dominance of the VHS format in the video business).

Part One—Monopoly

Both the federal district court and the court of appeals in the *Microsoft* case concluded that the computer giant holds monopoly power in the Intel-compatible PC operating systems market. How did those courts reach that conclusion? How do we know when an organization is an unlawful monopolist? An extensive, sophisticated, yet imperfect system of analysis has emerged. [For the American Bar Association Antitrust section, see **http://www.abanet.org/antitrust**]

Principal Monopoly Legislation: Sherman Act, Section 2

> Every person who shall monopolize, or attempt to monopolize, or combine or conspire with any other person or persons, to monopolize any part of the trade or commerce among the several States, or with foreign nations, shall be deemed guilty of a felony punishable by a fine.

Section 5 of the Federal Trade Commission Act also applies to most antitrust violations.

From an economic viewpoint, a *monopoly* is a situation in which one firm holds the power to control prices and/or exclude competition in a particular market. The general legal test for monopolization is

1. The possession of monopoly power in the relevant market, and
2. The willful acquisition or maintenance of that power, as distinguished from growth or development as a consequence of a superior product, business acumen, or historic accident.[4]

Thus the critical inquiries are the percentage of the market held by the alleged monopolist and the behavior that produced and maintained that market share. Antitrust law does not punish efficient companies who legitimately earn and maintain large market shares.

Indeed, high market concentration often promotes competition, whereas a fragmented market of many small firms may produce higher prices. (Imagine a retail food market of many corner grocery stores and no supermarkets.) Nonetheless, the federal government continues to rely strongly on market concentration data (*structure*) in combination with evidence of actual behavior (*conduct*) to identify anticompetitive situations. Market share alone is highly unlikely to lead to antitrust action, but a high market share acquired and/or maintained via abusive conduct (as alleged in *Microsoft*) is likely to be challenged.

Oligopoly A few firms sharing monopoly power constitute an *oligopoly*. Scholar Thomas Piraino reminds us that oligopolistic markets are common in American life:

> The public accounting industry includes only four national firms; four automobile companies produce approximately 75 percent of the cars in the United States; seven national carriers control most domestic airline traffic; Visa and MasterCard together account for most of the transactions in the credit card market; four tobacco companies manufacture 97 percent of the cigarettes sold in the United States; and five pharmaceutical companies produce most of the nation's prescription drugs.[5]

Oligopolies may promote competition, but they also raise the threat of collusion. With a few firms controlling enormous markets, competitors may find value in unlawful cooperation. Because express collusion is illegal on its face (see Chapter 10), those rivals, as Piraino explains, may find other ways of communicating their anticompetitive messages:

> [O]ligopolists can engage in informal means of communicating and enforcing a consensus price, such as by signaling planned price increases in press releases or on the Internet.[6]

PRACTICING ETHICS   Apple a Monopolist?

An antitrust lawsuit filed against Apple in 2007 charged the company with monopolizing the digital music market. The complaint claimed that Apple controls 75 percent of the online video market, 83 percent of the online music market, more than 90 percent of the hard-drive based music player market and 70 percent of the Flash-based music player market. Beyond its large market shares, the complaint alleged that Apple uses anticompetitive measures to secure and retain its dominance:

- Apple's iPod, alone among successful digital music players, does not support the Windows Media Audio (WMA) format.
- Apple deliberately designed its iPod software so that it would play only Apple's format.
- Apple's iPod Shuffle is capable of playing WMA files, but Apple deliberately disabled that feature.
- Apple's pricing is "monopolistic, excessive, and arbitrary." The complaint cites a $5.52 wholesale price difference between a one-GB ($4.15) and four-GB ($9.67) flash memory module that results in a $100

retail price difference between the one-GB iPod Nano and the four-GB Nano.[7]

The legal merits of the complaint are debatable particularly in that music listeners have many options should they not want to do business with Apple. Further, changing technology seems likely to address some of the alleged problems. For the moment, however, we will leave the law aside and think about ethics; the right and wrong of Apple's alleged monopolistic behavior.

Questions

1. Is it unethical for Apple to control 70 to 90 percent of the music player markets? Explain.
2. Would it be unethical of Apple to design its music players so they are incompatible with competing systems such as those of its big rival, Microsoft? Explain.
3. Would it be unethical of Apple to price its iPod Nano in an "excessive" or "arbitrary" manner not reflecting the underlying costs of the Nano? Explain.

Monopolization Analysis

Although the case law is not a model of clarity, a rather straightforward framework for monopoly analysis has emerged:

1. Define the relevant *product market*.
2. Define the relevant *geographic market*.
3. Compute the defendant's *market power*.
4. Assess the defendant's *intent* (predatory or coercive conduct).
5. Raise any available *defenses*.

1. Product Market

Here the court seeks, effectively, to draw a circle that encompasses categories of goods in which the defendant's products or services compete and that excludes those not in the same competitive arena. The fundamental test is *interchangeability* as determined primarily by the price, use, and quality of the product in question.

An analysis of cross-elasticity of demand is a key ingredient in defining the product market. Assume that two products, X and Y, appear to be competitors. Assume that the price of X doubled and Y's sales volume was unchanged. What does that tell us about whether X and Y are, in fact, in the same product market?

Defining the product market is really the process we all go through in routine purchasing decisions. Let us assume that you feel a rather undefined hunger for salty snack food. You go to the nearby convenience store. Many options confront you, but for simplicity, let's confine them to chips, nuts, and popcorn. Of course, each of those food types is composed of variations. As you sort through the choices—corn chips, cheese curls, peanuts, potato chips, and so on—you employ the criteria of price, use, and quality in focusing your decision. In so doing, you are defining the product market for "salty junk food." Products closely matched in price, use, and quality are interchangeable, and thus are competitors in the same product market. But, for example, an imported salty cheese at $10 per quarter pound presumably is not in the same product market as salted sunflower seeds.

Expressed as a matter of elasticity, the critical question becomes something like the following: If the price of potato chips, for example, falls by 10 percent, does the sales volume of salted nuts likewise fall? If so, we have a strong indication that potato chips and salted nuts lie in the same product market and thus are competitors.

2. Geographic Market

Once the product market has been defined, we still must determine where the product can be purchased. The judicial decisions to date offer no definitive explanation of the geographic market concept. A working definition might be "any section of the country where the product is sold in commercially significant quantities." From an economic perspective, the geographic market is defined by elasticity. If prices rise or supplies are reduced within the geographic area in question (New England, for example) and demand remains steady, will products from other areas enter the market in a quantity sufficient to affect price and/or supply? If so, the geographic market must be broadened to embrace those new sources of supply. If not, the geographic market is not larger than the area in question (New England). Perhaps a better approach is to read the cases and recognize that each geographic market must simply be identified in terms of its unique economic properties.

3. Market Power

Market Share

Does the market share held by the defendant threaten competition? How large that share must be to raise monopoly concerns depends on a variety of considerations including how fragmented or concentrated the market is. The *Harvard Law Review,* however, notes some approximate boundaries:

> Market share above 70 percent typically suffices to support an inference of monopoly power. Conversely, courts have rarely found monopoly power when a firm's market share is below 50 percent, leaving some uncertainty as to market shares between 50 and 70 percent.[8]

Market share alone, however, does not establish monopoly power. Barriers to entry, economies of scale, the strength of the competition, trends in the market, and pricing patterns all help to determine whether the market remains competitive despite a single firm's large share. (Why are the courts interested in barriers to entry?)

4. Intent (Predatory or Coercive Conduct)

Assuming a threatening market share is established, the next requirement is proof of an intent to monopolize. Remember that a monopoly finding requires a showing of both market power (*structure*) and willful acquisition or maintenance of that power (*conduct*). Antitrust law is not designed to attack legitimately earned market power. Rather, the concern lies with those holding monopoly power that was earned or is maintained wrongfully. Thus a showing of deliberate, predatory, coercive, or unfair conduct (such as collusion leading to price fixing) will normally suffice to establish the requisite intent.

5. Defenses

The defendant may yet prevail if the evidence demonstrates that the monopoly was innocently acquired via "superior skill, foresight, or industry"; that is, the monopoly was earned. Sometimes a monopoly may be "thrust upon" the monopolist because the competition failed or because of "natural monopoly" conditions where the market will support only one firm or where large economies of scale exist (such as for electricity suppliers). [For an antitrust law professors blog, see **http://lawprofessors.typepad.com/antitrustprof_blog**]

Attempted Monopolization

The Sherman Act forbids attempts to monopolize as well as monopoly itself. In the 1993 *Spectrum Sports* decision,[9] the Supreme Court set out a three-part test for attempted monopolization: (1) that the defendant has engaged in predatory or anticompetitive conduct with (2) a specific intent to monopolize and (3) a dangerous probability of achieving monopoly power (by which the court was insisting upon evidence of some "realistic" likelihood that monopoly would actually follow).

Monopoly Case I

The case that follows is a private antitrust action involving soft drink giant PepsiCo's claim that rival giant Coca-Cola monopolized a particular portion of the soft drink market.

PepsiCo v. The Coca-Cola Company
315 F.3d 101 (2d Cir. 2002; as amended 2003)

PER CURIAM

PepsiCo appeals from the judgment of the United States District Court for the Southern District of New York, granting summary judgment in favor of The Coca-Cola Company on PepsiCo's claims that Coca-Cola's enforcement of loyalty provisions in its distributorship agreements with independent food service distributors ("IFDs") that prohibit the IFDs from delivering PepsiCo products to any of their customers constitutes monopolization and attempted monopolization in violation of Section 2 of the Sherman Act....

BACKGROUND

Coca-Cola and PepsiCo, in addition to selling their famous beverages in bottles and cans, sell fountain syrup to numerous customers, including large restaurant chains, movie theater chains, and other "on-premise" accounts. PepsiCo and Coca-Cola bid for agreements to supply fountain syrup and negotiate a price directly with the customer, and then pay a fee to a distributor to deliver the product. Historically, PepsiCo delivered fountain syrup primarily through bottler distributors; Coca-Cola delivered fountain syrup through bottler distributors as well as IFDs, who can offer customers one-stop shopping for all of their restaurant supplies. In the late 1990s, PepsiCo decided it wanted to start delivering fountain syrup via IFDs, but when it sought to do so, Coca-Cola began to enforce the so-called "loyalty" or "conflict of interest" policy contained in its agreements with IFDs, which provides that distributors who supply customers with Coca-Cola may not "handle[] the soft drink products of [PepsiCo]." IFDs who breach the loyalty policy risk termination by Coca-Cola....

DISCUSSION
Section 2 of the Sherman Act
A. The Relevant Market

The parties do not dispute that the relevant geographic market is the United States. A relevant product market consists of "products that have reasonable interchangeability for the purposes for which they are produced—price, use, and qualities considered." *United States v. E.I. DuPont de Nemours & Co.* Products will be considered to be reasonably interchangeable if consumers treat them as "acceptable substitutes."

In its complaint, PepsiCo defined the relevant market as the "market for fountain-dispensed soft drinks distributed through [IFDs] throughout the United States." Pepsico sought to narrow this market definition by confining it to customers with certain characteristics, specifically "large restaurant chain accounts that are not 'heavily franchised' with low fountain 'volume per outlet.'" The district court rejected this definition....

[T]he district court held that fountain syrup delivered by bottler distributors was an "acceptable substitute" for fountain syrup delivered by IFDs—and thus had to be included in the relevant product market—because none of the numerous customers . . . said that the availability of delivery via IFDs was determinative of its choice of fountain syrup. . . . PepsiCo's internal strategy documents, moreover, repeatedly explain that Coca-Cola has several advantages over PepsiCo in the fountain syrup business, only some of which relate to flexible delivery methods.

The district court also rejected PepsiCo's argument that the relevant market should be confined to certain customers. . . . The district court found that, although. . . . many customers have a preference for receiving fountain syrup through IFDs because of the advantages provided by one-stop-shopping, these customers did not constitute a discrete group, but rather were included in various groups of fountain syrup customers.

* * * * *

[T]he evidence established that there is no discrete class of customers that has such a strong preference for IFDs that it would not consider substitutes if other factors (especially price) changed; the competition between PepsiCo and Coca-Cola demonstrates that there is a high sensitivity to price change between IFD-delivered and bottler-distributor–delivered fountain syrup; and there is no industry recognition of fountain syrup delivered by IFDs as a separate market. . . . In short, as the district court observed, "the evidence shows that Coca-Cola viewed PepsiCo as a competitor, and vice versa, and that both they and fountain syrup purchasers viewed systems distribution as a competitive advantage, not a separate market."

B. Monopoly Power

* * * * *

The core element of a monopolization claim is market power, which is defined as "the ability to raise price by restricting output.". . . The pertinent inquiry in a monopolization claim, then, is whether the defendant has engaged in improper conduct that has or is likely to have the effect of controlling prices or excluding competition, thus creating or maintaining market power.

* * * * *

PepsiCo has failed to adduce direct evidence that Coca-Cola has market power (i.e., that it can control prices or exclude competition). To the contrary, the result of PepsiCo's stepped-up attack on the fountain syrup market resulted in numerous bidding wars between PepsiCo and Coca-Cola. PepsiCo was successful in obtaining several accounts, and in those cases where it lost out to Coca-Cola, it nevertheless forced Coca-Cola to drastically reduce its price and profitability to keep the account. As the district court stated, moreover, it is "most compelling, [that] no customer testified that Coca-Cola's loyalty policy prevented the customer from obtaining Pepsi."

* * * * *

In sum, we conclude, as did the district court, that PepsiCo's Section 2 antitrust claim fails because fountain syrup distributed by IFDs is not a separate submarket. Moreover, PepsiCo has not sought to argue that Coca-Cola has monopoly power in the broader fountain syrup market. Nor could it; according to PepsiCo's own figures, in 1998, the year it filed this lawsuit, IFDs accounted for only 50.2 percent of all fountain syrup deliveries by the three largest suppliers (Coca-Cola, PepsiCo, and Dr. Pepper/Seven-Up), and Coca-Cola had only a 64 percent share of the total fountain syrup sales by these three suppliers. Absent additional evidence, such as an ability to control prices or exclude competition, a 64 percent market share is insufficient to infer monopoly power. See *Tops Mkts.*, 142 F.3d at 99 (holding that "a share between 50 percent and 70 percent can occasionally show monopoly power," but only if other factors support the inference). . . .

[Affirmed.]

Questions

1. *a.* Explain PepsiCo's monopoly complaint.
   b. Define the product market from PepsiCo's point of view.
   c. How did the court respond to PepsiCo's product market definition?
2. Why did PepsiCo lose this case?
3. Why didn't PepsiCo allege that Coca-Cola was a monopolist in the total fountain syrup market?
4. The U.S. government sued DuPont, claiming monopolization of the cellophane market. DuPont produced almost 75 percent of the cellophane sold in the United States. Cellophane constituted less than 20 percent of the "flexible packaging materials" market. The lower court found "[g]reat sensitivity of customers in the flexible packaging markets to price or quality changes."
   a. What is the relevant product market?
   b. Who wins the case? Explain. See *United States v. E. I. DuPont de Nemours & Co.*, 351 U.S. 377 (1956).

Monopoly Case II

The *Syufy* case that follows reflects what is probably the dominant "ideological" view of monopoly among federal court judges. The decision embodies the free market philosophy of the Reagan and Bush administrations and their judicial appointees, and it suggests an increasing judicial acceptance of the position that dominant market shares may be earned and maintained legitimately—particularly where competition can easily enter the market. Remember, however, the *Microsoft* lesson that a dominant share gained and/or maintained by anticompetitive practices is impermissible.

The *Syufy* case is also notable because Judge Kozinski, in the spirit of the facts, managed to insert the titles of nearly 200 movies in his 25-page opinion (only a small portion of which is reprinted here).

LEGAL BRIEFCASE

U.S. v. Syufy Enterprises
903 F.2d 659 (9th Cir. 1990)

Circuit Judge Kozinski

Suspect that giant film distributors like Columbia, Paramount, and Twentieth Century–Fox had fallen prey to Raymond Syufy, the canny operator of a chain of Las Vegas, Nevada, movie theaters, the U.S. Department of Justice brought this civil antitrust action to force Syufy to disgorge the theaters he had purchased in 1982–84 from his former competitors. The case is unusual in a number of respects: The Department of Justice concedes that moviegoers in Las Vegas suffered no direct injury as a result of the allegedly illegal transactions; nor does the record reflect complaints from Syufy's bought-out competitors, as the sales were made at fair prices and not precipitated by any monkey business; and the supposedly oppressed movie companies have weighed in on Syufy's side. The Justice Department nevertheless remains intent on rescuing this platoon of Goliaths from a single David.

After extensive discovery and an eight-and-a-half day trial, the learned district judge entered comprehensive findings of fact and conclusions of law, holding for Syufy. He found, *inter alia,* that Syufy's actions did not injure competition because there are no barriers to entry—others could and did enter the market—and that Syufy therefore did not have the power to control prices or exclude the competition. . . .

FACTS

Gone are the days when a movie ticket cost a dime, popcorn a nickel, and theaters had a single screen: This is the age of the multiplex. With more than 300 new films released every year— each potentially the next *Batman* or *E.T.*—many successful theaters today run a different film on each of their 6, 12, or 18 screens. . . .

Raymond Syufy understood the formula well. In 1981 he entered the Las Vegas market with a splash by opening a six-screen theater. Newly constructed and luxuriously furnished, it put existing facilities to shame. Syufy's entry into the Las Vegas market caused a stir, precipitating a titanic bidding war. Soon theaters in Las Vegas were paying some of the highest license fees in the nation, while distributors sat back and watched the easy money roll in.

It is the nature of free enterprise that fierce, no-holds-barred competition will drive out the least effective participants in the market, providing the most efficient allocation of productive resources. And so it was in the Las Vegas movie market in 1982. After a hard-fought battle among several contenders, Syufy gained the upper hand. Two of his rivals, Mann Theatres and Plitt Theatres, saw their future as rocky and decided to sell out to Syufy. While Mann and Plitt are major exhibitors nationwide, neither had a large presence in Las Vegas. Mann operated two indoor theaters with a total of three screens; Plitt operated a single theater with three screens. Things were relatively quiet until September 1984; in September Syufy entered into earnest negotiations with Cragin Industries, his largest remaining competitor. Cragin sold out to Syufy midway through October, leaving Roberts Company, a small exhibitor of mostly second-run films, as Syufy's only competitor for first-run films in Las Vegas.

It is these three transactions—Syufy's purchases of the Mann, Plitt, and Cragin theaters—that the Justice Department claims amount to antitrust violations. As government counsel explained at oral argument, the thrust of its case is that "you may not get monopoly power by buying out your competitors.". . .

DISCUSSION

*　*　*　*　*

[O]f significance is the government's concession that Syufy was only a monopsonist, not a monopolist. Thus the government argues that Syufy had market power, but that he exercised this power only against suppliers (film distributors), not against consumers (moviegoers). This is consistent with the record, which demonstrates that Syufy always treated moviegoers fairly: The movie tickets, popcorn, nuts, and the Seven-Ups cost about the same in Las Vegas as in other, comparable markets. While it is theoretically possible to have a middleman who is a monopolist upstream but not downstream, this is a somewhat counterintuitive scenario. Why, if he truly had significant market power, would Raymond Syufy have chosen to take advantage of the big movie distributors while giving a fair shake to ordinary people? And why do the distributors, the alleged victims of the monopolization scheme, think that Raymond Syufy is the best thing that ever happened to the Las Vegas movie market?

*　*　*　*　*

There is universal agreement that monopoly power is the power to exclude competition or control prices. . . .

1. Power to Exclude Competition

It is true, of course, that when Syufy acquired Mann's, Plitt's, and Cragin's theaters he temporarily diminished the number of competitors in the Las Vegas first-run film market. But this does not necessarily indicate foul play; many legitimate market arrangements diminish the number of competitors. . . . If there are no significant barriers to entry, however, eliminating competitors will not enable the survivors to reap a monopoly profit; any attempt to raise prices above the competitive level will lure into the market new competitors able and willing to offer their commercial goods or personal services for less. . . .

*　*　*　*　*

The district court. . . . found that there were no barriers to entry in the Las Vegas movie market. . . . Our review of the record discloses that the district court's finding is amply supported by the record.

*　*　*　*　*

Immediately after Syufy bought out the last of his three competitors in October 1984, he was riding high, having captured 100 percent of the first-run film market in Las Vegas. But this utopia proved to be only a mirage. That same month, a major movie distributor, Orion, stopped doing business with Syufy, sending all of its first-run films to Roberts Company, a dark-horse competitor previously relegated to the second-run market. Roberts Company took this as an invitation to step into the major league and, against all odds, began giving Syufy serious competition in the first-run market. Fighting fire with fire, Roberts opened three multiplexes within a 13-month period, each having six or more screens. By December 1986, Roberts was operating 28 screens, trading places with Syufy, who had only 23. At the same time, Roberts was displaying a healthy portion of all first-run films. In fact, Roberts got exclusive exhibition rights to many of its films, meaning that Syufy could not show them at all.

By the end of 1987, Roberts was showing a larger percentage of first-run films than was the Redrock multiplex at the time Syufy bought it. Roberts then sold its theaters to United Artists, the largest theater chain in the country, and Syufy continued losing ground. It all boils down to this: Syufy's acquisitions did not short-circuit the operation of the natural market forces; Las Vegas's first-run film market was more competitive when this case came to trial than before Syufy bought out Mann, Plitt, and Cragin.

The Justice Department correctly points out that Syufy still has a large market share, but attributes far too much importance to this fact. In evaluating monopoly power, it is not market share that counts, but the ability to *maintain* market share. . . . Syufy seems unable to do this. In 1985 Syufy managed to lock up exclusive exhibition rights to 91 percent of all the first-run films in Las Vegas. By the first quarter of 1988, that percentage had fallen to 39 percent; United Artists had exclusive rights to another 25 percent, with the remaining 36 percent being played on both Syufy and UA screens.

Syufy's share of box office receipts also dropped off, albeit less precipitously. In 1985 Syufy raked in 93 percent of the gross box office from first-run films in Las Vegas. By the first quarter of 1988, that figure had fallen to 75 percent. The government insists that 75 percent is still a large number, and we are hard-pressed to disagree; but that's not the point.

* * * * *

The numbers reveal that Roberts/UA has steadily been eating away at Syufy's market share: In two and a half years, Syufy's percentage of exclusive exhibition rights dropped 52 percent and its percentage of box office receipts dropped 18 percent. During the same period, Roberts/UA's newly opened theaters evolved from absolute beginners, barely staying alive, into a big business.

* * * * *

2. Power to Control Prices

The crux of the Justice Department's case is that Syufy, top gun in the Las Vegas movie market, had the power to push around Hollywood's biggest players, dictating to them what prices they could charge for their movies. The district court found otherwise. This finding too has substantial support in the record.

Perhaps the most telling evidence of Syufy's inability to set prices came from movie distributors, Syufy's supposed victims. At the trial, distributors uniformly proclaimed their satisfaction with the way the Las Vegas first-run film market operates; none complained about the license fees paid by Syufy. . . . Particularly damaging to the government's case was the testimony of the former head of distribution for MGM/UA that his company "never had any difficulty . . . in acquiring the terms that we thought were reasonable,". . . explaining that the license fees Syufy paid "were comparable or better than any place in the United States. And in most cases better.". . .

The documentary evidence bears out this testimony. Syufy has at all times paid license fees far in excess of the national average, even higher than those paid by exhibitors in Los Angeles, the Mecca of Moviedom. In fact, Syufy paid a higher percentage of his gross receipts to distributors in 1987 and 1988 than he did during the intensely competitive period just before he acquired Cragin's Redrock.

While successful, Syufy is in no position to put the squeeze on distributors. . . .

* * * * *

It is a tribute to the state of competition in America that the Antitrust Division of the Department of Justice has found no worthier target than this paper tiger on which to expend limited taxpayer resources. Yet we cannot help but wonder whether bringing a lawsuit like this, and pursuing it doggedly through 27 months of pretrial proceedings, about two weeks of trial, and now the full distance on appeal, really serves the interests of free competition.

* * * * *

Affirmed.

Questions

1. At one point, Syufy held 100 percent of the first-run market. Why was Syufy not a monopolist?

2. Is this decision rooted more in structural (market share) or conduct (predatory pricing) considerations? Explain.

3. What role did the issue of Syufy's intent to monopolize play in this case? Explain.

4. Assume we have historical data showing that when the price of rolled steel has increased, the sales volume of rolled aluminum has remained constant. What, if anything, does that fact tell us about the product market for rolled steel?

5. Define the product market for championship boxing matches. See *United States v. International Boxing Club of New York, Inc.,* 358 U.S. 242 (1959).

6. Adidas provides cash, sporting goods, and the like to universities in exchange for various promotional rights, including the team's or coach's agreement to wear Adidas clothing in athletic activities. National Collegiate Athletic Association (NCAA) rules limit the amount of advertising that may appear on a uniform being used in competition.

Adidas sued the NCAA claiming, among other things, that the advertising restrictions constitute an attempted monopoly by the NCAA. In pursuing its monopoly claim, Adidas defined the relevant market as "the market for the sale of NCAA Promotional Rights." The NCAA responded by saying that a market consisting solely of the sale of promotional rights by NCAA member institutions (colleges and universities) on athletic apparel used in intercollegiate activity is not a plausible relevant market.

   a. Define the relevant product market from the NCAA point of view.

   b. How would the court decide where the product market actually lies? See *Adidas America, Inc v. NCAA,* 64 F. Supp. 2d 1097 (1999).

PRACTICING ETHICS Is Bigness Bad?

That question in decades past was a great source of debate, but today the question sounds almost naïve or quaint. In this era of consolidation and globalization, colossal corporations are a fact of life and, apparently, a competitive necessity. Nonetheless, enormous, concentrated power can be abused. *The Wall Street Journal* recently described increasing fears about *monopsony*, the monopoly variant that was the subject of the *Syufy* case:

> As more of the world's markets become dominated by a few big companies, a rare form of antitrust abuse is raising new concern: when corporations illegally drive *down* the prices of their suppliers. On the coast of Maine, blueberry growers alleged last year that four big processors conspired to push down the price they would pay for fresh wild berries. A state court jury agreed last year and awarded millions in damages. . . . In Alabama and Pennsylvania, federal antitrust enforcers last year targeted insurance companies that imposed contracts forcing down fees charged by doctors and hospitals. The insurers abandoned the practice.[10]

Questions

1. Is bigness bad? Explain.

2. Is it wrong of Wal-Mart to drive its suppliers' prices as low as possible? Explain.

3. Under what circumstances, if any, should monopsony be unlawful? Explain.

Questions—Part One

1. *a.* The *Harvard Law Review* argued, "In the New Economy (information technology) . . . there will inevitably be an increasing number of markets with only a few dominant players."[11] Why would that be so?

   b. Are we mistaken in pursuing Microsoft and other "new economy" giants with "old economy" antitrust principles? Explain.

2. Worldwide Basketball Sports Tours promoted early-season, NCAA-certified basketball tournaments. The National Collegiate Athletic Association's Two in Four Rule

limited college basketball teams to "not more than one certified basketball event in one academic year, and not more than two certified basketball events every four years." The promoters sued the NCAA on antitrust grounds, claiming the Two in Four rule hampered their ability to make money. The NCAA argued that the limit on games was academically motivated.

   a. Does antitrust law apply to Division I collegiate basketball? Explain.

   b. Define the product market in this case. See *Worldwide Basketball & Sports Tours, Inc. v. NCAA,* 388 F. 3d 955 (6th Cir. 2004).

3. *a.* A traditional concern about monopolies is that a lack of competition discourages efficiency and innovation. Argue that monopolies may actually *encourage* innovation.

   b. Even if monopolies do not discourage invention, we have firm economic grounds for opposing monopolies. Explain.

4. Real estate developer Ernest Coleman built an apartment complex in Stilwell, Oklahoma (population 2,700), and ordered electric service from an out-of-town utility, Ozark Electric. Stilwell officials said they would deny him city water and sewer service if he did not buy his electricity from the city-owned utility service. Because he could not buy water or sewer service elsewhere, Coleman decided to switch to Stilwell's utility.

   In 1996 the federal Justice Department sued Stilwell. Explain the federal government's complaint and decide the case. See Bryan Gruley, "Little Town Becomes First Municipality Sued by U.S. for Antitrust," *The Wall Street Journal,* June 3, 1996, p. A1.

5. Historically, perhaps the most important interpretation of the Sherman Act's proscription of monopolization was Judge Learned Hand's opinion in the *Alcoa* case. After finding that Alcoa controlled 90 percent of the aluminum ingot market, Hand had to determine whether Alcoa possessed a general intent to monopolize. Hand concluded that Alcoa's market dominance could have resulted only from a "persistent determination" to maintain control [148 F.2d 416, 431 (2d Cir. 1945)]:

> It was not inevitable that it should always anticipate increases in the demand for ingots and be prepared to supply them. Nothing compelled it to keep doubling and redoubling its capacity before others entered the field. It insists that it never excluded competitors; but we can think of no more effective exclusion than progressively to embrace each new opportunity as it opened, and to face every newcomer with new capacity already geared into a great organization.

Comment on Judge Hand's remarks.

6. Several smaller airlines sued the two giants, United and American, claiming that the two violated the Sherman Act through their computerized reservation systems (CRSs). The heart of the plaintiffs' position was that United and American were monopolists who violated the law by denying other airlines reasonable access to their CRSs. American and United had the largest CRSs, but other airlines also maintained CRSs. Neither had blocked any other airline's access to its CRS, but they had charged fees (in American's case, $1.75 per booking to the airline that

secured a passenger through American's CRS). United and American each controlled about 12 to 14 percent of the total air transportation market. According to the court, the plaintiffs were "unhappy" about United and American's ability to extract booking fees from them for the use of the CRSs. The U.S. Ninth Circuit Court of Appeals ruled for the defendants, and the Supreme Court declined to review this case.

a. Explain why the plaintiffs felt wronged by American and United.

b. Explain the defendants's argument that they could not successfully charge "excessive" prices for the use of the CRSs. See *Alaska Airlines v. United Airlines*, 948 F.2d 536 (9th Cir. 1991), cert. den. 112 S.Ct. 1603 (1992).

Part Two—Mergers

Merger activity tends to occur in cycles. At this writing, a new boom has emerged. United States' merger volume in 2007 totaled a record $1.57 trillion, but for the first time in five years, merger volume in Europe ($1.78 trillion) was greater than in America.[12] Global mergers also reached a record in 2007 at $4.38 trillion, a 21 percent increase over 2006.[13] Google's controversial $3.1 billion acquisition of Web advertising giant, DoubleClick, approved by American and European regulators in 2007–08, illustrates the efficiency advantages that often accompany mergers along with some of the risks in increasingly concentrated economic power. Closer perhaps to our personal lives is the 2007–08, $5 billion merger of XM and Sirius satellite radio companies uniting America's only two such services and their 17 million subscribers. The merger was approved in 2008 by the federal Justice Department, which concluded the merged firm would not unlawfully monopolize the market, in part, because iPods and other devices offer increasing options for listening to programming in our cars. The decision likely was also influenced by the fact that both companies have lost billions of dollars in their fierce battle. At this writing, the Federal Communications Commission must yet decide whether to challenge the merger or to insist on attaching consumer protection conditions to it. [For a brief analysis of the Google-DoubleClick merger, see **http://iblsjournal.typepad. com/illinois_ business_law_soc/2008/03/google-doublecl.html**]

Why? Technological change, efficiency enhancement, and piles of available cash are often important motivators for merger activity; but the big drivers at the moment appear to be growth opportunities and cost cutting. Many companies have extracted maximum value from their own products and thus can achieve growth only by purchasing new lines, and cost savings have become essential in fierce global competition. For example, at this writing, brewers SABMiller and Molson Coors are in the process of combining their U.S. operations in a deal that is expected to reduce costs by about $500 million by the third year.[14] The merger is not expected to be challenged by the government because the industry is considered highly competitive and the combined Miller-Molson 30 percent market share should strengthen the challenge to Anheuser-Busch's market leading 48 percent share.[15]

Merger Virtues

Of course, mergers often have clearly beneficial effects. Some of the potential virtues of mergers include these:

1. Mergers permit the replacement of inefficient management, and the threat of replacement disciplines managers to be more productive.
2. Mergers may permit stronger competition with previously larger rivals.
3. Mergers may improve credit access.
4. Mergers may produce efficiencies and economies of scale.
5. Mergers frequently offer a pool of liquid assets for use in expansion and in innovation.
6. Very often, mergers offer tax advantages.
7. Growth by merger is often less expensive than internal growth.
8. Mergers help to satisy the personal ambitions and needs of management.

Managers

> Job security appears to have evaporated

For American bosses, this deal-making fever has profound professional and personal consequences. Job security appears to have evaporated. On the other hand, rapid change means new opportunities. In this volatile managerial setting, experts now say that personal, managerial conditions have become a major factor in merger negotiations. *Across the Board* explains:

> You can't talk about the quest for bigness without discussing ego, which has played a role since the beginning of time. So what's different *today* in the land of ego that's driving today's merger mania? Big Money and Celebrity Status.
>
> According to Pearl Meyer & Partners' study of the top 200 U.S. companies, 90 percent of a CEO's pay is tied to performance, and more than half of that pay is in stock option grants. . . . Big equity stakes mean CEOs are inspired to shake things up, to acquire, to merge, to divest—anything to boost numbers and the company's stock.[16]

PRACTICING ETHICS) Greed?

James Kilts, chairman and CEO at Gillette, was expected to personally earn about $153 million when his firm was acquired by Procter & Gamble. He also was scheduled to receive a $1.2 million annual pension. Much of the $153 million was attributed to value Kilts was presumed to have added to Gillette during his tenure, but $23.9 million was, according to *The Wall Street Journal,* a "one-time sweet-ener from P&G." That money was accompanied by a $12.6 million "change in control" payment.[17]

Question
Could we fairly apply the label "greedy" to Kilts? That is, how do we know when the market has provided an "excessive" or "unfair" reward? Explain.

Merger Problems

| Mergers often are failures | From a shareholder's point of view, mergers often are failures. *BusinessWeek* merger investigations in 2002 and 2004 found that 61 per- |

From a shareholder's point of view, mergers often are failures. *BusinessWeek* merger investigations in 2002 and 2004 found that 61 percent of big deals hurt the acquiring firm's shareholders.[18] A study of worldwide mergers from 1997 to 1999 found 31 percent of the mergers actually reducing shareholder value, whereas 33 percent increased shareholder value. On the other hand, three-quarters of the companies involved considered the mergers successful because they were looking at results such as profitability and increasing market share.[19] In addition to the frequent financial failures with mergers, other hazards should also be noted:

1. Too much power is being concentrated in too few hands.
2. A particular merger, while not threatening in and of itself, may trigger a merger movement among industry competitors.
3. Higher market concentration may lead to higher prices.
4. Innovation may be harmed.
5. Some companies are so large that they can significantly shape political affairs.
6. Some companies may have become so large that we cannot allow them to fail.[20]

Broadly, critics argue that major elements of the American economy—communications, credit cards, energy, and so on—are becoming too concentrated for market forces to work as theorized. For example, a 2004 report from the Consumer Federation of America and the Consumers Union claims that oil industry consolidation has driven household energy costs up by an average of $1,000 annually.[21] The report blames the Federal Trade Commission for failing to block giant mergers. A General Accounting Office study in 2004 reached similar conclusions,[22] but the Federal Trade Commission's own study found that market concentration in the oil industry is "low to moderate" and is not responsible for rising gasoline prices.[23]

When Should the Government Intervene? The U.S. Justice Department faced that question in deciding against challenging the 2006 acquisition of the United States' third largest home appliance manufacturer, Maytag, by the market leader, Whirlpool. Maytag was staggering economically, but some antitrust authorities thought the merger was threatening because of the firms' combined market share of 50 to 75 percent, depending on the product. In addition to concerns about Maytag's struggling condition, the Justice Department apparently was convinced that the home appliance market would remain competitive. Justice officials pointed to the rapidly emerging strength of Asian appliance manufacturers, and the power of four giant retailers—Sears, Lowe's, Home Depot, and Best Buy—who control 65 percent of retail home appliance sales and thus could be expected to discipline Whirlpool's conduct.[24]

Merger Law: Overview

Mergers are addressed by the Sherman Act, Section 1; but the Clayton Act, Section 7, offers the primary legislative oversight:

That no person engaged in commerce shall acquire the whole or any part of the stock or the assets of another person engaged also in commerce where the effect of such acquisition may be substantially to lessen competition, or to tend to create a monopoly.

Technically, a *merger* involves the union of two or more enterprises wherein the property of all is transferred to the one remaining firm. However, antitrust law embraces all those situations in which previously independent business entities are united—whether by acquisition of stock, purchase of physical assets, creation of holding companies, consolidation, or merger.

Mergers fall, somewhat awkwardly, into three categories:

1. A *horizontal merger* involves firms that are in direct competition and occupy the same product and geographic markets. A merger of two vodka producers in the same geographic market would clearly fall in the horizontal category. Would the merger of a vodka producer and a gin producer constitute a horizontal merger?

2. A *vertical merger* involves two or more firms at different levels of the same channel of distribution, such as a furniture manufacturer and a fabric supplier.

3. A *conglomerate merger* involves firms dealing in unrelated products. Thus the conglomerate category embraces all mergers that are neither horizontal nor vertical. An example of such a merger would be the acquisition of a pet food manufacturer by a book publisher. (Conglomerate mergers currently receive little attention from the government, and we will not examine them further.)

Premerger Notification   Under the Hart–Scott–Rodino Antitrust Improvements Act (HSR), mergers and acquisitions must be reported to the Federal Trade Commission and the Justice Department if those deals exceed certain dollar thresholds which change annually in accord with the gross national product. [For more HSR threshold details, see **www.fenwick.com/docstore/Publications/Corporate/Corp_Sec_01-18-08.pdf**] The parties are barred from closing the merger until 30 days after they have made the required HSR filing unless the waiting period is shortened (as it often is) or lengthened by the FTC or the Justice Department. The merging firms are required to provide documentation about the merger's impact on competition. The waiting period gives the government time and information by which to determine whether the merger should be challenged.

Remedies   After the HSR review, the government may decide that the merger is not threatening, and it will be allowed to proceed. The government may, on the other hand, conclude that the merger is anticompetitive. The government could file suit to block the merger, but the preferred action is to work out an agreeable settlement. A settlement might involve one of the parties selling some of its assets or agreeing to forgo business in some geographic segment of the market for a while.

Critics argue that the government effectively has veto power over mergers. If merger partners do not agree to government demands, the government can sue, which results in a long, expensive process for both sides. During the eight years of the George W. Bush administration, however, government resistance to mergers has been slight, reflecting both Republican Party free market principles and a highly competitive global market.

FTC resistance was the critical consideration in Blockbuster's 2005 decision to withdraw its nearly $1 billion offer to buy video rental rival Hollywood Entertainment

Nonetheless, FTC resistance was the critical consideration in Blockbuster's 2005 decision to withdraw its nearly $1 billion offer to buy video rental rival Hollywood Entertainment. From the FTC point of view, perhaps the fatal flaw with the proposed merger was that Hollywood had located about 75 percent of its stores near those of Blockbuster in an effort to "steal" some of Blockbuster's business. A merger arguably would have reduced competition and harmed consumer welfare in many of those localized markets. Further, Blockbuster was already the market leader. The FTC's Blockbuster decision, in turn, cleared the way for the nation's number three video rental company, Movie Gallery, to acquire Hollywood, a move the FTC approved. The resulting firm was expected to challenge Blockbuster, but since the acquisition, Movie Gallery has struggled and, at this writing, is closing hundreds of stores. Thus we can see that the real story here, as is ordinarily the case, is not the power of government intervention, but the power of the market. Online rentals, such as Netflix, are threatening the Blockbuster video store model while DVD kiosks are an emerging success and small independent video rental stores are enjoying a bit of a renaissance where they occupy a healthy niche such as foreign films, and they give close attention to customer service.

In cases where negotiation fails and the government decides to sue, it can ask the court for a remedy, such as an order stopping the merger or an order requiring divestiture of certain assets. Government litigation is infrequent, but the resulting message to the business community is powerful. Furthermore, private parties commonly use the antitrust laws to sue for treble damages when they believe a merger has harmed them unlawfully. The threat of those private actions as well as government oversight helps to maintain a marketplace where consumers are offered the benefits of vigorous competition including lower prices, improved quality, and innovation.

Horizontal Analysis

Horizontal mergers raise anticompetitive risks because direct competitors seek to join together. Three recent lower federal court decisions have caused some experts to speculate that the courts may be demanding increased proof when challenging horizontal mergers in concentrated markets.[25] Whether proof expectations have escalated remains to be seen, but horizontal merger analysis will continue to follow the FTC/Justice Department merger guidelines, which focus on a pair of concerns:

1. **Coordinated effects/collusion:** Will the merger facilitate cooperation so that the parties might fix prices, reduce output, reduce quality, or otherwise coordinate their activities rather than competing against each other? Broadly, the government takes the position that fewer firms and thus greater market concentration increases the likelihood of collusion—a position the courts often, but not always, embrace.

2. **Unilateral effects:** Will the merger allow a firm to unilaterally raise prices, restrict output, or control innovation? Normally, unilateral effects arise with products that significantly restrain each other prior to the merger. For example, in evaluating the

merger of paper products manufacturers Scott and Kimberly-Clark, the Justice Department found that Scott's facial tissue brand, Scotties, and Kimberly-Clark's facial tissue brand, Kleenex, had significantly constrained each other's prices prior to the merger and that the merger would therefore allow unilateral and profitable price increases for both Scotties and Kleenex. In response, Kimberly-Clark agreed to divest itself of Scott's facial tissue brands.[26]

Market Power

Broadly, the guidelines are designed to identify mergers that may result in *market power,* defined as the ability of a seller "profitably to maintain prices above competitive levels for a significant period of time." The guidelines set out a five-step methodology for analyzing horizontal mergers:

1. Market definition.
2. Measurement of market concentration.
3. Identification of likely anticompetitive effects.
4. Liklihood of future entrants to the market.
5. Appraisal of efficiencies and other possible defenses.

Market   The market will be defined as the smallest product and geographic market in which a hypothetical monopolist could raise prices a small but significant and nontransitory amount (usually set at 5 percent above current prices).

Market Concentration   The Herfindahl–Hirschman Index (HHI) is employed to measure market concentration. Notwithstanding the formidable title, the index is computed quite easily. The market share of each firm is squared and the results are summed. Thus if five companies each had 20 percent of a market, the index for that market would be 2,000. The HHI is useful because it measures both concentration and dispersion of market share between big and small firms. If 10 firms each have 10 percent of the market, the resulting HHI is 1,000. The larger the HHI, the more concentrated the market. In general, a postmerger HHI below 1,000 ordinarily would not be challenged while a postmerger concentration of more than 1,800 accompanied by a change in the HHI above 50 (from the premerger HHI) is potentially threatening. In the middle ground involving postmerger HHI figures of 1,000 to 1,800 accompanied by changes in the HHI above 100, the guidelines find that the potential for competitive concerns depends on the analysis of other factors, such as adverse effects and ease of entry, as explained below. Broadly, the government's guidelines reject the older notion of market size *alone* as a threat to the welfare of the economy.

Adverse Effects   The basic point here is the government's worry that the merger may permit monopoly behavior in the merged firm's market.

Ease of Entry   If new competitors can readily enter the postmerger market, the existing firms will be forced to charge competitive prices and otherwise conform to the discipline of the market.

Defenses An otherwise unacceptable merger may be saved by certain defenses. The *failing company doctrine* permits a merger to preserve the assets of a firm that would otherwise be lost to the market. *Efficiencies* include such desirable economic results as economies of scale or reduced transportation costs as a result of the merger.

"I Am Going to Destroy You."

Whole Foods, the natural foods chain, in 2007 acquired its chief competitor, Wild Oats Market. Whole Foods had about 12 percent of the natural foods market, and Wild Oats held about three percent. Whole Foods had 197 stores and added 110 by purchasing Wild Oats. About 72 percent of Wild Oats' sales were in markets where the two overlapped.

Prior to the purchase, Whole Foods cofounder and CEO John Mackey reportedly shouted, "I am going to destroy you," to Wild Oats CEO, Perry Odak. For nearly eight years until discovered in 2007, Mackey, using an alias, posted more than 1,100 messages on Yahoo Finance's bulletin board bashing his competitors and boosting Whole Foods. According to court records, Mackey allegedly said that the proposed merger would end "forever, or almost forever" the possibility of a big grocery chain buying an existing natural foods chain to compete with Whole Foods. Mackey also allegedly said that buying Wild Oats would prevent "price wars."

The Federal Trade Commission challenged the Whole Foods purchase of Wild Oats concluding that Whole Foods was using the deal as a way to eliminate its major competition in dozens of cities and apparently feeling that Mackey's remarks effectively compelled government action.

Questions
1. What was the primary issue facing the federal courts that reviewed the FTC challenge?
2. Decide the case. Explain.

Sources: Federal Trade Commission v. Whole Foods Market, 502 F. Supp. 2d 1 (2007), *Federal Trade Commission v. Whole Foods Market,* 2007 U.S. App. LEXIS 20539, and David Kesmodel and Jonathan Eig, "A Grocer's Brash Style Takes Unhealthy Turn," *The Wall Street Journal,* July 20, 2007, p. A1.

Vertical Analysis

A vertical merger typically involves an alliance between a supplier and a purchaser. The primary resulting threat to competition is labeled *market foreclosure*. As illustrated in Figure 11.1, a vertical merger may deny a source of supply to a purchaser or an outlet for sale to a seller, thus potentially threatening competition in violation of the Clayton Act. The government would then look closely at that foreclosure to determine whether it actually has an anticompetitive effect. In addition to foreclosing sources of supply or outlets for sale, the government may be concerned about other anticompetitive effects such as raising rivals' costs, facilitating collusion, raising barriers to entry, increasing

FIGURE 11.1
Vertical
Merger

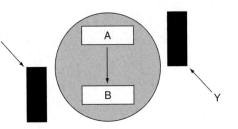

A supplies B. A and B merge. X (A's competitor) had traditionally sold
to B, and Y (B's competitor) had traditionally purchased from A. How
do we decide the legality of such a merger?

access to competitively sensitive information, encouraging discrimination in access to
products and services, and reducing incentives for innovation.

The government holds a generally lenient attitude toward vertical mergers, but under
some conditions they will be challenged.

The Federal Trade Commission in late 2000 insisted on a consent agreement before
allowing the $111 billion AOL–Time Warner vertical merger to go forward. The agree-
ment assured that competitors would have access to AOL–Time Warner markets. The
merger joined Time Warner assets CNN, HBO, *Time* magazine, the Atlanta Braves,
and Bugs Bunny, among others, with AOL's online service to 26 million consumers.
AOL was easily the largest Internet service provider, while Time Warner provided
much of the news and entertainment content for cable and Internet service. Time
Warner also owned vast cable systems that reached about 20 percent of all cable subscribers. So the general fear was that the merged company would effectively become
a monopoly in telecommunications, and Time Warner customers would be forced to
accept AOL's services while AOL customers would be forced to accept Time Warner's
news and entertainment products.[27] That result would have foreclosed vital marketing opportunities to competitors of Time Warner and AOL. The FTC was worried that
Time Warner might refuse to sell its products to competing cable television companies, or it might sell to them only at discriminatorily higher prices. Likewise,
AOL–Time Warner might have refused to carry programming produced by its rivals,
thus harming competition in the production of video content. The FTC had to balance those anticompetitive considerations against the efficiencies that were expected
from the merger. At this writing eight years later, the AOL-Time Warner merger has
proven to be a financial failure. [For political cartoons about the AOL-Time Warner
merger see **http://cagle.msnbc.com/news/aol**]

Horizontal Merger Case

The Staples–Office Depot litigation that follows illustrates the standard horizontal merger
analysis.

Judge Hogan

BACKGROUND

* * * * *

Staples is the second largest office superstore chain in the United States with approximately 550 retail stores located in 28 states and the District of Columbia, primarily in the Northeast and California. In 1996 Staples' revenues from those stores were approximately $4 billion through all operations. Office Depot, the largest office superstore chain, operates over 500 retail office supply superstores that are located in 38 states and the District of Columbia, primarily in the South and Midwest. Office Depot's 1996 sales were approximately $6.1 billion. OfficeMax, Inc., is the only other office supply superstore firm in the United States.

On September 4, 1996, defendants Staples and Office Depot . . . entered into an "Agreement and Plan of Merger" whereby . . . Office Depot would become a wholly owned subsidiary of Staples. . . . The FTC filed this suit on April 9, 1997, seeking a temporary restraining order and preliminary injunction against the merger. . . .

I. Discussion

Analysis of the likely competitive effects of a merger requires determinations of (1) the "line of commerce" or product market in which to assess the transaction, (2) the "section of the country" or geographic market in which to assess the transaction, and (3) the transaction's probable effect on competition in the product and geographic markets.

II. The Geographic Market

One of the few issues about which the parties to this case do not disagree is that metropolitan areas are the appropriate geographic markets for analyzing the competitive effects of the proposed merger. In its first amended complaint, the FTC identified 42 such metropolitan areas as well as future areas which could suffer anticompetitive effects from the proposed merger. . . .

III. The Relevant Product Market

* * * * *

The Commission defines the relevant product market as "the sale of consumable office supplies through office superstores," with "consumable" meaning products that consumers buy recurrently, i.e., items which "get used up" or discarded. For example, under the Commission's definition, "consumable office supplies" would not include capital goods such as computers,

fax machines, and other business machines or office furniture, but does include such products as paper, pens, file folders, self-stick notes, computer disks, and toner cartridges. The defendants characterize the FTC's product market definition as "contrived" with no basis in law or fact, and counter that the appropriate product market within which to assess the likely competitive consequences of a Staples–Office Depot combination is simply the overall sale of office products, of which a combined Staples–Office Depot accounted for 5.5 percent of total sales in North America in 1996.

* * * * *

The general rule when determining a relevant product market is that "[t]he outer boundaries of a product market are determined by the reasonable interchangeability of use [by consumers] or the cross-elasticity of demand between the product itself and substitutes for it." Interchangeability of use and cross-elasticity of demand look to the availability of substitute commodities, i.e., whether there are other products offered to consumers which are similar in character or use to the product or products in question. . . .

[T]he Commission has argued that a slight but significant increase in Staples–Office Depot's prices will not cause a considerable number of Staples–Office Depot's customers to purchase consumable office supplies from other nonsuperstore alternatives such as Wal-Mart, Best Buy, Quill, or Viking. On the other hand, the Commission has argued that an increase in price by Staples would result in consumers turning to another office superstore, especially Office Depot, if the consumers had that option. Therefore, the Commission concludes that the sale of consumable office supplies by office supply superstores is the appropriate relevant product market in this case, and products sold by competitors such as Wal-Mart, Best Buy, Viking, Quill, and others should be excluded. . . .

The Court acknowledges that there is, in fact, a broad market encompassing the sale of consumable office supplies by all sellers of such supplies, and that those sellers must, at some level, compete with one another. However, the mere fact that a firm may be termed a competitor in the overall marketplace does not necessarily require that it be included in the relevant product market for antitrust purposes. The Supreme Court has recognized that within a broad market, "well-defined submarkets may exist which, in themselves, constitute product markets for antitrust purposes."

* * * * *

[In defining the submarket] the FTC focused on what it termed the "pricing evidence.". . . First, the FTC presented evidence comparing Staples' prices in geographic markets where Staples is the only office superstore, to markets where Staples competes with Office Depot or OfficeMax, or both. Based on the FTC's calculations, in markets where Staples faces no office superstore competition at all, something which was termed a one-firm market during the hearing, prices are 13 percent higher than in three-firm markets where it competes with both Office Depot and OfficeMax.

* * * * *

This evidence suggests that office superstore prices are affected primarily by other office superstores and not by nonsuperstore competitors such as mass merchandisers like Wal-Mart, Kmart, or Target, wholesale clubs such as BJ's, Sam's, and Price Costco, computer or electronic stores such as Computer City and Best Buy, independent retail office supply stores, mail-order firms like Quill and Viking, and contract stationers.

* * * * *

In addition, Staples' own pricing information shows that warehouse clubs have very little effect on Staples' prices.

* * * * *

There is similar evidence with respect to the defendants' behavior when faced with entry of another competitor. The evidence shows that the defendants change their price zones when faced with entry of another superstore, but do not do so for other retailers.

* * * * *

Despite the high degree of functional interchangeability between consumable office supplies sold by the office superstores and other retailers of office supplies, the evidence presented by the Commission shows that even where Staples and Office Depot charge higher prices, certain consumers do not go elsewhere for their supplies. This further demonstrates that the sale of office supplies by nonsuperstore retailers is not responsive to the higher prices charged by Staples and Office Depot in the one-firm markets. This indicates a low cross-elasticity of demand between the consumable office supplies sold by superstores and those sold by other sellers.

* * * * *

The Court has observed that office supply superstores look far different from other sellers of office supplies. Office supply superstores are high-volume, discount office supply chain stores averaging in excess of 20,000 square feet, with over 11,000 of those square feet devoted to traditional office supplies, and carrying over 5,000 SKUs of consumable office supplies in addition to computers, office furniture, and other nonconsumables. In contrast, stores such as Kmart devote approximately 210 square feet to the sale of approximately 250 SKUs of consumable office supplies. Kinko's devotes approximately 50 square feet to the sale of 150 SKUs. Both Sam's Club and Computer City each sell approximately 200 SKUs.

In addition to the differences in SKU numbers and variety, the superstores are different from many other sellers of office supplies due to the type of customer they target and attract. The superstores' customer base overwhelmingly consists of small businesses with fewer than 20 employees and consumers with home offices. In contrast, mail-order customers are typically midsized companies with more than 20 employees. . . .

* * * * *

[T]he Court finds that the unique combination of size, selection, depth, and breadth of inventory offered by the superstores distinguishes them from other retailers.

* * * * *

While it is clear to the Court that Staples and Office Depot do not ignore sellers such as warehouse clubs, Best Buy, or Wal-Mart, the evidence clearly shows that Staples and Office Depot each consider the other superstores as the primary competition.

* * * * *

[T]he Court finds that the sale of consumable office supplies through office supply superstores is the appropriate relevant product market for purposes of considering the possible anticompetitive effects of the proposed merger between Staples and Office Depot.

* * * * *

IV. Probable Effect on Competition

[T]he Court next must consider the probable effect of a merger between Staples and Office Depot in the geographic markets previously identified. One way to do this is to examine the concentration statistics and HHIs within the geographic markets. If the relevant product market is defined as the sale of consumable office supplies through office supply superstores, the HHIs in many of the geographic markets are at problematic levels even before the merger. Currently, the least concentrated market is that of Grand Rapids–Muskegon–Holland, Michigan, with an HHI of 3,597, while the most concentrated is Washington, D.C., with an HHI of 6,944. In contrast, after a merger of Staples and Office Depot, the least concentrated area would be Kalamazoo–Battle Creek, Michigan, with an HHI of 5,003, and many areas would have HHIs of 10,000. The average increase in HHI caused by the merger would be 2,715 points. The concentration statistics show that a merged Staples–Office Depot would have a dominant market share in 42 geographic markets across the country. The combined shares of Staples and Office Depot in the office superstore market would be 100 percent in 15 metropolitan areas. It is in these markets the postmerger HHI would be 10,000. In 27 other metropolitan areas, where the number of office superstore competitors would drop from three to two, the postmerger market shares would range from 45 percent to 94 percent, with postmerger HHIs ranging from 5,003 to 9,049. Even the lowest of these HHIs indicates a "highly concentrated" market.

* * * * *

The HHI calculations and market concentration evidence, however, are not the only indications that a merger between Staples and Office Depot may substantially lessen competition. Much of the evidence already discussed with respect to defining the relevant product market also indicates that the merger would likely have an anticompetitive effect. The evidence of the defendants' own current pricing practices, for example, shows that an office superstore chain facing no competition from other superstores has the ability to profitably raise prices for consumable office supplies above competitive levels. The fact that Staples and Office Depot both charge higher prices where they face no superstore competition demonstrates that an office superstore can raise prices above competitive levels. The evidence also shows that defendants also change their price zones when faced with entry of another office superstore, but do not do so for other retailers.

* * * * *

V. Entry into the Market

"The existence and significance of barriers to entry are frequently, of course, crucial considerations in a rebuttal analysis. . . ."

* * * * *

The Commission offered Office 1 as a specific example of the difficulty of entering the office superstore arena. Office 1 opened its first two stores in 1991. By the end of 1994, Office 1 had 17 stores, and grew to 35 stores operating in 11 Midwestern states as of October 11, 1996. As of that date, Office 1 was the fourth largest office supply superstore chain in the United States. Unfortunately, also as of that date, Office 1 filed for Chapter 11 bankruptcy protection. Brad Zenner, president of Office 1, testified through declaration that Office 1 failed because it was severely undercapitalized in comparison with the

industry leaders, Staples, Office Depot, and OfficeMax. In addition, Zenner testified that when the three leaders ultimately expanded into the smaller markets where Office 1 stores were located, they seriously undercut Office 1's retail prices and profit margins. Because Office 1 lacked the capitalization of the three leaders and lacked the economies of scale enjoyed by those competitors, Office 1 could not remain profitable.

For the reasons discussed above, the Court finds it extremely unlikely that a new office superstore will enter the market and thereby avert the anticompetitive effects from Staples' acquisition of Office Depot.

* * * * *

VI. Efficiencies

* * * * *

First, the Court notes that the cost savings estimate of $4,947 billion over five years which was submitted to the Court exceeds by almost 500 percent the figures presented to the two Boards of Directors in September 1996, when the Boards approved the transaction. The cost savings claims submitted to the Court are also substantially greater than those represented in the defendants' Joint Proxy Statement/Prospectus "reflecting the best currently available estimate of management," and filed with the Securities and Exchange Commission on January 23, 1997. . . .

* * * * *

[T]he Court cannot find that the defendants have rebutted the presumption that the merger will substantially lessen competition . . .

CONCLUSION

* * * * *

[T]he Court finds that the Commission has shown a likelihood that it will succeed in proving, after a full administrative trial on the merits, that the effect of the proposed merger between Staples and Office Depot "may be substantially to lessen competition" in violation of Section 7 of the Clayton Act. . . . The FTC's motion for a preliminary injunction shall be granted.

AFTERWORD

Citing the time and money involved in battling the federal government, Staples and Office Depot officially called off their proposed merger days after Judge Hogan's decision.

Questions

1. *a.* What "general rule" did the *Staples* court employ in determining the relevant product market?

b. What evidence supported the use of the "office supply superstore submarket" as the relevant product market?

2. *a.* What evidence supported the FTC's claim that the merger would lead to anticompetitive effects?

   b. In weighing the "public and private equities," why did the court come down on the side of the government?

3. Analysts have argued that in the *Staples* case the government was less worried about market shares than about the price impact of the merger were it to be approved. Explain what those analysts meant.

4. Three firms controlled the $1 billion U.S. baby food market (Gerber—65 percent, Heinz—17.4 percent, and Beech-Nut—15.4 percent). Gerber was sold in over 90 percent of American supermarkets, and it had greater brand loyalty than any other product sold in the United States. Heinz was sold in 40 percent of the supermarkets and Beech-Nut in 45 percent. The baby food HHI was 4775, which would increase by 510 HHI points if Heinz and Beech-Nut were to merge. Heinz and Beech-Nut agreed to merge. The Federal Trade Commission opposed the merger.

   a. What other facts would you want to know to decide the legality of this proposed merger?

   b. Defend the merger.

   c. Decide. Explain. See *Federal Trade Commission v. H. J. Heinz Co.,* 246 F.3d 708 (D.C. Cir. 2001).

5. In 1958 Pabst Brewing Company acquired Blatz Brewing Company. Pabst was America's 10th largest brewer, while Blatz was the 18th largest. After the merger, Pabst had 4.49 percent of the nationwide beer market and was the fifth largest brewer. In the regional market of Wisconsin, Michigan, and Illinois, the merger gave Pabst 11.32 percent of the sales. After the merger, Pabst led beer sales in Wisconsin with 23.95 percent of that statewide market. The beer market was becoming increasingly concentrated, with the total number of brewers declining from 206 to 162 during the years 1957 to 1961. In *United States v. Pabst Brewing Co.,* 384 U.S. 546 (1966), the Supreme Court found the merger violated the Clayton Act, Section 7. The Court did not choose among the three geographic market configurations, saying that the crucial inquiry is whether a merger may substantially lessen competition anywhere in the United States. Thus the Court held that, under these facts, a 4.49 percent share of the market was too large.

   Respected scholar and jurist Richard Posner labeled the *Pabst* decision an "atrocity" and the product of a "fit of nonsense" on the part of the Supreme Court.[28] What economic arguments would support Posner's colorful complaint?

CEO Respects Regulators

Staples CEO Thomas Stemberg was interviewed following the *FTC v. Staples* battle:

Q: Should a company expect to be treated fairly by staff members of the antitrust regulators?

A: I do believe that the people in these agencies are well-intentioned and are trying to do the right thing for the consumer. As one who has spent the last decade or more of his business career fighting cartels and trying to induce procompetitive activity in the marketplace, their goals are very much the same as ours, which is to give the consumer the best deal possible. The antitrust regulators are some of the hardest-working people I have ever seen. They are extremely dedicated, and if you aren't prepared to go 15 rounds, you're picking a bad fight. Some of the mergers that are out there today that they are contesting, I'd be contesting if I were them, too.

Source: Del Jones, "Today's Issue: Some Lessons Learned in an Antitrust Fight," *USA TODAY,* March 30, 1998, p. 5B.

Part Three—American Antitrust Laws and the International Market

America's commercial market embraces the entire globe. Antitrust questions can become extremely complex in transactions involving multiple companies in multiple nations, where those transactions are potentially governed by U.S. and foreign antitrust laws. U.S. antitrust laws are, of course, applicable to foreign firms doing business here. The Sherman, Clayton, and FTC acts, among others, are all potentially applicable to American business abroad.

Sherman Act

The Sherman Act applies to the conduct of American business abroad when that business has a direct effect on American commerce. That the business was conducted entirely abroad or that the agreement was entered into in another nation does not excuse an American firm from the reach of the Sherman Act (assuming American courts can achieve the necessary jurisdiction).

Clayton Act

Section 7 of the Clayton Act is clearly applicable to acquisitions combining domestic and foreign firms and is potentially applicable to acquisitions not involving American firms if the effect would harm competition in the American market.

Federal Trade Commission Act

As noted earlier, the FTC shares antitrust enforcement authority with the Justice Department, and Section 5 of the act strengthens Clayton 7.

Enforcement

Under its Business Review Procedure, the Justice Department sometimes will prepare a statement of its likely response to a proposed transaction, either foreign or domestic, so that the parties will have advance notice of the government's antitrust stance.

International Antitrust Enforcement

Markets increasingly extend around the globe encouraging antitrust enforcement as an international effort to achieve both consumer welfare and market efficiency. Economic analysis, as practiced in the United States, is being embraced by the European Union and other nations as a more effective and rational antitrust regime than the more politicized models of the past. Most antitrust enforcement occurs in the United States and the European Union, but other nations are taking a more aggressive stance, usually by employing laws that largely mimic those of the United States or the European Union. Until recent years, antitrust behavior such as price fixing was not illegal in many nations, but the emergence of global markets, increased economic understanding and U.S. pressure have generated growing antitrust attention worldwide. U.S. regulators have been concerned that American consumers will be harmed by price fixing abroad since Americans buy more and more foreign-made goods. As a result, while American officials are encouraging strengthened antitrust enforcement by other nations, U.S. enforcers, when necessary, are willing to aggressively assert American laws globally.

Extraterritoriality

America's most controversial expression of antitrust in trade policy was the Justice Department decision, announced in 1992, to more broadly apply American antitrust law abroad. The general idea is to sue foreign firms that violate U.S. antitrust laws even when the anticompetitive actions take place entirely overseas (extraterritorial application). In practice, the Justice Department files suit in U.S. courts against foreign companies operating in the United States if those foreign companies are taking action abroad that (1) harms competition in the United States or (2) limits American access to markets in other nations. Those lawsuits are permissible under U.S. law only where the conduct abroad has a "direct, substantial, and reasonably foreseeable" effect on the United States' domestic market. Extraterritoriality does not mean, however, that the United States will become the world's antitrust police department.

European Union Antitrust Enforcement   At the beginning of this chapter, we saw that the European Union arguably took a firmer stance toward Microsoft's allegedly monopolistic conduct than did the United States. Similarly, the European Union blocked the proposed merger of General Electric and Honeywell even though the United States had earlier approved the merger—marking the first time EU regulators had stopped a deal already approved in the United States. EU regulators have indicated that they intend to move toward the American antitrust model of

> The European Union blocked the proposed merger of General Electric and Honeywell

concern for consumer welfare rather than attacking dominant companies just because competitors may be harmed, but differences remain, and in general, the European Union seems to be practicing a more aggressive attitude towards possible corporate market abuse. Given the European Union's powerful economic role, the antitrust decisions of EU regulators necessarily influence business practice worldwide. [For EU and competition law news, see **http://www.roschiers.com/Roschier/rhawwwnew.nsf/sivut/ Pub272200815/$File/EUNews_270208_HTML.htm**]

Other Nations   South Korea, Russia, Hong Kong, Japan and others are either introducing new antitrust laws or adjusting existing laws and practices. China's new antitrust rules are of particular interest given the Asian giant's increasingly influential role in the global economy. American corporations and regulators hope the rules will bring greater consistency and transparency to China's antitrust oversight, but some observers fear China will use the law to exclude foreign competition. [For an overview of China's new Antimonopoly Law, see **http://mondaq.com/article.asp?articleid=60816**]

Internet Exercise	What evidence might suggest to the consumer that antitrust laws are being violated? For an answer, see the U.S. Department of Justice, Antitrust Division, brochure, "Antitrust Enforcement and the Consumer" [**http://www.usdoj.gov/atr/public/div_stats/211491.htm**].

Chapter Questions

1. The Chicago Skyway, a toll bridge connecting Chicago and Indiana, was owned and operated by the City of Chicago. Chicago earned $52 million in tolls beyond the amount needed to meet bond payments and to maintain the Skyway. The excess was used to pay for other transportation expenses. Skyway tolls were higher than those of other area highways. Endsley, a bridge user, joined others in a class action against Chicago claiming that the city's control of the Skyway provided monopoly power in high-speed limited access travel between Indiana and Chicago and that the city was abusing that power by collecting excessive fees. Chicago demonstrated that at least two alternative, if less desirable, routes were in competition with the Skyway. Is Chicago a monopolist? Explain. See *Endsley v. City of Chicago*, 230 F.3d 276 (7th Cir. 2000); cert. den. 532 U.S. 972 (2001).

2. Major League Soccer (MLS) was the exclusive Division I professional soccer league in the United States, as recognized by the U.S. Soccer Federation (USSF), the national soccer governing body. MLS owned all of the league's 12 teams, set all schedules, negotiated all stadium leases, controlled all intellectual property rights, and controlled all player contracts. Partial control over some teams was transferred by MLS to certain investors. The investors did not hire their own players. Each employment contract was between the player and the league. MLS assigned the players in a manner designed to maintain competitive balance. MLS had been preceded in U.S. professional soccer by the North American Soccer League, which had failed financially. A group of players sued the MLS on antitrust grounds.

   a. What were the players' antitrust claims?

   b. Decide those claims. Explain. See *Fraser v. Major League Soccer*, 284 F.3d 47 (1st Cir. 2002).

3. Poplar Bluff is a city of 17,000 people in southeastern Missouri. Sikeston and Cape Girardeau, Missouri, both towns with populations of over 40,000, are 40 and 60 miles away from Poplar Bluff. Tenet Healthcare owns Lucy Lee Hospital in Poplar Bluff and proposed to buy Doctors' Regional Medical Center, also in Poplar Bluff. Both hospitals are profitable, but both are underutilized and have had trouble attracting specialists. The Federal Trade Commission filed suit to block the acquisition. The key question involved definition of the geographic market. The FTC proposed a relevant geographic market that essentially matched the service area: a 50-mile radius of downtown Poplar Bluff. Ninety percent of the two hospitals' patients come from that area. Four other hospitals are in that area. The merged hospital would have 84 percent of the patients in that geographic market. Tenet argues that the geographic market should encompass a 65-mile radius from downtown Poplar Bluff. That area includes 16 hospitals. How should the Court of Appeals decide where the geographic market lies? See *FTC v. Tenet Health Care Corp.*, 186 F.3d 1045 (8th Cir. 1999).

4. Staples CEO Thomas Stemberg was asked, based on his experience, "Which mergers will be contested and which ones will sail through?"

How do you think the government decides which mergers to challenge? See Del Jones, "Today's Issue: Some Lessons Learned in an Antitrust Fight," *USA TODAY,* March 30, 1998, p. 5B.

5. A major concern with horizontal mergers is the increased potential for collusion. List the structural conditions that would encourage coordinated interaction between competitors.

6. Critics are concerned that increasing mergers, especially those involving media firms, threaten democracy.

   a. Explain that argument.

   b. Do you agree? Explain.

7. In 1986 distinguished economist William Shepherd argued,

   It may not be too late to turn back from this road to serfdom by reviving the case for antitrust, but the odds aren't favorable. More probably, antitrust will continue to sink.[29]

   a. What did Shepherd mean about "this road to serfdom?"

   b. In reading this chapter, do you think antitrust has been revived? Explain.

   c. Is bigness bad, or is it necessary in today's global economy? Explain.

8. Antitrust attorney Joel Davidow said that four policy measures have been critical to the success of formerly socialist nations that moved to a market economy: privatization, restructuring, deregulation, and adoption of competition legislation (antitrust). Now almost all of the industrial nations of the world, including former Soviet states Russia, Poland, and Hungary are taking all of these measures.

   a. Why is antitrust law important to the success of the new market economies in these formerly collectivist nations?

   b. Is antitrust important to developing nations such as India, Argentina, and Brazil? Explain. See Joel Davidow, "The Relevance of Antimonopoly Policy for Developing Countries," *Antitrust Bulletin* 37, no. 1 (Spring 1992), p. 277.

9. Is the influence of big business so persuasive that it nullifies the effective enforcement of the antitrust laws? Explain.

10. Antitrust authorities must address a critical and empirically difficult policy problem: Does seller concentration in a market ordinarily result in increased prices? That is, in a particular market, are fewer firms with larger shares likely to produce higher prices than would be the case with a more fragmented market? Free market theorists are generally untroubled by concentration. What do you think? Explain.

11. Is a monopolist required to deal with its competitors? That question was the core of a 2004 Supreme Court decision in *Verizon Communications v. Law Offices of Curtis V. Trinko.*[30] The Trinko law firm bought its local phone service from AT&T. Trinko brought a class action claiming Verizon maintained a monopoly by exclusionary practices. Trinko contended that local phone services had difficulty connecting with the giant regional Bell operating companies' (Verizon, Qwest, Bell South, and SBC) local exchange facilities, thus harming competition and consumers. The Telecommunications

Act of 1996 specifically requires the regional Bell companies to provide the local phone services with fair, reasonable access. The Supreme Court, however, ruled in favor of Verizon and concluded that antitrust liability in these telephone situations would apply only where a telephone monopolist discontinues a voluntary business relationship with a competitor for the purpose of destroying that competitor. Explain why the Supreme Court decided that Verizon, a telephone monopolist, had no duty to deal with those telephone competitors with whom it had not previously dealt. See Matthew Cantor, "Is Trinko the Last Word on a Telephone Monopolist's Duty to Deal?" *New York Law Journal* 96 (May 19, 2004), p. 4.

12. In the period 1917—19, DuPont acquired 23 percent of the stock in the then-fledgling General Motors Corporation. By 1947 DuPont supplied 68 percent of GM's automotive finish needs and 38 percent of its fabric needs. In 1955 General Motors ranked first in sales and second in assets among all U.S. industrial corporations, while accounting for approximately two-fifths of the nation's annual automobile sales. In 1949 the Justice Department challenged Dupont's 1917—19 acquistions of GM stock.

    a. Why did the government challenge DuPont's acquisition?

    b. May an acquisition be properly challenged 30 years after the fact, as in DuPont? Explain.

    c. Given your general understanding of finishes and fabrics, how would you defend DuPont?

    d. Decide. Explain. See *United States v. E. I. DuPont de Nemours & Co.,* 353 U.S. 586 (1957).

13. How can a merger benefit society?

14. Which economic considerations support the view that unilateral growth is preferable to growth by merger?

15. Excel, a division of Cargill, was the second largest firm in the beef-packing market. It sought to acquire Spencer Pack, a division of Land-O-Lakes and the third largest beef packer. After the acquisition, Excel would have remained second ranked in the business, but its market share would have been only slightly smaller than that of the leader, IBP. Monfort, the nation's fifth largest beef packer, sought an injunction to block the acquisition, claiming a violation of Clayton Section 7. In effect, Monfort claimed the merger would result in a dangerous concentration of economic power in the beef-packing market, with the result that Excel would pay more for cattle and charge less for its processed beef, thus placing its competitors in a destructive and illegal price–cost squeeze. Monfort claimed Excel's initial losses in this arrangement would be covered by its wealthy parent, Cargill. Then, when the competition was driven from the market, Monfort claimed, Excel would raise its processed beef prices to supracompetitive levels. Among other defenses, Excel averred that the heavy losses Monfort claimed were merely the product of intense competition, a condition that would not constitute a violation of the antitrust laws. The district court found for Monfort, and the appeals court, considering the cost–price squeeze a form of predatory pricing, affirmed. Excel appealed to the Supreme Court. Decide. Explain. See *Cargill, Inc. v. Monfort of Colorado, Inc.,* 479 U.S. 104 (1986).

Notes

1. See *United States v. Microsoft Corporation*, 87 F. Supp. 2d 30 (D.D.C. 2000), and *Microsoft v. United States*, 253 F.3d 34 (D.C. Cir. 2001); cert. den. 122 S.Ct. 350 (2001).

2. Catherine Rampell, "Extension of Microsoft Antitrust Pact Requested," *Washington Post*, September 12, 2007, p. D02.

3. Alan Murray, "Microsoft Foe Quits Antitrust Crusade—with Check in Hand," *The Wall Street Journal*, December 7, 2004, p. A4.

4. *United States v. Grinnell*, 384 U.S. 563, 570-1 (1966).

5. Thomas Piraino, "Regulating Oligopoly Conduct under the Antitrust Laws," *Minnesota Law Review* 89 (November 2004), p. 9.

6. Piraino, "Regulating Oligopoly Conduct," p.11.

7. Thomas Claburn, "Antitrust Lawsuit Charges Apple with Monopolizing Online Music," *InformationWeek*, January 3, 2008 [**http://www.informationweek.com/news/showArticle.jhtml?articleID=205207895**].

8. Note, "Antitrust and the Information Age: Section 2 Monopolization Analyses in the New Economy," *Harvard Law Review* 114 (March 2001), p. 1623.

9. *Spectrum Sports, Inc. v. Shirley McQuillan*, 506 U.S. 447 (1993).

10. John R. Wilke, "How Driving Prices Lower Can Violate Antitrust Statutes," *The Wall Street Journal*, January 27, 2004, p. A1.

11. Note, "Antitrust and the Information Age," pp. 1623, 1645.

12. "M&A Deals Hit Record $1.57 Trillion in 2007," *The New York Times*, December 21, 2007 [**http://dealbook.blogs.nytimes.com**].

13. Ibid.

14. David Kesmodel and Deborah Ball, "Miller, Coors to Shake Up U.S. Beer Market," *The Wall Street Journal*, October 10, 2007, p. A1.

15. Ibid.

16. Peter Krass, "Why Do We Do It?" *Across the Board*, May/June 2001, pp. 22, 26.

17. Richard Cohen, "My Avaricious Hero," *Des Moines Register*, February 10, 2005, p. 9A.

18. David Henry, "Have Dealmakers Wised Up?" *BusinessWeek*, February 21, 2005, p. 36.

19. "KPMG Study Finds One-Third of Mergers, Acquisitions Boost Shareholder Returns," *AFX News Limited*, April 29, 2001 [**http://web.lexis-nexis.com/universe/doc...1&_md5=8efdeffc8d0c08b4fe812afdfa8399b9**].

20. See Michael J. Mandel, "All These Mergers Are Great, But . . . ," *BusinessWeek*, October 18, 1999, p. 48; and Jeffrey Garten, "Megamergers Are a Clear and Present Danger," *BusinessWeek*, January 25, 1999, p. 28.

21. Jaret Seiberg, "Consumer Groups Slam FTC," *Daily Deal/The Deal*, September 15, 2004.

22. Dar Haddix, "Oil Mergers May Raise Prices, Alter Market," *United Press International*, May 28, 2004.

23. "Mergers Not Driving Up Gas Prices, Says FTC," *AFX.COM*, August 13, 2004.

24. Diana B. Henriques, "U.S. Antitrust Review Backs Whirlpool-Maytag Merger," *New York Times*, March 30, 2006 [**http://www.nytmes.com/2006/03/30/business/30whirlpool.html**].

25. Jon B. Dubrow, "Antitrust Defeats May Spur Concentrated-Market Deals," *Mergers and Acquisitions Journal*, January 1, 2005.

26. Note, "Analyzing Differentiated-Product Mergers: The Relevance of Structural Analysis," *Harvard Law Review* 111 (June 1998), p. 2420.

27. News Services, "FTC Gains Consumer Safeguards in AOL Deal; Time Warner Merger Has Only One More Step Left in Approval Process," *St. Louis Post-Dispatch,* December 15, 2000, p. A1.

28. Richard Posner, *Antitrust Law* (Chicago: The University of Chicago Press, 1976), p. 130.

29. William G. Shepherd, "Bust the Reagan Trustbusters," *Fortune,* August 4, 1986, pp. 225, 227.

30. 540 U.S. 398 (2004).

Employer–Employee Relations

CHAPTER TWELVE

Employment Law I: Employee Rights

After completing this chapter, students will be able to:

1. Distinguish between an employee and independent contractor.

2. Identify potential legal challenges an employer faces in the hiring process.

3. Describe employers' liability under the doctrine of "respondeat superior."

4. Analyze claims of negligent hiring, supervision, and retention.

5. Explain employees' rights under the Fair Labor Standards Act.

6. Describe the role of the Occupational Safety and Health Administration (OSHA) in protecting employees' health and safety at work.

7. Describe the benefits, coverage, and requirements for bringing a successful claim under workers' compensation law.

8. Discuss workplace drug testing and the legal challenges it faces.

9. Describe the Family and Medical Leave Act (FMLA).

10. Distinguish between defined benefit and defined contribution pension plans.

11. Analyze whether a dismissed at-will employee may bring a claim of wrongful discharge.

12. Recognize the purpose and requirements of the employment eligibility verification form (I-9).

Introduction

Scott Rodrigues was fired in 2006 by The Scotts Company, the lawn care giant, because a required drug test revealed nicotine in his urine. Company policy forbade employee smoking both on and off the job. Scotts announced in 2005 that it would no longer hire smokers, and it gave its employees one year to comply with the new policy; a policy designed to improve employee wellness and reduce company healthcare costs. Rodrigues was a pack-a-day smoker when he was hired. He was aware of the no-smoking policy, and he had been warned to quit when a supervisor saw a pack of cigarettes on the dashboard of his car. Rodrigues acknowledged his smoking habit, but said he was trying to quit smoking when he was fired. Rodrigues complained that the company had not offered to help him quit smoking. The Scotts' plan does, however, pay for smoking cessation programs for its employees. Scotts said they were not interested in influencing workers' behavior in their free time, except in the case of smoking.[1] Rodrigues decided to file suit against Scotts because:

> What's to make them stop at just cigarettes? If they're a Republican company, can they try and figure out who you vote for and if you vote for the Democrats, they'll fire you?..."[2]

The National Workrights Institute [**www.workrights.org**] says that firing workers who won't stop smoking is illegal, under various statutes, in 30 states.[3] Massachusetts law, however, does not provide explicit protection for smokers. Therefore, Rodriguez brought suit in a U.S. federal district court in Massachusetts claiming, among other things, that his right to privacy was violated. Section 1B, Chapter 214 of the Massachusetts General Laws provides: "A person shall have a right against unreasonable, substantial or serious interference with his privacy."

Questions

1. How would you rule on Rodrigues' right to privacy claim?
2. Should employers be able to fire employees who smoke off the job? Explain. See *Rodrigues v. The Scotts Company,* 2008 U.S. Dist. LEXIS 6682.

Managing Lawsuits Managers have always had tough, demanding jobs, but in recent years the law has added complicated, frustrating new expectations. The threat of lawsuits, like Rodrigues', has become an important consideration in management decision making. As union strength has declined (see Chapter 14), government rules and court decisions protecting employees have expanded. Those increased legal protections, a volatile economy, downsizing, decreased employer–employee loyalty, and other forces have led to unprecedented levels of employee litigation. [For an extensive employment law database, see **http://dir. yahoo.com/Government/Law/employment_Law**]

Part One—Selection

Job Classification The nature of the selection (hiring) process and the laws governing it depend on the type of relationship the employer decides to build with the worker. The traditional, stable model of long-term direct employer–employee relationships now is often replaced with new, flexible, nontraditional staffing arrangements including outsourcing and employee leasing, along with the use of freelancers, temporary agencies, and professional employer organizations. (Firms save money and increase expertise by contracting with these PEOs to administer the firms' human resource services.) These *contingent workers,* along with *independent contractors,* who are increasingly relied on to perform specific, shorter-term, nonrecurring jobs, permit employers to rapidly and inexpensively inflate or shrink their workforces as competitive and regulatory conditions change. Employers who choose to provide health and retirement benefits for their traditional employees need not do so for their contingent workers. Nor must they withhold income, Social Security, Medicare, and unemployment taxes. With fringe benefit costs skyrocketing, benefits reduction has become an important consideration for most firms.

Employee or Independent Contractor?   The impact of many legal themes discussed in this chapter depends, initially, on whether the worker in question is an employee (whether long-term or contingent) or an independent contractor: a worker under contract to the organization to do a specific task but not, legally, a part of that organization.

Degree of control is the dominant test in settling the employee–independent contractor question. Where a worker's performance is controlled by an employer or where the employer has the right or the ability to control that work, the worker is likely to be considered an employee. A business that hires an independent contractor generally is not required to comply with a wide range of employment and labor law standards that would apply were the worker an employee. Thus a business must provide unemployment insurance, workers' compensation coverage, minimum wages, and so on to employees, but generally would not need to do so for independent contractors. Further, employers generally are not liable for discrimination claims by independent contractors; nor are they liable for most torts committed by independent contractors in the course of work. [For a sample of independent contractor agreements, see **http://www.toolkit.cch.com/tools/indcon_m.asp**]

Classification Problems   Employers anxious to reduce financial and legal burdens sometimes improperly classify workers as independent contractors rather than employees. In 2007, a California federal district court ordered a house cleaning service to pay $4.5 million to provide minimum wages and overtime pay for workers who had been misclassified as independent contractors. Employees, unlike independent contractors, are protected by the Fair Labor Standards Act (detailed later in this chapter), which requires, among other things, the payment of the federal minimum wage and overtime pay. The employer claimed that the workers were independent contractors and thus not covered by the FLSA, but the court pointed to a variety of considerations, including control and supervision, that confirmed the workers' correct status as employees.[4] At this writing, some 14,000 FedEx drivers in 36 states have been granted class action status in their lawsuit claiming they have been illegally classified as independent contractors thus depriving them of important legal rights, medical and pension benefits, and so on.[5]

Hiring and the Law   In recent years, potential legal problems in the hiring process have become increasingly troublesome:

- ***Résumé Fraud:*** David J. Edmondson resigned as chief executive of Radio Shack in 2006 a few days after a newspaper reported that Edmondson had not earned either of the two college degrees he had claimed on his résumé when he was hired more than 10 years previously.[6] Résumé inaccuracies are not unusual. ResumeDoctor.com checked the accuracy of more than 1,000 résumés in its database in 2006 and found "significant inaccuracies" in nearly 43 percent of them.[7]

- ***Background Checks:*** The 9/11 terrorist attack, lawsuit fears and careful management have dramatically increased employers' attention to background and security checks. A recent survey found that about 80 percent of companies conducted criminal background checks in 2003.[8] As has been vividly publicized, some job applicants have undermined their hiring prospects by online postings of inappropriate information about themselves. *The New York Times* reported one such episode involving the president of a small consulting company who was doing a background check on a promising applicant for a summer internship:

  At Facebook . . . the executive found the candidate's Web page with this description of his interests: "smokin' blunts . . . shooting people and obsessive sex, all described in vivid slang.[9] He didn't get the internship.

He didn't get the internship

- ***Inappropriate Questions:*** About 21 percent of 1,000 workers in a national survey said they had been asked inappropriate questions in a job interview.[10] Often these questions, such as "How old are you?" and "Are you married?" raise discrimination concerns. The questions themselves are not unlawful under federal law, but discrimination based on the answers to those questions would be illegal. (See Chapter 13.) But what about the enormous array of awkward, intrusive, but nondiscriminatory interview questions that might leave the candidate feeling uncomfortable if not wronged? For example:

  Following a job interview this year, Megan Johnson sent a handwritten thank-you note on fine stationery. But she didn't make the impression she intended. "You aren't a Republican, are you?" asked the hiring manager during a follow-up phone call. Ms. Johnson was stumped until she remembered the small blue elephant with an upturned trunk engraved along the upper margin of her note card.[11]

The elephant was, in fact, supposed to represent good luck, but Johnson did not get the job. Furthermore, she cannot sue the company because questions about politics break no employment laws.[12]

- ***Noncompete Clauses:*** Accountant Stephen Fitzgerald quit his employer, Brett Senior & Associates in Pennsylvania, and moved to Fesnak & Associates, an accounting firm, that Senior considered a competitor. Among other things, Fitzgerald called 20 clients before he left Senior, and 15 of them followed him to Fesnak. At this writing, Fitzgerald is being sued for his alleged breach of fiduciary duty for soliciting at least a portion of those clients.[13] To address problems like these, employers sometimes require employees to sign agreements providing they will not compete with their employer, solicit its customers or employees, pass trade secrets to others, and so on for a specified period of time. Fitzgerald had not signed such a pact, but a recent survey found that 30 percent of companies now require employees to sign noncompete agreements, and 51 percent require nondisclosure agreements.[14] Those agreements are fully enforceable if reasonable in their requirements.

- ***Arbitration:*** New hires are sometimes expected to sign agreements specifying that disputes with the employer will be settled by arbitration (see Chapter 4) rather than by litigation. Employers like arbitration because it can be cheaper, faster and less adversarial than a trial. Employees, on the other hand, argue that arbitration is stacked in favor of corporate interests and amounts to a denial of the fundamental right of access to the legal system. An important U.S. Supreme Court decision in the *Circuit City* case upheld the enforceability of legitimate, equitable employment arbitration agreement,[15] although recent court decisions have found some of those agreements unconscionable and thus unenforceable.[16] In any case, the federal government's Equal Employment Opportunity Commission (see Chapter 13) retains authority to file discrimination lawsuits on behalf of employees despite an arbitration agreement.[17]

- *References:* As a manager, you decide to fire an employee, Brown, because of what

> You decide to fire an employee

you believe to be convincing evidence that he had sexually harassed a coworker. Brown applies for a new job, and that employer seeks your evaluation of Brown's work. What should you do? If you tell what you know, you and your employer fear Brown might sue you for *defamation* (*slander* when spoken; *libel* when written). If you fail to say what you know, you fear you might be sued for *misrepresentation* or *negligent referral* if Brown is hired and commits further harassment on his new job. Because of those risks, employers often limit their references to purely factual details such as the date of hire, date of departure, and job title.

Broadly, a successful defamation suit requires the following conditions:

1. A false statement.
2. The statement must be "published" to a third party.
3. The employer must be responsible for the publication.
4. The plaintiff's reputation must be harmed.

Truth is a complete defense in defamation cases, and managers sticking to the facts and honest professional judgments are unlikely to have problems. Indeed, defamation and other reference fears may have been overblown because relatively few lawsuits have actually emerged. Further, many state courts provide the protection of what is labeled a *qualified privilege*. Under the privilege, legitimate business communications, with some exceptions, would be shielded from litigation. Similarly, a number of states have passed statutes protecting legitimate reference communications from defamation claims.

Part Two—Liability

Once hired, what happens when employees make mistakes or engage in misconduct on the job that hurts others? Must the employer bear the loss in these situations? Job classification is an important first question in determining company liability for workers' job-related injuries, harm to others, and crimes. An enterprise ordinarily will not be liable for the acts of its *independent contractors*. Employers, on the other hand, often bear legal responsibility for *employees'* accidents or wrongs. That liability may spring from the doctrine of *respondeat superior* (let the master answer), a form of *vicarious liability* (sometimes called *imputed liability*).

Scope of Employment Employer liability for employee injuries, accidents, or wrongs is largely dependent on whether the employee was on the job at the time of the incident in question. Employers will be held liable under respondeat superior/vicarious liability reasoning for harm to third parties caused by the intentional or negligent acts of their employees when those acts occur within the *scope of employment* (on the job). A finding of employer liability, of course, does not excuse the employee from her personal liability, but the respondeat superior reasoning does have the potential effect of opening the employer's deeper pockets to the plaintiff. The following questions ordinarily determine whether the harm occurred in the scope of employment:

1. Was the employee subject to the employer's supervision?
2. Was the employee motivated, at least in part, by a desire to serve the employer's business interests?
3. Did the problem arise substantially within normal working hours and in a work location?
4. Was the act in question of the general kind the employee had been hired to perform?

In *Mary M. v. City of Los Angeles*,[18] the city was held liable under the doctrine of respondeat superior for a sexual assault committed by a police officer. At 2:30 AM on October 3, 1981, Sergeant Leigh Schroyer was

> The City was held liable for a sexual assault committed by a police officer

on duty, in uniform, carrying a gun, and patrolling in his marked police car. He stopped Mary M. for erratic driving. She pleaded not to be arrested. He ordered her to enter his patrol car and took her to her home. He entered her home and said that he expected "payment" for not arresting her. He raped her and was subsequently sentenced to a term in state prison.

Mary M. sued the City of Los Angeles. The general inquiry was whether Schroyer was acting within the scope of his employment during the rape episode. The jury found for Mary M. and awarded $150,000 in damages. The Court of Appeals reversed, saying that Schroyer was not acting within the scope of his employment. The case went to the California Supreme Court. The city argued that Schroyer was acting on behalf of his own interests rather than those of the city, and that the city had not authorized his conduct. Therefore, Schroyer could not have been acting within the scope of employment. However, the court said that the correct question was not whether the rape was authorized but whether it happened in the course of a series of acts that were authorized. The court reversed, saying that a jury could find the city vicariously liable (imputed to the principal from the agent) given the unique authority of police officers in our society. [For an employment law overview, see **www.employlaw.com**]

Questions

1. Gonzalez, working for Land Transport, was driving his employer's tractor-trailer behind Nichols, who was driving his pickup. Gonzalez followed at an unsafe distance and twice attempted to pass in no-passing zones. Nichols responded with "predictable obscene gestures." While both drivers were stopped at a red light, Gonzalez left the company truck and attacked Nichols with a rubber-coated metal cable and a knife. Gonzalez was convicted of assault. Nichols sued Land Transport.

   a. What is his claim?

   b. Decide the case. Explain. See *Nichols v. Land Transport,* 233 F.3d 21 (1st Cir. 2000).

2. Williams, Hemphill, Dixon, and Osborne, while driving in Chicago, noticed some pizza boxes on top of a car parked in front of the Italian Fiesta Pizzeria. Dixon and Hemphill jumped out, discovered the boxes were empty, dropped them, and reentered their Jeep. Hall, a driver for Italian Fiesta, observed Dixon and Hemphill, yelled at them to return the pizza boxes, and then followed them in his vehicle. Dixon turned the wrong way onto a one-way street and Hall followed. Dixon then collided with another vehicle. Williams died and Hemphill was injured. Italian Fiesta was subsequently sued on negligent hiring (see below) and vicarious liability claims. The negligent hiring claim was rejected by the judge, but the vicarious liability theme was allowed to proceed to trial. The defendants provided evidence showing the pizzeria specifically informed employees that they were not to attempt to recover stolen property or punish perpetrators. Rather, the pizzeria's policy was for supervisors to contact police. Further, drivers were not penalized if property was stolen.

   a. What was the central issue in this case?

   b. Decide the case. Explain. See *Williams v. Hall*, 681 N.E.2d 1037 (Ill. App. 1997).

3. What policy justifications support the imposition of liability on an employer for the wrongs of an employee operating within the scope of employment?

Hiring/Retention/Training/Supervision

Negligence

In addition to respondeat superior situations, employers may be liable for negligence in hiring an employee or retaining an employee who subsequently causes harm to a third party, or for careless training or supervision. Typically, the employer is liable on negligence grounds for hiring or retaining an employee whom the employer knew or should have known to be dangerous, incompetent, dishonest, or the like where that information was directly related to the injury suffered by the plaintiff. Note that under negligence liability an employer may be liable for acts *outside* the scope of employment. The case that follows examines the law of negligent hiring, supervision, and retention.

LEGAL BRIEFCASE

Yunker v. Honeywell, Inc.
496 N.W.2d 419 (Minn.App. 1993)

Judge Lansing

FACTS

Honeywell employed Randy Landin from 1977 to 1979 and from 1984 to 1988. From 1979 to 1984 Landin was imprisoned for the strangulation death of Nancy Miller, a Honeywell coemployee. On his release from prison, Landin reapplied at Honeywell. Honeywell rehired Landin as a custodian in Honeywell's General Offices facility in South Minneapolis in August 1984. Because of workplace confrontations Landin was twice transferred, first to the Golden Valley facility in August 1986, and then to the St. Louis Park facility in August 1987.

Kathleen Nesser was assigned to Landin's maintenance crew in April 1988. Landin and Nesser became friends and spent time together away from work. When Landin expressed a romantic interest, Nesser stopped spending time with Landin. Landin began to harass and threaten Nesser both at work and at home. At the end of June, Landin's behavior prompted Nesser to seek help from her supervisor and to request a transfer out of the St. Louis Park facility.

On July 1, 1988, Nesser found a death threat scratched on her locker door. Landin did not come to work on or after July 1, and Honeywell accepted his formal resignation on July 11, 1988. On July 19, approximately six hours after her Honeywell shift ended, Landin killed Nesser in her driveway with a close-range shotgun blast. Landin was convicted of first degree murder and sentenced to life imprisonment.

Jean Yunker, as trustee for the heirs and next-of-kin of Kathleen Nesser, brought this wrongful death action based on theories of negligent hiring, retention, and supervision of a dangerous employee. Honeywell moved for summary judgment and, for purposes of the motion, stipulated that it failed to exercise reasonable care in the hiring and supervision of Landin. The trial court concluded that Honeywell owed no legal duty to Nesser and granted summary judgment for Honeywell.

ISSUE

Did Honeywell have a duty to Kathleen Nesser to exercise reasonable care in hiring, retaining, or supervising Randy Landin?

ANALYSIS

In determining that Honeywell did not have a legal duty to Kathleen Nesser arising from its employment of Randy Landin, the district court analyzed Honeywell's duty as limited by its ability to control and protect its employees while they are involved in the employer's business or at the employer's place of business. Additionally, the court concluded that Honeywell could not have reasonably foreseen Landin's killing Nesser.

Incorporating a "scope of employment" limitation into an employer's duty borrows from the doctrine of *respondeat superior*. However, of the three theories advanced for recovery, only negligent supervision derives from the *respondeat superior* doctrine, which relies on connection to the employer's premises or chattels. We agree that negligent supervision is not a viable theory of recovery because Landin was neither on Honeywell's premises nor using Honeywell's chattels when he shot Nesser.

The remaining theories, negligent hiring and negligent retention, are based on direct, not vicarious, liability. Negligent hiring and negligent retention do not rely on the scope of employment but address risks created by exposing members of the public to a potentially dangerous individual. These theories of recovery impose liability for an employee's intentional tort, an action almost invariably outside the scope of employment, when the employer knew or should have known that the employee was violent or aggressive and might engage in injurious conduct.

I

Minnesota first explicitly recognized a cause of action based on negligent hiring in *Ponticas* in 1983. *Ponticas* involved the employment of an apartment manager who sexually assaulted a tenant. The supreme court upheld a jury verdict finding the apartment operators negligent in failing to make a reasonable investigation into the resident manager's background before providing him with a passkey. The court defined negligent hiring as

> predicated on the negligence of an employer in placing a person with known propensities, or propensities which should have been discovered by reasonable investigation, in an employment position in which, *because of the circumstances of the employment,* it should have been foreseeable that the hired individual posed a threat of injury to others.

Honeywell argues that under *Ponticas* it is not liable for negligent hiring because, unlike providing a dangerous resident manager with a passkey, Landin's employment did not enable him to commit the act of violence against Nesser. This argument has merit, and we note that a number of jurisdictions have expressly defined the scope of an employer's duty of reasonable care in hiring as largely dependent on the type of responsibilities associated with the particular job. See *Connes,* 831 P.2d at 1321 (employer's duty in hiring is dependent on anticipated degree of contact between employee and other persons in performing employment duties).

Ponticas rejected the view that employers are required to investigate a prospective employee's criminal background in every job in which the individual has regular contact with the public. Instead, liability is determined by the totality of the circumstances surrounding the hiring and whether the employer exercised reasonable care. The court instructed that

> [t]he scope of the investigation is directly related to the severity of the risk third parties are subjected to by an incompetent employee. Although only slight care might suffice in the hiring of a yardman, a worker on a production line, or other types of employment where the employee would not constitute a high risk of injury to third persons, when the prospective employee is to be furnished a passkey permitting admittance to living quarters of tenants,

the employer has the duty to use reasonable care to investigate his competency and reliability prior to employment.

Applying these principles, we conclude that Honeywell did not owe a duty to Nesser at the time of Landin's hire. Landin was employed as a maintenance worker whose job responsibilities entailed no exposure to the general public and required only limited contact with coemployees. Unlike the caretaker in *Ponticas,* Landin's duties did not involve inherent dangers to others, and unlike the tenant in *Ponticas,* Nesser was not a reasonably foreseeable victim at the time Landin was hired.

To reverse the district court's determination on duty as it relates to hiring would extend *Ponticas* and essentially hold that ex-felons are inherently dangerous and that any harmful acts they commit against persons encountered through employment will automatically be considered foreseeable. Such a rule would deter employers from hiring workers with a criminal record and "offend our civilized concept that society must make a reasonable effort to rehabilitate those who have erred so they can be assimilated into the community."

Honeywell did not breach a legal duty to Nesser by hiring Landin because the specific nature of his employment did not create a foreseeable risk of harm, and public policy supports a limitation on this cause of action. The district court correctly determined that Honeywell is not liable to Nesser under a theory of negligent hiring.

II

In recognizing the tort of negligent hiring, *Ponticas* extended established Minnesota case law permitting recovery under theories of negligent retention.

* * * * *

The difference between negligent hiring and negligent retention focuses on when the employer was on notice that an employee posed a threat and failed to take steps to ensure the safety of third parties. The Florida appellate court has provided a useful definition:

> Negligent hiring occurs when, prior to the time the employee is actually hired, the employer knew or should have known of the employee's unfitness, and the issue of liability primarily focuses upon the adequacy of the employer's pre-employment investigation into the employee's background. Negligent retention, on the other hand, occurs when, during the course of employment, the employer becomes aware or should have become aware of problems with an employee that indicated his unfitness, and the employer fails to take further action such as investigating, discharge, or reassignment.

. . . The record contains evidence of a number of episodes in Landin's postimprisonment employment at Honeywell that demonstrate a propensity for abuse and violence toward coemployees.

While at the Golden Valley facility, Landin sexually harassed female employees and challenged a male coworker to fight. After his transfer to St. Louis Park, Landin threatened to kill a coworker during an angry confrontation following a minor car accident. In another employment incident, Landin was hostile and abusive toward a female coworker after problems developed in their friendship. Landin's specific focus on Nesser was demonstrated by several workplace outbursts occurring at the end of June, and on July 1 the words "one more day and you're dead" were scratched on her locker door.

Landin's troubled work history and the escalation of abusive behavior during the summer of 1988 relate directly to the foreseeability prong of duty. The facts . . . show that it was foreseeable that Landin could act violently against a coemployee, and against Nesser in particular.

This foreseeability gives rise to a duty of care to Nesser that is not outweighed by policy considerations of employment opportunity. An ex-felon's "opportunity for gainful employment may spell the difference between recidivism and rehabilitation," but it cannot predominate over the need to maintain a safe workplace when specific actions point to future violence.

Our holding is narrow and limited only to the recognition of a legal duty owed to Nesser arising out of Honeywell's continued employment of Landin. It is important to emphasize that in reversing the summary judgment on negligent retention, we do not reach the remaining significant questions of whether Honeywell breached that duty by failing to terminate or discipline Landin, or whether such a breach was a proximate cause of Nesser's death. These are issues generally decided by a jury after a full presentation of facts . . .

DECISION

We affirm the entry of summary judgment on the theories of negligent hiring and supervision, but reverse the summary judgment on the issue of negligent retention.

AFTERWORD

Published reports indicate the *Yunker* case was settled out of court soon after this decision was handed down.

Questions

1. What did the court mean when it said that "negligent hiring and negligent retention are based on direct, not vicarious, liability"?
2. Why did the court reject the negligent supervision claim?
3. Why did the court reject the negligent hiring claim?

4. Why did the court allow the negligent retention issue to go to trial?

5. L.M. sued Iglesia Cristiana La Casa Del Senor, Inc., an Assemblies of God Church in Florida, among others, because she allegedly was sexually assaulted at age 16 by the then church pastor, Ali Pacheco. The assault occurred at a hotel where Pacheco took the victim for lunch and for a conversation about the marital problems of the victim's parents. Pacheco testified that L.M. consented to the sexual act. The local church had not investigated Pacheco's background because that duty resided exclusively in the church's district offices. Pacheco had been involved in a consensual extramarital affair, but that relationship had not been discovered during the district's background check. Pacheco was president of the church corporation and his wife was vice president. Mrs. Pacheco learned that her husband had sent gifts to the victim, but the record is unclear as to whether she knew about the gifts prior to the sexual assault.

a. What causes of action against the local church and the district church could legitimately arise from these facts?

b. Decide the case. Explain. See *Iglesia Cristiana La Casa Del Senor, Inc. v. L.M.,* 783 So.2d 360 (Fl. Ct. App. 2001).

Part Three—Fair Labor Standards Act

A note was passed to President Franklin D. Roosevelt in 1936 from a young girl:

> I wish you could do something to help us girls. We have been working in a sewing factory . . . getting our minimum pay of $11 a week. Today, the 200 of us girls have been cut down to $4 and $5 and $6 a week.[19]

Roosevelt reportedly remarked that something needed to be done about child labor. The Depression and its tragic suffering, even of those working hard, shattered many Americans' faith in the free market and led to government intervention including, in 1938, the Fair Labor Standards Act (FLSA), which is directed to these major objectives:

1. The establishment of a minimum wage that provides at least a modest standard of living for employees.

2. A flexible ceiling on hours worked weekly, the purpose of which is to increase the number of employed Americans.

3. Child labor protection.

4. Equal pay for equal work regardless of gender. (See Chapter 13.)

[For the U.S. Department of Labor home page, see **http://www.dol.gov**]

Minimum Wage   For the first time in a decade, the federal government in 2007 increased the federally mandated minimum wage to $7.25 an hour from $5.15 in three stages concluding in 2009. Various business interests lobbied against the change, and the National Restaurant Association argued that the most recent increase in 1997 had caused a reduction of 146,000 jobs in their industry alone.[20] Critics feel that the government should not interfere in the marketplace, and they argue that the increase threatens not only job growth but the livelihoods of many small business owners. Some evidence supports those critics, but a recent study found that states with a minimum wage higher than the federal minimum had job growth equal to or greater than those states with the federal minimum.[21] More than 100 communities, many where living costs are particularly high, have adopted their own "living wage" requirements. Maryland in 2007 became the first state to adopt a living wage standard, requiring all state government contractors in urban areas to pay their employees a minimum of $11.30 per hour.[22] A 2002 study found that the higher minimums have been effective in reducing poverty despite some increase in unemployment.[23] [For state minimum wage laws, see **http://www.dol.gov/esa/minwage/america.htm**]

Overtime   Most workers are entitled to Fair Labor Standards Act protections, including the minimum wage and overtime, but certain occupational classes are *exempt* (managers and some professionals, for example) and therefore are not protected by the FLSA. IBM was sued for allegedly violating the FLSA by misclassifying thousands of tech support workers as exempt professionals (thus not entitled to overtime wages); a claim that IBM settled in 2006 for $65 million. IBM then decided those tech workers needed to be reclassified as hourly workers eligible for overtime in order to comply with the FLSA. The story became heated, however, in 2008 when IBM decided to pay for the change in compensation by cutting those employees' wages by 15 percent. IBM says those employees will earn as much under the new overtime arrangements as when salaried, but the workers disagree.[24]

> **Wal-Mart has been swamped with wage and hour lawsuits**

Wal-Mart has been swamped with about 80 wage and hour lawsuits and has lost jury decisions of $172 million to a group of California employees and $78.5 million to Pennsylvania workers.[25] Similarly, at this writing, Starbucks is defending overtime lawsuits in Florida and Texas, after settling with store managers for $18 million in a 2003 California case.[26] Like many of these cases, the California Starbucks managers claimed they were given the title of store manager or assistant manager in an effort to make them ineligible for overtime, but most of their work was of an hourly nature, such as preparing and serving drinks.[27] Simply calling them managers did not make them so, they claimed, if their work was not of a managerial character.

These *misclassification* cases are one of two primary areas of overtime contention; the other being *off-the-clock* claims in which employers are accused of not giving employees recorded credit for all of the time they have worked. For example, Wal-Mart employees claim that the company's relentless pressure to cut costs causes managers to expect employees to work through their lunch breaks without pay. In another off-the-clock case, eventually settled for $7.2 million, Hollywood Video stores' work practices required employees to boot the store computer before they could punch in, and they had to punch out before they could close the register and do the daily tally.[28] Wage and hour cases, like these, have exploded in recent years such that defense attorneys regard them as much more financially damaging to the business community than more highly publicized conflicts such as sexual harassment claims.[29]

New Rules   In response to corporate pleas for relief from lawsuits, the Bush administration approved a 2004 revision of overtime rules. While still complicated, the new rules attempt to clarify the murky distinction between exempt and nonexempt employees.

At the simplest level, nearly all workers making less than $23,660 per year will be nonexempt (entitled to time and one–half overtime pay), whereas very few of those making $100,000 or more will be entitled to that pay. The tens of millions in between may or may not receive overtime depending on some rather vague rules. Those who fall in one of the following classes may, after close analysis of their duties, prove to be exempt from the overtime protections: executives, administrators, professional/creative workers, computer professionals, and outside salespeople. Some workers such as police officers, firefighters, and better-paid blue-collar workers are expressly granted the right to overtime pay. Others, such as insurance adjusters, dental hygienists, pharmacists, and journalists, are expressly exempt and thus not entitled to overtime. Critics say millions of workers will be ineligible for overtime pay under the new rules, but at this writing the impact is unclear. [For more details about the new overtime rules, see the federal Department of Labor guidance at **http://www.dol.gov/esa/regs/compliance/whd/fairpay/main.htm**]

Question

Answer this person's complaint: "I work at a business that offers overtime. There are two employees, myself and one other, who do the same job. The other person is always offered overtime, and I'm left working regular hours only. Is there a law that requires an employer to equally distribute overtime? Is there some place I can complain to?"[30]

Part Four—Health and Safety at Work

Alatorre was overcome by hydrogen sulfide gas

Jose Alatorre An illegal Mexican immigrant, Jose Alatorre, took a job for $8.75 an hour as a welder at a dairy farm in the California Central Valley. He was 22. On his first wedding anniversary (February 22, 2001) his wife asked him to stay home, but he said he had to go to work for the morning to repair a machine. The farm's 1,700 cattle produced 200,000 gallons of waste per day. That day the waste pump clogged. Alatorre went down a 30-foot shaft, was overcome by hydrogen sulfide gas, plunged headfirst into standing manure, and drowned. Another worker died trying to rescue him.

At the time of their deaths *The New York Times* reported that the two men's lungs were packed with cow manure, and they had eight pennies and one dime in their pockets. In telling Alatorre's story, the *Times* reported on his first encounter with his wife-to-be:

> It was not a promising pickup line. "I don't own a car, I'm not legally here, and I don't earn much money," he said, flashing a smile. "It's up to you." Angelica Acevedo Hernandez followed Jose Alatorre onto the dance floor.[31]

15 Die in Refinery Blast Jose Alatorre died doing what he took to be his occupational duty. At the giant BP oil refinery in Texas City, Texas in 2005, workers were doing their day's work by restarting a unit that had been down for repair when a gasoline overflow exploded injuring 170 and killing 15. BP attributed the disaster primarily to operator error and six employees were fired, but government investigators found problems "just about everywhere they looked," according to a *60 Minutes* investigation.[32] Carolyn Merritt, the chief of the government investigation, says that management authorized the restart knowing that three key pieces of equipment were not working properly:

> These things do not have to happen. They are preventable. They are predictable, and people do not have to die because they're earning a living.[33]

Lax federal oversight and cost cutting were among the key factors in the explosion, according to the government inquiry.[34] The Department of Labor announced stepped-up inspections in the refinery industry in response to a string of 36 incidents of hazardous chemical releases since 1992 resulting in 52 deaths and 250 injuries.[35] BP reportedly set aside $1.6 billion to settle lawsuits resulting from the explosion.[36]

Deaths, Illnesses, and Injuries Some workplaces are unacceptably risky, but America has achieved considerable progress in building safety on the job. Workplace fatalities that totaled 6,632 in 1995 fell to 5,734 in 2005 and 5,703 in 2006, and the rate of fatalities per 100,000 workers fell to 3.9 in 2006, the lowest since data were first collected in 1992.[37] Nonfatal injuries and illnesses have also declined from 4.6 per 100 workers in 2005 to 4.4 in 2006.[38] A striking contrast to that generally improving picture is the persistent increase in deaths among Latinos, reaching a total of 937 in 2006.[39] Of course, Latino numbers in the workforce are likewise steadily increasing, and Latinos often occupy the most dangerous working roles. As to the overall job safety improvement, we should remember that America's job profile has been moving from more dangerous jobs such as manufacturing and mining to service roles where safety is ordinarily a less pressing issue.

OSHA

A federal agency, the Occupational Safety and Health Administration (OSHA), is responsible for ensuring safe workplaces. The 1970 Occupational Safety and Health Act imposes a *general duty* on most employers to provide a workplace free of "recognized hazards causing or likely to cause death or serious physical harm to employees." Employers have an absolute duty to remove any serious and preventable workplace hazards that are generally recognized in the industry and are known to the employer or should be known to the employer. That general duty is then supplemented with numerous, detailed, and demanding *specific standards*. [For the OSHA home page, see **www.osha.gov**]

Standards

OSHA, through the secretary of labor, promulgates and enforces health and safety standards that identify and seek to correct specific workplace hazards and problems. These can range from exposure to cancer-causing agents (such as the chemical benzene) to the surprisingly commonplace problem of one worker restarting a machine while another is servicing it. Following eight years of pressure from the courts, Congress and labor unions, OSHA announced a rare, new standard, effective in 2008, requiring that employers pay for all OSHA-mandated personal protective equipment (safety-specific eyewear, skin creams, clothing, etc.).

More New Standards?

The eight-year battle over personal protective equipment (PPE) typifies the ongoing ideological and practical conflict over imposing additional safety rules in American workplaces. Some of the competing considerations are illustrated by recent disputes over ergonomics and violence.

Ergonomics Repetitive motion and over exertion injuries, such as carpal tunnel syndrome and back strains, account for about one-third of workplace injuries and a big part of the total workplace injury bill, which in 2003 amounted to about $1 billion per week.[40] Employers often try to address these problems with ergonomics, "the science of fitting the job to the worker"[41] (for example, changing the height of a workstation). After years of work, OSHA issued ergonomics standards in 2000, but Congress repealed those rules in 2001 after business complaints about the costs of implementation. Now OSHA employs a system of voluntary ergonomics guidelines, but critics consider them weak and vague. OSHA also can apply its general duty authority to the repetitive motion and over exertion situations. As it turns out, however, those injuries seem to be falling on their own. For example, the notorious carpal tunnel syndrome (often wrist or hand pain from repetitive stress, such as keyboard use) fell among professional and business service workers by one half between 2005 and 2006.[42] Experts now believe the carpal tunnel fears about keyboarding may have been exaggerated, although many blue-collar, assembly-line workers certainly are at risk. [For advice on measures to reduce repetitive stress problems for students, see **http://ergo.human.cornell.edu**]

Violence

> **"Going postal"**

"Going postal" has become, probably unfairly, a readily recognizable shorthand expression for violence in the workplace. In fact, however, homicides on the job have been declining steadily in recent years with the 2006 total at 516, down from 567 in 2005 and from a high of 1,080 in 1994.[43] While that trend is quite encouraging, violence remains a concern in the workplace, perhaps particularly for women for whom homicide has been the second leading cause of death on the job.[44]

Do we need firmer rules (OSHA standards) to address problems like workplace violence and ergonomics programs? Would those rules be effective? Or will the market and naturally evolving workplace conditions provide the most effective and efficient protection?

An interesting 2007 federal district court decision did affirm OSHA's dominant, unifying role in setting violence-prevention standards in the workplace.[45] A 2004/05 Oklahoma state statute affirmed individual gun possession rights by forbidding employers from banishing weapons from the workplace. The Oklahoma weapons law was challenged, and the federal court ruled that the Oklahoma law conflicted with and was preempted by (see Chapter 5) the Occupational Safety and Health Act. Thus federal safety standards nullified the Oklahoma state law, pending a possible appeal.

Variances

Employers may seek both permanent and temporary variances (exceptions) from OSHA standards. A permanent variance may be granted only if the workplace will be as safe as if the standard were enforced. A temporary variance permits additional time to put in place the necessary compliance measures. Employees have a right to a hearing to contest variances.

Fatal Accidents: The Bright Side?

Every day some new do-gooder is trying to save us from ourselves. We have so many laws and safety commissions to ensure our safety that it seems nearly impossible to have an accident. The problem is that we need accidents, and lots of them.

Danger is nature's way of eliminating stupid people. Without safety, stupid people die in accidents. Since the dead don't reproduce, our species becomes progressively more intelligent (or at least less stupid).

With safety, however well-intentioned it may be, we are devolving into half-witted mutants, because idiots, who by all rights should be dead, are spared from their rightful early graves and are free to breed even more imbeciles.

Let's do away with safety and improve our species. Take up smoking. Jaywalk. Play with blasting caps. Swim right after a big meal. Stick something small in your ear. Take your choice of dangerous activity and do it with gusto. Future generations will thank you.

Source: This letter to the editor by Lawrence A. Bullis, originally published in the *Arizona Republic,* appeared in issue number 49 of *View from the Ledge,* a 'zine published by Chuck Shepherd in St. Petersburg, Florida. Bullis lives in Phoenix.

OSHA Information Requirements

Right to Know

OSHA has adopted an employee *hazard communication standard* to protect employees from the dangers associated with chemicals and other toxins in the workplace. Chemical manufacturers and importers must develop *material safety data sheets* (MSDS) for all chemicals. Employers must then label all chemical containers so that employees will know about the chemical and its dangers, and employers must educate employees about chemical hazards and how to deal with them.

Records

Businesses must maintain records listing and summarizing injuries, illnesses, and deaths on the job. A summary of those records must be posted at the job. Notice of any OSHA citations of imminent dangers on the job must also be posted at the job site. OSHA recently reformed and simplified the record-keeping process. Some smaller companies, especially in nonhazardous activities, do not need to meet the record-keeping requirements.

Enforcement

OSHA's most publicized enforcement mechanism is the unannounced on-site inspection. Inspections arise at the initiative of the agency itself or at the request of employees or their representatives. The inspections must be conducted in a reasonable manner during working hours or other reasonable times, and ordinarily they must not be announced in advance. Employers can demand a warrant prior to inspection. With proper justification, warrants can easily be secured from a federal magistrate. Employer and employee representatives may accompany the inspector.

To enhance efficiency, OSHA practices a targeted, site-specific inspection plan designed to identify and monitor the workplaces most likely to have safety and health problems.

Citations

Citations may be issued if violations are discovered during the inspection process. Immediate, serious threats can be restrained with a court order. Following a citation, the employer may ask to meet with an area OSHA official to discuss the problem. Often a settlement emerges from these meetings. Failing a settlement, the employer can appeal to the independent OSHA Review Commission and thereafter to the federal court of appeals. Violations may lead to fines and/or imprisonment.

> OSHA can inspect each American workplace only once each century

> "Weak enforcement, minimal fines and dwindling inspections"

Firmer Enforcement? The business community criticizes OSHA for unfairly increasing the cost of production by imposing inflexible and overzealous expectations. Labor organizations and job safety advocates, on the other hand, see OSHA as a timid, faltering safety shield. The AFL–CIO estimates that OSHA can inspect each American workplace only once each century.

After years of lean funding, the Bush administration, at this writing, has proposed a significant increase in OSHA's budget and enforcement staff, perhaps signaling a new respect for the government's role in job safety. But OSHA practice in recent years has been discouraging to critics. A 2008 *Charlotte Observer* investigation found "weak enforcement, minimal fines and dwindling inspections" in poultry plants, noting, for example, that 2006 inspections of the 500 U.S. poultry plants totaled 94, about half the number of 1999.[46] The *New York Times* harshly criticized OSHA policies during the George W. Bush years:

> . . . Across Washington, political appointees—often former officials of the industries they now oversee—have eased regulations or weakened enforcement of rules. . . . Since George W. Bush became president, OSHA has issued the fewest significant standards in its history. . . . The agency has killed dozens of existing and proposed regulations and delayed adopting others. . . .

"The people at OSHA have no interest in running a regulatory agency," said Dr. David Michaels, an occupational health expert at George Washington University. . . . The concern about protecting workers has gone out the window.[47]

But perhaps the market remains the best vehicle for achieving job safety?

Workers' Compensation

> Korey Stringer, a 27-year-old Pro Bowl tackle, died of heatstroke complications

Korey Stringer, a 27-year-old Pro Bowl tackle, died of heatstroke complications on August 1, 2001, after going through a preseason Minnesota Vikings workout.[48] Normally, when an employee is injured or dies on the job, the employee or the estate may not sue for damages. Rather, recovery is limited to the fixed sum provided for by the workers' compensation statute, regardless of fault. Stringer's family, however, filed a wrongful death suit trying to hold the Vikings and various individuals responsible for gross negligence and other wrongs in responding to Stringer's heatstroke. The Vikings argued that the Stringer suit was barred by the state workers' compensation law. Minnesota is one of a number of states, however, that recognize an exception to workers' compensation exclusivity provisions in cases of gross negligence by the defendants.[49] The Stringers' case reached the Minnesota Supreme Court in 2005 where the 4–2 majority ruled on technical grounds against the family's gross negligence claim, thus limiting their remedy to workers' compensation, a sum much beneath Stringer's projected commercial worth.[50]

Early in the twentieth century, the states began enacting workers' compensation laws to provide an administrative remedy for those, like Stringer, who are injured or killed on the job. Previously, employers' superior financial resources and various technical legal defenses meant that employees often could not successfully sue to recover damages for their on-the-job injuries. Thus all states now provide some form of workers' compensation not requiring a lawsuit. Workers or their families simply apply for compensation based on illness, injury, or death. Typically, the system is governed by a state board or commission. Most decisions are routine and are accomplished by completing the necessary forms. Often a claims examiner will verify the nature and severity of the injury. In return for the ease and predictability of the system, however, workers and families are, by law, denied the right to sue, barring unusual circumstances such as gross negligence (as alleged in the *Stringer* case).

In most states, employers are compelled to participate in workers' compensation, depending on state law, either by purchasing insurance privately, by contributing to a state-managed fund, or by being self-insured (paying claims directly from their own funds). Firms with good safety records are rewarded with lower premium payments.

A Sticky Moment

A woman went to the bathroom at the Mall of the Bluffs in Council Bluffs, Iowa, where she noticed what she thought was a clear liquid on the toilet seat. She wiped it away, sat down, and then realized she was stuck to the toilet seat. Mall employees unsuccessfully used fingernail polish remover to try to free her from the seat. Firefighters were called. They began to unbolt the seat when the woman decided to try to stand up. She came loose from the seat, embarrassed and having sustained minor burns. Had she been a mall employee, would she have been entitled to workers' compensation? Explain.

Source: Meghan V. Malloy, "Pit Stop Becomes Sticky Situation," *The Des Moines Register,* August 4, 2006, p. 1A.

Benefits

Medical and rehabilitation expenses along with partial income replacement are provided according to state law. The amount of the income award is normally a percentage of the worker's salary either for a specified period or indefinitely, depending on the severity of the injury. Injury benefits normally amount to one-half to two-thirds of regular wages. Death benefits ordinarily are tied to the wages of the deceased.

Coverage

Certain employment classifications such as agriculture may be excluded from workers' compensation, but about 90 percent of the labor force is covered. Most on-the-job injuries are covered, but those that are self-inflicted (including starting a fight) and others such as those springing from alcohol or drug use may not be.

Legal Requirements

In general, injuries, illnesses, and deaths are compensable where the harm (1) *arose out of the employment,* and (2) *arose in the course of employment.* (explained next in *Ciha*). Proof of employer negligence is not required, and the traditional defenses such as contributory negligence are not available to the employer. Thus workers' compensation provides a form of no-fault protection in the workplace. Workers give up the right to sue, and employers participate in an insurance system that recognizes the inevitability of workplace harm.

Although workers' compensation recovery is the exclusive remedy for workplace injury, illness, or death, some jurisdictions allow litigation in cases of intentional torts and/or gross negligence, as noted earlier. [For the Workers' Compensation Research Institute, see **http://www.wcrinet.org**]

Litigation

Notwithstanding its no-fault character, workers' compensation has generated many lawsuits. For example, Manuel Guico had worked for two years in an Excel meat packing plant until he was fired after sustaining an injury on the job. Guico's knife slipped, cutting his thumb and a finger, and causing an 11 percent permanent partial disability. Guico had repeatedly been told to wear his steel-mesh gloves and mesh apron whenever he was using his knife, but he was not doing so when he was injured. Guico applied for and received workers' compensation benefits. Excel appealed to the courts but lost when the Nebraska Supreme Court ruled that Excel failed to show that Guico was willfully negligent.[51] The *Ciha* case that follows raises some key workers' compensation themes.

Chief Justice McGiverin

I. BACKGROUND FACTS

In May 1991, petitioner Bradley Ciha was employed by defendant Quaker Oats Company at its Cedar Rapids plant as an area maintenance supervisor. . . . By all accounts, Ciha was considered an excellent employee. Ciha's normal workweek at Quaker Oats was Monday through Friday. On a typical weekend including Saturday and Sunday, Ciha was not on duty and was not expected to be on call to drive to the plant for emergency maintenance purposes.

For the first 48 hours on Memorial Day weekend in 1991, Ciha was assigned as "204 supervisor" for Quaker Oats. In that capacity, he was required to be on call for mechanical emergencies anywhere in the plant.

While preparing dinner at his home on Sunday, May 26, Ciha was contacted at approximately 4:15 PM through a company electronic paging device. He was informed that several large cooling fans at the plant were malfunctioning. Ciha responded to the breakdown by electing to drive his motorcycle to the plant to remedy the problem himself. To reach the plant, Ciha drove a direct route (of approximately four and a half miles) on Johnson Avenue. After reaching the plant without incident, he personally remedied the problem by cooling the fans with an air hose. At approximately 5:45 PM, Ciha telephoned his wife and informed her that she could resume dinner preparations because he was about to return home.

Ciha drove a different route from the plant to home than he drove earlier from his home to the plant. The return-home route was on Ellis Road and was admittedly not the most direct route from the plant to Ciha's home. The Ellis Road route (approximately nine miles) was scenic and subject to less traffic and traffic signals than the direct route Ciha commonly drove from home to the plant. Apparently, the Ellis Road route took approximately five to seven minutes longer to drive than the direct, Johnson Avenue route.

On his return trip from the plant to home along Ellis Road, Ciha was involved in a serious motor vehicle accident in which he suffered a broken neck and was rendered a quadriplegic. At the time of the accident, Ciha was married and resided in a home in Cedar Rapids with his wife, Kim.

Following the accident, Ciha was admitted to St. Luke's Hospital in Cedar Rapids until June 12, 1991, when he requested transfer to a specialized care facility, Craig Hospital, located in Englewood, Colorado.

In addition to the health care Ciha received while at Craig, the hospital also provided Kim specialized training in order for her to be able to care for Ciha upon his return home.

Ciha was discharged from Craig Hospital on September 14, 1991, to his home in Cedar Rapids. Since his discharge, Kim has performed necessary, extensive home nursing services. Ciha requires assistance in dressing, changing urine bags, and transferring between his wheelchair and his bed. At night, he must be repositioned in bed one to four times in order to prevent him from developing pressure sores.

Ciha first returned to work at Quaker Oats in January 1992 in a new position as materials supervisor. In this position, he works at a computer (with the aid of an adaptive device and telephone headset) in the company's purchasing department. With the aid of a modified computer, Ciha analyzes inventory and makes purchases on behalf of Quaker Oats. Quaker Oats greatly aided in Ciha's return to work by adapting the workplace and position in order for Ciha to be able to perform the job.

In his position as materials supervisor, he receives the same base salary, not including raises, as that of an area maintenance supervisor. Ciha no longer has the same opportunity, however, to earn overtime as he had as an area maintenance supervisor.

In order to return to work, Ciha relied on the county's disabled persons transportation service to and from Quaker Oats. Based on the hours of the transportation service, however, Ciha was not able to return to work full-time.

Ciha was readmitted to Craig for one week in March 1992 for a comprehensive evaluation. At the time of his readmittance, Ciha did not own a van and did not drive. While at Craig, Ciha had his driving potential assessed. A driving specialist from the hospital concluded Ciha would need to purchase a specially modified van in order to be able to drive independently. At some time thereafter, Ciha purchased the recommended van.

Many of Ciha's medical expenses from the accident were paid for through a group health and accident insurance plan available to Ciha through his employer Quaker Oats. However, there were significant limitations in coverage under the group plan. For example, in addition to a lifetime cap on medical expenses, the group plan did not provide Ciha coverage for necessary home health care services, home modifications, or motor vehicle conversions.

II. WORKERS' COMPENSATION LITIGATION

In November 1991, Ciha filed a claim for permanent partial disability benefits with the Iowa industrial commissioner's office against his employer, Quaker Oats.

Ciha's claim proceeded to an arbitration hearing.

* * * * *

[At arbitration, the deputy industrial commissioner reached several conclusions favorable to Ciha. Quaker Oats then appealed to the industrial commissioner who agreed with the deputy. Quaker Oats next took the case to the district court, which affirmed. The Iowa Supreme Court then undertook this review.]

* * * * *

IV. GOING AND COMING RULE, THE "SPECIAL ERRAND" AND "REQUIRED VEHICLE" EXCEPTIONS, AND DEVIATION

In Iowa,

> [e]very employer, not specifically excepted by the provisions of [Iowa Code chapter 85], shall provide, secure, and pay compensation according to the provisions of this chapter for any and all personal injuries sustained by an employee arising out of and in the course of the employment. . . .

To obtain such compensation, an injured employee has the burden of proving by a preponderance of the evidence that his injuries arose out of and in the course of his employment. An injury arises "out of" the employment when there is a causal relationship between the employment and the injury. "In the course of" the employment concerns the time, place, and circumstances of the injury. Stated more specifically,

> [a]n injury occurs in the course of the employment when it is within the period of employment at a place where the employee reasonably may be in performing his duties, and while he is fulfilling those duties or engaged in doing something incidental thereto. An injury in the course of employment embraces all injuries received while employed in furthering the employer's business and injuries received on the employer's premises, provided that the employee's presence must ordinarily be required at the place of the injury, or, if not so required, employee's departure from the usual place of employment must not amount to an abandonment of employment or be an act wholly foreign to his usual work. An employee does not cease to be in the course of his employment merely because he is not actually engaged in doing some specifically prescribed task, if, in the course of his employment, he does some act which he deems necessary for the benefit or interest of his employer.

First and foremost, Quaker Oats contends Ciha did not sustain his injury in the course of his employment because the injury was sustained away from the employer's premises and while Ciha was on his way home from the plant. The employer relies on the well-established "going and coming" rule, which generally provides, "[A]bsent special circumstances, injuries occurring off the employer's premises while the employee is on the way to or from work are not compensable."

Under the going and coming rule, Ciha admittedly did not sustain an injury in the course of his employment: He was injured while driving his motorcycle home from the Quaker Oats plant.

There are, however, several exceptions to the going and coming rule. . . .

The first exception to the going and coming rule relied on by the commissioner is the "special errand" exception.

Under the exception, if an employee is on a special errand or mission for his or her employer at the time of the injury, the injury is held to have arisen in the course of employment.

* * * * *

After considering all arguments raised by the parties, we believe substantial evidence supports the commissioner's conclusion that Ciha was on a special errand at the time of his injury.

[I]n answer to the question "[w]hose business was [the employee] pursuing at the time of the injury?" the answer must be Quaker Oats' business. The fact that Ciha was contacted on Sunday while he was on 204 duty was truly "special." It was unusual, sudden, and unexpected.

* * * * *

Deviation

Notwithstanding our conclusion that the special errand exception to the going and coming rule applies in the present case, Quaker Oats contends Ciha had "deviated" from his trip home from the plant to such an extent that he abandoned his employment at the time of the accident. The commissioner and district court rejected this argument, and we do the same.

* * * * *

In concluding Ciha did not deviate from his special errand, the commissioner stated,

> [Ciha] testified that he often took [the Ellis Road] route home because it was more scenic, it had less traffic, it had fewer stoplights, and the actual difference in miles between this route and the more direct route was minimal. [Ciha's] call to his wife from the plant to start the grill for their meal shows that his purpose was to return home, and that he had no other destination other than to return to his residence. The record does not show a deviation from the course of the employment.

V. CLAIMED EXPENSES UNDER IOWA CODE SECTION 85.27

Of the expenses awarded by the commissioner under Iowa Code section 85.27, Quaker Oats only challenges the award of costs for home modifications, van conversion, and home nursing services. The commissioner and district court found the home modification and van conversion expenses to be reasonable "appliances" under section 85.27. In addition, the commissioner found the claimed expenses for home nursing services and the claimed value of those services to be reasonable.

Iowa Code section 85.27 provides in pertinent part,

> The employer, for all injuries compensable under this chapter or chapter 85A, shall furnish reasonable surgical, medical, dental, osteopathic, chiropractic, podiatric, physical rehabilitation, nursing, ambulance, and hospital services and supplies therefor and shall allow reasonably necessary transportation expenses incurred for such services. The employer shall also furnish reasonable and necessary crutches, artificial members, and appliances. . . .

* * * * *

A. Home Modifications and Van Conversion

In order for Ciha to have been able to access his house in a wheelchair upon his return from Craig Hospital, various home modifications were required. The home modifications included widened doorways, a ramp into the home, a special shower, an elevator, and other items necessitated by Ciha's wheelchair-bound status. He also incurred van conversion expenses in order to be able to return to work full-time.

In his workers' compensation claim, Ciha sought and was awarded $20,788 in home modification expenses and $24,509 in van conversion expenses under Iowa Code section 85.27. The deputy concluded the home modification expenses incurred by Ciha "relate to items designed to substitute for function lost in [his] work injury." Relying on past agency decisions, the commissioner also held Quaker Oats responsible for the van conversion expenses. The commissioner further concluded,

> [Ciha's] need for a ramp to enter his home, and for a special shower designed to accommodate a wheelchair, are held to be necessary and reasonable medical expenses. All of the items are related to accommodating [Ciha's] wheelchair. An appliance has been held to be a device that serves to replace a physical function lost by the injury. Just as a wheelchair seeks to replace the lost functions of standing and walking, a wheelchair ramp, a wheelchair shower, etc. also seek to replace physical functions claimant possessed before the work injury but has now lost.

Quaker Oats contends on appeal that the claimed home modification and van conversion costs are not compensable as "appliances."

* * * * *

We begin with the unusually strong medical evidence of necessity and of the record that [the claimant's] family status and past lifestyle reveal no other use for the van. That evidence refutes any contention that the van is a frill or luxury and reveals what can be described as an appliance, not greatly different from crutches or a wheelchair. The point is that a van is necessary in order to make [the claimant's] wheelchair fully useful.

* * * * *

B. Home Nursing Services

In addition to the claimed home modification and van conversion expenses, Ciha also sought $58,447 in home nursing services performed by his wife after his return home from the hospital in Colorado. At the arbitration hearing, Quaker Oats unsuccessfully contended the claimed home nursing services were not reasonable expenses under section 85.27, and also that the claimed amount of the services set forth in an affidavit prepared by Kim Ciha was unreasonable.

On appeal, Quaker Oats does not dispute that it had a duty under Iowa Code section 85.27 to provide reasonable nursing services to Ciha if his injury was compensable (which we have concluded it is). In addition, Quaker Oats agrees the services performed by Kim were "nursing" services as contemplated by section 85.27. Quaker Oats contends, however, that $58,447 in home nursing expenses claimed by Ciha is unreasonable. The commissioner and district court disagreed.

In ordering Quaker Oats to pay Ciha's home nursing services, the commissioner stated the following:

> In the instant case, [Ciha's] spouse, although not a nurse or LPN, did have to receive special training to perform the services. The services themselves are clearly medical nursing services and not general care services such as dressing, bathing, feeding, etc.

We believe the affidavit and Kim's testimony establish the reasonableness of the claimed home nursing care expenses. . . .

Industrial Disability

As a final issue, Quaker Oats contends the commissioner erred in ruling that Ciha had sustained an 80 percent permanent partial industrial disability. Quaker Oats argues Ciha's disability is only 50 to 60 percent because it, Ciha's employer, went to great lengths to accommodate claimant and also that claimant has suffered no loss of earnings.

As we have stated on many occasions, "[i]ndustrial disability measures an injured worker's lost earning capacity." Factors that should be considered include the employee's functional disability, age, education, qualifications, experience, and the ability of the employee to engage in employment for which the employee is fitted.

As a result of the accident and resulting quadriplegia, Ciha is wheelchair-bound, cannot control his bowel functions, and his lifestyle has been severely limited from that prior to the injury. He requires extensive, daily care and attention by his wife, relatives, and coworkers as he no longer has the ability to perform many basic daily living functions. Also, as a 38-year-old man, it cannot be reasonably disputed that Ciha's employability outside of the Quaker Oats workforce has been significantly and negatively affected by his injury. Although we applaud the efforts of Quaker Oats in modifying the workplace to accommodate Ciha's disability, such efforts are not determinative of Ciha's industrial disability rating. *See Thilges v. Snap–On Tools Corp.,* 528 N.W.2d 614, 617 (Iowa 1995) ("[W]e are satisfied that the commissioner was correct in viewing loss of earning capacity in terms of the injured worker's present ability to earn in the competitive job market without regard to the accommodation furnished by one's present employer.").

* * * * *

We conclude there is substantial evidence to support the commissioner's decision on this issue.

Affirmed.

Questions

1. The Iowa Supreme Court in *Quaker Oats* (and most courts in workers' compensation cases) required a two-part showing that the injury must "arise out of" and "in the course of" employment.

   a. Explain those two standards.

   b. Must an employee be engaged in a prescribed task in order to be "in the course of employment?" Explain.

   c. Why did the court conclude that Ciha was on a "special errand?"

2. Why did the court conclude that Ciha had suffered an 80 percent permanent partial industrial disability?

3. Fernandez, an exotic dancer, left her job drunk and was seriously injured in a crash while riding as a passenger in a car driven by another dancer. The crash came within one hour of leaving work. Her intoxication led to her decision to ride with her intoxicated coworker. Fernandez sought workers' compensation. She claimed that her employer, Bottoms Up Lounge in Council Bluffs, Iowa, required her to socialize with male customers when not dancing and to generate at least two drinks per hour from customers. Dancers were not required to drink, but most dancers consumed six to eight drinks per night or more. Did Fernandez's injury arise out of and in the course of employment so that she can recover workers' compensation? Explain. See *2800 Corp. v. Fernandez,* 528 N.W.2d 124 (Ia. S.Ct. 1995).

4. Joseph Smyth, a college mathematics instructor, was killed while driving his personal auto home from work. At the time, Smyth had student papers with him, which he intended to grade that evening. He often worked at home. Many faculty members took work home in the evenings. However, the college did not require that practice. Indeed, the college neither encouraged nor discouraged working at home.

   The widely adopted "going and coming rule" provides that employees injured while commuting to and from work, in general, are not covered by workers' compensation.

   a. Should Smyth (and other teachers) be exempted from the going and coming rule, thus permitting recovery by Smyth's family? Explain. See *Santa Rosa Junior College v. Workers' Compensation Appeals Board and Joann Smyth,* 708 P.2d 673 (Cal. S.Ct. 1985).

   b. Would you reach a different conclusion had a student been accompanying Smyth? Explain.

5. Casimer Gacioch worked at a Stroh Brewery. The company provided free beer at work. When he began work in 1947 he drank only three to four beers on the weekend. He was fired in 1974, by which time he was drinking 12 bottles of beer daily. After Gacioch's death, his wife sought workers' compensation benefits. The evidence indicated that Gacioch had a predisposition to alcoholism but was not an alcoholic at the time he was hired. How would you rule on the widow's workers' compensation claim? Explain. See *Gacioch v. Stroh Brewery,* 466 N.W. 2d 303 (Mich Ct. of Appeals, 1991).

Part Five—Employee Privacy

Privacy on the Job? Forty percent of Americans between 26 and 40 have tattoos, but that number drops to 10 percent for those over 40; often the ones making business decisions.[52] Will you have to give up that tongue stud or that butterfly tattoo on your ankle when you move on to the "real world" of professional employment? PricewaterhouseCoopers specifies only that employees must wear "professional" attire. Boeing Co. employees can display tattoos so long as they are not "offensive," but Von's wants tattoos completely covered.[53] In general, the law gives employers wide latitude to establish dress and grooming codes in accord with their business goals.

> Will you have to give up that tongue stud?

Beyond appearance concerns, employers are engaging in an array of testing and monitoring procedures both before and after hiring. Drug testing, integrity tests, personality tests, spying, television and computer monitoring of work performance, and so forth are routine personnel practices in many firms. Employers have an interest in these strategies not only to hire better employees and improve productivity but to protect coworkers, reduce insurance claims, and shield consumers from poor products and service. On the other hand, job applicants and employees resist parking their personal being at the office door.

Privacy Off the Job? Work for Indiana-based hospital chain, Clarian Health Partners, and you might pay a penalty of up to $30 every two weeks unless you meet specified health guidelines including weight control.[54] Or if IBM is your employer, you could earn an extra $300 annually by participating in various health programs.[55] If you work for Weyko, a Michigan employee benefits company, and you smoke on or off the job, you might be fired, or you might have to pay an $80 monthly fee until your spouse is able to pass a nicotine test.[56] The law offers only limited shelter for employees with off-the-job privacy concerns. About half the states provide some form of "smoking discrimination" protection, and the federal Health Insurance Portability and Accountability Act (HIPAA) generally forbids discrimination based on health status or conditions. Of course, for employers, money is the issue. Obese patients, according to an Emory University study, cost 37 percent more than those of normal weights.[57] Critics, such as Randall Wilson, legal director of the Iowa Civil Liberties Union, worry that employers could extend their demands to, for example, rock climbing or other dimensions of individual choice and build ever more authority over employee lives. As Wilson explained:

> The concern is that with the rise of corporate power, we're beginning to feel at the mercy of a government operating outside a government.[58]

> Robert Barbee was fired for dating Melanie Tomita

And what about office romance? Robert Barbee, former national sales manager for Household Automotive Finance, sued HAF after he was fired for dating Melanie Tomita, an HAF salesperson. They worked in different locations, and he did not directly supervise her. He claimed that the dismissal violated his right to privacy, but a California appeals court ruled for HAF in part on the grounds that the company needed to prevent conflicts of interest, sexual harassment claims, and the appearance of favoritism.[59] While relatively few office romance cases have reached the courts, the law in most states clearly provides substantial employer latitude in dealing with these situations.

Search and Seizure in the Office   Do employees have privacy rights in their office computers? The *Ziegler* case that follows examines that important question. (See Chapter 5 for a discussion of privacy rights under the Fourth Amendment prohibition against unreasonable searches and seizures.)

LEGAL BRIEFCASE

United States of America v. Ziegler   474 F.3d 1184 (9th Cir. 2007)

FACTS

Frontline processes online electronic payments in Bozeman, Montana. The FBI received a tip from Frontline's Internet service provider that a Frontline employee, Jeff Ziegler, accessed child pornography from his office computer. Additional evidence confirmed that tip. Frontline employees understood FBI agent James Kennedy to have instructed them to copy Ziegler's hard drive. (Kennedy disputed that understanding.) Those employees got a key to Ziegler's office from Ronald Reavis, Frontline's chief financial officer, entered the office and made two copies of the hard drive. Thereafter, Frontline's corporate counsel told the FBI that the company would voluntarily turn over Ziegler's computer, thus implicitly suggesting, as Kennedy said, that a search warrant was unnecessary. The FBI searched the hard drive and discovered many child pornography images. Ziegler was charged with various child pornography crimes. Ziegler filed a motion to suppress the evidence acquired in the computer search claiming that his Fourth Amendment right to be free of unreasonable searches and seizures had been violated. The district court denied Ziegler's motion, and he was sentenced to two years of probation and a fine of $1,000. Ziegler appealed.

Circuit Judge O'Scannlain

II (I OMITTED.)

A

Ziegler argues that "[t]he district court erred in its finding that Ziegler did not have a legitimate expectation of privacy in his office and computer." He likens the workplace computer to the desk drawer or file cabinet given Fourth Amendment protection in cases such as *O'Connor v. Ortega*, 480 U.S.709 (1987).

* * * * *

[A] criminal defendant may invoke the protections of the Fourth Amendment only if he can show that he had a *legitimate* expectation of privacy in the place searched or the item seized.

* * * * *

The threshold question then is whether Ziegler had a legitimate expectation of privacy in the area searched or the object seized. If he had no such expectation, we need not consider whether the search was reasonable.

1
The government does not contest Ziegler's claim that he had a subjective expectation of privacy in his office and the computer. The use of a password on his computer and the lock on his private office door are sufficient evidence of such expectation.

* * * * *

[I]n the private employer context, employees retain at least some expectation of privacy in their offices.

Ziegler's expectation of privacy in his office was reasonable on the facts of this case. His office was not shared by coworkers, and kept locked. And while there was a master key, the existence of such will not necessarily defeat a reasonable expectation of privacy in an office given over for personal use.

Because Ziegler had a reasonable expectation of privacy in his office, any search of that space and the items located therein must comply with the Fourth Amendment.

III

The next step is to inquire whether there was a search or seizure by the government. While the two Frontline employees may not have scoured the desk drawers and cabinets for evidence, they undoubtedly "searched" Ziegler's office when they entered to make a copy of the hard drive of his computer.

* * * * *

IV

A

The remaining question is whether the search of Ziegler's office and the copying of his hard drive were "unreasonable" within the meaning of the Fourth Amendment. [T]he government does not deny that the search and seizure were without a warrant, and "it is settled for purposes of the Amendment that 'except in certain carefully defined classes of cases, a search of private property without proper consent is 'unreasonable' unless it has been authorized by a valid search warrant.'" . . .

One well-settled exception is where valid consent is obtained by the government. . . .

B

We first consider whether Frontline exercised common authority over the office and the workplace computer such that it could validly consent to a search. . . . [E]ven where a private employee retains an expectation that his private office will not be the subject of an unreasonable government search, such interest may be subject to the possibility of an employer's consent to a search of the premises which it owns.

We are also convinced that Frontline could give valid consent to a search of the contents of the hard drive of Ziegler's workplace computer because the computer is the type of workplace property that remains within the control of the employer "even if the employee has placed personal items in [it]."

* * * * *

Although use of each Frontline computer was subject to an individual log-in, Schneider and other IT-department employees "had complete administrative access to anybody's machine." The company had also installed a firewall, which, according to Schneider, is "a program that monitors Internet traffic . . . from within the organization to make sure nobody is visiting any sites that might be unprofessional." Monitoring was routine, and the IT department reviewed the log created

by the firewall "[o]n a regular basis," sometimes daily if Internet traffic was high enough to warrant it. Finally, upon their hiring, Frontline employees were apprised of the company's monitoring efforts through training and an employment manual, and they were told that the computers were company-owned and not to be used for activities of a personal nature.

In this context, Ziegler could not reasonably have expected that the computer was his personal property, free from any type of control by his employer. The contents of his hard drive were work-related items that contained business information and which were provided to, or created by, the employee in the context of the business relationship. Ziegler's downloading of personal items to the computer did not destroy the employer's common authority. Thus, Frontline, as the employer, could consent to a search of the office and the computer that it provided to Ziegler for his work.

C

The remaining question is, given Frontline's ability to consent to a search, did it consent to a search of the office and the computer[?]. . .

[The] testimony makes clear that Ziegler's superiors at Frontline, in particular Reavis, an officer of the company, gave consent to a search of the property that the company owned and which was not of a personal nature.

Although Ziegler retained a legitimate expectation of privacy in his workplace office, Frontline retained the ability to consent to a search of Ziegler's office and his business computer. And because valid third party consent to search the office and computer located therein was given by his employer, the district court's order denying suppression of the evidence of child pornography existing on Ziegler's computer.

Affirmed.

Questions
1. *a.* Why did Ziegler have a reasonable expectation of privacy in his office computer?
   b. Why was a search warrant not required in this situation?
   c. Why was Ziegler's employer, Frontline, able to lawfully consent to the search of Ziegler's office computer?
2. Young was the pastor of Ft. Caroline United Methodist Church in Florida. Young was provided with a private office and a computer in that office. The computer was not networked to any other computers. Young and the church administrator had keys to the office. No one was permitted in the office without Young's permission, and the church administrator was not permitted to log on to the computer unless Young was present.

The church administrator received notice from the church's Internet service provider that spam was linked to the church's Internet address. The administrator ran a "spybot" program on the church computers and found questionable Web addresses. The church's district supervisor and bishop were contacted and permission was given to involve police officials. Officers came to the church, the administrator unlocked Young's office and signed "consent to search" forms for the office and the computer. Officers searched the office and computer and found proscribed images and Web sites.

Young subsequently filed a trial court motion to suppress the evidence gained from the office and computer search. The trial judge granted that motion ruling that the search violated Young's Fourth Amendment right to be free of unreasonable searches and seizures. The state appealed. Rule on that appeal. *See State v. Young,* 974 So.2d 601 (Fla. App. 1 Dist. 2008).

Drug Testing

Mary Wells decided that she had to institute an employee drug testing program for her Chagrin Falls, Ohio landscaping company. One job applicant at Wells' company told the interviewer that he would have no problem with the drug test. Then according to Wheeler: "While filling out his paperwork, the interviewer asked the applicant for a driver's license. The applicant reached into his pocket, and by accident pulled out a small bag of cocaine."[60] That episode certainly confirmed Wheeler's judgment that workplace drug tests were necessary for her company, and the data support Wheeler's fears. The federal government estimates that companies lose $82 billion in productivity each year because of substance abuse.[61] More than three quarters of America's 14.8 million drug users are employed, and they are nearly four times as likely to be involved in a workplace accident.[62] One employee high on marijuana dropped his forklift five feet off a loading dock and employees at another job built a meth lab in the back of a truck.[63]

In an effort to address those workplace drug problems, over 60 percent of companies reported drug testing programs in 2004, down from 81 percent in 1996.[64] Perhaps because of testing, drug use by applicants and employees has fallen steadily from 13.6 percent positive results in 1988 to a low of 3.8 percent in 2006.[65] Companies without drug testing programs reported a nearly 50 percent higher incidence of illicit drug use than those companies with testing programs.[66] Some companies have backed away from drug testing because of the expense and the sense that the risk does not justify that expenditure while others feel they must conduct drug testing to protect themselves against liability claims and to comply with the federal Drug-Free Workplace Act. [For more details on drug testing results, see **www.questdiagnostic.com/employersolutions/drug_and _alcohol_es.html**]

Drug-Free Workplace

The Drug-Free Workplace Act of 1988 applies to employers who have contracts of $100,000 or more with the federal government or who receive aid from the government. Those employers are required to develop an antidrug policy for employees. They must provide drug-free awareness programs for employees, and they must acquaint employees with available assistance for those with drug problems, while also warning them of the penalties that accompany violation of the policy. The act requires employees to adhere to the company policy and to inform the company within five days if they are convicted of or plead no contest to a drug-related offense in the workplace. [For more drug testing information, see **http://www.courttv.com/legalcafe/work/drug_testing**]

Drug Testing in Law and Practice

Drug testing is regulated primarily by state law so generalizations are difficult. Broadly, we can say, however, that private sector drug testing, properly conducted, ordinarily is lawful in the following five situations:

1. *Pre-employment testing.* State and local law may impose some restrictions.
2. *In association with periodic physical examinations.* Advance notice is often required.
3. *For cause.* An employer has probable cause or reasonable suspicion.
4. *Postaccident testing* where drug use is suspected.
5. *Follow-up testing* for those returning from drug (or alcohol) rehabilitation.

Random testing, on the other hand, sometimes produces significant legal problems. A number of states forbid random drug testing or limit it to safety-sensitive situations. The Supreme Court has upheld such testing for public-sector employees where public safety is involved and for those having access to particularly sensitive information.[67] The legality of drug testing often reduces to a balancing test where the employee's right to privacy is balanced against the employer's business needs. Where safety and security are involved and when notice is provided, the courts are more supportive of testing. Particularly intrusive or careless testing often tilts that balance toward employees. Beyond the balancing test, a number of other legal considerations influence employer drug testing practices, particularly in public sector jobs:

1. **Federal constitution:** As explained in Chapter 5, the Fourth Amendment to the United States Constitution forbids unreasonable searches and seizures. Thus government officials ordinarily cannot conduct a search without individualized suspicion—that is, without probable cause. Certain exceptions, however, have been recognized in cases involving safety, national security, athletic participation, and other special needs. Remember that the Constitution protects us from the government, not from private-sector employers (with limited exceptions).
2. **State constitutions:** Many state constitutions offer privacy protection, but court decisions, to date, have generally not extended those protections to private-sector employers. On the other hand, certain states, such as California and Massachusetts, explicitly offer constitutional protection to private-sector employees.
3. **Federal statutes:** Drug testing could violate Title VII of the Civil Rights Act of 1964 or the Americans with Disabilities Act (see Chapter 13) if the testing fails to treat all individuals equally. The ADA protects *recovering* drug addicts and those erroneously believed to be drug users.
4. **State and local statutes:** Historically, most state and local drug testing legislation placed limits on that testing; but in recent years, fears about drug use in the workplace and often intense business community lobbying have, in some cases, relaxed those testing restraints.

5. **Common law claims:** Some of the more prominent judge-made (common law) claims that might provide a challenge to drug testing include invasion of privacy, defamation (dissemination of erroneous information about an employee), negligence (in testing or in selecting a test provider), intentional infliction of emotional distress, and wrongful discharge (discussed later in this chapter).

Monitoring

The New York Post recently argued that America's workplaces are now in the "era of the overwatched worker, or Big Boss meets Big Brother":

> When you're sitting behind the walls of a cubicle or making deliveries in a company car, you might be working in solitude, but chances are you're not alone.[68]

Workplace privacy expert, Lewis Maltby, responded to a *Post* question about companies monitoring their workers with GPS-equipped cellphones:

> All cellphones are now GPS-equipped, and so many employers are giving out company phones . . . What's probably going to happen is, picture a driver for FedEx driving through Manhattan (New York City) in the middle of August. He pulls over for five minutes to get an iced tea, and before he gets his foot on the asphalt, he hears his boss's voice saying, "Get your ass back in that truck."[69]

GPS tracking remains relatively uncommon, however. A 2007 survey of 300 companies, from small to large, found only 8 percent of them tracking company vehicles with GPS technology and 3 percent using GPS to monitor cellphones.[70] Other forms of electronic monitoring are increasingly routine. Two-thirds of the survey respondents monitor employee Internet connections, while 43 percent monitor e-mail.[71] Twenty-eight percent of the companies reported firing workers for e-mail misuse and 30 percent for Internet misuse.[72]

Employees are, of course, concerned about privacy, while employers' worries include reduced productivity and company liability for criminal or tortious conduct (such as sexual harassment or defamation).

The Law

In general, employers can lawfully monitor workers' attendance, performance, e-mail, use of the Internet, and so on; but uncertainty remains. Certainly the prudent course of action is to expect employees to sign an agreement such as the following language from the Principal Financial Group employee handbook:

> The corporation's electronic mail system is business property and is to be used for business purposes. The corporation reserves the right to monitor all electronic mail messages.[73]

The primary federal legislation, the 1986 Electronic Communications Privacy Act, prohibits private individuals and organizations from intercepting wire, oral, or electronic communications. The act provides for two exceptions, however: (1) prior consent by one of the parties to the communication, and (2) employer monitoring in the "ordinary course of business" by telephone or other device furnished by a provider of wire or electronic communication service. Thus workplace monitoring of phone calls (except for purely private conversations), workplace computers, voice mail, e-mail, and Internet use are all likely to be considered lawful at this point if approached in a reasonable manner.

"Kill the Backstabbing Bastards"

Smyth was fired by his employer Pillsbury for transmitting what it deemed to be inappropriate and unprofessional comments over the company e-mail system. Pillsbury claimed the messages addressed company practices and included, among other things, a threat to "kill the backstabbing bastards." Pillsbury had repeatedly assured its employees that all e-mail communications would be confidential and would not be intercepted or used against employees. Smyth sued Pillsbury claiming that his termination violated his right to privacy.

Question
Was Smyth's right to privacy violated ? Explain.

Source: Smyth v. Pillsbury Co., 914 F. Supp. 97 (E.D. Pa. 1996). [For more information on e-mail and privacy, see **http://www. hrlawindex.com/email/email.html**].

Part Six—Employee Benefits and Income Maintenance

Have we reached that uncomfortable and perhaps socially destabilizing moment when the generous benefits (health insurance, life insurance, pensions) we have come to expect from our jobs are beginning a permanent decline? For decades employers used benefits to attract and retain the best employees, but the economic downturn in recent years forced employers to shift benefit burdens to employees by raising insurance deductibles and copayments, for example. Indeed, the portion of firms providing health insurance fell to 60 percent in 2007, from 66 percent in 1999.[74] Fifteen percent of the population, 47 million Americans, including nine million children, were without health insurance in 2007.[75] The average annual health insurance premium in 2007 for family coverage was $12,106, with workers contributing $3,281.[76] While wages rose 19 percent from 2001 to 2007, family coverage premium costs rose 78 percent.[77] These spiraling health care costs threaten family welfare, but they also threaten corporate financial competitiveness. General Motors, for example, says that health care costs add $1,500 to the price of each car it makes, and the company helps support two-and-one-half retirees and dependents for every active employee.[78]

One of the consequences of this health care crisis is that millions of Americans are caught in what is being labeled "job lock"; shackled to a job only for the purpose of retaining health insurance when they would like to move on; the preferred result in an efficient, fluid economy.[79] A federal law, COBRA (Consolidated Budget Reconciliation Act), is designed to help with this problem by requiring employers with 20 or more employees to permit departing employees to retain group health coverage at their own expense for up to 18 months as long as they are not terminated for gross misconduct. Unfortunately, COBRA policies for a family of four start at $700 a month; a sum affordable for only about seven percent of those who lose their jobs.[80]

Even as benefits decline, American employees try harder. We often hear that Americans live to work while Europeans work to live. The numbers support that assessment, as *The Wall Street Journal* explained:

> By almost every measure, Europeans do work less and relax more than Americans. According to data from the Organization for Economic Co-operation and Development, Americans work 25% more hours each year than the Norwegians or the Dutch. The average retirement age for European men is 60.5, and its even lower for European women. Our vacations are pathetically short by comparison: The average U.S. worker takes 16 days of vacation each year, less than half that typically taken by Germans (35 days), the French (37 days) or the Italians (42 days).[81]

The New York Times reports that even when Americans do go on vacation, they maintain an unbreakable electronic connection to work:

> "I never go on vacation," said Ellen Kapit, a real estate agent in Manhattan. "And when I do, I have my computer, my Palm, my e-mail and my phone with me at all times." Ms. Kapit's habits are typical of today's employees, who check for e-mail messages from work in between parasailing or floating in the hotel pool. . . .[82]

Family Leave

The 1993 Family and Medical Leave Act (FMLA) requires up to 12 weeks of *unpaid* leave in any 12-month period for family needs such as the birth or adoption of a child, caring for a child or parent, or for the employee's own serious illness. An employee may also be entitled to leave to help meet some needs, including health care, of family members serving in the U.S. military. Employees taking leave are entitled to reinstatement to the same or equivalent job. The law applies to all companies employing 50 or more workers and covers about 50 percent of the workforce. The business community has opposed the FMLA from the beginning, and experience with the law has not decreased that opposition, as *The Wall Street Journal* reported:

> Companies say more workers are using it to take time off for vague and chronic maladies and doing so intermittently, rather than in blocks of time, which makes scheduling and staffing difficult. Many of them have begun to clamp down on employees, hiring outsiders to screen applications for leave and at times to videotape workers to make sure they aren't moonlighting or vacationing.[83]

Employees, on the other hand, say managers often do not comply with the letter and the spirit of the FMLA, as *The Wall Street Journal* explained:

> Workers, for their part, say companies are making it more difficult to qualify for leave and requiring second or third opinions from healthcare providers. Some are fired or punished with worse assignments when they return to their jobs, they charge.[84]

In any case, as many as 13 million employees took FMLA leave in 2005,[85] but males have taken leave no more frequently than they did before the FMLA was enacted, and females have done so only slightly more frequently.[86] Lost wages often make FMLA leave unattractive, but California, New Jersey, and Washington have begun to address that problem by becoming the first states to require private employers to provide *paid* time off. California's program, for example, is financed by employee payroll deductions and allows up to six weeks of leave at 55 percent of wages up to $840 per week. [For more on the FMLA, see **http://www.dol.gov/esa/whd/fmla**]

Work Abroad?

A 2004 study found that workers in most nations around the world have greater legal rights to time off for family and medical matters than do American workers. Likewise, most of the 168 nations in the study mandate *paid* leave for pregnancy and illness.

Source: Associated Press, "Harvard Study: U.S. Policies on Time Off Rank at Bottom," *Waterloo/Cedar Falls Courier,* June 17, 2004, p. C10.

Unemployment Compensation

The tragedy of the Depression, when up to 25 percent of the workforce was unemployed, led in 1935 to the passage of the Social Security Act, one portion of which provided for an unemployment insurance program. Today all 50 states and the federal government are engaged in a cooperative system that helps protect the temporarily jobless. The system is financed through a payroll tax paid by employers.

The actual state tax rate for each employer varies, depending on the employer's *experience* ratings—the number of layoffs in its workforce. Thus employers have an incentive to retain employees.

Rules vary by state, but in general, employees qualify for unemployment benefits by reaching a specified total of annual wages. Those losing their jobs must apply to a state agency for unemployment compensation, which varies by state. Benefits may be collected up to a specified maximum period, usually 26 weeks. During that time, those collecting compensation must be ready to work and must make an effort to find suitable work. Workers who quit or who are fired for *misconduct* are ineligible for unemployment compensation. The episodes that follow illustrate the foolish and often funny cases where compensation has been denied:

- The Swiss Valley Farms dairy worker who led her coworkers in an after-hours swim in the cheese vat (filled with water at the time).[87]
- The bored production worker who removed her underwear, put the garment on the production line, and asked a supervisor if he "wanted to sniff them."[88]
- The 25-year-old Sheraton hotel worker who used her employer's computer to write a 300-page manuscript describing her successful efforts to avoid doing any work: "Once lunch is over, I will come right back to writing to piddle away the rest of the afternoon. . . . It's noon already and I don't feel like I have accomplished a damn thing. Accomplishment is overrated, anyway. . . . I am only here for the money and, lately, for the printer access."[89]

WARN

The Worker Adjustment and Retraining Notification Act (WARN) requires firms with 100 or more employees to provide 60 days notice if they lay off one-third or more of their workers at any site employing at least 150 workers, drop 500 employees at any site, or close a plant employing at least 50 workers. A General Accounting Office study concluded, however, that the law had been ineffectual, with half of plant closings not covered by the law.

Pensions

Employees of some of America's biggest, most prestigious companies have seen their pension benefits shrink or disappear in recent years:

> Sean Schuback, a 15-year veteran of Verizon, arrived at work one morning last December to unsettling news: A company e-mail sent the night before announced that the telecommunications giant was freezing its pension plan. In an instant, Schuback, 33, who joined the company as a phone operator right out of high school, saw the $469,286 payout he was told he could receive by working another 15 years sliced to $245, 494, where it would stay no matter how many more years he put in. What happened to Schuback's pension is part of a long-running trend, as otherwise healthy companies—not only Verizon Communications Inc., but also International Business Machines Corp. and . . . DuPont Co.—freeze, terminate, or alter the terms of their employees' retirement packages. Most of these companies increased other retirement offerings, which don't include fixed payouts.[90]

Many companies have reduced retirement benefits, in most cases entirely legally

Under intense financial pressure from a tough, global market, many companies have reduced retirement benefits, in most cases entirely legally. The result is that only about 19 percent of active private-sector workers now enjoy the security of traditional, guaranteed payout pension plans, as opposed to 39 percent three decades ago.[91] Many workers have been switched to less secure plans, often of the 401(k) variety, and over 40 percent of workers, age 21 and older, have no workplace pension plan whatsoever.[92]

Broadly, pensions take two forms: defined benefit plans and defined contribution plans. *Defined benefit* pensions are of the traditional form providing specified monthly payments upon retirement. Although Schuback and many others have lost those pensions in recent years, some 40 million Americans still are protected by defined benefit plans.[93] *Defined contribution* plans, such as the popular 401(k), specify in advance the "match" the employer will provide to go with the employee's own contributions and allow the employee a menu of investment options for that retirement money; but no promises are made about the amount that will be paid upon retirement. Defined contribution plans are now much more common than defined benefit plans. Defined contribution plans can be attractive to employees because the money vests (the point at which the employee has nonforfeitable right to the funds) quickly and follows the employee who changes jobs. From the employer's point of view, the defined contribution plans are less expensive to manage, and they shift the risk from employer to employee. [See **www.401khelpcenter. com** and **www.ebri.org** for large databases on 401(k) and other retirement topics.]

Pension Law   The federal Employee Retirement Income Security Act (ERISA) regulates pension funds to help ensure their long-term financial security by reducing fraud and mismanagement. ERISA requires that fund managers keep detailed records, engage in prudent investments, and provide an annual report that has been certified by qualified, impartial third parties. ERISA also establishes strict vesting rights to ensure that employees actually receive the pensions to which they are entitled. Employer contributions typically vest after three years or in a six-year, graduated system. The Pension Benefit Guaranty Corporation (PBGC), funded by company contributions, was created as an element of ERISA to insure defined benefit plans so that vested persons will be paid up to a specified maximum if their plan cannot meet its obligations. Defined contribution arrangements are not covered by the PBGC.

Fears that companies were not sufficiently funding their traditional pension plans led to provisions in the federal Pension Protection Act of 2006 requiring companies to more adequately fund those plans. Now experts are concerned that the stiffer financial expectations will cause more companies to freeze or drop their plans entirely. The PPA also made a somewhat revolutionary legal change in allowing companies to automatically enroll workers in company 40l(k) or similar plans; forcing workers to affirmatively opt out of the plan (rather than the previous system that allowed workers to enroll or not as they saw fit). The new rules also allow for contributions to automatically increase as pay rises, and they make it easier for plan providers to offer investment advice to their employees; something that had previously been forbidden on the theory that the advice might favor the company's interests rather than those of the employee.

Now millions of Americans depend upon their own investment wisdom and the reliability of their 40l(k) plan for their retirement security. In 2008, the U.S. Supreme Court strengthened that security a bit by finding that retirement account holders can sue if the manager of their plan fails to follow their investment instructions.[94]

The Future?   Substantial and expanding legal guidelines cannot address the primary impediment to comfortable retirement for millions of American workers: money. Employer-provided pension and health care benefits for retirees increasingly are at risk. As expenses, including pensions and health care, continue to rise, can American companies compete successfully with lower-cost foreign competition? Will we see something of a generational battle between the young and the old about how big a slice of American wealth each will receive? Will you need to work years longer than your parents in order to maintain comfortable elderly years?

> Will you need to work years longer than your parents?

Part Seven—Termination: Protection from Wrongful Discharge

> Wagenseller declined to participate in a "Moon River" skit

Catherine Wagenseller, an Arizona nurse, her boss, Kay Smith, and some coworkers joined a Colorado River rafting trip where Wagenseller declined to participate in a "Moon River" skit in which the group allegedly "mooned" the audience. Likewise,

Wagenseller did not join Smith in the heavy drinking, "grouping up," public urination, and similar behaviors that allegedly marked the trip. Despite favorable job evaluations preceding the trip, Wagenseller's relationship with Smith deteriorated following the trip, and eventually she was terminated. Wagenseller, an at-will employee, sued claiming that she was wrongfully discharged. An *at-will employee,* by definition, is not under contract for a definite period of time, and as such can be fired at any time. Wagenseller, however, argued that Arizona should adopt the *public policy exception* to the at-will doctrine. She claimed that she was fired because she refused to engage in behaviors that might have violated the Arizona indecent exposure statute. The state Supreme Court agreed with Wagenseller by finding in the statute a public policy favoring privacy and decency. The case was returned to the trial level, giving Wagenseller the opportunity to prove that her refusal to violate state public policy by engaging in public indecency led to her dismissal.[95]

The *Wagenseller* decision is an exception to the long-standing American rule that at-will employees can be fired for good reasons, bad reasons, or no reason at all. Of course, the employee is likewise free to quit at any time. Furthermore, both employer and employee freely entered the bargain understanding its terms, and thus the court should, in general, enforce those terms. Critics, however, argue that the doctrine ignores the historic inequality of bargaining power between employers and employees. In recent decades the at-will rule has been softened in most states by legislative and judicially imposed limitations. Statutory exceptions to the at-will rule include our labor laws protecting union workers (see Chapter 14) and the equal employment opportunity laws that forbid the dismissal of an employee for discriminatory reasons (see Chapter 13).

Judicial Limitations on At-Will Principles

An increasing number of court decisions provide grounds for dismissed at-will employees to claim that they have been *wrongfully discharged.* Those judicial decisions were often provoked by transparently unjust dismissals including, for example, whistle-blowers who exposed their employers' misdeeds and employees who declined to commit perjury on behalf of their employers. Those judicial limitations to the at-will doctrine fall into three categories: (1) express or implied contracts, (2) an implied covenant of good faith and fair dealing, and (3) the tort of violating an established public policy, as in *Wagenseller.* Additional tort claims may substitute for or supplement wrongful discharge claims.

1. **Express or implied employment contracts:** A number of states have adopted a contract protection for at-will employees that arises, typically, either from the employee handbook or from employer conduct and oral representations. The notion here is that the courts will recognize a contract based either on language in the handbook or on such assurances of continued employment as routine promotions, no notice of poor performance, longevity, and oral communications.

2. **Implied covenant of good faith and fair dealing:** A few state courts have held that neither party to a contract may *act in bad faith* to deprive the other of the benefits of the contract. For example, Bruce Rubenstein gave up his job with Arbor Mortgage

and took an at-will position with Huntington Mortgage with the understanding that he would be manager of a new branch office in central New Jersey. After a few weeks, however, Huntington decided on a downsizing strategy that included not opening the new branch. Rubenstein was offered a job as a loan originator, but he declined. He sued Huntington asserting, among other things, that Huntington had breached the covenant of good faith and fair dealing. Reubenstein believed that Huntington knew of the possibility of downsizing before hiring him. The court agreed that Rubenstein may have had a viable claim for breach of the implied covenant of good faith and fair dealing if the facts, at trial, proved to be as Rubenstein alleged.[96]

3. **Public policy:** Most states have now adopted some form of public policy (the general preference of the citizenry) exception providing that a dismissal is wrongful if it results from employee conduct that is consistent with the will of the people as expressed in statutes, constitutions, and the like. Those exceptions are established case by case, and they differ from state to state. In addition to reporting illegal activity (whistle blowing) and refusing to commit an illegal act (e.g., perjury), as noted above, the exception often protects, for example, those fired for pursuing a lawful claim (like workers' compensation) and those fired for fulfilling a civic responsibility (like jury duty).

Additional Torts Dismissed employees are increasingly turning to a variety of tort actions (often labeled *tag-along torts*) to enhance potential financial recovery, including punitive damages. Those tort possibilities include, among others, defamation, intentional infliction of emotional distress, interference with contract, and invasion of privacy. The following case raises public policy issues following an employment termination.

LLOYD V. DRAKE UNIVERSITY

LEGAL BRIEFCASE 686 N.W. 2d 225 (Iowa S.Ct. 2004)

JUSTICE STREIT

* * * * *

FACTS

Nicholas Lloyd was a Drake University security guard on duty at the annual Drake Relays street-painting event on April 20, 2002. A student told Lloyd about an apparent altercation between Philippe Joseph, a Drake football player, and Erin Kane. Lloyd and Kane were white; Joseph was black. Joseph was holding Kane in the air with her feet kicking. Lloyd and another security guard, Steven Smith, thought Joseph was holding

Kane in a headlock. Although Kane later claimed she and Joseph were just friends engaged in horseplay, Lloyd alleges Joseph's girlfriend called Lloyd and said Joseph had admitted to her that he and Kane were fighting. Lloyd ordered Joseph to release Kane. After Lloyd's second command, Joseph did so. Joseph suddenly made a 180-degree turn and lunged toward Lloyd with his fists raised to his chest and "an angry look on his face." Lloyd feared for his own safety and pepper sprayed Joseph. Smith reached for his pepper spray at the same time and would have sprayed Joseph if Lloyd had not done so first. Another Drake security guard, Sergeant Risvold, attempted to handcuff Joseph, but was unable to do so—Joseph was still writhing from the pepper spray. Lloyd hit Joseph on the thigh with his baton, forcing him to the ground.

Des Moines police officers took Joseph to the police station, where he was charged with disorderly conduct. Meanwhile, witnesses began screaming "racist, racist" at Lloyd. Students immediately discussed the incident with Drake's president, David Maxwell. Maxwell obtained Joseph's release and took him for medical treatment, even though he had not previously complained about any injuries resulting from the arrest. Joseph later pled guilty to disturbing the peace. He also received a settlement from Drake.

As local media reported on the street-painting episode, Lloyd's actions became the subject of a heated controversy. After the NAACP and Black Student Coalition demanded an investigation, Drake organized a panel to study the incident and related topics. The panel concluded Lloyd had overreacted and used unnecessary force. Although the panel determined Lloyd's actions at the street-painting event were not overtly racially motivated, the panel discovered some prior complaints against Lloyd involving minority students. (Lloyd, however, points out he was never reprimanded on any of those occasions.) The panel also criticized Drake for insufficiently training its security guards and its "ambiguous philosophy for security." During the investigation, Drake assigned Lloyd to a desk job. Maxwell assured Lloyd he would not lose his job. One of Lloyd's supervisors told Lloyd he was still in line for a promotion. Nonetheless, Drake fired Lloyd from his security position on June 16, 2002. . . .

WRONGFUL DISCHARGE

Lloyd does not dispute he was an at-will employee. As a consequence, Drake could fire him for any lawful reason, or for no reason at all. A discharge is not lawful, however, when it violates public policy. Lloyd claims Drake violated public policy and thereby committed the tort of wrongful discharge when it fired him simply for upholding the criminal laws, i.e., attempting to arrest Joseph, a man he thought was assaulting a student.

The district court dismissed Lloyd's wrongful-discharge claim. . . . ruling Drake had fired Lloyd for a variety of other lawful reasons, including (1) a desire to capitulate to outside pressures in the hopes of forestalling a lack of public confidence in Drake's security system; and (2) a determination—based upon newly rediscovered prior complaints and the panel's conclusion Lloyd used premature and excessive force in subduing Joseph—that Lloyd lacked the appropriate demeanor of a security guard. (On appeal, Drake also points out Lloyd's conduct affected its relationships with a variety of constituencies, and his retention could have cost it essential financial support.) . . .

We take a different route than the district court, but reach the same conclusion. . . . Even assuming Lloyd was fired simply for upholding the law, we think his claim still fails because the public policy against discharge that Lloyd asserts is neither clearly defined nor well recognized.

. . . [I]n order to prevail on his wrongful-discharge claim Lloyd must first identify a clearly defined and well-recognized public policy that would be undermined by his dismissal. . . . Only such policies are weighty enough "to overcome the employer's interest in operating its business in the manner it sees fit," which we have long and vigorously protected. Over the years we have recognized a number of clearly defined public policies. . . . To date, however, we have not held that a private security guard's actions in "enforcing the criminal laws of the state" to be a well-recognized and clearly defined public policy.

. . . [Lloyd's] argument mostly consists of vague generalizations about the social desirability of upholding the criminal laws of the state. . . . Lloyd also points out that there need not be an express statutory prohibition against discharge to underpin the public policy. In a number of cases, we have "found an implied prohibition against retaliatory discharge based on an employee's exercise of a right conferred by a clearly articulated legislative enactment." The gist of Lloyd's argument is that because upholding the criminal laws is important and socially desirable conduct, this court should find a public-policy exception to the at-will employment doctrine for a private security guard who tried to effectuate an arrest of a suspected criminal.

Lloyd's argument is not well taken. We have little quarrel, however, with one of the basic premises of Lloyd's argument: namely, that the criminal laws of the state reflect a general public policy against crime, and in favor of the protection of the public. That said, the public policy asserted here is far too generalized to support an argument for an exception to the at-will doctrine. In short, the public policy is not *clearly defined*. Apart from a vague reference to the whole of the criminal law, Lloyd cites no statutory or constitutional provision to buttress his claim. Divorced from any such provision or equivalent expression of public policy, we cannot find a well recognized and clearly defined public policy in such vague generalizations. "Any effort to evaluate the public policy exception with generalized concepts of fairness and justice will result in an elimination of the at-will doctrine itself."

* * * * *

[W]e can find no origin for the well-recognized and clearly defined public policy essential to carve out an exception to the at- will employment doctrine. There is nothing, then, to sustain the tort of wrongful discharge on these facts—however encouraged or frequently beneficial it may be to have private citizens take it upon themselves to enforce the criminal laws. . . . The point is simply this: while we might be persuaded that society would be better off if private security personnel investigated and attempted to stop crimes in progress, we are not convinced it is a clear and well-recognized public policy of this state "that we all become citizen crime fighters."

Affirmed.

Questions

1. *a.* Why did Lloyd lose this lawsuit?
   b. Why did the Iowa Supreme Court decide that Lloyd had failed to establish the public policy exception?
   c. Are you more convinced by the Iowa Supreme Court's reasoning, or the rationale offered by Drake to the District Court and on appeal? Explain.

2. Was Drake's decision to terminate Lloyd an appropriate response to this difficult situation? Explain.

3. Schuster worked, in an at-will relationship, for Derocili for 15 months, during which time she claims he touched her inappropriately and made numerous sexual comments despite her repeated rejections of those behaviors. Schuster received bonuses and good evaluations, but in a meeting between Schuster, Derocili, and Schuster's direct supervisor, Goff, she was fired for poor performance. Schuster's sexual harassment complaint with the Delaware Department of Labor was rejected as unsubstantiated. She sued Derocili for breach of contract, but the trial court dismissed that complaint. She appealed.
   a. Does Schuster have a legitimate wrongful discharge claim? Explain.
   b. Does she have any other plausible causes of action? Explain. See Schuster *v. Derocili,* 775 A.2d 1029 (Del. S. Ct. 2000).

4. Gilmartin took a job as station manager at a Texas television station. He was hired on a year-to-year basis under an oral agreement providing that his employment would continue as long as his work was satisfactory. Gilmartin was subsequently blamed for declining profits, and he was fired. Gilmartin sued. In his pleadings, Gilmartin said that he was informed of his annual salary, vacation time, and possible future raises, that his contract was to be renewed from year to year contingent on satisfactory performance, and that a commitment by KVTV for one to three years was "very doable." He was also told that a written agreement was not necessary. Was Gilmartin wrongfully discharged? Explain. See *Gilmartin v. KVTV-Channel 13,* 985 S.W.2d 553 (Ct. App. Tex. 1998).

5. IBP operated a large hog-processing plant in Storm Lake, Iowa. IBP prohibited possession of "look-alike drugs" on company property. An employee, Michael Huegerich, was randomly and lawfully inspected as he was entering the plant. The inspection revealed an asthma medication, Maxalert, which was identical in appearance to an illegal street drug, "speed." Maxalert contained the stimulant ephedrine. The pills actually belonged to his girlfriend and were in his possession by accident. Huegerich was terminated for possessing a look-alike drug in violation of company policy. Huegerich admitted that he was generally aware of IBP drug policies, but since he was a transfer from another IBP division, he had not gone through the company orientation program where new employees were advised of the policy against look-alike drugs. About six months after his dismissal, two IBP employees told Huegerich that they had heard he was fired for possessing speed. Huegerich then sued IBP for, among other claims, wrongful discharge and defamation.

   At trial, Huegerich provided no evidence as to how, when, and from whom the IBP employees had heard that he was terminated for possession of speed. The district court found for Huegerich in the amount of $24,000 on the wrongful discharge claim and $20,000 on the defamation claim. The court said that IBP was guilty of negligent discharge in failing to inform Huegerich about its drug policy. IBP appealed to the Iowa Supreme Court. Iowa law recognizes the doctrine of at-will employment with "narrow" exceptions for public policy violations and where a contract is created by an employer's handbook. Decide. Explain. See *Huegerich v. IBP,* 547 N.W.2d 216 (Iowa S.Ct. 1996).

6. Freeman, a television anchorperson employed by KSN, gave birth to her second child. On the day she returned from the hospital, she was notified that she had been dismissed. Six weeks later, she became unable to lactate. She sued KSN for wrongful discharge, tortious interference with contract, and negligent infliction of emotional distress. Decide. Explain. See *Freeman v. Medevac Midamerica of Kansas, Inc.,* 719 F. Supp. 995 (D Kan. 1989).

PRACTICING ETHICS)   Afraid to Fire?

BusinessWeek magazine recently ran a lengthy cover story entitled, "Fear of Firing?—How the Threat of Litigation Is Making Companies Skittish about Axing Problem Workers." *BusinessWeek* asked: "Would you have dared to fire Hermant K. Mody?"[97] Mody's story according to *BusinessWeek:*

In February 2003, the longtime engineer had returned to work at a General Electric Co. facility in Plainville, Conn., after a two-month medical leave. He was a very unhappy man. For much of the prior year, he and his superiors had been sparring over his performance and promotion prospects. According to court documents, Mody's bosses claimed he spoke disparagingly of his coworkers, refused an assignment as being beneath him, and was abruptly taking days off and coming to work late.[98]

Mody, born in India, was an at-will employee, 49 years old, and in need of daily dialysis for a chronic kidney problem. He accused his bosses of discriminating against him. (See Chapter 13 for a detailed overview of discrimination law.) After the discrimination accusation, Mody claims he was mistreated. He said that his boss began complaining that Mody was absent and tardy too often, and that he was given a very poor review just six weeks after receiving a very favorable review. Mody also said that he was given meaningless, demeaning assignments, and that his boss at

one point said: "There are things I can ask you to do that if I asked you to do them, you would just quit."[99] How would you have handled this situation? Consider some evidence about the risks of a lawsuit (based on 10,000 employment suits):

- 7,000 are settled out of court at an average cost to the employer of $10,000.
- 2,400 are resolved in pretrial motions at an average cost to the employer of $100,000.
- 600 go to trial where the average cost to the employer reaches $175,000 at the beginning of the trial.
- 186 are won by plaintiffs at an average cost to the employer of $250,000 at the end of a typical five-day trial.
- 13 of those plaintiffs' victories survive on appeal with an average total cost to the employer of $300,000.[100]

Questions

1. *a.* Would you fire Mody? Explain.
   b. Would that be the ethically proper thing to do? Explain.
   c. Would Mody win a lawsuit based upon these facts? Explain.

Part Eight—Immigration

Immigration is a vital fuel for America's economic and cultural growth, but immigration is also a source of deep divisions in national opinion—especially since "9/11." One in eight people living in the United States is an immigrant (about 40 million people), and immigration has surged to the highest level in the nation's history with 10.3 million new immigrants arriving from 2000 to 2007; more than half of them without legal status.[101] Illegal immigrants in the United States total about 11.3 million.[102]

Illegal immigrants total about 11.3 million

Immigration policy is one of the most divisive issues in American public life. Something of a backlash against Mexican and Central American immigration, in particular, has emerged in recent years with some cities and states taking steps to curb the Latino culture and presence by, for example, requiring the use of English or manning volunteer border watches in Texas and Arizona.[103] The backlash, in part, reflects resistance to changing ways of life and to the perception that illegal immigrants are an economic burden. A recent study found that illegal immigrants living in the United States used $2,700 in government services per person more than they paid in taxes.[104] But the evidence on the pluses and minuses of immigration is quite mixed. Immigrants to California appear to drive wages up and those immigrants are incarcerated at far lower rates than native-born citizens[105] A group of 500 economists wrote to Congress in 2006 arguing that immigration is, overall, a "modest" net gain for the American economy[106] In a more subjective sense, advocates claim that we must benefit from immigration's steady pipeline of new talent and energy including thousands of unaccompanied young children annually; many of whom literally walk to the United States from Central America.[107] The *Los Angeles Times* asked if our "sheltered and chaperoned children" could manage that feat on their own.[108]

American Immigration Law   Foreign workers seeking permanent residence in the United States on the basis of employment must have an offer of a permanent, full-time job. If so, the employer and the foreign national employee apply to the appropriate state Department of Labor for *labor certification,* which affirms that no one is available for the job and the hiring will not harm wages and working conditions in similar jobs. Some exceptions are provided for people in occupations where shortages exist and for those with exceptional abilities.

In hiring those already in the United States, federal immigration law, including the 1986 Immigration Reform and Control Act, requires employers to verify that each new hire is a U.S. citizen, a permanent resident, or a foreign national with permission to work in this country. To meet this requirement, employers must complete an employment eligibility verification form (I–9) for each new employee. New employees must present documents establishing the employee's identity and eligibility to work in the United States. The employer must examine the documents and complete the I–9 if the documents appear legitimate. Of course, employers cannot knowingly hire illegal immigrants, but neither can they discriminate against legal immigrants because of national origin and similar factors. [For links to the I–9 form and other immigration information, see **http://www.uscis.gov/portal/site/uscis**]

Crackdown?   Bending to pressure from the business community seeking cheap labor, immigrant rights groups and others, the federal government in recent years has been reluctant to prosecute businesses for unlawfully employing immigrants. Now lawmakers in Washington, DC and around the nation are scrambling to satisfy growing public demands to curb illegal immigration and to maintain the necessary flow of new labor, both skilled and unskilled, into the United States. The centerpiece of the reenergized federal effort is aggressive enforcement of the *no match* policy that requires employers to fire workers who cannot resolve mismatches between their names and their social security numbers.[109]

At this writing, the federal government is struggling to improve the accuracy of its electronic database, *E-Verify,* relied upon to identify the mismatches by comparing new hires' I–9 identity information with social security and immigration services records.

More broadly, the federal government announced plans in 2007 to raise fines for knowingly hiring illegal workers, and to build border defenses, including 370 miles of fencing, 300 miles of vehicle barriers and 1,700 new border patrol agents.[110] Meanwhile more than 100 states and municipalities, impatient with what they perceive to be federal inaction, have implemented their own plans to stem illegal immigration.[111] Arizona has been particularly aggressive by imposing a suspension of the license to operate a business in the state for up to 10 days if caught knowingly employing an undocumented worker. The license would then be lifted permanently (the "business death penalty") if caught a second time.[112] [For overviews of many of the employment law topics in this chapter, see **http://topics.law.cornell.edu/wex/category/employment_law**]

Internet Exercise

Using the Frequently Asked Questions portion of the Occupational Safety and Health Administration (OSHA) Web site [**http://www.osha.gov/as/opa/osha-faq.html**], answer the following:

1. What is OSHA's budget, and how many inspectors does the agency have?
2. How can I get help from OSHA to fix hazards in my workplace?
3. What cooperative programs does OSHA offer?

Chapter Questions

1. In general, employers are forced to bear (or at least share) the legal burden for their employees' negligent conduct on the job.

   a. Why do we force employers to bear that responsibility?

   b. Should we do so? Explain.

2. Abplanalp, a five-year employee of Com-Co Insurance, signed an employment agreement including a restrictive covenant providing that, should he leave Com-Co, he would not use Com-Co customer lists or solicit business from Com-Co clients for three years. Abplanalp moved to Service Insurance, where he sold insurance to some friends and relatives. He did not sell to any other persons whom he came to know while working for Com-Co. Abplanalp was sued by Com-Co for violating the restrictive covenant. Decide. Explain. See *Com-Co Insurance Agency v. Service Insurance Agency,* 748 N.E.2d 298 (Ill. App. Ct. 2001).

3. Many companies refer to credit reports when investigating job applicants. The Fair Credit Reporting Act requires employers to notify applicants if they are rejected because of information in a credit report.

   a. In your judgment, does evidence of failure to pay debts constitute useful information in the job selection process? Explain.

   b. Is the use of that information an "invasion of privacy" as you understand it? Explain.

4. A group of Fargo, North Dakota, nurses were paid a subminimum wage for their "on-call" time. When on call, the nurses were required to be able to report to their hospital within 20 minutes, they were required to provide a phone number where they could be reached, and they were not to consume alcohol or drugs. After being called, nurses returned to regular pay. In three years, 36 of the 135 nurses who sued had been called in more than once. The nurses sued the hospital for violating the Fair Labor Standards Act's minimum wage provision. Decide. Explain. See *Reimer v. Champion Healthcare Corp.*, 258 F.3d 720 (8th Cir. 2001).

5. Simons, an engineer at the CIA, downloaded child pornography on his workplace computer. The computer was to be used only for work. The pornography was discovered by a search of employee computers. Simons was then convicted of receiving and possessing child pornography. Simons appealed on Fourth Amendment grounds. Decide. Explain. See *United States v. Simons,* 206 F.3d 392 (4th Cir. 2000); cert. den. 122 S.Ct. 292 (2001).

6. Guz, a longtime Bechtel employee, was dismissed during what Bechtel said was a business slump. Bechtel's personnel policy included a provision saying employees "may be terminated at the option of Bechtel." Guz sued for wrongful dismissal claiming, among other things, that Bechtel breached an implied contract to be terminated only for good cause, and that Bechtel breached the implied covenant of good faith and fair dealing. A lower court concluded that Guz's promotions, raises, favorable performance reviews, together with Bechtel's progressive discipline policy and Bechtel officials' statements of company practices supported Guz's position. Bechtel appealed. Decide. Explain. See *Guz v. Bechtel National Inc.,* 8 P.3d 1089 (Cal. S.Ct. 2000).

7. Kang worked for PB Fasteners for 30 years. In January 2003, PB laid off Kang and three others in the same department while keeping another worker who was considered more proficient at the job. The employee handbook said that all employment was at-will. Kang sued accusing his employer of breach of contract.

   a. Explain Kang's breach of contract claim.

   b. Decide the case. Explain. See *Kang v. PB Fasteners,* 2008 U.S. App. Lexis 9694.

8. As explained in this chapter, many states have adopted one or more exceptions (express/implied contracts, good faith and fair dealing, and public policy) to the at-will doctrine. What effect, if any, would you expect those exceptions to have on employment levels, and company performance?

9. Safeway in Denver hosted a picnic for its employees. Safeway bought a 40-pound gas tank to use with a grill that was designed for a 20-pound tank. A label on the grill warned against that use. The grill failed to operate properly and a manager asked Lewis to try to fix it. When Lewis did so a "ball of fire" erupted and Lewis was badly burned. The Occupational Safety and Health Administration then issued a citation against Safeway. Safeway appealed to the courts.

   a. Defend Safeway.

   b. Decide the case. Explain. See *Safeway, Inc. v. Occupational Safety & Health Rev. Comm.,* 382 F.3d 1189 (10th Cir. 2004).

10. In most drug testing cases, courts have balanced the employee's privacy interests against the employer's need for information. What business justifications are likely to be most persuasive to a court reviewing the legality of employee drug testing?

11. Millions of workers can be regarded as telecommuters. As such, they bring new legal problems to the workplace. As a manager, what legal difficulties would you want to anticipate and protect against as more and more of your employees work off-premises and often from their own homes?

12. A reader sent the following story to a newspaper question and answer forum:

    I was fired recently by my employer, an architecture firm, immediately after serving for one month on a federal grand jury. From the moment I informed my boss . . . I was harassed . . . and told I was not putting the company first. I was told to get out of my jury service, "or else." . . . I was fired exactly one week after my service ended.[113]

    Was the dismissal of this at-will employee lawful? Explain.

13. Katherine Born and Rick Gillispie were employed by a Blockbuster Video store in Iowa. Blockbuster maintained a policy that forbade dating between supervisors and their subordinates. Born and Gillispie were dismissed for violating the policy. They denied that they were romantically involved and filed suit for wrongful dismissal. Under Iowa law, an at-will employee can be discharged at any time for any reason, but Iowa law does recognize the public policy exception. To prevail in this lawsuit, what must the plaintiffs show about Iowa law? See *Katherine Born and Rick Gillispie v. Blockbuster Videos, Inc.,* 941 F.Supp. 868 (S. D. Ia. 1996).

14. A pregnant employee at a retail store was operating a buffing machine when propane gas that powered the machine led to a carbon monoxide buildup, causing the worker and others to be taken to a hospital. The worker's fetus sustained oxygen deprivation, resulting in injuries including abnormal motor functions, cerebral palsy, and a seizure disorder. The worker sued on negligence grounds for her child's injuries. The employer defended by arguing that workers' compensation provides the exclusive remedy in such situations. Does workers' compensation bar the child's suit? Explain. See *Snyder v. Michael's Stores, Inc.,* 945 P.2d 781 (Cal. S.Ct. 1997).

15. Lang, a white male working in a factory, called a black coworker such names as "watermelon" and "buckwheat." The coworker told Lang to stop. Lang continued the racist name-calling and his coworker then called Lang a "cracker" and a "honkey." Later, while Lang was talking with his supervisor, the coworker twice struck Lang, who then filed a workers' compensation claim.

    a. Is Lang entitled to workers' compensation?

    b. What is the key issue? Explain. See *Redman Industries v. Lang,* 326 Or. 32 (Or. S.Ct. 1997).

16. LaTourette worked for a California college and was attending a conference for work purposes when he suffered a heart attack. He underwent various operations including bypass surgery, subsequent to which he died in the hospital from a bacterial

infection. His estate sought workers' compensation, claiming that his heart attack was a response to job stress. Is his estate entitled to workers' compensation? Explain. See *LaTourette v. Workers' Compensation Appeals Board*, 72 Cal. Rptr. 2d 217 (Cal. S.Ct. 1998).

Notes

1. Sacha Pfeiffer, "Off-the-Job Smoker Sues over Firing," *The Boston Globe*, November 30, 2006 [**www.boston.com**].

2. Ibid.

3. Ilan Brat, "A Company's Threat: Quit Smoking or Leave," *The Wall Street Journal*, December 20, 2005, p. D1.

4. *Chao v. Southern California Maid Services & Carpet Cleaning, Inc.*, No. CV-06-3903 (C.D. Cal. 2007).

5. "FedEx Drivers Gain Class-Action Status," *Des Moines Register*, October 19, 2007, p. 5C.

6. Floyd Norris, "RadioShack Chief Resigns after Lying," *The New York Times*, February 21, 2006, sec. C, p. 1.

7. Lore Croghan, "Almost Half of Job Applicants Lied on Résumé, Study Says," *Waterloo/Cedar Falls Courier*, March 5, 2006, p. D10.

8. Kris Maher, "The Jungle," *The Wall Street Journal*, January 20, 2004, p. B8.

9. Alan Finder, "For Some, Online Persona Undermines a Résumé," *The New York Times*, June 11, 2006 [**www.nytimes.com**].

10. Carlos Tejada, "They Asked What?" *The Wall Street Journal*, March 27, 2001, p. A1.

11. Kris Maher, "The Jungle," *The Wall Street Journal*, September 28, 2004, p. B10.

12. Maher, "The Jungle," p. B10.

13. Joann Lublin, "Watch for Legal Traps When You Quit a Job to Work for a Rival," *The Wall Street Journal*, November 6, 2007, p. B1.

14. Kris Maher, "The Jungle," *The Wall Street Journal*, June 8, 2004, p. B4.

15. *Circuit City Stores, Inc. v. Adams*, 532 U.S. 105 (2001).

16. Steven J. Burton, "The New Judicial Hostility to Arbitration: Federal Preemption, Contract Unconscionability, and Agreements to Arbitrate," *The Journal of Dispute Resolution* (forthcoming).

17. See Sidney L. Gold and Hyman Lovitz, "Arbitration Agreements Don't Supersede Authority to Recover Damages," *The Legal Intelligencer*, June 6, 2002, p. 6.

18. 814 P.2d 1341 (Cal. S.Ct. 1991).

19. Jenny B. Davis, "Still Working after All These Years," *ABA Journal*, October 2001, p. 67.

20. Stephen Labaton, "Congress Passes Increase in the Minimum Wage," *The New York Times*, May 25, 2007 [**www.nytimes.com**].

21. For a study involving 12 of the higher minimum wage states, see Gwendolyn Bounds, "Argument for Minimum-Wage Boost," *The Wall Street Journal*, July 27, 2004, p. B3.

22. John Wagner, "O'Malley Makes 'Living Wage' a Law," *Washington Post*, May 9, 2007, p. B01.

23. Associated Press, "Study Shows 'Living Wage' Helping to Reduce Poverty," *Waterloo/Cedar Falls Courier*, March 14, 2002, p. A2.

24. Brian Bergstein, "IBM Riles Employees with Base Pay Cuts," January 23, 2008, Boston.com [**http://www.boston.com**].

25. Michael Orey, "Wage Wars," *BusinessWeek,* October 1, 2007, p. 50.

26. Ibid.

27. Ibid.

28. Ibid.

29. Ibid.

30. "Call the *Courier,*" *Waterloo/Cedar Falls Courier,* February 4, 2001, p. C1.

31. David Barstow, "California Leads in Making Employer Pay for Job Deaths," *The New York Times,* December 23, 2003, p. A1.

32. "The Explosion at Texas City," *60 Minutes,* CBS News, October 29, 2006 [**http://www.cbsnews.com/stories/2006/10/26/60minutes**].

33. Ibid.

34. Associated Press, "Federal Probe of Fatal Texas Plant Explosion Cites Oversight," *Waterloo/Cedar Falls Courier,* March 21, 2007, p. B4.

35. Ana Campoy, "Refinery Safety Will Face Expanded OSHA Scrutiny," *The Wall Street Journal,* June 11, 2007, p. A8.

36. "The Explosion at Texas City," *60 Minutes.*

37. "Current Injury, Illness and Fatality Data," Federal Bureau of Labor Statistics [**www.bls.gov/iif/home.htm**].

38. "Workplace Injuries and Illnesses in 2006," *Bureau of Labor Statistics News* [**http://www.bls.gov/iif/oshwc/osh/os/osnr0028.pdf**].

39. "Current Injury, Illness and Fatality Data," Federal Bureau of Labor Statistics.

40. Megan O'Rourke, "The Impact of Workplace Injuries," *Risk Management Magazine* 52, Issue 11 (November 1, 2005).

41. Robert J. Grossman, "Making Ergonomics," *HR Magazine,* April 2000, p. 36.

42. Associated Press, "Carpal Tunnel Injuries at Work Decline," *The Des Moines Register,* March 17, 2008, p. 1D.

43. "Workplace Homicides Drop to New Low," *In Your State,* August 15, 2007 [**http://hr.blr.com/news.aspx?id=76887**].

44. U.S. Department of Labor, Bureau of Labor Statistics. Census of Fatal Occupational Injuries: Table 4. "Fatal Occupational Injuries by Worker Characteristics and Event or Exposure," 2003.

45. *ConocoPhillips v. Henry,* 520 F. Supp. 2d 1282 (N.D. Okla. 2007).

46. Ames Alexander, Kerry Hall, Ted Mellnik, Franco Ordonez, "Workplace Inspections at 15-Year Low," *Charlotte Observer,* February 14, 2008 [**http://www.charlotte.com/716/v-print/story/494390.html**].

47. Stephen Labaton, "OSHA Leaves Worker Safety in Hands of Industry," *The New York Times,* April 25, 2007 [**http://www.nytimes.com**].

48. For more on the Stringer story, see Mark A. Cohen, "MN Supreme Court Upholds Dismissal of Stringer Family's Wrongful-Death Suit," *The Minnesota Lawyer,* November 21, 2005.

49. At this writing, the Stringer family has sued the NFL and Riddell, a football equipment maker, claiming the defendants had not done enough to protect players from heat-related injuries and deaths.

50. *Stringer v. Minnesota Vikings,* 705 N.W. 2d 746 (Minn. S.Ct.2005).

51. *Guico v. Excel Corp.,* 619 N.W.2d 470 (Neb. S.Ct. 2000).

52. Marilyn Gardner, " 'Body Art' Gains Acceptance in Workplace," *The Christian Science Monitor,* December 3, 2007 [**http://www.csmonitor.com/2007/1203/p13s05-wmgn.html**].

53. Molly Selvin, "Better Hide the Tattoo If You Want the Job," *Los Angeles Times,* July 5, 2007 [**http://www.latimes.com/news/la-fi-tattoo5jul05,0,3084603.story?coll=la-tot-topstories&track=ntottext**].

54. *Los Angeles Times,* "Shape Up or Pay Up, More Employers Tell Workers," *Waterloo/Cedar Falls Courier,* July 29, 2007, p. A1.

55. M.P. McQueen, "Wellness Plans Reach Out to the Healthy," *The Wall Street Journal,* March 28, 2007, p. D1.

56. Amy Joyce, "Life Outside Work Can Tinge Job Prospects," *Des Moines Register,* October 30, 2006, p. 10C.

57. S.P. Dinnen, "Employers Slap Fees on Workers Who Smoke," *The Des Moines Register,* November 20, 2005. p. 1A.

58. Ibid.

59. *Robert Barbee v. Household Automotive Finance,* 113 Cal. App. 4th 525 (2003).

60. "Just Say Yes to Tests," *Crain's Cleveland Business,* May 14, 2007, News, p. 11.

61. Dalia Fahmy, "Aiming for a Drug-Free Workplace," *The New York Times,* May 10, 2007, Sec. C, p. 6.

62. Ibid.

63. Ibid.

64. George Lenard, "Employers Falling Off Drug Testing Bandwagon," February 28, 2005 [**http://www.employmentblawg.com/2005**].

65. "Diagnostics; Drug Use Hits New Low Among U.S. Workers in 2006," *Biotech Business Week,* March 26, 2007, Sec. Expanded Reporting, p. 191.

66. Ibid.

67. See, e.g., *National Treasury Employees Union v. Von Raab,* 109 S.Ct. 1385 (1989).

68. Chris Erikson, "Keeping Watch—Lewis Maltby Is the Country's Top Advocate for Worker Privacy," *The New York Post,* June 25, 2007, p. 39.

69. Ibid.

70. American Management Association, "2007 Electronic Monitoring & Surveillance Survey," *AMA Press Release* [**http://press.amanet.org/press-releases/177/2007-monitoring**].

71. Ibid.

72. Ibid.

73. Mark P. Couch, "Eyes Are on Your E-Mail," *Des Moines Register,* January 26, 1997, p. 1G.

74. Molly Selvin and Daniel Costello, "Workers Paying More for Coverage," *Los Angeles Times,* September 12, 2007 [**http://www.latimes.com/business/la-fi-premiums12sep12,0,4321950.story?coll=la-tot-business&track=ntottext**].

75. Ibid.

76. Ibid.

77. Ibid.

78. "Medical Bills Bury Businesses," *Des Moines Register,* December 5, 2005, p. 6A.

79. Michelle Conlin, "Held Hostage by Health Care," *BusinessWeek,* January 29, 2007, p. 82.

80. Ibid.

81. Arthur C. Brooks, "Happy for the Work," *The Wall Street Journal,* June 20, 2007, p. A16.

82. Stephanie Rosenbloom, "Please Don't Make Me Go to Vacation," *The New York Times,* August 10, 2006 [**http://www.nytimes.com/2006/08/10/fashion/10vacation.html**].

83. Kris Maher, "Is Family Leave Act Too Soft or Too Tough?" *The Wall Street Journal,* November 21, 2007, p. D1.

84. Ibid.

85. Ibid.

86. Knight Ridder Newspapers, "Study: New Parents' Leave Is Unchanged," *Waterloo/Cedar Falls Courier,* February 21, 2003, p. A10.

87. Patt Johnson, "Getting the Boot," *Des Moines Register,* May 4, 2003, p. 1D.

88. Johnson, "Getting the Boot."

89. Clark Kauffman, "Diary of a Goof-Off: No Work, No Pay," *Des Moines Register,* January 19, 2007, p. 1A.

90. Kathleen Day, "Retirement, Squeezed," *Washington Post,* September 17, 2006, p. F01.

91. Ibid.

92. David Wessel, "How Will the U.S. Fill Its Benefits Gap?" *The Wall Street Journal,* April 13, 2006, p. A2.

93. Mark Trumbull, "Reform Erodes the Future of US Pensions," *The Christian Science Monitor,* August 18, 2006 [**http://www.csmonitor.com/2006/0818/p02s02-usec.html**].

94. *LaRue v. DeWolff, Boberg & Associates, Inc.,* 128 S.Ct. 1020 (2008).

95. *Wagenseller v. Scottsdale Memorial Hospital,* 710 P.2d 1025 (Az. S.Ct. 1985).

96. *Rubenstein v. Huntington Mortgage Company,* N. J. Sup. Ct., App. Div., 1997. For a journalistic account of the case, see Pitney, Hardin, Kipp, and Szuch, "Employers Must Be Cautious about Failing to Disclose Business Plans that Will Affect the Jobs of New Hires," *New Jersey Employment Law Letter,* September 1997.

97. Michael Orey, "Fear of Firing," *BusinessWeek,* April 23, 2007, p. 52.

98. Ibid.

99. Ibid.

100. Ibid.

101. Julia Preston, "Immigration at Record Level, Analysis Finds," *The New York Times,* November 29, 2007 [**http://www.nytimes.com**].

102. Ibid.

103. Patrik Jonsson, "Backlash Emerges Against Latino Culture," *The Christian Science Monitor,* July 19, 2006 [**http://www.csmonitor.com/2006/0719/p03s03-ussc.html**].

104. Ibid.

105. Teresa Watanabe, "Immigrants Boost Pay, Not Prison Populations, New Studies Show," *Los Angeles Times,* February 28, 2007 [**http://www.latimes.com/news/local/la-me-immigstudy28feb28,0,7851813.story?track=ntottext**].

106. David Streitfeld, "Illegal—but Essential," *Los Angeles Times,* October 1, 2006 [**http://www.latimes.com/business/la-fi-immigecon1oct01,0,2945710.story?track=tottext**].

107. Rosa Brooks, "How Immigrants Improve the Curve," *Los Angeles Times,* June 29, 2007 [**http://www.latimes.com/news/opinion/la-oe-brooks29jun29,0,1106152.column?coll=la-tot-opinion&track=ntottext**].

108. Ibid.

109. Associated Press, "Cost of Crackdown on Illegals Questioned," *Waterloo/Cedar Falls Courier,* April 25, 2008, p. C1.

110. N.C. Aizenman, "Bush Moves to Step Up Immigration Enforcement," *Washington Post,* August 11, 2007, p. A01.

111. Jane Sasseen, "Hire an Illegal Worker, Lose Your Business," *BusinessWeek,* December 24, 2007, p. 064.

112. Ibid.

113. *Washington Post,* "The Boss Can't Fire You for Doing Your Civic Duty," *Waterloo/Cedar Falls Courier,* May 26, 1999, p. C8.

CHAPTER THIRTEEN

Employment Law II: Discrimination

After completing this chapter, students will be able to:

1. Discuss the purpose and history of legal protections against employment discrimination.

2. Compare and contrast the protections offered under the federal statutes prohibiting employment discrimination: Title VII of the Civil Rights Act of 1964; the Equal Pay Act; the Americans with Disabilities Act; and the Age Discrimination in Employment Act.

3. Explain the role of the Equal Employment Opportunity Commission (EEOC) in enforcing federal statutes prohibiting employment discrimination.

4. Identify remedies available to victims of unlawful employment discrimination.

5. Distinguish the forms of employment discrimination analysis, disparate treatment and disparate impact.

6. Identify when unlawful sexual harassment has occurred.

7. Identify when employers are liable for unlawful sexual harassment.

8. Describe protections against retaliation offered under the federal statutes prohibiting employment discrimination.

9. Discuss the purposes and development of affirmative action.

10. Describe the concept of reasonable accommodation as applied to religious and disability-based discrimination claims.

11. Discuss the current status of protections against sexual orientation discrimination in the workplace.

Introduction

Have you shopped at Abercrombie & Fitch? Many Americans do so routinely, but as of November 2004, those customers learned that their shopping may have contributed to alleged racial and sexual discrimination. Basically, the retailer was accused of maintaining a virtually all-white image by discriminating in recruiting, hiring, and promoting women and minorities. A nationwide class action was filed claiming that Abercrombie disproportionately assigned minority employees to stockrooms and other jobs out of the public eye, while white employees were conspicuously on display as a means of projecting the company's "clean-cut, classic" image.

Abercrombie denied the charges, but it decided to settle before trial by agreeing to pay a $40 million settlement along with $10 million in attorney fees and other expenses. The settlement also required the company to promote diversity in its workforce.[1] Additionally, Abercrombie agreed to manifest a more diverse image in its marketing materials, including its catalogs, shopping bags, and store posters.[2]

Questions

1. The conservative *California Patriot* at the University of California at Berkeley:

   If Abercrombie & Fitch Co. wants to promote a certain image, that is its prerogative. The goal of any business is to make a profit, and Abercrombie & Fitch may have found it profitable to use a "white image" in order to promote its clothing.

   a. The law aside, is Abercrombie simply wrong to project a "white image," if, indeed, it did so? Explain.

   b. Would it be wrong for Abercrombie to build its business plan on an ethnic or black or "hip-hop" image in its products?

2. Is discrimination based on appearance an ethical wrong? Explain.

3. Katie Hollenbeck, a junior graphic arts major, was thinking of applying for a job at Abercrombie & Fitch, but she decided that she didn't feel "appropriate" for the job after she observed all of the store's "tall, skinny white girls." Hollenbeck says that, in the long run, hiring only attractive employees will "hurt Abercrombie."[3]

   a. Would the market punish Abercrombie, even if the law had not intervened? Explain.

   b. Should the market punish Abercrombie? Explain. Put another way, should you decline to shop at Abercrombie stores? Explain.

Continuing Discrimination   The ethical issues raised by Abercrombie & Fitch's hiring and staffing practices highlight the challenges of enforcing legal protections against employment discrimination, often referred to as Equal Employment Opportunity (EEO) laws.

Employers compare, distinguish, and choose among applicants and employees based on many factors. However, EEO laws forbid those considerations that would undermine equal employment opportunity. Prohibited factors, also called "protected categories," include an applicant's or employee's race, color, and gender, among other characteristics. Generally, EEO laws protect all employees and are not restricted to certain groups such as women or racial minorities.

Do we still need EEO laws in the United States? Consider a recent study in which black and white men applied for the same entry-level jobs with nearly identical résumés. Some of the white men were instructed to tell the employer that they had felony drug convictions. Who would receive the employer's call—the white ex-convict or the black with no criminal record? Most likely, the study found, the white applicant with the criminal record would be preferred over the black applicant with no criminal record.[4] As diversity grows in the United States, EEO laws may serve to support and sustain a more inclusive, and ultimately, more productive workplace.[5]

Diversity Grows throughout the United States

With the exception of West Virginia, diversity is growing in each state, according to the U.S. Census Bureau's 2005 American Community Survey. Hispanics are the country's largest minority group, making up 14.5 percent of the U.S. population, while non-Hispanic whites are the minority in Hawaii, New Mexico, California, Texas, and the District of Columbia. 12.8 percent of the U.S. population is black. Immigrants, both legal and undocumented, made up 12.4 percent of the population in 2005.

Source: (CBSNews.com, "Census: Diversity Growing in 49 States," August 15, 2006 (**http://www. cbsnews. com/stories/2006/08/15/national/main1895117.shtml**).

Part One—Employment Discrimination: The Foundation in Law

History

In the Reconstruction Era following the Civil War, Congress passed the Civil Rights Act of 1866 to provide the newly freed black slaves with the same right to make and enforce contracts as was enjoyed by white citizens. This law still exists today, with updated language emphasizing its protection against racial discrimination. The Civil Rights Act of 1866 has been interpreted to forbid discrimination on the basis of race in employment, which is essentially a contractual relationship.

However, this legal protection did not prevent discriminatory practices in housing, education, business, and employment. In 1941 A. Philip Randolph, president of the predominantly black Brotherhood of Sleeping Car Porters, organized black leaders who threatened a massive march in Washington, DC, protesting employment discrimination. In response, President Franklin Roosevelt issued Executive Order 8802, which created a Fair Employment Practice Committee. Congress limited the committee's budget, but Roosevelt's action was a striking step for the federal government in addressing racial discrimination.

The next big step toward racial equality was the landmark *Brown v. Board of Education*[6] decision in 1954, in which the Supreme Court forbade "separate but equal" schools. Following *Brown,* citizens engaged in sit-ins, freedom rides, boycotts, and the like to press claims for racial equality. It was a turbulent, sometimes violent, era, but those activities were critical ingredients in subsequent advances for the black population. With the passage of the 1964 Civil Rights Act, the campaign against discrimination solidified as one of the most energetic and influential social movements in American history.[7] The Civil Rights Act of 1964 changed American life by forbidding discrimination in education, housing, public accommodation, and, perhaps most importantly, employment. [For the National Civil Rights Museum, see **http://www.civilrightsmuseum.org**]

Civil Rights Act of 1964

Reflecting the increased diversity of the U.S. workforce, in which women had gone beyond traditional roles and where immigrants from around the world could be found, Title VII of the Civil Rights Act of 1964 ("Title VII") marked a new era in employment practices. Title VII forbids discrimination in employment on the basis of race, color, religion, sex, or national origin. Relying on its authority to regulate commerce, Congress applied Title VII to private-sector employers with 15 or more employees, employment agencies, labor unions with 15 or more members as well as those operating a hiring hall, state and local governments, and most of the federal government. Private clubs are exempt from Title VII, and religious organizations may discriminate in employment on the basis of religion. Broadly, Title VII forbids discrimination in hiring, firing, and all aspects of the employment relationship.

Other Legislation and Orders

Title VII is the core of EEO laws in the United States. Other federal statutes, such as the Americans with Disabilities Act of 1990 (ADA) and the Age Discrimination in Employment Act of 1967 (ADEA), have established additional protected categories. The Equal Pay Act of 1963 and the Civil Rights Act of 1991 address particular issues in employment discrimination. For example, the Civil Rights Act of 1991 provides that U.S. citizens working abroad for American-owned or American-controlled companies are protected from discrimination under Title VII and the ADA unless such protection would require the employer to violate the laws of its host nation. These federal laws will be discussed further later in this chapter.

The Constitution

As explained in Chapter 5, the federal Constitution, among other purposes, protects us from wrongful government action. The Fourteenth Amendment to the Constitution provides that no state shall deny to any person life, liberty, or property without *due process of law* or deny him or her the *equal protection of the laws.* Thus citizens are protected from discrimination via state government action. Similarly, the Supreme Court has interpreted the Due Process Clause of the Fifth Amendment ("nor shall any person . . . be deprived of life, liberty, or property, without due process of law") to forbid discrimination by the federal government.

Employment Discrimination Enforcement

EEOC and State Fair Employment Practice Agencies

The Equal Employment Opportunity Commission (EEOC), an independent federal agency, has the authority to issue regulations and guidelines as well as to receive, initiate, and investigate charges of discrimination against employers covered by federal antidiscrimination statutes such as Title VII [see the Equal Employment Opportunity Commission's Web site at **http://www/eeoc.gov**].

Several states enacted fair employment practices legislation that mirrors or expands the antidiscrimination protections found in federal statutes such as Title VII. State fair employment practice agencies may serve the same function as the EEOC in enforcing these laws. [For an example, see California Department of Fair Employment and Housing's Web site at **http://www.dfeh.ca.gov**]. Municipal ordinances may also address employment discrimination, enforced by a particular branch of the city's government. [For the San Francisco Human Rights Commission, see **http://www.sfgov.org/site/sfhumanrights_index.asp**]

Litigation

The first step in lawsuits claiming employment discrimination is not taken in a courthouse. A victim of employment discrimination, usually referred to as the "charging party," will file a complaint within a limited period of time with either the EEOC or, where applicable, the local or state fair employment practices agency.

What if the allegedly discriminatory act is ongoing rather than an incident occurring on a certain date—at what moment does the clock start ticking on the victim's time to file an EEOC complaint? After 19 years as a Goodyear employee, Lily Ledbetter discovered that her wages were much lower than her male coworkers. She filed an EEOC complaint alleging gender discrimination, and later won a jury verdict for back pay and punitive damages. In 2007, the U.S. Supreme Court held in *Ledbetter v. Goodyear Tire & Rubber Co.* that Ledbetter's claim should have been brought within 180 days of the first paycheck at issue.[8] At this writing, the U.S. Senate is considering the Ledbetter Fair Pay Act, passed by the U.S. House of Representatives in July 2007, which will clarify that each paycheck issued by an employer engaged in pay discrimination is a discriminatory act, meaning that the clock resets on a potential discrimination claim each time the employee is paid.[9]

Typically, the EEOC will refer the charging party and employer for mediation. If mediation does not resolve the complaint, then the EEOC will investigate. If the EEOC finds no cause for the complaint, then the EEOC will issue a *right-to-sue letter,* thus removing itself from the matter and releasing the grievant to file his or her own lawsuit because all administrative remedies have been exhausted. If grounds for complaint are found, the case will first be referred to conciliation. That failing, the commission may file a civil suit or issue a right-to-sue letter to the grievant.

Many potential employment discrimination lawsuits no longer reach the judicial system because they are resolved in arbitration. Many businesses are now including binding arbitration agreements in job offers, requiring job seekers, as a condition of employment, to waive the right to trial and turn any grievance over to arbitration. A series of U.S. Supreme Court decisions has firmly established the enforceability of those agreements when the arbitration process provided for is legitimate and fair. The Court has also ruled, however, that the EEOC retains its right to sue on behalf of an employee even if the worker has signed away his or her own rights.[10]

When job discrimination suits reach the courts, only about 30 percent of those claims are successful for plaintiffs.[11] By contrast, plaintiffs win about 43 percent of all categories of civil federal district court cases.[12] Broadly, job discrimination claims are harder to win, at least in the federal courts, than virtually all other kinds of civil suits.

Remedies

Recognizing the gravity and nature of injuries caused by *intentional* discrimination in the workplace, Congress expanded the remedies available for such injury under Title VII and the Americans with Disabilities Act (ADA) to include compensatory damages as well as punitive damages in some cases. Compensatory damages may be sought to redress, for example, emotional pain and suffering, but combined compensatory and punitive damages are capped at $50,000 to $300,000, depending on the size of the employer's workforce. Damages are not capped for front pay (awarded for future earnings) or in cases of intentional discrimination based on race. At this writing, the proposed Civil Rights Act of 2008, also known as the Equal Remedies Act of 2008, would eliminate the caps on compensatory and punitive damages for intentional employment discrimination.[13] The EEOC often negotiates consent decrees that may require new procedures to correct wrongful practices. [For the Civil Rights Division of the U.S. Justice Department, see **http://www.usdoj.gov/crt/crt-home.html**]

Part Two—"Types of Discrimination"

There are three basic types of illegal employment discrimination: disparate treatment, disparate impact, and harassment. Additionally, Title VII and other antiemployment discrimination statutes prohibit retaliation for opposing an employment practice reasonably believed to be discriminatory, or for participating in a claim of employment discrimination. Plaintiffs may raise claims of more than one type of employment discrimination, as well as retaliation, against an employer.

Disparate Treatment and Disparate Impact

Title VII of the 1964 Civil Rights Act provides two primary theories of recovery for individuals—disparate treatment and disparate impact (sometimes labeled *adverse impact*). A disparate treatment claim addresses *intentional* discrimination by an employer who has purposefully treated an employee or applicant less favorably because of his/her race, color, religion, national origin, gender, or membership in a group under another protected category. Disparate impact claims arise from "unintentional" discrimination where an employment practice appearing to be neutral has the effect of adversely impacting a particular group under a protected category more than it impacts other groups.

As we turn now to a close look at disparate treatment and disparate impact analysis, keep in mind the various constitutional, statutory, and executive order protections just outlined.

Disparate Treatment

Employees or applicants making claims of disparate treatment must prove their employers' intent to discriminate with either direct or indirect evidence. For example, a company president's remarks that "women were simply 'not tough enough' to supervise collections and that it was a 'man's job,'" even if tempered by his statement that "I felt that a woman was not competent enough to do this job, but I think maybe you're showing me that you can do it," may constitute direct evidence of intentional sex discrimination, as a federal court of appeals found.[14] A warehouse company seeking truck loaders might write a letter to an employment agency offering that "women would not be welcome as applicants for this physically taxing job," which could be used as *direct evidence* of the employer's intent to treat female applicants adversely compared to male applicants. More often, however, disparate treatment claims must be established by relying on *indirect evidence* in accord with the following test.

1. **Plaintiff's (employee's) prima facie case** (sufficient to be presumed true unless proven otherwise) is confirmed by proving each of the following ingredients:

    a. Plaintiff belongs to a protected class.
    b. Plaintiff applied for a job for which the defendant was seeking applicants.
    c. Plaintiff was qualified for the job.
    d. Plaintiff was denied the job.
    e. The position remained open, and the employer continued to seek applicants.

2. **Defendant's (employer's) case:** If the plaintiff builds a successful prima facie case, the defendant must "articulate some *legitimate, nondiscriminatory reason* for the employee's rejection" (for example, greater work experience). However, the defendant need not prove that its decision not to hire the plaintiff was, in fact, based on that legitimate, nondiscriminatory reason. The defendant simply must raise a legitimate issue of fact disputing the plaintiff's discrimination claim.

3. **Plaintiff's response:** Assuming the defendant was successful in presenting a legitimate, nondiscriminatory reason for its action, the plaintiff must show that the reason offered by the defendant was false and thus was merely a *pretext* to hide discrimination. [For an overview of disparate treatment analysis, see **http://www.hr-guide. com/data/G701.htm**]

Question

Stalter, an African American, was fired for theft after working at a Wal-Mart loading dock for four months. Stalter ate a handful of taco chips from an open bag on the countertop in the break room. As he was eating, Ellenbecker entered the room, took the bag from Stalter, and placed it in her locker. Stalter later apologized to Ellenbecker and offered to buy a new bag. She said the incident was "no big deal" and told him to "forget about it." Management then investigated, concluded Stalter had stolen the chips, and fired him. Stalter sued, claiming his termination was race based. At court Stalter argued (a) Wal-Mart could not have reasonably believed that he committed theft, especially since the owner told him to forget about it; (b) the punishment was grossly excessive; (c) a similarly situated Caucasian employee who committed a similar offense was treated much more leniently; and (d) Wal-Mart did not investigate his claims of racial harassment. Resolve this case. Explain your reasoning. See *Stalter v. Wal-Mart Stores,* 195 F.3d 285 (7th Cir. 1999).

Disparate Impact

Disparate impact analysis involves situations in which employers use legitimate employment standards that, despite their apparent neutrality, impose a heavier burden on a protected class than on other employees. For example, a preemployment test, offered with the best of intentions and constructed to be a fair measurement device, may disproportionately exclude members of a protected class and thus be unacceptable (barring an effective defense). Alternatively, an employer surreptitiously seeking to discriminate may establish an apparently neutral, superficially valid employment test that has the effect of achieving the employer's discrimination goal. For example, a tavern might require its "bouncer" to be at least 6 feet 2 inches tall and weigh at least 200 pounds. Generally, height and weight are not protected classes. However, the tavern's requirement will disproportionately exclude women, and perhaps members of certain ethnic groups as well. Was this the tavern's intent? Most likely it was not, but remember that while disparate treatment requires proof of intent, disparate impact does not.

The Test

Disparate impact analysis requires the following:

1. The plaintiff/employee must identify the *specific employment practice or policy* (such as test score, skill, or height) that caused the alleged disparate impact on the protected class.
2. The plaintiff must prove (often with statistical evidence) that the protected class is suffering an adverse or disproportionate impact caused by the employment practice or policy in question. The statistical analysis to establish a disparate impact (against black job applicants, for example) must be based on a comparison of the racial composition of the group of persons actually holding the jobs in question versus the racial composition of the *job-qualified* population in the relevant labor market.
3. Assuming a prima facie case is established in steps 1 and 2, the plaintiff/employee wins unless the defendant/employer demonstrates that the employment practice/policy is (a) *job related* and (b) *consistent with business necessity*. In the "bouncer" example above, the tavern would have to demonstrate that the height and weight requirements were related to the job in accordance with the needs of taverns.
4. If the defendant/employer succeeds in demonstrating job relatedness and business necessity, the employer wins unless the plaintiff/employee demonstrates *that an alternative, less discriminatory business practice is available and that the employer refuses to adopt it.*

   The following classic case examines disparate impact analysis.

LEGAL BRIEFCASE

Griggs v. Duke Power Co.
401 U.S. 424 (1971)

Chief Justice Burger

We granted the writ in this case to resolve the question whether an employer is prohibited by the Civil Rights Act of 1964, Title VII, from requiring a high school education or passing of a standardized general intelligence test as a condition of employment in or transfer to jobs when (a) neither standard is shown to be significantly related to successful job performance, (b) both requirements operate to disqualify Negroes at a substantially higher rate than white applicants, and (c) the jobs in question formerly had been filled only by white employees as part of a longstanding practice of giving preference to whites.

Congress provided, in Title VII of the Civil Rights Act of 1964, for class actions for enforcement of provisions of the Act and this proceeding was brought by a group of incumbent Negro employees against Duke Power Company. . . .

The district court found that prior to July 2, 1965, the effective date of the Civil Rights Act of 1964, the company openly discriminated on the basis of race in the hiring and assigning of employees at its Dan River plant. The plant was organized into five operating departments: (1) Labor, (2) Coal Handling, (3) Operations, (4) Maintenance, and (5) Laboratory and Test. Negroes were employed only in the Labor Department where the highest-paying jobs paid less than the lowest-paying jobs in the other four "operating" departments in which only whites were employed. Promotions were normally made within each department on the basis of job seniority. Transferees into a department usually began in the lowest position.

In 1955 the company instituted a policy of requiring a high school education for initial assignment to any department except Labor, and for transfer from the Coal Handling to any "inside" department (Operations, Maintenance, or Laboratory). When the company abandoned its policy of restricting Negroes to the Labor Department in 1965, completion of high school also was made a prerequisite to transfer from Labor to any other department. From the time the high school requirement was instituted to the time of trial, however, white employees hired before the time of the high school education requirement continued to perform satisfactorily and achieve promotions in the "operating" departments. Findings on this score are not challenged.

The company added a further requirement for new employees on July 2, 1965, the date on which Title VII became effective. To qualify for placement in any but the Labor Department it became necessary to register satisfactory scores on two professionally prepared aptitude tests, as well as to have a high school education. Completion of high school alone continued to render employees eligible for transfer to the four desirable departments from which Negroes had been excluded if the incumbent had been employed prior to the time of the new requirement. In September 1965 the company began to permit incumbent employees who lacked a high school education to qualify for transfer from Labor or Coal Handling to an "inside" job by passing two tests—the Wonderlic Personnel Test, which purports to measure general intelligence, and the Bennett Mechanical Comprehension Test. Neither was directed or intended to measure the ability to learn to perform a particular job or category of jobs. The requisite scores used for both initial hiring and transfer approximated the national median for high school graduates.

The District Court had found that while the company previously followed a policy of overt racial discrimination in a period prior to the Act, such conduct had ceased. The District Court also concluded that Title VII was intended to be prospective only and, consequently, the impact of prior inequities was beyond the reach of corrective action authorized by the Act.

. . . The Court of Appeals concluded there was no violation of the Act.

* * * * *

The objective of Congress in the enactment of Title VII is plain from the language of the statute. It was to achieve equality of employment opportunities and remove barriers that have operated in the past to favor an identifiable group of white employees over other employees. Under the Act, practices, procedures, or tests neutral on their face, and even neutral in terms of intent, cannot be maintained if they operate to "freeze" the status quo of prior discriminatory employment practices.

The Court of Appeals' opinion, and the partial dissent, agreed that, on the record in the present case, "whites register far better on the company's alternative requirements" than Negroes. This consequence would appear to be directly traceable to race. Basic intelligence must have the means of articulation to manifest itself fairly in a testing process. Because they are Negroes, petitioners have long received inferior education in segregated schools.

. . . Congress did not intend by Title VII, however, to guarantee a job to every person regardless of qualifications. In short, the Act does not command that any person be hired simply because he was formerly the subject of discrimination, or because he is a member of a minority group. Discriminatory preference for any group, minority or majority, is precisely and only what Congress has proscribed. . . .

. . . The Act proscribes not only overt discrimination but also practices that are fair in form, but discriminatory in operation. The touchstone is business necessity. If an employment practice which operates to exclude Negroes cannot be shown to be related to job performance, the practice is prohibited.

On the record before us, neither the high school completion requirement nor the general intelligence test is shown to bear a demonstrable relationship to successful performance of the jobs for which it was used. Both were adopted, as the Court of Appeals noted, without meaningful study of their relationship to job-performance ability. Rather, a vice president of the company testified, the requirements were instituted on the company's judgment that they generally would improve the overall quality of the workforce.

The evidence, however, shows that employees who have not completed high school or taken the tests have continued to perform satisfactorily and make progress in departments for which the high school and test criteria are not used. . . .

The Court of Appeals held that the company had adopted the diploma and test requirements without any "intention to discriminate against Negro employees." We do not suggest that either the District Court or the Court of Appeals erred in examining the employer's intent; but good intent or absence of discriminatory intent does not redeem employment procedures or testing mechanisms that operate as "built-in headwinds" for minority groups and are unrelated to measuring job capability.

* * * * *

The facts of this case demonstrate the inadequacy of broad and general testing devices as well as the infirmity of using diplomas or degrees as fixed measures of capability. . . .

The company contends that its general intelligence tests are specifically permitted by § 703(h) of the Act. That section authorizes the use of "any professionally developed ability test" that is not "designed, intended *or used* to discriminate because of race. . . ." (Emphasis added.)

The Equal Employment Opportunity Commission, having enforcement responsibility, has issued guidelines interpreting § 703(h) to permit only the use of job-related tests. The administrative interpretation of the Act by the enforcing agency is entitled to great deference. Since the Act and its legislative history support the commission's construction, this affords good reason to treat the guidelines as expressing the will of Congress.

. . . From the sum of the legislative history relevant in this case, the conclusion is inescapable that the EEOC's construction of § 703(h) to require that employment tests be job related comports with congressional intent.

Nothing in the Act precludes the use of testing or measuring procedures; obviously they are useful. What Congress has forbidden is giving these devices and mechanisms controlling force unless they are demonstrably a reasonable measure of job performance. Congress has not commanded that the less qualified be preferred over the better qualified simply because of minority origins. Far from disparaging job qualifications as such, Congress has made such qualifications the controlling factor, so that race, religion, nationality, and sex become irrelevant. What Congress has commanded is that any tests used must measure the person for the job and not the person in the abstract.

The judgment of the Court of Appeals is . . . reversed.

Questions

1. According to the Supreme Court, what was Congress's objective in enacting Title VII?
2. Had Duke Power been able to establish that its reasons for adopting the diploma and test standards were entirely without discriminatory intent, would the Supreme Court have ruled differently? Explain.
3. What is the central issue in this case?
4. Why was North Carolina's social and educational history relevant to the outcome of the case?
5. Statistical evidence showed that 35 percent of new hires in grocery and produce at Lucky Stores, a retail grocery chain, were women, while 84 percent of new hires in deli, bakery, and general merchandise were women. Statistical evidence also showed that 31 percent of those promoted into apprentice jobs in grocery and produce were women, while women comprised 75 percent of those promoted into apprentice jobs in deli, bakery, and general merchandise. Grocery and produce jobs generally were higher-paying jobs than those in deli, bakery, and general merchandise. Women received significantly fewer overtime hours than men.

   Do these facts regarding Lucky Stores suggest discrimination? Explain. See *Stender v. Lucky Stores, Inc.* 803 F. Supp. 259 (DC Cal. 1992).
6. Gregory, a black male, was offered employment by Litton Systems as a sheet metal worker. As part of a standard procedure he completed a form listing a total of 14 nontraffic arrests but no convictions. Thereupon the employment offer was withdrawn. Gregory then brought suit, claiming he was a victim of racial discrimination.

   a. Explain the foundation of his argument.
   b. Decide the case. See *Gregory v. Litton,* 412 F.2d 631 (9th Cir. 1972).
7. Eighty-one percent of the hires at Consolidated Service Systems, a small Chicago janitorial company, were of Korean origin. The EEOC brought a disparate treatment claim, saying the firm discriminated in favor of Koreans by relying primarily on word-of-mouth recruiting. Hwang, the owner, is Korean. Seventy-three percent of the job applicants were Korean. One percent of the Chicago-area workforce is Korean, and not more than 3 percent of the janitorial workforce for the area is Korean. The court found no persuasive evidence of intentional discrimination, although the government claimed that 99 applicants were denied jobs because they were not Koreans.

   a. Does restricting hiring to members of one ethnic group constitute discrimination where hiring is accomplished by word of mouth? Explain.
   b. What if a firm, using the word-of-mouth approach, hired only white applicants? Explain.
   c. In this case, the EEOC brought but dropped a disparate impact claim. Analyze the case using the disparate impact test. See *Equal Employment Opportunity Commission v. Consolidated Service Systems,* 989 F.2d 233 (7th Cir. 1993).

Statutory Defenses

In addition to the aforementioned defenses against disparate treatment and disparate impact claims, Title VII also affords specific exemptions or defenses, three of which are of particular note: (1) seniority, (2) employee testing, and (3) bona fide occupational qualification. Bona fide occupational qualifications are addressed in the next section as part of the sex discrimination discussion.

Seniority

Differences in wages and conditions of employment are permissible under the Civil Rights Act of 1964 where those differences are the result of a bona fide (good faith) seniority system, as long as the system was not intended to hide or facilitate discrimination. Seniority is important because it often determines who is laid off first and who gets promotions, vacations, and so forth. Because white people often have greater seniority than blacks, the result is that seniority may perpetuate the effects of historical discrimination. The Supreme Court has made it clear, however, that a bona fide seniority system that perpetuates past wrongs is illegal only if discriminatory intent is proven.[15]

Job-Related Employee Testing

Many employers use testing in making hiring and promotion decisions. The availability of online applications has contributed to an increase in this practice.[16] In order to avoid a disparate impact created by employee testing, an employer must be able to show that the test in question is job-related and consistent with business necessity; that is, the test must evaluate an individual's skills as they relate to the relevant employment opportunity. To prevent unlawful disparate treatment, an employer's test must be uniformly applied regardless of an applicant's or employee's race, sex, or other protected categories. For example, Title VII prohibits an employer from testing the reading ability of African-American applicants or employees while not requiring the same test of their white counterparts.[17]

Division I College Athletics and Discrimination

In 1992 the National Collegiate Athletic Association (NCAA) Division I schools adopted Proposition 16, which determined athletic eligibility based on the student athlete's GPA and standardized test score (ACT/SAT). For example, a student athlete with a 2.0 high school GPA needed a 1010 SAT score to ensure athletic eligibility as a college freshman. Kelly Pryor, an African American, signed a National Letter of Intent (NLI) to play soccer on scholarship at San Jose State University in the fall of 1999. Warren Spivey, an African American, signed an NLI to play football on scholarship at the University of Connecticut. Neither Pryor nor Spivey met the Proposition 16 requirements. They sued, claiming the NCAA intentionally discriminated against them because of their race. Essentially, the plaintiffs claimed that Proposition 16 achieved the NCAA goal of improving graduation rates for black athletes relative to white athletes simply by screening out greater numbers of black athletes than white athletes. The plaintiffs provided evidence indicating that the

NCAA knew that Proposition 16 would disqualify black athletes in greater proportions than white athletes. In effect, the NCAA, according to the plaintiffs, had intentionally established explicit race-based goals rather than providing a racially neutral way of deciding who would qualify for scholarship eligibility. How would you rule on the case? Explain.

Source: Pryor v. NCAA, 288 F.3d 548 (3d Cir. 2002).

The Four-Fifths Rule and Disparate Impact

If the selection rate (such as the percentage passing a test, being hired, or being promoted) for any protected class is less than 80 percent of the selection rate for the group with the highest selection rate, then the employment practice in question will be presumed to create a disparate impact. An employer falling below that standard must prove the job relatedness of the employment practice in question and demonstrate that a good-faith effort was made to find a selection procedure that lessened the disparate impact on protected classes. [For an extensive employment discrimination database, see **http://topics. law.cornell.edu/wex/Employment_discrimination**]

National Origin: Special Issues

Employment discrimination often reflects larger social issues that come to influence workplace relations. A dramatic example is found in the aftermath of the September 11, 2001 terrorist attacks on the United States. Between September 11, 2001 and September 11, 2004, the EEOC processed over 900 claims of national origin discrimination associated with the September 11 attacks, resulting in approximately $3.2 million in monetary relief.[18]

In 2005, the EEOC settled a claim it brought against Pesce, an upscale Houston-based restaurant on behalf of Karim El-Raheb, former Pesce general manager. In his August 2001 review, El-Raheb had been told he was doing very well. After business declined following the September 11 terrorist attacks, Pesce's coowners speculated that customers may be frightened by El-Raheb's appearance and name, suggesting that he could "pass for Hispanic" and should change his name to "something Latin." In November 2001, El-Raheb was fired because "things weren't working out." El-Raheb received $150,000 in monetary relief.[19]

Speak English Only?

Reflecting a national debate over whether English should be the official language of the United States, "Speak English Only" rules in the workplace have generated controversy as well as national origin discrimination claims based on the disparate impact these rules may have on members of ethnic groups whose primary language is not English.

Employers argue that the rules are necessary when dealing with customers, to maintain job safety, and to encourage congenial worker relations. EEOC guidelines prohibit employers from imposing a blanket ban on employees speaking their primary language in the workplace, but an English-only rule at certain times is permissible if justified by business necessity and if adequately explained to the employees.

In *Garcia v. Spun Steak Co.,* the employer, a producer of meat products, instituted an English-only rule for its bilingual employees to enhance safety and product quality and to address allegations that some employees were making rude comments in Spanish to English-speaking employees. The English-only rule applied to work but not to lunch, breaks, or employees' own time. The employer's rule was upheld by a federal appellate court on the grounds that it was narrowly defined and did not create a discriminatory atmosphere.[20]

Question

Rodriguez, a FedEx employee of Hispanic origin, informed FedEx's Regional Human Resources Manager Adkinson that he wanted to obtain a promotion to a supervisory position. After applying and interviewing for an available supervisory position, Rodriguez was rejected. The manager who interviewed Rodriguez found him to be qualified, but did not hire him because of Adkinson's expressed concerns that Rodriguez's "accent and speech pattern" would undermine his ability to rise through the corporate ranks. Another FedEx manager stated that when he asked Adkinson why Rodriguez had not received the promotion, Adkinson made derogatory comments about Rodriguez's "language" and "how he speaks." Is FedEx liable for national origin discrimination based on its failure to promote Rodriguez? Decide. Explain. See *Rodriguez v. FedEx Freight East, Inc.,* 487 F.3d 1001 (6th Cir. 2007).

Harassment: The Example of Racial Harassment

The hangman's noose, perhaps the most hurtful and disgraceful expression of racism, sometimes appears in America's increasingly integrated workplaces. On January 24, 2008, the EEOC announced the $465,000 settlement of a racial harassment lawsuit on behalf of African-American employees of Henredon Furniture Industries. The lawsuit alleged that these employees had for years been subjected to a persistent racially hostile work environment that included the display of hangman's nooses. Racial harassment charges filed with the EEOC, some of which similarly involve hangman's nooses as well as verbal threats of lynching, more than doubled between 1991 and 2007.[21]

Legal requirements and the evolving standards for analyzing harassment claims will be explored later in the context of sexual harassment—perhaps the most familiar form of workplace harassment.

Recent court decisions suggest that the Supreme Court's reasoning in sexual harassment cases will likely apply to cases of racial or national origin harassment. In addition to overt forms of harassment such as racial slurs, some decisions suggest that the use of more subtle "code words" may constitute racial and/or national origin harassment. In *Aman v. Cort Furniture Rental Corporation,*[22] two black employees claimed that they were subjected to a racially hostile work environment in part because black employees were labeled by coworkers and managers with racist "code words" such as "all of you," "one of them," and "poor people." The court, in finding for the employees, ruled that certain phrases in the employment setting cannot be excused as mere rudeness and may, in the totality of the circumstances, add up to discrimination so severe that it creates an abusive work environment. In addition to those mentioned in *Aman,* a number of other code phrases might bring legal problems: "They're all stupid and lazy." "Your type." "All they're interested in is drugs." "You people don't understand how to save money."[23]

KKK

"Auburn University said ... it has indefinitely suspended 15 students who wore Ku Klux Klan costumes and blackface to fraternity Halloween parties."

Source: Associated Press, "Racist Costumes Draw Suspensions," *Waterloo/Cedar Falls Courier,* November 16, 2001, p. A2.

Part Three—Sex Discrimination

Equality for Women

In 2006, more than 40 years after the 1963 passage of the Equal Pay Act, American women working full-time earn about 77 cents for every dollar earned by men; up dramatically from the 59 cents of the early 1960s, but still far short of equality.[24] Of course, factors beyond discrimination, including decisions to interrupt careers for child rearing, account for some of that disparity; but allegations of sex discrimination remain common.

The power and limits of statutory protections against sex discrimination are seen in recent Title VII class-action lawsuits brought by female employees alleging disparity in pay, work assignments, and promotion. In 2007, a federal judge approved a $46 million settlement of a class-action lawsuit brought against Morgan Stanley representing 3,000 female financial advisers and trainees claiming discrimination in compensation, promotion, and work assignments.[25] At this writing, Wal-Mart faces a Title VII class action based on its allegedly discriminatory pay and promotion policies.[26]

Glass Ceiling?   Critics say a "glass ceiling" of prejudice holds women back from roles of power and career advancement. In 2005, women held almost 15 percent of the board seats at the 500 largest companies in the United States, but less than 2 percent of *Fortune* 500 companies had a female chief executive officer.[27] According to a 2006 survey, most women would agree that a glass ceiling restricts their upward professional mobility; however, they enjoy the same level of satisfaction with their professional advancement as men.[28] The importance women typically place on such factors as relationships with coworkers, as found in a 2005 study, might explain why the glass ceiling does not necessarily create job dissatisfaction among women.[29]

A Double Standard?

Linda Hamburger is no wallflower, and she was working at a Florida utility company when the "F-bomb" escaped her mouth in a moment of frustration. It would not have been a big deal if it had come from a man, but Hamburger says it got her fired for insubordination.

Women in business argue that their careers can be destroyed by language that is routine when uttered by men. Further, experts argue that women may unintentionally distract men and give men ammunition for laughs at the expense of women by uttering legitimate language with a sexual subtext such as "screwed up," "stay abreast," and "get it off my chest."

Source: Del Jones, "Watch What You Say, Women Are Told," *Des Moines Register*, December 6, 2004, p. 8C

Analysis of Sex Discrimination: Current Issues

Sex discrimination claims brought under Title VII include disparate treatment and disparate impact, as well as sexual harassment. Employee training and policies targeting sex discrimination have become common in the American workplace. However, the number of Title VII sex-based discrimination charges filed with the EEOC remained relatively steady from 1997—2007. Thus, sex discrimination claims remain a critical area of Title VII analysis.

PRACTICING ETHICS   More Evidence in the Ongoing Gender Struggle

- Department of Education statistics reveal that men, whatever their race or socioeconomic status, are less likely than women to earn bachelor's degrees—and those who do take longer to complete their programs than women. Young men from low-income families are the most underrepresented on college campuses. Federal data show, however, that when it comes to gaining a college education, the gap between whites and blacks or Hispanics is larger than the gender gap.

- According to the 2005 National Survey of Student Engagement, male college students were more likely to spend at least 11 hours a week relaxing or socializing compared to their female counterparts, who said they spent at least that much time preparing for class. Men also admitted they frequently come to class unprepared. Another study conducted by the National Endowment for the Arts indicates that reading rates are falling three times as fast among young men as among young women.

- Researchers at *US News & World Report* magazine concluded that, based on data from more than 1,400 colleges and universities, many four-year institutions have maintained gender balance among students by admitting many more men than women, even when women candidates were more qualified. Admissions directors want to maintain gender balance to, among other things, attract the best candidates of both sexes: when the gender balance on campus tilts out of balance in favor of either gender, students lose interest in attending.

- Harvard University president Lawrence Summers, in a spectacularly successful effort to be provocative, reportedly said in 2005 that women may be underrepresented in senior math and science posts because women *may* be, on average, innately inferior to men in advanced mathematics. Summers later apologized and announced a new initiative to recruit women for the sciences.

Questions

1. *a.* Should we be concerned about the declining proportion of men who are graduating from college? Explain.

   b. Should we be more concerned with economic, racial, and ethnic disparities in college graduation rates than with declining rates for males?

2. *a.* Given his highly influential position in higher education, was it wrong of President Summers even to suggest that women *might* be innately inferior to men in mathematics?

   b. Is it wrong of some colleges and universities to favor men in admissions over women?

Sources: Tamar Lewin, "At Colleges, Women Are Leaving Men in the Dust," *New York Times*, July 9, 2006 (**http://www.nytimes.com/2006/07/09/education**); David Brooks, "The Gender Gap at School," *New York Times*, June 11, 2006, p. 12; "Gender Bias in College Admissions," *Christian Science Monitor*, July 24, 2007 (**http://www.csmonitor.com/2007/0724/p08s01-comn.html**) and Kingsley R. Browne, "Women in Science: Biological Factors Should Not Be Ignored," *Cardozo Women's Law Journal* 11 (2005) 509-528 at 509 (citations omitted).

Sex Discrimination: Disparate Impact

The following case illustrates the analysis of a sex discrimination claim alleging disparate impact.

LEGAL BRIEFCASE

Pietras v. Farmingville Fire District   180 F.3d 468 (2d Cir. 1999); cert. den. 528 U.S. 948 (1999)

Circuit Judge Calabresi

The district court found that Farmingville's physical agility test ("PAT"), which all probationary volunteer firefighters were required to pass in order to become full-fledged volunteer firefighters, had a disparate impact on women.

*   *   *   *   *

BACKGROUND

Farmingville is the governing body of a volunteer fire department that has approximately 100 members. Pietras was a probationary (i.e., trainee) firefighter in the Farmingville Department. Even as a probationary volunteer, Pietras was entitled to numerous firefighter benefits under state law and the by-laws of the de-

partment. These included (1) a retirement pension, (2) life insurance, (3) death benefits, (4) disability insurance, and (5) some medical benefits.

Before Pietras could become a full member of the department, however, she and all other probationary volunteers were required to pass a newly instituted PAT.[1] The PAT consisted of a series of physical tasks that the applicants had to complete within a specified time limit. The most difficult of these nine labors was the "charged hose drag," which involved dragging a water-filled hose—weighing approximately 280 pounds—over a distance of 150 feet.

---

[1] Pietras passed both a medical exam and a written exam that were also preconditions to becoming a full firefighter.

To determine the appropriate time limit for the PAT, Farmingville officials asked various members of the department to take the test. Forty-four firefighters participated in these trials. Of the 44 test-takers, 33 were males who served as full firefighters, 6 were male probationary members, 3 were male junior members, one was Jeanine Serpe, a female full firefighter, and one was Pietras. The average times of these subgroups were:

Sample Pool	Average Time
Full males (33)	3:12
Probationary males (6)	2:47
Junior males (3)	2:52
Full female (Serpe)	5:30
Probationary female (Pietras)	5:21

From these results, Farmingville set four minutes as the time within which the labors had to be completed. The four-minute threshold was determined by taking the average of all the (mostly male) test runs (approximately 3:30) and then adding an extra half-minute "to have some leeway." There was some concern expressed at a 1993 Farmingville Board meeting that neither Serpe nor Pietras had been able to finish the PAT in anything close to four minutes, but Farmingville nevertheless instituted the four-minute cutoff.

Following the implementation of the PAT, Pietras tried and failed the test twice. During this same period, six other female probationary firefighters took the test. Four of these women completed the PAT in under four minutes and therefore passed. One woman failed to complete the test for an unknown reason. And one woman did not complete the test despite repeated efforts to drag the water-filled hose over the required distance. All of the 24 male probationary volunteers who took the test at about this time passed.

Following her second failure to pass the PAT, Pietras was fired from her volunteer position at Farmingville.

*   *   *   *   *

Pietras filed suit in district court, alleging that Farmingville had violated Title VII of the Civil Rights Act of 1964.

*   *   *   *   *

At trial . . . , Pietras presented testimony from Dr. Robert Otto, an expert exercise physiologist. Dr. Otto conducted an extensive review of the physical agility tests administered by various volunteer and paid fire departments and concluded (a) that the four-minute limit in the Farmingville test had a disparate impact on women, and (b) that it was not job related.

After reviewing the evidence, the district court ruled for Pietras.

*   *   *   *   *

[T]he court concluded that "the record is bereft of any evidence" that a four-minute time limit to finish the PAT was job related.[2]

In support of its finding of disparate impact, the court noted that the male pass rate on the PAT was 95 percent (63 out of 66) while the female pass rate was only 57 percent (4 out of 7). Relying on the "four-fifths" rule set forth in the EEOC Guidelines, the court reasoned that "a pass rate for women which is less [than] four-fifths (or 80 percent) of the pass rate for men typically signifies disparate impact sufficient to establish a *prima facie* case. . . . Therefore, the gender imbalance [in this case] more than satisfies the 80 percent standard." This statistical evidence (which was corroborated by Dr. Otto's testimony concerning the effect of the PAT on women) was deemed by the district court to be enough to establish disparate impact.

Farmingville appeals.

DISCUSSION

*   *   *   *   *

Disparate Impact

*   *   *   *   *

Farmingville asserts that, even if the statistical figures before the district court were correct, a sample of seven female test takers is simply too small to support a disparate impact finding.

*   *   *   *   *

In the case before us, however, Pietras presented more than just statistics. After conducting an exhaustive analysis of the practices of other fire departments, Dr. Otto provided expert testimony on the disparate impact of Farmingville's PAT. This expert testimony, combined with the statistics Pietras did present, comfortably tips the scales in favor of the district court's finding of disparate impact.

Affirmed.

Questions

1. *a.* Why did the court conclude that the Farmingville Fire Department had discriminated against Pietras?
   b. Did the court conclude that Farmingville intended to discriminate? Explain.
   c. What, if anything, could Farmingville have done differently to win this case?
2. *a.* Shouldn't we always choose the strongest, fastest firefighters as long as they are otherwise well qualified? Explain.

---

[2][T]here is no evidence at all to indicate that the time chosen for the test reflected the needs of the job. In fact, the record makes clear that Farmingville selected the four-minute figure simply by taking the average of all the test scores and then arbitrarily adding some extra time.

b. Do the firefighters' rescue efforts at the World Trade Center on September 11, 2001, indicate that only men should serve as firefighters? Explain.

3. *a.* How would you argue that Women's Workout World, a health and exercise club, should be able to lawfully decline to accept men as customers and/or employees?

b. Decide the case. Explain. See *U.S. EEOC v. Sedita,* 816 F.Supp. 1291 (N.D. Ill. 1993).

4. Dianne Rawlinson sought employment as a prison guard in Alabama. She was a 22-year-old college graduate with a degree in correctional psychology. She was denied employment because she failed to meet the 120-pound weight requirement for the job. The state also required such employees to be at least 5 feet 2 inches tall. Alabama operated four all-male, maximum security prisons. The district court characterized the Alabama prison system as one of "rampant violence." Rawlinson sued, claiming employment discrimination. Decide. Explain. See *Dothard v. Rawlinson,* 97 S.Ct. 2720 (1977).

Pietras **or** *SEPTA?*

The Southeastern Pennsylvania Transportation Authority (SEPTA) was sued on sex discrimination grounds by several female job applicants who had been rejected for employment as police officers. The women were unable to run 1.5 miles in 12 minutes, a job requirement. A disparate impact was established with evidence that 56 percent of the men passed the test, while 93 percent of women could not pass, but the Third Circuit Federal Court of Appeals ruled that the standard was consistent with business necessity and therefore did not violate Title VII. SEPTA was able to satisfy the court that running up and down subway stairs and pursuing wrongdoers required fitness like that measured by the test. Evidence also established that minimal training would allow most women to qualify.

The case against SEPTA had been pursued for a number of years by President Clinton's Justice Department, but President Bush's Justice Department decided to withdraw its support from the case, saying that officer fitness is critical to public safety.

Source: Lanning v. SEPTA, 308 F.3d 286 (3d Cir. 2002).

Bona Fide Occupational Qualification

Often in intentional sex discrimination cases, the key inquiry involves the *bona fide occupational qualification (BFOQ)* defense provided by Title VII. Discrimination is lawful where sex, religion, or national origin is a BFOQ reasonably necessary to the normal operation of that business. The exclusion of race and color from the list suggests Congress thought those categories always unacceptable as bona fide occupational qualifications. The BFOQ was meant to be a very limited exception applicable to situations where specific inherent characteristics are necessary to the job (for example, wet nurse) or where authenticity (actors), privacy (nurses), or safety (guards) are required. Broadly, the BFOQ defense rests on this question: Is being a female, for example, necessary to perform the *essence* of the job?

Essence

An employer can lawfully insist on a woman to fill a woman's modeling role because being female goes to the essence of the job. Airlines, on the other hand, cannot hire only women as flight attendants even if customers prefer females and even if females perform the supplementary elements of the job (like charming passengers) better than most men. Those duties "are tangential to the essence of the business involved"[30] (the essence being the maintenance of safe, orderly conditions, providing service as needed, etc). Presumably, gender has little to do with the ability to perform those essential ingredients of the job.

Many employers have simply assumed that women could not perform certain tasks. For example, women were thought to be insufficiently aggressive for sales roles, and women were denied employment because they were assumed to have a higher turnover rate due to the desire to marry and have children. Those stereotypes are at the heart of sex discrimination litigation generally and do not support a BFOQ defence.

Hooters

Can the 40-state restaurant chain Hooters lawfully decline to hire men to be food servers? The article that follows explains the 1997 settlement of a lawsuit addressing that question.

READING Hooters Agrees to Hire Men in Support Roles, But It Will Still Hire Scantily Clad Women; Discrimination

CHICAGO—Hooters of America Inc. said that it will not change its policy of hiring scantily clad "Hooters girls" to serve customers despite its tentative $3.75 million settlement with male applicants who sued it for sex discrimination after being turned down for jobs because of their gender.

Several class-action lawsuits were filed around the country beginning in 1993 on behalf of rejected male applicants, and the suits were consolidated in Chicago.

"We've settled the entire issue," said Mike McNeil, vice president of marketing for the privately held, 204-restaurant Hooters chain. The settlement "preserves the integrity of the Hooters concept—the service of food and beverages will continue to be performed by the Hooters girls." The settlement allows Atlanta-based Hooters to continue luring customers with an exclusively female staff of Hooters Girls, but the chain agreed to create a few other support jobs, such as bartenders and hosts, that must be filled without regard to gender.

"Our business is on the female sex appeal side," McNeil said. "Over the years, there have been lots of people who have suggested [offering some male sex appeal]. Our answer is, if you think that's a good, economically viable idea, get your capital together and go ahead and do it."

In the agreement the restaurant chain agreed to set aside $2 million as compensation for men who were turned away from jobs because of their gender. Lawyers will get $.75 million. The agreement is subject to U.S. District Court approval.

The Equal Employment Opportunity Commission investigated the discrimination complaint for four years, then dropped it in 1996, saying it had more important cases to pursue. The EEOC did, however, suggest that the chain hire men. The recommendation drew snickers and ridicule. The chain put on a mock advertising campaign featuring a burly, mustachioed man wearing a blond wig, short shorts, and stuffed shirt, with the slogan "Come on, Washington. Get a grip."

The private lawsuit settled a consolidation of legal action brought by seven men from Illinois and Maryland who argued that their failure to get jobs at Hooters was a violation of federal law.

Source: *Baltimore Sun*, October 1, 1997, p. 3C. Reprinted by permission of the copyright holder, The Associated Press.

AFTERWORD

According to published accounts, the parties agreed that a woman would continue to work behind each Hooters bar, but an assistant could be either male or female. Likewise, men or women could serve as greeters and do work such as clearing tables.

Questions

1. *a.* Explain the plaintiffs' view that Hooters' hiring policy constitutes impermissible sexual discrimination.

   b. Explain Hooters' claim that it does not violate Title VII.

2. Is Hooters' hiring policy better left to the market than to the courts? Explain.

Appearance Policies: An Unequal Burden?

Harrah's Reno, Nevada casino instituted a "Personal Best" appearance policy requiring its female bartenders to wear makeup while prohibiting their male counterparts from wearing any. After a successful twenty-year career as a Harrah's bartender, Darlene Jespersen was fired for refusing to wear makeup under the policy. Ms. Jespersen brought a Title VII lawsuit. Decide.

Source: Jespersen v. Harrah's, 444 F.3d 1104 (9th Cir. 2006).

Parent and Manager?

Antidiscrimination law has been critical in allowing women to pursue careers and in providing some refuge from the professional disadvantages of pregnancy experienced at some workplaces. The Pregnancy Discrimination Act (PDA) amended Title VII of the Civil Rights Act of 1964 so that discrimination with regard to pregnancy is treated as a form of sex discrimination. Broadly, the PDA requires that pregnant employees be treated the same as all other employees with temporary disabilities. In general, an employer should not ask job applicants about pregnancy, and applicants have no duty to reveal that pregnancy. Nor can a pregnant employee be forced to take time off or be forced to quit due to pregnancy. Pregnancy discrimination complaints to the EEOC and local Fair Employment Practices agencies have been among the fastest-rising claims, with an increase of over 40 percent from 1997 to 2007.[31]

In a variation on pregnancy discrimination, a federal court of appeals in 2004 recognized a particular form of gender bias that might be thought of as "maternal" or "caregiver" discrimination. In that case, the court ruled that a lower court must hear a woman's complaint that she was discriminated against merely because she is a mother. Elana Back, a school psychologist, claims that she was denied tenure, despite high performance, because her bosses doubted her ability to do her job and be a mother.[32]

Questions

1. Waitresses at the Rustic Inn were prohibited under a written policy from waiting tables past their fifth month of pregnancy and required either to suspend working or to switch to working as cashiers or hostesses, who are paid less since they do not receive gratuities. The EEOC filed a lawsuit against the employer on behalf of a class of three aggrieved employees, alleging that the policy violated the PDA. Decide. See *EEOC v. W&O Inc.,* 213 F.3d 600 (11th Cir. 2000).

2. "Family Responsibilities Discrimination" (FRD) is gaining recognition. While no express antidiscrimination statutory protection is afforded to parents or caregivers, FRD claims may be based on existing statutes such as Title VII. For example, mothers may face a "maternal wall" in their professional advancement created by sex-based stereotypes, which may result in unlawful disparate treatment based on sex. In May 2007, the EEOC issued an Enforcement Guidance regarding FRD claims [see EEOC *Enforcement Guidance: Unlawful Disparate Treatment of Workers with Caregiving Responsibilities* at **http://www.eeoc.gov/policy/docs/caregiving.html**]. Besides avoiding FRD liability, how might an employer benefit from effectively supporting employees' balancing of work and life responsibilities? Should parents and other caregivers be given express statutory protection against employment discrimination? Explain.

Equal Pay

Title VII affords broad protection from discrimination in pay because of sex. The Equal Pay Act of 1963 directly forbids discrimination on the basis of sex by paying wages to employees of one sex at a rate less than the rate paid to employees of the opposite sex for equal work on jobs requiring equal skill, effort, and responsibility and performed under similar working conditions (*equal* has been interpreted to mean "substantially equal"). The act provides for certain exceptions. Unequal wage payments are lawful if paid pursuant to (1) a seniority system, (2) a merit system, (3) a system that measures earnings by quantity or quality of production, or (4) a differential based on "any . . . factor other than sex." The employer seeking to avoid a violation of the Equal Pay Act can adjust its wage structure by raising the pay of the disfavored sex. Lowering the pay of the favored sex violates the act.

Women's Basketball Coach

Former University of Southern California head women's basketball coach Marianne Stanley sued the university for violating the Equal Pay Act because she was not as well paid as then head men's basketball coach George Raveling. Both coaches had successful won/lost records. The university defended the pay differential by pointing to Raveling's 14 years of coaching experience beyond Stanley's, his having coached the U.S. Olympic team, his marketing experience outside of coaching, and his books on basketball. Stanley could not point to similar credentials. Did the university violate the Equal Pay Act? See *Stanley v. University of Southern California,* 178 F. 3d 1069 (9th Cir. 1999); cert.den. 528 U.S. 1022 (1999).

Sexual Harassment

Sexual harassment is a form of sex discrimination actionable under Title VII. As the following article clearly warns, addressing sexual harassment in the workplace has become an important component of management practice.

Settlement OKd in Smith Barney Bias Suit

Times **Staff and Wire Reports**

A federal judge approved a unique settlement of the sex bias case against Salomon Smith Barney, allowing the investment house to close an ugly chapter in its treatment of women.

* * * * *

[T]he settlement of the class-action bias case does not constitute an admission by Smith Barney of any wrongdoing. The firm will bear all costs associated with notifying 22,000 potential claimants about the settlement.

"We believe the settlement focuses on effecting real change and progress, rather than simply delivering monetary awards," Smith Barney said in a statement.

Marianne Dalton, 37, of Westlake Village[, CA] was one of 23 women who filed the initial class-action bias complaint. A retail broker for Smith Barney's Los Angeles office in 1995, she said she repeatedly witnessed her boss changing his clothes.

"I would hear unbelievably lewd comments about his personal life" while he would strip to his underwear, Dalton said. When she reported her experiences to management, she said she was transferred to the Beverly Hills office. But she said her reputation for speaking against her boss preceded her. When she quit a year later, she could not get a similar position elsewhere.

"I was blacklisted . . . because of this case," Dalton said.

* * * * *

Dalton and the 22 other original complainants will receive a total of $1.9 million as part of the settlement, which does not include punitive damages.

Women employees alleged that they were harassed and intimidated by senior male workers who engaged in fraternity-house antics in the "boom-boom room," a basement space in a Smith Barney branch in Garden City, N.Y., on Long Island.

The suit also alleged that women were denied promotions at Smith Barney and that the firm ignored complaints of abuse and unwanted sexual advances and investigated claims in a way that subjected female workers to retaliation.

The settlement allows the women to resolve discrimination claims using an independent arbitrator instead of being forced to go to mandatory industry-sponsored arbitration.

In the settlement, the firm will spend more than $15 million over four years on programs to recruit and promote women and minorities. That figure could rise under a penalty provision of the settlement.

* * * * *

Source: *Los Angeles Times,* July 25, 1998, part D, p. 2, Reprinted by permission of the copyright holder, The Associated Press.

What Is It?   Often we are not sure which behaviors constitute sexual harassment. A 1992 Roper Poll summarized 22 situations and asked the respondents which of them amounted to sexual harassment. Clear majorities found sexual harassment in only three of the situations. Those involved direct questions about sexual practices and being required to sleep with the boss in exchange for a raise. Strong majorities rejected a finding of sexual harassment in such situations as these:

• A compliment about a coworker's appearance.
• Asking a coworker for a date.
• A woman looking a man "up and down" as he walks by.
• Referring to women as "girls."

A middle ground of great confusion included such situations as these:

• A male boss calling a female "honey."
• A man looking a woman "up and down" as she walks by.
• Men in the office repeatedly discussing the appearance of female coworkers.[33]

Male Worker Harassed at Domino's

For five months, David Papa's boss at a Domino's Pizza made comments about his body, touched him, and told him she loved him. Six days after he told her to stop, she fired him.

A federal judge ordered the pizza chain to pay Papa $237,000 in damages in the first case the U.S. Equal Employment Opportunity Commission ever took to trial involving a man harassed by a woman.

Source: Associated Press, "Male Worker Harassed at Domino's, Judge Rules," *Des Moines Register,* November 23, 1995, p. 4A.

The Law of Sexual Harassment

In brief, sexual harassment, as a form of discrimination, consists of unwelcome sexual advances, requests for sexual favors, and other verbal or physical conduct of a sexual nature that (1) becomes a condition of employment, (2) becomes a basis for employment decisions, or (3) unreasonably interferes with work performance or creates a hostile working environment.

Sexual harassment cases have been divided into a pair of categories, *quid pro quo* (this for that, such as a sexual experience in exchange for keeping one's job) and *hostile environment* (a workplace rendered offensive and abusive by sexual comments, pictures, jokes, sexual aggression, and the like where no employment benefit is gained or lost). Note that hostile work environments may be created by offensive or abusive conduct involving protected categories other than sex, including race, religion, national origin, and disability. The law of sexual harassment, particularly in regard to hostile work environments, may apply to these cases.

The Test

Once we have some idea of behavior that constitutes sexual harassment, our concern turns to which remedies are available for the victims. Although the question is not settled, most federal courts to date have ruled that victims of sexual harassment seeking recovery under Title VII cannot sue the person who actually committed the harassment. The victim might be able to sue the wrongdoer under a state statute or by using a tort claim such as assault, but under Title VII, *personal liability* appears not to be available. This result, if the current judicial pattern continues, is not as unfair as might at first appear because well-settled principles of justice hold the employer and not the employer's agents or employees, generally responsible for workplace wrongdoing. The victim, therefore, can seek damages from the employer as the responsible party. A pair of 1998 U.S. Supreme Court decisions in the *Burlington Industries* and *Faragher*[34] cases considerably clarified the circumstances under which an employer is liable for sexual harassment in the workplace. The analysis proceeds as follows:

1. **Proof of sexual harassment**—The plaintiff/employee/victim must prove items *a–c:*

   a. Harassment unwelcome.

b. Harassment because of sex.

c. Harassment resulted in a tangible employment action, or was sufficiently severe or pervasive as to unreasonably alter the conditions of employment and create a hostile, abusive working environment.

If the plaintiff is unable to prove items *a–c*, her/his claim fails. If the plaintiff proves items *a–c*, the inquiry then turns to Part 2 and the question of whether the employer bears responsibility for the harassment.

2. Employer liability

a. If the wrongdoer was a coworker, the plaintiff/employee can bring a negligence claim seeking to prove that the employer unreasonably failed to prevent or remedy the discriminatory harassment of the coworker where management knew or should have known about the harassment.

b. If the wrongdoer was a supervisor with authority over the plaintiff/employee, and if the employee suffered a *tangible employment action* (job loss, demotion) because of the harassment, the employer is vicariously liable (*indirect* liability—see Chapter 12) for the employee's losses. That is, the employer is automatically liable for the employee's wrong and cannot offer a defense regardless of lack of knowledge, absence of negligence, or any other factor.

c. If the wrongdoer was a supervisor with authority over the plaintiff/employee, but the employee suffered no tangible employment action, the employer can avoid liability by proving both elements of the following affirmative defense:

(1) The employer exercised reasonable care to prevent and correct the harassment promptly (by instituting antiharassment training programs, having a policy for reporting harassment, and so on, and (2) the employee unreasonably failed to take advantage of those opportunities. See *Pennsylvania State Police v. Suders,* 542 U.S. 129 (2005) for an analysis of the affirmative defense.

The case that follows illustrates sexual harassment analysis, and the application of the employer's affirmative defense.

Craig v. M & O Enterprises, d/b/a Mahoney Group

LEGAL BRIEFCASE   496 F.3d 1047 (9th Cir. 2007)

Circuit Judge Bybee

Eileen Craig appeals the district court's grant of summary judgment in favor of M&O Agencies (dba The Mahoney Group),

Leon Byrd and Patricia Roberts (collectively "Appellees") in her sexual harassment suit.

* * * * *

I. BACKGROUND

Craig worked for The Mahoney Group as the branch manager in Tucson and reported to Byrd who was the interim president. Over the course of several months, Byrd made repeated inappropriate comments to Craig about her legs and how she should wear shorter skirts. Although Craig thought the comments were obnoxious, she was not particularly offended. The situation took a turn for the worse on August 8, 2003, when at Byrd's invitation, Craig met him for drinks after work at (a local) Border restaurant, She had previously been to other happy hours and lunches with Byrd to discuss work related matters and thought this would be a similar meeting. Craig and Byrd drank wine and at one point, Byrd asked Craig "if she had ever thought of making love to him" and told her that he would like to take off the blue dress she was wearing. Later Byrd invited her back to his house to drink more wine in his hot tub and told her that "it's not a matter of if but when" something would happen between them. Craig laughed and shook her head at Byrd's comments but did not leave the restaurant.

Around 8:00 PM, Craig excused herself to go to the restroom, and moments later Byrd followed her into the women's bathroom. When Craig exited the stall, Byrd approached her, grabbed her arms, "gave her an open-mouthed kiss and stuck his tongue in her mouth." The kiss ended when someone walked into the restroom. Byrd exited and Craig remained in the restroom for five minutes to compose herself, after which she left the restaurant alone while Byrd was paying the check. Byrd called Craig's phone later that night, but hung up when her husband answered. Craig's husband urged her to report the incident, but she refused.

Approximately one week after the happy-hour incident Byrd called Craig from the golf course, told her she was beautiful and asked her out for another drink, which she declined. Undeterred, Byrd later called Craig from a hotel room in Wisconsin and upon his return to Tucson went into Craig's office and repeatedly asked her if she would like to make love to him. Craig's response was consistently and emphatic "no." On August 14, 2003, Byrd told Craig that he "wanted' her and asked her if she remembered telling him that she "wanted to make love to him." Craig denied ever telling him that she "wanted to make love to him."

Shortly thereafter Byrd apologized to Craig and told her that he wanted to remain friends, . . . but two days later asked Craig why she was cold and distant toward him. He again asked her why she didn't remember saying that she wanted to "make love to him," and told her that he still had feelings for her, but said that if she wanted him to leave her alone, he would do so. At some point Byrd told Craig that he didn't think he could work with her anymore, but never explicitly conditioned her continued employment or promotion on entering a sexual relationship with him. On August 27, 2003, Craig finally reported Byrd's conduct to Dawn Zimbleman, one of the individuals (in addition to Byrd) listed on the company's sexual harassment policy to whom complaints should be made. Reporting the claim spurred the company to immediate action. Byrd was instructed to stay away from Craig and to stop making sexual coments to her, and Craig began reporting to John McEvoy, another company executive. Additionally, the company appointed a senior executive to investigate the complaint, but replaced him with the Group's outside corporate counsel, Denis Fitzgibbons, when it was brought to the company's attention that the executive had previously been investigated for sexual harassment. . . .

After investigating, Fitzgibbons recommended that (1) the Group offer Craig and her husband counseling sessions at the company's expense; (2) Byrd receive a severe written reprimand (stating) that if he engaged in this type of behavior again, he would be terminated; (3) Byrd attend sexual harassment sensitivity training; and (4) all of the Group managers and supervisors receive sexual harassment training in the near future.

In late September 2003, Craig was told that the investigation was complete, and she began reporting to Byrd again. . . .

Craig filed a complaint, which she later amended, alleging (among other claims) sex discrimination under Title VII. . . .

II. DISCUSSION

* * * * *

1. Liability under a *quid pro quo* theory

To prove actionable harassment under a *quid pro quo* or "tangible employment action" theory, Craig must show that Byrd "explicitly or implicitly condition[ed] a job, a job benefit, or the absence of a job detriment, upon an employee's acceptance of sexual conduct." If a plaintiff is able to make such a showing, the employer is strictly liable for the supervisor's conduct. . . .

Craig does not allege that Byrd explicitly conditioned her continued empoyment with The Mahoney Group on her acquiescing to sexual relations with him. She did testify that she felt she had to consent if she wanted to keep her job, yet she offers little else to support her contention. Byrd's comment "I just don't think I can work with you anymore" is merely a "vague and unsupported allegation,"which we have held is insufficient to cause a reasonable woman to believe that retaining her job was conditioned on having sex with her supervisor. Additionally, several other senior executives approached Craig after she reported the harassment and reassured her that her job was not in jeopardy. Because Craig, who did not acquiesce to Byrd's demands, was neither demoted nor fired, nor did she suffer any other "tangible employment action," we agree with the district court that Craig has not made out a prima facie case for liability under Title VII on a theory of *quid pro quo* harassment.

2. Liability under a hostile environment theory

Craig alternatively could sustain her Title VII action under a hostile work environment theory of liability. To make a prima facie case of a hostile work environment, a person must show "that: (1) she was subjected to verbal or physical conduct of a sexual nature, (2) this conduct was unwelcome, and (3) the conduct was sufficiently severe or pervasive to alter the conditions of the victim's eimployment and create an abusive working envionment. Additionally, "[t]he working environment must both subjectively and objectively be perceived as abusive." Objective hostility is determined by examining the totality of the circumstances and whether a reasonable person with the same characteristics as the victim would perceive the workplace as hostile. Finally, to find a violation of Title VII, "conduct must be extreme to amount to a change in the terms and conditions of employment."

An employer may be vicariously liable under a hostile environment theory when the harassment is perpetrated by a supervisor "with immediate (or successively higher) authority over the employee." When no "tangible employment action" (such as firing or demotion) is taken, an emplyer may avoid liability by asserting a "reasonable care" defense. An employer can sustain the affirmative defense if it shows "(a) that the employer exercised reasonable care to prevent and correct promptly any sexually harassing behavior, and (b) that the plaintiff employee unreasonably failed to take advantage of any preventive or corrective opportunities provided by the employer or to avoid harm otherwise." [W]e conclude that there are sufficient triable issues of fact to overcome summary judgment with respect to Craig's prima facie case, and that The Mahoney Group did not successfully assert the "reasonable care" affirmative defense.

a. Craig's prima facie case

Byrd's behavior was explicitly sexual in nature, and unwelcome, as Craig repeatedly rebuffed his advances and eventually reported his conduct to the company. We also find that Byrd's conduct meets the requirement of being both subjectively and objectively abusive. Craig testified that she felt Byrd's comments and actions—particularly the incident in the bathroom—were abusive and made her feel uncomfortable. The conduct also met the objective standard: A reasonable woman in Craig's position could feel that Byrd's comments and actions were hostile, demeaning and abusive.

Craig's prima facie showing turns on whether or not Byrd's actions were pervasive and serious enough to amount to "a change in the terms and conditions of employment."

* * * * *

Byrd's conduct falls somewhere between mere isolated incidents or offhand comments, which do not amount to a Title VII claim, and serious and pervasive harassment, that clearly comes within Title VII . . .

Craig alleges that Byrd's actions resulted in a concrete change in her working environment. Specifically, she alleges she was removed from many of her duties, received budgets late, had some of her duties reassigned, and was forced to interact with Byrd despite his continued propositions. She claims that these additional stresses in the workplace made her nervous, spawned anxiety attacks and affected her health. Each of her complaints standing alone might not satisfy the standard, but in the aggregate, they are sufficiently serious to amount to an alteration in her condition of employment. . . .

b. The Mahoney Group's affirmative defense

The Mahoney Group argues that even if Craig has alleged sufficient facts to support her Title VII claim, because Craig did not suffer "tangible employment action," it is entitled to assert an affirmative defense. *See Pa. State Police v. Suders*, 542 U.S. 129, 148-49 . . .

[W]e hold that The Mahoney Group satisfied the first prong of the affirmative defense---that the company "exercised reasonable care to prevent and correct promptly any sexually harassing behavior." Specifically, the company had a mechanism in place for filing complaints about sexual harassment. When Craig finally did complain, The Mahoney Group addressed the situation promptly: It told Byrd to stay away from Craig, hired outside counsel to investigate and make recommendations, had Craig report to another individual other than Byrd and conducted sexual harassment training.[1] These responsible and prompt actions satisfy the first prong of the test.

The company's affirmative defense fails on the second prong, however, because The Mahoney Group cannot show that Craig "unreasonably failed to take advantage of any preventive or corrective opportunities provided by the employer." The Mahoney Group argues that Craig unreasonably delayed reporting the harassment because she waited until August 27, 2003 to file a complaint with the company, some 19 days after the incident at the restaurant; it suggests that if Craig had reported the behavior earlier, it is quite possible that Byrd would not have made the subsequent phone calls or repeatedly propositioned her at work. However, we do not think that in this situation a 19-day delay is unreasonable; an employee in Craig's position may have hoped the situation would resolve itself without the need of

---

[1]Craig alleges that the investigation the company undertook was a "sham" and alleges that outside counsel failed to interview several individuals Craig claimed had also been harassed by Byrd. Because The Mahoney Group's affirmative defense fails on the second prong, we need not address this issue, although it may be a relevant inquiry on remand.

filing a formal complaint, and she justifiably may have delayed reporting in hopes of avoiding what she perceived could be adverse—or at least unpleasant—employment consequences.

We cannot see how a delay of a mere seven days (including the weekend) rises to the level of being "unreasonable." Craig's delay is markedly different from cases where victims have allowed the harassment to continue for a period of months or years before finally reporting it to the appropriate authority.

We hold that The Mahoney Group's affirmative defense fails, as Craig's minor delay in reporting the behavior did not meet the stringent standard outlined in *Faragher*. Consequently, we reverse the district court's grant of summary judgment for The Mahoney Group and remand for further proceedings.

* * * * *

Questions

1. *a.* According to the court, Craig did not prove *quid pro quo* harassment based on Byrd's conduct. Do you agree or disagree? Explain. Describe a situation which might meet the court's evidentiary requirements for *quid pro quo* harassment claims.

   b. The court asserted that if taken alone, Craig's individual complaints about the change in her working environment would not meet the standard for a hostile work environment. Do you agree? Should the standard be lowered? Explain.

   c. How did the Mahoney Group satisfy the first prong of the affirmative defense? Why did the affirmative defense ultimately fail? What should employers learn from this? What should employees learn?

   d. Craig brought individual claims against Byrd, for which the court affirmed the district court's summary judgment citing its prior decisions that Title VII does not provide for separate causes of action against individuals. Do you think that Title VII liability should be extended to supervisors? To coworkers? Why or why not?

2. Truck driver Lesley Parkins claimed that she was a victim of hostile environment sexual harassment while employed by Civil Constructors beginning in 1994. Parkins alleged that coworkers subjected her to foul language, sexual stories, and touching. Parkins complained to her dispatcher, Tim Spellman, and to one of her purported harassers, Robert Strong. She saw the job superintendent and the company EEO officer almost daily, but she did not complain to either. In 1996 Parkins filed a grievance with her union—

Teamsters Local 325. The union contacted the company EEO officer, who immediately launched an investigation that led to punishment for the employees. Parkins conceded that she was not harassed following the company punishment. Parkins filed suit charging Civil Constructors with sexual harassment. Parkins claimed that two of her harassers, Strong and Charles Boeke, were foremen who supervised her work. Assuming Parkins can prove that she was, in fact, sexually harassed, what must she prove in order to hold Civil Constructors liable? See *Parkins v. Civil Constructors of Illinois,* 163 F.3d 1027 (7th Cir. 1998).

3. Rena Lockard worked for a Pizza Hut franchise in Atoka, Oklahoma, in September 1993. Two male customers made sexually offensive comments to her such as, "I would like to get in your pants." Lockard told her supervisor she did not like waiting on the men, but she did not mention the sexual comments. In November 1993, the men returned to the Pizza Hut, and Lockard was instructed to wait on them. One of them asked what kind of cologne she was wearing, and Lockard replied that it was none of his business. The customer then grabbed her by the hair. Lockard told her supervisor what had happened and said that she did not want to wait on the two men. The supervisor ordered her to do so. Lockard returned to the table where one of the men pulled her by the hair, grabbed one of her breasts, and put his mouth on her breast. Lockard then quit her job and later sued the local franchise and Pizza Hut.

   a. What is the central issue(s) in this case?

   b. Is the franchise and/or Pizza Hut responsible for sexual harassment by a *customer* against an employee? Explain. See *Lockard v. Pizza Hut,* 162 F.3d 1062 (10th Cir. 1998).

4. A female employed as an Installation and Repairs Technician claimed a hostile work environment was created in the garage in which she worked by the routine use of profanity, crude humor, vulgar graffiti depicting sexual acts, and especially by sexually demeaning conversations conveying a profound disrespect for women. While the comments and graffiti demeaned some male employees, the conduct was directed at all the women working in the garage.

   a. In deciding whether the conduct constituted hostile environment sexual harassment, should the court evaluate the facts from the point of view of a "reasonable person" or a "reasonable woman"? Explain.

   b. Why does it matter? See *Petrosino v. Bell Atlantic,* 385 F. 3d 210 (2d Cir. 2004); see also *Ellison v. Brady,* 924 F. 2d 872 (9th Cir. 1991).

***Friends* Writers Accused of Sexual Harassment**

Amaani Lyle, hired to be a writers' assistant for the *Friends* television show, said her initial excitement gave way to feelings of degradation when the writers' conversations turned sexually explicit. At times, she felt nauseated.

> They would basically sit like teenagers in a locker room, talking about, you know . . . things they wanted to do to the cast and walking around pretending to masturbate and just ridiculous conduct.

After being told she was fired for typing too slowly, Lyle sued in 1999, claiming the writers created a hostile working environment. In sworn depositions, some of the writers admitted they told stories of oral sex, talked about anal sex, and simulated masturbation as a way of saying they were wasting time.

On April 20, 2006, the California Supreme Court ruled against Lyle, concluding that the sexual and vulgar language was not aimed at Lyle or other women in the workplace. Rather, the conduct was part of the creative activity of generating scripts for a situation comedy featuring sexual themes.

Questions

1. Briefs were filed in this case from a variety of organizations, including the California Newspaper Publishers Association.
   a. Why do you think newspaper publishers were interested in this case involving writers for a television show?
   b. What might they have argued in their brief? Explain.
2. Do you agree with the court's decision? Explain.

Sources: Los Angeles Times, " . . . Sex Harassment Collide," Waterloo/Cedar Falls Courier, November 14, 2004, p. A3; Matthew J. Heller, "'Friends' Ruling Seen as Victory for Employers," Workplace Management, May 10, 2006 [http://www.workforce.com/section/00/article/24/36/37.html]; Associated Press, "Friends' Lawsuit Tossed," Waterloo/Cedar Falls Courier, April 21, 2006, p. A2.

Same Sex?

Joseph Oncale, a heterosexual who worked on an offshore oil rig, charged a supervisor and two male coworkers with sexually harassing him, including repeated taunts and several sexual assaults, one with a bar of soap while Oncale was showering. Oncale complained to superiors, but to no avail. He then quit his job and sued his employer for sexual harassment. The case went to the U.S. Supreme Court, which unanimously ruled that same-sex harassment is actionable under Title VII.[35] Oncale then settled out of court for an undisclosed amount of money. Justice Scalia, who wrote the Supreme Court opinion, explained that the harassment must be "because of sex" (that is, gender); that harassment can be motivated by hostility as well as by desire; and that common sense and social context count. Thus, smacking a football teammate on the rear end, horseplay, rough-housing, or occasional gender-related jokes, teasing, and abusive language normally would not constitute harassment. Ordinarily, plaintiffs in same-sex harassment cases must show that the behavior was motivated by (a) sexual desire, (b) general hostility to one or other gender, or (c) the victim's failure to conform to sexual stereotypes (such as effeminate behavior by a male). [For an analysis of the significance of the *Oncale* case, see **http://www.reason.com/news/show/28636.html**]

> What if the harasser bothers both genders equally?

Oncale settles the big question of protection against same-sex harassment, but it raises other puzzles. For example, what if the harasser bothers both genders equally?

After Oncale, a husband and wife, who were also coworkers, brought a Title VII claim against their employer alleging that their supervisor had harassed both of them by soliciting sex from each of them on separate occasions. The federal appeals court affirmed the district court's dismissal, concluding that the "equal opportunity harasser" does not give rise to a Title VII sex discrimination complaint.[36]

Sexual Harassment in Other Nations

American managers working abroad must deal with international differences in attitudes toward sexual behavior in the workplace, although a general shift in harassment law in the direction of the American model is evident. This shift is significant for the American manager working abroad for a U.S.-based company, or a foreign employer controlled by an American company. The Civil Rights Act of 1991 extends Title VII's protection to American employees working abroad for such employers, but offers a "foreign law defense" under which the employer would not be required to comply with Title VII if to do so would violate the host country's law.[37] Now the European Union has adopted laws requiring harassment-free workplaces.[38] In Japan recent rule changes make sexual harassment law very much like the U.S. model.[39] Mexico, Taiwan, Venezuela, and other nations make sexual harassment a crime under some circumstances: Managers can go to jail.[40]

Retaliation Claims

The power in an employment relationship is imbalanced in favor of the employer. In bringing a discrimination claim, an employee is vulnerable to the employer's retaliatory action. In order to protect against an employer's abuse of power and to encourage exercise of employees' rights, Title VII's antiretaliation provision prohibits an employer from discriminating against an employee for engaging in a "protected activity." Protected activities include opposing an employment practice that is reasonably believed to violate Title VII, or participating in any manner in a charge made under Title VII, including offering testimony on behalf of a coworker. Other civil rights laws, including the Americans with Disabilities Act (ADA), the Age Discrimination in Employment Act (ADEA), and the Civil Rights Act of 1866, offer similar protections against retaliation.

A prima facie case of retaliation requires:

1. Participation in a protected activity known to the defendant;
2. An employment action disadvantaging the plaintiff; and
3. A causal connection between the protected activity and the adverse employment action.

In the 2006 case of *Burlington Northern & Santa Fe Railway v. White,*[41] the U.S. Supreme Court held that a Title VII retaliation claim may be based on assigning a complainant to less desirable duties, since this action by the employer might dissuade a reasonable employee from making or supporting a discrimination claim.

Part Four—Affirmative Action

I do not like the sea of white faces in the audience. We have too many middle-aged white Anglo-Saxon males, and that needs to change.[42]

Former Ford Motor Co. CEO Jacques Nasser allegedly made those remarks in explaining his efforts to bring greater diversity to the Ford workforce. That evidence was provided in support of several lawsuits charging Ford with race, sex, and age discrimination as part of an effort to elevate more women and minorities to higher decision-making roles at the auto company while reducing the number of white males. Among the claims in one of the suits:

- Women and minorities were routinely promoted or hired over more qualified white males.
- Bonuses for Ford executives were tied in part to hiring and promoting more women and minorities.
- Ford Credit internal documents ... stated "diversity candidate preferred" or "female candidate preferred."[43]

Ford denied the allegations and settled with 620 claimants for $10.5 million.[44]

For years, we have been struggling with *affirmative action* as a means of remedying past and present discriminatory wrongs. In following an affirmative action plan, employers consciously take positive steps to seek out minorities and women for hiring and promotion opportunities, and they often employ goals and timetables to measure progress toward a workforce that is representative of the qualified labor pool.

Affirmative action efforts arise in four ways: (1) Courts may order the implementation of affirmative action after a finding of wrongful discrimination, (2) employers may voluntarily adopt affirmative action plans, (3) some statutes require affirmative action, and (4) employers may adopt affirmative action to do business with government agencies. Federal contractors must meet the affirmative action standards of the Office of Federal Contract Compliance Programs. [For criticisms of affirmative action, see the Center for Equal Opportunity at **http://www.ceousa.org**]

"Crying 'Foul'" in the NBA?

According to a 2007 academic study, white referees in professional basketball games call fouls at a greater rate against black players than against white players. Analyzing National Basketball Association (NBA) box scores from the 13 seasons from 1991 through 2004, the study found that players who were similar in all ways except skin color drew foul calls at a different rate, depending on the racial composition of the NBA game's three referees. Fouls called on black players could increase 4.5 percent when the number of white referees went from zero to three. The study also found that black officials called fouls more frequently against white players, but that tendency was less pronounced.

Questions
1. In your opinion, should the NBA act on the study's findings? What actions might the NBA take? Explain.

2. In another 2007 study, the NBA was found to have the highest percentages of minority vice presidents and office personnel in the history of men's sports—15 percent and 34 percent, respectively. Further, the study found that 40 percent of the head coaches were black. Do these findings change your response to Question 1? Explain.

Sources: Alan Schwarz, "Study of N.B.A. Sees Racial Bias in Calling Fouls," *New York Times,* May 2, 2007 [**http://nytimes/com/2007/05/02/sports/basketball/02refs**]; Associated Press, "Racial Bias? Players Don't See It," *Washington Post*, May 3, 2007, p. E10; and News Services, "More Minority Execs in NBA," *Washington Post*, May 10, 2007, p. E2.

The Early Law

For nearly 20 years, judicial decisions were firmly supportive of affirmative action. A massive system of relief emerged at all levels of government and in the private sector. In a 1979 case, *United Steelworkers of America v. Weber,*[45] the Court set out perhaps its most detailed "recipe" for those qualities that would allow a *voluntary affirmative action plan in the private sector* to withstand scrutiny. Weber, a white male, challenged the legality of an affirmative action plan that set aside for black employees 50 percent of the openings in a training program until the percentage of black craft workers in the plant equaled the percentage of blacks in the local labor market. The plan was the product of a collective bargaining agreement between the Steelworkers and Kaiser Aluminum and Chemical. In Kaiser's Grammercy, Louisiana, plant, only 5 of 273 skilled craft workers were black, whereas the local workforce was approximately 39 percent black. In the first year of the affirmative action plan, seven blacks and six whites were admitted to the craft training program. The most junior black employee accepted for the program had less seniority than several white employees who were not accepted. Weber was among the white males denied entry to the training program.

Weber filed suit, claiming Title VII forbade an affirmative action plan that granted a racial preference to blacks where whites dramatically exceeded blacks in skilled craft positions but where there was no proof of discrimination. The federal district court and the federal court of appeals held for Weber, but the U.S. Supreme Court reversed. Several qualities of the Steelworkers' plan were instrumental in the Court's favorable ruling:

1. The affirmative action was part of a *plan.*
2. The plan was designed to "open employment opportunities for Negroes in occupations which have been traditionally closed to them."
3. The plan was temporary.
4. The plan did not unnecessarily harm the rights of white employees. That is,

   a. The plan did not require the discharge of white employees.

   b. The plan did not create an absolute bar to the advancement of white employees.

Then, in an important 1987 public-sector decision, *Johnson v. Transportation Agency,*[46] the Supreme Court approved the extension of affirmative action to women.

The political tides were turning, however. The 1980s were politically conservative years. Appointments to the Supreme Court and to the lower federal courts, by President Reagan in particular, reflected that mood. Affirmative action was under attack.

Rethinking Affirmative Action

From the late 1980s to the present, a series of judicial decisions and increasing public and political skepticism have challenged the legality and the wisdom of affirmative action, at least where the government is involved. The 1989 *City of Richmond v. J. A. Croson Co.*[47] case struck down Richmond, Virginia's, minority "set-aside" program that required prime contractors who were doing business with the city to subcontract at least 30 percent of the work to minority businesses. The Court said such race-conscious remedial plans were constitutional only if (1) the city or state could provide specific evidence of discrimination against a particular protected class in the past (rather than relying on proof of general societywide discrimination) and (2) its remedy was "narrowly tailored" to the needs of the situation.

Then in *Adarand Constructors v. Pena,* a landmark 1995 decision, the Supreme Court struck down a federal highway program that extended bidding preferences to "disadvantaged" contractors.[48] The suit was brought by Randy Pech, a white contractor whose low bid on a Colorado guardrail project was rejected in favor of the bid of a minority firm. The Supreme Court ruled that the government's preference program denied Pech his right to equal protection under the law as guaranteed by the Fifth Amendment to the federal Constitution. [For a "Timeline of Affirmative Action Milestones," see **http://www. infoplease.com/spot/affirmativetimeline1.html**]

The case that follows illustrates the courts' current reasoning about the constitutionality of affirmative action in a public-sector employment case involving preferences for minority and female firefighters in Chicago.

Reynolds v. City of Chicago   296 F.3d 524 (7th Cir. 2002)

LEGAL BRIEFCASE

Judge Posner

This suit by white Chicago police sergeants and lieutenants challenges, as a denial of equal protection of the laws, the promotion in 1990 and 1991 of 20 black, Hispanic, and female sergeants and lieutenants to the rank of lieutenant and captain, respectively. The challenged promotions were made pursuant to an affirmative action plan by which blacks, Hispanics, and women could be promoted "out of rank"—that is, promoted even though they had a lower score than a white male on the test for the promotion. The district judge entered judgment after a jury trial. . . . The judgment was for the city with respect to all the promotions except that of the one Hispanic in the pool, who was promoted from sergeant to lieutenant. The plaintiffs appeal the ruling that the promotions of the blacks and women ahead of them did not deny the equal protection of the laws, while the city appeals the ruling that the promotion of the Hispanic sergeant ahead of the plaintiff sergeants was a denial of equal protection.

*   *   *   *   *

The findings of fact made by the jury in this case are neither clearly erroneous nor unreasonable, and what they reveal, so far as the black and female affirmative-action promotions are concerned, is the following. Until Orlando Wilson became the City of Chicago's police commissioner in 1960, black and white police officers were segregated, with black officers being confined to the parts of Chicago that were predominantly black. However, blacks were hired roughly in proportion to their share of the Chicago population. Wilson desegregated the police force. The city presented evidence that this resulted in a *decline* in the hiring of blacks. That may seem a paradoxical consequence of desegregation, but the evidence dispels the paradox. The evidence shows that white officers didn't want to serve with blacks. There were numerous acts of racial harassment of blacks, and black applicants flunked the police medical exam at rates suspiciously higher than whites. As a result of these circumstances, applications of blacks to the police force plummeted. After reforms in the mid-1970s that are acknowledged to have eliminated or at least greatly reduced racial discrimination in the Chicago police department, the rate of black applications climbed, and black applicants no longer flunked the medical exam at rates significantly higher than whites.

The evidence that we have briefly summarized justified a finding that discrimination by members of the police force depressed the hiring of blacks during the 1960s, leading in turn to a deficit of blacks in senior positions in the 1980s. The affirmative-action promotions of blacks challenged here, promotions designed to remedy the discrimination that we have just described, involved the promotion of 11 black sergeants out of a total of 182 promotions of sergeants and 3 black lieutenants out of a total of 50 promotions of lieutenants. These affirmative-action promotions resulted in percentages of black sergeants and lieutenants that still were lower than would have been expected had there not been that decline in the entry-level hiring of blacks in the 1960s.

The evidence that the decline was the result of discrimination was not conclusive. The plaintiffs presented evidence that

the decline was the result of racial tensions in the 1960s that made blacks reluctant to become police officers because it would make them unpopular with other blacks. Against this the city presented evidence that although racial tensions were not limited to Chicago during the 1960s, other cities did not experience a drop-off in black hiring for their police forces, which suggests that something other than racial tensions probably accounted for the drop-off in Chicago; that something other may have been discrimination. The conflict over this issue was one for the jury to resolve. Since remedying past discrimination is a recognized justification for affirmative action, and since the action taken was modest—the promotion out of rank of a mere handful of blacks, resulting merely in delayed promotion for some whites rather than in anyone's losing his job or failing (eventually) to get the promotion he sought and was entitled to—the conclusion that the defendant had not violated the equal protection clause followed directly from the jury's factual findings.

The case for the affirmative-action promotion of the five women was even stronger. Until the 1970s women were formally barred from being hired for most jobs in the police department, including patrol officer. As a result, few were hired and many were deterred from applying because of the truncated career opportunities.

*   *   *   *   *

The city defends the affirmative-action promotions of the blacks and the women on the further, alternative ground that they were justified by the operational needs of the police force—a ground completely different from the remedial ground that we have been discussing. One ground is enough, so we need not consider the alternative ground except with regard to the Hispanic who the district court determined had been improperly promoted. For the city's argument is not that his promotion was justifiable as a remedy against past discrimination against Hispanics—the disparity between the percentage of Hispanic policemen and the percentage of Hispanic Chicagoans in 1990 was due largely to the rapid growth of the city's Hispanic population in the 1980s—but that it was justifiable in order to make the police force more effective in performing its duties. By 1990 the population of Chicago was almost 20 percent Hispanic, but fewer than 5 percent of police lieutenants were Hispanic. Because there were only 14 Hispanic lieutenants before the affirmative-action promotion of Sergeant Denk and the police work in three shifts with the result that the number of lieutenants per shift is small, on any given shift in 1990 only two or three Hispanic lieutenants were on duty in the entire city, with its population of 2.78 million in 1990 of whom more than 500,000 were Hispanic.

The evidence presented by the city, including the testimony of a competent expert witness, established a twofold need for a larger number of Hispanic lieutenants. First, lieutenants and captains are the principal supervisors in the police department. They set the tone for the department. If there are negligible numbers of Hispanics in these ranks (and in 1990 the percentage of Hispanic captains was only half the percentage of Hispanic lieutenants), non-Hispanic police officers are less likely to be sensitized to any special problems in policing Hispanic neighborhoods. Second, the lieutenants and captains act as "ambassadors" to the various communities that make up Chicago, of which the Hispanic community is an important one. Effective police work, including the detection and apprehension of criminals, requires that the police have the trust of that community, and they are more likely to have it if they have "ambassadors" to the community of the same ethnicity.

Justifications of discrimination that are based on a public employer's operational needs are suspect because they seem to have no natural limits, unlike remedial justifications, which cease when the last traces of the discrimination that gave rise to the remedy have been eliminated. Some discrimination, whether of the old-fashioned kind or the modern "affirmative action" kind, is vicious, ignorant, political, or otherwise invidious, but much is not.

As we pointed out in *Builders Ass'n of Greater Chicago v. Cook County,* the question whether nonremedial justifications for affirmative action can ever satisfy the equal protection clause has in the absence of definitive resolution by the Supreme Court caused bitter divisions in the lower federal courts. Many courts, however, including our own, have at least left open a small window for forms of discrimination that are supported by compelling public safety concerns, such as affirmative action in the staffing of police departments and correctional institutions. Especially in a period of heightened public concern with the dangers posed by international terrorism, effective police work must be reckoned a national priority that justifies some sacrifice of competing interests. If it is indeed the case that promoting one Hispanic police sergeant out of order is important to the effectiveness of the Chicago police in protecting the people of the city from crime, the fact that this out-of-order promotion technically is "racial discrimination" does not strike us as an impressive counterweight.

The imperative need for this discrimination had, however, to be proved and not merely conjectured. [The city] had to substantiate its position with evidence. It did so. It proved that it has a compelling need to increase the number of Hispanic lieutenants; and the increase it defended—the promotion of one Hispanic sergeant—is the smallest increase it could have made.

Affirmed in part and reversed in part, and the case is remanded.

Questions

1. *a.* Why did the court uphold the constitutionality of the Chicago Police Department's affirmative action program?

   b. Do you agree with the judgment of the court?

   c. How did the court's analysis of the constitutionality of the Hispanic promotion differ from the analysis applied to blacks and women?

2. Frederick Claus, a white man with a degree in electrical engineering and 29 years of experience with Duquesne Light Company, was denied a promotion in favor of a black man who had not earned a bachelor's degree and did not have the required seven years of experience. Only 2 of 82 managers in that division of Duquesne Light were black. Claus sued, claiming in effect that he was a victim of "reverse discrimination." At trial, both sides conceded that the black candidate was an outstanding employee and that he was qualified to be a manager. Decide the case. Explain. See *Claus v. Duquesne Light Co.,* 46 F.3d 1115 (1994); cert. den. 115 S.Ct. 1700 (1995).

3. In 1974, Birmingham, Alabama, was accused of unlawfully excluding blacks from management roles in its fire department. After several years of litigation, Birmingham adopted an affirmative action plan that guaranteed black firefighters one of every two available promotions. The city, the Justice Department, and others applauded the arrangement, but a group of 14 white firefighters claimed they were victims of reverse discrimination. After years of wrangling, the white firefighters' claim reached the 11th Circuit Federal Court of Appeals. Was the affirmative action plan lawful? Explain. See *In re Birmingham Reverse Discrimination Employment Litig.,* 20 F.3d 1525 (11th Cir. 1994) cert. den. sub nom.; *Martin v. Wilks,* 115 S.Ct. 1695 (1995).

So Where Are We?

The Law?

Reynolds, a recent case, illustrates that affirmative action in employment remains lawful if carefully justified. On the other hand, government preference programs that push contracts toward minorities and women (as in *Croson* and *Adarand*) are reviewed with judicial skepticism. Confusion also results from differences in analysis depending on whether the cases in question are based on the Constitution or on Title VII (Title VII cases appear to allow racial preferences to a greater extent than do those analyzed under the Constitution),[49] and whether those cases address employment questions, set-asides, or other issues. The law simply is not clear; but we can be certain that the courts will now take a very close look at racial and gender preferences in employment. We can also say that both quotas and affirmative action justified broadly by "societal discrimination" are unconstitutional.

> Quotas are unconstitutional

A lawful affirmative action remedy in employment cases apparently will be evaluated, in most cases, by the following considerations:

- The plan addresses a compelling interest such as remedying past or present discrimination or correcting the underutilization of women and minorities.
- The plan is temporary.
- The plan is narrowly tailored to minimize layoffs and other burdens.

Part Five—Additional Discrimination Topics

Religious Discrimination

Managers must reasonably accommodate employees' religious beliefs and practices. *The Wall Street Journal* pointed to the example of a Whirlpool factory near Nashville, Tennessee, where 200 employees, 10 percent of the workforce, were Muslims of six nationalities. To maintain their religious principles, many devout Muslim men must wear beards and skull caps, and many women must wear loose-fitting clothes and head scarves in public. Muslims pray five times daily and must first wash their hands and feet. The clothing requirements raised safety concerns. Prayers disrupted assembly line schedules. The before-prayer washing left restrooms wet and slippery. Other workers sometimes resented the rituals and worried that production would decline and the factory might not be able to remain competitive in the fierce appliance market. As the law requires, Whirlpool made efforts to accommodate the religious needs of its workers. Substitutes were available during prayer times. Washrooms were mopped more frequently. Scarves were retained, but had to be tucked in tightly. Sometimes accommodations could not be reached, as in workers' preference for sandals where steel-toed shoes were required. And Muslim men were expected to respectfully take instructions from female managers even though their own culture and religion left the men uncomfortable in that subordinate role.[50]

The Law

Title VII forbids discrimination on the basis of religion. That religious faith must be sincere and meaningful, not merely a sham to achieve advantages. Employers must take reasonable steps to prevent and remedy religious harassment. But the much more common challenge is that of reasonable accommodation, as seen in the above example from Whirlpool.

The leading religious discrimination case is *Trans World Airlines, Inc. v. Hardison,* in which the plaintiff, who celebrated his religion on Saturdays, was unable to take that day off from his work in a parts warehouse.[51] Efforts to swap shifts or change jobs were unsuccessful. The company rejected Hardison's request for a four-day week because it would have required the use of another employee at premium pay. The Supreme Court's ruling in the case reduced the employer's duty to a very modest standard: "To require TWA to bear more than a *de minimis cost* in order to give Hardison Saturdays off is an *undue hardship.*" Saturdays off for Hardison would have imposed extra costs on TWA and would have constituted religious discrimination against other employees who would have sought Saturday off for reasons not grounded in religion. So any accommodation imposing more than a de minimis cost on the employer represents an undue hardship and is not required by Title VII. Of course, the lower courts have differed considerably on what constitutes a de minimis cost and an undue hardship. For example, an Ohio court ruled that an employee, a Seventh Day Adventist, was discriminated against when he was fired for refusing to work from sundown Friday to sundown Saturday. The employee could have been moved to an earlier shift at no cost.[52] [For links to religious discrimination in the workplace materials, see **http://www.hrhero.com/topics/reldiscrim.html**]

Question

Resolving job-related religious conflicts can be among the most emotionally demanding management dilemmas. For example, what, if anything, would you do as a manager if one of your subordinates, as an expression of her religious beliefs, wore to work an antiabortion button displaying a picture of a fetus? See *Wilson v. U.S. West Communications,* 58 F.3d 1337 (8th Cir. 1995).

The Americans with Disabilities Act (ADA)

A Fuddruckers restaurant in St. Louis Park, Minnesota, says it fired a cook, Barbara Andresen, in 2002 because managers had received three complaints from customers about Andresen's "excessive salivation" and because coworkers allegedly saw her spitting and drooling into food. New managers had been brought in because the public perceived the restaurant to be unsanitary.

> Coworkers allegedly saw her spitting and drooling into food

Andresen says she was fired because of her disability: excessive stuttering. The record indicated that Andresen had a great deal of trouble speaking, and she avoided situations that would require her to speak to strangers. Andresen also indicated that she heard one manager tell another that he was going to "find a way to get rid of Barb." The firing, Andresen claims, violated the Americans with Disabilities Act. Fuddruckers responded that stuttering does not constitute a disability under the ADA and that her "excessive salivation" constituted a "direct threat" to the health and safety of others (a defense provided for in the ADA). A federal judge denied Fuddruckers' motion for a summary judgment, noting, among other things, that Andresen's termination notice indicated that she was fired for failing to properly prepare lettuce for salad and said nothing about drooling or spitting.[53]

This situation illustrates the general purpose of the 1990 ADA, which seeks to remove barriers to a full, productive life for disabled Americans. The ADA forbids discrimination in employment, public accommodations, public services, transportation, and telecommunications. Small businesses with fewer than 15 employees are exempted from the employment portions of the ADA. The Rehabilitation Act of 1973 protects disabled workers in the public sector from employment discrimination.

Under the ADA, a disabled person (1) has a physical or mental impairment that substantially limits one or more major life activities, (2) has a record of such an impairment, or (3) is regarded as having such an impairment. The nature of major life activities (walking, seeing, hearing, performing an array of manual tasks) is addressed in the *Williams* case that follows this discussion. One who has a history of cancer might "have a record of such an impairment." And one might be regarded by others as impaired because of a physical deformity when, in fact, that condition does not impair job performance in any material way.

Disabilities

Blindness, hearing loss, mental retardation, cosmetic disfigurement, anatomical loss, and disfiguring scars are examples of covered disabilities. Alcoholism, drug abuse, and AIDS are covered. However, the act specifically excludes job applicants and employees who *currently* use illegal drugs when the employer acts on the basis of such use. Thus the act covers those who are rehabilitated and no longer using illegal drugs, those in rehabilitation and no longer using illegal drugs, and those erroneously regarded as using illegal drugs. Employers may expect the same performance and behavior from alcoholics and drug abusers as from all other employees. In sum, the ADA treats alcoholism and drug addiction as medical conditions and protects those who are overcoming their impairments.

> The act specifically excludes job applicants and employees who *currently* use illegal drugs

Specifically excluded as disabilities are homosexuality, bisexuality, exhibitionism, gambling, kleptomania, and pyromania, among others. Questions regarding which conditions constitute disabilities will continue to require litigation. For example, in interpreting the federal Rehabilitation Act and state disability laws, some courts have treated severe obesity as a disability, whereas others have not. Jennifer Portnick, a 240-pound, size 16–18, San Francisco aerobics instructor brought national publicity to job disadvantages for those who are overweight. Portnick sought to work for Jazzercise but was rejected because of her size and the company's expectation that its instructors look fit. Portnick filed a complaint under a San Francisco ordinance forbidding discrimination on the basis of weight and height, and Jazzercise agreed to change its policy. Portnick almost certainly could not have been considered disabled under the ADA, and few jurisdictions provide the protection offered in San Francisco.

Accommodation

An employer may not discriminate in hiring or employment against a *qualified person with a disability.* A qualified person is one who can perform the *essential functions* of the job. The act requires employers to make *reasonable accommodations* for disabled employees and applicants. Reasonable accommodations might include structural changes in the workplace, job reassignment, job restructuring, or new equipment. [For EEOC advice about small employers and reasonable accommodation, see **http://www.eeoc. gov/facts/accommodation.html**]

The ADA and a Golf Cart

Casey Martin, a young golfer with a degenerative circulatory disorder in one leg, requested that the Professional Golfers Association (PGA) waive its rule requiring walking in tournaments so that Martin could ride in a cart. The request was denied, Martin sued claiming a violation of the ADA, and the case reached the U.S. Supreme Court. The primary substantive question before the Court was whether the requested accommodation (riding in a cart) would fundamentally alter the nature of the Tour tournaments. Relying on a trial court finding that Martin suffered greater fatigue even while riding than competitors who walk, the Court ruled 7–2 that Martin has a legal right to the use of the cart.

What lessons might an employer derive from the Martin decision?

Source: PGA Tour, Inc. v. Casey Martin, 532 U.S. 661(2001).

Defenses

The employer's primary defense is *undue hardship.* The employer need not make an accommodation for a disabled person if that adjustment would be unduly expensive, substantial, or disruptive.

Further, unqualified applicants need not be hired, and one who cannot perform the essential functions of the job after reasonable accommodations may be discharged. The BFOQ defense does not apply to the ADA. However, employers may assert safety qualifications as a "business necessity" defense.

Question

United Parcel Service (UPS) required all its "package-car drivers" to pass a U.S. Department of Transportation (DOT) hearing standard. DOT's standard applies only to those vehicles weighing over 10,001 pounds when loaded with cargo, but UPS' requirement applied to all UPS drivers. A class of UPS employees and applicants unable to pass the DOT hearing standard brought an ADA claim against UPS. Decide the case. Explain. See *Bates v. UPS,* 511 F.3d 974 (9th Cir. 2007).

The ADA in Practice

Approximately 12 percent of working-age Americans have a disability.[54] The employment rate for this group is approximately 38 percent,[55] while the overall U.S. labor participation rate at this writing is nearly 66 percent.[56] According to some disability advocates, the low employment rate for those with disabilities may be due to several factors, including managers' negative attitudes and inadequate job training.[57]

Compliance Costs

The expense of dealing with ADA expectations had been a great worry to the employment community, but the data show that those costs are quite modest:

JAN (the President's Job Accommodation Network) reports that the median accommodation under ADA costs $500 or less. The BPA (Berkeley Planning Associates) study found that the average cost of an accommodation is very low—approximately $900—and that 51 percent of accommodations cost nothing.[58]

Further, tax credits to hire and provide access to individuals with disabilities, as well as tax deductions to remove architectural barriers to make its facilities more accessible, also ease the ADA's compliance costs.[59]

What Is a Disability?

The important 9–0 Supreme Court decision that follows clarifies the question of when impairments must be treated as disabilities under the ADA.

Toyota Motor Manufacturing, Kentucky v. Ella Williams

LEGAL BRIEFCASE   534 U.S. 184 (2002)

Justice O'Conner

Under the Americans with Disabilities Act of 1990 (ADA or Act), a physical impairment that "substantially limits one or more . . . major life activities" is a "disability." Respondent (Williams), claiming to be disabled because of her carpal tunnel syndrome and other related impairments, sued petitioner (Toyota), her former employer, for failing to provide her with a reasonable accommodation as required by the ADA.

* * * * *

I

Respondent began working at petitioner's automobile manufacturing plant in Georgetown, Kentucky, in August 1990. She was soon placed on an engine fabrication assembly line, where her duties included work with pneumatic tools. Use of these tools eventually caused pain in respondent's hands, wrists, and arms. She sought treatment at petitioner's in-house medical service, where she was diagnosed with bilateral carpal tunnel syndrome and bilateral tendinitis. Respondent consulted a personal physician who placed her on permanent work restrictions that precluded her from lifting more than 20 pounds or from "frequently lifting or carrying of objects weighing up to 10 pounds," engaging in "constant repetitive . . . flexion or extension of [her] wrists or elbows," performing "overhead work," or using "vibratory or pneumatic tools."

* * * * *

[Later] petitioner placed respondent on a team in Quality Control Inspection Operations (QCIO). QCIO is responsible for four tasks: (1) "assembly paint"; (2) "paint second inspection"; (3) "shell body audit"; and (4) "ED surface repair." Respondent was initially placed on a team that performed only the first two of these tasks, and for a couple of years, she rotated on a weekly basis between them. In assembly paint, respondent visually inspected painted cars moving slowly down a conveyor. She scanned for scratches, dents, chips, or any other flaws that may have occurred during the assembly or painting process, at a rate of one car every 54 seconds. When respondent began working in assembly paint, inspection team members were required to open and shut the doors, trunk, and/or hood of each passing car. Sometime during respondent's tenure, however, the position was modified to include only visual inspection with few or no manual tasks. Paint second inspection required team members to use their hands to wipe each painted car with a glove as it moved along a conveyor. The parties agree that respondent was physically capable of performing both of these jobs and that her performance was satisfactory.

During the fall of 1996, petitioner announced that it wanted QCIO employees to be able to rotate through all four of the QCIO processes. Respondent therefore received training for the shell body audit job, in which team members apply a highlight oil to the hood, fender, doors, rear quarter panel, and trunk of passing cars at a rate of approximately one car per minute. The highlight oil has the viscosity of salad oil, and employees spread it on cars with a sponge attached to a block of wood. After they wipe each car with the oil, the employees visually inspect it for flaws. Wiping the cars required respondent to hold her hands and arms up around shoulder height for several hours at a time. [Williams experienced pain and asked to return to her original two jobs.]

* * * * *

According to respondent, petitioner refused her request and forced her to continue working in the shell body audit job, which caused her even greater physical injury. According to petitioner, respondent simply began missing work on a regular basis. Regardless, it is clear that on December 6, 1996, the last day respondent worked at petitioner's plant, she was placed under a no-work-of-any-kind restriction by her treating physicians. On January 27, 1997, respondent received a letter from petitioner that terminated her employment, citing her poor attendance record.

Respondent filed a charge of disability discrimination with the Equal Employment Opportunity Commission (EEOC).

Respondent based her claim that she was "disabled" under the ADA on the ground that her physical impairments substantially limited her in (1) manual tasks; (2) housework; (3) gardening; (4) playing with her children; (5) lifting; and (6) working, all of which, she argued, constituted major life activities under the Act. Respondent also argued, in the alternative, that she was disabled under the ADA because she had a record of a substantially limiting impairment and because she was regarded as having such an impairment.

* * * * *

The District Court held that respondent had suffered from a physical impairment, but that the impairment did not qualify as a disability because it had not "substantially limited" any "major life activity." The court rejected respondent's arguments that gardening, doing housework, and playing with children are major life activities. Although the court agreed that performing manual tasks, lifting, and working are major life activities, it found the evidence insufficient to demonstrate that respondent had been substantially limited in lifting or working.

* * * * *

The Court of Appeals for the Sixth Circuit reversed the District Court's ruling on whether respondent was disabled at the time she sought an accommodation. The Court of Appeals held that in order for respondent to demonstrate that she was disabled due to a substantial limitation in the ability to perform manual tasks at the time of her accommodation request, she had to "show that her manual disability involved a 'class' of manual activities affecting the ability to perform tasks at work." Respondent satisfied this test, according to the Court of

Appeals, because her ailments "prevented her from doing the tasks associated with certain types of manual assembly line jobs, manual product handling jobs and manual building trade jobs (painting, plumbing, roofing, etc.) that require the gripping of tools and repetitive work with hands and arms extended at or above shoulder levels for extended periods of time."

* * * * *

III [II OMITTED]

The question presented by this case is whether the Sixth Circuit properly determined that respondent was disabled ... at the time that she sought an accommodation from petitioner. The parties do not dispute that respondent's medical conditions, which include carpal tunnel syndrome, myotendinitis, and thoracic outlet compression, amount to physical impairments. The relevant question, therefore, is whether the Sixth Circuit correctly analyzed whether these impairments substantially limited respondent in the major life activity of performing manual tasks. . . .

Our consideration of this issue is guided first and foremost by the words of the disability definition itself. "Substantially" in the phrase "substantially limits" suggests "considerable" or "to a large degree."

"Major" in the phrase "major life activities" means important. "Major life activities" thus refers to those activities that are of central importance to daily life. In order for performing manual tasks to fit into this category—a category that includes such basic abilities as walking, seeing, and hearing—the manual tasks in question must be central to daily life. If each of the tasks included in the major life activity of performing manual tasks does not independently qualify as a major life activity, then together they must do so.

That these terms need to be interpreted strictly to create a demanding standard for qualifying as disabled is confirmed by the first section of the ADA. When it enacted the ADA in 1990, Congress found that "some 43,000,000 Americans have one or more physical or mental disabilities." If Congress intended everyone with a physical impairment that precluded the performance of some isolated, unimportant, or particularly difficult manual task to qualify as disabled, the number of disabled Americans would surely have been much higher.

We therefore hold that to be substantially limited in performing manual tasks, an individual must have an impairment that prevents or severely restricts the individual from doing activities that are of central importance to most people's daily lives. The impairment's impact must also be permanent or long-term.

It is insufficient for individuals attempting to prove disability status under this test to merely submit evidence of a medical diagnosis of an impairment. . . . That the Act defines "disability" "with respect to an individual" makes clear that Congress intended the existence of a disability to be determined in such a case-by-case manner.

* * * * *

An individualized assessment of the effect of an impairment is particularly necessary when the impairment is one whose symptoms vary widely from person to person. Carpal tunnel syndrome, one of respondent's impairments, is just such a condition. While cases of severe carpal tunnel syndrome are characterized by muscle atrophy and extreme sensory deficits, mild cases generally do not have either of these effects and create only intermittent symptoms of numbness and tingling. Studies have further shown that, even without surgical treatment, one-quarter of carpal tunnel cases resolve in one month, but that in 22 percent of cases, symptoms last for eight years or longer. When pregnancy is the cause of carpal tunnel syndrome, in contrast, the symptoms normally resolve within two weeks of delivery. Given these large potential differences in the severity and duration of the effects of carpal tunnel syndrome, an individual's carpal tunnel syndrome diagnosis, on its own, does not indicate whether the individual has a disability within the meaning of the ADA.

IV

The Court of Appeals' analysis of respondent's claimed disability suggested that in order to prove a substantial limitation in the major life activity of performing manual tasks, a "plaintiff must show that her manual disability involves a 'class' of manual activities," and that those activities "affect the ability to perform tasks at work." Both of these ideas lack support.

When addressing the major life activity of performing manual tasks, the central inquiry must be whether the claimant is unable to perform the variety of tasks central to most people's daily lives, not whether the claimant is unable to perform the tasks associated with her specific job.

* * * * *

[T]he manual tasks unique to any particular job are not necessarily important parts of most people's lives. As a result, occupation-specific tasks may have only limited relevance to the manual task inquiry. In this case, "repetitive work with hands and arms extended at or above shoulder levels for extended periods of time," the manual task on which the Court of Appeals relied, is not an important part of most people's daily lives. The court, therefore, should not have considered respondent's inability to do such manual work in her specialized assembly line job as sufficient proof that she was substantially limited in performing manual tasks.

At the same time, the Court of Appeals appears to have disregarded the very type of evidence that it should have focused

upon. It treated as irrelevant "the fact that [respondent] can . . . tend to her personal hygiene [and] carry out personal or household chores." Yet household chores, bathing, and brushing one's teeth are among the types of manual tasks of central importance to people's daily lives, and should have been part of the assessment of whether respondent was substantially limited in performing manual tasks.

[A]t the time respondent sought an accommodation from petitioner, she admitted that she was able to do the manual tasks required by her original two jobs in QCIO. In addition, even after her condition worsened, she could still brush her teeth, wash her face, bathe, tend her flower garden, fix breakfast, do laundry, and pick up around the house. The record also indicates that her medical conditions caused her to avoid sweeping, to quit dancing, to occasionally seek help dressing, and to reduce how often she plays with her children, gardens, and drives long distances. But these changes in her life did not amount to such severe restrictions in the activities that are of central importance to most people's daily lives that they establish a manual-task disability as a matter of law.

Reversed and remanded.

Questions

1. *a.* What is the central issue in the *Williams* case?

    b. What is the Court's holding?

    c. Does a diagnosis of carpal tunnel syndrome mean that an individual is disabled for ADA purposes?

    d. What test did the Court articulate for determining whether an individual can fulfill the major life activity of performing manual tasks?

2. Does the *Williams* decision leave workers like her unprotected in the workplace? Explain.

3. *a.* Do correctable impairments such as high blood pressure or poor vision constitute disabilities?

    b. Should they? See *Sutton and Hinton v. United Air Lines*, 119 S.Ct. 2139 (1999).

4. Chenoweth worked for Hillsborough County, Florida, reviewing files of hospital patients. She had to drive to hospitals to examine some of the records. She suffered a seizure, was diagnosed as having epilepsy, and was told not to drive at all until six months had passed without a seizure. She asked her employer to accommodate her by allowing her to work at home two days per week and by eliminating the requirement that she drive to hospitals. Her employer agreed to the former but not the latter. She sued, claiming a violation of the ADA. Decide. Explain. See *Chenoweth v. Hillsborough County*, 250 F.3d 1328 (11th Cir. 2001); cert.den. 534 U.S. 1131 (2002).

ADA Disabled?

Several recent Supreme Court decisions, in addition to *Williams,* appear to have significantly limited the impact of the ADA. For example, the Supreme Court in 2003 upheld Raytheon's refusal to rehire a recovered drug user who had been discharged for violating workplace rules. The worker argued that his addiction was a disability.[60] A leading ADA advocate has referred to the act as the "incredible shrinking law." [61] However, at this writing the proposed ADA Restoration Act would expand the definition of "disability" by eliminating the requirement that the disability "substantially limit" one or more "major life activities."[62]

Genetic Testing

Genetic testing in the workplace, and its discriminatory effects, has been addressed by the EEOC. In 2002, the Burlington Northern & Santa Fe Railway Co. agreed to pay 36 workers $2.2 million for the railway's use of a genetic testing program which, without the workers' knowledge, identified predispositions to carpal tunnel syndrome. In 2008, Congress and the president approved the Genetic Information Nondiscrimination Act (GINA) that prohibits employers from discriminating because of genetic information.[63]

Age Discrimination

Can a clothing store featuring styles designed for the college market lawfully prefer youthful salespersons? May a marketing firm reject older applicants in an effort to bring "new blood" into its workforce? While these questions are not definitively resolved, employers taking such actions might face liability for age discrimination.

Downhill after 43?

Eighty-eight percent of CEOs surveyed anonymously report that they see a connection between a worker's age and productivity. In a poll of 773 chief executives in 23 countries, consultants Watson Wyatt Worldwide found that most think productivity peaks around age 43.

While short-term memory may decrease with age, crystallized abilities such as verbal skills and knowledge mastery get better over time.

Sources: Glenn Burkins, "Aging Workforce: Issues Companies Would Rather Not Talk About," *The Wall Street Journal,* March 24, 1998, p. A1; and Robert J. Grossman, "Keeping Pace with Older Workers: Use It or Lose It," *HR Magazine* 53, no. 5 (May 2008) [**http://www.shrm.org/hrmagazine/articles/0508/0508grossman_use.asp**].

ADEA Claims   Basically, an Age Discrimination in Employment Act (ADEA) plaintiff claiming disparate treatment must show that she or he is 40 years of age or older, is qualified for the position in question, and either was not hired or was terminated or demoted while a younger person received more favorable treatment, or alternatively she or he must offer direct evidence of discriminatory intent. Disparate treatment, as well as harassment, under the ADEA are established under analysis similar to that under Title VII. The U.S. Supreme Court endorsed the disparate impact approach to age discrimination analysis in an important 2005 case[64] that increases the possibility that employment practices (such as layoffs) disproportionately impacting those 40 years of age or older may create age discrimination liability. At this writing, the proposed Civil Rights Act of 2008 would, among other things, amend the ADEA to set forth requirements for proving disparate impact claims similar to those brought under Title VII.[65]

Defenses The employer may defend against an age discrimination claim by showing that the termination was based on a legitimate, nondiscriminatory reason (such as poor performance) or that age is a bona fide occupational qualification (BFOQ). To establish age as a BFOQ, an employer must demonstrate that only employees of a certain age can safely and/or efficiently complete the work in question (such as piloting airplanes). The ADEA also provides that an employer can defeat an age discrimination claim by demonstrating that a "reasonable factor other than age" (like poor attendance) was the actual reason for terminating or otherwise disfavoring an older worker. But what is reasonable? Is saving money by dismissing higher-paid older workers a "reasonable factor other than age?" The Supreme Court has yet to address this question, but a reduction in force that strikes a disproportionate number of older worker may create an unlawful disparate impact on older workers.

Too Young for a Job?

Being young is cool, but the job market may prefer a little gray. Jeremy Pepper, 31, became discouraged in his job search after being laid off: "I know it sounds like Generation X whining, but this discrimination is real," says Pepper of Scottsdale, Arizona. Younger workers say they have to hide their age: "During my job search, I had much more of a challenge making myself look older, since I am often mistaken for 16," says Patricia Froelich, 21, a publicist in Orlando, Florida. "I tried my hardest to look older—using everything from fake reading glasses (to) more conservative clothing and carrying a briefcase."

Federal law protects only those 40 years of age and older, but a number of state age discrimination laws do not specify an age, while others set a cutoff at 18.

Question
Should the ADEA protect against age discrimination, regardless of age? Explain.

Source: Stephanie Armour, "Young Workers Say Their Age Holds Them Back," *USA TODAY,* October 7, 2003 [**http://www.usatoday.com/money/workplace/2003-10-07-reverseage_x.htm**].

Questions

1. Metz alleged that he was fired in violation of the ADEA. He had been a plant manager for a company, Transit Mix, that was experiencing financial problems. His employer notified him that the plant would be closed and he would be laid off. The company then sent the assistant manager of another plant, Burzloff, to Metz's plant to inspect it and make repairs. Burzloff requested that he be allowed to manage Metz's plant; the employer approved this request and discharged Metz. At the time of his

layoff, the 54-year-old Metz had a salary of $15.75 an hour; when the 43-year-old Burzloff replaced Metz, his salary was $8.05 per hour.[66]

Metz had worked for Transit for 27 years. He had received raises each year, even though the company was not profitable during some of those years. The company decided its poor financial performance did not justify retaining Metz, whose salary was comparatively high. Metz was not asked to take a pay cut before he was dismissed. The court framed the issue in the case in this manner:

> The sole issue on appeal is whether the salary savings that can be realized by replacing a single employee in the ADEA age-protected range with a younger, lower-salaried employee constitutes a permissible, nondiscriminatory justification for the replacement.[67]

Resolve that issue. Explain. See *Metz v. Transit Mix, Inc.,* 828 F.2d 1202 (7th Cir. 1987).

2. The Insurance Company of North America (ICNA) sought to hire a "loss control representative." The ad called for a B.S. degree, two years of experience, and other qualities. The plaintiff, who had 30 years of loss control experience, applied for the job but was not interviewed. ICNA hired a 28-year-old woman with no loss control experience. The plaintiff sued claiming age discrimination. ICNA said the plaintiff was overqualified.

   a. Explain the plaintiff's argument.

   b Decide the case. Explain. See *EEOC v. Insurance Co. of N. Am.,* 49 F.3d 1418 (9th Cir. 1995).

Sexual Orientation

A Davenport, Iowa, care center manager allegedly fired six employees because they were homosexual and, in his view, did not exhibit acceptable "moral character."[68] The manager explained,

> When I first came here, there was probably at least three—excuse my French—faggots working here and I had at least three dykes working here.[69]

Are those dismissed employees protected by our expansive network of employment antidiscrimination law? At this writing, neither federal law nor the law of most states offers protection against discrimination on the basis of an employee's sexual orientation. The courts have consistently ruled that Title VII's prohibition of discrimination based on sex refers to gender only and thus does not offer protection to gays. However, at this writing, the Employment Non-Discrimination Act (ENDA) has passed the House of Representatives, and awaits a vote in the Senate. ENDA would prohibit employers from discriminating on the basis of an employee's actual or perceived sexual orientation.[70] At this writing, 20 states and the District of Columbia prohibit employment discrimination based on sexual orientation. Thirteen of those states, along with the District of Columbia, also prohibit employment discrimination based on gender identity/expression.[71]

Gay Rights at Wal-Mart

After receiving "heartfelt" letters from employees, Wal-Mart's management decided in 2003 to include sexual orientation in its corporate antidiscrimination policy. Gays and lesbians will be protected against harassment, although domestic partners of gays and lesbians will not receive corporate benefits. With Wal-Mart's sudden shift in policy, 49 of America's 50 largest companies now provide antidiscrimination protection for gay and lesbian employees. Exxon-Mobil does not do so.

Source: Ann Zimmerman, "Wal-Mart Adds Sexual Lifestyle to Its Antidiscrimination Policy," *The Wall Street Journal,* July 3, 2003, p. B3.

Internet Exercise

Using UCLA law professor Eugene Volokh's Web site [**http://www.law.ucla.edu/faculty/volokh/harass**], explain how sexual harassment law is regarded by some as a threat to freedom of speech.

Chapter Questions

1. Blockbuster established a grooming policy forbidding long hair for men but allowing it for women. Four men, who were fired for refusing to cut their long hair, sued Blockbuster for sex discrimination. Has Blockbuster violated title VII? Explain. See *Kenneth Harper, et al. v. Blockbuster,* 139 F.3d 1385 (11th Cir. 1998; cert. den. 525 U.S. 1000 (1998).

2. In 2006, the EEOC filed a class action against Lawry's Restaurants including Lawry's The Prime Rib, Five Crowns, and The Tam O'Shanter Inn, on behalf of all male applicants for server positions who were systematically rejected because of their gender. Since 1938, Lawry's hired only females as servers, and did not update their policy after the passage of Title VII. Servers' uniforms are antiquated women's costumes. What might Lawry's defense be? Will this defense be successful? Explain. See EEOC Press Release, "Lawry's Restaurants Sued for Sex Bias in Hiring" [**http://www.eeoc.gov/press/4-4-06a.html**].

3. Emma, a Chinese-American, applies for an available server position in a Mexican restaurant and is rejected. She suspects it is because of her national origin. What might the Mexican restaurant say in defense of a national origin discrimination complaint made by Emma? Will this defense be successful? Explain. See EEOC Compliance Manual (2002) at 13-II-C [**http://www.eeoc.gov/policy/docs/national-origin.html**].

4. Edwin, a restaurant manager, abused male and female employees alike. However, Edwin singled out female subordinates for especially cruel treatment that included frequent and repeated sexual jokes, crude comments about their bodies, and questions such as whether they "liked to be spanked." One of these female employees, Shelby, asked him to stop making sexual comments, but he persisted despite her visible distress. When Shelby resumed work after quitting due to Edwin's conduct, Edwin continued his behavior toward her. Shelby made several complaints to managers, one of whom advised her that she was overreacting. Though the restaurant

conducted an investigation, neither Shelby nor Edwin was interviewed. No disciplinary action was taken. Resolve this case. Explain. See *EEOC v. R&R Ventures, d/b/a Taco Bell,* 244 F.3d 334 (4th Cir. 2001).

5. Breeden, a female employee, met with two male coworkers to review the psychological evaluation reports for four job applicants. Breeden's supervisor read aloud a comment in one of the reports that the applicant had once said to a coworker, "I hear making love to you is like making love to the Grand Canyon." The men chuckled. Breeden complained, and eventually filed a sexual harassment complaint with supervisory personnel. Soon thereafter, she was transferred to another position, a move that had been contemplated for some time. Breeden brought Title VII claims against her employer. What claims might she have asserted? Decide the case. Explain. See *Clark County School District v. Breeden,* 533 U.S. 912 (2001).

6. Rodriguez managed a Wal-Mart store at Fajardo, Puerto Rico. Following an evaluation, his performance was considered unsatisfactory, and he was demoted to assistant manager at another store. Rodriguez filed suit claiming race and national origin discrimination. Rodriguez pointed to two favorable previous performance evaluations, and he argued that he was evaluated in a different manner than non–Puerto Rican managers. Rodriguez was evaluated with the use of an opinion survey given to all of his subordinates. Rodriguez claimed that non–Puerto Rican managers at other stores were not subject to opinion surveys. Assuming that claim is true, would Rodriguez be able to prevail on a disparate treatment cause of action? Explain. See *Rodriguez-Cuervos v. Wal-Mart Stores,* 181 F.3d 15 (1st Cir. 1999).

7. Define *affirmative action.*

8. Diane Piantanida went on maternity leave. While absent, her employer discovered tasks that she had not completed. Before her return, Piantanida was informed that she was being reassigned to a lesser job because of her inability to keep up in her former job. Upon objecting to the change, Piantanida claims she was told that she was being given a position "for a new mom to handle." Piantanida admits that her demotion was not based on her pregnancy or her maternity leave. Piantanida declined the offer and sued, claiming a violation of the Pregnancy Discrimination Act stemming from her status as a new mother. Decide. Explain. See *Piantanida v. Wyman Center,* 116 F.3d 340 (8th Cir. 1997).

9. Thornton worked as a manager at a Connecticut retail store. In accordance with his religious beliefs, Thornton notified his manager that he could no longer work on Sundays as required by company (Caldor, Inc.) policy. A Connecticut statute provided that "No person who states that a particular day of the week is observed as his Sabbath may be required by his employer to work on such day. An employee's refusal to work on his Sabbath shall not constitute grounds for his dismissal." Management offered Thornton the options of transferring to a Massachusetts store where Sunday work was not required or transferring to a lower-paying supervisory job in the Connecticut store. Thornton refused both, and he was transferred to a lower-paying clerical job in the Connecticut store. Thornton claimed a violation of the Connecticut statute. The store argued that the statute violated the Establishment Clause (see Chapter 5) of the First Amendment, which forbids establishing an official state

religion and giving preference to one religion over another or over none at all. Ultimately the case reached the U.S. Supreme Court.

a. Decide. Explain.

b. Do the religious accommodation provisions of Title VII of the Civil Rights Act violate the Establishment Clause? See *Estate of Thornton v. Caldor, Inc.,* 472 U.S. 703 (1985).

10. Sanchez worked as a host and food server at a pair of Azteca restaurants. Throughout his work experience, male coworkers and a supervisor referred to him as "she" and "her." He was mocked for walking and carrying his serving tray "like a woman." He was called a "faggot" and a "female whore." This abuse occurred repeatedly.

    a. Make the argument that Sanchez was *not* a victim of sexual harassment.

    b. Decide the case. Explain. See *Nichols v. Azteca Restaurant Enterprises,* 256 F.3d 864 (9th Cir. 2001).

11. Must your local country club admit qualified applicants regardless of race, religion, sex, or other protected categories? Explain.

12. A new Texas airline, flying out of Dallas's Love Field, was in a precarious financial posture. A campaign was mounted to sell itself as "the airline personification of feminine youth and vitality." In commercials, its customers, who were primarily businessmen, were promised "in-flight love," including "love potions" (cocktails), "love bites" (toasted almonds), and a ticketing process (labeled a "quickie machine") that delivered "instant gratification." A male was denied a job with the airline because of his sex. He filed a Title VII action. The airline argued that attractive females were necessary to maintain its public image under the "love campaign," a marketing approach that the company claimed had been responsible for its improved financial condition. Decide. Explain. See *Wilson v. Southwest Airlines Co.,* 517 F. Supp. 292 (ND Tex. 1981).

13. Vanderbilt is among a few American universities that acknowledge actively recruiting Jewish students for admission. About 4 percent of Vanderbilt's students are Jewish, as compared with more than 20 percent at Ivy League schools. About 2 percent of the national population is Jewish. Gordon Gee, a Mormon and the Vanderbilt chancellor, has applauded the ability and liveliness of Jewish students and the contribution they make to campus intellectual life. Assistant to the provost at Vanderbilt David Davis explained, "We want the best students to come to Vanderbilt. Jews score well on the SAT." Last year's college-bound Jewish seniors averaged 1,161 out of a possible 1,600 on the SAT, second only to Unitarians (1,209) among 35 religions while the national average was 1,020. Vanderbilt characterizes its Jewish recruitment effort as part of a broader diversity strategy. In targeting Jews for special recruitment efforts, are Vanderbilt and other universities engaging in a form of profiling or stereotyping that amounts to discrimination? Explain. See John Gerome, "Vanderbilt Recruitment Produces Unease," *Boston Globe,* May 18, 2002, p. A3.

14. On balance, have the feminist movement and accompanying legal victories improved the quality of life for American women? For American men? Explain.

15. Taylor, a black woman, worked for the Burlington County, New Jersey, sheriff's office. She heard the sheriff, in speaking to another supervisor, refer to her as a

"jungle bunny." She complained to her superiors. She suffered mental distress. She discussed the matter with the media. She was shunned at work. Was Taylor a victim of a hostile working environment? Explain. See *Taylor v. Metzger,* 706 A.2d 685 (N.J.S.Ct. 1998).

16. Linda Tarr-Whelan at the Center for Policy Alternatives says, "In this economy we have a diminished sense that the work women do with people is worth the same amount as the work men do with machines and dollars."

    a. Why are jobs that may be described as traditionally "women's jobs" be considered "worth less" than "men's"?

    b. Should we insist on pay equity by requiring equal pay for work of comparable value? Explain. See Ellen Goodman, "Gender Pay Gap Is Real: $200 Billion," *Des Moines Register,* March 17, 1999, p. 9A.

17. The author of a *Harvard Law Review* article argues for discrimination claims based on appearance:

    The most physically unattractive members of our society face severe discrimination.… The unattractive ("those individuals who depart so significantly from the most commonly held notions of beauty that they incur employment discrimination") are poorly treated in such diverse contexts as employment decisions, criminal sentencing, and apartment renting. Although appearance discrimination can have a devastating economic, psychological, and social impact on individuals, its victims have not yet found a legal recourse.

    Should we treat some aspects of appearance (for example, shortness, obesity, and unattractive facial characteristics) as disabilities, thus forbidding discrimination based on those characteristics? Explain. See Note, "Facial Discrimination: Extending Handicap Law to Employment Discrimination on the Basis of Physical Appearance," *Harvard Law Review* 100, no. 8 (June 1987), p. 2035.

18. Should American firms abroad adhere to American antidiscrimination policies even if those policies might put the American firms at a competitive disadvantage or offend the values and mores of the host country? Explain.

19. John D. Archbold Memorial Hospital excluded all job applicants whose weight exceeded the maximum desirable weight (based on Metropolitan Life's actuarial survey) for large-framed men and women plus 30 percent of that weight. Sandra Murray claimed she was denied a job as a respiratory therapist because her height-to-weight ratio did not meet the guidelines. Murray did not claim to be morbidly obese.

    a. Explain the plaintiff's argument.

    b. Did the hospital violate the ADA? Explain. See *Murray v. John D. Archbold Memorial Hospital,* 50 F. Supp. 2d 1368 (M.D. Ga. 1999).

Notes

1. AFJustice.com Web site of Lieff Cabraser Heimann & Bernstein, LLP [**http://www. afjustice.com**].

2. See Jenny Strasburg, "Abercrombie to Pay $50 Million in Bias Suits," *San Francisco Chronicle,* November 10, 2004, p. C1; and Julie Tamaki, "Judge Accepts Abercrombie Plan to Settle Hiring Lawsuits," *Los Angeles Times,* November 17, 2004, p. C2.

3. Michael Lopardi, "Minority Groups Sue Abercrombie for $40 M," *University Wire,* January 27, 2005.

4. Devah Pager, "The Mark of a Criminal Record," *American Journal of Sociology* 105, no. 5, (March 2003), pp. 937–975 [**www.northwestern.edu/ipr/publications/papers/2003/pagerajs.pdf**].

5. General Accounting Office, Diversity Management: Expert-Identified Leading Practices and Agency Examples, GAO-05-90 (Washington, D.C., Jan. 14, 2005) [**http://www.gao.gov/htext/d0590.html**].

6. 347 U.S. 483 (1954).

7. A portion of this paragraph is drawn from William P. Murphy, Julius G. Getman, and James E. Jones Jr., *Discrimination in Employment,* 4th ed. (Washington: Bureau of National Affairs, 1979), pp. 1–4.

8. 127 S. Ct. 2162 (2007).

9. Janel Johnson, "Senate Committee Holds Hearing on Ledbetter Bill," Civilrights.org, February 6, 2008 [**http://www.civilrights.org/press_room/buzz_clips/civilrightsorg-stories/senate-committee-holds.html**].

10. *EEOC v. Waffle House, Inc.,* 534 U.S. 279 (2002).

11. Jess Bravin, "U.S. Courts Are Tough on Job-Bias Suits," *The Wall Street Journal,* July 16, 2001, p. A2.

12. Bravin, "U.S. Courts Are Tough on Job-Bias Suits."

13. GovTrack.us. S. 2554–110th Congress (2008): Civil Rights Act of 2008, *GovTrack.us (database of federal legislation)* [**http://www.govtrack.us/congress/bill.xpd?tab=summary&bill=s110-2554**]

14. *Haynes v. W.C. Caye & Co.,* 52 F.3d 926 (11th Cir. 1995).

15. See *International Brotherhood of Teamsters v. United States,* 97 S.Ct. 1843 (1977); *American Tobacco v. Patterson,* 456 U.S. 63 (1982); *Firefighters Local Union No. 1784 v. Stotts,* 467 U.S. 561 (1984).

16. Tresa Baldas, "Employment Tests May Fail Legal Exam," *National Law Journal,* February 18, 2008, p. 4.

17. Equal Employment Opportunity Commission Fact Sheet on Employment Tests and Selection Procedures [**http://www.eeoc.gov/policy/docs/factemployment_procedures.html**].

18. EEOC Receives Award for Post-9/11 Efforts," HR.BLR.com (October 4, 2004) [**http://hr.blr.com/news.aspx?id=10396**].

19. EEOC Litigation Settlements March 2005 [**http://www.eeoc.gov/litigation/settlements/settlement03-05.html**].

20. *Garcia v. Spun Steak Co.,* 998 F.2d 1480, cert. den. 114 S. Ct. 2726 (1994).

21. The U.S. Equal Employment Opportunity Commission, *Henredon Furniture Industries to Pay $465,000 for Racial Harassment, Hangman's Nooses* (January 24, 2008) [**http://www.eeoc.gov/press/1-24-08.html**].

22. *Aman v. Cort Furniture Rental Corp.,* 85 F.3d 1074 (3d Cir. 1996).

23. *HR Focus* 74, no. 2 (February 1997), p. 11.

24. Genaro Armas, "Gender Economics: Men Still Earn More," *Des Moines Register,* June 4, 2004, p. 1A; National Committee on Pay Equity, Citing U.S. Census Bureau Current Population Survey, 2007 Annual Social and Economic Supplement, Series PINC-05.

25. Associated Press, "Judge Approves $46 Million Settlement of Gender Discrimination Claims against Morgan Stanley," *San Jose Mercury News*, October 11, 2007 [**http://www.mercurynews.com/portlet/article/html/fragments**].

26. *Dukes v. Wal-Mart*, 509 F.3d 1168 (9th Cir. 2007).

27. Phred Dvorak, "Women Slowly Break into Boardroom," *The Wall Street Journal*, March 27, 2006, p. B3.

28. Hannah Clark, "Are Women Happy under the Glass Ceiling?" *Forbes.com*, March 8, 2006 [**http://www.forbes.com/2006/03/07/glass-ceiling-opportunities**].

29. *Id.*

30. See, generally, *Diaz v. Pan American World Airways, Inc.*, 442 F.2d 385 (5th Cir.), cert. den. 404 U.S. 950 (1971).

31. "Pregnancy Discrimination Charges EEOC and FEPAs Combined: FY 1997–FY2007" [**http://www.eeoc.gov/stats/pregnanc.html**].

32. *Elana Back v. Hastings on Hudson Union Free School District*, 365 F.3d 107 (2d Cir. 2004).

33. Allen Otten, "Uncertainty Persists on Sexual Harassment," *The Wall Street Journal*, July 29, 1992, p. B1.

34. *Burlington Industries v. Ellerth*, 524 U.S. 742 (1998); and *Faragher v. Boca Raton*, 524 U.S. 775 (1998).

35. *Oncale v. Sundowner Offshore Services*, 523 U.S. 75 (1998).

36. *Holman v. State of Indiana*, 211 F.3d 299 (7th Cir. 2000).

37. Kiren Dosanjh, "Crossing Boundaries: Sexual Harassment Liability of U.S.-Based Multi-National Corporations in Developing Countries," [**www.sba.muohio.edu/abas/2001/brussels/Dosanjh_Crossing_Boundaries.pdf**].

38. Stephen Miller. "Sexual Jokes No Laughing Matter," *Glasgow Herald*, June 7, 2002, p. 4.

39. Gerald L. Maatman Jr. "A Global View of Sexual Harassment," *HRMagazine* July 2000. p. 151.

40. Maatman, "A Global View."

41. 548 U.S. 53 (2006).

42. Tom Brown, "Ford Settles Suit Alleging Bias against White Males" [**wysiwyg://38/http://www.auto.com/industry/iwirg28_20020328.htm**].

43. Mark Truby, "Lawsuits Accuse Ford of Job Bias," *Detroit News* [**wysiwyg://35/http://detnews.com/2001/autos/0106/22b01-239087.htm**].

44. Earle Eldridge. "Ford Settles 2 Lawsuits by White Male Workers," *USA TODAY*, December 19, 2001, p. 3B.

45. 443 U.S. 193 (1979).

46. 480 U.S. 616 (1987).

47. 488 U.S. 469 (1989).

48. 115 S.Ct. 2097 (1995).

49. Charles A. Sullivan, "Circling Back to the Obvious: The Convergence of Traditional and Reverse Discrimination in Title VII Proof," *William and Mary Law Review* 46 (December 2004), p. 1031.

50. Timothy Schellhardt, "In a Factory Schedule, Where Does Religion Fit In?" *The Wall Street Journal*, March 4, 1999, p. B1.

51. 423 U.S. 63 (1977).

52. *Franks v. National Lime & Stone Co.*, 740 N.E. 2d 694 (Ohio Ct. App. 2000).

53. *Andresen v. Fuddruckers, Inc.*, No. 03-3294, 2004 WL 2931346 (D. Minn. 2004). For a journalistic account, see Donna Higgins, "Fuddruckers Loses Health Defense in 'Drooling Cook' Disability Case," *FindLaw*, January 11, 2005 [**http://news.findlaw.com**].

54. Rehabilitation Research and Training Center on Disability Demographics and Statistics (2005). 2004 Disability Status Reports. Ithaca, NY: Cornell University [**http://digitalcommons.ilr. cornell.edu/cgi/viewcontent.cgi?filename=0&article=1180&context=edicollect&type= additional**].

55. Kris Maher, "Disabled Face Scarcer Jobs, Data Show," *The Wall Street Journal,* October 5, 2006, p. D2.

56. Bureau of Labor Statistics, "Employment Situation Summary" [**http://www.bls.gov/ news.release/empsit.nr0.htm**].

57. Maher, "Disabled Face Scarcer Jobs," p. D2.

58. Thomas E. Deleire, "The Unintended Consequences of the Americans with Disabilities Act," *Regulation* 23, no. 1 (2000), p. 21.

59. Equal Employment Opportunity Commission, "Facts About Disability-Related Tax Provisions" [**http://www.eeoc.gov/facts/fs-disab.html**].

60. *Raytheon v. Hernandez,* 537 U.S. 1187 (2003).

61. Joan Biskupic, "High Court Raises Bar for ADA," *USA TODAY,* January 9, 2002, p. 3A.

62. GovTrack.us. S. 1881—110th Congress (2007): Americans with Disabilities Act Restoration Act of 2007, *GovTrack.us (database of federal legislation)* [**http://www.govtrack.us/ congress/bill.xpd?bill=s110-1881**].

63. GovTrack.us. H.R. 493—110th Congress (2007): Genetic Information Nondiscrimination Act of 2008, *GovTrack.us (database of federal legislation)* [**http://www.govtrack.us/congress/ bill.xpd?tab=summary&bill=h110-493**].

64. *Smith v. City of Jackson,* 2005 US LEXIS 2931.

65. GovTrack.us. S. 2554—110th Congress (2008): Civil Rights Act of 2008, *GovTrack.us (database of federal legislation)* [**http://www.govtrack.us/congress/bill.xpd?tab=summary &bill=s110-2554**].

66. "Age Discrimination," 56 *U.S.L.W.* 2155 (1987), summarizing *Metz v. Transit Mix, Inc.*

67. *Metz v. Transit Mix, Inc.,* 828 F.2d 1202, 1205 (7th Cir. 1987).

68. John Carlson, "Six Care Center Workers Are Fired," *Des Moines Register,* June 8, 1997, p. 1B.

69. Carlson, "Six Care Center Workers," p. 1B.

70. GovTrack.us. H.R. 3685—110th Congress (2007): Employment Non-Discrimination Act of 2007, *GovTrack.us (database of federal legislation)* [**http://www.govtrack.us/congress/ bill.xpd?tab=summary&bill=h110-3685**].

71. See Jon W. Davidson, "Celebrating Recent LGBT Legislative Advances," *Lambda Legal,* May 30, 2007 [**http://www.lambdalegal.org/our-work/publications/facts-backgrounds/ recent-lgbt-advances.html**]; and National Gay and Lesbian Task Force [**http://www. thetaskforce.org/reports_and_research/nondiscrimination_laws**].

CHAPTER FOURTEEN

Employment Law III: Labor–Management Relations

After completing this chapter, students will be able to:

1. Describe both the decline of labor unions and their hopes for renewal.

2. Describe the goals of the National Labor Relations Act (NLRA).

3. Identify unfair labor practices by management and unions.

4. Describe the role of the National Labor Relations Board (NLRB) in enforcing the NLRA.

5. Describe the process of union organizing and the related legal issues.

6. Describe "bargaining in good faith."

7. Distinguish between "unfair labor practice strikes" and "economic strikes."

8. Compare and contrast "primary picketing" and "secondary picketing/boycotts."

9. Describe employees' rights within or against unions.

10. Explain the impact of "right to work" laws on union security agreements.

Introduction

Manuel Alvarez is the type of worker that service-sector unions are eager to attract. After 11 years as a houseman at the Hilton Hotel at Los Angeles International Airport, he earns $9.95 an hour, about $20,000 a year.

"It's not enough to live on." said Mr. Alvarez, an immigrant from Mexico who vacuums halls and flips mattresses. "I go to two churches each week to pick up donated food." On his days off, he collects bottles and cans for the deposit, adding $200 a month to his income. His hope is to join a union, and soon.[1]

If America's unions have a robust future, it probably lies with people like Manuel Alvarez. Global economic shifts have split America's private sector unions in two pieces; one, the old-line manufacturing organizations represented by the United Auto Workers (UAW), for example; the other, the emerging service sector organized most notably by the Service Employees International Union (SEIU) which represents 1.8 million nurses, security guards, janitors, and others. Traditional union power in manufacturing has been deeply undercut by the outsourcing of jobs abroad to take advantage of cheaper wages. Only two million manufacturing workers currently belong to unions, a decline from three-and-one-half million 10 years ago.[2] By contrast, low-wage service jobs—for the most part not subject to outsourcing—look ripe for organizing by unions. Currently, three million such workers belong to unions.[3] Service jobs are growing, while one sixth of American manufacturing jobs, three million in total, disappeared from 2000 to 2006.[4]

Union Division   One of the results of the changing manufacturing to service composition of the American workforce is that the union movement itself has split. The AFL-CIO is maintaining its traditional role in manufacturing, construction, transportation, and the like, but the SEIU, Unite Here and other unions have broken away from the AFL-CIO to form the rival Change to Win federation that, in total, represents some six million workers. [For the Change to Win home page, see **http://www.changetowin.org**]

Manufacturing Decline   Union problems in the manufacturing sector were vividly illustrated by the 2007 settlements of new labor agreements between the UAW and the Big Three American automobile manufacturers: General Motors, Ford, and Chrysler. In return for automakers' promises of investments to maintain manufacturing jobs in the United States, UAW members approved dramatic contract changes that are expected to allow the American Big Three to compete more effectively with their nonunion competitors, Toyota, Honda, and others. Average wages were substantially frozen for a few years at about $28 per hour, and a two-tier wage structure was accepted with all new workers receiving a reduced starting rate averaging $14–$16 per hour. A major element of the new contracts is the transfer of retiree health care liabilities from the auto companies to voluntary employees' beneficiary associations (VEBAs) run by the UAW. The automakers will contribute billions to partially fund the VEBAs, but will thereafter be free of continuing health care responsibilities which will rest with the union. For the union, the two-tier wage structure and other concessions were designed to preserve auto jobs. For the manufacturers, the VEBAs along with other recent changes are expected to reduce the Japanese cost advantage in manufacturing to as little as $250 per car, down from about $2,500 in 2003.[5]

Union Hopes?   Public support for unions is quite high, with 58 percent of eligible workers saying they would join a union if they could.[6] Worker productivity jumped a record 20 percent between 2000 and 2006, but real wages increased only two percent.[7] Health and pension coverage are falling for many, and the gap between rich and poor is growing. Despite these favorable conditions, union membership continues to fall. Changing economic conditions and union corruption have certainly played a big role in union struggles, but union supporters say corporate resistance has made organizing very difficult. When Honda, for example, announced in 2006 that it would be opening a new manufacturing plant in southeastern Indiana, laid-off union workers were elated. Honda, however, limited hiring to 20 nearby, primarily rural counties, thereby excluding thousands of laid-off union workers in the other 72 Indiana counties. Honda said the geographic policy was designed to assure that workers could reach the job, even in bad weather, but union leaders believe the strategy was explicitly antiunion.[8] Indeed, of the 33 automobile, engine and transmission plants in the United States that are wholly owned by foreign companies, none have been successfully organized by the UAW.[9] In the 1980s, Honda had employed similar geographic preferences in hiring for its two rural Ohio plants, but the policy, which excluded the city of Columbus, Ohio, led to discrimination complaints from the federal Equal Employment Opportunity Commission. Honda settled the dispute by offering jobs to 370 women and minorities and paying them several million dollars.[10] To assure a "diverse and inclusive" workplace at the new Indiana plant, Honda included the city of Indianapolis in the eligible geographic area, which is otherwise approximately 96 percent white.[11]

Union Membership   The Honda episode is only one example of the many struggles unions have faced in the United States in recent decades. As recently as 1983, unions represented 20.1 percent of the American wage and salary labor force.[12] A glimmer of hope emerged in 2007 when union membership rose to 12.1 percent, up slightly from 12.0 in 2006.[13] Only 7.5 percent of private-sector workers belong to unions, but in the public sector, about 36.0 percent are union members.[14] [For more on union membership, see **http://www.ncpa.org/pd/unions/membership.html**]

Questions

1. Do we need labor unions to counterbalance the power of big corporations? Explain.
2. Harvard economics professor Richard Freeman commented on America's "apartheid economy,"

> From all points on the political map comes the message that something is wrong with the U.S. economy. Indeed, income inequality has jumped in the past two decades in almost every category: College graduates have gained in comparison with high school graduates, older workers in comparison with younger ones, professionals in comparison with laborers. The list goes on.

Is the declining power of labor unions a factor in the growing income inequality in America? Explain. See Richard Freeman, "Toward an Apartheid Economy," *Harvard Business Review,* September/October 1996, p. 114. [For the federal Bureau of Labor Statistics, see **http://stats.bls.gov/**]

Greater Union Power in China?

Unions have spread rapidly across the more than 100 Wal-Mart stores in China, and the Chinese government, through the All-China Federation of Trade Unions, is encouraging foreign corporations to embrace unions. Of course, those unions are much different than here in America. They are controlled by the Chinese Communist Party, and the union locals often are headed by plant managers. A new Chinese labor law that went into effect in January 2008 strengthened protections for Chinese workers. Unions have increased power to negotiate terms of worker contracts, workplace rules, job safety and other matters. Chinese workers do not, however, have the right to strike. Prior to passage of the new law, the American Chamber of Commerce, the U.S.-China Business Council and others aggressively lobbied the Chinese government to weaken the law's worker protection provisions. Still, the law is regarded as an important step forward in Chinese workplace rights.

Question

Are American corporations wrong to oppose the strengthening of unions in China? Explain.

Sources: David Barboza, "China Drafts Law to Boost Unions and End Abuse," *The New York Times,* October 13, 2006 [**http://www.nytimes.com**]; Shi Jiangtao, "'Sacred Duty' for Unions to Protect Workers, Says Hu," *South China Morning Post,* January 8, 2008, p.6; and Harold Meyerson, "In Fear of Chinese Democracy," *Washington Post,* April 4, 2007, p. A13.

Part One—History

As the United States moved from an agrarian to an industrial society in the late 1880s, business competition was fierce. Costs had to be cut. By paying workers as little as possible and making them work 14- to 18-hour days, employers could prosper. Farmers began moving to the city to be near their jobs and thus left their safety net of gardens, chickens, and cows. Similarly, immigrants streamed into the big cities, and competition for jobs became heated. Wages fell, and deplorable working conditions were the norm.[15] Some of those immigrants brought with them ideas and experiences in labor conflict and class struggle that would soon contribute to dramatic changes in the American workplace.

A Grim Picture

To say that working conditions for many people at this time were unpleasant or even dismal would be a vast understatement. The term *desperate* better describes the problem. Children were impressed into service as soon as they were big enough to do a job and then made to work 12- and 14-hour days.[16] In fact, small children were employed in coal mines for 10–12 hours each day, and at a rate of $1–3 per week, because they were small enough to fit in the confined spaces.[17] Textile companies sent men called *slavers* to New England and southern farm communities to gather young women to work in the mills.[18]

> Children were employed in coal mines because they were small enough to fit in the confined spaces

The following first-hand report from the early 20th century reveals the grim picture:

When I moved from the North to the South in my search for work, I entered a mill village to work in a cotton mill as a spinner. There I worked 11 hours a day, five and a half days a week, for $7 a week. In a northern mill I had done the same kind of work for $22 a week, and less hours. I worked terribly hard. . . .

The sanitary conditions were ghastly. When I desired a drink of water, I had to dip my cup into a pail of water that had been brought into the mill from a spring in the fields. It tasted horrible to me. Often I saw lint from the cotton in the room floating on top of the lukewarm water. All of the men chewed tobacco, and most of the women used snuff. Little imagination is needed to judge the condition of the water which I had to drink, for working in that close, hot spinning room made me thirsty. Toilet facilities were provided three stories down in the basement of the mill in a room without any ventilation. Nowhere was there any running water. . . .

Everything in the village is company owned. The houses look like barns on stilts, and appear to have been thrown together. When I would go inside one of them, I could see outside through the cracks in the walls. The workers do all of their trading at the company store and bank, and use the company school and library for they have no means of leaving the village.[19]

[For a history of women in the labor movement, see **http://www.afscme.org/ otherlnk/whlinks.htm**]

Compare these working-class conditions with those of John D. Rockefeller, the great tycoon of the same era. Although Rockefeller was notoriously frugal, his estate at Pocantico Hills, New York contained

. . . more than 75 buildings. . . .Within his estate were 75 miles of private roads on which he could take his afternoon drive; private golf links on which he could play his morning game; and anywhere from 1,000 to 1,500 employees, depending on the season.

. . . Rockefeller also owned an estate at Lakewood, [New Jersey] which he occupied in the spring; an estate at Ormond Beach in Florida for his winter use; a townhouse . . . in New York; an estate at Forest Hill, Cleveland which he did not visit; and a house on Euclid Avenue in Cleveland, likewise unused by him.[20]

These conditions enable us to better understand the sense of injustice felt by many workers and the belief that a redistribution of wealth might provide the only solution to class conflict.

Organizing Labor

The Knights of Labor, the first major labor organization in the United States, had a large following during the 1870s and 1880s.[21] The order admitted any workers to its ranks, regardless of occupation, gender, or nationality; in fact, the only people excluded from the group were gamblers, bankers, stockbrokers, and liquor dealers.[22] The Knights of Labor dedicated itself to principles of social reform, including the protection of wage and hour laws, improved health care systems, and mandatory education.[23] However, the goals of the Knights of Labor were perhaps too broad and far-reaching to bring workers any relief from their immediate problems. Great philosophical divisions within the Knights of Labor brought about its rapid decline.[24]

Skilled Workers

Samuel Gompers, who built and developed the American Federation of Labor (AFL), had more practical, attainable goals in mind for his organization. Gompers, a worker in the cigar industry, saw the need to organize workers along craft lines (such as plumbers, electricians, and machinists) so that each craft group could seek higher wages and better working conditions for its own workers, all of whom had the same type of skills and, presumably, shared the same occupational goals.[25] This approach, a national association of local unions directed to workers' pragmatic needs rather than the more politically motivated activities of the Knights of Labor, proved to be a successful formula for union organization.

Laborers

The Congress of Industrial Organizations (CIO) was organized in response to the needs of ordinary laborers not working in the skilled trades to which the AFL was devoted. The CIO was organized in 1935 and served assembly-line workers and others who often performed repetitive, physically demanding tasks. The AFL and CIO were fierce competitors, but after years of bitter conflict, the two groups united forces in 1955. They function together today as the AFL–CIO. [For the AFL–CIO home page, see **http://www.aflcio.org**]

Unions and the Developing Law

Labor Protection

Responding to mounting public pressure, Congress passed the Norris–LaGuardia Act in 1932 making clear that the terminology "restraint of trade," which was the heart of the 1890 Sherman Antitrust Act (see Chapter 10), was not meant to include labor organizations or activities.

From 1932 to 1935, labor tensions continued to mount. The nation was still caught in the Great Depression. Believing that one element essential to economic recovery was stability in the workforce, Congress addressed the labor question with the Wagner Act of 1935. This legislation gave workers for the first time the unequivocal right to organize and engage in concerted activities for their mutual aid and benefit. To protect this right, Congress identified and made illegal a number of unfair labor practices. Through the Wagner Act, Congress also established the National Labor Relations Board (see below).

Management Protection

Unions grew rapidly with the passage of the Wagner Act, and by 1947 Congress decided management might need a little help in coping with ever-growing labor organizations.[26] Congress enacted the Taft–Hartley Act, identifying as unfair labor practices certain activities unions used to exercise economic leverage over employers as part of the collective bargaining process. The Taft–Hartley Act also ensured employers' right to speak out in opposition to union organizing—in effect, protecting their First Amendment right to freedom of speech. Thus the Taft–Hartley Act signaled a move by the government away from unconditional support for labor toward a balance of rights between labor and management.[27]

Corrupt Union Leaders

In response to the growing evidence that union leaders were benefiting at the expense of the membership, Congress in 1959 enacted the Landrum–Griffin Act, requiring unions to keep records of their funds. It also prohibits unions from lending money except under specified circumstances and procedures; all of which must be reported annually to the government.

Members' Rights

The Landrum–Griffin Act also contains a set of provisions often referred to as the "Bill of Rights" for individual union members. These provisions are designed to protect union members by requiring that union meetings be held, that members be permitted to speak and vote at these meetings, that every employee covered by a collective bargaining agreement has the right to see a copy of that agreement, and that a union member be informed of the reasons and given a chance for a hearing if the union wishes to suspend or take disciplinary action against that member, unless he or she is being suspended for non-payment of dues.[28]

The law has also regulated the manner in which unions represent employees in the collective bargaining process. Because a union serves as employees' exclusive bargaining representative, the courts have devised a *duty of fair representation*.[29] To fulfill this duty, a union must represent employees, both in negotiating and enforcing the collective bargaining agreement, "without hostility or discrimination . . . [and] . . . with complete good faith and honesty [so as to] avoid arbitrary conduct."[30]

PRACTICING ETHICS   Fairness in the Workplace?

Workplace Fairness, a nonprofit advocate for "workplace policies and practices that work for everyone," argues that America's workers are "short-changed" by "giving more and getting less":

> Whether you look at job security, career opportunity, income, time spent on the job, health care, retirement security, or the right to organize, it's clear that working people are worse off today than they were several decades ago. . . . Is this because America has fallen on hard times? Hardly. Our economy is stronger than it has ever been. . . . Today's workplace has winners as well as losers. Executives and investors are winning and winning big. Workers trying to earn their livelihoods are losing.

Question

Is America now unfair to its ordinary workers? Explain.

Source: "Short-Changed, America's Workers Are Giving More and Getting Less," *Workplace Fairness* [http://www.workplacefairness.org/sc/].

Part Two—Labor Legislation Today

Today labor–management relations are governed by the National Labor Relations Act (NLRA), as enforced by the NLRB.[31] This act includes within it the Wagner Act, the Taft–Hartley Act, and portions of the Landrum–Griffin Act. The remaining provisions of the Landrum–Griffin Act make up the Labor–Management Reporting and Disclosure Act and the Bill of Rights of Members of Labor Organizations.

Right to Organize

The NLRA gives employees the right to engage in concerted activity, including strikes and collective bargaining. Section 7 of the NLRA states,

> Employees shall have the right to self-organization, to form, join, or assist labor organizations, to bargain collectively through representatives of their own choosing, and to engage in other concerted activities for the purpose of collective bargaining or other mutual aid or protection, and shall also have the right to refrain from any and all of such activities except to the extent that such right may be affected by an agreement requiring membership in a labor organization as a condition of employment.

[For a vast database of federal labor law statutes, regulations, state codes, and so on, see **http://topics.law.cornell.edu/wex/labor**]

Nudes Organize

Complaining of low pay, cold rooms, and air laden with paint fumes and charcoal dust, models who pose nude at a Philadelphia art school voted . . . to join a union. "We were at a loss about how to get the school to pay attention to us," said Claire Hankins, 39, who led the effort to organize.

Source: "Nudes Organize," *Des Moines Register,* May 8, 2003, p. 8C.

Unfair Labor Practices by Management

The NLRA describes and outlaws certain activities by employers that would hamper or discourage employees from exercising the rights granted to them in Section 7. Thus Section 8(a) of the act makes it an unfair labor practice for an employer to

1. Interfere with, restrain, or coerce employees in the exercise of the rights given to them by Section 7.
2. Dominate, interfere, or assist with the formation of any labor organization, including contributing financial support to it.
3. Encourage or discourage membership in any labor organization by discrimination in regard to hiring, tenure of employment, promotion, salary, or any other term of employment.
4. Discharge or take any other action against an employee because he or she has filed charges or given testimony under the act.
5. Refuse to bargain collectively with a duly certified representative of the employees.

These five provisions are designed to allow employees to organize in an atmosphere free from intimidation by the employer. In addition, if employees have chosen a union as their exclusive collective bargaining representative, Section 8(a) regulates the bargaining between the employer and the union. The provisions also ensure that the employer will not be able to interfere with union activities by either seizing control of the union or rendering it impotent by refusing to bargain collectively.

Unfair Labor Practices by Unions

Section 8(b) lists activities constituting unfair labor practices by a labor organization. Some of these provisions mirror some of the activities prohibited to employers. Moreover, at least since the enactment of the Taft–Hartley Act, the law is not sympathetic to labor organizations that try to use certain coercive tactics, threats of the loss of livelihood, or any other strong-arm methods. Finally, Section 8(b) also regulates the union's collective bargaining practices, including economic action. Thus a labor organization is not permitted to

1. Restrain or coerce any employee in the exercise of his or her rights as granted by Section 7.
2. Cause or attempt to cause an employer to discriminate against an employee who has chosen not to join a particular labor organization or has been denied membership in such an organization.
3. Refuse to bargain collectively with an employer on behalf of the bargaining unit it is certified to represent.
4. Induce or attempt to induce an employer to engage in secondary boycott activities.
5. Require employees to become union members and then charge them excessive or discriminatory dues.
6. Try to make an employer compensate workers for services not performed.
7. Picket or threaten to picket an employer in an attempt to force the employer to recognize or bargain with a labor organization that is not the duly certified representative of a bargaining unit.

Representation Matters

Section 9 of the NLRA also sets forth the election procedures by which employees may choose whether to be represented by a particular union or no union at all.

Smell a Rat?

Workers at the Asbestos, Lead, and Hazardous Waste Laborers Local 78 in New York put a 30-foot inflatable rat on a flatbed truck and stuck its nose in the third-story windows of CBS Television's Manhattan office to protest against the network's use of nonunion labor on a construction project. Police deflated and confiscated the rat. CBS had no comment.

Source: Stacy Kravetz "Ratted Out," *The Wall Street Journal,* May 11, 1999, p. A1.

National Labor Relations Board (NLRB)

The NLRB is an administrative agency responsible for regulating labor–management relations. Its primary tasks are designating appropriate bargaining units of workers (deciding which workers have a sufficient community of interest so that their needs can best be acknowledged and so that collective bargaining is efficient for the employer and the union); conducting elections for union representation within the chosen bargaining unit; certifying the results of such elections; and investigating, prosecuting, and adjudicating charges of unfair labor practices.[32]

Although the congressional mandate by which the NLRB was formed gives the agency jurisdiction theoretically to the full extent of the interstate commerce powers vested in Congress, the agency has neither the funding nor the staff to administer its duties to all of American industry. Some smaller businesses, government employees, railroad and airline workers covered by the Railway Labor Act, agricultural workers, domestic workers, independent contractors, and supervisors and other managerial employees are not protected by the board.[33]

Over the years, the NLRB has been criticized for sometimes reaching decisions based upon political/philosophical considerations rather than legal reasoning and Board precedent. Decisions often "seesaw" according to changes in power in Washington. Those criticisms were particularly loud in late 2007 when the three-member Republican majority reversed or substantially altered several longstanding precedents (some of which are noted below) in ways that favored corporate interests and harmed unions. Critics claimed that the Republican majority on the Board was hurrying to set a labor climate more favorable to the business community before the terms expired for three of the five board members. The Board majority, however, pointed to its duty to enforce the law, whether helpful to employer or employee. [For the NLRB, see **www.nlrb.gov**]

Strippers' Rights?

Two strippers claimed they lost their jobs because of their association with the Exotic Dancers Alliance, an organization in San Francisco that tries to improve working conditions in strip clubs. The women asked the NLRB to rule on the dispute, but the board concluded, by a 2–1 vote, that it did not have jurisdiction in the case. The revenue for the strip club was about $352,200, and the jurisdictional minimum for NLRB action in retail cases is $500,000. The strippers argued that $162,000 in tips should be included in the revenue total, but the NLRB disagreed.

Source: Carlos Tejada, "No Tips: Exotic Dancers Lose a Round before the Labor Board," *The Wall Street Journal,* January 22, 2002, p. A1.

Part Three—Elections

Choosing a Bargaining Representative

Representation elections are the process by which the NLRB achieves the first of the two statutory goals under the act—employee freedom of choice. That goal, however, is sometimes in conflict with the other statutory goal—stable collective bargaining. The

NLRB has devised rules to resolve such conflicts. [For the AFL–CIO view of why workers should join unions, see **http://www.workingamerica.org/issues**]

Election Petition

A union, employee, or employer initiates the formal organizing process by filing an election petition with the NLRB. The petition is sent to the employer, thus providing notice of union activity. Also, the employer must post notices supplied by the NLRB so that employees are aware of the petition. The NLRB then assumes its authority to closely oversee the conduct of employer and union. Of course at that point, the employer is free to simply acknowledge its employees' interest in joining a particular union and to engage in bargaining with that union; a decision normally called *voluntary recognition.*

Sometimes an employer enters an agreement with a union specifying that the employer will voluntarily recognize the union if the union can demonstrate that it has majority support among the employees. Majority support is often established by a *card check* method where employees signify their interest in the union simply by signing authorization cards. The card check approach thus bypasses the secret ballot election and can greatly ease union organizing. One of the controversial NLRB decisions of 2007, however, overturned 40 years of precedent and made the card check method less useful for union organizing. In *Dana Corporation/Metaldyne,*[34] the NLRB ruled that where an employer voluntarily recognizes a union based on a card check majority, antiunion employees now have 45 days to petition the board for a federally supervised, secret ballot election to *decertify* the newly recognized union or to support a petition by a rival union. Under previous rulings, that election ordinarily would not have been permitted until at least 12 months had passed. The NLRB majority believed that elections are more accurate representations of employee preferences than the more open, and easily influenced card check.

Failing voluntary recognition, the process proceeds according to NLRB rules. The NLRB will accept only those election petitions supported by a substantial showing of interest, which, at a minimum, must include the signatures of at least 30 percent of the employees in the bargaining unit. (In practice today, most unions will not proceed toward an election without 50 to 65 percent of the employees' signatures.) Those signatures accompany the petition, or they may appear on the authorization cards.

Procedure

Prior to an election, the NLRB ordinarily will first attempt to settle certain issues such as whether a union contract already covers the employees or whether the election should be delayed. In determining the timing of the election, the two statutory goals of employee free choice and stable collective bargaining may conflict. For example, if the employees are already covered by a collective bargaining agreement, should they be able to choose again during the term of the agreement? Similarly, if the employees have rejected a union in an election, can they be prohibited from voting again in the name of stable collective bargaining? Alternatively, what if the employees choose to unionize in an election, but reconsider before a collective bargaining agreement is reached? Can they have another election?

The crucial issue to be addressed at this point, however, is normally whether the proposed bargaining unit (the designated employee group—for example, all hourly workers, all welders, or all craftspersons) is appropriate for the election.

Appropriate Bargaining Unit

The key consideration in establishing an appropriate employee bargaining unit is the community of interest among the employees. The NLRB searches for an appropriate bargaining unit because collective bargaining will not be stable and efficient if it involves employees with diverse interests. Therefore, the bargaining unit may range from a portion of a plant to multiple employers in multiple plants. Plants may have more than one appropriate bargaining unit, depending on the composition of the workforce. The NLRB makes the decision regarding the appropriate bargaining unit on the basis of such considerations as physical location of the plants; physical contact among employees; similarity of wages, benefits, and working conditions; differences in skill requirements among job categories; and common supervision.

Certain classes of employees, such as supervisors, are excluded from the bargaining unit. Obviously supervisors are excluded because they act on behalf of the employer and, through their power to direct and assign work and to discipline and discharge employees, exert control over their subordinates who are or may be in the bargaining unit. Often labor and management do not agree about the classification of workers as supervisors. In another decision outraging union activists, the NLRB in 2006 substantially expanded the range of employees who might lawfully be considered supervisors and thus ineligible for union membership.[35] The three-person Republican majority ruled, among other things, that an employee assigned supervisory duties just 10 or 15 percent of the time could be deemed a supervisor. The result, according to some experts, is that more than eight million workers could be affected by the decision, but others say that number is vastly inflated.[36]

Solicitation

A 1992 Supreme Court decision in the *Lechmere* case[37] made union organizing much more difficult by ruling that employers do not have to allow on their property union organizers who are not employees. One of the results of that decision has been an increase in *salting,* the practice of union organizers applying for jobs with the intent of unionizing the other employees from the inside. The Supreme Court's 1995 *Town & Country* decision[38] held that salts are employees, thus affording them NLRA protection that forbids discrimination based on union affiliation, but a 2007 NLRB decision limited protection under the NLRA to those salts who are "genuinely interested" in obtaining employment.[39] Many employers saw the *Town & Country* decision as an unfair intrusion on their property rights and on their preference to remain union-free. The case that follows involves a Wal-Mart employee's efforts to interest coworkers in joining a union.

Wal-Mart Stores, Inc. v. National Labor Relations Board   400 F.3d 1093 (8th Cir. 2005)

Circuit Judge Melloy

Petitioner appeals the National Labor Relations Board's order finding that it violated the National Labor Relations Act by punishing employee Brian Shieldnight for union solicitation.

I.

This case arises from efforts to unionize employees at the Wal-Mart store in Tahlequah, Oklahoma. The store, like all Wal-Mart stores, maintains and enforces a policy that prohibits solicitation during employees' work time, regardless of the cause or organization.

Brian Shieldnight, an employee of the Tahlequah Wal-Mart, contacted the United Food and Commercial Workers Union, Local 1000 ("Union") about possible union representation. He obtained authorization cards from the union to organize employees at the Tahlequah store.

On January 29, 2001, Shieldnight entered the store while off-duty. He wore a T-shirt that read "Union Teamsters" on the front and "Sign a card . . . Ask me how!" on the back. Assistant Store Manager John Lamont and Assistant Night Manager Tammy Flute saw Shieldnight's T-shirt and saw him speak to an associate. Flute told the associate to return to work, and Lamont ordered Shieldnight to leave associates alone. Lamont then consulted a Wal-Mart "union hotline." The hotline representative told Lamont that Shieldnight's shirt constituted solicitation and that Shieldnight should be removed from the store. Lamont and Flute sought out Shieldnight. They found him in the jewelry department talking to two friends who were not associates. Lamont informed Shieldnight that his shirt constituted a form of solicitation and that he would have to leave the store immediately. Lamont escorted Shieldnight to the front door of the store and instructed him to leave the store and Wal-Mart property.

The next incident occurred on January 30, 2001. While on duty at the store, Shieldnight invited Department Manager Debra Starr and associates Patricia Scott and James Parsons, all of whom were also on duty, to a union meeting. Shieldnight asked Starr to come to the meeting and stated that he would like her to consider signing a union authorization card. Shieldnight separately asked Scott and Parsons to attend the meeting to hear "the other side of the story."

Based on these two incidents, Co-Manager Rick Hawkins and Assistant Manager John Lamont held a written "coaching session" with Shieldnight for violating the no-solicitation rule. A "coaching session" is part of Wal-Mart's progressive discipline process. Verbal coaching and written coaching are the first two steps in a four-step process. Hawkins and Lamont explained to Shieldnight that he had violated the solicitation policy on January 29 by soliciting on the sales floor with his T-shirt and on January 30 by verbally soliciting employees while on-duty and on the sales floor. Lamont told Shieldnight that it was wrong to have sent Shieldnight off Wal-Mart property completely. Lamont clarified that while Shieldnight could not solicit on the sales floor, he could do so in the parking lot while not on duty. Hawkins, Lamont, and Shieldnight also discussed Shieldnight's questions and concerns regarding Wal-Mart employment policies, such as health insurance for associates. Lamont suggested Shieldnight should raise the matter in "grassroots" meetings that all Wal-Mart stores hold to identify the top three companywide issues. The three men arranged a time to meet in the future. That meeting never occurred.

The union subsequently filed an unfair labor practice charge against Wal-Mart. . . .

[A] divided Board panel found that Shieldnight had not engaged in solicitation when he (1) wore the T-shirt during his shift; (2) asked on-duty employees to attend a union meeting; or (3) asked a coworker to sign a union card. . . . Wal-Mart appeals. . . .

II

* * * * *

A. The T-Shirt

The union contends that Shieldnight's T-shirt did not constitute solicitation, but rather was a "union insignia." Wal-Mart argues that by encouraging people to approach him, Shieldnight's T-shirt was a form of solicitation. In *NLRB v. W. W. Grainger, Inc.,* the board held,

> "Solicitation" for a union usually means asking someone to join the union by signing his name to an authorization card in the same way that solicitation for a charity would mean asking an employee to contribute to a charitable organization . . . or in the commercial context asking an employee to buy a product or exhibiting the product for him. . . .

Ordinarily, employees may wear union insignia while on their employer's premises. . . .

The board stated that the T-shirt should be treated as union insignia because "it did not 'speak' directly to any specific individual . . . and it did not call for an immediate response, as would an oral person-to-person invitation to accept or sign an authorization card." The board found that there was "no claim or evidence that Shieldnight did anything in furtherance of the T-shirt message. . . . He merely walked around and socialized . . . about nonunion matters." Anyone, including any Wal-Mart employee who saw Shieldnight was free to ignore both Shieldnight and the message on the T-shirt. In contrast, a solicitation to sign an authorization card requires more interaction, likely a direct yes or no answer. Absent further evidence of direct inquiry by Shieldnight, the board's conclusion was supported by substantial evidence.

Wal-Mart alleges that the panel's conclusion is not reasonable because it ignores both Shieldnight's purpose and the long-held rule that an employer may implement rules against solicitation during work time to prevent interference with work productivity.

* * * * *

Wal-Mart failed to demonstrate how the T-shirt interfered in any manner with the operation of the store. Accordingly, substantial evidence supports the board's conclusion that Shieldnight's T-shirt did not constitute solicitation.

B. The Coworker Conversations

* * * * *

Shieldnight invited three coworkers to a union meeting. . . . Shieldnight's statements did not require an immediate response from the three coworkers. Instead of a solicitation that required a response, the record shows that Shieldnight's statements were more akin to a statement of fact that put his coworkers on notice that there was to be a union meeting that night and that they were welcome to attend. Nothing in the record suggests that the environment at Wal-Mart made Shieldnight's actions uniquely disruptive. Accordingly, the panel's conclusion regarding Shieldnight's conversations was supported by substantial evidence. Furthermore, the panel acted reasonably when it concluded that "simply informing another employee of an upcoming meeting or asking a brief, union-related question does not occupy enough time to be treated as a work interruption in most settings."

C. Asking Coworker to Sign a Card

The board concluded that it was not solicitation when Shieldnight asked a coworker to sign a union authorization card. . . .

In light of the totality of the circumstances, Shieldnight's actions constituted solicitation even though he did not actually offer Starr a card at the time he asked her to sign. Shieldnight had contacted the union about obtaining union representation and had obtained cards from the union for the purpose of organizing employees at the Tahlequah store. There is little doubt as to Shieldnight's intent in the words he spoke to Starr. The record indicates that Shieldnight did not have a card in his hand at the time he spoke to Starr. It is silent as to whether he had a card on his person. The fact that he did not place a card directly in front of Starr at the time of his statement makes little difference in regard to the nature of his conversation. Further, Shieldnight's actions in this instance are more analogous to a direct solicitation than when he asked his coworkers to attend the union meeting. Asking someone to sign a union card offers that individual person the choice to be represented by a union. Informing coworkers about a union meeting merely puts fellow employees on notice that a meeting is going to take place.

Accordingly, there is insufficient evidence to support the board's conclusion that Shieldnight's actions were not solicitation, and thus we reverse the board regarding the authorization card issue.

* * * * *

Questions

1. Why was the T-shirt not a form of solicitation?
2. Would statements at work such as "support the union" or "there is a meeting tonight" constitute solicitation? Explain.
3. Why was Shieldnight's invitation to three coworkers to attend a union meeting not a form of solicitation, whereas asking a coworker to sign a card was considered impermissible solicitation?

The Election for Union Representation

If the parties have agreed to conduct an election, or alternatively, the NLRB has directed that an election be conducted following a hearing, the board will require that the employer post notices and conduct the election. The union may be selected only by a majority of the votes cast by the employees. The NLRB oversees the election to ensure the process is carried on under "laboratory conditions."[40] In other words, elections must be held under circumstances that, to the extent possible, are free from undue or unfair influence by either the employer or by unions vying for the right to represent the bargaining unit.

For both employers and employees, the circulation of racist propaganda is grounds for setting aside an election. Historically, the board set aside elections tainted by trickery such as falsehoods, allegations, misstatements, and the like but its current position is that misrepresentation alone will not constitute grounds for overturning an election. The burden is on the parties to correct misrepresentations and sort out the truth via the marketplace of ideas. The board will intervene only if the deceptive manner of the misrepresentation (such as a forged document) makes it impossible for the parties themselves to discern the truth. Some courts have endorsed the NLRB view; others have not.

Employers have the right to speak out against unions in the form of ads, speeches, and the like. Section 8(c) of the Taft–Hartley Act is designed to ensure employers' and labor organizations' traditional First Amendment rights as long as they do not overstep certain bounds:

> The expressing of any views, argument, or opinion, or the dissemination thereof, whether in written, printed, graphic, or visual form, shall not constitute or be evidence of an unfair labor practice . . . if such expression contains no threat of reprisal or force or promise of benefit.

Gooseplay?

During a union organizing campaign, a goose wandered from a company pond into the work area where a worker "talked" to the goose and determined that it favored the union. Workers then put a "Vote Yes" card around the goose's neck and drove the goose around the plant on a forklift. The workers were fired for disrupting work and creating a safety hazard. The union claimed the company illegally fired the workers for engaging in union organizing. An administrative law judge agreed with the union, but the NLRB reversed, saying, "Placing a 'Vote Yes' sign on a wild animal does not transform otherwise unprotected 'gooseplay' into activity protected by the National Labor Relations Act."

Source: NACCO Materials Handling Group, Inc., 331 NLRB No. 164 (Aug. 25, 2000).

Threats of Reprisal or Force

As noted above in our discussion of salts, employers cannot discriminate in employment to encourage or discourage union membership. Clearly, an employer who tells employees that, for example, they will all be discharged if they engage in union activity, has interfered with their rights. Similarly, an employer who interrogates employees about their activities or spies on them while they attend union meetings has engaged in unlawful interference. Problems often arise, however, in determining whether antiunion arguments by an employer are legitimate or whether they contain veiled threats. Suppose, for instance, that a company owner warns her employees that if she has to pay higher wages, she will be forced to go out of business and the employees will all lose their jobs. Such statements of economic forecast by employers are more likely to be lawful if based on objective facts not under management's control.

Promise of Benefit

Although threats of force or reprisal are clearly unlawful in union campaigns, the rationale behind the prohibition against promises of benefit is not as intuitively obvious. In a

> The union can't put any of those things in your envelope

dispute that reached the U.S. Supreme Court, Exchange Parts sent its employees a letter shortly before a representation election that spoke of "the empty promises of the union" and "the fact that it is the company that puts things in your envelope." After mentioning a number of benefits, the letter said, "The union can't put any of those things in your envelope—only the company can do that." Further on, the letter stated, "It didn't take a union to get any of those things and . . . it won't take a union to get additional improvements in the future." Accompanying the letter was a detailed statement of the benefits granted by the company and an estimate of the monetary value of such benefits to the employees.

In the representation election two weeks later, the union lost, but the outcome was challenged in court. Eventually the Supreme Court ruled that the employer's actions constituted an unfair labor practice reasoning that "well-timed increases in benefits" provide a clear message that those who provide advantages are the same people who can withdraw those benefits should their wishes not be followed.[41]

Buying Votes?

An Atlantic City, New Jersey, limousine service held a union election-day raffle for a TV/VCR. The NLRB ruled, 3–2, that the raffle was an unfair labor practice that might reasonably be interpreted to be a reward that would influence voting. A new election was ordered. The NLRB order banned election-day raffles, but minor "gifts" such as food, drinks, and buttons would be considered case-by-case if an objection were lodged.

Source: Carlos Tejada, "Bad Draw," *The Wall Street Journal,* September 5, 2000, p. A1.

The case that follows involves allegations that a company illegally interfered with union organizing activity.

Multi-Ad Services v. NLRB

255 F.3d 363 (7th Cir. 2001)

Judge Ripple

This petition asks us to review whether Multi-Ad Services, Incorporated ("Multi-Ad") violated the National Labor Relations Act ("Act") by interfering with its employees' efforts to form a union. The National Labor Relations Board ("Board") concluded that Multi-Ad violated the Act. . . .

BACKGROUND

Multi-Ad employs 450 workers at its full-service advertising art production facility in Peoria, Illinois. Multi-Ad hired Steele in 1989 to work in the bindery department. Fifteen employees work in the department, which manufactures loose-leaf, three-ring binders. The bindery department is a small operation, accounting for a limited percentage of the company's sales and profits. Steele's performance evaluations were above average throughout his tenure at the company.

* * * * *

On July 29, 1996, Multi-Ad held a quarterly meeting for employees of the bindery, press, and finishing departments. After discussing the company's financial performance, plant production manager Jerry Ireland announced the company's plan to implement a new drug-testing policy. Following this announcement, Steele spoke up and openly criticized the policy, contending in a loud and persistent manner that such testing violated employees' right to privacy. Other employees also voiced their displeasure with the policy. Steele and Larry Clore, Multi-Ad's president, then began to argue about the policy's legality. At the end of this exchange, Steele requested a copy of Multi-Ad's laws and bylaws. Clore told Steele that he could have these materials after the meeting.

Later that day, the quarterly meeting split into separate departmental meetings. The bindery department meeting commenced around 3:00 PM, the normal quitting time for day-shift employees. At this meeting, Clore gave Steele a summary plan description of Multi-Ad's corporate structure. After Steele pointed out that he wanted the complete bylaws and not a summary, Clore responded, "Have your lawyer get them." Clore then told Steele that if he did not like the company's drug policy, "Why don't you think about leaving the company?" Steele responded that he would not give Clore the pleasure of quitting. After Clore departed, Ireland tried to continue with the meeting, but Steele announced that he was leaving because "he was on his own time now." Steele testified that Ireland said, "Okay." Ireland, however, testified that Steele's remark had shocked him and that he had said nothing

in response. Ireland also testified that he had apologized to the group for Steele's behavior. Steele, however, was not ordered to remain for the rest of the meeting, which ended shortly after his exit.

Two days later, Steele and Ireland met at Steele's request. Steele apologized for his conduct at the department meeting and then told Ireland that hourly shop workers were dissatisfied with company policies. Steele told Ireland that "management needed to just sit down with the hourly employees and work some things out." Ireland replied, "That could not be done." Steele then told Ireland that, if they could not sit down and discuss these problems, he would organize a union. Ireland asked Steele to wait until Ireland returned from his vacation to discuss the issue further. Steele agreed and made no effort to contact a union while Ireland was away.

On August 16, 1996, Steele met with Ireland and bindery department manager Marty Heathcoat in Heathcoat's office. During this meeting, the two managers asked Steele why he would want to bring a union into the company. Steele told them that it would be nice to have seniority rights, better working conditions, and raises when possible. Ireland then asked what Steele could do to improve Steele's own situation at the company and pointed out that Multi-Ad posted job openings. After Steele expressed interest in a maintenance position, Ireland told him that he would set up an interview, even though the company did not have an opening for a maintenance position. At the end of the meeting, Ireland asked Steele "what it would take to satisfy him." Steele replied that it would satisfy him if management "would sit down with the hourly employees and work something out." After Ireland responded that he could not do that, Steele informed the two managers that he was leaving the meeting and was going to attempt to organize a union. Ireland asked Steele to come back and talk some more, but Steele responded that there was nothing left to talk about. Steele left at 3:30 PM, 30 minutes after his shift had ended. No one told Steele to stay, nor was he reprimanded for having left the meeting. The next day, Steele interviewed for a maintenance position, but the interview revealed that he lacked the necessary qualifications. In any event, Steele said that he did not want the job.

Steele twice met with union officials in late August. During this time, employees began to talk about Steele's efforts at organizing a union. At a meeting of bindery department employees in late August, Heathcoat addressed rumors about a union and asked employees why they wanted a union. In response, Steele stated that everyone knew that Heathcoat was referring to Steele's desire to look into unionization. Ted DeRossett, Steele's supervisor, then warned that the bindery department would be the "first to go" if the company unionized. Steele immediately challenged the legality of closing the bindery department in such a fashion. After Steele and DeRossett began to argue heatedly, Heathcoat ended the meeting.

At another bindery department meeting in late August, management informed employees that they would be working mandatory 10-hour shifts. Steele protested that it was unfair to require employees to work overtime when in the past they had been able to decline overtime. Steele also stated that it was decisions like this that caused him to explore bringing in a union.

Shortly after the meeting, Multi-Ad announced that it was adding a second shift in the bindery department and that Steele would be the lead man. On August 29, 1996, Heathcoat and DeRossett asked Steele if he would work the second shift with a positive attitude. The two assured Steele that he could still take his scheduled vacation days from August 30 through September 3. Steele told them that he would go to the second shift, do the job, and represent the company as was expected of him.

The next day, while Steele was on vacation, Multi-Ad received a letter from Steele requesting copies of the company's policies and bylaws. When Steele returned from his vacation on September 4, Heathcoat and DeRossett were waiting for him at the plant's garage door. The two asked Steele if he still wanted to see the materials that he had requested in the letter. Steele said yes, and the two told him that he could pick up the materials in the office of Bruce Taylor, Multi-Ad's vice president of finance. Steele punched the time clock and, as he started to walk toward Taylor's office, noticed DeRossett and Heathcoat accompanying him. Steele told them that he did not need them to pick up the papers. The two replied that they were tagging along in case he had any questions. Steele told them that he could not possibly have any questions because he had not yet read the materials. Nevertheless, both managers followed Steele into Taylor's office. Ireland entered the office shortly thereafter. Steele first asked Taylor for the documents. Taylor replied that Steele already had been given the summary statement at the quarterly meeting. Steele responded that he was not asking for a summary but for complete documents. After again requesting the documents and receiving no response, Steele announced that he would no longer participate in the meeting and walked out. Heathcoat ordered him to remain or be fired. Steele ignored this command and walked back to the plant, pursued by Heathcoat and Ireland. Heathcoat repeated his order that Steele return to the office or be fired. Steele, again, refused. Ireland then told

Steele that "this is the third meeting you have walked out of, you are gone." Steele immediately demanded a termination letter.

Even though Ireland had made the decision to fire Steele, Heathcoat prepared the letter. The letter spells out the purported reasons for Steele's termination:

> He [Steele] said that he didn't come for a meeting, [sic] and then walked out of the room. I told him to get back in Bruce's [Taylor's] office to discuss this with us. He repeated himself again saying that he didn't want a meeting. Jerry Ireland then Fired [sic] him.
>
> Ted Steele has walked out of three meetings within a month because he didn't feel like hearing what was being said to him. He has said that he does not agree with corporate policies set for all the employees of Multi[-]Ad. He has interrupted the work flow of the Bindery Department by persuading it's [sic] employees that this is not a good place to work. Ted will never see eye to eye with Multi[-]Ad's policies and goals for it's [sic] employees and will not even conduct himself in a professional manner when talking to management about his concerns. Ted is terminated on 9-4-96 because of his unwillingness to abide to [sic] corporate policies.

Ireland testified that he fired Steele because he was totally disrespectful to management. Ireland also testified that Steele's exit from the meeting on September 4 was an act of insubordination, particularly after he ignored Heathcoat's order to return.

THE ADMINISTRATIVE PROCEEDINGS

On September 26, 1996, Graphic Communications Union, Local 68C, and Graphic Communications International Union, AFL–CIO, filed an unfair labor charge against Multi-Ad on behalf of its employees, including Steele. Soon thereafter, the Board's General Counsel issued a complaint and a notice of hearing. The complaint alleged that Multi-Ad violated the Act by (1) coercively interrogating Steele about his interest in forming a union during the August 16 meeting with Heathcoat and Ireland; (2) impliedly promising at the August 16 meeting to help Steele improve his employment situation without the need for representation; and (3) threatening to close the bindery department if its employees unionized. The complaint also alleges that Multi-Ad violated the Act by discharging Steele because it believed that he might contact a union to organize employees.

On May 29, 1997, the Administrative Law Judge (ALJ) conducted a hearing on the board's complaint. Based on the evidence presented at the hearing, the ALJ issued his decision on December 2, 1997, and found that Multi-Ad had committed the charged unfair labor practices. On August 25,

2000, the board issued a decision and order affirming the ALJ's conclusions.

On October 10, 2000, Multi-Ad filed this petition for review.

Substantial Evidence

Multi-Ad first challenges the Board's determination that Multi-Ad coercively interrogated Steele on August 16 in violation of the Act.

* * * * *

Substantial evidence supports the Board's conclusion that management coercively interrogated Steele on August 16. The closed-door meeting was conducted in a manager's office by Heathcoat and Ireland, two people who had authority to fire Steele. The two managers questioned Steele regarding why he would want to bring a union into the company.... Moreover, Ireland immediately thereafter asked Steele about his own career advancement and arranged an interview for a maintenance position, even though no such opening existed. The managers did not assure Steele that reprisals would not be taken against him for his answers, adding to the potentially coercive nature of the inquiry. Further, this meeting was conducted after company managers had expressed uneasiness over union activity. These circumstances are more than enough evidence to sustain the Board's findings.

Multi-Ad next challenges the Board's finding that it made an implied promise of benefits by asking Steele how he could help his own situation and by arranging the job interview.... Here, Ireland asked Steele why he wanted to form a union and then asked Steele how Steele could improve his own situation. Steele expressed an interest in a maintenance position, and Ireland arranged for an interview immediately, even though there were no such openings. The context in which this occurred is significant. Because the managers made this overture during a conversation about the need for a union, the Board reasonably could have concluded that the company was willing to confer a benefit to deter Steele from contacting a union....

Next, Multi-Ad argues that substantial evidence does not support the Board's conclusion that Multi-Ad threatened to close the bindery department. Unlike an interrogation, which is coercive only if reasonable employees would perceive it as such, a threat of plant closure is per se a violation of § 8(a)(1). In this case, three employees testified unequivocally that DeRossett said that the bindery department would be the "first to go" if they brought in a union, and this evidence is more than sufficient to establish a violation.

Finally, Multi-Ad disputes the Board's conclusion that Steele's discharge violates §§ 8(a)(1) and (3). An employer violates §§ 8(a)(1) or (3) of the Act by firing employees because of their union activities. To prove a violation, the Board must prove that antiunion animus was a substantial or motivating factor in the employer's decision to make the adverse employment decision. If the Board proves such a motivation by a preponderance of the evidence, the employer can avoid a finding of an unfair labor practice by showing that it would have taken the action regardless of the employee's union activities.

[S]ubstantial evidence supports a finding that the company harbored animus, including (1) the timing of Steele's firing, which coincided with his increased efforts to organize a union; (2) the coercive interrogation of Steele regarding his interest in forming a union; (3) management's questioning of other employees about their interest in forming a union; and (4) DeRossett's warning that the bindery department would close if employees unionized. Thus, the Board met its burden of establishing antiunion animus.

Multi-Ad claims as an affirmative defense that it fired Steele for leaving three meetings without permission. The Board concluded, however, that Multi-Ad's proffered reason was pretextual and that the company fired Steele because of his efforts to unionize. That conclusion is supported by substantial evidence, including (1) Multi-Ad's written explanation of termination stating a different reason—that he was discharged because he refused to abide by corporate policies; (2) the September 4 encounter was not a "meeting"—Steele entered the office to pick up materials to which he was legally entitled and twice denied access; and (3) no manager instructed Steele to remain at the previous two meetings, both of which occurred after shift hours....

Order enforced.

Questions

1. *a.* List the four unfair labor practices identified by the court.

   b. What test did the court employ in determining whether the employer coercively interrogated Steele?

   c. What evidence supported the court's conclusion that Steele's firing was motivated by antiunion animus?

   d. Why did the court conclude that the employer's stated reason for dismissing Steele was pretextual?

2. Jose Ybarra was a labor consultant for Met West. A union election was pending at the company. An employee allegedly told Ybarra that his promised raise had not been delivered. Ybarra later allegedly told the employee that management had decided that wages could not be adjusted with an election pending. The union lost the election and filed suit claiming that Ybarra's statement was an

unfair labor practice. Decide. Explain. See *Met West Agribusiness, Inc.,* 334 NLRB No. 14 (May 23, 2001).

3. During an election campaign, the general manager's office was used to interview employees in small groups of five or six. The employees had previously visited that office to discuss grievances and obtain loans. That office was the only space available for the conversations. The general manager's remarks were temperate and noncoercive. The union lost the election. Should that result be set aside for unlawful campaigning? Explain. See *NVF Company, Hartwell Division,* 210 NLRB 663 (1974).

Union Persuasion

Unions, like employers, are restricted in the type of preelection persuasion they employ. In cases involving promises of benefits made by the union, the NLRB has been more reluctant to set aside elections than it has when such promises have been made by management. The Board's reasoning is that employees realize that union preelection promises are merely expressions of a union platform, so to speak. Employees recognize that these are benefits for which the union intends to fight. Employers, on the other hand, really do hold the power to confer or withdraw benefits. Nonetheless, a union promise to employees to provide "the biggest party in the history of Texas" if the union won the next day's election was an unfair labor practice.[42]

> "The biggest party in the history of Texas"

Remedies for Election Misconduct

Unfair labor practices during a representation election can result in the imposition of penalties and remedies. If the union loses the election and the employer engaged in wrongful behavior, a new election or other remedies may be ordered.

Decertification

After a union has been certified or recognized, an employee or group of employees may continue to resist the union or may lose confidence in it. If so, they can file a decertification petition with the NLRB. The employees must be able to demonstrate at least - 30 percent support for their petition. Once a decertification petition is properly filed with the board the usual election rules are followed to determine whether the union enjoys continuing majority support. If not, the union is decertified, and ordinarily at least one year must pass before a new representation election can be conducted. [For management advice about decertification, see **http://www.nrtw.org/d/decert.htm**]

Withdrawal of Recognition

An employer may unilaterally withdraw recognition of a union only where the union has, in fact, lost the support of a majority of its members. A mere suspicion or even a good-faith doubt of declining union support among workers does not meet the legal standard for withdrawal of recognition. One way of demonstrating that a union does not hold majority support is to file a petition (called an RM petition) with the NLRB for an employer-requested election. The employer may file the RM petition where the facts support a "good-faith reasonable uncertainty" about whether the union enjoys majority support. Normally, however, a union's majority status cannot be challenged during the term of a collective bargaining agreement (up to three years).

Escape the Union?

If a union clearly is about to win a representation election or already has done so, thus establishing its right to collective bargaining, management sometimes continues to resist. One strategy is to declare bankruptcy. That tactic may be lawful but only after bargaining sincerely with the union and only after convincing the bankruptcy court that fairness requires modification or rejection of the collective bargaining agreement. Similarly, a company may simply choose to shut down its business rather than engage in collective bargaining. Going out of business is fully lawful unless the reason for doing so was to discourage union efforts at plants in other locations. Likewise, companies sometimes employ

> Companies sometimes employ the *runaway shop* strategy

the *runaway shop* strategy in which the about-to-be-unionized plant is simply shut down and replaced by another in a location less responsive to union interests. If that move was made for the purpose of thwarting union interests, it is an unfair labor practice; but if the move reflected legitimate economic goals such as reduced wages or taxes, the move is probably lawful.

The Union as Exclusive Bargaining Agent

Once a union has been elected and certified as the representative of a bargaining unit, it becomes the exclusive agent for all of the employees within that bargaining unit, whether they voted for the union or not. The exclusivity of the union's authority has a number of implications, but one is particularly relevant in determining whether an employer has failed to demonstrate good faith at the bargaining table. Specifically, the employer must deal with the certified representative who acts on behalf of all employees in the bargaining unit. The employer commits an unfair labor practice if she or he attempts to deal directly with the employees or recognizes someone other than the workers' chosen representative. In both instances, the issue is fairly straightforward. The employer is undermining the position of the representative by ignoring him or her.

Part Four—Collective Bargaining

Section 8(a)(5) of the NLRA requires an employer to engage in *good-faith* collective bargaining with a representative of the employees, and Section 8(b)(3) imposes the same duty on labor organizations. Failure to bargain by either an employer or representative of the employees constitutes an unfair labor practice.

What is collective bargaining? What must one do to discharge the duty imposed? According to Section 8(d) of the NRLA,

> To bargain collectively is the performance of the mutual obligation of the employer and
> the representatives of the employees to meet at reasonable times and confer in good faith

with respect to wages, hours, and other terms and conditions of employment . . . but such obligation does not compel either party to agree to a proposal or require the making of a concession.

Note what is *not* included. The duty to bargain in good faith does not require that the parties reach agreement. The NLRB and the courts recognize that collective bargaining, like any negotiation, is consensual. Thus the act governs only the process, not the result, of collective bargaining.

Bargaining in Good Faith

Good faith is a murky area with no definitive answers. Over the years, various factors (none of which is conclusive in and of itself) have been identified by the board and the courts as being suggestive of good-faith bargaining. Some of these include the following:[43]

1. The employer must make a serious attempt to adjust differences and to reach an acceptable common ground; that is, one must bargain with an open mind and a sincere desire to reach agreement.

2. Counterproposals must be offered when another party's proposal is rejected. This must involve the give and take of an auction system.[44]

3. A position regarding contract terms may not be constantly changed.[45]

Mandatory Bargaining Subjects   Although employers and labor representatives are free to discuss whatever lawful subjects they mutually choose Section 8(d) of the NLRA clearly sets out some mandatory subjects over which the parties must bargain. These are wages, hours, and "other terms and conditions of employment." Although these topics for mandatory bargaining seem simple enough, questions still arise frequently. For example, suppose the union and employer bargain over wages and agree to institute merit increases for employees. Must the employer also bargain over which employees are entitled to receive these increases or who will make the decision at the time they are to be given? What about a decision to close a plant?

Generally, the board and the courts will balance three factors. First, they look at the effect of a particular decision on the workers—how direct is it and to what extent is the effect felt? Second, they consider the degree to which bargaining would constitute an intrusion into entrepreneurial interest or, from the opposite side, an intrusion into union affairs. Third, they examine the practice historically in the industry or the company itself.[46] [For an online collection of labor contracts, see **http://www.irle.berkeley.edu/library/index.php?page=3**]

Permissive and Prohibited Bargaining Subjects   Those matters not directly related to wages, hours, and terms and conditions of employment and not falling within the category of prohibited subjects are considered permissive. Either party may raise permissive subjects during the bargaining process, but neither may pursue them to the point of a bargaining impasse. Refusal to bargain over a permissive subject does not constitute an NLRA violation, and permissive subjects must simply be dropped if the parties do not

> Whether a union has a right to bargain over management's placement of hidden surveillance cameras in the workplace

reach agreement. Permissive subjects ordinarily would include such items as alteration of a defined bargaining unit, internal union affairs, and strike settlement agreements. Prohibited bargaining subjects are those that are illegal under the NLRA or other laws.

In the case that follows the NLRB had to decide whether a union has a right to bargain over management's placement of hidden surveillance cameras in the workplace.

LEGAL BRIEFCASE

Colgate–Palmolive Co.
323 NLRB No. 82 (1997)

FACTS

Colgate–Palmolive's Jeffersonville, Indiana, plant employed approximately 750 workers. Colgate and the employees had a collective bargaining arrangement for over 20 years. In 1994 an employee discovered a surveillance camera in a restroom air vent. The union president later discussed the matter with Colgate's human resources officer, who indicated that the camera had been placed in the vent because of theft concerns and that the camera had been removed after employees objected to it. The Union filed a grievance over the matter, and the parties met for discussion where Colgate argued that it had the absolute right to install internal surveillance cameras. Later, the Union sent a letter to Colgate demanding to bargain over the subject of cameras within the plant. Colgate did not respond, and the Union filed an unfair labor practice charge. The case was heard by an administrative law judge. Evidence indicated that Colgate had installed 11 secret cameras over four years to address problems of theft and misconduct, including sleeping on the job. The cameras were placed in several offices, a fitness center, a restroom, and as a monitor for an overhead door that was not a proper exit from the building. The Union and some employees were aware of various "unhidden" cameras in the workplace and in some instances fortuitously discovered some of the hidden cameras.

The Administrative Law Judge (ALJ) concluded that the use of hidden surveillance cameras is a mandatory subject of bargaining and by failing to do so, Colgate–Palmolive violated

the National Labor Relations Act. The ALJ's ruling was then appealed to the National Labor Relations Board. The NLRB decision follows.

CHAIRMAN GOULD AND MEMBERS FOX AND HIGGINS

In *Ford Motor Co. v. NLRB,* the Supreme Court described mandatory subjects of bargaining as such matters that are "plainly germane to the 'working environment'" and "not among those 'managerial decisions, which lie at the core of entrepreneurial control.'" As the judge found, the installation of surveillance cameras is both germane to the working environment, and outside the scope of managerial decisions lying at the core of entrepreneurial control.

As to the first factor—germane to the working environment—the installation of surveillance cameras is analogous to physical examinations, drug/alcohol testing requirements, and polygraph testing, all of which the Board has found to be mandatory subjects of bargaining. They are all investigatory tools or methods used by an employer to ascertain whether any of its employees has engaged in misconduct.

The Respondent [Colgate–Palmolive] acknowledges that employees caught involved in theft and/or other misconduct are subject to discipline, including discharge. Accordingly, the installation and use of surveillance cameras has the potential to affect the continued employment of employees whose actions are being monitored.

Further, as the judge finds, the use of surveillance cameras in the restroom and fitness center raises privacy concerns which add to the potential effect upon employees. We agree that these areas are part of the work environment and that the use of hidden cameras in these areas raises privacy concerns which impinged upon the employees' working conditions. The use of cameras in these or similar circumstances is unquestionably germane to the working environment.

With regard to the second criterion, we agree with the judge that the decision is not a managerial decision that lies at the core of entrepreneurial control.

* * * * *

The use of surveillance cameras is not entrepreneurial in character, is not fundamental to the basic direction of the enterprise, and impinges directly upon employment security. It is a change in the Respondent's methods used to reduce workplace theft or detect other suspected employee misconduct with serious implications for its employees' job security, which in no way touches on the discretionary "core of entrepreneurial control."

The Respondent urges that bargaining before a hidden camera is actually installed would defeat the very purpose of the camera. The very existence of secret cameras, however, is a term and condition of employment, and is thus a legitimate concern for the employees' bargaining representative. Thus, the placing of cameras, and the extent to which they will be secret or hidden, if at all, is a proper subject of negotiations between the Respondent and the union. Concededly, the Respondent also has a legitimate concern. However, bargaining about hidden cameras can embrace a host of matters other than mere location. And, even as to location, mutual accommodations can and should be negotiated. The vice in the instant case was the respondent's refusal to bargain.

* * * * *

Accordingly, we affirm the judge's finding that the union has the statutory right to engage in collective bargaining over the installation and continued use of surveillance cameras, including the circumstances under which the cameras will be activated, the general areas in which they may be placed, and how affected employees will be disciplined if improper conduct is observed.

ORDER

The National Labor Relations Board adopts the recommended Order of the administrative law judge as modified and set forth in full below and orders that the Respondent, its officers, agents, successors, and assigns, shall

1. Cease and desist from

    a. Failing and refusing to bargain with Local 15, International Chemical Workers Union, AFL–CIO with respect to the installation and use of surveillance cameras and other mandatory subjects of bargaining.

2. Take the following affirmative action necessary to effectuate the policies of the Act.

    a. On request, bargain collectively with the Union as the exclusive bargaining representative of the Respondent's employees with respect to the installation and use of surveillance cameras and other mandatory subjects of bargaining.

    b. Within 14 days after the service by the Region, post at its facility in Jeffersonville, Indiana, copies of the attached notice.

Notice to Employees
Posted by Order of the
National Labor Relations Board
An Agency of the United States Government

The National Labor Relations Board has found that we violated the National Labor Relations Act and has ordered us to post and abide by this notice. Section 7 of the Act gives employees these rights.

To organize
To form, join, or assist any union
To bargain collectively through representatives of their own choice
To act together for other mutual aid or protection

To choose not to engage in any of these protected concerted activities.

We will not fail and refuse to bargain with Local 15, International Chemical Workers Union, AFL–CIO over the installation and use of surveillance cameras within our facility and other mandatory subjects of bargaining.

We will not in any like or related manner interfere with, restrain, or coerce you in the exercise of the rights guaranteed you by Section 7 of the Act.

We will, on request, bargain collectively with the Union as the exclusive bargaining representative of our employees with respect to the installation and use of surveillance cameras within our facility and other mandatory subjects of bargaining.

Colgate–Palmolive Company.

Questions

1. What test did the ALJ and the NLRB employ to determine whether the placement of hidden surveillance cameras was a mandatory subject of bargaining?

2. Why did the union win this case?

3. If you were managing a workplace where theft, sleeping on the job, and other misconduct were at a worrisome level, would you employ hidden, secret cameras to monitor restrooms, fitness areas, and the like? Explain.

4. A mirror fell off the wall in a Consolidated Freightways bathroom. Employees discovered that management had installed cameras behind two-way bathroom mirrors in order to address "ongoing drug abuse." The employees sued, saying the cameras violated California state privacy laws.

A federal court of appeals labeled the two-way mirrors "a direct violation" of California criminal law. Consolidated argued that its collective bargaining agreement (CBA) permitted the surveillance. The CBA provided that Consolidated could not use video cameras to discipline or discharge employees for reasons other than theft or dishonesty. Consolidated also claimed that the Labor Management Relations Act preempts the employees' state claims because the claims required interpretation of the collective bargaining agreement. The lower court ruled for Consolidated. The case was appealed. How would you rule? Explain. See *Cramer v. Consolidated Freightways*, 255 F.3d 683 (2001); cert. den. 122 S.Ct. 806 (2002).

Administering the Agreement

Union–management bargaining does not end with the negotiation of a labor agreement. Rather, bargaining continues daily as the parties work out the disputes and confusions and conflicting interpretations that are bound to arise and that cannot be entirely provided for in the labor agreement. Often this process of contract maintenance takes the form of resolving *grievances,* as in the *Colgate–Palmolive* case. Those problems are addressed through the grievance procedure that is included in collective bargaining agreements. Often the grievance procedure involves a series of steps beginning with informal discussion mechanisms. Failing there, the dissatisfied employee typically files a written complaint (the grievance). Normally, grievances are presented to management by a union representative, often with the worker also present.

Arbitration

If, after negotiation, the parties cannot resolve their dispute, the collective bargaining agreement ordinarily provides for *final and binding arbitration.* Many court decisions have vigorously supported the arbitration process as the means of settling labor–management contract maintenance disputes and tend to find disputes arbitrable unless the labor agreement explicitly and unambiguously exempts the subject at issue from the arbitration process. Further, but for rare exceptions, neither the company nor the union can turn to the courts to set aside arbitration decisions.

Fair Representation

Because grievance processing is part of a union's bargaining responsibility, the union might breach its duty if it declined to represent an employer's grievance. An employee who feels wronged when a union does not process his or her grievance has the option of appealing to the NLRB or to the courts.

Part Five—Labor Conflict

PRACTICING ETHICS   Union Loyalty, Employee Loyalty or Money?

The Writers Guild of America, the union for show business writers, struck the television and movie industries in 2007–08 pushing for a bigger share of revenues, particularly revenues from movies and television shows distributed over the new media, such as the Internet. The late night talk shows featuring David Letterman, Jay Leno, Conan O'Brien, Jimmy Kimmel, and others respected the union for weeks by confining their telecasts to reruns. After six weeks, Letterman's production company, Worldwide Pants, was able to reach its own agreement with the striking union, thus allowing Letterman to return to the air with his full staff, including writers. The other talk shows decided to return to the air without their writers although their network and studio owners had not reached agreements with the Writers' Guild. Many stars, however, declined to appear as talk show guests since they would have been forced to cross the striking writers' picket lines (explained below) to appear on the shows.

Leno and others argued that they needed to return to the air even without a strike settlement because they

wanted to avoid laying off their many staff members who would have been without work if the shows stayed off the air. Indeed, some of those shows and hosts had paid their staffs while not working during the rerun period, but that financial burden reportedly could not be sustained. O'Brien, a strong union supporter, said he had to decide whether to "go back to work and keep my staff employed or stay dark and allow 80 people, many of whom have worked for me for 14 years, to lose their jobs."[47]

The 100-day strike was settled in February, 2008.

Questions

1. Was it wrong of Leno, Kimmel and the others to return to the air rather than continuing to honor the writers' strike? Explain.

2. Assume you are a Jimmy Kimmel fan, and you received tickets to the show during the strike. Would you support the writers by refusing to attend the Kimmel show? Explain.

Strikes

For many, the initial image of labor conflict is one of employees on strike, picketing a store or factory. Striking is, however, an extremely drastic measure under which employees must bear an immediate loss of wages and, in many instances, risk job loss. Similarly, employers bear the loss of a disruption to continued operations. As Table 14.1 shows, work stoppages have declined dramatically since World War II.

We will address two kinds of strikes:

1. *Unfair labor practice strikes* are those instituted by workers in response to the employer's commission of an unfair labor practice such as interfering with legitimate union activities or failure to bargain in good faith. These strikers can be temporarily, but not permanently, replaced.

2. *Economic strikes* are those used purely as economic weapons to persuade employers to provide more favorable benefits or better working conditions. All strikes not involving unfair labor practices fall into this category. With some exceptions, economic strikers cannot be fired, but they can be permanently replaced. In what has been

TABLE 14.1 U.S. Work Stoppages Involving 1,000 or More Workers

Year	Number	Workers (thousands)	Days Idle (thousands)	Percentage of Estimated Working Time
1948	245	1,435	26,127	.22
1958	332	1,587	17,900	.13
1968	392	1,855	35,367	.20
1978	219	1,006	23,774	.11
1988	40	387	4,381	.02
1998	34	387	5,116	.02
2005	22	100	1,736	.01
2007	21	189	1,265	.005

Source: [http://stats.bls.gov/news.release/wkstp.htm].

labeled "the most significant change in collective bargaining to occur since the passage of the Wagner Act in 1934," employers are now increasingly willing to permanently replace economic strikers.[48] Employers had enjoyed that right where necessary "in an effort to carry on the business" since a 1938 Supreme Court decision, but for practical reasons they had rarely exercised it.[49] Later decisions imposed some limitations on that right. For example, any striker who is permanently replaced is put on a preferential hiring list and will have priority to be selected to fill subsequent vacancies. However, President Reagan's 1981 dismissal of 11,300 striking air traffic controllers effectively crushed their union (PATCO) and caused private-sector employers to reassess their long-standing reluctance to use replacements during and after strikes.[50] Thus recent years have seen some major employers like Hormel, Caterpillar, Greyhound Bus Lines, Firestone/Bridgestone, the National Football League, and Major League Baseball use, or threaten to use, strike replacements.

The following case examines when employers can legitimately decline to reinstate strikers.

LEGAL BRIEFCASE

Diamond Walnut Growers, Inc. v. NLRB
113 F.3d 1259 (D.C. Cir. 1997); cert. den. 118 S.Ct.1299 (1998)

Circuit Judge Silberman

I

Diamond Walnut processes and packages walnuts for national and international distribution. . . . Diamond's employees have for years been represented by Cannery Workers, Processors, Warehousemen, and Helpers Local 601 of the International Brotherhood of Teamsters, AFL–CIO (the union). In September of 1991, following expiration of the most recent collective bargaining agreement between Diamond and the union, nearly 500 of Diamond's permanent and seasonal employees went on strike. Diamond hired replacement workers to allow it to continue operations.

By all accounts, the strike was, and remains, a bitter affair. The strikers are alleged to have engaged in various acts of violence against the replacement workers. . . . In addition, as part of its effort to exert economic pressure on Diamond, the union undertook an international boycott of its product. The boycott included a well-publicized national bus tour during which union members distributed to the public leaflets which described Diamond's workforce as composed of "scabs" who packaged walnuts contaminated with "mold, dirt, oil, worms, and debris."

Approximately one year into the strike, the Board held a representation election. The union lost the election, but its objections prompted the Board to order a rerun to be held in October of 1993. Just over two weeks prior to the new election, a group of four striking employees, represented by a union official, approached Diamond with an unconditional offer to return to work. According to the letter presented to the company at that time by their representative, the employees were convinced that "a fair election [was] simply impossible." Nonetheless, the employees "fe[lt] that it [was] important that the replacement workers . . . have an opportunity to hear from Union sympathizers." Thus, the group of strikers was "available and willing to return to immediate active employment." The following day, the union notified Diamond that pursuant to the above-quoted letter, two additional strikers were willing to return to work.

It is undisputed that for three of the returning strikers, neither the permanent jobs they held before the strike, nor substantially equivalent ones, were available at the time of their return. Diamond placed these three in various seasonal jobs. Prior to the strike, Willa Miller was a quality control supervisor; she was placed in a seasonal packing position even though a seasonal inspection job was available. Alfonsina Munoz had been employed as a lift truck operator and, despite the availability of a seasonal forklift job, was given a seasonal job cracking and inspecting nuts in the growers' inspection department at the front end of the production process. Mohammed Kussair, formerly an air separator machine operator, was, like Munoz, placed in a seasonal cracking and inspecting position in the growers' inspection department. . . .

The rerun election took place as scheduled, and the union lost. Following that election, the General Counsel filed a complaint alleging that Diamond had violated the National Labor Relations Act by unlawfully discriminating against Miller, Munoz, and Kussair. The General Counsel alleged that because of their protected activity, Diamond declined to put them in certain available seasonal positions for which they were qualified and that were preferable to the positions in which they were actually placed. After a hearing, an administrative law judge recommended that the charges be dismissed. He found that Diamond had "discriminated" insofar as it had placed the employees at least in part because of their protected activity, but he did not think that discrimination "unlawful."

* * * * *

[The NLRB reversed saying] "although [Diamond] was under no legal obligation . . . to reinstate the strikers . . ., once it voluntarily decided to reinstate them, it was required to act in a nondiscriminatory fashion toward the strikers." Diamond had discriminated against Miller, Munoz, and Kussair, in the Board's view, by declining "to place them in the [seasonal] positions of quality control assistant, lift truck operator, and loader, respectively, because of their union status and/or because of certain protected union activity they engaged in while on strike.". . . The Board rejected the contention that the placements were warranted by the employer's concern that the replacement workers might instigate violence against the three and thus justified placement in well-supervised jobs, since "there [was] no evidence that Miller, Munoz, or Kussair were involved" in the strike-related violence allegedly causing Diamond's concern. The Board also dismissed the notion that the placements of Miller and Munoz were justified by their participation in the boycott and the circulation of disparaging leaflets: "[T]he strikers' conduct constituted protected . . . activity and there is no evidence indicating that such protection was lost because of threats made by Miller and Munoz to damage or sabotage [Diamond's] equipment or products." Since Diamond had failed to justify its discrimination, the Board found unfair labor practices.

* * * * *

[Diamond sought judicial review of the NLRB ruling.]

II

Diamond Walnut challenges the Board's determination that it lacked substantial business justification for refusing to place the three employees in the specific jobs they sought—quality control assistant, lift truck operator, and loader. It is undisputed that the *Fleetwood* framework governs this case. The General Counsel under *Fleetwood* must make out a *prima facie* case that the employer discriminated within the meaning of the Act, which means the employer's decision as to how to treat the three returning strikers was attributable to their protected activity. *Rose Printing* establishes that a struck employer faced with an unconditional offer to return to work is obliged to treat the returning employee like any other applicant for work (unless the employee's former job or its substantial equivalent is available, in which case the employee is preferred to any other applicant). But Miller and Munoz were not treated like any other applicant for work. Miller was qualified for a seasonal position in quality control that paid 32 cents per hour more than the packing job to which she was assigned. And Munoz was qualified to fill a forklift operating job, a position that paid between $2.75 and $5.00 per hour more than the walnut cracking and inspecting job she received. Diamond admits that it took into account Miller's and Munoz's protected activity in choosing to place them in jobs that were objectively less desirable than those for which they were qualified. Petitioner [Diamond], although it contended that the discrimination was comparatively slight, does not dispute that its action discriminated against Munoz and Miller within the meaning of the Act.

* * * * *

Under *Fleetwood,* after discrimination is shown, the burden shifts to the employer to establish that its treatment of the employees has a legitimate and substantial business justification. Petitioner declined to give Munoz the forklift driver job because of its concern that driving that piece of equipment throughout the plant would be unduly risky in two respects. First, because of the bad feeling between strikers and replacements, Munoz would be endangered if confronted by hostile replacement workers in an isolated area. Second, since Munoz had participated in the bus tour during which the union had accused the company of producing tainted walnuts, Munoz would be tempted to engage in sabotage by using the 11,000 pound vehicle to cause unspecified damage. As for Miller, who was also on the bus tour, the company declined to put her in the "sensitive position of quality control assistant" where "the final visual inspection of walnuts is made prior to leaving the plant." In that position, she would have "an easy opportunity to let defective nuts go by undetected . . . or to place a foreign object into the final product, thereby legitimizing the Union's claim of tainted walnuts."

* * * * *

A. Munoz

The Board rejected petitioner's proffered justifications for its placement of Munoz on the same ground as did the ALJ. As to Diamond's purported fear for her safety, no evidence had been produced that Munoz was thought to be responsible for any violence, so there was no reason to believe she would have been a special target. The Board said, "[T]here is no specific evidence that any replacements harbored hostility toward these three strikers, and, if such evidence did exist as [Dia-

mond] claims, we fail to see how placing them in the positions to which they were assigned would lessen the perceived danger of retaliatory acts being committed against them." The Board discounted Diamond Walnut's contention that Munoz would be under greater protection if closely supervised, noting that petitioner had admitted that "Munoz freely roamed the plant unsupervised during her breaks."

* * * * *

As for the possibility that Munoz would engage in forklift sabotage, the Board was more terse, stating only that "the strikers' conduct [referring to the bus tour] constituted protected . . . activity," and there was no evidence indicating that such protection was lost because of threats made by Miller and Munoz. If Munoz had uttered specific threats of sabotage, however, she would have lost her protected status. . . . [T]he Board necessarily concluded that the possibility of Munoz engaging in future sabotage by misuse of her forklift was simply not a sufficient risk to constitute a substantial business justification for her treatment.

* * * * *

Similarly, the Board was reasonable in its determination that the risk of Munoz engaging in sabotage while riding around on her 11,000 pound forklift—the petitioner seems to most fear her crashing the forklift into machinery—is not a substantial business justification for her disadvantageous placement in another job. Strikes tend to be hard struggles, and although this one may have been more bitter than most, there is always a potential danger of returning strikers engaging in some form of sabotage. There is therefore undeniably some risk in employing returning strikers during a strike. But it could not be seriously argued that an employer cannot be forced to assume *any* risk of sabotage, because that would be equivalent to holding that an employer need not take back strikers during an ongoing strike at all. . . .

* * * * *

B. Miller

The Miller case is another matter. It will be recalled that petitioner declined to assign her to the post of quality control assistant, the job responsible for the final inspection of walnuts leaving the plant (she received a job paying 32 cents an hour less). The Board rejected the employer's justification, which was based on Miller's participation in the product boycott and bus tour leafleting, saying only "the strikers' conduct constituted protected . . . activity and there is no evidence indicating that such protection was lost because of threats made by Miller and Munoz to damage or sabotage . . . equipment or products." With respect to Miller, we think the Board's determination that petitioner's business justification is insubstantial is flatly unreasonable.

All strikes are a form of economic warfare, but when a union claims that a food product produced by a struck company is actually tainted it can be thought to be using the strike equivalent of a nuclear bomb; the unpleasant effects will long survive the battle. . . . The company's ability to sell the product . . . could well be destroyed.

* * * * *

The Board's counsel argues that it is unfair to assume that an employee would behave in a disloyal and improper fashion. It is unnecessary, however, for us to make that assumption to decide the Board was unreasonable. The Board accepted petitioner's contention that Miller would have been placed "in the sensitive position . . . where final visual inspection of walnuts is made prior to leaving the plant." Miller would therefore have been put in a rather acute and unusual conflict of interest in which her job for her employer could be thought to have as a function the rebutting of her union's claim. A similar conflict would be raised if she wished a bargaining unit job in the company's public relations department. This conflict makes all too likely the possibility that Miller would be *at least* inattentive to her product quality duties. . . . To make matters worse, any "mistake" by Miller on the product quality control line would not be easily attributable to her unless petitioner paid someone to stand all day looking over Miller's shoulder. . . . If Munoz ran her forklift into valuable machinery, she would run a risk of being discovered and would therefore be deterred. But Miller, as a quality control assistant, could simply avert her eye and cause the damage with apparently little risk of discovery. . . .

In short, she would have had a special motive, a unique opportunity, and little risk of detection to cause severe harm. Both the risk Diamond faced in its placement of Miller was qualitatively different than a normal risk of sabotage, and the deterrence to Miller's possible misbehavior was peculiarly inadequate.

* * * * *

[W]e are obliged to ask in the last analysis whether the Board's decision, as to whether the employer's action was substantially justified by business reasons, falls within the broad stretch of reasonableness. In this case, at least with respect to one part of the Board's decision, we conclude the Board exceeded the reasonableness limits.

So ordered.

AFTERWORD

After nearly 14 years of bitter struggle, the Diamond Walnut strike was settled in March 2005. The settlement allowed strikers to return to work with full seniority and benefits, although many of them had already returned to Diamond Walnut or had moved to other jobs. [For a time line of the Diamond Walnut strike, see **http://www.teamster.org/divisions/foodprocessing/diamondwalnut/dwtimeline.htm**]

Questions

1. Set out the two-part test the court employed to determine whether Diamond Walnut violated the National Labor Relations Act by discriminating against its employees because of their participation in protected union activities.

2. Explain why the court found that Munoz had been wronged by Diamond but Miller had not.

3. *a.* How would you vote on federal legislation banning the practice of permanently replacing economic strikers? Explain.

   b. Is there any reason to distinguish between economic strikers and unfair labor practice strikers? Any reason not to do so? Explain.

4. A pilots' union, Airline Professionals Association, had a collective bargaining agreement with freight carrier Airborne Express (ABX). The union and ABX had a dispute about time-off provisions in the CBA. The union applied pressure to ABX by asking all pilots not to bid on open flying time not covered in the regular monthly schedule. ABX says it lost jobs due to the lack of pilots and filed a complaint saying the union was engaging in an illegal strike. A district court agreed with ABX, and the union appealed. Decide the case. Explain. See *ABX Air, Inc. v. Airline Professionals Assn.,* 266 F.3d 392 (2001); cert. den. 122 S.Ct. 1459 (2002).

Picketing and Boycotts

Primary Picketing   In addition to striking, unions often picket or boycott to publicize their concerns and pressure employers during the negotiating process. Picketing is the familiar process of union members gathering and sometimes marching, placards in hand, at a place of business. Peaceful, informational picketing for a lawful purpose is protected by the NLRA. Some kinds of picketing, however, are forbidden, and all picketing can be regulated by the government to ensure public safety. Primary picketing is expressed directly to the employer with whom the picketers have a dispute. Primary picketing enjoys broad constitutional and statutory protection, but it may be unlawful if violent or coercive.

Secondary Picketing/Boycotts   Secondary picketing or boycotting is directed to a business other than the primary employer, and ordinarily it is unlawful. That is, unions are engaging in an unfair labor practice if they threaten or coerce a third party with whom they are not engaged in a dispute in order to cause that third party to put pressure on the firm that is the real target of the union's concern. Consider, however, the mock funeral case summarized below.

Mock Funeral

The Sheet Metal Workers' union staged a mock funeral outside a Florida hospital in 2004. One person dressed in a "Grim Reaper" costume carrying a plastic sickle and four "pallbearers" carried a prop coffin and handed out leaflets. Various somber tunes played in the background on a portable audio system. The leaflets detailed several malpractice lawsuits against the hospital with the implication that the malpractice was linked to the hospital's decision to contract with nonunion labor. The demonstration was designed to pressure the hospital, a neutral entity, to stop doing business with the picketers' actual target, the nonunion contractors. The "funeral" was conducted about 100 feet from the entrance and was separated from it by a street, a strip of grass, a hedge, and a parking lot. The hospital filed an unfair labor practice charge against the union claiming the funeral constituted illegal secondary picketing in violation of the NLRA. The NLRB issued an order commanding the union to cease and desist. That decision was reviewed by the federal District of Columbia Court of Appeals.

Questions
1. What constitutional law defense would you offer on behalf of the Sheet Metal Workers' union?
2. Decide the case. Explain.

Source: Sheet Metal Workers' International Association, Local 15, AFL-CIO v. National Labor Relations Board, 2007 U.S. App. LEXIS 14361.

Lockouts

Sometimes management takes the initiative in labor disputes by locking its doors to some or all of its employees. Both the NLRB and the courts allow lockouts as defensive acts to protect businesses against sudden strikes and to prevent sabotage or violence. Some court decisions have also expanded lawful lockouts to include those of an offensive nature designed to improve management's bargaining position. Lockouts, however, are clearly not lawful if designed to interfere with bargaining rights and other legitimate union activity.

Sports fans have learned some labor law in recent years. National Hockey League owners locked out the players and eventually cancelled the entire 2004–05 season. Since 1972 baseball has had three lockouts and five player strikes. Owners locked out National Football League game officials during the final week of the pre-season 2001 schedule, then settled with them in mid-September after using college officials in the interim. National Basketball Association team owners locked out their players in 1998 and reached a settlement in 1999.

> Since 1972 baseball has had three lockouts and five player strikes.

Question

George A. Hormel & Co. and the United Food and Commercial Workers Union settled a long labor dispute. Thereafter, an unhappy employee drove his car in a parade and attended a rally, both of which were designed to encourage a nationwide boycott of Hormel Products. The employee did nothing to signal his feelings beyond his presence at the two events.

Employees may lawfully be dismissed for disloyalty to their employer. Supporting a boycott of an employer's products ordinarily constitutes disloyalty except where (1) the boycott is related to an ongoing labor dispute and (2) the support does not amount to disparagement of the employer's product.

Was this Hormel employee engaged in protected activity such that his dismissal was unlawful? Explain. See *George A. Hormel and Company v. National Labor Relations Board*, 962 F.2d 1061 (D.C. Cir. 1992).

Part Six—Employees' Rights within or against the Union

The Union's Duty of Fair Representation

As you have seen in previous sections of this chapter, the union is given statutory authority to be the exclusive bargaining agent for the employees in the designated bargaining unit. This means that even if an individual employee in the bargaining unit does not agree with union policies or is not a member of the union, he or she cannot bargain individually with the employer. Such an employee is bound by the terms of the collective bargaining agreement, and the union has a duty to fairly represent that employee and all members of the bargaining unit, whether or not they become members of the union.

The Bill of Rights of Labor Organization Members

The Bill of Rights for members of labor organizations is contained in Title 1, Section 101 of the Labor–Management Reporting and Disclosure Act (LMRDA or Landrum–Griffin Act). The Bill of Rights was designed to ensure equal voting rights, the right to sue the union, and the rights of free speech and assembly. These rights of union members are tempered by the union's right to enact and enforce "reasonable rules governing the responsibilities of its members." [51]

Union Security Agreements and Right-to-Work Laws

To maintain their membership, unions typically seek a collective bargaining clause requiring all employees to become union members after they have been employed for some period—generally 30 days (*union shop agreements*)—or, at the least, requiring them to pay union dues and fees (*agency shop agreements*). These union security arrangements are lawful under the NLRA.

Under the 1988 Supreme Court decision in *Communications Workers of America v. Beck*[52] nonunion employees can be compelled to pay union dues and fees only for core collective bargaining activities. Thus nonunion employees' agency shop dues and fees must be reduced by an amount equal to that applied to such noncore purposes as lobbying and political campaigning. [For the Communications Workers of America home page, see **http://www.cwa-union.org**]

Right-to-Work   Twenty-two states, primarily in the South and West, have enacted right-to-work laws that prohibit union security arrangements in collective bargaining agreements. In these states, nonmembers do not pay dues or fees, but as members of the bargaining unit, they must be represented by the union. Unions regard those employees as free riders, but right-to-work supporters see the matter as one of personal freedom. [For questions and answers on right-to-work laws, see **http://www.nrtw.org/a/a_prime.htm**]

Closed Shop   At one time, powerful unions insisted on *closed-shop* arrangements wherein employers could hire only individuals who already belonged to unions, but those arrangements are now forbidden by the NLRA.

Part Seven—Other Unions

Public-Sector Unions

The public sector is a growth area for union membership. Legal regulation of public-sector labor–management relations begins with state law. Although the specific provisions of those laws vary, many NLRA concepts are applicable. Some fundamental policies and doctrines are quite different, however. A particular distinction lies in the ability of public-sector employees to strike.

Some states prohibit those strikes and others permit them only under restricted conditions. In either case, the rationale for treating public employees differently than private-sector employees is the role of public employees as servants of the voters. Public servants arguably have a higher duty than private employees. In addition, certain public employees, including police officers and fire-fighters, work in positions that clearly involve public safety, and to permit them to strike might endanger the citizenry.

Internet Exercise

Using the United Auto Workers' frequently asked questions [**http://www.uaw.org/about/faqs.html**],

1. Explain "how union pay compares to nonunion pay."

2. Explain how union dues are used.

Chapter Questions

1. *a.* In your opinion, what are the average blue-collar worker's biggest sources of job dissatisfaction? Can they be eliminated through collective bargaining? Explain.

   b. In your opinion, what are the average white-collar worker's biggest sources of job dissatisfaction? What means do such workers have for eliminating those sources of dissatisfaction? Explain.

2. *a.* Imagine what the world will be like 50 years from now. In what ways do you picture the work life of the average American to have changed? Explain.

   b. Imagine the ideal work world. How close does that picture come to the one you conjured up in response to the previous question? What types, if any, of labor or other legislation would bring society closer to that ideal? Explain.

3. You are the human resources manager for a manufacturing firm that is presently the subject of an organizing campaign by a union that has filed an election petition with the NLRB just 30 days ago. Your plant manager has come to you and said that she wishes to discharge one of her employees. She further explains that the employee in question has worked for the company for three years and throughout that time has had a terrible attendance record. She adds that up to this point the employee has not received any discipline for his attendance. Upon inquiry, the plant manager tells you that the employee has been seen on the plant floor wearing a button that says "Union Yes!" In addition, the plant manager tells you that she knows that the employee is an outspoken union activist. What would you advise the plant manager to do? Why?

4. ACE/CO, a Milwaukee automobile parts manufacturer, was accused of a series of unfair labor practices springing from company conduct both before and after a disputed union representation election. Among the charges were the following:

   - ACE/CO declined to grant its usual across-the-board wage increases and told employees that the union was responsible for the failure to grant a raise.
   - ACE/CO distributed a memorandum asking employees to inform supervisors whenever they felt pressured to sign a union authorization card. One employee testified that union representatives had visited his home 13 times and that he did feel "pressured" to support the union.
   - ACE/CO included in its employee handbook a statement indicating the company's "intention to do everything possible to maintain our company's union-free status for the benefit of both our employees and [the company]."

   a. Why might ACE/CO legitimately decline to offer a wage increase during an organizing campaign?

   b. Do any of these company behaviors constitute unfair labor practices? See *NLRB v. Aluminum Casting & Engineering Co.*, 230 F.3d 286 (7th Cir. 2000).

5. When assistant manager Diane Gorrell was fired from a Bob Evans restaurant in East Peoria, Illinois, most of the employees walked off the job in protest. They stood outside the restaurant for a time and discouraged customers from entering. The restaurant was left in some disarray and problems persisted for a number of days, clearly harming business. Later all but one of the employees asked to return to their jobs, but were refused. The employees filed an unfair labor practices charge with the NLRB.

   a. Justify, as a matter of law, management's decision not to allow the employees to return to work.

   b. Explain the employees' unfair labor practices charge.

   c. Decide the case. Explain. See *Bob Evans Farms, Inc. v. NLRB,* 163 F.3d 1012 (7th Cir. 1998).

6. Seawin, an Ohio fittings manufacturer, was forced to lay off 17 employees. The company's net income had declined by 88 percent, it had lost some major customers, and it had excess inventory. At the time of the layoffs, a company vice president said that he "hoped that business . . . would turn around soon." Asked when they would be called back, employees remembered the vice president saying "probably" around two weeks to a month. Others, however, indicated that the layoffs were intended to be permanent, and the company made significant equipment and computer improvements to enhance efficiency. Soon thereafter the NLRB held a representation election at Seawin that resulted in a 31–21 vote in favor of a union. Eleven of the laid-off workers had been allowed to vote in the election. Seawin challenged the election results saying the laid-off employees should not have been allowed to vote. Was Seawin correct? Explain. See *NLRB v. Seawin, Inc.,* 248 F.3d 551 (6th Cir. 2001).

7. Midwestern Personnel Services provided truck drivers to employers in Indiana, Kentucky, and other locations. Midwestern wanted the drivers to join a union so they would be allowed to enter a unionized workplace, AK Steel, where they were to deliver cement. Midwestern management favored Teamsters Local 836 in Middletown, Ohio, for their drivers, but a majority of the drivers voted to join Teamsters Local 215 in Evansville, Indiana. Midwestern refused to recognize Local 215; management and the drivers could not reach agreement about pension rights and contract length; and the drivers went on strike. The drivers later made an unconditional offer to return to work, but Midwestern would not allow them to return because, in its view, the drivers were economic strikers. The NLRB concluded that the drivers were motivated in part by unfair labor practices, and thus should be reinstated to their jobs. Were the drivers entitled to reinstatement? Explain. See *NLRB v. Midwestern Personnel Services,* 322 F.3d 969 (7th Cir. 2003).

8. Local 582 engaged in an economic strike against Broadview Dairy of Spokane, Washington. Local 582 tried to distribute handbills at several Albertson's groceries in the Spokane area. The handbills urged customers to refrain from buying Broadview products, which Albertson's sold. Albertson's formal policy forbade all solicitations, but some groups, such as Boy Scouts and area schools, were allowed on company property to make solicitations. Albertson's ordered the union members off

its property. Later, Albertson's ordered union organizers off its property where they were trying to encourage Albertson's employees to join their union. Local 582 filed an unfair labor practices charge against Albertson's. Does Albertson's have the right to exclude from its property nonemployee union representatives who engage in either nonorganizing or organizing activities? Explain. See *Albertson's Inc. v. National Labor Relations Board,* 301 F.3d 441 (6th Cir. 2002).

9. A union–management dispute led to an economic strike, at which point the employer hired replacement workers. At the end of the strike, the workforce consisted of 25 former strikers and 69 replacement workers. The agreement settling the strike provided that strikers would be recalled as vacancies arose. However, the employer did not follow the agreement when it recalled four workers (three of whom were replacements) and failed to consider any of 28 strikers who remained out of work.

   Well-settled labor law provides that "economic strikers who have been permanently replaced but who have unconditionally offered to return to work are entitled to reinstatement upon the departure of the replacements." The NLRB found a violation of the National Labor Relations Act, and framed the issue as follows: "How should the layoff of the permanent replacement worker—who has a contractual right to recall—affect the reinstatement rights of unreinstated strikers?" The NLRB ruled that it would require a showing that the laid-off replacements had no "reasonable expectancy of recall." Then the burden of proof would shift to the employer to justify its failure to recall strikers when vacancies arose. The NLRB decision was appealed. Decide. Explain. See *Aqua-Chem, Inc. v. NLRB,* 910 F.2d 1487 (7th Cir., 1990); cert. den. 111 S.Ct. 2871 (1991).

10. Suzi Prozanski, a union president and an employee of the Eugene, Oregon *Register-Guard,* sent three union-related messages on the company e-mail system. She was warned her use of the company system to send those messages violated the company's communications policy. The e-mail dispute ultimately reached the National Labor Relations Board in 2007 where, by a 3–2 vote, the board ruled that an employer has a basic right to restrict employee use of company property. The ruling provided that restrictions on union messages on the company e-mail system are lawful so long as employers also barred employees from sending e-mail for "non-job related solicitations" for outside organizations generally. Personal, non-work-related postings (e.g., wedding announcements) remained permissible under company policy. Historically, the board had ruled that employers were engaging in discrimination if they permitted personal messages on bulletin boards and telephones, but did not permit union messages. The NLRB decision in the *Register-Guard* situation was one of several in 2006 and 2007 (some of which were explained earlier in this chapter) that changed the direction of labor law in ways that significantly weakened union rights.

   a. In your judgment, did the NLRB rule correctly in the *Register-Guard* dispute? Explain.

   b. In light of the *Register-Guard* decision and others favoring employer interests, do you think the NLRB has unwisely shifted the balance of labor–management power? Explain. See *Register-Guard,* 351 NLRB No. 70 (December 16, 2007).

11. In October 1998, members of the Graphic Communications International Union, representing employees of *The San Diego Union-Tribune,* distributed leaflets urging a boycott of Robinsons-May, a department store that advertised in the newspaper. The protest was conducted at the privately owned, upscale Fashion Valley Mall. Mall owners stopped the leaflet distribution as it was being conducted in front of the department store. Does the Mall have the legal right to stop that distribution? Explain. See *Fashion Valley Mall v. National Labor Relations Board,* 2007 WL 4472241 (Cal.).

12. Jerry Kirby was discharged from his job at Ford Motor Company, allegedly because of "being under the influence of alcohol, absenteeism, and threatening management." The United Auto Workers union (UAW) immediately filed a grievance on Kirby's behalf. Kirby lost through the first three steps of the grievance process, and the UAW declined to appeal to arbitration on Kirby's behalf. The UAW said that Kirby had no right to appeal because he had allowed his union membership to lapse. Kirby then filed an unfair labor practice charge against the union. Decide. Explain. See *International Union v. NLRB,* 168 F.3d 509 (D.C. Cir. 1999).

13. *a.* Can an employer lawfully discharge a group of employees who walk out in protest of working conditions?

    b. Would it matter if the collective bargaining agreement contains a no-strike clause? Explain.

14. What steps can an employer lawfully take to provide the labor necessary to keep a plant operative during a strike?

Notes

1. Steven Greenhouse, "The New Face of Solidarity," *The New York Times,* June 16, 2006 [**www.nytimes.com**].

2. Ibid.

3. Ibid.

4. Ibid.

5. Joseph Szczesny, "Big Three-UAW Contracts Even the Playing Field—Eventually," *Auto Observer,* November 18, 2007 [**http://www.autoobserver.com/2007/11/big-three-uaw-c.html**].

6. Harley Shaiken, "Stronger Unions Mean a Strong Middle Class," *Los Angeles Times,* February 17, 2007 [**http://www.latimes.com/news/opinion/la-oe-shaiken17feb17,0,312807.story?track=tottext**].

7. Ibid.

8. Neal E. Boudette, "Honda and UAW Clash Over New Factory Jobs," *The Wall Street Journal,* October 10, 2007, p. A1.

9. Ibid.

10. Ibid.

11. Ibid.

12. "Union Membership Continues Steady Decline in 2006" [**http://hr.cch.com/topic-spotlight/emplaw/021607b.asp**].

13. "Union Members Summary," Bureau of Labor Statistics *News,* January 25, 2008 [**http://www.bls.gov/news.release/union2.nr0.htm**].

14. Ibid.

15. Isaac A. Hourwich, *Immigration and Labor* (New York: Arno Press, 1969), pp. 125–45.

16. John J. Flagler, *The Labor Movement in the United States* (Minneapolis: Lerner Publications, 1972), pp. 26–28.

17. Alan Glassman, Naomi Berger Davidson, and Thomas Cummings, *Labor Relations: Reports from the Firing Line* (New York: Business Publications, Inc., 1988), pp. 5–6.

18. Flagler, *Labor Movement,* pp. 26–28.

19. Eli Ginzberg and Hyman Berman, *The American Worker in the Twentieth Century: A History through Autobiographies* (New York: Free Press, 1963), pp. 193–95, in *I Am a Woman Worker,* ed. Andria Taylor Hourwich and Gladys L. Palmer, Affiliated Schools for Workers, 1936, pp. 17 ff.

20. Flagler, *Labor Movement,* pp. 33 and 36, quoting Frederick Lewis Allen, *The Big Change:.. America Transforms Itself, 1900–1950* (New York: Harper, 1952).

21. Flagler, *Labor Movement,* p. 47.

22. J. David Greenstone, *Labor in American Politics* (New York: Alfred A. Knopf, 1969), p. 21.

23. Archibald Cox, with Derek Bok and Robert A. Gorman, *Cases and Materials on Labor Law,* 8th ed. (Mineola, NY: Foundation Press, 1977), pp. 7–8.

24. Greenstone, *Labor in American Politics,* p. 22.

25. Greenstone, *Labor in American Politics,* p. 23.

26. Patrick Hardin, *The Developing Labor Law* (Washington, DC: Bureau of National Affairs, 1992), pp. 31–32.

27. Hardin, *The Developing Labor Law,* p. 94.

28. Hardin, *The Developing Labor Law,* pp. 1, 108.

29. *Steele v. Louisville and Nashville Railroad,* 323 U.S. 192 (1944).

30. *Vaca v. Sipes,* 386 U.S. 171 (1967); *Miranda Fuel Co.,* 140 NLRB 181 (1962).

31. The National Labor Relations Act is found in Title 29 U.S.C. § 151 et seq.

32. Cox, *Labor Law,* pp. 113–22.

33. Cox, *Labor Law,* pp. 99–101.

34. 351 NLRB No. 28 (2007).

35. *Oakwood Healthcare, Inc.,* 348 NLRB No. 37 (2006).

36. Molly Selvin, "U.S. Ruling Could Eliminate Union Eligibility for Millions," *Los Angeles Times,* October 4, 2006 [**http://www.latimes.com/business/la-fi-labor4oct04,0,5076104. story?track=tottext**].

37. *Lechmere, Inc. v. NLRB,* 502 U.S. 527 (1992).

38. *NLRB v. Town & Country Electric, Inc.,* 516 U.S. 85 (1998).

39. *Toering Electric Company,* 351 NLRB No. 18 (2007).

40. See *Sewell Mfg. Co.,* 138 NLRB 66 (1962), which states that the board's goal is to conduct elections "in a laboratory under conditions as nearly ideal as possible to determine the uninhibited desires of employees" and "to provide an atmosphere conducive to the sober and informed exercise of the franchise free from . . . elements which prevent or impede reasonable choice."

41. *NLRB v. Exchange Parts Co.,* 375 U.S. 405 (1964).

42. *Trencor, Inc. v. National Labor Relations Board,* 110 F.3d 268 (5th Cir. 1997).

43. Benjamin J. Taylor and Fred Whitney, *Labor Relations Law,* 4th ed. (Englewood Cliffs, NJ: Prentice Hall, 1983), p. 406.

44. *Majure Transport Co. v. NLRB,* 198 F.2d 735 (5th Cir. 1952).

45. *NLRB v. Norfolk Shipbuilding & Drydock Corp.,* 172 F.2d 813 (4th Cir. 1949).

46. See *First National Maintenance Corporation v. NLRB,* 101 S.Ct. 2573 (1981).

47. Matea Gold, Maria Elena Fernandez, and Richard Verrier, "Jay Leno, Conan O'Brien to Return to the Air Jan. 2," *Los Angeles Times,* December 18, 2007 [**http://www.latimes.com/news/la-fi-strike18dec18,0,3643358.story?coll=la-tot-topstories&track=ntothtml**].

48. Littler, Mendelson Fastiff and Tichy *The 1990 Employer* (San Francisco: Littler Mendelson, Fastiff and Tichy, P.C., 1990), p. V6.

49. *NLRB v. Mackay Radio & Tel. Co.,* 304 U.S. 333 (1938).

50. Littler, et al., *The 1990 Employer,* p. V6.

51. *United Steelworkers of America v. Sadlowski,* 457 U.S. 102 (1982).

52. 487 U.S. 735 (1988).

Selected Topics in Government–Business Relations

CHAPTER FIFTEEN

Consumer Protection

After completing this chapter, students will be able to:

1. Identify some consumer protections offered under common law.

2. Describe "lemon laws" as an example of state consumer regulation.

3. Explain the purpose, roles, and power of the federal consumer protection agencies including the Federal Trade Commission (FTC), the Consumer Product Safety Commission (CPSC), and the Food and Drug Administration (FDA).

4. Identify the circumstances in which the Truth in Lending Act (TILA) applies to a consumer loan.

5. Identify protections offered under the Fair Credit Reporting Act (FCRA).

6. Describe the protections offered by the Fair Credit Billing Act (FCBA).

7. Recognize the purpose of the Electronic Fund Transfer Act (EFTA).

8. Explain the purpose of the Equal Credit Opportunity Act (ECOA).

9. Identify debt collection practices forbidden by the Fair Debt Collection Practices Act (FDCPA).

10. Explain the purpose and effect of filing a Chapter 7 liquidation or "straight" bankruptcy.

Introduction

Fans of Miss Cleo the "Jamaican" television "psychic" must be suffering withdrawal pains since the famous seer packed her tarot cards in the fall of 2002. Miss Cleo, who reportedly was more a California Valley Girl than the Jamaican shaman she claimed, evidently did not foresee the weight of the American legal system coming down on her. Under pressure from the U.S. Federal Trade Commission, two companies associated with Cleo, Access Resource Services and Psychic Readers Network, Inc., agreed to pay a $5 million fine and cancel $500 million in billings. Smaller settlements were subsequently reached with at least five states. Before her legal problems, Miss Cleo had been a spectacular financial success:

> Her honeyed words persuaded millions to pick up the phone and call, bringing in millions of dollars. . . . But the calls also generated 2,000 complaints across the United States

from people who said they had been the victims of duplicitous marketing and outright fraud. Miss Cleo herself has not been charged, as it turns out she rarely answered the phone. Instead callers were farmed out to contract workers. . . . At $4.99 a minute, the numbers quickly added up. . . . People who had asked to be placed on a "do not call" list were contacted, while others received up to 10 calls a day, usually automated messages telling them, "Miss Cleo had a dream about them and they should call back."[1]

Doubtless the government should not always protect us from our own foolishness, but costly consumer fraud and other forms of consumer abuse (invasion of privacy, dangerous products, identity theft, false advertising, and so on) are not unusual in our consumption-driven lives. Historically we relied on the market to address those problems; but in recent decades legislatures, courts, and administrative agencies have developed laws and rulings to protect us where the market arguably has failed. This chapter surveys some of those legal interventions.

Part One—Common Law Consumer Protection

Later in this chapter we will explore government efforts to protect consumers from dangerous products, unfair lending practices, and the like. Before turning to that legislation, we need to appreciate the common law (judge-made law) that preceded and, in some respects, provided the foundation for the many federal, state, and local initiatives of recent years. In addition to the product liability protection (negligence, warranties, and strict liability) discussed in Chapter 7, injured consumers can look to several common law protections, including actions for fraud, misrepresentation, and unconscionability. [For an extensive menu of consumer law sites, see **http://www.lectlaw.com/ files/cos19.htm**]

Fraud and Innocent Misrepresentation

If the market is to operate efficiently, the buyer must be able to rely on the truth of the seller's affirmations regarding a product. Regrettably, willful untruths appear to be common in American commerce. A victim of fraud is entitled to rescind the contract in question and to seek damages, including, in cases of malice, a punitive recovery. Although fraud arises in countless situations and thus is difficult to define, the legal community has generally adopted the following elements, each of which must be proven:

1. Misrepresentation of a material fact.
2. The misrepresentation was intentional.
3. The injured party justifiably relied on the misrepresentation.
4. Injury resulted.

In identifying a fraudulent expression, the law distinguishes between statements of objective, verifiable facts and simple expressions of opinion. The latter ordinarily are not fraudulent even though they are erroneous. Thus normal sales puffing ("This baby is the greatest little car you're ever gonna drive") is fully lawful, and consumers are expected to exercise good judgment in responding to such claims. If a misleading expression of opinion comes from an expert, however, and the other party does not share that expertise (such as in the sale of a diamond engagement ring), a court probably would offer a remedy.

Of course, fraud can involve false conduct as well as false expression. A familiar example is the car seller who rolls back an odometer with the result that the buyer is misled.

A variation on the general theme of fraud is innocent misrepresentation, which differs from fraud only in that the falsehood was unintentional. The wrongdoer believed the statement or conduct in question to be true, but he or she was mistaken. In such cases, the wronged party may secure rescission of the contract, but ordinarily damages are not awarded. The following case involves a fraud claim against Harley-Davidson.

Tietsworth v. Harley-Davidson

LEGAL BRIEFCASE 677 N. W.2d 233 (Wis. S.Ct. 2004)

Justice Diane S. Sykes

The circuit court dismissed the entire action for failure to state a claim. [T]he court of appeals reinstated [the claims.]

* * * * *

FACTS AND PROCEDURAL HISTORY
Plaintiff Steven C. Tietsworth and the members of the proposed class own or lease 1999 or early-2000 model year Harley motorcycles equipped with Twin Cam 88 or Twin Cam 88B engines. Harley's marketing and advertising literature contained the following statement about the TC-88 engines:

> Developing [the TC-88s] was a six-year process. . . . The result is a masterpiece. We studied everything from the way oil moves through the inside, to the way a rocker cover does its job of staying oil-tight. Only 21 functional parts carry over into the new design. What does carry over is the power of a Harley-Davidson™ engine, only more so.

Harley also stated that the motorcycles were "premium" quality, and described the TC-88 engine as "eighty-eight cubic inches filled to the brim with torque and ready to take you thundering down the road."

On January 22, 2001, Harley sent a letter to Tietsworth and other owners of Harley motorcycles informing them that "the rear cam bearing in a small number of Harley-Davidson's Twin Cam 88 engines has failed. While it is unlikely that you will ever have to worry about this situation, you have our assurance that Harley-Davidson is committed to your satisfaction." The letter went on to explain that the company was extending the warranty on the cam bearing from the standard one-year/unlimited mileage warranty to a five-year/50,000 mile warranty. Separately, Harley developed a $495 "cam bearing repair kit" and made the kit available to its dealers and service departments "to expedite rear cam bearing repair."

* * * * *

The amended complaint alleges that the cam bearing mechanism in the 1999 and early-2000 model year TC-88 engines is inherently defective, causing an unreasonably dangerous propensity for premature engine failure. [T]he amended complaint alleged that Harley's failure to disclose the cam bearing defect induced the plaintiffs to purchase their motorcycles by causing them to reasonably rely upon Harley's representations regarding the "premium" quality of the motorcycles.

The amended complaint further alleges that if the plaintiffs had known of the engine defect, they either would not have purchased the product or would have paid less for it. The amended complaint does not allege that the plaintiffs' motorcycles have actually suffered engine failure, have malfunctioned in any way, or are reasonably certain to fail or malfunction. Nor does the amended complaint allege any property damage or personal injury arising out of the engine defect. Rather, the amended complaint alleges that the plaintiffs' motorcycles have diminished value, including diminished resale value, because Harley motorcycles equipped with TC-88 engines have demonstrated a "propensity" for premature engine failure and/or fail prematurely.

* * * * *

DISCUSSION
Common-Law Fraud Claim

The plaintiffs' common-law fraud claim is premised on the allegation that Harley failed to disclose or concealed the existence of the cam bearing defect prior to the plaintiffs' purchases of their motorcycles. It is well established that a nondisclosure is not actionable as a misrepresentation tort unless there is a duty to disclose. *Ollerman v. O'Rourke Co., Inc.,* 94 Wis. 2d 17, 26, 288 N.W. 2d 95 (1980). Our decision in *Ollerman* outlined the three categories of misrepresentation in Wisconsin law—intentional misrepresentation, negligent misrepresentation, and strict responsibility misrepresentation—and described the common and distinct elements of the three torts.

All misrepresentation claims share the following required elements: (1) the defendant must have made a representation of fact to the plaintiff; (2) the representation of fact must be false; and (3) the plaintiff must have believed and relied on the misrepresentation to his detriment or damage. The plaintiffs here allege intentional misrepresentation, which carries the following additional elements: (4) the defendant must have made the misrepresentation with knowledge that it was false or recklessly without caring whether it was true or false; and (5) the defendant must have made the misrepresentation with intent to deceive and to induce the plaintiff to act on it to his detriment or damage.

Ollerman reiterated the general rule that in a sales or business transaction, "silence, a failure to disclose a fact, is not an intentional misrepresentation unless the seller has a duty to disclose." The existence and scope of a duty to disclose are questions of law for the court. *Ollerman* held that "a subdivider–vendor of a residential lot has a duty to a 'noncommercial' purchaser to disclose facts which are known to the vendor, which are material to the transaction, and which are not readily discernible to the purchaser." We specified that this was a "narrow holding," premised on certain policy considerations present in noncommercial real estate transactions.

The transactions at issue here, however, are motorcycle purchases, not residential real estate purchases, and it is an open question whether the duty to disclose recognized in *Ollerman* extends more broadly to sales of consumer goods. . . .

No Legally Cognizable Injury

Ollerman also held that damages in intentional misrepresentation cases are measured according to the "benefit of the bargain" rule, "typically stated as the difference between the value of the property as represented and its actual value as purchased." . . .

[W]e have generally held that a tort claim is not capable of present enforcement (and therefore does not accrue) unless the plaintiff has suffered actual damage. . . . Actual damage is harm that has already occurred or is "reasonably certain" to occur in the future. . . . Actual damage is not the mere possibility of future harm. . . . [T]he amended complaint must adequately plead an actual injury—a loss or damage that has already occurred or is reasonably certain to occur—in order to state an actionable fraud claim. . . .

The injury complained of here is diminution in value only—the plaintiffs allege that their motorcycles are worth less than they paid for them. However, the amended complaint does not allege that the plaintiffs' motorcycles have diminished value because their engines have failed, will fail, or are reasonably certain to fail as a result of the TC-88 cam bearing defect. The amended complaint does not allege that the plaintiffs have sold their motorcycles at a loss because of the alleged engine defect. The amended complaint alleges only that the motorcycles have diminished value—primarily diminished potential resale value—because Harley motorcycles equipped with TC-88 engines have demonstrated a "propensity" for premature engine failure and/or will fail as a result of the cam bearing defect. This is insufficient to state a legally cognizable injury for purposes of a fraud claim.

Diminished value premised upon a mere possibility of future product failure is too speculative and uncertain to support a fraud claim. The plaintiffs do not specifically allege that their particular motorcycles will fail prematurely, only that the Harley product line that consists of motorcycles with TC-88 engines has demonstrated a propensity for premature engine failure. An allegation that a particular product line fails prematurely does not constitute an allegation that the plaintiffs' particular motorcycles will do so, only that there is a possibility that they will do so.

We certainly agree with the court of appeals that the damage allegations in a fraud complaint are not evaluated against a standard of "absolute certainty" for purposes of a motion to dismiss for failure to state a claim. But an allegation that a product is diminished in value because of an event or circumstance that might—or might not—occur in the future is inherently conjectural and does not allege actual benefit-of-the-bargain damages with the "reasonable certainty" required to state a fraud claim.

* * * * *

[Reversed.] [The plaintiffs' additional claims are omitted.—Ed.]

Questions

1. *a.* According to the Wisconsin Supreme Court, under what circumstances might the nondisclosure by a seller of a defect constitute misrepresentation?

   b. Did the court find that Harley-Davidson had a duty to disclose in this case? Explain.

2. *a.* What injury, if any, do the plaintiffs claim they suffered in this episode?

   b. According to the Wisconsin Supreme Court, must a plaintiff in a fraud action prove that he or she has suffered actual damages prior to bringing a claim? Explain.

   c. What is the "benefit of the bargain" rule?

3. Why did the Wisconsin Supreme Court rule for the defendant Harley-Davidson in this case?

4. Robert McGlothlin, an employee of Thomson Consumer Electronics in Bloomington, Indiana, was injured while loading televisions into a semi-trailer when the trailer's "landing gear" (retractable legs that support the front of the trailer when it is not attached to the semi-tractor) collapsed. McGlothlin sued the owner of the trailer, among others, claiming that the defendants' repair and inspection procedures for *latent* (hidden) defects were inadequate. Should the court treat latent defects differently than *patent* (observable) defects in determining when a legal duty exists? Explain. See *McGlothlin v. M & U Trucking,* 688 N.E.2d 1243 (Ind. S.Ct. 1997).

Unconscionable Contracts

The doctrine of unconscionability emerged from court decisions where jurists concluded that some contracts are so unfair or oppressive as to demand intervention. (Unconscionability is also included in state statutory laws via the Uniform Commercial Code 2—302.) The legal system intrudes on contracts only with the greatest reluctance. Mere foolishness or want of knowledge does not constitute grounds for unconscionability, nor is a contract unconscionable and hence unenforceable merely because one party is spectacularly clever and the other is not. Unconscionability can take either or both of two forms:

1. *Procedural unconscionability* is a situation where the bargaining power of the parties was so unequal that the agreement, as a practical matter, was not freely entered. Procedural unconscionability usually arises from lack of knowledge (e.g., fine print) or lack of choice (e.g., urgent circumstances).

2. *Substantive unconscionability* is a situation where the clause or contract in question was so manifestly one-sided, oppressive, or unfair as to "shock the conscience of the court." A contract that does not provide a remedy for a breach, or contract terms completely out of line with the relative risks assumed by the parties are among the conditions that might lead to a finding of substantive unconscionability.

PRACTICING ETHICS   Brewers Target Teens?

Lynne and Reed Goodwin's daughter was killed in an accident involving a teenager who was driving under the influence of alcohol. The Goodwins sued Anheuser-Busch and Miller Brewing alleging that the brewers targeted underage teens by placing advertisements in print, radio, and television venues with a high percentage of teen consumers. Among others, the plaintiffs raised public nuisance (in brief, an injury to health affecting a considerable number of persons) and unjust enrichment claims (enriched by illegally selling beer to minors). Under California law, the defendants market their products through a distribution chain, but they cannot lawfully sell directly to consumers.

Questions

1. How would you rule on the public nuisance and unjust enrichment claims? Explain.

2. Do you believe that brewers unethically target underage teens? Explain.

Source: *Goodwin v. Anheuser Busch and Miller Brewing,* 2005 WL 280330 (Cal. Superior Ct.).

Part Two—The Consumer and Government Regulation of Business

State Laws

Having looked at the common law foundation of consumer protection, we turn to some of the many governmental measures that provide shelter in the marketplace. Many states have enacted comprehensive consumer protection statutes. States also have specific statutes addressing such problems as door-to-door sales, debtor protection, and telemarketing fraud. We will look at only one of those, the so-called lemon laws, which address the particularly frustrating problem of a hopelessly defective vehicle.

Lemon Laws New car purchases are covered by warranty laws (see Chapter 7 for a discussion of UCC warranty provisions and the federal Magnuson—Moss Warranty Act); in addition, all 50 states have some form of law designed to provide recourse for consumers whose new vehicles turn out to be defective such that they cannot be repaired after a reasonable effort. The quarrel, of course, is about when a car is truly a lemon. Lemon laws differ significantly from state to state, but they often cover new cars for one to two years or up to 24,000 miles after purchase. Typically state laws provide that the vehicle must have been returned to the manufacturer or dealer three or four times to repair the same defect and that defect must substantially impair the value or safety of the vehicle, *or* the vehicle must have been unavailable to the consumer for a total of at least 30 days in a 12-month period. Such a vehicle is a lemon, and the purchaser is entitled to a replacement vehicle or full refund of the purchase price. In some states, used cars may also be treated as lemons. In almost all states, the determination about whether a car is a lemon is handled by an arbitration panel. If dissatisfied with the ruling, the consumer may then file suit.

> The quarrel, of course, is about when a car is truly a lemon.

Suzuki Sucks?

Clearly one Suzuki purchaser thinks so:

> Eric Wiedemer, a 32-year-old Cincinnati auto painter, incurred corporate wrath when he created a Web gripe site to complain about a $20,000 Suzuki Verona car he bought from

an Alabama dealer. From the day he drove it home, he said, the engine stalled repeatedly. Unable to resolve the problem at a local Suzuki dealership, he hired a lawyer and created the Web site **www.suzukiveronasucks.com.** American Suzuki Motors Corp. bought back the car but wouldn't pay Wiedemer's legal bill and threatened possible legal action.

Suzuki said that Wiedemer's Web site contained defamatory, misleading, and inaccurate information. Several consumers have been sued because of their Web gripe sites. Consumers have often prevailed to date, but corporations do have legal rights, and false statements about verifiable facts do, in general, constitute defamation whether the victim is a person or a corporation. [For another current gripe site, see **www.myvwlemon.com**]

Source: James McNair, "Big Business Avenges Web Gripe Sites," *Des Moines Sunday Register,* February 27, 2005, p. 6D.

The case that follows examines Connecticut's lemon law requirements. [For lemon laws in all 50 states, see **http://www.lemonlawusa.com**]

LEGAL BRIEFCASE

General Motors Corporation v. Dohmann
722 A.2d 1205 (Conn. S.Ct. 1998)

Chief Justice Callahan

The sole issue in this appeal is whether the Connecticut "lemon law" requires the plaintiff, General Motors Corporation, to provide the defendant, Eugene Dohmann, with a replacement vehicle.

* * * * *

On October 26, 1996, the defendant purchased a new Chevrolet S-10 pickup truck (truck) from Maritime Motors (Maritime), a General Motors dealership located in South Norwalk. The following day, the defendant noticed defects in the paint on the truck's hood, roof, and bumpers. The defendant promptly notified Maritime of the defects and requested that the dealership provide him with a replacement vehicle. Maritime agreed to inspect the truck for defects, but refused the defendant's request for a replacement vehicle.

After inspecting the truck, Maritime agreed that the truck's paint was defective, but again refused to provide a different vehicle. Instead, the dealership offered to replace the truck's hood, the part of the truck on which the paint defects were most visible, with a hood taken from another vehicle of the same color. The defendant allowed Maritime to undertake that repair attempt. The replacement hood, however, did not fit properly and the paint was not an exact match. Dissatisfied with the repair attempt, the defendant told Maritime to reinstall the original hood, and Maritime complied.

Maritime subsequently suggested two other possible methods of curing the defects in the paint: (1) wet sanding and (2) repainting the affected areas of the truck. The defendant, however, rejected these suggestions because he believed that both wet sanding and repainting would remove the truck's original factory finish. In the defendant's view, the factory process produces a paint finish superior to that of a body shop. . . .

Thereafter, the defendant initiated an arbitration proceeding against the plaintiff. After a hearing, a three-member arbitration panel determined that (1) the truck had been subject to a reasonable number of unsuccessful repair attempts, and (2) the defective paint substantially impaired the truck's value to the defendant. Consequently, the panel concluded that the defendant was entitled to a new, comparably equipped replacement vehicle.

On appeal, the plaintiff claims that the trial court improperly affirmed the decision of the arbitration panel. Specifically, the plaintiff maintains that the record does not contain substantial evidence to support the arbitrators' findings that (1) the truck had been subject to a reasonable number of repair attempts, and (2) the defects in the paint substantially impaired the value of the truck to the defendant.

Our analysis begins with a brief overview of Connecticut's lemon law legislation. In 1982, the Connecticut legislature enacted Public Acts 1982, No. 82—287 (Lemon Law I). For consumer buyers of new motor vehicles, the act provides supplemental remedies of repair, replacement, and refund to facilitate the enforcement of express warranties made by the manufacturers of such vehicles. These supplemental remedies come into play whenever a manufacturer or authorized dealer, after a reasonable number of repair attempts, is unable substantially to conform a new vehicle to the terms of the express warranty. . . .

In 1984, the legislature enacted Public Acts 1984, No. 84–338 (Lemon Law II). The purpose of Lemon Law II is to provide, for consumer purchasers of new motor vehicles, an alternative to civil litigation. The key provision authorizes the department of consumer protection to establish 'an independent arbitration procedure for the settlement of disputes between consumers and manufacturers of motor vehicles which do not conform to all applicable warranties.'

* * * * *

II

The plaintiff first claims . . . that, because the additional repairs suggested by the dealership were capable of producing a paint finish that met factory standards, the single attempt to cure the defect by replacing the truck's hood was insufficient to constitute the requisite reasonable number of repair attempts. We disagree.

Section 42—179 provides in relevant part: "(d) If the manufacturer, or its agents or authorized dealers, are unable to conform the motor vehicle to any applicable express warranty by repairing or correcting any defect or condition which substantially impairs the use, safety, or value of the motor vehicle to

the consumer *after a reasonable number of [repair] attempts,* the manufacturer shall replace the motor vehicle with a new motor vehicle acceptable to the consumer . . . (e) It shall be presumed that a reasonable number of [repair] attempts have been undertaken . . . if . . . the same nonconformity has been subject to repair four or more times. . . . No claim shall be made under this section unless at least one attempt to repair a nonconformity has been made."

* * * * *

[T]he legislative program and review committee's report read in relevant part, "Generally a reasonable number of repair attempts is defined as four attempts during the first 18,000 miles or two years and the problem continues to exist. . . . In some instances, less than four repair attempts is allowed if the problem is one for which evidence exists that no repair will bring the vehicle back into conformance." The report further states, "In cases involving problems with the paint on a vehicle, a determination may be made that it is impossible for any dealer to repaint the vehicle in a manner that would match the type of finish originally achieved at the manufacturer's plant when the car was built." Consequently, if the record contains substantial evidence to support a finding that proposed additional repair attempts would not have produced a paint finish that satisfied factory paint specifications, arbitrators reasonably may find that a single repair attempt is sufficient.

The record before us reveals the following regarding the utility of additional repair attempts. The plaintiff presented affidavits of two automobile body experts who stated that body shop paint processes are capable of producing results equal to, and in some cases superior to, those produced by the original factory paint process. The state's technical expert, Gregory Carver, however, testified that the conditions under which the factory originally paints a vehicle are superior to those that exist in a body shop. Specifically Carver stated that paint bonds to the surface of a vehicle most successfully the first time it is applied, and that, therefore, it is impossible for a body shop to duplicate the bond achieved at the factory. Carver further stated that the finish of a repainted vehicle is less durable than the finish applied at the factory.

. . . [O]n the basis of Carver's testimony, the arbitration panel reasonably could have concluded that the suggested additional repair attempts would not have produced a finish that met factory paint specifications. We conclude, therefore, that the record contains substantial evidence to support the panel's conclusion that, under the circumstances, Maritime's attempt to replace the truck's hood constituted a reasonable number of repair attempts.

III

The plaintiff next claims that the arbitrators improperly concluded that the paint defects substantially impaired the value of the truck to the defendant.

* * * * *

During the arbitration hearing, the defendant testified that he takes great pride in the appearance of the vehicles that he owns and maintains the finish of those vehicles in factory condition. Moreover, he stated that appearance was a major factor in his decision to purchase a new truck rather than a used one. On the basis of that testimony, the arbitrators reasonably could have concluded that, had the defendant known of the defects in the paint before accepting delivery, he would not have purchased the truck, and that the statutory requirement of . . . substantial impairment had been satisfied.

Carver, the state's technical expert, testified that, on a scale of 1 to 10, with 10 representing the worst amount of damage, the damage to the truck constituted a 3. Carver further stated that the paint defects could not be removed easily. Moreover, Carver corroborated the defendant's contention that wet sanding and repainting the truck would remove its finish. Finally, Carver stated that the paint defects possibly could affect the resale value of the vehicle and that if the vehicle was not maintained meticulously, the affected areas could deteriorate further. Thus, on the basis of Carver's testimony, the arbitrators reasonably could have concluded that the statutory requirement of . . . substantial impairment had been satisfied.

We conclude, therefore, that the record contains substantial evidence to support a finding that the defects in the truck's paint substantially impaired its value to the defendant.

Affirmed.

Questions

1. How did the court determine when a "reasonable" number of repair attempts had been undertaken?
2. Why did General Motors lose this case?
3. Dieter and Hermes agreed to buy a new 1996 Dodge Ram pickup truck from Fascona Chrysler-Plymouth-Dodge Trucks on December 12, 1995. They requested the installation of some after-market accessories—a tonneau cover, a bug shield, and rustproofing. When Dieter and Hermes returned to take delivery of the truck, they noticed it had been scratched during the installation of the accessories. The salesperson told them the scratches would be repaired. Four months later the dealership sent the truck to a body shop for repairs. After repair, Dieter and Hermes noticed swirl marks in the truck's finish. Dieter then demanded that Frascona repurchase the truck. Eight months later Dieter and Hermes sued Chrysler Corporation under Wisconsin's lemon law.

   a. Make the argument that the lemon law does not apply to the facts of this case.

   b. Decide the case. Explain. See *Dieter and Hermes v. Chrysler Corporation,* 610 N.W. 2d 832 (Wis. S.Ct. 2000).

Federal Laws and Consumer Protection Agencies

The Federal Trade Commission (FTC)

The Federal Trade Commission was created in 1914 to prevent "unfair methods of competition and unfair or deceptive acts or practices in and affecting commerce." In conducting its business, the FTC performs as a miniature government with extensive and powerful quasi-legislative and quasi-judicial roles. [For the FTC's Bureau of Consumer Protection home page, see **http://www.ftc.gov/bcp/bcp.htm**]

Rule Making

The FTC's primary legislative direction is in issuing trade regulation rules to enforce the intent of broadly drawn congressional legislation. That is, the rules specify particular acts or practices that the commission deems deceptive.

The FTC's quasi-legislative or rule-making power is extensive, as evidenced by the following examples:

- The Federal Trade Commission's Do Not Call Registry forbids telemarketers, with certain exceptions, from placing calls to the 157 million Americans who have added their phone numbers to the Federal Trade Commission's list. Of course, some companies are charged with violating the list restrictions. Six of those companies settled FTC complaints in 2007 that they had called consumers on the list. One of them, the adjustable bed maker, Craftmatic, paid a $4.4 million fine. [For more details on the Do Not Call settlements, see **http://redtape.msnbc.com/2007/11/ftc-rings-up--1.html**] [Those wanting to be added to the Do Not Call list and those wanting to file complaints can visit **www.donotcall.gov**]

| A "Do Not Track" list | Now consumer groups have proposed a "Do Not Track" list that would allow the FTC to prevent companies from keeping track of which Web sites people visit. |

- Internet advertiser ValueClick agreed to pay $2.9 million in 2008 to settle FTC charges of deceptive claims in online ads and e-mails. For example, in order to induce consumers to open its e-mail messages, ValueClick and its subsidiary allegedly sent e-mails with subject lines that misrepresented the actual content of the message. Those subject lines allegedly included falsehoods such as announcing that the recipients had won products when, in fact, they were not winners. [For the FTC press release on the ValueClick case, see **http://www.ftc.gov/opa/2008/03/vc.shtm**]

Adjudication

On its own initiative or as a result of a citizen complaint, the FTC may investigate suspect trade practices. At that point the FTC may drop the proceeding, settle the matter, or issue a formal complaint.

Where a formal complaint is issued, the matter proceeds essentially as a trial conducted before an administrative law judge. The FTC has no authority to impose criminal sanctions.

Fraud and Deception

Unfair and deceptive trade practices, including those in advertising, are forbidden under Section 5 of the Federal Trade Commission Act. An unfair trade practice (1) must be likely to cause substantial injury to consumers, (2) must not be reasonably avoidable by consumers themselves, and (3) must not be outweighed by countervailing benefits to consumers or to competition. The FTC test for deception requires that the claim is (1) false or likely to mislead the reasonable consumer and (2) material to the consumer's decision making. Deception can take many forms, including, for example, testimonials by celebrities who do not use the endorsed product or do not have sufficient expertise to evaluate its quality. The primary areas of dispute involve quality and price.

Quality Claims

"Fewer calories," "faster acting," and "more effective" are the kinds of claims that may lead to allegations of deception unless they are factually supportable. Under the FTC's ad substantiation program, advertisers are engaging in unfair and deceptive practices if they make product claims without some reasonable foundation for those claims. For example, credible survey evidence must be in hand if an advertiser says, "Consumers prefer our brand two to one." Indeed, in recent years the FTC has brought a number of charges and settled many of them. In 2007, the FDA challenged four weight-loss drugs, whose makers were fined a total of $25 million for false advertising claims. Some of the ads promised permanent and fast weight loss or increases in metabolism. Others even claimed effectiveness in reducing Alzheimer's and cancer. The pills, Xenadrine EFX, CortiSlim, One-A-Day WeightSmart and TrimSpa will remain on the shelves.[2]

Pricing

Deception in price advertising sometimes takes the form of the so-called *bait and switch* practice, where a product is advertised at a very low price to attract customers although the seller actually has no intention of selling at that price. Once the customer is in the door (having taken the bait), the strategy is to switch the customer's attention to another, higher-priced product.

> When is a sale not truly a sale?

Sale pricing also sometimes leads to claims of deception. When is a sale not truly a sale? Do some retailers offer phony markdowns based on inflated "original" or "regular" prices? The FTC has long maintained guidelines for proving that a former price was genuine, but the problem is one that has been left largely to the states.

The Consumer Product Safety Commission (CPSC)

Another reason to avoid sleeping with an ex: fear of contracting lead poisoning. Just ask Barbie, who got it from Ken. That's according to "Toxic Toys: A Poisonous Affair," a YouTube attack on the Consumer Product Safety Commission produced by the nonprofit Campaign for America's Future.[3]

The Consumer Product Safety Commission (CPSC) is the federal agency charged with protecting us from "unreasonable risks of injury and death" from consumer products. The YouTube attack was a product of frustration with the CPSC's response to a 2007 wave of toy recalls; largely because of dangerous levels of lead. More than 25 million toys and children's items, most of them made in China, were recalled in 2007.[4] Toy making giant, Mattel, for example, learned of problems from one of its retailers and then, as required by law, filed a report with the CPSC which initiated a "fast track"

> Parents were frantic and furious.

recall of the toys. Nonetheless, parents were frantic and furious. California has filed suit against Mattel, Toy's R Us, and 18 other companies for making or selling products that contain unlawful quantities of lead. The problems, however, did not reside entirely in China. Mattel itself apologized to China saying its own design flaws were actually responsible for the bulk of its 20 million-toy, 2007 recall and that it had recalled more toys for lead problems than was justified by the facts. Some of the recalled toys actually met American lead safety standards.[5]

Lawsuits and apologies will not be the answer, however, in these situations. The CPSC was created precisely to address product safety problems where for various reasons the market has not provided the degree of immediate protection demanded by consumers. With responsibility for 15,000 product types but only 400 staffers, half the force of 30 years ago, the CPSC is struggling to meet its duties.[6] Furthermore, political/philosophical divisions about the wisdom of government intervention in the market have split politicians and expanded the gap between consumer groups and the regulated industries. As a result, support for the CPSC has been mixed and CPSC oversight has been limited for decades. At this writing in 2008, Congress and President Bush have approved the Consumer Product Safety Improvement Act to strengthen the agency that *BusinessWeek* labeled, "overwhelmed and underfunded."[7] The act essentially bans lead and certain phthalates (a class of chemicals) from children's products while providing the agency a big budget boost, stronger penalties, more recall authority and new whistleblower protections for its employees. [For the Consumer Product Safety Commission Web site, see **http://www.cpsc.gov**].

Reducing Risk   The CPSC, created in 1972, is responsible for reducing the risks in using consumer products such as toys, lawn mowers, washing machines, bicycles, fireworks, pools, portable heaters, and household chemicals. The CPSC pursues product safety, initially, by *collecting data* and *issuing rules*. The commission conducts research and collects information as a foundation for regulating product safety. Via its rule-making authority, the CPSC promulgates mandatory consumer product safety, performance, and labeling standards. Public comments and suggestions are encouraged, but industry trade associations appear to have the bigger voice with the commission.

To enforce its policies and decisions, the CPSC holds both *compliance* and *enforcement* powers. In seeking compliance with safety expectations, the commission can exert a number of expectations. Manufacturers must certify before distribution that products meet federal safety standards. Manufacturing sites may be inspected, and specific product safety testing procedures can be mandated. Businesses other than retailers are required to keep product safety records. In cases of severe and imminent hazards, the CPSC may enforce its decisions by seeking a court order to remove a product from the market. In less urgent circumstances, the commission may proceed with its own administrative remedy. Preferring voluntary compliance, the commission may negotiate with the company to issue notice of its defective product or to repair or replace the product.

Where voluntary negotiations fail, the commission may proceed with an adjudicative hearing before an administrative law judge or members of the commission. That decision may be appealed to the full commission and thereafter to the federal court of appeals. Civil or criminal penalties may result. Only a few products have actually been banned from the market.

The Food and Drug Administration

The FDA plays a broad, vital role in the health and welfare of America, but the agency has been the focus of relentless criticism in recent years. At the FDA's rather tardy insistence, huge-selling pain killers, Vioxx and Bextra, were removed from the market. Scientific evidence satisfied the FDA that the drugs dangerously raise the risk of heart attacks and strokes and may have caused, in the case of Vioxx alone, as many as 139,000 heart attacks, strokes, and deaths. [8] The withdrawals, while clearly in the public interest, did little to inspire public confidence in the agency since critics, particularly in Congress, could not help but wonder why the drugs were allowed on the market in the first place.

Confidence in consumer safety was not enhanced by the U.S. Supreme Court's 2008 ruling that patients injured by medical devices that have passed the FDA's most rigorous review cannot sue for damages.[9] The 8–1 decision said that federal law preempts any imposition of liability under state law leaving the FDA to protect consumers' interests in this area. Congress, of course, can revise the law to restore consumers' opportunities to sue when damaged by products like implanted defibrillators, heart pumps, catheters and other medical devices. The decision does not apply to the FDA's drug approval process.

Trust the Market or Strengthen the FDA?   Historically, the FDA was criticized for being too cautious and slow in allowing potentially helpful, new drugs on the market. Drug industry and free market advocates have long argued for greater faith in the market, and the agency has accelerated its drug approval process so that approval time fell from 27 to 14 months. Unfortunately, the proportion of new drugs removed from the market for safety reasons has jumped from 1.5 percent to 5 percent.[10] At the same time, FDA officials have long complained that they do not have the financial resources to fully monitor drugs following their market entry, and federal approval of new drugs sank in 2007 to its lowest level in five years.[11] The agency is supposed to guarantee public safety with 1,311 fewer workers in 2008 than it had in 1994 while its budget fell during the same period by $400 million in inflation-adjusted dollars.[12]

Are consumers at risk? A 2004 survey found about two-thirds of FDA scientists are less than fully confident about the FDA's safety monitoring of prescription drugs now on the market, and one-third have some doubts about the process of approving new drugs.[13] *The New York Times* recently argued that a "slew" of authoritative reports "have found serious defects in the agency's management, scientific capabilities and information technologies, as well as shortages of personnel and funding, all of which weaken its ability to protect the public."[14] So at the moment, the free market reforms seem to have lost some of their energy, but neither should we expect Congress to comfortably shower the FDA with new money, given grave doubts about the agency's ability to manage its affairs.

> **Are consumers at risk?**

Consumer Privacy

As *The Wall Street Journal* reported, identity theft has exploded in recent years:

> The biggest known theft of credit card numbers in history began two summers ago outside a Marshalls discount clothing store near St. Paul, Minnesota. There, investigators now believe, hackers pointed a telescope-shaped antenna toward the store and used a

laptop computer to decode data streaming through the air between handheld price-checking devices, cash registers and the store's computers. That helped them hack into the central database of Marshalls' parent, TJX Cos. in Framingham, Mass., to repeatedly purloin information about customers.

The $17.4-billion retailer's wireless network had less security than many people have on their home networks, and for 18 months the company . . . had no idea what was going on.[15]

> **200 million card numbers may have been grabbed.**

Investigators think as many as 200 million card numbers may have been grabbed from TJX over four years.[16] The Federal Trade Commission estimated that 8.3 million adult Americans were identity theft victims in 2005.[17] The typical loss was $500 and total theft-related loss in 2005 was $15.6 billion.[18] [For Federal Trade Commission advice on fighting ID theft, see **http://www.consumer.gov/idtheft**]

Consumers' identity-theft fears typically focus on malicious strangers probing the Internet, but the greater risk is from those who know us. [19] Stolen mail, lost wallets, checkbooks and credit cards, dumpster diving or a credit card application improperly disposed of can lead to big financial losses and a nightmare of months or more. In most cases, consumers learn about such theft only after their Social Security numbers, credit card numbers, and other vital information have been used to make purchases, drain bank accounts, and so on.

These identity theft scandals have critics calling for government intervention in the lightly regulated information industry. More than half of the states have approved laws permitting individuals to "freeze" their credit files with the three giant credit-reporting agencies, Equifax, Experian, and TransUnion. The freeze shuts down access to an individual's credit report so that no new credit lines can be opened without the individual's decision to "thaw" the report.

Smoothly flowing information, on the other hand, is vital to efficiency in a free market economy. In some sense, we must pay for our privacy because tighter protection for consumers likely would mean higher costs since the flow of information would be restricted. Furthermore, emerging evidence suggests that ID theft may be "more hype than harm," as *BusinessWeek* argued.[20] Losing one's personal information is bound to be traumatic, but one study pointed out that the odds of having stolen data actually misused is about 0.09 percent or one in 1,020 individuals.[21] [For a privacy database and links, see **http://www.privacyrights.org**]

Part Three—Debtor/Creditor Law

Credit Regulations

> **Angelique Trammel decided to buy a laptop on a "low weekly payment plan."**

According to *The New York Times,* Angelique Trammel, a single mother and telephone operator, decided to buy a laptop for her son on a "low weekly payment plan." She paid $99 down and agreed to have $41 per week withdrawn from her bank account. After six months, a broken computer arrived. Having spent well over $1,000 and after having received two nonworking computers, she demanded a refund from the retailer, Blue-Hippo. Under her agreement, Ms. Trammel allegedly would have paid more than $2,000 for a computer worth much less.[22] Describing sales schemes directed to the poor, Better Business Bureau spokesman Steve Cox said: "The way these companies operate is simply another form of predatory lending."[23] BlueHippo, on the other hand, said that, "before, during and after the sales transaction we fully disclose the total price and all shipping guidelines" to customers.[24]

Situations like Trammel's and broad fears of abuse in credit and lending led Congress and the state legislatures to supplement the market's powerful messages with a substantial array of protective legislation. We will turn now to a look at several particularly important pieces of federal lending practices law. [For a debtor/creditor law database, see **http://www.law.cornell.edu/topics/debtor_creditor.html**]

Truth in Lending Act (TILA)

As we increasingly turned to credit financing, consumers often did not understand the full cost of buying on credit. The TILA is part of the Consumer Credit Protection Act of 1968. Having been designed for consumer protection, it does not cover all loans. The following standards determine the TILA's applicability:

1. The debtor must be a "natural person" rather than an organization.
2. The creditor must be regularly engaged in extending credit and must be the person to whom the debt is initially payable.
3. The purpose of the credit must be "primarily for personal, family, or household purposes" not in excess of $25,000. However, "consumer real property transactions" are covered by the act. Hence home purchases fall within TILA provisions.
4. The credit must be subject to a finance charge or payable in more than four installments.

The TILA and Regulation Z interpreting the act were designed both to protect consumers from credit abuse and to assist them in becoming more informed about credit terms and costs so they could engage in comparison shopping. Congress presumed the increased information would stimulate competition in the finance industry. The heart of the act is the required conspicuous disclosure of the amount financed, the finance charge (the actual dollar sum to be paid for credit), the annual percentage rate (APR—the total cost of the credit expressed at an annual rate), and the number of payments. The finance charge includes not just interest but service charges, points, loan fees, carrying charges, and other costs. The TILA covers consumer loans generally, including credit cards and auto purchases, [For consumer information on "abusive lending," see **http://www.ftc.gov/bcp/menu-lending.htm**]

The case that follows examines the application of TILA to a department store purchase.

Justice White

John E. Bell appeals from summary judgment entered against him and in favor of Respondent, the May Department Stores Company, d/b/a/ Famous Barr Company.

I. FACTUAL BACKGROUND

Bell purchased a ceiling fan on August 2, 1992, at Famous Barr and charged the purchase price of $132.16 to his Famous Barr credit card account. After installing it a few weeks later, Bell determined the fan was defective because it made an unacceptable level of noise at all speeds and he was unable to fix it. Famous Barr never inspected the fan to dispute Bell's determination.

Famous Barr billed Bell for the cost of the fan on September 1, 1992, with payment due on September 25. On or about September 23, 1992, Bell told a Famous Barr representative his fan was defective and he did not intend to pay for it. Bell also sent Famous Barr a letter memorializing this conversation, dated October 27, 1992, following the directives on the back of his Famous Barr billing statement and making a general reference to "Regulation Z." Famous Barr wrote Bell acknowledging its receipt of his letter. Famous Barr later contacted Bell in November and agreed to locate a replacement fan and reimburse Bell for the installation cost. They never discussed the details, nor did they agree when Bell should ultimately pay for the fan. Bell waited for Famous Barr to locate a replacement fan and notify him, but he was never notified.

Bell again notified Famous Barr when his November 1992 statement contained a past due notice for the unpaid fan. Famous Barr assured Bell it had simply made a mistake. From May through October 1993, however, Bell's monthly statement showed past due notices, late fees, and finance charges. Except for the disputed price of the fan, Bell *always* paid his balance in full each month. On May 4, 1993, Famous Barr informed Bell it was sending his account to three credit reporting agencies, including TRW. It made similar written threats to Bell . . . and threatened to report the most derogatory rating of "R9." Bell contacted Famous Barr to explain the dispute numerous times. He was assured no further action would be taken to collect the disputed amount and that the matter would not affect his credit rating.

* * * * *

In August 1993, the parties reached a provisional settlement agreement. Famous Barr agreed to credit Bell's account with all finance and late fee charges and reinstate his credit line. Bell agreed to pay for the fan if Famous Barr sent a letter permitting the imminent buyer of Bell's house to exchange the fan. Nevertheless, on September 1, 1993, Famous Barr assessed late fees and finance charges for nonpayment, closed Bell's account, and reported derogatory information to the credit reporting agencies.

After memorializing this settlement agreement and sending a copy to Famous Barr on September 13, 1993, Bell received written confirmation that Famous Barr would "delete all derogatory information." On October 4, 1993, Bell re-dated his September 1993 letter and mailed it with a check for the price of the fan. Later that month, however, Bell found his Famous Barr account closed due to "poor prior payment history." Bell wrote a letter to Famous Barr quoting the pertinent sections of Regulation Z and demanding the deletion of adverse or derogatory credit history from his file. Famous Barr reinstated Bell's account, faxed letters to the credit reporting agencies to that effect, and sent Bell a copy. The parties later discovered the corrective letters that Famous Barr sent to the credit reporting agencies contained the wrong account number.

In early summer 1994, Bell applied to the European American Bank ("EAB") for a TWA credit card, hoping to earn frequent flyer miles with his purchases. EAB refused to extend credit based upon derogatory Famous Barr information contained in a credit report from TRW. TRW's report did not reflect Famous Barr's request to delete all derogatory credit information. Bell also discovered Famous Barr had requested other credit reporting agencies to delete his entire 22-year credit history with Famous Barr, the large majority of which was positive. Bell sued.

II. REGULATION Z OF THE TRUTH IN LENDING ACT

Count I in Bell's petition claims Famous Barr violated [the Federal Truth in Lending Act (TILA)] by reporting him delinquent to various credit reporting agencies after receiving notice of a "billing error" and prior to resolving that error. Count I also claims Famous Barr violated [TILA] by restricting and closing his Famous Barr account after receiving notice of a "billing error" and prior to resolving that error.

* * * * *

Famous Barr argues the "billing error" alleged by Bell and essential to his claim did not occur because Bell accepted the fan.

* * * * *

Famous Barr argues Bell accepted the fan because he did not reject it. For an effective rejection, the buyer must notify the seller in accordance with the contract or within a reasonable time if the contract is silent.

* * * * *

A reasonable jury could find Bell did not accept the fan. He properly notified Famous Barr and Famous Barr duly received notice of the defective fan. Bell's rejection of the fan within three months of purchase was reasonable, especially since Bell did not install it until some weeks after he bought it and tried to fix it. Bell also notified Famous Barr of his rejection within the 60-day period prescribed by both [Regulation Z] and Famous Barr's own billing statement. In addition, Bell did not commit acts inconsistent with Famous Barr's ownership of the rejected fan. Bell neither used the fan, nor prevented Famous Barr from removing it. Famous Barr even encouraged Bell to retain it pending replacement.

Also contrary to the decision of the trial court, summary judgment is improper because a reasonable jury could find Bell attempted to resolve his dispute with Famous Barr in good faith. Bell claimed he long awaited the availability of a replacement fan. . . .

If a reasonable jury finds Bell did not accept the fan, and acted in good faith, then it can find a "billing error" existed. If a "billing error existed," Famous Barr violated the Federal Truth in Lending Act by closing Bell's account and reporting him to credit agencies. The decision of the trial court granting Famous Barr's motion for summary judgment on Count I is reversed.

* * * * *

Questions

1. *a.* In what sense did Famous Barr violate Regulation Z and the TILA?

    b. Why was the court concerned about whether Bell had accepted the fan?

2. Green Tree Financial financed Randolph's mobile home purchase. Randolph sued, claiming that Green Tree's financing document contained an arbitration clause that violated TILA because it did not provide the same level of protection as TILA accords. If the arbitration clause provided lesser protection than that provided for by TILA, as Randolph claimed, should the arbitration go forward? Explain. See *Randolph v. Green Tree Financial Corp.*, 531 U.S. 79 (2000).

3. Sarah Hamm sued Ameriquest Mortgage Company claiming a violation of the Truth in Lending Act (TILA). Hamm borrowed money secured by a 30-year mortgage from Ameriquest. She signed a "Disclosure Statement" specifying, among other things, that she was responsible for 359 payments at a specified amount and one payment for the last month of a slightly smaller amount. The Statement did not, however, explicitly specify, as required by the TILA, the total payments due (360). Was the TILA violated? Explain. See *Hamm v. Ameriquest Mortgage*, 506 F.3d 525 (7th Cir. 2007).

Credit and Charge Cards

Nearly 76 percent of college students report stopping at campus tables to apply for credit cards and nearly one-third were offered gifts for signing up.[25] Colleges increasingly ban those practices, but students are loaded down with cards and high balances, nonetheless. Seniors whose parents were not helping them with expenses reported an average balance due of $2,623, and about one quarter of students report paying a late fee at some point.[26]

> Students are loaded down with cards and high balances.

The law offers substantial protections for credit card users. The TILA provides that credit cards cannot be issued to a consumer unless requested. Cardholder liability for unauthorized use (lost or stolen card) cannot exceed $50, and the cardholder bears no liability after notifying the issuer of the missing card. The Fair Credit and Charge Card Disclosure Act requires notification of various cost factors when applications are solicited. Details vary, depending on whether the solicitation was by mail, phone, or "take ones" (e.g., magazine insert), but in general, issuers must disclose key cost features, including APR, annual membership fees, minimum finance charges, late payment fees, and so on.

Expressing frustration with the slow pace of voluntary reforms in the credit card industry, Congress at this writing in 2008 is considering new legislation to curb alleged abuses, and the Federal Reserve Board, along with other federal agencies, has proposed new rules to further protect consumers. The rules in their final form may yet be changed or withdrawn, but at this writing some of the key provisions include:

- Credit card companies would be barred from increasing the annual percentage rate on an outstanding balance, except for certain instances.
- Billing statements would be delivered at least 21 days prior to their due dates.
- Where existing balances are subject to differing interests rates, credit card companies could not apply all payments to the balance with the lowest rate.[27]

Question

How would you argue that further government intervention in the credit card market, like the proposed Federal Reserve rules, is not in the best interest of consumers generally and college students in particular?

Credit Card Suicide

Sean Moyer, a University of Oklahoma junior, had earned the minimum wage as a part-time salesman and gift wrapper in a department store. Yet by the time he hanged himself in his bedroom closet, he had 12 credit cards and had amassed $10,000 in debt on them.

Source: Associated Press, "Hooked on Credit," *Waterloo/Cedar Falls Courier*, June 9, 1999, p. C7.

Consumer Credit Reports

Having a favorable credit rating is a vital feature of consumer life, and having reliable credit information is essential to efficient business practice. Thus the three national credit information giants, Equifax, Experian, and TransUnion, as well as local credit bureaus, provide retailers, employers, insurance companies, and so on with consumers' detailed credit histories. The federal Fair Credit Reporting Act (FCRA) affords consumers the following credit reporting protections, among others:

- Anyone using information from a credit reporting agency (CRA), such as Equifax, to take "adverse action" against you (denying you credit, a job, insurance) must notify you and tell you where it secured the information.
- At your request, a CRA must give you the information in your file and a list of all those who have recently sought information about you.
- If you claim that your credit file contains inaccurate information, the CRA must investigate your complaint and give you a written report. If you remain unsatisfied, you can include a brief statement in your credit file. Notice of the dispute and a summary of your statement normally must accompany future reports.

- All inaccurate information must be corrected or removed from the file, usually within 30 days.

- In most cases, negative information more than seven years old must not be reported.

- You must provide written consent before a CRA can provide information to your employer or prospective employer.

- You can sue for damages if your rights under the act have been violated.[28]

[For an extensive set of practical questions and answers about consumer rights under the Fair Credit Reporting Act, see **http://www.ftc.gov/bcp/conline/pubs/credit/fcra.htm**]

To provide consumers a ready opportunity to check the accuracy of their own credit information, the federal Fair and Accurate Credit Transactions Act of 2003 (FACT Act) guarantees consumers the right to receive free annual copies of their credit reports. One place to request a report is the Web site [**www.annualcreditreport.com**].

Fair Credit Billing Act (FCBA)

The FCBA provides a mechanism to deal with the billing errors that accompany credit card and certain other "open-end" credit transactions. A cardholder who receives an erroneous bill must complain in writing to the creditor within 60 days of the time the bill was mailed. The creditor must acknowledge receipt of the complaint within 30 days. Then, within two billing cycles but not more than 90 days, the creditor must issue a response either by correcting the account or by forwarding a written statement to the consumer explaining why the bill is accurate. The creditor cannot threaten the consumer's credit rating or report the consumer as delinquent while the bill is in dispute, although the creditor can report that the bill is being challenged. Where a "reasonable investigation" determines the bill was correct but the consumer continues to contest it, the consumer may refuse to pay, and the creditor will then be free to commence collection procedures after giving the consumer 10 days to pay the disputed amount. If the bill is reported to a credit bureau as delinquent, that report must also indicate the consumer's belief that the money is not owed, and the consumer must be told who received the report. Penalties for a creditor in violation of the act are quite modest. The creditor forfeits the right to collect the amount in question and any accompanying finance charges, but the forfeiture cannot exceed $50 for each charge in dispute.

Electronic Fund Transfers

With ATMs, point-of-sale machines, electronic deposits, and the like we are deeply immersed in an era of "electronic money." The Electronic Fund Transfer Act (EFTA) provides remedies for consumers confronting electronic banking problems such as liability for lost or stolen cards and billing errors. Notably, debit card losses are less well-protected than those involving credit cards. Under the EFTA, debit card liability is capped at $50 if the consumer provides notice within two business days after learning of the loss. The loss could reach $500 if notice is provided within 60 days and could exceed $500 thereafter. [Space constraints preclude further examination of this topic, but the Federal Trade Commission has provided a detailed and readable summary of those protections at **http://www.ftc.gov/bcp/conline/pubs/credit/elbank.htm**]

Equal Credit Opportunity

The Equal Credit Opportunity Act is designed to combat bias in lending. Credit must be extended to all creditworthy applicants regardless of sex, marital status, age, race, color, religion, national origin, good-faith exercise of rights under the Consumer Credit Protection Act, and receipt of public assistance (like food stamps). ECOA was in large part a response to anger over differing treatment of women and men in the financial marketplace. Creditors often would not lend money to married women in the women's own names, and single, divorced, and widowed women were similarly disadvantaged in securing credit. [For more details about ECOA, see **http://www.ftc.gov/bcp/conline/pubs/ credit/ecoa.htm**] The case that follows applies the ECOA to a "cross-dressing" male.

> ECOA was in large part a response to anger over differing treatment of women and men in the financial marketplace.

LEGAL BRIEFCASE

Lucas Rosa v. Park West Bank & Trust Co. 214 F.3d 213 (1st Cir. 2000)

Judge Lynch

I

[O]n July 21, 1998, [Lucas] Rosa came to the [Park West] Bank to apply for a loan. A biological male, he was dressed in traditionally feminine attire. He requested a loan application from Norma Brunelle, a bank employee. Brunelle asked Rosa for identification. Rosa produced three forms of photo identification: (1) a Massachusetts Department of Public Welfare Card; (2) a Massachusetts Identification Card; and (3) a Money Stop Check Cashing ID Card. Brunelle looked at the identification cards and told Rosa that she would not provide him with a loan application until he "went home and changed." She said that he had to be dressed like one of the identification cards in which he appeared in more traditionally male attire before she would provide him with a loan application and process his loan request.

II

Rosa sued the Bank. Rosa charged that "by requiring [him] to conform to sex stereotypes before proceeding with the credit transaction, [the Bank] unlawfully discriminated against [him] with respect to an aspect of a credit transaction on the basis of sex." He claims to have suffered emotional distress.

Without filing an answer to the complaint, the Bank moved to dismiss. . . . The district court granted the Bank's motion. The court stated,

> The issue in this case is not [Rosa's] sex, but rather how he chose to dress when applying for a loan. Because the Act does not prohibit discrimination based on the manner in which someone dresses, Park West's requirement that Rosa change his clothes does not give rise to claims of illegal discrimination. Further, even if Park West's statement or action were based upon Rosa's sexual orientation or perceived sexual orientation, the Act does not prohibit such discrimination.

PriceWaterhouse v. Hopkins, which Rosa relied on, was not to the contrary, according to the district court, because that case "neither holds, nor even suggests, that discrimination based merely on a person's attire is impermissible."

On appeal, Rosa says that the district court "fundamentally misconceived the law as applicable to the Plaintiff's claim by concluding that there may be no relationship, as a matter of law, between telling a bank customer what to wear and sex discrimination."

The Bank says that Rosa loses for two reasons. First, citing cases pertaining to gays and transsexuals, it says that the ECOA does not apply to cross-dressers. Second, the Bank says that its employee genuinely could not identify Rosa, which is why she asked him to go home and change.

III

The ECOA prohibits discrimination, "with respect to any aspect of a credit transaction[,] on the basis of race, color, religion, national origin, sex or marital status, or age." Thus to prevail, the alleged discrimination against Rosa must have been "on the basis of . . . sex."

While the district court was correct in saying that the prohibited bases of discrimination under the ECOA do not include style of dress or sexual orientation, that is not the discrimination alleged. It is alleged that the Bank's actions were taken, in whole or in part, "on the basis of . . . [the appellant's] sex." . . . Whatever facts emerge, and they may turn out to have nothing to do with sex-based discrimination, we cannot say at this point that the plaintiff has no viable theory of sex discrimination consistent with the facts alleged.

The evidence is not yet developed, and thus it is not yet clear why Brunelle told Rosa to go home and change. It may be that this case involves an instance of disparate treatment based on sex in the denial of credit. . . . It is reasonable to infer that Brunelle told Rosa to go home and change because she thought that Rosa's attire did not accord with his male gender: in other words, that Rosa did not receive the loan application because he was a man, whereas a similarly situated woman would have received the loan application. That is, the Bank may treat, for credit purposes, a woman who dresses like a man differently than a man who dresses like a woman. If so, the Bank concedes, Rosa may have a claim. Indeed, under *PriceWaterhouse*, "stereotyped remarks [including statements about dressing more 'femininely'] can certainly be evidence that gender played a part." It is also reasonable to infer, though, that Brunelle refused to give Rosa the loan application because she thought he was gay, confusing sexual orientation with cross-dressing. If so, Rosa concedes, our precedents dictate that he would have no recourse under the federal Act. It is reasonable to infer, as well, that Brunelle simply could not ascertain whether the person shown in the identification card photographs was the same person that appeared before her that day. If this were the case, Rosa again would be out of luck. It is reasonable to infer, finally, that Brunelle may have had mixed motives, some of which fall into the prohibited category.

It is too early to say what the facts will show; it is apparent, however, that, under some set of facts within the bounds of the allegations and nonconclusory facts in the complaint, Rosa may be able to prove a claim under the ECOA.

We reverse and remand.

Questions

1. *a.* Did the court of appeals find that Park West Bank had violated the ECOA? Explain.

   b. If at trial, the facts reveal that the bank employee thought Rosa was gay and demanded that he change clothes for that reason, who will win this case? Explain.

   c. According to the court of appeals, how did the lower court misunderstand this case?

2. *a.* Does federal law protect bank customers based on their style of dress? Explain.

   b. Should it offer that protection? Explain.

Debtor Protection

Personal debt is at an all-time high in America, and one of the predictable consequences is aggressive, even abusive, debt collection practices. From 1999 to 2005, debt collection complaints to the Federal Trade Commission increased six-fold. The FTC reports collectors calling at all hours of the night, spewing obscenities, contacting family members or employers and falsely threatening property seizures or imprisonment.[29] As a result, federal and state laws offer considerable protection for wronged debtors.

> The FTC reports collectors spewing obscenities.

Debt Collection Law   The federal Fair Debt Collection Practices Act (FDCPA) is designed to shield debtors from unfair debt collection tactics by debt collection agencies and attorneys who routinely operate as debt collectors. The act does not extend to creditors who are themselves trying to recover money owed to them. Several thousand debt collection agencies nationwide pursue those who are delinquent in their debts. The agencies are normally paid on a commission basis and are often exceedingly aggressive and imaginative in their efforts. The FDCPA requires the collector to include a warning in the first communication with the debtor that the communication is an attempt to collect a debt, and any information obtained will be used for that purpose. In any subsequent communication except a court pleading, the collector must always disclose his or her role as a collector.

The FDCPA forbids, among others, the following practices:

- Use of obscene language.
- Contact with third parties other than for the purpose of locating the debtor. (This provision is an attempt to prevent harm to the debtor's reputation.)
- Use of or threats to use physical force.
- Contact with the debtor during "inconvenient" hours. For debtors who are employed during "normal" working hours, the period from 9 PM to 8 AM would probably be considered inconvenient.
- Repeated phone calls with the intent to harass.
- Contacting the debtor in an unfair, abusive, or deceptive manner.

The Federal Trade Commission is responsible for administering the FDCPA. A wronged debtor may also file a civil action to recover all actual damages (for example, payment for job loss occasioned by wrongful debt collection practices as well as damages for associated embarrassment and suffering). [For more details about the FDCPA, see **http://www.ftc.gov/bcp/conline/pubs/credit/fdc.htm**]

The case that follows suggests some of the confusion that arises in debt collection.

LEGAL BRIEFCASE

Williams v. OSI Educational Services   505 F.3d 675 (7th Cir. 2007)

Circuit Judge Ripple

Sandra Williams . . . sought relief under the Fair Debt Collection Practices Act ("FDCPA"). The district court granted the defendant, OSI Educational Services, Inc., ("OSI"), summary judgment. Ms. Williams then filed a timely appeal to this court.

I. BACKGROUND

A.

Ms. Williams is a consumer whose debt was incurred for personal, family or household purposes. OSI is a debt collection agency; it was hired by Great Lakes Higher Education Guaranty Corp. ("Great Lakes") to collect its debts. OSI sent Ms. Williams a letter and a debt validation notice, dated March 28, 2005. The letter sought to collect a sum of $807.89 labeled as "Total Due," which was the outstanding balance owed to Great Lakes. The letter breaks down the amount owed as follows:

Date:	03/28/05
Principal:	$683.56
Interest:	16.46
Fees:	107.87
Total Due:	$807.89

The letter further states:

> The balance may not reflect the exact amount of interest which is accruing daily per your original agreement with your creditor. Contact us to find out your exact payout balance.

B.

The district court . . . determined that the letter apprised Ms. Williams of the total amount due, including the amount of the principal, interest and fees due. The district court stated that, . . . the letter clearly advises that additional interest is accruing on a daily basis and that, therefore, additional interest may be added." Comparing this case to *Taylor v. Cavalry Investment, L.L.C.*, the district court took the view that the letter complied with the statute because OSI's "letter states the amount of the debt clearly enough so that an unsophisticated recipient would not misunderstand it."

II. DISCUSSION

Ms. Williams submits that there is an issue of material fact as to whether OSI's letter clearly states the amount of the debt, as required by the FDCPA. In examining that contention, we begin with the wording of the statute. The FDCPA requires that debt collectors state "the amount of the debt" that they are seeking to collect from the consumer. The debt collector's letter must state the amount of the debt "clearly enough that the recipient is likely to understand it." *Chuway v. Nat'/Action Fin.Servs. Inc.* To ensure that this statutory command is implemented properly, we must evaluate the letter to determine whether it causes any "confusion" or "misunderstand[ing]" as to the amount due. In making this determination, we evaluate the letter from the perspective of an "unsophisticated consumer or debtor." The unsophisticated consumer is "uninformed, naive, [and] trusting," but possesses "rudimentary knowledge about the financial world, is wise enough to read collection notices with added care, possesses 'reasonable intelligence,' and is capable of making basic logical deductions and inferences." *Pettit v. Retrieval Masters Creditors Bureau, Inc.* Notably, we have rejected explicitly the notion that we should employ the *least* sophisticated debtor standard, the "very last rung on the sophistication ladder" *Pettit*.

* * * * *

Our past cases indicate that summary judgment may be avoided by showing that the letter, on its face, will "confuse a substantial number of recipients." We also have said that, absent a showing that the face of the letter will precipitate such a level of confusion, the "plaintiff must come forward with evidence beyond the letter and beyond [her] own self-serving assertions that the letter is confusing in order to create a genuine issue of material fact for trial." *Durkin* (noting that evidence may consist of "carefully designed and conducted consumer survey[s]" or expert witnesses).

Ms. Williams chooses to base her case on the first of these options. She focuses on the following language from OSI's letter:

> The balance may not reflect the exact amount of interest which is accruing daily per your original agreement with your creditor. Contact us to find out your exact payout balance.

In her view, there are three reasons why OSI's letter would confuse a substantial number of recipients. We shall examine each.

First, Ms. Williams argues that the language in OSI's letter is more confusing than that in *Chuway*, which we held could "confuse a substantial number of recipients." *Chuway*. In that case, the letter stated the "balance" and also contained the following language: "Please remit the balance listed above in the return envelope provided. To obtain your most current balance information, please call [phone number]." We held that the letter violated the FDCPA. There, the confusion arose because the letter did not state why the "current balance" would be different than the stated "balance." The plaintiff could have thought that "the reference to the 'current balance' meant that the defendant was trying to collect an additional debt [without] telling her how large an additional debt and thus violating the statute." In contrast, the language in OSI's letter links the difference between the "total due" and the "exact payout balance" to the "interest which is accruing daily per your original agreement with your creditor." OSI's letter thus provides the information that created the confusion in the *Chuway* letter.

Ms. Williams' second and third arguments are best treated together. She submits that the letter's language leaves open the possibility that the actual amount due is less than the amount stated on the letter. She further suggests that the sentence's use of the present tense makes it possible to conclude that the stated amount due was not accurate on the date that the letter was written. In our view, both these contentions are based on a strained reading of the sentence. It would be "unrealistic, peculiar, [and] bizarre" to read OSI's letter in this way. *Durkin*. The common sense reading of the letter is that the balance is accurate as of the date the letter is written, but that the amount due will increase because of interest that is accruing daily. This construction is supported by the letter's itemization of "PRINCIPAL," "INTEREST," "FEES" and "TOTAL DUE" in a box with, and immediately below, the "DATE." Under a natural reading, the language conveys, even to an unsophisticated consumer, that interest will accrue after the letter is sent and therefore that the consumer should call to find out the "*exact* payout balance."

As we said in *Chuway*, "It is impossible to draft a letter that is certain to be understood by every person who receives it; only if it would confuse a significant fraction of the persons to whom it is directed will be defendant be liable."

We believe that the language in this letter is closer to the language in *Taylor* than to the language in *Chuway*. In *Taylor*, the letter similarly set forth the total due and broke down that total into principal and interest. If further stated: "[I]f applicable, your account may have or will accrue interest at a rate specified in your contractual agreement with the original creditor." Three plaintiffs in *Taylor* had submitted affidavits stating that this sentence confused them about the amount of debt that the debt collector was trying to collect. We held that the language was "entirely clear on its face." . . .

As we noted earlier, in opposing summary judgment, Ms. Williams relied solely on OSI's letter. She submitted no other evidence to support her view that OSI's letter is confusing. Without more, Ms. Williams' unsupported assertion that OSI's letter is confusing is insufficient to create a genuine issue of fact as to confusion.

* * * * *

CONCLUSION

The letter set forth the amount of the debt with sufficient clarity and accuracy to comply with the requirements of the statute.

Affirmed.

Questions

1. *a.* A debt collection letter must be evaluated to determine whether it causes confusion or misunderstanding for the consumer. What level of consumer sophistication was employed by the court to determine whether the debt collection letter to Williams caused confusion or misunderstanding?

   b. Is confusion on the part of an individual consumer conclusive evidence of a violation of the Fair Debt Collection Practices Act? Explain.

   c. Describe the two ways by which a plaintiff/consumer can establish that a debt collection letter caused an impermissible level of confusion or misunderstanding.

2. Miller owed $2,501.61 to the Star Bank of Cincinnati. Payco attempted to collect the debt by sending a one-page collection form to Miller. The front side of the form included, among other words, in very large capital letters a demand for IMMEDIATE FULL PAYMENT, the words PHONE US TODAY, and the word NOW in white letters nearly two inches tall against a red background. At the bottom of the page in the smallest print on the form was the message: NOTICE: SEE REVERSE SIDE FOR IMPORTANT INFORMATION. The reverse side contained the validation notice required under the FDCPA. Does the form conform to FDCPA requirements? Explain. See *Miller v. Payco-General American Credits, Inc.*, 943 F. 2d 482 (4th Cir. 1991).

3. Why shouldn't debt collectors be able to use aggressive tactics to encourage payment of legitimate bills?

New Rules for the Lending Industry?

The American economy is reeling at this writing in 2008; suffering particularly from the collapse of the housing bubble. Many borrowers are unable to repay their subprime mortgage loans (home loans at very high interest rates often to borrowers with weak credit credentials) and are losing their homes as a result. Certainly the borrowers themselves bear responsibility for their financial struggles, but the evidence suggests that unscrupulous lending practices are also a factor. In an effort to curb predatory loans, North Carolina in 2007 strengthened its already substantial protections for borrowers which, among other things, require that borrowers receive independent counseling before taking high interest loans and allow borrowers to sue lenders if they are directed toward high interest loans that are inappropriate for their financial circumstances. About half of the states have passed similar laws and the federal government is considering something of the same.

Questions

1. How might consumers be harmed if the federal government were to impose restrictions on the lending market like those in North Carolina?

2. Would you favor new federal laws protecting consumers from predatory lenders? Explain.

Source: Christopher Conkey, "Predatory Lending: Hard to Tame," *The Wall Street Journal,* May 7, 2007, p. A5.

Part Four—Bankruptcy

Fresh Start?   Should we lend a hand to those who are down on their luck? Bankruptcy law was specifically designed to provide a fresh start for those whose financial problems were insurmountable. We believed that both the debtor and society benefited from the new beginning, but as bankruptcy filings skyrocketed, we downsized the fresh start by reforming federal bankruptcy law in 2005 to force more bankrupt parties to repay their creditors. Following the reform, bankruptcies did fall somewhat in 2006, but in 2007 consumer and business bankruptcies rose sharply to a total of 850,912, doubtless reflecting difficult economic conditions at the time.[30]

Interestingly, bankruptcy patterns vary dramatically by region, with the highest rates in the southeast (such as Tennessee, with one household in every 38.7 filing for bankruptcy in one 12-month period) and the lowest rates in parts of the West and Midwest along with the Northeast (one in 156.2 households in Vermont filed for bankruptcy).[31] The credit industry sees the bankruptcies as more evidence of declining personal responsibility, while consumer advocates say the bankruptcies are the product of tragedies spurred by medical emergencies, job losses, and an explosion of credit cards:

> "How is it that the person who wants to do right ends up so worse off?" asked Cleveland municipal judge Robert Triozzi . . . when he ruled against Discover in the company's breach-of-contract suit against another struggling credit cardholder, Ruth Owens.
>
> Owens tried for six years to pay off a $1,900 balance on her Discover card, sending the credit company a total of $3,492 in monthly payments between 1997 and 2003. Yet her balance grew to $5,564.28, even though . . . she never used the card to buy anything more. Of that total, over-limit penalty fees alone were $1,158.
>
> Triozzi denied Discover's claim, calling its attempt to collect more money from Owens "unconscionable."[32]

The Reform Law   In brief, the new legislation forces some bankruptcy filers to enter their claim under Chapter 13 of the bankruptcy code rather than the more forgiving Chapter 7 (see below). Those with income above their state's median who can pay $6,000 over five years—$100 per month—probably would be forced into Chapter 13, where the court would order a repayment plan. Those not meeting that test could file under Chapter 7, thereby achieving a fresh start by escaping most repayment responsibilities while their nonessential property would be sold to pay debtors. The new law also requires those filing for bankruptcy to pay for credit counseling. Supporters of the new law argue that it will reduce the cost of credit for all Americans, whereas opponents see the bill as a punitive assault on those already down on their luck. [For the American Bankruptcy Institute, see **http://www.abiworld.org**]

Question

Would you expect bankruptcy to rehabilitate debtors thus providing them a "fresh start" in the economy?

Bankruptcy Rules

Bankruptcy in the United States is governed exclusively by federal law; the states do not have the constitutional authority to enact bankruptcy legislation, but they do set their own rules within the limits provided by Congress. Our attention will be limited to the principal federal statute, the Bankruptcy Reform Act of 1978, as amended.

Bankruptcy is an adjudication relieving a debtor of all or part of his or her liabilities. Any person, partnership, or corporation may seek debtor relief. Three forms of bankruptcy action are important to us:

1. **Liquidation (Chapter 7** of the Bankruptcy Act), in which most debts are forgiven and all assets except exemptions are distributed to creditors.
2. **Reorganization (Chapter 11)**, in which creditors are kept from the debtor's assets while the debtor, under the supervision of the court, works out a plan to continue in business while paying creditors.
3. **Adjustment of debts** of an individual with regular income (**Chapter 13**), in which individuals with limited debts are protected from creditors while paying their debts in installments. [For links to bankruptcy sites on the Internet, see **http://www.lawtrove. com/bankruptcy**]

Liquidation

A Chapter 7 liquidation petition can be *voluntarily* filed in federal court by the debtor (individual, partnership, or corporation), or creditors can seek an *involuntary* bankruptcy judgment. A Chapter 7 liquidation is commonly called a "straight" bankruptcy.

In a voluntary action, the debtor files a petition with the appropriate federal court. The court then has jurisdiction to proceed with the liquidation, and the petition becomes the *order for relief*. The debtor need not be insolvent to seek bankruptcy.

Creditors often can compel an involuntary bankruptcy. The debtor may challenge that bankruptcy action. The court will enter an order for relief if it finds the debtor has not been paying his or her debts when due or if most of the debtor's property is under the control of a custodian for the purpose of enforcing a lien against that property.

After the order for relief is granted, voluntary and involuntary actions proceed in a similar manner. Creditors are restrained from reaching the debtor's assets. An interim bankruptcy trustee is appointed by the court. The creditors then hold a meeting, and a permanent trustee is elected. The trustee collects the debtor's property and converts it to money, protects the interests of the debtor and creditors, may manage the debtor's business, and ultimately distributes the estate proceeds to the creditors. Debtors are allowed to keep exempt property, which varies from state to state but typically includes a car, a homestead, some household or personal items, life insurance, and other "necessities." Normally a dollar maximum is attached to each.

The debtor's nonexempt property is then divided among the creditors according to the priorities prescribed by statute. Secured creditors are paid first. If funds remain, "priority" claims, such as employees' wages and alimony/child support, are paid. Then, funds permitting, general creditors are paid. Each class must be paid in full before a class of lower priority will be compensated. Any remaining funds will return to the debtor.

When distribution is complete, the bankruptcy judge may issue an order *discharging* (relieving) the debtor of any remaining debts except for certain statutorily specified claims. Those include, for example, taxes and educational loans. The debtor might fail to receive a discharge if he or she had received one in the previous six years, if property was concealed from the court, or if good faith in the bankruptcy process was lacking in other respects.

Reorganization

Chapter 11 is available to individuals and most businesses. The basic thrust of this type of bankruptcy is to allow financially troubled enterprises to continue in operation while debtor adjustments are arranged. Thus both debtor and creditor may ultimately benefit more than from a straight liquidation. The debtor may voluntarily seek reorganization, or the creditors may petition for an involuntary action. When a reorganization petition is filed with the court and relief is ordered, one or more committees of creditors are appointed to participate in bankruptcy procedures. Typically the debtor continues to operate the business, although the court may appoint a trustee to replace the debtor if required because of dishonesty, fraud, or extreme mismanagement. The company, its bankers, and its suppliers will meet to work out a method for continuing operations. A plan must be developed that will satisfy the creditors that their interests are being served by the reorganization. Perhaps new capital is secured, or perhaps creditors receive some shares in the company. The plan must be approved by the creditors and confirmed by the court. The company is then required to carry out the plan.

Adjustment of Debts

Under Chapter 13, individuals (not partnerships or corporations) can seek the protection of the court to arrange a debt adjustment plan. Chapter 13 permits only voluntary bankruptcies and is restricted to those with steady incomes and somewhat limited debts. The process can begin only with a voluntary petition from the debtor. Creditors are restrained from reaching the debtor's assets. The debtor develops a repayment plan. If creditors' interests are sufficiently satisfied by the plan, the court may confirm it and appoint a trustee to oversee the plan. The debtor may then have three to five years to make the necessary payments. [For an extensive bankruptcy law database, see **http://www.law.cornell.edu/topics/bankruptcy.html**]

PRACTICING ETHICS Bankruptcy—Who Is to Blame?

Commenting on the 2005 bankruptcy reform law, Todd Zywicki, a George Mason University law professor, said, "This is a matter of morality and personal responsibility." Consumer advocates, on the other hand, say the bankruptcy problem lies with the "enablers"—the credit card companies who encourage deeper and deeper indebtedness by bombarding consumers with billions of credit card solicitations annually.

Question

Who bears the moral blame for America's bankruptcy epidemic? Explain.

Source: Michael Schroeder and Suein Hwang, "Sweeping New Bankruptcy Law to Make Life Harder for Debtors," *The Wall Street Journal*, April 6, 2005, p. A1.

Part Five—Consumer Protection Abroad

Aggressive consumer protection measures of the kind we have studied in this chapter are unknown to much of the world, but change is coming. Because a staggering amount of American consumer goods come from China, we are pressing for more vigorous product safety efforts by Chinese exporters and government regulators. Most notoriously, Americans have been alarmed by the recall of millions of lead-tainted toys (explained in the Consumer Product Safety Commission materials earlier in this chapter), but the problems reach to pet food, tires, toothpaste, seafood, drugs, and other imports from China. At this writing, for example, hundreds of serious reactions and scores of deaths in the United States have been tentatively linked by the FDA to contaminated lots of the blood thinner heparin that were imported from China. Chinese officials, however, deny those findings.[33] The difficulty of maintaining product safety in a booming, export-driven economy along with the struggle to sustain 1.3 billion people and to navigate the treacherous transition from communism to elements of a free market is evident in the extraordinary story of Zheng Xiaoyu.

> China executed its former top food and drug safety regulator.

Bribery China executed its former top food and drug safety regulator, Zheng Xiaoyu, in 2007 after he was convicted of accepting more than $850,000 in bribes to help pharmaceutical companies avoid regulatory hurdles. At least 10 people died and dozens became seriously ill after consuming an antibiotic produced by a company that allegedly bribed Mr. Zheng.[34] More than 100 people reportedly died in Panama after consuming a cough syrup manufactured in China.[35] *The New York Times* detailed Mr. Zheng's disgrace:

> In his confession, Mr. Zheng acknowledged that during his eight-year tenure, he had accepted gifts and bribes from eight drug companies that sought special favors: a car, a villa, furniture, cash. . . . All told, he and his family accepted gifts valued at more than $850,000—in a country where the average worker earns less than $2,000 a year. . . .
>
> The rise and fall of Mr. Zheng offers a rare glimpse inside China's flawed regulatory system. He started out as an idealistic reformer. Concerned about China's unsafe drug supply, he lobbied for the creation of the State Food and Drug Administration. But in the end, according to friends and associates, he was corrupted by the very system he sought to change—even enlisting his wife and son to solicit bribes.[36]

Reform? Now China is anxious to improve consumer safety and avoid further damage to its export reputation. In 2007, the United States and China reached agreement on new policies to enhance safety for food, animal feed, drugs and medical devices exported to America. And the United States Food and Drug Administration has received State Department approval to open satellite offices in American embassies in China to help increase the safety of products exported to the United States. That initiative is expected to begin in 2008 following final Chinese goverment approval.

Pierce the Chinese Curtain?

When Mark Lanier, a liability lawyer in Houston took the case of a 6-year-old girl who choked to death on a toy, he tried suing everybody in the supply chain; the fast-food restaurant that sold the toy in a children's meal, the American importer and the toy's Chinese manufacturer. The restaurant chain, Whataburger, and the importer settled for an undisclosed amount, but Lanier said he could not even find the proper entity in China to serve with a lawsuit.

"Your're spitting in the wind," Lanier said of attempting to sue Chinese companies in U.S. courts. Lanier said his firm has seen a 500 percent increase in the number of inquiries over Chinese goods, but he will rarely take a case unless there is an American defendant as well.

Acquiring jurisdiction over a Chinese company is very difficult unless it actually does business on American soil. Simply finding the original supplier of the product in question and getting necessary records, lawyers say, can be virtually impossible, and the cost of litigation is high because of the many barriers. Further, the United States and China do not have an agreement enforcing each other's court judgments. While some lawsuits against Chinese companies are proceeding, injured U.S. consumers' best hopes may be in negotiation, political pressure, and adverse publicity.

Source: Xiyun Yang, "Liability Lawyers Struggle to Pierce the Chinese Curtain," *Washington Post,* July 28, 2007, p. D01.

Internet Exercise

Go to the Center for Auto Safety Web site [**http://www.autosafety.org/**] and find your way to your state's lemon law. Read the brief summary of the law of your state. Read the summary for the states of Texas, Virginia, and West Virginia.

a. Explain the differences in the laws of the states.

b. Which of those three or four states, in your view, provides the "fairest" protection considering the viewpoints of both consumers and dealers?

Chapter Questions

1. A group of parents sued Gerber claiming its "Fruit Juice Snacks" product packaging was misleading. The words "Fruit Juice" appeared on the package beside images of fruits such as peaches and cherries. In fact, the only fruit juice in the "Snacks" was white grape from concentrate. A side panel statement said the product was made "with real fruit juice and other all natural ingredients," but the primary ingredients were corn syrup and sugar. The side panel also displayed the statement, "one of a variety of nutritious Gerber Graduates foods and juices that have been specifically designed to help toddlers grow up strong and healthy." The actual ingredients were correctly listed in "small print" on the side of the box. Is a "reasonable consumer" "likely to be deceived" by the Gerber packaging? Explain. See *Williams v. Gerber Products,* 523 F.3d 934 (9th Cir. 2008).

2. Two-thirds of American adults are either obese or overweight. The rate of overweight children ages 6 to 11 has more than doubled since 1980, and the rate for adolescents has tripled. Timothy Muris, chairman of the Federal Trade Commission, objected to proposals to ban television commercials for "junk food" directed at kids:

"Banning junk food ads on kids' programming is impractical, ineffective, and illegal." Explain what Muris meant. See Timothy J. Muris, "Don't Blame TV," *The Wall Street Journal,* June 25, 2004, p. A10.

3. DeSantis sued a debt collection agency, Computer Credit. DeSantis apparently owed $319.50 to Dr. Jeffrey A. Stahl, who assigned the debt to CC for collection. On April 27, 2000, CC sent the following collection letter to DeSantis:

> This notice will serve to inform you that your overdue balance with Dr. Jeffrey A. Stahl has been referred to Computer Credit, Inc., a debt collector. *[The] doctor insists on payment or a valid reason for your failure to make payment.* The law prohibits us from collecting any amount greater than the obligation stated above. Unless you notify us to the contrary, we will assume the amount due is correct. This communication is sent to you in an attempt to collect this debt. Any information obtained will be used for that purpose. *In the absence of a valid reason for your failure to make payment, pay the above debt or contact the doctor to settle this matter.* Payment can be sent directly to the doctor. [Italics added.]

The Fair Debt Collection Practices Act specifies that the consumer may dispute the alleged debt, in which case the debt collector must desist from collection until the debt collector obtains verification regarding the amount of the debt, if any. Given that statutory requirement, was the FDCPA violated by the italicized sentences in the collection letter? Explain. See *DeSantis v. Computer Credit, Inc.,* 269 F.3d 159 (2d Cir. 2001).

4. A *New York Times* editorial recently argued that college students are taken advantage of by credit card companies:

> The credit card industry has made a profitable art of corralling consumers into ruinous interest rates and hidden penalties that keep even people who pay their bills permanently mired in debt. The companies are especially eager to target freshly minted college students, who are naïve in money matters and especially vulnerable to credit card offers that are too good to be true. [37]

   a. Do you think beginning college students are often "vulnerable" to manipulation by credit card companies?

   b. Are you vulnerable to that alleged manipulation?

   c. Should the federal government provide more protection against credit card deception? Explain.

5. Snow wrote a $23.12 check to a convenience store, Circle K. The check bounced, and Circle K sent the check to its attorney, Riddle, for collection. Riddle sent Snow a letter demanding payment along with a $15 service fee. Snow paid the $23.12, but refused to pay the $15. Then Snow sued Riddle for violating the Fair Debt Collection Practices Act because the collection letter did not include the required "validation notice" telling him about his legal rights under the FDCPA. Riddle responded by saying that the FDCPA does not apply to dishonored checks. Does a dishonored check constitute a debt such that the FDCPA would apply? Explain. See *Snow v. Riddle,* 143 F.3d 1350 (10th Cir. 1998).

6. Jenny Craig, Inc., reached a 1997 agreement with the Federal Trade Commission providing that the company must include the following statement in most ads: "For many dieters, weight loss is temporary." In your view, is that requirement a wise use of FTC authority? Explain.

7. Under 1998 federal rules, golf carts with a maximum speed of 25 miles per hour are exempt from most federal safety regulations and are allowed to use some public roads. The carts must be equipped with seat belts, windshields, headlights, and turn signals. The carts are widely used in retirement communities. The rules have been heavily criticized.

   a. What factors would you consider in deciding on the wisdom of this golf cart rule?

   b. How would you vote? Explain.

8. Recent studies suggest that consumer bankruptcies are much more common in some states than others. Aside from income levels, what socioeconomic factors would you expect to be closely correlated with high bankruptcy rates?

9. Playtex manufactures the market-leading spillproof cup for children, which a child uses by sucking on a spout to cause a valve to open. Gerber introduced its own version and ran ads showing an unnamed competitor's product and claiming that "Gerber's patented valve makes our cup more than 50 percent easier to drink from than the leading cup." Gerber's claims for the superiority of its cup were backed by tests from an independent laboratory. Playtex said the unnamed cup obviously was its brand and that the superiority claims were false and misleading. Playtex sought an injunction to block the Gerber ads. Would you grant that injunction? Explain. See *Playtex Products v. Gerber Products,* 981 F. Supp. 827 (S.D.N.Y. 1997).

10. Maguire, a credit card holder at Bradlees Department Store, fell behind in her payments. She received a series of dunning letters from Citicorp, which managed Bradlees' accounts, demanding that she pay the overdue amount. Later Maguire received a letter from "Debtor Assistance," which said that "your Bradlees account has recently [been] charged off." Debtor Assistance is a unit of Citicorp, but was not identified as such in the letter, beyond the phrase "a unit of CRS." The back of each Bradlees' account statement includes a notice that Citicorp Retail Services was the creditor that handled Bradlees' accounts. In general, creditors are not subject to the requirements of the Fair Debt Collections Practices Act, but Maguire sued claiming the Debtor Assistance letter violated the FDCPA. Is she correct? Explain. See *Maguire v. Citicorp Retail Services, Inc.,* 147 F.3d 232 (2d Cir. 1998).

11. A door-to-door salesman representing Your Shop at Home Services, Inc., called on Clifton and Cora Jones, who were welfare recipients. The Jones couple decided to buy a freezer from the salesman for $900. Credit charges, insurance, and so on were added to that $900 base so that the total purchase price was $1,439.69. Mr. and Mrs. Jones signed a sales agreement that accurately stipulated the price and its ingredients. The Joneses sued to reform the contract on unconscionability grounds. They had paid $619.88 toward the total purchase price. At trial, the retail value of the new freezer at the time of purchase was set at approximately $300.

    a. What is the issue in this case?

    b. Decide. Explain. See *Jones v. Star Credit Corp.,* 298 N.Y.S. 2d 264 (1969).

12. Roseman resigned from the John Hancock Insurance Company following allegations of misuse of his expense account. He reimbursed the account. Subsequently he was denied employment by another insurance firm after that firm read a Retail Credit Company credit report on him. The credit report included accurate information regarding Roseman's resignation. Was Retail Credit in violation of the Fair Credit

Reporting Act in circulating information regarding the resignation? Explain. See *Roseman v. Retail Credit Co., Inc.*, 428 F. Supp. 643 (Pa. 1977).

13. Once the government decided to intervene in the free market on behalf of consumers, two broad product safety options presented themselves: (*a*) the government could have limited its effort to generating and distributing information to consumers, or (*b*) the government could have set safety standards for all products. Assuming the government was forced to choose one or the other but not elements of both, which option should it have chosen? Explain.

14. Consumers sometimes abuse sellers. One familiar technique is shoplifting. Of course, shoplifting is a crime. However, the criminal process is cumbersome and often does not result in monetary recoveries for sellers. As a result, at least 43 states now have laws permitting store owners to impose civil fines, the collection of which is usually turned over to a lawyer or collection agency with a threat to sue in civil court, file criminal charges, or both if payment is not forthcoming. Fines may range from $50 to $5,000 or more, depending on the value of the item stolen.

    a. Defense lawyers say this civil fine system is unfair. Why?

    b. On balance, is the civil fine approach to shoplifting a good idea? Explain.

    c. Cite some other examples of consumers abusing businesspeople.

15. Goswami failed to pay her $900 credit card bill. A collection agency, ACEI, mailed her a collection letter with a blue bar across the envelope saying "Priority Letter." The letter did not, in fact, constitute priority mail. The purpose of the bar was to encourage Goswami to open the envelope. Was the bar a deceptive practice in violation of the Fair Debt Collection Practices Act? Explain. See *Goswami v. American Collections Enterprise, Inc.*, 377 F.3d 488 (5th Cir. 2004); cert. den. 2005 U.S. LEXIS 5511.

Notes

1. Araminta Wordsworth, "Miss Cleo Didn't See $5M Fine in Her Future," *National Post,* November 16, 2002, p. A21.

2. Donna De La Cruz, "Diet-Pill Companies Fined $25 Million," *Des Moines Register,* January 5, 2007, p. 5A.

3. Monica Hesse, "Barbie Tells CPSC to Get the Lead Out in Viral Video," *Washington Post,* November 24, 2007, p. C01.

4. M.P. McQueen, "Retailers Face the Test of Testing," *The Wall Street Journal*, November 26, 2007, p. A6.

5. Alexa Olesen, Associated Press, "Mattel Apologizes to China over Recalls," *USA TODAY*, September 21, 2007 [**http://www.usatoday.com/money/topstories/2007-09-21-1717639957_x.htm**].

6. David Lazarus, "Gaping Holes in Product Safety Net," *Los Angeles Times*, August 19, 2007 [**http://www.latimes.com/business/la-fi-lazarus19aug19,0,7044608.column?coll=la-tot-business&track=ntottext**].

7. Tom Lowry and Lorraine Woellert, "More Paper Tiger than Watchdog?" *BusinessWeek*, September 3, 2007, p. 45.

8. Knight Ridder Newspapers, "Merck Accused of Concealing Side Effects of Vioxx during Senate Hearings," *Waterloo/Cedar Falls Courier,* November 19, 2004, p. A1.

9. *Riegel v. Medtronic*, 128 S.Ct. 999 (2008).

10. Marie McCullough, "Journal Speaks Out against FDA," *Des Moines Register,* November 23, 2004, p. 3A.

11. Julie Schmit, "FDA Caution, 'Research Drought' Cut Drug Approvals," *USA TODAY,* February 4, 2008, p. 1A.

12. Editorial, "Condition Critical at the FDA," *The Boston Globe,* February 3, 2008, p. C8.

13. Paul Recer, "Most FDA Scientists Critical of Drug Monitoring," *Des Moines Register,* December 17, 2004, p. 3A.

14. Editorial, "No Recourse for the Injured," *The New York Times,* February 22, 2008 [**http://www.nytimes.com/2008/02/22/opinion/22fri1.html?th&emc=th**].

15. Joseph Pereira, "How Credit-Card Data Went Out Wireless Door," *The Wall Street Journal,* May 4, 2007, p. A1.

16. Ibid.

17. Christopher Conkey, "Assessing Identity-Theft Costs," *The Wall Street Journal,* November 28, 2007, p. D3.

18. Ibid.

19. Russ Wiles, "ID Theft Risk Underestimated," *Des Moines Sunday Register*, June 10, 2007, p. 3D.

20. Dean Foust, "ID Theft: More Hype than Harm," *BusinessWeek,* July 3, 2006, p. 34.

21. Ibid.

22. Erik Eckholm, "Enticing Ad, Little Cash and Then a Lot of Regret," *The New York Times,* July 14, 2007 [**www.nytimes.com**].

23. Ibid.

24. Ibid.

25. *Washington Post*, "College Students Get Too Much Credit," *Waterloo/Cedar Falls Courier,* April 13, 2008, p. A1.

26. Ibid.

27. Michael R. Crittenden, "Credit-Card Plan Includes Rate Curbs," *The Wall Street Journal,* May 2, 2008, p. C3.

28. This summary of FCRA requirements was drawn largely from the FTC document, "A Summary of Your Rights under the Fair Credit Reporting Act" [**http://www.ftc.gov/bcp/conline/edcams/fcra/summary.htm**].

29. Editorial, "When a Stranger Calls," *New York Times*, July 9, 2006 [**www.nytimes.com**].

30. Reuters, "Bankruptcy Filings Rise 38% in 2007," *Los Angeles Times*, April 16, 2008 [**http://www.latimes.com/business/la-fi-bankrupt16apr16,1,5994895.story**].

31. Constance Mitchell Ford, "Creditor-Friendly South Offers Preview of Bankruptcy Changes," *The Wall Street Journal,* March 10, 2005, p. A1.

32. *Washington Post,* "Punitive Charges Dog Credit Card Users," *Waterloo/Cedar Falls Courier,* March 7, 2005, p. A1.

33. Marc Kaufman, "New Data Link Heparin Deaths to Chinese Batches, FDA Says," *Washington Post*, April 22, 2008, p. A02.

34. Editorial, "Rough Justice," *washingtonpost.com,* July 14, 2007, p. A16.

35. Walt Bogdanich and Jake Hooker, "From China to Panama, a Trail of Poisoned Medicine," *The New York Times,* May 6, 2007 [**http://www.nytimes.com/2007/05/06/world/americas/06poison.html?pagewanted=1**].

36. David Barboza, "A Chinese Reformer Betrays His Cause, and Pays," *The New York Times*, July 13, 2007 [**http://www.nytimes.com/2007/07/13/business/worldbusiness/13corrupt.html**].

37. Editorial, "The College Credit Scam," *The New York Times,* August 27, 2007 [**www.nytimes.com**].

CHAPTER SIXTEEN

International Ethics and Law

After completing this chapter, students will be able to:

1. Discuss the role of the World Trade Organization (WTO) in reducing global trade barriers.

2. Compare and contrast an American firm's social responsibility to its host country with its social responsibility to its home country.

3. Provide a brief overview of Islamic criminal law.

4. Evaluate arguments in favor of global social responsibility standards.

5. Describe the basic forms of global business expansion.

6. Describe examples of the law governing international business in sales of goods, trade in services, employment, and intellectual property.

7. Describe the purpose and effect of the General Agreement on Tariffs and Trade (GATT).

8. Identify means of resolving international disputes.

9. Explain the "act of state" doctrine.

10. Describe the doctrine of sovereign immunity and its exceptions as codified under the Foreign Sovereign Immunities Act (FSIA).

Introduction

The preceding chapters have addressed law and ethics primarily in an American context. However, ours is an increasingly global economy. Evidence of our global economy is everywhere. For example, it is possible to travel the world accessing automated teller machines (ATMs) for local currency. Through online banking, you can see the cash obtained, say in Japanese yen, instantaneously debited from your domestic bank account. Watch as you drive on local roads and you can spot Subarus and Toyota Priuses (from Japan), Mercedes (Germany), MINI Coopers (England), Volvos (Sweden), and Hyundais and Kias (South Korea). In cities around the world, you will find adorning shops and buildings such American logos as Starbucks, McDonalds, and KPMG. Back at home, on streets and in malls you can see branches and outlets for HSBC (the world's largest banking group, headquartered in London), T-Mobile (part of the German Deutsche Telekom) and H&M clothing stores (Swedish). From national news outlets you can hear that foreign sovereign wealth funds (government-run investment funds) have bought stakes in such Wall Street icons as Merrill Lynch and Citicorp, as well as that China is now the largest source of foreign investment in Venezuela. Indeed, funds from China have been invested in projects around the globe including, for example, the building of four dams in Jordan. The process of globalization is the breaking down of national boundaries and rules to allow free interchange around the world—the free interchange, as just illustrated, of people, communications, services, goods, businesses, investments, and ideas.

But what are the implications of this networked global economy? To what laws are companies subject? The laws of their "home" country? The laws of the host country? The laws where their suppliers or customers reside? What results if the laws of the host country and the home country conflict? And what happens when a corporation changes its home country? When the German corporation, Daimler Benz, merged with Chrysler, becoming Daimler Chrysler, did the laws to which it was subject change? Did those changes have to be unwound when Daimler later sold Chrysler to Cerberus Capital Management, an American private equity fund, in 2007? When Yahoo! bought a 40 percent stake in the Chinese Alibaba Group (which includes alibaba.com), to what extent did that purchase subject Yahoo! to Chinese law? As firms become companies of the world, rather than of one nation, difficult issues of ethics and law arise.

The International Environment

Ever since Adam Smith wrote *The Wealth of Nations* in 1776, many have argued that it is axiomatic that a decrease in trade barriers between any number of countries will stimulate the total world economy, not simply the economies of the countries involved in the specific trade agreement. This principle has been resoundingly affirmed in recent years by the 151 countries that have, as of this writing, joined the World Trade Organization (WTO) since it was created January 1, 1995. A fundamental principle set forth in the preamble to the 1994 Marrakesh Agreement establishing the WTO is that "the substantial reduction of tariffs and other barriers to trade" will contribute to the objectives of "raising standards of living, ensuring full employment and a large and steadily growing volume of real income."[1] Member countries in the WTO represent a diverse array of the world's governments: from communist to socialist to capitalist, from Buddhist to Jewish to Christian to Muslim, and from all points around the globe. The most recent countries to have become members are Saudi Arabia (2005) and Viet Nam (2007). Thus the value of decreasing trade barriers is a widely shared belief in the international community.

The strength of this belief, however, is being tested as the WTO member states continue to struggle with the current round of multilateral trade negotiations (MTN), known as the Doha Round (after the city in Qatar where the round was initiated). The Doha Round deadlocked at a 2003 meeting in Cancun, Mexico. A significant cause was extensive domestic farm subsidy programs maintained by both the United States and the European Union (E.U.). Because the WTO talks are based on consensus, not on votes, even less powerful nations, particularly when they act in concert, can make their concerns felt. "Developing nations, led by Brazil and India, . . . contended that massive subsidies allow rich nations to flood global markets with farm products, depressing prices and impeding the economic development of poor countries that rely on agriculture as their primary source of exports. For example, African nations complain that American cotton subsidies contribute to the impoverishment of thousands of African growers."[2] Some commentators have wondered whether the deadlock might signal an end to viable WTO multilateral trade negotiations and a return to bilateral trade talks, in which the imbalance of power between rich and poor nations is more pronounced. That eventuality seemed to have been sidestepped by a 2004 deal brokered by Brazil, the United States, and the EU, in which wealthier nations agreed to abolish all agricultural export subsidies ultimately, but no firm deadlines were imposed. But the talks collapsed again in 2006. The United States and European Union are pushing, in exchange for a reduction in agricultural subsidies, for developing nations to lower their own tariffs on industrial goods and give broader access to foreign financial firms. Twenty developing countries, led by Brazil, thus far have refused, leaving the talks in limbo. [The WTO maintains an extensive online presence, including full text documents, through its Web site at **www.wto.org**]

> African nations complain that American cotton subsidies contribute to the impoverishment of thousands of African growers.

To the extent the WTO continues to be successful in reducing trade barriers to the free flow of goods and services, the global economy grows and the ethical and legal issues addressed in this chapter are magnified. However, the desire to reach some common legal ground in international business is not a recent development. For example, U.S. commercial treaties (largely bilateral), negotiated as early as 1778, have long regulated shipping and trading rights and rules between individuals of different countries. In the 20th century an unprecedented expansion of world trade was facilitated by the development of many regional trade agreements, such as the General Agreement on Tariffs and Trade (GATT—now a foundation agreement of the WTO) and the North American Free Trade Agreement (NAFTA), as well as the development of regional common markets such as the EU, the MERCOSUR Common Market (created by Argentina, Brazil, Paraguay, and Uruguay) and the East African Community (created by Kenya, Tanzania, and Uganda), among others. New international trade agreements continue to be reached. For example, China has concluded a free trade agreement with New Zealand, and Libya has made an agreement allowing it to grow wheat in the Ukraine in exchange for including the latter in construction and gas deals.

Consider the European Union, which continues to grow as an economic powerhouse. As of this writing, it has 27 member countries (most recently, Bulgaria and Romania) and three candidate countries: Croatia, Macedonia, and Turkey. Its population far surpasses that of the United States (497 million compared to 304 million, as of this writing) and its GDP has surpassed that of the United States ($11 trillion compared to $10 trillion). As does the United States, the European Union has a robust domestic regulatory regime that impacts foreign companies seeking to do business there, both large and small. For example, in late 2007, Microsoft abandoned its appeal of an adverse antitrust ruling against it by the European Union; United States chicken growers lost a

$63 million market in Romania when in 2007 Romania joined the European Union and imposed certain E.U. food safety standards, which differ from those approved by the United States Food and Drug Administration. [EUROPA is the portal site of the European Union, found at **http://europa.eu/index_en.htm**]

In the coming years, it may prove useful to watch the international economic roles and relationships among the United States, the European Union, and China. In 2008, a foreign-policy scholar, Parag Khanna, published a book, *The Second World*, that forecasts "a multipolar and multicivilizational world of three distinct superpowers competing on a planet of shrinking resources." By population, China is first, the European Union third and the United States fourth in size. (India is second.) By current size of its domestic economy, the European Union is first, the United States second and China third. In this context remember that the E.U. is not, and does not always act like, a single country with a single voice. It is more unified as to economics and trade and less so as to foreign policy. For example, all 27 European Union member countries are individually members of the WTO (and, thus, collectively, have 27 votes). If and when the European Union becomes more politically united, its position as a superpower will similarly strengthen.

Countervailing Forces

While many nations are finding common ground in important respects, other forces are slowing globalization. One concern is for the protection of historical, social, and cultural identities. Other concerns are economic and political. Many countries—Australia, Canada, China, Germany, Japan, Russia, South Korea, and the United States among them—are considering or have imposed restrictions on domestic investment by foreign government-owned funds. "Public support of immigration restrictions is growing in countries from the United States to India."[3] Although the majority of Americans still favor free trade, a recent survey found a growing number believes it costs more jobs than it creates.[4] As evidenced by the following article, there is widespread consensus that globalization has not been uniformly beneficial.

READING

Global Capitalism: Can It Be Made to Work Better?

Pete Engardio

The plain truth is that market liberalization by itself does not lift all boats, and in some cases, it has caused severe damage. What's more, there's no point denying that multinationals have contributed to labor, environmental, and human rights abuses.

For global capitalism to move into the next stage will require a much more sophisticated look at the costs and benefits of open markets . . . .

. . . The real question isn't whether free markets are good or bad. It is why they are producing such wildly different results in different countries. Figuring out that answer is essential before all the benefits of global markets are realized.

* * * * *

The downside of global capitalism is the disruption of whole societies. While the industrialized countries have enacted all sorts of worker and environmental safeguards since the turn of the [twentieth] century, the global economy is pretty much still in the robber-baron age. Yet if global capitalism's flaws aren't addressed, the backlash could grow more severe.

The longer-term danger is that if the world's poor see no benefits from free trade . . . political support for reform could erode . . . .

A more realistic view is now gaining hold. It begins with a similar premise: that trade and inflows of private capital are still essential to achieving strong sustainable growth and to reducing poverty. But it acknowledges that multinationals—which account for the bulk of direct cross-border investment and one-third of trade—have social responsibilities in nations where the rule of law is weak. And this view dispenses with the erroneous notion that open markets will magically produce prosperity in all conditions. . . .

Source: *BusinessWeek*, November 6, 2000, pp. 72–75. Reprinted by permission.

Questions

1. Consider the people from the United States and elsewhere that have expressed concern about continued globalization. What do you think they are most concerned about—the free interchange of people, businesses, goods, services, investments, communications, or ideas? Explain.

2. If, as this article suggests, multinational corporations have affirmative social responsibilities in "nations where the rule of law is weak," who should select and impose those responsibilities? If you believe that it is a matter for corporate management, what forces might cause management to act more responsibly? What forces exist that might impede more corporate social responsibility on the part of multinationals? On the other hand, if you believe that social responsibilities should be imposed upon multinationals, what body should do so? How will that body obtain the power to legislate and enforce such responsibilities?

A Contributing Factor Globalization is not uniformly beneficial, and recognition seems to be growing that promotion of free trade divorced from social concerns is also problematic. WTO's own Web site, in its general introduction, acknowledges the concern: "But the WTO is not just about liberalizing trade, and in some circumstances its rules support maintaining trade barriers—for example to protect consumers or prevent the spread of disease. . . . The system's overriding purpose is to help trade flow as freely as possible—so long as there are no undesirable side-effects . . . ."[5]

PRACTICING ETHICS) Globally, the Rich Are Getting Richer and the Poor, Poorer

A recent study found that global wealth rose by 7.5 percent from 2005 to 2006, the fifth consecutive year of growth. However, in those same five years, assets held by nonwealthy households (defined in the study as less than $100,000 in assets) actually declined.[6]

Question

When the globalization process is evaluated and values in addition to free trade are weighed, should global wealth distribution be a concern? Why or why not?

The Intercultural Environment: Ethics across International Borders

The events of September 11, 2001, served to highlight the ethical and legal divide between two cultures: American and Islamic. America's continued presence in Iraq has kept these cultural divisions in the public eye. The first step in creating an effective working relationship is to attempt to understand cultural differences. Language is an

obvious cultural difference. Chinese diplomats in Arab-speaking countries "show deference to local culture by learning Arabic and even taking Arabic names."[7]

Religion often provides the foundation of a culture's ethical structure. Thus two countries with different religious heritages are likely to have divergent
ethical and legal norms. For example, a basic precept in the United
States is the separation of church and state. In contrast, in Islamic
countries, religion is the basis for many legal, as well as ethical,
standards. In reading the following article, consider what rights you
believe to be "fundamental." Keep in mind that different cultures have different concepts
of those rights that should be protected.

> In Islamic countries, religion
> is the basis for many legal, as
> well as ethical, standards

READING   Islamic Law: Myths and Realities

**Dennis J. Wiechman, Jerry D. Kendall,
and Mohammad K. Azarian**

. . . Mohammed Salam Madkoar explains the theoretical assumptions of Islamic Law:

> In order to protect the five important indispensables in
> Islam (religion, life, intellect, offspring, and property),
> Islamic Law has provided a worldly punishment in addition
> to that in the hereafter. Islam has, in fact, adopted two
> courses for the preservation of these five indispensables:
> the first is through cultivating religious consciousness in the
> human soul and the awakening of human awareness
> through moral education; the second is by inflicting
> deterrent punishment, which is the basis of the Islamic
> criminal system. Therefore "Hudoud," Retaliation (Qesas),
> and Discretionary (Tazir) punishments have been
> prescribed according to the type of the crime committed.

Islamic Law and Jurisprudence are not always understood by
the Western press. Although it is the responsibility of the mass
media to bring to the world's attention violations of human
rights and acts of terror, many believe that media stereotyping
of all Muslims is a major problem. The recent bombing at the
World Trade Center in New York City is a prime example. The
media often used the term "Islamic Fundamentalists" when
referring to the accused in the case. They also referred to the
Egyptian connections in that case as "Islamic Fundamentalists."
The media have used the label of "Islamic Fundamentalist" to
imply all kinds of possible negative connotations: terrorists,
kidnappers, and hostage takers. Since the media do not use

the term "Fundamentalist Christian" each time a Christian
does something wrong, the use of such labels is wrong for any
group, Christians, Muslims, or Orthodox Jews.

A Muslim who is trying to live his religion is indeed a true
believer in God. This person tries to live all of the tenets of his
religion in a fundamental way. Thus, a true Muslim is a fundamentalist in the practice of that religion, but a true Muslim is
not radical, because the Quran teaches tolerance and moder-
ation in all things. When the popular media generalize from the
fundamentalist believer to the "radical fundamentalist" label
they do a disservice to all Muslims and others.

NO SEPARATION OF CHURCH AND STATE

To understand Islamic Law one must first understand the assumptions of Islam and the basic tenets of the religion. The
meaning of the word *Islam* is "submission or surrender to Allah's
(God's) will." Therefore, Muslims must first and foremost obey
and submit to Allah's will. Mohammed the Prophet was called by
God to translate verses from the Angel Gabriel to form the most
important book in Islam, the Quran, Muslims believe.

* * * * *

The most difficult part of Islamic Law for most Western-
ers to grasp is that there is no separation of church and state.
The religion of Islam and the government are one. Islamic
Law is controlled, ruled, and regulated by the Islamic religion. The theocracy controls all public and private matters.
Government, law, and religion are one. There are varying degrees of this concept in many nations, but all law, government,

and civil authority rest upon it and it is a part of Islamic religion. There are civil laws in Muslim nations for Muslim and non-Muslim people. Sharia [Islamic law] is only applicable to Muslims.... The U.S. Constitution (Bill of Rights) prohibits the government from "establishing a religion." The U.S. Supreme Court has concluded in numerous cases that the U.S. Government can't favor one religion over another. That concept is implicit, for most U.S. legal scholars and many U.S. academicians believe that any mixture of "church and state" is inherently evil and filled with many problems.

* * * * *

CRIMES IN ISLAM

Crimes under Islamic Law can be broken down into three major categories.

1. Had crimes (most serious).
2. Tazir crimes (least serious).
3. Qesas crimes (revenge crimes restitution).

Had crimes are the most serious under Islamic Law, and Tazir crimes are the least serious. Some Western writers use the felony analogy for Had crimes and misdemeanor label for Tazir crimes. The analogy is partially accurate, but not entirely true. Common law has no comparable form of Qesas crimes....

Had Crimes

Had crimes are those which are punishable by a preestablished punishment found in the Quran. These most serious of all crimes are found by an exact reference in the Quran to a specific act and a specific punishment for that act. There is no plea-bargaining or reducing the punishment for a Had crime....

The Had crimes are

1. Murder.
2. Apostasy from Islam (making war upon Allah and his messengers).
3. Theft.
4. Adultery.
5. Defamation (false accusation of adultery or fornication).
6. Robbery.
7. Alcohol drinking.

* * * * *

Had crimes have fixed punishments because they are set by God and are found in the Quran. Had crimes are crimes against God's law and Tazir crimes are crimes against society. There are some safeguards for Had crimes that many in the media fail to mention. Some in the media only mention that if you steal, your hand is cut off. The Islamic judge must look at a higher level of proof and reasons why the person committed the crime. A judge can only impose the Had punishment when a person confesses to the crime or there are enough witnesses to the crime. The usual number of witnesses is two, but in the case of adultery four witnesses are required....

Tazir Crimes

Tazir crimes are less serious than the Had crimes found in the Quran. Some common law writers use the analogy of misdemeanors, which is the lesser of the two categories (felony and misdemeanor) of common law crimes.

* * * * *

Tazir crimes are acts which are punished because the offender disobeys God's law and word. Tazir crimes can be punished if they harm the societal interest. [Islamic] Law places an emphasis on the societal or public interest.

* * * * *

In some Islamic nations, Tazir crimes are set by legislative parliament. Each nation is free to establish its own criminal code and there is a great disparity in punishment of some of these crimes. Some of the more common Tazir crimes are bribery, selling tainted or defective products, treason, usury, and selling obscene pictures. The consumption of alcohol in Egypt is punished much differently than in Iran or Saudi Arabia because they have far different civil laws. Islamic law has much greater flexibility than the Western media portray.

Qesas Crimes and Diya

Islamic Law has an additional category of crimes that common law nations do not have. A Qesas crime is one of retaliation. If you commit a Qesas crime, the victim has a right to seek retribution and retaliation. The exact punishment for each Qesas crime is set forth in the Quran. If you are killed, then your family has a right to seek Qesas punishment from the murderer. Punishment can come in several forms and also may include "Diya." Diya is paid to the victim's family as part of punishment. Diya is an ancient form of restitution for the victim or his family. The family also may seek to have a public execution of the offender or the family may seek to pardon the offender. Traditional Qesas crimes include

1. Murder (premeditated and nonpremeditated).
2. Premeditated offenses against human life, short of murder.
3. Murder by error.
4. Offenses by error against humanity, short of murder.

Some reporters in the mass media have criticized the thought of "blood money" as barbaric. They labeled the practice as undemocratic and inhumane. Qesas crimes are based upon the criminological assumption of retribution. The concept of retribution was found in the first statutory "Code of Hammurabi" and in the Law of Moses in the form of "an eye for an eye." Muslims add to that saying "but it is better to forgive." Contemporary common law today still is filled with the assumptions of retribution. . . . The idea of retribution is fixed in the U.S. system of justice. Qesas crime is simple retribution: if one commits a crime he knows what the punishment will be.

Diya has its roots in Islamic Law and dates to the time of the Prophet Mohammed. . . . Today, the Diya is paid by the offender to the victim if he is alive. If the victim is dead, the money is paid to the victim's family or to the victim's tribe or clan.

* * * * *

Each victim has the right to ask for retaliation, and, historically, the person's family would carry out that punishment. Modern Islamic law now requires the government to carry out the Qesas punishment. . . .

CONCLUSIONS

Islamic Law is very different from English Common Law or the European Civil Law traditions. Muslims are bound to the teachings of the Prophet Mohammed whose translation of Allah or God's will is found in the Quran. Muslims are held accountable to the Sharia Law, but non-Muslims are not bound by the same standard (apostasy from Allah). Muslims and non-Muslims are both required to live by laws enacted by the various forms of government such as tax laws, traffic laws, white-collar crimes of business, and theft. These and many other crimes similar to Common Law crimes are tried in modern "Mazalim Courts." The Mazalim Courts can also hear civil law, family law, and all other cases. Islamic Law does have separate courts for Muslims for "religious crimes" and contemporary nonreligious courts for other criminal and civil matters.

Source: Office of International Criminal Justice, *Criminal Justice International Online,* 12, no. 3 (May 1996) found at **http://www.iol.ie/ ~afifi/Articles/law.htm** and reprinted by permission of *Criminal Justice International Online.*

Questions

1. Do the laws discussed here make logical sense to you? On what basis should you judge them?

2. Would conflicts in cultural issues such as those addressed by the laws discussed in this article impact your decision as a manager about where to conduct your business? *Should* they impact your decisions? Explain.

3. If your job required that you live in a country that had laws with which you disagreed on moral grounds, would you follow those laws? Explain.

4. Consider the difference between fundamental rights and culturally based rights. Conduct a Web search of responses and/or criticisms of the implementation of Islamic laws and identify those that seem culturally based and those that seem based on some concept of fundamental, universally recognized rights.

Social Responsibility to Host Country

Where a firm is involved in business abroad, does that firm have social responsibilities to the host country beyond those required by the market and the law of that country? This issue has arisen in many contexts, including child labor. For instance, many of the world's soccer balls are made in the Pakistani city of Sialkot. Nearly all of those balls are hand-stitched and sold to companies such as Adidas, Nike, and Puma. In 1996, in advance of the European soccer championships, the press widely reported that child labor was common in Sialkot and working conditions poor. The end result, following a public outcry, was implementation of an agreement among the United Nations Children's Fund (UNICEF), the International Labour Organization and all Sialkot manufacturers that banned all child labor.

Some in Sialkot, however, are not so approving of the agreement. Prior to the agreement, many balls were made locally in villages. In order to ensure compliance with the agreement, manufacturing has largely been centralized in large halls. Workers now have to commute, but the piecework rate was not increased. Some women, as well as the children, lost their livelihood because in the Islamic culture of Pakistan many feel it is inappropriate for women to work in the same environment as men. Global competition is also taking its toll: Sialkot's hand-stitched balls now have to compete with cheap, mechanically stitched balls from China and high-tech, glued balls from Thailand.[8]

How have the corporate purchasers of these goods responded? Adidas, like many public corporations these days, provides its corporate responsibility reports online. It has adopted a workplace standard on child labor which provides that "Business partners must not employ children who are less than 15 years old, or less than the age for completing compulsory education in the country of manufacture where such age is higher than 15."[9] Online you can also read Adidas' specific case study on Sialkot, entitled "Independent review of compliance practices in football production, Pakistan."[10] [For Adidas' corporate responsibility reports generally, see **http://www.adidas-group.com/en/sustainability/welcome.asp**.] [For more information on child labor, see the International Labour Organization's Web site at **http://www.ilo.org/global/Themes/Child_Labour/lang--en/index.htm**]

> Adidas has adopted a workplace standard on child labor.

Substandard Working Conditions

Under the moniker "sweatshops," some corporations have also been chastised for allowing working conditions in their foreign operations or suppliers that Western cultures would consider substandard. Such sweatshops pose a host of commercial, economic, ethical, political, and social questions.

Traditionally, free market economists have believed that sweatshops are necessary and beneficial—that sweatshops allow the economies of developing countries to improve because their export sectors expand, and consumers in global markets are better off because they pay less for the products they buy. This belief is based on the concept of *comparative advantage,* that developing countries typically have a comparative competitive advantage in cheap labor, while developed countries have comparative advantages in such things as an educated workforce, a manufacturing infrastructure and expertise, certain particularly well-developed industries, and so on. Sweatshops have been an element of every developed country's transformation from an agrarian society to an urban-based, highly industrialized economy. If poor countries want to develop, these economists argue, a sweatshop stage is necessary.

Other economists disagree that all developing countries must necessarily endure a sweatshop phase. Neither industrialized countries nor the developing world actually have true free market, or hands-off, economies. Governments often play a role in creating comparative advantages. Recall the discussion of the stalled Doha round of WTO talks in which developing countries object to the domestic agricultural subsidy programs maintained by the United States and the European Union. Dani Rodrik, a Harvard professor and an expert in helping developing countries organize export industries, offers the example of Costa Rica, which "is not a natural place to manufacture semiconductors," but it "got Intel to come in and do just that."[11] China is another example. "It nurtured the manufacture of electronic products and auto parts. It forced foreign investors into joint ventures with domestic producers. Beijing lowered trade barriers . . . 'only after it developed a relatively sophisticated manufacturing capacity.'"[12] [For sweatshop Web sites, see Sweatshop Watch at **www.sweatshopwatch.org** and Global Exchange at **www.globalexchange.org/campaigns/sweatshops/background.htm**]

Question

If you were the vice president for supply chain management for a large manufacturer or retailer, what type of labor standards would you impose on suppliers from other countries, if any?

Social Responsibility to Home Country?

Notwithstanding a potential responsibility to the countries in which a firm does business, does that firm have any special obligation to its home country? A social responsibility to a home country might necessitate imposing the values of one's home country throughout the world. The United States exports its values structure in a variety of ways, including through the extraterritorial application of its laws. When the U.S. Supreme Court declared that antidiscrimination provisions of United States statutes such as Title VII of the Civil Rights Act of 1964 did not apply extraterritorially,[13] Congress reversed the decision with its 1991 Amendments to Title VII. Accordingly, American firms that do not maintain certain Title VII standards abroad will be subject to liability in their home country.

The Foreign Corrupt Practices Act (FCPA)

Consider the problem of bribery and other forms of corruption in certain countries. Some in those countries may contend that there is nothing wrong with bribery, while other nations criticize it greatly. How would you define *bribery*? What is the main problem with it? For years, U.S. firms have tackled this problem in their own and other countries. On a governmental scale, Congress has attempted to respond harshly to corruption in other governments and to support U.S. firms that do not participate in foreign corruption.

As we saw in Chapter 2, the FCPA prohibits U.S. business from making certain payments or gifts to government officials for the purpose of influencing business decisions. Although the FCPA appears to be well motivated, some critics argue that it is inappropriate for the United States to unilaterally try to impose its sense of morality on others via foreign trade. Others argue that the FCPA unduly restricts American companies operating abroad and prevents them from effectively competing with other firms. However, other countries have now adoped similar provisions.

Question

Is it ethical for the U.S. Congress to seek to enforce federal laws on the operations of U.S. corporations abroad? Why or why not?

Social Responsibility to Humanity?

Are we in fact evolving toward the identification of common international ethical standards, that can be supported and implemented globally? Is this a natural progression from national standards? For example, there was a time in history when agreement was achieved only at a city level, which evolved to state-level agreement, which then developed to agreement among federated states. Is such a progression to global standards inevitable? Does a framework that divides ethical issues between those of the "host" country and those of the "home" country remain a useful analytical tool?

> If we are moving to a concept of global social responsibility, can we do so without sacrificing the existence of wonderfully diverse and unique cultures?

If we are moving to a concept of global social responsibility, can we do so without sacrificing the existence of wonderfully diverse and unique cultures? Do we have to become the same? Or can we agree on fundamentals, but still appreciate diversity, as a garden is enriched by the presence of a wide selection of grasses, flowers, bushes, trees, and birds?

Consider the evidence. Not only are businesses interacting with stakeholders of ever more diverse nationalities (investors/owners/shareholders, customers/clients, suppliers, general citizenry impacted by business decisions), but the cultural identity of businesses themselves may be unclear. Consider the "Big Four" accounting firms: Deloitte, Ernst & Young, KPMG, and PricewaterhouseCoopers. Although each of these firms started in the United States, they are each now a global network with partners from a wide variety of nationalities.

There is considerable evidence of voluntary international cooperation to establish acceptable business practices. Only a few of them are listed here:

- As far back as 1948, the United Nations (UN) General Assembly adopted its Universal Declaration of Human Rights. Inherent in the structure of the Declaration is a recognition of the connection between work, and by extension business, and the protection of fundamental human values. Article 23 declares that everyone has a right "to just and favourable conditions of work" and "to just and favourable remuneration ensuring for himself and his family an existence worthy of human dignity."[14] More recently, in 2000 the UN launched a voluntary initiative to promote corporate social responsibility globally. The ten principles of the Global Compact address human rights, labor standards, the environment, and corruption. Over 4,000 businesses from 120 countries have joined the Compact. Further, in 2003, the UN offered for consideration by its members its nonbinding, draft "Norms on the Responsibilities of Transnational Corporations and Other Business Enterprises with Regard to Human Rights."[15] [For more on the Global Compact, see **http://www.unglobalcompact.org**]

- Social Accountability International (formerly the Council on Economic Priorities Accreditation Agency) has developed SA8000, a voluntary social accountability standard that companies can adopt to develop and assure an equitable and safe workplace for their employees and those of their suppliers. [For more on SAI and SA8000, see **http://www.sa-intl.org**]

- The Council of the Bars and Law Societies of the European Union published an updated report for EU lawyers to use in advising clients on matters of corporate social responsibility. The 2005 report is entitled "Corporate Social Responsibility and the Role of the Legal Profession."[16]

- In 1994 a group of business leaders from Europe, Japan, and the United States developed a code of ethical conduct for global firms, known as the Caux Round Table Principles.[17]

PRACTICING ETHICS   Individual Social Responsibility to Humanity?

Consider the following excerpt from a speech delivered September 28, 2001, by Jose Ramos-Horta, Nobel Peace Prize Laureate (1996) and Minister for Foreign Affairs and Cooperation for the East Timor Transition Government:

There is no dispute that abject poverty, child labor, and prostitution are a moral indictment of all humanity.

However, poverty should not only touch our conscience: It is also a matter of peace and security because it destabilizes entire countries and regions. In turn it threatens the integration of the global economy that is vital if the rich are to stay rich or if the poor are to move up, if only an inch.

Peace will be illusory as long as the rich ignore the clamor of the poor for a better life, as long as hundreds of millions of people live below the poverty line, cannot afford a meal a day, do not have access to clean water and a roof.[18]

Questions

Do most of us, not just active international businesses, accept a social responsibility to humanity? If we answer yes to this question how might our actions as students, employees, employers, and investors change?

Laws Governing Cross-Border Business

All businesses must, of course, follow the laws of the countries in which they are physically present and operating. (Whether a business with no physical presence that solicits or performs business in a foreign country electronically must follow the laws of the foreign country will be examined in Chapter 18). Thus when Disney opened its amusement park in France, it became subject to the labor laws of France. Similarly, U.S. businesses operating abroad will be subject to the property and contract law provisions of those countries, as well as an array of other laws.

> When Disney opened its amusement park in France, it became subject to the labor laws of France.

Conversely, foreign firms often wish to establish operations in the United States, in part because Americans are more inclined to buy goods made in this country. Doing business in the United States brings with it the requirement that these foreign businesses comply with U.S. laws and regulations.

Businesses may also be required, even in their foreign operations, to continue to follow certain laws of their home country, as previously discussed with regard to the application of American antidiscrimination laws and the Foreign Corrupt Practices Act to U.S. corporations operating abroad. Interestingly, although there is a presumption against the extraterritorial application of U.S. criminal law, where Congress has clearly indicated an intent to cover actions outside of the United States, U.S. citizens can be held accountable for their criminal actions abroad.[19]

Finally, businesses operating across national borders will also be subject to international law. The foundation and some examples of international business law will be discussed soon, but first it will be useful to explore some of the different forms of business available to companies wishing to expand their operations into foreign countries.

Forms of Global Business Expansion

Multinational Enterprise (MNE)

The term *multinational enterprise* traditionally refers to a company that conducts business in more than one country. Any of the following operations, except for a direct contract with a foreign purchaser, may qualify a company as an MNE.

Direct Contract   A firm may expand its business across territorial borders using a variety of methods. The simplest, from a contractual perspective, occurs where a firm in one country enters an agreement with a firm or individual in another country. Using the example of sales, a firm might decide to sell its product to a purchaser in another country through a basic contractual agreement. This is called a *direct sale* to a foreign purchaser. In this situation, the parties agree on the terms of the sale and record them in the contract.

Where the contract is silent as to a term of the sale, the law that will apply to the missing term will be the law specified in the contract; where none is specified, the applicable law will depend on the country in which the court is located. Some courts will apply the *vesting of rights doctrine,* where the applicable law is the law of the jurisdiction in which the rights in the contract vested. Other courts may apply the *most significant relationship doctrine,* where the applicable law is that of the jurisdiction that has the most significant relationship to the contract and the parties. Finally, some courts will apply the *governmental interest doctrine,* where the court will apply the law either of its own jurisdiction or of the jurisdiction that has the greatest interest in the outcome of the issue.

> One of the most complicated issues pertaining to direct sales is that of payment.

One of the most complicated issues pertaining to direct sales is that of *payment.* The seller should and usually does require an *irrevocable letter of credit,* which the buyer obtains from a bank after paying that amount to the bank (or securing that amount of credit). The bank then promises to pay the seller the amount of the contract after conforming goods have been shipped. The "irrevocable" component is that the bank may not revoke the letter of credit without the consent of both the buyer and the seller. In this way the seller is protected because the buyer already has come up with adequate funds for the purchase, confirmed by a bank. The buyer is protected because the funds are not turned over to the seller until it has been determined that the goods conform to the contract. It is important to the buyer, however, that the letter of credit be specific as to the conformance of the goods because the bank will only ensure that the goods conform to the letter of credit and not to the contract itself.

Foreign Representation   A second type of foreign expansion is a sale through a representative in the foreign country, whether it is through a distributor, agent, or other type of representative. A firm may decide to sell through an *agent*—that is, it hires an individual who will remain permanently in the foreign country, negotiate contracts, and assist in the performance of the contracts. Agents are generally compensated on a commission basis. On the other hand, the firm may act through a *representative,* who may solicit and take orders but, unlike an agent, may not enter into contracts on behalf of the firm. *Distributors* purchase the goods from the seller, then negotiate sales to foreign purchasers on their own behalf. In so doing, a distributor may be more likely to invest resources to develop the foreign market for the good.

Exclusive dealing agreements with distributors, where a distributor agrees to sell only the goods of one manufacturer and the manufacturer agrees to sell only to that distributor in that area, are generally not allowed abroad, although they often are legal in the United States.

Export trading companies are firms that specialize in acting as the intermediary between business and purchasers in foreign countries. The trading company will take title to the goods being sold and then complete the sale in the foreign country. *Export management companies,* on the other hand, merely manage the sale but do not take title to the goods; consequently they do not share in any of the risk associated with the sale.

Joint Venture   Foreign expansion may also occur through a *joint venture* agreement between two or more parties. This type of agreement is usually for one or several specific projects and is in effect for a specified period. For instance, several Japanese automobile manufacturers have entered joint ventures with American firms to manufacture some or all of certain models in America.

Branch Office or Subsidiary   A *branch office* is a wholly owned extension of a corporate entity in a foreign country. A *subsidiary* is a separate corporation formed in a foreign country and owned in whole or in part by the parent company. For example, an Indian paper company may open a branch office in London to market and sell its products. That office would be a mere extension of the offices already established in India. On the other hand, the Indian firm may create a separate subsidiary to handle its British orders, which might then have an office in London. A subsidiary or branch office relationship may also come about through an acquisition of an existing firm in the foreign country.

The primary difference between branch offices and subsidiaries comes into play with the question of liability. In most situations where a subsidiary is sued, the parent company is not liable. For example, in *U.S. v. Philip Morris, Inc.,*[20] the United States district court dismissed British American Tobacco (BAT) from the federal government's suit against various cigarette manufacturers for recovery of health care expenses. BAT was the British parent company of the U.S. company Brown & Williamson. The subsidiary, B&W, remained a part of the suit. In contrast, the liabilities of a branch office immediately become the liabilities of the main office. In addition, the income of a branch office is considered income to the parent firm and must be reported on that firm's income tax return. Income to a subsidiary remains on the balance sheet of the subsidiary. On the other hand, there is a benefit to opening a branch office. The branch office is considered by all dealing with it as merely an arm of the parent firm. In this respect, loans and insurance may be easier to obtain for a branch, as opposed to a subsidiary.

Licensing   Where a company has no interest in commencing operations in a foreign country but instead merely wants to have its product or name on the market there, the company may decide to license the rights to the name or to manufacturing the product to another company.

The benefit to this type of relationship is that the licensor (holder of the right) has the opportunity to enter the foreign market, while the licensee assumes all of the obligations of running the business.

Franchising In a franchise agreement, the franchisee pays the franchisor for a license to use trademarks, formulas, and other trade secrets. The difference between a franchising agreement and a licensing contract is that a franchise agreement may be made up of a number of licensing arrangements, as well as other obligations. For instance, in a typical fast-food franchise agreement, the franchisor will license to the franchisee the right to use its trademark, name, logo, recipes, menus, and other recognized resources.

Question

Assume that you are interested in importing silk blouses from Bangkok, Thailand to France. What facts might persuade you to enter into an agency agreement with a Thai blouse manufacturer rather than a distributorship or vice versa?

Foundations of International Law

A firm with manufacturing plants in Argentina and Thailand, and corporate headquarters in Bangkok, enters into a contract with a French firm to distribute its products produced in the Argentinean plant. The French firm is not satisfied with the quality of the products being sent. What law would apply to this situation? Argentinean? Thai? French? Or are there, perhaps, specific provisions of international law that will govern? The answer to this question is not simple, even for seasoned lawyers; yet the firms involved will be greatly affected by the decision.

> What law would apply to this situation? Argentinean? Thai? French?

The source of law applicable to an international issue depends on the issue involved. In general, private parties are free to form agreements in whatever manner they wish. The parties to the agreement can determine, for instance, which nation's law shall govern the contract, where disagreements in connection with the contract shall be settled, and even in which language the transactions shall be made. This is considered *private law*. Whenever the parties to a transaction are from different jurisdictions and are involved in a lawsuit, the court will look to the agreement of the parties to resolve these issues. Otherwise, where the contract is silent as to the choice of law, jurisdiction, and other questions, the court must decide. Generally, the law of the jurisdiction in which the transaction occurred is applied. If the transaction is done by mail, as are many international trade negotiations, most often the law of the jurisdiction of the seller's place of business applies. Recall, however, that the parties to the contract may always reach an agreement on the law to be applied.

Public law, on the other hand, includes those rules of each nation that regulate the contractual agreement between the parties—for instance, import and export taxes, packaging requirements, and safety standards. In addition, public law regulates the relationships between nations.

Public law derives from a number of sources. The most familiar source of international public law is a *treaty* or *convention* (a contract between nations). For example, the United States, Canada, and Mexico have entered into the North American Free Trade

Agreement (NAFTA), a convention regarding free trade between those countries. Some treaties and conventions are *self-executing,* which means that once the United States has signed them, a business can rely on and directly enforce their terms in court. The United Nations Convention on Contracts for the International Sale of Goods (CISG), which will be discussed soon, is an example of this. On the other hand, some treaties and conventions apply only to government signatories and not directly to private parties. Such a convention may, for example, require the United States to amend its federal statutory law to accomplish the purposes of the convention. Whether the Paris Convention (addressing international trademark issues) is self-executing or not is one of the issues the district court had to resolve in the *Piaggio* case, which appears later in this chapter.

Public law is also found in *international custom* or *generally accepted principles of law.* These terms refer to practices that are commonly accepted as appropriate business or commercial practices between nations. For instance, sovereign immunity, discussed later in this chapter, is an accepted principle of international law. A *custom* is derived from consistent behavior over time that is accepted as binding by the countries that engage in that behavior.

The Development of Customs

One might better understand the concept of *custom* if it is analogized to the law of sales in the United States. For years, merchants would follow certain accepted customs or principles in connection with the sale of goods. These customs or manners of dealing between merchants were later codified in the Uniform Commercial Code (UCC) that regulates the sale of goods and has certain provisions specifically related to the sale of goods between merchants. In this way, customs or practices traditionally followed by merchants have become accepted principles of law.

On the other hand, in the international legal arena, customary practices are still developing. For instance, in connection with personal privacy or information flow between countries, the custom had been that personal information moves freely between countries to encourage the free flow of information in the business world. However, the European Union in 1998 established minimum standards for the protection of personal data that must be maintained by any country receiving information from an EU country. (See Chapter 18 for more on the EU's Directive on Data Protection.)

Two factors are used to determine whether a custom exists: (1) consistency and repetition of the action or decision and (2) recognition by nations that this custom is binding. The first merely holds that the action or decision must be accepted by a number of nations for a time long enough to establish uniformity of application. The second dictates that the custom be accepted as binding by nations observing it. If the custom is accepted as merely persuasive, it does not rise to the level of a generally accepted principle of law. Through persistent objections, any nation may ensure that certain customs are not applied to cases in which it is involved.

Comity

The unique aspect of public international law is that countries are generally not subject to law in the international arena unless they consent to such jurisdiction. For instance, a country is not bound by a treaty unless that country has signed the treaty. A country is not bound by international custom unless it has traditionally participated in that custom. And prior judicial decisions are only persuasive where a country is convinced by and accepts these decisions as precedent. In fact, perhaps the most critical element in understanding international law is recognizing that it is not actually "law" in the way that we generally consider law. Countries are not bound to abide by it except through comity. *Comity* is the concept that countries *should* abide by international custom, treaties, and other sources of international direction because that is the civil way to engage in relationships. Nations must respect each other and respect some basic principles of dealing in order to have effective relationships.

The concept of comity also includes the respect one country gives to the actions another country takes in its own territory. Specifically, as stated by the Second Circuit in *Finanz AG Zurich v. Banco Economico S.A.*,[21] comity includes "the recognition which one nation allows within its territory to the legislative, executive, or judicial acts of another nation." Under this principle, U.S. courts "ordinarily refuse to review acts of foreign governments and defer to proceedings taking place in foreign countries." Thus the *Finanz* court held that a creditor could not sue in the United States to collect a debt that was subject to the jurisdiction of a bankruptcy proceeding in Brazil.

> Some believe that the origins of law are in religion.

Although some believe that the origins of law are in religion and its commandments, others have argued that, instead, law derives from a natural tendency to prevent chaos. International law is that attempt to prevent chaos in the international marketplace through the application of universal principles, and comity is the means by which it is encouraged.

Regulation of International Trade

As just explained, there is no such thing as one body of international law per se that regulates international contracts and trade. Instead, a contract between firms in different countries may be subject to the laws of one country or the other, depending on (1) whether it is a sales contract subject to the U.N. CISG, discussed below, (2) whether the contract itself stipulates the applicable law and forum in which a dispute will be heard, and (3) the rules regarding conflict of laws in each jurisdiction.

Additionally, every country has domestic laws that regulate business conducted within its borders and that sometimes regulate its domestic firms outside of its borders. These laws govern the areas of employment-related activities and discrimination, product liability, intellectual property, antitrust and trade practices, and import taxes, to name a few. Consequently, a business owner may actually decide to market a good in one country over another simply because of that country's laws relating to the particular good or to commercial contracts in general. What follows is a brief look at several specific examples of the law governing international business. [For an extensive international trade law database, see **www.jus.uio.no/lm**]

U.N. Convention on Contracts for the International Sale of Goods (CISG)

In 1988, 10 nations signed and became bound by the U.N. Convention on Contracts for the International Sale of Goods. At this writing, the CISG is enforceable in 70 nations. The CISG applies to contracts between parties of countries that have signed the convention and provides uniform rules for the sale of goods.

The CISG contains rules regarding the interpretation of contracts and negotiations and the form of contracts. Many obligations of the parties are enunciated by the CISG. For instance, the seller is required to deliver the goods and any documents relating to the goods, as well as to make sure that the goods conform to the contract terms. The buyer, on the other hand, is required to pay the contract price and to accept delivery of the goods. [For the Pace University CISG database, see **http://cisgw3.law.pace.edu**]

The CISG, however, does not answer all questions that may arise in a transaction. For instance, questions of a contract's validity are left to national law. We saw in Chapter 6, under American law, an enforceable contract requires five elements:

- *Capacity* to enter the contract.
- *Offer* and *acceptance* of the terms of the contract.
- *Consideration* for the promises in the contract.
- *Genuineness of assent.*
- *Legality of purpose* of the contract.

Countries with civil law systems do not, however, require consideration for a valid contract.

Generally, once a contract has been created, it is enforceable according to its terms by all parties to the contract. In the following case, read carefully to see what law the judge applies. He considers first the *private law* of the parties (that is, the express terms of the contract); then he looks to *custom;* and finally he applies the concept of *commercial impracticability.*

Transatlantic Financing Corporation v. United States

LEGAL BRIEFCASE · 363 F.2d 312 (D.C. Cir. 1966)

Judge Skelly Wright

[In 1956, Transatlantic Financing, a steamship operator, contracted with the United States to ship wheat from Texas to Iran. Six days after the ship left port for Iran, the Egyptian government was at war with Israel and blocked the Suez Canal to shipping. The steamer therefore was forced to sail around the Cape of Good Hope. Transatlantic accordingly sued the United States for its added expenses as a result of this change of circumstances. Transatlantic contended that it had contracted only to travel the "usual and customary" route to Iran and that the United States had received a greater benefit than that for which it contracted. The district court held for the United States; Transatlantic appealed.]

Transatlantic's claim is based on the following train of argument. The charter was a contract for a voyage from a Gulf port to Iran. Admiralty principles and practices, especially stemming from the doctrine of deviation, require us to [infer] into the contract the term that the voyage was to be performed by the "usual and customary" route. The usual and customary route from Texas to Iran was, at the time of contract, via Suez, so the contract was for a voyage from Texas to Iran via Suez. When Suez was closed this contract became impossible to perform. Consequently, appellant's argument continues, when Transatlantic delivered the cargo by going around the Cape of Good Hope, in compliance with the Government's demand under claim of right, it conferred a benefit upon the United States for which it should be paid on quantum meruit.

The contract in this case does not expressly condition performance upon availability of the Suez route. Nor does it specify "via Suez" or, on the other hand, "via Suez or Cape of Good Hope." Nor are there provisions in the contract from which we may properly [infer] that the continued availability of Suez was a condition of performance. Nor is there anything in custom or trade usage, or in the surrounding circumstances generally, which would support our constructing a condition of performance. The numerous cases requiring performance around the Cape when Suez was closed indicate that the Cape route is generally regarded as an alternative means of performance. So the implied expectation that the route would be via Suez is hardly adequate proof of an allocation to the promisee of the risk of closure. In some cases, even an express expectation may not amount to a condition of performance. The doctrine of deviation supports our assumption that parties normally expect performance by the usual and customary route, but it adds nothing beyond this that is probative of an allocation of the risk.

If anything, the circumstances surrounding this contract indicate that the risk of the Canal's closure may be deemed to have been allocated to Transatlantic. We know or may safely assume that the parties were aware, as were most commercial men with interest affected by the Suez situation, that the Canal might become a dangerous area. No doubt the tension affected freight rates, and it is arguable that the risk of closure became part of the dickered terms. We do not deem the risk of closure so allocated, however. Foreseeability or even recognition of a risk does not necessarily prove its allocation. Parties to a contract are not always able to provide for all the possibilities of which they are aware, sometimes because they cannot agree, often simply because they are too busy. Moreover, that some abnormal risk was contemplated is probative but does not necessarily establish an allocation of the risk of the contingency which actually occurs. In this case, for example, nationalization by Egypt of the Canal Corporation and formation of the Suez Users Group did not necessarily indicate that the Canal would be blocked even if a confrontation resulted. The surrounding circumstances do indicate, however, a willingness by Transatlantic to assume abnormal risks, and this fact should legitimately cause us to judge the impracticability of performance by an alternative route in stricter terms than we would were the contingency unforeseen.

We turn then to the question whether occurrence of the contingency rendered performance commercially impracticable under the circumstances of this case. The goods shipped were not subject to harm from the longer, less temperate Southern route. The vessel and crew were fit to proceed around the Cape. Transatlantic was no less able than the United States to purchase insurance to cover the contingency's occurrence. If anything, it is more reasonable to expect owner–operators of vessels to insure against the hazards of war. They are in the best position to calculate the cost of performance by alternative routes (and therefore to estimate the amount of insurance required), and are undoubtedly sensitive to international troubles which uniquely affect the demand for and cost of their services. The only factor operating here in appellant's favor is the added expense, allegedly $43,972.00 above and beyond the contract price of $305,842.92, of extending a 10,000-mile voyage by approximately 3,000 miles. While it may be an overstatement to say that increased cost and difficulty of performance never constitute impracticability, to justify relief there must be more of a variation between expected cost and the cost of performing by an available alternative than is present in this case, where the promisor can legitimately be presumed to have accepted some degree of abnormal risk, and where impracticability is urged on the basis of added expense alone.

We conclude, therefore, as have most other courts considering related issues arising out of the Suez closure, that performance of this contract was not rendered legally impossible.

Affirmed.

Questions

1. *a.* What did the court find with respect to the private law of the parties?

   b. What did it find with respect to the application of custom?

2. Would the result in this case be different if the shipment had been tomatoes as opposed to wheat? Explain.

3. Would the result in this case be different if the United States and Transatlantic agreed by contract that shipment was to arrive in Iran within a period of time that was only possible if the shipper used the canal route? Explain.

4. What do you think it would take for a court to render a contract commercially impracticable? In this case, the shipper was forced to spend almost $44,000 more than it had expected to spend in performing the $306,000 contract. What if the added cost had amounted to $100,000? Would you be persuaded that the contract was then commercially impracticable? What if the closing of the canal doubled the price of the contract? Explain.

International Trade in Services

Services, as opposed to goods, are a large component of the world's gross domestic product, accounting for 64 percent in 2007.[22] In the United States this percentage is even higher—services were 78.5 percent of gross national product (GNP) in 2007.[23] Further, trade in services represents about 30 percent of the total dollar value of U.S. exports.[24] And the United States isn't the only country exporting services. The popular press continues to report on the "outsourcing" and "offshoring" of U.S. service sector jobs. *Outsourcing* generally refers to the contracting by U.S. companies of such services as call centers, accounting, and customer services to foreign companies located in low-wage markets. *Offshoring* refers to U.S. companies setting up their own offices in foreign low-wage markets to perform services previously done by U.S. employees. Economists argue about whether the net effect on jobs in the United States is negative (through the direct loss of jobs) or positive (through corporate and consumer cost savings that permit job growth in the United States).[25]

What international agreements exist to regulate such trade in services? Although international trade in goods has been the subject of international agreement since shortly after WWII, until 1994 no similar agreement existed covering international trade in services. This was remedied with the creation of the General Agreement on Trade in Services (GATS), which is now one of the foundation agreements, with the General Agreement on Tariffs and Trade (GATT) to which all member countries of the World Trade Organization (WTO) must subscribe. [The foundation agreements can be found at the WTO Web site, in the document area, at **www.wto.org**]

The GATS agreement, still in its infancy, sets forth the general principles for the future of trade in services across borders, but at this time requires very little of member countries in moving toward the realization of those principles. Rather, it sets the stage for future negotiations to reduce barriers to trade in services. The services covered by GATS, and therefore by such negotiations, are broad: "any service in any sector except services supplied in the exercise of governmental authority."[26]

Two important general principles that govern international services negotiations include these:

- *Most favored nation (MFN) status:* WTO members get treatment by the host country no less favorable than that given to suppliers from any other country, whether or not the other country is a member of the WTO.

- *National treatment:* The national treatment standard calls for a comparison of the treatment accorded to suppliers from WTO member countries to the treatment accorded to domestic suppliers. As a general rule, the treatment is to be "no less favorable" than that received by domestic suppliers.

Question

The WTO member nations have only recently turned their consideration to the barriers between nations that impede the flow of services across boundaries. In the professions, such as medicine, law, and accounting, substantial barriers currently exist, some in the form of domestic licensure requirements, which in turn often require a particular educational background for the applicant. Would establishing a clearinghouse for educational equivalencies around the world and requiring WTO members to honor the educational achievements received by applicants in other member countries be a good idea? Why or why not?

Employment-Related Regulations

When the U.S. Congress passed the Civil Rights Act of 1991, it expressly provided for *extraterritorial* application of Title VII's antidiscrimination provisions. In doing so, Congress extended American firms' liability for discrimination against their employees to situations that occur outside the United States. For instance, if a firm conducts operations in Saudi Arabia, where women are not expected to hold certain management positions, that firm is still held to Title VII's prohibition against gender discrimination. Extraterritorial application of Title VII is considered essential because over 5 million Americans work abroad. Compliance with American civil rights laws is not required, however, where doing so would violate the host country's laws.

One of the few internationally applied, employment-related laws is the European Works Council Directive, implemented in 1996 by 17 European nations. This directive provides that any multinational firm with at least 1,000 workers in the countries covered by the directive must comply with its regulations. The regulations include an employee voice in company deliberations, prior consultation with works councils over a wide range of employment issues, and specific rules of engagement for negotiations that are similar to the U.S. National Labor Relations Act (see Chapter 14).

Compulsory Retirement

In late 2007, the European Court of Justice ruled that the European Framework Directive on Equal Treatment, which prohibits unjustified age discrimination in the workplace, applied to national laws requiring age-based compulsory retirement. The case challenged a Spanish law permitting employers to impose a compulsory retirement age. Although the Court held the Directive applied to the Spanish law, it nevertheless ruled that the Spanish legislation was a lawful, appropriate means of achieving a legitimate government aim. In this case, the law had been passed during a period of high unemployment in Spain and was intended to further a national policy for a better distribution of work between generations.

In the United States, the Age Discrimination in Employment Act prohibits discrimination on the basis of age of individuals who are 40 or older. It applies to decisions to hire or fire, as well as to discriminatory compensation or other terms or conditions of employment. Interestingly, a narrow exception allows colleges and universities to require retirement of tenured faculty who reach the age of 70. Another exception permits the compulsory retirement of business executives who have reached 65, so long as they are entitled to "an immediate nonforfeitable annual retirement benefit" of at least $44,000. The ADEA specifically applies to American citizens employed overseas by American companies.

Questions

1. A U.S. corporation operates a branch in Spain. Consistent with Spanish law, it adopts a compulsory retirement age of 62. Is this a violation of the ADEA?

2. Which policy do you favor—the Spanish or the American approach to compulsory retirement? Why? Is this an issue over which countries should be allowed to differ?

Intellectual Property Regulations

Intellectual property generally refers to copyrights, patents, and trademarks. Intellectual property is one form of personal property or *personalty,* which is the legal term used to denote all forms of property, both tangible and intangible, other than real property or *realty.* Realty is comprised only of land or real estate and items permanently affixed to the land, such as buildings.

Trademarks

A *trademark* is what identifies a product, whether it is the trade name, the packaging, the logo, or other distinguishing mark. When the law protects a trademark, it grants to the holder of the mark a limited monopoly: No one else may use that mark without the holder's permission. Under section 526 of the Tariff Act of 1930, it is unlawful to import goods bearing a trademark that has been registered with the Patent Office and that is "owned by a citizen of, or by a corporation or association . . . organized within the United States" without the permission of the mark holder.

This provision regulates the importation of goods that would infringe on a trademark holder's rights in the United States. But what about an American company that wants to obtain trademark protection in other countries? Each country has distinct trademark regulations and different levels of protection offered marks registered in other countries.

Paris Convention   In 1883 several countries entered an agreement called the International Convention for the Protection of Industrial Property, which was last revised in 1979. As of this writing, 172 countries, including the United States, are parties to the agreement, now called the *Paris Convention.* In short, according to the Paris convention, member countries ensure trademark protection to marks registered in other member countries. The convention also provides for *national treatment* requiring that any individual claiming infringement will have the same protection as would a national of that country. Thus a member country may not favor its own nationals over foreigners. The Madrid Agreement Concerning the International Registration of Marks, established after the Paris Convention, attempts to create an international trademark system. If a holder registers a trademark with the World Intellectual Property Organization (WIPO) in Switzerland, that mark is protected in all member countries requested by the holder. A Protocol relating to the agreement was concluded in 1989, with the "aim of rendering the Madrid system more flexible and more compatible with the domestic legislations of certain countries which had not been able to accede to the Agreement."[27] As of 2003, the United States became a party to the Protocol but it has not acceded to the Agreement. [For extensive information on WIPO, see **www.wipo.int**]

The following case offers a good example of the interplay between the trademark protection offered by the Lanham Act in the United States and the global protection offered through the Paris Convention. As you read this case, also pay attention to what the judge says about the self-executing nature of the Paris Convention.

Piaggio & C.S.p.A. v. Scooterworks USA, Inc., et al.

LEGAL BRIEFCASE

1999 U.S. Dist. LEXIS 13296 (N.D. IL 1999)

Judge Marovich

Plaintiff Piaggio & C.S.p.A. ("Piaggio") has filed this action against Defendants Scooterworks USA, Inc. ("Scooterworks"), Vesparts International, L.L.C. ("Vesparts"), and Philip S. McCaleb ("McCaleb"), alleging trademark and copyright infringement. For the reasons set forth below, Scooterworks' and Vesparts' motion is granted in part and denied in part, and McCaleb's motion is denied.

BACKGROUND

Piaggio is an Italian corporation with its principal place of business in Pontedera, Italy. Scooterworks is an Illinois corporation with its principal place of business in Chicago, Illinois. Vesparts is a Nevada corporation with its principal place of business in Chicago, Illinois. McCaleb is an officer, president, and co-shareholder, together with his wife, of Scooterworks. He is also an officer, president, and shareholder of Vesparts.

Piaggio is engaged in the business of manufacturing, distributing, and selling motor scooters, motorcycles, mopeds, and light transport vehicles, as well as related parts and accessories, throughout the world, including the United States. Piaggio owns the common law rights and registration for . . . the "PIAGGIO Trademarks." Piaggio has used, for over 50 years, the PIAGGIO Trademarks on and in connection with the distribution, marketing, and sale of motorized vehicles.

In 1948, Piaggio introduced a new line of motorized scooters under trademarks using the term VESPA ("VESPA scooters"). VESPA scooters have been in continuous production since their introduction. Piaggio owns the common law rights and registration of the word mark VESPA, VESPA with Design, and other Piaggio trademarks containing the term VESPA (the "VESPA Trademarks"). Piaggio has always used its VESPA Trademarks on and in connection with the distribution, marketing, and sale of VESPA scooters, with over 16 million units produced and sold in over 150 countries, including the United States, and it has had exclusive use of the VESPA Trademarks in connection with the sale of its motor scooters.

Piaggio also owns a family of VESPA trademarks registered under Italian law. The word mark VESPA, the VESPA logo, and other Piaggio trademarks containing the term VESPA are extremely well known in Italy.

Piaggio continuously utilized VESPA trademarks on and in connection with the manufacture, distribution, and sale of VESPA scooters in the United States up through approximately 1987, at which time, for various reasons, Piaggio "temporarily suspended" sales of its VESPA scooters in the United States. Nonetheless, Piaggio has continued to aggressively market and distribute VESPA scooters all over the world and to sell parts and promote its marks in the United States. Piaggio plans to resume VESPA scooter sales in the United States within the next 12 months.

McCaleb, Scooterworks, and Vesparts are in the business of selling replacement parts and accessories for VESPA scooters, as well as other goods and services of interest to fans of VESPA scooters. Beginning in approximately 1992, McCaleb attempted, but was unsuccessful, to establish some type of business relationship between Piaggio and McCaleb's start-up business, Scooterworks.

In 1995, without Piaggio's prior approval, Scooterworks filed an application with the United States Patent and Trade Office ("PTO") to register a VESPA mark for use in connection with the sale of key chains, posters, clothes, labels, models, and related goods. The PTO refused to register Scooterworks' application because the trademark in the application was deemed identical to trademarks previously registered by Piaggio. Thereafter, Piaggio applied to register the same trademark, based upon an assignment from Scooterworks to Piaggio of Scooterworks' rights in its prior application, and was approved.

In January 1996, Piaggio and Scooterworks entered into a License Agreement dated January 4, 1996. Pursuant to the License Agreement, Piaggio gave Scooterworks the exclusive right to produce and market in the United States under the VESPA Trademark, models of VESPA scooters, for a two-year period. Throughout 1996, Scooterworks attempted to secure from Piaggio a broader agreement providing for exclusive rights to distribute the VESPA scooter and related parts under the VESPA trademark. However, no definite agreement was ever reached, and negotiations were abandoned in January 1997.

Piaggio claims that Defendants have improperly used Piaggio's PIAGGIO and VESPA Trademarks in several ways. For example, Piaggio alleges that McCaleb and Scooterworks, on their Web site and in the free catalog offered through their Web site, "repeatedly assert and imply they have an exclusive arrangement with Piaggio to import and distribute authentic VESPA replacement parts in the United States" and display the VESPA and PIAGGIO Trademarks in such a manner as "to imply that Scooterworks is sponsored, supervised, endorsed, or otherwise connected with Piaggio." However, Piaggio alleges, McCaleb and Scooterworks are not sponsored, supervised, or endorsed by Piaggio; their only connection to Piaggio is that

Scooterworks markets and sells replacement parts and accessories for VESPA scooters. Piaggio also alleges that McCaleb and Scooterworks "wrongfully offer miniature VESPA motor scooters for sale" and "repeatedly misuse VESPA Trademarks by using VESPA as a generic name of a product rather than as a brand name for scooters." Piaggio asserts that although it has requested that Defendants cease their willful and wrongful acts, Defendants have refused to cooperate with Piaggio and continue in their improper and infringing activities.

On November 24, 1998, Piaggio filed its Complaint in this Court asserting 13 claims: trademark infringement, false designation, unfair competition, and antidilution under the Lanham Act, 15 U.S.C. § 1051, et seq.; trademark infringement and unfair competition under the International Convention for the Protection of Industrial Property of March 20, 1883, 21 U.S.T. 1583, as amended (the "Paris Convention"); trademark infringement, unfair competition, violation of the Uniform Deceptive Trade Practices Act, and antidilution under Illinois state law; breach of contract; copyright infringement and declaratory judgment. On January 27, 1999, Scooterworks filed a counterclaim seeking, inter alia, to cancel Piaggio's federal trademark registrations.

II. Paris Convention Claims—Counts IV and V

In Counts IV and V of the Complaint, Piaggio alleges claims under Articles 6 *bis* and 10 *bis,* respectively, of the Paris Convention. The Paris Convention, to which both the United States and Italy are signatories, is an international agreement which prohibits, among other things, unfair competition. Scooterworks argues that Counts IV and V should be dismissed because (1) the Paris Convention is not a self-executing treaty and there is no private right of action under the Paris Convention, and (2) even if there was a private right of action, such claims are duplicative of those asserted under the Lanham Act. This Court finds that Section 44 of the Lanham Act implements the Paris Convention but that the Paris Convention does not provide a relief distinct from that of the Lanham Act. Accordingly, Scooterworks' motion to dismiss Counts IV and V is granted.

The Lanham Act, which prohibits specific types of unfair competition, provides in section 44(b):

Any person whose country of origin is a party to any convention or treaty relating to trademarks . . . to which the

United States is also a party . . . shall be entitled to the benefits of this section under the conditions expressed herein to the extent necessary to give effect to any provisions of such convention [or] treaty . . . in addition to the rights to which any owner of a mark is otherwise entitled by this chapter.

Section 44(h) of the Lanham Act extends to foreign citizens such as Piaggio "effective protections against unfair competition, and the remedies provided in this chapter for infringement of marks . . . so far as they may be appropriate in repressing acts of unfair competition."

Piaggio argues that it has pleaded acts of unfair competition over and above those acts which constitute unfair competition under the Lanham Act, and thus, its Paris Convention claims are not duplicative and should not be dismissed. However, this Court agrees with the reasoning of the courts that hold that "subsections 44(b) and 44(h) [of the Lanham Act] work together to provide foreign nationals with rights under United States law which are coextensive with the substantive provisions of the treaty involved." . . . In other words, "the Paris Convention does not provide substantive rights in the United States, [instead] Section 44 [of the Lanham Act] merely extends existing Lanham Act and state law protections to foreign nationals conducting business in the United States.". . .

Therefore, as the Court finds that the Paris Convention does not create a separate and distinct cause of action than that already available under the Lanham Act, Counts IV and V are duplicative and, accordingly, are dismissed.

Questions

1. Should it have mattered to the disposition of the case that Scooterworks filed an application with the United States PTO without Piaggio's prior approval to register a VESPA mark for use in connection with the sale of paraphernalia?
2. According to Judge Marovich, is the Paris Convention a self-executing treaty? Explain.
3. If the Lanham Act implements the Paris Convention through its section 44 but offers no new relief, why would anyone bring a claim under the Paris Convention if she or he already has a claim under the Lanham Act?

Patents

A *patent* is a monopoly on a product, process, or device where the item or process claimed is an innovation, unique and inventive, and useful. The Paris Convention refers to patents as well as trademarks; however, it does not establish a worldwide network of protection.

Instead, it requires that member countries follow simplified procedures for registration. The most important provision provides the *right of priority,* which grants the first person to obtain a patent in any member country priority over other individuals seeking to register the same patent. In addition, because a patent must be original to be registered in any country, many countries hold that patents previously awarded in other countries automatically preclude additional patent registration. The European Patent Convention was established in 1978 to create an international registration procedure for patents. Individuals who obtain patents through the European Patent Office have valid patents in each member country.

At the start of this decade, considerable international controversy existed between drug companies holding patents on medicines for the treatment of HIV/AIDS and developing nations, which wanted to be able to manufacture, buy, and import cheap generics of these medicines to combat the AIDS epidemic. By various accounts, the cost of generics is 80 to 90 percent less than the cost of purchases from the patent holders. At the WTO summit in Qatar in November 2001, the public health argument ultimately carried the day when WTO members agreed to recognize a public health exception to patent protection. Although the United States had previously been a strong supporter of patent recognition, its promotion of that position was significantly weakened when, in light of the anthrax scares in the fall of 2001, it threatened to break Bayer's patent for the anthrax drug Cipro if that became necessary to protect the public health. Brazil, which had permitted the manufacture of AIDS/HIV generics, by some accounts has become a model for many developing countries. Through widespread dissemination of the generics, Brazil has cut the number of AIDS-related deaths and the new infection rate by half.[28]

> WTO members agreed to recognize a public health exception to patent protection.

Copyrights

A *copyright* is a government grant giving the copyright holder exclusive control over the reproduction of a literary, musical, or artistic work. Most developed nations provide copyright protection within their borders, but many also belong to international copyright protection pacts. The Berne Convention of 1886 and the Universal Copyright Convention (UCC) of 1952 both provide a measure of international protection against the unauthorized reproduction of books, photos, drawings, movies, and the like. Copyright protection extends for a period provided by national law. For example, in the United States, a copyright currently spans the author's life plus 70 years. The United States is a party to the UCC and the Berne Convention. Thus the Second Circuit Court of Appeals upheld the application of Russian copyright law when a Russian news agency sued a Russian-language newspaper located in New York for copyright violation of an article that had originally been published in Russia.[29]

Although we should recognize that we have not yet succeeded in establishing a solid international system of protection for intellectual property, some progress was made by the WTO adoption of the Agreement on Trade-Related Aspects of Intellectual Property Rights (the TRIPS agreement) in the mid-1990s. The TRIPS agreement establishes certain minimum levels of protection for copyrights, trademarks, and patents and also requires WTO members to adopt effective enforcement measures. In furtherance of its obligations under the TRIPS agreement, the United States passed federal legislation. The validity of that legislation was upheld by the Eleventh Circuit in *U.S. v. Moghadam,*[30] when it affirmed a criminal conviction for selling bootleg CDs featuring live performances of such groups as the Beastie Boys.

Libel Tourists: American Authors Beware

Libelous statements are false statements that may damage the reputation of the subject of the statements and which are communicated to a third person, in writing or another medium. (Such statements when spoken are classified as slander.) Many countries permit the harmed party to seek damages from the maker of the statements. What law should apply to, and what court should be able to hear, libel cases brought by persons referenced by writers and publishers of books and newspapers that are widely available through the Internet? Consider the following two scenarios:

1. In a book published in the United States in 2003, an American author identified a billionaire Saudi businessman as having financed Osama bin Laden. Twenty-three copies of the book were purchased in England over the Internet. The Saudi sued the American in a British court, which court asserted jurisdiction over the American author based on the availability of the book to British citizens through the Internet. British libel law is considerably more plaintiff-friendly than U.S. libel law, in part because of the free speech protections in the U.S. Constitution. Britain requires defendants to prove the truth of their statements, while restricting what can be provided as evidence. In the United States, the plaintiff first has to convince a jury the statements were false before the defendant has to present evidence of truth. The American author did not appear before the British court and in 2004 the Saudi won a default judgment of about $230,000 against the author.[31] Some Britons have expressed dissatisfaction with their reputation as a destination for "libel tourists," a phrase coined by a member of the House of Lords in 2003 when a Russian tycoon successfully sued *Forbes*, an American magazine. In 2006, Britain's highest court recognized a new defense against libel for statements made in the "public interest."

2. In the United States, celebrities have difficulty winning libel suits against gossip and rumors appearing in U.S. publications. Public figures, such as celebrities, have to prove "actual malice" on the part of the defendant to win. Because E.U. courts may assert jurisdiction over a defendant based on distribution of the libel through publication or the Internet, many U.S. celebrities (including Cameron Diaz, Jennifer Lopez, and Britney Spears) have gone abroad to sue U.S.-based publications, particularly to Britain where, as noted above, the libel law is more plaintiff-friendly.

Questions

1. Should an American author be required to defend a libel lawsuit in Great Britain? Is it appropriate for British libel law to apply to the American author? What facts might make you feel such a suit would be appropriate? What facts do you believe should be insufficient to permit suit in Britain or the application of British law?

2. Should an American be permitted to sue an American author or publisher in Great Britain? Is it appropriate for British libel law to apply to such a case? What facts might make you feel that such a suit would be appropriate? What facts do you believe should be insufficient to permit suit in Britain or the application of British law?

3. Based on your answers in Questions 1 and 2, can you create a single rule that would satisfy your sense of justice about both of these situations?

Regulation of Multinational Enterprises (MNEs)

With globalization, the number of MNEs has vastly expanded; and precisely because MNE operations span the globe, regulating their activities has become quite difficult. In the absence of effective international regulatory regimes, which do not currently exist, MNEs are subject to many different overlapping, and often contradictory, national regulatory schemes. Countries that impose regulatory requirements on MNEs may, in any given circumstance, be viewed with approval or be accused of "regulatory imperialism"[32] or be charged with domestic protectionism.[33] Consider four areas: securities regulation, imposition of financial accounting and auditing standards, anticompetitive restraints of trade, and mergers. The U.S. law covering each of these areas has previously been presented in Chapters 9 through 11, but here we want to specifically look at their international dimensions, particularly with regard to the oversight of the behavior of MNEs.

Anyone reading the business news over the past decade is quite aware of the many corporate financial scandals that have rocked the world: Enron and WorldCom in the United States; Lernout & Hauspie in Belgium; HIH Insurance in Australia; and Barings Bank in the UK. In the United States the SEC has played a major role in uncovering and pursuing financial corporate wrongdoing. But it also has a reputation outside of the United States, as one commentator put it, "as the cop on the beat for the world's securities markets."[34] For example, in recent years the SEC has imposed a $120 million fine on the Royal Dutch/Shell Group (UK and the Netherlands); investigated and settled charges against Parmalat (Italy); and, using a provision enacted as part of the Sarbanes–Oxley Act, blocked a $25 million severance payment to the former chairman of the French corporation Vivendi Universal SA. The SEC has a broad reach because of its jurisdiction to regulate all companies that choose to list their stocks or bonds on any U.S. securities market, such as the New York Stock Exchange. It is generally conceded that, worldwide, the United States has the most stringent securities laws and enforcement.

> The United States has the most stringent securities laws and enforcement.

Another aspect of the regulation of securities is the imposition of financial accounting standards. In the United States these standards also come under the regulatory authority of the SEC. However, the growth in the number of MNEs and the integration of the world's capital markets have propelled the development of internationally recognized and accepted financial accounting standards. In 2001 a set of such standards (International Financial Reporting Standards—IFRS) were offered for adoption under the auspices of the International Accounting Standards Board (IASB). Over 100 countries have now implemented these standards, although many of them have adopted local variations. The process of further harmonizing financial reporting standards is continuing along several fronts: In February 2006, the IASB and the SEC initiated a harmonization project between U.S. Generally Accepted Accounting Principles (GAAP) and the IFRS standards, a process which is expected to continue for a number of years;[35] in November 2007, the SEC ruled that foreign corporations using IFRS standards (although not the local variations) would be permitted to file financial statements with the SEC using those same standards, without requiring them to reconcile those statements to U.S. GAAP;[36] there is currently a proposal before the

European Union to allow U.S. companies to file financial reports there using only GAAP, without requiring reconciliation to IFRS standards;[37] and, finally, the SEC has taken testimony on a proposed rule that would permit U.S. companies to select IFRS reporting for their SEC filings.[38] [For more information on the IASB, see **www.iasb.org**]

Moving to international antitrust issues, Microsoft is the subject of undoubtedly the most notorious international antitrust controversy. At its heart the argument is about the identification of unacceptable trade practices by a company with monopoly market power—in this case, Microsoft's Windows operating system. In the United States alone Microsoft has faced three successive bouts of litigation brought by the U.S. Department of Justice, as well as numerous suits for damages by private plaintiffs. All of these suits apply U.S. antitrust law. However, Microsoft has also found itself being scrutinized by the European Commission for violations of the E.U.'s Competition Law. While increasingly convergent in practice, the policies behind the U.S. and E.U. laws remain distinct, and Microsoft has discovered that activity not violative of one law may nevertheless be objectionable under the other.[39] After an adverse decision by the European Commission in 2004 and losing on appeal, in the fall of 2007, Microsoft announced it would not seek further appeal. Since the beginning of the dispute in 1998, the Commission has levied fines totaling about $2.5 billion against Microsoft (if measured at 2008 exchange rates). The cease-fire didn't last long, however. In January 2008 the Commission opened another investigation of Microsoft for abuse of its monopoly power. This time the question is whether Microsoft unfairly bundled Internet Explorer with Windows, to the detriment of other Web browsers, such as Opera, produced by a Norwegian company, Opera Software.[40]

Finally, we come to merger law. The 70 or so countries with merger review systems as yet do not have an agreement coordinating these processes—not even at the level of coordinating review thresholds, timetables, and required filings.[41] Some bilateral agreements are in place, but they are simply inadequate to address the issues faced by proposed mergers among MNEs. China is now entering the fray, with its new antimonopoly law set to take effect in August 2008. There is speculation as to its potential effect on Microsoft's takeover bid for Yahoo!, if that bid goes forward, because Yahoo! has a dollar investment in China's largest e-commerce business, Alibaba.com.[42]

Imports

The General Agreement on Tariffs and Trade (GATT), now governed by the WTO, regulates import duties among signatory countries to reduce barriers to trade and to ensure fair treatment. Without GATT, it is argued, countries with stronger markets would be able to secure better deals on imports than would other countries. In addition, countries with strong market economies could use the threat of higher import taxes as a bargaining chip in other negotiations. To limit such discriminatory practices, the concepts of MFN status and national treatment are integral to GATT, just as they are to GATS, as discussed earlier in the context of international trade in services. Thus, under GATT, a reduced tariff offered to one WTO member country must be offered to all WTO members, and once a good has been imported, it must be treated just as domestic goods are treated. That, at any rate, is the ideal. In practice, GATT has not actually done away with nonconforming tariffs.

Rather, it prohibits countries from moving further away from the ideal, while providing successive rounds of multilateral trade negotiations to encourage countries to collectively move forward on achieving these goals.

A Closer Look at U.S. Tariffs

In addition to the fact that the imposition of any tariffs run counter to the avowed goal of free trade, little logic or defense seems to exist for the disparities in the U.S. system of tariffs. For example, an 8.5 percent duty is imposed on imported women's wool suits, but no duties are imposed on men's suits. Further, when a broader view is taken that incorporates whether U.S.-imposed tariffs hit imports from all countries fairly evenly, it is readily discovered that they do not. In 2006, both France and Cambodia paid $367 million in duties to the United States; but for its payment, France was able to import $36.8 billion in goods, while Cambodia paid the same duties for the importation of only $2.2 billion in goods.[43]

Questions
1. Who is hurt in the United States by the tariffs described above? Who in the United States is advantaged by them?
2. Why might U.S. tariffs be friendlier to French products than Cambodian goods?

To promote fair trade, the WTO prohibits the practice of *dumping.* Dumping occurs where a manufacturer sells its goods in a foreign country for less than their normal value. If this practice causes or threatens material injury to a domestic or established foreign manufacturer in the foreign country, the act is prohibited. The price is considered less than normal value if it is less than the price charged in the producer's home country. A firm may want to dump its goods in a foreign market for two reasons. First, its home market may be saturated and cannot support any further supply. Second, in an effort to establish itself and perhaps drive other firms out of the market, the firm may sell its goods in a foreign market at a price below other competitors and support that price with higher prices in its home country. In this way its competitors may be forced from the market; the producer may then raise prices to the normal level or above. GATT permits retaliatory duties to be imposed on countries that have dumped goods in other member countries. In theory, antidumping duties are to be imposed only to bring prices on the dumped goods back in line with what they should be. However, some commentators have argued that the computations can be manipulated and that the actual antidumping duties are just as abusive as the harm they were intended to remedy. A better approach, they argue, would be to subject imports to the same domestic predatory pricing rules that the country employs against domestic companies, as is done in Australia and New Zealand.[44]

The WTO also prohibits the payment of *unfair subsidies* by governments. This occurs where a government, in an effort to encourage growth in a certain industry, offers subsidies to producers in that industry. The producers are therefore able to sell their goods at a price lower than the prices of their worldwide competitors. Subsidies are considered unfair where governments use them to promote export trade that harms another country.

Where unfair subsidization or dumping has been found, the WTO permits the harmed country to impose *countervailing duties* on those products in an amount sufficient to counteract the effect of the subsidy. If a country feels such countervailing duties have been illegally imposed, it must either sue in the courts of the country imposing the duties based on that country's law or take the dispute through the adjudication process provided by the WTO, which is discussed later in this chapter.

The existence and level of import duties can have substantial impacts both on the volume of international trade itself and on the political and public relations between countries. Thus, when Congress passed the Africa Growth and Opportunity Act in June 2000, which gives 23 sub-Saharan countries the opportunity to ship certain textile products to the United States duty-free, it gave a considerable boost to foreign investment and the economy in Madagascar. In fact, exports to the United States in the first half of 2001 were up 115 percent from exports in all of 2000.[45] Conversely, when the United States increased duties on such French imports as Roquefort cheese in response to France's refusal to allow the import of American hormone-treated beef, it kicked off a reaction in France that resulted in, among other things, $100,000 of damage to a McDonald's restaurant in the town of Millau in the south of France.[46]

> $100,000 of damage to a McDonald's restaurant

Question

Why do developed countries like the United States impose import duties? Why would a less developed country do so?

Exports

Whereas imports are regulated to protect American businesses, exports by these businesses may also be regulated. Export regulation serves several purposes, articulated in the Export Administration Act of 1979, which states the following:

> It is the policy of the United States to use export controls only after full consideration of the impact on the economy of the United States and only to the extent necessary
>
> *a.* to restrict the export of goods and technology that would make a significant contribution to the military potential of any other country . . . which could prove detrimental to the national security of the United States;
> *b.* to restrict the export of goods and technology where necessary to further significantly the foreign policy of the United States or to fulfill its declared international obligations; and
> *c.* to restrict the export of goods where necessary to protect the domestic economy from the excessive drain of scarce materials and to reduce the serious inflationary impact of foreign demand.

Under the act, anyone wishing to export any type of goods or technology from the United States to a foreign country must obtain a license. Violations of the licensing requirement may bring imprisonment of up to 10 years and/or fines of up to $250,000, or five times the value of the export or $1 million, whichever is higher.

Two types of licenses are available, *general* or *validated* licenses. The shipper is responsible for determining which type is required. A commodity control list is published that specifies which goods are controlled and for which countries a validated license is required. Otherwise, a general license is available if no specific export license is required. To obtain a general license, the shipper must merely fill out a declaration form at the time of shipping. A validated license is required when a firm exports certain goods or technology to specified controlled countries. Firms must apply for the license at the Bureau of Industry and Security in the Department of Commerce prior to shipping. [For the Bureau of Industry and Security, see **www.bis.doc.gov**]

In determining whether to award a license, the Department of Commerce will look at several factors, including the type and amount of the exported good, the importing country, the good's use or purpose, the unrestricted availability of the same or comparable item in the importing country, and the intended market in the importing country. [To learn more about U.S. import and export practices, see **www.customs.gov/xp/cgov/trade**]

Other countries also exercise export controls. In the spring of 2008, food riots occurred in Cameroon, Egypt, Ethiopia, Guinea, Ivory Coast, Mauritania, Mexico, Morocco, Senegal, Uzbekistan, and Yemen. The cause was both the cost and scarcity of basic staples. The price of rice on international markets, for example, nearly doubled during the first three months of the year. The response by many rice exporting countries was to impose export controls to maintain domestic supplies and hold down domestic prices. These countries included Cambodia, Egypt, India, and Vietnam. This may, however, exacerbate the problem in countries dependent on rice imports, such as the Philippines and Senegal. "In countries where buying food requires half to three-quarters of a poor person's income, 'there is no margin for survival'," [Robert Zoellick, World Bank President] said.[47]

International Dispute Resolution

As we have seen to this point, international ethical/legal relationships are highly complex. Disputes are inevitable. Resolution of these international disputes often faces several roadblocks. In the international arena, three significant international dispute resolution bodies presently exist: the International Court of Justice, the European Court of Justice, and the WTO Dispute Settlement Body. Each is discussed in turn here.

The only court that is devoted entirely to hearing cases of international public law is the International Court of Justice (ICJ) in the United Nations. The ICJ is made up of 15 judges from 15 different member countries. It may issue two types of decisions, depending on its jurisdiction. It has *advisory jurisdiction* where the United Nations asks the court for an opinion on a matter of international law. These opinions do not bind any party. It has *contentious jurisdiction* where two or more nations (not individual parties) have consented to its jurisdiction and have requested a binding opinion. Such opinions are not, however, precedent for the ICJ in later cases. [For more information about the ICJ, see **www.icj-cij.org**]

How Binding Are ICJ Decisions?

Just how binding an ICJ contentious case decision actually is on U.S. state and federal courts has been called into question by the recent U.S. Supreme Court decision in *Medellin v. Texas*.[48] The Supreme Court, in a 6–3 decision, held that a Texas court did not have to give effect to an ICJ ruling in spite of the fact that the case was submitted to the ICJ pursuant to a treaty obligation specifying that the ICJ has "compulsory jurisdiction" for all "disputes arising out of the interpretation or application" of the treaty. In the view of the majority, the "most natural reading of the ["compulsory jurisdiction" language of the treaty] is as a bare grant of jurisdiction. . . . The [treaty] says nothing about the effect of an ICJ decision and does not itself commit signatories to comply with an ICJ judgment." In his dissent, Justice Breyer observed:

> In the majority's view, the [treaty] simply sends the dispute to the ICJ . . . and the U. N. Charter contains no more than a promise to "'undertak[e] to comply'" with that judgment. Such a promise, the majority says, does not as a domestic law matter . . ."operat[e] of itself without the aid of any legislative provision." Rather, here (and presumably in any other ICJ judgment rendered pursuant to any of the approximately 70 U.S. treaties in force that contain similar provisions for submitting treaty-based disputes to the ICJ for decisions that bind the parties) Congress must enact specific legislation before ICJ judgments entered pursuant to our consent to compulsory ICJ jurisdiction can become domestic law. . . . In my view, . . . we must look instead to our own domestic law, in particular, to the many treaty-related cases interpreting the Supremacy Clause. Those cases . . . lead to the conclusion that the ICJ judgment before us is enforceable as a matter of domestic law without further legislation.

The European Court of Justice (ECJ) hears cases involving European Community law. Although not required, one judge from each member nation traditionally sits on the ECJ. At first glance, the ECJ may not seem a particularly important court for American business. But in an age of MNEs, its decisions can be very important. For example, PricewaterhouseCoopers (PWC) sought to develop consulting firms in Europe that combine under one roof the services of both accountants and lawyers, an organizational structure that has been referred to as a *multidisciplinary practice* (*MDP*). Its efforts were prohibited under the law of the Netherlands, and PWC responded that such a prohibition would violate European Community law. Unfortunately for PWC, the ECJ ruled against it and held that the Netherlands could regulate the practice of the professions to protect the public interest and that disallowing MDPs could be in the public interest.[49] [For information on the ECJ, see **http://curia.europa.eu/en/index.htm**]

While the WTO Dispute Settlement Body (DSB) is not a true court, it is a significant forum for the resolution of international trade disputes between WTO members. The DSB is made up of all member governments, usually represented by ambassadors or the equivalent. The DSB establishes a panel to hear a particular dispute brought by a member state. The panel then reports back to the DSB, which can either accept or reject the panel's findings. Either side can then appeal to the WTO Appellate Body. Again, the DSB can either accept or reject the appeals report. If a WTO member fails to comply with the final decision of the DSB, the opposing party may seek compensation. If compensation is not agreed upon between the parties within 20 days, the complaining party can seek authorization for retaliation—that is, the suspension of favorable trade concessions to the noncompliant party. The reality of this power was aptly demonstrated by the DSB's 2002 authorization of $4 billion of import duties against U.S. goods by the EU based on objections to certain provisions in the U.S. corporate tax laws. [For more information on the WTO dispute resolution function and dispute documents, see **www.wto.org/english/tratop_e/dispu_e/dispu_e.htm**]

In addition to these three dispute resolution bodies, other treaties may also implement specific dispute resolution processes for disputes under the treaty between signatories to the agreement. For example, NAFTA provides for special tribunals before which corporations can, and have, brought complaints against governments for actions perceived to be unfair or inequitable to them as foreign investors. Of concern to some commentators is the fact that a tribunal under NAFTA can as a practical matter operate as a further review of the decision of a domestic court. Thus, after the U.S. Supreme Court declined to review a Massachusetts case brought by a Canadian real estate company, the company took its dispute to a NAFTA tribunal (which decided that Massachusetts had not violated international law).[50] [For information on proceedings before NAFTA tribunals against the governments of Canada, Mexico, and the United States, see the U.S. State Department site at **www.state.gov/s/l/c3439.htm**, as well as a private site, **www.NaftaClaims.com**]

Of course, national courts may also rule on matters of international law and on matters involving business in international settings. In fact, because of the absence of any international courts of general jurisdiction, national courts are where most international business disputes are heard. When the underlying dispute seems to have little association with the forum state, and the national court agrees to rule on the substantive claim, legal commentators may lay charges of "judicial imperialism."[51]

The Long Road to Court

In the summer of 2007, twelve banana plantation workers from Nicaragua got their day or, rather, their four months in court.

The workers were employed by Dole Food Co. on banana plantations in Nicaragua, where a pesticide known as DBCP, manufactured by Dow Chemical Co. was used to increase the weight of the banana harvest and help with rodent and pest control. In 1977, the U.S. government suspended the use of the chemical after complaints arose of sterility in California workers. When Dow informed Dole that it would no longer be producing the chemical, the two companies came to an agreement that Dow would sell Dole the more than 500,000 gallons that had been returned to it by other purchasers, for Dole's use in Central America.

The plaintiffs in the case were some of the workers that were exposed to the DBCP while working for Dole in Nicaragua; workers who then became sterile.

After a successful suit was brought in the United States in the early 1980s on behalf of affected California workers, U.S. law firms began suing in U.S. courts on behalf of workers from other countries. Nearly every case ended when American courts ruled that the principle of *forum non conveniens* required the lawsuits to be maintained in the countries where the workers had suffered their injuries. So the workers tried again at home. After lengthy delays and, ultimately, a change in Nicaraguan law to facilitate the DBPC lawsuits, in 2002 a Nicaraguan court awarded nearly $490 million in damages, and other judgments followed. But so far Dole and Dow have successfully blocked all enforcement of the judgments in U.S. courts. The new laws in Nicaragua have meant, however, that Dole and Dow have ceased invoking the *forum non conveniens* argument against new suits in the United States.

After a month of deliberations in the 2007 case, the jury awarded six of the Nicaraguan workers a total of $3.3 million. Following a number of posttrial motions, the companies successfully reduced the award to $1.58 million to be shared among four of the plaintiffs. The jury decision as to one plaintiff was overturned and Dole was granted a new trial as to another.[52]

Questions

1. Why do you think Dole and Dow did not object to the new suits brought in the United States?
2. Do you think the Nicaraguan judgments should be enforceable in the United States? Why or why not?

Arbitration

In light of the difficulty of litigation between parties with diverse nationalities, and the desire for more certainty and expediency in business transactions, parties to an international contract may prefer to insert a clause that calls for international arbitration in case of a dispute. As previously discussed in Chapter 4, arbitration is a nonjudicial means to settle a conflict where the parties agree to a hearing in front of a third party who will issue a binding award decision.

Government Defenses

"Some evil acts don't violate international law unless they are performed by someone acting with government authority."[53] Even where such governmental action exists, two additional doctrines, accepted as general principles of international law, may pose barriers to the judicial enforcement of a party's rights. They are the *act of state doctrine* and the *doctrine of sovereign immunity.*

Act of State Doctrine

It is generally accepted that a country has absolute rule over what occurs within its borders. Consequently, the act of state doctrine holds that a judge in one country does not have the authority to examine or challenge the acts of another country within that country's borders. For instance, an American court may not declare the acts of the British government invalid because it is presumed that the foreign country (Britain) acted legally within its own territory.

One area that has caused a great deal of dispute in connection with the act of state doctrine is *expropriation.* Expropriation is the taking by a national government of property and/or rights of a foreign firm within that government's borders. The United States contends that international law dictates that an individual or firm be compensated for the taking by the government. Not all governments agree with this statement of law.

Doctrine of Sovereign Immunity

The doctrine of sovereign immunity is based on the concept that "the king can do no wrong." In other words, if the king makes the rules, how could the king ever be wrong? As Chief Justice Marshall explained in *The Schooner Exchange v. McFaddon*,[54] "The jurisdiction of the nation within its own territory is necessarily exclusive and absolute. It is susceptible of no limitation not imposed by itself; deriving validity from an external source would imply a diminution of its sovereignty to the extent of the restriction, and an investment of that sovereignty to the same extent in that power which could impose such restriction."

The doctrine has been codified in the United States by the Foreign Sovereign Immunities Act of 1976 (FSIA), which provides that foreign countries may not be sued in American courts, subject to several exceptions. Accordingly, U.S. citizens generally could not sue Britain in the U.S. courts. A foreign country may be sued in American courts, however, if the claim falls into one of the following FSIA exceptions:

1. The foreign countries have waived their immunity (they have consented to be sued in another country's courts).
2. The legal action is based on a *commercial activity* by the foreign country in the United States or outside the United States but having a direct effect in the United States.
3. The legal action is based on personal injuries "caused by an act of torture, extrajudicial killing, aircraft sabotage, hostage taking, or the provision of material support or resources" for such acts.[55]

Therefore, a country that conducts a commercial activity in a foreign country may not hide behind sovereign immunity if sued, while a country acting on its own behalf and not for a commercial purpose would be able to avail itself of the protection. This "restrictive theory of immunity" is to be contrasted with the policies of some countries, which contend that immunity is absolute—no exceptions exist. The following case examines sovereign immunity.

Butters v. Vance International, Inc.

LEGAL BRIEFCASE 225 F.3d 462 (4th Cir. 2000)

Chief Judge Wilkinson

Appellant Nyla Butters brought suit against her employer, Vance International, claiming that Vance discriminated against her on the basis of gender. The district court held that

Vance was entitled to immunity from Butters' suit under the Foreign Sovereign Immunities Act, 28 U.S.C. §§ 1602–1611, because Vance's client, the Kingdom of Saudi Arabia, was responsible for Butters not being promoted.

I.

Vance International, headquartered in Oakton, Virginia, provides security services to corporations and foreign sovereigns. In October 1994, Saudi Arabia hired Vance to augment the security provided to Princess Anud, a wife of Saudi King Fhad, while the Princess was undergoing medical treatments in California. The Saudi military was responsible for protecting Princess Anud. The Princess' residence in Bel Air, California, was referred to as "Gold." Saudi Arabian Colonel Mohammed Al-Ajiji supervised all security at the site—three Saudi military officers and the Vance agents. Saudi Captain Abdullah was second in command. The Saudi government paid Vance for its services.

In August 1995, Vance hired Nyla Butters as a part-time, at-will security agent. From 1995 until April 14, 1998, . . . [on] several occasions, Butters temporarily worked in Gold's command post.

In early April 1998, Vance supervisors at Gold recommended that Butters serve a full rotation in the command post. In Colonel Mohammed's absence, Captain Abdullah rejected the recommendation. When Colonel Mohammed returned, Gregg Hall, the Vance detail leader, spoke with Mohammed. Colonel Mohammed denied Hall's request for Butters to serve a rotation in the command post. Colonel Mohammed told Hall that such an assignment was unacceptable under Islamic law, and Saudis would consider it inappropriate for their officers to spend long periods of time in a command post with a woman present. This in turn could have political ramifications at home for the Saudi royal family. Mohammed also informed Hall that the Princess and her contingent wanted to speak only to male officers when they called the command post. In total, three Vance supervisors recommended Butters for the assignment. Saudi military officers denied every request.

* * * * *

On May 28, 1998, Butters filed a charge of gender discrimination with the California Department of Fair Employment and Housing. On October 15, 1998, Butters filed suit . . . for discriminatory constructive termination, retaliatory constructive termination, and wrongful constructive termination in violation of public policy under California's Fair Employment and Housing Act. Vance filed a motion for summary judgment with respect to these counts.

On July 30, 1999, the district court granted Vance's motion, finding Vance immune from Butters' suit under the Foreign Sovereign Immunities Act (FSIA). Under the FSIA, "a foreign state shall be immune from the jurisdiction of the courts of the United States and of the States except as provided in sections 1605 to 1607 of this chapter." 28 U.S.C. § 1604. The district court

held that derivative FSIA immunity attached to Vance because it was "acting under the direct military orders of Colonel Mohammed when [it] did not allow the plaintiff to work a full rotation in the command center." Butters appeals.

II.

Butters first contends that FSIA immunity does not attach to Vance because the action here was a "commercial activity." Section 1605(a)(2) provides, "A foreign state shall not be immune from the jurisdiction of courts of the United States or of the States in any case in which the action is based upon a commercial activity carried on in the United States by the foreign state. . . ."

The FSIA defines "commercial activity" as "a regular course of commercial conduct or a particular commercial transaction or act. The commercial character of an activity shall be determined by reference to the nature of the course of conduct or particular transaction or act, rather than by reference to its purpose." 28 U.S.C. § 1603(d). In *Saudi Arabia v. Nelson,* the Supreme Court stated, "a state is immune from the jurisdiction of foreign courts as to its sovereign or public acts (jure imperii), but not as to those that are private or commercial in character (jure gestionis)." 507 U.S. 349, 359–60 (1993). The Court elaborated on the distinction: "[A] state engages in commercial activity . . . where it exercises 'only those powers that can also be exercised by private citizens,' as distinct from those 'powers peculiar to sovereigns.'" Id. At 360 (quoting *Republic of Argentina v. Weltover, Inc.*, 504 U.S. 607, 614 (1992)).

The relevant act here—a foreign sovereign's decision as to how best to secure the safety of its leaders—is quintessentially an act "peculiar to sovereigns." . . . Indeed, it is difficult to imagine an act closer to the core of a nation's sovereignty. Providing security for the royal family in this country is not a commercial act in which the state is acting "in the manner of a private player within the market." Id. at 360. . . .

One of the main concerns of the immunity framework adopted by the FSIA is to accommodate "the interests of foreign states in avoiding the embarrassment of defending the propriety of political acts before a foreign court." . . . These acts often have political, cultural, and religious components. Judicial interference with them would have serious foreign policy ramifications for the United States. We thus decline to require the Saudi government to justify to us the arrangements it believes are best suited to ensure the safety of its royal family.

III.

Butters next argues that Vance is not entitled to immunity since Vance, as opposed to the Saudi officials, was responsible for the decision not to promote Butters.

A.

If Vance was following Saudi Arabia's orders not to promote Butters, Vance would be entitled to derivative immunity under the FSIA. . . .

. . . To abrogate immunity would discourage American companies from entering lawful agreements with foreign governments and from respecting their wishes even as to sovereign acts. Under the circumstances here, imposing civil liability on the private agents of Saudi Arabia would significantly impede the Saudi government's sovereign interest in protecting its leaders while they are in the United States.

* * * * *

IV.

Any type of governmental immunity reflects a trade-off between the possibility that an official's wrongdoing will remain unpunished and the risk that government functions will be impaired. See *Harlow v. Fitzgerald,* 457 U.S. 800, 813–14 (1982)

("The resolution of immunity questions inherently requires a balance between the evils inevitable in any available alternative."). FSIA immunity presupposes a tolerance for the sovereign decisions of other countries that may reflect legal norms and cultural values quite different from our own. Here Saudi Arabia made a decision to protect a member of its royal family in a manner consistent with Islamic law and custom. The Act requires not that we approve of the diverse cultural or political motivations that may underlie another sovereign's acts, but that we respect them. We thus affirm the judgment.

Questions

1. Why did the court hold that Vance, a U.S. corporation, could avoid Butters' claim of discrimination based on a claim of sovereign immunity? Why did Butters argue that sovereign immunity would not apply?
2. How do you feel about the end result of this decision? Did Butters suffer discrimination?

Enforcement of Decisions

As we have just seen, even if a harmed party in an international dispute is successful initiating a judicial proceeding, many procedural hurdles are likely to be encountered. Recall the *forum non conveniens* principle that initially kept the Nicaraguan workers from obtaining substantive hearings in U.S. courts, as well as the more stringent evidentiary rules faced by defendants in libel suits in Britain, as compared with the United States. What about after a successful conclusion of such a suit? Do challenges arise in the enforcement of the court's decision?

The answer is yes, particularly in those cases where the losing defendant has insufficient or no assets located in the same jurisdiction as the court awarding the plaintiff monetary relief. In those cases, the plaintiff may need to present the judgment to a court in a country where assets of the defendant are located and seek local enforcement of that decision. This is an added expense for successful plaintiffs, both in terms of time and money. But, even more, it may be difficult or impossible to obtain enforcement.

When a plaintiff is successful in a California court, but the defendant's assets are in New York, the plaintiff may have to seek enforcement from a New York court. In that situation, the U.S. Constitution requires the New York court to give "full faith and credit" to the decision of the California court. No such broad policy exists in U.S. law with respect to decisions of foreign courts; nor does such a broad policy exist in international law. Instead, the court from which enforcement is being requested is likely to consider whether the original judgment violates local notions of justice and morality, or is otherwise contrary to public policy, so as not to be entitled to enforcement. This is also true of foreign arbitration awards if the losing party has refused to satisfy the award—even if both countries are among the 142 current signatories of the United Nations Convention on the Recognition and Enforcement of Foreign Arbitral Awards.[56]

To illustrate the problem, consider the previously discussed Nicaraguan banana plantation workers. After U.S. courts largely refused to allow substantive hearings in the 1980s based on *forum non conveniens*, the workers took their claims back to Nicaragua, which was exactly what U.S. courts had told them to do. Although resolution of claims in Nicaragua took a long time, some plaintiffs obtained substantial judgments there. In response to plaintiffs' applications to U.S. courts for recognition and enforcement of these Nicaraguan judgments, however, the defendant U.S. corporations have thus far been successful in avoiding the requested enforcement.

Now consider the American author with the outstanding $230,000 British libel judgment against her in favor of the Saudi businessman. The British judgment was a *default judgment*, that is, the Saudi won because the American author did not appear in court to defend the suit. In this case, no defense was made because of the cost of doing so, an expectation that the British court would not assert personal jurisdiction over the author (who was not a British citizen and who had no contacts to Britain other than the 23 copies of her book which had been ordered over the Internet), and a concern that under British libel law there was a substantial risk that she would lose even with a substantive hearing. As the author's assets are in the United States, to obtain enforcement of the British judgment, the Saudi would have to request recognition of the award from a U.S. court. Believing that the British libel decision would not be enforced by a U.S. court, in part because it offends the fundamental value of free speech protected by the Bill of Rights in the U.S. Constitution, the author filed a *declaratory judgment* action in a federal district court in New York, requesting a ruling on her constitutional claim and seeking to have the issue finally resolved. The Saudi businessman argued that the district court did not have personal jurisdiction over him and, thus, could not hear the author's substantive claim; the district court agreed. The author appealed to the Second Circuit, which said the issue was a matter of *first impression* under New York law, that the New York high court, its Court of Appeals, had never ruled on similar facts. Thus, the Second Circuit certified the question to the New York Court of Appeals for a determination. On December 20, 2007, that court agreed with the federal district court.[57] Thus, the American author is still left in limbo—not knowing whether the British judgment is enforceable in the United States and simply left to wait until the Saudi actually seeks enforcement to resolve the matter. (If an enforcement action is begun in the United States, she will be able to raise her constitutional claims at that time.)

Similar problems can arise when a U.S. citizen obtains a judgment from a U.S. court against a foreign national, which judgment is then sought to be enforced by the home courts of the foreign national. One aspect of American law, the granting of *punitive damages*, over and above solely *compensatory damages*, to private plaintiffs is viewed with considerable distaste in many countries. Consider the case of a mother of a 15-year-old, who died in an accident when the buckle of his motorcycle helmet failed. The helmet was made by an Italian company. The mother sued and won a $1 million judgment. The company refused to pay and the mother presented the judgment to an Italian court for enforcement. The Italian Supreme Court found the award of punitive damages so offensive to its notion of justice that it refused to enforce any of the award, as the U.S. court had not specified how much of the award was compensatory and how much was punitive.[58]

Question

On balance, do you think it would be better for countries to agree mutually to simply enforce judgments in favor of private citizens (nationals or nonnationals) obtained from foreign courts, respecting the effort and delay the plaintiff has already undergone in obtaining the judgment and without applying culturally based notions of justice? Why or why not? If not, try generating a list of principles you think should permit a court to refuse enforcement of a foreign judgment.

Internet Exercise

Identify a multinational firm that conducts business with suppliers in developing countries. Find its code of vendor conduct on the Web and evaluate the areas of enforcement that might prove to be the most difficult.

Chapter Questions

1. Why do you think China, one of the most communist of nations, wanted to join the WTO? Would it surprise you to learn that Afghanistan, Iraq, Russia, and Uzbekistan, while not currently WTO members, are all formally enrolled as observer countries? This means they are (or are considering) pursuing accession negotiations to become WTO member states. The most recent state to become an observer country is Iran. Why might it have now decided to become involved with the WTO?

2. Judge Leo Strine, the Vice Chancellor of the Delaware Court of Chancery (the Delaware Court with original jurisdiction over state corporate law cases), has suggested that effective regulation of corporate behavior will require nations to give up some of their sovereignty to international institutions in exchange for regulation of the global product and financial markets in which multinational corporations conduct their business.[59] Do you agree? Will some form of corporate global regulation be necessary to protect all of the stakeholders of such corporations?

3. America has embraced fast food. This may be part of the reason that, in the United States, obesity has risen at an epidemic rate during the past 30 years. According to the Center for Disease Control, currently one third of the adults in the United States are considered obese. Seventeen percent of those between 12 and 19 are overweight. [For more on obesity in the United States, see the Web site for the Center for Disease Control, **www.cdc.gov/nccdphp/dnpa/obesity/index.htm**] Should other countries be concerned about the influx of American fast-food chains? Why or why not? What about countries that provide universal health care? If a country is concerned about its citizens' dietary changes, what actions should it take in response? Explain.

4. Cultural values can sometimes come into conflict with outside values spread through the process of globalization. The following story originated in India.

   A group called the Hindu Jagran Manch, or the Hindu Awakening Platform, said Valentine's Day was an affront to Indian traditional culture and warned against Feb. 14 celebrations in the city. Many conservative segments of Indian society view the day—a celebration of romantic love—as indecent.

   "Valentine's Day, Mother's Day, and Father's Day . . . these are all the gimmicks of multinational companies to market their products. Valentine's Day is against the culture and ethics of Indian society," said Vinay Tewari, a Manch leader.[60]

As a result of threatened attacks by Manch, many shopkeepers in India's largest state closed for Valentine's Day. Should the shopkeepers have closed their doors? Do you understand how a celebration of "romantic love" might be offensive to some? Do you think that Valentine's Day and other U.S. holidays are promoted more for their commercial value than to further the stated purpose for the day? Consider the dates when Halloween, Thanksgiving, and Christmas decorations go up in U.S. stores.

5. Thomas Friedman, in his 2005 book, *The World Is Flat: A Brief History of the Twenty-First Century,* offers his opinion that countries with connected manufacturing supply chains won't go to war with each other. He offers an example of Dell's multicountry supply chain for the manufacture of its laptops. On balance, do you think globalization is a catalyst for bringing world peace or a tinderbox that may set international disputes on fire through the collision of differing ideals?

6. What are the relative advantages and disadvantages of each form of doing business in a foreign country? Why would a firm choose one form over another?

7. What may look to one observer like the application of objective standards may appear to another observer as improper protectionism. NAFTA, originally signed in the mid-1990s, calls for an open border for commercial truck traffic among Canada, the United States, and Mexico. But in early 2005 Mexican trucks were still not allowed into the United States, due in part to litigation brought by environmental and labor groups. Their claim was that the United States hadn't appropriately considered the environmental impact of letting Mexican trucks roll on American roads because there are no standardized emissions rules for commercial vehicles. On balance, does this argument sound to you more like a principled objection or like protection for U.S. jobs? Why? See *Dept. of Transportation v. Public Citizen,* 541 U.S. 752 (2004).

8. Original Appalachian Artworks (OAA) is the manufacturer and license holder of Cabbage Patch Kids dolls. Granada Electronics imported and distributed Cabbage Patch Kids dolls to the United States that were made in Spain by Jesmar under a license from OAA. Jesmar's license permitted manufacture and distribution of the dolls in Spain, the Canary Islands, Andorra, and Ceuta Melilla. Under the license, Jesmar agreed not to make, sell, or authorize any sale of the dolls outside its licensed territory and to sell only to those purchasers who would agree not to use or resell the licensed products outside the territory as well. Jesmar's argument that Granada's sales do not constitute "gray market" sales is that OAA's dolls sold in the United States have English-language adoption papers, birth certificates, and instructions while Granada's dolls come equipped with Spanish-language adoption papers, birth certificates, and instructions. In addition, Granada argues that the role of trademark law is to prevent an infringer from passing off its goods as being those of another. Such is not the case here. Are these sales prohibited? Explain. See *Orig. Appalachian Artworks v. Granada Electronics,* 816 F.2d 68 (2d Cir. 1987); cert. den. 484 U.S. 847 (1987).

9. Camel Manufacturing imported nylon tents to the United States. The tents held nine people and weighed over 30 pounds. The tents' floors ranged from 8 feet by 10 feet to 10 feet by 14 feet. The tents were to be used as shelter during camping. The importer categorized the goods as "sports equipment," which carried a 10 percent

import duty, whereas the U.S. Customs Service considered the tents "textile articles not specifically provided for," with a duty of $.25 per pound plus 15 percent import duty. The importer appealed the decision. What should be the result? Explain. See *Camel Manufacturing Co. v. United States,* 686 F.Supp. 912 (C.I.T. 1988); aff'd 861 F.2d 1266 (Fed. Cir. 1988).

10. Should a Mexican citizen who bought a Chrysler vehicle in Mexico be allowed to sue the manufacturer in a U.S. court under U.S. product liability laws when the plaintiff's three-year-old son was killed when the passenger-side air bag deployed during an accident in Mexico? See *Gonzalez v. Chrysler Corp.,* 301 F. 3d 377 (5th Cir. 2002); cert. den. 538 U.S. 1012 (2003).

11. Prior to 1941, Kalmich owned a business in Yugoslavia. In 1941 the Nazis confiscated his property as a result of Kalmich's Jewish heritage and faith. Bruno purchased the business from the Nazis in 1942 without knowledge of the potential unlawful conversion. Kalmich contends that because the confiscation was in violation of well-defined principles of international law prior to the German occupation, the transfer to Bruno was ineffective. Kalmich seeks to apply a 1946 Yugoslavian law called "Law Concerning the Treatment of Property Taken Away from the Owner." That law provides that where property is taken from its owners, the owner may bring an action against "responsible persons" for recovery. Does the act of state doctrine apply here? If not, what should be the result in an American court? Explain. See *Kalmich v. Bruno,* 450 F. Supp. 227 (N.D. IL 1978).

12. Zedan received a telephone call from a Saudi Arabian organization offering him an engineering position at a construction project in Saudi Arabia. The Ministry of Communications, an agency of the government, guaranteed payment to Zedan for any work he performed there, whether for the government or for a nonsovereign third party. After three years, Zedan left the country without being fully paid. After he returned to the United States, he filed an action in federal court seeking to enforce the ministry's guarantee. The ministry argued that it was protected under the Foreign Sovereign Immunities Act. Was Zedan's recruitment in the United States a commercial activity as required by the act? Did this action have a direct effect in the United States as required by the act? Explain. See *Zedan v. Kingdom of Saudi Arabia,* 849 F.2d 1511 (1988).

13. From time to time courts are called upon to determine the enforceability of an arbitration clause contained in a contract. One such case was *DiMercurio v. Sphere Drake Insurance,* 202 F.3d 71 (1st Cir. 2000). DiMercurio was injured in 1994 when the commercial fishing vessel in which he was working sank. The vessel was owned by R&M, which was found by a court to be liable to DiMercurio for his injuries and ordered to pay $350,000 in compensation. However, because R&M had no other assets, it assigned to DiMercurio all the rights it had against Sphere Drake, the London-based insurer of the fishing vessel. When DiMercurio looked to Sphere Drake for payment, it denied the claim and invoked the arbitration clause in its insurance policy with R&M, which required the arbitration to take place in England. Should DiMercurio be required to pursue his claim through arbitration in England?

Notes

1. "Agreement Establishing the World Trade Organization," found at [**www.wto.org/english/docs_e/legal_e/legal_e.htm**].

2. Bill Sing, "Deal to Loosen Trade Reached," *Los Angeles Times,* August 1, 2004, p. A1.

3. Bob Davis, "Rise of Nationalism Frays Global Ties," *The Wall Street Journal,* April 28, 2008, p. A1.

4. Marc Champion, "Americans' Support for Free Trade Declines," *The Wall Street Journal,* December 6, 2007.

5. [**http://www.wto.org/english/thewto_e/whatis_e/tif_e/fact1_e.htm**].

6. Reuters News Service, "Study Finds Rich Getting Richer, More Numerous," *The Wall Street Journal,* October 4, 2007.

7. Parag Khanna, *The Second World* (Random House 2008), as quoted by Raymond Bonner, "Guess Who's Coming to Power," *New York Times*, March 30, 2008.

8. Much of this discussion was based on Jess Smee, "Rights: Workers Score with Fair-Trade Soccer Balls," *Inter Press Service,* April 3, 2006; and Uwe Buse, "Balls and Chains," *Spiegel Online*, May 26, 2006.

9. [**http://www.adidas-group.com/en/sustainability/suppliers_and_workers/exploring_labour_standards/position_on_child_labour.asp**].

10. [**http://www.adidas-group.com/en/sustainability/suppliers_and_workers/case_studies/independent_review_football_production_pakistan.asp**].

11. Louis Uchitelle, "Economist Wants Business and Social Aims to Be in Sync," *New York Times,* January 30, 2007.

12. *Id.*

13. *EEOC v. Arabian American Oil Co.,* 499 U.S. 244 (1991).

14. A copy of the Declaration can be found in the University of Minnesota's Human Rights Library at [http://www1.umn.edu/humanrts/instree/b1udhr.htm].

15. A copy of the draft can be found in the University of Minnesota's Human Rights Library [**www1.umn.edu/humanrts/links/NormsApril2003.html**].

16. A copy of the report can be downloaded from [**http://www.ccbe.eu/fileadmin/user_upload/NTCdocument/csr_guidelines_0405_1_1182254964.pdf**].

17. The Principles can be found at [**www.cauxroundtable.org/principles.html**].

18. Jose Ramos-Horta, "Speech to the Northern Medical Foundation Tribute to Military Medicine and Lt-Gen. P. Cosgrove," Sydney, Australia, September 28, 2001. Copy with author's work papers.

19. See, for example, *U.S. v. Kim,* 246 F. 3d 186 (2d Cir. 2001), where a New York resident was convicted of wire fraud while working for the United Nations in Croatia.

20. 116 F. Supp. 2d 116 (D.D.C. 2000).

21. 192 F. 3d 240 (2d Cir. 1999).

22. From the CIA's World Factbook at [**https://www.cia.gov/library/publications/the-world factbook/geos/xx.html#Econ**].

23. From the CIA's World Factbook at [**https://www.cia.gov/library/publications/the-world factbook/geos/us.html#Econ**].

24. From the US Census Bureau, Foreign Trade Division at [**http://www.census.gov/foreign-trade/statistics/historical/gands.pdf**].

25. Michael Schroeder, "Outsourcing May Create U.S. Jobs," *The Wall Street Journal,* March 30, 2004, p. A2.

26. GATS, Art. I, para. 3(b).

27. Summary of the Madrid Agreement Concerning the International Registration of Marks (1891) and the Protocol Relating to That Agreement (1989) at [**www.wipo.int/treaties/en/registration/madrid/summary_madrid.html**].

28. G. Winestock and H. Cooper, "Activists Outmaneuver Drug Makers at WTO," *The Wall Street Journal,* November 14, 2001, p. A2, A13.

29. *Itar-Tass Russian News Agency v. Russian Kurier, Inc.,* 153 F.3d 82 (2d Cir. 1998).

30. 175 F.3d 1269 (11th Cir. 1999); cert. den. 529 U.S. 1036 (2000).

31. See *Ehrenfeld v. Mahfouz,* 881 N.E.2d 830 (NY 2007) and Michael J. Broyde and Deborah E. Lipstadt, "Home Court Advantage," *New York Times,* October 11, 2007.

32. Michael Schroeder and Silvia Ascarelli, "New Role for SEC: Policing Companies beyond U.S. Borders," *The Wall Street Journal,* July 30, 2004, p. A1.

33. "European Imperialism," *The Wall Street Journal,* October 31, 2007, p. A20.

34. Schroeder and Ascarelli, "New Role for SEC."

35. Thomas Jaworski, "IASB Official Sees Worldwide Concern Over SEC's Influence in Global Accounting Standards," *Tax Notes Today,* November 30, 2007.

36. Floyd Norris, "SEC Says Foreign Companies Do Not Have to Adjust to U.S. Accounting," *New York Times,* November 16, 2007.

37. Darryl Tait, "EU Official Will Soon Propose Elimination of Reconciliation Requirement for Users of U.S. GAAP," *Tax Notes Today,* December 4, 2007.

38. "Closing the GAAP," *The Wall Street Journal,* December 12, 2007, p. A18.

39. Amanda Cohen, "Surveying the Microsoft Antitrust Universe," *Berkeley Technology Law Journal* 19 (2004), p. 333.

40. Charles Forelle, "EU Regulators Begin New Microsoft Probes," *The Wall Street Journal,* January 15, 2008, p. A3.

41. For a good comparison of U.S. and EU merger analysis and enforcement, see Cento Veljanovski, "EC Merger Policy after GE/Honeywell and Airtours," *Antitrust Bulletin* 49 (Spring 2004), p.153.

42. John Markoff, "China Law Could Impede Microsoft Deal for Yahoo," *New York Times,* March 28, 2008.

43. Editorial, "The Other Boot," *New York Times,* May 4, 2007.

44. "Against Anti-Dumping," *The Economist* 349, no. 8093 (November 7, 1998), p. 18.

45. Helene Cooper, "Can African Nations Use Duty-Free Deal to Revamp Economy?" *The Wall Street Journal,* January 2, 2002, pp. A1, A4.

46. Keith B. Richburg, "McDonald's Attacker Convicted in France," *Washington Post,* September 14, 2000, p. A28.

47. Bob Davis and Douglas Belkin, "Food Inflation, Riots Spark Worries for World Leaders," *The Wall Street Journal,* April 14, 2008, p. A1. See also, Keith Bradsher, "High Rice Cost Creating Fears of Asia Unrest," *New York Times,* March 29, 2008.

48. 128 S. Ct. 1346 (2008).

49. *J.C.J. Wouters, J.W. Savelbergh, Price Waterhouse Belastingadviseurs BV and Algemene Raad Van de Nederlandse Orde Van Advocaten,* C-309/99, 2002 TNT 37–62 (EU Ct. 2002).

50. Adam Liptak, "NAFTA Tribunals Stir U.S. Worries," *The New York Times,* April 18, 2004.

51. Klaus-Heiner Lehne, "Hands Off Our Torts," *The Wall Street Journal,* November 18, 2003, p. A20.

52. Based on information from T. Christian Miller, "Plantation Workers Look for Justice in the North," *Los Angeles Times*, May 27, 2007; Justin Rebello, "U.S. District Court in Calif. Rules against Dow Chemical in Pesticide Exposure Case," *Lawyers USA*, December 2007; and "Dole Food Co. Inc. Wins Court Rulings," *Business Wire*, March 10, 2008.

53. Steve Garmisa, "U.S. Courts Handle International Law," *Chicago Sun-Times*, September 24, 1997.

54. 11 U.S. (7 Cranch) 116 (1812).

55. *Sutherland v. Islamic Republic of Iran*, 151 F. Supp. 2d 27 (D.D.C. 2001).

56. Current information on the status of the convention, as well as additional information, can be found at [**http://www.uncitral.org/uncitral/en/uncitral_texts/arbitration/NYConvention.html**].

57. See *Ehrenfeld v. Mahfouz*, 881 N.E.2d 830 (NY 2007).

58. Adam Liptak, "Foreign Courts Wary of U.S. Punitive Damages," *New York Times*, March 26, 2008.

59. Leo E. Strine, "Human Freedom and Two Friedmen: Musings on the Implications of Globalization for the Effective Regulation of Corporate Behavior," *University of Pennsylvania Law School Law and Economics Research Paper Series*, November 1, 2007.

60. Rupan Bhattacharya, "Valentine's Day Menace Causes Shop Closings," *Des Moines Register*, February 14, 2001, p. 2A.

CHAPTER SEVENTEEN

Environmental Protection

After completing this chapter, students will be able to:

1. Identify market incentives for businesses to prevent and correct environmental problems.

2. Discuss environmental protection in the context of cost-benefit analysis, impact on future generations, and causation.

3. Describe the National Environmental Policy Act (NEPA).

4. Identify duties of the Environmental Protection Agency (EPA).

5. Describe the Clean Air Act (CAA).

6. Describe the Clean Water Act (CWA).

7. Discuss regulation of land pollution.

8. Discuss the purpose and effect of the Comprehensive Environmental Response, Compensation, and Liability Act of 1980 (CERCLA), commonly known as "the Superfund."

9. Identify penalties and other enforcement mechanisms under federal and state regulations as well as common law.

10. Evaluate the competing arguments regarding the wisdom of the Endangered Species Act.

11. Describe the primary common law remedies for environmental damage.

Introduction

From local issues such as routing a new highway around a wetland or allowing leaf burning to colossal fears such as global warming, environmental issues mark our lives in a manner that was unimaginable a few decades ago. From the moment a firm begins to produce, service, manufacture, or create, its operations affect the environment. Imagine the small decisions made by a company: Does it pack its glassware in plastic bubbles or corrugated wrapping? Does it publish a catalog once a month or once a year? Is that catalog published on paper or only through the Internet? Does it meet with the community before choosing a disposal system? Each of these decisions will have an impact on our physical world; so it is critical to understand the law as it relates to the environment and to be aware of the ethical component of each decision.

The Global Picture

It is also important to have an understanding of the magnitude of the environmental problems we face, that their scope often extends beyond political boundaries and that all countries are affected. Consider the following:

- "New glimpses of Earth from space show air pollution wrapping around the planet, spreading haze and hazardous gases across oceans and continents and posing new challenges for cleanup. . . . Increasingly, researchers are discovering air pollution is not a transient phenomenon. Emissions climb high into the atmosphere, borne on trade winds that circumnavigate the globe."[1]

- In the summer of 2007, the Arctic ice cap melted one million square miles more than the average summer melt since 1979 when satellite measurements began, opening up the famed Northwest Passage over Canada. One million square miles is equivalent to six Californias.[2] Antarctica and Greenland are both losing ice overall—about 125 billion metric tons a year combined.[3] [For an interactive map showing the extent of the Arctic sea ice on September 16 each year from 2001 through 2007, see **www .nytimes.com/interactive/2007/10/01/science/20071002_ARCTIC_GRAPHIC.html#**].

- There is a dead zone (an oxygen-starved area devoid of fish) in the Gulf of Mexico, caused in part by run-off of fertilizers into the Mississippi River, which varies in size from year to year and can cover more than 8,000 square miles (that is, almost the size of New Jersey).[4] According to the United Nations Environment Program, there are nearly 150 such dead zones around the globe, double the number existing in 1990, covering some 27,000 square miles.[5]

As China's presence on the global economic stage has increased, its environmental problems have also taken center stage in environmental reporting. It is probably accurate to say that, in the two years prior to this writing, global warming and China's environmental problems have been the most reported on environmental issues in the American press. Part Five of this chapter takes a look at global warming and responses to it. Below are a few illustrations of some of China's environmental challenges.

- A 2007 report from the World Bank identified the world's 30 most polluted cities— 20 of which are in China.[6]

- China suffers simultaneously from a shrinking supply of water and a growing demand for it, coupled with rampant water pollution. For example, the underground water table is sinking about four feet a year in an area in northern China about the size of New Mexico and most natural streams in the area have disappeared.[7] China's textile industry is one of its dirtiest, spinning off such pollutants as heavy metals and various carcinogens. In 2007, one textile factory was discovered to have a pipe buried underneath the factory floor, daily dumping tons of contaminated water into a nearby river.[8] Nearly 500 million people in China lack access to safe drinking water.[9] The Yangtze River's white dolphins may have become extinct[10] and portions of China's coastline suffers so much from red algal tides that no marine life survives in large sections of the ocean.[11]

- "Heart disease and respiratory problems linked to air pollution are among the leading causes of death in China. . . . [A]cid rain now fall[s] on 30 percent of the country."[12] China's coal-fired plants are also responsible for acid rain in Seoul, South Korea and Tokyo, Japan.[13] And "[o]n some days, almost a third of the air over Los Angeles and San Francisco can be traced directly" to China and other parts of Asia.[14]

"For two decades, China has made economic growth a priority. The results have been impressive as the country becomes a bigger player on the global stage and hundreds of millions of its people are lifted out of extreme poverty."[15] As has been the case in all countries which have previously industrialized, part of the cost of China's economic prosperity has been paid by the environment. The question is whether this necessarily has to be so.

Consider the following. As will be discussed more fully in Part Five, many countries are acting to address carbon emissions through a multilateral carbon-trading program (where pollution rights are traded globally to bring down overall carbon levels by funding least-cost controls first, regardless of where the least-cost opportunities exist). China could be an immediate beneficiary of this approach by permitting foreign industry to reduce carbon emissions through funding of the clean up of China's carbon sources. This creates a win-win-win situation where total world carbon emissions decrease, China's own air pollution decreases and foreign corporations have to pay less to meet their carbon reduction requirements. Many least-cost opportunities exist in China because, by and large, Chinese industry has not undertaken even the most cost-effective pollution controls. Some evidence indicates the Chinese are becoming more open to foreign investments of this type.

Food for Thought

Each of the following observations was made by Jeff Gersh in "Seeds of Chaos," *Amicus Journal* 21, no. 2 (Summer 1999), p. 36.

- "Because hunger and misery cannot afford to make the distinctions of the well-fed— to choose between cutting a tree or saving it—poverty is among the greatest environmental threats in the world."
- The process of development and industrialization has always been accompanied by environmental degradation. "Still, many economists counsel patience. If these emerging markets stay on the prescribed path of development, . . . they will eventually raise their per capita incomes to the threshold at which economic and political capital takes an interest in environmental reforms."
- Some pollutants, such as carbon dioxide, seem to grow as incomes rise.

Questions
1. What do you think is the most significant source of environmental degradation globally: Impoverished populations in the world's poorest countries, countries which are struggling to develop economically, or already industrialized countries? Explain.
2. Is environmental degradation a necessary companion to economic progress? Explain.

Part One—A Return to Fundamentals: The Market, Government Regulation, and Self-Regulation

The first three chapters of this text set up a framework for analyzing the substantive law topics that followed: (1) consideration of how well market forces achieve the goals we have for our society; (2) investigation of whether government intervention, through laws and regulations, can bring and has brought us closer to those societal goals; and (3) reflection on the role that self-regulation, through ethical decision making and corporate social responsibility, can and does play in realizing our goals. We will look at each of these forces in our exploration of the interplay between business and our natural environment.

Market Failure?

Without regulation, a firm may consider that dumping its garbage into a nearby canal is no big deal. In fact, perhaps the slight amount of garbage the firm dumps *is* no big deal. However, if every firm were allowed to dump that amount, the canal might become thoroughly polluted. Or consider the possibility that we may all prefer less costly cars that pollute more. Would future generations concur?

As discussed in Chapter 8, pollution in these cases would be categorized by economists as a negative "externality." Wilfred Beckerman described the economic analysis as follows:

> [T]he costs of pollution are not always borne fully, if at all, by the polluter. . . . Naturally, he has no incentive to economize in the use [of the environment] in the same way that he has for other factors of production that carry a cost, such as labor or capital. . . . This defect of the price mechanism needs to be corrected by governmental action in order to eliminate excessive pollution.[16]

Thus environmentalists claim the market has failed to protect us from pollution and rules are necessary. The public and Congress have apparently agreed: The United States has enacted a substantial number of environmental laws since the early 1970s, addressing air pollution, pollution of our waterways, protection of rare plant and animal species, and hazardous and toxic wastes. Many of these laws will be discussed in Part Two of this chapter.

Market Incentives

As we will see, one form our federal regulation has taken is to dictate standards with which businesses must comply. Such legislation has in fact led to steady, and at times even spectacular, strides forward in environmental protection in the United States. But this progress has not dispelled the view, particularly among economists and businesspeople, that standard-setting regulation may not be the best approach to remedy environmental problems. They believe that pollution control is not so much a matter of law as of economics. It follows that with proper incentives, the market will, in some instances, prove superior to traditional regulation in preventing and correcting environmental problems. Some examples of market incentives follow.

Pollution Credits

Perhaps the most prominent and successful example of the U.S. government employing free market tactics to address an environmental issue is the government-created market in pollution credits. In the early 1990s the United States set a cap on the number of tons of pollutants to be permitted in the air, a cap lower than the actual amount then being emitted. Pollution credits were issued to several hundred of the biggest power plants and certain factories. Credit recipients could either reduce their discharges to within their credit limit or they could buy credits from other companies who had reduced their emissions below their own credit amounts. Companies with a relatively low cost to reduce their emissions made plant improvements and then paid for some of their own improvements by selling their excess credits. Companies with a relatively high cost to reduce emissions found it more economical to help pay to reduce another company's emissions (by purchasing that plant's excess credits) than incur their own higher-cost pollution reduction.[17] Electric utilities in 1999 produced about 41 percent more electricity than in 1980 while emitting 25 percent fewer tons of sulfur dioxide, a major factor in the creation of acid rain.[18]

Taxes

Tax provisions can also affect behavior, either to encourage particular behavior through tax incentives or to discourage other behavior through application of additional taxes. For example, in the environmental area we have provided an income tax credit for purchasing certain new hybrid cars, such as the Mazda Tribute or the Ford Escape. Another example is the tax-free fringe benefit allowed to employees through a payroll deduction purchase of commuter vouchers or transit passes. The EPA in 2000 began actively seeking major employers in urban areas to enroll in the program so that the environmental benefits from the incentive would be realized.[19]

Global Examples Some European countries, such as Norway and Sweden, had substantial success in reducing sulfur and carbon emissions with pollution taxes in the 1990s. More recently, in January 2008, the European Commission adopted new targets of a 20 percent renewable energy use and a 20 percent reduction in carbon dioxide emissions by 2020. Member countries will face fines if they do not meet their individual country targets, which has inspired many of them to provide additional subsidies for renewable energy projects.[20] On another front, Australia, Greenland, Iceland, New Zealand, and the Netherlands have all also been quite successful using market incentives to address overfishing. "Government authorities cap the total allowable catch and then allocate quotas among fishermen, usually based on the historical catch. The quotas become a 'property right' that can be bought and sold among fishermen—helping to reduce fleet capacity. And because fishermen have access to a guaranteed share of the catch, they don't race to compete, . . . prices rise and fish stocks grow."[21] Ireland has successfully addressed a different urban pollutant—plastic and paper shopping bags. Starting with the imposition of a tax in 2002 on shopping bags, which is now 33 cents per bag, nearly everyone now brings their own,

A tax on shopping bags

reusable cloth bags for shopping. In the beginning merchants were skeptical of the new tax, but it was illegal for them to pay for customers' bags themselves, forcing individual consumers to choose between bringing reusable bags or paying the tax. The collected taxes go to pay for environmental enforcement and cleanup programs.[22] [For more on the environmental impact of paper and plastic bags, see **www.reusablebags. com**]

The Kyoto Protocol on global warming, which will be discussed in Part Five, also uses market incentives to achieve its goal of lower global greenhouse gas emissions.

Question

Suggested free market incentives for pollution control include government taxes or fees on pollution and government rules mandating refundable deposits on hazardous materials. Explain how those incentives might work.

Ethical Business Decision Making

On a particularly busy corner in a suburb of Auckland, New Zealand, the proprietors of a small café, Triniti of Silver, do a brisk breakfast, lunch, and coffee trade. Their menu declares their philosophy: Only organic eggs of free-range chickens are used here; only paddock-reared pigs; only certified organic beef—"we do not feel happy to encourage the inhumane treatment of animals." Just one example of grassroots, intentional, ethical business decision making.

But what can we expect in the environmental area from managers of publicly held corporations? Can we find significant examples of corporate social responsibility (discussed in Chapter 3)? The answer is a resounding yes—all one has to do is review a sampling of corporate Web sites. Why are corporate giants voluntarily doing now what they haven't done in the past? What has changed? In part, the answer may be that the market has changed and market forces are operating to reward corporate responsibility. For example, managers may believe that being "green," or being seen as being green by consumers and investors, will improve the corporate bottom line. Or a manager may believe that a proactive approach may lessen the likelihood of future regulation on an issue that is becoming increasingly visible.[23] This is one example of a pay-now-or-pay-later management analysis. Managers may take a more socially responsible approach to an environmental issue now because they think the future cost of not doing so could be enormously larger—in negative publicity, in the cost of more stringent future regulation—than the present actual cost of the action.

But does the market actually reward sound environmental practices? We cannot yet be sure, but an interesting 1997 study found a strong relationship between environmental high performance and high profitability.[24] Some companies simply comply with environmental laws, whereas others take affirmative steps to improve their environmental performance. The study's authors theorize that the latter companies build more skillful workers by expecting them to cope with the complexities of "clean technologies." Prevention and improvement are more complicated than mere compliance, so perhaps the environmentally active firms are actually building their performance "muscles" by their activist approach, while the compliance firms are expending their energies on the external world in an effort to fend off new rules. [For many examples of environmentally responsible actions of business, see **www.bsr.org/about/in-the-news.cfm**]

Having reviewed both market forces and ethical business decision making, we turn now in Part Two to government regulation as an approach for meeting our societal environmental goals.

Question

"The single most important and pervasive moral obligation facing mankind is to ensure survival of a healthy planet for our grandchildren and theirs."[25] Do you agree? Why or why not?

Part Two—Laws and Regulations

The United States has developed a wide variety of environmental protection laws and remedies, some of which are discussed in this section. Throughout this discussion, keep in mind the following concepts:

- **Cost–benefit analysis:** Environmental protection can be expensive. How much as a society are we willing to pay? Do we want clean air at any cost? We may (or may not) be able to estimate the cost of a particular pro-environment action, but how do

  How do we value human life?

  we measure the benefit of taking the action? How do we value human life, represented by a statistical decrease in deaths or illness from exposure to environmental pollutants? Does environmental protection cause the sacrifice of short-term economic development? How can this cost be measured? These are not easy questions, and any answer will necessarily be inexact and require subjective judgments and the use of estimates. A 2003 study by the Office of Management and Budget concluded that a prior toughening of clean air regulations was well worth the cost to industry and consumers, that the "value of reductions in hospitalization and emergency room visits, premature deaths, and lost workdays resulting from improved air quality" was estimated between $120 and $193 billion over a 10-year period, where the cost to comply was only $23 to $26 billion.[26] Industry critics, however, argue that the costs of compliance were greatly understated. [For more information on cost–benefit analysis and environmental protection, see the Georgetown Environmental Law and Policy Project at **www.law.georgetown.edu/gelpi/research_archive/cost_benefit_analysis**]

- **Impact on future generations:** When performing a cost–benefit analysis, how do we deal with the cost to future generations of our not taking action? And how can we measure the value of the action to those generations? In some cases, the future generations will bear the brunt of the decision, whatever choice we make. For example, if greenhouse gases cause global warming, how do we measure that impact on future generations? This is a complex question about which there is no scientific consensus, let alone economic consensus.

- **Proving causation:** If event A occurs and event B follows, is it necessarily true that event A *caused* event B? It could simply be a coincidence that first A was observed and then B. Or there could in fact be a *correlation* between events A and B, but no actual causation. For example, event Z might cause both A and B, but no causal link may exist between A and B. In the environmental area, issues of coincidence, correlation, and causation may be extremely difficult to determine. For example, does exposure to secondhand smoke cause lung cancer in some nonsmokers? Is the observed increase in greenhouse gases a contributor to current weather patterns, such as the unusually severe hurricane season in 2004?[27] If, in the example of Z, A, and B, we spend a lot of effort trying to stop A to prevent B occurring, we will be wasting our money. On the other hand, how long can we wait to determine definitively whether a causal link exists between A and B? Our answer may depend on the severity of the harm we believe is associated with B.

- **Who pays?** Even if we decide to correct an environmental problem, who should pay for the correction? If we require corporate America to invest in pollution control devices, the cost may be shared between consumers (through increased prices) and investors (through a reduced corporate profit). If habitats of endangered species are to be preserved, current land owners may simply lose all or a portion of their investment, and workers employed on the land may lose their jobs. Who should pay? Sometimes the issue is where a particular facility, such as for hazardous waste, should be located. Not surprisingly, a common response of citizens near a proposed location is,

"Not in my backyard!"   "yes, it's necessary, but **not in my backyard**!" This response is so common, that it is now referred to as NIMBY.

- **The impact of politics:** Environmental protection in the United States has not been just a matter of science and cost assessment and social policy; it has also been a matter of politics. An administration has considerable impact on the enforcement of our environmental laws, particularly through the regulations it chooses to pursue under the authority of the various environmental statutes. In that regard, the Bush administration was seen as more pro-business than pro-environment.[28]

Question

What environmental issue do you care about most? Greenhouse gases? Deforestation? The dead zone in the Gulf of Mexico or the Chesapeake Bay? The loss of salmon in the Pacific Northwest? Select an issue you care about (if it's global warming, select a particular possible response to it, such as sharing environmental technologies with developing countries, increasing mileage requirements, requiring the use of energy-efficient lightbulbs, etc.), do some online research for related data and then explore your issue in light of the five concepts discussed above.

The Federal Role

The federal government has long maintained a role in the protection of the environment—some would argue too great a role. As early as 1899, Congress enacted a law that required a permit to discharge refuse into navigable waters. As it became apparent that private, state, and local environmental efforts were not adequate to address the burgeoning problems, in the early 1970s Congress began to take more aggressive legislative initiatives.

National Environmental Policy Act (NEPA)

The 1970 National Environmental Policy Act (NEPA) established a strong federal presence in the promotion of a clean and healthy environment. NEPA represents a general commitment by the federal government to "use all practicable means" to conduct federal affairs in a fashion that both promotes "the general welfare" and operates in "harmony" with the environment.

> The CEQ is a watchdog of sorts

NEPA established the Council on Environmental Quality (CEQ), which serves as an adviser to the president. The CEQ is a watchdog of sorts. It is required to conduct studies and collect information regarding the state of the environment. The council then develops policy and legislative proposals for the president and Congress. [For more on the CEQ, see **www.whitehouse.gov/ceq**]

But NEPA's primary influence results from its *environmental impact statement* (EIS) requirements. With few exceptions, "proposals for legislation and other major federal action significantly affecting the quality of the human environment" must be accompanied by an EIS explaining the impact on the environment and detailing reasonable alternatives. Completing an EIS requires undertaking a cost–benefit analysis. It also requires consideration of cause and effect links. Major federal construction projects (highways, dams, nuclear reactors) would normally require an EIS; but less visible federal programs (ongoing timber management or the abandonment of a lengthy railway) may also require EIS treatment. Although the focus here is on *federal* actions, thus exempting solely private acts from this scrutiny, a major private-sector action supported by federal funding or by one of several varieties of federal permission may also require an EIS. Hence private companies receiving federal contracts, funding, licenses, and the like may be parties to the completion of an EIS.

Questions

Should a state be required to prepare an EIS if it wants to use federal funds to promote statewide tourism? Does it matter which state it is? Consider Iowa and then consider Hawaii.[29]

Environmental Protection Agency (EPA)

The private sector was not left without regulation or constraint. The Environmental Protection Agency (EPA) was created in 1970 to mount a coordinated attack on environmental problems. EPA duties include, among other things, (1) gathering information, particularly by surveying pollution problems, (2) conducting research on pollution problems, (3) assisting state and local pollution control efforts, and (4) administering many of the federal laws directed to environmental concerns. [For the EPA home page, see **www.epa.gov**]

Regulation of Air Pollution

We depend on (indeed, we emotionally embrace) the automobile. In doing so, we have opened vistas of opportunity not previously imagined. However, motor vehicles also discharge carbon monoxide, nitrogen oxide, and hydrocarbons as by-products of the combustion of fuel, thus fouling our air. Industrial production and the combustion of fossil fuels in homes and industry are also significant contributors to the dilemma of dirty air.

Clean Air Act of 1990 (CAA)

Early clean air legislation in 1963 and 1965 afforded the government limited authority. The Clean Air Act amendments of 1970 and 1977 gave the EPA the power to set air quality standards and to ensure that those standards were achieved according to a timetable prescribed by the agency. Politics brought clean air to the fore in 1990, and a new Clean Air Act followed. The Clean Air Act of 1990, which phased in new standards over a period of years, generally required tougher auto emission controls, cleaner-burning gasoline, and new equipment to capture industrial and business pollution, all of which worked toward the general goal of reducing airborne pollutants by about 50 percent. Under the CAA, air quality standards are set federally, but the states are required to establish implementation plans to achieve and maintain those standards.

In recent years, there has been considerable high profile litigation over clean air standards. Three of these cases are discussed below. In the first, Massachusetts and a number of other states, cities and private organizations argued that the EPA had abdicated its responsibility under §202(a)(1) of the CAA to "prescribe . . . standards applicable to the emission of any air pollutant" when it refused to regulate greenhouse gas emissions from new motor vehicles.

LEGAL BRIEFCASE

Massachusetts v. Environmental Protection Agency   127 S. Ct. 1438 (2007)

Justice Stevens

A well-documented rise in global temperatures has coincided with a significant increase in the concentration of carbon dioxide in the atmosphere. Respected scientists believe the two trends are related. For when carbon dioxide is released into the atmosphere, it acts like the ceiling of a greenhouse, trapping solar energy and retarding the escape of reflected heat. It is therefore a species—the most important species—of a "greenhouse gas."

Calling global warming "the most pressing environmental challenge of our time," a group of States, local governments, and private organizations, alleged in a petition for certiorari that the . . . EPA has abdicated its responsibility under the Clean Air Act to regulate the emissions of four greenhouse gases, including carbon dioxide. Specifically, petitioners asked us to answer two questions concerning the meaning of § 202(a)(1) of the Act: whether EPA has the statutory authority to regulate greenhouse gas emissions from new motor vehicles; and if so, whether its stated reasons for refusing to do so are consistent with the statute.

I

Section 202(a)(1) of the Clean Air Act . . . provides:

The [EPA] Administrator shall by regulation prescribe (and from time to time revise) in accordance with the provisions of this section, standards applicable to the emission of any air pollutant from any class or classes of new motor vehicles or new motor vehicle engines, which in his judgment cause, or contribute to, air pollution which may reasonably be anticipated to endanger public health or welfare . . .

The Act defines "air pollutant" to include "any air pollution agent or combination of such agents, including any physical, chemical, biological, radioactive . . . substance or matter which is emitted into or otherwise enters the ambient air." "Welfare" is also defined broadly: among other things, it includes "effects on . . . weather . . . and climate."

* * * * *

II

On October 20, 1999, a group of 19 private organizations filed a rulemaking petition asking EPA to regulate "greenhouse gas emissions from new motor vehicles under § 202 of the Clean Air Act." . . . As to EPA's statutory authority, the petition observed that the agency itself had already confirmed that it had the power to regulate carbon dioxide. In 1998, Jonathan Z. Cannon, then EPA's General Counsel, prepared a legal opinion concluding that "CO[2] emissions are within the scope of EPA's authority to regulate," even as he recognized that EPA had so far declined to exercise that authority. Cannon's successor, Gary S. Guzy, reiterated that opinion before a congressional committee just two weeks before the rulemaking petition was filed.

* * * * *

On September 8, 2003, EPA entered an order denying the rulemaking petition. The agency gave two reasons for its decision: (1) that contrary to the opinions of its former general counsels, the Clean Air Act does not authorize EPA to issue mandatory regulations to address global climate change; and (2) that even if the agency had the authority to set greenhouse gas emission standards, it would be unwise to do so at this time.

* * * * *

Having reached that conclusion, EPA believed it followed that greenhouse gases cannot be "air pollutants" within the meaning of the Act. . . . The agency bolstered this conclusion by explaining that if carbon dioxide were an air pollutant, the only feasible method of reducing tailpipe emissions would be to improve fuel economy. But because Congress has already created detailed mandatory fuel economy standards subject to Department of Transportation (DOT) administration, the agency concluded that EPA regulation would either conflict with those standards or be superfluous.

Even assuming that it had authority over greenhouse gases, EPA explained in detail why it would refuse to exercise that authority. The agency began by recognizing that the concentration of greenhouse gases has dramatically increased as a result of human activities, and acknowledged the attendant increase in global surface air temperatures. EPA nevertheless gave controlling importance to the [National Resource Council] Report's statement that a causal link between the two cannot be unequivocally established. Given that residual uncertainty, EPA concluded that regulating greenhouse gas emissions would be unwise.

The agency furthermore characterized any EPA regulation of motor-vehicle emissions as a "piecemeal approach" to climate change and stated that such regulation would conflict with the president's "comprehensive approach" to the problem. That approach involves additional support for technological innovation, the creation of nonregulatory programs to encourage voluntary private-sector reductions in greenhouse gas emissions, and further research on climate change—not actual regulation. According to EPA, unilateral EPA regulation of motor-vehicle greenhouse gas emissions might also hamper the president's ability to persuade key developing countries to reduce greenhouse gas emissions.

III

Petitioners, now joined by intervenor States and local governments, sought review of EPA's order in the U.S. Court of Appeals for the District of Columbia Circuit. Although each of the three judges on the panel wrote a separate opinion, two judges agreed "that the EPA Administrator properly exercised his discretion under § 202(a)(1) in denying the petition for rule making." The court therefore denied the petition for review.

* * * * *

V

* * * * *

EPA concluded in its denial of the petition for rulemaking that it lacked authority . . . to regulate new vehicle emissions because carbon dioxide is not an "air pollutant" as that term is defined in [the CAA]. In the alternative, it concluded that even if it possessed authority, it would decline to do so because regulation would conflict with other administration priorities. . . . We . . . "may reverse any such action found to be . . . arbitrary, capricious, an abuse of discretion, or otherwise not in accordance with law."

VI

On the merits, the first question is whether § 202(a)(1) of the Clean Air Act authorizes EPA to regulate greenhouse gas emissions from new motor vehicles in the event that it forms a "judgment" that such emissions contribute to climate change. We have little trouble concluding that it does. . . .

The statutory text forecloses EPA's reading. The Clean Air Act's sweeping definition of "air pollutant" includes "*any* air pollution agent or combination of such agents, including *any* physical, chemical . . . substance or matter which is emitted into or otherwise enters the ambient air. . . . " On its face, the definition embraces all airborne compounds of whatever stripe, and underscores that intent through the repeated use of the word "any." Carbon dioxide, methane, nitrous oxide, and hydrofluorocarbons are without a doubt "physical [and] chemical . . . substance[s] which [are] emitted into . . . the ambient air." The statute is unambiguous.

* * * * *

EPA finally argues that it cannot regulate carbon dioxide emissions from motor vehicles because doing so would require it to tighten mileage standards, a job (according to EPA) that Congress has assigned to DOT. But that DOT sets mileage standards in no way licenses EPA to shirk its environmental responsibilities. EPA has been charged with protecting the public's "health" and "welfare," a statutory obligation wholly independent of DOT's mandate to promote energy efficiency. The two obligations may overlap, but there is no reason to think the two agencies cannot both administer their obligations and yet avoid inconsistency.

* * * * *

VII

The alternative basis for EPA's decision—that even if it does have statutory authority to regulate greenhouse gases, it would be unwise to do so at this time—rests on reasoning divorced from the statutory text. While the statute does condition the exercise of EPA's authority on its formation of a "judgment," that judgment must relate to whether an air pollutant "cause[s], or contribute[s] to, air pollution which may reasonably be anticipated to endanger public health or welfare." Put another way, the use of the word "judgment" is not a roving license to ignore the statutory text. It is but a direction to exercise discretion within defined statutory limits.

If EPA makes a finding of endangerment, the Clean Air Act requires the agency to regulate emissions of the deleterious pollutant from new motor vehicles. . . . EPA no doubt has significant latitude as to the manner, timing, content, and coordination of its regulations with those of other agencies. But once EPA has responded to a petition for rulemaking, its reasons for action or inaction must conform to the authorizing statute. Under the clear terms of the Clean Air Act, EPA can avoid taking further action only if it determines that greenhouse gases do not contribute to climate change or if it provides some reasonable explanation as to why it cannot or will not exercise its discretion to determine whether they do. To the extent that this constrains agency discretion to pursue other priorities of the administrator or the president, this is the congressional design.

EPA has refused to comply with this clear statutory command. Instead, it has offered a laundry list of reasons not to regulate. For example, EPA said that a number of voluntary executive branch programs already provide an effective response to the threat of global warming, that regulating greenhouse gases might impair the president's ability to negotiate with "key developing nations" to reduce emissions, and that curtailing motor-vehicle emissions would reflect "an inefficient, piecemeal approach to address the climate change issue."

Although we have neither the expertise nor the authority to evaluate these policy judgments, it is evident they have nothing to do with whether greenhouse gas emissions contribute to climate change. Still less do they amount to a reasoned justification for declining to form a scientific judgment. . . .

Nor can EPA avoid its statutory obligation by noting the uncertainty surrounding various features of climate change and concluding that it would therefore be better not to regulate at this time. If the scientific uncertainty is so profound that it precludes EPA from making a reasoned judgment as to whether greenhouse gases contribute to global warming, EPA must say so. That EPA would prefer not to regulate greenhouse gases because of some residual uncertainty . . . is irrelevant. The statutory question is whether sufficient information exists to make an endangerment finding.

In short, EPA has offered no reasoned explanation for its refusal to decide whether greenhouse gases cause or contribute to climate change. Its action was therefore "arbitrary, capricious, . . . or otherwise not in accordance with law." . . .

VIII

[Reversed and remanded.]

Questions

1. Under what conditions did the Supreme Court say it had the power to reverse the EPA's decision not to regulate the carbon dioxide emissions of new vehicles?
2. What did the petitioners, including the State of Massachusetts, want the EPA to do?
3. The EPA said that, even if it had the authority to regulate greenhouse gas emissions from motor vehicles, it would not do so. What reasons did the EPA give for this refusal? What did the Supreme Court say about those reasons?
4. Following this decision of the Supreme Court, what must the EPA now do? Is the EPA required to set a standard for greenhouse gas emissions from new vehicles?
5. Look back at the discussion about proving causation at the start of Part Two of this chapter. Did the Supreme Court say that greenhouse gas emissions from vehicles caused global warming? What did the Court observe about causation?

Motor Vehicle Emission Standards

Americans have long been noted for our love affair with automobiles. Gas shortages in the early 70s, knowledge of the air pollution created by motor vehicles, even the substantial rise in gas prices following hurricane Katrina, did not seem to change our use of cars or interest in large vehicles, such as sports utility vehicles (SUVs) and the Hummer. Between an uncertain economy and gas prices approaching $4 per gallon, with no expectation of a return to the lower prices of just a few years ago, the tide may now have turned. In the spring of 2008, the percentage of new car sales represented by small cars substantially increased and sales of SUVs dropped dramatically. In 2008, American drivers are projected to consume less gas than in 2007—its first annual drop in 17 years.[30]

As identified in the above opinion, the U.S. Department of Transportation (DOT) is charged with setting fuel economy standards for new motor vehicles. In 2006, DOT set standards for light trucks and SUVs for the 2008–2011 model years, requiring an increase from 22.2 to 23.5 miles per gallon. A number of public interest groups, led by the Center for Biological Diversity, as well as 11 states, sued, arguing the increase was "trivial," that the government's cost/benefit analysis should be required to include the benefit of reducing greenhouse gas carbon emissions, that light trucks and SUVs should not be held to a lesser standard than passenger cars and that the agency should be required to set standards for heavy trucks and SUVs, for which no fuel economy standards currently exist. The Ninth Circuit agreed in a November, 2007 decision.[31] Thus, once again, a federal court ruled that federal agencies cannot look the other way to avoid addressing the issues of greenhouse gases and global warming. The DOT has submitted a request for an en banc reconsideration by the Ninth Circuit of the three-judge panel's decision.[32]

In the meantime, in December 2007, Congress set a new minimum fuel efficiency goal for auto manufacturers. The goal is to reach a fleet average of 35 miles per gallon by 2020, compared to a current average of about 25 miles per gallon. The DOT was directed to set interim goals for the ultimate accomplishment of the 2020 goal. The proposed interim goal for 2015 was announced in April 2008—for passenger cars, the interim goal is 35.7 (up from 27.5) and, for light trucks, the interim goal is 28.6 (up from 23.5—the standard currently under review by the Ninth Circuit).[33]

Major Modification versus Routine Maintenance and Repair

Not satisfied with air quality progress, the EPA in the late 1990s took an increasingly aggressive stance. Among other actions, in late 1999, the EPA under the Clinton administration signaled its growing frustration by taking legal action against 32 coal-fired power plants operating in 10 states (Alabama, Florida, Georgia, Illinois, Indiana, Kentucky, Mississippi, Ohio, Tennessee, and West Virginia). Some were given administrative citations and warnings, but seven utilities (for operations at 17 plants) were sued for violating EPA regulations. Most of the plants were built before the Clean Air Act of 1970 and were allowed, under "grandfather" clauses, to meet less stringent air quality requirements unless they underwent major modifications. The supposition was that the old plants would soon be phased out, but that has not happened. The EPA claimed that major renovations have been made to extend the useful lives of the plants without making the required CAA upgrades.

As the Justice Department was pursuing these cases, the Bush administration took office and the EPA issued new regulations, which in part broadened the definition of "routine maintenance" thereby allowing plant improvements that were not subject to the "major modification" standard and its required CAA upgrades.[34] Cases questioning, directly or indirectly, the validity of the new routine maintenance definition reached the federal courts. In one of those cases, the DC Circuit ruled against the new definition. In another, the Seventh Circuit upheld the earlier regulation by ruling that energy utility, Cinergy, had violated the CAA when it made major modifications without installing modern pollution controls. Then, in a unanimous decision, the Supreme Court ruled against Duke Energy Corp., striking down a Fourth Circuit Court of Appeals decision which had invalidated the original Clinton Administration regulation.[35] In sum, these several court rulings renewed pressure on the energy companies to make the CAA upgrades, as a step toward cleaner air.

Regulation of Water Pollution

As with the air, we often treat our water resources as free goods. Rather than paying the full cost of producing goods and services, we have simply dumped a portion of that cost into the nearest body of water. The waste from production—indeed from the totality of our life experience—has commonly been disposed of in the water at a cost beneath that required to dispose of the waste in an ecologically sound fashion. The results range from smelly to dangerous to tragic.

- *Runoff.* Much of America's water pollution is directly attributable to our personal habits. Surface water runoff is polluted with lawn fertilizer, pet waste, grease and oil from vehicles, and all the other sludge from our modern lives. That runoff, of course, eventually debases our waterways. One of the significant problems with such runoff is that the EPA's system of tracking water pollution focuses on pollution from large facilities, which are more visible and easier to police, rather than dirty runoff from farms, storms and roads, which are known to be major sources of water pollution. (See the following discussion of "point source" discharges.) This is still true in spite of the new rules put in place in 1999 to reduce runoff from large hog, cattle, and poultry farms.

- *Beaches.* According to a report by the nonprofit National Resource Defense Council, pollution-related closings and health advisories were more numerous in 2006 at our national beaches than ever in their 17-year survey period, representing a 28 percent increase over 2005.[36] The report covers ocean, gulf, and Great Lakes beaches. A significant portion of the closings were related to sewage, debris and other pollutants carried into coastal waters as rainwater runoff—part of the problem just discussed.

Federal Policy

The Clean Water Act (CWA), designed to "restore and maintain the chemical, physical, and biological integrity of the nation's waters," establishes two national goals: (1) achieving water quality sufficient for the protection and propagation of fish, shellfish, and wildlife and for recreation in and on the water; and (2) eliminating the discharge of pollutants into navigable waters. The states have primary responsibility for enforcing the CWA, but the federal government, via the Environmental Protection Agency, is empowered to assume enforcement authority if necessary.

The goals of the Clean Water Act are implemented primarily by imposing limits on the amount of pollutants that may lawfully enter the water of the United States from any "point source" (typically a pipe). The National Pollutant Discharge Elimination System (NPDES) requires all pollutant dischargers to secure an EPA permit before pouring effluent into a navigable stream. The permit specifies maximum permissible levels of effluent. Typically the permit also mandates the use of a particular pollution control process or device and requires the permit holder to monitor its own performance and report on that performance to the state or the EPA, as appropriate.

In the following 2001 case, the Supreme Court looked at what qualifies as "navigable waters" for purposes of regulation under the CWA. You should be aware that this decision was made by a bare majority (five) of the justices; the other four dissented. In 2006, the Supreme Court took another look at the same issue, which decision will be discussed following this case.

Solid Waste Agency of Northern Cook County v. U.S. Army Corps of Engineers

LEGAL BRIEFCASE 531 U.S. 159 (2001)

Chief Justice Rehnquist

Section 404(a) of the Clean Water Act (CWA or Act), 33 U.S.C. § 1344(a), regulates the discharge of dredged or fill material into "navigable waters." The United States Army Corps of Engineers (Corps) has interpreted § 404(a) to confer federal authority over an abandoned sand and gravel pit in northern Illinois which provides habitat for migratory birds. We are asked to decide whether the provisions of § 404(a) may be fairly extended to these waters, and, if so, whether Congress could exercise such authority consistent with the Commerce Clause, U.S. Const., Art. I, § 8, cl. 3. We answer the first question in the negative and therefore do not reach the second.

Petitioner, the Solid Waste Agency of Northern Cook County (SWANCC), is a consortium of 23 suburban Chicago cities and villages that united in an effort to locate and develop

a disposal site for baled nonhazardous solid waste. The Chicago Gravel Company informed the municipalities of the availability of a 533-acre parcel, bestriding the Illinois counties Cook and Kane, which had been the site of a sand and gravel pit mining operation for three decades up until about 1960. Long since abandoned, the old mining site eventually gave way to a successional stage forest, with its remnant excavation trenches evolving into a scattering of permanent and seasonal ponds of varying size (from under one-tenth of an acre to several acres) and depth (from several inches to several feet).

The municipalities decided to purchase the site for disposal of their baled nonhazardous solid waste. By law, SWANCC was required to file for various permits from Cook County and the State of Illinois before it could begin operation of its balefill project. In addition, because the operation called for the filling of some of the permanent and seasonal ponds,

SWANCC contacted federal respondents (hereinafter respondents), including the Corps, to determine if a federal landfill permit was required under § 404(a) of the CWA.

Section 404(a) grants the Corps authority to issue permits "for the discharge of dredged or fill material into the navigable waters at specified disposal sites." *Ibid.* The term "navigable waters" is defined under the Act as "the waters of the United States, including the territorial seas." § 1362(7). The Corps has issued regulations defining the term "waters of the United States" to include

> waters such as intrastate lakes, rivers, streams (including intermittent streams), mudflats, sandflats, wetlands, sloughs, prairie potholes, wet meadows, playa lakes, or natural ponds, the use, degradation or destruction of which could affect interstate or foreign commerce. 33 CFR§ 328.3(a)(3) (1999).

In 1986, in an attempt to "clarify" the reach of its jurisdiction, the Corps stated that § 404(a) extends to intrastate waters

> *a.* Which are or would be used as habitat by birds protected by Migratory Bird Treaties; or
>
> *b.* Which are or would be used as habitat by other migratory birds which cross state lines; or
>
> *c.* Which are or would be used as habitat for endangered species; or
>
> *d.* Used to irrigate crops sold in interstate commerce. 51 Fed. Reg. 41217.

This last promulgation has been dubbed the "Migratory - Bird Rule."

The Corps initially concluded that it had no jurisdiction over the site because it contained no "wetlands," or areas which support "vegetation typically adapted for life in saturated soil conditions[.]" However, after the Illinois Nature Preserves Commission informed the Corps that a number of migratory bird species had been observed at the site, the Corps reconsidered and ultimately asserted jurisdiction over the balefill site pursuant to subpart (b) of the "Migratory Bird Rule." The Corps found that approximately 121 bird species had been observed at the site, including several known to depend upon aquatic environments for a significant portion of their life requirements. Thus, on November 16, 1987, the Corps formally "determined that the seasonally ponded, abandoned gravel mining depressions located on the project site, while not wet-lands, did qualify as 'waters of the United States' ... based upon the following criteria: (1) the proposed site had been abandoned as a gravel mining operation; (2) the water areas and spoil piles had developed a natural character; and (3) the water areas are used as habitat by migratory bird *[sic]* which cross state lines."

* * * * *

Despite SWANCC's securing the required water quality certification from the Illinois Environmental Protection Agency, the Corps refused to issue a § 404(a) permit. The Corps found that SWANCC had not established that its proposal was the "least environmentally damaging, most practicable alternative" for disposal of nonhazardous solid waste; that SWANCC's failure to set aside sufficient funds to remediate leaks posed an "unacceptable risk to the public's drinking water supply"; and that the impact of the project upon area-sensitive species was "unmitigatable since a landfill surface cannot be redeveloped into a forested habitat."

Petitioner filed suit under the Administrative Procedure Act, 5 U.S.C. § 701 *et seq.,* in the Northern District of Illinois challenging ... the Corps' jurisdiction over the site. ... On appeal to the Court of Appeals for the Seventh Circuit, petitioner renewed its attack on respondents' use of the "Migratory Bird Rule" to assert jurisdiction over the site. Petitioner argued that respondents had exceeded their statutory authority in interpreting the CWA to cover nonnavigable, isolated, intrastate waters based upon the presence of migratory birds and, in the alternative, that Congress lacked the power under the Commerce Clause to grant such regulatory jurisdiction.

The Court of Appeals ... held that the CWA reaches as many waters as the Commerce Clause allows and, given its earlier Commerce Clause ruling, it therefore followed that respondents' "Migratory Bird Rule" was a reasonable interpretation of the Act.

We granted certiorari and now reverse.

Congress passed the CWA for the stated purpose of "restoring and maintaining the chemical, physical, and biological integrity of the Nation's waters." 33 U.S.C. § 1251(a). In so doing, Congress chose to "recognize, preserve, and protect the primary responsibilities and rights of States to prevent, reduce, and eliminate pollution, to plan the development and use (including restoration, preservation, and enhancement) of land and water resources, and to consult with the Administrator in the exercise of his authority under this chapter." § 1251(b). Relevant here, § 404(a) authorizes respondents to regulate the discharge of fill material into "navigable waters," which the statute defines as "the waters of the United States, including the territorial seas," § 1362(7). Respondents have interpreted these words to cover the abandoned gravel pit at issue here because it is used as habitat for migratory birds. We conclude that the "Migratory Bird Rule" is not fairly supported by the CWA.

This is not the first time we have been called upon to evaluate the meaning of § 404(a). In *United States v. Riverside Bayview Homes, Inc.,* 474 U.S. 121 (1985), we held that the Corps had § 404(a) jurisdiction over wetlands that actually abutted on a navigable waterway. In so doing, we noted that the term "navigable" is of "limited import" and that Congress evidenced its intent to "regulate at least some waters that would not be deemed 'navigable' under the classical understanding of that term." *Id.* at 133. But our holding was based in large measure upon Congress' unequivocal acquiescence to, and approval of, the Corps' regulations interpreting the CWA to cover wetlands adjacent to navigable waters. We found that Congress' concern for the protection of water quality and aquatic ecosystems indicated its intent to regulate wetlands "inseparably bound up with the 'waters' of the United States." 474 U.S. at 134.

It was the significant nexus between the wetlands and "navigable waters" that informed our reading of the CWA in *Riverside Bayview Homes.* . . . In order to rule for respondents here, we would have to hold that the jurisdiction of the Corps extends to ponds that are *not* adjacent to open water. But we conclude that the text of the statute will not allow this.

Indeed, the Corps' *original* interpretation of the CWA, promulgated two years after its enactment, is inconsistent with that which it espouses here. Its 1974 regulations defined § 404(a)'s "navigable waters" to mean "those waters of the United States which are subject to the ebb and flow of the tide, and/or are presently, or have been in the past, or may be in the future susceptible for use for purposes of interstate or foreign commerce." 33 CFR § 209.120(d)(1). The Corps emphasized that "it is the water body's capability of use by the public for purposes of transportation or commerce which is the determinative factor." § 209.260(e)(1). Respondents put forward no persuasive evidence that the Corps mistook Congress' intent in 1974.

* * * * *

We hold that 33 CFR § 328.3(a)(3) (1999), as clarified and applied to petitioner's balefill site pursuant to the "Migratory Bird Rule," 51 Fed. Reg. 41217 (1986), exceeds the authority granted to respondents under § 404(a) of the CWA. The judgment of the Court of Appeals for the Seventh Circuit is therefore Reversed.

Questions

1. Summarize the arguments made by the Army Corps of Engineers for finding that the government had the power to regulate this site under the CWA.

2. Explain the Supreme Court's response to each of the Army Corps of Engineers' arguments previously identified.

3. Did the Supreme Court hold that the government could not regulate this type of site or only that Congress had not in fact sought to extend its regulation to this type of site?

4. In your view, should the federal government be able to regulate bodies of water that are of significant use by migratory birds? Explain.

Navigable Waters Revisited   As we saw in *Solid Waste Agency,* the Supreme Court evaluated a regulation of the Army Corps of Engineers (Corps) and determined that it exceeded the Corps' scope of authority under the Clean Water Act. All nine justices agreed that the term "navigable waters" should be interpreted more broadly than its literal meaning, but only four of the justices would have approved the Corps' expansive reading of the statute.

In 2006, the Supreme Court, in *Repanos v. United States,* once again reviewed the breadth of the Corps' authority under the CWA.[37] The same four justices again dissented, arguing that the broad authority asserted by the Corps was permissible under the statute. This time, however, the remaining five justices did not agree on the reach of the CWA, but only agreed that the Corps was still asserting an authority broader than allowable under the statute. The result was that the five, as a majority, remanded the case for "further proceedings" without settling upon a standard on which to base those proceedings. Four of those five justices held that the scope of the CWA did not reach to channels with intermittent water flows or those that periodically provided rainfall drainage and that only wetlands with a continuous surface connection to "navigable waters" were covered by the CWA. Justice Kennedy, the fifth of the five "remanders," took a middle position stating that the proper test is whether the property sought to be covered has a "significant nexus" to "navigable waters" and that wetlands bordering a ditch or drain with only a remote or insubstantial flow into "navigable waters" should not be covered, but that a continuous surface connection was not a necessary requirement and some intermittent flows might have such a significant nexus. As a result of these decisions, the Corps once again must define the scope of its regulatory authority, narrowing it at least within the boundaries Justice Kennedy described.

Regulation of Land Pollution

Pollution does not fit tidily into the three compartments (air, water, land) used for convenience in this text. Acid rain debases air and water as well as the fruits of the water and land, such as fish and trees. Similarly, the problems of land pollution addressed in this section often damage the fullness of the natural world. For most of recorded history, we felt safe and comfortable in using the Earth as a garbage dump.

Garbage

Our lifestyles result in mountains of solid waste that grow higher every year. Indeed, New York City's Fresh Kills Landfill is one of the world's largest man-made structures and one of the highest points of land on the East Coast. In 2006, each of us, on average, produced about 4.6 pounds of garbage daily, nearly 34 percent of which came in the form of paper and paperboard.[38] Of course, we pay an immediate price to dispose of all of the leftovers of our lives, but the long-term concern is that the waste will come back to haunt us. Even state-of-the-art landfills can leak, with the result that toxic elements can enter our groundwater. We had long assumed that much of the waste would simply decompose, but studies show that does not happen. The leading "garbologist," Professor William Rathje, explains, "The thought that after 30 or so years newspapers and food would disintegrate is off-track. Things become mummified. We found hot dogs that could be recooked and perfectly legible newspapers."[39] The suggested solution, of course, is to "reduce, reuse, recycle."

> We had long assumed that much of the waste would simply decompose, but studies show that does not happen

Recycling

Recycling turns materials that would otherwise become waste into usable resources, which can reduce dependence on new materials (reducing deforestation, for example). Recycling can also reduce the amount of waste that is burned in incinerators, reducing particulate matter and other pollutants that would otherwise be released into the air. The EPA reported that the number of solid waste landfills fell to 1,754 in 2006 from 3,091 in 1996. The national goal of recycling 25 percent of municipal garbage was reached in 1995 and the agency targeted a 35 percent standard for 2005.[40] As of 2006, we had reached 32.5 percent.

In light of the fact that one-third by weight of our garbage is paper and paperboard, Forest Ethics, an environmental group, has been working to encourage companies to increase their use of recycled paper. In December 2005, it launched a campaign against

Victoria's Secret to switch to recycled paper for the 395 million catalogs (over

Forest Ethics launched a campaign against Victoria's Secret.

a day) it prints and mails each year. Forest Ethics is also t develop a Do Not Mail campaign, to allow individuals to c whether to receive junk mail.[41] The ultimate recycling appr may be that taken by a group of anticonsumerists who call the selves freegans (as compared to vegans)—who attempt to live totally on free goods found in dumpsters and at "freemeets."[42] [For sites identifying the availability of free goods, see **www.epa.gov/jtr/comm/exchange** (the EPA's Materials and Waste Exchanges directory), **www.craigslist.org** (in the free section), and **http:// freecycle.org**]

Recycle Cars

Western European nations have generally been much more aggressive than the United States in demanding recycling. In 2000 the European Union approved new rules that require manufacturers to take back used cars for recycling with an expectation of 80 percent reuse and recycling by 2006. Studies indicate the recycling bill may reach $200 per car for collecting, transporting, dismantling, separating plastics and metals for recycling, and shredding the remainder.

Sources: "Green Light for End of Life Vehicles Directive" [**http://global.ihs.com/news/a4-2.html**] and "EU Wants Automakers to Recycle All Old Cars," *Ottawa Citizen,* July 30, 1999, p. C5.

Solid Waste Disposal Act

To attack the massive garbage problem, Congress approved the Solid Waste Disposal Act of 1965. The act, in brief, leaves solid waste problems to states and localities, but the federal government offers research and financial support.

Toxic Substances Control Act (TSCA)

In 1976 Congress approved the Toxic Substances Control Act (TSCA) to identify toxic chemicals, assess their risks, and control dangerous chemicals. Under the terms of the TSCA, the EPA requires the chemical industry to report any information it may have suggesting that a chemical poses a "substantial risk." The EPA is empowered to review and limit or stop the introduction of new chemicals. [For more on programs under TSCA, see **www.epa.gov/opptintr/index.html**]

Pollution in the Movies

Surprisingly, toxic pollution provided the central theme in two major Hollywood movies: *Erin Brockovich* and *A Civil Action*. The 2000 movie *Erin Brockovich* tells the story of a California community's battle against Pacific Gas & Electric for allegedly causing groundwater

'on resulting in extensive illness. [For more information about the movie, see **www
·ockovich.com**; for more on the pollutant at issue in the movie, see the National In-
.·tes of Health site, **www.niehs.nih.gov/centers/2001news/ctrnews9.html**] In the 1998
Disney movie *A Civil Action,* John Travolta plays a plaintiff's lawyer in a true story about
some middle-class families who sued two corporate giants, Beatrice Food and W. R. Grace &
Co., for allegedly polluting the groundwater in East Woburn, Massachusetts, where eight
children died of leukemia. [For more information about the movie from the corporate
perspective, see **http://www.civil-action.com**]

Question

Look back at the discussion of proving causation at the start of Part Two of this chapter.
Using the terminology from that discussion, describe the causation issues that had to be
addressed in the real-life counterparts to these movies.

Resource Conservation and Recovery Act (RCRA)

By 1976 the dangers of hazardous substances were becoming apparent to all, and Congress complemented the TSCA with the Resource Conservation and Recovery Act (RCRA).
The act addresses both solid and hazardous wastes. Its solid waste provisions are more supportive than punitive in tone and approach. The federal government is authorized, among
other strategies, to provide technical and financial assistance to states and localities; to prohibit future open dumping; and to establish cooperative federal, state, local, and private-
enterprise programs to recover energy and valuable materials from solid waste.

Subtitle C of the RCRA is designed to ensure the safe movement and disposal of hazardous wastes. The generator of the waste must determine if that waste is hazardous
under EPA guidelines and, if so, report the waste site and waste activities to the government. The waste generator must then create a manifest to be used in tracking the
waste from its creation to its disposal. Along the cradle-to-grave path of the waste, all
those with responsibility for it must sign the manifest and safely store and transport the
waste. Once the waste reaches a licensed disposal facility, the owner or manager of that
site signs the manifest and returns a copy of it to the generator.

Disposal Sites

Owners and operators of hazardous waste disposal sites must obtain government permits
to begin operation. Those sites must be operated according to EPA standards, and remedial action must be taken should hazardous wastes escape from the sites. [For more
information, see the EPA Web site at **www.epa.gov/epawaste/hazard/index.htm**]

Environmental justice is another issue that can come up in the siting of hazardous
waste disposal facilities. A 1987 study, "Toxic Wastes and Race in the United States,"
demonstrated a statistical link between race and income on the one hand and exposure
to levels of environmental and industrial risk on the other. A recent report has found the
same relationship exists today and that "the most potent predictor of where these facilities are sited is not how much income you have; it's race." For example, the new study
found that in Los Angeles 1.2 million people live less than two miles from a hazardous
waste facility, 1.1 million of whom are minorities.[43]

Question

Should environmental justice issues be a required component of the analysis that goes into an environmental impact statement under NEPA?

Superfund—Comprehensive Environmental Response, Compensation, and Liability Act of 1980 (CERCLA)

December 2005 marked the 25th anniversary of CERCLA, more commonly known as the Superfund, which is designed to help clean up hazardous dumps and spills. "Under CERCLA, the EPA may take actions to clean up a site from which hazardous substances have been released or where there is the threat of such a release. CERCLA also authorizes the federal government to order private parties to undertake the cleanup activities. The government and private parties who incur response costs cleaning up a site may seek recovery of those costs from liable parties."[44] Potentially responsible parties include present owners of the site as well as past owners who operated the site when the hazardous wastes were deposited; parent firms can be liable for actions of subsidiaries; and

> Any parties found to be responsible are strictly liable.

transferors (successive owners of businesses discharging hazardous wastes) are also liable. Any parties found to be responsible are strictly liable—that is, liability attaches without proof of either intent or negligence.

Cleanup tends to be very expensive and generally requires considerable time to accomplish. The first listed Superfund site, Love Canal in Niagara Falls, New York, was finally clean enough to be delisted in 2004.[45] Originally the government began the Superfund by creating a trust fund from taxes on chemicals and petroleum; but that taxing authority lapsed in 1995, and subsequently the Superfund program has been running on annual appropriations and reserve funds.

How Does Your Community Compare?

What do you know about the pollution in your community? Find out by logging onto **www.scorecard.org** and inserting your zip code.

Questions
1. Do you have any Superfund sites in your community?
2. How does your home rate with regard to the industrial release of toxic chemicals?
3. How does your air quality stack up with other communities in the United States?
4. How clean are your rivers and lakes?

Small Business Liability Relief and Brownfields Revitalization Act

There has been considerable dissatisfaction over CERCLA for many years for a number of reasons, including the percentage of Superfund dollars that have gone to administration expenses and litigation. Another complaint was that so-called *brownfields* (less contaminated former industrial and commercial sites that are not on the Superfund priority list) were covered by the successor–owner liability provisions of CERCLA, creating a disincentive for any developers to take them over and reestablish them as productive property. This complaint was largely addressed by the passage of the Small Business Liability Relief and Brownfields Revitalization Act (Brownfields Act), which President Bush signed into law on January 11, 2002. This law provides liability protection for prospective purchasers and contiguous property owners and authorizes increased funding for state and local programs that assess and clean up brownfields. [For more on brownfields, see **www.epa.gov/swerosps/bf/about.htm**]

PRACTICING ETHICS   Environmentally Aware Decision Making

You've just been hired as the business manager for a chain of restaurants in your state. During the interview process you were told that part of your responsibilities would be to develop more environmentally friendly practices to be implemented at all 10 locations, while making sure that the changes overall either have a neutral or a positive impact on the business' bottom line. A local business school professor is interested in having her students do semester projects on the feasibility of various green projects for local businesses. Develop a list of possible practices your restaurants could implement to share with the professor for further development by her students.

Part Three—Penalties and Enforcement under Federal Law

Civil/Criminal Actions

Because of the risks associated with pollution, environmental protection agencies have been given strong enforcement authority. Often violators initially are warned and a compliance schedule is set out. If corrective action is not forthcoming, sterner measures follow, including an administrative order to comply. Where problems persist or the difficulties are more serious, the government may initiate civil or criminal actions against both firms and managers. Penalties vary with the act in question, but civil and criminal fines are provided for. Individuals may be jailed for one year or more. In some instances, an entire operation may be shut down.

Fines have long been the standard remedy in governmental pollution enforcement, but in recent years both federal and state regulators have increasingly turned to Supplemental Environmental Projects (SEPs) to settle wrongs.[46] Normally, the SEP will involve some environmental "good work" in place of a fine, such as 11 Los Angeles–area corporations, accused of polluting the drinking supply of the San Gabriel Valley, agreeing to pay $85 million for the construction of a water treatment plant to remove dangerous chemicals from the aquifer running beneath the valley floor.[47] [For more on SEPs, see **www.epa.gov/compliance/civil/seps/**]

Our environmental laws are at times enforced with criminal suits against corporate officers. "The EPA employs more than 200 criminal investigators and works closely with 36 environmental prosecutors at the Justice Department. In 2001 alone, the EPA obtained

> The owner of a chemical reprocessing plant received a 17-year sentence.

prison sentences totaling 256 years." In one of the most publicized cases, the owner of a chemical reprocessing plant received a 17-year sentence for "disposing of hazardous waste without a permit, knowing that his actions placed others in imminent danger of death or serious bodily injury."[48] A 20-year-old employee of the facility was overcome by cyanide gas while cleaning sludge from the bottom of a 25,000 gallon tank. As a consequence of his exposure, he has been left in a Parkinson's-like condition, able to speak only with great difficulty and he struggles with even the simplest physical tasks, such as brushing his teeth.[49] However, according to Justice Department and EPA data, "criminal cases against polluters . . . dropped off sharply during the Bush administration, with the number of prosecutions, new investigations and total convictions all down by more than a third."[50]

Question

Are prison sentences for officers of corporate polluters a good idea or not? Explain.

Additional Enforcement Mechanisms

Many environmental statutes require companies to monitor their own environmental performance and report that information, including violations, to the government. Government agencies generally have broad authority to conduct environmental inspections of both plants and records as necessary, although they must obtain search warrants if criminal prosecutions are anticipated. Finally, many environmental statutes allow *citizen suits,* wherein an individual is empowered to challenge government environmental decisions, such as the granting of a permit, and generally to demand both governmental and private-sector compliance with the law. *Massachusetts v. EPA,* the Clean Air Act case set out above, was brought by a group of states, local governments and private organizations as a citizen suit.

In the case that follows, a citizens' group brought suit seeking to have the Cook Inlet beluga whale listed as endangered under the Endangered Species Act.

LEGAL BRIEFCASE

Cook Inlet Beluga Whale v. Daley   156 F. Supp. 2d 16 (D.C.D.C. 2001)

Judge James Robertson

This Administrative Procedure Act (APA) case presents a challenge to the decision of the Secretary of Commerce and the National Marine Fisheries Service (NMFS) to list the Cook Inlet (CI) Beluga Whale as "depleted" under the Marine Mammal Protection Act, but not as "endangered" or "threatened" under the Endangered Species Act (ESA). The Secretary determined that the recent Beluga Whale population decrease, which everyone agrees is attributable almost exclusively to over-hunting, can be arrested using the statutory protection afforded "depleted" marine mammal species and a legislative moratorium on Native American takings. Because the plaintiffs have not sustained their burden of showing that that determination was "arbitrary, capricious, an abuse of discretion, or otherwise not in accordance with law," summary judgment will be entered in favor of the government.

FACTUAL AND PROCEDURAL BACKGROUND

The Cook Inlet Beluga Whale (Delphinapterus leucas) is a genetically distinct, geographically isolated marine mammal with a remnant population that inhabits Cook Inlet from late April or early May until October or November. NMFS estimates that in the mid-1980s, between 1,000 and 1,300 whales inhabited the inlet. Today, the population is estimated at between 300 and 400 whales. It is not disputed that the single most significant factor in the population decline has been Native American hunting: NMFS estimates that between 1995 and 1997 the Native American subsistence harvest averaged 77 whales per year. That is why, in March 1999, the plaintiffs filed a petition to list the Cook Inlet Beluga Whale under the Endangered Species Act (ESA).[1]

The Endangered Species Act delegates to the Secretary of Commerce the authority to determine whether fish, wildlife, or plant species should be listed as endangered or threatened. A species is "endangered" when it is in "danger of extinction throughout all or a significant part of its range," and it is "threatened" when it is "likely to become an endangered species within the foreseeable future."16 U.S.C. §§ 1532(6), (20), 1533(c). The Secretary's ESA determination is made on the basis of five statutorily prescribed factors, any one of which is sufficient to support a listing determination. 16 U.S.C. 1533(a)(1).

Within 30 days of plaintiffs' request for an ESA listing, the NMFS published formal notice that action under the ESA "may be warranted." That notice triggered a one-year status review period. On October 19, 1999, the NMFS published a proposed rule, not under the ESA, but under the Marine Mammal Protection Act (MMPA), to list the whale as "depleted." (The final rule was issued May 31, 2000.) Under the MMPA, 16 U.S.C. § 1362, the Secretary can designate a species as "depleted" if the species is listed as endangered or threatened under the ESA or if the Secretary determines that the stock is below its Optimum Sustainable Population. Once a marine mammal has been listed as "depleted," the Secretary is authorized to promulgate regulations limiting takings by Native Americans, but a listing under the MMPA does not have the regulatory, economic, and environmental fallout of a listing as "threatened" or "endangered" under the ESA.

On June 22, 2000, the NMFS determined that an ESA listing was "not warranted." It is that determination which, in plaintiffs' submission, was "arbitrary, capricious, an abuse of discretion, or otherwise not in accordance with law."

ARGUMENT

"In exercising its narrowly defined duty under the APA, the Court must consider whether the agency acted within the scope of its legal authority, adequately explained its decision, based its decision on facts in the record, and considered the relevant factors." *National Park and Conservation Ass'n v. Stanton,* 54 F. Supp. 2d 7, 11 (D.D.C. 1999). Plaintiffs argue that the agency decision in this case improperly applied the law and facts to the five-factor determination; failed to apply the best scientific and commercial data available; and improperly considered political and economic factors.

I. Statutory Factors

A decision whether or not to list a species shall be made "solely on the basis of the best scientific and commercial data available . . . after conducting a review of the status of the species and after taking into account those efforts, if any, being made by any State or foreign nation." 16 U.S.C. § 1533(b). Applying this standard, the Secretary must list a species as endangered or threatened if "any of § 1533(a)(1)'s five factors are sufficiently implicated." *Southwest Center for Biological Diversity v. Babbitt,* 215 F.3d 58, 60 (D.C. Cir. 2000). Each of the five factors is considered below.

(A) The Present or Threatened Destruction, Modification, or Curtailment of the Species' Habitat or Range   The agency's conclusion that "no indication exists that the range has been, or is threatened with being modified or curtailed to an extent that appreciably diminishes the value of the habitat for both survival and recovery of the species," was not arbitrary or capricious. There is no dispute that the Cook Inlet, the whale's habitat, has changed over time in response to the increasing demand of municipal, industrial, and recreational activities, but there is no record basis for concluding that these changes have had a deleterious effect on the whale. Plaintiffs can point only to the fact that the whales have increasingly inhabited the upper inlet in recent

---

[1]The naming of the Cook Inlet Beluga Whale itself as a plaintiff is acknowledged by the Court as a beau geste, but it has no legal significance.

decades. The agency concedes that this change in whale behavior might be in response to human activities, but no data suggest that the change threatens extinction. The agency is not required to conduct further testing to determine the effect of various environmental factors, such as oil drilling, on the whale population. "The 'best available data' requirement makes it clear that the Secretary has no obligation to conduct independent studies." *Southwest Center for Biological Diversity,* 215 F.3d at 60.

(B) Overutilization   All agree that Native American harvesting has been the most significant factor in the declining whale population. The agency has found "that a failure to restrict the subsistence harvest would likely cause CI beluga whales to become in danger of extinction in the foreseeable future." But the agency has also concluded that "overutilization" does not support ESA listing because it has been stopped—by designating the whale as "depleted" under the MMPA. Plaintiffs attack that conclusion as unreasonable.

If the moratorium fails to control Native American harvesting in the future, ESA listing will be warranted. That much is agreed. But plaintiffs have been unable to point to anything in the record indicating that the current whale population is unsustainable if the harvest is indeed restricted successfully. . . .

Plaintiffs argue that harvesting will still occur even after the MMPA "depleted" listing because some hunting will be permitted under co-management agreements between the agency and Native American organizations and some hunting will occur illegally. Proposed regulations governing co-management agreements, however, limit Native American hunts to two strikes annually, and there is no reason to believe that the MMPA's enforcement mechanisms, which are identical to those of the ESA, will be less effective in controlling illegal takings. Plaintiffs' concerns are reasonable, and enforcement should be carefully monitored, but the record contains support for the agency's conclusion that future takings will be minimal and that the current population is sustainable.

(C) Disease or Predation   The agency concedes that both disease or predation "occur in the CI beluga population and may affect reproduction and survival," but it has concluded that these factors are not causing the stock to be threatened or endangered. Plaintiff has not shown that conclusion to be arbitrary or capricious. . . .

(D) Inadequacy of Existing Regulatory Mechanisms   We have found nothing in the record, and plaintiff has identified nothing,

showing that there are inadequacies in existing regulatory mechanisms or, if there were, what the effects of such inadequacies would be. Plaintiffs argue that the MMPA is inadequate to ensure that illegal hunting does not occur and to adequately protect Cook Inlet from damaging development activities, but that argument simply asserts plaintiffs' policy preference for a remedy under the ESA and begs the question of whether ESA listing is required.

(E) Other Natural or Manmade Factors Affecting Its Continued Existence   Plaintiffs argue that there are many other factors—strandings, oil spills, takings through commercial fishing, effects of pollutants, ship strikes, noise, urban runoff, etc.—that put the species at risk and that it was arbitrary and capricious for the agency to determine that "the best available information . . . indicates that these activities, alone or cumulatively, have not caused the stock to be in danger of extinction and are not likely to do so in the foreseeable future." They point to a snippet in the record indicating that "other factors could be contributing to the decline," AR-D545, at P 5, and argue that the agency failed to adequately consider the cumulative effects of all of the potential factors combined with the small population size of the Cook Inlet Beluga Whale.

It is true that the absence of "conclusive evidence" of a real threat to a species does not justify an agency's finding that ESA listing is not warranted. *Defenders of Wildlife,* 958 F. Supp. at 679. But neither is listing required simply because the agency is unable to rule out factors that could contribute to a population decline. It was not arbitrary or capricious for the agency to place its principal reliance on the cessation of Native American hunts and the Breiwick and DeMaster conclusion that the Cook Inlet Beluga Whale population could sustain itself, even accounting for stochastic events.

[Plaintiffs' remaining arguments have been omitted.]

Ordered that defendant's motion for summary judgment is granted.

Further ordered that plaintiffs' motion for summary judgment is denied.

Questions

1. Why did the plaintiffs want this beluga whale listed as endangered under the Endangered Species Act?

2. What was the standard of review that the court applied to the agency's decision?

3. What five factors are to be considered in the listing of a species as endangered under the Endangered Species Act?

Endangered Species Act

The *Cook Inlet* decision and the Endangered Species Act (ESA) are at the heart of some of the most interesting and poignant disputes of the long struggle between environmentalists and business. Should we save the grizzly bear, nine populations of Pacific Northwest salmon, the Delhi Sands flower-loving fly? Each is among the nearly 1,200 species officially protected by the Endangered Species Act. During the writing of this chapter, the polar bear became listed as a threatened species, specifically because of the impact of global warming on the Arctic sea ice.[51]

> Should we save the grizzly bear?

Most Americans don't want to lose those creatures, but as usual the question is who pays? As written, the ESA effectively forces landowners to bear the cost because the ESA forbids any practice, such as cutting trees, that results in the "taking" of any creature that is part of an endangered species. The ESA also forbids the degradation of the habitat of those species. As a result, affected communities face a dramatic decline in the economic use of property: no building, no logging, and no pesticides, for example.

Salmon or Jobs?

A general scientific consensus has emerged that four lower Snake River dams have played a major role in the well-documented decline of the salmon population in the Pacific Northwest.[52] Five percent of the region's hydroelectric power comes from the dams. Farmers depend on the dams for irrigation water and for shipping their grain and fruit to market. Ralph Broetje's 4,000-acre apple and cherry orchard in eastern Washington, for example, employs 700 people full time and 600 part time.[53] Without concerted action, either to mitigate the impact of the dams or remove them, extinction of the salmon by 2017 is forecast.[54] The Clinton administration developed the 2000 Federal Salmon Plan, which enumerated 199 actions to be taken to restore salmon populations, but also acknowledged that removing the dams would be the most effective method of restoration (although a method of last resort). A coalition led by the National Wildlife Federation, however, sued the government on the grounds that the 2000 plan was based on too many uncertainties and was therefore insufficient to protect the salmon. A federal judge agreed and ordered the plan rewritten.[55] When the Bush administration published its revision in 2004, environmentalists and conservationists protested, among other things, that instead of a plan to restore salmon populations, it was only a plan to prevent further reduction. This second plan was again challenged in court; the federal district court again ruled that the plan was flawed and ordered it rewritten for the third time; the government appealed and lost before the Ninth Circuit in early 2007. Once again, the government was ordered to rewrite the plan, which was released as this chapter was being written. Although it is too soon to predict what will occur next, those concerned with salmon preservation are no happier with this plan than with the preceding plans and are urging Congress to intervene.[56] The clock of extinction is still ticking. [To read the latest plan, see **www.nwr.noaa.gov/ Salmon-Hydropower/Columbia-Snake-Basin/final-BOs.cfm**; for more information from a salmon preservation point of view, see **www.salmonrecovery.gov** and **www .wildsalmon.org**]

Question

Reducing the use of lawn chemicals and retarding development near waterways would help save endangered salmon. To save those salmon, should we limit citizens' rights to live as they see fit and as they can afford to live? Explain.

State and Local Regulation

Under many of the federal environmental laws, the states have a substantial role to play, particularly in developing local plans to meet federal standards. But federal law permits state enforcement under statutes such as the Clean Water Act only if that enforcement equals federal standards. This point was reinforced by the 2004 Supreme Court ruling in *Alaska Dept. of Environmental Conservation v. EPA,*[57] in which the Court upheld an EPA order directing Alaska to withhold permits for the expansion of a zinc mine, which the state had approved. The EPA had determined the expansion would violate the Clean Air Act because it did not require the use of best available technology to limit air pollution.

In addition to their powers and obligations under federal environmental laws, state and local governments have the right to impose various controls on citizens to protect and maintain public health, safety, and general welfare. In constitutional law, these powers are referred to as a state's *police power.*

State and local governments have become increasingly aggressive in pursuing environmental concerns, particularly with respect to carbon dioxide and other greenhouse gas emissions in light of global warming concerns. Viewing the federal government as having seriously failed in its leadership role, states and even more local governments are attempting to fill the void. To give a few examples, a consortium of northeast states is planning to hold the nation's first auction of greenhouse gas emission permits in 2008[58] as part of their joint agreement to stabilize emissions at 2002–04 levels by 2015 and then reduce those levels another 10 percent by 2020. On another front, California is leading an effort that includes 16 other states to set state standards for carbon dioxide emissions from new automobiles. California has routinely been granted waivers by the EPA from the Clean Air Act to set more stringent standards than the federal standards with regard to other auto emissions, after which other states are allowed to piggyback on California's waiver. California established state standards for carbon dioxide in 2004 and then sought a waiver from the EPA. After delaying the ruling for years, at the end of 2007 the EPA denied California's request. California intends to go to court to contest the decision.[59] In another arena, at least 22 states have set standards for utility companies on the percentage of energy that must come from renewable sources by 2020. In October 2007, Kansas became the first government in the United States to refuse a permit for a proposed coal-fired electricity generating plant on the basis of carbon dioxide emissions.[60]

Another joint initiative was started by Seattle's mayor in 2005. Over 500 mayors have now joined the U.S. Mayors Climate Protection Agreement by pledging to have their cities meet the Kyoto Protocol's standard of cutting greenhouse gas emissions by 7 percent below 1990 levels by 2012. The approaches cities are taking to accomplish this goal are quite varied; in Austin, Texas, by 2015 all new single family homes must use 60 percent less energy than today's standards; Boulder, Colorado has imposed the first "carbon tax" on electric bills to encourage more efficient power use and fund a switch to alternative fuels; Chicago is distributing compact fluorescent light bulbs and encouraging the creation of rooftop gardens, which can cut summer rooftop temperatures in half from as high as 160 degrees and help keep the buildings cooler; Denver plans to plant an average of 140 trees a day for the next 20 years; Fargo, North Dakota is selling methane produced at its landfill to run the boilers of a soybean processing plant; New York City has ordered the city's 13,000 yellow cabs to go green within five years; in Portland, Oregon the water flowing through the city's drinking system is being used to generate hydroelectricity.[61] The Mayors are partnering with the American Institute of Architects to reach a goal by 2010 to halve the fossil fuels used to construct and operate both commercial and residential buildings. The energy used to heat, cool and light buildings, and in the construction phase, generates more greenhouse gas emissions than either the transportation or industrial sectors.[62] [For more on the Mayors Agreement, see **www.coolmayors.org**]

Part Four—Common Law Remedies

Long before the federal government became actively involved in environmental issues, courts were grappling with the problem. As early as the 1500s, city officials were ordered by a court to keep the streets clean of dung deposited by swine allowed to run loose; the air was said to be "corrupted and infected" by this practice. Legal arguments have typically revolved around the extent of a person's right to use and enjoy private property if such usage causes harm to a neighbor's property or the use of public property. More recently, tort actions of negligence and strict liability have been pursued by injured individuals. Successful plaintiffs may recover monetary damages for the harm suffered or obtain an injunction to prevent similar conduct (and therefore harm) by the defendant in the future, or both.

Nuisance   A *private nuisance* is a substantial and unreasonable invasion of the private use and enjoyment of one's land; a *public nuisance* is an unreasonable interference with a right common to the public. Harmful conduct may be both a public and private nuisance simultaneously; the case law distinctions between the two are often blurred. A classic nuisance dispute is a 1970 New York case, *Boomer v. Atlantic Cement Co.*[63] Neighboring landowners sued the operator of a cement plant for injury to their properties from the plant's dirt, smoke, and vibration. The court recognized the wrong done and ordered the operator to pay damages. In a more recent Rhode Island case, the state sued various manufacturers of lead paint, under a public nuisance theory as well as several other theories, for injuries to itself (medical costs) and to its lead-poisoned residents. The trial resulted in a hung jury.[64]

Trespass   A *trespass* occurs and liability is imposed with any *intentional* invasion of an individual's right to the exclusive use of his or her own property. For example, in a 1959 Oregon case, *Martin v. Reynolds Metals Co.*, the plaintiffs successfully sued in trespass for damages caused by the operation of an aluminum reduction plant, which caused certain fluoride compounds in the form of gases and particulates to become airborne, settle on the plaintiffs' land, contaminate their forage and water, and poison their cattle.[65]

Negligence   The elements of a negligence case have been previously discussed in Chapter 7. In the environmental area, a negligence claim may be based on such occurrences as carelessly fouling a neighbor's water, flooding another's land, or causing damage through the emission of excessive noise, smell, or particulate matter. A claim might also be based on the failure to correct a pollution problem where the necessary technology and resources were available to do so, where the defendant owed a duty to the harmed individual. Particularly troubling cases arise where a plaintiff claims injury from a toxic substance manufactured or otherwise supplied by defendant. Plaintiffs may have significant problems establishing *causation*. For example, does smoking cause lung cancer? Did the use of DES by pregnant women cause birth defects? Does DES cause infertility in daughters born to mothers who took DES during their pregnancy?

Strict Liability   Certain activities, such as the use of toxic chemicals, may be seen as so abnormally dangerous as to give rise to a strict liability claim (previously discussed in Chapter 7). In an environmental law context, strict liability has been considered in circumstances in which crop dusting contaminated adjacent properties,[66] poisonous gases used for fumigation spread,[67] toxic chemicals were improperly disposed of,[68] and oil contaminated a nearby water well.[69]

Several of these causes of action can sometimes be triggered by the same set of facts. In an interesting 2007 case in West Virginia, a jury found DuPont was negligent in its use of a 112-acre site that for 90 years had been a zinc-smelting plant. The jury also ruled that DuPont had created both a public and a private nuisance, had committed trespass, and should be held strictly liable for exposing local residents to various toxic substances. Residents and property owners had sued, claiming that the company had deliberately dumped toxic heavy metals, particularly zinc, on the site. The medical problems caused by such toxins include cancer, damage to internal organs, and decreased fertility.[70]

Part Five—Global Warming

Without question, the most debated environmental issue has been global warming. The phenomenon at issue is the projected overall increase in surface temperatures around the globe caused by the release of manmade carbon dioxide and other greenhouse gases into the atmosphere, largely through the burning of fossil fuels, especially in gasoline engines and coal-fired plants. Both the politics and the science of global warming have been controversial—a particularly potent example of the issues of coincidence, correlation, and causation discussed at the beginning of Part Two. The 2007 United Nations report on climate change seems to have all but ended the scientific dispute, but the political debate continues. The report concluded that global warming is unequivocal and that it is very likely (meaning 90 percent) due primarily to manmade greenhouse gas emissions. It found that the probability that the observed warming is only a natural phenomenon is less than 5 percent. [For a copy of the final Synthesis Report, see **www.ipcc.ch/ipccreports/ ar4-syr.htm**]

The governments of the world, realizing that global action is required to have any significant impact on overall emissions, adopted the Kyoto Protocol on December 11, 1997.

Specifically, the protocol calls for a 5 percent reduction from 1990 levels of greenhouse gas emissions to be achieved by 2012. The protocol became binding when countries accounting for at least 55 percent of total emissions ratified, which occurred with Russia's ratification in late 2004. The United States is not among the 180 ratifying countries, President Bush having announced in March 2001 that the protocol was "fatally flawed." [For additional information about the protocol, see the official Web site for the United Nations Framework convention on Climate Change at **http:// unfccc.int/essential_background/kyoto_protocol/items/2830.php**]

> President Bush announced in March 2001 that the protocol was "fatally flawed"

The Kyoto Protocol uses market incentives to achieve emission reductions. It permits industrialized countries, and the companies in them, to "generate credits toward their quotas by bankrolling projects that reduce emissions. . . . The theory is that because global warming is global, the atmosphere doesn't care whether emissions occur in, say, Germany or China. For a German company . . . financing an emissions reduction project in China is likely to be a lot cheaper than doing so at home, because in Germany, the cheap emissions improvements already have been made."[71]

The Kyoto Protocol has long been recognized as only the first step in the development of a global emission reduction program to stabilize greenhouse gases. Formal discussions for a post-Kyoto international framework began in Bali, Indonesia in December 2007. They are expected to last through 2009, at least partially, it seems, to provide a year of negotiations after the Bush administration leaves the White House. Thus far, the United States has prevented specific emissions targets from being included in the plan, but did finally agree to the funding by developed nations of clean technology for developing nations. In turn, developing nations have agreed to take as yet unspecified actions to mitigate global warming.[72]

What's Your Carbon Footprint?

One indication of how much global warming has become a grassroots issue in the United States is the entry of carbon footprint considerations into everyday conversation. A carbon footprint is a measurement of how much carbon dioxide is emitted into the atmosphere as the result of a particular product, activity or lifestyle. It is a way to measure the carbon "cost" of a particular activity or the carbon "savings" of changing that activity.

Question
What's your carbon footprint? Find out from **www.bp.com/extendedsectiongenericarticle .do?categoryId=9006010&contentId=7012265**. Compare that with your ecological footprint—that is, how many earths we would have to have if everyone lived as you do. Go to **www.earthday.net/Footprint/index.asp**

Going Green

Apart from governmental responses, a widespread acceptance of the necessity to control greenhouse gases has spawned many individual and corporate initiatives. (State and local government initiatives are discussed above in Part Three.) In some cases the corporate impetus to act may be a belief that voluntary action now may minimize the cost of required action in the future.[73] In other cases, a consensus that manmade emissions are contributing to the warming of the planet may cause corporate boards to seriously evaluate potential costs and risks to their companies, both from global warming itself and from their responses to it.[74] Some examples of corporate initiatives include DuPont, which made its first commitment to cutting its greenhouse gas emissions in 1994. It met its initial goal and set another—a 65 percent reduction in its 1990 levels by 2010—which it had achieved by 2006, despite a 30 percent higher production level. Its actions actually saved it more than $2 billion.[75] Wal-Mart, which owns one of the largest truck fleets in the United States, set a two-year goal to make its trucking operations 25 percent more efficient, with a longer term 50 percent goal over ten years.[76] Waste Management is capturing landfill gases for residential electricity generation.[77] And Frito-Lay has started a "net zero" project to take its Casa Grande, Arizona factory off the power grid, running it almost entirely on renewable fuels and recycled water. The project to convert the plant, which is larger than two football fields, is to be completed by 2010.[78]

PRACTICING ETHICS ⟩ Voluntarily Reduce Greenhouse Gas Emissions?

In spite of the nonparticipation of the United States in the Kyoto Protocol, many U.S. multinationals will come under its provisions because of their operations in ratifying countries. Other U.S. businesses, however, are voluntarily developing emission reduction strategies.

Question

Imagine that you are a vice president of a corporation that burns significant fossil fuels in the production process but operates solely in the United States. What stance would you take on global warming? Why?

Internet Exercise

Using the EPA's "Superfund Reforms" Web page [**www.epa.gov/oerrpage/superfund/programs/reforms/faqs.htm**], answer the following questions:

1. How have the Superfund reforms changed the Superfund program?
2. Which reforms, if any, have not been successful, and why?

Chapter Questions

1. Economist B. Peter Pashigian:

   It is widely thought that environmental controls are guided by the public-spirited ideal of correcting for "negative externalities"—the pollution costs that spill over from private operations. This view is not wrong by any means. But it is suspiciously incomplete.

   After all, there are numerous studies of regulatory programs in other fields that show how private interests have used public powers for their own enrichment.[79]

   In addition to correcting negative externalities, what forces might be influencing federal pollution control?

2. How might the government's ever-increasing environmental regulations, along with the public's call for a new environmental consciousness, favor big business interests over those of small business owners?

3. "The Aral Sea is going, gone. Once the world's fourth largest inland body of water, the Aral has shriveled to half its former area and a third of its volume. As for the region's drinking water, even the local vodka has a salty tang."[80] The Aral is the victim of the former Soviet Union's central planners, who decreed that the area would be the nation's main source of cotton. To achieve that goal, intense irrigation was required, with the result that only a trickle of fresh water was left to feed the Aral. Refilling the Aral would require tremendous dislocations in the agriculture of the vast region. If you were a member of a commission charged with developing a plan for the future of the Aral Sea, what issues would you cover?

4. Professor and business ethics scholar Norman Bowie:

> Environmentalists frequently argue that business has special obligations to protect the environment. Although I agree with the environmentalists on this point, I do not agree with them as to where the obligations lie. Business does not have an obligation to protect the environment over and above what is required by law; however, business does have a moral obligation to avoid intervening in the political arena in order to defeat or weaken environmental legislation.[81]

   a. Explain Professor Bowie's reasoning.

   b. Do you agree with him? Explain.

5. A 2002 report from the EPA concludes that we have not realized the benefits from the 1990 amendments to the Clean Air Act because it is not being enforced effectively. For example, by July 2001 "only 63 percent of the 19,025 major sources of industrial pollution in the United States had obtained permits, although the law imposed a deadline of 1997." The report further noted that several states "lacked sufficient resources to run the program and . . . many states had difficulties getting EPA guidance on how the agency's regulations should be applied to a specific polluter."[82] Instead of passing additional clean air standards, should we simply vigorously enforce the standards already on the books?

6. Mexico is quickly running short of water.

> 85 percent of Mexico's economic growth and 75 percent of its 100 million people are in the north, and the water is far to the south. . . . [P]oliticians facing elections are reluctant to ask voters to spend more on any utility, let alone water. Agriculture uses 80 percent of the water and pays nothing, although it only ranks seventh in contribution to the gross national product. . . . Less than half of the capital's wastewater is treated. The rest sinks into underground lakes or flows toward the Gulf of Mexico, turning rivers into sewers. . . . Well over half of irrigation water is lost to evaporation or seepage."[83]

Brainstorm as many possible contributions to the solution of Mexico's water problem as you can.

7. Due to the spread of the West Nile virus in the state of New York, an insecticide spraying program was implemented to control the mosquitoes responsible for its

spread. Several groups sued, arguing that the spray was a pollutant that damaged waters in violation of the Clean Water Act. What criteria should the court use to decide the outcome? See *No Spray Coalition, Inc. v. The City of New York,* 2000 U.S. Dist. LEXIS 13919, 51 ERC (BNA) 1508 (S.D.N.Y. 2000).

8. Ott Chemical Co. polluted the ground at its Michigan plant. CPC International created a wholly owned subsidiary to buy Ott, which was accomplished in 1965. CPC retained the original Ott managers. Pollution continued through 1972 when CPC sold Ott. In 1981 the U.S. EPA began a cleanup of the site. To recover some of the tens of millions in cleanup costs, the EPA sued CPC (now called Bestfoods) among other potentially responsible parties. The Superfund law places responsibility on anyone who "owned or operated" a property when pollution was deposited. The district court held that CPC was liable because of its active participation in Ott's business and its control of Ott's decisions in that it selected the Ott board of directors and placed some CPC managers as executives at Ott.

   a. Do you think CPC should be held liable? Why or why not?

   b. What test would you employ to determine whether a parent corporation should be liable for a subsidiary's pollution? See *United States v. Bestfoods,* 524 U.S. 51 (1998).

9. William Tucker:

   > [Environmentalism is] essentially aristocratic in its roots and derives from the land and nature-based ethic that has been championed by upper classes throughout history. Large landowners and titled aristocracies . . . have usually held a set of ideals that stresses "stewardship" and the husbanding of existing resources over exploration and discovery. This view favors handicrafts over mass production and the inheritance ethic over the business ethic.[84]

   Tucker went on to argue that environmentalism favors the economic and social interests of the well-off. He said people of the upper middle class see their future in universities and the government bureaucracy, with little economic stake in industrial expansion. Indeed, such expansion might threaten their suburban property values. Comment.

10. Americans' commitment to the car obviously raises serious environmental problems. The vast parking areas required to house those cars are themselves a significant environmental hazard. Explain some of the environmental problems created or encouraged by parking lots.

11. The Endangered Species Act provides that all federal agency actions are to be designed so that they do not jeopardize endangered or threatened species. The act had been interpreted to reach to federal agency work or funding in foreign countries, but the federal government changed that interpretation in 1986 to limit the act's reach to the United States and the high seas. A group labeled Defenders of Wildlife filed suit, seeking to reinstate the original interpretation. The case reached the U.S. Supreme Court, where Justice Scalia wrote that Defenders of Wildlife would have to submit evidence showing that at least one of its members would be "directly" affected by the interpretation. In response, one member of Defenders of Wildlife wrote that she had visited Egypt and observed the endangered Nile crocodile and

hoped to return to do so again but feared that U.S. aid for the Aswan High Dam would harm the crocodiles.

a. Why did Scalia call for that evidence?

b. Do you think Defenders of Wildlife should be permitted to sue? Why or why not? See *Lujan v. Defenders of Wildlife*, 112 S.Ct. 2130 (1992).

12. Economist Robert Crandall:

> [O]ur best chances for regulatory reform in certain environmental areas, particularly in air pollution policy, come from the states. Probably, responsibility for environmental regulation belongs with the states anyway, and most of it ought to be returned there.[85]

a. What reasoning supports Crandall's notion that responsibility for environmental regulation belongs with the states?

b. How might one reason to the contrary?

c. If the power were yours, would environmental regulation rest primarily at the state, federal, or international level? Explain.

13. Prior to the days of more than $3 per gallon gas, the United States seemed to be quite enamored with sport utility vehicles (SUVs), in spite of the fact that their gas mileage is considerably poorer than most sedans. To graphically bring home the environmental irresponsibility of SUV owners, two men in the San Francisco Bay area dreamed up a scheme to address what they perceived as a market failure. Uninvited, on hundreds of SUVs they have stuck homemade bumper stickers that read, "I'm changing the environment! Ask me how!"[86]

a. What effect do you think these self-appointed environmental police want from their actions?

b. What effect do you think they are likely to actually have?

14. Airplanes are a significant contributor to greenhouse gases. Comment on the following proposal: Each person receives an annual allowance for flights, fuel, gas and electricity. If a person's use exceeds the allowance, he will have to purchase "carbon points" from someone under their limit.[87]

Notes

1. "Satellite Findings Reveal Massive Global Pollution," *Waterloo/Cedar Falls Courier,* May 31, 2001, p. A5.

2. Andrew C. Revkin, "Arctic Melt Unnerves the Experts," *New York Times,* October 2, 2007.

3. Nicholas D. Kristof, "The Big Melt," *New York Times,* August 16, 2007.

4. John Roach, "Gulf of Mexico 'Dead Zone' Is Size of New Jersey," *National Geographic News,* May 25, 2005.

5. "Ocean 'Dead Zones' Top Environmental Problem," *Waterloo/Cedar Falls Courier,* March 29, 2004, p. A4.

6. Mark Magnier, "UN Report Raises Pressure on China to Cut Pollution," *Los Angeles Times,* April 8, 2007.

7. Jim Yardley, "Beneath Booming Cities, China's Future Is Drying Up," *New York Times,* September 28, 2007.

8. Jane Spencer, "China Pays Steep Price as Textile Exports Boom," *The Wall Street Journal,* August 22, 2007, p. A1.

9. Joseph Kahn and Jim Yardley, "As China Roars, Pollution Reaches Deadly Extremes," *New York Times,* August 26, 2007.

10. Shai Oster, "It May Be Too Late for China to Save The Yangtze Goddess," *The Wall Street Journal,* December 6, 2006.

11. Kahn and Yardley, "As China Roars, Pollution Reaches Deadly Extremes."

12. Mark Magnier, "UN Report Raises Pressure on China to Cut Pollution."

13. Kahn and Yardley, "As China Roars, Pollution Reaches Deadly Extremes."

14. Robert Lee Hotz, "Huge Dust Plumes from China Cause Changes in Climate," *The Wall Street Journal,* July 20, 2007, p. B1.

15. Mark Magnier, "UN Report Raises Pressure on China to Cut Pollution."

16. Wilfred Beckerman, cited in Robert Solomon, *The New World of Business* (Lanham, MD: Rowman & Littlefield, 1994), p. 319.

17. Susan Lee, "How Much Is the Right to Pollute Worth?" *The Wall Street Journal,* August 1, 2001, p. A15.

18. Mark Golden, "Dirty Dealings," *The Wall Street Journal,* September 13, 1999, p. R13.

19. John Fialka, "EPA Plans to Offer Incentives to Curb 'Sprawl' Pollution," *The Wall Street Journal,* October 18, 2000, p. A4.

20. "Europe Gains on U.S. as Best for Renewable Energy Invest-Report," *The Wall Street Journal,* March 19, 2008.

21. "Review and Outlook: A Fish Story," *The Wall Street Journal,* November 6, 2003, p. A14.

22. Elisabeth Rosenthal, "Motivated by a Tax, Irish Spurn Plastic Bags," *New York Times,* February 2, 2008.

23. Jon J. Fialka and Jeffrey Ball, "Companies Get Ready for Greenhouse-Gas Limits," *The Wall Street Journal,* October 26, 2004, p. A2.

24. Michael V. Russo and Paul A. Fouts, "A Resource-Based Perspective on Corporate Environmental Performance and Profitability," *Academy of Management Journal* 40, no. 3 (1997), p. 534.

25. Bill Leonard, "Someday We'll Regret Damage to Our Planet," *Des Moines Register,* September 20, 2004, p. 7A.

26. Eric Pianin, "Environmental Rules Worth Their Cost, Study Says," *Des Moines Register,* September 28, 2003, p. 3A.

27. *The Baltimore Sun,* "Predicting the Global-Warming Weather: Art, Science, or Neither?," *Waterloo/Cedar Falls Courier,* November 7, 2004, p. A7.

28. Seth Borenstein, "Bush Eases Rules, Angers Environmentalists," *Des Moines Register,* September 8, 2003, p. 4A.

29. Ellen Goodman, "Can Tourists Love a Place to Death?" *Des Moines Register,* March 31, 2001, p. 7A.

30. Jad Mouawad, "Gas Reaches $3.50, with Little Hope for Relief," *New York Times,* April 22, 2008.

31. "Ninth Circuit Rejects NHTSA Mileage Standards for Light Trucks; Agency Must Achieve 'Maximum Feasible' Fuel Economy," *Planning & Environmental Law* 60, No. 2 (February 2008), p. 15.

32. Harry Stoffer, "Bush Seeks to Save 2008-11 CAFE Rules," *Automotive News* 82, Iss. 6295 (February 18, 2008), p. 16.

33. Department of Transportation, "Secretary Peters Proposes 25 Percent Increase in Fuel Efficiency Standards over 5 Years for Passenger Vehicles, Light Trucks," [**www.dot.gov/ affairs/dot5608.htm**].

34. *Los Angeles Times,* "EPA Eases Clean Air Act," *Waterloo/Cedar Falls Courier,* August 28, 2003, p. A1.

35. Associated Press, "Court Backs Environmentalists on Power Plant Cleanup," *New York Times,* April 2, 2007.

36. [**www.nrdc.org/water/oceans/ttw/titinx.asp**].

37. *Rapanos v. United States,* 547 U.S. 715 (2006).

38. [**www.epa.gov/epaoswer/non-hw/muncpl/pubs/msw06.pdf**].

39. Bernard Gavzer, "Take Out the Trash, and Put It . . . Where?" *Parade,* June 13, 1999, p. 4.

40. Scripps-Howard News Service, "White House Delays Notice of Welfare Cuts," *Waterloo/Cedar Falls Courier,* September 15, 1996, p. F3.

41. Jeremy Caplan, "Paper War," *Time,* January 2006, p. A11.

42. Steven Kurutz, "Not Buying It," *New York Times,* June 21, 2007.

43. Janet Wilson, "State Has Most Minorities Near Toxic Facilities," *Los Angeles Times,* April 12, 2007.

44. Rachel A. Schneider, *Federal Environmental Laws,* American Bar Association [**www.abanet.org/genpractice/magazine/1998/jul-aug/98julschneid.html**].

45. Anthony DePalma, "Love Canal Declared Clean, Ending Toxic Horror," *The New York Times,* March 18, 2004, P. A1.

46. John Milliman and John Grosskopf, "Improving the Regulatory Enforcement Settlement Process: Applying Collaborative Solutions for Businesses and Environmental Regulatory Agencies," *Environmental Quality Management* 13 (Spring 2004), p. 25.

47. Richard Winton, "Firms to Pay $200 Million to Clean Up Water Supply," *Los Angeles Times,* September 16, 1999, p. B1.

48. "Criminal Prosecution: The Latest Threat to Help You Get Management on Board," *IOMA's Safety Director's Report* 4 (February 2004), p. 1.

49. Tom Kenworthy, "It's a New World: Polluters Go to Prison," *USA Today,* April 21, 2000, p. 3A.

50. *Washington Post,* "Bush's EPA Pursuing Fewer Polluters," *Waterloo/Cedar Falls Courier,* September 30, 2007, p. A3.

51. Associated Press, "Polar Bear to Be a Protected Species," *New York Times,* May 14, 2008.

52. Fredreka Schouten, "Dam-Breaking Idea Spawns Fierce Debate about Fish," *USA TODAY,* November 24, 1999, p. 22A.

53. Schouten, "Dam-Breaking Idea."

54. Paul VanDevelder, "A Political Football . . . with Fins; Clock Is Ticking as Salmon in the Pacific Northwest Face Extinction," *Los Angeles Times,* April 3, 2005, p. M6.

55. See [**http://www.wildsalmon.org/library/fed-salmon-plan.cfm**].

56. [**www.wildsalmon.org/pressroom/press-detail.cfm?docID=766**].

57. 540 U.S. 461 (2004).

58. Ian Bowles, "Want to Buy Some Pollution?," *New York Times,* March 15, 2008.

59. John M. Broder and Felicity Barringer, "EPA Says 17 States Can't Set Emission Rules," *New York Times,* December 20, 2007.

60. Steven Mufson, "Power Plant Rejected over Carbon Dioxide for First Time," *Washington Post,* October 19, 2007, p. A1.

61. Anthony Faiola and Robin Shulman, "Cities Take Lead on Environment as Debate Drags at Federal Level," *Washington Post,* June 9, 2007, p. A1 and Stephanie Simon, "Global Warming, Local Initiatives," *Los Angeles Times,* December 10, 2006.

62. Ronald Brownstein, "Local Governments Get Serious about the Environment," *Los Angeles Times,* October 1, 2006.

63. 257 N.E. 2d 870 (N.Y. 1970).

64. *State v. Lead Indus. Ass'n, Inc.,* 2001 R.I. Super. LEXIS 37 (R.I. Super. Ct. 2001) and *Whitehouse v. Lead Indus. Ass'n,* 2003 R.I. Super. LEXIS 50 (R.I. Super. Ct. 2003).

65. 342 P.2d 790 (Or. 1959).

66. *Langan v. Valicopters, Inc.,* 567 P. 2d 218 (Wash. S. Ct. 1977).

67. *Luthringer v. Moore,* 190 P. 2d 1 (Cal. S. Ct. 1948).

68. *State Dep't of Envtl. Prot. v. Ventron,* 468 A. 2d 150 (N.J. S. Ct. 1983).

69. *Branch v. W. Petroleum, Inc.,* 657 P. 2d 267 (Utah 1982).

70. Associated Press, "DuPont Found Negligent In Waste-Site Lawsuit," *The Wall Street Journal,* October 3, 2007.

71. Jeffrey Ball, "As Kyoto Protocol Comes Alive, So Do Pollution-Permit Markets," *The Wall Street Journal,* November 8, 2004, p. A2.

72. Thomas Fuller and Andrew C. Revkin, "Climate Plan Looks Beyond Bush's Tenure," *New York Times,* December 16, 2007.

73. John J. Fialka and Jeffrey Ball, "Companies Get Ready for Greenhouse-Gas Limits," *The Wall Street Journal,* October 26, 2004, p. A2.

74. Jeffrey Ball, "Conference Board Stiffens Global-Warming Stance," *The Wall Street Journal,* September 8, 2004, p. A2.

75. Adam Aston and Burt Helm, "The Race against Climate Change," *BusinessWeek,* December 12, 2005.

76. John Fialka, "Big Businesses Have New Take on Warming," *The Wall Street Journal,* March 28, 2006.

77. Michael S. Rosenwald, "Showcasing the Growth of the Green Economy," *Washington Post,* October 16, 2006, p. D1.

78. Andrew Martin, "In Eco-Friendly Factory, Low-Guilt Potato Chips," *New York Times,* November 15, 2007.

79. B. Peter Pashigian, "How Large and Small Plants Fare under Environmental Regulation," *Regulation,* March–April 1983, p. 19.

80. Hugh Pope, "Uzbeks Manage to Endure Amid Ruins of the Aral Sea," *The Wall Street Journal,* February 5, 1998, p. A18.

81. Norman Bowie, with Kenneth Goodpaster, "Corporate Conscience, Money and Motorcars," in *Business Ethics Report, Highlights of Bentley College's Eighth National Conference on Business Ethics,* ed. Peter Kent, 1989, pp. 4, 6.

82. John Fialka, "EPA Report Says Pollution-Control Effort Is Hurt by Bureaucracy, Lack of Funds," *The Wall Street Journal,* March 12, 2002, p. A28.

83. "Profligate Past, Poor Planning Created Mexican Water Crisis," *Associated Press,* August 22, 2002.

84. "Tucker Contra Sierra," *Regulation,* March–April 1983, pp. 48–49.

85. Robert Crandall, "The Environment," in "Regulation—The First Year," *Regulation,* January–February 1982, pp. 19, 29, 31.

86. "'Mad Taggers' Leave Their Mark on SUV Culture," *Waterloo/Cedar Falls Courier,* December 26, 2000, p. B5.

87. "Save the Planet: Stop Flying," *Parade Magazine,* January 7, 2007, p. 22.

CHAPTER EIGHTEEN

Internet Law and Ethics

After completing this chapter, students will be able to:

1. Evaluate ethical dilemmas emerging from widespread Internet access.

2. Apply the requirements of jurisdiction to a dispute arising in cyberspace.

3. Analyze free speech issues in the context of the Internet.

4. Provide examples of online privacy concerns.

5. Describe "cyberstalking" and other Internet-related crimes.

6. Explain the impact of the Electronic Signatures in Global and National Commerce Act (E-SIGN).

7. Identify UCITA.

8. Compare and contrast intellectual property rights in patents, copyrights, trademarks, and domain names in cyberspace.

9. Recognize tax issues arising in cyberspace.

Introduction: The Internet and Globalization

The Internet has changed our lives. The extraordinary power of nearly instantaneous communication around the globe promises remarkable new opportunities and challenges, creating and facilitating relationships (whole new "communities" of interest) among individuals, businesses, and governments that could never have occurred without it. The Internet is itself a substantial catalyst for continuing globalization, breaking down national boundaries and rules to allow free interchange of communications, ideas, goods and services around the world. In a recent survey, 52 percent of responders indicated agreement with the assertion that by 2020, the free flow of information on the Internet "will completely blur current national boundaries as they are replaced by . . . geographically diverse and reconfigured human organizations tied together by global networks."[1]

As we enter our last chapter, we have the opportunity to consider against the backdrop of a global stage such fundamentals as what substantive law we want to govern our Internet activities and what process we should use to establish global standards. For example, now that 1.4 billion of the world's 6.7 billion inhabitants have Internet access, it seems more pressing for the world community to come to agreement on certain fundamental principles, everything from what characters should be usable in a domain name suffix (the characters that appear after the "dot," as in .com, .org, and so forth)[2] to when and how electronic attacks are allowable weapons of war.[3]

On the other hand, the most interesting question raised by the Internet's creation and facilitation of these new relationships may be what process is going to develop to create a consensus over what the substantive law should be. Can national governments legitimately impose standards and sanctions? Will international forums, such as the United Nations Internet Governance Forum, be necessary to resolve what are global issues? Will such international bodies be able to act fast enough and have enough legitimacy to secure U.S. compliance? Might international enforcement tools need to be developed? Is grassroots use among individuals, business and government driving the development of this new medium so vigorously that its worldwide expansion may act as a catalyst for some fundamental restructuring of our global relationships?

Introduction: Law and the Market

Policy makers, users, and posters are all concerned about the degree to which we need to impose the force of law on Internet activities. The question is familiar: Can we count on the free market and ethics to govern Internet conduct or are government rules necessary? Put another way, which model is best for the Internet—market regulation, government regulation, self-regulation, or some combination of the three? [For links to many Internet law Web sites, see **www.willyancey.com/internet_law.htm**]

Certainly the law will play a great role in the future of the Internet. Experience confirms that a framework of law will be necessary for predictability, efficiency, and trust in the new global economy. Many of the problems law addresses in the conventional commercial world must now be revisited in the virtual world. Digital signatures, privacy, copyright infringement, freedom of speech, fraud, and taxes are among the issues that are likely to require attention from the law. The question is how much law? Even the firmest free market advocates recognize the necessity for clear contractual principles and effective means to prevent fraud and other criminal behavior. The key regulatory question is how to maintain the vigor of the free market while establishing a limited array of binding legal standards that will bring confidence to the global Internet market.

Critical Thinking

> The Internet is a superhighway not only for information, but also for misinformation.

The Internet is a superhighway not only for information, but also for misinformation. Not only can posted information be sadly out of date, it is possible that the "information" was never accurate. Because Internet publishing is so cheap and so accessible, readers and users of the Internet must build their critical assessment skills for evaluating the worth of the information found. For example, one should always investigate who or what organization is responsible for the posted information. Information posted by an individual may not have been investigated as thoroughly as information posted by a traditional news service. In addition, the identity of the poster may indicate a particular bias or slant on the information presented. We would not expect, for example, to get a neutral evaluation of a particular lawsuit from the Web pages of the corporate defendant.

Introduction: Ethics

So we see that market forces and law will blend in some uncertain, emerging formula to provide the security and confidence necessary for effective e-commerce. Now we ask what role ethics—that is, self-regulation—can play in this equation. The anonymity, the speed, the elusiveness, and the global reach of the Internet suggest very difficult new ethical problems (or old problems in a new venue). Some of those problems such as privacy, consumer fraud, and crime of all kinds will be discussed later in this chapter.

Selected Ethical Dilemmas

The Digital Divide

For some time there has been a concern that the Internet may worsen the income/wealth gap that splits both Americans and the globe. In the United States, some programs developed to address the digital divide seem to be paying off. Between 2005 and 2007, African American households with broadband access increased from 14 percent to 40 percent, while the U.S. average increased only from 30 percent to 47 percent; 73 percent of African Americans online have used the Internet for school or training and 67 percent have used it to seek jobs, while only 54 percent and 39 percent of whites, respectively, have used the Internet for these purposes. On the other hand, only 30 percent of households with an income under $30,000 have a broadband connection, while 76 percent of households with income above $75,000 have such connections.[4] Another digital divide, that is being addressed both voluntarily and through litigation, is access for the blind. One estimate is that more than a third of Internet content is not accessible to blind users, often because it is not compatible with software that can vocalize text and computer graphics. The most common problem faced by the blind is the lack of labeling for links and images. Another issue is the use of visual verification tools, such as the requirement to retype visually distorted characters.[5] The applicable federal law for addressing such issues is the Americans with Disabilities Act.

But the most serious accessibility imbalance is at the global level. For example, only 5.3 percent of the population in Africa has access to the Internet, while 73.1 percent in North America has access. Out of the 1.4 billion with access worldwide, only 246 million are in North America. Asia has by far the most users (530 million), while Europe has 382 million. [For current statistics on world Internet usage, see **www.internet-worldstats.com/stats.htm**]

In recognition of this global imbalance, the United Nations (UN) held a World Summit on the Information Society in two phases. In December 2003, representatives from 175 countries adopted a Declaration of Principles including a "commitment to build a people-centred, inclusive, and development-oriented Information Society, where everyone can create, access, utilize, and share information and knowledge, enabling individuals, communities, and peoples to achieve their full potential in promoting their sustainable development and improving their quality of life." Out of the second phase, held in November 2005, grew the UN Internet Governance Forum, which lays the foundation for policy changes but cannot itself result in binding decisions. Its work is expected to run from 2006–2010. Topics for discussion include expanding access in less developed countries and blocking online child pornography, as well as reducing U.S. control over a medium with many more users outside of the United States than in.[6] [For more information on the Internet Governance Forum, see **www.intgovforum .org**. For more information on the World Summit on the Information Society, see **www.itu.int/wsis/index.html**]

Community

We cannot know what our lives will be like as the Internet begins to assert its full technological potential, but we can be sure that much will be different. One commentator, Thomas Naylor, argues that what we really need are "more town squares and village greens where people can sit and talk, have a coffee, pass the time away, and experience real community." But what he sees is a medium, pushed by "our universities with their frantic rush to the Web," that "encourages instant gratification, superficial research, poor writing, sloppy analysis, uncritical thinking, and unrelenting conformity."[7] On the other side is the argument that "Technology has not devalued individual human life; it has elevated it, creating new opportunities, new connections, new freedoms. The human imagination has not been suppressed; it has been liberated, in ways unimaginable even a decade or two ago. . . . [T]he new technologies ensure better opportunities for a larger number. More people will have more access to more information than ever before. And that information is power."[8] [For more on the intersection of the Internet and society, see **http://cyber.law .harvard.edu**]

> More people will have more access to more information than ever before. And that information is power.

Net Neutrality

At this writing, if an individual or business wishes to connect to the Internet, they contract with an Internet service provider (ISP) (e.g., AOL, Comcast, Verizon), pay a fee for the type (such as dial-up or broadband) and level of service (such as length of term and total volume) they desire, and they then have access to any content provider (e.g., Craigslist, Google, YouTube). This uniform access is referred to as net neutrality. Some ISPs, particularly telephone and cable companies providing broadband access, want to change that and begin charging certain content providers for access to the ISP's subscribers. Specifically, these ISPs want to charge content providers with heavy traffic for the substantial bandwidth used to access their sites, products and services. The consequence of nonpayment would be either blocking access or degrading the speed at which access is provided. Arguments against such tiered pricing include that ISP customers already pay for the distribution system (paying higher fees for various broadband connections), that some ISPs compete with content providers (cable companies provide content as well as Internet access) and might discriminate either in price or speed to favor their own content, and that such pricing might make it difficult for new content providers to succeed

(Amazon had high volume traffic long before it became profitable). Arguments for such tiered pricing, in addition to the claim that large bandwidth content providers pay for the volume of traffic they induce, are frequently based on a belief that the market will determine if tiered pricing is appropriate. That is, customers will be able to select ISPs that don't degrade the speed of certain connections, and there will be enough competition that ISPs will differentiate themselves on this dimension. Another argument presumes that any prohibition of tiered pricing would require regulatory oversight. The concern is that the regulatory agency would ultimately be "captured" by the regulated ISPs and turn the regulatory process to their own advantage through lavish spending on lobbyists and lawyers.[9]

Marketing and the Internet

As anyone regularly using the Internet can tell you, marketing efforts are pervasive. Where once marketing amounted to putting up Web pages where potential customers could get product and service information, it has grown into banner ads on news sites, pop-up windows that have to be affirmatively closed to escape the advertisement, online tracking systems for pitching specific ads at individual users,[10] and whole Web sites designed to hook kids with interactive games that themselves promote the posters' products.[11] Even more aggressive marketing gambits are available, including "typo-piracy" (use of misspellings or derivations of a popular brand to divert traffic to an unintended site), "astroturfing" (fake users on discussion forums and in chat rooms to create the impression of a grassroots buzz for a particular product), "meat puppets" (fictional posters on social networks like Facebook used to collect e-mail addresses for sending product ads),[12] and spyware (software unknowingly downloaded by the user that can deliver volumes of pop-up ads, redirect browsers to undesired search engines, or steal personal information).[13] And who has not received unsolicited e-mail advertisements offering low mortgage rates, as well as many much less savory devices and services?

Questions

1. *a.* Can you think of any imaginative ways to provide widespread Internet access in developing countries?

   b. How would you deal with the reality that most Internet content is in English?

2. *a.* In your experience, has access to the Internet encouraged "superficial research, poor writing, sloppy analysis, uncritical thinking, and unrelenting conformity"? Or do you think it has given "more access to more information than ever before"?

   b. Has the issue of information reliability been raised at your college or university in the context of accessing information off the Internet?

3. Both net neutrality and the marketing practices described above raise the question of whether legislation (government regulation) is appropriate or necessary to restrict unwanted market behavior. Would you favor a law imposing net neutrality? Why or why not? What law could you design to prevent the described marketing abuses? Is it necessary for an agency to be created or designated to enforce any of your proposed laws?

Part One—Jurisdiction to Adjudicate

Business in the cyberworld raises puzzling new legal problems. The Internet, after all, is borderless. We can and do communicate and conduct transactions around the world. When a dispute arises from one of those billions of communications and transactions, where will that dispute be litigated? If an American Web site provides child pornography viewed by a German on the Internet, which nation will have the authority to prosecute the offense?[14] If a Massachusetts resident posts an arguably libelous article on an Internet bulletin board sited in New York, may the Texas resident who claims harm from the libel sue the author and the bulletin board host in a Texas court?[15] These are jurisdiction questions. A party filing suit over an Internet dispute must take that claim to a court that has both *subject-matter jurisdiction* (the authority and power to address the particular kind of legal problem being raised) and *personal jurisdiction* (the power to make the defendant respond to the court). (For a general discussion of jurisdiction, see Chapter 4.)

In the United States, where the plaintiff and defendant are both residents of the forum state, personal jurisdiction ordinarily is not an issue. However, personal jurisdiction over nonresidents depends on the constitutional requirement of *due process.* In practice, the test is one of *minimum contacts:* Did the defendant have sufficient contact with the forum state that being sued there would be fair and just? Put another way, was the defendant's contact with the forum state such that he or she should expect to be subject to the state's courts? Thus, the more business a defendant does in a state, the more likely that personal jurisdiction will be found. The Internet, of course, raises special problems because the "contacts" often are electronic and fleeting.

Several cases have arisen in the United States that begin to answer this question. For example, the Fifth Circuit held that, in a case of alleged copyright violation, Texas did not have personal jurisdiction over a Vermont corporation merely because the corporation's Web site was accessible from Texas.[16] It reached this conclusion, in part, because it found that there was no specific connection between the existence of the corporation's Web site and the harm complained of by the plaintiff. Thus the Vermont corporation could be sued in Texas only if it had contacts with Texas that were sufficiently "continuous and systematic" to subject the corporation generally to suit in Texas. A passive Web site could not do this. When the defendant has more contact with the forum state than mere creation of a passive Web site available to forum state computer users, the due process analysis becomes more complex and hinges on an evaluation of the defendant's specific additional contacts with the forum state. The existing decisions are often hard to reconcile and many cases have been reversed on appeal, indicating that judgments as to jurisdiction are challenging.[17]

Jurisdiction in International Suits

Jurisdictional issues like these also arise across national boundaries. In January 2001 an Italian court ruled that Italy can try to close down foreign-based Web sites that break Italian law.[18] Similarly, Germany has brought criminal actions to prevent persons from providing German residents with access to pornographic Internet sites.[19] In these international contexts, it may be useful to distinguish among three types of jurisdiction: jurisdiction to prescribe (legislate), jurisdiction to adjudicate (judicial personal jurisdiction), and jurisdiction to enforce.[20] Most countries have long had laws that prohibit or regulate expression and commerce, such as pornography, gambling, alcohol, and so on. But when they seek to apply those laws to various classes of foreigners, what is in question is their jurisdiction to adjudicate. Section 421 of the Restatement (Third) of Foreign Relations Law of the United States attempts to identify the circumstances under which countries have exercised their jurisdiction to adjudicate. It enumerates, among other circumstances, (1) when a person is present in the territory, other than transitorily; (2) when a person is domiciled, a resident, or a national of that country; (3) when a person regularly carries on business in that country; (4) when a person has carried on an activity in the country, where that activity is the subject of the dispute; and (5) when a person has done something outside the country, but it has a "substantial, direct, and foreseeable effect within" the country and that effect forms the subject of the suit.

Consider both the French court's approach and the U.S. district court's approach to the issue of jurisdiction to adjudicate in the following dispute.

YAHOO! v. La Ligue Contre Le Racisme Et L'Antisemitisme

LEGAL BRIEFCASE

169 F. Supp. 2d 1181 (N.D. Cal. 2001)

Judge Jeremy Fogel

I. PROCEDURAL HISTORY

Defendants La Ligue Contre Le Racisme Et L'Antisemitisme ("LICRA") and L'Union Des Etudiants Juifs De France, citizens of France, are nonprofit organizations dedicated to eliminating anti-Semitism. Plaintiff Yahoo!, Inc. ("Yahoo!") is a corporation organized under the laws of Delaware with its principal place of business in Santa Clara, California. Yahoo! is an Internet service provider that operates various Internet Web sites and services that any computer user can access at the Uniform Resource Locator ("URL") **http://www.yahoo.com**. Yahoo! services ending in the suffix ".com," without an associated country code as a prefix or extension (collectively, "Yahoo!'s U.S. Services"), use the English language and target users who are residents of, utilize servers based in, and operate under the laws of the United States. Yahoo! subsidiary corporations operate regional Yahoo! sites and services in 20 other nations, including, for example, Yahoo! France, Yahoo! India,

and Yahoo! Spain. Each of these regional Web sites contains the host nation's unique two-letter code as either a prefix or a suffix in its URL (Yahoo! France is found at **http://www.yahoo.fr** and Yahoo! Korea at **http://www.yahoo.kr**). Yahoo!'s regional sites use the local region's primary language, target the local citizenry, and operate under local laws.

Yahoo! provides a variety of means by which people from all over the world can communicate and interact with one another over the Internet. . . . As relevant here, Yahoo!'s auction site allows anyone to post an item for sale and solicit bids from any computer user from around the globe. Yahoo! records when a posting is made and after the requisite time period lapses sends an e-mail notification to the highest bidder and seller with their respective contact information. Yahoo! is never a party to a transaction, and the buyer and seller are responsible for arranging privately for payment and shipment of goods. Yahoo! monitors the transaction through limited regulation by prohibiting particular items from being sold (such as stolen goods, body parts, prescription and illegal drugs, weapons, and goods violating U.S. copyright laws or the Iranian and Cuban embargos). . . . Yahoo! informs auction sellers that they must comply with Yahoo!'s policies and may not offer items to buyers in jurisdictions in which the sale of such item violates the jurisdiction's applicable laws. Yahoo! does not actively regulate the content of each posting, and individuals are able to post, and have in fact posted, highly offensive matter, including Nazi-related propaganda and Third Reich memorabilia, on Yahoo!'s auction sites.

On or about April 5, 2000, LICRA sent a "cease and desist" letter to Yahoo!'s Santa Clara headquarters informing Yahoo! that the sale of Nazi and Third Reich–related goods through its auction services violates French law. LICRA threatened to take legal action unless Yahoo! took steps to prevent such sales within eight days. Defendants subsequently utilized the United States Marshal's Office to serve Yahoo! with process in California and filed a civil complaint against Yahoo! in the Tribunal de Grande Instance de Paris (the "French Court").

The French Court found that approximately 1,000 Nazi and Third Reich–related objects, including Adolf Hitler's *Mein Kampf, The Protocol of the Elders of Zion* (an infamous anti-Semitic report produced by the Czarist secret police in the early 1900s), and purported "evidence" that the gas chambers of the Holocaust did not exist, were being offered for sale on Yahoo.com's auction site. Because any French citizen is able to access these materials on Yahoo.com directly or through a link on Yahoo.fr, the French Court concluded that the Yahoo.com auction site violates Section R645-1 of the French Criminal Code, which prohibits exhibition of Nazi propaganda and artifacts for sale. On May 20, 2000, the French Court entered an order requiring Yahoo! to (1) eliminate French citizens' access to any material on the Yahoo.com auction site that offers for sale any Nazi objects, relics, insignia, emblems, and flags; (2) eliminate French citizens' access to Web pages on Yahoo.com displaying text, extracts, or quotations from *Mein Kampf* and *Protocol of the Elders of Zion;* (3) post a warning to French citizens on Yahoo.fr that any search through Yahoo.com may lead to sites containing material prohibited by Section R645-1 of the French Criminal Code, and that such viewing of the prohibited material may result in legal action against the Internet user; (4) remove from all browser directories accessible in the French Republic index headings entitled "negationists" and from all hypertext links the equation of "negationists" under the heading "Holocaust." The order subjects Yahoo! to a penalty of 100,000 Euros for each day that it fails to comply with the order. . . .

The French Court also provided that penalties assessed against Yahoo! Inc. may not be collected from Yahoo! France.

Defendants again utilized the United States Marshal's Office to serve Yahoo! in California with the French Order.

Yahoo! subsequently posted the required warning and prohibited postings in violation of Section R645-1 of the French Criminal Code from appearing on Yahoo.fr. Yahoo! also amended the auction policy of Yahoo.com to prohibit individuals from auctioning:

> Any item that promotes, glorifies, or is directly associated with groups or individuals known principally for hateful or violent positions or acts, such as Nazis or the Ku Klux Klan. Official government-issue stamps and coins are not prohibited under this policy. Expressive media, such as books and films, may be subject to more permissive standards as determined by Yahoo! in its sole discretion.

Yahoo Auction Guidelines (visited Oct. 23, 2001) [**http://user . auctions.Yahoo.com/html/guidelines.html**]. Notwithstanding these actions, the Yahoo.com auction site still offers certain items for sale (such as stamps, coins, and a copy of *Mein Kampf*) which appear to violate the French Order. . . .

Yahoo! claims that because it lacks the technology to block French citizens from accessing the Yahoo.com auction site to view materials which violate the French order or from accessing other Nazi-based content of Web sites on Yahoo.com, it cannot comply with the French order without banning Nazi-related material from Yahoo.com altogether. Yahoo! contends that such a ban would infringe impermissibly upon its rights under the First Amendment to the United States Constitution. Accordingly, Yahoo! filed a complaint in this Court seeking a declaratory judgment that the French Court's orders are neither cognizable nor enforceable under the laws of the United States.

Defendants immediately moved to dismiss on the basis that this Court lacks personal jurisdiction over them. That motion was denied. . . .

II. OVERVIEW

As this Court and others have observed, the instant case presents novel and important issues arising from the global reach of the Internet. Indeed, the specific facts of this case implicate issues of policy, politics, and culture that are beyond the purview of one nation's judiciary. Thus it is critical that the Court define at the outset what is and is not at stake in the present proceeding.

This case is *not* about the moral acceptability of promoting the symbols or propaganda of Nazism. Most would agree that such acts are profoundly offensive. By any reasonable standard of morality, the Nazis were responsible for one of the worst displays of inhumanity in recorded history. . . .

Nor is this case about the right of France or any other nation to determine its own law and social policies. A basic function of a sovereign state is to determine by law what forms of speech and conduct are acceptable within its borders. . . .

What *is* at issue here is whether it is consistent with the Constitution and laws of the United States for another nation to regulate speech by a United States resident within the United States on the basis that such speech can be accessed by Internet users in that nation. In a world in which ideas and information transcend borders and the Internet in particular renders the physical distance between speaker and audience virtually meaningless, the implications of this question go far beyond the facts of this case. The modern world is home to widely varied cultures with radically divergent value systems. There is little doubt that Internet users in the United States routinely engage in speech that violates, for example, China's laws against religious expression, the laws of various nations against advocacy of gender equality or homosexuality, or even the United Kingdom's restrictions on freedom of the press.

* * * * *

The French order prohibits the sale or display of items based on their association with a particular political organization and bans the display of Web sites based on the authors' viewpoint with respect to the Holocaust and anti-Semitism. A United States court constitutionally could not make such an order. The First Amendment does not permit the government to engage in viewpoint-based regulation of speech absent a compelling governmental interest, such as averting a clear and present danger of imminent violence.

* * * * *

Comity

No legal judgment has any effect, of its own force, beyond the limits of the sovereignty from which its authority is derived. . . . The extent to which the United States, or any state, honors the judicial decrees of foreign nations is a matter of choice, governed by "the comity of nations." United States courts generally recognize foreign judgments and decrees unless enforcement would be prejudicial or contrary to the country's interests.

As discussed previously, the French order's content and viewpoint-based regulation of the Web pages and auction site on Yahoo.com, while entitled to great deference as an articulation of French law, clearly would be inconsistent with

the First Amendment if mandated by a court in the United States. . . . The reason for limiting comity in this area is sound. "The protection to free speech and the press embodied in [the First] amendment would be seriously jeopardized by the entry of foreign judgments granted pursuant to standards deemed appropriate in [another country] but considered antithetical to the protections afforded the press by the U.S. Constitution." *Bachchan*, 585 N.Y.S.2d at 665. Absent a body of law that establishes international standards with respect to speech on the Internet and an appropriate treaty or legislation addressing enforcement of such standards to speech originating within the United States, the principle of comity is outweighed by the Court's obligation to uphold the First Amendment.

* * * * *

CONCLUSION

Yahoo! seeks a declaration from this Court that the First Amendment precludes enforcement within the United States of a French order intended to regulate the content of its speech over the Internet. . . . Accordingly, the motion for summary judgment will be granted.

AFTERWORD

The Ninth Circuit, in a 2006 decision, ruled by a vote of eight to three that the district court in California had personal jurisdiction over the French defendants, but six judges also held that Yahoo! could not pursue its declaratory judgment action. Three of those six said the declaratory judgment action was not "ripe" for decision, while the other three were the minority that held that the court had no personal jurisdiction.[21] The Supreme Court declined to review the decision.[22]

Questions

1. As relayed by the district court, we do not know why the French court believed it had jurisdiction to adjudicate against Yahoo!, as opposed to Yahoo! France. Look back at the discussion of the Restatement (Third) of Foreign Relations Law of the United States immediately before this case. Why do you think the French court had jurisdiction over Yahoo! France? Yahoo!, Inc.?

2. If you were sitting on the court of appeals for the rehearing, how would you decide the jurisdiction question? Consider both the U.S. rule of minimum contacts and the restatement provision.

Speech

The district court opinion in *Yahoo! v. La Ligue Contre Le Racisme Et L'antisemitisme* illustrates one of the free speech issues the Internet raises. In addition to international disputes, Internet content has also raised free speech issues here at home. The Internet's anonymity, ease of use, relatively low costs, and global reach make it a natural vehicle for transporting speech messages. As we saw in Chapter 5, the First Amendment protects us from government restraints on the *content* of speech, although reasonable restraints on the context (time, place, and manner) of that speech are sometimes constitutionally permissible. Thus a court will not restrain free speech by enjoining someone from posting defamatory or copyrighted material, but the damaged parties may, of course, sue for defamation or copyright infringement after the fact.[23] [For many articles on cyberlaw free speech, search for "free speech" at **www.jcil. org/journal/search**]

One of the most troublesome issues for free speech and the Internet is how or whether children can be protected from content that is inappropriate, while adult access to that content is nevertheless protected by the First Amendment. According to a recent survey, 34 percent of Internet users aged 10 to 17 experienced "unwanted exposure to online pornography, up from 25 percent" in a similar survey five years earlier.[24] A sixth-grader "was worried about stumbling onto inappropriate sites on the Net when she uses it for school-work. 'Maybe instead of having dot-com, they should put a dot-x or something, so we wouldn't accidentally get there,' she suggested."[25]

That said, Congress has struggled to enact legislation eliminating access by minors to pornographic information on the Web. In 1997, the Supreme Court held that certain provisions of the Communications Decency Act of 1996 were overbroad and therefore violated the First Amendment. "[I]n order to deny minors access to potentially harmful speech, the [Act] effectively suppresses a large amount of speech that adults have a constitutional right to receive."[26]

In response, Congress passed the Child Online Protection Act, seeking to criminalize online content "harmful to minors" based on "contemporary community standards." In 2002, the Supreme Court held that reference to "contemporary community standards" did not make the standard unconstitutional.[27] But then in 2004 the Court approved the continuation of the temporary injunction (imposed in 1999), which prohibited the government from enforcing the law until a trial on the merits could determine whether it was the least restrictive means available for the government to achieve its purpose.[28] In 2007, the federal district court hearing the case found the law unconstitutional and permanently enjoined its enforcement. The court found that the law would not be effective in protecting children from online pornography, in part because about 50 percent of sexually explicit Web pages originate overseas which the law would not reach. Further, the court found that parents could shield their children using software filters and other, less restrictive means.[29] The government has not appealed this decision.

In another 2002 decision, the Supreme Court found the 1996 Child Pornography Prevention Act unconstitutional. This Act prohibited not just actual child pornography, but also material that depicts persons who "appear to be minors" (although in fact they may just be computer-generated images) or that is presented so it "conveys the impression" that the person depicted is a minor. The Court reasoned in part that the government had failed to show a causal link between computer-generated images of child porn and harm to actual children.[30]

The PROTECT Act, Congress' latest effort to curb child pornography distribution, may have turned the tide because the Supreme Court in 2008 ruled that the Act meets First Amendment free speech standards. (For more details, see Chapter 5.)

PRACTICING ETHICS   Government Control of Web Content

Governments seem intent on restricting content, or access to certain content, on the Web—from Congress' repeated attempts to prohibit pornography from reaching minors, to the French court's ordering Yahoo! to prevent access by French citizens to auctions of Nazi memorabilia, to China's insistence that if Microsoft, Yahoo!, and Google want to provide Internet services in China they agree to help it censor information on democracy as well as the Tiananmen Square massacre.

Questions

Do you think any government can effectively stop its citizens' access to particular Web content? Should any government try to do so? Should Internet service providers voluntarily aid governments in their attempts? Is it more ethical for an ISP to provide such aid only if ordered to do so by a court with jurisdiction? Should an ISP operating in a host country seek to impose only those speech restrictions allowable in its home country, or is it permissible to impose the standards of the host country?

Commercial Speech

You will remember from Chapter 5 that commercial speech has been accorded reduced but significant First Amendment protection. Thus online advertising is subject to the same kinds of government oversight as that in print and on television. One form of online commercial message receiving special attention is so-called *spam* (mass e-mailings). This electronic junk mail may be a legitimate form of commercial message at times, but it may also be an annoyance, a threat to the efficiency of the Internet because of its volume, or deceptive; or it may contain objectionable content (obscenity, viruses).

The federal CAN-SPAM Act of 2003 establishes both civil and criminal penalties for violations of its provisions, which (among other things) prohibit false or misleading header and subject line information on e-mail, require that recipients be given a method to opt out of receipt of future e-mail, mandate that commercial e-mail be clearly labeled as advertisements, and specify that a valid "snail mail" address for the sender be identified. The Federal Trade Commission (FTC) is charged with enforcing the act and brought its first criminal actions under the act in April 2004.[31] [For more information on the CAN-SPAM Act and the FTC's enforcement, see **www.ftc.gov/spam**]

Privacy

Americans cherish the right to privacy, but the Internet opens up previously uncontemplated possibilities for intrusion. Some of the information now available online has in fact been public for decades, but most people were not aware that it was public, did not know how to obtain it, or simply never bothered. For example, local governments keep property, tax, and court records on file, all of which are open to the public, generally through visits to the local courthouse. Now, however, local governments are making this data available online, so that anyone who is simply curious can explore it.[32] Similarly, licensing bodies now often have online membership lists and sometimes also information on complaints filed and disciplinary actions taken.

But other information that may now be collected on individuals is unique to the phenomenon of the Internet. The public got a glimpse of how much personal information can be collected and stored by ISPs when AOL released 36 million search queries from 657,000 unidentified customers in 2006 and the *New York Times* was able to trace searches back to specific individuals.[33] Then in September 2007 the *Los Angeles Times* reported that the privacy policy California subscribers agree to when signing up for Time Warner's combination phone, cable, Internet package indicates the company can track what you watch on TV, the Internet addresses you visit and how long you stay there, and purchases you make. It reserves the right "to disclose personally identifiable information to others," as well as store all this information for "as long as you are a subscriber and up to 15 additional years."[34]

Privacy in Europe

The European Union has taken quite a different tack from America's market-driven approach to online privacy. The EU's 1998 Data Protection Directive basically allows individuals to decide how their collected data can be used. Thus, if a European consumer provides personal information such as an address when buying from an online store, that store cannot legally send an ad to the purchaser without first seeking permission.[35] The directive also prohibits the transfer of data to countries outside the European Union that do not have "adequate" privacy rules.[36] The United States was one of the nations deemed inadequate, but by mid-2000 European and U.S. negotiators had reached an agreement providing U.S. companies with three voluntary safe-harbor options to choose among that, if implemented, will shield them from prosecution by EU governments under the Data Protection Directive.[37] In mid-2007 the EU started an investigation into whether Google is complying with these rules.[38]

Privacy concerns have also been raised in the context of the Patriot Act, which was passed in the wake of the events of September 11, 2001 to strengthen the government's ability to deal with terrorism threats. The act provided much broader authority for the government to issue National Security Letters (NSLs). In essence, an NSL is an administrative subpoena order requiring appearance in court, issuable without any review by a court as to its reasonableness or probable cause. The American Civil Liberties Union (ACLU) brought suit on behalf of an unidentified ISP, which had been presented with an NSL by the FBI ordering it to turn over certain of its subscribers' records. In 2004 a federal district court found the provision unconstitutional under both the First and Fourth Amendments.[39] On appeal, the Second Circuit Court of Appeals remanded the case for further First Amendment proceedings.[40] The district court then held the relevant NSL provision was unconstitutional under the First Amendment.[41]

> COPPA prohibits Web sites from collecting personal information from children under 13 without parental permission.

Another area of concern is the privacy of our children online. In 1998 Congress passed the Children's Online Privacy Protection Act (COPPA), which prohibits Web sites from collecting personal information from children under 13 without parental permission and requires that parents be allowed to review and correct any information collected about their children. The FTC is charged with primary enforcement responsibility for COPPA. [To take a look at the complaints, and other information, in the cases brought by the FTC under COPPA, go to **www.ftc.gov/privacy/privacyinitiatives/childrens_enf.html**]

Yet another area drawing interest is whether employers are allowed to access e-mail sent from or received on office computers and files stored on those computers. "In a recent survey of 840 U.S. companies by the American Management Association, 60 percent said they now use some type of software to monitor their employees' incoming and outgoing e-mail, up from 47 percent in 2001."[42] Today's software can be customized to look for such things as company officers' and competitors' names, as well as inappropriate language. Software is also available that can "track every keystroke, file download, and Internet page that appears on an employee's computer screen."[43] In part, companies may adopt some of these strategies to protect themselves from lawsuits. For example, Continental Airlines was sued for defamation and workplace harassment based on derogatory and insulting remarks posted about one employee by other coworkers on Continental's electronic bulletin board.[44] Employers wishing to implement such monitoring programs should, however, advise their employees of that fact and have all employees sign an acknowledgment so there is no question about whether an employee has any expectation of privacy on company systems.

Question

Explain why employers might want to monitor their employees' computer activities.

Freedom of Speech and the Right to Anonymity

One unique characteristic of the Internet and electronic communication through the Internet is the sender's or poster's ability to be and remain anonymous. Anonymity, of course, makes it more likely that individuals will feel free to say things about which they would otherwise keep silent. This may be a positive aspect, where the anonymous speech is truthful. But anonymity may also make individuals bolder about asserting untruths—misleading, fraudulent, or otherwise unprotected speech. So we find ever more numerous situations where one side argues to preserve its anonymity, while the other side argues that abuse of anonymity gives the right to remove the speaker's anonymity. A user's Internet service provider (ISP) has the ability to reveal the identity of the sender or poster, based on information provided by the user when contracting for service from the ISP.

In the case that follows, a Yahoo! poster asserts the First Amendment to prevent Yahoo! from responding to a subpoena from Immunomedics, a corporation claiming the anonymous poster is or was an employee who violated the company's confidentiality agreement by posting company information on a Yahoo! message board.

Immunomedics v. Jean Doe

LEGAL BRIEFCASE 775 A. 2d 773 (N.J. Super. 2001)

Judge Fall

Defendant Jean Doe, a/k/a "moonshine_fr," appeals from an order entered on December 20, 2000, denying her motion to quash a subpoena issued to Yahoo! by plaintiff, Immunomedics, Inc., seeking all personally identifiable information relating to the person or identity who posted messages on the Yahoo! Finance Message Board under the identifier "moonshine_fr" which may identify or lead to the identification of that person or entity.

Immunomedics is a publicly held biopharmaceutical Delaware corporation, with its principal place of business located at 300 American Road in Morris Plains, New Jersey. Immunomedics is focused on the development, manufacture, and commercialization of diagnostic imaging and therapeutic products for the detection and treatment of cancer and infectious diseases.

Yahoo! is an Internet Service Provider (ISP) that maintains a Web site that includes a section called Yahoo! Finance. Yahoo! Finance maintains a message board for every publicly traded company, including Immunomedics. Visitors to the Immunomedics site can obtain up-to-date information on the company, and can post and exchange messages about issues related to the operation or performance of the company.

On October 12, 2000, Immunomedics filed a complaint against Jean Doe, also known by the computer screen name "moonshine_fr" ("Moonshine"). The complaint alleged that Moonshine had "posted a message on Yahoo! Finance." Immunomedics claimed that message contained information confidential and proprietary to Immunomedics. As a result, Immunomedics asserted it had sustained injury and that Moonshine should be held liable under theories of breach of contract, breach of duty of loyalty, and negligently revealing confidential and proprietary information.

* * * * *

Of the two messages in question, the first, with Moonshine describing herself as "[a] worried employee," stated that

Immunomedics was "out of stock for diagnostic products in Europe" and claimed that there would be "no more sales if [the] situation [did] not change." The second message, allegedly posted by Moonshine after the initial complaint was filed, reported that Chairman of the Company Dr. Goldenberg was going to fire the Immunomedics "european manager." In her certification to the trial court, Immunomedics' Executive Vice President and Chief Operations Officer Cynthia L. Sullivan admitted that the statements were true, but that, as an employee, Moonshine had violated the company's confidentiality agreement and "several provisions" of the company's Employee Handbook.

On or about October 20, 2000, Immunomedics served a subpoena on Yahoo!, seeking discovery of Moonshine's true identity. Yahoo!, in turn, contacted Moonshine. In response, Moonshine filed a motion to quash the subpoena on or about November 15, 2000.

The motion to quash was argued before Judge Zucker-Zarett on December 15, 2000. After considering the arguments, the judge denied Moonshine's motion, stating, in pertinent part,

> We have two issues here. We have an issue, she's an employee, she signed a confidential document saying that she was not going to speak freely about information she learned at the company. So she contracted away her right of free speech if she's an employee. Number two, free speech, anonymous, but if it harms another individual, that is another way that we have a little bit of a dent in our rights for free speech.

* * * * *

Moonshine contends the motion judge erred in denying her motion to quash the subpoena, as anonymous speech is constitutionally protected and Immunomedics' complaint is insufficient to warrant a breach of that anonymity. Immunomedics argues that, while anonymous speech is constitutionally protected, that protection can be overcome if a defendant uses that freedom in an unlawful manner. . . .

In *Dendrite International, Inc. v. John Doe No. 3* (2001), another case involving an application for expedited discovery to disclose the identity of an anonymous user of an ISP message board, we concluded that courts must decide such applications by striking a balance between the First Amendment right of an individual to speak anonymously and the right of a company to protect its proprietary interest in the pursuit of claims based on actionable conduct by the ISP message board user.

* * * * *

We hold that when such an application is made, the trial court should first require the plaintiff to undertake efforts to notify the anonymous posters that they are the subject of a subpoena or application for an order of disclosure, and withhold action to afford the fictitiously named defendants a reasonable opportunity to file and serve opposition to the application. These notification efforts should include posting a message of notification of the identity discovery request to the anonymous user on the ISP's pertinent message board.

The court shall also require the plaintiff to identify and set forth the exact statements purportedly made by each anonymous poster that plaintiff alleges constitute actionable speech.

The complaint and all information provided to the court should be carefully reviewed to determine whether plaintiff has set forth a prima facie cause of action against the fictitiously named anonymous defendants. In addition to establishing that its action can withstand a motion to dismiss for failure to state a claim upon which relief can be granted, the plaintiff must produce sufficient evidence supporting each element of its cause of action, on a prima facie basis, prior to a court ordering the disclosure of the identity of the unnamed defendant.

Finally, assuming the court concludes that the plaintiff has presented a prima facie cause of action, the court must balance the defendant's First Amendment right of anonymous free speech against the strength of the prima facie case presented and the necessity for the disclosure of the anonymous defendant's identity to allow the plaintiff to properly proceed.

The application of these procedures and standards must be undertaken and analyzed on a case-by-case basis. The guiding principle is a result based on a meaningful analysis and a proper balancing of the equities and rights at issue.

. . . Here, Immunomedics' cause of action is based on Moonshine's status as an employee and her alleged violation of a confidentiality agreement, and Moonshine's alleged breach of her common law duty of loyalty. . . .

Applying the procedure and test outlined in *Dendrite,* we conclude Judge Zucker-Zarett properly analyzed the disclosure issue, and we affirm substantially for the reasons articulated by the judge in her oral opinion delivered on December 15, 2000. We add the following. Immunomedics presented sufficient evidence that Moonshine is, or was, an employee of Immunomedics. Ms. Sullivan indicated in her certification that "all employees are bound by several Company policies and a confidentiality agreement." Within its "Confidentiality and Assignment Agreement," Immunomedics includes the following language:

> This Agreement and any disputes arising under or in connection with it shall be governed by the laws of the State of New Jersey and each of the parties hereto hereby submits to the jurisdiction of any Federal or state court sitting in the State of New Jersey over any such dispute.

Accordingly, Immunomedics clearly established a prima facie cause of action for breach of the confidentiality agreement founded on the content of Moonshine's posted messages.

In balancing Moonshine's right of anonymous free speech against the strength of the prima facie case presented and the necessity for disclosure, it is clear that the motion judge struck the proper balance in favor of identity disclosure. With evidence demonstrating Moonshine is an employee of Immunomedics, that employees execute confidentiality agreements, and the content of Moonshine's posted messages providing evidence of the breach thereof, the disclosure of Moonshine's identity, which can be reasonably calculated to be achieved by information obtained from the subpoena, was fully warranted. Although anonymous speech on the Internet is protected, there must be an avenue for redress for those who are wronged. Individuals choosing to harm another or violate an agreement through speech on the Internet cannot hope to shield their identity and avoid punishment through invocation of the First Amendment.

* * * * *

Affirmed.

Questions

1. In your opinion, should employers, police, and others who have been damaged by anonymous postings be able to obtain the identity of the poster from the hosting site or the poster's ISP? Explain.

2. An FBI agent monitored an AOL chat room suspected of being a site for exchanging child pornography. The agent did not participate in the chat room conversations. Charbonneau allegedly distributed child pornography to the chat room participants, including the FBI agent. Charbonneau was arrested.

    a. Did Charbonneau have a First Amendment free speech right to transmit child pornography online?

    b. Does the Fourth Amendment's prohibition on unreasonable searches and seizures protect the statements made in the AOL chat room? Explain. See *United States of America v. Kenneth Charbonneau*, 979 F.Supp. 1177 (S.D.Ohio, 1997).

Part Three—Crime

Crimes facilitated by the Internet include both truly new types and some old, familiar crimes in somewhat new clothing. Some of the laws already discussed in this chapter provide criminal penalties for violations of their provisions, most notably the CAN-SPAM Act and the Child Pornography Prevention Act. Other laws criminalizing specific online behavior exist as well, such as the Computer Pornography and Child Exploitation Prevention Act of 1999, which makes it unlawful to use a computer to solicit, lure, or entice a child or otherwise engage in sexual offenses with a child.

But many of our long-standing, pre-Internet criminal laws can be applied to both online and offline behavior. For example, theft of a laptop is still theft. On the other hand, if the thief connects the laptop to the Internet and the necessary antitheft software is installed, the police may be informed of the log-on location, complete with phone number and owner's name—particularly helpful if the thief has logged on from home.[45] Similarly, it is a federal crime to transport stolen property across state lines, even if that property is a detailed litigation strategy e-mailed by a law firm's employee to opposing counsel in another state.[46]

Computer Security   As just illustrated, both computers and the information kept in them can be the objects of theft. Often the stored information is much more valuable than the hardware, generating a whole new category of thieves, so called hackers. Thanks to the Internet, hackers can break into others' computers from the privacy of their own home (even if it's in the Ukraine) and traffic in such data as credit card numbers, personal identities, eBay accounts and bank funds. Hacking can also just be malicious—destroying data or whole computer networks.[47] The notion that it may take a thief to catch a thief has even led to classes for "ethical" hackers that train computer security professionals about the psychology and skills used by actual hackers.[48]

Computing power can also be the object of theft. Sophisticated hackers can create botnets by taking control of multiple computers (zombie computers) through software robots (bots) installed via worms and software backdoors. A particular botnet can involve thousands of individual computers. It is estimated that 11 percent of computers connected to the Internet are so infected. Precautions such as upgrading software, using firewalls and running antivirus software can significantly reduce the risk of such unintended use.[49]

Fraud   Botnets have also been used in a new type of fraud, so-called click fraud. Online advertising is a growing business as vendors move away from traditional media in an attempt to reach Web surfers and to pay for access to more targeted audiences (those who actually click on a display ad). Click fraud ranges from repeated clicks on a competitor's ad to run up its advertising bill to enlisting others in "paid to read" rings to generate income for the Web sites hosting ads. Clickbots have been used to automatically generate page hits. Both Google and Yahoo! have settled class-action lawsuits based on click fraud, brought by advertisers that were charged based on the number of clicks the ads Google and Yahoo! placed for them received. It has been estimated that 10 to 15 percent of ad clicks are fake.[50]

First there was phishing and now there's spear phishing. "In a phishing attack, scammers send e-mails that purport to be from a bank . . . directing customers to a site where they are asked to enter vital information, such as passwords, bank account numbers or credit card details. The scams are so effective because the bogus e-mails and Web sites look so legitimate." It is also a global phenomenon, having affected banks in Australia, Germany, Malaysia, New Zealand, Spain, and the United Kingdom, as well as the United States.[51] In spear phishing, scammers enter social networking sites, such as MySpace and Facebook, and mine posted profiles for such information as addresses, birthdates, and friends names, allowing them to "tap into [posters'] network of trust." Once connected as "friends," spear-phishers can send e-mail messages "containing malicious code that infects the computer with a virus, which then tracks every user name and password entered on other legitimate sites. . . . 'Then parents use the same computer for their banking. . . . It could be months before they realize their bank accounts have been hacked.'"[52]

With e-commerce thriving, we know that e-fraud cannot be far behind. According to the Internet Fraud Watch, false check scams result in the highest number of reported incidents of online fraud—29 percent in 2007. Nondelivery or misrepresentation of general merchandise was the next highest reported category at 23 percent. Third place, with 11 percent of the total, was nondelivery or misrepresentation associated with online auctions. Nigerian money offers came in fourth, at 11 percent, but the average loss was greater than with the first three categories.[53] The highest percentage of perpetrators come from outside the United States and Canada. The Internet Fraud Watch collects its statistics based on complaints reported to it, either online [see **www.fraud.org**] or by phone. It then forwards the complaints to federal, state, and local law enforcement agencies, including a database maintained by the FTC. [International fraud events can be reported at **www.econsumer.gov**]

Online securities fraud has also been in the news, although perhaps not as much recently as in the late 1990s when the stock market was booming. One type is an online version of a classic "pump and dump" scheme—when someone holding a stock artificially drives its share price up by floating exaggerated or false reports of its value through Web sites, online postings, or e-mail. When the stock price jumps, the promoter sells shares at the inflated price. One of the most notorious examples was reported in 2000 when the SEC accused a 15-year old from New Jersey of stock manipulation, issued a cease and desist order, and required him to turn over his profit, plus interest—a tidy $285,000.[54]

Cyberstalking   In a recent Illinois case, a former electronics store employee was sentenced to four years in prison for sending lewd photos and threatening e-mail and phone messages to a 22-year-old woman who had brought her computer in for repair.[55] This is just one example of cyberstalking—the repeated use of electronic media (such as e-mail or chat rooms) to harass or threaten another person. It has been publicly recognized as a problem at least since 1999, when the U.S. Attorney General prepared a formal report on the growing problem.[56] Every state has laws criminalizing traditional physical stalking, although the first such law was passed only in 1990. Most of these laws require that the perpetrator make a credible threat of violence for the action to be a violation; many do not expressly include cyberstalking, although under appropriate facts it might be covered.

> Cyberstalking—the repeated use of electronic media (such as e-mail or chat rooms) to harass or threaten another person.

International Crimes   On the international front, the Council of Europe has drafted the Convention on Cybercrime, which 40 member states and several nonmember states, including the United States, have signed, although only 22 countries have ratified it.[57] For those states, the convention went into force July 1, 2004, and requires "the criminalization of a long list of computer activities—everything from breaking into a computer to the 'deterioration' of computer data. . . . It also requires countries to make sure they can snoop through Internet data in real time. And it obliges nations to assist each other's investigations by monitoring Net communications."[58]

Apparently one country's crime is often another country's business opportunity. Every country criminalizes certain behaviors in support of its moral attitudes and historical experiences. Some proscribed behaviors such as murder, seem fairly universal. But other behaviors are acceptable in some countries while criminalized in others. Where such crimes are facilitated by the Internet, international disputes over the appropriate reach of such laws have arisen. We have already seen one example in the *Yahoo! v. La Ligue Contre Le Racisme Et L'Antisemitisme* case in Part One of this chapter, where France sought to enforce its ban on the sale of Nazi memorabilia to French citizens. Both the United Kingdom and Germany have criminal laws that they have enforced based on pornographic materials posted on Web sites outside their geographic boundaries. The United Kingdom convicted a U.K. citizen operating out of his home in the United Kingdom for "publication" of pornographic materials on Web sites located in the United States.[59] Germany convicted the German head of CompuServe for allowing German citizens access to pornographic Web sites hosted outside Germany, despite the fact that he had no technological way to block access. (Blocking access required the U.S. corporation to block access to all its customers worldwide.)[60]

PRACTICING ETHICS

Internet Gambling Bans—Necessary to Protect Public Morals or Discrimination against Foreign Gambling Operations?

The U.S. government has long held the position that Internet gambling is illegal in the United States. It has pressured U.S. businesses not to open Internet gambling sites and U.S. credit card companies not to permit charges from foreign gambling operations. The United States made processing such credit card transactions illegal in October 2007.

In 2003 the Caribbean nation of Antigua and Barbuda filed a dispute with the WTO arguing that "if bricks-and-mortar casinos can operate in the United States, it would be illegal to stop Internet casinos from providing essentially the same service."[61] Antigua is a country "with no natural resources and a population of only about 68,000, [which] built up its Internet gambling industry to supplement its tourism-driven economy." The 2005 decision of the WTO gave something to both parties. It ruled that some

U.S. laws violated WTO trade agreements, but that others were appropriate to "protect public morals or maintain public order." The United States' appeal of the decision was denied in 2007, which opens the door to retaliation by Antigua and Barbuda as allowed under WTO rules. Income from its online casinos dropped from $1 billion in 2000 to $130 million.[62]

Questions
1. What ethical arguments can you identify to allow Antigua to actively market its online gambling to U.S. citizens?
2. What ethical arguments support the position of the U.S. government against permitting its residents to participate in gambling online?

Part Four—Commercial Law

Contracts and Uniform Laws

Internet sales have grown significantly, but for the Internet to reach its commercial potential a routine, well-settled contracts structure is essential. The basic ingredients of a binding contract, as we saw in Chapter 6, also apply to Internet transactions.

- *Capacity* to enter the contract.
- *Offer and acceptance* of the terms of the contract.
- *Consideration* for the promises in the contract.
- *Genuineness* of assent.
- *Legality* of purpose of the contract.

Thus an exchange of e-mail meeting the traditional contract requirements should result in an enforceable agreement. But what about acceptance by providing an "electronic signature" (a digital code unique to an individual), downloading some information, opening a shrink-wrap package, or clicking an "Accept" button?

E-Signature   Electronic signatures can take a variety of forms (voice prints, distinctive marks, mathematical codes), but the key is that they are electronic symbols, sounds, or processes intended to have the same effect as a signature affixed by hand. Electronic signatures obviously will be central to trust and efficiency in online contracting. On June 30, 2000, President Clinton signed into law the Electronic Signatures in Global and National Commerce Act (E-SIGN), giving electronic signatures the same legal stature as handwritten ones, at least for most commercial purposes.[63] Consumers, however, cannot be forced to accept electronic signature agreements or to receive records and documents electronically instead of in paper form. [For a look at the digital signature laws of the United Nations, European Union, and United Kingdom, see **http://law.richmond. edu/jolt/v11i2/article6.pdf**]

UCITA   In 1999 the National Conference of Commissioners on Uniform State Laws (NCCUSL) approved a model law designed to achieve uniformity across the United States in the law governing software and Internet transactions. The proposed law reaches all deals involving computer information or goods and is designed to address the special problems of the electronic market, including software licensure (right to use). The Uniform Computer Information Transactions Act (UCITA) addresses the substance of computer information transactions, rather than procedural aspects such as electronic signatures.

To this point, UCITA has been amended twice (2000 and 2002), but has not been well received, having been adopted in only Maryland and Virginia.[64] Until it or some other such legislation is widely approved, the Uniform Commercial Code (UCC), other applicable state and federal laws, and the common law of contracts (judge-made law) will govern electronic contractual arrangements. (The UCC, having been approved in 49 of the 50 states, is designed to provide nationwide consistency, predictability, and fairness in contract law where a sale of goods is involved.)

Click-Wrap Agreements   Today software is typically downloaded with license terms provided onscreen during the installation process. Those terms often say that in using the software the buyer agrees to the terms. Whether all of those terms are enforceable in court is the subject of dispute. The likelihood is that many terms will be enforceable if the buyer has a reasonable opportunity to review those terms and can abort the installation (and the charge) if the terms are unacceptable. The court in *Caspi v. Microsoft Network,* 732 A.2d 528 (N.J. Super. 1999), applying a traditional contract law analysis, held the choice of forum provision in an online click-wrap agreement to be enforceable.

There is growing concern, however, over just how voluntary some provisions of such standard-form contracts are, that is, the genuineness of the purchaser's consent. It can appear that retailers are, perhaps deliberately, obscuring one-sided terms.[65] Who has not wondered at the presentation of contract terms in a 2-by-4-inch scrollable window with an "Agree" button prominently displayed below? Recall also the online 3,000-word privacy agreement for Time Warner's packaged phone, cable, and Internet services in California (described in Part Two's section on Privacy). The article that follows identifies some surprising terms that appeared in one such electronic, standard-form contract.

Megalomania   How Much Does Microsoft Have the

READING   Right to Control?

E. J. Heresniak

* * * * *

I have a driver's license, which warrants that I have the basic knowledge and skill to maintain my right to maneuver a ton and a half of metal and plastic at high speeds in traffic while drinking coffee and talking on the phone. . . . Having a license usually indicates you have permission to do something based on demonstrated ability or under terms you find acceptable. Those licenses I understand.

When you buy a computer program—any computer program—you don't own the program in the sense that you can do whatever you want with it. You buy a paid-up license. Nobody expects you to give the program back at the end of a term, but by retaining ownership, the maker of the software is afforded a bit of legal protection from thievery. Common sense would lead you to expect limitations in the license to prevent stealing ideas or copying the programs and handing them out on the street. But Microsoft has taken it a step further.

Microsoft's End User License Agreement, or EULA, is the fine print on Microsoft products. When you install a Microsoft

program on your computer, the EULA is the thing you skip over and check "I agree" before you can continue with the installation of the program you bought or downloaded from the Web. If you check "no," that you do not agree with something in the EULA, installation stops. This is not an agreement that you reach after negotiating. The EULA is a one-way deal, and it can be dangerous and overreaching.

Here's some interesting language from the EULA for FrontPage, Microsoft's easy-to-use Web-design software package: "You may not use the Software in connection with any site that disparages Microsoft, MSN, MSNBC, Expedia, or their products or services, infringe any intellectual property or other rights of these parties, violate any state, federal, or international law, or promote racism, hatred, or pornography."

What constitutes pornography and other socially obnoxious behavior is often in the eye of the beholder. Last August, the U.S. Postal Service shut down a child-pornography ring operating a Web site in Texas. . . .

If the offending Texas Web site were produced with the Microsoft product FrontPage, the Microsoft license police could have shut down the site—after all, it violated the terms of their software license. So if Postal Service inspectors or the FBI ever get distracted, help is on the way. . . .

* * * * *

I do, in fact, use FrontPage to develop my Web site. Microsoft has special deals with Internet service providers so you can get cheap rates for hosting your site with easy and automatic ways to make changes. If I decided to post this column on my Web site, I could get in trouble—not because my editors claim all the rights to the column, but because Microsoft lawyers say you can't use their Web page software for anything they might find disparaging to Microsoft or, surprisingly, to the travel site Expedia, to the cable TV network, or to MSNBC. I'm not kidding. Interestingly, after four weeks of inquiries, Microsoft public relations people hadn't figured out quite what to say about their practice—and if they've had occasion to enforce it.

* * * * *

Putting a critic in the same club as lawbreakers, copyright infringers, racists, and pornographers is stupid. Apparently, whether my Web site stays or goes depends on the meaning of the word *disparage*. Well, I think the Microsoft crowd are a bunch of monopolists who want to control the world, and plan to keep stuffing everything anyone does with a computer into an operating system that only they control. Was that disparaging?

Source: *Across the Board,* Nov/Dec 2001, p. 83.

Questions

1. Do you think Microsoft should be able to tell the licensees of its software that the software cannot be used to "disparage" Microsoft? What about its attempt to prevent its products from being used to "promote racism, hatred, or pornography"?

2. If Microsoft brought a lawsuit against one of its licensees for in fact using one of its products to "disparage" Microsoft, or to "promote racism, hatred, or pornography," what do you think the outcome would be?

Intellectual Property

Continuing expansion of electronic commerce depends to a significant extent on the business community's success in protecting its technology from theft, copying, infringement, and the like. Intellectual property, broadly, is composed of creative ideas that are the products of the human mind. Songs, computer programs, new medicines, a novel, and so on are forms of intellectual property. Recalling our discussion of market failure in Chapter 8, you may recognize that intellectual property, from an economics point of view,

> **Intellectual property, from an economics point of view, is a public good.**

is a public good. Clearly, the market alone cannot effectively protect those ideas from theft and exploitation. Intellectual property law preserves the rights to those ideas for those who developed them. In doing so, we hope to provide justice by rewarding those whose ingenuity and hard work developed those ideas and their

tangible results (recordings, movies, and the like), and we want to provide an incentive to produce those imaginative advances. At least that is the American and Western view of intellectual property. Some cultures remain reluctant to recognize property rights of this kind, but globalization seems certain to generate relatively consistent intellectual property standards for most of the world. Inclusion of the agreement on Trade-Related Aspects of Intellectual Property Rights (TRIPS Agreement) as one of the WTO's foundation agreements supports this projection. [For more on intellectual property law, see **www.ipmall.fplc.edu**]

Patents   Exactly what role patents will play in the future development of the Internet seems uncertain at this time. The grant of some early patents associated with basic methods of doing business online (such as Amazon.com's "one-click" method for making Internet purchases and Priceline.com's process of "reverse" auctions) raised considerable controversy, sufficiently so that in 2000 the U.S. Patent and Trademark Office announced it was overhauling the way it processes and awards patents for many online processes.[66] It is currently operating under a set of interim guidelines governing subject matter eligibility. [For more on business methods patents, see **www.uspto.gov/web/menu/ pbmethod**]

Copyrights In America and much of the world, anyone who creates "original works of authorship," whether in print or digital form, is, in most cases, automatically protected by copyright laws if the "works" are original and are "fixed in tangible form" (written down on paper, for example). Consequently, the author has exclusive rights for a period of years to commercially exploit those works. Virtually all of the information available online is protected by the U.S. Copyright Act and includes such intellectual creations as data, databases, literature, music, software, photos, and multimedia works. While original works of authorship are automatically copyrighted, the full protection of the law can be achieved by placing a copyright notice on the work (such as "copyright 2006 McGraw-Hill") and registering the copyright with the U.S. Copyright Office. International protection is provided by the principal copyright treaty, the Berne Convention. [Information on the U.S. Copyright Office can be found at **www.copyright.gov**]

The copyright holder possesses the exclusive right to (1) reproduce the copyrighted work, (2) prepare adaptations based on the copyrighted material, (3) distribute the material by sale or otherwise, and (4) perform or display the material. When anyone other than the copyright holder or one acting with the holder's permission makes use of one of those rights, the copyright has been *infringed* unless the use falls within a series of exceptions. Perhaps the most notable of those exceptions is the *fair use* doctrine, which allows use of copyrighted material without permission under some conditions, such as limited, nonprofit use in a classroom.

The electronic age has spawned some new disputes arising out of applications of new technologies. Under the Digital Millennium Copyright Act (DMCA), passed in 1998, Webcasters can play copyrighted music over the Internet as long as they pay standard royalties and meet certain criteria, such as ensuring that the broadcasts are not interactive.[67] But some researchers are claiming that the act is too broadly written and as a result impinges on First Amendment free speech rights—for example, in attempting to prohibit scientific discussions of certain technologies.[68]

The most visible Internet copyright dispute has been the ongoing battle of the music recording industry to protect its copyrights. Music file sharing took off in the late 1990s through the use of the Napster Web site, where users could swap digital music. The recording industry successfully obtained an injunction against Napster's facilitation of such file sharing;[69] but the practice continued, aided by peer-to-peer computer programs such as KaZaA and Grokster, which are installed on users' computers. So the recording industry sued Grokster and other file-sharing software distributors. The defendants prevailed at the district and circuit court levels.[70] Then, in the following unanimous Supreme Court decision, the recording industry gained a big victory.

Justice Souter

I

A

Respondents, Grokster, Ltd., and StreamCast Networks, Inc., defendants in the trial court, distribute free software products that allow computer users to share electronic files through peer-to-peer networks, so called because users' computers communicate directly with each other, not through central servers. . . .

A group of copyright holders (MGM for short, but including motion picture studios, recording companies, songwriters, and music publishers) sued Grokster and StreamCast for their users' copyright infringements, alleging that they knowingly and intentionally distributed their software to enable users to reproduce and distribute the copyrighted works in violation of the Copyright Act.

Grokster's software employs what is known as FastTrack technology. . . . StreamCast distributes a very similar product except that its software, called Morpheus, relies on what is known as Gnutella technology. A user who downloads and installs either software possesses the protocol to send requests for files directly to the computers of others using software compatible with FastTrack or Gnutella.

*   *   *   *   *

Although Grokster and StreamCast do not know when particular files are copied, a few searches using their software would show what is available on the networks the software reaches. MGM commissioned a statistician to conduct a systematic search, and his study showed that nearly 90 percent of the files available for download on the FastTrack system were copyrighted works. Grokster and StreamCast dispute this figure. . . . They also argue that potential noninfringing uses of their software are significant in kind, even if infrequent in practice. Some musical performers, for example, have gained new audiences by distributing their copyrighted works for free across peer-to-peer networks, and some distributors of unprotected content have used peer-to-peer networks to disseminate files, Shakespeare being an example. . . .

But MGM's evidence gives reason to think that the vast majority of users' downloads are acts of infringement, and because well over 100 million copies of the software in question are known to have been downloaded, and billions of files are shared across the FastTrack and Gnutella networks each month, the probable scope of copyright infringement is staggering.

Grokster and StreamCast concede the infringement in most downloads, and it is uncontested that they are aware that users employ their software primarily to download copyrighted files, even if the decentralized FastTrack and Gnutella networks fail to reveal which files are being copied, and when. . . .

Grokster and StreamCast are not, however, merely passive recipients of information about infringing use. The record is replete with evidence that from the moment Grokster and StreamCast began to distribute their free software, each one clearly voiced the objective that recipients use it to download copyrighted works, and each took active steps to encourage infringement.

After the notorious file-sharing service, Napster, was sued by copyright holders for facilitation of copyright infringement, StreamCast gave away a software program of a kind known as OpenNap, designed as compatible with the Napster program and open to Napster users for downloading files from other Napster and OpenNap users' computers. Evidence indicates that "it was always [StreamCast's] intent to use [its OpenNap network] to be able to capture e-mail addresses of [its] initial target market so that [it] could promote [its] StreamCast Morpheus interface to them." . . .

*   *   *   *   *

StreamCast developed promotional materials to market its service as the best Napster alternative. One proposed advertisement read, "Napster Inc. has announced that it will soon begin charging you a fee. That's if the courts don't order it shut down first. What will you do to get around it?" Another proposed ad touted StreamCast's software as the "#1 alternative to Napster" and asked "when the lights went off at Napster . . . where did the users go?"

*   *   *   *   *

In addition to this evidence of express promotion, marketing, and intent to promote further, the business models employed by Grokster and StreamCast confirm that their principal object was use of their software to download copyrighted works. Grokster and StreamCast receive no revenue from users, who obtain the software itself for nothing. Instead, both companies generate income by selling advertising space, and they stream the advertising to Grokster and Morpheus users while they are employing the programs. As the number of users of each program increases, advertising opportunities become worth more.

Finally, there is no evidence that either company made an effort to filter copyrighted material from users' downloads or otherwise impede the sharing of copyrighted files. . . .

B

The District Court . . . granted summary judgment in favor of Grokster and StreamCast as to any liability arising from distribution of the then current versions of their software. Distributing that software gave rise to no liability in the court's view, because its use did not provide the distributors with actual knowledge of specific acts of infringement.

The Court of Appeals affirmed. In the court's analysis, a defendant was liable as a contributory infringer when it had knowledge of direct infringement and materially contributed to the infringement. But the court read *Sony Corp. of America v. Universal City Studios, Inc.,* 464 U.S. 417, 78 L. Ed. 2d 574, 104 S. Ct. 774 (1984), as holding that distribution of a commercial product capable of substantial noninfringing uses could not give rise to contributory liability for infringement unless the distributor had actual knowledge of specific instances of infringement and failed to act on that knowledge. The fact that the software was capable of substantial noninfringing uses in the Ninth Circuit's view meant that Grokster and StreamCast were not liable, because they had no such actual knowledge, owing to the decentralized architecture of their software. The court also held that Grokster and StreamCast did not materially contribute to their users' infringement because it was the users themselves who searched for, retrieved, and stored the infringing files, with no involvement by the defendants beyond providing the software in the first place.

II
A

*   *   *   *   *

The argument for imposing indirect liability in this case is . . . a powerful one, given the number of infringing downloads that occur every day using StreamCast's and Grokster's software. When a widely shared service or product is used to commit infringement, it may be impossible to enforce rights in the protected work effectively against all direct infringers, the only practical alternative being to go against the distributor of the copying device for secondary liability on a theory of contributory or vicarious infringement.

B

*   *   *   *   *

In *Sony Corp. v. Universal City Studios* this Court addressed a claim that secondary liability for infringement can arise from the very distribution of a commercial product. There, the product, novel at the time, was what we know today as the videocassette recorder or VCR. Copyright holders sued Sony as the manufacturer, claiming it was contributorily liable for infringement that occurred when VCR owners taped copyrighted programs because it supplied the means used to infringe, and it had constructive knowledge that infringement would occur. At the trial on the merits, the evidence showed that the principal use of the VCR was for "'time-shifting,'" or taping a program for later viewing at a more convenient time, which the Court found to be a fair, not an infringing, use. There was no evidence that Sony had expressed an object of bringing about taping in violation of copyright or had taken active steps to increase its profits from unlawful taping. Although Sony's advertisements urged consumers to buy the VCR to "'record favorite shows'" or "'build a library'" of recorded programs, neither of these uses was necessarily infringing.

On those facts, with no evidence of stated or indicated intent to promote infringing uses, the only conceivable basis for imposing liability was on a theory of contributory infringement arising from its sale of VCRs to consumers with knowledge that some would use them to infringe. But because the VCR was "capable of commercially significant noninfringing uses," we held the manufacturer could not be faulted solely on the basis of its distribution.

*   *   *   *   *

Because the Circuit [Court of Appeals] found the StreamCast and Grokster software capable of substantial lawful use, it concluded on the basis of its reading of *Sony* that neither company could be held liable, since there was no showing that their software, being without any central server, afforded them knowledge of specific unlawful uses.

This view of *Sony,* however, was error. . . .

C

[N]othing in *Sony* requires courts to ignore evidence of intent if there is such evidence. . . . Thus, where evidence goes beyond a product's characteristics or the knowledge that it may be put to infringing uses, and shows statements or actions directed to promoting infringement, *Sony's* . . . rule will not preclude liability. The classic case of direct evidence of unlawful purpose occurs when one induces commission of infringement by another, or "entices or persuades another" to infringe, as by advertising.

*   *   *   *   *

[T]he inducement rule is a sensible one for copyright. We adopt it here, holding that one who distributes a device with the object of promoting its use to infringe copyright, as shown by clear expression or other affirmative steps taken to foster infringement, is liable for the resulting acts of infringement by third parties. We are, of course, mindful of the need to keep from trenching on regular commerce or discouraging the development of technologies with lawful and unlawful potential. Accordingly, just as *Sony* did not find intentional inducement despite the knowledge of the VCR manufacturer that its device could be used to infringe, mere knowledge of infringing potential or of actual infringing uses would not be enough here to subject a distributor to liability. Nor would ordinary acts incident to product distribution, such as offering customers technical support or product updates, support liability in themselves. The inducement rule, instead, premises liability on purposeful, culpable expression and conduct, and thus does nothing to compromise legitimate commerce or discourage innovation having a lawful promise.

III
A

The only apparent question about treating MGM's evidence as sufficient to withstand summary judgment under the theory of inducement goes to the need on MGM's part to adduce evidence that StreamCast and Grokster communicated an inducing message to their software users.

* * * * *

Here, the . . . record is replete with evidence that Grokster and StreamCast, unlike the manufacturer and distributor in *Sony*, acted with a purpose to cause copyright violations by use of software suitable for illegal use.

Three features of this evidence of intent are particularly notable. First, each company showed itself to be aiming to satisfy a known source of demand for copyright infringement, the market comprising former Napster users.

* * * * *

Second, this evidence of unlawful objective is given added significance by MGM's showing that neither company attempted to develop filtering tools or other mechanisms to diminish the infringing activity using their software.

Third, [it] is useful to recall that StreamCast and Grokster make money by selling advertising space, by directing ads to the screens of computers employing their software. . . .

B

In addition to intent to bring about infringement and distribution of a device suitable for infringing use, the inducement theory of course requires evidence of actual infringement by recipients of the device, the software in this case. As the account of the facts indicates, there is evidence of infringe-

ment on a gigantic scale, and there is no serious issue of the adequacy of MGM's showing on this point. . . . There is substantial evidence in MGM's favor on all elements of inducement, and summary judgment in favor of Grokster and StreamCast was error.

[Vacated and remanded.]

Questions

1. *a.* Explain how the Court was able to hold software distributors like Grokster liable for the misconduct of others (those who actually used the peer-to-peer networks to download copyrighted materials).

   b. What does the Court mean by "contributory" and "vicarious" copyright infringement?

   c. Why did the Supreme Court overrule the Court of Appeals decision?

2. Will this decision effectively stop illegal downloading of copyrighted material? Explain.

3. As a consequence of this decision, is peer-to-peer technology now unlawful? Explain.

4. In your judgment do Grokster and other peer-to-peer software distributors have a moral responsibility regarding the unlawful use of their products by third parties? Explain.

AFTERWORD

The recording industry has not limited itself to suing file-sharing facilitators such as Grokster, it has also pursued the file sharers themselves, including many university students. According to one source, in 2006 "college students illegally obtained two-thirds of their music and accounted for 1.3 billion illegal downloads."[71] Under the DMCA, the recording industry can subpoena universities (or other ISPs) and require they identify the students who are believed to be violating copyright laws. A university will not be liable for its students' violations, as long as it responds expeditiously to remove, or disable access to, the copyrighted material when notified of the violations. Some members of Congress have suggested that universities might lose that protection if they don't take more effective means to reduce copyright infringement. Thus, many universities have signed contracts with legal providers giving students download rights for modest flat fees. Others have installed campuswide filters to stop the download of copyrighted material.

While record labels continue to pursue copyright infringers, some of the largest online music stores are removing usage restrictions from their downloaded music files. In mid-2007, both Apple and Amazon.com announced that they would start offering music in their online stores that would no longer be locked to certain players or programs. Both have the support of EMI, one of the largest record labels. The restrictions on placing purchased and downloaded music on multiple computers and personal devises, restrictions that aren't imposed when a CD is purchased, have long annoyed consumers. It has also drawn the unfavorable attention of regulators in the EU, who see it as a form of unfair competition.[72]

Grokster Redux?

In March 2007 Viacom filed a complaint against Google's YouTube video-sharing service claiming over $1 billion in damages. Viacom claims YouTube willfully facilitates the infringement of its video copyrights on a massive scale.[73] One defense YouTube has open to it, that Grokster did not, is the same safe harbor used by universities described above—Viacom can identify the offending material and YouTube can escape liability by expeditiously prohibiting further access to it.

Trademarks and Domain Names   Words, names, symbols, devices, or combinations thereof that are used to distinguish one seller's products from those of another are called *trademarks* when associated with products (like IBM, Coke, or Pepsi Cola) and *service marks* when associated with service businesses (United Airlines).

The Internet address for a Web page is called its *domain name.* Ordinarily, a business engaging in electronic commerce will want to use the simplest form of its name as its domain name. Rights to a domain name are secured simply by being the first to request a name and paying a registration fee. In 1999 Congress approved the Anticybersquatting Consumer Protection Act, which created a cause of action where a trademark has been infringed upon by the registration of a domain name. The trademark holder must show a bad-faith intention on the part of the registrant to profit from the registration, traffic in the name, or use the name. To date, many successful suits have been brought under this act, protecting such names as vw.net,[74] sportys.com,[75] and ClassicVolvo.com.[76] The Third Circuit has held that registration of deliberate misspellings of famous marks is also a violation of the act.[77] [For information on the United Nations' World Intellectual Property Organization, which provides arbitrations pursuant to ICANN's domain name arbitration policy, see **www.wipo.int**]

Domain Name Disputes

"The Internet grew rapidly over the last decade as a place to do business, although no international legal standards existed to resolve domain name disputes. . . . The process of negotiating a new international treaty was considered too slow, and new national laws would most likely be too diverse. What was needed were internationally uniform and mandatory procedures to deal with what are frequently cross-border disputes." Ultimately, ICANN adopted the arbitration approach to dispute resolution. A number of organizations have been approved as arbitrators of domain name disputes. Carmen Electra, Michael Crichton, Kevin Spacey, Pamela Anderson, Celine Dion, and Bruce Springsteen have all used the process to have domain name versions of their names transferred to them, all of which were previously registered by the same Canadian company.

Sources: WIPO, "Frequently Asked Questions: Internet Domain Names" [**http://www.wipo.int/amc/en/ center/faq/ domains.html**]; "People: News/Gossip/Scoops," *St. Louis Post–Dispatch,* January 17, 2004, p. 41.

Taxes

We close this chapter, and the book, with an interesting public policy question raised by the remarkable confusion (and profusion) of the Internet. It is a policy issue, like many raised by the Internet and discussed in this chapter, that crosses traditional jurisdictional lines—both state boundaries in the United States and national boundaries around the world. Its resolution, either at the national level or at the international level, will require substantial negotiation, compromise and, ultimately, consensus building.

What is the issue? We start with a national example: If you buy a CD on the Internet, your neighborhood retailer will not receive your business and your state and local governments often will not receive sales taxes as they would have if you had made the purchase at that local store. To address that issue and others, the federal government undertook a study of e-commerce tax policy and imposed a moratorium on Internet taxes that expired in October 2007. Resolution, however, has proven elusive. In pre-Internet days, the Supreme Court had ruled that an out-of-state vendor cannot be required to collect sales taxes for any state in which that vendor does not have some significant presence, including a physical presence.[78] The Court held that it would be an undue burden on interstate commerce for states to be able to require out-of-state vendors to comply with each unique set of state and local sales tax rules. Thus, while the initial Internet tax moratorium was in effect, many states joined an effort to streamline, simplify, and coordinate their sales tax laws. The idea was that if state sales taxes were more uniform, the burden on interstate commerce from requiring compliance from out-of-state vendors would disappear.

As of this writing, of the 44 states that have been involved in the project, 22 have conformed their state laws to the requirements of the negotiated agreement, which became operational in 2005. An additional six states have introduced legislation to do so in 2008. Participation on the part of vendors is voluntary, but over 1000 have registered and are now remitting taxes to member states. The primary incentive for voluntary participation is a grant of amnesty for any prior unpaid taxes which might have been owed.[79]

The problem is just as complex, if not more so, on an international scale. Here the issue spans the whole range of taxes, paralleling both our income tax laws and our sales tax laws. In a nutshell, what nation is entitled to tax cross-border transactions? In the international arena, certain key principles were adopted by the 30 countries that comprise the Organization for Economic Cooperation and Development (OECD) in 1998, including the principle that consumption taxes (like our sales taxes) should be collected by the jurisdiction where consumption takes place. But finding workable arrangements to effectuate general principles has proven elusive. The European Union amended its Value-Added Tax (VAT) to require non-EU-resident vendors to apply the VAT (for each of the EU countries) when selling "digital goods" within the EU.[80] [For more on the international taxation of e-commerce, see **www.internetpolicy.net/taxation**]

Reprise: Who Governs Cyberspace?

We end this chapter with some of the same questions with which we started: What substantive law should govern the taxation of international transactions (or, for that matter,

> And what government can legitimately impose standards and sanctions for violations of those standards?

the protection of intellectual property internationally, or any of the other international issues brought to the fore by the rapid development and expansion of the Internet)? What process should be used to develop international consensus over those substantive laws? And what government can legitimately impose standards and sanctions for violations of those standards?

Question

Comment on the following portion of John Perry Barlow's "Cyberspace Declaration of Independence":

> Governments of the Industrial World, you weary giants of flesh and steel, I come from Cyberspace, the new home of Mind. On behalf of the future, I ask you of the past to leave us alone. You are not welcome among us. You have no sovereignty where we gather.
>
> We have no elected government, nor are we likely to have one, so I address you with no greater authority than that with which liberty itself always speaks. I declare the global social space we are building to be naturally independent of the tyrannies you seek to impose on us. You have no moral right to rule us nor do you possess any methods of enforcement we have true reason to fear.[81]

Internet Exercise

Review the materials on privacy issues in this chapter and then log on to the Website for an Internet vendor that you, or someone you know, has used. Can you find the vendor's privacy policy? Is it easy to find? Is it easy to access and read? How long is it? How complicated? Do any of its provisions surprise you? What control do you have over the use of your personal information? Is that information easy to find? Can you tell when the policy was last updated and what changes were made in it? Has the policy received approval from TRUSTe.org (indicated by a seal displayed on the policy page)? Would you purchase again from this vendor?

Chapter Questions

1. *a.* Germany, France, the Netherlands, and Austria have laws that allow publishing groups to specify the price at which new books are to be sold at retail. That is, anyone selling one of those books at retail in those countries must sell it at the price specified by publishers or they won't be supplied with the books. Why would those countries support price fixing in book sales?

   b. Germany's *Rabattgesetz* (discount law) requires that all customers pay precisely the same price for a product. Thus an Internet concept like *Priceline.com* where buyers specify a price they are willing to pay for a product is unlawful. Why would Germany insist on identical pricing for products?

   c. How would you expect the Internet to affect those laws forbidding discounts on books and other products? See Neal Boudette, "In Europe, Surfing a Web of Red Tape," *The Wall Street Journal,* October 29, 1999, p. B1.

2. The United Nations recently warned that the worldwide growth of e-commerce may constitute a threat to the well-being of the world's developing nations as well as parts of Europe. Explain the UN concerns.

3. Psychologists are worried that the Internet will make shopping too easy. Explain their concern.

4. Bensusan Restaurant Corporation owns the famous New York City jazz club "The Blue Note," and in 1985 it registered the name as a federal trademark. Since 1980, King has operated a small club in Columbia, Missouri, also named "The Blue Note." Around 1993, Bensusan wrote to King demanding that he discontinue use of "The Blue Note" name. King's attorney responded by saying that Bensusan had no legal right to make the demand. In 1996 King created, in Missouri, a Web site for "The Blue Note," which also contained a hyperlink to the New York club's Web site. Bensusan then sued in the Southern District of New York, alleging Lanham Act and trademark violations, among other things. The New York court dismissed the case for lack of personal jurisdiction. Bensusan appealed. Decide. Explain. See *Bensusan Restaurant Corp. v. King,* 126 F.3d 25 (2d Cir. 1997).

5. Are online bloggers (that is, authors of topical Web logs) entitled to protection as journalists under the First Amendment with regard to the confidentiality of their sources? What if those sources have illegally revealed corporate trade secrets?[82]

6. America Online (AOL), an Internet service provider, sued TSF Marketing and Joseph Melle, who founded TSF. AOL claimed that Melle and TSF sent unauthorized bulk e-mail advertisements (spam) to AOL subscribers. The e-mail contained the letters "aol.com" in the headers. AOL claimed that the e-mail totaled some 60 million messages over a 10-month period. Melle allegedly continued the mailings after he was notified in writing by AOL to stop. AOL received over 50,000 complaints from subscribers. AOL claimed, among other things, that Melle had diluted its trademark.[83] The case arose before the passage of the CAN-SPAM Act. Would Melle have been liable under that Act? Explain.

7. McLaren was an employee of Microsoft Corporation. In December 1996, Microsoft suspended McLaren's employment pending an investigation into accusations of sexual harassment and "inventory questions." McLaren requested access to his electronic mail to disprove the allegations against him. According to McLaren, he was told he could access his e-mail only by requesting it through company officials and telling them the location of a particular message. By memorandum, McLaren requested that no one tamper with his Microsoft office workstation or his e-mail. McLaren's employment was terminated on December 11, 1996.

   Following the termination of his employment, McLaren filed suit against the company alleging as his sole cause of action a claim for invasion of privacy. In support of his claim, McLaren alleged that, on information and belief, Microsoft had invaded his privacy by "breaking into" some or all of the personal folders maintained on his office computer and releasing the contents of the folders to third parties. According to McLaren, the personal folders were part of a computer application created by Microsoft in which e-mail messages could be stored. Access to the e-mail system was obtained through a network password. Access to personal folders could be additionally restricted by a "personal store" password created by the individual user. McLaren created and used a personal store password to restrict access to his personal folders.

McLaren concedes in his petition that it was possible for Microsoft to "decrypt" his personal store password. McLaren alleges, however, that "[b]y allowing [him] to have a personal store password for his personal folders, [McLaren] manifested and [Microsoft] recognized an expectation that the personal folders would be free from intrusion and interference." McLaren characterizes Microsoft's decrypting or otherwise "breaking in" to his personal folders as an intentional, unjustified, and unlawful invasion of privacy.

Did Microsoft unlawfully invade McLaren's privacy? Explain. See *McLaren v. Microsoft,* 1999 Texas App. LEXIS 4103 (5th Dist., Dallas).

8. In March 1992 Danish police seized the business records of BAMSE, a computer bulletin board system based in Denmark that sold child pornography over the Internet. The records included information that Mohrbacher, who lived in Paradise, California, had downloaded two graphic interface format (GIF) images from BAMSE in January 1992.

In March 1993 police executed a search warrant at Mohrbacher's workplace and found, among other images, two files that had been downloaded from BAMSE, one of a nude girl and one of a girl engaged in a sex act with an adult; both girls were under 12. During the execution of the warrant, Mohrbacher was cooperative, confessing that he had downloaded the two images from BAMSE. Mohrbacher was charged with transporting or shipping images by computer as prohibited by 18 U.S.C. 2252(a)(1). Mohrbacher argued that downloading is properly characterized as receiving images by computer, which is proscribed by section 2252(a)(2). He was not charged under (a)(2).

Does downloading from a computer bulletin board constitute shipping or transporting within the meaning of 18 U.S.C. section 2252(a)(1)? Explain. See *United States of America v. Mohrbacher,* 182 F.3d 1041 (9th Cir. 1999).

9. Enza and Richard Hill ordered a Gateway 2000 computer by telephone and paid by credit card. The computer was delivered in a box that also contained the terms of sale. Those terms were to be effective unless the computer was returned within 30 days. Among those terms was a clause providing for arbitration of any problems. The Hills kept the computer for more than 30 days before complaining about its performance and components. They filed suit, and Gateway argued that the arbitration clause should be enforced. The Hills conceded that they noticed the statement of terms, but they did not read those terms closely enough to notice the arbitration provision. Should the arbitration clause be enforced? Explain. See *Hill v. Gateway 2000,* 105 F.3d 1147 (7th Cir. 1997); cert. den. 522 U.S. 808 (1997).

10. Plaintiff Marobie-FL, Inc., released software of copyrighted clip art for use in the fire service industry. Robisheaux administered the National Association of Fire Equipment Distributors (NAFED) Web page. He received the clip art from a source that he could not remember. He placed the clip art on NAFED's Web page. At that point, the clip art could be readily accessed and downloaded by any Web user.

Marobie claimed copyright infringement. Among other arguments, NAFED claimed that its display of the clip art constituted a fair use, within the meaning of federal copyright law. Decide. Explain. See *Marobie-FL v. National Ass'n of Fire Equip. Dist.*, 983 F.Supp. 1167 (N.D. Ill. 1997).

11. Recently journalist John Snell remarked, "Not long ago you couldn't turn around in cyberspace without bumping into a tech geek. Now you're no more than a mouse click away from a lawyer. Attorneys are everywhere."[84] What factors account for the dramatic increase in lawyers addressing Internet issues?

Notes

1. Janna Quitney Anderson and Lee Rainie, "The Future of the Internet II," *Pew Internet & American Life Project,* September 24, 2006.

2. Christopher Rhoads, "What's the Hindi Word for Dot-Com?," *The Wall Street Journal,* October 11, 2007, p. B1.

3. Duncan B. Hollis, "E-War Rules of Engagement," *Los Angeles Times,* October 8, 2007.

4. Roger O. Crockett and Spencer E. Ante, "Equal Opportunity Speedway," *BusinessWeek,* May 21, 2007, p. 44.

5. James Covert, "Advocates for Web Access for Blind Pass Legal Hurdle," *The Wall Street Journal,* October 4, 2007, p. B4.

6. Jack Chang, "Many Nations Want to End U.S. Control of Internet," *Des Moines Register,* November 11, 2007, p. 1A; and Michael Astor, "Internet Forum Yields No Action on U.S. Control," *Des Moines Register,* November 16, 2007, p. 2A.

7. Thomas Naylor, "Trading Our Souls for Virtual Reality," *Across the Board,* July/August 2001, p. 19.

8. "Who Wins in the New Economy?" *The Wall Street Journal,* June 27, 2000, p. B1.

9. Editorial, "Protecting Internet Democracy," *New York Times,* January 3, 2007; Ryan McGeeney, "Consumers Would Lose Out with Internet Privatization," *The Oracle,* April 19, 2006; Timothy B. Lee, "Entangling the Web," *New York Times,* August 3, 2006; and "Neutral Net: A Battle for Control of the Web," *The Wall Street Journal,* June 24, 2006, p. A9.

10. Louise Story, "Online Marketers Joining Internet Privacy Efforts," *New York Times,* October 31, 2007.

11. Matt Richtel and Brad Stone, "Doll Web Sites Drive Girls to Stay Home and Play, *New York Times,* June 6, 2007.

12. Frank Ahrens, "'Puppets' Emerge as Internet's Effective, and Deceptive, Salesmen," *Washington Post,* October 7, 2006, p. D1.

13. See Bill Bane, "Spyware Taking Toll on Computer Firms, Users," *Waterloo/Cedar Falls Courier,* November 1, 2004, p. B6; Michael Totty, "Pesky Pop-Up Ads Go Mainstream, as 'Adware' Gains Acceptance," *The Wall Street Journal,* June 22, 2004, p. B1.

14. "Ex-CompuServe Chief's Conviction Overturned; German Case Involved Child Porn Sites," *Houston Chronicle,* November 18, 1999, p. 3. The head of CompuServe Germany was convicted in 1998 of violating German law by failing to block CompuServe's customers' access to child pornography Web sites. At the time the only technical way for CompuServe to comply was to block all of its worldwide users from access. The conviction was reversed in 1999.

15. See *Revell v. Lidov,* 317 F.3d 467 (5th Cir. 2002). Lidov posted an article he wrote on the "bombing of Pan Am Flight 103, which exploded over Lockerbie, Scotland, in 1988. The article alleges that a broad politically motivated conspiracy among senior members of the Reagan administration

lay behind their willful failure to stop the bombing despite clear advance warnings. Further, Lidov charged that the government proceeded to cover up its receipt of advance warning. . . . Specifically, the article singles out Oliver "Buck" Revell, then Associate Deputy Director of the FBI, for severe criticism, accusing him of complicity in the conspiracy and cover-up." The article was posted on an Internet bulletin board maintained by Columbia University's School of Journalism. "At the time he wrote the article, Lidov had never been to Texas, except possibly to change planes, or conducted business there, and was apparently unaware that Revell then resided in Texas." "Columbia, since it began keeping records, never received more than 20 Internet subscriptions to the *Columbia Journalism Review* from Texas residents." The Fifth Circuit found that neither general nor specific jurisdiction existed in the Texas courts.

16. *Mink v. AAAA Development,* 190 F. 3d 333 (5th Cir. 1999).

17. See, for example, *Pavlovich v. DVD Copy Control Association.* A California appeals court held that a Texas resident was subject to California's jurisdiction for the knowing posting of trade secrets of a California company on an Indiana Web site (91 Cal. App. 4th 409, 109 Cal. Rptr. 2d 909 (Cal. Ct. App. 2001)). But the California Supreme Court reversed (58 P. 3d 2 (Cal. 2002)). See also *Gator.com Corp. v. L.L.Bean, Inc.,* where the district court held that L.L.Bean could not be sued in California where it had no stores or agents, although it did sell merchandise to California residents through its Web site (2001 U.S. Dist. LEXIS 19373 (N.D. Cal. 2001)). A three-judge panel of the Ninth Circuit reversed, finding in part that the volume of Internet business done by L.L.Bean with California residents made it subject to California's jurisdiction (341 F. 3d 1072 (9th Cir. 2003)). That decision was vacated, however, when the Ninth Circuit decided to rehear the case *en banc* (366 F. 3d 789 (9th Cir. 2004)). After oral argument on the rehearing, however, Gator.com and L.L.Bean settled their substantive dispute, and thus the Ninth Circuit dismissed the appeal because of the lack of a continuing case or controversy (398 F. 3d 1125 (2005)).

18. Kevin Delaney, "Local Rules: Jean-Jacques Gomez Believes that If a Web Site Appears on a French Computer, France Should Be Able to Regulate It. The Internet World Is Aghast," *The Wall Street Journal,* October 1, 2001, p. R3.

19. "Ex-CompuServe Chief's Conviction Overturned," p.3.

20. Stephan Wilske and Teresa Schiller, "International Jurisdiction in Cyberspace: Which States May Regulate the Internet?" *Federal Communications Law Journal* 50 (December 1997), p. 117.

21. 433 F. 3d 1199 (9th Cir. 2006).

22. 126 S. Ct. 2332 (2006).

23. See, for example, *Ford Motor Co. v. Lane,* 67 F. Supp. 2d 745 (E.D. Mich. 1999).

24. "42% of Youths Report Exposure to Porn on Web," *Des Moines Register,* February 5, 2007, p. 5A.

25. Kara Swisher, "Forget Wall Street, Main Street Still Thinks the Internet Is Hot," *The Wall Street Journal,* October 30, 2000, p. B1.

26. *Reno v. ACLU,* 521 U.S. 844 (1997).

27. *Ashcroft v. ACLU,* 122 S. Ct. 1700 (2002).

28. *Ashcroft v. ACLU,* 124 S. Ct. 2783, 159 L. Ed. 2d 690 (2004).

29. *ACLU v. Gonzales,* 478 F. Supp. 775 (ED Pa. 2007); and Ellen Nakashima and Sam Diaz, "Judge Rejects Law Aimed at Internet Porn," *Washington Post,* March 23, 2007, p. D1.

30. *Ashcroft v. Free Speech Coalition,* 122 S. Ct. 1389 (2002).

31. "FTC Announces First Can-Spam Act Cases," *Federal Trade Commission,* April 29, 2004 [**www.ftc.gov/opa/2004/04/040429canspam.htm**].

32. Jim Stanton, "From Where Your House Is to How Much You Paid for It—It's All on the Internet for Anyone to See," *Waterloo/Cedar Falls Courier,* August 27, 2000, p. A1.

33. Editorial, "Watching Your Every Move," *New York Times,* June 13, 2007; and Sam Diaz, "Google to Tighten Privacy," *Washington Post,* March 15, 2007, p. D3.

34. David Lazarus, "Your Loss of Privacy Is a Package Deal," *Los Angeles Times,* September 12, 2007.

35. Glenn Simpson, "U.S., EU Negotiators Reach Agreement on Electronic-Commerce Privacy Rules," *The Wall Street Journal,* March 15, 2000, p. B4.

36. Carter Manny, "Privacy Controls on Transborder Flows of Personal Data from Europe," *Business Law Review,* Spring 2001, pp. 101–20.

37. "U.S., Europe Move to Net Privacy Pact," *Waterloo/Cedar Falls Courier,* June 5, 2000, p. B5.

38. Associated Press, "EU Panel Questions Google on Protecting Its Users' Privacy," *Washington Post,* May 26, 2007, p. D2.

39. *John Doe v. Ashcroft,* 334 F. Supp. 2d 471 (SD NY 2004).

40. *John Doe v. Gonzales,* 449 F. 3d 415 (2d Cir. 2006).

41. *John Doe v. Gonzales,* 500 F. Supp. 2d 379 (SD NY 2007).

42. Pui-Wing Tam, Erin White, Nick Wingfield, and Kris Maher, "Snooping E-Mail by Software Is Now a Workplace Norm," *The Wall Street Journal,* March 9, 2005, p. B1.

43. Ibid.

44. *Blakey v. Continental Airlines,* 751 A. 2d 538 (Sup. Ct. N.J. 2001).

45. Tom Alex, "Stolen Laptop Sends up a Flare," *Des Moines Register,* October 18, 2005, p. 1A.

46. *US v. Farraj,* 142 F. Supp. 2d 484 (SD NY 2001).

47. Spencer E. Ante and Brian Grow, "Meet The Hackers," *BusinessWeek,* May 29, 2006, p. 58.

48. Yigal Schleifer, "Want to Outwit Hackers? Hire an Ethical One," *Christian Science Monitor,* June 21, 2006.

49. Editorial, "Wake Up Your Computer," *New York Times,* January 12, 2007.

50. Brian Grow and Ben Elgin, "Click Fraud: The Dark Side of Online Advertising," *Business-Week,* October 2, 2006, p. 46; and Sara Kehaulani Goo, "Google Says Worries about Click Fraud Are Overblown," *Washington Post,* August 9, 2006.

51. Jeanette Borzo, "Something's Phishy," *The Wall Street Journal,* November 15, 2004, p. R8.

52. Kim Hart, "Phish-Hooked," *Washington Post,* July 16, 2006, p. F1.

53. [**www.fraud.org/internet/2007internet.pdf**]

54. Susan Pulliam, "Moving the Market—Tracking the Numbers/Street Sleuth: Online Stock Pickers—and Hype—Are Back," *The Wall Street Journal,* January 12, 2004, p. C3.

55. "Former Worker Gets 4 years for Cyberstalking," *Chicago Tribune,* March 18, 2005, p. 13.

56. "The 1999 Report on Cyberstalking: A New Challenge for Law Enforcement and Industry" can be found at [**www.cybercrime.gov/cyberstalking.htm**].

57. Current status of the convention can be found at [**http://conventions.coe.int/Treaty/Commun/ ChercheSig.asp?NT=185&CM=&DF=&CL=ENG**].

58. Thomas Weber, "Treaty on Cybercrime Flew under the Radar despite Potential Risks," *The Wall Street Journal,* December 3, 2001, p. B1.

59. Alan S. Reid and Nic Ryder, "The Case of Richard Tomlinson: The Spy Who E-Mailed Me," *Information & Communications Technology Law* 9 (March 2000), p. 61.

60. "Ex-CompuServe Chief's Conviction Overturned," p.3.

61. Jeffrey Sparshott, "WTO Lets U.S. Limit Internet Gambling," *Knight Ridder Tribune Business News,* April 8, 2005, p. 1.

62. Warren Giles, "U.S. Ban on Web Gambling Rejected," *Washington Post,* March 31, 2007, p. D1.

63. P. Liddell, M. Moore, and R. Moore, "Just Sign on the Electronic Line," *Journal of the Academy of Marketing Science,* Winter 2001, p. 110.

64. [**www.nccusl.org/Update/uniformact_factsheets/uniformacts-fs-ucita.asp**].

65. Ronald J. Mann and Travis Siebeneicher, "Just One Click: The Reality of Internet Retail Contracting," University of Texas Law, *Law and Econ Research Paper No. 104,* May 2007 [available at SSRN: **http://ssrn.com/abstract=988788**].

66. Anna Mathews, "U.S. Will Give Web Patents More Scrutiny," *The Wall Street Journal,* March 29, 2000, p. B1.

67. Shannon Lafferty, "Personalized Webcasting Spawns Copyright Feud," *Law.com,* September 27, 2001.

68. David Hamilton, "Digital-Copyright Law Faces New Fight," *The Wall Street Journal,* June 7, 2001, p. B10.

69. *A&M Records, Inc. v. Napster, Inc.,* 284 F.3d 1091 (9th Cir. 2002) and *A&M Records, Inc. v. Napster, Inc.,* 239 F.3d 1004 (9th Cir. 2001).

70. *Metro-Goldwyn-Mayer Studios, Inc. v. Grokster, Ltd.,* 380 F. 3d 1154 (9th Cir. 2004).

71. Amy Brittain, "Universities Strike Back in Battle over Illegal Downloads," *Christian Science Monitor,* June 18, 2007.

72. Rob Peoraro, "The Sound of Copy Restrictions Crashing," *Washington Post,* May 17, 2007, p. D1; and Michelle Quinn, Alana Semuels, and Dawn C. Chmielewski, "Apple Seeks to Unchain Melodies," *Los Angeles Times,* February 7, 2007.

73. Lawrence Lessig, "Make Way for Copyright Chaos," *New York Times,* March 18, 2007.

74. *Virtual Works v. Volkswagen of America,* 238 F. 3d 264 (4th Cir. 2001).

75. *Sporty's Farm LLC v. Sportsman's Market,* 202 F. 3d 489 (2d Cir. 2000).

76. A. Latour and S. Miller, " 'Pirate' Is Caught in a War with Ford over Volvo Site," *The Wall Street Journal,* October 23, 2000, p. A 31.

77. *Shields v. Zuccarini,* 254 F. 3d 476 (3d Cir. 2001).

78. *Quill Corporation v. North Dakota,* 504 U.S. 298 (1992).

79. Michelle Blackson, "Closing the Online Tax Loophole," *State Legislatures* 34, Issue 4 (April 2008), p. 24.

80. [**www.gipiproject.org/taxation**].

81. John Perry Barlow, "Cyberspace Declaration of Independence" [**http://hobbes.ncsa.uiuc.edu/ sean/declaration.html**].

82. See documents filed in *Apple Computer v. John Does* [**www.eff.org/Censorship/ Apple_v_Does**]. For a blogger's perspective, see Benny Evangelista, "Net Buzzing on Bloggers' Status; First Amendment Issues Become Hot Topic in Chat Rooms," *San Francisco Chronicle,* March 9, 2005, p. C1.

83. See *America Online, Inc. v. IMS,* 24 F. Supp. 2d 548 (ED Va. 1998).

84. John Snell, "Lawyers Drawn to Unsettled Internet; Lots of Legal Issues, Large and Small, Must Be Sorted Out," *Minneapolis Star Tribune,* November 29, 1999, p. 6D.

The Constitution of the United States of America

Preamble

We the People of the United States, in Order to form a more perfect Union, establish Justice, insure domestic Tranquility, provide for the common defence, promote the general Welfare, and secure the Blessings of Liberty to ourselves and our Posterity, do ordain and establish this Constitution for the United States of America.

Article I

Section 1. All legislative Powers herein granted shall be vested in a Congress of the United States, which shall consist of a Senate and House of Representatives.

Section 2. (1) The House of Representatives shall be composed of Members chosen every second Year by the People of the several States, and the Electors in each State shall have the Qualifications requisite for Electors of the most numerous Branch of the State Legislature.

(2) No Person shall be a Representative who shall not have attained to the Age of twenty-five Years, and been seven Years a Citizen of the United States, and who shall not, when elected, be an Inhabitant of that State in which he shall be chosen.

(3) Representatives and direct Taxes shall be apportioned among the several States which may be included within this Union, according to their respective Numbers, which shall be determined by adding to the whole Number of free Persons, including those bound to Service for a Term of Years, and excluding Indians not taxed, three fifths of all other Persons.[1] The actual Enumeration shall be made within three Years after the first Meeting of the Congress of the United States, and within every subsequent Term of ten Years, in such Manner as they shall by Law direct. The Number of Representatives shall not exceed one for every thirty Thousand, but each State shall have at Least one Representative; and until such enumeration shall be made, the State of New Hampshire shall be entitled to chuse three, Massachusetts eight, Rhode Island and Providence Plantations one, Connecticut five, New York six, New Jersey four, Pennsylvania eight, Delaware one, Maryland six, Virginia ten, North Carolina five, South Carolina five, and Georgia three.

---

[1] Refer to the Fourteenth Amendment.

(4) When vacancies happen in the Representation from any State, the Executive Authority thereof shall issue Writs of Election to fill such Vacancies.

(5) The House of Representatives shall chuse their Speaker and other Officers; and shall have the sole Power of Impeachment.

Section 3. (1) The Senate of the United States shall be composed of two Senators from each State, chosen by the Legislature thereof,[2] for six Years; and each Senator shall have one Vote.

(2) Immediately after they shall be assembled in Consequence of the first Election, they shall be divided as equally as may be into three Classes. The Seats of the Senators of the first Class shall be vacated at the Expiration of the Second Year, of the second Class at the Expiration of the fourth Year, and of the third Class at the Expiration of the sixth Year, so that one third may be chosen every second Year; and if Vacancies happen by Resignation, or otherwise, during the Recess of the Legislature of any State, the Executive thereof may make temporary Appointments until the next Meeting of the Legislature, which shall then fill such Vacancies.[3]

(3) No Person shall be a Senator who shall not have attained to the Age of thirty Years, and been nine Years a Citizen of the United States, and who shall not, when elected, be an Inhabitant of that State for which he shall be chosen.

(4) The Vice President of the United States shall be President of the Senate, but shall have no Vote, unless they be equally divided.

(5) The Senate shall chuse their other Officers, and also a President pro tempore, in the Absence of the Vice President, or when he shall exercise the Office of President of the United States.

(6) The Senate shall have the sole Power to try all Impeachments. When sitting for that Purpose, they shall be on Oath or Affirmation. When the President of the United States is tried, the Chief Justice shall preside: And no Person shall be convicted without the Concurrence of two thirds of the Members present.

(7) Judgment in Cases of Impeachment shall not extend further than to removal from Office, and disqualification to hold and enjoy any Office of honor, Trust, or Profit under the United States: but the Party convicted shall nevertheless be liable and subject to Indictment, Trial, Judgment, and Punishment, according to Law.

Section 4. (1) The Times, Places and Manner of holding Elections for Senators and Representatives, shall be prescribed in each State by the Legislature thereof; but the Congress may at any time by Law make or alter such Regulations, except as to the Places of chusing Senators.

(2) The Congress shall assemble at least once in every year, and such Meeting shall be on the first Monday in December, unless they shall by Law appoint a different Day.[4]

Section 5. (1) Each House shall be the Judge of the Elections, Returns, and Qualifications of its own Members, and a Majority of each shall constitute a Quorum to do Business; but a smaller Number may adjourn from day to day, and may be authorized to compel the Attendance of absent Members, in such Manner, and under such Penalties as each House may provide.

---

[2]Refer to the Seventeenth Amendment.

[3]Ibid.

[4]Refer to the Twentieth Amendment.

(2) Each House may determine the Rules of its Proceedings, punish its Members for disorderly Behavior, and, with the Concurrence of two thirds, expel a Member.

(3) Each House shall keep a Journal of its Proceedings, and from time to time publish the same, excepting such Parts as may in their Judgment require Secrecy; and the Yeas and Nays of the Members of either House on any question shall, at the Desire of one fifth of those Present, be entered on the Journal.

(4) Neither House, during the Session of Congress, shall, without the Consent of the other, adjourn for more than three days, nor to any other Place than that in which the two Houses shall be sitting.

Section 6. (1) The Senators and Representatives shall receive a Compensation for their Services, to be ascertained by Law, and paid out of the Treasury of the United States. They shall in all Cases, except Treason, Felony and Breach of the Peace, be privileged from Arrest during their Attendance at the Session of their respective Houses, and in going to and returning from the same; and for any Speech or Debate in either House, they shall not be questioned in any other Place.

(2) No Senator or Representative shall, during the Time for which he was elected, be appointed to any civil Office under the Authority of the United States, which shall have been created, or the Emoluments whereof shall have been encreased during such time; and no Person holding any Office under the United States, shall be a Member of either House during his Continuance in Office.

Section 7. (1) All Bills for raising Revenue shall originate in the House of Representatives; but the Senate may propose or concur with Amendments as on other Bills.

(2) Every Bill which shall have passed the House of Representatives and the Senate, shall, before it becomes a Law, be presented to the President of the United States; If he approve he shall sign it, but if not he shall return it, with his Objections to the House in which it shall have originated, who shall enter the Objections at large on their Journal, and proceed to reconsider it. If after such Reconsideration two thirds of that House shall agree to pass the Bill, it shall be sent together with the Objections, to the other House, by which it shall likewise be reconsidered, and if approved by two thirds of that House, it shall become a Law. But in all such Cases the Votes of both Houses shall be determined by yeas and Nays, and the Names of the Persons voting for and against the Bill shall be entered on the Journal of each House respectively. If any Bill shall not be returned by the President within ten Days (Sundays excepted) after it shall have been presented to him, the Same shall be a Law, in like Manner as if he had signed it, unless the Congress by their Adjournment prevent its Return in which Case it shall not be a Law.

(3) Every Order, Resolution, or Vote, to Which the Concurrence of the Senate and House of Representatives may be necessary (except on a question of Adjournment) shall be presented to the President of the United States; and before the same shall take Effect, shall be approved by him, or being disapproved by him, shall be repassed by two thirds of the Senate and House of Representatives, according to the Rules and Limitations prescribed in the Case of a Bill.

Section 8. (1) The Congress shall have Power To lay and collect Taxes, Duties, Imposts and Excises, to pay the Debts and provide for the common Defence and general Welfare of the United States; but all Duties, Imposts and Excises shall be uniform throughout the United States;

(2) To borrow money on the credit of the United States;

(3) To regulate Commerce with foreign Nations, and among the several States, and with the Indian Tribes;

(4) To establish a uniform Rule of Naturalization, and uniform Laws on the subject of Bankruptcies throughout the United States;

(5) To coin Money, regulate the Value thereof, and of foreign Coin, and fix the Standard of Weights and Measures;

(6) To provide for the Punishment of counterfeiting the Securities and current Coin of the United States;

(7) To Establish Post Offices and Post Roads;

(8) To promote the Progress of Science and useful Arts, by securing for limited Times to Authors and Inventors the exclusive Right to their respective Writings and Discoveries;

(9) To constitute Tribunals inferior to the Supreme Court;

(10) To define and punish Piracies and Felonies committed on the high Seas, and Offenses against the Law of Nations;

(11) To declare War, grant Letters of Marque and Reprisal, and make Rules concerning Captures on Land and Water;

(12) To raise and support Armies, but no Appropriation of Money to that Use shall be for a longer Term than two Years;

(13) To provide and maintain a Navy;

(14) To make Rules for the Government and Regulation of the land and naval Forces;

(15) To provide for calling forth the Militia to execute the Laws of the Union, suppress Insurrections and repel Invasions;

(16) To provide for organizing, arming, and disciplining, the Militia, and for governing such Part of them as may be employed in the Service of the United States, reserving to the States respectively, the Appointment of the Officers, and the Authority of training the Militia according to the discipline prescribed by Congress;

(17) To exercise exclusive Legislation in all Cases whatsoever, over such District (not exceeding ten Miles square) as may, by Cession of particular States, and the Acceptance of Congress, become the Seat of the Government of the United States, and to exercise like Authority over all Places purchased by the Consent of the Legislature of the State in which the Same shall be, for the Erection of Forts, Magazines, Arsenals, dock-Yards, and other needful Buildings;—And

(18) To make all Laws which shall be necessary and proper for carrying into Execution the foregoing Powers, and all other Powers vested by this Constitution in the Government of the United States, or in any Department or Officer thereof.

Section 9. (1) The Migration or Importation of Such Persons as any of the States now existing shall think proper to admit, shall not be prohibited by the Congress prior to the Year one thousand eight hundred and eight, but a Tax or duty may be imposed on such Importation, not exceeding ten dollars for each Person.

(2) The privilege of the Writ of Habeas Corpus shall not be suspended, unless when in Cases of Rebellion or Invasion the public Safety may require it.

(3) No Bill of Attainder or ex post facto Law shall be passed.

(4) No Capitation, or other direct, Tax shall be laid, unless in proportion to the Census or Enumeration herein before directed to the taken.[5]

[5]Refer to the Sixteenth Amendment.

(5) No Tax or Duty shall be laid on Articles exported from any state.

(6) No Preference shall be given by any Regulation of Commerce or Revenue to the Ports of one State over those of another; nor shall Vessels bound to, or from, one State be obliged to enter, clear, or pay Duties in another.

(7) No money shall be drawn from the Treasury, but in Consequence of Appropriations made by Law; and a regular Statement and Account of the Receipts and Expenditures of all public Money shall be published from time to time.

(8) No Title of Nobility shall be granted by the United States; And no person holding any Office of Profit or Trust under them, shall, without the Consent of the Congress, accept of any present, Emolument, Office or Title, of any kind whatever, from any King, Prince, or foreign State.

Section 10. (1) No State shall enter into any Treaty, Alliance, or Confederation; grant Letters of Marque and Reprisal; coin Money; emit Bills of Credit; make any Thing but gold and silver Coin a Tender in Payment of Debts; pass any Bill of Attainder, ex post facto Law, or Law impairing the Obligation of Contracts, or grant any Title of Nobility.

(2) No State shall, without the Consent of the Congress, lay any Imposts or Duties on Imports or Exports, except what may be absolutely necessary for executing its inspection Laws: and the net Produce of all Duties and Imposts, laid by any State on Imports or Exports, shall be for the Use of the Treasury of the United States; and all such Laws shall be subject to the Revision and Controul of the Congress.

(3) No State shall, without the Consent of Congress, lay any Duty of Tonnage, keep Troops, or Ships of War in time of Peace, enter into any Agreement or Compact with another State, or with a foreign Power, or engage in War, unless actually invaded, or in such imminent Danger as will not admit of delay.

Article II

Section 1. (1) The executive Power shall be vested in a President of the United States of America. He shall hold his Office during the Term of four Years, and, together with the Vice President, chosen for the same Term, be elected as follows:

(2) Each State shall appoint, in such Manner as the Legislature thereof may direct, a Number of Electors, equal to the whole Number of Senators and Representatives to which the State may be entitled in the Congress; but no Senator or Representative, or Person holding an Office of Trust or Profit under the United States, shall be appointed an Elector.

(3) The Electors shall meet in their respective States, and vote by Ballot for two Persons, of whom one at least shall not be an Inhabitant of the same State with themselves. And they shall make a list of all the Persons voted for, and of the Number of Votes for each; which List they shall sign and certify, and transmit sealed to the Seat of the Government of the United States, directed to the President of the Senate. The President of the Senate shall, in the Presence of the Senate and House of Representatives, open all the Certificates, and the Votes shall then be counted. The Person having the greatest Number of Votes shall be the President, if such Number be a Majority of the whole Number of Electors appointed; and if there be more than one who have such Majority, and have an equal Number of Votes, then the House of Representatives shall immediately chuse by Ballot one of them for President; and if no Person have a Majority, then from the five highest on the List the said House shall in like Manner chuse the President. But in chusing the President, the Votes

shall be taken by States, the Representation from each State have one Vote; A quorum for this Purpose shall consist of a Member or Members from two thirds of the States, and a Majority of all the States shall be necessary to a Choice. In every Case, after the Choice of the President, the Person having the greater Number of Votes of the Electors shall be the Vice President. But if there should remain two or more who have equal Votes, the Senate shall chuse from them by Ballot the Vice President.[6]

(4) The Congress may determine the Time of chusing the Electors, and the Day on which they shall give their Votes; which Day shall be the same throughout the United States.

(5) No person except a natural born Citizen, or a Citizen of the United States, at the time of the Adoption of this Constitution, shall be eligible to the Office of President; neither shall any Person be eligible to that Office who shall not have attained to the Age of thirty-five Years, and been fourteen Years a Resident within the United States.

(6) In case of the removal of the President from Office, or of his Death, Resignation or Inability to discharge the Powers and Duties of the said Office, the Same shall devolve on the Vice President, and the Congress may by Law provide for the Case of Removal, Death, Resignation or Inability, both of the President and Vice President, declaring what Officer shall then act as President, and such Officer shall act accordingly, until the Disability be removed, or a President shall be elected.[7]

(7) The President shall, at stated Times, receive for his Services, a Compensation, which shall neither be encreased nor diminished during the Period for which he shall have been elected, and he shall not receive within that Period any other Emolument from the United States, or any of them.

(8) Before he enter on the Execution of his Office, he shall take the following Oath or Affirmation: "I do solemnly swear (or affirm) that I will faithfully execute the Office of President of the United States, and will to the best of my Ability, preserve, protect, and defend the Constitution of the United States."

Section 2. (1) The President shall be Commander in Chief of the Army and Navy of the United States, and of the militia of the several States, when called into the actual Service of the United States; he may require the Opinion, in writing, of the principal Officer in each of the executive Departments, upon any Subject relating to the Duties of their respective Offices, and he shall have Power to grant Reprieves and Pardons for Offenses against the United States, except in Cases of Impeachment.

(2) He shall have Power, by and with the Advice and Consent of the Senate, to make Treaties, provided two thirds of the Senators present concur; and he shall nominate, and by and with the Advice and Consent of the Senate, shall appoint Ambassadors, other public Ministers and Consuls, Judges of the supreme Court, and all other Officers of the United States, whose Appointments are not herein otherwise provided for, and which shall be established by Law; but the Congress may by Law vest the Appointment of such inferior Officers, as they think proper, in the President alone, in the Courts of Law, or in the Heads of Departments.

---

[6]Refer to the Twelfth Amendment.

[7]Refer to the Twenty-Fifth Amendment

(3) The President shall have Power to fill up all Vacancies that may happen during the Recess of the Senate, by granting Commissions which shall expire at the End of their next Session.

Section 3. He shall from time to time give to the Congress Information of the State of the Union, and recommend to their Consideration such Measures as he shall judge necessary and expedient; he may, on extraordinary Occasions, convene both Houses, or either of them, and in Case of Disagreement between them, with Respect to the Time of Adjournment, he may adjourn them to such Time as he shall think proper; he shall receive Ambassadors and other public Ministers; he shall take Care that the Laws be faithfully executed, and shall Commission all the Officers of the United States.

Section 4. The President, Vice President and all civil Officers of the United States, shall be removed from Office on Impeachment for, and Conviction of, Treason, Bribery, or other high Crimes and Misdemeanors.

Article III

Section 1. The judicial Power of the United States, shall be vested in one supreme Court, and in such inferior Courts as the Congress may from time to time ordain and establish. The Judges, both of the supreme and inferior Courts, shall hold their Offices during good Behaviour, and shall, at stated Times, receive for their Services a Compensation, which shall not be diminished during their Continuance in Office.

Section 2. (1) The judicial Power shall extend to all Cases, in Law and Equity, arising under this Constitution, the Laws of the United States, and Treaties made, or which shall be made, under their Authority;—to all Cases affecting Ambassadors, other public Ministers and Consuls;—to all Cases of admiralty and maritime Jurisdiction;—to Controversies to which the United States shall be a Party;—to Controversies between two or more States;—between a State and Citizens of another State,[8]—between Citizens of different states;—between Citizens of the same State claiming Lands under the Grants of different States, and between a State, or the Citizens thereof, and foreign States, Citizens or Subjects.

(2) In all Cases affecting Ambassadors, other public Ministers and Consuls, and those in which a State shall be a Party, the supreme Court shall have original Jurisdiction. In all the other Cases before mentioned, the supreme Court shall have appellate Jurisdiction, both as to Law and Fact, with such Exceptions, and under such Regulations as the Congress shall make.

(3) The trial of all Crimes, except in Cases of Impeachment, shall be by Jury; and such Trial shall be held in the State where the said Crimes shall have been committed; but when not committed within any State, the Trial shall be at such Place or Places as the Congress may by Law have directed.

Section 3. (1) Treason against the United States, shall consist only in levying War against them, or, in adhering to their enemies, giving them Aid and Comfort. No Person shall be convicted of Treason unless on the Testimony of two Witnesses to the same overt Act, or on Confession in open Court.

[8]Refer to the Eleventh Amendment.

(2) The Congress shall have Power to declare the Punishment of Treason, but no Attainder of Treason shall work Corruption of Blood, or Forfeiture except during the Life of the Person attainted.

Article IV

Section 1. Full Faith and Credit shall be given in each State to the public Acts, Records, and judicial Proceedings of every other State. And the Congress may by general Laws prescribe the Manner in which such Acts, Records and Proceedings shall be proved, and the Effect thereof.

Section 2. (1) The Citizens of each State shall be entitled to all Privileges and Immunities of Citizens in the several States.

(2) A Person charged in any State with Treason, Felony, or other Crime, who shall flee from Justice, and be found in another State, shall on demand of the executive Authority of the State from which he fled, be delivered up, to be removed to the State having Jurisdiction of the Crime.

(3) No Person held to Service or Labour in one State, under the Laws thereof, escaping into another, shall, in Consequence of any Law or Regulation therein, be discharged from such Service or Labour, but shall be delivered up on Claim of the Party to whom such Service or Labour may be due.[9]

Section 3. (1) New States may be admitted by the Congress into this Union; but no new State shall be formed or erected within the Jurisdiction of any other State; nor any State be formed by the Junction of two or more States, or Parts of States without the Consent of the Legislatures of the States concerned as well as of the Congress.

(2) The Congress shall have Power to dispose of and make all needful Rules and Regulations respecting the Territory or other Property belonging to the United States; and nothing in this Constitution shall be so construed as to Prejudice any Claims of the United States, or of any particular State.

Section 4. The United States shall guarantee to every State in this Union a Republican Form of Government, and shall protect each of them against Invasion; and on Application of the Legislature, or of the Executive (when the Legislature cannot be convened) against domestic Violence.

Article V

The Congress, whenever two thirds of both Houses shall deem it necessary, shall propose Amendments to this Constitution, or, on the Application of the Legislatures of two thirds of the several States, shall call a Convention for proposing Amendments, which, in either Case, shall be valid to all Intents and Purposes, as part of this Constitution, when ratified by the Legislatures of three fourths of the several States, or by Conventions in three fourths thereof, as the one or the other Mode of Ratification may be proposed by the Congress; Provided that no Amendment which may be made prior to the Year One thousand eight hundred and eight shall in any Manner affect the first and fourth Clauses in the Ninth Section

---

[9]Refer to the Thirteenth Amendment.

of the first Article; and that no State, without its Consent, shall be deprived of its equal Suffrage in the Senate.

Article VI

(1) All Debts contracted and Engagements entered into, before the Adoption of this Constitution shall be as valid against the United States under this Constitution, as under the Confederation.

(2) This Constitution, and the Laws of the United States which shall be made in Pursuance thereof; and all Treaties made, or which shall be made, under the Authority of the United States, shall be the supreme Law of the Land; and the Judges in every State shall be bound thereby, any Thing in the Constitution or Laws of any State to the Contrary notwithstanding.

(3) The Senators and Representatives before mentioned, and the Members of the several State Legislatures, and all executive and judicial Officers, both of the United States and of the several States, shall be bound by Oath or Affirmation, to support this Constitution, but no religious Test shall ever be required as a Qualification to any Office or public Trust under the United States.

Article VII

The Ratification of the Conventions of nine States shall be sufficient for the Establishment of this Constitution between the States so ratifying the Same.

[Amendments 1–10, the Bill of Rights, were ratified in 1791.]

Amendment I

Congress shall make no law respecting an establishment of religion, or prohibiting the free exercise thereof; or abridging the freedom of speech, or of the press; or the right of the people peaceably to assemble, and to petition the Government for a redress of grievances.

Amendment II

A well regulated Militia, being necessary to the security of a free State, the right of the people to keep and bear Arms, shall not be infringed.

Amendment III

No Soldier shall, in time of peace be quartered in any house, without the consent of the Owner, nor in time of war, but in a manner to be prescribed by law.

Amendment IV

The right of the people to be secure in their persons, houses, papers, and effects, against unreasonable searches and seizures, shall not be violated, and no Warrants shall issue, but upon probable cause, supported by Oath or affirmation, and particularly describing the place to be searched, and the persons or things to be seized.

Amendment V

No person shall be held to answer for a capital, or otherwise infamous crime, unless on a presentment or indictment of a Grand Jury, except in cases arising in the land or naval forces, or in the Militia, when in actual service in time of War or public danger; nor shall any person be subject for the same offence to be twice put in jeopardy of life or limb; nor shall be compelled in any criminal case to be a witness against himself, nor be deprived of life, liberty, or property, without due process of law; nor shall private property be taken for public use, without just compensation.

Amendment VI

In all criminal prosecutions, the accused shall enjoy the right to a speedy and public trial, by an impartial jury of the State and district wherein the crime shall have been committed, which district shall have been previously ascertained by law, and to be informed of the nature and cause of the accusation; to be confronted with the witness against him; to have compulsory process for obtaining witnesses in his favor, and to have the Assistance of Counsel for his defence.

Amendment VII

In Suits at common law, where the value in controversy shall exceed twenty dollars, the right of trial by jury shall be preserved, and no fact tried by jury, shall be otherwise re-examined in any Court of the United States, than according to the rules of the common law.

Amendment VIII

Excessive bail shall not be required, nor excessive fines imposed, nor cruel and unusual punishments inflicted.

Amendment IX

The enumeration in the Constitution, of certain rights, shall not be construed to deny or disparage others retained by the people.

Amendment X

The powers not delegated to the United States by the Constitution, nor prohibited by it to the States, are reserved to the States respectively, or to the people.

Amendment XI [1798]

The Judicial power of the United States shall not be construed to extend to any suit in law or equity, commenced or prosecuted against one of the United States by Citizens of another State, or by Citizens or Subjects of any Foreign State.

Amendment XII [1804]

The Electors shall meet in their respective states and vote by ballot for President and Vice-President, one of whom, at least, shall not be an inhabitant of the same state with themselves; they shall name in their ballots the person voted for as President, and in distinct ballots the person voted for as Vice-President, and they shall make distinct lists of all persons voted for as President, and of all persons voted for as Vice-President, and of the number of votes for each, which lists they shall sign and certify, and transmit sealed to the seat of the government of the United States, directed to the President of the Senate;—The President of the Senate shall, in the presence of the Senate and House of Representatives, open all the certificates and the votes shall then be counted;—The person having the greatest number of votes for President, shall be the President, if such number be a majority of the whole number of Electors appointed; and if no person have such majority, then from the persons having the highest numbers not exceeding three on the list of those voted for as President, the House of Representatives shall choose immediately, by ballot, the President. But in choosing the President, the votes shall be taken by states, the representation from each state having one vote; a quorum for this purpose shall consist of a member or members from two-thirds of the states, and a majority of all the states shall be necessary to a choice. And if the House of Representatives shall not choose a President whenever the right of choice shall devolve upon them before the fourth day of March next following, then the Vice-President shall act as President, as in the case of the death or other constitutional disability of the President.[10]—The person having the greatest number of votes as Vice-President, shall be the Vice-President, if such number be a majority of the whole number of Electors appointed, and if no person have a majority, then from the two highest numbers on the list, the Senate shall choose the Vice-President; a quorum for the purpose shall consist of two-thirds of the whole number of Senators, and a majority of the whole number shall be necessary to a choice. But no person constitutionally ineligible to the office of President shall be eligible to that of Vice-President of the United States.

Amendment XIII [1865]

Section 1. Neither slavery nor involuntary servitude, except as a punishment for crime whereof the party shall have been duly convicted, shall exist within the United States, or any place subject to their jurisdiction.

Section 2. Congress shall have power to enforce this article by appropriate legislation.

---

[10]Refer to the Twentieth Amendment.

Amendment XIV [1868]

Section 1. All persons born or naturalized in the United States, and subject to the jurisdiction thereof, are citizens of the United States and of the State wherein they reside. No State shall make or enforce any law which shall abridge the privileges or immunities of citizens of the United States; nor shall any State deprive any person of life, liberty, or property, without due process of law; nor deny to any person within its jurisdiction the equal protection of the laws.

Section 2. Representatives shall be apportioned among the several States according to their respective numbers, counting the whole number of persons in each State, excluding Indians not taxed. But when the right to vote at any election for the choice of electors for President and Vice President of the United States, Representatives in Congress, the Executive and Judicial officers of a State, or the members of the Legislature thereof, is denied to any of the male inhabitants of such State, being twenty-one years of age,[11] and citizens of the United States, or in any way abridged, except for participation in rebellion, or other crime, the basis of representation therein shall be reduced in the proportion which the number of such male citizens shall bear to the whole number of male citizens twenty-one years of age in such State.

Section 3. No person shall be a Senator or Representative in Congress, or elector of President and Vice President, or hold any office, civil or military, under the United States, or under any State, who having previously taken an oath, as a member of Congress, or as an officer of the United States, or as a member of any State legislature, or as an executive or judicial officer of any State, to support the Constitution of the United States, shall have engaged in insurrection or rebellion against the same, or given aid or comfort to the enemies thereof. But Congress may by a vote of two thirds of each House, remove such disability.

Section 4. The validity of the public debt of the United States, authorized by law, including debts incurred for payment of pensions and bounties for services in suppressing insurrection or rebellion, shall not be questioned. But neither the United States nor any State shall assume or pay any debt or obligation incurred in aid of insurrection or rebellion against the United States, or any claim for the loss or emancipation of any slave; but all such debts, obligations and claims shall be held illegal and void.

Section 5. The Congress shall have power to enforce, by appropriate legislation, the provisions of this article.

Amendment XV [1870]

Section 1. The right of citizens of the United States to vote shall not be denied or abridged by the United States or by any State on account of race, color, or previous condition of servitude.

Section 2. The Congress shall have power to enforce this article by appropriate legislation.

---

[11]Refer to the Twenty-Sixth Amendment.

Amendment XVI [1913]

The Congress shall have power to lay and collect taxes on incomes, from whatever source derived, without apportionment among the several States, and without regard to any census or enumeration.

Amendment XVII [1913]

(1) The Senate of the United States shall be composed of two Senators from each State, elected by the people thereof, for six years; and each Senator shall have one vote. The electors in each State shall have the qualifications requisite for electors of the most numerous branch of the State legislatures.

(2) When vacancies happen in the representation of any State in the Senate, the executive authority of such State shall issue writs of election to fill such vacancies: *Provided,* That the legislature of any State may empower the executive thereof to make temporary appointments until the people fill the vacancies by election as the legislature may direct.

(3) This amendment shall not be so construed as to affect the election or term of any Senator chosen before it becomes valid as part of the Constitution.

Amendment XVIII [1919]

Section 1. After one year from the ratification of this article the manufacture, sale, or transportation of intoxicating liquors within, the importation thereof into, or the exportation thereof from the United States and all territory subject to the jurisdiction thereof for beverage purposes is hereby prohibited.

Section 2. The Congress and the several States shall have concurrent power to enforce this article by appropriate legislation.

Section 3. This article shall be inoperative unless it shall have been ratified as an amendment to the Constitution by the legislatures of the several States, as provided in the Constitution, within seven years from the date of the submission hereof to the States by the Congress.[12]

Amendment XIX [1920]

(1) The right of citizens of the United States to vote shall not be denied or abridged by the United States or by any State on account of sex.

(2) Congress shall have power to enforce this article by appropriate legislation.

Amendment XX [1933]

Section 1. The terms of the President and Vice President shall end at noon on the 20th day of January, and the terms of Senators and Representatives at noon on the 3rd day of

[12]Refer to the Twenty-First Amendment.

January, of the years in which such terms would have ended if this article had not been ratified; and the terms of their successors shall then begin.

Section 2. The Congress shall assemble at least once in every year, and such meeting shall begin at noon on the 3rd day of January, unless they shall by law appoint a different day.

Section 3. If, at the time fixed for the beginning of the term of the President, the President elect shall have died, the Vice President elect shall become President. If the President shall not have been chosen before the time fixed for the beginning of his term or if the President elect shall have failed to qualify, then the Vice President elect shall act as President until a President shall have qualified; and the Congress may by law provide for the case wherein neither a President elect nor a Vice President elect shall have qualified, declaring who shall then act as President, or the manner in which one is to act shall be selected, and such person shall act accordingly until a President or Vice President shall have qualified.

Section 4. The Congress may by law provide for the case of the death of any of the persons from whom the House of Representatives may choose a President whenever the right of choice shall have devolved upon them, and for the case of the death of any of the persons from whom the Senate may choose a Vice President whenever the right of choice shall have devolved upon them.

Section 5. Sections 1 and 2 shall take effect on the 15th day of October following the ratification of this article.

Section 6. This article shall be inoperative unless it shall have been ratified as an amendment to the Constitution by the legislatures of three-fourths of the several States within seven years from the date of its submission.

Amendment XXI [1933]

Section 1. The eighteenth article of amendment to the Constitution of the United States is hereby repealed.

Section 2. The transportation or importation into any State, Territory, or possession of the United States for delivery or use therein of intoxicating liquors, in violation of the laws thereof, is hereby prohibited.

Section 3. This article shall be inoperative unless it shall have been ratified as an amendment to the Constitution by conventions in the several States, as provided in the Constitution, within seven years from the date of the submission hereof to the States by the Congress.

Amendment XXII [1951]

Section 1. No person shall be elected to the office of the President more than twice, and no person who has held the office of President, or acted as President, for more than two years of a term to which some other person was elected President shall be elected to the office of President more than once. But this Article shall not apply to any person holding the office of President when this Article was proposed by the Congress, and shall not prevent any person who may be holding the office of President, or acting as President, during the term within which this Article becomes operative from holding the office of President or acting as president during the remainder of such term.

Section 2. This article shall be inoperative unless it shall have been ratified as an amendment to the Constitution by the legislatures of three-fourths of the several States within seven years from the date of its submission to the States by the Congress.

Amendment XXIII [1961]

Section 1. The District constituting the seat of Government of the United States shall appoint in such manner as the Congress may direct:

A number of electors of President and Vice President equal to the whole number of Senators and Representatives in Congress to which the District would be entitled if it were a State, but in no event more than the least populous state; they shall be in addition to those appointed by the states, but they shall be considered, for the purposes of the election of President and Vice President, to be electors appointed by a state; and they shall meet in the District and perform such duties as provided by the twelfth article of amendment.

Section 2. The Congress shall have power to enforce this article by appropriate legislation.

Amendment XXIV [1964]

Section 1. The right of citizens of the United States to vote in any primary or other election for President or Vice President, for electors for President or Vice President, or for Senator or Representative in Congress, shall not be denied or abridged by the United States or any State by reason of failure to pay any poll tax or other tax.

Section 2. The Congress shall have power to enforce this article by appropriate legislation.

Amendment XXV [1967]

Section 1. In case of the removal of the President from office or of his death or resignation, the Vice President shall become President.

Section 2. Whenever there is a vacancy in the office of the Vice President, the President shall nominate a Vice President who shall take office upon confirmation by a majority vote of both Houses of Congress.

Section 3. Whenever the President transmits to the President pro tempore of the Senate and the Speaker of the House of Representatives his written declaration that he is unable to discharge the powers and duties of his office, and until he transmits to them a written declaration to the contrary, such powers and duties shall be discharged by the Vice President as Acting President.

Section 4. Whenever the Vice President and a majority of either the principal officers of the executive departments or of such other body as Congress may by law provide, transmit to the President pro tempore of the Senate and the Speaker of the House of Representatives their written declaration that the President is unable to discharge the powers and duties of his office, the Vice President shall immediately assume the powers and duties of the office as Acting President.

Thereafter, when the President transmits to the President pro tempore of the Senate and the Speaker of the House of Representatives his written declaration that no inability exists, he shall resume the powers and duties of his office unless the Vice President and a majority of either the principal officers of the executive departments or of such other body as Congress may by law provide, transmit within four days to the President pro tempore of the Senate and the Speaker of the House of Representatives their written declaration that the President is unable to discharge the powers and duties of his office. Thereupon Congress shall decide the issue, assembling within forty-eight hours for that purpose if not in session. If the Congress, within twenty-one days after receipt of the latter written declaration, or, if Congress is not in session, within twenty-one days after Congress is required to assemble, determines by two-thirds vote of both Houses that the President is unable to discharge the powers and duties of his office, the Vice President shall continue to discharge the same as Acting President; otherwise, the President shall resume the powers and duties of his office.

Amendment XXVI [1971]

Section 1. The right of citizens of the United States, who are eighteen years of age or older, to vote shall not be denied or abridged by the United States or by any State on account of age.

Section 2. The Congress shall have power to enforce this article by appropriate legislation.

Amendment XXVII [1992]

No law, varying the compensation for the services of the Senators and Representatives, shall take effect, until an election of Representatives shall have intervened.

Uniform Commercial Code 2000 Official Text, Article 2

Table of Sections

Part 3. *General Obligation and Construction of Contract*

Part 4. *Title, Creditors, and Good-Faith Purchasers*

Part 5. *Performance*

Article 2. Sales

Part 1. Short Title, General Construction, and Subject Matter

§ 2–101. Short Title

This Article shall be known and may be cited as Uniform Commercial Code—Sales.

§ 2–102. Scope; Certain Security and Other Transactions Excluded from This Article

Unless the context otherwise requires, this Article applies to transactions in goods; it does not apply to any transaction which although in the form of an unconditional contract to sell or present sale is intended to operate only as a security transaction; nor does this Article impair or repeal any statute regulating sales to consumers, farmers, or other specified classes of buyers.

§ 2–103. Definitions and Index of Definitions

(1) In this Article unless the context otherwise requires

    (a) "Buyer" means a person who buys or contracts to buy goods.

    (b) "Good faith" in the case of a merchant means honesty in fact and the observance of reasonable commercial standards of fair dealing in the trade.

    (c) "Receipt" of goods means taking physical possession of them.

    (d) "Seller" means a person who sells or contracts to sell goods.

(2) Other definitions applying to this Article or to specified Parts thereof, and the sections in which they appear, are:

"Acceptance"	Section 2–606.
"Banker's credit"	Section 2–325.
"Between merchants"	Section 2–104.
"Cancellation"	Section 2–106(4).
"Commercial unit"	Section 2–105.
"Confirmed credit"	Section 2–325.
"Conforming to contract"	Section 2–106.
"Contract for sale"	Section 2–106.
"Cover"	Section 2–712.
"Entrusting"	Section 2–403.
"Financing agency"	Section 2–104.
"Future goods"	Section 2–105.
"Goods"	Section 2–105.
"Identification"	Section 2–501.
"Installment contract"	Section 2–612.
"Letter of credit"	Section 2–325.
"Lot"	Section 2–105.
"Merchant"	Section 2–104.
"Overseas"	Section 2–323.
"Person in position of seller"	Section 2–707.
"Present sale"	Section 2–106.
"Sale"	Section 2–106.
"Sale on approval"	Section 2–326.
"Sale or return"	Section 2–326.
"Termination"	Section 2–106.

(3) The following definitions in other Articles apply to this Article:

"Check"	Section 3–104.
"Consignee"	Section 7–102.
"Consignor"	Section 7–102.
"Consumer goods"	Section 9–102.
"Dishonor"	Section 3–502.
"Draft"	Section 3–104.

(4) In addition Article 1 contains general definitions and principles of construction and interpretation applicable throughout this Article.

§ 2–104. Definitions: "Merchant"; "Between Merchants"; "Financing Agency"

(1) "Merchant" means a person who deals in goods of the kind or otherwise by his occupation holds himself out as having knowledge or skill peculiar to the practices or

goods involved in the transaction or to whom such knowledge or skill may be attributed by his employment of an agent or broker or other intermediary who by his occupation holds himself out as having such knowledge or skill.

(2) "Financing agency" means a bank, finance company, or other person who in the ordinary course of business makes advances against goods or documents of title or who by arrangement with either the seller or the buyer intervenes in ordinary course to make or collect payment due or claimed under the contract for sale, as by purchasing or paying the seller's draft or making advances against it or by merely taking it for collection whether or not the documents of title accompany the draft. "Financing agency" includes also a bank or other person who similarly intervenes between persons who are in the position of seller and buyer in respect to the goods (Section 2–707).

(3) "Between merchants" means in any transaction with respect to which both parties are chargeable with the knowledge or skill of merchants.

§ 2–105. Definitions: Transferability; "Goods"; "Future" Goods; "Lot"; "Commercial Unit"

(1) "Goods" means all things (including specially manufactured goods) which are movable at the time of identification to the contract for sale other than the money in which the price is to be paid, investment securities (Article 8), and things in action. "Goods" also includes the unborn young of animals and growing crops and other identified things attached to realty as described in the section on goods to be severed from realty (Section 2–107).

(2) Goods must be both existing and identified before any interest in them can pass. Goods which are not both existing and identified are "future" goods. A purported present sale of future goods or of any interest therein operates as a contract to sell.

(3) There may be a sale of a part interest in existing identified goods.

(4) An undivided share in an identified bulk of fungible goods is sufficiently identified to be sold although the quantity of the bulk is not determined. Any agreed proportion of such a bulk or any quantity thereof agreed upon by number, weight, or other measure may to the extent of the seller's interest in the bulk be sold to the buyer who then becomes an owner in common.

(5) "Lot" means a parcel or a single article which is the subject matter of a separate sale or delivery, whether or not it is sufficient to perform the contract.

(6) "Commercial unit" means such a unit of goods as by commercial usage is a single whole for purposes of sale and division of which materially impairs its character or value on the market or in use. A commercial unit may be a single article (as a machine) or a set of articles (as a suite of furniture or an assortment of sizes) or a quantity (as a bale, gross, or carload) or any other unit treated in use or in the relevant market as a single whole.

§ 2–106. Definitions: "Contract"; "Agreement"; "Contract for Sale"; "Sale"; "Present Sale"; "Conforming" to Contract; "Termination"; "Cancellation"

(1) In this Article unless the context otherwise requires "contract" and "agreement" are limited to those relating to the present or future sale of goods. "Contract for sale" includes both a present sale of goods and a contract to sell goods at a future time. A

"sale" consists in the passing of title from the seller to the buyer for a price (Section 2–401). A "present sale" means a sale which is accomplished by the making of the contract.

(2) Goods or conduct including any part of a performance are "conforming" or conform to the contract when they are in accordance with the obligations under the contract.

(3) "Termination" occurs when either party pursuant to a power created by agreement or law puts an end to the contract otherwise than for its breach. On "termination" all obligations which are still executory on both sides are discharged, but any right based on prior breach or performance survives.

(4) "Cancellation" occurs when either party puts an end to the contract for breach by the other, and its effect is the same as that of "termination" except that the cancelling party also retains any remedy for breach of the whole contract or any unperformed balance.

§ 2–107. *Goods to Be Severed from Realty: Recording*

(1) A contract for the sale of minerals or the like (including oil and gas) or a structure or its materials to be removed from realty is a contract for the sale of goods within this Article if they are to be severed by the seller; but until severance a purported present sale thereof which is not effective as a transfer of an interest in land is effective only as a contract to sell.

(2) A contract for the sale apart from the land of growing crops or other things attached to realty and capable of severance without material harm thereto but not described in subsection (1) or of timber to be cut is a contract for the sale of goods within this Article whether the subject matter is to be severed by the buyer or by the seller even though it forms part of the realty at the time of contracting, and the parties can by identification effect a present sale before severance.

(3) The provisions of this section are subject to any third party rights provided by the law relating to realty records, and the contract for sale may be executed and recorded as a document transferring an interest in land and shall then constitute notice to third parties of the buyer's right under the contract for sale.

Part 2. Form, Formation, and Readjustment of Contract

§ 2–201. *Formal Requirements; Statute of Frauds*

(1) Except as otherwise provided in this section, a contract for the sale of goods for the price of $500 or more is not enforceable by way of action or defense unless there is some writing sufficient to indicate that a contract for sale has been made between the parties and signed by the party against whom enforcement is sought or by his authorized agent or broker. A writing is not insufficient because it omits or incorrectly states a term agreed upon, but the contract is not enforceable under this paragraph beyond the quantity of goods shown in such writing.

(2) Between merchants, if within a reasonable time a writing in confirmation of the contract and sufficient against the sender is received and the party receiving it has reason to know its contents, it satisfies the requirements of subsection (1) against such party unless written notice of objection to its contents is given within 10 days after it is received.

(3) A contract which does not satisfy the requirements of subsection (1) but which is valid in other respects is enforceable

    (a) if the goods are to be specially manufactured for the buyer and are not suitable for sale to others in the ordinary course of the seller's business and the seller, before notice of repudiation is received and under circumstances which reasonably indicate that the goods are for the buyer, has made either a substantial beginning of their manufacture or commitments for their procurement; or

    (b) if the party against whom enforcement is sought admits in his pleading, testimony, or otherwise in court that a contract for sale was made, but the contract is not enforceable under this provision beyond the quantity of goods admitted; or

    (c) with respect to goods for which payment has been made and accepted or which have been received and accepted (Section 2–606).

§ 2–202. Final Written Expression: Parol or Extrinsic Evidence

Terms with respect to which the confirmatory memoranda of the parties agree or which are otherwise set forth in a writing intended by the parties as a final expression of their agreement with respect to such terms as are included therein may not be contradicted by evidence of any prior agreement or of a contemporaneous oral agreement but may be explained or supplemented

    (a) by course and dealing or usage of trade (Section 1–205) or by course of performance (Section 2–208); and

    (b) by evidence of consistent additional terms unless the court finds the writing to have been intended also as a complete and exclusive statement of the terms of the agreement.

§ 2–203. Seals Inoperative

The affixing of a seal to a writing evidencing a contract for sale or an offer to buy or sell goods does not constitute the writing a sealed instrument and the law with respect to sealed instruments does not apply to such a contract or offer.

§ 2–204. Formation in General

(1) A contract for sale of goods may be made in any manner sufficient to show agreement, including conduct by both parties which recognizes the existence of such a contract.

(2) An agreement sufficient to constitute a contract for sale may be found even though the moment of its making is undetermined.

(3) Even though one or more terms are left open a contract for sale does not fail for indefiniteness if the parties have intended to make a contract and there is a reasonably certain basis for giving an appropriate remedy.

§ 2–205. Firm Offers

An offer by a merchant to buy or sell goods in a signed writing which by its terms gives assurance that it will be held open is not revocable, for lack of consideration, during the time stated or if no time is stated for a reasonable time, but in no event may such period of irrevocability exceed three months; but any such term of assurance on a form supplied by the offeree must be separately signed by the offerer.

§ 2–206. Offer and Acceptance in Formation of Contract

(1) Unless otherwise unambiguously indicated by the language or circumstances

    (a) an offer to make a contract shall be construed as inviting acceptance in any manner and by any medium reasonable in the circumstances;

    (b) an order or other offer to buy goods for prompt or current shipment shall be construed as inviting acceptance either by a prompt promise to ship or by the prompt or current shipment of conforming or nonconforming goods, but such a shipment of nonconforming goods does not constitute an acceptance if the seller seasonably notifies the buyer that the shipment is offered only as an accommodation to the buyer.

(2) Where the beginning of a requested performance is a reasonable mode of acceptance, an offerer who is not notified of acceptance within a reasonable time may treat the offer as having lapsed before acceptance.

§ 2–207. Additional Terms in Acceptance or Confirmation

(1) A definite and seasonable expression of acceptance or a written confirmation which is sent within a reasonable time operates as an acceptance even though it states terms additional to or different from those offered or agreed upon, unless acceptance is expressly made conditional on assent to the additional or different terms.

(2) The additional terms are to be construed as proposals for addition to the contract. Between merchants such terms become part of the contract unless

    (a) the offer expressly limits acceptance to the terms of the offer;

    (b) they materially alter it; or

    (c) notification of objection to them has already been given or is given within a reasonable time after notice of them is received.

(3) Conduct by both parties which recognizes the existence of a contract is sufficient to establish a contract for sale although the writings of the parties do not otherwise establish a contract. In such case the terms of the particular contract consist of those terms on which the writings of the parties agree, together with any supplementary terms incorporated under any other provisions of this Act.

§ 2–208. Course of Performance or Practical Construction

(1) Where the contract for sale involves repeated occasions for performance by either party with knowledge of the nature of the performance and opportunity for objection to it by the other, any course of performance accepted or acquiesced in without objection shall be relevant to determine the meaning of the agreement.

(2) The express terms of the agreement and any such course of performance, as well as any course of dealing and usage of trade, shall be construed whenever reasonable as consistent with each other; but when such construction is unreasonable, express terms shall control course of performance and course of performance shall control both course of dealing and usage of trade (Section 1–205).

(3) Subject to the provisions of the next section on modification and waiver, such course of performance shall be relevant to show a waiver or modification of any term inconsistent with such course of performance.

§ 2–209. Modification, Rescission, and Waiver

(1) An agreement modifying a contract within this Article needs no consideration to be binding.

(2) A signed agreement which excludes modification or rescission except by a signed writing cannot be otherwise modified or rescinded, but except as between merchants such a requirement on a form supplied by the merchant must be separately signed by the other party.

(3) The requirements of the statute of frauds section of this Article (Section 2–201) must be satisfied if the contract as modified is within its provisions.

(4) Although an attempt at modification or rescission does not satisfy the requirements of subsection (2) or (3) it can operate as a waiver.

(5) A party who has made a waiver affecting an executory portion of the contract may retract the waiver by reasonable notification received by the other party that strict performance will be required of any term waived, unless the retraction would be unjust in view of a material change of position in reliance on the waiver.

§ 2–210. Delegation of Performance; Assignment of Rights

(1) A party may perform his duty through a delegate unless otherwise agreed or unless the other party has a substantial interest in having his original promisor perform or control the acts required by the contract. No delegation of performance relieves the party delegating of any duty to perform or any liability for breach.

(2) Except as otherwise provided in Section 9–406, unless otherwise agreed all rights of either seller or buyer can be assigned except where the assignment would materially change the duty of the other party, or increase materially the burden or risk imposed on him by his contract, or impair materially his chance of obtaining return performance. A right to damages for breach of the whole contract or a right arising out of the assignor's due performance of his entire obligation can be assigned despite agreement otherwise.

(3) The creation, attachment, perfection, or enforcement of a security interest in the seller's interest under a contract is not a transfer that materially changes the duty of or increases materially the burden or risk imposed on the buyer or impairs materially the buyer's chance of obtaining return performance within the purview of subsection (2) unless, and then only to the extent that, enforcement actually results in a delegation of material performance of the seller. Even in that event, the creation, attachment, perfection, and enforcement of the security interest remain effective, but (i) the seller is liable to the buyer for damages caused by the delegation to the extent that the damages could not reasonably be prevented by the buyer, and (ii) a court having jurisdiction may grant other appropriate relief, including cancellation of the contract for sale or an injunction against enforcement of the security interest or consummation of the enforcement.

(4) Unless the circumstances indicate the contrary a prohibition of assignment of "the contract" is to be construed as barring only the delegation to the assignee of the assignor's performance.

(5) An assignment of "the contract" or of "all my rights under the contract" or an assignment in similar general terms is an assignment of rights and unless the language or the circumstances (as in an assignment for security) indicate the contrary, it is a delegation of performance of the duties of the assignor and its acceptance by the assignee constitutes a promise by him to perform those duties. This promise is enforceable by either the assignor or the other party to the original contract.

(6) The other party may treat any assignment which delegates performance as creating reasonable grounds for insecurity and may without prejudice to his rights against the assignor demand assurances from the assignee (Section 2–609).

Part 3. General Obligation and Construction of Contract

§ 2–301. *General Obligations of Parties*

The obligation of the seller is to transfer and deliver and that of the buyer is to accept and pay in accordance with the contract.

§ 2–302. *Unconscionable Contract or Clause*

(1) If the court as a matter of law finds the contract or any clause of the contract to have been unconscionable at the time it was made the court may refuse to enforce the contract, or it may enforce the remainder of the contract without the unconscionable clause, or it may so limit the application of any unconscionable clause as to avoid any unconscionable result.

(2) When it is claimed or appears to the court that the contract or any clause thereof may be unconscionable the parties shall be afforded a reasonable opportunity to present evidence as to its commercial setting, purpose, and effect to aid the court in making the determination.

§ 2–303. *Allocation or Division of Risks*

Where this Article allocates a risk or a burden as between the parties "unless otherwise agreed," the agreement may not only shift the allocation but may also divide the risk or burden.

§ 2–304. *Price Payable in Money, Goods, Realty, or Otherwise*

(1) The price can be made payable in money or otherwise. If it is payable in whole or in part in goods each party is a seller of the goods which he is to transfer.

(2) Even though all or part of the price is payable in an interest in realty the transfer of the goods and the seller's obligations with reference to them are subject to this Article, but not the transfer of the interest in realty or the transferor's obligations in connection therewith.

§ 2–305. *Open Price Term*

(1) The parties if they so intend can conclude a contract for sale even though the price is not settled. In such a case the price is a reasonable price at the time for delivery if

    (a) nothing is said as to price; or

    (b) the price is left to be agreed by the parties and they fail to agree; or

(c) the price is to be fixed in terms of some agreed market or other standard as set or recorded by a third person or agency and it is not so set or recorded.

(2) A price to be fixed by the seller or by the buyer means a price for him to fix in good faith.

(3) When a price left to be fixed otherwise than by agreement of the parties fails to be fixed through fault of one party the other may at his option treat the contract as cancelled or himself fix a reasonable price.

(4) Where, however, the parties intend not to be bound unless the price be fixed or agreed and it is not fixed or agreed there is no contract. In such a case the buyer must return any goods already received or if unable so to do must pay their reasonable value at the time of delivery and the seller must return any portion of the price paid on account.

§ 2–306. Output, Requirements, and Exclusive Dealings

(1) A term which measures the quantity by the output of the seller or the requirements of the buyer means such actual output or requirements as may occur in good faith, except that no quantity unreasonably disproportionate to any stated estimate or in the absence of a stated estimate to any normal or otherwise comparable prior output or requirements may be tendered or demanded.

(2) A lawful agreement by either the seller or the buyer for exclusive dealing in the kind of goods concerned imposes unless otherwise agreed an obligation by the seller to use best efforts to supply the goods and by the buyer to use best efforts to promote their sale.

§ 2–307. Delivery in Single Lot or Several Lots

Unless otherwise agreed all goods called for by a contract for sale must be tendered in a single delivery and payment is due only on such tender; but where the circumstances give either party the right to make or demand delivery in lots the price if it can be apportioned may be demanded for each lot.

§ 2–308. Absence of Specified Place for Delivery

Unless otherwise agreed

(a) the place for delivery of goods is the seller's place of business or if he has none his residence; but

(b) in a contract for sale of identified goods which to the knowledge of the parties at the time of contracting are in some other place, that place is the place for their delivery; and

(c) documents of title may be delivered through customary banking channels.

§ 2–309. Absence of Specific Time Provisions; Notice of Termination

(1) The time for shipment or delivery or any other action under a contract if not provided in this Article or agreed upon shall be a reasonable time.

(2) Where the contract provides for successive performance but is indefinite in duration it is valid for a reasonable time but unless otherwise agreed may be terminated at any time by either party.

(3) Termination of a contract by one party except on the happening of an agreed event requires that reasonable notification be received by the other party and an agreement dispensing with notification is invalid if its operation would be unconscionable.

§ 2–310. Open Time for Payment or Running of Credit; Authority to Ship under Reservation

Unless otherwise agreed

 (a) payment is due at the time and place at which the buyer is to receive the goods even though the place of shipment is the place of delivery; and

 (b) if the seller is authorized to send the goods he may ship them under reservation, and may tender the documents of title, but the buyer may inspect the goods after their arrival before payment is due unless such inspection is inconsistent with the terms of the contract (Section 2–513); and

 (c) if delivery is authorized and made by way of documents of title otherwise than by subsection (b) then payment is due at the time and place at which the buyer is to receive the documents regardless of where the goods are to be received; and

 (d) where the seller is required or authorized to ship the goods on credit the credit period runs from the time of shipment, but postdating the invoice or delaying its dispatch will correspondingly delay the starting of the credit period.

§ 2–311. Options and Cooperation Respecting Performance

(1) An agreement for sale which is otherwise sufficiently definite (subsection (3) of Section 2–204) to be a contract is not made invalid by the fact that it leaves particulars of performance to be specified by one of the parties. Any such specification must be made in good faith and within limits set by commercial reasonableness.

(2) Unless otherwise agreed specifications relating to assortment of the goods are at the buyer's option and except as otherwise provided in subsections (1) (c) and (3) of Section 2–319 specifications or arrangements relating to shipment are at the seller's option.

(3) Where such specification would materially affect the other party's performance but is not seasonably made or where one party's cooperation is necessary to the agreed performance of the other but is not seasonably forthcoming, the other party in addition to all other remedies

 (a) is excused for any resulting delay in his own performance; and

 (b) may also either proceed to perform in any reasonable manner or after the time for a material part of his own performance treat the failure to specify or to cooperate as a breach by failure to deliver or accept the goods.

§ 2–312. Warranty of Title and against Infringement; Buyer's Obligation against Infringement

(1) Subject to subsection (2) there is in a contract for sale a warranty by the seller that

 (a) the title conveyed shall be good, and its transfer rightful; and

(b) the goods shall be delivered free from any security interest or other lien or encumbrance of which the buyer at the time of contracting has no knowledge.

(2) A warranty under subsection (1) will be excluded or modified only by specific language or by circumstances which give the buyer reason to know that the person selling does not claim title in himself or that he is purporting to sell only such right or title as he or a third person may have.

(3) Unless otherwise agreed a seller who is a merchant regularly dealing in goods of the kind warrants that the goods shall be delivered free of the rightful claim of any third person by way of infringement or the like; but a buyer who furnishes specifications to the seller must hold the seller harmless against any such claim which arises out of compliance with the specifications.

§ 2–313. Express Warranties by Affirmation, Promise, Description, Sample

(1) Express warranties by the seller are created as follows:

(a) Any affirmation of fact or promise made by the seller to the buyer which relates to the goods and becomes part of the basis of the bargain creates an express warranty that the goods shall conform to the affirmation or promise.

(b) Any description of the goods which is made part of the basis of the bargain creates an express warranty that the goods shall conform to the description.

(c) Any sample or model which is made part of the basis of the bargain creates an express warranty that the whole of the goods shall conform to the sample or model.

(2) It is not necessary to the creation of an express warranty that the seller use formal words such as "warrant" or "guarantee" or that he have a specific intention to make a warranty, but an affirmation merely of the value of the goods or a statement purporting to be merely the seller's opinion or commendation of the goods does not create a warranty.

§ 2–314. Implied Warranty: Merchantability; Usage of Trade

(1) Unless excluded or modified (Section 2–316), a warranty that the goods shall be merchantable is implied in a contract for their sale if the seller is a merchant with respect to goods of that kind. Under this section the serving for value of food or drink to be consumed either on the premises or elsewhere is a sale.

(2) Goods to be merchantable must be at least such as

(a) pass without objection in the trade under the contract description; and

(b) in the case of fungible goods, are of fair average quality within the description; and

(c) are fit for the ordinary purposes for which such goods are used; and

(d) run, within the variations permitted by the agreement, of even kind, quality, and quantity within each unit and among all units involved; and

(e) are adequately contained, packaged, and labeled as the agreement may require; and

(f) conform to the promises or affirmations of fact made on the container or label if any.

(3) Unless excluded or modified (Section 2–316) other implied warranties may arise from course of dealing or usage of trade.

§ 2–315. Implied Warranty: Fitness for Particular Purpose

Where the seller at the time of contracting has reason to know any particular purpose for which the goods are required and that the buyer is relying on the seller's skill or judgment to select or furnish suitable goods, there is unless excluded or modified under the next section an implied warranty that the goods shall be fit for such purpose.

§ 2–316. Exclusion or Modification of Warranties

(1) Words or conduct relevant to the creation of an express warranty and words or conduct tending to negate or limit warranty shall be construed wherever reasonable as consistent with each other, but subject to the provisions of this Article on parol or extrinsic evidence (Section 2–202) negation or limitation is inoperative to the extent that such construction is unreasonable.

(2) Subject to subsection (3), to exclude or modify the implied warranty of merchantability or any part of it the language must mention merchantability and in case of a writing must be conspicuous, and to exclude or modify any implied warranty of fitness the exclusion must be by a writing and conspicuous. Language to exclude all implied warranties of fitness is sufficient if it states, for example, that "There are no warranties which extend beyond the description on the face hereof."

(3) Notwithstanding subsection (2)

    (a) unless the circumstances indicate otherwise, all implied warranties are excluded by expressions like "as is," "with all faults," or other language which in common understanding calls the buyer's attention to the exclusion of warranties and makes plain that there is no implied warranty; and

    (b) when the buyer before entering into the contract has examined the goods or the sample or model as fully as he desired or has refused to examine the goods there is no implied warranty with regard to defects which an examination ought in the circumstances to have revealed to him; and

    (c) an implied warranty can also be excluded or modified by course of dealing or course of performance or usage of trade.

(4) Remedies for breach of warranty can be limited in accordance with the provisions of this Article on liquidation or limitation of damages and on contractual modification of remedy (Sections 2–718 and 2–719).

§ 2–317. Cumulation and Conflict of Warranties Express or Implied

Warranties whether express or implied shall be construed as consistent with each other and as cumulative, but if such construction is unreasonable the intention of the parties shall determine which warranty is dominant. In ascertaining that intention the following rules apply:

    (a) Exact or technical specifications displace an inconsistent sample or model or general language of description.

    (b) A sample from an existing bulk displaces inconsistent general language of description.

(c) Express warranties displace inconsistent implied warranties other than an implied warranty of fitness for a particular purpose.

§ 2–318. Third Party Beneficiaries of Warranties Express or Implied

Note: *If this Act is introduced in the Congress of the United States this section should be omitted. (States to select one alternative.)*

Alternative A   A seller's warranty whether express or implied extends to any natural person who is in the family or household of his buyer or who is a guest in his home if it is reasonable to expect that such person may use, consume, or be affected by the goods and who is injured in person by breach of the warranty. A seller may not exclude or limit the operation of this section.

Alternative B   A seller's warranty whether express or implied extends to any natural person who may reasonably be expected to use, consume, or be affected by the goods and who is injured in person by breach of the warranty. A seller may not exclude or limit the operation of this section.

Alternative C   A seller's warranty whether express or implied extends to any person who may reasonably be expected to use, consume, or be affected by the goods and who is injured by breach of the warranty. A seller may not exclude or limit the operation of this section with respect to injury to the person of an individual to whom the warranty extends.

§ 2–319. F.O.B. and F.A.S. Terms

(1) Unless otherwise agreed the term F.O.B. (which means "free on board") at a named place, even though used only in connection with the stated price, is a delivery term under which

(a) when the term is F.O.B. the place of shipment, the seller must at that place ship the goods in the manner provided in this Article (Section 2–504) and bear the expense and risk of putting them into the possession of the carrier; or

(b) when the term is F.O.B. the place of destination, the seller must at his own expense and risk transport the goods to that place and there tender delivery of them in the manner provided in this Article (Section 2–503);

(c) when under either (a) or (b) the term is also F.O.B. vessel, car, or other vehicle, the seller must in addition at his own expense and risk load the goods on board. If the term is F.O.B. vessel the buyer must name the vessel and in an appropriate case the seller must comply with the provisions of this Article on the form of bill of lading (Section 2–323).

(2) Unless otherwise agreed the term F.A.S. vessel (which means "free alongside") at a named port, even though used only in connection with the stated price, is a delivery term under which the seller must

(a) at his own expense and risk deliver the goods alongside the vessel in the manner usual in that port or on a dock designated and provided by the buyer; and

(b) obtain and tender a receipt for the goods in exchange for which the carrier is under a duty to issue a bill of lading.

(3) Unless otherwise agreed in any case falling within subsection (1)(a) or (c) or subsection (2) the buyer must seasonably give any needed instructions for making delivery, including when the term is F.A.S. or F.O.B. the loading berth of the vessel and in an appropriate case its name and sailing date. The seller may treat the failure of needed instructions as a failure of cooperation under this Article (Section 2–311). He may also at his option move the goods in any reasonable manner preparatory to delivery or shipment.

(4) Under the term F.O.B. vessel or F.A.S. unless otherwise agreed the buyer must make payment against tender of the required documents and the seller may not tender nor the buyer demand delivery of the goods in substitution for the documents.

§ 2–320. C.I.F. and C. & F. Terms

(1) The term C.I.F. means that the price includes in a lump sum the cost of the goods and the insurance and freight to the named destination. The term C. & F. or C.F. means that the price so includes cost and freight to the named destination.

(2) Unless otherwise agreed and even though used only in connection with the stated price and destination, the term C.I.F. destination or its equivalent requires the seller at his own expense and risk to

(a) put the goods into the possession of a carrier at the port for shipment and obtain a negotiable bill or bills of lading covering the entire transportation to the named destination; and

(b) load the goods and obtain a receipt from the carrier (which may be contained in the bill of lading) showing that the freight has been paid or provided for; and

(c) obtain a policy or certificate of insurance, including any war risk insurance, of a kind and on terms then current at the port of shipment in the usual amount, in the currency of the contract, shown to cover the same goods covered by the bill of lading and providing for payment of loss to the order of the buyer or for the account of whom it may concern; but the seller may add to the price the amount of the premium for any such war risk insurance; and

(d) prepare an invoice of the goods and procure any other documents required to effect shipment or to comply with the contract; and

(e) forward and tender with commercial promptness all the documents in due form and with any endorsement necessary to perfect the buyer's rights.

(3) Unless otherwise agreed the term C. & F. or its equivalent has the same effect and imposes upon the seller the same obligations and risks as a C.I.F. term except the obligation as to insurance.

(4) Under the term C.I.F. or C. & F. unless otherwise agreed the buyer must make payment against tender of the required documents and the seller may not tender nor the buyer demand delivery of the goods in substitution for the documents.

§ 2–321. C.I.F. or C. & F.: "Net Landed Weights"; "Payment on Arrival"; Warranty of Condition on Arrival

Under a contract containing a term C.I.F. or C. & F.

(1) Where the price is based on or is to be adjusted according to "net landed weights," "delivered weights," "out turn" quantity or quality, or the like, unless otherwise agreed the seller must reasonably estimate the price. The payment due on tender of the documents called for by the contract is the amount so estimated, but after final adjustment of the price a settlement must be made with commercial promptness.

(2) An agreement described in subsection (1) or any warranty of quality or condition of the goods on arrival places upon the seller the risk of ordinary deterioration, shrinkage, and the like in transportation but has no effect on the place or time of identification to the contract for sale or delivery or on the passing of the risk of loss.

(3) Unless otherwise agreed where the contract provides for payment on or after arrival of the goods the seller must before payment allow such preliminary inspection as is feasible; but if the goods are lost delivery of the documents and payment are due when the goods should have arrived.

§ 2–322. Delivery "Ex-Ship"

(1) Unless otherwise agreed a term for delivery of goods "ex-ship" (which means from the carrying vessel) or in equivalent language is not restricted to a particular ship and requires delivery from a ship which has reached a place at the named port of destination where goods of the kind are usually discharged.

(2) Under such a term unless otherwise agreed

   (a) the seller must discharge all liens arising out of the carriage and furnish the buyer with a direction which puts the carrier under a duty to deliver the goods; and

   (b) the risk of loss does not pass to the buyer until the goods leave the ship's tackle or are otherwise properly unloaded.

§ 2–323. Form of Bill of Lading Required in Overseas Shipment; "Overseas"

(1) Where the contract contemplates overseas shipment and contains a term C.I.F. or C. & F. or F.O.B. vessel, the seller unless otherwise agreed must obtain a negotiable bill of lading stating that the goods have been loaded on board or, in the case of a term C.I.F. or C. & F., received for shipment.

(2) Where in a case within subsection (1) a bill of lading has been issued in a set of parts, unless otherwise agreed if the documents are not to be sent from abroad the buyer may demand tender of the full set; otherwise only one part of the bill of lading need be tendered. Even if the agreement expressly requires a full set

   (a) due tender of a single part is acceptable within the provisions of this Article on cure of improper delivery (subsection (1) of Section 2–508); and

   (b) even though the full set is demanded, if the documents are sent from abroad the person tendering an incomplete set may nevertheless require payment upon furnishing an indemnity which the buyer in good faith deems adequate.

(3) A shipment by water or by air or a contract contemplating such shipment is "overseas" insofar as by usage of trade or agreement it is subject to the commercial, financing, or shipping practices characteristic of international deep water commerce.

§ 2–324. *"No Arrival, No Sale" Term*

Under a term "no arrival, no sale" or terms of like meaning, unless otherwise agreed,

- (a) the seller must properly ship conforming goods and if they arrive by any means he must tender them on arrival but he assumes no obligation that the goods will arrive unless he has caused the nonarrival; and
- (b) where without fault of the seller the goods are in part lost or have so deteriorated as no longer to conform to the contract or arrive after the contract time, the buyer may proceed as if there had been casualty to identified goods (Section 2–613).

§ 2–325. *"Letter of Credit" Term; "Confirmed Credit"*

(1) Failure of the buyer seasonably to furnish an agreed letter of credit is a breach of the contract for sale.

(2) The delivery to seller of a proper letter of credit suspends the buyer's obligation to pay. If the letter of credit is dishonored, the seller may on seasonable notification to the buyer require payment directly from him.

(3) Unless otherwise agreed the term "letter of credit" or "banker's credit" in a contract for sale means an irrevocable credit issued by a financing agency of good repute and, where the shipment is overseas, of good international repute. The term "confirmed credit" means that the credit must also carry the direct obligation of such an agency which does business in the seller's financial market.

§ 2–326. *Sale on Approval and Sale or Return; Rights of Creditors*

(1) Unless otherwise agreed, if delivered goods may be returned by the buyer even though they conform to the contract, the transaction is

- (a) a "sale on approval" if the goods are delivered primarily for use, and
- (b) a "sale or return" if the goods are delivered primarily for resale.

(2) Goods held on approval are not subject to the claims of the buyer's creditors until acceptance; goods held on sale or return are subject to such claims while in the buyer's possession.

(3) Any "or return" term of a contract for sale is to be treated as a separate contract for sale within the statute of frauds section of this Article (Section 2–201) and as contradicting the sale aspect of the contract within the provisions of this Article on parol or extrinsic evidence (Section 2–202).

§ 2–327. *Special Incidents of Sale on Approval and Sale or Return*

(1) Under a sale on approval unless otherwise agreed

- (a) although the goods are identified to the contract the risk of loss and the title do not pass to the buyer until acceptance; and
- (b) use of the goods consistent with the purpose of trial is not acceptance but failure seasonably to notify the seller of election to return the goods is acceptance, and if the goods conform to the contract acceptance of any part is acceptance of the whole; and

    (c) after due notification of election to return, the return is at the seller's risk and expense but a merchant buyer must follow any reasonable instructions.

(2) Under a sale or return unless otherwise agreed

    (a) the option to return extends to the whole or any commercial unit of the goods while in substantially their original conditions, but must be exercised seasonably; and

    (b) the return is at the buyer's risk and expense.

§ 2–328. *Sale by Auction*

(1) In a sale by auction if goods are put up in lots each lot is the subject of a separate sale.

(2) A sale by auction is complete when the auctioneer so announces by the fall of the hammer or in other customary manner. Where a bid is made while the hammer is falling in acceptance of a prior bid the auctioneer may in his discretion reopen the bidding or declare the goods sold under the bid on which the hammer was falling.

(3) Such a sale is with reserve unless the goods are in explicit terms put up without reserve. In an auction with reserve the auctioneer may withdraw the goods at any time until he announces completion of the sale. In an auction without reserve, after the auctioneer calls for bids on an article or lot, that article or lot cannot be withdrawn unless no bid is made within a reasonable time. In either case a bidder may retract his bid until the auctioneer's announcement of completion of the sale, but a bidder's retraction does not revive any previous bid.

(4) If the auctioneer knowingly receives a bid on the seller's behalf or the seller makes or procures such a bid, and notice has not been given that liberty for such bidding is reserved, the buyer may at his option avoid the sale or take the goods at the price of the last good faith bid prior to the completion of the sale. This subsection shall not apply to any bid at a forced sale.

Part 4. Title, Creditors, and Good-Faith Purchasers

§ 2–401. *Passing of Title; Reservation for Security; Limited Application of This Section*

Each provision of this Article with regard to the rights, obligations, and remedies of the seller, the buyer, purchasers, or other third parties applies irrespective of title to the goods except where the provision refers to such title. Insofar as situations are not covered by the other provisions of this Article and matters concerning title become material the following rules apply:

(1) Title to goods cannot pass under a contract for sale prior to their identification to the contract (Section 2–501), and unless otherwise explicitly agreed the buyer acquires by their identification a special property as limited by this Act. Any retention or reservation by the seller of the title (property) in goods shipped or delivered to the buyer is limited in effect to a reservation of a security interest. Subject to these provisions and to the provisions of the Article on Secured Transactions (Article 9), title to goods passes from the seller to the buyer in any manner and on any conditions explicitly agreed on by the parties.

(2) Unless otherwise explicitly agreed title passes to the buyer at the time and place at which the seller completes his performance with reference to the physical delivery of the goods, despite any reservation of a security interest and even though a document of title is to be delivered at a different time or place; and in particular and despite any reservation of a security interest by the bill of lading

    (a) if the contract requires or authorizes the seller to send the goods to the buyer but does not require him to deliver them at destination, title passes to the buyer at the time and place of shipment; but

    (b) if the contract requires delivery at destination, title passes on tender there.

(3) Unless otherwise explicitly agreed, where delivery is to be made without moving the goods.

    (a) if the seller is to deliver a document of title, title passes at the time when and the place where he delivers such documents; or

    (b) if the goods are at the time of contracting already identified and no documents are to be delivered, title passes at the time and place of contracting.

(4) A rejection or other refusal by the buyer to receive or retain the goods, whether or not justified, or a justified revocation of acceptance revests title to the goods in the seller. Such revesting occurs by operation of law and is not a "sale."

§ 2–402. *Rights of Seller's Creditors against Sold Goods*

(1) Except as provided in subsections (2) and (3), rights of unsecured creditors of the seller with respect to goods which have been identified to a contract for sale are subject to the buyer's rights to recover the goods under this Article (Sections 2–502 and 2–716).

(2) A creditor of the seller may treat a sale or an identification of goods to a contract for sale as void if as against him a retention of possession by the seller is fraudulent under any rule of law of the state where the goods are situated, except that retention of possession in good faith and current course of trade by a merchant–seller for a commercially reasonable time after a sale or identification is not fraudulent.

(3) Nothing in this Article shall be deemed to impair the rights of creditors of the seller

    (a) under the provisions of the Article on Secured Transactions (Article 9); or

    (b) where identification to the contract or delivery is made not in current course of trade but in satisfaction of or as security for a preexisting claim for money, security, or the like and is made under circumstances which under any rule of law of the state where the goods are situated would apart from this Article constitute the transaction a fraudulent transfer or voidable preference.

§ 2–403. *Power to Transfer; Good-Faith Purchase of Goods; "Entrusting"*

(1) A purchaser of goods acquires all title which his transferor had or had power to transfer except that a purchaser of a limited interest acquires rights only to the extent of the interest purchased. A person with voidable title has power to transfer a good title to a good-faith purchaser for value. When goods have been delivered under a transaction of purchase the purchaser has such power even though

    (a) the transferor was deceived as to the identity of the purchaser, or

(b) the delivery was in exchange for a check which is later dishonored, or

(c) it was agreed that the transaction was to be a "cash sale," or

(d) the delivery was procured through fraud punishable as larcenous under the criminal law.

(2) Any entrusting of possession of goods to a merchant who deals in goods of that kind gives him power to transfer all rights of the entruster to a buyer in ordinary course of business.

(3) "Entrusting" includes any delivery and any acquiescence in retention of possession regardless of any condition expressed between the parties to the delivery or acquiescence and regardless of whether the procurement of the entrusting or the possessor's disposition of the goods have been such as to be larcenous under the criminal law.

(4) The rights of other purchasers of goods and of lien creditors are governed by the Articles on Secured Transactions (Article 9). [Bulk Transfers/Sales (Article 6)* and Documents of Title (Article 7)].

Part 5. Performance

§ 2–501. Insurable Interest in Goods; Manner of Identification of Goods

(1) The buyer obtains a special property and an insurable interest in goods by identification of existing goods as goods to which the contract refers even though the goods so identified are nonconforming and he has an option to return or reject them. Such identification can be made at any time and in any manner explicitly agreed to by the parties. In the absence of explicit agreement identification occurs

(a) when the contract is made if it is for the sale of goods already existing and identified;

(b) if the contract is for the sale of future goods other than those described in paragraph (c), when goods are shipped, marked, or otherwise designated by the seller as goods to which the contract refers;

(c) when the crops are planted or otherwise become growing crops or the young are conceived if the contract is for the sale of unborn young to be born within 12 months after contracting or for the sale of crops to be harvested within 12 months or the next normal harvest season after contracting, whichever is longer.

(2) The seller retains an insurable interest in goods so long as title to or any security interest in the goods remains in him; and where the identification is by the seller alone he may until default or insolvency or notification to the buyer that the identification is final substitute other goods for those identified.

(3) Nothing in this section impairs any insurable interest recognized under any other statute or rule of law.

§ 2–502. Buyer's Right to Goods on Seller's Insolvency

(1) Subject to subsections (2) and (3) and even though the goods have not been shipped, a buyer who has paid a part or all of the price of goods in which he has a special property under the provisions of the immediately preceding section may on making

and keeping good a tender of any unpaid portion of their price recover them from the seller if

- (a) in the case of goods bought for personal, family, or household purposes, the seller repudiates or fails to deliver as required by the contract; or
- (b) in all cases, the seller becomes insolvent within 10 days after receipt of the first installment on their price.

(2) The buyer's right to recover the goods under subsection (1)(a) vests upon acquisition of a special property, even if the seller had not then repudiated or failed to deliver.

(3) If the identification creating his special property has been made by the buyer he acquires the right to recover the goods only if they conform to the contract for sale.

§ 2–503. *Manner of Seller's Tender of Delivery*

(1) Tender of delivery requires that the seller put and hold conforming goods at the buyer's disposition and give the buyer any notification reasonably necessary to enable him to take delivery. The manner, time, and place for tender are determined by the agreement and this Article, and in particular

- (a) tender must be at a reasonable hour, and if it is of goods they must be kept available for the period reasonably necessary to enable the buyer to take possession; but
- (b) unless otherwise agreed the buyer must furnish facilities reasonably suited to the receipt of the goods.

(2) Where the case is within the next section respecting shipment tender requires that the seller comply with its provisions.

(3) Where the seller is required to deliver at a particular destination tender requires that he comply with subsection (1) and also in any appropriate case tender documents as described in subsections (4) and (5) of this section.

(4) Where goods are in the possession of a bailee and are to be delivered without being moved

- (a) tender requires that the seller either tender a negotiable document of title covering such goods or procure acknowledgment by the bailee of the buyer's right to possession of the goods; but
- (b) tender to the buyer of a nonnegotiable document of title or of a written direction to the bailee to deliver is sufficient tender unless the buyer seasonably objects, and receipt by the bailee of notification of the buyer's rights fixes those rights as against the bailee and all third persons; but risk of loss of the goods and of any failure by the bailee to honor the nonnegotiable document of title or to obey the direction remains on the seller untill the buyer has had a reasonable time to present the document or direction, and a refusal by the bailee to honor the document or to obey the direction defeats the tender.

(5) Where the contract requires the seller to deliver documents

- (a) he must tender all such documents in correct form, except as provided in this Article with respect to bills of lading in a set (subsection (2) of Section 2–323); and

(b) tender through customary banking channels is sufficient and dishonor of a draft accompanying the documents constitutes nonacceptance or rejection.

§ 2–504. Shipment by Seller

Where the seller is required or authorized to send the goods to the buyer and the contract does not require him to deliver them at a particular destination, then unless otherwise agreed he must

(a) put the goods in the possession of such a carrier and make such a contract for their transportation as may be reasonable having regard to the nature of the goods and other circumstances of the case; and

(b) obtain and promptly deliver or tender in due form any document necessary to enable the buyer to obtain possession of the goods or otherwise required by the agreement or by usage of trade; and

(c) promptly notify the buyer of the shipment.

Failure to notify the buyer under paragraph (c) or to make a proper contract under paragraph (a) is a ground for rejection only if material delay or loss ensues.

§ 2–505. Seller's Shipment under Reservation

(1) Where the seller has identified goods to the contract by or before shipment,

(a) his procurement of a negotiable bill of lading to his own order or otherwise reserves in him a security interest in the goods. His procurement of the bill to the order of a financing agency or of the buyer indicates in addition only the seller's expectation of transferring that interest to the person named.

(b) a nonnegotiable bill of lading to himself or his nominee reserves possession of the goods as security but except in a case of conditional delivery (subsection (2) of Section 2–507) a nonnegotiable bill of lading naming the buyer as consignee reserves no security interest even though the seller retains possession of the bill of lading.

(2) When shipment by the seller with reservation of a security interest is in violation of the contract for sale it constitutes an improper contract for transportation within the preceding section but impairs neither the rights given to the buyer by shipment and identification of the goods to the contract nor the seller's powers as a holder of a negotiable document.

§ 2–506. Rights of Financing Agency

(1) A financing agency by paying or purchasing for value a draft which relates to a shipment of goods acquires to the extent of the payment or purchase and in addition to its own rights under the draft and any document of title securing it any rights of the shipper in the goods including the right to stop delivery and the shipper's right to have the draft honored by the buyer.

(2) The right to reimbursement of a financing agency which has in good faith honored or purchased the draft under commitment to or authority from the buyer is not impaired by subsequent discovery of defects with reference to any relevant document which was apparently regular on its face.

§ 2–507. Effect of Seller's Tender; Delivery on Condition

(1) Tender of delivery is a condition to the buyer's duty to accept the goods and, unless otherwise agreed, to his duty to pay for them. Tender entitles the seller to acceptance of the goods and to payment according to the contract.

(2) Where payment is due and demanded on the delivery to the buyer of goods or documents of title, his right as against the seller to retain or dispose of them is conditional upon his making the payment due.

§ 2–508. Cure by Seller of Improper Tender or Delivery; Replacement

(1) Where any tender or delivery by the seller is rejected because nonconforming and the time for performance has not yet expired, the seller may seasonably notify the buyer of his intention to cure and may then within the contract time make a conforming delivery.

(2) Where the buyer rejects a nonconforming tender which the seller had reasonable grounds to believe would be acceptable with or without money allowance the seller may if he seasonably notifies the buyer have a further reasonable time to substitute a conforming tender.

§ 2–509. Risk of Loss in the Absence of Breach

(1) Where the contract requires or authorizes the seller to ship the goods by carrier

    (a) if it does not require him to deliver them at a particular destination, the risk of loss passes to the buyer when the goods are duly delivered to the carrier even though the shipment is under reservation (Section 2–505); but

    (b) if it does require him to deliver them at a particular destination and the goods are there duly tendered while in the possession of the carrier, the risk of loss passes to the buyer when the goods are there duly so tendered as to enable the buyer to take delivery.

(2) Where the goods are held by a bailee to be delivered without being moved, the risk of loss passes to the buyer

    (a) on his receipt of a negotiable document of title covering the goods; or

    (b) on acknowledgment by the bailee of the buyer's right to possession of the goods; or

    (c) after his receipt of a nonnegotiable document of title or other written direction to deliver, as provided in subsection (4)(b) of Section 2–503.

(3) In any case not within subsection (1) or (2), the risk of loss passes to the buyer on his receipt of the goods if the seller is a merchant; otherwise the risk passes to the buyer on tender of delivery.

(4) The provisions of this section are subject to contrary agreement of the parties and to the provisions of this Article on sale on approval (Section 2–327) and on effect of breach on risk of loss (Section 2–510).

§ 2–510. Effect of Breach on Risk of Loss

(1) Where a tender or delivery of goods so fails to conform to the contract as to give a right of rejection the risk of their loss remains on the seller until cure or acceptance.

(2) Where the buyer rightfully revokes acceptance he may to the extent of any deficiency in his effective insurance coverage treat the risk of loss as having rested on the seller from the beginning.

(3) Where the buyer as to conforming goods already identified to the contract for sale repudiates or is otherwise in breach before risk of their loss has passed to him, the seller may to the extent of any deficiency in his effective insurance coverage treat the risk of loss as resting on the buyer for a commercially reasonable time.

§ 2–511. Tender of Payment by Buyer; Payment by Check

(1) Unless otherwise agreed tender of payment is a condition to the seller's duty to tender and complete any delivery.

(2) Tender of payment is sufficient when made by any means or in any manner current in the ordinary course of business unless the seller demands payment in legal tender and gives any extension of time reasonably necessary to procure it.

(3) Subject to the provisions of this Act on the effect of an instrument on an obligation (Section 3–310), payment by check is conditional and is defeated as between the parties by dishonor of the check on due presentment.

§ 2–512. Payment by Buyer before Inspection

(1) Where the contract requires payment before inspection nonconformity of the goods does not excuse the buyer from so making payment unless

    (a) the nonconformity appears without inspection; or

    (b) despite tender of the required documents the circumstances would justify injunction against honor under this Act (Section 5–109(b)).

(2) Payment pursuant to subsection (1) does not constitute an acceptance of goods or impair the buyer's right to inspect or any of his remedies.

§ 2–513. Buyer's Right to Inspection of Goods

(1) Unless otherwise agreed and subject to subsection (3), where goods are tendered or delivered or identified to the contract for sale, the buyer has a right before payment or acceptance to inspect them at any reasonable place and time and in any reasonable manner. When the seller is required or authorized to send the goods to the buyer, the inspection may be after their arrival.

(2) Expenses of inspection must be borne by the buyer but may be recovered from the seller if the goods do not conform and are rejected.

(3) Unless otherwise agreed and subject to the provisions of this Article on C.I.F. contracts (subsection (3) of Section 2–321), the buyer is not entitled to inspect the goods before payment of the price when the contract provides

    (a) for delivery "C.O.D." or on other like terms; or

    (b) for payment against documents of title, except where such payment is due only after the goods are to become available for inspection.

(4) A place or method of inspection fixed by the parties is presumed to be exclusive but unless otherwise expressly agreed it does not postpone identification or shift the place for delivery or for passing the risk of loss. If compliance becomes impossible, inspection

shall be as provided in this section unless the place or method fixed was clearly intended as an indispensable condition, failure of which avoids the contract.

§ 2–514. *When Documents Deliverable on Acceptance; When on Payment*

Unless otherwise agreed documents against which a draft is drawn are to be delivered to the drawee on acceptance of the draft if it is payable more than three days after presentment; otherwise, only on payment.

§ 2–515. *Preserving Evidence of Goods in Dispute*

In furtherance of the adjustment of any claim or dispute

- (a) either party on reasonable notification to the other and for the purpose of ascertaining the facts and preserving evidence has the right to inspect, test, and sample the goods including such of them as may be in the possession or control of the other; and
- (b) the parties may agree to a third-party inspection or survey to determine the conformity or condition of the goods and may agree that the findings shall be binding upon them in any subsequent litigation or adjustment.

Part 6. Breach, Repudiation, and Excuse

§ 2–601. *Buyer's Rights on Improper Delivery*

Subject to the provisions of this Article on breach in installment contracts (Section 2–612) and unless otherwise agreed under the sections on contractual limitations of remedy (Sections 2–718 and 2–719), if the goods or the tender of delivery fail in any respect to conform to the contract, the buyer may

- (a) reject the whole; or
- (b) accept the whole; or
- (c) accept any commercial unit or units and reject the rest.

§ 2–602. *Manner and Effect of Rightful Rejection*

(1) Rejection of goods must be within a reasonable time after their delivery or tender. It is ineffective unless the buyer seasonably notifies the seller.

(2) Subject to the provisions of the two following sections on rejected goods (Sections 2–603 and 2–604),

- (a) after rejection any exercise of ownership by the buyer with respect to any commercial unit is wrongful as against the seller; and
- (b) if the buyer has before rejection taken physical possession of goods in which he does not have a security interest under the provisions of this Article (subsection (3) of Section 2–711), he is under a duty after rejection to hold them with reasonable care at the seller's disposition for a time sufficient to permit the seller to remove them; but
- (c) the buyer has no further obligations with regard to goods rightfully rejected.

(3) The seller's rights with respect to goods wrongfully rejected are governed by the provisions of this Article on Seller's remedies in general (Section 2–703).

§ 2–603. Merchant Buyer's Duties as to Rightfully Rejected Goods

(1) Subject to any security interest in the buyer (subsection (3) of Section 2–711), when the seller has no agent or place of business at the market of rejection a merchant buyer is under a duty after rejection of goods in his possession or control to follow any reasonable instructions received from the seller with respect to the goods and in the absence of such instructions to make reasonable efforts to sell them for the seller's account if they are perishable or threaten to decline in value speedily. Instructions are not reasonable if on demand indemnity for expenses is not forthcoming.

(2) When the buyer sells goods under subsection (1), he is entitled to reimbursement from the seller or out of the proceeds for reasonable expenses of caring for and selling them, and if the expenses include no selling commission then to such commission as is usual in the trade or if there is none to a reasonable sum not exceeding 10 percent on the gross proceeds.

(3) In complying with this section the buyer is held only to good faith and good-faith conduct hereunder is neither acceptance nor conversion nor the basis of an action for damages.

§ 2–604. Buyer's Options as to Salvage of Rightfully Rejected Goods

Subject to the provisions of the immediately preceding section on perishables if the seller gives no instructions within a reasonable time after notification of rejection the buyer may store the rejected goods for the seller's account or reship them to him or resell them for the seller's account with reimbursement as provided in the preceding section. Such action is not acceptance or conversion.

§ 2–605. Waiver of Buyer's Objections by Failure to Particularize

(1) The buyer's failure to state in connection with rejection a particular defect which is ascertainable by reasonable inspection precludes him from relying on the unstated defect to justify rejection or to establish breach

  (a) where the seller could have cured it if stated seasonably; or
  (b) between merchants when the seller has after rejection made a request in writing for a full and final written statement of all defects on which the buyer proposes to rely.

(2) Payment against documents made without reservation of rights precludes recovery of the payment for defects apparent on the face of the documents.

§ 2–606. What Constitutes Acceptance of Goods

(1) Acceptance of goods occurs when the buyer

  (a) after a reasonable opportunity to inspect the goods signifies to the seller that the goods are conforming or that he will take or retain them in spite of their nonconformity; or
  (b) fails to make an effective rejection (subsection (1) of Section 2–602), but such acceptance does not occur until the buyer has had a reasonable opportunity to inspect them; or

    (c) does any act inconsistent with the seller's ownership; but if such act is wrongful as against the seller it is an acceptance only if ratified by him.

  (2) Acceptance of a part of any commercial unit is acceptance of that entire unit.

§ 2–607. *Effect of Acceptance; Notice of Breach; Burden of Establishing Breach after Acceptance; Notice of Claim or Litigation to Person Answerable Over*

  (1) The buyer must pay at the contract rate for any goods accepted.

  (2) Acceptance of goods by the buyer precludes rejection of the goods accepted and if made with knowledge of a nonconformity cannot be revoked because of it unless the acceptance was on the reasonable assumption that the nonconformity would be seasonably cured; but acceptance does not of itself impair any other remedy provided by this Article for nonconformity.

  (3) Where a tender has been accepted

    (a) the buyer must within a reasonable time after he discovers or should have discovered any breach notify the seller of breach or be barred from any remedy; and

    (b) if the claim is one for infringement or the like (subsection (3) of Section 2–312) and the buyer is sued as a result of such a breach he must so notify the seller within a reasonable time after he receives notice of the litigation or be barred from any remedy over for liability established by the litigation.

  (4) The burden is on the buyer to establish any breach with respect to the goods accepted.

  (5) Where the buyer is sued for breach of a warranty or other obligation for which his seller is answerable over

    (a) he may give his seller written notice of the litigation. If the notice states that the seller may come in and defend and that if the seller does not do so he will be bound in any action against him by his buyer by any determination of fact common to the two litigations, then unless the seller after seasonable receipt of the notice does come in and defend he is so bound.

    (b) if the claim is one for infringement or the like (subsection (3) of Section 2–312) the original seller may demand in writing that his buyer turn over to him control of the litigation including settlement or else be barred from any remedy over and if he also agrees to bear all expense and to satisfy any adverse judgment, then unless the buyer after seasonable receipt of the demand does turn over control the buyer is so barred.

  (6) The provisions of subsection (3), (4), and (5) apply to any obligation of a buyer to hold the seller harmless against infringement or the like (subsection (3) of Section 2–312).

§ 2–608. *Revocation of Acceptance in Whole or in Part*

  (1) The buyer may revoke his acceptance of a lot or commercial unit whose nonconformity substantially impairs its value to him if he has accepted it

    (a) on the reasonable assumption that its nonconformity would be cured and it has not been seasonably cured; or

(b) without discovery of such nonconformity if his acceptance was reasonably induced either by the difficulty of discovery before acceptance or by the seller's assurances.

(2) Revocation of acceptance must occur within a reasonable time after the buyer discovers or should have discovered the ground for it and before any substantial change in condition of the goods which is not caused by their own defects. It is not effective until the buyer notifies the seller of it.

(3) A buyer who so revokes has the same rights and duties with regard to the goods involved as if he had rejected them.

§ 2–609. *Right to Adequate Assurance of Performance*

(1) A contract for sale imposes an obligation on each party that the other's expectation of receiving due performance will not be impaired. When reasonable grounds for insecurity arise with respect to the performance of either party the other may in writing demand adequate assurance of due performance and until he receives such assurance may if commercially reasonable suspend any performance for which he has not already received the agreed return.

(2) Between merchants the reasonableness of grounds for insecurity and the adequacy of any assurance offered shall be determined according to commercial standards.

(3) Acceptance of any improper delivery or payment does not prejudice the aggrieved party's right to demand adequate assurance of future performance.

(4) After receipt of a justified demand failure to provide within a reasonable time not exceeding 30 days such assurance of due performance as is adequate under the circumstances of the particular case is a repudiation of the contract.

§ 2–610. *Anticipatory Repudiation*

When either party repudiates the contract with respect to a performance not yet due the loss of which will substantially impair the value of the contract to the other, the aggrieved party may

(a) for a commercially reasonable time await performance by the repudiating party; or

(b) resort to any remedy for breach (Section 2–703 or Section 2–711), even though he has notified the repudiating party that he would await the latter's performance and has urged retraction; and

(c) in either case suspend his own performance or proceed in accordance with the provisions of this Article on the seller's right to identify goods to the contract notwithstanding breach or to salvage unfinished goods (Section 2–704).

§ 2–611. *Retraction of Anticipatory Repudiation*

(1) Until the repudiating party's next performance is due he can retract his repudiation unless the aggrieved party has since the repudiation cancelled or materially changed his position or otherwise indicated that he considers the repudiation final.

(2) Retraction may be by any method which clearly indicates to the aggrieved party that the repudiating party intends to perform, but must include any assurance justifiably demanded under the provisions of this Article (Section 2–609).

(3) Retraction reinstates the repudiating party's rights under the contract with due excuse and allowance to the aggrieved party for any delay occasioned by the repudiation.

§ 2–612. *"Installment Contract"; Breach*

(1) An "installment contract" is one which requires or authorizes the delivery of goods in separate lots to be separately accepted, even though the contract contains a clause "each delivery is a separate contract" or its equivalent.

(2) The buyer may reject any installment which is nonconforming if the nonconformity substantially impairs the value of that installment and cannot be cured or if the nonconformity is a defect in the required documents; but if the nonconformity does not fall within subsection (3) and the seller gives adequate assurance of its cure the buyer must accept that installment.

(3) Whenever nonconformity or default with respect to one or more installments substantially impairs the value of the whole contract there is a breach of the whole. But the aggrieved party reinstates the contract if he accepts a nonconforming installment without seasonably notifying of cancellation or if he brings an action with respect only to past installments or demands performance as to future installments.

§ 2–613. *Casualty to Identified Goods*

Where the contract requires for its performance goods identified when the contract is made, and the goods suffer casualty without fault of either party before the risk of loss passes to the buyer, or in a proper case under a "no arrival, no sale" term (Section 2–324) then

    (a) if the loss is total the contract is avoided; and

    (b) if the loss is partial or the goods have so deteriorated as no longer to conform to the contract the buyer may nevertheless demand inspection and at his option either treat the contract as voided or accept the goods with due allowance from the contract price for the deterioration or the deficiency in quantity but without further right against the seller.

§ 2–614. *Substituted Performance*

(1) Where without fault of either party the agreed berthing, loading, or unloading facilities fail or an agreed type of carrier becomes unavailable or the agreed manner of delivery otherwise becomes commercially impracticable but a commercially reasonable substitute is available, such substitute performance must be tendered and accepted.

(2) If the agreed means or manner of payment fails because of domestic or foreign governmental regulation, the seller may withhold or stop delivery unless the buyer provides a means or manner of payment which is commercially a substantial equivalent. If delivery has already been taken, payment by the means or in the manner provided by the regulation discharges the buyer's obligation unless the regulation is discriminatory, oppressive, or predatory.

§ 2–615. *Excuse by Failure of Presupposed Conditions*

Except so far as a seller may have assumed a greater obligation and subject to the preceding section on substituted performance,

(a) delay in delivery or nondelivery in whole or in part by a seller who complies with paragraphs (b) and (c) is not a breach of his duty under a contract for sale if performance as agreed has been made impracticable by the occurrence of a contingency the nonoccurrence of which was a basic assumption on which the contract was made or by compliance in good faith with any applicable foreign or domestic governmental regulation or order whether or not it later proves to be invalid.

(b) where the causes mentioned in paragraph (a) affect only a part of the seller's capacity to perform, he must allocate production and deliveries among his customers but may at his option include regular customers not then under contract as well as his own requirements for further manufacture. He may so allocate in any manner which is fair and reasonable.

(c) the seller must notify the buyer seasonably that there will be delay or nondelivery and, when allocation is required under paragraph (b), of the estimated quota thus made available for the buyer.

§ 2–616. *Procedure on Notice Claiming Excuse*

(1) Where the buyer receives notification of a material or indefinite delay or an allocation justified under the preceding section he may by written notification to the seller as to any delivery concerned, and where the prospective deficiency substantially impairs the value of the whole contract under the provisions of this Article relating to breach of installment contracts (Section 2–612), then also as to the whole,

(a) terminate and thereby discharge any unexecuted portion of the contract; or

(b) modify the contract by agreeing to take his available quota in substitution.

(2) If after receipt of such notification from the seller the buyer fails so to modify the contract within a reasonable time not exceeding 30 days the contract lapses with respect to any deliveries affected.

(3) The provisions of this section may not be negated by agreement except in so far as the seller has assumed a greater obligation under the preceding section.

Part 7. Remedies

§ 2–701. *Remedies for Breach of Collateral Contracts Not Impaired*

Remedies for breach of any obligation or promise collateral or ancillary to a contract for sale or not impaired by the provisions of this Article.

§ 2–702. *Seller's Remedies on Discovery of Buyer's Insolvency*

(1) Where the seller discovers the buyer to be insolvent he may refuse delivery except for cash including payment for all goods therefore delivered under the contract, and stop delivery under this Article (Section 2–705).

(2) Where the seller discovers that the buyer has received goods on credit while insolvent he may reclaim the goods upon demand made within 10 days after the receipt, but if misrepresentation of solvency has been made to the particular seller in writing within three months before delivery the 10-day limitation does not apply. Except as provided in this subsection the seller may not base a right to reclaim goods on the buyer's fraudulent or innocent misrepresentation of solvency or of intent to pay.

(3) The seller's right to reclaim under subsection (2) is subject to the rights of a buyer in ordinary course or other good-faith purchaser under this Article (Section 2–403). Successful reclamation of goods excludes all other remedies with respect to them.

§ 2–703. Seller's Remedies in General

Where the buyer wrongfully rejects or revokes acceptance of goods or fails to make a payment due on or before delivery or repudiates with respect to a part or the whole, then with respect to any goods directly affected and, if the breach is of the whole contract (Section 2–612), then also with respect to the whole undelivered balance, the aggrieved seller may

    (a) withhold delivery of such goods;

    (b) stop delivery by any bailee as hereafter provided (Section 2–705);

    (c) proceed under the next section respecting goods still unidentified to the contract;

    (d) resell and recover damages as hereafter provided (Section 2–706);

    (e) recover damages for nonacceptance (Section 2–708) or in a proper case the price (Section 2–709);

    (f) cancel.

§ 2–704. Seller's Right to Identify Goods to the Contract Notwithstanding Breach or to Salvage Unfinished Goods

(1) An aggrieved seller under the preceding section may

    (a) identify to the contract conforming goods not already identified if at the time he learned of the breach they are in his possession or control;

    (b) treat as the subject of resale goods which have demonstrably been intended for the particular contract even though those goods are unfinished.

(2) Where the goods are unfinished an aggrieved seller may in the exercise of reasonable commercial judgment for the purposes of avoiding loss and of effective realization either complete the manufacture and wholly identify the goods to the contract or cease manufacture and resell for scrap or salvage value or proceed in any other reasonable manner.

§ 2–705. Seller's Stoppage of Delivery in Transit or Otherwise

(1) The seller may stop delivery of goods in the possession of a carrier or other bailee when he discovers the buyer to be insolvent (Section 2–702) and may stop delivery of carload, truckload, planeload, or larger shipments of express or freight when the buyer repudiates or fails to make a payment due before delivery or if for any other reason the seller has a right to withhold or reclaim the goods.

(2) As against such buyer the seller may stop delivery until

    (a) receipt of the goods by the buyer; or

    (b) acknowledgment to the buyer by any bailee of the goods except a carrier that the bailee holds the goods for the buyer; or

    (c) such acknowledgment to the buyer by a carrier by reshipment or as warehouseman; or

    (d) negotiation to the buyer of any negotiable document of title covering the goods.

(3) (a) To stop delivery the seller must so notify as to enable the bailee by reasonable diligence to prevent delivery of the goods.

(b) After such notification the bailee must hold and deliver the goods according to the directions of the seller, but the seller is liable to the bailee for any ensuing charges or damages.

(c) If a negotiable document of title has been issued for goods, the bailee is not obliged to obey a notification to stop until surrender of the document.

(d) A carrier who has issued a nonnegotiable bill of lading is not obliged to obey a notification to stop received from a person other than the consignor.

§ 2–706. Seller's Resale Including Contract for Resale

(1) Under the conditions stated in Section 2–703 on seller's remedies, the seller may resell the goods concerned or the undelivered balance thereof. Where the resale is made in good faith and in a commercially reasonable manner the seller may recover the difference between the resale price and the contract price together with any incidental damages allowed under the provisions of this Article (Section 2–710), but less expenses saved in consequence of the buyer's breach.

(2) Except as otherwise provided in subsection (3) or unless otherwise agreed resale may be at public or private sale including sale by way of one or more contracts to sell or of identification to an existing contract of the seller. Sale may be as a unit or in parcels and at any time and place and on any terms but every aspect of the sale including the method, manner, time, place, and terms must be commercially reasonable. The resale must be reasonably identified as referring to the broken contract, but it is not necessary that the goods be in existence or that any or all of them have been identified to the contract before the breach.

(3) Where the resale is at private sale the seller must give the buyer reasonable notification of his intention to resell.

(4) Where the resale is at public sale

(a) only identified goods can be sold except where there is a recognized market for a public sale of futures in goods of the kind; and

(b) it must be made at a usual place or market for public sale if one is reasonably available and except in the case of goods which are perishable or threaten to decline in value speedily the seller must give the buyer reasonable notice of the time and place of the resale; and

(c) if the goods are not to be within the view of those attending the sale the notification of sale must state the place where the goods are located and provide for their reasonable inspection by prospective bidders; and

(d) the seller may buy.

(5) A purchaser who buys in good faith at a resale takes the goods free of any rights of the original buyer even though the seller fails to comply with one or more of the requirements of this section.

(6) The seller is not accountable to the buyer for any profit made on any resale. A person in the position of a seller (Section 2–707) or a buyer who has rightfully rejected or justifiably revoked acceptance must account for any excess over the amount of his security interest, as hereinafter defined (subsection (3) of Section 2–711).

§ 2–707. *"Person in the Position of a Seller"*

(1) A "person in the position of a seller" includes as against a principal an agent who has paid or become responsible for the price of goods on behalf of his principal or anyone who otherwise holds a security interest or other right in goods similar to that of a seller.

(2) A person in the position of a seller may as provided in this Article withhold or stop delivery (Section 2–705) and resell (Section 2–706) and recover incidental damages (Section 2–710).

§ 2–708. *Seller's Damages for Nonacceptance or Repudiation*

(1) Subject to subsection (2) and to the provisions of this Article with respect to proof of market price (Section 2–723), the measure of damages for nonacceptance or repudiation by the buyer is the difference between the market price at the time and place for tender and the unpaid contract price together with any incidental damages provided in this Article (Section 2–710), but less expenses saved in consequence of the buyer's breach.

(2) if the measure of damages provided in subsection (1) is inadequate to put the seller in as good a position as performance would have done then the measure of damages is the profit (including reasonable overhead) which the seller would have made from full performance by the buyer, together with any incidental damages provided in this Article (Section 2–710), due allowance for costs reasonably incurred and due credit for payments or proceeds of resale.

§ 2–709. *Action for the Price*

(1) When the buyer fails to pay the price as it becomes due the seller may recover, together with any incidental damages under the next section, the price

> (a) of goods accepted or of conforming goods lost or damaged within a commercially reasonable time after risk of their loss has passed to the buyer; and
> (b) of goods identified to the contract if the seller is unable after reasonable effort to resell them at a reasonable price or the circumstances reasonably indicate that such effort will be unavailing.

(2) Where the seller sues for the price he must hold for the buyer any goods which have been identified to the contract and are still in his control except that if resale becomes possible he may resell them at any time prior to the collection of the judgment. The net proceeds of any such resale must be credited to the buyer, and payment of the judgment entitles him to any goods not resold.

(3) After the buyer has wrongfully rejected or revoked acceptance of the goods or has failed to make a payment due or has repudiated (Section 2–610), a seller who is held not entitled to the price under this section shall nevertheless be awarded damages for nonacceptance under the preceeding section.

§ 2–710. *Seller's Incidental Damages*

Incidental damages to an aggrieved seller include any commercially reasonable charges, expenses, or commissions incurred in stopping delivery, in the transportation, care, and custody of goods after the buyer's breach in connection with return or resale of the goods, or otherwise resulting from the breach.

§ 2–711. Buyer's Remedies in General; Buyer's Security Interest in Rejected Goods

(1) Where the seller fails to make delivery or repudiates or the buyer rightfully rejects or justifiably revokes acceptance then with respect to any goods involved, and with respect to the whole if the breach goes to the whole contract (Section 2–612), the buyer may cancel and whether or not he has done so may in addition to recovering so much of the price as has been paid

- (a) "cover" and have damages under the next section as to all the goods affected whether or not they have been identified to the contract; or
- (b) recover damages for nondelivery as provided in this Article (Section 2–713).

(2) Where the seller fails to deliver or repudiates the buyer may also

- (a) if the goods have been identified recover them as provided in this Article (Section 2–502); or
- (b) in a proper case obtain specific performance or replevy the goods as provided in this Article (Section 2–716).

(3) On rightful rejection of justifiable revocation of acceptance a buyer has a security interest in goods in his possession or control for any payments made on their price and any expenses reasonably incurred in their inspection, receipt, transportation, care, and custody and may hold such goods and resell them in like manner as an aggrieved seller (Section 2–706).

§ 2–712. "Cover"; Buyer's Procurement of Substitute Goods

(1) After a breach within the preceding section the buyer may "cover" by making in good faith and without unreasonable delay any reasonable purchase of or contract to purchase goods in substitution for those due from the seller.

(2) The buyer may recover from the seller as damages the difference between the cost of cover and the contract price together with any incidental or consequential damages as hereinafter defined (Section 2–715), but less expenses saved in consequence of the seller's breach.

(3) Failure of the buyer to effect cover within this section does not bar him from any other remedy.

§ 2–713. Buyer's Damages for Nondelivery or Repudiation

(1) Subject to the provisions of this Article with respect to proof of market price (Section 2–723), the measure of damages for nondelivery or repudiation by the seller is the difference between the market price at the time when the buyer learned of the breach and the contract price together with any incidental and consequential damages provided in this Article (Section 2–715), but less expenses saved in consequence of the seller's breach.

(2) Market price is to be determined as of the place for tender or, in cases of rejection after arrival or revocation of acceptance, as of the place of arrival.

§ 2–714. Buyer's Damages for Breach in Regard to Accepted Goods

(1) Where the buyer has accepted goods and given notification (subsection (3) of Section 2–607) he may recover as damages for any nonconformity of tender the loss resulting

in the ordinary course of events from the seller's breach as determined in any manner which is reasonable.

(2) The measure of damages for breach of warranty is the difference at the time and place of acceptance between the value of the goods accepted and the value they would have had if they had been as warranted, unless special circumstances show proximate damages of a different amount.

(3) In a proper case any incidental and consequential damages under the next section may also be recovered.

§ 2–715. *Buyer's Incidental and Consequential Damages*

(1) Incidental damages resulting from the seller's breach include expenses reasonably incurred in inspection, receipt, transportation, and care and custody of goods rightfully rejected, any commercially reasonable charges, expenses, or commissions in connection with effecting cover, and any other reasonable expense incident to the delay or other breach.

(2) Consequential damages resulting from the seller's breach include

    (a) any loss resulting from general or particular requirements and needs of which the seller at the time of contracting had reason to know and which could not reasonably be prevented by cover or otherwise; and

    (b) injury to person or property proximately resulting from any breach of warranty.

§ 2–716. *Buyer's Right to Specific Performance or Replevin*

(1) Specific performance may be decreed where the goods are unique or in other proper circumstances.

(2) The decree for specific performance may include such terms and conditions as to payment of the price, damages, or other relief as the court may deem just.

(3) The buyer has a right of replevin for goods identified to the contract if after reasonable effort he is unable to effect cover for such goods or the circumstances reasonably indicate that such effort will be unvailing or if the goods have been shipped under reservation and satisfaction of the security interest in them has been made or tendered. In the case of goods bought for personal, family, or household purposes, the buyer's right of replevin vests upon acquisition of a special property, even if the seller had not then repudiated or failed to deliver.

§ 2–717. *Deduction of Damages from the Price*

The buyer on notifying the seller of his intention to do so may deduct all or any part of the damages resulting from any breach of the contract from any part of the price still due under the same contract.

§ 2–718. *Liquidation or Limitation of Damages; Deposits*

(1) Damages for breach by either party may be liquidated in the agreement but only at an amount which is reasonable in the light of the anticipated or actual harm caused by the breach, the difficulties of proof of loss, and the inconvenience of nonfeasibility of otherwise obtaining an adequate remedy. A team fixing unreasonably large liquidated damages is void as a penalty.

(2) Where the seller justifiably withholds delivery of goods because of the buyer's breach, the buyer is entitled to restitution of any amount by which the sum of his payments exceeds

    (a) the amount to which the seller is entitled by virtue of terms liquidating the seller's damages in accordance with subsection (1), or

    (b) in the absence of such terms, 20 percent of the value of the total performance for which the buyer is obligated under the contract or $500, whichever is smaller.

(3) The buyer's right to restitution under subsection (2) is subject to offset to the extent that the seller establishes

    (a) a right to recover damages under the provisions of this Article other than subsection (1), and

    (b) the amount or value of any benefits received by the buyer directly or indirectly by reason of the contract.

(4) Where a seller has received payment in goods their reasonable value or the proceeds of their resale shall be treated as payments for the purposes of subsection (2); but if the seller has notice of the buyer's breach before reselling goods received in part performance, his resale is subject to the conditions laid down in this Article on resale by an aggrieved seller (Section 2–706).

§ 2–719. *Contractual Modification or Limitation of Remedy*

(1) Subject to the provisions of subsections (2) and (3) of this section and of the preceding section on liquidation and limitation of damages,

    (a) the agreement may provide for remedies in addition to or in substitution for those provided in this Article and may limit or alter the measure of damages recoverable under this Article, as by limiting the buyer's remedies to return of the goods and repayment of the price or to repair and replacement of non-conforming goods or parts; and

    (b) resort to a remedy as provided is optional unless the remedy is expressly agreed to be exclusive, in which case it is the sole remedy.

(2) Where circumstances cause an exclusive or limited remedy to fail of its essential purpose, remedy may be had as provided in this Act.

(3) Consequential damages may be limited or excluded unless the limitation or exclusion is unconscionable. Limitation of consequential damages for injury to the person in the case of consumer goods is prima facie unconscionable but limitation of damages where the loss is commercial is not.

§ 2–720. *Effect of "Cancellation" or "Rescission" on Claims for Antecedent Breach*

Unless the contrary intention clearly appears, expressions of "cancellation" or "rescission" of the contract or the like shall not be construed as renunciation or discharge of any claim in damages for an antecedent breach.

§ 2–721. *Remedies for Fraud*

Remedies for material misrepresentation or fraud include all remedies available under this Article for non-fraudulent breach. Neither rescission or a claim for rescission of the contract for sale nor rejection or return of the goods shall bar or be deemed inconsistent with a claim for damages or other remedy.

§ 2–722. *Who Can Sue Third Parties for Injury to Goods*

Where a third party so deals with goods which have been identified to a contract for sale as to cause actionable injury to a party to that contract

(a) a right of action against the third party is in either party to the contract for sale who has title to or a security interest or a special property or an insurable interest in the goods; and if the goods have been destroyed or converted a right of action is also in the party who either bore the risk of loss under the contract for sale or has since the injury assumed that risk as against the other;

(b) if at the time of the injury the party plaintiff did not bear the risk of loss as against the other party to the contract for sale and there is no arrangement between them for disposition of the recovery, his suit or settlement is, subject to his own interest, as a fiduciary for the other party to the contract;

(c) either party may with the consent of the other sue for the benefit of whom it may concern.

§ 2–723. *Proof of Market Price: Time and Place*

(1) If an action based on anticipatory repudiation comes to trial before the time for performance with respect to some or all of the goods, any damages based on market price (Section 2–708 or Section 2–713) shall be determined according to the price of such goods prevailing at the time when the aggrieved party learned of the repudiation.

(2) If evidence of a price prevailing at the times or places described in this Article is not readily available the price prevailing within any reasonable time before or after the time described or at any other place which in commercial judgment or under usage of trade would serve as a reasonable substitute for the one described may be used, making any proper allowance for the cost of transporting the goods to or from such other place.

(3) Evidence of a relevant price prevailing at a time or place other than the one described in this Article offered by one party is not admissible unless and until he has given the other party such notice as the court finds sufficient to prevent unfair surprise.

§ 2–724. *Admissibility of Market Quotations*

Whenever the prevailing price or value of any goods regularly bought and sold in any established commodity market is in issue, reports in official publications or trade journals or in newspapers or periodicals of general circulation published as the reports of such market shall be admissible in evidence. The circumstances of the preparation of such a report may be shown to affect its weight but not its admissibility.

§ 2–725. *Statute of Limitations in Contracts for Sale*

(1) An action for breach of any contract for sale must be commenced within four years after the cause of action has accrued. By the original agreement the parties may reduce the period of limitation to not less than one year but may not extend it.

(2) A cause of action accrues when the breach occurs, regardless of the aggrieved party's lack of knowledge of the breach. A breach of warranty occurs when tender of

delivery is made, except that where a warranty explicitly extends to future performance of the goods and discovery of the breach must await the time of such performance the cause of action accrues when the breach is or should have been discovered.

(3) Where an action commenced within the time limited by subsection (1) is so terminated as to leave available a remedy by another action for the same breach such other action may be commenced after the expiration of the time limited and within six months after the termination of the first action unless the termination resulted from voluntary discontinuance or from dismissal for failure or neglect to prosecute.

(4) This section does not alter the law on tolling of the statute of limitations nor does it apply to causes of action which have accrued before this Act becomes effective.

A

absolute privilege   In libel and slander law, situations where a defendant is entirely excused from liability for defamatory statements because of the circumstances under which the statements were made.

acceptance   The actual or implied receipt and retention of that which is tendered or offered.

accord and satisfaction   A legally binding agreement to settle a disputed claim for a definite amount.

accredited investors   Financially sophisticated and/or wealthy individuals and institutions who understand and can withstand the risk associated with securities investments.

act of state doctrine   The view that a judge in the United States or another country does not have the authority to challenge the legality of acts by a foreign government within that foreign government's own borders.

actus reus   Wrongful act or omission.

ad substantiation   Under Federal Trade Commission policy, product claims for which reasonable evidentiary support does not exist. Constitute unfair and deceptive trade practices.

ad valorem   According to value. Hence an ad valorem tax would be based on the value of the item in question rather than, for example, a fixed rate for all such items.

adjudication   The formal pronouncement of a judgment in a legal proceeding.

adjustment of debts   Individuals with limited debts are protected from creditors while paying their debts in installments (Chapter 13 bankruptcy).

administrative agency   An agency of the government charged with administering particular legislation.

administrative law   That branch of public law addressing the operation of the government's various agencies and commissions. Also the rules and regulations established by those agencies and commissions.

administrative law judge   An officer who presides at the initial hearing on matters litigated before an administrative agency. He or she is independent of the agency staff.

Administrative Procedure Act   A federal statute specifying the procedural rules under which the government's agencies and commissions conduct their business.

adverse impact   An employee may make a prima facie case for adverse impact where the employer's facially neutral rule may result in a different impact on one protected group than on another.

adverse possession   Open and notorious possession of real property over a given length of time that denies ownership in any other claimant.

advisory jurisdiction   Power of the International Court of Justice (ICJ) to hear a dispute and to render an advisory opinion on the matter. The opinion is not binding on any party.

affidavit   A written statement sworn to by a person officially empowered to administer an oath.

affirmative action   A government or private-sector program, springing from the civil rights movement, designed to *actively promote* the employment or educational opportunities of protected classes rather than merely forbidding discrimination.

affirmative defense   A portion of a defendant's answer to a complaint in which defendant presents contentions that, if proved true, will relieve the defendant of liability even if the assertions in the complaint are correct.

agent   A person entrusted by a principal to act on behalf of that principal; one who is authorized to carry out the business of another.

agreement   A meeting of the minds based on an offer by one party and acceptance by another.

alternate dispute resolution   The growing practice of employing strategies other than conventional litigation to solve conflicts. Those strategies include negotiation, arbitration, and mediation with variations such as "minitrials" and "rent-a-judge" arrangements.

amicus curiae   A "friend of the court" who, though not a party to the case, files a brief because of a strong interest in the litigation.

annual percentage rate (APR)   The rate of interest charged for borrowing money as expressed in a standardized, yearly manner allowing for comparison among lenders' fees.

annual percentage yield (APY)   The rate of interest paid on a deposit as expressed in a standardized, yearly manner allowing for comparison of returns among institutions.

answer   The defendant's first pleading in a lawsuit, in which the defendant responds to the allegations raised in the plaintiff's complaint.

anticipatory breach   A contracting party's indication before the time for performance that he cannot or will not perform the contract. Same as **anticipatory repudiation**.

appeal   The judicial process by which a party petitions a higher court to review the decisions of a lower court or agency to correct errors.

appellant   The party filing an appeal.

appellee   The party against whom an appeal is filed.

appraisal   Assessment of the value of property by one with appropriate qualifications for the task.

appropriation   Making commercial use of an individual's name or likeness without permission.

arbitrary trademark   A trademark that is a new word or a common word that bears no relation to the product to which it is applied.

arbitration   An extrajudicial process in which a dispute is submitted to a mutually agreeable third party for a decision.

arraignment   A criminal law proceeding in which a defendant is brought before a judge to be informed of the charges and to file a plea.

assault   A show of force that would cause reasonable persons to believe that they are about to receive an intentional, unwanted, harmful physical touching.

assignee   A person to whom an assignment is made.

assignment   A transfer of property, or some right or interest therein, from one person to another.

assignor   The maker of an assignment.

assumption of risk   An affirmative defense in a negligence case in which the defendant seeks to bar recovery by the plaintiff by showing that the plaintiff knowingly exposed himself or herself to the danger that resulted in injury.

attachment   As to secured transactions, the process by which a security interest in the property of another becomes enforceable.

at-will employee   An individual not under contract for a specified term and therefore, under the general rule, subject to discharge by the employer at any time and for any reason.

B

bait-and-switch advertising   An unlawful sales tactic in which the seller attracts buyer interest by insincerely advertising a product at a dramatically reduced price while holding no genuine intent to sell the product at that price. The seller then disparages the "bait" and diverts the buyer's attention to a higher-priced product (the switch), which was the sales goal from the first.

barriers to entry   Economic or technological conditions in a market making entry by a new competitor very difficult.

battery   An intentional, unwanted, harmful physical touching.

beyond a reasonable doubt   The level of proof required for conviction in a criminal case.

bilateral contract   A contract formed by an offer requiring a reciprocal promise.

blacklists   Lists of union organizers or participants in labor activities circulated to companies to dissuade the companies from hiring the listed individuals.

blue laws   Laws forbidding certain kinds of business on Sundays.

blue sky laws   Statutes regulating the sale of stocks and other securities to prevent consumer fraud.

bona fide   In good faith; honestly.

bona fide occupational qualification (BFOQ)   A defense in a discrimination claim where the employer argues that a particular religion, sex, or national origin is a necessary qualification for a particular job.

boycott   A confederation or conspiracy involving a refusal to do business with another or an attempt by the confederation to stop others from doing business with the target person or organization.

breach of contract   Failure, without legal excuse, to perform any promise that forms the whole or part of a contract.

breach of warranty   Failure, without legal excuse, to fulfill the terms of the guarantee.

bribe   Anything of value given or taken with the corrupt intent to influence an official in the performance of her or his duties.

brief   A written document setting out for the court the facts, the law, and the argument of a party to the lawsuit.

burden of proof   The party with the burden of proof (normally the plaintiff in a civil suit and the state in a criminal case) is required to prove the truth of a claim or lose on that issue.

business judgment rule   A rule protecting business managers from liability for making bad decisions when they have acted prudently and in good faith.

bylaws   A document that governs the maintenance and operation of an organization.

C

capacity   The ability to incur legal obligations and acquire legal rights.

capitalism   Private ownership of the means of production with a largely unrestricted marketplace in goods and services.

cause in fact   The actual cause of an event. One of the required elements in a negligence claim.

cause of action   The legal theory on which a lawsuit is based.

caveat emptor   Let the buyer beware.

cease and desist order   An instruction from an agency instructing a party to refrain from a specified goal.

certificate of incorporation   An instrument from the state bestowing the right to do business under the corporate form of organization. Same as **charter**.

certiorari   A legal procedure affording an appellate court the opportunity to review a lower court decision. Also a writ asking the lower court for the record of the case.

choice of law rule   A rule of law in each jurisdiction that determines which jurisdiction's laws will be applied to a case. For instance, one state may have a choice of law rule that says that the law of the jurisdiction where the contract was signed shall govern any dispute, while another state may apply a different rule.

civil law   The branch of law dealing with private rights. Contrast with **criminal law**.

class action   A legal action brought by one on behalf of himself or herself and all others similarly situated.

Clean Air Act   Amended in 1990, establishes air quality standards and enforcement procedures for the standards.

Clean Water Act   Establishes standards for water quality relating to the protection of water life as well as for safe recreation, and the enforcement of those standards.

closed-end loan   Credit arrangement where a specified sum is borrowed and a repayment plan usually is established.

closing date   The date on which a transfer of property is made.

Code of Federal Regulations   A compilation of final federal agency rules.

codetermination   German corporate governance and labor law system in which board representation by labor unions is required.

Colgate doctrine   Sellers may lawfully engage in resale price maintenance if they do nothing more than specify prices at which their products are to be resold and unilaterally refuse to deal with anyone who does not adhere to those prices.

collateral   Property pledged as security for satisfaction of a debt.

comity   Courtesy. Nations often recognize the laws of other nations not because they must do so but because of the tradition of comity: that is, goodwill and mutual respect.

Commerce Clause   The portion of the U.S. Constitution that provides for federal regulation of foreign and interstate trade.

commercial impracticability   The standard used by the UCC to relieve a party of his or her contract obligations because of the occurrence of unforeseeable, external events beyond his or her control.

commercial speech   Speech directed toward a business purpose. Advertising is an example of commercial speech. Such speech is protected by the First Amendment, but not to the degree that we protect other varieties of speech.

Commodity Futures Trading Commission (CFTC) Federal regulatory agency responsible for overseeing futures trading.

common law   Judge-made law. To be distinguished from statutory law as created by legislative bodies.

common shares   Most universal type of corporate stock.

community property   Property acquired during marriage through the labor or skill of either spouse.

comparable worth   The legal theory that all employees should be paid the same wages for work requiring comparable skills, effort, and responsibility and having comparable worth to the employer.

comparative negligence   Defense in a negligence suit in which the plaintiff's recovery is reduced by an amount equivalent to her contribution to her own injury.

compensatory damages   Damages that will compensate a party for actual losses due to an injury suffered.

complaint   The first pleading filed by the plaintiff in a civil lawsuit.

comp time   Compensatory time. Giving an employee time off from work in place of cash for hours of overtime worked.

concerted activity   Organizing, forming, joining, or assisting labor organizations, bargaining collectively through representatives of the employees' choosing, or other activities taken for the purpose of collective bargaining or other mutual aid or protection.

concurrent conditions   When each party's obligation to perform under a contract is dependent on the other party's performance.

condemning   To appropriate land for public use.

conditions precedent   Conditions that operate to give rise to a contracting party's duty to perform.

conditions subsequent   Conditions that operate to discharge one from an obligation under a contract.

condominium or cooperative ownership   An interest in property where owners retain individual control and specific ownership over a precise segment of real estate, but own common areas as tenants in common.

confession of judgment clause   A clause stipulating that the lessee grants judgment in any action on the contract to the landlord without the formality of an ordinary proceeding.

conglomerate merger   A merger between firms operating in separate markets and having neither buyer–seller nor competitive relationships with each other.

conscious parallelism   Conduct by competitors that is very similar or identical but that is not the product of a conspiracy and thus is not, in and of itself, illegal.

consent decree   A settlement of a lawsuit arrived at by agreement of the parties. Effectively, an admission by the parties that the decree is a just determination of their rights.

consent order   The order administrative agencies issue when approving the settlement of an administrative action against some party.

consequential damages   Damages that do not flow directly and immediately from an act but rather flow from the results of the act.

consideration   A required element in an enforceable contract. The thing of value passing between the parties that results in a benefit to the one making the promise or a detriment to the one receiving the promise.

conspiracy   An agreement between two or more persons to commit an unlawful act.

constructive eviction   A breach of duty by the landlord that makes the property uninhabitable or otherwise deprives the tenant of the benefit of the lease and gives rise to the tenant's right to vacate the property and to terminate the lease.

consumer goods   Under the UCC, goods used or bought primarily for personal, family, or household purposes.

contentious jurisdiction   Power of the ICJ to hear a dispute and to render a binding opinion on the issue and the parties involved. All parties must give prior consent to contentious jurisdiction.

contingent fee   An arrangement wherein an attorney is compensated for his or her services by receiving a percentage of the award in a lawsuit rather than receiving an hourly wage or specified fee.

contingent workers   Workers that do not have an implicit or explicit contract for ongoing employment.

contract   An agreement that is legally enforceable by the courts.

contract bar rule   The NLRB prohibits an election during the term of a collective bargaining agreement, for a maximum of three years.

contract firm workers   Workers employed by a company that provides them or their services under contract or leases. Usually are assigned to only one customer and work at the customer's worksite.

contract of adhesion   One in which all the bargaining power (and all the contract terms) are unfairly on one side. This often occurs when buyers have no choice among sellers of a particular item, and when the seller uses a preprinted form contract.

contributory negligence   A defense in a negligence action wherein the defendant attempts to demonstrate that the plaintiff contributed to the harm on which the litigation was based. Contrast with. **comparative negligence**.

conversion   Wrongfully exercising control over the personal property of another.

copyright   The creator's (artist, author, or the like) right to control the copying and distribution of his or her work for a period of time specified by statute.

corporate opportunity   A doctrine that prevents corporate officials from personally appropriating an opportunity that belongs to the corporation.

corporation   A form of business organization that is owned by *shareholders* who have no inherent right to manage the business, and is managed by a board of directors elected by the shareholders.

Council on Environmental Quality   Serves as an adviser to the president in connection with the preparation of the annual Environmental Quality Report.

counterclaim   A cause of action filed by the defendant in a lawsuit against the plaintiff in the same suit.

counteroffer   Response by the offeree that, in its legal effect, constitutes a rejection of the original offer and proposes a new offer to the offerer.

countervailing duties   Duties imposed by a government against the products of another government that has offered subsidies to its own producers.

covered disabilities   A physical or mental impairment that substantially limits one or more major life activities of an individual; a record of such impairment or being regarded as having such impairment.

creditor   A person to whom a debt is owed.

creditor beneficiary   Person who has given consideration, who is an intended beneficiary of a contract though not a party, and thus is entitled to enforce the contract.

crime   A public wrong, an act punishable by the state.

criminal law   Wrongs against society that the state has seen fit to label as crimes and that may result in penalties against the perpetrator(s). Contrast with **civil law**.

cumulative voting   A procedure for voting for directors that permits a shareholder to multiply the number of shares he or she owns by the number of directors to be elected and to cast the resulting total of votes for one or more directors.

curtesy interest   The right of a husband upon the death of his wife to receive all of the wife's real property as long as the two had a child between them.

D

d.b.a.   Doing business as.

de facto   In fact. Actually. As in *de facto* school segregation, which is caused by social and economic conditions rather than by government act.

de jure   Legitimate. Lawful. Of right. As in *de jure* school segregation, which is caused by government order and thus is legally correct even if morally wrong.

debenture   Any long-term debt instrument, such as a bond, issued by a company or institution, secured only by the general assets of the issuer.

deceit   A tort involving intentional misrepresentation to deceive or trick another.

deception   Trade claim that is either false or likely to mislead the reasonable consumer and that is material to the consumer's decision making.

deceptive advertising   Advertising practices likely to mislead the reasonable consumer where the practice in question is material in that it affected consumer choice.

decertification petition   Election petition stating that a current bargaining representative no longer has the support of a majority of the employees in the bargaining unit.

declaration   A document that defines the rights, responsibilities, and powers of property owners in a condominium.

declaratory judgment or order   A judicial or agency action expressing an opinion or articulating the rights of the parties without actually requiring that anything be done.

deed   An instrument transferring title to property.

deed of trust   A three-party instrument used to create a security interest in real property in which the legal title to the real property is placed in one or more trustees to secure the repayment of a sum of money or the performance of other conditions.

defamation   A false and intentional verbal or written expression that damages the reputation of another.

default   A party fails to pay money when due or when lawfully demanded.

defeasible fee simple   A title to property that is open to attack, that might be defeated by the performance of some act, or that is subject to conditions.

defendant   The party in a civil suit against whom the cause of action was brought and, in a criminal case, the party against whom charges have been filed.

delegatee   The one to whom a duty is delegated.

delegator   The one who delegates a duty.

deontological ethics   The rightness of an action depends on its conformance with duty, obligation, and moral requirements regardless of outcome.

deposition A discovery procedure wherein a witness's sworn testimony is taken out of court, prior to trial, for subsequent use at trial.

deregulation Returning authority to the free market by shrinking government bureaucracies and reducing government rules.

derivative suit A lawsuit by a stockholder on behalf of the corporation where the corporation declines to act to protect the organization's rights against the conduct of an officer, director, or outsider.

derivatives Specialized trading contracts tied to underlying assets such as bonds or currencies.

descriptive mark A trademark that is merely descriptive of the product or its qualities.

dicta Statements in a judicial opinion that are merely the views of the judge(s) and are not necessary for the resolution of the case.

directed verdict A party to a lawsuit makes a motion asking the judge to instruct the jury to reach a particular decision because reasonable minds could not differ about the correct outcome of the case.

discharged Released from liability.

disclaimer As to warranties, a contract term wherein a party attempts to relieve itself of potential liability under that contract.

discovery Legal procedures by which one party to a litigation may obtain information from the other party. Depositions and interrogatories are examples of discovery procedures.

disparate impact Employment discrimination theory in which a facially neutral employment practice (such as requiring a high school diploma for new hires) results in an unfair and adverse impact on a protected class.

disparate treatment Theory of employment discrimination wherein an individual or group is intentionally disfavored via actual discriminatory policies and practices.

dissolution In partnership law, the change in the relation of the partners caused by any partner ceasing to be associated with the carrying on of the business.

diversity of citizenship One standard by which federal courts may gain jurisdiction over a lawsuit. Plaintiffs and defendants must be from different states and more than $50,000 must be at issue.

divestiture In antitrust law, a remedy wherein the court orders a defendant to dispose of specified assets.

dividend A shareholder's earnings from his or her stock in a corporation.

doctrine of sovereign immunity Principle that a foreign nation may not be sued in American courts, with certain exceptions.

dominant estate The property accessed through an easement appurtenant or implied easement.

donee beneficiary Person who has not given consideration, but is an intended beneficiary of a contract, though not a party, and is entitled to enforce the contract.

double jeopardy The United States Constitution provides that the same individual may not be tried twice in the same tribunal for the same criminal offense.

dower interest The right of a wife upon the death of her husband to receive a life estate in one-third of her husband's real property.

dramshop law State laws imposing liability on the seller of intoxicating liquors when a third party is injured as a result of the intoxication of the buyer where the sale has caused or contributed to that intoxication.

due care and diligence Corporate officers and directors must act in good faith and in a prudent manner.

due diligence A defense against a securities violation claim where the defendant used ordinary prudence and still failed to find an error or omission in the registration statement.

due process A constitutional principle requiring fairness in judicial proceedings and that government laws and conduct be free of arbitrariness and capriciousness.

dumping The commercial practice of selling goods in a foreign market at a price substantially beneath that charged in the domestic market.

duress Overpowering of the will of a person by force or fear.

duty of due care Standard of conduct expected of a reasonable, prudent person under the circumstances.

E

easement The right to use property without taking anything away from the property.

easement or profit appurtenant The right of an owner of adjacent land to enter or to enter and take away from property next to it.

economies of scale Expansion of a firm or industry's productive capacity resulting in a decline in long-run average costs of production.

efficiencies   A defense to an otherwise unlawful merger in which costs of production are reduced because of the merger.

election year or certification year bar   The NLRB prohibits an election for 12 months following a prior election.

elective share   Legislative mandate that a spouse receive a specific percentage interest in a deceased spouse's estate.

embargo   Government order prohibiting importation of some or all products from a particular country.

embezzlement   The fraudulent and unauthorized taking of the money of another while charged with the care of that money.

Emergency Planning and Community Right-to-Know Act of 1986   Amended Superfund requiring companies to inform the government upon release of any hazardous chemicals into the environment and to provide to the government an inventory of their hazardous chemicals. The act also requires states to establish emergency procedures for chemical discharges.

eminent domain   The state's power to take private property for public use.

employer identification number   Number issued to employer by federal and state governments for the purpose of record keeping associated with income and Social Security tax collections.

en banc   All of the judges hearing a case as a group rather than individually or in panels.

enabling legislation   Law that establishes an administrative agency and grants power to that agency.

enjoin   To require. A court issues an injunction requiring a certain act or ordering a party to refrain from a certain act.

enterprise law   Legal doctrine treating all companies in a corporate group as one giant organization rather than a collection of smaller, independent units.

entity law   Legal doctrine treating each company in a corporate group as a separate, independent unit.

environmental impact statement   Statement of the anticipated impact on the environment of legislation or other major federal action, and suggestions for reasonable alternatives.

Environmental Protection Agency   Created in 1970 to gather information relating to pollution and to assist in pollution control efforts and sanctions.

equal protection   The Fourteenth Amendment to the U.S. Constitution provides that all similarly situated individuals are entitled to the same advantages and must bear the same burdens under the law.

equitable remedies   Injunction, specific performance, restraining orders, and the like, as opposed to money damages.

equity   Fairness; a system of courts that developed in England. A chancellor presided to mete out fairness in cases that were not traditionally assigned to the law courts headed by the king.

essential functions of a position   Those tasks that are fundamental, as opposed to marginal or unnecessary, to the fulfillment of the position's objectives.

establishment clause   The First Amendment to the U.S. Constitution forbids the U.S. government from creating a government-supported church or religion.

estate   An interest in land or property owned by a decedent at the time of her or his death.

estate per *autre vie*   A life estate that is measured by the life of someone other than the possessor.

estoppel   A legal doctrine providing that one may not assert facts that are in conflict with one's own previous acts or deeds.

eviction   Depriving a tenant of the possession of leased premises.

excise taxes   Taxes imposed at both the state and federal levels on the sale of particular commodities, especially alcohol, tobacco, and gasoline.

exclusive dealing   Agreement to deal only with a particular buyer or a particular seller.

exculpatory clause   Portion of a contract that seeks to relieve one of the parties to the contract from any liability for breach of duty under that contract.

executed   In contract law, full performance of the terms of the bargain.

executed contract   Performances are complete.

executory contract   Not yet fully performed or completed.

exemplary damages   Same as **punitive damages**.

exempt property   Specified classes of property that are unavailable to the creditor upon default of the debtor.

exempt security   Certain kinds of securities and certain transactions involving securities are not required to meet federal registration requirements under the 1933 act.

existentialism A philosophy emphasizing the individual's responsibility to make herself what she is to become. Existence precedes essence.

express authority Corporate officers' powers as expressed in the bylaws or conferred by the board of directors.

express authorization In contract law, offerer specifies a means of communication by which the offeree can accept.

express conditions Conditions within contracts that are clear from the language.

express contract Contract whose terms are clear from the language.

express warranty A guarantee made by affirmation of fact or promise, by description of the goods, or by sample or model.

expropriation A government's taking of a business's assets, such as a manufacturing facility, usually without just compensation.

extraterritoriality The application of U.S. laws on persons, rights, or relations beyond the geographic limits of this country and even though the parties involved are not American citizens.

F

failing company doctrine A defense to an otherwise unlawful merger in which the acquired firm is going out of business and no other purchaser is available.

fair use A doctrine that permits the use of copyrighted works for purposes such as criticism, news reporting, training, or research.

false imprisonment Tort of intentionally restricting the freedom of movement of another.

false light Falsely and publicly attributing certain characteristics, conduct, or beliefs to another such that a reasonable person would be highly offended.

featherbedding A labor law term describing the practice where workers were paid even though they did not perform any work. Featherbedding is a violation of federal labor law.

federal question Litigation involving the federal constitution, statutes, and treaties. The federal courts have jurisdiction over cases involving federal questions.

Federal Register Daily publication of federal agency regulations and other legal materials coming from the executive branch of government.

Federal Sentencing Guidelines Standards established by the U.S. Sentencing Commission that rank the seriousness of individual and organizational federal crimes and provide sentences that, with little flexibility, must be applied to those crimes.

Federal Trade Commission Agency of the federal government responsible for promoting fair trade practices in interstate commerce.

federalism The division of authority between the federal government and the states to maintain workable cooperation while diffusing political power.

fee simple A form of land ownership that gives the owner the right to possess and to use the land for an unlimited period of time, subject only to governmental or private restrictions, and unconditional power to dispose of the property during his or her lifetime or upon death.

felony A crime of a serious nature ordinarily involving punishment by death or imprisonment in a penitentiary.

fiduciary One who holds a relationship of trust with another and has an obligation to act in the best interests of the other—for example, one who manages property on behalf of another.

fiduciary duty The responsibility of one in a position of trust with another to act in the best interests of the other.

financing statement Document notifying others that the creditor claims an interest in the debtor's collateral. Must be filed as provided for by law to perfect a security interest.

firm offer Under the Uniform Commercial Code, a signed, written offer by a merchant containing assurances that it will be held open, and which is not revocable for the time stated in the offer, or for a reasonable time if no such time is stated.

fixture A thing that was originally personal property and that has actually or constructively affixed to the soil itself or to some structure legally a part of the land.

foreclose To terminate the mortgagor's rights in the property covered by the mortgage.

franchise A marketing arrangement in which the franchisor permits the franchisee to produce, distribute, or sell the franchisor's product using the franchisor's name or trademark.

franchisee A holder of a franchise.

franchisor A party granting a franchise.

fraud An intentional misrepresentation of a material fact with intent to deceive where the misrepresentation is justifiably relied on by another and damages result.

fraud-on-the-market theory   Misleading statements distort the market and thus defraud a securities buyer whether the buyer actually relies on the misstatement or not. Based on the assumption that the price of a stock reflects all of the available information about that stock.

Free Exercise Clause   First Amendment provision guaranteeing all Americans the right to pursue their religious beliefs free of government intervention (with limited exceptions).

free riders   Those who lawfully benefit from goods or services without paying a share of the cost of those goods or services.

Full Faith and Credit Clause   Provision of the U.S. Constitution requiring each state to recognize the laws and judicial decisions of all other states.

futures   Contracts to deliver or take delivery of specified quantities of commodities at a previously specified price.

G

G8   An association embracing eight of the world's leading industrial powers (Canada, France, Italy, Germany, Japan, Russia, the United Kingdom, and the United States) designed to improve worldwide economic and political conditions.

garnishment   Action by a creditor to secure the property of a debtor where that property is held by a third party.

General Agreement on Tariffs and Trade   Establishes and regulates import duties among signatory countries.

general duty   An OSHA provision requiring that employers furnish to each employee a place of employment free from recognized hazards that cause or are likely to cause death or serious physical harm to the employee.

general warranty deed   A deed that carries with it certain warranties or guarantees.

generic mark   A trademark employing a common descriptive name for a product.

genuineness of assent   In contract law, the parties knowingly agreed to the same thing.

going public   Selling shares in a company on the open market.

good faith   Honesty; an absence of intent to take advantage of another.

goods   All things that are movable at the time of identification to the contract for sale except the money in which the price is to be paid, investment securities, and so forth.

grand jury   A body of people convened by the state to determine whether the evidence is sufficient to bring a criminal indictment (formal accusation) against a party.

grant deed   A deed that does not have the warranties contained in a warranty deed.

gray market   Transactions conducted outside the usual supplier-approved channels of distribution. These transactions (unlike *black market* sales) are lawful but are often discouraged by suppliers. The gray market operates parallel to the "officially" authorized chain of distribution.

grease   Payments to low-ranking authorities for the purpose of facilitating business in another nation. Not forbidden by the Foreign Corrupt Practices Act if legal in the host nation.

greenmail   Takeover defense involving the target corporation's repurchase of a takeover raider's stock at a premium not offered to other shareholders.

group boycott   An agreement among traders to refuse to deal with one or more other traders.

guarantor   A person who promises to perform the same obligation as the principal if the principal should default.

H

Herfindahl–Hirschman Index (HHI)   Calculation used by the Justice Department to determine the degree of economic concentration in a particular market and to determine the degree to which a proposed horizontal merger would further concentrate that market. Computed by squaring the market share of each firm in a market and summing those totals.

holdover lease   The tenancy that exists where a tenant subject to a term lease is allowed to remain on the premises after the term has expired.

horizontal divisions of the market   Competitors agree to share their market geographically or to allocate customers or products among themselves.

horizontal merger   Acquisition by one company of another company competing in the same product and geographic markets.

hostile environment   A form of sexual harassment in which sexual conduct, sexual remarks, sexual depictions, and the like render the workplace offensive and intimidating such that performance is affected even though no tangible employment action has occurred.

hostile takeover   The acquisition of a formerly independent business where the acquired business resists the union.

I

Immigration Reform and Control Act (IRCA)   Enacted by Congress, IRCA's purpose is to discourage the entry of illegal aliens to the United States.

implied authority   Corporate officers' powers to take actions that are reasonably necessary to achieve their express duties.

implied authorization   In contract law, where the offerer's behavior or previous dealings with the offeree suggest an agreeable means of communicating an acceptance.

implied easement   Also called easement by prescription or way of necessity. An interest created where someone has openly used an adjoining piece of property for access with no complaint from the owner for a statutorily determined period of time.

implied warranty of fitness for a particular purpose   A warranty that arises by operation of law and promises that the good warranted is reasonably useful for the buyer's purpose where the buyer was relying on the seller's expertise in making the purchase.

implied warranty of habitability   Implied warranty arising in lease or sale of residential real estate that the property will be fit for human habitability.

implied warranty of merchantability   A warranty that arises by operation of law and promises that the good warranted is at least of average, fair, reasonable quality.

implied-in-fact conditions   Conditions derived from the parties' conduct and the circumstances of the bargain.

implied-in-fact contract   Contract whose terms are implicitly understood based on the behavior of the parties.

implied-in-law conditions or constructive conditions   Conditions imposed by the court to avoid unfairness.

in personam jurisdiction   The power of the court over a person.

incidental beneficiary   Person who is not a party to a contract, who benefits indirectly from the contract, who was not contemplated by the parties, and who may not enforce the contract.

incidental damages   Collateral damages that are incurred because of a breach; damages that compensate a person injured by a breach of contract for reasonable costs incurred in an attempt to avoid further loss.

incorporators   Those who initiate a new corporation.

indemnification   Corporate policy to compensate officers and directors for losses sustained in defending themselves against litigation associated with their professional duties where those duties were performed with reasonable business judgment.

indemnify   Reimburse one who has suffered a loss.

indenture   Agreement governing the conditions under which bonds are issued.

indenture trustee   Person or institution holding legal title to trust property and charged with carrying out the terms of the indenture.

independent contractor   A person who contracts with a principal to perform some task according to his or her own methods, and who is not under the principal's control regarding the physical details of the work.

indictment   A grand jury's formal accusation of a crime.

Industry Guides   Published advice to industry and the public providing Federal Trade Commission interpretations of the likely legality of specific marketing practices.

information   A prosecutor's formal accusation of a crime.

initial public offering (IPO)   A security offered for sale to the public for the first time.

injunction   A court order commanding a person or organization to do or not do a specified action.

injurious falsehood   Intentional tort based on a false statement made with malice that disparages the property of another.

innocent misrepresentation   An unintentional misrepresentation of material fact where the misrepresentation is justifiably relied on by another and damages result.

insider   In securities law, anyone with a fiduciary duty who has knowledge of material facts not available to the general public.

insider trading   Trading securities while in possession of material nonpublic information, in violation of a fiduciary duty.

intellectual property   Intangible personal property.

intent   A conscious and purposeful state of mind.

intentional infliction of emotional distress   Intentional tort based on outrageous conduct that causes severe emotional distress in another.

intentional tort   Voluntary civil wrong causing harm to a protected interest.

interference with contractual relations   Improperly causing a third party to breach or fail to perform its contract with another.

interference with prospective advantage   Improperly causing a third party not to enter a prospective contractual relationship.

interpretive rules   In administrative law, an agency's view of the meaning of statutes governing agency action.

interrogatories   An ingredient in the discovery process wherein one party in a lawsuit directs written questions to another party in the lawsuit.

intrastate offerings   Registration exemption for securities sold only to residents of the state in which the issuer is organized and doing business.

intrusion   Wrongfully entering upon or prying into the solitude or property of another.

invasion of privacy   Violation of the right to be left alone.

invitee   One who comes on the premises of another by invitation of the owner, in connection with the owner's business, and for the benefit of the owner or for the mutual benefit of the invitee and the owner.

J

joint and several liability   Liability of a group of persons in which the plaintiff may sue all members of the group collectively or one or more individuals for the entire amount.

joint liability   Liability of a group of persons in which, if one of these persons is sued, he can insist that the other liable parties be joined to the suit as codefendants, so that all must be sued collectively.

joint tenancy   An estate held by two or more jointly with an equal right in all to share in the enjoyment of the land during their lives.

joint venture   A form of business organization essentially identical to a partnership, except that it is engaged in a single project, not carrying on a business.

judgment notwithstanding the verdict (judgment n.o.v.)   A judge's decision overruling the finding of the jury.

judgment proof   Describes those against whom money judgments will have no effect because they are insolvent or their assets are beyond the reach of the court.

judicial review   A court's authority to review statutes and, if appropriate, declare them unconstitutional. Also refers to appeals from administrative agencies.

jurisdiction   The power of a judicial body to adjudicate a dispute. Also the geographical area within which that judicial body has authority to operate.

jurisprudence   The philosophy and science of law.

jury instructions   A judge's directions to the jury explaining the law that must be applied in the case at hand.

K

keiretsu   Japanese cartels of vertically related firms working together in a collaborative fashion.

L

land contract   Typically, an installment contract for the sale of land wherein the purchaser receives the deed from the owner on payment of the final installment.

landlord/lessor   A party to a lease contract who allows a tenant to possess and to use his or her property in return for rent payments.

latent defects   Imperfections that are not readily apparent upon reasonable inspection.

lease   A contract for the possession and use of land or other property, including goods, on one side, and a recompense of rent or other income on the other.

leasehold estate   A right to occupy and to use land pursuant to a lease or contract.

legal detriment   Any act or forbearance by a promisee.

legal impossibility   A party to a contract is relieved of his or her duty to perform when that performance has become objectively impossible because of the occurrence of an event unforeseen at the time of contracting.

legality of purpose   The object of the contract does not violate law or public policy.

legitimate nondiscriminatory reason (LNDR)   An employer's justification for taking adverse action against an employee or applicant where the basis for the action is something other than the individual's membership in a protected class (such as termination for dishonesty or theft).

lemon laws   State statutes providing remedies for those buying vehicles which turn out to be so thoroughly defective that they cannot be repaired after reasonable efforts.

letter of credit   A statement from a financial institution such as a bank guaranteeing that it will pay the financial obligations of a particular party.

libel   Tort of defaming or injuring another's reputation by a published writing.

license   A contractual right to use property in a certain manner.

licensee   A person lawfully on land in possession of another for purposes unconnected with business interests of the possessor.

licenses   Government-granted privileges to do some act or series of acts. Authorization to do what, without a license, would be unlawful. Same as **permits**.

lien   A claim against a piece of property in satisfaction of a debt; the financial interest of the lienholder in the property as a result of a debt or other obligation of the landowner.

life estate   A property interest that gives a person the right to possess and to use property for a time that is measured by her or his lifetime or that of another person.

life tenant   The possessor of a life estate interest.

limited liability   Maximum loss normally limited to the amount invested in the firm.

limited liability company (LLC)   Hybrid of limited partnership and corporation receiving partnership tax treatment with the operating advantages of a corporation.

limited liability partnership   A special partnership form providing some of the advantages of limited liability.

limited partnership   A form of business organization that has one or more general partners who manage the business and have unlimited liability for the obligations of the business and one or more limited partners who do not manage and have limited liability.

liquidated damages   Damages made certain by the prior agreement of the parties.

liquidation   "Straight" bankruptcy action in which all assets except exemptions are distributed to creditors (Chapter 7 bankruptcy).

lockout defense   Takeover defense where the target company manipulates its assets, shares, and so on, to make the company unattractive as a takeover candidate.

lockouts   Where employees are kept from the workplace by the employer. Where the landlord deprives the tenant of the possession of the premises by changing the locks on the property.

long-arm statute   A state enactment that accords the courts of that state the authority to claim jurisdiction over people and property beyond the borders of the state as long as certain "minimum contacts" exist between the state and the people or property.

M

mailbox rule   Rule holding that a mailed acceptance is effective upon dispatch when the offerer has used the mail to invite acceptance; the rule has been expanded to include the use of any reasonable manner of acceptance.

malice   A required element of proof in a libel or slander claim by a public figure. Proof of a defamatory statement expressed with actual knowledge of its falsity or with reckless disregard for the truth would establish malice.

malicious prosecution   Criminal prosecution carried on with malice and without probable cause with damages resulting.

malpractice   Improper or negligent conduct in the performance of duties by a professional such as a doctor or lawyer.

market failure   Economic theory arguing that the free market works imperfectly because of certain allegedly inherent defects such as monopoly, public goods, and so forth.

market foreclosure   In vertical mergers, the concern that the newly combined firm will close its doors to potential suppliers and purchasers such that competition will be harmed.

market share liability   Product liability action by which plaintiffs may be able to recover against manufacturers of defective products based on those manufacturers' market shares even though proof of causation cannot be established.

material breach   In contract law, performance that falls beneath substantial performance and does not have a lawful excuse.

mechanic's lien or materialman's lien   A claim created by law for the purpose of securing a priority of payment of the price or value of work performed and materials furnished in erecting or repairing a structure.

mediation An extrajudicial proceeding in which a third party (the mediator) attempts to assist disputing parties to reach an agreeable, voluntary resolution of their differences.

mens rea Evil intent.

merger The union of two or more business organizations wherein all of the assets, rights, and liabilities of one are blended into the other with only one firm remaining.

misappropriation In securities law, taking material, nonpublic information and engaging in insider trading in violation of a fiduciary duty.

misdemeanor A criminal offense less serious than a felony normally requiring a fine or less than a year in a jail other than a penitentiary.

misrepresentation The innocent assertion of a fact that is not in accord with the truth.

mitigation Obligation of a person who has been injured by a breach of a contract to attempt to reduce the damages.

Model Business Corporation Act (MBCA) Drafted by legal experts, the MBCA is designed to improve corporate law and to serve as a model for state legislatures in drafting their corporate laws.

mommy track An employment track, whether formally or informally instituted, in some firms that allows for slower upward mobility for mothers who must divide their attention between their positions and their families.

monopoly Market power permitting the holder to fix prices or exclude competition.

monopsony Only one buyer to purchase the output of several sellers. A "buyer's monopoly."

moot An issue no longer requiring attention or resolution because it has ceased to be in dispute.

mortgage An interest in land formalized by a written instrument providing security for the payment of a debt.

mortgagee One who receives a mortgage to secure repayment of a debt.

mortgagor One who pledges property for a particular purpose such as security for a debt.

most favored nation status (MFN) Preferential status offered to certain countries under the GATT or WTO, which allows the MFN country to obtain the lowest applicable tariff on goods.

motion A request to a court seeking an order or action in favor of the party entering the motion.

motion for a directed verdict A request by a party to a lawsuit arguing that the other party has failed to prove facts sufficient to establish a claim and that the judge must, therefore, enter a verdict in favor of the moving party.

multinational enterprise A company that conducts business in more than one country.

mutual mistake Where both parties to the contract are in error about a material fact.

N

National Environmental Policy Act Requires that the government "use all practicable means" to conduct federal affairs in harmony with the environment.

National Pollutant Discharge Elimination System Requires that all who discharge pollutants obtain an EPA permit before adding pollutants to a navigable stream.

National Priorities List A list of hazardous dump or spill sites scheduled to be cleaned using CERCLA funds.

national treatment Concept that requires that, once goods have been imported into a country, they must be treated as if they were domestic goods (that is, no tariff may be imposed other than that at the border).

nationalization A country taking over a private business often without adequate compensation to the ex-owners.

necessaries That which is reasonably necessary for a minor's proper and suitable maintenance.

negative externality A spillover in which all the costs of a good or service are not fully absorbed by the producer and thus fall on others.

negligence Failure to do something that a reasonable person would do under the circumstances, or an action that a reasonable and prudent person would not take under the circumstances.

negligence per se Action violating a public duty, particularly where that duty is specified by statute.

negligent tort Unintentional, civil wrong causing harm to a protected interest. Injury to another resulting from carelessness.

nolo contendere A no-contest plea in a criminal case in which the defendant does not admit guilt but does submit to such punishment as the court may accord.

nominal damages   Small damages, oftentimes $1, awarded to show that there was a legal wrong even though the damages were very slight or nonexistent.

noncompetition clause   Employee agrees not to go into business in competition with employer.

nonpossessory interest   An interest in real property that is not sufficient to be an ownership or possessory interest.

nonprice restraints   Resale limitations imposed by manufacturers on distributors or retailers in any of several forms (such as territorial or customer restraints) that do not directly affect price.

nonreversionary interest   The interest held by the remainderman. It is called *nonreversionary* because it does not revert to the original grantor.

nonvoting stock   Owners of nonvoting stock participate in firm profits and dividends but may not vote at shareholder meetings.

novation   A mutual agreement between all parties concerned for the discharge of a valid existing obligation by the substitution of a new valid obligation on the part of the debtor or another, or a like agreement for the discharge of a lessee to a landlord by the substitution of a new lessee.

nuisance   A class of wrongs that arises from the unreasonable, unwarrantable, or unlawful use by a person of his or her property that produces material annoyance, inconvenience, discomfort, or hurt.

O

obligee   A person to whom another is bound by a promise or other obligation; a promisee.

obligor   A person who is bound by a promise or other obligation; a promisor.

offer   A proposal by one person to another that is intended to create legal relations on acceptance by the person to whom it is made.

oligopoly   An economic condition in which the market for a particular good or service is controlled by a small number of producers or distributors.

on-call workers   Workers who report to work only when called.

open-end loan   Credit arrangement not involving a lump sum but permitting repeated borrowing where payment amounts are not specified.

option contract   A separate contract in which an offerer agrees not to revoke her or his offer for a stated period in exchange for some valuable consideration.

ordinance   A law, rule, or regulation enacted by a local unit of government (such as a town or city).

output restriction   An agreement to limit production, which is a per se violation of the Sherman Act and may have the effect of artificially stabilizing or raising prices.

over-the-counter securities   Stocks, bonds, and like instruments sold directly from broker to customer rather than passing through a stock exchange.

P

parol evidence   When the written document is intended as the parties' final expression of their contract, oral evidence of prior agreements or representations cannot be used to vary the terms of the document.

partial ownership interest   An interest that may revert back to the original grantor.

partition   A legal proceeding that enables joint tenants or tenants in common to put an end to the tenancy and to vest in each tenant a sole estate in specific property or an allotment of the lands and buildings. If division is impossible, the estate may have to be sold and the proceeds divided.

partnership   An association of two or more persons where they agree to work together in a business designed to earn a profit.

past consideration   Performance that is not bargained for and was not given in exchange for the promise.

patent   A right conferred by the federal government allowing the holder to restrict the manufacture, distribution, and sale of the holder's invention or discovery.

patent defects   Imperfections that are visible and obvious.

per curiam   By the court. Refers to legal opinions offered by the court as a whole rather than those instances where an individual judge authors the opinion.

per se   By itself; inherently.

per se doctrine   Certain antitrust violations are considered so harmful to competition that they are always unlawful and no proof of actual harm is required.

peremptory challenge   An attorney's authority to dismiss prospective members of the jury without offering any justification for that dismissal.

perfection   Process by which a secured party obtains a priority claim over other possible claimants to certain collateral belonging to a debtor.

periodic tenancy   The tenancy that exists when the landlord and tenant agree that the rent will be paid in regular successive intervals until notice to terminate is given but do not agree on a specific duration of the lease.

personal jurisdiction   The authority of a particular court over the parties to a lawsuit.

personal property   Movable property. All property other than real estate.

piercing the corporate veil   Holding a shareholder responsible for acts of a corporation due to a shareholder's domination and improper use of the corporation.

plaintiff   One who initiates a lawsuit.

pleadings   The formal entry of written statements by which the parties to a lawsuit set out their contentions and thereby formulate the issues on which the litigation will be based.

police power   The government's inherent authority to enact rules to provide for the health, safety, and general welfare of the citizenry.

political action committee   A legally defined lobbying group that uses funds and activities to support certain political views.

possibility of reverter   An interest that is uncertain or may arise only upon the occurrence of a condition.

precedent   A previously decided lawsuit that may be looked to as an authoritative statement for resolving current lawsuits involving similar questions of law.

predatory pricing   Selling of goods below cost for the purpose of harming competition.

preemption doctrine   Constitutional doctrine providing that the federal government "preempts the field" where it passes laws in an area, thus denying the states the right to pass conflicting laws or, in some cases, denying the states the right to pass any laws in that area.

preemptive right   A shareholder's option to purchase new issuances of shares in proportion to the shareholder's current ownership of the corporation.

preexisting duty   Prior legal obligation or commitment, performance of which does not constitute consideration for a new agreement.

preferred shares   Shares having dividend and liquidation preferences over other classes of shares.

pretext   After an employee has established a prima facie case of discrimination and the employer has articulated a BFOQ or LNDR, the employee must show that the proffered defense is pretextual—that is, that the BFOQ is not actually bona fide (or not applied in all situations) or that the LNDR has been applied differently to this individual compared to another.

price discrimination   Selling goods of like grade and quality to different buyers at different prices without justification where competitive harm results.

price fixing   An agreement among competitors to charge a specified price for a particular product or service. Also any agreement that prevents a seller from independently setting a price or from independently establishing the quantity to be produced.

prima facie case   A litigating party may be presumed to have built a prima facie case when the evidence is such that it is legally sufficient unless contradicted or overcome by other evidence.

principal   In agency law, one under whose direction an agent acts and for whose benefit that agent acts.

private law   Individually determined agreement of the parties relating to choice of laws, where disagreements shall be settled, and the language of the transactions.

private placements   Securities sold without a public offering, thus excusing them from SEC registration requirements.

privatization   The many strategies for shifting public-sector activities back to private enterprise. Those strategies include contracting out government work to private parties, raising the user fees charged for public services, selling state-owned property and enterprises, and returning government services such as garbage collection to the private sector.

privity of contract   The legal connection that arises when two or more parties enter a contract.

procedural due process   Constitutional principle requiring that the government ensure fundamental fairness to all in the execution of our system of laws.

procedural rules   In administrative law, an agency's internal operating structure and methods.

product liability   Refers to legal responsibility of manufacturers and sellers to compensate buyers, users, and, in some cases, bystanders for harm from defective products.

profit à prendre   The right to enter property and to take something away from it, such as crops.

promisee   The person to whom a promise is made.

promisor   A person who makes a promise to another.

promissory estoppel   An equitable doctrine that protects those who foreseeably and reasonably rely on the promises of others by enforcing such promises when enforcement is necessary to avoid injustice.

promoter   A person who incorporates a business, organizes its initial management, and raises its initial capital.

prospectus   A communication, usually in the form of a pamphlet, offering a security for sale and summarizing the information needed for a prospective buyer to evaluate the security.

proximate cause   Occurrences that in a natural sequence, unbroken by potent intervening forces, produce an injury that would not have resulted in the absence of those occurrences.

proxy   Written permission from a shareholder to others to vote his or her share at a stockholders' meeting.

public disclosure of private facts   Public disclosure of private facts where disclosure of the matter in question would be highly offensive to a reasonable person.

public goods   Goods or services usually provided by government when underproduced by markets.

public law   Rules of national law that regulate transactions between parties, as well as the relationships between nations.

public policy   That which is good for the general public, as gleaned from a state's constitution, statutes, and case law.

puffing   An expression of opinion by a seller not made as a representation of fact.

punitive damages   Damages designed to punish flagrant wrongdoers and to deter them and others from engaging in similar conduct in the future.

purchase money security interest   A security interest that is (1) taken or retained by the seller of collateral to secure all or part of its purchase price or (2) taken by a debtor to acquire rights in or the use of the collateral if the value is so used.

Q

qualified person with a disability   An individual with a covered disability who can perform the essential functions of her or his position, with or without reasonable accommodation.

qualified privilege   In libel and slander law, situations where a defendant is excused from liability for defamatory statements except where the statements were motivated by malice.

quantum meruit   As much as he deserves. Describes a plea for recovery under a contract implied by law. Fair payment for work performed.

quasi-contract   The doctrine by which courts imply, as a matter of law, a promise to pay the reasonable value of goods or services when the party receiving such goods or services has knowingly done so under circumstances that make it unfair to retain them without paying for them.

quid pro quo   Exchanging one thing of value for another. In sexual harassment law, quid pro quo cases are those where employment benefits are conditioned on the subordinate's submission to sexual advances.

quitclaim deed   A deed conveying only the right, title, and interest of the grantor in the property described, as distinguished from a deed conveying the property itself.

R

ratified   The adoption or affirmance by a person of a prior act that did not previously bind her or him.

ratify   Adopting or affirming a prior, nonbinding act.

real property   Land, buildings, and things permanently attached to land or buildings.

real property or real estate   The earth's crust and all things firmly attached to it.

reasonable accommodation   An accommodation to an individual's disability or religion that does not place an undue burden on the employer, which may be determined by looking to the size of the employer, the cost to the employer, the type of employer, and the impact of the accommodation on the employer's operations.

reasonable expectations test   Measure of negligence holding that a product is negligently designed if it is not safe for its intended use and also for any reasonably foreseeable use.

reasonable person   Fictitious being the law constructs to determine whether a person's behavior falls short of what a "reasonable person" would do under the circumstances.

red herring   A preliminary securities prospectus that provides information but does not constitute an offer to sell.

redlining   Most commonly, the practice of refusing to make loans in economically unstable areas with the result that minorities are sometimes discriminated against in securing credit.

reformation   An equitable remedy in which a court effectively rewrites the terms of a contract.

registration statement   Document filed with the SEC upon issuance of a new security detailing the information investors need to evaluate that security.

Regulation Z   Rules of the Federal Reserve Board implementing provisions of the Federal Truth-in-Lending Act.

release   Agreement to relinquish a right or a claim. Sometimes labeled a *waiver* or a *hold harmless* clause.

remainderman   One who is entitled to the remainder of the estate after a particular estate carved out of it has expired.

remand   To send back. For example, a higher court sends a case back to the lower court from which it came.

rent   The consideration paid by a lessee to a lessor in exchange for the right to possess and to use property.

rent-strike statutes   Legislation that allows a tenant to deduct from the rent payment the cost of property repairs that are otherwise the responsibility of the landlord.

reorganization   A bankruptcy action in which creditors are kept from the debtor's assets while the debtor, under court supervision, works out a repayment plan and continues operations (Chapter 11 bankruptcy).

res   A thing, object, or status.

res ipsa loquitur   The thing speaks for itself. Rule of evidence establishing a presumption of negligence if the instrumentality causing the injury was in the exclusive control of the defendant, the injury would not ordinarily occur unless someone was negligent, and there is no evidence of other causes.

res judicata   A thing decided. A doctrine of legal procedure preventing the retrial of issues already conclusively adjudicated.

resale price maintenance   Manufacturer's effort to restrict the price at which its product is resold.

rescission   Canceling a contract; its effect is to restore the parties to their original position.

Resource Conservation and Recovery Act   Authorizes the federal government to provide assistance to states and localities in connection with solid waste, to prohibit open dumping, and to establish programs to recover energy and valuable materials from solid waste.

respondeat superior   Let the master respond. Doctrine holding the employer liable for negligent acts committed by an employee while in the course of employment.

Restatement of Contracts   A collection of the rules of contract law created by the American Law Institute to provide guidance to lawyers and judges.

restitution   A remedy whereby one is able to obtain the return of that which he has given the other party, or an equivalent amount of money.

restraints of trade   Contracts, combinations, or conspiracies resulting in obstructions of the marketplace, including monopoly, artificially inflated prices, artificially reduced supplies, or other impediments to the natural flow of commerce.

restrictive covenant   An agreement restricting use of real property.

retaliation   Various statutes, including Title VII of the Civil Rights Act of 1964, forbid employers from punishing employees who legitimately exercise their legal rights.

reverse   Overturn the decision of a court.

RICO   Federal organized crime law making it illegal to acquire or operate an enterprise by a pattern of racketeering behavior.

right of survivorship   A feature of a joint tenancy that causes a co-owner's interest in property to be transferred on her or his death to the surviving co-owner(s).

right-of-way   Where an easement appurtenant refers to the right to physically cross property.

right-to-know laws   Federal and state laws and regulations requiring employers to assume the affirmative responsibility of acquainting employees with hazardous substances and conditions in the workplace.

risk–utility test   Measure of negligence holding that a product is negligently designed if the benefits of that product's design are outweighed by the risks that accompany that design.

RM petition   Employer-filed request to the National Labor Relations Board seeking an election to demonstrate that a union is no longer supported by a majority of the employees.

rule of reason   For antitrust purposes, reviewing an agreement in its specific factual setting, considering its pro- and anticompetitive features, to determine if it is harmful to competition.

runaway shop   An employer closes in one location and opens in another to avoid unionization.

S

scienter   Intent to commit a legal wrong. Guilty knowledge.

scope of employment   Limitation on master's liability to only those torts that a servant commits while "about the master's business."

scorched earth defense   Takeover defense where the target corporation takes on new debt, sells assets, and so on in an effort to make itself a less attractive target.

secondary boycott   Typically a union strategy that places pressure not on the employer with whom the union has a dispute but rather with a supplier or customer of that employer in the hope that the object of the boycott will persuade the employer to meet the union's expectations.

Securities and Exchange Commission (SEC)   Federal regulatory agency responsible for overseeing the securities markets.

security   A stock, bond, note, or other investment interest in an enterprise designed for profit and operated by one other than the investor.

As to loans, refers to lien, promise, mortgage, or the like, given by a debtor to assure payment or performance of her debt.

security interest   A lien given by a debtor or his creditor to secure payment or performance of a debt or obligation.

self-employment tax   A Social Security tax on people who are self-employed.

separate property   Property held by either spouse at the time of marriage or property received by either spouse through a gift or inheritance.

separation of powers   The strategy of dividing government into separate and independent executive, legislative, and judicial branches, each of which acts as a check on the power of the others.

service mark   A word, mark, symbol, design, picture, or combination thereof that identifies a service provider.

servient estate   The property subject to an easement appurtenant or implied easement.

sexual harassment   Unwelcome sexual advances, requests for sexual favors, and other unwanted physical or verbal conduct of a sexual nature.

shareholder   One holding stock in a corporation.

shark repellant   Various kinds of corporate behaviors designed to make a company unattractive to potential acquirers.

shelf registration   IPO registration that permits the issuer to hold the securities for sale until favorable market conditions emerge or the issuer needs the proceeds.

short-swing profits   Profits made by an insider through sale of company stock within six months of acquisition.

slander   A defamatory statement orally communicated to at least one third party.

slander per se   Category of oral defamation not requiring proof of actual harm to recover.

small claims courts   Courts of limited powers designed to hear cases involving modest sums of money (typically limited to $2,000–$7,500, but some states permit recoveries of $15,000 or more) in hearings free of many of the formalities and burdens associated with the more conventional judicial process.

small issues   Registration exemption for securities issued in small amounts.

sole proprietorship   A form of business under which one person owns and controls the business.

sovereign immunity   The government's right to exclude itself from being sued for damages in all but those situations where it consents to be sued. In international law, sovereign immunity permits a nation to decline to be sued in the courts of other nations.

specific performance   A contract remedy whereby the defendant is ordered to perform precisely according to the terms of his contract.

standing   A stake in a dispute sufficient to afford a party the legal right to bring or join a litigation exploring the subject of the dispute.

stare decisis   Let the decision stand. A doctrine of judicial procedure expecting a court to follow precedent in all cases involving substantially similar issues unless extremely compelling circumstances dictate a change in judicial direction.

state action   Situation of a sufficiently close relationship between the state and the action in question that the action can reasonably be treated as that of the state itself.

statute   A legislative enactment.

statute of frauds   A statute specifying that certain contracts must be in writing to be enforceable.

statute of limitations   A statute requiring that certain classes of lawsuits must be brought within defined limits of time after the right to begin them accrued or the right is lost.

straight voting   A form of voting for directors that ordinarily permits a shareholder to cast a number of votes equal to the number of shares he or she owns for as many nominees as there are directors to be elected.

strict liability   Civil wrong springing from defective and "unreasonably dangerous" products where responsibility automatically attaches without proof of blame or fault.

sub S corporation   A close corporation whose shareholders have elected to be taxed essentially as partners are taxed under federal income tax law.

subject-matter jurisdiction   The authority of a particular court to judge a particular kind of dispute.

sublease   A transfer of some but not all of a tenant's remaining right to possess property under a lease.

subpoena   An order from a court or administrative agency commanding that an individual appear to give testimony or produce specified documents.

substantial performance   Performance with minor, unimportant, and unintentional deviation.

substantive due process   The Due Process Clause of the Constitution requires that a statute be fair and reasonably related to a legitimate government purpose so that persons are not improperly deprived of their property rights.

suggestive mark   A trademark that suggests the product or its qualities; one that is more than merely descriptive.

summary judgment   A judicial determination prior to trial finding that no factual dispute exists between the parties and that, as a matter of law, one of the parties is entitled to a favorable judgment.

summons   A document originating in a court and delivered to a party or organization indicating that a lawsuit has been commenced against him, her, or it. The summons constitutes notice that the defendant is expected to appear in court to answer the plaintiff's allegations.

sunset legislation   A statute providing that a particular government agency will automatically cease to exist as of a specified date unless the legislative body affirmatively acts to extend the life of the agency.

Superfund/CERCLA   Established to help pay for the cleanup of hazardous dumps and spills.

Supremacy Clause   An element of the U.S. Constitution providing that all constitutionally valid federal laws are the paramount law of the land and, as such, are superior to any conflicting state or local laws.

surety   A person who promises to perform the same obligation as the principal and is jointly liable with the principal for that performance.

suretyship   A third party agrees to answer for the debt of another.

T

takeover bid   A tender offer designed to assume control of a corporation.

teleological ethics   The rightness of an action depends on its contribution to an end; often the maximum good.

temporary workers   Workers paid by a temporary help or staffing company.

tenancy at sufferance   The leasehold interest that occurs when a tenant remains in possession of property after the expiration of a lease.

tenancy at will   A leasehold interest that occurs when a property is leased for an indefinite period and is terminable at the will of either party to the lease.

tenancy by the entirety   A form of co-ownership of property by a married couple that gives the owners a right of survivorship.

tenancy in partnership   The manner in which partners co-own partnership property, much like tenancy in common, except that partners have a right of survivorship.

tenant/lessee   A party to a lease contract who pays rent in return for the right to possess and to use property.

tenants in common   Co-owners of real property who have undivided interests in the property and equal rights to possess it.

tender offer   A public bid to the shareholders of a firm offering to buy shares at a specified price for a defined period of time.

term tenancy   The tenancy that exists where a landlord and tenant have agreed to the terms of the lease period and a specific termination date for the lease.

test of nonobviousness   Determines whether the development described in a patent application would have been obvious to an ordinary skilled worker in the art at the time the invention was made.

third-party beneficiaries   People who are not parties to a contract but who have the right to enforce it because the contract was made with the intent to benefit them.

thrust upon   Company holds a monopoly innocently because of superior performance, the failure of competition, or changing market conditions.

tippee   In securities law, one who receives inside information from another.

tipper   In securities law, one who conveys inside information to another.

tombstone ad   A securities advertisement that does not constitute an offer and that usually appears in the financial press set inside heavy black borders suggestive of a tombstone.

tort A civil wrong, not arising from a contract, for which a court will provide a remedy.

totalitarianism A rigid, undemocratic government according power to a particular political group and excluding all others from access to political influence. The Soviet Union, Nazi Germany, and Fascist Italy were totalitarian states.

Toxic Substances Control Act Requires chemical manufacturers to report information relating to chemicals that pose a "substantial risk" and allows the EPA to review and limit, or to stop, the introduction of new chemicals.

Trade Regulation Rules Directives from the Federal Trade Commission interpreting the will of Congress and specifying those practices that the commission considers unfair or deceptive.

trademark A word, name, or other distinctive symbol registered with the government and used exclusively by the owner to identify its product.

trademark infringement Unauthorized use of the trademark of another.

treaty or convention A contract between nations.

treble damages An award of damages totaling three times the amount of actual damages, authorized by some statutes in an effort to discourage further wrongful conduct.

trespass Entering the property of another without any right, lawful authority, or invitation.

trespasser A person who enters the property of another without any right, lawful authority, or invitation.

tying arrangement Dealer agrees to sell or lease a product (the tying product) only on the condition that the buyer also purchases or leases another product (the tied product).

U

ultra vires Corporate conduct beyond the scope of activities provided for under the terms of incorporation.

unconscionable A contract so one-sided and oppressive as to be unfair.

underwriter Professional who helps sell new securities or buys those securities for the purpose of resale.

undivided share A share of the interest in property that is not subject to division into parts.

undue hardship A burden imposed on an employer by accommodating an individual's disability or religion that

would be too onerous for the employer to bear. See **reasonable accommodation**.

undue influence Dominion that results in a right to rescind a contract.

unemployment taxes Federal and state (most) taxes paid by employers as a percentage of the total payroll to fund benefits for those who have lost their jobs.

unenforceable contract Meets basic requirements, but remains faulty.

unfair labor practice Activities identified by Congress that employers might use to thwart workers' attempts to unionize and to undermine the economic power that would come from the workers' right to concerted activities and to unionize.

unfair subsidies Subsidies offered to producers in a certain industry by a government to spur growth in that industry. These subsidies are considered unfair if they are used to promote export trade that harms another country.

Uniform Partnership Act (UPA) Original uniform act for creation and operation of partnerships.

unilateral contract A contract wherein the only acceptance of the offer that is necessary is the performance of the act.

unilateral mistake Where one party to a contract is in error about a material fact.

union shop In labor law, the situation where all employees of a company must join a union to retain employment. Forbidden in right-to-work states.

unjust enrichment An unearned benefit knowingly accepted.

unsecured Refers to a loan not backed by some kind of security.

use taxes Normally, taxes imposed on the use, storage, or consumption of tangible personal property bought outside of the state imposing the taxes.

usury Charging an interest rate exceeding the legally permissible maximum.

V

valid contract Effective; sufficient in law.

venture capital funds Organizations designed to invest in new and often risky business enterprises.

venue The specific geographic location in which a court holding jurisdiction should properly hear a case, given the convenience of the parties and other relevant considerations.

verdict   The jury's decision as to who wins the litigation.

vertical merger   A union between two firms at different levels of the same channel of distribution.

vesting rights   The right of an individual to a present or future fixed benefit.

vicarious liability   Legal responsibility for the acts of another person because of some relationship with the person; for example, the liability of an employer for the acts of an employee.

void contract   Entirely null; no contract at all.

voidable contract   Capable of being made void; enforceable but can be canceled.

voir dire   The portion of a trial in which prospective jurors are questioned to determine their qualifications, including absence of bias, to sit in judgment in the case.

voting stock   Owners of voting stock have the right to vote at shareholder meetings.

W

waiver   Relinquishing a legal right—as in the situation where one agrees not to sue if injured while participating in a particular activity, such as attending a baseball game.

warranty   Any promise, expressed or implied, that the facts are true as specified. For example, in consumer law, the warranty of merchantability is a guarantee that the product is reasonably fit for the general purpose for which it was sold.

watered stock   Inadequate consideration received for stock.

white-collar crime   Law violations by corporations or by managerial and executive personnel in the course of their professional duties.

white knight   In a takeover battle, a friendly company that rescues the target company from a hostile takeover. Often the rescue is accomplished by a merger between the target and the white knight.

winding up   In partnership and corporation law, the orderly liquidation of the business's assets.

without reserve   At an auction advertised as "without reserve," the seller is not free to withdraw an item before the high bid is accepted.

workers' compensation laws   State statutes providing fixed recoveries for injuries and illnesses sustained in the course of employment. Under those statutes, workers need not establish fault on the part of the employer.

wrongful discharge   Tort of dismissing another from employment in violation of public policy or for other illegal reasons.

Y

yellow dog contract   An employment agreement by an employee not to become a member of a union.

Z

zoning   Restriction on the use of land as a result of public land use regulation.

zoning ordinances   Dividing a city or a county into geographical areas of restriction—for example, only residential housing would be permitted in an area zoned R.

CASE INDEX

SUBJECT INDEX